A GUIDE TO TREATMENTS THAT WORK

ADVISORY BOARD

A GUIDE TO
TREATMENTS
THAT WORK

EDITED BY

PETER E. NATHAN

JACK M. GORMAN

New York   Oxford
Oxford University Press
1998

Oxford University Press

Oxford   New York
Athens   Auckland   Bangkok   Bogota   Bombay   Buenos Aires
Calcutta   Cape Town   Dar es Salaam   Delhi   Florence   Hong Kong
Istanbul   Karachi   Kuala Lumpur   Madras   Madrid   Melbourne
Mexico City   Nairobi   Paris   Singapore   Taipei   Tokyo   Toronto   Warsaw

and associated companies in
Berlin   Ibadan

Published by Oxford University Press, Inc.
198 Madison Avenue, New York, New York 10016

Oxford is a registered trademark of Oxford University Press

Library of Congress Cataloging-in-Publication Data
A guide to treatments that work / edited by Peter E. Nathan, Jack M.
Gorman.
p.   cm.
Includes bibliographical references.
ISBN 0-19-510227-4
1. Mental illness—Treatment—Evaluation.   I. Nathan, Peter E.
II. Gorman, Jack M.
RC480.5.G85   1997
616.89'1—dc21   97-36492

3 5 7 9 8 6 4

Printed in the United States of America
on acid-free paper

Foreword—A Purpose

Martin E. P. Seligman

This volume emanates from a task force of the Board of Directors of Division 12 (Clinical Psychology) of the American Psychological Association (APA) established in 1993 during my presidency of that division. When it became known that this volume was in the offing, it was deemed so controversial and so potentially destructive to some constituencies within APA that grave doubts were expressed about its publication as an APA document. The worry was that if this were an "official" document of Division 12, it might imply APA endorsement of its contents; this raised the spectre that this book would never find its way into print. That it now appears is not only a major service to mental health practitioners and their patients, but it is also a testimony to the doggedness, even the courage, of its authors, editors, and supporters.

In this foreword, I want to tell the history of this volume: how and why it came about and what its purpose is. Oddly, I also find it necessary to write an afterword to be found, aptly, at the end of the volume. I do this to explain why this was such a controversial project and to propose a resolution to the controversy. I consider the work before you enormously valuable but incomplete. Once you have digested the chapters herein, I want to tell you why I consider them to be a most useful but nonetheless partial answer to "Which treatments work?" The afterword is a plea for a project and a resolution that now urgently needs doing. This was not a project I anticipated when I established the task force, but it arose in the interim when I went through an intellectual odyssey about treatment efficacy and effectiveness. So, the afterword tells the story of my own odyssey.

HISTORY AND PURPOSE OF THE VOLUME

I have always believed that the practice of psychotherapy should be shaped by the hard facts of treatment effectiveness. We should not shape the research to justify what we already do in practice, but rather we should shape what we do in practice to conform to what is discovered in research on therapy. So, at the top of my list of worthy projects for the Division of Clinical Psychology to undertake when I became its president-elect in 1993 was a scholarly review of the outcome studies of psychotherapy and medications for each major disorder.

I was no stranger to such an endeavor. I had published a small book, *What You Can Change and What You Can't* (1994) which attempted to present a "Guide Michelin" for several disorders, and for the different psychotherapies and drugs used to treat them. In preparing the book, I read a very large number of "efficacy" studies of drugs and of psychotherapy. A well-done efficacy study involves, at minimum, a manualized treatment compared to a control group, random assignment of patients to control groups or to therapy, prospective observation across time, up-to-date diagnostic interviews, and blindness about group assignment by the evaluators of outcome. I was convinced that the efficacy method was the gold standard for judging whether a treatment worked and the crown jewel in the tiara of research on treatment. I was further convinced that an exhaustive, disinterested, and scholarly review of this literature for the entire range of disorders would demonstrate to professionals and to the general public alike that the treatment of mental illness had come out of the dark ages and that there was at last a panoply of effective psychotherapies and drugs for much of mental illness.

So, with the approval of the Board of Directors of Division 12, I created a task force with the concern "treatments that work." The mission statement of the Task Force on Treatments That Work read as follows:

To publish information for both the practitioner and the general public on the random assignment, controlled outcome study literature of psychotherapy and of psychoactive medications.

Its product was to be:

First, an edited volume for the practitioner, entitled "Psychotherapies and Drugs That Work: A Review of the Outcome Studies." This will review, disorder by disorder, the well-done, random-assignment controlled outcome studies and recommend a "treatment of choice" when such is clearly indicated. Disorders in which there are insufficient well-done, controlled outcome studies will be noted and omitted. Major types of treatments for which there are insufficient well-done, controlled outcome studies for a given disorder will likewise be so noted.

The work was to be interdisciplinary, combining the best efforts of outcome researchers in psychotherapy with those of outcome researchers in psychopharmacology. It was to be a joint product of distinguished psychologists and psychiatrists, distinctly not a product of one of these two all-too-often warring guilds. I was fortunate enough to secure two of the most respected researchers in psychology and psychiatry, respectively, as editors in chief: Peter E. Nathan, Ph.D., and Jack M. Gorman, M.D. An advisory board consisting of some of the most distinguished outcome researchers in the two fields was formed, and they are listed on page ii.

The work was to be a disinterested review of outcome studies, not a lobbying effort:

These volumes are intended to be scientific documents of a high order. It is essential that their integrity be unimpeachable. Here is what is needed to avoid the documents losing their scientific integrity to lobbying interests: (1) The chairs, advisory board members, editors, and authors must avoid the appearance and actuality of conflict of interest. Drug companies and their employees, and practitioners who derive substantial income from the practice of a particular kind of therapy, may not serve in these positions. (2) While companies, groups, and individuals who have a financial interest in the findings should be consulted for advice, they must have no say in the choice of the above personnel. Nor should they be able to control or censor in any way the content of the documents. This must be so both in appearance and actuality. (3) No editorial control shall be exerted by any groups or individuals other than the members of the advisory board and the editors. This incudes the various governing bodies, officers, and employees of Division 12 and of the American Psychological Association.

My greatest worry was that "efficacy imperialism" would reign. I knew that much of psychotherapy as it is actually practiced in the field—psychodynamic therapy, family therapy, humanistic therapy, and long-term eclectic therapy—had not been evaluated by the efficacy method. These therapies are long, difficult to manualize, and often have broader and deeper aims than just removing a disorder, and all of these considerations make the efficacy method a poor fit for such treatments. So, I was concerned that in addition to concluding that the specific medications and psychotherapies were efficacious, scholars and more casual readers would be tempted to conclude that psychodynamic therapy, family therapy, humanistic therapy, and long-term eclectic therapy did not work. And I knew that such a facile inference was on the agenda of more than a handful of scholars. Hence, this caveat:

THE INCOMPLETENESS
OF THE DOCUMENTS

These documents will not be the final word on effectiveness of treatments for two reasons. First, I intend them partly as a spur to further research, particularly on disorders and treatments that have been underinvestigated. These documents will call for their own revision as more information becomes available. A second major lacuna will be the evaluation of treatments for which there is as yet insufficient controlled-outcome research. In present-day medicine, many of the treatments meeting current, acceptable "standards of care" have not been subjected to the "gold standard" of random-assignment, controlled-outcome research. The absence of such research does not invalidate their use. Similarly, I believe that many psychotherapies have not been subjected to controlled-outcome study. There is, for example, a dearth of controlled-outcome studies of psychodynamic treatments and of family therapy—two widely used modalities. The absence of such research does not invalidate these treatments. On the contrary, it should make controlled-outcome studies an urgent research priority.

APA's lawyers suggested the following disclaimers and caveats to minimize the organization's legal exposure. I reproduce them here in full because they are sensible and reflect the intention of the volume:

DISCLAIMERS AND CAVEATS

This book does not represent an official statement by APA, or any of its divisions, but rather the personal views of the authors based upon their review of the scientific literature relative to therapeutic techniques and drugs for various psychological disorders. This book recites the literature and describes the controlled outcome studies relative to therapies but it is not intended to recommend "treatments of choice," establish standards or guidelines for "care" or provide advice on the efficacy of the therapies listed. The effectiveness of therapy depends on many factors which are beyond the scope of this book. Such factors may include the adequacy of assessment of the patient, patient-therapist rapport, skill and experience of the therapist, patient compliance, stressors in the patient's environment, and other factors. Therapies that are not widely proven effective in the literature may nevertheless work, and those proven effective in the literature may not work. This book does not purport to address all the studies and literature reviews which may have been conducted on a given therapy. Similarly, studies and literature reviews are continuously evolving and may not have been addressed in the book as of the date of publication. The reader is, therefore, advised that other uncited literature reviews or studies may have been conducted. Although this book may provide useful information relative to studies and reviews of the literature relative to therapies for various psychological disorders, health care providers and members of the public are advised that this book should not be definitively relied upon in making choices for appropriate care and treatment."

To further ensure against the perception that this book is a statement of guidelines or standards promulgated by APA, we decided that the book would be published by Oxford University Press, contracting only with the editors and authors. It represents only the opinions of these esteemed scholars and not the views of Division 12.

References

Seligman, M. (1993). Mission Statement: Task Force on Treatments That Work. Unpublished document, Division 12, American Psychological Association.

Seligman, M. (1994). *What You Can Change and What You Can't.* New York: Knopf.

Preface

In the absence of science, opinion prevails.

This simple truism clearly applies to the treatment of mental disorders. There are abundant treatment approaches to the various conditions listed in the fourth edition of the *Diagnostic and Statistical Manual* (*DSM-IV*) of the American Psychiatric Association. Some of them are viewed by their proponents with nearly religious fervor. We are told that some treatments actually "get to the bottom" of the illness, alleging, one supposes, that we actually know where that bottom is for most of the conditions. Others insist that their treatment works with virtually no failures. I can still remember sheepishly approaching a senior clinician when I was in training with the embarrassing confession that my patient had failed to respond to his most cherished treatment option. "You made the wrong diagnosis," I was strongly told. "It is already well known that patients with the diagnosis your patient actually has don't respond to my treatment." Looking back, there is little doubt that it was the treatment, not the diagnosis, that was wrong.

We get interesting responses when we ask advocates of particular treatment approaches if they have scientific proof that their approach really does work. Perhaps the most interesting we have heard was "of course we don't have proof using *your* scientific method. We use our own scientific method." Another fascinating response to the challenge to prove a treatment for mental illness works was "you are too concerned with getting the patient better. That is not the only thing to be interested in."

It is no wonder that treatments rendered by psychiatrists, psychologists, and other mental health–care practitioners have been often looked upon with skepticism. If the simple question "do you have proof?" is dodged, patients and the public in general are justified in being wary. Many medical interventions, once thought *de rigueur* have fallen by the wayside with scientific investigation. How many children had needless tonsillectomies, for example, before the impassioned belief that removal of the tonsils would lead to a reduction in pharyngitis was proven mythical? Yet in the 1950s pediatricians and surgeons recommended the procedure with little doubt; it seemed so logical. This example is a sobering reminder that human biology and psychology only occasionally follow logic.

To appreciate this book, one must accept its basic principles. First, we assert that the very most important test any treatment should meet is whether the patient gets better. Rigorously defining what "better" means is crucial, although at times controversial. But merely seeking "self-awareness" is more appropriate for religion than treatment for illness.

Second, we assert that the scientific method is the only way to establish definitively whether a treatment works. This does not necessarily mean, as we discuss below, that all treatments lacking proof by the standard scientific method must immediately be discredited. Nevertheless, it does mean that without proof we must remain cautious and skeptical in recommending or applying a particular treatment.

Finally, we insist that mental disorders are indeed amenable to rigorous scientific experimentation. It is probably the case that research into treatments of mental disorders is as difficult as that of any other condition. The brain, our organ of interest, is infinitely more complex and elusive than any other organ of the body, giving us major difficulties in establishing diagnosis and knowing when a treatment has worked or failed. Yet despite the difficulties we now know that a broad variety of mental health therapies can and have been studied rigorously and many have been shown to be effective using the standard scientific method of proof.

The design of this book is fairly simple. First, we selected all of the *DSM-IV* categories for which there are known treatments. Then, we asked whether there were psychosocial or psychopharmacological treatments, or both. We selected a distinguished group of internationally known clinical scientists to serve on an editorial board. The editors worked with members of the editorial board to select outstanding scientists to write chapters on the treatment of each of the *DSM-IV* disorders, commissioning two chapters for each disorder in the many cases in which both psychosocial and psychopharmacological therapies exist.

Our instructions to the authors were as follows: "The purpose of these chapters is to present the most rigorous, scientifically based evidence for the efficacy of treatments that is available. At the same time, it is clear that for some disorders there are treatments widely recognized by experienced clinicians to be useful that may not have been subjected to rigorous investigation for a variety of reasons. Our aim is to be clear with readers what treatments have been scientifically validated, what treatments are felt by a large number of experts to be valuable but have never been properly scientifically examined, and what treatments are known to be of little value."

Note that we did not instruct the authors to ignore therapies that are in common practice but bear less than optimal scientific proof. It is true, for example, that we currently lack the technology to submit psychoanalysis to rigorous scientific exploration: what would serve as the control treatment for a multiyear intervention? Rather, we asked the authors to be brutally honest in noting when commonly used approaches lack scientific proof and whether there is even a shred of evidence to validate them.

We asked the authors to think about the following classification of research studies when reviewing the evidence for a particular treatment:

TYPE 1 STUDIES: These are the most rigorous and involve a randomized, prospective clinical trial. Such studies must involve comparison groups with random assignment, blinded assessments, clear presentation of exclusion and inclusion criteria, state-of-the-art diagnostic methods, adequate sample size to offer statistical power, and clearly described statistical methods.

TYPE 2 STUDIES: These are clinical trials in which an intervention is made, but some aspect of the Type 1 study requirement is missing. For example, a trial in which a double-blind cannot be maintained; a trial in which two treatments are compared but the assignment is not randomized; and a trial in which there is a clear but not fatal flaw such as a period of observation that is felt to be too short to make full judgments on treatment efficacy. Such studies clearly do not merit the same consideration as Type 1 studies, but often make important contributions and generally should not be ignored.

TYPE 3 STUDIES: These are clearly methodologically limited. Generally, Type 3 studies are open treatment studies aiming at obtaining pilot data. They are highly subject to observer bias and can usually do little more than indicate if a treatment is worth pursuing in a more rigorous design. Also included in this category are case-control studies in which patients are identified and then information about treatment is obtained from them retrospectively. Such studies can, of course, provide a great deal of naturalistic information but are prone to all of the problems of uncontrolled data collection and retrospective recall error.

TYPE 4 STUDIES: Reviews with secondary data analysis can be useful, especially if the data analytic techniques are sophisticated. Modern methods of meta-analysis attempt to account for the fact that, for example, negative studies tend to be reported at a substantially lower rate than positive outcome studies.

TYPE 5 STUDIES: Reviews without secondary data analysis are helpful to give an impression of the literature but are clearly subject to the writer's opinion and sometimes are highly biased.

TYPE 6 STUDIES: This encompasses a variety of reports that have marginal value, such as case studies, essays, and opinion papers.

One may ask why we felt that this was the time to put such a volume together. The answer is simple: there are now plenty of treatments that have been proven to work and it is critical at this juncture to review them carefully. Treatment of all conditions is now under intense review as patients and payers both demand to know how likely it is that a particular therapy is actually going to work. We feel this is exactly the moment to take a sober look at the state of treatment for mental illness.

One important aspect of this book is that it brings together psychologists and psychiatrists and also those whose main approach is psychosocial or psychopharmacological. There is surely competition and sometimes disagreement among these disciplines, but there is also much collaboration and agreement. In this book we find psychologists advocating medication for some conditions and psychiatrists advocating psychotherapy. We feel this is a genuine advantage and hope that this volume will be seen as an attempt to rise above interdisciplinary rivalries to arrive at a consensus based on hard scientific proof. As the volume was prepared, the American Psychiatric Association and the American Psychological Association agreed to be partners in producing a new electronic journal on clinical issues. Perhaps our book fits into a new era of cooperation in the service of bettering care for the millions of Americans and people worldwide who suffer from mental illness.

Iowa City, Iowa   P. E. N.
New York, New York   J. M. G.
August 1997

Contents

Contributors

Abikoff, Howard, M.D.: Professor of Psychiatry, Long Island Jewish Medical Center, and Schneider Children's Hospital, New Hyde Park, New York

Althof, Stanley, Ph.D.: Associate Professor, Department of Psychiatry, Case Western Reserve School of Medicine

Barlow, David H., Ph.D.: Professor and Director, The Boston Center for Anxiety and Related Disorders, Boston University

Butler, Lisa D.: Department of Psychiatry and Behavioral Sciences, Stanford University School of Medicine

Buysse, Daniel J.: Associate Professor, Department of Psychiatry and Sleep and Chronobiology Center, University of Pittsburgh School of Medicine.

Cowley, Deborah S., M.D.: Associate Professor, Department of Psychiatry and Behavioral Sciences, University of Washington School of Medicine at Harborview Medical Center

Craighead, Linda Wilcoxon, Ph.D.: Associate Professor, Department of Psychology, University of Colorado at Boulder

Craighead, W. Edward, Ph.D.: Professor and Director of Clinical Training, Department of Psychology, University of Colorado at Boulder

Crits-Christoph, Paul, Ph.D.: Associate Professor of Psychology in Psychiatry and Director, Center for Psychotherapy Research, Department of Psychiatry, University of Pennsylvania Health System

Esler, Jeanne Lawton, B.A.: The Boston Center for Anxiety and Related Disorders, Boston University

Fairburn, Christopher G., Ph.D.: Professor, Department of Psychiatry, Oxford University

Finney, John W., Ph.D.: Associate Director, Center for Health Care Evaluation and Program Evaluation and Resource Center, VA Palo Alto Health Care System and Stanford University Medical Center

Foa, Edna B., Ph.D.: Professor and Director, Center for the Treatment and Study of Anxiety, Department of Psychiatry, Allegheny University Hospitals

Frank, Ellen, Ph.D.: Professor of Psychiatry, Department of Psychiatry, University of Pittsburgh School of Medicine

Franklin, Martin E., Ph.D.: Assistant Professor, Department of Psychiatry, Allegheny University Hospitals

Giller, Earl L., Jr., M.D.: Adjunct Associate Professor and Senior Associate Director, CNS Clinical Research, Department of Psychiatry, College of Physicians & Surgeons of Columbia University

Gorman, Jack M., M.D.: Professor of Psychiatry, College of Physicians & Surgeons of Columbia University, and Deputy Director, New York State Psychiatric Institute

Greenhill, Laurence L., M.D.: Associate Professor of Clinical Psychiatry, College of Physicians & Surgeons of Columbia University

Hinshaw, Stephen P., Ph.D.: Professor, Department of Psychology, University of California, Berkeley

Ilardi, Stephen S., Ph.D.: Senior Instructor, Department of Psychology, University of Colorado at Boulder

Jenike, Michael A., M.D.: Professor, Department of Psychiatry, Harvard Medical School, and Associate Chief of Psychiatry, Massachusetts General Hospital

Kazdin, Alan E., Ph.D.: Professor, Department of Psychology, Yale University

Keane, Terence M., Ph.D.: Chief, Psychology Service, Boston VA Medical Center/Outpatient Clinics, and Professor of Psychiatry (Psychology), Tufts University School of Medicine

Keck, Paul E., Jr., M.D.: Associate Professor, Departments of Psychiatry and Pharmacology, University of Cincinnati College of Medicine

Kinon, Bruce J., M.D.: Clinical Research Physician, U.S. Affiliate Medical Operations, Eli Lilly & Co.

Klein, Rachel G., Ph.D.: Professor, Department of Psychiatry, College of Physicians & Surgeons of Columbia University

Kopelowicz, Alex, M.D.: Department of Psychiatry, UCLA School of Medicine

Kupfer, David J.: Thomas Detre Professor and Chairman, Department of Psychiatry, University of Pittsburgh School of Medicine

Liberman, Robert Paul, M.D.: Professor, Department of Psychiatry, UCLA School of Medicine

Lieberman, Jeffrey A., M.D.: Professor and Vice Chairman, Department of Psychiatry, School of Medicine, The University of North Carolina at Chapel Hill

Maldonado, Jose R., M.D.: Assistant Professor and Director, Medical Psychotherapy Clinic, Department of Psychiatry and Behavioral Sciences, Stanford University School of Medicine

Maletzky, Barry M., M.D.: Professor of Clinical Psychiatry and Director of the Sexual Abuse Clinic, Oregon Health Sciences University

Marshall, Randall, M.D.: Clinical Fellow, Department of Psychiatry, College of Physicians & Surgeons of Columbia University

McElroy, Susan L., M.D.: Assistant Professor, Department of Psychiatry, University of Cincinnati College of Medicine

McKay, James, M.D.: Assistant Professor, Department of Psychiatry, University of Pennsylvania School of Medicine

Miklowitz, David J., Ph.D.: Associate Professor, Department of Psychology, University of Colorado at Boulder

Moos, Rudolph H., Ph.D.: Director, Center for Health Care Evaluation and Program Evaluation and Resource Center, VA Palo Alto Health Care System and Stanford University Medical Center

Morin, Charles M., Ph.D.: Professor, School of Psychology, Universite Laval

Nathan, Peter E., Ph.D.: University of Iowa Foundation Distinguished Professor, Department of Psychology, University of Iowa

Nemeroff, Charles B., M.D.: Reunette W. Harris Professor and Chairman, Department of Psychiatry and Behavioral Sciences, Emory University School of Medicine

Niederehe, George, Ph.D.: National Institute of Mental Health, Rockville, Maryland

Nowell, Peter D., M.D.: Fellow, Department of Psychiatry and Sleep and Chronobiology Center, University of Pittsburgh School of Medicine

O'Brien, Charles P., M.D.: Professor, Department of Psychiatry, University of Pennsylvania School of Medicine

Rauch, Scott L., M.D.: Assistant Professor, Department of Psychiatry, Harvard Medical School and Massachusetts General Hospital

Reynolds, Charles F., III, M.D.: Professor, Department of Psychiatry and Sleep and Chronobiology Center, University of Pittsburgh School of Medicine

Ridgway, Beth A., M.D.: Research Psychiatrist, Dorothea Dix Hospital, Raleigh, NC

Roy-Byrne, Peter P., M.D.: Professor and Vice-Chairman, Department of Psychiatry and Behavioral Sciences, University of Washington School of Medicine at Harborview Medical Center

Schatzberg, Alan F., M.D.: Kenneth T. Norris Professor and Chairman, Department of Psychiatry and Behavioral Sciences, Stanford University School of Medicine

Schneider, Lon S., M.D.: Professor, Department of Psychiatry, University of Southern California School of Medicine

Segraves, Robert T., M.D., Ph.D.: Professor, Department of Psychiatry, Case Western Reserve School of Medicine

Seligman, Martin E. P., Ph.D.: Professor, Department of Psychology, University of Pennsylvania

Sheitman, Brian B., M.D.: Assistant Professor, Department of Psychiatry, School of Medicine, The University of North Carolina at Chapel Hill

Siever, Larry J., M.D.: Professor, Department of Psychiatry, Mount Sinai School of Medicine

Simon, Gregory E., M.D.: Investigator, Center for Health Studies, Group Health Cooperative, and Research Assistant Professor, Department of Psychiatry and Behavioral Sciences, University of Washington School of Medicine

Spiegel, David, M.D.: Professor, Department of Psychiatry and Behavioral Sciences, Stanford University School of Medicine

Tune, Larry, M.D.: Professor, Department of Psychiatry and Behavioral Sciences, Emory University School of Medicine

Vajk, Fiona C., Ph.D.: Graduate Student, Department of Psychology, University of Colorado

Vitali, Amy E., B.A.: The Boston Center for Anxiety and Related Disorders, Boston University

Wilson, G. Terence, Ph.D.: Oscar K. Buros Professor of Psychology, Graduate School of Applied & Professional Psychology, Rutgers University

Woo-Ming, Ann Marie, M.D.: Associate Professor, Department of Psychiatry, Mount Sinai School of Medicine

Yehuda, Rachel, Ph.D.: Associate Professor, Department of Psychiatry, Mount Sinai School of Medicine

Summary of Treatments
That Work

Syndromes	Treatments	Standards of Proof	References
Alcohol use disorders	Several cognitive-behavioral treatments (notably, social skills training, community reinforcement, behavioral marital therapy) helped patients shape and adapt to their life circumstances; an effective treatment strategy for many patients may be to provide lower intensity treatment for a longer duration	Several Type 1 and a larger number of Type 2 random clinical trials (RCTs)	Finney & Moos, chapter 7
	Twelve-step treatment has been shown to be as effective as cognitive-behavioral and motivational-enhancement treatment	Two large-scale, multi-site, comparative evaluations	
	Naltrexone is now an FDA-approved therapy for alcohol abuse and dependence; it diminishes craving during the early stages of abstinence. It works best when accompanied by psychosocial and/or twelve-step interventions	A limited number of Type 1 and Type 2 RCTs	O'Brien & McKay, chapter 6
Avoidant personality disorder	A group-administered behavioral intervention (either graded exposure, standard social skills training, or in-	A single Type 2 RCT, which compared the 3 group-administered	Crits-Christoph, chapter 27

Syndromes	Treatments	Standards of Proof	References
Avoidant personality disorder (*cont.*)	timacy-focused social skills training) was more efficacious than a wait-list control	behavioral interventions with a wait-list control	
Bipolar disorders	While pharmacological interventions are treatments of choice, psychosocial treatments, including psychoeducation and cognitive-behavior therapy for medication adherence, have also shown promise	Several Type 2 and Type 3 studies of psychoeducation and a single Type 1 study of cognitive-behavior therapy	Craighead, Miklowitz, Vajk, & Frank, chapter 12
	Lithium reduced the symptoms of acute mania in bipolar I disorder	Five Type 1 and Type 2 RCTs, four of them crossover trials, in comparison with placebo, and seven Type 1 and Type 2 RCTs, in comparison with antipsychotics	Keck & McElroy, chapter 13
	More recently, Valproate has also shown effectiveness in reducing the symptoms of acute mania in bipolar I disorder	Six Type 1 and Type 2 RCTs, in comparison with placebo, with antipsychotics, or with lithium	
	Carbamazepine has also demonstrated effectiveness in treating the symptoms of acute mania	At least 14 Type 1 RCTs, in comparison with placebo and other medications	
	Lithium has been effective with a substantial percentage of bipolar patients (e.g., 35–50%) in preventing or reducing the frequency of recurrent affective episodes; however, side effects have interfered with drug compliance	A large number of Type 1 and Type 2 RCTs, in comparison with placebo	
	Lithium and several antidepressants have also shown moderate effectiveness with acute and chronic bipolar depression	A moderate number of Type 2 RCTs and Type 3 case reports, in comparison with placebo or each other	

Syndromes	Treatments	Standards of Proof	References
Body dysmorphic disorder	Cognitive-behavior therapy helped patients identify and challenge distorted body perceptions and interrupted self-critical thoughts, especially when employed in conjunction with guided exposure and response prevention	A few Type 2 RCTs and Type 3 case reports	Simon, chapter 21
Borderline personality disorder	Dialectical behavioral therapy (DBT) produced lower attrition, fewer and less severe episodes of parasuicidal behavior, and fewer days of hospitalization compared to a control condition	A single Type 2 RCT which randomized 44 women to either DBT or usual treatment in the community	Crits-Christoph, chapter 27
	Noradrenergic agents tended to improve mood but not irritability or dyscontrol, whereas serotonergic agents may act to decrease impulsivity; there are inconsistent data for the utility of antipsychotic and anticonvulsive agents	Four Type 1 RCTs, 2 Type RCTs, and 4 Type 3 case reports	Woo-Ming & Siever, chapter 28
Bulimia nervosa (BN)	Several different classes of antidepressant drugs produced significant, short-term reductions in binge eating and purging	A large number of Type 1 and Type 2 RCTs, in comparison to placebo treatment	Wilson & Fairburn, chapter 25
	Manual-based cognitive-behavioral therapy (CBT) was most effective in eliminating the core features of BN; roughly half the patients receiving CBT reduced binge eating and purging; long-term maintenance of improvement was reasonably good	A very substantial number of Type 1 and Type 2 RCTs	
Childhood attention deficit hyperactivity disorder (ADHD)	Contingency management produced impressive behavioral and academic gains in specialized classrooms when contingencies were enforced; at times, it permitted reduced doses of the stimulants needed for optimal classroom behavior	Several substantial reviews of post-1980 case reports (Type 3 studies)	Hinshaw, Klein, & Abikoff, chapter 2

Syndromes	Treatments	Standards of Proof	References
Childhood attention deficit hyperactivity disorder (ADHD) (cont.)	Psychostimulants (e.g., methyphenidate, dexedrine, and magnesium pemoline) have shown marked efficacy in the short-term in reducing overactivity, increasing concentration and prosocial behavior, and eliminating disruptive classroom behavior; however, the long-term benefits of the psychostimulants have not yet been adequately assessed	More than 100 Type 1 RCTs, in comparison with placebo	Greenhill, chapter 3
Conduct disorder in children	Cognitive Problem-Solving Skills Training (CPSST) with impulsive, aggressive, and conduct disordered (CD) children and adolescents, Parent Management Training (PMT) with the parents of disturbed children and adolescents, Functional Family Therapy (FFT) with difficult-to-treat CD populations, and Multisystemic Therapy (MST) with troubled families and their disordered adolescents have all shown success	Several Type 1 and Type 2 RCTs of CPSST, a large number of Type 1 and Type 2 RCTs of PMT, a few Type 1 and Type 2 RCTs of FFT, and several Type 1 and Type 2 RCTs of MST	Kazdin, chapter 4
Dementia	The efficacy of dihydroergotoxine mesylate (Hydergine), one of two drugs currently approved by the FDA for alleviation of the cognitive deterioration of dementia, remains in question	A few small, double-blind investigations	Tune, chapter 5
	An acetylcholinesterase inhibitor (Tacrine) is the other FDA-approved drug for this disorder; it has shown modest clinically significant benefit	Four Type 1 RCTs	
Depression and anxiety in the aged	The primary classes of antidepressant medications were effective in both the acute and maintenance phases of late-life depression, although they represented a heightened risk of adverse side effects	A very large number of Type 1 RCTs	Niederehe & Schneider, chapter 14

Syndromes	Treatments	Standards of Proof	References
	Electroconvulsive therapy (ECT) has shown its effectiveness and safety in the short-term management of late-life, severe psychotic depression and mania	A large number of Type 1 and Type 2 RCTs	
	Psychosocial interventions were efficacious in treating major depressive disorder in the aged	A moderate number of Type 1 and Type 2 RCTs	
Dissociative disorders	Psychodynamic psychotherapy, hypnosis, and amytal narcosynthesis are treatments of choice for these conditions based on case reports	No RCTs; in the case of Dissociative Identity Disorders (DID or Multiple Personality Disorder), several longitudinal outcome studies have been reported during the last 15 years	Maldonado, Butler, & Spiegel, chapter 22
Generalized anxiety disorder	Most treatment outcome studies have shown active treatments to be superior to non-directive approaches, and uniformly superior to no treatment; however, most of these studies failed to demonstrate differential rates of efficacy among active treatments	A large number of Type 1 and Type 2 RCTs, comparing active treatments to non-directive treatments and/or no treatment	Barlow, Esler, & Vitali, chapter 15
	Recent studies suggested cognitive-behavioral therapy (combining relaxation exercises and cognitive therapy), with the goal of bringing the worry process under control, to be most efficacious	Twelve Type 1 and Type 2 RCTs comparing CBT to other treatments or wait-list controls	
	The benzodiazepines reduced the anxiety and worry symptoms of GAD	Numerous placebo-controlled Type 1 RCTs	Roy-Byrne & Cowley, chapter 16
	Buspirone appeared comparable to the benzodiazepines in alleviating GAD symptoms	Several placebo-controlled Type 1 RCTs	

Syndromes	Treatments	Standards of Proof	References
Generalized anxiety disorder (*cont.*)	The tricyclic antidepressants showed utility in the treatment of GAD	Three Type 1 RCTs	
Hypochondriasis	Cognitive-behavior therapy has proven helpful in correcting the misinformation and exaggerated beliefs as well as pointing out the cognitive processes maintaining disease fears in hypochondriasis	Several Type 3 case series and uncontrolled studies	Simon, chapter 21
Major depressive disorder (MDD)	Tricyclic antidepressants (TCAa), the first antidepressants to be studied extensively, were consistently more efficacious than placebo both in reducing the complex of symptoms of MDD and managing the disorder over the long term	Many placebo-controlled Type 1 RCTs	Nemeroff & Schatzberg, chapter 10
	Because of their narrow safety margin and significant drug-induced adverse side effects, TCAs have now been largely replaced for the treatment of MDD by selective serotonin reuptake inhibitors (SSRIs), including fluoxetine, sertraline, and paroxetine and the new compounds, venlafaxine, bupropion, and nefazodone	Several placebo-controlled Type 1 RCTs for each SSRI	
	Because of adverse side effects, monoamine oxidase inhibitors (MAOIs) are generally reserved for treatment-refractory MDD patients	A large number of placebo-controlled Type 1 RCTs	
	Interventions utilizing behavior therapy, cognitive-behavior therapy, and interpersonal therapy have all yielded substantial reductions in scores on the two major depression rating scales, as well as in the percentage of patients meeting MDD criteria post-treatment; all three treatments have also shown significant maintenance of effect post-treatment	At least two Type 1 and Type 2 RCTs (7 in the case of cognitive-behavior therapy) for each of these psychosocial interventions, as well as two major meta-analytic reports of the literature	Craighead, Craighead, & Ilardi, chapter 11

Syndromes	Treatments	Standards of Proof	References
Mixed personality disorder (excluding Cluster A disorders)	An average of 40 weeks of brief dynamic therapy yielded substantial symptomatic improvement at both the end of treatment and after 1.5 years	A single Type 2 RCT, which randomized 81 patients to two forms of brief dynamic therapy, and a wait-list control condition	Crits-Christoph, chapter 27
	Medications may be useful for several of these disorders, although many methodological problems remain to be worked out	A few Type 1, Type 2, and Type 3 studies	Woo-Ming & Siever, chapter 28
Obsessive compulsive disorder (OCD)	Cognitive-behavioral therapy involving exposure and ritual prevention methods reduced or eliminated the obsessions and behavioral and mental rituals of OCD	A very substantial number of Type 1 and Type 2 RCTs	Franklin & Foa, chapter 17
	Approximately 40–60% of OCD patients respond to serotonergic reuptake inhibitors (SRIs), including chlomipramine, fluoxamine, paroxetine, fluoxetine, and sertraline, with mean improvement in obsessions and compulsions of approximately 20–40%	A very large number of Type 1 RCTs which randomized patients to SRI and non-SRI antidepressant treatments in both placebo-controlled and non-placebo-controlled studies	Rauch & Jenike, chapter 18
Panic disorder with and without agoraphobia	Situational in vivo exposure substantially reduced symptoms of panic disorder with agoraphobia	A substantial number of Type 1 RCTs	Barlow, Esler, & Vitali, chapter 15
	Cognitive-behavioral treatments which focused on education about the nature of anxiety and panic and provided some form of exposure and coping skills acquisition significantly reduced symptoms of panic disorder without agoraphobia	A substantial number of Type 1 RCTs	
	Tricyclic antidepressants and monoamine oxidase inhibitors reduced the number of panic attacks and also reduced anticipatory anxiety and phobic avoidance, although side effects caused some patients to drop from clinical trials	A large number of Type 1 and Type 2 RCTs with comparisons primarily to placebos	Roy-Byrne & Cowley, chapter 16

Syndromes	Treatments	Standards of Proof	References
Panic disorder with and without agoraphobia (cont.)	The benzodiazepines (e.g., Alprazolam) eliminated panic attacks in 55% to 75% of patients	Eight Type 1 and Type 2 RCTs, with comparisons to placebo	
	More recently, Serotonin Reuptake Inhibitors (SRIs), including selective SRIs, have produced reductions in panic frequency, generalized anxiety, disability and phobic avoidance	Several Type 1 and Type 2 RCTs, with comparisons to placebo	
Paraphilias	Cognitive, behavioral, and cognitive behavioral treatments have been reported to lower rates of recidivism, although methodological difficulties in carrying out this research have reduced confidence in its results	A few Type 2 RCTs, a larger number of Type 3 open trials, and several Type 4 reviews	Maletzky, chapter 24
	Hormonal treatments to lower testosterone levels have also been reported; however, most offenders treated with hormones show a rapid return to deviant arousal following their discontinuation	Several Type 3 case series and uncontrolled studies	
Post-traumatic stress disorder (PTSD)	Monoamine oxidase inhibitors reduced intrusive thoughts, improved sleep, and moderated anxiety and depression in PTSD patients	One Type 1 and one Type 2 RCTs; three Type 3 open trials	Yehuda, Marshall, & Giller, chapter 19
	Tricyclic antidepressants reduced intrusive thoughts and obsessions and moderated depression in these patients	Two Type 1 and one Type 2 RCTs; three Type 3 open trials	
	Selective Serotonin Reuptake Inhibitors (SSRIs) markedly reduced intrusive thoughts, avoidance, and sleep problems	One Type 1 RCT and six Type 3 open trials	
	Exposure therapies (systematic desensitization, flooding, prolonged exposure, and implosive therapy)	A substantial number of Type 1 and Type 2 RCTs, as well as sev-	Keane, chapter 20

Syndromes	Treatments	Standards of Proof	References
	and, to a lesser extent, anxiety management techniques (utilizing cognitive-behavioral strategies) reduced PTSD symptoms, including anxiety and depression, and increased social functioning	eral open trials and literature reviews	
Schizophrenia	Conventional antipsychotic medications (e.g., chlorpromazine, fluphenazine, haloperidol, loxapine, perphenazine, trifluoperazine, thiothixene, and thioridazine) markedly reduced the positive symptoms of schizophrenia and significantly decreased the risk of symptomatic relapse and rehospitalization; however, serious neurological side effects made these drugs difficult to tolerate for many patients with schizophrenia	More than 100 Type 1 RCTs	Sheitman, Kinon, Ridgway, & Lieberman, chapter 8
	More recently, a group of "atypical" antipsychotic drugs (e.g., clozapine, risperidone, and olanzapine) have demonstrated comparable—or better—efficacy with schizophrenic symptoms with significantly less risk of adverse neurological events; these drugs may be especially effective in treating the negative symptoms of schizophrenia	A number of Type 1 RCTs, with both placebo and active drug treatment comparisons	
	Behavior therapy and social learning/token economy programs helped structure, support, and reinforce prosocial behaviors in treatment refractory persons with schizophrenia; structured, educational family interventions helped maintain gains achieved with medication and customary case management; social skills training enabled persons with schizophrenia to acquire instrumental and affiliative skills to improve functioning in their communities	Five Type 1 RCTs and hundreds of Type 3 studies of behavior therapy and social learning/token economy programs; several Type 1 RCTs of educational family interventions; more than 40 Type 1 and Type 2 RCTs of social skills training	Kopelowicz & Liberman, chapter 9

Syndromes	Treatments	Standards of Proof	References
Schizotypal personality disorder (and other Cluster A disorders)	Dopamine antagonists may be useful in reducing some of the symptoms of these disorders	Two Type 1 and 2 Type 2 RCTs, and one Type 3 case study	Woo-Ming & Siever, chapter 28
Sexual dysfunctions	A variety of techniques, including those labelled as "Masters & Johnson," "neo-Masters & Johnson," and psychobiological have been reported to be useful for several of the categories of sexual dysfunction; some long-term follow-up studies have shown the positive sustained effect of therapy on individuals' and couples' subjective sense of sexual satisfaction	Few controlled trials have been reported, in part because of the methodological problems associated with evaluating the effects of these treatments	Segraves & Althof, chapter 23
Sleep disorders	The benzodiazepines and zolpidem typically reduced sleep onset by 15–30 minutes, decreased the number of awakenings to an absolute level of 1–3 per night, and increased total sleep time by about 15–45 minutes; these pharmacological agents act more reliably than behavioral interventions in the short-term	A large number of Type 1 and, especially, Type 2 RCTs, in comparison to placebo and a variety of pharmacological agents	Nowell, Buysse, Morin, Reynolds, & Kupfer, chapter 26
	Over the long-term, behavioral interventions, including stimulus control, sleep restriction, relaxation strategies, and cognitive behavioral therapy reduced sleep onset, decreased awakenings, and increased total sleep time; these behavioral interventions produced more sustained effects than pharmacological agents	A moderate number of Type 2 RCTs, in comparison to wait-list controls, partial behavioral interventions, and pharmacological agents	
Social phobia	Exposure-based procedures, which reduced or eliminated symptoms of the disorder, have been shown to be efficacious; other common treatment approaches to social phobia include social skills training, relaxation techniques, and multicomponent cognitive-behavioral treatments	A large number of Type 1 RCTs for exposure-based procedures; Type 2 RCTs and Type 3 case reports for the other common treatments	Barlow, Esler, & Vitali, chapter 15

Syndromes	Treatments	Standards of Proof	References
	Medications from three different drug families (an MAOI, benzodiazepine, and two SSRIs) have been shown to be effective in treating the symptoms of social phobia	Three Type 1 RCTs indicated that the monoamine oxidase inhibitor phenelzine relieved symptoms of social phobia; one Type 1 RCT found clonazepam, a benzodiazepine, to be superior to placebo in treating social phobia symptoms; two Type 1 RCTs suggested the effectiveness of fluvoxamine and sertraline, both of them SSRI's, for some aspects of the symptoms of social phobia	Roy-Byrne & Cowley, chapter 16
Somatoform pain disorder	Individual and group cognitive-behavior therapy reduced pain-related distress and disability	Several Type 2 RCTs	Simon, chapter 21
	Antidepressants decreased pain intensity	A large number of Type 1 and 2 placebo-controlled RCTs	
Specific phobias	Exposure-based procedures, particularly *in vivo* exposure, reduced or eliminated phobic behavior	A very large number of Type 1 RCTs	Barlow, Esler, & Vitali, chapter 15
Substance use disorders	In the treatment of nicotine addiction, nicotine gum and the nicotine patch assisted with smoking cessation	Five large-scale Type 1 RCTs and a comprehensive review of 17 additional studies	O'Brien & McKay, chapter 6
	Methadone treatment has proven to be an effective maintenance option following detoxification from opiates, especially when combined with psychosocial treatment designed to facilitate retention and compliance and address the many psychological and social problems that accompany addiction	A substantial number of Type 1 and Type 2 RCTs	

Syndromes	Treatments	Standards of Proof	References
Substance use disorders (*cont.*)	While naltrexone is also FDA-approved for the maintenance treatment of opiate addiction, it has been underutilized because it is more complicated to prescribe than methadone and most physicians have not been trained in its use	Several Type 1 and Type 2 RCTs	

A GUIDE TO TREATMENTS THAT WORK

1

Treatments That Work—and What Convinces Us They Do

Peter E. Nathan

Jack M. Gorman

The history of systematic efforts to identify empirically validated treatments for mental disorders is a short one. Only at midcentury, coincident with Eysenck's influential article, "The Effects of Psychotherapy: An Evaluation," was treatment research first subjected to rigorous methodological scrutiny in an effort to distinguish effective from ineffective mental health treatments. Since then, research designs increasingly capable of discriminating efficacious psychosocial and pharmacological treatments have been developed. Their development was facilitated by the publication in 1980 of a substantially more reliable diagnostic system, the *Diagnostic and Statistical Manual of Mental Disorders (DSM-III)*, accompanied by a series of structured diagnostic interviews that made it easier for treatment researchers to assemble diagnostically homogeneous patient groups. With Eysenck's 1952 article as a starting point, this chapter reviews several important efforts to distinguish empirically validated treatments over the past half century.

Practice guidelines, reflecting more potent outcome methodology and more effective treatments, have recently been proposed by both the American Psychiatric Association and the Division of Clinical Psychology of the American Psychological Association, as well as by the U.S. Agency for Health Care Policy and Research (AHCPR) and several managed care companies. The guidelines are controversial, however, because they are new and untested and because they have the potential to encroach on the clinical decision-making role that has traditionally been solely the treating clinician's. Differences in the standards of proof on which the practice guidelines rest are explored in the chapter; they stem from differences in the methodological criteria used to judge outcome studies, as well as the degree to which clinical experience and judgment are accorded emphasis.

These reviews of empirically validated treatments, practice guidelines, and standards of proof provide a helpful background to a succinct examination of the recommendations of the volume's chapter authors to determine the extent to which their views on *treatments that work* derive from accepted standards and fit into the evolving history of research on empirically validated treatments.

EMPIRICALLY VALIDATED TREATMENTS

The emphasis of this review of research on empirically validated treatments is on psychotherapy research, although some of the 50-year history we trace relates as well to research on the effectiveness of psychopharmacological treatments. However, the debates on whether and how to examine psychotherapy outcomes have been both fundamentally different from and a good deal more extensive than those in the history of psycho-pharmacology outcome research (in part because psychosocial researchers have had to wrestle with the unavailability of a true placebo control and the impossibility of a meaningful double blind). From the beginning of the modern era of psychopharmacology research (e.g., over the past four decades), most scientists recognized the necessity to submit new drugs to clinical trials using standard methodology, the most highly valued of which has become the prospectively randomized, double-blind, placebo control design (Klein & Davis, 1969).

Of course, debates on methodological issues also occupy a prominent position in the history of psychopharmacological research. Among the most pressing current issues are how well the blind has been maintained; whether patients who qualify for and agree to participate in clinical drug trials represent a highly selective sample, thereby yielding restricted information about clinical populations in general; and whether it is ethical to use placebos when drugs of known efficacy (e.g., antidepressants and antipsychotics) are available. Common to both psychosocial and psychopharmacological treatments are concerns about the failure of many clinicians to attend to the research evidence on empirically validated treatments (e.g., Wilson, 1996a, 1996b). Some of these issues, and others, are taken up by the authors of the volume's chapters on psychopharmacology.

Although our examination of efforts to identify empirically validated treatments could have begun before or after 1952 or with someone other than British psychologist Hans Eysenck, the impact of his review of psychotherapy effectiveness published that year was so marked—and his survey so far-reaching and prescient—that we have chosen to begin our own overview of this extensive literature with Eysenck's landmark critique of psychotherapy effectiveness. Another reason to begin with this paper is that the modern era of psychopharmacological treatment and research also began at about the same time with the discovery of the phenothiazines as breakthrough treatments for schizophrenia (Yamamoto & Meltzer, 1995).

"The Effects of Psychotherapy," Eysenck, 1952

Eysenck was not alone in questioning the effectiveness of psychotherapy for what were then called the neuroses; Landis (1937), Denker (1946), and Zubin (1953),

among others, raised similar concerns. Nonetheless, Eysenck's 1952 evaluation of the effects of psychotherapy, updated and extended in 1960 and 1969, was undoubtedly the most important single impetus to research in the outcomes of treatment that unfolded over the next 40 years.

A number of Eysenck's key observations in 1952 were derived from his reanalysis of data initially gathered and reported by Landis (1937) and Denker (1946) from 24 treatment studies of 7,000 treated patients. Of several notable conclusions in Eysenck's 1952 review, two stand out. Estimating the spontaneous remission rate of the neuroses as a benchmark against which to compare the effects of psychotherapy, Eysenck determined that "roughly two-thirds of a group of neurotic patients will recover or improve to a marked extent within about two years of the onset of their illness" (1952, p. 322). Although Bergin (1971) disputed the figure of two thirds, putting it closer to 30%, his critique of Eysenck's position on the spontaneous remission of the neuroses has been thoroughly criticized, most tellingly by Rachman and Wilson (1980).

Reanalyzing data from Landis (1937) and Denker (1946), Eysenck (1952) also provocatively calculated that "patients treated by means of psychoanalysis improved to the extent of 44%; patients treated eclectically improved to the extent of 64%; patients treated only custodially or by general practitioners improved to the extent of 72%. There thus appears to be an inverse correlation between recovery and psychotherapy" (1952, p. 322). Eysenck's controversial 1952 conclusion was elaborated in 1960 and 1969: the psychotherapies in widest use at midcentury were largely ineffective.

In response to his review's numerous critics, Eysenck acknowledged that the inadequate methodology of most of the treatment outcome studies of the time required him to qualify his most provocative conclusions, although he did not withhold them. Few of the treatment outcome studies Eysenck examined were controlled, making comparisons across studies extremely difficult. Moreover, the nature and severity of patients' illnesses were inadequately described, due in part to the low reliability of the *Diagnostic and Statistical Manual of Mental Disorders (DSM-I)* (1952); the length and specifics of the treatments provided tended to be insufficiently detailed; and treatment follow-up data were often skimpy and unidimensional. Nonetheless, Eysenck persisted in believing that his calculations, despite the shortcomings of their methodological base, consistently pointed in one direction: "They fail to prove that psychotherapy, Freudian or otherwise, facilitates the recovery of neurotic patients" (Eysenck, 1952, p. 323).

Reactions to Eysenck's review were predictable. The psychoanalysts and psychoanalytic psychotherapists who accounted for the majority of the psychotherapists of the time accused Eysenck of bias and misinterpretation of weak data and urged that his findings be consigned to oblivion (e.g., Rosenzweig, 1954; Sanford, 1953). Others (e.g., Malan, Bacal, Heath, & Balfour, 1968), however, weighed Eysenck's findings more objectively, accepting some conclusions, questioning others, and suggesting ways to build on what Eysenck had been the first to do.

In his 1960 reexamination of the psychotherapy outcome literature, Eysenck had access to data from better designed, better controlled studies. The most important were the Cambridge-Somerville delinquency prevention project (Powers & Witmer, 1951; Teuber & Powers, 1953), for its time a state-of-the-art prevention/treatment study, and Rogers and Dymond's (1954) investigation of the process and outcomes of nondirective therapy, which broke new ground by utilizing a double control group and multiple, newly developed outcome measures. Despite the substantial improvement in research methodology these and a handful of other contemporary studies represented, Eysenck's 1960 conclusions were strikingly similar to those he had reached eight years earlier.

Two major conclusions from the 1960 review stand out. The first reiterates the most controversial finding in Eysenck's 1952 review: "When untreated neurotic control groups are compared with experimental groups of neurotic patients treated by means of psychotherapy, both groups recover to approximately the same extent" (1960, p. 17). The second is the following prescient observation:

> With the single exception of psychotherapeutic methods based on learning theory, results of published research with military and civilian neurotics, and with both adults and children, suggest that the therapeutic effects of psychotherapy are small or non-existent, and do not in any demonstrable way add to the non-specific effects of routine medical treatment, or to such events as occur in patients' every-day experience. (Eysenck, 1960, p. 19)

Here Eysenck unsurprisingly reaffirmed his views on the ineffectiveness of psychotherapy. What is surprising in the quotation is Eysenck's recognition, at the very beginning of the behavioral revolution, of the potential of the evolving behavioral therapies both to lend themselves better to structured empirical examination and ultimately to yield better outcomes than the popular psychotherapies of the time. A number of this volume's chapters, written more than 35 years after Eysenck's 1960 review, bear out his prophecy.

"Evaluation of Psychological Therapies," American Psychopathological Association, 1973

Responses to Eysenck's reviews of psychotherapy outcomes varied from very positive and admiring to strongly negative to dismissive. The 1973 meeting of the American Psychopathological Association, "Evaluation of Psychological Therapies," represented one of the most curious of the latter reactions. Edited and published in 1976 by Spitzer and Klein, the proceedings of the meeting showcase current comparative studies of psychotherapy, behavior therapy, and drug therapy. Given its title and focus, it is surprising that the proceedings volume fails to reference any of Eysenck's three influential reviews of psychotherapy effectiveness. Nonetheless, the volume—and, presumably, the 1973 meeting it chronicles—reflect a number of the themes familiar to those conversant with Eysenck's critiques.

In the volume's foreword, Max Fink, president of the American Psychopathological Association in 1973, noted that "despite a popular acceptance of psychiatric therapy, there remains a gnawing professional suspicion that treatment methods leave much to be desired, with neither the process well defined nor the outcome assured. . . . For the psychological therapies, the observers noted that little outcome data were available, much of it uncontrolled" (Fink, 1976, p. xi). Aside from his euphemistic reference to "a gnawing professional suspicion" that psychotherapy outcomes in the mid-1970s were not terribly encouraging, Fink's assessment of the data on psychotherapy outcomes in 1976 differs little from Eysenck's in 1952.

With a nod to Lewis Carroll's dodo bird, the volume's lead paper (Luborsky, Singer, & Luborsky, 1976) is titled, "Comparative Studies of Psychotherapies: Is It True That 'Everyone Has Won and All Must Have Prizes?'" The central premise of this review, modified from both a journal article published a year earlier (Luborsky, Singer, & Luborsky, 1975) and a paper given at the 1973 American Psychopathological Association meeting, echoes a familiar theme—that more adequate research methodologies for examining, weighing, and comparing treatment efficacy must be developed before an unencumbered picture of psychotherapy effectiveness is possible:

> Our title implies what I think many of us believe— that all psychotherapies produce some benefits for some patients. What we do not know is whether there are psychotherapies which produce significantly better results and whether certain psychotherapies are especially well suited to certain patients. (Luborsky et al., 1976, p. 3)

Luborsky and his colleagues compared outcomes from group versus individual psychotherapy, time-limited versus open-ended psychotherapy, and client-centered versus other traditional psychotherapies, concluding that "most comparative studies of different forms of psychotherapy found insignificant differences in proportions of patients who improved by the end of psychotherapy" (1976, p. 12). Utilizing a system for grading methodological adequacy extending from A ("the main principles of research design were satisfied") to E ("the deficiencies were so serious that the results were not worth considering and the study therefore was not included"), Luborsky and his colleagues reviewed "only studies in which some attention was paid to the main requirements of controlled comparative research." Those requirements included many of the design elements we expect today, including random assignment of subjects, suitable controls, and blind outcome assessment. Missing were current expectations that the form of treatment be carefully specified and monitored, preferably by treatment manual, that follow-up be appropriately extended, and that follow-up assessments focus on specific rather than more general behaviors.

The 1976 proceedings volume contains additional discussions of methodological issues associated with treatment outcome research; Kernberg (1976) reported on the Menninger Foundation's Psychotherapy Research Project and Wilson (1976) examined research on outcomes of behavior therapy with alcoholics. The members of the American Psychopathological Association who attended the 1973 annual meeting should certainly have understood the importance of improvements in the methodology of therapy outcome research; roughly 20 years after Eysenck's initial plea

for better outcome studies and about 20 years before publication of this volume, the methodology of therapy effectiveness studies had clearly begun to receive center-stage attention.

"Meta-Analysis of Psychotherapy Outcome Studies," Smith and Glass, 1977

A year after Luborsky and his colleagues published their review, Smith and Glass (1977) reported on the use of a new statistical procedure, called meta-analysis, to determine the effectiveness of psychotherapy independently from the methodological shortcomings that burdened many of the therapy outcome studies of the time. Despite the seeming advantages of their controversial new method, Smith and Glass concluded, as had Luborsky and his colleagues, that while psychotherapy is generally effective, it is not possible to differentiate among therapies in effectiveness.

Smith and Glass's 1977 meta-analysis integrated the findings of independent studies to determine an overall "effect size" for each outcome measure; effect size was defined as the mean difference between treated and control subjects divided by the standard deviation of the control group. The 833 effect sizes Smith and Glass examined as dependent variables were derived from the outcome measures in the studies they analyzed. Also, 16 variables descriptive of each study were considered independent variables; they included the type of therapy, its duration, and whether it was group or individual; the professional identity and experience level of the therapists; the age, IQ, and diagnosis of patients; and the reactivity of outcome measures and internal validity of the study's research design.

Smith and Glass calculated that "the average study showed a .68 standard deviation superiority of the treated group over the control group" (1977, p. 756), which convinced them that psychotherapy works, especially when they extrapolated the finding to signify that the average patient in the studies they reviewed achieved a better outcome than 75% of untreated controls. Of 10 types of therapy evaluated, Smith and Glass reported that the average effect size for systematic desensitization was highest, at .90, followed by rational-emotive therapy at .77, and behavior modification at .76. Client-centered therapy achieved an effect size of .63, while the effect size for psychodynamic therapy was .59. After some additional calculations designed to reduce the 10 therapies to 2 superclasses, the authors concluded that, despite the apparent difference in effect size among them, they could not distinguish among the 10, or even between the 2 superclasses, in effectiveness. Thus, even though the effect size differences Smith and Glass computed suggested that behavioral treatments yielded best outcomes (as Eysenck had anticipated 25 years earlier), they did not report that conclusion.

Smith and Glass's 1977 meta-analysis received a great deal of attention. Praised for its very substantial sample size and an innovative statistical methodology that appeared capable of both overlooking the methodological shortcomings of contemporary therapy outcome studies and reducing qualitative judgments to quantitative ones, their meta-analysis method was also roundly criticized. Among the most telling was Cooper's (1979), which lamented the conceptual and methodological spread of the almost 400 studies Smith and Glass included in their analysis, as well as the method's bias potential at this early stage in its development. Rachman and Wilson (1980) took strong exception to Smith and Glass' uncritical acceptance of the flawed methodology of many of the studies they included in their analysis; their agreement, despite apparently insufficient evidence, with Luborsky, Singer, and Luborsky's (1976) positive views on the general effects of psychotherapy; and their unexplained failure to include some of the best-designed behavior therapy outcome studies of the early 1970s in their analysis.

The 1977 meta-analysis of Smith and Glass, like more recent efforts to apply meta-analysis to the study of therapy outcomes, remains controversial. Nonetheless, their effort almost certainly helped accelerate the development of better designs for outcome studies, as well as better statistical means to evaluate them.

Diagnostic and Statistical Manual of Mental Disorders, Third Edition

The 1980 publication of *DSM-III* marked a breakthrough of considerable magnitude in efforts to heighten the reliability and validity of syndromal diagnosis. In format, as well as in the empirical base on which much of it was developed, *DSM-III* constituted a marked advance over its 1952 and 1968 predecessors. According to Robert Spitzer (American Psychiatric Association [APA], 1980), principal architect of *DSM-III*, one of the principal goals for the new instrument was to enhance the diagnostic homogeneity of patient groups in treatment outcome studies.

The roots of *DSM-III*'s advances lay, in part, in the research, which began in the late 1960s, on syndromal diagnostic processes by Spitzer and his colleagues at the New York State Psychiatric Institute. Their studies led to the development of a series of structured diagnostic interviews capable of gathering the exhaustive data on signs and symptoms on which an empirically based nomenclature could be built. These instruments included the Mental Status Schedule (Spitzer, Fleiss, Endicott, & Cohen, 1967) and the Psychiatric Status Schedule (Spitzer, Endicott, Fleiss, & Cohen, 1970).

Along with many others interested in more systematic approaches to diagnosis, Spitzer was impressed by a paper published by researchers at Washington University in St. Louis (Feighner et al., 1972) that proposed explicit criteria for the 16 major diagnostic categories for which the Washington University group felt sufficient empirical data had been assembled to ensure validity. The intent of the paper of the Feighner group was to substitute more precise, formally organized diagnostic criteria for the vague and nonspecific admixture of signs and symptoms condensed in *DSM-I* and *DSM-II*. The format of these criteria both anticipated and heavily influenced the format for diagnostic criteria adopted by the drafters of *DSM-III*.

Publication of the criteria of Feighner et al. in 1972 was followed in 1975 by the Research Diagnostic Criteria (RDC) (Spitzer, Endicott, & Robins, 1975), designed to allow empirical testing of the assumptions of the criteria, including their superior reliability. Not surprisingly in view of their prescriptive format, the reliability of the RDC proved to be substantially greater than that for diagnoses from the 1968 *DSM-II* (Helzer, Clayton, et al., 1977; Helzer, Robins, et al., 1977), thereby anticipating the heightened reliability of the *DSM-III* diagnostic criteria. The development of the RDC also brought an explosion of research through the rest of the decade of the 1970s into the signs and symptoms of the 16 RDC syndromes, thereby preparing the way for a more empirically based *DSM-III*.

The *DSM-III* operational criteria, which benefited greatly from the 1970s research on the RDC, represent the instrument's most far-reaching departure from its predecessors. Modeled closely after the RDC, the operational criteria organized each syndrome's associated signs and symptoms within a format designed to induce each clinician to approach the diagnosis of that syndrome in precisely the same way, defining each sign and symptom consistently and processing the resultant diagnostic information uniformly. As most of the studies of the diagnostic reliability of *DSM-III* have demonstrated, the reliability of its diagnoses did improve, albeit selectively.

Another result of the *DSM-III* developmental process of special relevance to treatment outcome research was the creation of several structured and semistructured diagnostic interviews. The best known of these instruments is the National Institute of Mental Health (NIMH) Diagnostic Interview Schedule (DIS) (Robins, Helzer, Croughan, & Ratcliff, 1981), which can be administered reliably by nonclinician interviewers and scored by computer. Test-retest studies of the DIS (Helzer et al., 1985; Robins et al., 1981; Robins, Helzer, Ratcliff, & Seyfried, 1982) showed that interrater agreement was quite good for alcohol abuse/dependence and major depression, adequate for schizophrenia, and poor for panic disorder. The Structured Clinical Interview for DSM-III (SCID) (Spitzer, 1983; Spitzer & Williams, 1986), also based on the *DSM-III*, was developed around the same time.

The first direct tests of the interrater reliability of *DSM-III* diagnostic criteria took place during the *DSM-III* field trials conducted in the late 1970s (Hyler, Williams, & Spitzer, 1982; Spitzer, Forman, & Nee, 1979; Williams & Spitzer, 1980). Volunteer clinicians working in pairs used the draft criteria to evaluate new patients. Results from two large field trials indicated that reliability was improved over that of the instrument's predecessors, with overall *kappa* values of 0.68 and 0.72 for chance-correct agreement on Axis I disorders. The reliability of diagnoses for substance use disorder, schizophrenia, and organic mental disorder was significantly higher than that for the adjustment and anxiety disorders.

The reliability of draft criteria for disorders of childhood and adolescence, traditionally troublesome, were also examined during this time. Their reliability turned out to be somewhat disappointing, in part due to diagnosticians' unfamiliarity with the new system (Cantwell, Russell, Mattison, & Will, 1979; Mattison, Cantwell, Russell & Will, 1979). However, reliability studies utilizing translations of semistructured research interviews based on *DSM-III* diagnostic criteria in Norway (Larsen & Vaglum, 1986) and Japan (Hanada & Takahashi, 1983) yielded reliability estimates comparable to those of the U.S. field trials.

Reliability studies of *DSM-III* (and its successors *DSM-III-R* and *DSM-IV*) have continued. They continue to show that these instruments produce greater diagnostic stability over time and greater interclinician agreement than their predecessors, especially for such diagnostic categories as schizophrenia, bipolar disorder, major depression, and substance abuse. However, the reliability of a few other diagnoses, notably the personality disorders, some of the disorders of childhood and adolescence, and some of the anxiety disorders, remains significantly less encouraging.

The Effects of Psychological Therapy, 2nd Edition, Rachman and Wilson, 1980

Rachman and Wilson's *The Effects of Psychological Therapy* (1980) provides a comprehensive, well-informed evaluation of the research literature on psychotherapy outcomes published during the decades of the 1950s, 1960s, and 1970s. The volume evaluates, in depth and often on a study-by-study basis, much of the available outcome literature on the effects of psychoanalytic treatment, Rogerian psychotherapy, psychotherapy with psychotic patients, behavior therapy, and cognitive behavior therapy.

Summarizing this substantial literature but emphasizing research completed during the 1970s (following the first edition of the book; Rachman, 1971), Rachman and Wilson concluded their effort with a distinctly underwhelming assessment of the effectiveness of psychotherapy circa 1980:

> Since the First Edition was published (in 1971), some slight progress has been made in the attempt to produce evidence to support the claims made on behalf of psychotherapy in general. . . . Nevertheless, it is our view that modest evidence now supports the claim that psychotherapy is capable of producing some beneficial changes—but the negative results still outnumber the positive findings, and both of these are exceeded by reports that are beyond interpretation. (Rachman & Wilson, 1980, p. 259)

In other words, after agreeing, in the first edition of their book, with Eysenck's earlier judgments that psychotherapy had not been shown to be effective in the 1950s and 1960s, in 1980 Rachman and Wilson concluded that the improved methodology of outcome research in the 1970s, coupled with advances in behavioral treatment methods, give reason for guarded optimism.

Rachman and Wilson (1980) cited two reasons for their positive stance on behavior therapy, present and future:

1. The roots of much behavior therapy were in the experimental psychology laboratory. As a result, by 1980 behavioral treatment had fostered the development of a variety of empirically based therapy outcome tools:

> A significant contribution of behaviour therapy has been the development of innovative research strategies for the study of treatment outcome. These methodological strategies range from single-case experimental designs to a variety of different group designs, including highly controlled laboratory-based investigations, more applied evaluations of multifaceted therapy programmes, and improved comparative outcome studies. (p. 262)

2. The data on outcomes of behavior therapy for several conditions had become quite encouraging by 1980:

> It can safely be said that there are well-established methods for reducing anxieties and fears of various sorts, good progress has been made in establishing an equally powerful method for dealing with obsessions and compulsions, and significant advances have been made in dealing with some sexual dysfunctions. (p. 261)

On the issue of cognitive behavior therapy, by 1980 a promising but largely unproven therapeutic approach, Rachman and Wilson said the following:

> We firmly expect cognitive behaviour therapy to develop into a valuable and interesting addition to the methods for assisting people in difficulty, but hope that vigorous attempts will be made to avoid making the same unnecessary assumptions that interfered with the progress of behaviour therapy itself. (1980, p. 261)

On the future of cognitive behavior therapy, as several chapters of this volume confirm, Rachman and Wilson appear to have been remarkably prophetic.

Special Issue of the *American Psychologist* on Psychotherapy Outcome Research, 1986

Several articles in an early 1986 special issue of the *American Psychologist* on psychotherapy outcome research focused on familiar themes. Howard and his colleagues reported on a detailed analysis of a group of outcome studies (in a successful effort to quantify a dose-effect relationship) (Howard, Kopta, Krause, & Orlinsky, 1986), while Stiles, Shapiro, and Elliott weighed the methodological adequacy of contemporary outcome studies (finding it wanting). New issues, some of them presaging present-day concerns, were also addressed, including ethical issues in psychotherapy research (Imber et al., 1986) and the growing diversity in the uses to which research on psychotherapy outcomes was being put (Cohen, Sargent, & Sechrest, 1986; Morrow-Bradley & Elliott, 1986; Newman & Howard, 1986).

Referring to "a growing consensus in the psychotherapy research literature that psychotherapeutic treatment is generally beneficial to patients," Howard et al. (1986, p. 159) observed that the same literature, some of it their own, suggested that the amount of therapeutic benefit is positively associated with the amount of treatment. However, "to date, there has been no systematic attempt to specify the mathematical form of this dose-effect relationship or to determine its accuracy." Confirming this relationship would constitute strong additional evidence for the efficacy of psychotherapy. Selecting the therapy session as the dose unit and the percentage of patients improved as the effect, Howard and his colleagues undertook a "probit analysis" of 15 diverse therapy outcome studies. As a consequence, they reported that

> 10% to 18% of patients could be expected to have shown some improvement after the first session of psychotherapy . . . by eight sessions, 48% to 58% of patients would be expected to have measurably improved . . . [and] about 75% of patients should have shown measurable improvements by the end of six months of once-weekly psychotherapy. (Howard et al., 1986, p. 162)

While the confound of time with number of sessions and an exclusive reliance on global ratings of improvement by therapists and patients detract from the impact of these findings, the quantitative determination by Howard and his colleagues of a dose-effect relationship for psychotherapy, as it had previously been demonstrated for pharmacological treatment, constituted a strong empirical voice of support for psychotherapy more than a decade ago.

The title of Stiles, Shapiro, and Elliott's 1986 article, "Are All Psychotherapies Equivalent?" intentionally echoes the title of the important review, "Comparative Studies of Psychotherapies: Is It True That 'Everybody Has Won and All Must Have Prizes'?" by Luborsky and his colleagues (1975, 1976). Starting from the premise that the data to date still "appear to support the conclusion that outcomes of diverse therapies are generally similar," Stiles and his colleagues proceeded to explore some possible determinants of the paradox: "the lack of differential effectiveness contrasted with evident technical diversity; that is, outcome equivalence contrasted with content nonequivalence" (1986, p. 165). Although Stiles and his colleagues suggested several changes in the design of outcome studies (a few of which, like manualization of treatments and provision for multiple outcome measures, are now routine) to resolve the paradox of "outcome equivalence contrasted with content nonequivalence," those suggestions are not our prime concern here.

Instead, we want to point out that little more than a decade ago prominent clinical scientists were still debating, as they had since shortly after Eysenck's initial review of psychotherapy effectiveness in 1952, the continuing failure of their efforts to differentiate effective from ineffective treatments for specific disorders (even though, six years earlier in 1980, Rachman and Wilson marshalled strong evidence pointing to the superiority of behavior therapy for several common syndromes).

The 1995 *Consumer Reports* Survey of Psychotherapy: "Mental Health: Does Therapy Help?"

In 1994, the 180,000 subscribers to *Consumer Reports* were asked, in the largest survey to date of psychotherapy outcomes, to respond to a series of questions about their experiences with mental health professionals, physicians, medications, and self-help groups (*Consumer Reports* Editors, 1995). Responses were received from 7,000 readers of the magazine, detailing information about the persons from whom they sought help for emotional problems. Of the 7,000, about 3,000 had talked only to friends, family, or clergy; 4,100 had sought out a combination of mental health professionals, family doctors, and self-help groups. Of this group, 2,900 saw a mental health professional, 1,300 joined a self-help group, and 1,000 spoke to family doctors; some, clearly, sought help from more than one source. Of those who consulted a mental health professional, 37% saw a psychologist, 22% a

psychiatrist, 14% a social worker, and 9% a marriage counselor.

While the representativeness of the readership of *Consumer Reports* can be questioned (subscribers are older and better educated than Americans overall and may well be different in other ways as well), the 4,100 questionnaire respondents who sought help from mental health professionals, family doctors, and self-help groups were in clear emotional need: 43% admitted they were in a "very poor" ("I barely managed to deal with things") or "fairly poor" ("Life was usually pretty tough") emotional state when they sought help.

A mail survey of matters of this sensitivity and complexity, a substantially undefined and essentially undiagnosed group of respondents, and outcome questions that focused on generalized "improvement" rather than specific outcomes targeted to symptoms all raise concerns about this survey. Most troubling is the very low response rate to the mailed questionnaire, discussed below. Nonetheless, as the largest and most comprehensive inquiry into the results of psychotherapy ever reported, its findings deserve consideration.

The authors of the survey portrayed its principal findings as follows:

- Level of satisfaction with therapy was equivalent whether respondents saw a social worker, psychologist, or psychiatrist; those who saw a marriage counselor, however, were somewhat less likely to report having benefited from therapy.
- Respondents who sought therapy from a family doctor reported doing well, but those who saw a mental health professional for more than 6 months reported doing much better.
- Psychotherapy alone worked as well as combined psychotherapy and pharmacotherapy; while most persons who took prescribed medication found it helpful, many reported side effects.
- The longer psychotherapy lasted, the more it helped.
- Respondents who had tried self-help groups, especially Alcoholics Anonymous, felt especially good about the experience. (*Consumer Reports* Editors, 1995, p. 734)

As we indicated above, the *Consumer Reports* survey had some important limitations that cause us to question the validity of these findings. One of the most important was the absence of an untreated control group. This meant that respondents who reported having benefited from treatment (44% of those whose emotional state was "very poor" when treatment began reported feeling good after treatment, while 43% who felt "fairly poor" when therapy started also improved, though to a lesser extent) could simply have experienced a spontaneous remission of their symptoms with the passage of time, rather than as a result of psychotherapy. The issue of spontaneous remission, raised by Eysenck in 1952, necessitates the provision for untreated or waiting-list controls in studies of therapy.

The study's principal shortcoming, however, was its minimal response rate: 4,100 respondents from the 180,000 subscribers to the magazine to whom the survey was sent reported seeking professional help or joining groups; only 2,900 reported actually consulting a mental health professional. These numbers are low enough to raise the question of whether substantially more subscribers who had benefited from psychotherapy chose to respond to the questionnaire than those who did not, thereby skewing the findings in a positive direction. In the absence of data on the universe of *Consumer Reports* subscribers who sought professional help for their emotional problems, this serious design problem cannot be dismissed.

Given the *Consumer Reports* survey's substantial methodological shortcomings, our enthusiasm for its findings are distinctly restrained, although we can take some satisfaction from the finding that most of the subscribers who completed the survey found psychotherapy helpful.

While Martin Seligman (1995), a consultant to the project, acknowledged the gap between its methodology and that of other contemporary psychotherapy outcome studies, he nonetheless concluded that the *Consumer Reports* survey "complements the [more traditional] efficacy method, and that the best features of these two methods can be combined into a more ideal method that will best provide empirical validation of psychotherapy" (p. 965). Seligman urged his readers to appreciate the difference between *efficacy* studies, the traditional "gold standard" for judging psychotherapy outcomes, and *effectiveness* studies, feasibility and clinical utility in the real world, as epitomized by the *Consumer Reports* survey. The distinction between efficacy and effectiveness studies of psychotherapy is also considered in a recent article (Clarke, 1995) and elaborated in the *Template for Developing Guidelines* (American Psychological Association Task Force, 1995), reviewed below.

If efficacy studies show us only part of the psychotherapy elephant, it seems clear that effectiveness studies show us only another part. And while it seems likely that the two together reveal more about the outcomes of psychotherapy than either does separately, we must determine how to integrate the two — and that lesson will only be learned over time and with data from additional studies. It is clearly important, of course, that future effectiveness studies address the serious methodological problems that prevent us from according the *Consumer Reports* study more credence.

A Guide to Treatments That Work, Nathan and Gorman (Editors), 1998

The chapters of A *Guide to Treatments That Work*, their contents summarized in the front of the book, offer impressive testimony to gains made, in many instances in the last decade, in the number of effective treatments for an ever-broader range of the *DSM-IV* disorders. From a handful of somatic treatments for schizophrenia of questionable efficacy at midcentury, all with devastating side effects, this volume's chapters on pharmacological treatments reflect the availability today of safer and more effective drug treatments for the most common and disabling psychoses. Just as noteworthy is that a number of the "neuroses," conditions for which Eysenck despaired the lack of effective treatment more than 40 years ago, can now be treated, with good to excellent outcomes, by pharmacotherapy, often in combined treatment regimens with psychosocial treatments.

The contents of this volume confirm the even greater changes that characterize the psychosocial treatment domain. In 1952, Eysenck could find no evidence of psychotherapy's effectiveness. Now, as a number of our chapters document, psychosocial treatments, many of them cognitive behavioral, have shown clear efficacy for a range of diverse conditions. Moreover, and in many ways just as significant, psychosocial treatments have now been linked with pharmacological treatments in combined regimens that often demonstrate greater therapeutic effectiveness than either treatment by itself.

Empirically Validated Treatments: Summary and Conclusions

More than 40 years separate Eysenck's landmark 1952 paper, "The Effects of Psychotherapy," from this volume. Over that time, Eysenck's negative assessment of both the effects of psychotherapy and the informational value of research on psychotherapy outcomes has given way increasingly to positive evaluations of both psychotherapy outcomes and the methodological rigor of the outcome studies on which these evaluations are based. In like fashion, the field has also moved away from the judgment that all psychotherapies are equally effective. Today, as the contents of this volume suggest, we are closer than ever to being able to specify which psychotherapy delivered by which psychotherapist is most effective for which person in which treatment setting. While much progress remains to be made in outcome methodology and further elaboration of both efficacy and effectiveness, a great deal has already been made.

As the next section of this chapter suggests, these substantial advances have led to an outcome that Eysenck could not have anticipated: the controversial development of practice guidelines, the multiple potential uses of which are now as hotly debated as psychotherapy effectiveness only a few years ago.

PRACTICE GUIDELINES

As greater numbers of empirically validated treatments have been identified, pressures on providers of psychological and psychiatric services to use them have grown. Giving impetus to this development is the dramatic growth in recent years of managed care, which demands proof of efficacy whenever possible in return for payment for services (Pallack, 1995). As a consequence, practice guidelines that prescribe validated treatments have begun to appear, for the most part within the past 5 years. Created to meet a variety of needs and, accordingly, taking a variety of forms, virtually all practice guidelines nonetheless have a common goal: detailed specification of methods and procedures to ensure effective treatment for each disorder.

This section of the chapter reviews recently developed practice guidelines to illustrate one of the most important emerging contemporary uses of empirically validated treatments. The section examines in greatest detail the practice guidelines developed by two groups of mental health professionals, psychiatrists and clinical psychologists, in order to identify significant similarities and differences, especially in the standards of proof that lead a treatment to be included among other validated treatments.

National Institutes of Health Consensus Statement on Diagnosis and Treatment of Depression in Late Life, 1991

The *National Institutes of Health (NIH) Consensus Statement on the Diagnosis and Treatment of Depres-*

sion in Late Life (National Institutes of Health, 1991), written from an NIH-sponsored conference held in late 1991, represents one of the first practice guidelines for mental disorders. The NIH conference from which this 22-page pamphlet emerged was held in recognition of the frequent underdiagnosis and mistreatment of depression in late life. While the *Consensus Statement*'s brevity prevents it from detailing specific diagnostic approaches and elaborating on effective treatments for these vexing, multifaceted disorders, the document does summarize the principal diagnostic criteria by which these conditions can be differentiated from similar physical and psychological conditions, as well as the treatments for them that have been shown to be effective.

While this short document contains insufficient detail to aid clinicians unfamiliar with the diagnosis or treatment of depression in late life, it summarizes diagnostic and treatment standards in sufficient detail to permit evaluation of the appropriateness of care provided by a given clinician to a given patient. Perhaps its greatest value, though, comes from its precursor role in the development of the two subsequent, substantially more elaborate American Psychiatric Association practice guidelines dealing with major depressive disorder in adults and bipolar disorder.

American Psychiatric Association's *Practice Guidelines*, 1993, 1994, and 1995

Essentially identical prefaces introduce the *Practice Guideline for Major Depressive Disorders in Adults* (APA, 1993), *Practice Guideline for Treatment of Patients with Bipolar Disorder* (APA, 1994b), and *Practice Guideline for the Treatment of Patients with Substance Use Disorders: Alcohol, Cocaine, Opioids* (1995). The prefaces, "Statements of Intent," disavow any intention "to be construed or to serve as a standard of medical care" since "standards of medical care are determined on the basis of all clinical data available for an individual case and are subject to change as scientific knowledge and technological advance and patterns evolve" (APA, 1993, p. v; APA, 1994b, p. iv; APA, 1995, p. 4).

In other words, despite their hard-won empirical roots, these practice guidelines are to be considered suggestive rather than prescriptive. While reflecting the realities of clinical practice and the need for clinical flexibility depending on the patient's needs, this affirmation is also clearly designed to discourage use of the guidelines to monitor or restrict clinicians' clinical decision making when doing so is not in the best interests of their patients. This ambiguity in the role of practice guidelines—when are they suggestive rather than prescriptive and when, if ever, are they prescriptive rather than suggestive?—remains an unresolved issue, both for those who consult practice guidelines and those who develop them (Grady, 1995; Persons, 1995).

All three documents are lengthy. The *Guideline for Major Depressive Disorders in Adults* (APA, 1993) totals 26 pages, including almost 4 pages of references. The bipolar disorder practice guideline (APA, 1994b) totals 36 pages, including 6 pages of references. And the alcohol, cocaine, and opioids practice guideline (APA, 1995) is longest of all; it totals 59 pages and includes 481 references that require more than 10 pages to list.

Each guideline follows the same format: a brief section detailing disease definition, epidemiology, and natural history, followed by a lengthy section on treatment principles and alternatives, and concluding with a summary of research directions. A concise summary of recommendations accompanies each guideline.

The treatment principles and alternatives sections, key for most clinicians, are succinct, yet comprehensive. As an example, in the guideline for alcohol-related disorders, this section begins by considering the issue of choice of treatment setting; it provides empirical indications for in-or outpatient treatment, as well as the data on relationships between intensity of treatment and treatment outcomes. A consideration of pharmacological treatments for alcohol dependence and abuse follows; the empirical research on the efficacy of naltrexone, disulfiram (Antabuse), lithium, and the antidepressants is presented. The psychosocial treatment section next reviews outcome data from a broad array of alternative treatments, including cognitive-behavior therapy, behavior therapy, psychodynamic/interpersonal therapy, brief interventions, marital and family therapy, group therapy, aftercare, and self-help groups. A concluding section—clinical features influencing treatment—covers management of intoxication, management of withdrawal, comorbid psychiatric and general medical disorders, pregnancy, and the elderly. The coverage is comprehensive but telegraphic; the most convincing, methodologically sound studies are cited, and the coverage is generally balanced. While not adventuresome and, hence, generally conservative, the guidelines take an informed, contemporary view of the data on the most important

issues affecting treatment for the alcohol-related disorders.

The successive sets of practice guidelines that follow describe differing standards of proof and prescribe differing degrees of clinical decision making:

> Major review articles and standard psychiatric texts were consulted. Review articles and relevant prospective randomized clinical trials were reviewed in their entirety; other studies were selected for review on the basis of their relevance to the particular issues discussed in this guideline. Definitive standards are difficult to achieve, except in narrow circumstances where multiple replicated studies and wide clinical opinion dictate certain forms of treatment. In other areas much is left to the clinical judgment and expertise of the clinician. (APA, 1993, p. 1)

> Papers selected from these searches for further review included those published in English in peer-reviewed journals. Preference was given to those articles based on randomized, placebo-controlled clinical trials. Clinical reports involving descriptions of patients or groups of patients were reviewed when data from controlled trials were not available. Review articles, especially those published in well-regarded peer-reviewed journals, and book chapters were reviewed. (APA, 1994b, p. 1)

> The degree of specificity of recommendations in this guideline depends on the quality of available research and the degree of consensus among expert clinicians. By providing guidance in choosing among available treatment options and making specific recommendations whenever possible, the guideline reflects the variability in the availability of relevant research data and in the extent of clinical consensus. (APA, 1995, p. 5)

The greater qualification of the literature in the 1995 excerpt may reflect the greater number of empirically validated pharmacological and combined treatments for patients with major depressive disorder and bipolar disorder than for substance-abusing patients, although it is also possible that experience with the first two practice guidelines may have led the drafters of the third to be more cautious in emphasizing the primacy of empirical data as the dominant guide to practice.

Each guideline employs the same system for coding "categories of endorsement" that, for the most part, reflect on the methodological adequacy of the relevant empirical literature:

Each recommendation is identified as falling into one of three categories of endorsement, by a bracketed Roman numeral following the statement. The three categories represent varying levels of clinical confidence regarding the efficacy of the treatment for the disorder and conditions described. [I] indicates recommended with substantial clinical confidence; [II] indicates recommended with moderate clinical confidence; [III] indicates options that may be recommended on the basis of individual circumstances. (APA, 1993, p. 19)

Many alternative treatments are briefly described and evaluated in the guidelines. Efforts are made to weigh the cumulative evidence supporting the efficacy of each, although phrases such as "there is some evidence in controlled studies that treatment A is effective in reducing symptoms of X" and "research suggests that therapy B may reduce Y symptoms and the risk of relapse" make it difficult to know just how strongly a treatment has been supported by the empirical research. In contrast, the guidelines leave little doubt when they note that "therapy C has a high rate of therapeutic success, relative speed in inducing improvement in Z symptoms, and an excellent safety profile."

Persons, Thase, and Crits-Christoph (1996) recently published a combined evaluation of the 1993 American Psychiatric Association practice guideline for the treatment of major depression and the 1993 Agency for Health Care Policy and Research (AHCPR) practice guideline for the same syndrome. They concluded that while the APA guideline represents a laudable initial effort, it "understates the value of cognitive, behavioral, brief psychodynamic, and group therapies" (p. 283). Persons and her coworkers also wrote that "both guidelines understate the value of psychotherapy alone in the treatment of more severely depressed outpatients" and that the APA guideline "overvalues the role of combined psychotherapy-pharmacotherapy regimens . . . and makes recommendations about choosing among psychotherapies that are not well supported by empirical evidence" (p. 283). According to Persons and her colleagues, the principal reason for the APA guidelines' understatement of the value of the several psychosocial treatments is that "the AHCPR took a more empirical approach to its task than did the APA" (p. 288) (the AHCPR guidelines' assessment of the same treatments is a good deal more positive). Many have expressed similar concerns about all three of the APA guidelines, feeling that the weight given "clinical experience" and "clinical judgment" in them has the distinct potential to focus attention away from the weight of the empirical research, especially for the psychosocial treatments.

McIntyre, Zarin, and Pincus (1996), Rush (1996), Merriam and Karasu (1996), and Kocsis (1996) made a number of points in rebuttal, including that empirical data alone are insufficient to make judgments of this complexity; that the APA practice guideline is not a prescriptive standard of care; that the AHCPR guideline is intended for an audience of primary care physicians, who are substantially less knowledgable about the treatment of depression than the largely psychiatric audience for the APA guideline; and that treatment cost, which Persons and colleagues (1996) felt was inadequately weighted in the APA guideline, was appropriately underemphasized by the panel that wrote the APA guideline. This airing of these issues will not be the last time they are considered in the context of practice guidelines.

Could a neophyte clinician successfully treat alcohol, cocaine, or heroin dependence by attentively following the 1995 APA guideline for alcohol-related disorders? Probably not, because the nuances of clinical judgment required for the effective delivery of both psychosocial and psychopharmacological treatments are not—and cannot be—detailed in these few pages. Among the most important of these judgments are which treatment or treatments to choose initially and how long to utilize it or them before turning to alternate approaches. In contrast, the APA guideline for treatment of bipolar disorder (1994b), which emphasizes psychopharmacological treatment, would be a more effective treatment guide for the neophyte clinician.

To what extent would the APA practice guidelines permit a professional association's committee on practice standards—or a managed care organization—to judge the standard of care provided a given patient by a given clinician? Despite each guideline's prefatory statement that differences among patients require detailed knowledge of each patient's needs before a treatment plan is developed, each of the guidelines does endorse several treatments, most of them empirically validated. Substantial deviations from the guidelines' prescriptions would certainly require explanation and justification, so, like it or not, these prescriptive guidelines do establish a standard of practice from which most clinicians would likely prefer not to stray too markedly.

"Training In and Dissemination of Empirically Validated Psychological Treatments: Report and Recommendations," Division 12 Task Force, 1995

A task force of the Division of Clinical Psychology of the American Psychological Association recently published "Training In and Dissemination of Empirically Validated Psychological Treatments: Report and Recommendations" (Division 12 Task Force, 1995). While the task force was "to consider methods for educating clinical psychologists, third party payors, and the public about effective psychotherapies" (p. 3), its report and recommendations actually constitute a condensed, preliminary set of empirically validated psychosocial treatment guidelines.

Although the task force believed from the outset of its efforts that "from a research perspective, no treatment is ever fully validated," the empirical data it reviewed led it to propose three categories of treatment efficacy: well-established treatments, probably efficacious treatments, and experimental treatments (defined as treatments that have not yet been established as at least probably efficacious). The group used the criteria shown in Tables 1.1 and 1.2 to allocate treatments to the first two categories.

The task force identified 22 "well-established treatments" for 21 different *DSM-IV* syndromes; 7 "probably efficacious" treatments for the same number of

TABLE 1.1 Criteria for Empirically Validated Treatments: Well-Established Treatments

---

I. At least two good group design studies, conducted by different investigators, demonstrating efficacy in one or more of the following ways:
  A. Superior to pill or psychological placebo or to another treatment.
  B. Equivalent to an already established treatment in studies with adequate statistical power.

Or

II. A large series of single-case design studies demonstrating efficacy. These studies must have
  A. Used good experimental designs.
  B. Compared the intervention to another treatment as in I.A.

Further criteria for both I and II:
III. Studies must be conducted with treatment manuals.
IV. Characteristics of the client samples must be clearly specified.

Source: Division 12 Task Force, 1995, p. 21.

TABLE 1.2 Criteria for Empirically Validated Treatments: Probably Efficacious Treatments

---

I. Two studies showing the treatment is more effective than a waiting-list control group.

Or

II. Two studies otherwise meeting the well-established treatment criteria I, III, and IV, but both are conducted by the same investigator. Or one good study demonstrating effectiveness by these same criteria.

Or

III. At least two good studies demonstrating effectiveness but flawed by heterogeneity of the client samples.

Or

IV. A small series of single-case design studies otherwise meeting the well-established treatment criteria II, III, and IV.

Source: Division 12 Task Force, 1995, p. 22.

disorders are also listed. With the exception of family education programs for schizophrenia and interpersonal therapy for bulimia and for depression, all the remaining "well-established" psychosocial treatments are behavioral. Similarly, all but the brief psychodynamic therapies listed as "probably efficacious" are behavioral.

Why do behavioral approaches to treatment figure so prominently in these two lists of empirically validated treatments? One reason is that, as several chapters in this volume show, behavioral treatments have been shown to be effective for quite a number of disorders. However, these treatments are also designed to induce the discrete behavioral changes that are the target of many treatment outcome measures; they lend themselves especially well to manualized treatment programs; they are products of the behavioral movement's long history of respect for experimental validation; and they tend to induce desired changes within a brief enough duration to fit into the typical, time-limited outcome study. A continuing issue, then, will be whether treatments drawn from other traditions not so amenable to accepted outcome research will ultimately be empirically validated when the methodology for doing so has been developed or whether behavioral treatments will continue to predominate because they achieve positive outcomes other treatments will not.

The restricted number of empirically validated treatments listed in the Division 12 Task Force report contrasts sharply with the large number of treatments endorsed in the American Psychiatric Association practice guidelines (1993, 1994b, 1995). Differences in the standards of proof demanded by the two groups appear to be the primary reason for this marked difference in number of recommended treatments.

The three sets of American Psychiatric Association practice guidelines employ a rigorous rating system to reflect the methodological adequacy of the treatment outcome studies on which they base their judgments; the system is reviewed later in this chapter. At the same time, their inclusion of "clinical practice" and "expert clinical judgment" considerations along with the treatment outcome data provides latitude to include treatments for which consistently positive findings have not been reported. In contrast, the Division 12 practice guideline was shaped by very specific criteria (shown in Tables 1.1 and 1.2). While, as noted earlier, these criteria are not overly demanding, they nonetheless require that studies supporting the efficacy of a treatment meet specific methodological criteria (e.g., provision for the use of treatment manuals) that many therapy outcome studies until recently have not been able to meet.

These apparent differences in the standards of proof employed by the two associations' practice guidelines are important because they lead to divergent treatment recommendations. For this reason, we consider below the specific issue of standards of proof in greater detail.

Reactions to Practice Guidelines

Sol Garfield, a prominent psychotherapy researcher, has taken issue (1996) with several aspects of the Division 12 practice guidelines. A number of his criticisms relate as well to the American Psychiatric Association guidelines—or to most other prospective guidelines developed for the treatment of mental disorders.

[Garfield] judges "the language of the [Task Force] report [to be] overly strong and the recommendations premature." Most pointed of his criticisms is that "the emphasis on validated therapies for specific diagnostic entities seemingly implies a greater knowledge of the variables that produce or facilitate positive change" than he thinks is warranted by the state of our data and knowledge. . . . Garfield also questions the reliability and validity of DSM-IV (1994), asking whether they are adequate even now to ensure diagnostically-homogeneous treat-

ment groups. His concerns extend to the Task Force's requirement that studies pointing to "well-established treatments" utilize treatment manuals; manualized therapy, he believes, idealizes and, thus, distorts the psychotherapy setting. He is also convinced that psychotherapy patients in research studies are sufficiently different from their counterparts in the real world as to affect both therapy process and outcome. . . . Finally, Garfield laments the failure of the Task Force to acknowledge the important role common factors like therapist variance play in determining therapy outcome, in favor of the Task Force's emphasis on form of therapy. Garfield is convinced that psychotherapy research over several decades has revealed the primacy of these process variables over therapy form in determining therapy outcome. (Nathan, 1996, p. 251)

Nathan disagrees with Garfield's view that the Division 12 practice guidelines are premature, concluding instead that "the time has come to develop methodological criteria by which to identify strong studies validly reflecting effective treatments" (1996, p. 251). Acknowledging both that the methodology for assessing outcomes is not yet ideal and that more effective treatments for many conditions remain to be developed, Nathan nonetheless concludes that "we have made sufficient progress in both realms to justify taking a chance and beginning the process."

Besides Garfield, critics of practice guidelines include Davison and Lazarus, who are wary of the possibility that standards of practice will reduce clinical innovation, "the lifeblood of advances in the development of new therapeutic interventions" (1995, p. 96), by reducing the motivation of research workers to identify alternatives to empirically validated treatments.

Wilson (1995) and Persons (1995), supporters of efforts to establish empirically validated treatments, have compiled a list of reasons why empirically validated treatments have not been embraced by mental health professionals. Among the most important is the failure of programs training mental health professionals, by and large, to emphasize empirically validated therapeutic methods and, conversely, the tendency of these programs to continue to provide training in therapies that lack empirical evidence of efficacy. These authors also lament the paucity of mental health professionals familiar with the empirical data on therapeutic outcomes; the persistent view among many clinicians that all psychotherapies are more or less effective; and the fact that most consumers of mental health services, like most mental health professionals, are not well informed about effective treatments.

Nonetheless, more and more clinicians have begun to acknowledge the contributions empirically based therapy practice guidelines can make to clinical practice. Wilson (1995), Clinton, McCormick, and Besteman (1994), Schulberg and Rush (1994), Schooler, (1994), and Ogles, Lambert, and Sawyer (1995), among others, have written about the diverse benefits therapy practice guidelines could bring. Using bulimia nervosa, the focus of much of his clinical research, as an example, Wilson (1995) is particularly eloquent in making the case for the widest possible dissemination of empirically validated treatments:

> Moving aggressively in the direction of developing and implementing empirically-validated treatment methods would seem imperative in securing the place of psychological therapy in future health care policy and planning. . . . The development and implementation of empirically-validated treatments is seen by many mental health professionals as not only desirable but ethically imperative. It has been commonplace for some time now to emphasize patients' right to treatment and their right to refuse treatment. But patients should (also) have a right to safe and effective treatment. (Wilson, 1995, p. 163)

The drafters of both the American Psychiatric Association and Division 12 practice guidelines emphasize the importance of integrating training in empirically validated treatments into training programs for family physicians and mental health professionals. However, a recent survey (Crits-Christoph, Frank, Chambless, Brody, & Karp, 1995) conducted by the Task Force on Promotion and Dissemination of Psychological Procedures revealed that clinical psychology training programs vary enormously—from 0% to 96%—in the number of empirically validated psychotherapeutic treatments they teach. Furthermore, as Wilson lamented: "underscoring the lack of attention to empirically-validated treatments, the report revealed that more than one fifth of the programs did not teach anything about 75% or more of the treatment methods listed by the Task Force" (1995, p. 165). Although comparable data for training programs in psychiatry and social work are not available, there is no reason to believe that they differ in their degree of commitment to training in empirically validated treatments.

Beyond the compelling arguments in favor of training in the use of empirically validated treatments from both clinical and ethical perspectives, proponents of doing so also point to an economic justification. In the present managed care era, mental health practices that do not have strong empirical support—and do not yield the best possible outcomes—are unlikely to continue to be reimbursed (Barlow, 1994; Broskowski, 1995). Empirical validation of psychological treatments is especially important, Barlow has observed, since the public and federal and state policy makers mistakenly believe that few psychosocial treatments are efficacious. However, as many of this volume's chapters demonstrate (including the one on treatments for the anxiety disorders written by Barlow and colleagues), psychological treatments alone and in combination with drugs are now effective for a wide variety of conditions. Only when these empirical findings are more widely known will patients gain the fullest possible access to these treatments.

Practice Guidelines: Summary and Conclusions

As this volume demonstrates, a substantial number of empirically validated treatments, both pharmacological and psychosocial, are now available. As a consequence, the American Psychiatric Association, the Division of Clinical Psychology of the American Psychological Association, the Agency for Health Care Policy and Research, and the National Institutes of Health have proposed empirically validated practice guidelines. Somewhat unexpectedly, the guidelines' standards of proof of efficacy differ to some extent, with the result that the range of treatments suggested by the American Psychological Association guideline, for example, is substantially more limited than that suggested by the American Psychiatric Association guidelines for the same syndromes. While it seems likely that, as these groups gain greater experience with the creation and utilization of treatment guidelines, a greater correspondence of inclusion criteria may well develop, differences based on each group's view of its practice domain and sense of its own practice history may well remain.

The formal efforts to develop practice guidelines reviewed here draw on a lengthy history of efforts to develop methodological guidelines for outcome studies. During the past several decades, many research scientists (e.g., Fiske et al., 1970; Garfield, 1992; Kazdin & Wilson, 1978a, 1978b; Kiesler, 1971; Klein & Davis, 1969; Klein, Gittelman, & Quitkin, 1980; Klerman, Weissman, & Markowitz, 1994; Rachman & Wilson, 1980) have analyzed the outcome research of their day to identify its strengths and weaknesses and propose additional design features to make future studies more sensitive and selective. To this time, though, what has been well known to clinical scientists has been largely unknown and, hence, of little interest to practitioners and the public. The result, as noted above, has been that the best available data on the efficacy of treatments have been neither widely taught nor widely applied. With the appearance of practice guidelines developed by two groups of mental health professionals, clinical psychologists and psychiatrists, however, this situation seems destined to change. Moreover, the growing interest in the effectiveness and clinical utility of treatments, not simply their efficacy, represents an additional impetus for wider dissemination of these treatments beyond the clinical research community to that of the practice community. The following chapters represent a substantial additional effort in that desirable direction.

Practice guidelines are understandably controversial. While they establish, for the first time, an empirical standard by which the adequacy of a treatment can be judged, they also impose constraints on the decision making of clinicians, despite disclaimers to the contrary. Moreover, because they are available to managed care practice monitors, as well as to clinicians, they will almost certainly be used on occasion to assess the quality of practice of individual clinicians, contrary to the intentions of their developers. It is in connection with this possibility that the greatest current concerns about practice guidelines have understandably arisen.

STANDARDS OF PROOF

Efforts to translate the results of research on empirically validated therapies into therapy practice guidelines have a very recent history. Hence it is not surprising that the standards of proof used to establish the practice guidelines developed by leading groups of mental health professionals are somewhat divergent. This brief section compares and contrasts the differing standards of proof that the drafters of the American Psychiatric Association and Division 12 practice guide-

lines—as well as the authors of this volume—employed to guide their selection of effective treatments. The section concludes by considering a recent proposal to develop a common set of standards of proof; the proposal would increase the consistency of judgments of the methodological adequacy of outcome research and likely lead to greater agreement on which treatments meet the common standard.

American Psychiatric Association Practice Guidelines

The three American Psychiatric Association practice guidelines (APA, 1993, 1994b, 1995) describe the research criteria to which they give greatest credence—the standards of proof they used—in identical brief sections preceding the references:

The following coding system is used to indicate the nature of the supporting evidence in the summary recommendations and references:

[A] Randomized clinical trial. A study of an intervention in which subjects are prospectively followed over time; there are treatment and control groups; subjects are randomly assigned to the two groups; both the subjects and the investigator are blind to the assignment.

[B] Clinical trial. A prospective study in which an intervention is made and the results of that intervention are tracked longitudinally; study does not meet standards for a randomized clinical trial.

[C] Cohort or longitudinal study. A study in which subjects are prospectively followed over time without any specific intervention.

[D] Case-control study. A study in which a group of patients is identified in the present and information about them is pursued retrospectively or backward in time.

[E] Review with secondary data analysis. A structured analytic review of existing data, e.g., a meta-analysis or a decision analysis.

[F] Review. A qualitative review and discussion of previously published literature without a quantitative synthesis of the data.

[G] Other. Textbooks, expert opinion, case reports, and other reports not included above. (APA, 1995, p. 79)

Division of Clinical Psychology Practice Guidelines

The practice guidelines developed by the Division of Clinical Psychology of the American Psychological Association (Division 12 Task Force, 1995) included two sets of criteria, shown in Tables 1.1 and 1.2, designed to identify "well-established treatments" and "probably efficacious treatments." These criteria have been described as "rather modest (if not minimalist)" (Wilson, 1995, p. 165) for some of the reasons outlined in our discussion of them above. Nonetheless, they do represent a starting point from which more elaborate, demanding, and inclusive standards of proof can develop.

The Division 12 Task Force discusses the problems of defining empirically validated treatment in the early pages of its "Report and Recommendations." One of the most revealing of its comments on this subject is the following:

> Our criteria are summarized in Tables 1 and 2. We recognize that these criteria are somewhat arbitrary, and that other criteria might be equally important. For example, the clinical significance, as opposed to the statistical significance, of a treatment is important to consider. Additionally, in some cases a treatment for a disorder for which no other treatments have been shown to be successful may have been demonstrated to be extremely powerful by an open trial without a control condition. It could be argued that even without evidence from controlled outcome studies such a treatment should be disseminated, since the treatment appears very promising and no other treatments have been successful. However, controlled outcome studies, or a large series of single case designs, are likely to remain the source of most policy decisions and clinical recommendations. (Division 12 Task Force, 1995, pp. 4–5)

Despite these words, however, the task force's choices of empirically validated treatments appear to have been based almost entirely on the criteria in Tables 1.1 and 1.2. In that way, they differ from the decisions of the drafters of the American Psychiatric Association guidelines, which were more heavily influenced by the "clinical judgment and expertise of the clinician."

A Guide to Treatments That Work

The editors of this volume, A Guide to Treatments That Work, provided potential chapter authors the following brief advisory material for judging the methodological adequacy of the studies on which they were to base their conclusions. While the reader will note some similarity to the criteria by which the evidentiary

material in the three American Psychiatric Association practice guidelines was evaluated, the reader will also note that we went into greater detail on how and why the several categories of evidentiary material should be used. In writing this material, we attempted to walk a fine line—to achieve a more representative outcome—between the rigor of the Division 12 criteria and the apparently greater latitude, at least in application, of the American Psychiatric Association's standards of proof.

The purpose of these chapters is to present the most rigorous, scientifically-based evidence for the efficacy of treatments that is available. At the same time, it is clear that for some disorders there are treatments widely recognized by experienced clinicians to be useful that may not have been subjected to rigorous investigation for a variety of reasons. Our aim is to be clear with readers what treatments have been scientifically validated, what treatments are felt by a large number of experts to be valuable but have never been properly scientifically examined, and what treatments are known to be of little value.

To do this, it is useful to establish some criteria for evaluating the validity of articles in the literature that are reviewed in writing the chapters. We would like you to keep in mind the following classification when you are reviewing the literature and writing your chapter:

Type One Studies: These are the most rigorous and involve a randomized, prospective clinical trial. Such studies also must involve comparison groups with random assignment, blinded assessments, clear presentation of exclusion and inclusion criteria, state-of-the-art diagnostic methods, adequate sample size to offer statistical power, and clearly described statistical methods.

Type Two Studies: These are clinical trials in which an intervention is made, but some aspects of the Type One study requirement is missing. For example, a trial in which a double-blind cannot be maintained; a trial in which two treatments are compared but the assignment is not randomized; and the trial in which there is a clear but not fatal flaw such as a period of observation that is felt to be too short to make full judgments on treatment efficacy. Such studies clearly do not merit the same consideration as Type One studies, but often make important contributions and generally should not be ignored.

Type Three Studies: These are clearly methodologically limited. Generally, Type Three studies are open treatment studies aiming at obtaining pilot data. They are highly subject to observer bias and can usually do little more than indicate if a treatment is worth pursuing in a more rigorous design. Also included in this category are case-control studies in which patients are identified and then information about treatment is obtained from them retrospectively. Such studies can, of course, provide a great deal of naturalistic information, but are prone to all of the problems of uncontrolled data collection and retrospective recall error.

Type Four Studies: Reviews with secondary data analysis can be useful, especially if the data analytic techniques are sophisticated. Modern methods of meta-analysis attempt to account for the fact that, for example, negative studies tend to be reported at a substantially lower rate than positive outcome studies.

Type Five Studies: Reviews without secondary data analysis are helpful to give an impression of the literature, but are clearly subject to the writer's opinion and sometimes are highly biased.

Type Six Studies: This encompasses a variety of reports that have marginal value, such as case studies, essays, and opinion papers. (Personal communication, Nathan and Gorman letter to potential authors, 1995)

Template for Developing Guidelines, American Psychological Association Task Force, 1995

A task force of the American Psychological Association recently published the *Template for Developing Guidelines: Interventions for Mental Disorders and Psychosocial Aspects of Physical Disorders* (American Psychological Association Task Force, 1995) that makes substantially more clear than either the Division 12 or American Psychiatric Association practice guidelines important aspects of the process of selecting and utilizing standards of proof.

Developed "to assure comprehensiveness and consistency" of practice guidelines, the template has two features especially relevant to this discussion. The first is designed to ensure that the efficacy of a treatment does not depend only on whether the empirical tests of the treatment involved randomized clinical trials, but also on the nature of the *treatment comparisons* in those trials. To this time, the drafters of practice guidelines have emphasized the adequacy of research designs in making judgments about the efficacy of treatments. Adding the nature of the outcome comparison—to no treatment, to nonspecific treatment vari-

ables, or to treatments known to be effective—provides an additional powerful evaluative dimension: randomized clinical trials that compare the experimental treatment with established, effective treatments clearly offer a more powerful test than those that compare the experimental treatment with nonrobust comparison treatments or no treatment at all. While clinical scientists have known and generally followed this strategy when possible, making it explicit for the consumers of treatment research is a valuable contribution.

A second notable feature of the template is the distinction it draws (it is drawn as well by Seligman, 1995, in describing the *Consumer Reports* survey) between the efficacy of an intervention and its *effectiveness* or *clinical utility*:

Clinical practice guidelines for behavioral health care [should] be constructed on the basis of two simultaneous considerations or "axes." The first is that guidelines take into consideration a rigorous assessment of scientific evidence with the goal of measuring the efficacy of any given intervention [efficacy]. The second axis specifies that guidelines consider the applicability and feasibility of the intervention in the local setting where it is to be proffered [clinical utility]. (American Psychological Association Task Force, 1995, p. i)

While a series of well-designed studies might establish the efficacy of an intervention, unless it is effective in real-life clinical settings it will not be effective:

The clinical utility axis refers to the ability (and willingness) of practitioners to use, and of patients to accept, the treatment in question, and to the range of applicability of that treatment. It reflects the extent to which the intervention, regardless of the efficacy that may or may not have been demonstrated in the clinical research setting, will be effective in the practice setting in which it is to be applied. Among the factors that will be considered under this rubric are the generalizability of administering the intervention in various settings, the feasibility of the intervention across patients and settings, and the costs and benefits associated with the administration of the intervention. (American Psychological Association Task Force, 1995, p. 13)

To this time, the methodology for undertaking and evaluating efficacy studies is substantially more advanced than that for effectiveness studies. While studies on the generalizability of a treatment have been undertaken (Finney and Moos describe a series of such studies of alcoholism treatments in chapter 7 of this volume), the methodology for undertaking feasibility and costs and benefits studies requires substantial further development.

A GUIDE TO TREATMENTS
THAT WORK: EMPIRICALLY
VALIDATED TREATMENTS AND
STANDARDS OF PROOF

The practice guidelines reviewed above differ in both the numbers and the identity of the treatments they endorse for the syndromes they share, in part because of differences in standards of proof. By design, these guidelines are designed to reflect a concise summary of best practices as of their date of creation. By contrast, this volume's chapters reflect substantially more than the best practices as of 1997. Their extensive summaries of the history of treatment research on their syndrome, in some instances from midcentury, permit the reader to identify useful trends as more adequate standards of proof and more effective treatments appeared. It is on some of those observations that this final section of the chapter focuses.

The contents of this volume amply demonstrate that, from the early 1950s to the present, clinical scientists increasingly aware of the inadequacies of the methodology of treatment research worked hard to improve it. Discussions of the nature of those inadequacies and suggestions for needed improvements began to appear with greater regularity in monographs and journal articles from the early 1970s. From that time to the present, great progress has been made in designing outcome designs and measures that more accurately reflect the contributions of specific treatments, both pharmacological and psychosocial, to observed outcomes.

Our authors also make clear that accompanying these marked improvements in the methodology of outcome research have been equally dramatic advances in the effectiveness of treatments for a wide range of disorders. Just as some of our chapters document impressive advances in the psychosocial domain, for which few treatments of documented effectiveness were available 25 years ago, they also emphasize the magnitude of advances in psychopharmacological treatments—for example, in new drugs with more specific, targeted effects on specific neurotransmitter systems (e.g., the selective serotonergic reuptake inhibitors).

The contents of the volume also make clear that major discoveries in treatments for the psychoses characterized the 1950s and 1960s in both the pharmacological (e.g., the phenothiazines, lithium) and psychosocial (e.g., behavior modification, behavioral contracting) domains. Marked advances in psychosocial and pharmacological treatments for the anxiety disorders, many of the mood disorders, some of the somatoform disorders, and the eating disorders—Eysenck's neuroses—came later, during the 1970s and 1980s. Only now have promising treatments for such recalcitrant conditions as the substance-related disorders begun to be reported. Some disorders, most notably the personality disorders and the paraphilias, still await the development of effective treatments. Improvements in outcome research methodology and the advent of more effective treatments have tended to go hand in hand.

Both because of a lengthier history of success documenting efficacy and substantially fewer outcome measurement problems, the methodology of psychopharmacological research was markedly advanced over that of psychosocial research 25 years ago. By virtue of marked advances in the intervening years in the complex methodologies required to study psychosocial treatment outcomes, however, it is probably fair to say that this gap in methodological adequacy separating the psychosocial and psychopharmacological research domains has been reduced, although without real placebo control and use of the double blind in psychosocial treatment research a methodological gap nonetheless remains.

A divide of greater proportions distinguishes the methodological adequacy of research on behavioral and psychodynamic treatments. For a variety of reasons, as we noted above, behavior therapy lends itself better to outcome research than does psychodynamic therapy. Those reasons, which have to do with focus, duration, predictability, and complexity, help explain why so many more behavioral treatments than nonbehavioral treatments are included in contemporary practice guidelines. Another important reason, of course, may be underlying differences in efficacy and effectiveness. However, to date, a fully adequate methodology for the study of psychodynamic treatment has not been developed. Until and unless it is, it seems unlikely that the psychodynamic treatments will appear prominently on lists of effective treatments in practice guidelines.

Our authors point to yet another important trend in treatment. More and more combined treatments, in which psychosocial — usually behavioral — and psychopharmacological treatments are employed concurrently and produce behavioral and symptomatic gains greater than either treatment approach alone, have now been incorporated into the practice guidelines. The affective disorders, attention deficit hyperactivity disorder (ADHD), obsessive compulsive disorder, posttraumatic stress disorder (PTSD), and some of the phobic disorders all have clearly benefited from combined psychopharmacological and psychosocial treatment.

Although much hard work remains to develop even more effective outcome methodologies and an even broader range of efficacious treatments, the contents of this volume offer dramatic testimony to the gains that have been made during the past half century. As a result, more patients with a broader range of disorders than ever before now have the opportunity to return to productive lives.

References

American Psychiatric Association. (1952). *Diagnostic and statistical manual of mental disorders*. Washington, D.C.: Author.

———. (1968). *Diagnostic and statistical manual of mental disorders* (2nd ed.). Washington, D.C.: Author.

———. (1980). *Diagnostic and statistical manual of mental disorders* (3rd ed.). Washington, D.C.: Author.

———. (1987). *Diagnostic and statistical manual of mental disorders* (3rd ed., revised). Washington, D.C.: Author.

———. (1993). Practice Guideline for Major Depressive Disorders in Adults. *American Psychiatric Association, 150*(4, Supplement), v, 1–26.

———. (1994a). *Diagnostic and statistical manual of mental disorders* (4th ed.). Washington, D.C.: Author.

———. (1994b). Practice Guideline for Treatment of Patients with Bipolar Disorder. *American Journal of Psychiatry, 151*(12, Supplement), iv, 1–36.

———. (1995). Practice Guideline for the Treatment of Patients with Substance Use Disorders: Alcohol, Cocaine, Opioids. *American Journal of Psychiatry, 152*(11, Supplement), 1–59.

American Psychological Association Task Force. (1995). *Template for developing guidelines: Interventions for mental disorders and psychosocial aspects of physical disorders*. Washington, D.C.: Author.

Barlow, D. H. (1994). Psychological intervention in the era of managed competition. *Clinical Psychology: Science and Practice, 1*, 109–122.

Bergin, A. E. (1971). The evaluation of therapeutic outcomes. In A. E. Bergin and S. L. Garfield (Eds.), *Handbook of psychotherapy and behavior change*. New York: Wiley.

Broskowski, A. T. (1995). The evolution of health care: Implications for the training and careers of psychologists. *Professional Psychology: Research and Practice, 26*, 156–162.

Cantwell, D. P., Russell, A. T., Mattison, R., & Will, L. (1979). A comparison of *DSM-II* and *DSM-III* in the diagnosis of childhood psychiatric disorders. I. Agreement with expected diagnosis. *Archives of General Psychiatry, 36*, 1208–1213.

Clarke, G. N. (1995). Improving the transition from basic efficacy research to effectiveness studies: Methodological issues and procedures. *Journal of Consulting and Clinical Psychology, 63*, 718–725.

Clinton, J. J., McCormick, K., & Besteman, J. (1994). Enhancing clinical practice: The role of practice guidelines. *American Psychologist, 49*, 30–33.

Cohen, L. H., Sargent, M. M., & Sechrest, L. B. (1986). Use of psychotherapy research by professional psychologists. *American Psychologist, 41*, 198–206.

Consumer Reports editors. (1995). Mental health: Does therapy help? *Consumer Reports, 60*, 734–737.

Cooper, H. M. (1979). Statistically combining independent studies: A meta-analysis of sex differences in conformity research. *Journal of Personality and Social Psychology, 37*, 131–146.

Crits-Christoph, P., Frank, E., Chambless, D. L., Brody, C., & Karp, J. F. (1995). Training in empirically validated treatments: What are clinical psychology students learning? *Professional Psychology: Research and Practice, 26*, 514–522.

Davison, G. C., & Lazarus, A. A. (1995). The dialectics of science and practice. In S. C. Hayes, V. M. Follette, R. M. Dawes, & K. E. Grady (Eds.), *Scientific standards of psychological practice: Issues and recommendations* (pp. 95–120). Reno, Nev.: Context Press.

Denker, P. (1946). Results of treatment of psychoneuroses by the G.P. *New York State Journal of Medicine, 46*, 2164–2166.

Depression Guideline Panel. (1993). *Clinical Practice Guideline Number 5: Depression in Primary Care, 2: Treatment of Major Depression*. Rockville, Md.: U.S. Department of Health and Human Services, Agency for Health Care Policy and Research.

National Institutes of Health. (1991). *Diagnosis and treatment of depression in late life*. (Reprinted from NIH Consensus Development Conference Consensus Statement, 1991, November 4–6: 9(3).)

Division 12 Task Force. (1995). Training in and dissemination of empirically validated psychological treatments: Report and recommendations. *The Clinical Psychologist, 48,* 3–23.

Eysenck, H. J. (1952). The effects of psychotherapy: an evaluation. *Journal of Consulting Psychology, 16,* 319–324.

———. (1960). *Behavior therapy and the neuroses.* Oxford, U.K.: Pergamon Press.

———. (1969). *The effects of psychotherapy.* New York: Science House.

Feighner, J. P., Robins, E., Guze, S. B., Woodruff, R. A., Winokur, G., & Munoz, R. (1972). Diagnostic criteria for use in psychiatric research. *Archives of General Psychiatry, 26,* 57–63.

Fink, M. (1976). Foreword. In R. L. Spitzer & D. F. Klein (Eds.), *Evaluation of psychological therapies* (pp. xi–xii). Baltimore, Md.: Johns Hopkins University Press.

Fiske, D. W., Hunt, H. F., Luborsky, L., Orne, M. T., Parloff, M. B., Reiser, M. F., & Tuma, A. H. (1970). The planning of research on effectiveness of psychotherapy. (Report on workshop sponsored and supported by the Clinical Projects Research Review Committee, National Institute of Mental Health.) *Archives of General Psychiatry, 22,* 22–32; also *American Psychologist, 25,* 727–737.

Garfield, S. L. (1992). Major issues in psychotherapy research. In D. K. Freedheim (Ed.), *History of psychotherapy: A century of change* (pp. 335–359). Washington, D.C.: American Psychological Association.

———. (1996). Some problems associated with "validated" forms of psychotherapy. *Clinical Psychology: Science and Practice, 3,* 218–229.

Grady, K. E. (1995). Compliance with standards of care: Evidence from medical research. In S. C. Hayes, V. M. Follette, R. M. Dawes, & K. E. Grady (Eds.), *Scientific standards of psychological practice: Issues and recommendations* (pp. 83–91). Reno, Nev.: Context Press.

Hanada, K., & Takahashi, S. (1983). Multi-institutional collaborative studies of diagnostic reliability of *DSM-III* and *ICD-9* in Japan. In R. L. Spitzer, J. B. W. Williams, & A. E. Skodel (Eds.), *International perspectives on* DSM-III (pp. 273–290). Washington, D.C.: American Psychiatric Association.

Helzer, J. E., Clayton, P. J., Pambakian, R., Reich, T., Woodruff, R. A., & Reveley, M. A. (1977). Reliability of psychiatric diagnosis: II. The test/retest reliability of diagnostic classification. *Archives of General Psychiatry, 34,* 136–141.

Helzer, J. E., Robins, L. N., McEvoy, L. T., Spitznagel, E. L., Stoltzman, R. K., Farmer, A., & Brockington, I. F. (1985). A comparison of clinical and diagnostic interview schedule diagnoses. Physician reexamination of lay-interviewed cases in the general population. *Archives of General Psychiatry, 42,* 657–666.

Helzer, J. E., Robins, L. N., Taibleson, M., Woodruff, R. A., Reich, T., & Wish, E. D. (1977). Reliability of psychiatric diagnosis: I. Methodological review. *Archives of General Psychiatry, 34,* 129–133.

Howard, K. I., Kopta, S. M., Krause, M. S., & Orlinsky, D. E. (1986). The dose-effect relationship in psychotherapy. *American Psychologist, 41,* 159–164.

Hyler, S. E., Williams, J. B. W., & Spitzer, R. L. (1982). Reliability in the *DSM-III* field trials: Interview versus case summary. *Archives of General Psychiatry, 39,* 1275–1278.

Imber, S. D., Glanz, L. M., Elkin, I., Sotsky, S. M., Boyer, J. L., & Leber, W. R. (1986). Ethical issues in psychotherapy research: Problems in a collaborative clinical trials study. *American Psychologist, 41,* 137–146.

Kazdin, A. E., & Wilson, G. T. (1978a). Criteria for evaluating psychotherapy. *Archives of General Psychiatry, 35,* 407–418.

———. (1978b). *Evaluation of behavior therapy: Issues, evidence, and research strategies.* Cambridge, Mass.: Ballinger.

Kernberg, O. F. (1976). Some methodological and strategic issues in psychotherapy research: Research implications of the Menninger Foundation's psychotherapy research project. In R. L. Spitzer & D. F. Klein (Eds.), *Evaluation of psychological therapies* (pp. 23–38). Baltimore, Md.: Johns Hopkins University Press.

Kiesler, D. J. (1971). Experimental designs in psychotherapy. In A. E. Bergin & S. L. Garfield (Eds.), *Handbook of psychotherapy and behavior change* (pp. 36–74). New York: Wiley.

Klein, D. F., Gittelman, R., & Quitkin, F. (1980). *Diagnosis and drug treatment of psychiatric disorders: Adults and children* (2nd ed.). Baltimore, Md.: Williams & Wilkins.

Klein, D. K., & Davis, J. M. (Eds.) (1969). *Diagnosis and treatment of psychiatric disorders: Review of mood-stabilizing drug literature.* Baltimore, Md.: Williams & Wilkins.

Klerman, G. L., Weissman, M. M., & Markowitz, J. (1994). Medication and psychotherapy. In S. L. Garfield & A. E. Bergin (Eds.), *Handbook of psychotherapy and behavior change: An empirical analysis* (4th ed.) (pp. 734–782). New York: Wiley.

Kocsis, J. H. (1996). Commentary. *Archives of General Psychiatry, 53,* 303–304.

Landis, C. (1937). A statistical evaluation of psychotherapeutic methods. In L. E. Hinsie (Ed.), *Concepts and problems in psychotherapy.* New York: Columbia University Press.

Larsen, F., & Vaglum, S. (1986). Clinical experiences

with the *DSM-III* system of classification. Interrater reliability of the *DSM-III* diagnoses in two Norwegian studies on psychiatric and super-obese patients. *Acta Psychiatrica Scandinavia, 73*(Supplement 328), 18–21.

Luborsky, L., Singer, B., & Luborsky, L. (1975). Comparative studies of psychotherapies: Is it true that "everybody has won and all must have prizes"? *Archives of General Psychiatry, 32,* 995–1008.

———. (1976). Comparative studies of psychotherapies: Is it true that "everybody has won and all must have prizes"? In R. L. Spitzer & D. F. Klein (Eds.), *Evaluation of psychological therapies* (pp. 3–22). Baltimore, Md.: Johns Hopkins University Press.

Malan, D. H., Bacal, H., Heath, E., & Balfour, F. L. (1968). A study of psychodynamic changes in untreated neurotic patients. *British Journal of Psychiatry, 114,* 525–551.

Mattison, R., Cantwell, D. P., Russell, A. T., & Will, L. (1979). A comparison of *DSM-II* and *DSM-III* in the diagnosis of childhood psychiatric disorders. II. Interrater agreement. *Archives of General Psychiatry, 36,* 1217–1222.

McIntyre, J. S., Zarin, D. A., & Pincus, H. A. (1996). Commentary. *Archives of General Psychiatry, 53,* 291–293.

Merriam, A. E., & Karasu, T. B. (1996). Commentary. *Archives of General Psychiatry, 53,* 301–302.

Morrow-Bradley, C., & Elliott, R. (1986). Utilization of psychotherapy research by practicing psychotherapists. *American Psychologist, 41,* 188–197.

Nathan, P. E. (1996). Validated forms of psychotherapy may lead to better-validated psychotherapy. *Clinical Psychology: Science and Practice, 3,* 251–255.

Nathan, P. E., & Gorman, J. M. (Eds.) (1998). *A Guide to Treatments That Work.* New York: Oxford University Press.

Newman, F. L., & Howard, K. I. (1986). Therapeutic effort, treatment outcomes, and national health policy. *American Psychologist, 41,* 181–187.

Ogles, B. M., Lambert, M. J., & Sawyer, J. D. (1995). Clinical significance of the National Institute of Mental Health treatment of depression collaborative research program data. *Journal of Consulting and Clinical Psychology, 63,* 321–326.

Pallack, M. S. (1995). Managed care and outcomes-based standards in the health care revolution. In S. C. Hayes, V. M. Follette, R. M. Dawes, & K. E. Grady (Eds.), *Scientific standards of psychological practice: Issues and recommendations* (pp. 73–77). Reno, Nev.: Context Press.

Persons, J. B. (1995). Why practicing psychologists are slow to adopt empirically-validated treatments. In S. C. Hayes, V. M. Follette, R. M. Dawes, & K. E. Grady (Eds.), *Scientific standards of psychological practice: Issues and recommendations* (pp. 141–157). Reno, Nev.: Context Press.

Persons, J. B., Thase, M. E., & Crits-Christoph, P. (1996). The role of psychotherapy in the treatment of depression. *Archives of General Psychiatry, 53,* 283–290.

Powers, E., & Witmer, H. (1951). *An experiment in the prevention of delinquency: The Cambridge-Somerville youth study.* New York: Columbia University Press.

Rachman, S. (1971). *The effects of psychotherapy.* Oxford, U.K.: Pergamon Press.

Rachman, S., & Wilson, G. T. (1980). *The effects of psychological therapy* (2nd ed.). Oxford, U.K.: Pergamon Press.

Robins, L. N., Helzer, J. E., Croughan, J., & Ratcliff, K. S. (1981). National Institute of Mental Health Diagnostic Interview Schedule: Its history, characteristics, and validity. *Archives of General Psychiatry, 38,* 381–389.

Robins, L. N., Helzer, J. E., Ratcliff, K. S., & Seyfried, W. (1982). Validity of the Diagnostic Interview Schedule, version II: *DSM-III* diagnoses. *Psychological Medicine, 12,* 855–870.

Rogers, C. F., & Dymond, R. (1954). *Psychotherapy and personality change.* Chicago: University of Chicago Press.

Rosenzweig, S. (1954). A transvaluation of psychotherapy: A reply to Eysenck. *Journal of Abnormal and Social Psychology, 49,* 298–304.

Rush, A. J. (1996). Commentary. *Archives of General Psychiatry, 53,* 298–300.

Sanford, N. (1953). Psychotherapy. *Annual Review of Psychology, 4,* 317–342.

Schooler, N. R. (1994). Translating treatment research findings into clinical action. *American Journal of Psychiatry, 151,* 1719–1721.

Schulberg, H. C., & Rush, A. J. (1994). Clinical practice guidelines for managing major depression in primary care practice. *American Psychologist, 49,* 34–41.

Seligman, M. E. P. (1995). The effectiveness of psychotherapy: The *Consumer Reports* survey. *American Psychologist, 50,* 965–974.

Smith, M. L., & Glass, G. V. (1977). Meta-analysis of psychotherapy outcome studies. *American Psychologist, 32,* 752–760.

Spitzer, R. L. (1983). Psychiatric diagnosis: Are clinicians still necessary? *Comprehensive Psychiatry, 24,* 399–411.

Spitzer, R. L., Endicott, J., Fleiss, J. L., & Cohen, J. (1970). The Psychiatric Status Schedule: A technique for evaluating psychopathology and impairment of role functioning. *Archives of General Psychiatry, 23,* 41–55.

Spitzer, R. L., Endicott, J., & Robins, E. (1975). Research

Diagnostic Criteria (RDC) for a selected group of functional disorders. New York: New York State Psychiatric Institute.

Spitzer, R. L., Fleiss, J. L., Endicott, J., & Cohen, J. (1967). Mental Status Schedule: Properties of a factor-analytically derived scale. *Archives of General Psychiatry, 16,* 479–493.

Spitzer, R. L., Forman, J. B., & Nee, J. (1979). *DSM-III* field trials: I. Initial interrater diagnostic reliability. *American Journal of Psychiatry, 136,* 815–817.

Spitzer, R. L., & Klein, D. F. (1976). *Evaluation of psychological therapies: Psychotherapies, behavior therapies, drug therapies, and their interactions.* Baltimore, Md.: Johns Hopkins University Press.

Spitzer, R. L., & Williams, J. B. W. (1986). *Structured Clinical Interview for* DSM-III. New York: Biometrics Research Department, New York State Psychiatric Institute.

Stiles, W. B., Shapiro, D. A., & Elliott, R. (1986). "Are all psychotherapies equivalent?" *American Psychologist, 41,* 165–180.

Teuber, N., & Powers, E. (1953). Evaluating therapy in a delinquency prevention program. *Proceedings of the Association of Nervous and Mental Disease, 3,* 138–147.

Williams, J. B. W., & Spitzer, R. L. (1980). *DSM-III* field trials: Interrater reliability and list of project staff and participants. In American Psychiatric Association, *Diagnostic and statistical manual of mental disorders* (3rd ed.). Washington, D.C.: American Psychiatric Association.

Wilson, G. T. (1976). Outcome research strategies in behavior therapy: Issues and evidence from the treatment of alcoholics. In R. L. Spitzer & D. F. Klein (Eds.), *Evaluation of psychological therapies* (pp. 96–107). Baltimore, Md.: Johns Hopkins University Press.

———. (1995). Empirically validated treatments as a basis for clinical practice: Problems and prospects. In S. C. Hayes, V. M. Follette, R. M. Dawes, & K. E. Grady (Eds.), *Scientific standards of psychological practice: Issues and recommendations* (pp. 163–196). Reno, Nev.: Context Press.

———. (1996a). Empirically-validated treatments: Reality and resistance. *Clinical Psychology: Science and Practice, 3,* 241–244.

———. (1996b). Manual-based treatments: The clinical application of research findings. *Behaviour Research and Therapy, 34,* 295–314.

Yamamoto, B. K., & Meltzer, H. Y. (1995). Basic neuropharmacology of antipsychotic drugs. In G. O. Gabbard (Ed.), *Treatments of psychiatric disorders* (pp. 947–968). Washington, D.C.: American Psychiatric Press.

Zubin, J. (1953). Evaluation of therapeutic outcome in mental disorders. *Journal of Nervous and Mental Disease, 117,* 95–111.

2

Childhood Attention Deficit Hyperactivity Disorder: Nonpharmacological and Combination Treatments

Stephen P. Hinshaw

Rachel G. Klein

Howard Abikoff

Several substantial reviews of post-1980 case reports of direct contingency management with children with attention deficit hyperactivity disorder (ADHD) reveal impressive behavioral and academic gains in specialized classroom settings as long as contingencies are enforced. Although stimulant medication appears to improve both behavioral and academic outcomes to an even greater extent, contingency management procedures may effect a reduction in the stimulant dosage needed for optimal classroom behavior. The small number of key experimental investigations of clinical behavior therapy (generally, of Types 2 and 3) for children with ADHD reported since 1980, most often involving both consultation with teachers and parent management sessions, have tended to yield statistically significant improvement in child behavior as rated by parents and teachers but not as directly observed. The effect sizes of these interventions are, on average, smaller than those from stimulant medication. Two recent well-designed investigations with the potential to assess the effects of lengthier and more intensive multimodal treatments for ADHD that look at both the separate and combined effects of multicomponent psychosocial treatment and medications are nearing completion.

The prevalence, impairment, and poor outcomes associated with attention deficit hyperactivity disorder (ADHD) in childhood provide a clarion call for the application of effective treatment strategies to youngsters with this condition (e.g., Hinshaw, 1994). We feature nonpharmacological intervention strategies, the most effective of which for ADHD comprise behavioral approaches. We highlight at the outset that documented short-term efficacy of medication treatments for ADHD (Campbell & Cueva, 1995; Klein & Wender, 1995) provide a standard for judging other treatments (Hinshaw & Erhardt, 1991). Therefore, in addition to describing studies of nonpharmacological/ behavioral treatments themselves, we also examine (a)

comparisons of behavioral and medication treatments and (b) combined psychosocial-pharmacological intervention strategies for ADHD (see Greenhill, chapter 3, this volume, regarding medication treatments per se). Also, the frequent co-occurrence of ADHD with aggressive and antisocial behavior patterns (Abikoff & Klein, 1992; Fergusson, Horwood, & Lloyd, 1991; Hinshaw, 1987) dictates that intervention success for such outcome domains not be ignored; we refer the reader to Kazdin (chapter 4, this volume) for specific discussion of the treatment of conduct disorders. Finally, we note at the outset that whereas the overall efficacy of psychotherapeutic interventions for children and adolescents has been established (see

Weisz, Weiss, Han, Granger, & Morton, 1995), youth with ADHD have proven distressingly refractory to long-term treatment benefit, a point to which we return at the conclusion of the chapter.

BACKGROUND INFORMATION REGARDING ATTENTION DEFICIT HYPERACTIVITY DISORDER

Considerable knowledge has accumulated about ADHD, the latest title for a constellation of symptoms that has been described for well over a century and that has undergone many name changes over time (Barkley, 1990; Schachar, 1986). First, the constituent symptoms of this disorder fall into two main clusters: inattention-disorganization and overactivity-impulsivity (American Psychiatric Association, 1994; Barkley, 1996). Because such behavior patterns are ubiquitous in young children, clear impairment in academic, family, interpersonal, and self-related domains must be demonstrated to justify the diagnosis. Indeed, the diagnostic criteria for ADHD in the fourth edition of the *Diagnostic and Statistical Manual of Mental Disorders* (*DSM-IV*; American Psychiatric Association, 1994, pp. 83–85) mandate the presence, from early ages, of developmentally atypical levels of the constituent behaviors that yield impairment in multiple settings (see Table 2.1). Individuals can be classified as predominantly inattentive, predominantly hyperactive-impulsive, or combined subtypes. Distinctions between inattentive-type youth and those with inattention plus impulsive-hyperactive features have been found with respect to family history, gender distribution, neuropsychological profiles, and some aspects of treatment response (see Hinshaw, 1994).

When stringent diagnostic criteria are applied, the prevalence of childhood ADHD appears to be approximately 3–4% of elementary-school-aged boys and 1–2% of girls of the same age (Hinshaw, 1994). This gender disparity is even more pronounced in clinic samples, for which boys' higher rates of comorbidity with disruptive disorders (i.e., oppositional defiant disorder or conduct disorder) presumably lead to higher rates of referral. Attention deficit hyperactivity disorder has been shown to exist across multiple cultures and in multiple nations, but precise comparisons of prevalence rates are hampered by disparate screening thresholds and diverse diagnostic criteria (Schachar, 1991).

Crucially, children who meet criteria for ADHD are highly likely to show substantial impairment in key functional domains. They are prone to serious accidents and injuries; they are likely to be academic underachievers (even in the absence of formal learning disabilities); they are highly rejected by peers; their families are often in conflict; and, not surprisingly, they have lowered self-esteem (see, e.g., Barkley, 1990; Hinshaw, 1992; Hinshaw & Melnick, 1995; Slomkowski, Klein, & Mannuzza, 1995). Furthermore, prospective studies have shown that children with ADHD are likely to show persisting symptomatology and impairment into adolescence, with a minority also demonstrating marked problems in young adulthood (Barkley, 1996; Klein & Mannuzza, 1991; Weiss & Hechtman, 1993). In short, evidence for substantial impairment and a negative course speak to the clear need for concerted prevention and treatment efforts.

The underlying nature of ADHD remains an area of active contention. For many years, in keeping with earlier labels of *hyperactivity* or *hyperkinesis*, basic research focused on motoric overactivity and implicated subcortical brain regions in neural models (Laufer & Denhoff, 1957). Two decades ago, focus shifted to underlying attentional processes and deficient self-regulation (e.g., Douglas, 1983). Current work capitalizes on more precise and differentiated views of attentional style, cognitive processing, and behavioral regulation, with increasing recognition that children with ADHD show pronounced difficulties in response inhibition and in organization of motoric output (Schachar, Tannock, Marriott, & Logan, 1995). Frontal and prefrontal impairment is strongly (but nonspecifically) implicated (Barkley, 1996). The lack of agreement on basic mechanisms dictates that evaluation focus on behavioral ratings and structured interviews regarding key symptom areas, developmental history, and domains of impairment. As with nearly all other mental disorders, treatment approaches for ADHD remain empirically and behaviorally based.

The search for causal mechanisms has uncovered a host of potentially interacting risk factors but limited evidence for unimodal, overarching etiologies. Evidence is increasing for moderate heritability of both dimensional and categorical conceptions of ADHD (Faraone et al., 1992); and a host of nongenetic risk factors, such as prenatal and perinatal difficulties, appear to be nonspecifically linked with attentional deficits and hyperactivity (Breslau, 1995; Sprich-Buckminster, Biederman, Milberger, Faraone, & Lehman,

TABLE 2.1 Diagnostic Criteria for Attention Deficit Hyperactivity Disorder

A. Either (1) or (2):
    (1) Six (or more) of the following symptoms of *inattention* have persisted for at least 6 months to a degree that is maladaptive and inconsistent with developmental level:
         Inattention
         (a) often fails to give close attention to details or makes careless mistakes in schoolwork, work, or other activities
         (b) often has difficulty sustaining attention in tasks or play activities
         (c) often does not seem to listen when spoken to directly
         (d) often does not follow through on instructions and fails to finish schoolwork, chores, or duties in the workplace (not due to oppositional behavior or failure to understand directions)
         (e) often has difficulty organizing tasks and activities
         (f) often avoids, dislikes, or is reluctant to engage in tasks that require sustained mental effort (such as schoolwork or homework)
         (g) often loses things necessary for tasks or activities (e.g., toys, school assignments, pencils, books, or tools)
         (h) is often easily distracted by extraneous stimuli
         (i) is often forgetful in daily activities
    (2) Six (or more) of the following symptoms of *hyperactivity-impulsivity* have persisted for at least 6 months to a degree that is maladaptive and inconsistent with developmental level:
         Hyperactivity
         (a) often fidgets with hands or feet or squirms in seat
         (b) often leaves seat in classroom or in other situations in which remaining seated is expected
         (c) often runs or climbs excessively in situations in which it is inappropriate (in adolescents or adults, may be limited to subjective feelings of restlessness)
         (d) often has difficulty playing or engaging in leisure activities quietly
         (e) is always "on the go" or often acts as if "driven by a motor"
         (f) often talks excessively
         Impulsivity
         (g) often blurts out answers before questions have been completed
         (h) often has difficulty awaiting turn
         (i) often interrupts or intrudes on others (e.g., butts into conversations or games)
B. Some hyperactive-impulsive or inattentive symptoms that caused impairment were present before age 7 years.
C. Some impairment from the symptoms is present in two or more settings (e.g., at school [or work] and at home).
D. There must be clear evidence of clinically significant impairment in social, academic, or occupational functioning.
E. The symptoms do not occur exclusively during the course of a Pervasive Developmental Disorder, Schizophrenia, or other Psychotic Disorder and are not better accounted for by another mental disorder (e.g., Mood Disorder, Anxiety Disorder, Dissociative Disorder, or a Personality Disorder).

Attention deficit hyperactivity disorder, combined type: If both Criterion A1 and Criterion A2 are met for the past 6 months.

Attention deficit hyperactivity disorder, predominantly inattentive type: If Criterion A1 is met but Criterion A2 is not met for the past 6 months.

Attention deficit hyperactivity disorder, predominantly hyperactive-impulsive type: If Criterion A2 is met but Criterion A1 is not met for the past 6 months.

Source: American Psychiatric Association, 1994, pp. 83–85. Reprinted by permission.

1993). Some investigations of high-risk, low-income samples have implicated overly stimulating parenting during infancy and toddlerhood in the later display of ADHD (Carlson, Jacobvitz, & Sroufe, 1995; Jacobvitz & Sroufe, 1987), but child-rearing practices or attitudes are not likely candidates as "main effect" causes of ADHD. Indeed, bidirectional conceptions of parent-child influence are necessary. The clear role of coercive parenting styles in the development of

aggressive and antisocial behaviors that often accompany ADHD (Anderson, Hinshaw, & Simmel, 1994; Patterson, Reid, & Dishion, 1992) implicates family intervention as a cornerstone of psychosocial treatment approaches.

It is in the classroom setting that the constituent behaviors of ADHD often yield their most harmful effects. Nonfocused attention, disruptive behavior, and poor rule following place youth with ADHD at high risk for underachievement, peer rejection, and consequent decrements in self-esteem (Barkley, 1990). School-based intervention is thus a key aspect of psychosocial interventions.

In summary, ADHD is a persistent behavior disorder that yields substantial impairment. Comorbidity with aggressive-spectrum disorders is commonplace, and associations with emotional and learning disorders are above chance levels (Biederman, Newcorn, & Sprich, 1991). Prevalence is estimated to approach 3–5% of the school-aged population, with a male preponderance (American Psychiatric Association, 1994). Interacting causal factors include genetic predispositions and early biological triggers, with negative familial patterns serving as potential escalating variables. Home- and school-based intervention strategies comprise the backbone of psychosocial treatments.

HISTORICAL CONCEPTIONS
OF INTERVENTION

For many decades, the child guidance model and its underlying psychodynamic conceptualization held court as the primary approach for nearly all clinically referred children in the United States. Thus, play therapy constituted the predominant psychosocial treatment strategy for youngsters with ADHD. Evidence for the efficacy of such insight-oriented treatments for youngsters with ADHD is lacking. The application of behavioral, social learning approaches to youngsters specifically diagnosed as "hyperactive" began in the 1960s (e.g., Patterson, 1965). During the 1970s and 1980s, both behavioral and cognitive-behavioral interventions—which promised greater durability of treatment gains through self-management training—became far more widespread. Cognitive-behavioral treatments have not shown clinically significant benefits for children with ADHD (Abikoff, 1991; Hinshaw & Erhardt, 1991); systematically applied behavioral interventions are the focus of our review.

As discussed in greater detail by Greenhill (chapter 3, this volume), psychopharmacological approaches to ADHD have been scientifically appraised for nearly 60 years. Stimulants were first noted in the 1930s to yield impressive short-term benefits for youth with behavioral and emotional disturbances, and many hundreds of controlled intervention studies have continued to document impressive gains in core symptom

areas and in domains of associated impairment when youngsters with ADHD are treated with stimulants (Campbell & Cueva, 1995; Klein, 1987; Swanson, McBurnett, Christian, & Wigal, 1995). However, evidence for a relative prognostic advantage in children treated with medication has eluded empirical verification. As a result, evaluation of (a) more intensive psychosocial strategies and (b) integrations of psychosocial and pharmacological interventions is a priority (Pelham & Murphy, 1986; Richters et al., 1995).

PROGRAMMATIC AND
METHODOLOGIC ISSUES IN
DETERMINING TREATMENT BENEFITS

Before appraising specific evidence regarding the documented benefits of psychosocial treatments for ADHD, we discuss the different types of behavioral interventions, as well as the research designs and assessment methods used to evaluate these types of nonpharmacological treatments.

Direct Contingency Management Versus
Clinical Behavior Therapy

Two types of behavioral intervention approaches for youngsters with behavior disorders are salient: (a) direct contingency management, for which intensive reward and punishment procedures are established in specialized treatment facilities or demonstration classrooms, and (b) clinical behavior therapy procedures, for which consultation (via group or individual sessions) is provided to families and teachers, who in turn implement behavior management programs in the child's natural environment. With direct contingency management, a variety of systematic reward and response cost procedures is implemented with frequent and intensive schedules of administration. The heavy reinforcement schedules implemented in specialized settings, however, may not be readily applicable in the natural environment, and effects may not be generalizable to other settings. Furthermore, gains seen under conditions of direct prompting may dissipate without explicit programming for generalization. Thus, evaluation during explicitly prompted performance (e.g., in the presence of a teacher's aide who delivers strict contingencies) is likely to yield greater estimates of efficacy than appraisal during unprompted periods; in the vast majority of investigations of contingency management, treatment evaluation is made during the period of active contingencies.

Clinical behavior therapy procedures involve a structured curriculum of parent consultation, teacher consultation, or both. A prototypic sequence of activities for parent training involves (a) directing positive attention to the child; (b) targeting performance goals and collecting baseline data; (c) implementing individualized, systematic, and coordinated home- and school-based reinforcement programs; and (d) utilizing contingent, nonphysical punishment procedures such as time-out or response cost (e.g., Barkley, 1987). Teachers receive consultation in such areas as modifying expectations, classroom seating patterns, individualized reward programs, and coordination of home-school reinforcement systems. Clinical behavior therapy programs originated in the 1960s for children with oppositional or aggressive behavior patterns; during the 1970s, applications were targeted specifically to youth with ADHD (O'Leary, Pelham, Rosenbaum, & Price, 1976).

A key research issue is that the two types of behavioral treatment strategies are typically evaluated in different ways, confounding easy comparison across investigations. Specifically, direct contingency management interventions, which emanate from the applied behavior analysis tradition, usually employ single-case experimental designs (e.g., reversal, multiple baseline) to ascertain the causal effect of specific contingencies on the dependent measures of interest. Such interventions are appraised nearly exclusively in specialized programs containing only youth with ADHD (or other disruptive behavior disorders); these programs use extremely short periods of intervention (measured in hours or days). As a result, such investigations do not readily fit the standards-of-proof framework (i.e., Type 1, Type 2, Type 3) used in the current volume. Clinical behavior therapy procedures, on the other hand, are usually implemented in home and regular-education settings and are evaluated by means of randomized, parallel group clinical trials, with subjects assigned to contrasting treatments for periods of several months (or more). Note that we have designated most of the investigations of clinical behavior therapy as Type 2. That is, although they employ random assignment to treatment condition, they have relatively short intervention periods and no manualization of treatment procedures. We reserve Type 1 status for long-term randomized clinical trials with carefully manualized intervention procedures and objective observations or other blinded assessments as outcome measures (see the section on long-term multimodal treatments).

OUTCOME STUDIES

Our review focuses on investigations of direct contingency management or clinical behavior therapy for children diagnosed specifically with ADHD (or with earlier diagnostic conceptions that correspond with ADHD, e.g., attention deficit disorder or hyperactivity). For both direct contingency management and clinical behavior therapy studies, we include designs that (a) directly compare behavioral interventions with placebo treatments or contrasting psychosocial treatments, (b) contrast behavioral treatments with medication conditions, and/or (c) examine combinations of behavioral and pharmacological treatments in relation to single-treatment modalities. The comprehensive reviews of early studies in the field (see Mash & Dalby, 1979; Sprague, 1983) allow us to restrict our coverage to treatment investigations published from the year 1980. Finally, we exclude interventions that focus on cognitive mediational approaches as the systematic reviews of Abikoff (1987, 1991) and Hinshaw and Erhardt (1991) document their lack of efficacy for this population. In brief, despite their initial promise, self-instructional strategies have failed to produce any significant cognitive or behavioral gains for youngsters with ADHD even though more mildly impaired youth may respond. Because, however, the field is searching for any means possible of extending the gains of treatments for youth with ADHD, the potential for problem-solving, mediational approaches to extend benefits from structured contingency management programs is still worthy of study (Hinshaw, Henker, & Whalen, 1984).

Direct Contingency Management

Building on the explosion of research on single-case experiments in the 1960s and 1970s—in which it was repeatedly demonstrated that specific contingencies produced strong, acute effects on observed child behavior—more recent studies have focused on (a) comparisons of varying types of contingencies (e.g., positive versus negative consequences) and (b) contrasts between behaviorally oriented and medication-related strategies for children with ADHD. The large number of specific investigations precludes a study-by-study analysis (for a thorough review, see Pfiffner & O'Leary, 1993). We note that investigators of contingency management programs often de-emphasize formal diagnosis; thus, results pertain to a wide range of children who externalize.

The prototypic investigation of direct contingency management takes place in a specialized classroom in which all of the participating children have behavioral disorders. The teacher or "behavioral engineer" is trained to implement classroomwide contingencies, typically incorporating (a) such positive incentives as praise or individualized reward programs for targeted behaviors (see Pfiffner, Rosen, & O'Leary, 1985); (b) negative consequences such as reprimands, response cost contingencies (the subtraction of earned points; see Rapport, Murphy, & Bailey, 1982), or time-out; or (c) combinations of positive and negative contingencies (e.g., see Rosen, O'Leary, Joyce, Conway, & Pfiffner, 1984). The contingencies are altered over periods of hours or, at most, days; outcome measures are usually restricted to observations of on-task or disruptive classroom behavior (see Pelham, Carlson, Sams, Dixon, & Hoza, 1993, for a wider range of outcome measures); and single-case or within-subject experimental methodologies are typically employed to yield causal inferences. Given their specialized and time-restricted nature, most investigations of direct contingency management programs can best be viewed as demonstrations of the acute effects of reward-and-punishment procedures rather than as integrative treatments per se.

The behavioral gains reported in these studies are often impressive (e.g., see Robinson, Newby, & Ganzell, 1981). For instance, Rosen et al. (1984, Experiment 1) reported an average increase in on-task behavior (across 8 subjects), from 35% during no-contingency periods to 79% during intervals of active contingent reinforcement or punishment. Importantly, in some reports academic productivity has been found to parallel the behavioral improvements (e.g., Rapport et al., 1982). The systematic work of Susan O'Leary and colleagues has demonstrated that stringently implemented, individualized reward programs can yield benefits for youth who are hyperactive, disruptive, or both (see Pfiffner et al., 1985), but the use of prudent, low-intensity negative consequences (e.g., brief repri-

mands backed up with privilege loss; response cost) is an extremely valuable component of contingency management (Rosen et al., 1984; see also Rapport et al., 1982).

From another perspective, however, the experimental success of demonstrating stimulus control (i.e., improvements over baseline that remit when contingencies are removed) betrays a lack of sustained treatment-related clinical benefits. In other words, the lack of generalized and persisting gains when contingencies are lifted highlights the key deficiency of such behavioral intervention strategies (Pelham & Hinshaw, 1992).

In some early investigations, effects of behavioral manipulations appeared stronger than those from medication-related changes (Rapport et al., 1982). The more recent, systematic research of Pelham and colleagues (Carlson, Pelham, Milich, & Dixon, 1992; Pelham et al., 1993) in intensive summer treatment program settings, however, demonstrates otherwise. In both reports, systematic behavioral contingencies in special classroom settings produced a significant benefit (compared with nonsystematic contingencies) regarding observed classroom behavior but did not yield significant improvement in academic productivity or accuracy. Stimulant medication, on the other hand, improved both behavioral and academic outcome domains, with an effect size approximately twice that of the behavioral contingencies (Pelham et al., 1993). Furthermore, whereas stimulants added a significant benefit to direct contingency management, the converse was not the case. It is noteworthy, however, that contingency management procedures may effect a reduction in the stimulant dosage needed to yield optimal classroom behavior in specialized settings, with investigations suggesting that methylphenidate (MPH) dosages can be roughly halved (Carlson et al., 1992; see also Horn et al., 1991; Pelham, Schnedler, Bologna, & Contreras, 1980).

In summary, direct contingency management procedures produce significant short-term benefits regarding off-task and disruptive behavior patterns but are largely confined to specialized settings. The lack of maintenance of behavior change and the artificiality of the settings in which contingency management has been implemented are key limitations; in addition, even intensive, systemic classroom programs show significantly weaker overall effects than those from stimulant medication. Moreover, the addition of contingency procedures has not provided significant increments to medication-related gains (Carlson et al., 1992; Pelham et al., 1993). As noted above, the types of studies used to show the efficacy of direct contingency management for children with ADHD are not readily classifiable by the framework for standards of proof used in this volume. Whereas single-case demonstrations of contingency-related effects on observed behavior are heuristic, they do not, in and of themselves, translate into comprehensive interventions for groups of youngsters in natural settings. It is incumbent on future investigators to incorporate the power of direct contingency management approaches into generalizable treatment strategies.

Clinical Behavior Therapy

Table 2.2 lists key experimental investigations published in the 1980s and 1990s of clinical behavior therapy investigations for children with ADHD. Between-group clinical trials are included in this table. As can be seen, the typical treatment period spans several months, with parent training procedures and teacher consultation sessions comprising the key clinical activities. An important feature of many such programs is the establishment of a joint, home-school reward program such as a "daily report card" through which key school targets are monitored by the teacher with home reinforcement contingent on a positive teacher report or even with response cost contingent on a negative report.

The cited investigations are few in number and diverse in treatment methods and specific research design parameters. For example, some studies compare behavior therapy directly to medication (e.g., Gittelman et al., 1980; Firestone, Kelly, Goodman, & Davey, 1981), some evaluate combination medication-psychosocial treatments (Firestone et al., 1981; Gittelman et al., 1980; Pelham et al., 1988), and others employ either delayed treatment controls (Anastopoulos, Shelton, DuPaul, & Guevremont, 1993; Dubey, O'Leary, & Kaufman, 1983; Pisterman et al., 1989, 1992) or alternative treatment control groups (Barkley, Guevremont, Anastopoulos, & Fletcher, 1992; Dubey et al., 1983; Horn, Ialong, Popvich, & Perdatto, 1987; Horn, Ialong, Greenburg, Packard, & Smith-Winberry, 1990; Horn et al., 1991; Pelham et al., 1988). Several investigations, in fact, perform more than one type of comparison. Furthermore, some of the clinical behavior therapy interventions include

school consultation (Firestone et al., 1981; Gittelman et al., 1980; Pelham et al., 1988; Horn et al., 1990, 1991), whereas the majority consist solely of parent management. Several investigations are not included in Table 2.2 for reasons of sampling (e.g., Strayhorn & Weidman, 1989, who evaluated preventive parent-child interaction training for low-income preschoolers) or design (i.e., within-subject investigations of Pelham et al., 1980, and Pollard, Ward, & Barkley, 1983).

Despite the differences across the reported investigations, it is apparent from Table 2.2 that clinical behavior therapy procedures often yield statistically significant benefits with regard to ADHD-related problem behavior. In several cases, the effects reveal clinical significance as well (e.g., Anastopoulos et al., 1993; Pelham et al., 1988), for at least some domains of outcome.

Five key limitations are noteworthy. First, in our view, none of the studies in Table 2.2 qualifies strictly as a Type 1 investigation. We reserved this designation for rigorous, long-term, randomized clinical trials with assessment of multiple outcome domains. Our stringent standards for a Type 1 designation must be kept in mind while reviewing the contents of the table. The best controlled and most rigorous of the investigations in the table is the study of Gittelman et al. (1980), which is labeled "Type 2+" in the table. That is, despite its merits, the interventions tested were 8 weeks in duration, and treatment procedures were not fully manualized. Type 1 investigations of psychosocial treatments in the child-adolescent field are daunting (see discussion below of the National Institute of Mental Health [NIMH] Multimodal Treatment Study for Children with ADHD).

Second, significant effects are more often found on parent (or teacher) rating scales than for objectively observed behavior (e.g., Dubey et al., 1983; Gittelman et al., 1980). Although the best-established rating scales are well normed and treatment sensitive (see Hinshaw & Nigg, in press), the potential for bias is real in that the adults who determine child outcomes are precisely those individuals who receive active intervention. A parent's or teacher's increased sense of efficacy or coping resulting from training procedures may underlie improved behavior ratings of the child. Objective assessment procedures (e.g., direct observations, sociometric appraisals from peers, tests of academic performance) are needed to supplement rating scale measures.

Authors	N/M Age (years)	Behavioral Treatment	Study Design	Outcome Domains	Key Findings
Gittelman et al. (1980)	61/8.25	8 weeks: Weekly individual sessions with parents and with teacher augmented by child attendance when needed and by telephone contact	**Type 2+** 1. BT + placebo 2. MPH 3. BT + MPH (pre-post)	A. Behavior ratings (T) B. Classroom observations C. Global improvement ratings (M, T, Psy)	A. 3 = 2 > 1 B. Disruptive: 3 = 2 > 1 Minor motor: 3 > 2 = 1 C. M: 1 = 2 = 3; Tchr: 1 > 2 = 3; Psy: 1 > 3, with 2 = both 1 and 3[a]
Firestone et al. (1981)[b]	43/7.3	3 months: 3 individual and 6 group parent training sessions plus 2 teacher consultations	**Type 2** 1. BT + placebo 2. MPH 3. BT + MPH (pre-post)	A. Academic achievement B. Laboratory reaction time C. Behavior ratingss (P, T)	A. and B.: 2 = 3 > 1 C.:[c]
Dubey et al. (1983)	37/8.4	9 weeks: Weekly group parent training sessions	**Type 2** 1. BT 2. Parent effectiveness training 3. Delayed treatment control (prepost-9-month FU)	A. Behavior ratings (P) B. Videotaped PC interaction, scored for parent and child behavior	A. 1 = 2 > 3, with 1 and 2 both showing significant pre-post, and pre-FU change for several scales B. No effects
Horn et al. (1987)	19/9.7	8 weeks: 8 weekly group parent training sessions	**Type 2** 1. BT 2. SI 3. BT + SI (pre-post-1-month FU)	A. Child self-report and lab measures B. Behavior ratings (P, T) C. Classroom observations	Equal improvement across groups for all but 1 of 32 outcome measures[d]
Pelham et al. (1988)	30/[e]	5 months: M = 10 individual and group parent training sessions, plus M = 10 teacher consultations	**Type 2** 1. BT + social skills + MPH 2. BT + social skills + placebo 3. BT + MPH 4. BT + placebo 5. Social skills only (not assigned randomly) (pre-post)	A. Behavior ratings (P, T) B. Academic achievement C. Peer sociometrics D. Classroom observations	1 = 2 = 3 = 4 for A (parent), B, C, and D, with all 4 groups showing significant pre-post improvement (whereas 5 did not). For teacher ratings, 1 and 3 improved more than 2 and 4 during period of active medication.
Pisterman et al. (1989)	46/4.2	12 weeks: 10 group parent training sessions plus 2 individual sessions	**Type 2** 1. BT 2. Delayed-treatment control group (pre-post-3-month FU)	A. Videotaped PC interaction scored for parent and child behavior B. Behavior ratings (P)	A. 1 > 2 re: child compliance and several parenting measures. B. 1 = 2 re: Conners ratings[f]
Horn et al. (1990)	31/8.8	12 weeks: 12 group parent training sessions plus 3 teacher consultations	**Type 2** 1. BT 2. SI 3. BT + SI (pre-post-8-month FU)	A. Child achievement, attention, and self-concept B. Behavior ratings (P, T)	No treatment differences (no group × time interactions); all groups showed pre-post and pre-FU improvement[g].

(continued)

TABLE 2.2 (continued)

Authors	N/M Age (years)	Behavioral Treatment	Study Design	Outcome Domains	Key Findings
Horn et al. (1991)[h]	78/7–11	12 weeks: 12 group parent training sessions plus 12 child SI sessions plus 3 teacher consultations	**Type 2** 1. Placebo 2. Low-dose MPH 3. High-dose MPH 4. 1 + BT/SI 5. 2 + BT/SI 6. 3 + BT/SI (pre-post)	A. Child achievement, attention, and self-concept B. Classroom observations C. Behavior ratings (P, T)	Groups with MPH showed greater improvement than did those with placebo; Groups 5 and 6 did not outperform 2 and 3.[i]
Barkley et al. (1992)	61/13.9	10 weeks: 8–10 weekly parent sessions	**Type 2** 1. Behavioral parent training 2. Problem-solving and communication therapy 3. Structural family therapy (pre-post-3-month FU)	A. Behavior ratings (P, A) B. Family ratings (P, A) C. Videotaped P-A interaction D. Rated depression (M)	1 = 2 = 3 for all outcomes; all groups yielded pre-post improvement for A, B, and D (with maintenance at FU).[i]
Pisterman et al. (1992)	45/4.0	12 weekly group parent training sessions	**Type 2** 1. BT 2. Delayed treatment group (pre-post-3-month FU)	A. Behavior ratings (P) B. Videotaped PC interaction scored for parent and child behavior and attention	1 > 2 for pre-post and pre-FU comparisons regarding parent behavior and child behavior but not child attention.
Anastopoulos et al. (1993)	34/8.1	2 months: 9 sessions of parent training	**Type 3** 1. BT 2. Delayed treatment group	A. Behavior ratings (P) B. Parent-reported stress, parenting efficacy, ADHD knowledge, marital satisfaction	1 > 2 for pre-post comparisons regarding ADHD symptoms and some aspects of parental functioning; gains maintained at FU.

Notes: N = number of subjects completing the investigation. BT = clinical behavior therapy; FU = follow-up; SI = self-instructional training for child; MPH = methylphenidate; M = mother; P = parent; T = teacher; PC = parent-child; Psy = psychiatrist; A = adolescent; PA = parent-adolescent.

[a]Final N = 86 as reported in Klein and Abikoff (1989); overall findings identical to those reported here. For Treatments 2 and 3, MPH was individually titrated, averaging 38.2 mg/day. For all measures, each of the three treatments yielded significant within-subject change across the 8 weeks of treatment. Furthermore, Treatment 1 (combination) was the only one in which subjects were rated by teachers and observers as indistinguishable from normal comparison subjects after treatment.

[b]See also Firestone, Crowe, Goodman, and McGrath (1986) for presentation of 1-year (N = 52) and 2-year (N = 30) follow-up data for subsets of this sample who remained for assessment. At each follow-up period, no significant between-group differences were found for any outcome measure, in part because a noteworthy subgroup of parent training plus placebo subjects had "switched" to medication treatment.

[c]Results of covariance analysis are difficult to interpret, but it appears as though the medicated groups outperformed the behavior therapy plus placebo children for teacher Conners scores. The MPH was individually titrated, averaging 22 mg/day. All three groups showed significant within-subject change on Metropolitan Achievement Tests and on parent- and teacher-rated behavior but only the medicated youngsters improved on the Gates-MacGinitie Verbal Grade Level score.

[d]SI treatment involved weekly group sessions for the children. Follow-up data at 1 month showed persistence of within-subject changes across treatment groups for several outcome measures.

[e]For the 20 children in Groups 1–4 who received behavior therapy, Md age was reported to be 7 years; for the 10 children in Group 5, Md = 8 years. The MPH dosages were fixed at 0.3 mg/kg, with most children receiving b.i.d. dosages.

[f]Immediate posttreatment gains for the treated versus delayed-treatment control group were maintained at 3-month follow-up.

[g]Pre-FU changes were found, across groups, for parent ratings only.

[h]See also Ialongo et al (1993) for presentation of 9-month FU data, which revealed a general deterioration of performance for all groups and extremely limited evidence for Group 5 or to outperform Groups 2 or 3 (i.e., marginally significant finding and only for parental ratings).

[i]Low-dose MPH = 0.4 mg/kg; high-dose MPH = 0.8 mg/kg.

[j]When clinical significance of effects was ascertained via procedures of Jacobson and Truax (1991), only 5–30% improved sufficiently across treatment groups and only 5–20% "recovered" (rates did not differ across treatment groups).

Third, the average effects of clinical behavior therapy procedures are smaller in magnitude than those from stimulant medications (Firestone et al., 1981; Gittelman et al., 1980; Horn et al., 1991; see also Carlson et al., 1992; Pelham et al., 1993). Whether longer term benefits might accrue to systematically delivered and lengthier psychosocial interventions (as opposed to medication) is currently indeterminate.

Fourth, full normalization of problem behavior is rarely attained with behavior therapy programs. The analysis of Abikoff and Gittelman (1984), which utilizes data from the Gittelman et al. (1980) investigation, is heuristic in this regard. From direct observation procedures, the main behaviors relevant to ADHD (e.g., interference, off task, out of chair, noncompliance) did not show normalization for the behavior therapy condition, whereas medication normalized 3 of these 4 categories. Only aggressive behavior— which showed rather low initial levels—was brought into normative ranges with the clinical behavior therapy procedures. In addition, peer sociometric status has not been found to be normalized with behavior therapy (see Pelham et al., 1980, 1988), a limitation shared by medication treatment (Whalen et al., 1989).

Fifth, analysis of long-term carryover of effects has rarely been undertaken; those investigations with any follow-through data (ranging from 1 to 9 months) have yielded only tentative evidence for significant maintenance of gains following the end of treatment.

Can clinical behavior therapy procedures increment the effects of medication for youngsters with ADHD? The evidence is suggestive but not definitive. In Gittelman et al. (1980), only the combined medication-behavior therapy condition normalized all measures of behavior, although the differences between this combination treatment condition and the medication-only group were not statistically significant. Along this line, the within-subject study of Pelham et al. (1980) complements several of the studies reported in Table 2.2; it incorporated a 5-month regimen of clinical behavior therapy (parent training plus regular-classroom teacher consultation) with 3-week-long MPH probes performed at baseline and following 3 and 13 weeks of behavioral treatment. After 3 weeks of treatment, the high medication dosage yielded stronger effects than the low dosage level, but following 13 weeks, low and high medication dosages were

equivalent, with both leading to normalization of behavior. The suggestion is that, over time, concerted behavioral intervention can effect a reduction (by approximately 50%) in the dosage of stimulant medication that is required for optimal behavior.

Summary of Findings from Contingency Management and Behavior Therapy Studies

1. Direct contingency management, provided in special classroom settings over brief time periods, yields significant and large reductions in problem behavior and, in some cases, enhancement of academic performance for youngsters with ADHD. Such gains are transitory, however, and stimulants yield stronger effects than those from such classroom contingencies (Carlson et al., 1992; Pelham et al., 1993).

2. Clinical behavior therapy procedures, involving consultation with teachers and conducting parent management sessions, yield statistically significant improvement in child behavior as rated by parents and teachers (but not, typically, as directly observed). Benefits fall short of normalization of functioning, however, and are considerably weaker than those from medication. On occasion, clinical behavior therapy significantly increments the gains yielded from medication; while contingencies are in effect, behavioral programs combined with low-dosage medication appear to yield effects that are similar to benefits from higher doses of medication.

3. Because of the importance of defiant, aggressive, and antisocial behavior patterns for the persistence and magnification of ADHD-related impairment, it is essential that treatment studies document effects for this domain.

4. Intensive behavioral intervention blending (a) direct contingency management (through summer treatment program settings and in-class paraprofessional prompting and reinforcement) with (b) long-term clinical behavior therapy (through parent management classes and school consultation) has not been studied to date but is under investigation in a Type 1, multicenter clinical trial focusing on ADHD (Richters et al., 1995; see discussion below).

5. As reviewed elsewhere and noted above, cognitive approaches (particularly those emphasizing self-instructional therapies) have not yielded statistically or clinically significant benefits for youth with ADHD (Abikoff, 1987, 1991; Hinshaw & Erhardt, 1991). The

use of self-management procedures to extend the benefits of well-implemented behavioral intervention is worth systematic investigation, however, given the poor maintenance of gains from both behavioral and pharmacological treatments beyond active intervention periods.

Given these conclusions, we cannot offer a carte blanche endorsement of nonpharmacological interventions for ADHD as they are currently operationalized and delivered. Indeed, although benefits have been shown to accrue with well-delivered behavioral treatments, they are rarely long lasting or sufficient for the child and family. Despite their clear benefits, medication approaches have limitations as well (see Greenhill, chapter 3, this volume). More intensive and lengthy psychosocial treatments therefore require investigation as alternatives or adjuncts to pharmacological approaches.

Long-Term Multimodal Treatments

Regarding duration, even the longest trials of behavior therapy for children with ADHD have spanned periods of a few months at most (see Table 2.2), and integration of direct contingency management with intensive behavior therapy explicitly programmed for generalization and maintenance has not been undertaken in an experimental clinical trial. We therefore briefly describe two recent investigations that promise to answer questions regarding the effects of lengthier and more intensive psychosocial treatment. Before doing so, we point out that an important nonexperimental investigation of long-term, multimodality treatment—a Type 3 study involving tailored combinations of medication, family therapy, tutoring, marital therapy, and individual child therapy decided on by careful clinical appraisal—was undertaken over 15 years ago (Satterfield, Cantwell, & Satterfield, 1979). Because (a) random assignment of children and families to treatment combinations was not made, (b) a control group was not utilized, and (c) only a minority of families who began the intervention were available for follow-up assessments, attributions of decreased delinquency in adolescence (several years after the termination of treatment) to the multimodality intervention must be regarded with extreme caution (Satterfield, Satterfield, & Schell, 1987). Nonetheless, this investigation spurred the field to consider integrative interventions for youth with ADHD.

New York-Montreal Study

A dual-site, 2-year, randomized clinical trial of stimulant medication in combination with multimodal psychosocial treatment was undertaken to determine the additive effects of psychosocial treatment and to ascertain the viability of medication discontinuation after multimodal psychosocial treatment (Abikoff & Hechtman, 1994; Hechtman & Abikoff, 1995). This was a Type 1 study in New York and Montreal, but one that did not include a psychosocial treatment condition in the absence of medication. Positive responders ($N =$ 102) to stimulant medication, aged 7–9 years, were assigned to one of three treatments for 12 months: (a) optimal-dose MPH alone; (b) MPH in combination with active parent, child, and teacher intervention; or (c) MPH in combination with an attention control intervention. Maintenance therapy for 1 year followed the year-long intensive intervention phase. The mean daily dosage of MPH was 34 mg/day during the two years of active treatment.

Multimodal treatment included social skills training, remedial tutoring, organization skills training, and individual psychotherapy for the child; parent management training and counseling for the parents; and a home-based reinforcement program for targeted school behavior. As described in Abikoff and Hechtman (1996), multimodal and attention control treatments were held twice per week during the first year of intervention, decreasing to monthly booster sessions for the second year. Despite the intensity, scope, and duration of clinical, multimodal treatment, assessments from multiple sources (including parent and teacher ratings of child behavior, school observations, academic achievement, parental perceptions of parenting and self-efficacy, and child self-report measures) yielded no evidence of incremental efficacy for the psychosocial intervention. That is, children and parents in each condition improved in all outcome domains, maintaining gains during the 2 years of medication treatment; multimodal treatment did not provide any protection when medication was discontinued in that all children deteriorated and had to be placed back on active medication, with the majority requiring remediation within 2 weeks of placebo substitution at the end of 1 year of treatment. Thus, findings indicate that carefully monitored stimulant treatment is not incremented by the addition of a long-term, multimodal, intensive package of parent and child interventions. On the other hand, direct contingency management played only a small part of the psychosocial intervention (points were awarded during the child social skills groups).

Multimodal Treatment Study of Children with ADHD (MTA Study)

Following growing national concern regarding the need for systematic, long-term, multimodal treatment for ADHD (see Institute of Medicine, 1989), the Child and Adolescent Disorders Research Branch of the NIMH released a Request for Applications in 1992, soliciting proposals to design an optimal investigation. Six sites were awarded funding, and the MTA study began later that year.

Combining elements of efficacy and effectiveness studies (see Seligman, 1995), the MTA study is a Type 1 investigation of 576 children, ages 7 through 9.9, with ADHD who have a wide range of comorbidity. Random assignment is made to one of four intensive, 14-month-long treatments: (a) medication only, (b) psychosocial only, (c) combined medication and psychosocial, and (d) community comparison (assessment and referral only). The psychosocial treatment package in Conditions (b) and (c) involves a systematic integration of direct contingency management — implemented through the Summer Treatment Program (STP) of Pelham and Hoza (1996) and the Irvine Paraprofessional Program (IPP) of Swanson (1992) — with long-term clinical behavior therapy in the form of parent management training and teacher consultation (see Anastopoulos et al., 1993; O'Leary & Pelham, 1978).

These treatment components, focusing on the child, the family, and the teacher, are manualized and carefully integrated. Families begin treatment in the winter or spring of a given year with weekly parent management sessions — group as well as individual — and the same therapist commences teacher consultation. Children participate in the STP that summer; during the fall, teacher consultation and parent management continue, with the child receiving a half-day IPP aide to facilitate the school consultation (aides are the same individuals who serve as STP counselors). The next winter and spring are devoted to a systematic program aimed at maintenance of treatment gains. In all, 27 group and 8 individual parent training sessions, 20 teacher consultations, an 8-week STP, and 12 weeks of IPP aide facilitation are incorporated and integrated in the 14-month active treatment period.

This package of validated, intensive, and long-term intervention components will be tested for its comparability to and combination with stimulant medication strategies in the MTA investigation; it is unique in its integration of direct contingency management with extensive clinical behavior therapy. Finally, in keeping with the zeitgeist of psychotherapy research in general, a key goal for the MTA investigation is to ascertain the effectiveness of these treatment procedures for different domains of functioning in different types of individuals with ADHD, including those with and without antisocial-spectrum comorbidity (Richters et al., 1995). Outcome results await the completion of the trial in 1998.

CONCLUSIONS

As we have highlighted in this chapter, the traditional behavior therapy approaches fall short of clinically sufficient benefits for the treatment of children with ADHD. The emphasis has therefore moved to more intensive and ambitious programs — referred to as multimodal — that explicitly target multiple functions over extended periods of time in the hope of influencing posttreatment adjustment (see, e.g., Kazdin, 1987, who argues for a "chronic disease" model, requiring long-term treatment strategies, of externalizing behavior patterns). The sole experimentally controlled multimodal study completed to date (Abikoff & Hechtman, 1996) did not yield evidence for a significant advantage of a combination pharmacological-multimodal condition over and above medication alone. As noted, however, this investigation did not test a multimodal psychosocial intervention without medication. The MTA study, described above, the most elaborate study of its type ever undertaken, includes several novel features, such as participation of paraprofessional aides in the child's classroom, an intensive summer treatment program, and close integration of child, school, and family treatment components. The field is therefore in the advantageous position of looking forward to what is believed to be a rigorous test of the best effort yet undertaken to ameliorate the course of children with ADHD.

ACKNOWLEDGMENTS   Work on this chapter was supported, in part, by National Institute of Mental Health Grants R01 MH45064 and U01 MH50461 (Stephen P. Hinshaw), R01 MH35779 (Rachel G. Klein), and U01 MH50453 (Howard Abikoff).

References

Abikoff, H. (1987). An evaluation of cognitive behavior therapy for hyperactive children. In B. B. Lahey & A. E. Kazdin (Eds.), *Advances in clinical child psychology* (Vol. 10, pp. 171–216). New York: Plenum Press.

———. (1991). Cognitive training in ADHD children: Less to it than meets the eye. *Journal of Learning Disabilities, 24,* 205–209.

Abikoff, H., & Gittelman, R. (1984). Does behavior therapy normalize the classroom behavior of hyperactive children? *Archives of General Psychiatry, 41,* 449–454.

Abikoff, H., & Hechtman, L. T. (1994, October). Methylphenidate and multimodal treatment for ADHD. In B. Geller (Chair), *Advanced topics in psychopharmacology.* Paper presented at the annual meeting of the American Academy of Child and Adolescent Psychiatry, New York.

Abikoff, H., & Hechtman, L. (1996). Multimodal therapy and stimulants in the treatment of children with ADHD. In E. D. Hibbs & P. Jensen (Eds.), *Psychosocial treatment for child and adolescent disorders: Empirically based approaches* (pp. 341–369. Washington, D.C.: American Psychological Association.

Abikoff, H., & Klein, R. (1992). Attention-deficit hyperactivity and conduct disorder: Comorbidity and implications for treatment. *Journal of Consulting and Clinical Psychology, 60,* 881–892.

American Psychiatric Association. (1994). *Diagnostic and statistical manual of mental disorders* (4th ed.). Washington, D.C.: Author.

Anastopoulos, A. D., Shelton, T., DuPaul, G. J., & Guevremont, D. C. (1993). Parent training for attention-deficit hyperactivity disorder: Its impact on parent functioning. *Journal of Abnormal Child Psychology, 21,* 581–596.

Anderson, C. A., Hinshaw, S. P., & Simmel, C. (1994). Mother-child interactions in ADHD and comparison boys: Relationships to overt and covert externalizing behavior. *Journal of Abnormal Child Psychology, 22,* 247–265.

Barkley, R. A. (1987). *Defiant children: A clinician's manual for parent training.* New York: Guilford Press.

———. (1990). *Attention deficit hyperactivity disorder: A handbook for diagnosis and treatment.* New York: Guilford Press.

———. (1996). Attention-deficit hyperactivity disorder. In E. J. Mash & R. A. Barkley (Eds.), *Child psychopathology.* New York: Guilford Press.

Barkley, R. A., Guevremont, D. C., Anastopoulos, A. D., & Fletcher, K. E. (1992). A comparison of three family therapy programs for treating family conflicts in adolescents with attention-deficit hyperactivity disorder. *Journal of Consulting and Clinical Psychology, 60,* 450–462.

Biederman, J., Newcorn, J., & Sprich, S. (1991). Comorbidity of attention deficit hyperactivity disorder with conduct, depressive, anxiety, and other disorders. *American Journal of Psychiatry, 148,* 564–577.

Breslau, N. (1995). Psychiatric sequelae of low birth weight. *Epidemiologic Reviews, 17,* 96–104.

Campbell, M., & Cueva, J. E. (1995). Psychopharmacology in child and adolescent psychiatry: A review of the past seven years. *Journal of the American Academy of Child and Adolescent Psychiatry, 34,* 1124–1132.

Carlson, C. L., Pelham, W. E., Milich, R., & Dixon, J. (1992). Single and combined effects of methylphenidate and behavior therapy on the classroom performance of children with attention-deficit hyperactivity disorder. *Journal of Abnormal Child Psychology, 20,* 213–232.

Carlson, E. A., Jacobvitz, D., & Sroufe, L. A. (1995). A developmental investigation of inattentiveness and hyperactivity. *Child Development, 66,* 37–54.

Douglas, V. I. (1983). Attention and cognitive problems. In M. Rutter (Ed.), *Developmental neuropsychiatry* (pp. 280–329). New York: Guilford Press.

Dubey, D. R., O'Leary, S. G., & Kaufman, K. F. (1983). Training parents of hyperactive children in child management: A comparative outcome study. *Journal of Abnormal Child Psychology, 11,* 229–246.

Faraone, S., Biederman, J., Chen, W. J., Krifcher, B., Keenan, K., Moore, C., Sprich, S., & Tsuang, M. (1992). Segregation analysis of attention-deficit hyperactivity disorder: Evidence for single-gene transmission. *Psychiatric Genetics, 2,* 257–276.

Fergusson, D. M., Horwood, L. J., & Lloyd, M. (1991). Confirmatory factor models of attention deficit and conduct disorder. *Journal of Child Psychology and Psychiatry, 32,* 257–274.

Firestone, P., Crowe, D., Goodman, J. T., & McGrath, P. (1986). Vicissitudes of follow-up studies. Differential effects of parent training and stimulant medication with hyperactives. *American Journal of Orthopsychiatry, 56,* 184–194.

Firestone, P., Kelly, M. J., Goodman, J. T., & Davey, J. (1981). Differential treatment effects of parent training and stimulant medication with hyperactives. *Journal of the American Academy of Child Psychiatry, 20,* 135–147.

Gittelman, R., Abikoff, H., Pollack, E., Klein, D., Katz, S., & Mattes, J. (1980). A controlled trial of behavior modification and methylphenidate in hyperactive children. In C. K. Whalen & B. Henker (Eds.), *Hyperactive children: The social ecology of identification and treatment* (pp. 221–243). New York: Academic Press.

Hechtman, L., & Abikoff, H. (1995, October). Multimodal treatment plus stimulants v. stimulant treatment in ADHD children: Results from a two-year comparative treatment study. In R. J. Schachar (Chair), *Recent studies of the treatment of attention-deficit hyperactivity disorder.* Paper presented at the annual meeting of the American Academy of Child and Adolescent Psychiatry, New Orleans.

Hinshaw, S. P. (1987). On the distinction between attentional deficits/hyperactivity and conduct problems/aggression in child psychopathology. *Psychological Bulletin, 101,* 443–463.

———. (1992). Externalizing behavior problems and academic underachievement in childhood and adolescence: Causal relationships and underlying mechanisms. *Psychological Bulletin, 111,* 127–155.

———. (1994). *Attention deficits and hyperactivity in children.* Thousand Oaks, Ca.: Sage.

Hinshaw, S. P., & Erhardt, D. (1991). Attention-deficit hyperactivity disorder. In P. C. Kendall (Ed.), *Child and adolescent therapy: Cognitive-behavioral perspectives* (pp. 98–128). New York: Guilford Press.

Hinshaw, S. P., Henker, B., & Whalen, C. K. (1984). Cognitive-behavioral and pharmacologic interventions for hyperactive boys: Comparative and combined effects. *Journal of Consulting and Clinical Psychology, 52,* 739–749.

Hinshaw, S. P., & Melnick, S. M. (1995). Peer relationships in boys with attention-deficit hyperactivity disorder with and without comorbid aggression. *Development and Psychopathology, 7,* 627–647.

Hinshaw, S. P., & Nigg, J. T. (in press). Behavior rating scales in the assessment of disruptive behavior disorders in childhood. In D. Shaffer & J. Richters (Eds.), *Assessment in child and adolescent psychopathology* (2nd ed.). New York: Guilford Press.

Horn, W. F., Ialongo, N., Greenberg, G., Packard, T., & Smith-Winberry, C. (1990). Additive effects of behavioral parent training and self-control therapy with attention deficit hyperactivity disordered children. *Journal of Clinical Child Psychology, 19,* 98–110.

Horn, W. F., Ialongo, N. S., Pascoe, J. M., Greenberg, G. A., Packard, T., Lopez, M., Wagner, A., & Puttler, L. (1991). Additive effects of psychostimulants, parent training, and self-control therapy with ADHD children. *Journal of the American Academy of Child and Adolescent Psychiatry, 30,* 233–240.

Horn, W. F., Ialongo, N., Popvich, S., & Perdatto, D. (1987). Behavioral parent training and cognitive-behavioral self-control therapy with ADD-H children:

Comparative and combined effects. *Journal of Clinical Child Psychology, 16,* 57–68.

Ialongo, N. S., Horn, W. F., Pascoe, J. M., Greenberg, G., Packard, T., Lopez, M., Wagner, A., & Puttler, L. (1993). The effects of a multimodal intervention with attention-deficit hyperactivity disorder children: A 9-month follow-up. *Journal of the American Academy of Child and Adolescent Psychiatry, 32,* 182–189.

Institute of Medicine. (1989). *Research on children and adolescents with mental, behavioral, and developmental disorders.* Washington, D.C.: National Academy Press.

Jacobvitz, D., & Sroufe, L. A. (1987). The early caregiver-mother relationship and attention deficit disorder with hyperactivity in kindergarten: A prospective study. *Child Development, 58,* 1488–1495.

Jacobson, N. S., & Truax, P. (1991). Clinical significance: A statistical approach to defining meaningful change in psychotherapy research. *Journal of Consulting and Clinical Psychology, 59,* 12–19.

Kazdin, A. E. (1987). Treatment of antisocial behavior in children: Current status and future directions. *Psychological Bulletin, 102,* 187–203.

Klein, R. G. (1987). Pharmacotherapy of childhood hyperactivity: An update. In H. Y. Meltzer (Ed.), *Psychopharmacology: The third generation of progress* (pp. 1215–1224). New York: Raven Press.

Klein, R., & Abikoff, H. (1989). The role of psychostimulants and psychosocial treatments in hyperkinesis. In T. Sagvolden & T. Archer (Eds.), *Attention deficit disorder: Clinical and basic research* (pp. 167–180). Hillsdale, N.J.: Erlbaum.

Klein, R., & Mannuzza, S. (1991). Long-term outcome of hyperactive children: A review. *Journal of the American Academy of Child and Adolescent Psychiatry, 30,* 383–387.

Klein, R. G., & Wender, P. (1995). The role of methylphenidate in psychiatry. *Archives of General Psychiatry, 52,* 429–433.

Laufer, M. W., & Denhoff, E. (1957). Hyperkinetic behavior syndrome in children. *Journal of Pediatrics, 50,* 463–473.

Mash, E. J., & Dalby, J. T. (1979). Behavioral interventions for hyperactivity. In R. L. Trites (Ed.), *Hyperactivity in children: Etiology, measurement, and treatment implications* (pp. 161–216). Baltimore, Md.: University Park Press.

O'Leary, K. D., Pelham, W. E., Rosenbaum, A., & Price, G. H. (1976). Behavioral treatment of hyperkinetic children. *Clinical Pediatrics, 15,* 510–515.

O'Leary, S. G., & Pelham, W. E. (1978). Behavior therapy and withdrawal of stimulant medication in hyperactive children. *Pediatrics, 61,* 211–217.

Patterson, G. R. (1965). An application of conditioning

techniques to the control of a hyperactive child. In L. P. Ullmann & L. Krasner (Eds.), *Case studies in behavior modification* (pp. 370–375). New York: Holt, Rinehart & Winston.

Patterson, G. R., Reid, J. B., & Dishion, T. J. (1992). *Antisocial boys.* Eugene, Ore.: Castalia.

Pelham, W. E., Carlson, C., Sams, S. E., Dixon, M. J., & Hoza, B. (1993). Separate and combined effects of methylphenidate and behavior modification on boys with attention-deficit hyperactivity disorder in the classroom. *Journal of Consulting and Clinical Psychology, 61,* 506–515.

Pelham, W. E., & Hinshaw, S. P. (1992). Behavioral intervention for attention-deficit hyperactivity disorder. In S. M. Turner, K. S. Calhoun, & H. E. Adams (Eds.), *Handbook of clinical behavior therapy* (2nd ed., pp. 259–283). New York: Wiley.

Pelham, W. E., & Hoza, B. (1996). Comprehensive treatment for ADHD: A proposal for intensive summer treatment programs and outpatient follow-up. In E. Hibbs & P. Jensen (Eds.), *Psychosocial treatment research of child and adolescent disorders: Empirically-validated approaches* (pp. 311–340. Washington, D.C.: American Psychological Association Press.

Pelham, W. E., & Murphy, H. A. (1986). Behavioral and pharmacological treatment of attention deficit and conduct disorders. In M. Hersen (Ed.), *Pharmacological and behavioral treatment: An integrative approach* (pp. 108–148). New York: Wiley.

Pelham, W. E., Schnedler, R. W., Bender, M., Nilsson, D., Miller, J., Budrown, M., Ronnei, M., Paluchowski, C., & Marks, D. (1988). The combination of behavior therapy and methylphenidate in the treatment of attention deficit disorder: A therapy outcome study. In L. M. Bloomingdale (Ed.), *Attention deficit disorder* (Vol. 3, pp. 29–48). Oxford, U.K.: Pergamon.

Pelham, W. E., Schnedler, R. W., Bologna, N. C., & Contreras, J. A. (1980). Behavioral and stimulant treatment of hyperactivy children: A therapy study with methylphenidate probes in a within-subject design. *Journal of Applied Behavior Analysis, 13,* 221–236.

Pfiffner, L. J., & O'Leary, S. G. (1993). School-based psychological treatments. In J. L. Matson (Ed.), *Handbook of hyperactivity in children* (pp. 234–255). Boston: Allyn & Bacon.

Pfiffner, L. J., Rosen, L. A., & O'Leary, S. G. (1985). The efficacy of an all-positive approach to classroom management. *Journal of Applied Behavior Analysis, 18,* 257–261.

Pisterman, S., Firestone, P., McGrath, P., Goodman, J., Webster, I., Mallory, R., & Goffin, B. (1992). The role of parent training in treatment of preschoolers with ADDH. *American Journal of Orthopsychiatry, 62,* 397–408.

Pisterman, S., McGrath, P., Firestone, P., Goodman, J. T., Webster, I., & Mallory, R. (1989). Outcome of parent-mediated treatment of preschoolers with attention deficit disorder with hyperactivity. *Journal of Consulting and Clinical Psychology, 57,* 628–635.

Pollard, S., Ward, E., & Barkley, R. A. (1983). The effects of parent training and Ritalin on the parent-child interactions of hyperactive boys. *Child and Family Behavior Therapy, 5,* 51–69.

Rapport, M. D., Murphy, H. A., & Bailey, J. S. (1982). Ritalin v. response cost in the control of hyperactive children: A within-subject comparison. *Journal of Applied Behavior Analysis, 15,* 205–216.

Richters, J. E., Arnold, L. E., Jensen, P. S., Abikoff, H., Conners, C. K., Greenhill, L. L., Hechtman, L. T., Hinshaw, S. P., Pelham, W. E., & Swanson, J. M. (1995). The National Institute of Mental Health Collaborative Multisite Multimodal Treatment Study of Children with Attention-Deficit Hyperactivity Disorder (MTA): I. Background and rationale. *Journal of the American Academy of Child and Adolescent Psychiatry, 34,* 987–1000.

Robinson, P. W., Newby, T. J., & Ganzell, S. L. (1981). A token system for a class of underachieving hyperactive children. *Journal of Applied Behavior Analysis, 14,* 307–315.

Rosen, L. A., O'Leary, S. G., Joyce, S. A., Conway, G., & Pfiffner, L. J. (1984). The importance of prudent negative consequences for maintaining the appropriate behavior of hyperactive students. *Journal of Abnormal Child Psychology, 12,* 581–604.

Satterfield, J. H., Cantwell, D. P., & Satterfield, B. T. (1979). Multimodality treatment: A one-year follow-up of 84 hyperactive boys. *Archives of General Psychiatry, 36,* 965–974.

Satterfield, J. H., Satterfield, B. T., & Schell, A. M. (1987). Therapeutic interventions to prevent delinquency in hyperactive boys. *Journal of the American Academy of Child and Adolescent Psychiatry, 26,* 56–64.

Schachar, R. (1986). Hyperkinetic syndrome: Historical development of the concept. In E. A. Taylor (Ed.), *The overactive child* (pp. 19–40). London: MacKeith.

———. (1991). Childhood hyperactivity. *Journal of Child Psychology and Psychiatry, 32,* 155–191.

Schachar, R., Tannock, R., Marriott, M., & Logan, G. (1995). Deficient inhibitory control in attention deficit hyperactivity disorder. *Journal of Abnormal Child Psychology, 23,* 411–437.

Seligman, M. E. P. (1995). The effectiveness of psychotherapy: The *Consumer Reports* survey. *American Psychologist, 50,* 965–974.

Slomkowski, C., Klein, R. G., & Mannuzza, S. (1995). Is self-esteem an important outcome in hyperactive children? *Journal of Abnormal Child Psychology, 23,* 303–315.

Sprague, R. L. (1983). Behavior modification and educational techniques. In M. Rutter (Ed.), *Developmental neuropsychiatry* (pp. 404–421). New York: Guilford.

Sprich-Buckminster, S., Biederman, J., Milberger, S., Faraone, S. V., & Lehman, B. K. (1993). Are perinatal complications relevant to the manifestation of ADD? Issues of comorbidity and familiality. *Journal of the American Academy of Child and Adolescent Psychiatry, 32,* 1032–1037.

Strayhorn, J. M., & Weidman, C. S. (1989). Reduction of attention deficit and internalizing symptoms in preschoolers through parent-child interaction training. *Journal of the American Academy of Child and Adolescent Psychiatry, 28,* 888–896.

Swanson, J. (1992). *School-based assessments and interventions for ADD students.* Irvine, Ca.: K. C. Publications.

Swanson, J. M., McBurnett, K., Christian, D. L., & Wigal, T. (1995). Stimulant medications and the treatment of children with ADHD. In T. H. Ollendick & R. J. Prinz (Eds.), *Advances in clinical child psychology* (Vol. 17, pp. 265–322). New York: Plenum Press.

Weiss, G., & Hechtman, L. T. (1993). *Hyperactive children grown up* (2nd ed.). New York: Guilford Press.

Weisz, J. R., Weiss, B., Han, S. S., Granger, D. A., & Morton, T. (1995). Effects of psychotherapy with children and adolescents revisited: A meta-analysis of treatment outcome studies. *Psychological Bulletin, 117,* 450–468.

Whalen, C. K., Henker, B., Buhrmester, D., Hinshaw, S. P., Huber, A., & Laski, K. (1989). Does stimulant medication improve the peer status of hyperactive children? *Journal of Consulting and Clinical Psychology, 57,* 545–549.

3

Childhood Attention Deficit Hyperactivity Disorder: Pharmacological Treatments

Laurence L. Greenhill

More than 100 placebo-controlled investigations demonstrate that psychostimulants—methylphenidate, pemoline, and dextroamphetamine—are effective in reducing core symptoms of childhood attention deficit hyperactivity disorder (ADHD). (See Table 3.1 for common abbreviations used in this chapter.) Approximately 70% of patients respond to active medication compared with the response of only 10% to a placebo. Short-term efficacy is more pronounced for behavioral rather than cognitive and learning abnormalities associated with ADHD. In contrast, evidence for the efficacy of psychostimulants in the treatment of ADHD in adults is still regarded by many as inconclusive, with studies reporting very divergent rates of drug efficacy (23–75%). The main adverse side effects of psychostimulant therapy in trials have been insomnia, decreased appetite, stomachache, headache, and dizziness, each occurring significantly more frequently in patients on an active drug than on a placebo. Although psychostimulants are clearly effective in the short term, there is concern that long-term benefits have not yet been adequately assessed. Tricyclic antidepressants are considered the "second-line" therapy for childhood ADHD, with support coming from several controlled trials. Other nonstimulant agents for which there is limited evidence for efficacy include bupropion, buspirone, clonidine, and venlafaxine.

Attention deficit hyperactivity disorder (ADHD), as diagnosed in the United States, is regarded as a major public health problem because it is responsible for 30% to 50% of referrals to mental health services for children. The prevalence of ADHD may be gleaned from comprehensive reviews (Bauermeister, Camino, & Bird, 1994; Szatmari, 1992) of epidemiological studies conducted in Australia (Connell, Irvine, & Rodney, 1982); Norway (Vikan, 1985); the Netherlands (Verhulst, Eussen, & Berden, 1985); Ontario, Canada (Szatmari, Offord, & Boyle, 1989); Mannheim, Germany (Esser, Schmidt, & Woerner, 1996); New Zealand (Anderson, Williams, McGee, & Silva, 1987); Pittsburgh, Pennsylvania (Costello, 1989); Puerto Rico (Bird et al., 1988); and East London (Taylor, Sandberg, Thorley, & Rutter, 1991). Many have used a multimethod-multistage approach involving symptom checklists, followed by direct interviews of a subsample of children scoring above a predetermined cutoff. Rates for ADHD in school-age children ages 6–12 range between 1.7% (Taylor et al., 1991) and 9.5% (Bird et al., 1988), while the prevalence for all subtypes of ADHD shows a wider range, between 1.7% (Taylor et al., 1991) and 12.6% (Velez, Johnson, & Cohen, 1989).

Fortunately, ADHD has proven to be one of the most effectively treated child disorders. A quarter century of published treatment studies and clinical experience attest to the short-term effectiveness of pharmacological strategies (Richters et al., 1995). It has been estimated that between 2% and 2.5% of all school-age children in North America receive some pharma-

TABLE 3.1 Common Abbreviations in This Chapter

TABLE 3.1 Common Abbreviations in This Chapter

ADHD = attention deficit hyperactivity disorder
CLON = clonidine
DA = dopamine
DEX = dextroamphetamine
DMI = desipramine
MPH = methylphenidate
NE = norepinephrine
PEM = pemoline
RCT = randomized clinical trial
SE = side effects

cological intervention for hyperactivity (Bosco & Robin, 1980), with more than 90% being treated with the psychostimulant methylphenidate (MPH) (Greenhill, 1995; Wilens & Biederman, 1992). Estimates (Swanson et al., 1995b) suggest that, from 1990 to 1993, the number of outpatient visits for ADHD increased from 1.6 to 4.2 million per year and the amount of MPH manufactured increased from 1,784 to 5,110 kg per year. Experts and clinicians alike accept that psychostimulants are highly effective in reducing core ADHD symptoms in as many as 80% of children treated. This unusually high rate of drug response explains, to some degree, why published drug research in the past decade has focused on the two safe medications, MPH and DEX (dextroamphetamine), for study (Vitiello & Jensen, 1995). Rather than explore new compounds, published research has applied the randomized clinical trial (RCT) research strategy to special topics, including the treatment response of mentally retarded ADHD children, to the study of MPH's adverse effects, to the determination of "normalization" during drug treatment, and to the clearer delineation of patient characteristics among nonresponders to psychostimulants.

This chapter provides a review of the ADHD treatment literature over the past decade. As with other chapters in this volume, the study classification system listed below is used to guide the reader.

Types of Drug Studies

Type 1 = randomized clinical trials

Type 2 = quasi-experimental trials

Type 3 = pilot studies

Type 4 = review with meta-analyses

Type 5 = reviews without meta-analyses

Type 6 = retrospectives, case reports

Unlike other chapters, a thorough description of the *Diagnostic and Statistical Manual of Mental Disorders*, 4th edition (*DSM-IV*) (American Psychiatric Association [APA], 1994), syndrome of ADHD, its principal diagnostic criteria, and information on incidence, prevalence, epidemiology are not be given as they are well covered elsewhere (see chapter 2, this volume). Instead, the chapter includes (a) a brief historical perspective on ADHD drug treatment studies, using Type 5 reviews to highlight conceptual notions driving drug research; (b) a description of current psychopharmacological treatments of choice, supported by recently published Type 1 RCTs; and (c) a perspective on future areas of ADHD psychopharmacological investigation. New medications, current ongoing ADHD treatment studies involving drug treatments, and alternative new psychopharmacological agents are surveyed, drawing on Type 3 pilot studies.

HISTORICAL PERSPECTIVE: PHARMACOLOGICAL INTERVENTIONS FOR ATTENTION DEFICIT HYPERACTIVITY DISORDER

In 1937, Bradley serendipitously observed that disturbed children and adolescents in a residential treatment facility responded to treatment with sympathomimetics (Bradley, 1937). He administered benzedrine, a racemic form of amphetamine. This treatment produced a dramatic calming effect while simultaneously increasing compliance and academic performance. Benzedrine produced an increase in academic productivity and a "zest for work." Bradley published other Type 6 studies that reported the improvement of children during amphetamine treatment (Bradley, 1941; Bradley & Bowen, 1941). His careful clinical observations later would be verified by Type 1 randomized clinical trials.

The first controlled investigations of these drugs were carried out between 1960 and 1970. During that period, studies showed that psychostimulants increased the seizure threshold (Laufer, Denhoff, & Solomon, 1957), decreased oppositional behavior of boys with conduct disorder in a residential school (Eisenberg et al., 1961), and reliably improved the target symptoms of ADHD as measured using standardized rating forms filled out by parents and teachers (Conners, Eisenberg, & Barcai, 1967). These early studies lacked many refinements available today, such as the use of uniform diagnostic criteria, reliability measures, and multiple observers, so must be judged Type 2 studies.

Since those controlled studies in the early 1960s, there has been an explosion of published Type 1 ADHD psychostimulant studies. The rapid effects of these medications and the clinicians' growing knowledge of ADHD in children facilitated the publication of many well-controlled Type 1 RCTs, all confirming Bradley's initial observations. The drugs DEX and MPH, in particular, can produce statistically significant and clinically meaningful improvements in controlled studies within days. Starting in 1977 (Barkley, 1977), a series of Type 5 literature reviews summarized these studies. Wilens and Biederman's 1992 MEDLINE search retrieved over 990 psychostimulant treatment publications between 1982 and 1991. Summaries of these open-label and controlled studies (Barkley, 1977, 1982; Gittelman, 1987; Gittelman-Klein, 1980) all conclude that the psychostimulants have major beneficial effects on the behavior of children with ADHD over short time periods. Recent verification

of this agreement appeared in a Type 4 meta-analysis (Swanson, 1993) that utilized 250 reviews of psychostimulant studies of children with ADHD. These are enough subjects and studies to satisfy a rigorous Phase 3, premarketing, investigational new drug application to the Food and Drug Administration (FDA). A small sample of frequently cited reviews appears in Table 3.2.

These reviews summarize the overwhelming evidence that the psychostimulants MPH, DEX, and pemoline (PEM) dramatically reduce ADHD behaviors, such as task-irrelevant activity and classroom disturbance, in school-age children (Barkley, 1977; Gittelman-Klein, 1980; Greenhill, 1995; Jacobvitz, Srouge, Stewart, & Leffert, 1990). One such review in 1992 (Wilens & Biederman, 1992) encompassed 4 preschool, 96 school-age, 6 adolescent, and 6 adult controlled studies of psychostimulant treatment. Of these controlled trials, 85 compared MPH to a placebo, 21 compared DEX to a placebo, and 6 evaluated PEM. Treatment response occurred in 65–75% of 4,777 ADHD children treated.

TABLE 3.2 Selected Reviews of Psychostimulant Treatments for School-Age Children

Study (Year)	Type	Drugs	No. of Studies	Subjects	Response Rate	Placebo Response	References (Bibliographic)
Barkley (1977)	3	DEX	15	915	74%	29%	159
		MPH	14	866	77%	23%	
		PEM	2	105	73%	27%	
		PL	8	417	39%	—	
Klein & Wender[a] (1995)	3	DEX	6	225	Mod	Low	398
		MPH	18	528	69%	24%	
		PEM	4	228	69%	23%	
Gittelman[a] (1987)	3	MPH	25	777	N/A	N/A	82
		PEM	1	20	N/A	N/A	
Hinshaw (1991)	3	MPH	10	187	Situation[b]	N/A	82
Jacobvitz et al. (1990)	4	MPH	136	N/A	N/A	N/A	175
Wilens & Biederman (1992)	3	MPH	37	1113	73%	2–22%	121
Schachar & Tannock (1993)	4	MPH	18	531	Resp.[c]	26% attrition	88
Greenhill (1995)	3	MPH	15	236	70%	20%	229
		SR	7	181	75%	20%	
		DEX	2	2	High	Low	
		PEM	1	22	75%	20%	

Source: Based on Wilens and Biederman, 1992.

DEX = dextroamphetamine; MPH = methylphenidate; PEM = pemoline; PL = placebo; SR = sustained-release MPH.

[a]Author of both reviews is Rachel Klein, Ph.D.

[b]Hinshaw's review focuses on aggression and reports different rates, depending on age and setting.

[c]Resp. = Only responders included in Schachar et al.'s examination of long-term stimulant treatment.

These reviews conclude that psychostimulants demonstrate efficacy by reducing core ADHD behaviors (Barkley, 1977, 1982; DuPaul & Barkley, 1990). Other early papers discussed psychostimulant mechanisms of action (Solanto, 1984), the question of diagnostic specificity for stimulant response (Gittelman, 1980), and the ability of these medications to enhance other therapies (Gittelman, 1987). Other key treatment issues were considered, including dosing methods, paradoxical stimulant effects (Jacobvitz et al., 1990), and whether stimulants improved academic performance (DuPaul & Barkley, 1990; Jacobvitz et al., 1990).

Dosing methods and dose-response issues during stimulant treatments were brought to the fore by the seminal 1977 paper of Sprague and Sleator (1977), which reported dissociation of cognitive and behavioral MPH responses in ADHD children. Using weight-adjusted doses, Sprague and Sleator reported that children responded optimally to a memory task at a low dose (0.3 mg/kg) but needed higher doses (1.0 mg/kg) to attain behavioral control in the classroom. This paper set the customary weight-adjusted MPH dosing standard that permeates the ADHD drug treatment literature to the present and also raised the question of whether MPH doses optimized for behavior might not be best for learning.

Reviews of pre-1990 drug studies (Jacobvitz et al., 1990; Wilens & Biederman, 1992) concluded that there was no diagnostically specific positive response to stimulants for ADHD children. No differences in response were found among the stimulant-treated ADHD children, stimulant-treated normal children, or clinically referred non-ADHD children (Rapoport et al., 1980). Also rejected was the notion that ADHD children show a "paradoxical" slow-down response to stimulants. Rather, the literature shows a decrease in aimless activity, an increase in attention, and an increase in heart rate and blood pressure.

These reviews also grappled with the question of whether stimulants, so successful in short-term trials, lead to long-term improvements. Follow-up ADHD studies (Barkley et al., 1990a; Mannuzza, Klein, Bessler, Malloy, & LaPadula, 1993; Weiss & Hechtman, 1993) have shown that ADHD core symptoms persist into late adolescence and even into adult life. It is encouraging, then, that one review (Schachar & Tannock, 1993) finds evidence that drug treatment studies lasting 3 to 7 months show stimulants to be more effective than a placebo, nonpharmacological therapies, or no treatment in ameliorating core ADHD symptoms. Studies reporting no benefit over time suffer from major methodological weaknesses, such as lack of uniform diagnostic criteria, no use of standardized outcome measures, no random assignment, a high attrition rate, or no compliance checks.

The early psychostimulant treatment studies showed strong behavioral improvements and less impressive academic gains in ADHD children who were treated. Although there is evidence for short-term gains in arithmetic performance (Pelham, Bender, Codell, Booth, & Moorer, 1985), other work (Charles & Shain, 1979) shows no differences in long-term academic achievement when treated and untreated ADHD children were compared.

Despite the breadth and depth of the pre-1990 treatment literature, with its attention to concerns for finding an optimal dosage level, tracking compliance, understanding time-action effects of the psychostimulants (Hinshaw, 1994), interpreting concurrent interventions, and studying individual differences in response, a number of weaknesses exist (Pelham, 1993). These include the use of academic measures to test treatment response in a group of ADHD children heterogenous for learning disabilities and the use of global measures of improvement rather than objective measures of cognitive skill to adjust doses in titration. No mention is made of a tight standardization of dosing times for all subjects, so some subjects may have had greatly different times of dosing within the same study. Because most clinical studies treated behavioral targets, attempts were not made to synchronize the time of peak drug effectiveness with the child's daily academic tasks. The majority of drug studies covered by reviews in Table 3.2 lasted 6 weeks or less, too brief to generalize application to typical medication treatments, which average 3 years. No common definition of a categorical treatment responder existed much before 1985, so it was difficult to do meta-analytic studies that look across studies for identical response patterns in children.

**CURRENT
PSYCHOPHARMACOLOGICAL AGENTS:
EFFICACY AND UTILITY**

Three stimulants are currently approved by the FDA for treatment of ADHD in children and are available in both brand and generic forms. These include DEX,

MPH, and magnesium pemoline (PEM). Characteristics of these stimulants can be found in Table 3.3. While DEX and MPH are structurally related to the catecholamines (dopamine [DA] and norepinephrine [NE]), PEM has a different structure, although it too has strong DA effects in the central nervous system (CNS) (McCracken, 1991).

The term *psychostimulant* used for these compounds refers to their ability to increase CNS activity in some, but not all, brain regions. Psychostimulants are thought to release catecholamines and block their reuptake. Methylphenidate, like cocaine, has affinity for the dopamine transporter. Although the mechanism for psychostimulant enhancement of attention is unknown, positron emission tomography (PET) scan data show that [^{11}C]methylphenidate concentration in the brain is maximal in striatum (Volkow et al., 1995).

Psychostimulants have demonstrated short-term efficacy, compared to a placebo, reducing ADHD symptoms such as overactivity (fidgetiness, off-task behavior during direct observation) and eliminating behavior that disrupts the classroom (constant requests of the teacher during direct observation) (Jacobvitz et al., 1990). In experimental settings, stimulants have been shown to improve child behavior during parent-child interactions (Barkley & Cunningham, 1979) and problem-solving activities with peers (Whalen et al., 1989). The behavior of children with ADHD has a tendency to elicit negative, directive, and controlling behavior from parents (Campbell, 1973) and peers. When placed on stimulants, their mothers' rates of disapproval, commands, and control diminish to the extent seen between other mothers and their non-ADHD children (Barkley & Cunningham, 1979; Humphries, Kinsbourne, & Swanson, 1978). In the laboratory, stimulant-treated children with ADHD

demonstrate major improvements during experimenter-paced continuous performance tests (Halperin, Matier, Bedi, Sharma, & Newcorn, 1992), paired-associate learning, cued and free recall, auditory and reading comprehension, spelling recall, and arithmetic computation (Pelham & Bender, 1982; Stephens, Pelham, & Skinner, 1984). Some studies show correlations between plasma levels of MPH and performance of a laboratory task (Greenhill, 1995), but plasma levels rarely correlate with clinical response. Likewise, hyperactive conduct-disordered children and preadolescents show reductions in aggression behavior when treated with stimulants and observed in structured and unstructured school settings (Hinshaw, 1991). Stimulants also can reduce the display of covert antisocial behaviors such as stealing and property destruction (Hinshaw, Heller, & McHale, 1992).

No single theory explains the psychostimulant mechanism of action on the CNS that ameliorates ADHD symptoms. A drug's effect based on a single neurotransmitter has been discounted (Zametkin & Rapoport, 1987), as well as its ability to correct the ADHD child's under- or overaroused CNS (Solanto, 1984). More recently, a two-part theory of stimulant action has been postulated (McCracken, 1991) in which stimulants increase DA release, producing enhanced autoreceptor-mediated inhibition of ascending DA neurons while simultaneously increasing adrenergic-mediated inhibition of the noradrenergic-locus coeruleus via epinephrine activity. This theory awaits confirmation from basic research in animals and imaging studies in humans.

To date, brain imaging has shown few consistent psychostimulant effects on glucose metabolism. Theory would predict that psychostimulants might produce increased brain glucose metabolism in the stria-

TABLE 3.3 Stimulant Drugs, Doses, and Pharmacodynamics

Medication	D-Amphetamine	Methylphenidate	Pemoline
Tablets and Dosages Available in Brand Medications	5 mg tablets 5, 10, 15 mg spansule	5, 10, 20 mg tablets 20 mg SR	18.75, 37.5, 75 mg tablet; 37.5 mg chewable
Package Insert Dose Range	10–40 mg/day in split doses: bid	10–60 mg/day in split doses	37.75–112.5 mg/day
Administration	bid or tid	bid or tid	q AM or bid
Maximum Effect	1–3 hours	1–3 hours	2–4 hours
Length of Effect	3–5 hours	2–4 hours	7 hours

SR = sustained-release

tal and frontal regions of adults with ADHD (Ernst & Zametkin, 1995). Two studies using Positron emission tomography (PET) and [^{18}F]fluorodeoxyglucose (Matochik et al., 1993, 1994) of acute and chronic stimulant treatment in ADHD adults report no effect on global glucose metabolism. The PET reveals a significant difference in the pharmacokinetics of [^{11}C]methylphenidate and [^{11}C]cocaine (Volkow et al., 1995). Although both drugs display rapid uptake into striatum, MPH is more slowly cleared from the brain. The authors speculate that this low reversal of binding to the DA transporter means that MPH is not as reinforcing as cocaine and therefore does not lead to as much self-administration as does cocaine.

One of the most important findings in the stimulant treatment literature is the high degree of short-term efficacy for *behavioral* targets, with weaker effects for *cognition and learning*. (K. Conners, personal communication, 1993) notes that 0.8, 1.0, and 0.9 effect sizes are reported for behavioral improvements in Type 4 meta-analytic reviews of stimulant drug actions (Kavale, 1982; Ottenbach & Cooper, 1983; Thurber & Walker, 1983). These behavioral responses to stimulant treatment, when compared to treatment with a placebo, resemble the treatment efficacy of antibiotics. Less powerful effects are found for laboratory measures for cognitive changes, in particular on the Continuous Performance Task, for which effect sizes of these medications range between 0.6 and 0.5 for omissions and commissions, respectively, in a within-subject design (Milich, Licht, & Murphy, 1989) and 0.6 and 1.8 in a between-subject study (Schechter & Keuezer, 1985).

Psychostimulants continue to show behavioral efficacy in the Type 1 RCTs published over the last 10 years (see Table 3.4). These modern-day controlled trials have matured with the field and now utilize multiple-dose conditions with multiple stimulants (Elia, Borcherding, Rapoport, & Keysor, 1991), parallel designs (Spencer et al., 1995), and studies using a common definition of response as normalization (Abikoff & Gittelman, 1985; Rapport, Denney, DuPaul, & Gardner, 1994). These studies now test psychostimulants in special ADHD populations, including adolescents (Klorman, Brumagham, Fitzpatrick, & Brugstedt, 1990), adults (Spencer et al., 1995), the mentally retarded (Horn et al., 1991), ADHD subjects with anxiety disorders and internalizing disorders, and ADHD subjects with tic disorders (Gadow, Sverd, Sprafkin, Nolan, & Ezor, 1995). As shown in Table 3.4, 70% of school-age ADHD subjects respond to stimulants. The placebo response rate is much lower, estimated at between 5% and 20% (Pelham et al., 1990; Pelham, Swanson, Forman, & Schwint, 1995; Spencer et al., 1995; Ullmann & Sleator, 1986).

Recently, researchers have attempted to study stimulant nonresponders. In some drug trials (Douglas, Barr, Amin, O'Neill, & Britton, 1988), a 100% response rate is reported in small samples in which multiple doses of MPH were used. Others found that a trial involving two stimulants effectively lowered the nonresponse rate. Elia, Borcherding, Rapoport, and Keysor (1991) reduced the 32% nonresponse rate to a single psychostimulant to less than 4% when two stimulants, DEX and MPH, were titrated sequentially in the same subject. However, if one includes children with comorbidity in the sample, the rate of medication nonresponse might be higher. Finally, few studies have used the double-blind or single-blind placebo discontinuation model to determine if the child continues to respond to stimulants after being treated for 1 year or more. One study found that 80% of ADHD children relapsed when switched single blind from MPH to a placebo after 8 months of treatment (H. Abikoff, personal communication, 1994).

Currently, over 85% of psychostimulant prescriptions in the United States are written for MPH (Safer & Krager, 1984; Williams & Swanson, 1996). The rate of MPH prescription writing increased fourfold from 1990 to 1995. The indications, pharmacology, adverse effects, and usage directions for MPH are frequently highlighted in reviews (Dulcan, 1990; Greenhill, 1995; Wilens & Biederman, 1992). It has become the "first-line" psychostimulant for ADHD, followed by DEX and PEM (Richters et al., 1995). Within the group of stimulants, practitioners order MPH first, DEX second, and PEM third. The popularity of MPH as the first choice in psychostimulants is not supported by the literature, however. Both DEX and PEM have identical efficacy to MPH (Arnold, Christopher, Huestis, & Smeltzer, 1978; Elia et al., 1991; Pelham et al., 1990, 1995; Vyborova, Nahunek, Drtilkova, Balastikova, & Misurec, 1984; Winsberg, Press, Bialer, & Kupietz, 1974). Arnold has noted (Greenhill et al., 1996) that of the 141 subjects in these studies, 50 responded better to DEX and only 37 better to MPH.

Among the three stimulants, PEM has the poorest market share and is placed third in some drug decision algorithms for stimulant treatment of ADHD children (Greenhill et al., 1996). Pelham and colleagues (Pelham et al., 1995) attribute this to clinicians' percep-

TABLE 3.4 Type 1 Studies Showing Efficacy in ADHD Drug Treatments

Study (Year)	N	Age Range (Years)	Design	Drug (Dose)[a]	Duration	Response	Comment
Abikoff & Gittleman (1985)	28	6–12	ADHD × controls	MPH (PB, 41 mg)	8 weeks	80.9%	MPH normalized[b] activity, compliance
Barkley (1989)	74	6–13	Crossover 37 agg 37 nonagg	MPH (PB, 0.3, 0.5)	4 weeks	80%	Aggression did not affect MPH effects on activity
Barkley (1991)	40	6–12	Crossover 23 ADHD 17 ADHD-W	MPH bid (5, 10, 15 bid) PB bid	6 weeks	ADHD 95% ADD-H 76%	Fewer ADD-H respond to MPH, need lower dose
Biederman et al. (1989)	62	6–17	Parallel	DMI (4.6)	6 weeks	68% DMI 10% PB	DMI effective using CGI-improve scores
Douglas et al. (1988)	19	7–13	Crossover	MPH (PB, 0.15, 0.3, 0.6)	2 weeks	100%*	Linear D/R relationships: academic, cognitive, behavioral measures
Douglas (1995)	17	6–11	Crossover	MPH (0.3, 0.6, 0.9) PB	4 weeks	Behavior 70%	No cognitive toxicity at high doses, linear D/R curves for behavior
DuPaul & Rapport (1993)	31	6–12	Crossover 31 ADHD 25 normal	MPH (20 mg) PB bid	6 weeks	Behavior 78% Attention 61% Efficient 75%	MPH normalizes classroom behavior; 25% of ADHD Ss did not normalize academics
DuPaul et al. (1994)	40	6–12	Crossover 12 high internal 17 mid internal 11 low internal	MPH (5, 10, 15 mg) PB single dose	6 weeks	High 68% nor Mid 70% nor Low 82% nor	25% int. Ss deteriorated behavior on meds; ADHD Ss with int. disorders less likely to normalize or to respond to MPH
Elia et al. (1991)	48	6–12	Crossover	MPH (0.5; 0.8, 1.5) PB bid DEX (0.25, 0.5, 0.75)	6 weeks	MPH 79% DEX 86%	Behavioral response rate for two stimulants tried serially is 96%
Gadow et al. (1995)	34	6–12	Crossover + ADHD + tic disorder	MPH (0.1, 0.3, 0.5) PB bid	8 weeks	MPH 100%	No nonresponders to behavior; MD's increases 2 min MD rating of motor tics; Only shows effects of 8 weeks treatment

Study	N	Age	Design	Medication/dose[a]	Duration	Response[c]	Comments
Klorman et al. (1990)	48	12–18	Crossover	MPH tid (0.26) PB bid	6 weeks	MPH 60%	Fewer ADHD adolescents respond
Pelham et al. (1990)	22	8–13	Crossover	MPH 10 bid; PB bid; DEX spansules 10 mg PEM 56.25 g AM	24 days	Stim 68%	DEX spansules, PEM best for behavior / 27% did best on DEX; 18% on SR; 18% on PEM; 5% on MPH bid
Pelham et al. (1995)	28	5–12	Crossover	PEM (18.75, 37.5, 75, 112.5 mg) PB	7 weeks	PEM 89% PB resp 0%	PEM dose ≥ 37.5 mg/day act 2–7 hr / Efficacy and time course = MPH
Rapport (1988)	22	6–10	Crossover	MPH (PB, 5, 10, 15 mg)	5 weeks	72%	MPH response same in 2 settings
Rapport et al. (1994)	76	6–12	Crossover	MPH (5, 10, 15, 20 mg) PB bid	5 weeks	Behavior 94% Attention 53%	MPH normalizes behavior > academics / Higher doses better, linear D/R curve
Spencer et al. (1995)	23	18–60	Crossover	MPH (1 mg/kg day)	7 weeks	MPH resp 78% PB resp 4%	MPH at 1 mg/kg/d improves CGI equivalent to that seen from MPH in kids
Tannock et al. (1993)	40	6–12	Crossover 22 ADHD 17 ADHD-Anx	MPH (0.3, 0.6)	2 weeks	Memory 70% Activity 80%	Activity level better in both groups; working memory not better in anxious
Tannock et al. (1995)	28	6–12	Crossover	MPH (0.3, 0.6, 0.9) PB	2 weeks	Behavior 70% Resp inhib 70%	Effects on behavior D/R curve linear, but effects on resp inhibition U shaped suggest adjust dose on objective measures
Taylor (1987)	38	6–10	Crossover	MPH (PB, 0.2–1.4)	6 weeks	58%	Ss respond better if have severe ADHD Sx
Whalen et al. (1989)	25	6.3–12	Crossover	MPH (PB, 0.3, 0.5)	5 weeks	48–72%	MPH helps, not normalizes, peer status

Table listings arranged by author.

[a]Doses are mg/kg/dose and medication is given twice daily unless otherwise stated.

[b]Normalized means that ADHD children do not differ significantly on the same measure from children with no mental disorder.

[c]In response column means all patients selected to be responders.

agg = aggressive; nonagg = non-aggressive; nor = normalize; int = internalizing symptoms; stim = stimulants; resp = response; PB = placebo; CGI = clinical global impressions; D/R = dose response; MD = medical doctor; Ss = subjects; Sx = symptoms; ADHD-Anx = ADHD comorbid with anxiety disorder; ADD-H = attention deficit disorder with hyperactivity; ADHD = attention deficit disorder without hyperactivity.

tions that PEM is slow acting if used according to the manufacturer's dosing instructions, which suggest starting with a very low 18.75 mg/day dose and increasing in weekly steps. The use of PEM has been associated with abnormal liver function tests and liver damage, so PEM is the only medication that requires blood tests routinely every 3 months. Children with ADHD, especially those with needle phobias, may refuse the tests. Also, PEM is more expensive than the other psychostimulants. For these reasons, practitioners are reluctant to prescribe the drug. However, PEM is effective. Pelham's RCT (Pelham et al., 1995) comparing four doses of once-daily PEM with a placebo showed a 72% rate of response for PEM in doses of 37.5 mg or larger.

Stimulant responsiveness or rates of side effects may be affected by the presence of comorbid anxiety (ANX) symptoms. Pliszka (1989) treated 43 subjects with ADHD with MPH (0.25–0.4 mg/kg and 0.45–0.70 mg/kg) and a placebo for 4 weeks. The 22 subjects comorbid for anxiety symptoms and ADHD (the ADHD + ANX group) showed less efficacy when active stimulant treatment was compared with the placebo, as judged by teacher's global ratings, with no increase in side effects. This might be explained by strong placebo response in the ADHD + ANX group. Tannock, Ickowicz, and Schachar (1995) reported that children with ADHD, some with ($N = 18$) and some without ($N = 22$) comorbid anxiety symptoms, treated in a double-blind, randomized, crossover design with three MPH doses (0.3, 0.6, 0.9 mg/kg) showed equal decreases in motor activity, but the group with comorbid anxiety did poorer on a serial addition task and had a differential heart rate response to MPH. DuPaul, Barkley, and McMurray (1994) found that 40 children with ADHD and comorbid anxiety were less likely to respond to MPH and showed more side effects; 3 doses of MPH (5, 10, 15 mg) and placebo were used. However, the study did not collect ratings for anxiety symptoms, so the direct effect of MPH on such symptoms was not recorded. On the other hand, the one controlled study (Gadow et al., 1995) that tested the effects of MPH in children with comorbid anxiety disorders, rather than just comorbid symptoms, found equally good response in both those with and those without the anxiety disorder. These divergent data leave open the question about whether comorbid anxiety symptoms predict poor response to stimulant treatment.

Predicting drug response in the individual ADHD child is difficult. While pretreatment patient characteristics (young age, low rates of anxiety, low severity of disorder, and high IQ) may predict a good response to methylphenidate on global rating scales (Buitelaar, Gary, Swaab-Barneveld, & Kuiper, 1995), most research shows that no neurological, physiological, or psychological measures of functioning have been identified that are reliable predictors of response to psychostimulants (Pelham & Milich, 1991; Zametkin & Rapoport, 1987). Once a child responds, there has been no universally agreed-upon criterion for how much the symptoms must change before the clinician stops increasing the dose. Furthermore, there is no standard for the outcome measure. For example, should global ratings alone be used, or should they be combined with more "objective" academic seatwork measures such as percent correct or percent completed lists of math problems? Some have advocated a 25% reduction of ADHD symptoms, while others suggest that the dose continue to be adjusted until the child's behavior and classroom performance is normalized.

The concept of *normalization* has helped standardize the definition of a categorical responder across domains and across studies. Studies now determine if the improvement from treatment is clinically meaningful, using normal classroom controls, instead of just being statistically significant. Treatment was noted to remove differences between ADHD children and nonreferred classmates on measures of activity and attention (Abikoff & Gittelman, 1985), but not for positive peer nominations (Whalen et al., 1989). Further advances occurred when investigators used statistically derived definitions of clinically meaningful change during psychotherapeutic treatment (Jacobsen, Truax, 1991). Rapport and colleagues (1994) used this technique to calculate reliable change and normalization on a global rating scale used by parents or teachers to rate symptoms of ADHD (the Conners Abbreviated Rating Scale) using national norms. They determined that a child would be normalized when the child's score on this scale fell closer to the mean of the normal population than to the mean of the ADHD population. Using this technique, they found, in a controlled trial of 4 doses of MPH in ADHD children, that MPH normalized behavior and, to a lesser extent, academics (94% versus 53%) and the MPH dose-normalization response curve for MPH was linear. Similarly, DuPaul and Rapport (1993) found that MPH normalized behavior for all ADHD children treated, but only 75% of the ADHD children normalized for academics. In another study, DuPaul, Barkley, and McMurray (1994) reported that normalization in behavior and academics occurred less often when ADHD subjects were comorbid for high levels of internalizing disorders.

TREATMENT OF ADULTS WITH ATTENTION DEFICIT HYPERACTIVITY DISORDER

The prevalence of ADHD in adults, its severity, and indications for treatment are issues that are not settled among clinicians. Although it had been assumed that children with ADHD outgrow their problems, recent prospective follow-up studies have shown that ADHD signs and symptoms continue into adult life (APA, 1980). Adults with concentration problems, impulsivity, poor anger control, job instability, and marital difficulties sometimes seek help for problems they believe to be the manifestation of ADHD in adult life. Parents may decide that they are impaired by the same attentional and impulse control problems during an evaluation of their ADHD children.

The diagnosis attention deficit disorder, residual state (ADD-R) was placed in *DSM-III* (APA, 1980), to include patients over age 18, who had been diagnosed as children with ADD, and were no longer motorically hyperactive, but had impairment from residual impulsivity, overactivity, or inattention. The diagnosis of ADD-R was dropped from the 1987 *DSM-III-R* (APA, 1987). Since the publication of *DSM-III-R*, a small but steady stream of publications has supported the existence of the adult ADD disorder, and clinicians and parent groups find it to be a useful and realistic clinical condition. These clinicians requested that future manuals include ADHD descriptors that would cover both adults and children with ADD difficulties, not just those that applied only to children. These clinicians noted that ADHD is widely viewed as a disorder of childhood, so it may be overlooked in adults.

Although *DSM-IV* (APA, 1994) did not restore the diagnosis of ADD-R, the item lists for the ADHD syndrome are rephrased so that they can apply to adults. Furthermore, *DSM-IV* contains a category "in partial remission" that covers the adult with ADHD who retains some, but not all, of the childhood problems. This is because of the concern that a few ADHD symptoms in an adult might be as impairing as a larger number in a child. One method to discover the extent of residual disorders in this population is to follow ADHD children prospectively. A study carried out by Weiss and Hechtman (1985) compared adults who had ADHD as children (index group) with adults who had no mental disorder as children (control group) but did not compare rates of ADHD (either full syndrome or subthreshold) in the two groups. Compared to controls, the index group had higher rates of antisocial personality disorder, reported fewer years of education completed, and had more complaints of restlessness, sexual problems, and interpersonal problems. There was a higher incidence of antisocial personality disorder, and there were lower scores on clinician-rated global assessment scores. Mannuzza and colleagues (1991) found little evidence of a residual ADHD syndrome because approximately half of their ADHD sample had the full syndrome by age 18 and 8% had the full syndrome by age 25. The *DSM-IV* agrees with the Mannuza group's finding and does not specifically include a diagnostic category for this problem. Rather, the category "not otherwise specified" (NOS) allows adult patients whose past childhood histories are unclear but who have ADHD symptoms as adults to receive a diagnosis of ADHD NOS. Such patients might not recall if their ADHD symptoms had appeared before the age of 7 years (APA Workgroup on *DSM-IV*, 1991).

Shaffer, in an invited editorial (1994), urged clinicians to be wary of making the diagnosis and treating ADHD in adults. First, the diagnosis of "adult" ADD is difficult to make because adults cannot easily recall their own childhood history of ADHD symptoms with sufficient accuracy. The high incidence of Axis 1 (e.g., major depressive disorder) and Axis 2 (e.g., antisocial personality disorder) comorbid disorders makes it difficult to determine if the adult's current impairment is from the comorbid condition or from the ADHD. Shaffer further notes that adult ADHD may be an infrequent condition. The one controlled prospective follow-up study with low attrition rates (Mannuzza et al., 1993) showed that only 3% of 25-year-old adults with a childhood history of ADHD had impairment related to present ADHD symptoms.

Controlled stimulant treatment studies have been conducted with adults with ADHD including over 200 patients, some involving MPH (Gualtieri et al., 1981; Mattes & Boswell, 1984; Wender, Reimherr, & Wood, 1981). With the caveat that sample selection criteria differ greatly study to study, different pharmacological treatment strategies have been applied to ADHD in adults with varying success. Although Mattes and Boswell (1984) showed little benefit from MPH, others have found robust effects (Ratey, Greenberg, & Lindem, 1991; Wender, Reimherr, & Wood, 1985). In a study by Spencer and colleagues (Spencer et al., 1995), the response to MPH was independent of gender, comorbidity, or family history of psychiatric disorders. Treatment was generally well tolerated at the target dose of 1.0 mg/kg; side effects included loss of appetite, insomnia, and anxiety. Other drugs that have been reported as beneficial include fluoxetine (Sabelsky, 1990), nomifensine (Shekim, Masterson, Cantwell, & Hanna, 1989), pargyline (Wender, Wood, Reimherr, & Ward, 1994), bupropion (Wender & Reimherr, 1990), the monoamine oxidase (MAO) inhibitor selegiline (Ernst, Liebenauer, Jons, Murphy, & Zametkin, 1995), and the long-acting methamphetamine compound Desoxyn Gradumets (Wender, 1994).

Even with this level of investigation, evidence for the efficacy of psychostimulants in the treatment of ADHD in adults is regarded by Shaffer (1994) as inconclusive. The number of subjects involved is small; the findings are divergent, with widely varying drug efficacy (23–73%); and the reported treatment responses include nonspecific changes unrelated to ADHD, such as improvement in social functioning or reduction of comorbid conditions. Others (e.g., Wilens and Biederman, 1992) disagree with Shaffer's concerns. They point out that the initial studies of stimulant-treated adults were inconclusive because low stimulant dosages are used. A double-blind comparison of high-dose MPH (1 mg/kg/dose) and a placebo was carried out in 23 adult patients with ADHD, and 78% showed improvement on MPH versus 4% who responded to the placebo (Spencer et al., 1995). The same group (Wilens and coworkers), in a chart review study, reported that 32 adult patients with ADHD demonstrated a positive response to treatment with tricyclics (Wilens et al., 1994).

SIDE EFFECTS ASSOCIATED WITH STIMULANT USE

Both the risk-benefit and cost-benefit ratio for the psychostimulants are very favorable (Klein & Wender, 1995). Two recent double-blind, placebo-controlled studies (Ahmann et al., 1993; Barkley et al., 1990) identified only four side effects associated with MPH treatment. One study (Ahmann et al., 1993) involving 234 children ages 5–15 used the Barkley Side Effect Questionnaire and found that only five side effects during MPH treatment showed a significant increase over placebo use: insomnia (58.8% v. 36.7%), decreased appetite (55.7% v. 25.4%), stomachache (33.8% v. 18.4%), headache (30.4% v. 21.4%), and dizziness (12.5% v. 4.5%).

Motor or vocal tics have been reported to appear in as many as 1% of children taking MPH (Ickowicz, Tannock, Fulford, Purvis, & Schachar, 1992). A controlled trial of MPH in children with ADHD and chronic tic disorder (Gadow et al., 1995) reported significant improvement in ADHD symptoms for all subjects but no consistent worsening or increase in tic frequency. However, the total daily MPH doses used never exceeded 20 mg/day. These low doses and the short 8-week study do not resemble the higher doses or longer treatment duration found in clinical practice, in which tics may appear after several months of MPH administration. The clinical literature has held that MPH lowers the seizure threshold, although treatment of patients with ADHD and seizures with MPH shows no change in seizure frequency (Klein & Wender, 1995). As for growth, one large controlled study (Gittelman Klein, Landa, Mattes, & Klein, 1988) reported growth rate reductions among a subgroup of children, but growth resumed immediately when treatment was interrupted (Safer, Allen, & Barr, 1975).

Growth slowdown is another infrequent psychostimulant adverse reaction. Psychostimulant-induced reductions in growth velocity have been the most consistently researched long-term side effect for this type of medication (Greenhill et al., 1984). Even with the many studies in this area (Greenhill, 1981), myriad methodological difficulties prevent an easy interpretation. Few studies employ the optimal controls needed, which include untreated ADHD children, a psychiatric control group, and an ADHD group treated with a class of medications other than stimulants. Studies differ in quality of compliance measures, whether the children are off stimulants on weekends, and whether the stimulants are used through the summer.

Safer and Allen (Safer et al. 1975; Safer & Allen, 1973; Safer, Allen, & Barr, 1972) first reported that treatment for 2 or more years with MPH and DEX could produce decrements in weight velocity on age-adjusted growth rate charts; stopping the medication produced a quick return to baseline growth velocities. Dextroamphetamine, with a half-life two to three times that of MPH, produces more sustained effects than does MPH on weight velocity, as well as suppressing mean sleep-related prolactin concentrations (Greenhill, 1981). In MPH-treated ADHD children, followed for 2 to 4 years, dose-related decreases in weight velocity are seen (Gittelman/Klein et al., 1988; Satterfield, Cantwell, Schell, & Blaschke, 1979), with some tolerance to the suppressive effect developing in the second year (Satterfield et al., 1979). Hechtman and Weiss (1984) report that ADHD children not treated with psychostimulants attain expected heights, so that there was no suspected associated growth slowdown from the ADHD disorder itself.

The actual psychostimulant mechanism for any growth slowdown is unknown. Early theories blamed the drug's putative growth suppressant action for its effects on growth hormone or prolactin, but research studies on 13 children treated for 18 months with 0.8 mg/day of DEX (Greenhill et al., 1981) or on 9 children treated for 12 months on 1.2 mg/kg/day of MPH (Greenhill et al., 1984) failed to demonstrate a consistent change in growth hormone release. The most parsimonious explanation for this drug effect is the medication's suppression of appetite, leading to reduced caloric intake. No study, however, has collected the standardized diet diaries necessary to track calories consumed by ADHD children on psychostimulants (Greenhill, 1981).

In any case, the growth effects of MPH appear to be minimal. Satterfield et al. (1979) followed 110 children and found decreases in height velocity during the first year of psychostimulant treatment, but this reversed during the second year of treatment. An initial growth loss during MPH treatment was seen in 65 children followed to age 18, but these children "caught up" during adolescence and reached heights predicted from their parents' heights (Gittelman & Mannuzza, 1988). These results confirm the observations by Roche and colleagues (Roche, Lipman, Overall, & Hung, 1979) that psychostimulants have mild and transitory effects on weight and only rarely interfere with height acquisition. Height and weight should be measured at 6-month intervals during stimulant treatment and recorded on age-adjusted growth forms to determine the presence of a drug-related reduction in height or weight velocity. If such a decrement is discovered during maintenance therapy with psycho-stimulants, a reduction in dosage or change to another class of medication can be carried out.

LIMITATIONS OF STIMULANTS FOR THE TREATMENT OF ATTENTION DEFICIT HYPERACTIVITY DISORDER

Although treatment studies for 3 to 7 months carried out on groups of children with ADHD (Schachar & Tannock, 1993) show impressive reductions in ADHD symptoms, clinicians must manage individual ADHD children over years. Although psychostimulants produce moderate to marked short-term improvement in motor restlessness, on-task behavior, compliance, and classroom academic performance (DuPaul & Barkley, 1990), these effects have been demonstrated convincingly only in short-term studies. When examined over periods longer than 6 months, these medications fail to maintain academic improvement (Gadow, 1991) or to improve the social problem-solving deficits that accompany ADHD. Many of the long-term studies reporting lack of academic improvement have been uncontrolled, with many of the children followed not taking stimulants consistently, so it is not possible to draw conclusions about whether stimulant treatment reverses academic failure over time.

Although there are over 100 controlled studies of stimulant efficacy in the literature, only 18 studies lasted as long as 3 months according to a recent authoritative review (Schachar & Tannock, 1993). Because literally 4 million psychostimulant prescriptions were written in 1994 and because the duration of treatment extends from first grade through college, there is growing interest in showing that stimulant treatment is effective over the long run. A dual-site, multimodal treatment study (Abikoff, 1991) treated children over 2 years and found that medication-alone treatment is as effective as combination treatment involving medication plus psychosocial interventions. However, that study did not have a no-medication group. The National Institute of Mental Health Cooperative Multimodal Treatment Study of Children with Attention Deficit Hyperactivity Disorder (NIMH MTA study) (Richters et al., 1995), now under way, attempts to address long-term stimulant use by including a no-medication psychosocial treatment only arm in a sample of 576 children with ADHD.

There are other complications involving the use of psychostimulants for the treatment of children with

ADHD. The behavioral benefits from a single dose of a psychostimulant last only a few hours during its absorption phase (Perel, Greenhill, Curran, Feldman, & Puig-Antich, 1991) and are often gone by the afternoon if given in the morning. Second, even with the new understanding about the relatively small numbers of nonresponders (Elia et al., 1991), some patients may improve but experience unmanageable side effects. Approximately 25% of children with ADHD are not helped by the first psychostimulant given or experience side effects so bothersome that meaningful dose adjustments cannot be made (DuPaul & Barkley, 1990). Third, the indications for choosing a particular psychostimulant and the best methods for adjusting the dose remain unclear, and this may prove confusing to the clinician and family. Although MPH is regarded as the drug of choice for the treatment of ADHD, controlled treatment studies show no particular advantage for this medication over DEX or PEM.

In addition to the widely accepted short-term side effects of stimulants, there may be other effects, which may be subtle or only emerge over a longer period. Some of these have been substantiated, others not. A few studies indicate the response to MPH treatment may be diminished by the presence of comorbid internalizing disorders (Pliszka, 1989; Tannock, Schachar, & Logan, 1993). On the other hand, the worry has not been substantiated that causal attributions ADHD children attach to medication may offset any benefits the medication offers (Hinshaw, Henker, Whalen, Erhardy, & Dunnington, 1989). Third, investigators have sometimes found that stimulant effects may be influenced by the patient's IQ or age (Buitelaar et al., 1995).

Although the general literature deals with multiple studies involving groups of children with ADHD, the practitioner may find it difficult to cull specific guidelines about dosing the individual patient from these studies. There is no universally agreed-upon method for dosing with these medications; some practitioners use the child's weight as a guideline (dose by weight method), and others titrate each child's response through the approved dose range until a clinical response occurs or side effects limit further dose increases (stepwise titration method). These discrepancies are a result of the highly variable nature of the psychostimulant dose-response cognitive and behavioral effect curves (Solanto, 1991). Furthermore, MPH dose-response relationships vary from individual to individual. Rapport and colleagues (Rapport, DuPaul, & Kelly, 1989) have shown that there is no

consistent relationship between weight-adjusted MPH doses and behavioral responses, calling into question the widely accepted practice in research of standardizing MPH doses by weight adjustment. Some children with ADHD show dose responses that can be conceptualized as a simple linear function (Gittelman & Kanner, 1986), while others show curvilinear patterns. These relationships may vary in the same child, one type for cognitive performance and another type for the behavioral domain (Sprague & Sleator, 1977).

USING NONSTIMULANT MEDICATION TREATMENTS FOR ATTENTION DEFICIT HYPERACTIVITY DISORDER

There are times when nonstimulant medications are used in the treatment of ADHD. Short-acting stimulants require cooperation from school personnel for midday dosing, and this may not always be possible. Stimulants, which cause insomnia, cannot be given too late in the day. The attention-enhancing effects of MPH, which last only 3–4 hours, may be needed in the late evening to help school-age children with their homework, but delayed sleep onset may result. Adverse effect, including severe weight loss, headaches, insomnia, and tics, are also observed. March and colleagues (March, Erhardt, Johnston, & Conners, 1994) suggest a nonstimulant may be used when there is an unsatisfactory response to two different stimulants; this agrees with the studies of Elia et al. (1991).

Type 6 studies of alternative medications have appeared over the past 5 years. These are listed in Table 3.5.

The tricyclic antidepressants (TCAs) have been considered the second-line treatment for ADHD and are supported by well-designed, controlled-type RCTs (Biederman, Baldessarini, Wright, Keenan, & Faraone, 1989) of DMI, as shown in Table 3.2. The TCAs are long acting, allow flexible dosing, and are not drugs of abuse. Dosages can be checked with plasma levels. The TCAs affect cardiac conduction time, so electrocardiographic monitoring is necessary.

Bupropion, an antidepressant with noradrenergic activity, was reported to be effective for some of the symptoms of ADHD in placebo-controlled trials (Casat & Pleasants, 1989; Clay, Gualtieri, Evans, & Guillian, 1988; Simeon & Ferguson, 1986). Barrickman and colleagues (Barrickman et al., 1995) reported that bupropion was equivalent to MPH in the treatment of 15 children with ADHD, who showed equal improvements on both medications for overall improvement rated by a clinician, as well as improvements in the level of ADHD symptoms as rated by teacher and parent. The study showed an order effect, which suggests a carryover from one drug condition to the next. Also, subjects were not placed on a placebo in the crossover, so the study is not placebo controlled. Bupropion's efficacy was shown in a completed multisite controlled trial of bupropion (Conners, et al., 1996).

Buspirone is an anxiolytic compound with weak DA activity. Data to date for children with ADHD come from a small, 10-patient controlled study (McCormick, Rizzo, & Knickes, 1994) and case reports. One of these case reports (Quaison, Ward, & Kitchen, 1991) suggests that buspirone may reduce aggressivity, as well as ameliorate the symptoms of ADHD.

Clonidine (CLON) is an alpha-2 presynaptic receptor agonist indicated for adult hypertension. However, a recent review (Swanson et al., 1995a) reveals that, from 1990 to 1995, there was a fivefold increase in physicians writing CLON prescriptions for children with ADHD. Safety and efficacy issues have not been addressed in this age group. Only one small controlled study of 10 ADHD children (Hunt, Minderaa, & Cohen, 1985) suggests that CLON may be effective in ADHD, with reductions in hyperactivity and aggression. In postmarketing reports (MEDWATCH), 23 children treated simultaneously with CLON and MPH have been reported to have had drug reactions, including heart rate and blood pressure abnormalities. Among that group, 4 experienced severe adverse effects, including death (Swanson et al., 1995a). Guanfacine, a similar alpha-2 presynaptic agonist, has been studied in two open trials involving 23 children (Chappell et al., 1995; Hunt, Arnstan, & Asbell, 1995), but no efficacy or safety data are available. Much of the popularity for the off-label use of these antihypertensives in ADHD has come from their sedating effects, useful for counteracting stimulant-related insomnia (Wilens, Biederman, & Spencer, 1994).

Venlafaxine is a new antidepressant that acts as a reuptake inhibitor at both the serotonin and norepinephrine neuron. Investigators have begun reporting venlafaxine-related improvements in patients with ADHD (Adler, Resnick, Kunz, & McDevinsky, 1995; Hornig-Roher & Amsterdam, 1995; Reimherr, Hedges, Strong, & Wender, 1995; Wilens, Biederman, & Spencer, 1995), with symptom reductions in the 40% to 60% range. Other investigators have run small open trials with school-age children and adolescents (Luh, Pliszka, Olvera, & Taron, 1995; Pleak & Gornly, 1995) and found that venlafaxine was well tolerated while improving ADHD symptoms. Derivan and colleagues (Derivan, Aguir, Preskorn, D'Amico, & Troy, 1995) completed a pharmacokinetic study of 25 children and adolescents with ADHD and conduct disorder and showed that these youth need a higher oral dose than adults to achieve the same blood level. He also reported improvement in CGI (Clinical Global Impression Rating Form) scores for these children and adolescents. No direct comparison has been done between venlafaxine and stimulants, although early impressions suggest that it is less effective in reducing the symptoms of ADHD.

Selective serotonin reuptake inhibitors (SSRIs) enjoy a reputation for high efficacy and low adverse event reporting in adults with major depressive disorder. Costellanos (1996) found no signs of efficacy for SSRIs in the treatment of ADHD symptoms in children in the seven studies (68 children) he reviewed.

CONCLUSIONS

Psychostimulant medications have become a mainstay in the American medical community for the treatment of ADHD. This popularity may be a result of the proven efficacy of these compounds during short-term controlled studies, as shown by improvements in global ratings of ADHD symptoms by teachers and parents. In fact, the majority of children with ADHD will respond to either MPH or DEX, so that nonresponders are rare (Elia et al., 1991). Although the long-term response of ADHD children to psychostimulants has not been examined in a controlled study (Jacobvitz et al., 1990), anecdotal reports suggest that children with ADHD relapse when their medication is withdrawn and respond when the medication is restarted.

Psychostimulant treatment research has also flourished, but there is ample opportunity for more studies. Not all patients respond to psychostimulants, in particular, patients with comorbid psychiatric disorders. The aim of new pharmacological studies will be to target populations with comorbid disorders (e.g., the child with ADHD and generalized anxiety disorder) and to examine differential responses to medications in these patients versus patients without the additional psychi-

TABLE 3.5 Type 6 Studies Suggesting Efficacy for Alternative Medications for ADHD

Study (Year)	N	Age Range (Years)	Design	Drug (Dose)	Duration	Response	Comment
Simeon & Ferguson (1986)	17	7–13	Single blind	Bupropion (135 mg/day)	8 weeks	70% improved	CGI, Conners Rating scales
Casat et al. (1989)	30	6–12	Double-blind parallel	Bupropion (150–250 mg/day)	4 weeks	Moderate improve	Teacher, CGI improved
Clay et al. (1988)	33	6–12	Double-blind parallel	Bupropion (5.3 mg/kg/day)	3 weeks	Moderate improve	Teacher, parent, CGI improved
Jacobsen (1995)	1	7	Open-L	Bupropion (75 mg tid)	4 weeks	Moderate improved	Increased compulsions, so stopped BPR
Barrickman et al. (1995)	15	7–17	Crossover	Bupropion (3.3 mg/kg/day) MPH (0.7 mg/kg/day)	6 weeks	BPR = MPH	CGI, Iowa-Conners, CDI, RC-MAS, CPT No placebo group; order effects
McCormick et al. (1994)	10	6–12	Crossover	Buspirone (10 mg/day) PB	6 weeks	BPR > PB	Teacher ratings better
Quiason et al. (1991)	1	8	Open-L	Buspirone (15 mg tid)	10 days	Improved	Decreased aggression
Hunt et al. (1985)	10	11.6	Open	Clonidine	12 weeks	70%	Observers disagree about improvement
Schvehla et al. (1994)	18	6–12	Open	Clonidine (0.15–0.3 mg)	2 months	61% improved	Sedation transient; all subjects inpatients, so improvement may be due to ward milieux
Ernst & Zametkin (1995)	36	37.6	Crossover	l-Deprenyl (20 mg, 60 mg)	6 weeks	PB = active	High dose l-deprenyl decreased p-HVA

56

Study	N	Age	Type	Drug (dose)	Duration	Outcome	Comments
Chappel et al. (1995)	10	8–16	Open	Guanfacine (1.5 mg/day)	4–20 weeks	Improve tics 40% ADHD	ADHD + Tourette's patients 40% behavior improve
Hunt et al. (1995)	13	8–17	Open	Guanfacine (0.5–4.0 mg)	4 weeks	Improved	Compares baseline versus end point
Conners et al. (1995)	17	N/A	Crossover 11 nonsmokers vs 6 smokers	Nicotine patch (7-mg patch) (21-mg patch)	3 sessions	Improved	Improved CGI, reaction time
Hinton et al. (1995)	10	N/A	Crossover A-B-A	Nicotine patch (7-mg patch)	3 sessions	Improved	Improved deficits in timing accuracy
Spencer et al. (1996)	21	Adults	Crossover	Tomoxetin (76 mg/day)	6 weeks	52% active 10% placebo	Found mild appetite suppression for this NE reuptake inhibitor
Pleak & Gomly (1995)	1	11	Open-L	Venlafaxine (75 mg tid)	6 weeks	Improved	Diastolic blood pressure increased on 100 mg tid
Wilens et al. (1995)	2	45–48	Open	Venlafaxine (18.75 tid–75 bid)	2 months	Improved	52–60% reduction of ADHD symptoms
Reimherr et al. (1995)	20	35	Open	Venlafaxine (50–150 mg/day)	N/A	40% improved	8 patients unable to tolerate lowest dose
Adler et al. (1995)	12	19–59	Open	Venlafaxine (110.4 mg/day)	8 weeks	49.6% improved	4 dropped: sedation
Hornig-Rohan & Amsterdam (1995)	17	43	Open	Venlafaxine (N/A)	N/A	80% improved	Small samples, some on multiple medications
Luh et al. (1995)	15	8–17	Open	Venlafaxine (12.5–75 mg)	5 weeks	50% improved	Well tolerated
Derivan et al. (1995)	25	6–15	Open PK	Venlafaxine	6 weeks	Significant	AUC, clearance kids > adults
Costellanos (1996) (Review)	12	6–12	1 Crossover	CMI	3 weeks	N/A	CMI > MPH for depressive symptoms
	55	3–39	5 Open	Fluoxetine	6 weeks–3 months	Improvement	All open studies
	1	24	1 Open	Sertraline		Improvement	Temper, distractibility improved

Studies arranged alphabetically by drug generic name. Most studies open or letters (see "L" added to study type column).

CGI = Clinical Global Impressions Rating Form; BPR = bupropion; CDI = Child Depression Inventory Rating Form; CPT = Continuous Performance Test; RCMAS = Revised Children's Manifest Anxiety Scale; PB = placebo; PHVA = homovanillic acid; A-B-A = Design for drug study; PK = pharmacokinetic; AUC = area under curve, density of plasma drug level concentrations; CMI = clomipramine (Anafranil).

atric diagnoses. It is also important to determine medication effects on the acquisition of social skills in ADHD children (Hinshaw, 1991). Finally, it will be helpful to determine if the combination of behavioral and medication therapies is more effective than medication alone (Gittelman, 1987). Current and future studies of multimodal therapies will test whether combined treatment results in better long-term functioning and decreased appearance of comorbid conditions than does monomodal treatment with psychostimulants.

References

Abikoff, H. (1991). Interaction of methylphenidate and multimodal therapy in the treatment of attention deficit hyperactivity disorder. In B. Osman & L. L. Greenhill (Eds.), *Ritalin: Theory and patient management* (pp. 147–154). New York: Mary Ann Liebert.

Abikoff, H., & Gittelman, R. (1985). Hyperactive children treated with stimulants: Is cognitive training a useful adjunct? *Archives of General Psychiatry, 42,* 953–961

Adler, L., Resnick, S., Kunz, M., & McDevinsky, O. (1995) Open-label trial of venlafaxine (Effexor) in attention deficit disorder. *Psychological Bulletin, 31,* 544.

Ahmann, P., Waltonen, S., Olson, K., Theye, F., Van Erem, A., & LaPlant, R. (1993). Placebo-controlled evaluation of ritalin side effects. *Pediatrics, 91,* 1101–1106.

American Psychiatric Association. (1980). *Diagnostic and statistical manual of mental disorders (DSM-III),* 3rd ed. Washington, D.C.: Author.

———. (1987). *Diagnostic and statistical manual of mental disorders,* 3rd ed. Washington, D.C.: Author.

———. (1994). *Diagnostic and statistical manual of mental disorders (DSM-IV),* 4th ed. Washington, D.C.: Author.

American Psychiatric Association Workgroup on DSM-IV. (1991). *DSM-IV options book.* Washington, D.C.: Author.

Anderson, J., Williams, S., McGee, R., & Silva, P. (1987). DSM-III disorders in pre-adolescent children; prevalence in a large sample for the general population. *Archives of General Psychiatry, 44,* 69–76.

Arnold, L. E., Christopher, J., Huestis, R., & Smeltzer, D. (1978). Methylphenidate versus dextroamphetamine versus caffeine in minimal brain dysfunction. *Archives of General Psychiatry, 35,* 463–473.

Barkley, R. (1989). Hyperactive girls and boys; stimulant drug effects on mother-child interactions. *Journal of Child Psychology & Psychiatry, 30,* 379–390.

Barkley, R. (1991). Adolescents with ADHD: Patterns of behavioral adjustment, academic functioning, and treatment utilization. *Journal of the American Academy of Child & Adolescent Psychiatry, 30,* 752–761.

Barkley, R., Fischer, M., Edelbroch, C., & Smallish, L. (1990a). The adolescent outcome of hyperactive children diagnosed by research criteria: An 8-year prospective follow-up. *Journal of the American Academy of Child Psychiatry, 29,* 546–557.

Barkley, R., McMurray, M., Edelbroch, C., & Robbins, K. (1990b). Side effects of MPH in children with attention deficit hyperactivity disorder: A systematic placebo-controlled evaluation. *Pediatrics, 86,* 184–192.

Barkley, R. A. (1977). A review of stimulant drug research with hyperactive children. *Journal of Child Psychology and Psychiatry, 18,* 137–165.

———. (1982). *Hyperactive children: A handbook for diagnosis and treatment.* New York: Guilford Press.

Barkley, R. A., & Cunningham, C. E. (1979). The effects of methylphenidate on the mother-child interactions of hyperactive children. *Archives of General Psychiatry, 36,* 201–208.

Barrickman, L., Perry, P., Allen, A., Kuperman, S., Arndt, S., Herman, K., & Schumacher, E. (1995). A double-blind crossover trial of bupropion and methylphenidate. *Journal of the American Academy of Child and Adolescent Psychiatry, 34,* 649–657.

Bauermeister, J., Canino, G., & Bird, H. (1994). Epidemiology of disruptive behavior disorders. *Child & Adolescent Psychiatric Clinics of North America, 3,* 177–194.

Biederman, J., Baldessarini, R.J., Wright, V., Keenan, K., & Faraone, S. (1989). A double-blind placebo controlled study of desipramine in the treatment of ADD: I. Efficacy. *Journal of the American Academy of Child and Adolescent Psychiatry, 28*(5), 777–784.

Bird, H. R., Canino, G., Rubio-Stipec, M., Gould, M. S., Ribera, J., Sesman, M., Woodbury, M., Heurtas-Goldman, S., Pagan, A., Sanchez-Lacay, A., & Moscoso, M. (1988). Estimates of the prevalence of childhood maladjustment in a community sample in Puerto Rico. *Archives of General Psychiatry, 45,* 1120–1126.

Bosco, J., & Robin, S. (1980). Hyperkinesis: Prevalence and treatment. In C. Whalen & B. Henker (Eds.), *Hyperkinetic children: The social ecology of identification and treatment.* New York: Academic Press.

Bradley, C. (1937). The behavior of children receiving benzedrine. *American Journal of Psychiatry, 94,* 577–585.

———. (1941). The behavior of children receiving benzedrine. *American Journal of Orthopsychiatry, 11,* 92–103.

Bradley, C., & Bowen, M. (1941). Amphetamine (benzedrine) therapy of children's behavior disorders. *American Journal of Orthopsychiatry, 11,* 92–103.

Buitelaar, J., Gary, R., Swaab-Barneveld, H., & Kuiper, M. (1995). Prediction of clinical response to methylphenidate in children with attention deficit hyperactivity disorder. *Journal of the American Academy of Child and Adolescent Psychiatry, 34,* 1025–1032.

Campbell, S. (1973). Mother-child interaction in reflective, impulsive, and hyperactive children. *Developmental Psychology, 8,* 341–349.

Casat, C. D., Pleasants, D. Z., Schroeder, D., & Parker, D. (1989). Bupropion in children with attention deficit disorder. *Psychopharmacology Bulletin, 25*(2), 198–201.

Chappell, P., Riddle, M., Scahill, L., Lynch, K., Shultz, R., Arnsten, A., Leckman, J., & Cohen, D. (1995). Guanfacine treatment of comorbid ADHD and Tourette's syndrome: Preliminary clinical experience. *Journal of the American Academy of Child and Adolescent Psychiatry, 34,* 1140–1146.

Charles, L., Schain, R. J., & Guthrie, D. (1979). Long-term use and discontinuation of methylphenidate with hyperactive children. *Developmental Medicine and Child Neurology, 21*(6), 758–764.

Clay, T., Gualtieri, C., Evans, P., & Guillian, C. (1988). Clinical and neurophysiological effects of the novel antidepressant bupropion. *Psychological Bulletin, 24,* 143–148.

Connell, H., Irvine, L., & Rodney, J. (1982). Psychiatric disorder in Queensland primary school children. *Australian Pediatrics, 18,* 177–180.

Conners, C. K., Eisenberg, L., & Barcai, A. (1967). Effect of dextroamphetamine on children: Studies on subjects with learning disabilities and school behavior problems. *Archives of General Psychiatry, 17,* 478–485.

Conners, C. K., Casat, C. D., Gualtieri, C. T., Weller, E., Reader, M., Reiss, A., Weller, R., Khayrallah, M., & Ascher, J. (1996). Bupropion hydrochloride in attention deficit hyperactivity disorder with hyperactivity. *Journal of the American Academy of Child & Adolescent Psychiatry, 35,* 1314–1321.

Conners, C. K., Levin, E., March, J., Sparrow, E., & Erhardt, D. (1995). Neurocognitive and behavioral effects of nicotine in adult attention-deficit hyperactivity disorder (ADHD). *Psychopharmacology Bulletin, 31,* 559, abstract.

Costellanos, X. (1996). SSRIs in ADHD. Paper presented at NIMH meeting on Alternative Therapies for ADHD, January, 1996.

Costello, E. (1989). Child psychiatric disorders and their correlates: A primary care pediatric sample. *Journal of the Academy of Child & Adolescent Psychiatry, 28,* 851–858.

Derivan, A., Aquir, L., Preskorn, S., D'Amico, D., & Troy, S. (1995). A study of venlafaxine in children and adolescents with conduct disorder. In *Proceedings of the Annual Meeting of the American Academy of Child and Adolescent Psychiatry, 11,* 128.

Douglas, V. I., Barr, R. G., Amin, K., O'Neill, M. E., & Britton, B. G. (1988). Dose effects and individual responsivity to methylphenidate in attention deficit disorder. *Journal of Child Psychology and Psychiatry, 29,* 453–475.

Douglas, V., Barr, R., Desilets, J., & Sherman, E. (1995). Do high doses of stimulants impair flexible thinking in ADHD? *Journal of the American Academy of Child & Adolescent Psychiatry, 34,* 877–885.

Dulcan, M. (1990). Using psychostimulants to treat behavior disorders of children and adolescents. *Journal of Child and Adolescent Psychopharmacology, 1,* 7–20.

DuPaul, G., Barkley, R., & McMurray, M. (1994). Response of children with ADHD to methylphenidate: Interaction with internalizing symptoms. *Journal of the American Academy of Child and Adolescent Psychiatry, 33*(6), 894–903.

DuPaul, G., & Rapport, M. (1993). Does MPH normalize the classroom performance of children with attention deficit disorder? *Journal of the American Academy of Child and Adolescent Psychiatry, 32,* 190–198.

DuPaul, G. J., & Barkley, R. A. (1990). Medication therapy. In R. A. Barkley (Ed.), *Attention deficit hyperactivity disorder: A handbook for diagnosis and treatment* (2nd ed., pp. 573–612). New York: Guilford Press.

Eisenberg, L., Lachman, R., Molling, P., Lockner, A., Mizelle, J., & Conners, C. (1961). A psychopharmacologic experiment in a training school for delinquent boys: Methods, problems and findings. *American Journal of Orthopsychiatry, 33,* 431–447.

Elia, J., Borcherding, B., Rapoport, J., & Keysor, C. (1991). Methylphenidate and dextroamphetamine treatments of hyperactivity: Are there true non-responders? *Psychiatry Research, 36,* 141–155.

Ernst, M., Liebenauer, L., Jons, P., Murphy, D., & Zametkin, A. (1995). L-Deprenyl on behavior and plasma monoamine metabolites in hyperactive adults. *Psychopharmacology Bulletin, 31,* 565.

Ernst, M., & Zametkin, A. (1995). The interface of genetics, neuroimaging, and neurochemistry in attention-deficit hyperactivity disorder. In F. Bloom & D. Kupfer (Eds.), *Psychopharmacology: The fourth generation of progress* (4th ed., pp. 1643–1652). New York: Raven Press.

Esser, G., Schmidt, M., & Woerner, W. (1996). Epidemiology and course of psychiatric disorders in school-age children—results of a longitudinal study. *Journal of Child Psychology & Psychiatry, 31,* 243–253.

Gadow, K. (1991). Effects of stimulant drugs on academic

performance in hyperactive and learning disabled children. *Journal of Learning Disabilities, 16,* 190–199.

Gadow, K., Sverd, J., Sprafkin, J., Nolan, E., & Ezor, S. (1995). Efficacy of methylphenidate for attention deficit hyperactivity in children with tic disorder. *Archives of General Psychiatry, 52,* 444–455.

Gittelman, K. (1987). Pharmacotherapy of childhood hyperactivity: An update. In H. Y. Meltzer (Ed.), *Psychopharmacology: The third generation of progress* (3rd ed., pp. 1215–1224) New York: Raven.

Gittelman/Klein, R., Landa, B., Mattes, J. A., & Klein, D. F. (1988). Methylphenidate and growth in hyperactive children. *Archives of General Psychiatry, 45,* 1127–1130.

Gittelman, R. (1980). Drug treatment of child psychiatric disorders. In D. F. Klein, R. Gittelman, F. Quitkin, & A. Rifkin (Eds.), *Diagnosis and drug treatment of psychiatric disorders: Second Edition* (pp. 590–696). Baltimore, Md.: Williams and Wilkins.

Gittelman, R., & Kanner, A. (1986). Psychopharmacotherapy. In H. Quay & J. Werry (Eds.), *Psychopathological disorders of childhood* (3rd ed., pp. 455–495). New York: Wiley.

Gittelman, R., & Mannuzza, S. (1988). Hyperactive boys almost grown up: III. Methylphenidate effects on ultimate height. *Archives of General Psychiatry, 45,* 1131–1134.

Gittelman-Klein, R. (1980). Diagnosis and drug treatment of childhood disorders: Attention deficit disorder with hyperactivity. In D. F. Klein, R. Gittelman-Klein, F. Quitkin, & A. Rifkin (Eds.), *Diagnosis and drug treatment of psychiatric disorders: Adults and children* (2nd ed.) Baltimore, Md.: Williams and Wilkins.

Greenhill, L. (1995). Attention-deficit hyperactivity disorder: The stimulants. *Child and Adolescent Clinics of North America, 4*(1), 123–168.

Greenhill, L., Abikoff, H., Conners, C. K., Elliott, G., Hechtman, L., Hinshaw, S., Hoza, B., Jensen, P., Kraemer, H., March, J., Newcorn, J., Pelham, W., Richters, J., Schiller, E., Severe, J., Swanson, J., Vereen, D., & Wells, K. (1996). Medication treatment strategies in the MTA: Relevance to clinicians and researchers. *Journal of the American Academy of Child and Adolescent Psychiatry, 35,* 444–454.

Greenhill, L. L. (1981). Stimulant-relation growth inhibition in children: A review. In M. Gittelman (Ed.), *Strategic interventions for hyperactive children* (pp. 39–63). Armonk, N.Y.: M. E. Sharpe.

Greenhill, L. L., Pulg-Antich, J., Chambers, W., Rubinstein, B., Halpern, F., & Sachar, E. J. (1981). Growth hormone, prolactin, and growth responses in hyperkinetic males treated with D-amphetamine. *Journal of*

the American Academy of Child and Adolescent Psychiatry, 20, 84–103.

Greenhill, L. L., Puig-Antich, J., Novacenko, H., Solomon, M., Anghern, C., Florea, J., Goetz, R., Fiscina, B., & Sachar, E. J. (1984). Prolactin, growth hormone and growth responses in boys with attention deficit disorder and hyperactivity treated with methylphenidate. *Journal of the American Academy of Child and Adolescent Psychiatry, 23*(1), 58–67.

Gualtieri, C. T., Kanoy, R., Koriath, U., Schroeder, S., Youngblood, W., Breese, G. R., & Prange, A. J. (1981). Growth hormone and prolactin secretion in adults and hyperactive children relation to methylphenidate serum levels. *Psychoneuroendocrinology, 6*(4), 331–339.

Halperin, J. M., Matier, K., Bedi, G., Sharma, S., & Newcorn, J. H. (1992). Specificity of inattention, impulsivity, and hyperactivity to the diagnosis of attention-deficit disorder. *Journal of the Academy of Child and Adolescent Psychiatry, 31,* 190–196.

Hechtman, L., & Weiss, G. (1984). Hyperactives as young adults: Initial predictors of adult outcome. *Journal of the American Academy of Child and Adolescent Psychiatry, 23,* 250–260.

Hinshaw, S. (1991). Effects of methylphenidate on aggressive and antisocial behavior. *Proceedings of the Annual Meeting of the American Academy of Child and Adolescent Psychiatry, 7,* 31–32 (abstract).

———. (1994). *Attention deficits and hyperactivity in children.* Thousand Oaks, Ca.: Sage.

Hinshaw, S., Heller, T., & McHale, J. (1992). Covert antisocial behavior in boys with attention-deficit hyperactivity disorder: External validation and effects of methylphenidate. *Journal of Consulting and Clinical Psychology, 60,* 274–281.

Hinshaw, S., Henker, B., Whalen, C., Ehrardy, D., & Dunnington, R. E. (1989). Aggressive, prosocial and nonsocial behavior in hyperactive boys: Dose effects of MPH in naturalistic settings. *Journal of Consulting and Clinical Psychology, 57*(4), 636–643.

Hinton, S., Conners, C., Levin, E., & Meck, W. (1995). Nicotine and ADHD: Effects on temporal generalization. *Psychopharmacology Bulletin, 31,* 579, abstract.

Horn, W. F., Islongo, N. S., Pascoe, J. M., Greenberg, G., Packard, T., Lopez, M., Wagner, A., & Puttler, L. (1991). Additive effects of psychostimulants, parent training, and self-control therapy with ADHD children. *Journal of the American Academy of Child and Adolescent Psychiatry, 30*(2), 233–240.

Hornig-Roher, M., & Amsterdam, J. (1995). Venlafaxine versus stimulant therapy in patients with dual diagnosis of attention deficit disorder and depression. *Psychopharmacology Bulletin, 3,* 580 (abstract).

Humphries, T., Kinsbourne, M., & Swanson, J. (1978).

Stimulant effects on cooperation and social interaction between hyperactive children and their mothers. *Journal of Child Psychology and Psychiatry, 19*, 13–22.

Hunt, R., Arnstan, A., & Asbell, M. (1995). An open trial of guanfacine in the treatment of attention-deficit hyperactivity disorder. *Journal of the American Academy of Child and Adolescent Psychiatry, 34*, 41–50.

Hunt, R., Minderaa, R., & Cohen, D. (1985). Clonidine benefits children with attention deficit disorder and hyperactivity: Report of a double-blind placebo-crossover therapeutic trial. *Journal of the American Academy of Child and Adolescent Psychiatry, 24*, 617–629.

Ickowicz, A., Tannock, R., Fulford, P., Purvis, K., & Schachar, R. (1992). Transient tics and compulsive behaviors following methylphenidate: Evidence from a placebo controlled double blind clinical trial. In *American Academy of Child and Adolescent Psychiatry, Scientific Proceedings of the Annual Meeting*, Vol. 8 (p. 70).

Jacobsen, L., Chappell, P., & Woolish, J. (1995). Bupropion and compulsive behavior. *Journal of the American Academy of Child & Adolescent Psychiatry, 31*, 144 (abstract).

Jacobsen, N., & Truax, P. (1991). Clinical significance: A statistical approach to defining meaningful change in psychotherapy research. *Journal of Consulting and Clinical Psychology, 50*, 12–19.

Jacobvitz, D., Srouge, L. A., Stewart, M., & Leffert, N. (1990). Treatment of attentional and hyperactivity problems in children with sympathomimetic drugs: A comprehensive review. *Journal of the American Academy of Child and Adolescent Psychiatry, 29*(5), 677–688.

Kavale, K. (1982). The efficacy of stimulant drug treatment for hyperactivity: A meta-analysis. *Journal of Learning Disabilities, 15*, 280–289.

Klein, R., & Wender, P. (1995). The role of methylphenidate in psychiatry. *Archives of General Psychiatry, 52*, 429–433.

Klorman, R., Brumagham, J., Fitzpatrick, P., & Burgstedt, A. (1990). Clinical effects of a controlled trial of methylphenidate on adolescents with attention deficit disorder. *Journal of the American Academy of Child and Adolescent Psychiatry, 29*, 702–709.

Laufer, M. W., Denhoff, E., & Solomon, G. (1957). Hyperkinetic impulsive disorder in children's behavior problems. *Psychosomatic Medicine, 19*, 38–49.

Luh, J., Pliszka, S., Olvera, R., & Taton, R. (1995). An open trial of venlafaxine in the treatment of ADHD. *Proceedings of the Annual Meeting of the American Academy of Child and Adolescent Psychiatry, 11*, 122. Washington, DC.

Mannuzza, S., Klein, R., Bessler, A., Malloy, P., & LaPadula, M. (1993). Adult outcome of hyperactive boys: Educational achievement, occupational rank and psychiatric status. *Archives of General Psychiatry, 50*, 565–576.

Manuzza, S., Klein, R., Bonagura, N., Malloy, P., Giampino, T., & Addlii, K. (1991). Hyperactive boys almost grown up: V. Replication of psychiatric status. *Archives of General Psychiatry, 48*, 77–83.

March, J., Conners, C. K., Erhardt, D., & Johnston, H. (1994). Pharmacotherapy of attention-deficit hyperactivity disorder. *Annals of Drug Therapy, 2*, 187–213.

Matochik, J., Liebenauer, L., King, A., Szymanski, H., Cohen, R., & Zametkin, A. (1994). Cerebral glucose metabolism in adults with attention deficit hyperactivity disorder after chronic stimulant treatment. *American Journal of Psychiatry, 151*, 658–664.

Matochik, J., Nordahl, T., Gross, M., Semple, M., King, A., Cohen, R., & Zametkin, A. (1993). Effects of acute stimulant medication on cerebral metabolism in adults with hyperactivity. *Neuropsychopharmacology, 8*, 377–386.

Mattes, J., Boswell, L., & Oliver, H. (1984). Methylphenidate effects on symptoms of attention deficit disorder in adults. *Archives of General Psychiatry, 41*, 449–456.

McCormick, L., Rizzuo, G., & Knickes, H. (1994). A pilot study of buspirone in ADHD. *Archives of General Psychiatry, 3*, 68–70.

McCracken, J. (1991). A two-part model of stimulant action on attention-deficit hyperactivity disorder in children. *Journal of Neuropsychiatry and Clinical Neuroscience, 3*(2), 201–209.

Milich, R., Licht, B., & Murphy, D. (1989). Attention-deficit hyperactivity disordered boys evaluations of and attributions for task performance on medication versus placebo. *Journal of Abnormal Psychology, 98*, 280–284.

Ottenbach, J., & Cooper, H. (1983). Drug treatment of hyperactivity in children. *Developmental Medicine and Child Neurology, 25*, 358–366.

Pelham, W. (1993). Pharmacotherapy for children with attention-deficit hyperactivity disorder. *School Psychology Review, 23*, 199–227.

Pelham, W., Swanson, J., Forman, M., & Schwint, H. (1995). Pemoline effects on children with ADHD: A time response by dose-response analysis on classroom measures. *Journal of the American Academy of Child and Adolescent Psychiatry, 34*, 1504–1514.

Pelham, W. E., & Bender, M. E. (1982). Peer relationships in hyperactive children: Description and treatment. In K. D. Gadow, & I. Bailer (Eds.), *Advances in learning and behavioral disabilities*. Greenwich, Ct.: JAI Press.

Pelham, W. E., Bender, M. E., Cadell, J., Booth, S., & Moorer, S. (1985). The dose-response effects of methylphenidate on classroom academic and social behavior in children with attention deficit disorder. *Archives of General Psychiatry, 42,* 948–952.

Pelham, W. E., Greenslade, K. E., Vodde-Hamilton, M. A., Murphy, D. A., Greenstein, J. J., Gnagy, E. M., & Dahl, R. E. (1990). Relative efficacy of long-acting stimulants on ADHD children: A comparison of standard methylphenidate, Ritalin-SR, Dexedrine spansule, and pemoline. *Pediatrics, 86,* 226–237.

Pelham, W. E., & Milich, R. (1991). Individual differences in response to Ritalin in classwork and social behavior. In L. L. Greenhill & B. Osman (Eds.), *Ritalin: Theory and patient management* (pp. 203–222). New York: Mary Ann Liebert.

Perel, J., Greenhill, L. L., Curran, S., Feldman, B., & Puig-Antich, J. (1991). Correlates of pharmacokinetics and attentional measures in methylphenidate treated hyperactive children. Manuscript submitted for publication.

Pleak, R., & Gornly, L. (1995). Effects of venlafaxine treatment for ADHD in a child. *American Journal of Psychiatry, 152,* 1099.

Pliszka, S. R. (1989). Effect of anxiety on cognition, behavior, and stimulant response in ADHD. *Journal of the American Academy of Child and Adolescent Psychiatry, 28*(6), 882–887.

Quaison, N., Ward, D., & Kitchen, T. (1991). Buspirone for aggression. *Journal of the American Academy of Child and Adolescent Psychiatry, 30,* 1026.

Rapoport, J. L., Buchsbaum, M. S., Weingartner, H., Zahn, P., Ludlow, C., & Mikkelsen, E. J. (1980). Dextroamphetamine: Cognitive and behavioral effects in normal and hyperactive boys and normal men. *Archives of General Psychiatry, 37,* 933–943.

Rapport, M., Denney, C., DuPaul, G., & Gardner, M. (1994). Attention deficit disorder and methylphenidate: Normalization rates, clinical effectiveness and response prediction in 76 children. *Journal of American Academy of Child and Adolescent Psychiatry, 33*(6), 882–893.

Rapport, M. D., DuPaul, G. J., & Kelly, K. L. (1989). Attention deficit hyperactivity disorder and methylphenidate: The relationship between gross body weight and drug response in children. *Psychopharmacology Bulletin, 25*(2), 285–290.

Rapport, M., Stoner, G., DuPaul, G., Kelly, K., Tucker, S., & Shroeler, T. (1988). Attention deficit disorder and methylphenidate: A multilevel analysis of dose-response effects on children's impulsivity across settings. *Journal of the American Academy of Child & Adolescent Psychiatry, 27,* 60–69.

Ratey, J., Greenberg, M., & Lindem, K. (1991). Combination of treatments for attention deficit hyperactivity disorder in adults. *Journal of Nervous and Mental Disease, 179*(11), 699–701.

Reimherr, F., Hedges, D., Strong, R., & Wender, P. (1995). An open trial of venlafaxine in adult patients with ADHD. *Pharmacology Bulletin, 31,* 609–614.

Richters, J., Arnold, L., Abikoff, H., Conners, C., Greenhill, L., Hechtman, L., Hinshaw, S., Pelham, W., & Swanson, J. (1995). The National Institute of Mental Health Collaborative Multisite Multimodal Treatment Study of Children with Attention-Deficit Hyperactivity Disorder (MTA): I. Background and rationale. *Journal of the American Academy of Child and Adolescent Psychiatry, 34,* 987–1000.

Roche, A. F., Lipman, R. S., Overall, J. E., & Hung, W. (1979). The effects of stimulant medication on the growth of hyperactive children. *Pediatrics, 63*(6), 847–849.

Sabelsky, D. (1990). Fluoxetine in adults with residual attention deficit disorder and hypersomnolence. *Journal of Neuropsychiatry and Clinical Neuroscience, 2*(4), 463–464.

Safer, D., & Allen, R. (1973). Factors influencing the suppressant effects of two stimulant drugs on the growth of hyperactive children. *Pediatrics, 51,* 660–667.

Safer, D., Allen, R., & Barr, E. (1972). Depression of growth in hyperactive children on stimulant drugs. *New England Journal of Medicine, 287,* 217–220.

———. (1975). Growth rebound after termination of stimulant drugs. *Journal of Pediatrics, 86,* 113–116.

Safer, D. J., & Krager, J. M. (1984). Trends in medication treatment of hyperactive school children. In K. D. Gadow (Ed.), *Advances in learning and behavioral disabilities* (3rd ed.) Greenwich, Ct.: JAI Press.

Satterfield, J. H., Cantwell, D. P., Schell, A., & Blaschke, T. (1979). Growth of hyperactive children with methylphenidate. *Archives of General Psychiatry, 36,* 212–217.

Schachar, R., & Tannock, R. (1993). Childhood hyperactivity and psychostimulants: A review of extended treatment studies. *Journal of Child and Adolescent Psychopharmacology, 3,* 81–97.

Schechter, M., & Keuezer, E. (1985). Learning in hyperactive children: Are there stimulant-related and state-dependent effects? *Journal of Clinical Pharmacology, 25,* 276–280.

Schvehla, T., Mandoki, M., & Summer, G. (1994). Clonidine therapy for comorbid attention deficit hyperactivity disorder and conduct disorder: Preliminary findings in a children's inpatient unit. *Southern Medical Journal, 87,* 692–695.

Shaffer, D. (1994). Attention deficit hyperactivity disorder in adults. *American Journal of Psychiatry, 151*(5), 633–638.

Shekim, W., Masterson, A., Cantwell, D., & Hanna, G. (1989). Nomifensine maleate in adult attention deficit disorder. *Journal of Nervous and Mental Disease*, 177(5), 296–299.

Simeon, J. G., Ferguson, H. B., & Van Wyck Fleet, J. (1986). Bupropion effects in attention deficit and conduct disorders. *Canadian Journal of Psychiatry*, 31, 581–585.

Solanto, M. V. (1984). Neuropharmacological basis of stimulant drug action in attention deficit disorder with hyperactivity: a review and synthesis. *Psychology Bulletin*, 95, 387–409.

————. (1991). Dosage effects of ritalin on cognition. In B. Osman & L. L. Greenhill (Eds.), *Ritalin: Theory and patient management* (pp. 150–171). New York: Mary Ann Liebert.

Spencer, T., Biederman, J., Kerman, K., Steingard, R., & Wilens, T. (1993a). Desipramine in the treatment of children with tic disorder or Tourette's syndrome and attention deficit disorder. *Journal of the American Academy of Child & Adolescent Psychiatry*, 32, 354–360.

Spencer, T., Biederman, J., Wilens, T., Harding, M., O'Donnell, D., & Griffin, S. (1996). Pharmacotherapy of attention-deficit hyperactivity disorder across the life cycle. *Journal of the American Academy of Child and Adolescent Psychiatry*, 35, 409–432.

Spencer, T., Wilens, T., Biederman, J., Farone, S., Ablen, S., & Lapey, K. (1995). A double-blind, crossover comparison of methylphenidate and placebo in adults with childhood onset ADHD. *Archives of General Psychiatry*, 52, 434–443.

Spencer, T., Wilens, T., Steingard, R., & Geist, D. T. (1993b). Nortriptyline in the treatment of children with attention deficit disorder and tic disorder or Tourette's syndrome. *Journal of the American Academy of Child & Adolescent Psychiatry*, 32, 205–210.

Sprague, R. L., & Sleator, E. K. (1977). Methylphenidate in hyperkinetic children: differences in dose effects on learning and social behavior. *Science*, 198, 1274–1276.

Stephens, R., Pelham, W. E., & Skinner, R. (1984). The state-dependent and main effects of pemoline and methylphenidate on paired-associates learning and spelling in hyperactive children. *Journal of Consulting and Clinical Psychology*, 52, 104–113.

Swanson, J. (1993). Effect of stimulant medication on hyperactive children: A review of reviews. *Exceptional Child*, 60, 154–162.

Swanson, J., Flockhart, D., Udrea, D., Cantwell, D., Conner, D., & Williams, L. (1995a). Clonidine in the treatment of ADHD: Questions about the safety and efficacy. *Journal of Child and Adolescent Psychopharmacology*, 5, 301–305.

Swanson, J., Lerner, M., & Williams, L. (1995b). More

frequent diagnosis of attention deficit-hyperactivity disorder. *New England Journal of Medicine*, 333, 944.

Szatmari, P. (1992). The epidemiology of attention-deficit hyperactivity disorders. *Child & Adolescent Clinics of North America*, 1, 361–371.

Szatmari, P., Offord, D., & Boyle, M. (1989). Ontario child health study: Prevalence of attention deficit disorder with hyperactivity. *Journal of Child Psychology, Psychiatry & Allied Disciplines*, 30, 219–230.

Tannock, R., Ickowicz, A., & Schachar, R. (1995). Differential effects of MPH on working memory in ADHD children with and without comorbid anxiety. *Journal of the American Academy of Child and Adolescent Psychiatry*, 34, 886–896.

Tannock, R., Schachar, R., & Logan, R. (1993). Methylphenidate and working memory: Differential effects in attention-deficit hyperactivity disorder (ADHD) with and without memory. In *American Academy of Child and Adolescent Psychiatry, Scientific Proceedings of the Annual Meeting*, Vol. 9 (p. 42).

Taylor, E., Sandberg, S., Thorley, G., & Rutter, M. (1991). The epidemiology of childhood hyperactivity. In E. Taylor & M. Rutter (Eds.) *Child Psychiatry* (pp. 1–122). London: Oxford University Press.

Thurber, S., & Walker, C. (1983). Medication and hyperactivity: A meta-analysis. *Journal of General Psychiatry*, 108, 79–86.

Ullmann, R. K., & Sleator, E. K. (1986). Responders, nonresponders, and placebo responders among others during a treatment evaluation. *Clinical Pediatrics*, 25, 594–599.

Velez, C., Johnson, J., & Cohen, P. (1989). A longitudinal analysis of selected risk factors for childhood psychopathology. In *Journal of the American Academy of Child & Adolescent Psychiatry*, 28, 861–871.

Verhulst, F., Eussen, M., & Berden, G. (1992). Pathways of problem behaviors from childhood to adolescence. *Journal of the American Academy of Child & Adolescent Psychiatry*, 32, 388–392.

Vikan, A. (1985). Psychiatric epidemiology in a sample of 1,510 ten-year-old children. I. Prevalence. In (26th ed., pp. 55–60).

Vitiello, B., & Jensen, P. (1995). Developmental perspectives in pediatric psychopharmacology. *Psychopharmacology Bulletin*, 31, 75–81.

Volkow, N., Ding, J., Fowler, G., Wang, J., Logan, J., Gatley, J., Dewey, S., Ashby, C., Lieberman, J., Hitzemann, R., & Wolf, A. (1995). Is methylphenidate like cocaine? *Archives of General Psychiatry*, 52, 456–464.

Vyborova, L., Nahunek, K., Drtilkova, I., Balastikova, B., & Misurec, J. (1984). Intraindividual comparison of 21-day application of amphetamine and methylphenidate in hyperkinetic children. *Activas Nervosa Superior*, 26, 268–269.

Weiss, G., & Hechtman, L. (1993). *Hyperactive children grown up* (2nd ed.) New York: Guilford Press.

———. (1985). Psychiatric status of hyperactives as adults: A controlled prospective 15-year follow-up of 63 hyperactive children. *Journal of the American Academy of Child and Adolescent Psychiatry*, 24, 211–220.

Wender, P. (1994). Attention deficit/hyperactivity disorder in adults. Grand rounds, New York State Psychiatric Institute, September 9, 1994, New York. Unpublished.

Wender, P., & Reimherr, F. (1990). Bupropion treatment of attention-deficit hyperactivity disorder in adults. *American Journal of Psychiatry*, 147(8), 1018–1020.

Wender, P., Reimherr, F., & Wood, D. (1985). A controlled study of methylphenidate in the treatment of attention deficit disorder. *American Journal of Psychiatry*, 142, 547–552.

Wender, P., Wood, D., Reimherr, F., & Ward, M. (1994). An open trial of pargyline in the treatment of adult attention deficit disorder, residual type. *Psychiatry Research*, 9, 329–336.

Wender, P. H., Reimherr, F., & Wood, D. (1981). Attention deficit disorder in adults. *Archives of General Psychiatry*, 38, 449–456.

Whalen, C., Henker, B., Buhrmester, D., Hinshaw, S.,

Huber, A., & Laski, K. (1989) Does stimulant medication improve the peer status of hyperactive children? *Journal of Consulting and Clinical Psychology*, 57, 545–549.

Wilens, T., Biederman, J., Mick, E., & Spencer, T. (1994). Treatment of adult attention-deficit hyperactivity disorder (ADHD) with tricyclic antidepressants: Clinical experience with 23 patients. In *American Academy of Child and Adolescent Psychiatry, Scientific Proceedings of the Annual Meeting*, Vol. 9 (p. 45).

Wilens, T., Biederman, J., & Spencer, T. (1994). Clonidine for sleep disturbances associated with attention deficit hyperactivity disorder. *Journal of the American Academy of Child and Adolescent Psychiatry*, 33, 424–427.

———. (1995). Venlafaxine for adult ADHD. *American Journal of Psychiatry*, 152, 1099–1100.

Wilens, T. E., & Biederman, J. (1992). The stimulants. *Psychiatric Clinics of North America*, 15(1), 191–222.

Winsberg, B. G., Press, M., Bialer, I., & Kupietz, S. (1974). Dextroamphetamine and methylphenidate in the treatment of hyperactive/aggressive children. *Pediatrics*, 53, 236–241.

Zametkin, A. J., & Rapoport, J. L. (1987). Neurobiology of attention deficit disorder with hyperactivity: Where have we come in 50 years? *Journal of the American Academy of Child and Adolescent Psychiatry*, 26, 676–686.

4

Psychosocial Treatments for Conduct Disorder in Children

Alan E. Kazdin

Several Type 1 and Type 2 RCTs of cognitive problem-solving skills training (PSST) with impulsive, aggressive, and conduct disorder (CD) children and adolescents have been reported; PSST focuses on the cognitive processes that underlie social behavior and response repertoires in interpersonal situations. The RCTs, which included among control and comparison conditions no treatment, waiting list, and other treatments such as individual psychotherapy, significantly reduced aggressive and antisocial behavior at home, at school, and in the community.

A large number of RCTs of parent management training (PMT) have been completed over the past 25 years with youths varying in age and degree of severity of dysfunction; marked improvements in child behavior on measures including parent and teacher reports of deviant behavior, direct observation of behavior at home and at school, and institutional records have been reported.

A few Type 1 and Type 2 RCTs have evaluated the effectiveness of functional family therapy (FFT) with difficult-to-treat CD populations, including adjudicated delinquent adolescents and multiple offender delinquents; FFT has led to greater, more long-lasting positive change than comparison treatments or control techniques, including improved family communication and lower rates of referral to and contact with the courts.

A number of Type 1 and Type 2 RCTs have evaluated multisystemic therapy (MST), a multimodality, family-based treatment approach; goals of MST are to help parents develop positive behaviors in their adolescents, overcome marital difficulties that impede their ability to function as parents, eliminate negative interactions between parent and adolescent, and build cohesion and emotional warmth among family members. Multisystemic therapy has been shown to be superior in reducing delinquency and emotional and behavioral problems and improving family functioning in comparison to other methods of achieving these desirable goals.

Antisocial behaviors in children refer to a variety of acts that reflect social rule violations and actions against others. Such behaviors as fighting, lying, and stealing are seen in varying degrees in most children over the course of development. Conduct disorder, for present purposes, is used here to refer to antisocial behavior that is clinically significant and clearly beyond the realm of "normal" functioning. The extent to which antisocial behaviors are sufficiently severe to constitute conduct disorder depends on several characteristics of the behaviors, including their frequency, intensity, and chronicity; whether they are isolated acts or part of a larger syndrome with other deviant behaviors; and whether they lead to significant impairment of the child as judged by parents, teachers, or others.

Little in the way of effective treatment has been generated for the treatment of conduct disorder. This is unfortunate in light of the personal tragedy that conduct disorder can represent to children and their families and others who may be victims of aggressive and antisocial acts. From a social perspective, the absence of effective treatments is problematic as well. Conduct disorder is one of the most frequent bases of clinical referral in child and adolescent treatment services, has relatively poor long-term prognosis, and is transmitted across generations (see Kazdin, 1995b). Because children with conduct disorder often traverse multiple social services (e.g., special education, mental health, juvenile justice), the disorder is one of the most costly mental disorders in the United States (Robins, 1981).

There have been significant advances in treatment. The present chapter reviews research for four psychosocial treatments that have shown considerable promise in the treatment of conduct disorder in children and adolescents.[1] The treatments were selected because they have been carefully evaluated in controlled clinical trials. The chapter describes and evaluates the underpinnings, techniques, and evidence on behalf of these treatments. Critical issues that are raised in providing treatment to children with conduct disorder and their families also are examined.

CHARACTERISTICS OF CONDUCT DISORDER

Descriptive Features: Diagnosis and Prevalence

The overriding feature of conduct disorder is a persistent pattern of behavior in which the rights of others and age-appropriate social norms are violated. Isolated acts of physical aggression, destruction of property, stealing, and firesetting are sufficiently severe to warrant concern and attention in their own right. Although these behaviors may occur in isolation, several of these are likely to appear together as a constellation or syndrome and form the basis of a clinical diagnosis. For example, in the *Diagnostic and Statistical Manual of Mental Disorders* (*DSM-IV*; American Psychiatric Association [APA], 1994), the diagnosis of conduct disorder (CD) is reached if the child shows at least 3 of the 15 symptoms within the past 12 months, with at least 1 symptom evident within the past 6 months. The symptoms include bullying others, initiating fights, using a weapon, being physically cruel to others or to animals, stealing while confronting a victim, firesetting, destroying property, breaking into others' property, stealing items of nontrivial value, staying out late, running away, lying, deliberate firesetting, and truancy.

Using these diagnostic criteria or prior versions of the *DSM*, the prevalence of the disorder among community samples of school-age youth is approximately 2–6% (see Zoccolillo, 1993). One of the most frequent findings is that boys show approximately 3–4 times higher rates of CD than girls. Rates of conduct disorder tend to be higher for adolescents (approximately 7% for youths age 12–16 years) than for children (approximately 4% for children age 4–11 years) (Offord, Boyle, & Racine, 1991). The higher prevalence rate for boys is associated primarily with childhood-onset conduct disorder; the boy-to-girl ratio evens out in adolescence. Characteristic symptom patterns tend to differ as well. Child-onset conduct problems tend to reflect aggressive behavior, whereas adolescent-onset problems tend to reflect delinquent behavior (theft, vandalism).

The prevalence rates are only approximations of conduct disorder as a dysfunction among children and adolescents. The criteria for delineating individual symptoms as present and for delineating the diagnosis are somewhat arbitrary. Youths who approximate but fail to meet the diagnosis often are significantly impaired. Also, the symptom picture one obtains varies considerably as a function of source of information (e.g., parent, teacher, child). For these reasons, it is useful to retain the distinction between conduct disorder as a general pattern of behavior and the diagnosis of CD. The general pattern of conduct disorder behavior has been studied extensively using varied populations (e.g., clinical referrals and delinquent samples) and defining criteria (Kazdin, 1995b). There is widespread agreement and evidence that a constellation of antisocial behaviors can be identified and has correlates to child, parent, and family functioning. Moreover, antisocial behaviors included in the constellation extend beyond those recognized in diagnosis (e.g., substance abuse, associating with delinquent peers).

Causes and Long-Term Clinical Course

Conduct disorder is not the result of a single cause or simple set of antecedents. Current work tends to focus on characteristics, events, and experiences that influence the likelihood (increase the risk) of conduct disorder. The factors that predispose children and adolescents to conduct disorder have been studied extensively in the context of clinical referrals and adjudicated delinquents (see Kazdin, 1995b; Patterson, Reid, & Dishion, 1992; Robins & Rutter, 1990). Numerous factors have been implicated. Table 4.1 highlights several risk factors that have been studied along with general statements of the relations found.

Merely enumerating risk factors is misleading without conveying some of the complexities of their operation. These complexities have direct implications for interpreting the findings, for understanding the disor-

---

TABLE 4.1 Factors That Place Youths at Risk for the Onset of Conduct Disorder

---

Child Factors
  Child Temperament
    A more difficult child temperament (on a dimension of "easy-to-difficult"), as characterized by more negative mood, lower levels of approach toward new stimuli, and less adaptability to change
  Neuropsychological Deficits and Difficulties
    Deficits in diverse functions related to language (e.g., verbal learning, verbal fluency, verbal IQ), memory, motor coordination, integration of auditory and visual cues, and "executive" functions of the brain (e.g., abstract reasoning, concept formation, planning, control of attention)
  Subclinical Levels of Conduct Disorder
    Early signs (e.g., elementary school) of mild ("subclinical") levels of unmanageability and aggression, especially with early age of onset, multiple types of antisocial behaviors, and multiple situations in which they are evident (e.g., at home, school, the community)
  Academic and Intellectual Performance
    Academic deficiencies and lower levels of intellectual functioning
Parent and Family Factors
  Prenatal and Perinatal Complications
    Pregnancy- and birth-related complications including maternal infection, prematurity and low birth weight, impaired respiration at birth, and minor birth injury
  Psychopathology and Criminal Behavior in the Family
    Criminal behavior, antisocial personality disorder, and alcoholism of a parent
  Parent-Child Punishment
    Harsh (e.g., severe corporal punishment) and inconsistent punishment increase risk
  Monitoring of the Child
    Poor supervision, lack of monitoring of whereabouts, and few rules about where youth can go and when they can return
  Quality of the Family Relationships
    Less parental acceptance of their children: less warmth, affection, emotional support, and attachment
  Marital Discord
    Unhappy marital relationships, interpersonal conflict, and aggression of the parents
  Family Size
    Larger family size (i.e., more children in the family)
  Sibling with Antisocial Behavior
    Presence of a sibling, especially an older brother, with antisocial behavior
  Socioeconomic Disadvantage
    Poverty, overcrowding, unemployment, receipt of social assistance ("welfare"), and poor housing
School-Related Factors
  Characteristics of the Setting
    Attending schools in which there is little emphasis on academic work, little teacher time spent on lessons, infrequent teacher use of praise and appreciation for school work, little emphasis on individual responsibility of the students, poor working conditions for pupils (e.g., furniture in poor repair), unavailability of the teacher to deal with children's problems, and low teacher expectancies

---

Note: The list of risk factors highlights major influences. The number of factors and the relations of specific factors to risk are more complex than the summary statements noted here. For a more detailed discussion, other sources can be consulted (e.g., Kazdin, 1995b; Loeber, 1990; Mrazek & Haggerty, 1994).

der, and for identifying at-risk children for preventive interventions. First, risk factors tend to come in "packages." Thus, at a given point in time several factors may be present, such as low income, large family size, overcrowding, poor housing, poor parental supervision, parent criminality, and marital discord, to mention a few (Kazdin, 1995b). Second, over time several risk factors become interrelated because the presence of one factor can augment the accumulation of other risk factors. For example, early aggression can lead to poor peer relations, academic dysfunction, and dropping out of school, which further increase risk for conduct disorder.

Third, risk factors may interact with (i.e., be moderated or influenced by) each other and other variables (see Boyle & Offord, 1990). As one example, large family size has been repeatedly shown to be a risk factor for conduct disorder. However, the importance of family size as a predictor is moderated by income. If family income and living accommodations are adequate, family size is less likely to be a risk factor (West, 1982). As another example, risk factors often interact with age of the child (e.g., infancy, early or middle childhood). For example, marital discord or separation appear to serve as risk factors primarily when they occur early in the child's life (e.g., within the first 4 or 5 years) (Wadsworth, 1979). How risk factors exert an impact in childhood and why some periods of development are sensitive to particular influences underscore the importance of understanding normal developmental processes.

There are important conclusions resulting from risk-factor research. First, no single characteristic or factor seems to be necessary or sufficient for the onset of the disorder. Second, even though some risk factors are more important than others, the accumulation of factors (i.e., number present) itself is important. One or two risk factors may not increase risk very much; with several risk factors, the likelihood of the outcome may increase sharply (e.g., Rutter, Tizard, & Whitmore, 1970; Sanson, Oberklaid, Pedlow, & Prior, 1991) Third, even with the presence of multiple risk factors, the outcome is not determined. Some individuals at high risk may not show the dysfunction (Werner & Smith, 1992). Many factors that contribute to reducing risk, referred to as protective factors, have been studied and identified (see Kazdin, 1995b).

Longitudinal studies have consistently shown that conduct disorder identified in childhood predicts a continued course of social dysfunction, problematic behavior, and poor school adjustment. For example, antisocial child behavior predicts multiple problems in adulthood 30 years later (Robins, 1966). Youths who are referred for their antisocial behavior, compared with youths with other clinical problems or matched normal controls, as adults suffer dysfunction in psychiatric symptoms, criminal behavior, physical health, and social adjustment. Even though conduct disorder in childhood portends a number of other significant problems in adulthood, not all antisocial children suffer impairment as adults. Drawing from multiple samples, Robins (1978) noted that among the most severely antisocial children, less than 50% become antisocial adults. If diverse diagnoses are considered rather than serious antisocial behavior alone, the picture of impairment in adulthood is much worse. Among youths referred for antisocial behavior, 84% received a diagnosis of psychiatric disorder as adults (Robins, 1966). Similar patterns have been found in other follow-up studies of conduct-disordered youth. In brief, the data suggest that the majority of children with clinically referred antisocial behavior will suffer from a significant degree of impairment over the course of their lives.

The Scope of Dysfunction

If one were to consider "only" the symptoms of conduct disorder and the persistence of impairment, the challenge of identifying effective treatments would be great enough. However, the presenting characteristics of children and their families usually raise a number of other considerations that are central to treatment. Consider characteristics of children, families, and contexts that are associated with conduct disorder as a backdrop for comments below on treatment.

Child Characteristics

Children who meet criteria for CD are likely to meet criteria for other disorders as well. The coexistence of more than one disorder is referred to as comorbidity. In general, diagnoses involving disruptive or externalizing behaviors (CD, oppositional defiant disorder [ODD], and attention deficit hyperactivity disorder [ADHD]) often go together. In studies of community and clinic samples, a large percentage of youth with CD or ADHD (e.g., 45–70%) also meet criteria for the other disorder (e.g., Fergusson, Horwood, & Lloyd, 1991; Offord et al., 1991). The co-occurrence of CD and ODD is common as well. Among clinic-referred youth who meet criteria for CD, 84% to 96% also meet concurrent diagnostic criteria for ODD (see Hinshaw, Lahey, & Hart, 1993).[2] Conduct disorder is sometimes comorbid with anxiety disorders and depression (Hinshaw et al., 1993; Walker et al., 1991).

Several other associated features of CD are relevant to treatment. For example, children with conduct disorder are also likely to show academic deficiencies, as reflected in achievement level, grades, being left behind in school, early termination from school, and deficiencies in specific skill areas such as reading. Youths with the disorder are likely to evince poor interpersonal relations, as reflected in diminished social skills in relation to peers and adults and higher levels of peer rejection. Conduct-disordered youths also are likely to show deficits and distortions in cognitive problem-solving skills, attributions of hostile intent to others, and resentment and suspiciousness. Clearly, the disorder is pervasive in the scope of characteristics that are affected for the child with conduct disorder.

Parent and Family Characteristics

Several parent and family characteristics are associated with conduct disorder (see Kazdin, 1995b; Robins, 1991; Rutter & Giller, 1983). The above comments on risk factors convey major characteristics that are likely to be evident among families with a conduct-disordered child who is referred for treatment. Criminal behavior and alcoholism are two of the stronger and more consistently demonstrated parental characteristics. Parental disciplinary practices and attitudes are often characterized as especially harsh, lax, erratic, and inconsistent. Dysfunctional relations are also evident, as reflected in less acceptance of their children and less warmth, affection, emotional support, and attachment compared with parents of nonreferred youth. Less supportive and more defensive communications among family members, less participation in activities as a family, and more clear dominance of one family member are also evident. In addition, unhappy marital relations, interpersonal conflict, and aggression characterize the parental relations of antisocial children. Poor parental supervision and monitoring of the child and lack of knowledge of the child's whereabouts also are associated with conduct disorder.

Contextual Conditions

Conduct disorder is associated with a variety of untoward living conditions such as large family size, overcrowding, poor housing, and disadvantaged school settings (see Kazdin, 1995b). Many of the untoward conditions in which families live place stress on the parents or diminish their threshold for coping with everyday stressors. The net effect can be evident in parent-child interactions in which parents inadvertently engage in patterns that sustain or accelerate antisocial and aggressive interactions (e.g., Dumas & Wahler, 1985; Patterson, Capaldi, & Bank, 1991).

Quite often, the child's dysfunction is embedded in a larger context that cannot be neglected in conceptual views about the development, maintenance, and course of conduct disorder or in the actual delivery of treatment. For example, at our outpatient clinical service (Yale Child Conduct Clinic), it is likely that a family referred for treatment will experience a subset of these characteristics: financial hardship (unemployment, significant debt, bankruptcy), untoward living conditions (dangerous neighborhood, small living quarters), transportation obstacles (no car or car in frequent repair, state-provided taxi service), psychiatric impairment of one of the parents, stress related to significant others (former spouses, boyfriends, or girlfriends), and adversarial contact with an outside agency (schools, youth services, courts). Conduct disorder is conceived as a dysfunction of children and adolescents. The accumulated evidence regarding the symptom constellation, risk factors, and course over childhood, adolescence, and adulthood attests to the heuristic value of focusing on characteristics of the individual. At the same time, there is a gestalt of the child, parent, and family context that includes multiple and reciprocal influences that affect each participant (child and parent) and the systems in which they operate (family, school) (Kazdin, 1993). For treatment to be effective, it is likely that multiple domains will have to be addressed.

CHILD AND ADOLESCENT THERAPY

Overview of Research and Practice

The context for examining psychosocial treatments for conduct disorder is the broader child and adolescent therapy literature (see Kazdin, 1994b). Until recently, there has been a paucity of studies of child and adolescent psychotherapy. This stands in sharp contrast to therapy for adults, which has a rather extensive literature that focuses on multiple facets of treatment, clients, therapists, and domains of dysfunction (see Bergin & Garfield, 1994). Moreover, the focus of child therapy research has been restricted largely to questions of technique or approach, as reflected, for example, in studies comparing treatments with each other and with control conditions (Kazdin, Bass, Ayers, & Rodgers, 1990). These questions are obviously important but represent an early stage before questions about moderators and mechanisms of change can be pursued.

Even so, there has been much progress. A few hundred controlled outcome studies have emerged and have been reviewed in various qualitative and quantitative analyses (Kazdin, 1988; Weisz & Weiss, 1993). The conclusions have been uniformly positive in noting that child and adolescent therapy is effective; that is, effect sizes across multiple studies show that those who receive treatment show a greater reduction in symptoms than those who do not receive treatment. The conclusion might be tempered a bit. Effect sizes do not necessarily translate to meaningful or clinically important reductions in symptoms or improvement of adaptive functioning for those who have been treated. Also, characteristics of the studies themselves greatly limit what can be said about the effects of treatment in clinical application (Kazdin, Bass, et al., 1990). In the majority of cases, child and adolescent therapy research focuses on youths recruited, rather than referred, for treatment. This means that such characteristics as comorbid diagnoses, impairment in multiple domains of functioning, and parent and family dysfunction are likely to be appreciably less than cases seen in clinical work. Also, treatment research focuses on group treatments provided in the schools. The most commonly investigated treatments are behavioral or cognitive-behavioral interventions. Treatment is relatively brief (e.g., 8–10 hours) and does not involve the family or address many of the child, parent, and contextual characteristics noted above. Finally, most studies do not include follow-up assessment of treatment effects; when follow-up is conducted, the median duration is 5 months.

Surveys of clinical practice reveal that psychodynamic, psychoanalytic, family, and eclectic treatments are the most commonly used interventions for children and adolescents (Kazdin, Siegel, & Bass, 1990;

Koocher & Pedulla, 1977; Silver & Silver, 1983). Treatment is usually provided in individual psychotherapy and lasts an average of 6–12 months. Also, usually the parent is seen as part of the treatment, either as a supplement to child treatment or as part of family therapy. These are summarizations of clinical practice and do not convey the remarkable variation. At the same time, some general conclusions are clear. The treatments most frequently used in clinical practice are those that are the least well studied in research. The treatments investigated in research usually are applied to cases that may bear little resemblance to cases seen in treatment. There are some important exceptions, and these reflect programs of research that focus on clinical samples, discussed below.

Identifying Promising Treatments

Many different treatments have been applied to conduct-disordered youths, including psychotherapy; pharmacotherapy; psychosurgery; home-, school-, and community-based programs; residential and hospital treatment; and social services (see Brandt & Zlotnick, 1988; Dumas, 1989; Kazdin, 1985; U.S. Congress, 1991). Of the over 230 documented psychotherapies available for children and adolescents (Kazdin, 1988), the vast majority have not been studied. Among those that have, none has been shown to controvert conduct disorder and its long-term course. Many treatments might seem reasonable to apply to conduct disorder. Conduct disorder is a dysfunction with pervasive features so that one can point to virtually any domain (e.g., psychodynamics, family interaction patterns, cognitive deficiencies) and find aberrations, deficits, and deficiencies.

For present purposes, promising treatments are identified on the basis of multiple criteria. First, it is important for treatment to have some theoretical rationale that notes how the dysfunction, in this case conduct disorder, comes about and then how treatment redresses the dysfunction. Specification of the mechanisms leading to conduct disorder and leading to therapeutic change is required for this initial criterion. Second, basic research on these processes, too, would be very important to support the conceptualization. Basic research refers to studies that examine conduct problems and factors that lead to their onset, maintenance, exacerbation, amelioration, or attenuation. An example would be studies of the family that demonstrate specific interaction patterns among parents and children that exacerbate aggression within the home (Patterson et al., 1992). Third, outcome data that the treatment can achieve change are obviously central. In the present chapter, randomized, controlled outcome (Types 1 and 2) research is used as the criterion for delineating effective treatments. Finally, evidence from outcome research that shows a relation among processes hypothesized to be critical to therapeutic change and actual change would be very persuasive. Assessment of processes might be reflected in cognitions, family interaction, or core conflicts and defenses. Therapeutic change would be shown to covary with the extent to which these processes were altered in treatment. Very little research addresses this aspect of treatment, and hence this criterion is important to note as an objective toward which research might strive.

No single treatment among those available adequately traverses all of these criteria. Yet, a number of promising treatments have been identified for conduct disorder. Four treatment approaches with evidence on their behalf are illustrated below. In highlighting the approaches, the purpose is not to convey that only four promising treatments exist. Yet, these four are clearly among the most well developed in relation to the criteria highlighted here and the number of controlled clinical trials.[3]

PROMISING TREATMENT APPROACHES

Cognitive Problem-Solving Skills Training

Cognitive processes are a broad class of constructs that pertain to how the individual perceives, codes, and experiences the world. Individuals who engage in conduct-disordered behaviors, particularly aggression, show distortions and deficiencies in various cognitive processes. These deficiencies are not merely reflections of intellectual functioning. Although selected processes (recall, information processing) are related to intellectual functioning, their impact has been delineated separately and shown to contribute to behavioral adjustment and social behavior. A variety of cognitive processes have been studied, such as generating alternative solutions to interpersonal problems (e.g., different ways of handling social situations), identifying the means to obtain particular ends (e.g., making friends) or consequences of one's actions (e.g., what

could happen after a particular behavior), making attributions to others of the motivation of their actions; perceiving how others feel, expectations of the effects of one's own actions, and others (see Shirk, 1988; Spivack & Shure, 1982). Deficits and distortion among these processes relate to teacher ratings of disruptive behavior, peer evaluations, and direct assessment of overt behavior (e.g., Lochman & Dodge, 1994; Rubin, Bream, & Rose-Krasnor, 1991).

As an illustration, aggression is not merely triggered by environmental events, but rather through the way in which these events are perceived and processed. The processing refers to the child's appraisals of the situation, anticipated reactions of others, and self-statements in response to particular events. For example, attribution of intent to others represents a salient cognitive disposition critically important to understanding aggressive behavior. Aggressive youths tend to attribute hostile intent to others, especially in social situations in which the cues of actual intent are ambiguous (see Crick & Dodge, 1994). Understandably, when situations are initially perceived as hostile, youths are more likely to react aggressively. In general, research on cognitive processes, as illustrated by this example, has served as an important heuristic base for conceptualizing treatment and for developing specific treatment strategies.

Characteristics of Treatment

Cognitive problem-solving skills training (PSST) consists of developing interpersonal cognitive problem-solving skills. Although many variations of PSST have been applied to children with a conduct problem, several characteristics usually are shared. First, the emphasis is on how children approach situations, that is, the thought processes in which the child engages to guide responses to interpersonal situations. The children are taught to engage in a step-by-step approach to solve interpersonal problems. They make statements to themselves that direct attention to certain aspects of the problem or tasks that lead to effective solutions. Second, behaviors that are selected (solutions) to the interpersonal situations are important as well. Prosocial behaviors are fostered (through modeling and direct reinforcement) as part of the problem-solving process. Third, the treatment utilizes structured tasks involving games, academic activities, and stories. Over the course of treatment, the cognitive problem-solving skills are increasingly applied to real-life situations in which oppositional, aggressive, and antisocial behavior have been evident for the child. Fourth, therapists usually play an active role in treatment. They model the cognitive processes by making verbal self-statements, apply the sequence of statements to particular problems, provide cues to prompt use of the skills, and deliver feedback and praise to develop correct use of the skills. Finally, treatment usually combines several different procedures, including modeling and practice, role playing, and reinforcement and mild punishment (loss of points or tokens). These are deployed in systematic ways to develop increasingly complex response repertoires of the child.

Overview of the Evidence

Several randomized clinical trials (Type 1 and Type 2 studies) have been completed with impulsive, aggressive, and conduct-disordered children and adolescents and have been reviewed in meta-analyses (see Baer & Nietzel, 1991; Durlak, Furhman, & Lampman, 1991). Among the different studies, control and comparison conditions have included no treatment, waiting list, and other treatments such as individual psychotherapy. Cognitively based treatments have significantly reduced aggressive and antisocial behavior at home, at school, and in the community and have surpassed the impact of these other control and comparison conditions. At follow-up, these gains have been evident up to 1 year later. Many early (e.g., 1970-1980) studies in the field focused on impulsive children and nonpatient samples. Since that time, several additional (Types 1 and 2) studies have shown treatment effects with inpatient and outpatient samples (see Kazdin, 1993; Kendall, 1991; Pepler & Rubin, 1991).

There is only sparse evidence that addresses the child, parent, family, contextual, or treatment factors that influence treatment outcome. Some evidence suggests that older children profit more from treatment than younger children, perhaps due to their cognitive development (Durlak et al., 1991). However, the basis for differential responsiveness to treatment as a function of age has not been well tested. Conduct-disordered children who show comorbid diagnoses, academic delays and dysfunction, and lower reading achievement and who come from families with high levels of impairment (parent psychopathology, stress, and family dysfunction) respond less well to treatment than youths with less dysfunction in these domains (Kazdin, 1995a; Kazdin & Crowley, 1997). However,

these child, parent, and family characteristics may influence the effectiveness of several different treatments for conduct-disordered youths rather than PSST in particular. Much further work is needed to evaluate factors that contribute to responsiveness to treatment.

Overall Evaluation

There are features of PSST that make it an extremely promising approach for clinical use. Perhaps most importantly, several controlled outcome studies with clinic samples have shown that cognitively based treatment leads to therapeutic change. Second, basic research in developmental psychology continues to elaborate the relation of maladaptive cognitive processes among children and adolescents and conduct problems that serve as underpinnings of treatment (Crick & Dodge, 1994; Shirk, 1988). Third, and on a more practical level, many versions of treatment are available in manual form (e.g., Feindler & Ecton, 1986; Finch, Nelson, & Ott, 1993; Shure, 1992) to facilitate further evaluation and refinement in research and application in clinical practice.

Fundamental questions remain regarding the effects of cognitively based treatment for conduct disorders. To begin, the role of cognitive processes in clinical dysfunction and treatment warrants further evaluation. Evidence is not entirely clear showing that a specific pattern of cognitive processes characterizes youths with conduct disorder rather than with adjustment problems more generally. Also, although evidence has shown that cognitive processes change with treatment, evidence has not established that change in these processes is correlated with improvements in treatment outcome. This means that the bases for therapeutic change have yet to be established. Also, characteristics of children and their families and parameters of treatment that may influence outcome have not been carefully explored in relation to treatment outcome. Clearly, central questions about treatment and its effects remain to be addressed. Even so, PSST is highly promising because treatment effects have been replicated in several controlled studies with conduct-disordered youths.

Parent Management Training

Parent management training (PMT) refers to procedures in which parents are trained to alter their child's behavior in the home. The parents meet with a therapist or trainer who teaches them to use specific procedures to alter interactions with their child to promote prosocial behavior and to decrease deviant behavior. Training is based on the general view that conduct problem behavior is inadvertently developed and sustained in the home by maladaptive parent-child interactions. There are multiple facets of parent-child interaction that promote aggressive and antisocial behavior. These patterns include directly reinforcing deviant behavior, frequently and ineffectively using commands and harsh punishment, and failing to attend to appropriate behavior (Patterson, 1982; Patterson et al., 1992).

It would be misleading to imply that the parent generates and is solely responsible for the child-parent sequences of interactions. Influences are bidirectional, so that the child influences the parent as well (see Bell & Harper, 1977; Lytton, 1990). Indeed, in some cases, children engage in deviant behavior to help prompt the parent-child interaction sequences. For example, when parents behave inconsistently and unpredictably (e.g., not attending to the child in the usual ways), the child may engage in some deviant behavior (e.g., whining, throwing some object). The effect is to cause the parent to respond in more predictable ways (see Wahler & Dumas, 1986). Essentially, inconsistent and unpredictable parent behavior is an aversive condition for the child; the child's deviant behavior is negatively reinforced by terminating this condition. However, the result is also to increase parent punishment of the child.

Among the many interaction patterns, those involving coercion have received the greatest attention (Patterson et al., 1992). Coercion refers to deviant behavior on the part of one person (e.g., the child) that is rewarded by another person (e.g., the parent). Aggressive children are inadvertently rewarded for their aggressive interactions and their escalation of coercive behaviors as part of the discipline practices that sustain aggressive behavior. The critical role of parent-child discipline practices has been supported by correlational research, which relates specific discipline practices to children's antisocial behavior, and by experimental research, which shows that directly altering these practices reduces antisocial child behavior (see Dishion, Patterson, & Kavanagh, 1992).

The general purpose of PMT is to alter the pattern of interchanges between parent and child so that prosocial, rather than coercive, behavior is directly reinforced and supported within the family. This requires developing several different parenting behaviors, such as establishing the rules for the child to follow, providing positive reinforcement for appropriate behavior, delivering mild forms of punishment to suppress behavior, negotiating compromises, and other procedures. These parenting behaviors are systematically and progressively developed within the sessions in which the therapist shapes (develops through successive approximations) parenting skills. The programs that parents eventually implement in the home also serve as the basis for the focus of the sessions in which the procedures are modified and refined.

Characteristics of Treatment

Although many variations of PMT exist, several common characteristics can be identified. First, treatment is conducted primarily with the parent(s), who implement several procedures in the home. The parents meet with a therapist who teaches them to use specific procedures to alter interactions with their child, promoting prosocial behavior and decreasing deviant behavior. There usually is little direct intervention of the therapist with the child. With young children, the child may be brought into the session to help train both parent and child how to interact and especially to show the parent precisely how to deliver antecedents (prompts) and consequences (reinforcement, time out from reinforcement). Older youths may participate to negotiate and to develop behavior-changing programs in the home. Second, parents are trained to identify, define, and observe problem behaviors in new ways. Careful specification of the problem is essential for delivering reinforcing or punishing consequences and for evaluating if the program is achieving the desired goals. Third, the treatment sessions cover social learning principles and the procedures that follow from them, including positive reinforcement (e.g., the use of social praise and tokens or points for prosocial behavior), mild punishment (e.g., use of time out from reinforcement, loss of privileges), negotiation, and contingency contracting. Fourth, the sessions provide opportunities for parents to see how the techniques are implemented, to practice using the techniques, and to review the behavior-changing programs in the home. The immediate goal of the program is to develop specific skills in the parents. As the parents become more proficient, the program can address the child's most severely problematic behaviors and encompass other problem domains (e.g., school behavior). Over the course of treatment, more complex repertoires are developed for both the parents and the child. Finally, the child's functioning at school is usually incorporated into the program. Parent-managed reinforcement programs for child deportment and performance at school, completion of homework, and activities on the playground often are integrated into the behavior-changing programs. If available, teachers can play an important role in monitoring or providing consequences for behaviors at school.

Overview of the Evidence

Over the past 25 years, a large number of randomized, controlled (Types 1 and 2) studies of PMT have been completed with youths varying in age and degree of severity of dysfunction (e.g., oppositional, conduct disorder, delinquent youth) (see Kazdin, 1993; McMahon & Wells, 1989; Miller & Prinz, 1990; Patterson, Dishion, & Chamberlain, 1993). Treatment effects have been evident in marked improvements in child behavior on a wide range of measures, including parent and teacher reports of deviant behavior, direct observation of behavior at home and at school, and institutional (e.g., school, police) records. The effects of treatment have also been shown to bring problematic behaviors of treated children within normative levels of their peers who are functioning adequately in the community. Follow-up assessment has shown that the gains are often maintained 1 to 3 years after treatment. Longer follow-up assessment is rarely done, although one program reported maintenance of gains 10 to 14 years later (Forehand & Long, 1988; Long, Forehand, Wierson, & Morgan, 1994).

The impact of PMT can be relatively broad. The effects of treatment are evident for child behaviors that have not been a direct focus as part of training. Also, siblings of children referred for treatment improve, even though they are not a direct focus in treatment. This is an important effect because siblings of conduct-disordered youths are at risk for severe antisocial behavior. In addition, maternal psychopathology, particularly depression, decreases systematically following PMT (see Kazdin, 1985). These changes suggest that PMT alters multiple aspects of dysfunctional families.

Several characteristics of the treatment contribute to outcome. Duration of treatment appears to influence outcome. Brief and time-limited treatments (e.g., less than 10 hours) are less likely to show benefits

with clinical populations. More dramatic and durable effects have been achieved with protracted or time-unlimited programs extending up to 50 or 60 hours of treatment (see Kazdin, 1985). Second, specific training components, such as providing parents with in-depth knowledge of social learning principles and utilizing time out from reinforcement in the home, enhance treatment effects. Third, some evidence suggests that therapist training and skill are associated with the magnitude and durability of therapeutic changes, although this has yet to be carefully tested. Fourth, families characterized by many risk factors associated with childhood dysfunction (e.g., socioeconomic disadvantage, marital discord, parental psychopathology, poor social support) tend to show fewer gains in treatment and maintain the gains less well than families without these characteristics (e.g., Dadds & McHugh, 1992; Dumas & Wahler, 1983; Webster-Stratton, 1985). Some efforts to address parent and family dysfunction during PMT have led to improved effects of treatment outcome for the child in some studies (e.g., Dadds, Schwartz, & Sanders, 1987; Griest et al., 1982), but not in others (Webster-Stratton, 1994). Much more work is needed on the matter given the prominent role of parent and family dysfunction among many youths referred for treatment.

One promising line of work has focused on implementation of PMT in community, rather than clinic, settings. The net effect is to bring treatment to those persons least likely to come to, or remain in, treatment. In one study, for example, when PMT was delivered in small parent groups in the community, the effectiveness surpassed what was achieved with clinic-based PMT. Also, community-based treatment was considerably more cost effective (Cunningham, Bremner, & Boyle, 1995).

Conceptual development of processes underlying parent-child interaction and conduct disorder continues (e.g., Patterson et al., 1992). Also, recent research on processes in treatment represents a related and important advance. A series of studies on therapist-parent interaction within PMT sessions has identified factors that contribute to parent resistance (e.g., a parent saying, "I can't," "I won't"). The significance of this work is in showing that parent reactions in therapy relate to their discipline practices at home, that changes in resistance during therapy predict change in parent behavior, and that specific therapist ploys (e.g., reframing, confronting) can help overcome or contribute to resistance (Patterson & Chamberlain,

1994). This line of work advances our understanding of PMT greatly by relating in-session interactions of the therapist and parent to child functioning and treatment outcome.

Overall Evaluation

The extensive outcome evidence makes PMT one of the most promising treatments. The evidence is bolstered by related lines of work. First, the study of family interaction processes that contribute to antisocial behavior in the home and evidence that changing these processes alters child behavior provide a strong empirical base for treatment. Second, the procedures and practices that are used in PMT (e.g., various forms of reinforcement and punishment practices) have been widely and effectively applied outside the context of conduct disorder. For example, the procedures have been applied in regard to parents of children with autism, language delays, developmental disabilities, and medical disorders for which compliance with special treatment regimens is required, and in regard to parents who physically abuse or neglect their children (see Kazdin, 1994a). Third, a great deal is known about the procedures and the parameters that influence the reinforcement and punishment practices that form the core of PMT. Consequently, very concrete recommendations can be provided to change behavior and to alter programs when behavior change has not occurred.

Treatment manuals and training materials for PMT are available for parents and therapists (e.g., Forehand & McMahon, 1981; Sanders & Dadds, 1993). Also noteworthy is the development of self-administered videotapes of treatment. In a programmatic series of studies with young (3–8 years) children with conduct problems, Webster-Stratton and her colleagues have developed and evaluated videotaped materials to present PMT to parents; treatment can be self-administered in individual or group format supplemented with discussion (e.g., Webster-Stratton, 1994; Webster-Stratton, Hollinsworth, & Kolpacoff, 1989). Controlled studies have shown clinically significant changes at posttreatment and follow-up assessments with variations of videotaped treatment. The potential for extension of PMT with readily available and empirically tested videotapes presents a unique feature in child treatment.

Several limitations of PMT can be identified as well. First, some families may not respond to treatment. The treatment makes several demands on the parents, such as mastering educational materials that convey major principles underlying the program, systematically observing deviant child behavior and implementing specific procedures at home, attending weekly sessions, and responding to frequent telephone contacts made by the therapist. For some families, the demands may be too great to continue in treatment. Interestingly, within the approach several procedures (e.g., shaping parent behavior through reinforcement) provide guidelines for developing parent compliance and the desired response repertoire in relation to their children.

Second, perhaps the greatest limitation or obstacle in using PMT is that there are few training opportunities for professionals to learn the approach. Training programs in child psychiatry, clinical psychology, and social work are unlikely to provide exposure to the technique, much less opportunities for formal training. Mastery of social learning principles and multiple procedures that derive from them are required for PMT (Cooper, Heron, & Heward, 1987; Kazdin, 1994a). For example, the administration of reinforcement by the parent in the home (to alter child behavior) and by the therapist in the session (to change parent behavior) requires more than passing familiarity with the principle and the parametric variations that dictate its effectiveness (e.g., administration of reinforcement contingently, immediately, frequently; use of varied and high-quality reinforcers; use of prompts, shaping). The requisite skills in administering the procedures within the treatment sessions can be readily trained but they are not trivial.

Parent management training has been applied primarily to parents of preadolescents. Although treatment has been effective with delinquent adolescents (Bank, Marlowe, Reid, Patterson, & Weinrott, 1991) and younger adolescents with conduct problems who have not yet been referred for treatment (Dishion & Andrews, 1995), some evidence suggests that treatment is more effective with preadolescent youths (see Dishion & Patterson, 1992). Parents of adolescents may less readily change their discipline practices and also have higher rates of dropping out of treatment. The importance and special role of peers in adolescence and the greater amount of time that adolescents spend outside the home suggest that the principles and procedures may need to be applied in novel ways. At this point, few PMT programs have been developed specifically for adolescents, so conclusions about the effects for youths of different ages must be tempered. On balance, PMT is one of the most promising treatment modalities. No other intervention for conduct disorder has been investigated as thoroughly as PMT.

Functional Family Therapy

Functional family therapy (FFT) reflects an integrative approach to treatment that relies on systems, behavioral, and cognitive views of dysfunction (Alexander, Holtzworth-Munroe, & Jameson, 1994; Alexander & Parsons, 1982). Clinical problems are conceptualized from the standpoint of the functions they serve in the family as a system, as well as for individual family members. Problem behavior evident in the child is assumed to be the way in which some interpersonal functions (e.g., intimacy, distancing, support) are met among family members. Maladaptive processes within the family are considered to preclude a more direct means of fulfilling these functions. The goal of treatment is to alter interaction and communication patterns in such a way as to foster more adaptive functioning. Treatment is also based on learning theory and focuses on specific stimuli and responses that can be used to produce change. Social-learning concepts and procedures, such as identifying specific behaviors for change, reinforcing new adaptive ways of responding, and evaluating and monitoring change, are included in this perspective. Cognitive processes refer to the attributions, attitudes, assumptions, expectations, and emotions of the family. Family members may begin treatment with attributions that focus on blaming others or themselves. New perspectives may be needed to help serve as the basis for developing new ways of behaving.

The underlying rationale emphasizes a family systems approach. Specific treatment strategies draw on findings that underlie PMT in relation to maladaptive and coercive parent-child interactions, discussed in the previous section. Functional family therapy views interaction patterns from a broader systems view that focuses also on communication patterns and their meaning. As an illustration of salient constructs, research underlying FFT has found that families of delinquents show higher rates of defensiveness in their communications, both in parent-child and parent-parent interactions, blaming, and negative attributions, and also lower rates of mutual support compared with families of nondelinquents (see Alexander & Parsons,

1982). Improving these communication and support functions is a goal of treatment.

Characteristics of Treatment

Functional family therapy requires that the family see the clinical problem from the relational functions it serves within the family. The therapist points out interdependencies and contingencies among family members in their day-to-day functioning and with specific reference to the problem that has served as the basis for seeking treatment. Once the family sees alternative ways of viewing the problem, the incentive for interacting more constructively is increased.

The main goals of treatment are to increase reciprocity and positive reinforcement among family members, to establish clear communication, to help specify behaviors that family members desire from each other, to negotiate constructively, and to help identify solutions to interpersonal problems. In therapy, family members identify behaviors they would like others to perform. Responses are incorporated into a reinforcement system in the home to promote adaptive behavior in exchange for privileges. However, the primary focus is within the treatment sessions, in which family communication patterns are altered directly. During the sessions, the therapist provides social reinforcement (verbal and nonverbal praise) for communications that suggest solutions to problems, clarify problems, or offer feedback.

Overview of the Evidence

Relatively few outcome studies have evaluated FFT (see Alexander et al., 1994). However, the available studies (Types 1 and 2) have focused on populations that are difficult to treat (e.g., adjudicated delinquent adolescents, multiple-offender delinquents) and have produced relatively clear effects. In controlled studies, FFT has led to greater change than other treatment techniques (e.g., client-centered family groups, psychodynamically oriented family therapy) and various control conditions (e.g., group discussion and expression of feeling, no-treatment control groups). Treatment outcome has been reflected in improved family communication and interactions and lower rates of referral to and contact of youth with the courts. Moreover, gains have been evident in separate studies up to 2½ years after treatment.

Research has examined processes in therapy to identify in-session behaviors of the therapist and how these influence responsiveness among family members (Alexander, Barton, Schiavo, & Parsons, 1976; Newberry, Alexander, & Turner, 1991). For example, providing support and structure and reframing (recasting the attributions and bases of a problem) influence family member responsiveness and blaming of others. The relations among such variables are complex insofar as the impact of various types (e.g., supportive) of statements can vary as a function of gender of the therapist and family member. Evidence of changes in processes proposed to be critical to FFT (e.g., improved communication in treatment, more spontaneous discussion) supports the conceptual view of treatment.

Overall Evaluation

Several noteworthy points can be made about FFT. First, the outcome studies indicate that FFT can alter conduct problems among delinquent youths with varying severity and chronicity of antisocial behavior (e.g., youths with status offenses; others with multiple offenses and who have served in maximum security wards). The studies have produced consistent effects. Second, the evaluation of processes that contribute to family member responsiveness within the sessions, as well as to treatment outcome, represents a line of work rarely seen among treatment techniques for children and adolescents. Some of this process work has extended to laboratory (analogue) studies to examine more precisely how specific types of therapist statements (e.g., reframing) can reduce blaming among group members (e.g., Morris, Alexander, & Turner, 1991). Third, a treatment manual has been provided (Alexander & Parsons, 1982) to facilitate further evaluation and extension of treatment.

A number of limitations are worth mentioning. First, the primary focus of treatment has been with delinquent samples. Research is needed to extend treatment to clinically referred youths, to younger samples, and to youths with comorbid diagnoses. Clinical samples are not necessarily any more recalcitrant to treatment than are delinquents. Yet, delinquency and conduct disorder, despite overlap of selected characteristics, are not the same designations, and generalization from one population to another is not assured. Second, the child, parent, and family characteristics that may influence outcome have not been well stud-

ied. Third, further extensions are needed to replicate the treatment beyond the original program from which it emerged. One such effort demonstrated that delinquent youths who received FFT showed lower recidivism rates up to 2½ years later than a comparison group of lower risk delinquent youths (Gordon, Arbuthnot, Gustafson, & McGreen, 1988). These results suggest that FFT can be replicated. Further replication efforts in randomized controlled trials are needed.

Multisystemic Therapy

Multisystemic therapy (MST) is an approach to treatment based on family systems (Henggeler & Borduin, 1990). Family approaches maintain that clinical problems of the child emerge within the context of the family and focus on treatment at that level. Multisystemic therapy expands on that view by considering the family as only one, albeit very important, system. The child is embedded in multiple systems, including the family (immediate and extended family members), peers, schools, neighborhood, and so on. Also, within a given system, different subsystem issues may be relevant. For example, within the context of the family, some tacit alliance between one parent and child may contribute to disagreement and conflict between the parents over discipline. Treatment may be required to address the alliance and sources of conflict in an effort to alter the child's behavior. Also, a child's functioning at school may involve limited and poor peer relations; treatment may address these areas as well. Finally, the systems approach entails a focus on the individual's own behavior insofar as it affects others. Individual treatment of the child or parents may be included.

Because multiple influences are entailed by the focus of the treatment, many different treatment techniques are used. Thus, MST can be viewed as a package of interventions that are deployed with children and their families. Treatment procedures are used "as needed" to address individual, family, and system issues that may contribute to problem behavior. The conceptual view that focuses on multiple systems and their impact on the individual serves as a basis for selecting multiple and quite different treatment procedures.

Characteristics of Treatment

Central to MST is a family-based treatment approach. Several family therapy techniques (e.g., joining, reframing, enactment, paradox, and assigning specific tasks) are used to identify problems, increase communication, build cohesion, and alter how family members interact. The goals of treatment are to help the parents develop behaviors of the adolescent, to overcome marital difficulties that impede the parents' ability to function as parents, to eliminate negative interactions between parent and adolescent, and to develop or build cohesion and emotional warmth among family members.

Multisystemic therapy draws on many other techniques as needed, such as PSST, PMT, and marital therapy, to alter the response repertoire of the child, parent-child interactions at home, and marital communication, respectively. In some cases, practical advice and guidance are also given to address parenting issues (e.g., involving the adolescent in prosocial peer activities at school, restricting specific activities with a deviant peer group). Although MST includes distinct techniques of other approaches, it is not a mere amalgamation of them. The focus of treatment is on interrelated systems and how they affect each other. Domains are addressed in treatment (e.g., parent unemployment) if they raise issues for one or more systems (e.g., parent stress, increased alcohol consumption) and affect how the child is functioning (e.g., marital conflict, child discipline practices).

Overview of the Evidence

A number of randomized outcome studies (Types 1 and 2) have evaluated MST, primarily with delinquent youths with arrest and incarceration histories that include violent crime (e.g., manslaughter, aggravated assault with intent to kill). Thus, this is a group of extremely antisocial and aggressive youths. Results have shown MST to be superior in reducing delinquency and emotional and behavioral problems and in improving family functioning in comparison with other procedures, including "usual services" provided to such youths (e.g., probation; court-ordered activities that are monitored, such as school attendance), individual counseling, and community-based eclectic treatment (e.g., Borduin et al., 1995; Henggeler et al., 1986; Henggeler, Melton, & Smith, 1992). Followup assessments up to 2, 4, and 5 years later, in separate samples, have shown that MST youths have lower arrest rates than youths who receive other services (see Henggeler, 1994).

Research has also shown that treatment affects critical processes proposed to contribute to deviant behavior (Mann, Borduin, Henggeler, & Blaske, 1990). Specifically, parents and teenage youths show a reduction in coalitions (e.g., less verbal activity, conflict, and hostility) and increases in support, and the parents show increases in verbal communication and decreases in conflict. Moreover, decreases in adolescent symptoms are positively correlated with increases in supportiveness and decreases in conflict between the mother and father. This work provides an important link between theoretical underpinnings of treatment and outcome effects.

Overall Evaluation

Several controlled outcome studies are available for MST; they are consistent in showing that treatment leads to change in adolescents and that the changes are sustained. A strength of the studies is that many of the youths who are treated are severely impaired (delinquent adolescents with a history of arrest). Another strength is the conceptualization of conduct disorder as a problem involving multiple domains of dysfunction within and among individual, family, and extrafamilial systems. Multisystemic therapy begins with the view that many different domains are likely to be relevant; they need to be evaluated and then addressed as needed in treatment.

A challenge of the approach is deciding what treatments, among the many interventions encompassed by MST, to use in a given case. Guidelines are available to direct the therapist, although they are somewhat general (e.g., focus on developing positive sequences of behaviors between systems such as parent and adolescent, evaluate the interventions during treatment so that changes can be made; see Henggeler, 1994). Providing interventions as needed is very difficult, even among trained professionals, without a consistent way to assess what is needed, given inherent limits of decision making and perception. Related to this, the administration of MST is demanding in light of the need to provide several different interventions in a high-quality fashion. Individual treatments (e.g., PSST, PMT) alone are difficult to provide; multiple combinations invite problems related to providing treatments of high quality, strength, and integrity. Yet, there have been replications of MST beyond the original research program, indicating that treatment can be extended across therapists and settings (Henggeler, Schoenwald, & Pickrel, 1995).

On balance, MST is quite promising given the quality of evidence and consistency in the effects that have been produced. The promise stems from a conceptual approach that examines multiple domains (systems) and their contribution to dysfunction, evidence on processes in therapy and their relation to outcome, and the outcome studies themselves. The outcome studies have extended to youths with different types of problems (e.g., sexual offenses, drug use) and to parents who engage in physical abuse or neglect (e.g., Borduin, Henggeler, Blaske, & Stein, 1990; Brunk, Henggeler, & Whelan, 1987). Thus, the model of providing treatment may have broad applicability across problem domains among seriously disturbed children. In passing, it may be worth noting that other literature is relevant to MST. Some of the techniques included in treatment are variations of PSST and PMT, discussed above, which hence have evidence on their behalf as effective interventions.

Limitations of Promising Treatments

Each of the above treatments has had randomized controlled trials, includes replications of treatment effects in multiple studies, focuses on youths whose aggressive and antisocial behavior have led to impairment and referral to social services (e.g., clinics, hospitals, courts), and has assessed outcome over the course of follow-up, at least up to a year, but often longer. Even though these treatments have made remarkable gains, they also have limitations worth highlighting.

Magnitude of Therapeutic Change

Promising treatments have achieved change, but is the change enough to make a difference in the lives of the youths who are treated? Clinical significance refers to the practical value or importance of the effect of an intervention, that is, whether it makes any "real" difference to the patients or to others with whom they interact (see Kazdin, 1992). Clinical significance is important because it is quite possible for treatment effects to be statistically significant but not to have impact on most or any of the cases in a way that improves functioning or adjustment in daily life.

There are several ways to evaluate clinical significance. As an example, one way is to consider the extent to which youths function at normative levels at the end of treatment (i.e., compared to same age and sex peers who are functioning well). This is partic-

ularly useful as a criterion in relation to children and adolescents because base rates of emotional and behavioral problems can vary greatly as a function of age. Promising treatments occasionally have shown that treatment returns individuals to normative levels in relation to behavioral problems and prosocial functioning at home and at school (see Kazdin, 1995b). Yet, the majority of studies, whether of promising or less well evaluated treatments, have not examined whether youths have changed in ways that place them within the normative range of functioning or if they have made gains that would reflect clinically significant changes (Kazdin, Bass, et al., 1990).

Although the goal of treatment is to effect clinically significant change, other less dramatic goals are not trivial. For many conduct-disordered youths, symptoms may escalate, comorbid diagnoses (e.g., substance abuse, depression) may emerge, and family dysfunction may increase. Also, such youths are at risk for teen marriage, dropping out of school, and running away. If treatment were to achieve stability in symptoms and family life and prevent or limit future dysfunction, that would be a significant achievement. The reason evaluation is so critical to the therapeutic enterprise is to identify whether treatment makes a difference because "making a difference" can have many meanings that are important in the treatment of conduct disorder.

Maintenance of Change

Promising treatments have included follow-up assessment, usually up to a year after treatment. Yet, conduct disorder has a poor long-term prognosis, so it is especially important to identify whether treatment has enduring effects. Also, in evaluating the relative merit of different treatments, follow-up data play a critical role. When two (or more) treatments are compared, the treatment that is more (or most) effective immediately after treatment is not always the one that proves to be the most effective treatment in the long run (Kazdin, 1988). Consequently, the conclusions about treatment may be very different depending on the timing of outcome assessment. Apart from conclusions about treatment, follow-up may provide important information that permits differentiation among youths. Over time, youths who maintain the benefits of treatment may differ in important ways from those who do not. Understanding who responds and who responds more or less well to a particular treatment can be very helpful in understanding, treating, and preventing conduct disorder.

The study of long-term effects of treatment is difficult in general, but the usual problems are exacerbated by focusing on conduct disorder. Among clinic samples, families of conduct-disordered youths have high rates of dropping out during treatment and during the follow-up assessment period due in part to the many parent and family factors (e.g., socioeconomic disadvantage, stress) often associated with the problem (Kazdin, 1996b). As the sample size decreases over time, conclusions about the impact of treatment become increasingly difficult to draw. Nevertheless, evaluation of the long-term effects of treatment remains a high priority for research.

Limited Assessment of Outcome Domains

In the majority of child therapy studies, child symptoms are the exclusive focus of outcome assessment (Kazdin, Bass, et al., 1990). Other domains such as prosocial behavior and academic functioning are neglected, even though they relate to concurrent and long-term adjustment (e.g., Asher & Coie, 1990). Perhaps the greatest single deficit in the evaluation of treatment is the absence of attention to impairment. Impairment reflects the extent to which the individual's functioning in everyday life is impeded. Impairment can be distinguished from symptoms insofar as individuals with similar levels of symptoms (e.g., scores), diagnoses, and patterns of comorbidity are likely to be distinguishable based on their ability to function adaptively. School and academic functioning, peer relations, participation in activities, and health are some of the areas included in impairment. In the context of treatment, an intervention may significantly reduce symptoms. Yet, is there any change or reduction in impairment? The impact of treatment on impairment is arguably as important as the impact on the conduct disorder symptoms.

Beyond child functioning, parent and family functioning may also be relevant. Parents and family members of conduct-disordered youths often experience dysfunction (e.g., psychiatric impairment, marital conflict). Also, the problem behaviors of the child often are part of complex, dynamic, and reciprocal influences that affect all relations in the home. Consequently, parent and family functioning and the quality of life for family members are relevant outcomes and may be appropriate goals for treatment.

In general, there are many outcomes that are of interest in evaluating treatment. From existing research we already know that the conclusions reached about a given treatment can vary depending on the outcome criterion. Within a given study, one set of measures (e.g., child functioning) may show no differences between two treatments, but another measure (e.g., family functioning) may show that one treatment is clearly better than the other (e.g., Kazdin, Bass, Siegel, & Thomas, 1989; Kazdin, Siegel, & Bass, 1992; Szapocznik et al., 1989). Thus, in examining different outcomes of interest, we must be prepared for the different conclusions that these outcomes may yield.

General Comments

In light of the above comments, clearly even the most promising treatments have several limitations. Yet, it is critical to place these in perspective. The most commonly used treatments in clinical practice consist of "traditional" approaches including psychodynamic, relationship, play, and family therapies (other than those mentioned above) (Kazdin, Siegel, et al., 1990). These treatments have rarely been tested in controlled outcome studies showing that they achieve therapeutic change in referred (or nonreferred) samples of youths with conduct problems. Many forms of behavior therapy have rather extensive literature relating to them, showing that various techniques (e.g., reinforcement programs, social skills training) can alter aggressive and other antisocial behaviors (Kazdin, 1985; McMahon & Wells, 1989). Yet, the focus has tended to be on isolated behaviors rather than a constellation of symptoms. Also, durable changes among clinical samples rarely have been shown.

Pharmacotherapy represents a line of work of some interest. For one reason, stimulant medication (e.g., methylphenidate), frequently used with children diagnosed with attention deficit hyperactivity disorder, has some impact on aggressive and other antisocial behaviors (see Hinshaw, 1994). This is interesting in part because such children often have a comorbid diagnosis of conduct disorder. Still, no strong evidence exists that stimulant medication can alter the constellation of symptoms (e.g., fighting, stealing) associated with conduct disorder. A review of various medications for aggression in children and adolescents has raised possible leads, but the bulk of research consists of uncontrolled studies (Campbell & Cueva, 1995; Stewart, Myers, Burket, & Lyles, 1990). Controlled studies (e.g., random assignment, placebo controls) have shown antiaggressive effects with some medications (e.g., lithium; Campbell et al., 1995) but not others (e.g., carbamazepine; Cueva et al., 1996). Reliable psychopharmacological treatments for aggression, leaving aside the constellation of conduct disorder (e.g., firesetting, stealing, and so on), remain to be developed.

There is a genre of interventions that is worth mentioning in passing. Occasionally, interventions are advocated and implemented, such as sending conduct-disordered youths to a camp in the country where they learn how to "rough it," how to take care of horses, or experience military (e.g., basic training) regimens. The conceptual bases of such treatments and supportive research on the processes involved in the onset of conduct disorders are rarely provided. On the one hand, developing treatments that emerge outside the mainstream of the mental health professions is to be encouraged precisely because traditional treatments have not resolved the problem. On the other hand, this genre of intervention tends to eschew evaluation. Evaluation is key because well-intentioned and costly interventions can have little or no effect on youths they treat (Weisz, Walter, Weiss, Fernandez, & Mikow, 1990) and may actually increase antisocial behavior (e.g., see Lundman, 1984).

DEVELOPING MORE EFFECTIVE TREATMENTS

There are a number of issues that emerge in the treatment of conduct-disordered youths and decision making about what interventions to provide to whom. These issues reflect obstacles in delivering treatment, lacunae in our knowledge base, and limitations in the models of providing care. Addressing these issues in research is likely to increase the effectiveness of treatment, in both research and clinical applications.

Treatments That Do Not Work

With a few hundred or so treatments available for children, it would be quite helpful to know which among these do not work or do not work very well. Addressing the matter directly is not possible in light of the fact, noted above, that the vast majority of treatment approaches has not been evaluated empirically. Thus, there is no accumulated body of evidence

in which treatments have consistently emerged as weak or ineffective. Moreover, the nature of the dominant scientific research paradigm (inability to prove the null hypothesis) precludes firm demonstration of no effects of treatment. Treatments commonly used in clinical work (Kazdin, Siegel, et al., 1990), including psychodynamic therapy, relationship-based treatment, play therapy, and a plethora of eclectic combinations, have not been carefully evaluated (Kazdin, Bass, et al., 1990). Occasionally, variations of these treatments have been used as comparison or control conditions and have been shown to be less effective than one of the promising treatments noted above (e.g., Borduin et al., 1995; Kazdin, Esveldt-Dawson, French, & Unis, 1987a, 1987b). From this limited research, it is premature to conclude that these last treatments are ineffective. Yet, at best their benefits have yet to be demonstrated, and more promising treatments with firmer empirical bases currently are the treatments of choice.

The absence of empirical evidence is only one criterion, albeit an obviously important one. In advance of, and eventually along with, the evidence, scrutiny of the conceptual underpinnings of treatment and the treatment focus is important in relation to what we know about conduct disorder. We know, for example, that conduct-disordered youths usually show problems in multiple domains, including overt behavior, social relations (e.g., peers, teachers, family members), and academic performance. For a treatment to be effective, it is likely that several domains have to be addressed explicitly within the sessions or a conceptual model (with supporting evidence) is needed to convey why a narrow or delimited focus (e.g., on psychic conflicts or a small set of overt behaviors) is likely to have broad effects on domains not explicitly addressed in treatment. Although one cannot say for certain what techniques will not work, it is much safer to say that treatments that neglect multiple domains are likely to have limited effects.

Second, some evidence has emerged that is useful for selecting what treatments to avoid or to use with great caution. Often conduct-disordered youths are treated in group therapy. Yet, placing youths together could impede improvement. For example, Feldman, Caplinger, and Wodarski (1983) randomly assigned youths (age 8–17) to variations of group therapy. In one type of group, all members were referred for conduct disorder; in another type of group, conduct-disordered youths were placed with nonantisocial youths (without clinical problems). Those placed in a group of their deviant peers did not improve; those placed with non-deviant peers did improve. Interpretation of this is based on the likelihood that peer bonding to others can improve one's behavior if those peers engage in more normative behavior; bonding to a deviant group can sustain deviant behavior.

Similarly, Dishion and Andrews (1995) evaluated several interventions for nonreferred youths (age 10–14) with conduct problems. One of the treatment conditions included youths meeting in a group with a focus on self-regulation, monitoring, and developing behavior-changing programs. This condition, whether alone or in combination with parent training, was associated with increases in behavioral problems and substance use (cigarette smoking). Again, it appeared that placing teens with conduct problems in a group situation can exacerbate their problems. Other research has shown that individuals may become worse (e.g., increased arrest rates) through association with deviant peers as part of treatment (O'Donnell, 1992).

Treatments for conduct-disordered youths, in such settings as hospitals, schools, and correctional facilities, often are conducted in a group therapy format in which several youths with conduct problems are together to talk about or work on their problems or go to the country for some fresh air experience to get better. There may be conditions under which this arrangement is beneficial. However, current research suggests that placing several such youths together can impede therapeutic change and have deleterious effects.

Who Responds Well to Treatment

We have known for many years that the critical question of psychotherapy is not what technique is effective, but rather what technique works for whom, under what conditions, as administered by what type of therapists, and so on (Kiesler, 1971). The adult psychotherapy literature has focused on a range of questions to identify factors (e.g., patient, therapist, treatment process) that contribute to outcome. Child and adolescent therapy research has neglected the role of child, parent, family, and therapist factors that may moderate outcome (Kazdin, Bass, et al., 1990).

In the case of conduct disorder, a few studies have looked at who responds to treatment, mostly in the context of parent management training and problem-solving skills training. Although much more work is needed, current evidence suggests that risk factors for onset of conduct disorder and poor long-term prognosis (e.g., early onset, severe aggressive behavior, family adversity) are likely to influence responsiveness to treatment (Dumas & Wahler, 1983; Kazdin, 1995a; Kazdin & Crowley, 1997; Webster-Stratton, 1985). Our own work has shown that even those youths with multiple risk factors still improve with treatment, but the changes are not as great as those achieved for cases with fewer risk factors.

In current subtyping of conduct-disordered youths, early (childhood) and later (adolescent) onset conduct disorder are distinguished (Hinshaw et al., 1993; Moffitt, 1993). Early-onset conduct-disordered youths are characterized by aggressive behavior, neuropsychological dysfunction (in "executive" functions), a much higher ratio of boys to girls, and a poor long-term prognosis. Youths with a later onset (at about age 15) are characterized more by delinquent activity (theft, vandalism), a more even distribution of boys and girls, and a more favorable prognosis. The subtype and associated characteristics are by no means firmly established but reflect current conceptual and empirical work in the area (e.g., Moffitt, 1993; Patterson, DeBaryshe, & Ramsey, 1989). We can expect from this that youths with an early onset are more likely to be recalcitrant to treatment. At present and in the absence of very much treatment research on the matter, a useful guideline to predict responsiveness to treatment is to consider loading of the child, parent, and family with risk factors that portend a poor long-term prognosis (see Kazdin, 1995b; Robins, 1991).

A goal of research is to identify whether some children respond to one type of treatment more than another. At this point, the literature cannot address this issue. The characteristics that have been studied in relation to treatment outcome (e.g., comorbidity) have not been examined across different treatments. Consequently, we do not know whether these factors affect responsiveness to any treatment or to particular forms of treatment.

Combining Treatments

There is keen interest, both in clinical work and in research, in using combinations of treatment, that is, multiple psychosocial and/or pharmacological interventions (see Kazdin, 1996a). In the case of conduct disorder, impetus stems from the scope of impairment evident in children (e.g., comorbidity, academic dysfunction) and families (e.g., stress, conflict), as well as the limited effects of most treatments. The benefits of combined treatments can be identified in selected areas. For example, in the treatment of adult schizophrenia, combinations of treatment (e.g., medication and family counseling/therapy) surpass the effects of the constituent components alone (e.g., Falloon, 1988).

In the case of child and adolescent therapy, combined treatments have not been well studied. I have argued elsewhere that there are many reasons to expect combined treatments not to surpass the effects of any promising single treatment (Kazdin, 1996a). Among the reasons, we know very little about the parameters of a given treatment that influence its effectiveness and to whom the treatment is most suitably applied. Combining techniques of which we know relatively little, particularly in time-limited treatment, is not a firm base on which to build more effective treatments. Also, there are many obstacles in combining treatments that materially affect their likely outcome, such as decision rules regarding what treatments to combine, how to combine them (e.g., when, in what order), how to evaluate their impact, and others.

An important assumption for combined treatments is that individual treatments are weak and, if combined, they would produce additive or synergistic effects. This is a reasonable, even if poorly tested, assumption. An alternative assumption is that the way in which treatment, whether a single or a combined treatment, is usually administered inherently limits the likelihood of positive outcome effects, a point discussed further below. As a general point, combining treatments itself is not likely to be an answer to developing effective treatment without more thought and evidence about the nature of these combinations.

Some of the promising treatments reviewed in this chapter (MST, FFT) are combined treatments. For example, multisystemic therapy provides many different treatments for antisocial youths. Two points are worth noting. First, the constituent treatments that form a major part of treatment are those that have evidence on their behalf (e.g., PSST, PMT), so that not any combination is used. Second, we do not yet know that multisystemic therapy, as a combined treatment package, is more effective than the most effective constituent component administered for the same duration. The comparisons of multisystemic therapy

have mostly included ordinary individual psychotherapy and counseling, important comparison groups to be sure. Although treatment has surpassed traditional therapy practices, this is not the same as showing that combinations of treatment per se are necessary to achieve therapeutic changes.

Combined treatments may be very useful and should be pursued. At the same time, a rash move to combine treatments is unwarranted. The effects of combined treatment obviously depend very much on the individual treatments that are included in the combination. For example, mentioned already was a study in which parent training and a teen-focused group were evaluated alone and in combination (Dishion & Andrews, 1995). The combination of parent training with the teen-focused group led to worse outcomes than parent training alone. Obviously, one cannot assume that combined treatments will automatically be neutral or better than their constituent treatments. There is another more subtle and perhaps worrisome facet of combined treatments. A danger in promoting treatment combinations is to continue to use techniques with little evidence in their behalf as an ingredient in a larger set of techniques. Old wine in new bottles is not bad if the original wine has merit. However, without knowing if there is merit, the tendency to view the wine as new and improved would be unfortunate. With promising treatments available, we have a comparative base to evaluate novel treatments, treatment combinations, and unevaluated treatments in current use. If a promising treatment is not used in clinical work, we would want evidence that it has clearly failed, that other promising treatments for whatever reason cannot be used, and that the treatment that is to be applied has a reasonable basis for addressing the scope of dysfunctions.

Models of Delivering Treatment

The model of treatment delivery in current research is to provide a relatively brief and time-limited intervention. For several clinical dysfunctions or for a number of children with a particular dysfunction such as conduct disorder, the course of maladjustment may be long. In such cases, the notion of providing a brief, time-limited treatment may very much limit outcome effects. Even if a great combination of various psychotherapies were constructed, administration in the time-limited fashion might have the usual, checkered yield. More extended and enduring treatment in some form may be needed to achieve clinically important effects with the greatest number of youths. Two ways of delivering extended treatment illustrate the point.

The first variation is referred to as a *continued-care model*. The model of treatment delivery that may be needed can be likened to the model used in the treatment of diabetes mellitus. With diabetes, ongoing treatment (insulin) is needed to ensure that the benefits of treatment are sustained. The benefits of treatment would end with the discontinuation of treatment. Analogously, in the context of conduct disorder, a variation of ongoing treatment may be needed. Perhaps after the child is referred, treatment is provided to address the current crises and to have an impact on functioning at home, at school, and in the community. After improvement is achieved, treatment is modified rather than terminated. At that point, the child could enter into maintenance therapy, that is, continued treatment perhaps in varying schedules ("doses"). Treatment would continue but perhaps on a more intermittent basis. Continued treatment in this fashion has been effective as a model for treating recurrent depression in adults (see Kupfer et al., 1992).

The second variation is referred to as a *dental-care model* to convey a different way of extending treatment. After initial treatment and demonstrated improvement in functioning in everyday life, treatment is suspended. At this point, the child's functioning begins to be monitored regularly (e.g., every 3 months) and systematically (with standardized measures). Treatment could be provided *pro re nata* (PRN) based on the assessment data or emergent issues raised by the family, teachers, or others. The approach might be likened to the more familiar model of dental care in the United States in which "checkups" are recommended every 6 months; an intervention is provided if, and as, needed based on these periodic checks.

Obviously, the use of ongoing treatment is not advocated in cases for which there is evidence that short-term treatment is effective. A difficulty with most of the research on treatment (whether promising, poorly investigated, or combined treatments) of conduct disorder, is that the conventional treatment model of brief, time-limited therapy has been adopted. Without considering alternative models of delivery, current treatments may be quite limited in the effects they can produce. Although more effective treatments are sorely needed, the way of delivering currently available treatments ought to be reconsidered.

CONCLUSIONS

Many different types of treatment have been applied to conduct-disordered youths. Unfortunately, little outcome evidence exists for most of the techniques. Four treatments with the most promising evidence to date were highlighted: problem-solving skills training, parent management training, functional family therapy, and multisystemic therapy. Cognitive problem-solving skills training focuses on cognitive processes that underlie social behavior and response repertoires in interpersonal situations. Parent management training is directed at altering parent-child interactions in the home, particularly those interactions related to child-rearing practices and coercive interchanges. Functional family therapy utilizes principles of systems theory and behavior modification as the basis for altering interactions, communication, and problem solving among family members. Multisystemic therapy focus on the individual, family, and extrafamilial systems and their interrelations as a way to reduce symptoms and to promote prosocial behavior. Multiple treatments (e.g., PSST, PMT, family therapy) are used in combination to address domains that affect the child. Evidence on behalf of these four treatments was reviewed; each has multiple controlled outcome studies with follow-up data on its behalf.

We cannot yet say that one intervention can ameliorate conduct disorder and overcome the poor long-term prognosis. On the other hand, much can be said. Much of what is practiced in clinical settings is based on psychodynamically oriented treatment, general relationship counseling, various forms of family therapy (other than those reviewed above), and group therapy (with only antisocial youths as members). These and other procedures, alone and in various combinations in which they are often used, have not been evaluated carefully in controlled trials. Of course, absence of evidence is not tantamount to ineffectiveness. At the same time, promising treatments have advanced considerably, and a very special argument might be needed to justify administration of treatments that have neither basic research in their conceptual underpinnings in relation to conduct disorder nor outcome evidence from controlled clinical trials on their behalf.

Promising treatments, at best, leave important questions unanswered. Further development of treatments clearly is needed. Apart from treatment studies, further progress in understanding the nature of conduct disorder is likely to have very important implications for improving treatment outcome. Improved triage of patients to treatments that are likely to work will require understanding of characteristics of children, parents, and families that will make them more or less amenable to current treatments.

Notes

Completion of this paper was supported by a Research Scientist Award (MH00353) and a grant (MH35408) from the National Institute of Mental Health. Support for this work is gratefully acknowledged.

1. Children will be used to refer to both children and adolescents. When pertinent to the discussion, a distinction will be made and referred to accordingly.

2. In *DSM-IV*, if the child meets criteria for CD, ODD is not diagnosed because the former is likely to include many symptoms of the latter. Yet, invoking and evaluating the criteria for these diagnoses ignoring this consideration has been useful in understanding the relation and overlap of these diagnoses.

3. The rationale, empirical underpinnings, outcome research, and treatment procedures cannot be fully elaborated for each of the techniques. References are made to reviews of the evidence and to treatment manuals that elaborate each of the treatments.

References

Alexander, J. F., Barton, C., Schiavo, R. S., & Parsons, B. V. (1976). Systems-behavioral intervention with families of delinquents: Therapist characteristics, family behavior, and outcome. *Journal of Consulting and Clinical Psychology, 44*, 656–664.

Alexander, J. F., Holtzworth-Munroe, A., & Jameson, P. B. (1994). The process and outcome of marital and family therapy research: Review and evaluation. In A. E. Bergin & S. L. Garfield (Eds.), *Handbook of psychotherapy and behavior change* (4th ed., pp. 595–630). New York: John Wiley & Sons.

Alexander, J. F., & Parsons, B. V. (1982). *Functional family therapy*. Monterey, Ca.: Brooks/Cole.

American Psychiatric Association. (1994). *Diagnostic and statistical manual of mental disorders* (4th ed.). Washington, D.C.: Author.

Asher, S. R., & Coie, J. D. (Eds.) (1990). *Peer rejection in childhood*. New York: Cambridge University Press.

Baer, R. A., & Nietzel, M. T. (1991). Cognitive and behavioral treatment of impulsivity in children: A meta-analytic review of the outcome literature. *Journal of Clinical Child Psychology, 20*, 400–412.

Bank, L., Marlowe, J. H., Reid, J. B., Patterson, G. R., & Weinrott, M. R. (1991). A comparative evaluation of

parent-training interventions for families of chronic delinquents. *Journal of Abnormal Child Psychology, 19*, 15–33.

Bell, R. Q., & Harper, L. (1977). *Child effects on adults.* New York: John Wiley & Sons.

Bergin, A. E., & Garfield, S. L. (Eds.) (1994). *Handbook of psychotherapy and behavior change* (4th ed). New York: Wiley.

Borduin, C. M., Henggeler, S. W., Blaske, D. M., & Stein, R. (1990). Multisystemic treatment of adolescent sexual offenders. *International Journal of Offender Therapy and Comparative Criminology, 34*, 105–113.

Borduin, C. M., Mann, B. J., Cone, L. T., Henggeler, S. W., Fucci, B. R., Blaske, D. M., & Williams, R. A. (1995). Multisystemic treatment of serious juvenile offenders: Long-term prevention of criminality and violence. *Journal of Consulting and Clinical Psychology, 63*, 569–578.

Boyle, M. H., & Offord, D. R. (1990). Primary prevention of conduct disorder: Issues and prospects. *Journal of the American Academy of Child and Adolescent Psychiatry, 29*, 227–233.

Brandt, D. E., & Zlotnick, S. J. (1988). *The psychology and treatment of the youthful offender.* Springfield, Ill.: Charles C Thomas.

Brunk, M., Henggeler, S. W., & Whelan, J. P. (1987). A comparison of multisystemic therapy and parent training in the brief treatment of child abuse and neglect. *Journal of Consulting and Clinical Psychology, 55*, 311–318.

Campbell, M., Adams, P. B., Small, A. M., Kafantaris, V., Silva, R. R., Shell, J., Perry, R., & Overall, J. E. (1995). Lithium in hospitalized aggressive children with conduct disorder: A double-blind and placebo-controlled study. *Journal of the American Academy of Child and Adolescent Psychiatry, 34*, 445–453.

Campbell, M., & Cueva, J. E. (1995). Psychopharmacology in child and adolescent psychiatry: A review of the past seven years. Part II. *Journal of the American Academy of Child and Adolescent Psychiatry, 34*, 1262–1272.

Cooper, J. O., Heron, T. E., & Heward, W. L. (1987). *Applied behavior analysis.* Columbus, Ohio: Merrill.

Crick, N. R., & Dodge, K. A. (1994). A review and reformulation of social information processing mechanisms in children's social adjustment. *Psychological Bulletin, 115*, 74–101.

Cueva, J. E., Overall, J. E., Small, A. M., Armenteros, J. L., Perry, R., & Campbell, M. (1996). Carbamazepine in aggressive children with conduct disorder: A double-blind and placebo controlled study. *Journal of the American Academy of Child and Adolescent Psychiatry, 35*, 480–490.

Cunningham, C. E., Bremner, R., & Boyle, M. (1995). Large group community-based parenting programs for families of preschoolers at risk for disruptive behaviour disorders: Utilization, cost effectiveness, and outcome. *Journal of Child Psychology and Psychiatry*, 36, 1141–1159.

Dadds, M. R., & McHugh, T. A. (1992). Social support and treatment outcome in behavioral family therapy for child conduct problems. *Journal of Consulting and Clinical Psychology*, 60, 252–259.

Dadds, M. R., Schwartz, S., & Sanders, M. R. (1987). Marital discord and treatment outcome in behavioral treatment of child conduct disorders. *Journal of Consulting and Clinical Psychology*, 55, 396–403.

Dishion, T. J., & Andrews, D. W. (1995). Preventing escalation in problem behaviors with high-risk young adolescents: Immediate and 1-year outcomes. *Journal of Consulting and Clinical Psychology*, 63, 538–548.

Dishion, T. J., & Patterson, G. R. (1992). Age effects in parent training outcomes. *Behavior Therapy*, 23, 719–729.

Dishion, T. J., Patterson, G. R., & Kavanagh, K. A. (1992). An experimental test of the coercion model: Linking theory, measurement, and intervention. In J. McCord & R. E. Tremblay (Eds.), *Preventing antisocial behavior* (pp. 253–282). New York: Guilford.

Dumas, J. E. (1989). Treating antisocial behavior in children: Child and family approaches. *Clinical Psychology Review*, 9, 197–222.

Dumas, J. E., & Wahler, R. G. (1983). Predictors of treatment outcome in parent training: Mother insularity and socioeconomic disadvantage. *Behavioral Assessment*, 5, 301–313.

———. (1985). Indiscriminate mothering as a contextual factor in aggressive oppositional child behavior: "Damned if you do and damned if you don't." *Journal of Applied Behavior Analysis*, 13, 1–17.

Durlak, J. A., Fuhrman, T., & Lampman, C. (1991). Effectiveness of cognitive-behavioral therapy for maladapting children: A meta-analysis. *Psychological Bulletin*, 110, 204–214.

Falloon, I. R. (1988). Expressed emotion: Current status. *Psychological Medicine*, 18, 269–274.

Feindler, E. L., & Ecton, R. B. (1986). Adolescent anger control: Cognitive-behavioral techniques. Elmsford, N.Y.: Pergamon.

Feldman, R. A., Caplinger, T. E., & Wodarski, J. S. (1983). *The St. Louis conundrum: The effective treatment of antisocial youths*. Englewood Cliffs, N.J.: Prentice-Hall.

Fergusson, D. M., Horwood, L. J., & Lloyd, M. (1991). Confirmatory factor models of attention deficit and conduct disorder. *Journal of Child Psychology and Psychiatry*, 32, 257–274.

Finch, A. J., Jr., Nelson, W. M., & Ott, E. S. (1993). *Cognitive-behavioral procedures with children and adolescents: A practical guide*. Needham Heights, Mass.: Allyn & Bacon.

Forehand, R., & Long, N. (1988). Outpatient treatment of the acting out child: Procedures, long-term follow-up data, and clinical problems. *Advances in Behaviour Research and Therapy*, 10, 129–177.

Forehand, R., & McMahon, R. J. (1981). *Helping the noncompliant child: A clinician's guide to parent training*. New York: Guilford.

Gordon, D. A., Arbuthnot, J., Gustafson, K. E., & McGreen, P. (1988). Home-based behavioral-systems family therapy with disadvantaged juvenile delinquents. *American Journal of Family Therapy*, 163, 243–255.

Griest, D. L., Forehand, R., Rogers, T., Breiner, J., Furey, W., & Williams, C. A. (1982). Effects of parent enhancement therapy on the treatment outcome and generalization of a parent training program. *Behaviour Research and Therapy*, 20, 429–436.

Henggeler, S. W. (1994). *Treatment manual for family preservation using multisystemic therapy*. Charleston, S.C.: Medical University of South Carolina, South Carolina Health and Human Services Finance Commission.

Henggeler, S. W., & Borduin, C. M. (1990). *Family therapy and beyond: A multisystemic approach to teaching the behavior problems of children and adolescents*. Pacific Grove, Ca.: Brooks/Cole.

Henggeler, S. W., Melton, G. B., & Smith, L. A. (1992). Family preservation using multisystemic therapy: An effective alternative to incarcerating serious juvenile offenders. *Journal of Consulting and Clinical Psychology*, 60, 953–961.

Henggeler, S. W., Rodick, J. D., Borduin, C. M., Hanson, C. L., Watson, S. M., & Urey, J. R. (1986). Multisystemic treatment of juvenile offenders: Effects on adolescent behavior and family interaction. *Developmental Psychology*, 22, 132–141.

Henggeler, S. W., Schoenwald, S. K., & Pickrel, S. A. G. (1995). Multisystemic therapy: Bridging the gap between university-and community-based treatment. *Journal of Consulting and Clinical Psychology*, 63, 709–717.

Hinshaw, S. P. (1994). *Attention deficits and hyperactivity in children*. Thousand Oaks, Ca.: Sage.

Hinshaw, S. P., Lahey, B. B., & Hart, E. L. (1993). Issues of taxonomy and comorbidity in the development of conduct disorder. *Development and Psychopathology*, 5, 31–49.

Kazdin, A. E. (1985). *Treatment of antisocial behavior in children and adolescents*. Homewood, Ill.: Dorsey Press.

———. (1988). *Child psychotherapy: Developing and identifying effective treatments.* Needham Heights, Mass.: Allyn & Bacon.

———. (1992). *Research design in clinical psychology* (2nd ed.). Needham Heights, Mass.: Allyn & Bacon.

———. (1993). Treatment of conduct disorder: Progress and directions in psychotherapy research. *Development and Psychopathology, 5,* 277–310.

———. (1994a). *Behavior modification in applied settings* (5th ed.). Pacific Grove, Ca.: Brooks/Cole.

———. (1994b). Psychotherapy for children and adolescents. In A. E. Bergin & S. L. Garfield (Eds.), *Handbook of psychotherapy and behavior change* (4th ed., pp. 543–594). New York: Wiley & Sons.

———. (1995a). Child, parent, and family dysfunction as predictors of outcome in cognitive-behavioral treatment of antisocial children. *Behaviour Research and Therapy, 33,* 271–281.

———. (1995b). *Conduct disorder in childhood and adolescence* (2nd ed.). Thousand Oaks, Ca.: Sage.

———. (1996a). Combined and multimodal treatments in child and adolescent psychotherapy: Issues, challenges, and research directions. *Clinical Psychology: Science and Practice, 3,* 69–100.

———. (1996b). Dropping out of child psychotherapy: Issues for research and implications for practice. *Clinical Child Psychology and Psychiatry, 1,* 133–156.

Kazdin, A. E., Bass, D., Ayers, W. A., & Rodgers, A. (1990). Empirical and clinical focus of child and adolescent psychotherapy research. *Journal of Consulting and Clinical Psychology, 58,* 729–740.

Kazdin, A. E., Bass, D., Siegel, T., & Thomas, C. (1989). Cognitive-behavioral treatment and relationship therapy in the treatment of children referred for antisocial behavior. *Journal of Consulting and Clinical Psychology, 57,* 522–535.

Kazdin, A. E., & Crowley, M. (1997). Moderators of treatment outcome in cognitively based treatment of antisocial children. *Cognitive Therapy and Research, 21,* 185–207.

Kazdin, A. E., Esveldt-Dawson, K., French, N. H., & Unis, A. S. (1987a). The effects of parent management training and problem-solving skills training combined in the treatment of antisocial child behavior. *Journal of the American Academy of Child and Adolescent Psychiatry, 26,* 416–424.

———. (1987b). Problem-solving skills training and relationship therapy in the treatment of antisocial child behavior. *Journal of Consulting and Clinical Psychology, 55,* 76–85.

Kazdin, A. E., Siegel, T. C., & Bass, D. (1990). Drawing upon clinical practice to inform research on child and adolescent psychotherapy: A survey of practitioners.

Professional Psychology: Research and Practice, 21, 189–198.

———. (1992). Cognitive problem-solving skills training and parent management training in the treatment of antisocial behavior in children. *Journal of Consulting and Clinical Psychology, 60,* 733–747.

Kendall, P. C. (Ed.). (1991). *Child and adolescent therapy: Cognitive-behavioral procedures.* New York: Guilford.

Kiesler, D. J. (1971). Experimental designs in psychotherapy research. In A. E. Bergin & S. L. Garfield (Eds.), *Handbook of psychotherapy and behavior change: An empirical analysis* (pp. 36–74). New York: Wiley.

Koocher, G. P., & Pedulla, B. M. (1977). Current practices in child psychotherapy. *Professional Psychology, 8,* 275–287.

Kupfer, D. J., Frank, E., Perel, J. M., Cornes, C., Mallinger, A. G., Thase, M. E., McEachran, A. B., & Grochocinski, V. J. (1992). Five-year outcome for maintenance therapies in recurrent depression. *Archives of General Psychiatry, 49,* 769–773.

Lochman, J. E., & Dodge, K. A. (1994). Social-cognitive processes of severely violent, moderately aggressive, and nonaggressive boys. *Journal of Consulting and Clinical Psychology, 62,* 366–374.

Loeber, R. (1990). Development and risk factors of juvenile antisocial behavior and delinquency. *Clinical Psychology Review, 10,* 1–41.

Long, P., Forehand, R., Wierson, M., & Morgan, A. (1994). Does parent training with young noncompliant children have long-term effects? *Behaviour Research and Therapy, 32,* 101–107.

Lundman, R. J. (1984). *Prevention and control of juvenile delinquency.* New York: Oxford University Press.

Lytton, H. (1990). Child and parent effects in boys' conduct disorder: A reinterpretation. *Developmental Psychology, 26,* 683–697.

Mann, B. J., Borduin, C. M., Henggeler, S. W., & Blaske, D. M. (1990). An investigation of systemic conceptualizations of parent-child coalitions and symptom change. *Journal of Consulting and Clinical Psychology, 58,* 336–344.

McMahon, R. J., & Wells, K. C. (1989). Conduct disorders. In E. J. Mash & R. A. Barkley (Eds.), *Treatment of childhood disorders* (pp. 73–132). New York: Guilford.

Miller, G. E., & Prinz, R. J. (1990). Enhancement of social learning family interventions for child conduct disorder. *Psychological Bulletin, 108,* 291–307.

Moffitt, T. E. (1993). The neuropsychology of conduct problems. *Development and Psychopathology, 5,* 135–151.

Morris, S. M., Alexander, J. F., & Turner, C. W. (1991). Do reattributions reduce blame? *Journal of Family Psychology, 5,* 192–203.

Mrazek, P. J., & Haggerty, R. J. (Eds.). (1994). *Reducing risks for mental disorders: Frontiers of preventive intervention research*. Washington, D.C.: National Academy Press.

Newberry, A. M., Alexander, J. F., & Turner, C. W. (1991). Gender as a process variable in family therapy. *Journal of Family Psychology*, 5, 158–175.

O'Donnell, C. R. (1992). The interplay of theory and practice in delinquency prevention: From behavior modification to activity settings. In J. McCord & R. E. Tremblay (Eds.), *Preventing antisocial behavior* (pp. 209–232). New York: Guilford.

Offord, D. R., Boyle, M. H., & Racine, Y. A. (1991). The epidemiology of antisocial behavior. In D. J. Pepler & K. H. Rubin (Eds.). *The development and treatment of childhood aggression* (pp. 31–54). Hillsdale, N.J.: Erlbaum.

Patterson, G. R. (1982). *Coercive family process*. Eugene, Ore.: Castalia.

Patterson, G. R., Capaldi, D., & Bank, L. (1991). An early starter model for predicting delinquency. In D. J. Pepler & K. H. Rubin (Eds.), *The development and treatment of childhood aggression* (pp. 139–168). Hillsdale, N.J.: Erlbaum.

Patterson, G. R., & Chamberlain, P. (1994). A functional analysis of resistance during parent training therapy. *Clinical Psychology: Science and Practice*, 1, 53–70.

Patterson, G. R., DeBaryshe, B. D., & Ramsey, E. (1989). A developmental perspective on antisocial behavior. *American Psychologist*, 44, 329–335.

Patterson, G. R., Dishion, T. J., & Chamberlain, P. (1993). Outcomes and methodological issues relating to treatment of antisocial children. In T. R. Giles (Ed.), *Handbook of effective psychotherapy* (pp. 43–87). New York: Plenum.

Patterson, G. R., Reid, J. B., & Dishion, T. J. (1992). *Antisocial boys*. Eugene, Ore.: Castalia.

Pepler, D. J., & Rubin, K. H. (Eds.) (1991). *The development and treatment of childhood aggression*. Hillsdale, N.J.: Erlbaum.

Robins, L. N. (1966). *Deviant children grown up*. Baltimore, Md.: Williams & Wilkins.

———. (1978). Sturdy childhood predictors of adult antisocial behavior: Replications from longitudinal studies. *Psychological Medicine*, 8, 611–622.

———. (1981). Epidemiological approaches to natural history research: Antisocial disorders in children. *Journal of the American Academy of Child Psychiatry*, 20, 566–680.

———. (1991). Conduct disorder. *Journal of Child Psychology and Psychiatry*, 32, 193–212.

Robins, L., & Rutter, M. (Eds.). (1990). *Straight and devious pathways from childhood to adulthood*. Cambridge, U.K.: Cambridge University Press.

Rubin, K. H., Bream, L. A., & Rose-Krasnor, L. (1991). Social problem solving and aggression in childhood. In D. J. Pepler & K. H. Rubin (Eds.), *The development and treatment of childhood aggression* (pp. 219–248). Hillsdale, N.J.: Erlbaum.

Rutter, M., & Giller, H. (1983). *Juvenile delinquency: Trends and perspectives*. New York: Penguin Books.

Rutter, M., Tizard, J., & Whitmore, K. (Eds.). (1970). *Education, health and behaviour*. London: Longmans.

Sanders, M. R., & Dadds, M. R. (1993). *Behavioral family intervention*. Needham Heights, Mass.: Allyn & Bacon.

Sanson, A., Oberklaid, F., Pedlow, R., & Prior, M. (1991). Risk indicators: Assessment of infancy predictors of pre-school behavioural maladjustment. *Journal of Child Psychology and Psychiatry*, 32, 609–626.

Shirk, S. R. (Ed.). (1988). *Cognitive development and child psychotherapy*. New York: Plenum.

Shure, M. B. (1992). *I can problem solve (ICPS): An interpersonal cognitive problem solving program*. Champaign, Ill.: Research Press.

Silver, L. B., & Silver, B. J. (1983). Clinical practice of child psychiatry: A survey. *Journal of the American Academy of Child Psychiatry*, 22, 573–579.

Spivack, G., & Shure, M. B. (1982). The cognition of social adjustment: Interpersonal cognitive problem solving thinking. In B. B. Lahey & A. E. Kazdin (Eds.), *Advances in clinical child psychology*, Vol. 5 (pp. 323–372). New York: Plenum.

Stewart, J. T., Myers, W. C., Burket, R. C., & Lyles, W. B. (1990). A review of the psychopharmacology of aggression in children and adolescents. *Journal of the American Academy of Child and Adolescent Psychiatry*, 29, 269–277.

Szapocznik, J., Rio, A., Murray, E., Cohen, R., Scopetta, M., Rivas-Vasquez, A., Hervis, O., Posada, V., & Kurtines, W. (1989). Structural family versus psychodynamic child therapy for problematic Hispanic boys. *Journal of Consulting and Clinical Psychology*, 57, 571–578.

U.S. Congress, Office of Technology Assessment. (1991). *Adolescent health* (OTA-H-468). Washington, D.C.: U.S. Government Printing Office.

Wadsworth, M. (1979). *Roots of delinquency: Infancy, adolescence and crime*. New York: Barnes & Noble.

Wahler, R. G., & Dumas, J. E. (1986). Maintenance factors in coercive mother-child interactions: The compliance and predictability hypotheses. *Journal of Applied Behavior Analysis*, 19, 13–22.

Walker, J. L., Lahey, B. B., Russo, M. F., Christ, M. A. G., McBurnett, K., Loeber, R., Stouthamer-Loeber, M., & Green, S. M. (1991). Anxiety, inhibition, and conduct disorder in children: I. Relation to social impairment. *Journal of the American Academy of Child and Adolescent Psychiatry, 30,* 187–191.

Webster-Stratton, C. (1985). Predictors of treatment outcome in parent training for conduct disordered children. *Behavior Therapy, 16,* 223–243.

———. (1994). Advancing videotape parent training: A comparison study. *Journal of Consulting and Clinical Psychology, 62,* 583–593.

Webster-Stratton, C., Hollinsworth, T., & Kolpacoff, M. (1989). The long-term effectiveness and clinical significance of three cost-effective training programs for families with conduct-problem children. *Journal of Consulting and Clinical Psychology, 57,* 550–553.

Weisz, J. R., Walter, B. R., Weiss, B., Fernandez, G. A., & Mikow, V. A. (1990). Arrests among emotionally disturbed violent and assaultive individuals following minimal versus lengthy intervention through North Carolina's Willie M. Program. *Journal of Consulting and Clinical Psychology, 58,* 720–728.

Weisz, J. R. & Weiss, B. (1993). *Effects of psychotherapy with children and adolescents.* Newbury Park, Ca.: Sage.

Werner, E. E., & Smith, R. S. (1992). *Overcoming the odds: High risk children from birth to adulthood.* Ithaca, N.Y.: Cornell University Press.

West, D. J. (1982). *Delinquency: Its roots, careers and prospects.* Cambridge, Mass.: Harvard University Press.

Zoccolillo, M. (1993). Gender and the development of conduct disorder. *Development and Psychopathology, 5,* 65–78.

5

Treatments for Dementia

Larry Tune

The term *dementia* refers to a large number of disorders characterized by global cognitive deficits, including impairments of recent memory, and one or more of the following: aphasia, apraxia, agnosia, and disturbance of executive functioning. The fourth edition of the *Diagnostic and Statistical Manual of Mental Disorders* (*DSM-IV*; American Psychiatric Association, 1994) designates separate criteria (Criteria B) for many of these disorders with distinct etiologies, while retaining common criteria for the global cognitive deficits (Criteria A). The most common dementias are Alzheimer's disease (AD), vascular dementia, dementia due to general medical conditions (including HIV dementia), head trauma, Parkinson's disease (PD), Huntington's disease, Pick's disease, Creutzfeldt-Jacob disease, substance-induced persisting dementia, and multiple etiologies. Alzheimer's disease, alone or in combination with other conditions (e.g., stroke), is easily the most common. With the exception of dementia associated with Parkinson's disease, the remaining syndromes are either so rare or heterogeneous that it is difficult to find well-controlled studies that would meet diagnostic and clinical design criteria for standards defined for this book.

The principal focus of this chapter is on therapeutic interventions for Alzheimer's disease. Innumerable articles investigating patient populations defined as "geropsychiatric" or "gerontopsychiatric" have been excluded. Following this discussion, there is a brief review of therapeutic intervention for Parkinson's disease.

ALZHEIMER'S DISEASE

Alzheimer's disease accounts for approximately 70% of all patients suffering with dementia and affects approximately 2.5 million individuals in North America over the age of 65. Mortimer et al. (1992) found an incidence of 1% per year in the elderly. The prevalence increases with age. Approximately 10% of all patients over the age of 65 are demented, and 33–50% of adults over the age of 84 suffer from dementia.

The study of therapeutic interventions in AD has been affected by both our increased understanding of the pathophysiology of AD and by progressive refinement in diagnostic criteria. Clinicopathologic studies published in the last 10 years have shown a clinical diagnostic accuracy of approximately 90%. However, recent studies have shown that the more we understand about Alzheimer's disease, the more complicated the story becomes. For example, approximately one third of autopsy-confirmed AD cases have coexisting "Lewy body dementia" with associated clinical findings of extrapyramidal symptoms (Thal, 1994).

Other issues critical to the investigation of any drug for AD include the myriad rating instruments used to measure clinical outcome (in the accompanying tables, over 200 separate measures were used to assess clinical outcome), the absence of clinical diagnostic markers, the absence of compelling animal models for AD, and the variability in the course of illness. This is a slow, variably progressive illness in a patient population with markedly heterogeneous premorbid cognitive abilities. Most clinical trials are of relatively short duration and emphasize short-term clinical improvement as the principal outcome measure. Until recently, most investigations have excluded the possibility of slowing the rate of progression of illness. Several recent studies have focused on change in the rate of clinical deterioration, but most of these are studies of relatively short duration.

The choice of study design must be carefully considered. Three basic designs—crossover studies, randomized control parallel design, and enrichment designs (e.g., see U. S. multicenter tacrine study; Davis et al., 1992)—have all been used. All of these designs could satisfy criteria for Type 1 studies using the guidelines for this book. Nonetheless, each has significant strengths and weaknesses, particularly the long-term studies.

Vasodilators and Metabolic Enhancement Strategies

Most early clinical trials focused on the potential roles of vasodilators or (more recently) metabolic enhancers (Tables 5.1, 5.2) in the treatment of AD. By far the most popular of these was dihydroergotoxine mesylate (Hydergine). Hydergine is one of two drugs currently approved for use in dementia (actually for use in "idiopathic decline in mental capacity"). Despite its long (more than 40 years) and frequent use, its utility in the management of dementia is still in doubt.

Many small, double-blind investigations showed significant improvement in patients with dementia. Most of these early investigations suffered from several critical flaws, including poor diagnostic criteria and outcome measures that did not focus specifically on cognition (for full review, see Hollister & Yesavage, 1984, and Schneider & Olin, 1994). One recent investigation found that two ergot derivatives, nicergoline and ergoloid mesylate, were moderately effective in the management of mild to moderate dementia (Battaglia et al., 1989).

Nootrophic agents (e.g., piracetam, oxiracetam, aniracetam, pyrrolidone), derivatives of the excitatory amino acid neurotransmitter GABA, have been extensively investigated in the treatment of dementing illnesses. Animal studies have repeatedly shown these nootrophic compounds to facilitate learning and memory performance in animals. Although the exact mechanism of action is unclear, they are thought to serve as neuroprotective agents in the central nervous system (CNS) circulation. Table 5.2 summarizes several Type 2 and Type 3 studies of piracetam, oxiracetam, and vinpocetine. Most studies have failed to show significant clinical improvement with these drugs. One lingering experimental question is whether long-term nootrophic administration will affect the progression of disease (e.g., see Croisile et al., 1993).

Cholinergic Augmentation Strategies

The newer therapeutic approaches have followed our understanding of the pathophysiology of AD. The first of these, and by far the most extensively studied, focuses on selective impairments in cholinergic neurotransmission, which were first identified in 1976 (Tables 5.3–5.6). These cholinergic strategies have attempted to potentiate cholinergic neurotransmission in one of several ways: cholinergic precursor loading, acetylcholinesterase inhibition, and direct or indirect central cholinergic stimulation.

Precursor loading strategies are based on demonstrations that peripheral administration enhances brain acetylcholine levels in animal models. Few of the existing human studies, most of which involved lecithin or choline administration, show convincing clinical efficacy (Table 5.6 and 5.7, respectively). We found one Type 1 study (with significant improvement from bethanechol), eight Type 2 studies (five showing improvement), and two Type 3 studies (with one showing improvement). Two studies (one each of Types 2 and 3) of nicotinic agonists showed clinical improvement. Overall, the effects of this treatment strategy have been mixed. Many have suffered either from poor study design or small sample size.

Of these cholinergic augmentation strategies, the use of acetylcholinesterase inhibitors, particularly tacrine, physostigmine, and velnacrine (Tables 5.3 to 5.5, respectively), has provided promising data. The earliest studies focused on physostigmine. Physostigmine proved to be a difficult investigational compound, largely because of its relatively brief half-life ($T\frac{1}{2}$ = 30 minutes following oral ingestion) and high rate of side effects. However, Thal et al. (1983) showed

TABLE 5.1 Hydergine[a]

Authors	Design	N	Outcome Measures	Length of Study	Measure Results
Thompson et al. (1990)	DB, PC, random parallel group	80	DSY, WMS, SCAGS, IPSCE, GERRI	24 weeks	No significant improvement
Rouy et al. (1989)	DB, PC, random parallel group	97	SCAGS, NOISE	6 months	Significant improvement on SCAGS
Theinhaus et al. (1987)	DB, PC, random parallel group	41	IPSCE, GDS, BSRT, DSY, ZVT	12 weeks	Significant improvement on memory section of IPSCE
van Loveren-Huyben et al. (1984)	DB, PC, random parallel group	58	BDT, DS, DSY, SCAGS, BVRT, TMT, LT	24 weeks	Significant improvement on SCAGS
Hollingsworth (1980)	DB, PC, random parallel group	60	SCAGS, MSCL	3 months	Significant improvement on SCAGS
Matejcek et al. (1979)	DB, PC, random parallel group	16	EEG, SCAGS	12 weeks	Significant improvement on EEG only
Novo, Ryan, & Frazier (1978)	DB, PC, random parallel group	34	SCAGS, PNRS	16 weeks	Significant improvement on SCAGS and PNRS
Soni & Soni (1975)	DB, PC, random parallel group	78	CS	9 months	Significant improvement at 3-month evaluation only
Thibault (1974)	DB, PC, random parallel group	48	ADL, psychological, and physical states	12 weeks	Significant improvement on all three scales
Rechman (1973)	DB, PC, random crossover & parallel group	43, 60	CS	16 & 12 weeks	Significant improvement on para. group study only
McConnachie (1973)	DB, PC, random parallel group	58	ADL, physical, mood, and motor activity scales	12 weeks	Significant improvement in all but ADL
Jennings (1972)	DB, PC, random parallel group	50	CSCL, MSCL	12 weeks	Significant improvement on CSCL
Banen (1972)	DB, PC, random parallel group	78	Subtests from WAIS	12 weeks	No significant improvement on WAIS subtests
Tribolitti & Ferri (1969)	DB, PC, random parallel group	59	MSCL, "in-house" rating scales	12 weeks	Significant improvement on one subtest of MSCL

All studies were Type 1.
[a]Refer to "List of Acronyms," pp. 116–118, for definitions of abbreviations.

that the improvement in memory performance following multiple doses of physostigmine could persist up to 36 hours.

Recent investigations have used longer acting cholinesterase inhibitors. Tacrine hydrochloride alone or in combination with lecithin is the best studied of these long-acting AChEs, especially in large-scale studies. Four Type 1 studies showed that tacrine provides a modest, clinically significant effect. Three of nine Type 2, and three of four Type 3 studies report similar findings. Most of the Type 2 and 3 studies involve relatively small samples and are of relatively short duration. None of these has demonstrated a clear effect on the course of illness. Of particular interest is the U.S. multicenter tacrine study (Davis et al., 1992), which utilized a novel enrichment strategy combining aspects of both crossover and parallel design studies. All patients were initially treated with tacrine. Those patients showing a response in the open trial, following a drug washout period, participated in a randomization trial investigating either tacrine or placebo in a double-blind, parallel group study.

Schneider and Tariot (1994) reviewed the clinical trials involving tacrine and found that individualized dosing produced greater clinical results. Clinical response occurred at higher doses (>120 mg/day). Unfortunately, adequate dosing (>120 mg/day) often resulted in significant hepatotoxicity (approximately 30% of patients). Because of this, any treatment strategy must be diligently monitored with weekly determinations of hepatic enzymes. The clinical treatment strategy should be to attempt to administer higher doses of tacrine (120–160 mg/day in four divided doses).

Despite the problems inherent in tacrine therapy (hepatotoxicity, the requirement for QID dosing, and side effects), several recent findings from prolonged clinical trials have proven exciting. First, Knopman et al. (1996), in a 2-year open-label continuation trial, found that patients taking tacrine (>80 mg/day) were significantly less likely to have entered a nursing home than age-matched patients taking either a placebo or low-dose tacrine (<80 mg/day). Second, Kaufer et al. (1996) found that tacrine (doses >80 mg/day) had an independent, positive effect on behavioral symptoms associated with AD.

Other acetylcholinesterase inhibitors include velnacrine (a hydroxy metabolite of tacrine) and galanthamine (Table 5.5). The clinical effects of velnacrine are similar to those of tacrine. Three of four studies (two Type 1 studies) showed modest clinical improvement. Unfortunately, hepatotoxicity was a greater problem for velnacrine than for tacrine, affecting approximately 50% of patients. We were unable to find any Type 1 studies using galanthamine. Significant clinical improvement was found in 8 of 12 Type 2 studies and 5 of 7 Type 3 studies.

One of the more novel cholinergic strategies is a procholinergic strategy using high-dose infusions of thyrotropin in conjunction with physostigmine (Mellow et al., 1993). One Type 1 study investigating 4-aminopyridine showed no apparent therapeutic benefit (see "Other Treatment Strategies" section). Asthana et al. (1996) found that continuous intravenous infusion of physostigmine resulted in significant short-term improvement in five of nine patients with mild-to-moderate AD.

The overall clinical results of these cholinergic augmentation strategies, especially short-term trials with cholinesterase inhibitors, have not been compelling. However, this has been confounded by (a) impractical dosing requirements, (b) a high rate of side effects (except in a relatively small percentage of AD patients), and (c) the relatively short duration of most clinical trials. The largest and best-designed studies found modest clinical improvement with tacrine, but raised serious concerns about hepatotoxicity.

The "next generation" of cholinesterase inhibitors appears to be showing clinical efficacy similar to tacrine, but with less toxicity and greater ease of administration. Recently, donepezil (Aricept) has received approval for use in mild-to-moderate Alzheimer's disease. In one large, double-blind, placebo-controlled clinical trial (Rodgers et al., 1996), donepezil was found to have positive effects on measures of cognition (Mini-Mental State Exam [MMSE], Alzheimer's Disease Assessment Scale—Cognitive Scale [ADAS-Cog]) and clinical improvement (CIBIC) when compared with a placebo. Given the "history" of AChE therapy, perhaps most noteworthy in these studies was the clear demonstration of (a) once daily dosing, (b) absence of hepatotoxicity, and (c) low incidence of side effects traditionally associated with AChE therapy. This is the earliest of this new generation of AChE's; several more are in the final stages of development or Food and Drug Administration (FDA) approval. Most of this new wave of AChEs holds a similar promise.

The most exciting noncholinergic strategy focuses on reducing the accumulation of amyloid protein. This is an insoluble, fibrillary component of the senile plaques first described by Alzheimer in 1907. Amyloid protein accumulation is thought by many to be the central lesion in many forms of AD.

There are a number of studies that have used anti-amyloid treatment strategies (Table 5.8). One approach has been to focus on the possible role of nonsteroidal anti-inflammatory drugs (NSAIDs) as a means of primary prevention. A second strategy, summarized below, involves treatment with estrogenlike compounds. Breitner (1996) reviewed 15 studies examining the role of either glucocorticoids or NSAIDs as a means of delaying the onset or halting the progression of AD. Of these studies, 14 of 15 suggested that both strategies are effective, decreasing the risk of developing AD or delaying the onset of AD in patient populations for which these drugs are regularly administered for other purposes (e.g., NSAIDs for treatment of ar-

TABLE 5.2 Nootropics[a]

Authors	Drug	Type	Design	N	Outcome Measures	Length of Study	Measure Results
Ruther et al. (1994)	Cerebrolysin	1	DB, PC, random parallel group	120	MMSE, SCAGS, CGI, ADL, TMT	4 weeks	Significant improvement on CGI, TMT
Croisile et al. (1993)	Piracetam	2	DB, PC, random parallel group	33	MMSE, DS, AB, VVLT, SS, CFT	1 year	No significant improvement
Green et al. (1992)	Oxiracetam	2	DB, PC, random parallel group	24	BSRT, BVRT, BNT, COWGT, TT, BDT, ROCF	3 months	No significant improvement
Bottini et al. (1992)	Oxiracetam	2	DB, PC, random parallel group	58	QOL, RT, COWGT, SS, RPMT, TT, DS, WLL	12 weeks	Significant improvement on QOL, SS, RPM, COWGT
Villardita et al. (1987)	Oxiracetam	2	DB, PC, random cross-over	40	MMSE, ACPT, VCPT, WLL, LM, DS, BTT, VFT, RCFT, RPMT, LAS, MC, GS, IADL	90 days	Significant improvement on MMSE, ACPT, BTT, VFT, IADL
Sourander et al. (1987)	Aniracetam	2	DB, PC, random parallel group	44	FTT, TMT, BD, DS, SM, BVRT, SCAGS, PB, SVT, HP, VPM, OM, TG, WLL, SM, CN, SIM, ASMC, OR	3 months	Significant improvement on WLL only

Study	Drug		Design	N	Tests	Duration	Result
Growden et al. (1986)	Piracetam & physostigmine	2	DB, PC, random crossover	18	BPDP, DS, BS, SR, BNT, VFT, PWT, AF	2 to 8 weeks	No significant improvement
R. C. Smith et al. (1984)	Lecithin & piracetam plus lecithin	2	DB, PC, random crossover	11 & 11	BSRT, AST, DRS, PMSE	10 & 6 months	No significant improvement on lecithin; improvement on BSRT in 8/11 piracetam + lecithin
Claus et al. (1991)	Pramiracetam	3	SB, dose finding & DB, PC, random crossover	10	ADAS-Cog, BSRT, DS, VFT, LM, VSRT	5 & 4 weeks	Significant improvement on part of VSRT
Sinforiani et al. (1990)	Acetyl-L-carnitine & piracetam	3	SB, open label	12 & 12	DS, DSY, BTT, GS, VFT, WLL	2 week IV & 90 day oral	No significant improvement for piracetam
Falsaperla, Preti, & Oliani (1990)	Oxiracetam & selegiline	3	SB, random parallel group	40	BRS, RMT, DS, SR, VFT, GS	90 days	Significant improvement on all tests with oxiracetam
Thal, Salmon, et al. (1989)	Vinpocetine	3	Open label pilot study	19	VFT, BSRT, COWGT, BNT, CCSE, CGI	52 weeks	No significant improvement
Heiss et al. (1988)	Piracetam in Alzheimer's disease & MID	3	Open label	9 & 7	RCGM in PET	2 weeks	Inc. in RCGM in AD but not MID
Branconnier et al. (1983)	Pramiracetam	3	Open label	32	BSRT, VFT, RMPT, SCAGS	4 weeks	Significant improvement on SCAGS
Delwaide, Devoitille, & Ylieff[b] (1980)	Piracetam, lysin-vasopressin, & physostigmine	3	DB, crossover	13	AVLT	Acute injection	Significant improvement with piracetam and lysin-vasopressin

[a]Refer to "List of Acronyms," pp. 116–118, for definitions of abbreviations.
[b]See also Table 5.4.

TABLE 5.3 Cholinesterase Inhibitors: Tacrine[a]

Authors	Drug	Type	Design	N	Outcome Measures	Length of Study	Measure Results
Knapp et al. (1994)	Tacrine	1	DB, PC, random parallel group	263	CIBC, ADAS-Cog, FCCA	30 weeks	Significant difference on CIBC, ADAS-Cog, FCCA
Sahakian & Coull (1993)[b]	Tacrine	1	DB, PC, random cross-over	89	MMSE, AMTS, ADL, RNCP, KOL, CANTAB	30 weeks	Significant effect on MMSE, AMTS, CANTAB-attention
Wilcock et al. (1993)	Tacrine	1	DB, PC, random cross-over	79	MMSE, ADAS-NCog, FLS, ADL, KOL, LMT, DS, IADL, CAMCOG	24 weeks	Significant improvement on KOL & CAMCOG
Farlow et al. (1992)	Tacrine	1	DB, PC, rand parallel group	468	ADAS-Cog, CL-CGIC, CG-CGIC, MMSE, PDS, ADAS, ADAS-NCog	12 weeks	Significant improvement on ADAS-Cog, CL-CGIC, CG-CGIC
Maltby et al. (1994)	Tacrine & lecithin	2	DB, PC, random parallel group	41	MMSE, V&V SRT, WNA, LPRS, IADL	36 weeks	No significant difference between groups
Minthon et al. (1993)	Tacrine & lecithin	2	DB, PC, random cross-over	17	VOCT, KBD, VL, DS, RT, CFF, EEG, rCBF	26 weeks	6 patients classified as responders
Schneider et al. (1993)[c]	L-Deprenyl & tacrine or physostigmine	2	DB, PC, rand. X-over	10	ADAS-Cog, MMSE	8 weeks	Significant improvement on ADAS-Cog in those receiving drug first
Gustafson (1993)[d]	Physostigmine, tacrine, & lecithin	2	DB, PC, random cross-over	10 & 17	rCBF, EEG, OBS-DS, OBS-CS, CGI, RR	2-hr iv (P) 26 weeks (T&L)	No significant improvement compared with placebo
Davis et al. (1992)	Tacrine	2	DB, PC, random parallel group	215	ADAS, CCIC, MMSE, PDS, IADL, PSMS	14 weeks	Smaller decline in ADAS-Cog

Study	Drug		Design	N	Measures	Duration	Results
Molloy et al. (1991)	Tacrine	2	DB, PC, random cross-over	34	MMSE, MSQ, VFT, PWT, DS, LMT, CST, BVRT, BI, LS	9 weeks	No significant difference between groups
Weinstein, Teunisse, & van Gool (1991)	Tacrine & lecithin	2	DB, PC, random parallel group	12	CAMCOG, IDDD	12 weeks	No significant difference between groups
Chatiellier & Lacomblez (1990)	Tacrine & lecithin	2	DB, PC, random cross-over	67	MMSE, SGRS, MDS, LC, PVAS	8 weeks	Significant improvement on PVAS
Fitten et al. (1990)[e]	Tacrine & lecithin	2	DB, PC, random cross-over	10 & 6	MMSE, FOM, DS, TMT, NLT, ADL, IADL, NOSIE, GDS, COWGT, GERRI, ADAS	3 weeks & 10 weeks	3 weeks, no significant improvement; 10 weeks, mild improvement in some
Gauthier et al. (1990)	Tacrine & lecithin	2	DB, PC, random cross-over	52	MMSE, RDRS-II, HDS	20 weeks	Significant improvement on MMSE
Summers et al. (1986)	Tacrine	2	DB, PC, random cross-over	17	GAS, NLT, OT	6 weeks	Significant improvement on GAS, NLT, OT
Alhainen & Riekkinen (1993)	Tacrine	3	Pilot responder discrimination	25	QEEG, MMSE, ADAS-Cog, BRST, HVR, VFT, DS, TMT	7 weeks	Significant improvement on MMSE, TMT
Mellow et al. (1993)	Tacrine & TRH	3	Pilot SB, PB, X-over	6	BSRT, VFT, DS, PMT	Acute 2 days	Significant improvement on VFT
Kaye et al. (1982)[f]	Tacrine & lecithin	3	PC random crossover	10	SLT, BSRT, FR-subjects diagnosed with PDD	Acute 3 doses	No significant improvement
Summers & Viesselman (1981)	Tacrine	3	Pilot—1, 6, 24 hour post-iv	12	OT, NLT	Acute 1-hour iv	Significant improvement on OT in 6 of 12

[a] Refer to "List of Acronyms," pp. 116–118, for definitions of abbreviations.

[b] See also Eagger et al., 1991, 1992; Eagger, Levy, & Sahakain, 1992; for papers evaluating the same population.

[c] See also Table 5.9.

[d] See also Gustafson et al., 1987, for evaluation of the same population.

[e] See also Perryman & Fitten, 1993, for evaluation of the same population.

[f] See also Table 5.11.

TABLE 5.4 Cholinesterase Inhibitors: Physostigmine[a]

Authors	Drug	Type	Design	N	Outcome Measures	Length of Study	Measure Results
Gustafson (1993)[b]	Physostigmine, tacrine, & lecithin	2	DB, PC, random crossover	10 & 17	rCBF, EEG, OBS-DS, OBS-CS, CGI, RR	2-hr IV (P), 26-weeks (T&L)	No significant improvement compared with placebo
Sano et al. (1993)	Physostigmine	2	DB, PC, random crossover	29	BSRT	12 weeks	Significant difference on BSRT-Total Recall/Intrusions
Schneider et al. (1993)[c]	L-Deprenyl & tacrine or physostigmine	2	DB, PC, random crossover	10	ADAS-Cog, MMSE	8 weeks	Significant important on ADAS-Cog in those receiving drug first
Sevush, Gutterman, & Villalon (1991)	Physostigmine	2	DB, PC, random crossover	8	AVLT, DS, VFT	3 weeks	Significant improvement on AVLT
Harrell, Calloway, et al. (1990)	Physostigmine	2	DB, PC, random crossover	20	BSRT, COWGT, PRT, FTT	8 weeks	No significant improvement except for responder subgroup
Jenike et al. (1990)	Physostigmine	2	DB, PC, random crossover	12	DRST, BSRT, ADAS	8 days	No significant difference between groups
Thal, Salmon et al. (1989)	Physostigmine	2	DB, PC, random parallel group	16	BSRT, BICMT, MDS	12 weeks	Significant improvement on BSRT in 7/10 physostigmine subjects
Stern, Sano, & Mayeux (1988)	Physostigmine	2	DB, PC, random crossover	14	BSRT	36 weeks	Significant improvement compared with placebo
Stern, Sano, & Mayeux (1987)	Physostigmine	2	DB, PC, random crossover	22	BSRT, WAIS-R, WMS, RDT, mMMSE, CWAT, VFT	2 weeks	Significant improvement on WAIS-R Digit Span Subtest
Beller, Overall, & Swann (1985)	Physostigmine	2	DB, PC, random crossover	8	BSRT	8 days	Significant improvement on highest dose
Mohs et al. (1985)	Physostigmine	2	DB, PC, crossover	12	ADAS	6-10 days	Significant improvement in 3 subjects
Schwartz & Kohlstaedt (1986)	Physostigmine & lecithin	2	DB, PC, random crossover, & replication	11	BSRT	Acute injections	No significant improvement

Study	Drug		Design	N	Test	Duration	Outcome
Sullivan et al. (1982)	Physostigmine	2	DB, PC, random crossover	12	VPAL, NVPAL, BPDP, VRMT	Acute 30 min iv	No significant improvement
Davis & Mohs (1982)	Physostigmine	2	DB, PC, random crossover	10	DS, FFT, BSRT	Acute 30-min iv	Significant improvement in 8 subjects
Peters & Levin (1979)	Physostigmine & lecithin	2	DB, PC, random crossover	5	BSRT	Acute subQ injection	No significant improvement compared to baseline
Bierer et al. (1994)	Physostigmine & clonidine	3	SB, PC, random crossover	10	ADAS	2 weeks	No significant improvement
Beller et al. (1988)	Physostigmine	3	Open-label follow-up	5	BSRT	17 months to 3 years	4/5 BSRT scores at end same as at start
Thal et al. (1986)	Physostigmine	3	DB, PC, crossover, open-label follow-up	16 & 10	BSRT	1 week and 4–18 months	Significant improvement for responders
Muramoto, Sugishia, & Ando (1984)	Physostigmine	3	DB, SB, PC, random crossover	6	Figure copying	Acute injections	Significant improvement in 3/6 subjects
Wettstein (1983)	Physostigmine & lecithin	3	DB, PC, random crossover	8	Self-designed test battery	12 weeks	No significant improvement
Jotkowitz (1983)	Physostigmine	3	SB, PC, crossover	10	BRS	Up to 10 months	No significant improvement
Thal et al. (1983)	Physostigmine & lecithin	3	Open label, DB, PC, crossover	8	BSRT	6 days for each	Significant improvement in 6 of 8
Ashford et al. (1981)	Physostigmine	3	DB, PC, random crossover	6	BWLLT, BVRT subjects diagnosed with PDD	Acute 30-min iv	No significant improvement
Christie et al. (1981)[c]	Physostigmine & arecoline	3	DB, PC, random crossover	11 & 7	SPT	Acute 30-min iv	Significant improvement in both groups
Delwaide, Devoitille, & Ylieff (1980)[d]	Piracetam, lysin-vasopressin, & physostigmine	3	DB, crossover	13	AVLT	Acute injection	No significant improvement with physostigmine
Muramoto et al. (1979)	Physostigmine	3	DB, PC, case study	1	Figure copying, BSRT	Acute subQ injection	Significant improvement on figure copying

[a]Refer to "List of Acronyms," pp. 116–118, for definitions of abbreviations.

[b]See also Gustafson et al. 1987.

[c]See also Table 5.9.

[d]See also Table 5.2.

TABLE 5.5 Cholinesterase Inhibitors: Velnacrine[a]

Authors	Drug	Type	Design	N	Outcome Measures	Length of Study	Measure Results
Antuono (1995)	Velnacrine	1	DB, PC, random parallel group	449	ADAS-Cog, CGIC	24 weeks	Significantly less deterioration on ADAS-Cog and CGIC
Murphy et al. (1991)	Velnacrine maleate	1	DB, PC, random parallel group	105	ADAS-cog, CGI, IADL, PGIR, ADAS-NCog	15 weeks	No significant improvment
Ebmeier et al. (1992)	Velnacrine	2	DB, PC, random parallel group (SPECT)	12 & 21	ORT, WRT, SPECT	Single dose	Significant improvement on WRT and increase in frontal SPECT
Sigfried (1993)	Velnacrine	3	DB, PC, random crossover	35	ADAS-Cog, IWRT, CGII, CRTT	3 weeks	Significant improvement on ADAS-Cog, IWRT
Dal-Bianco et al. (1991)	Galanthamine	3	Open label	18	Neuropsychological battery	2–6 months	No significant improvement

[a]Refer to "List of Acronyms," pp. 116–118, for definitions of abbreviations.

thritis or leprosy, for which the rate of AD neuropathology is significantly less than for controls). One twin study (Breitner et al., 1994) has suggested that NSAIDs reduce the risk of AD. Table 5.8 lists several of the important studies (Types 2, 3).

Again, while most of these studies lack the scientific rigor of Type 1 clinical trials, all of these mainly retrospective studies have consistently suggested a role for NSAIDs in either reducing risk or slowing progression of AD. More conclusive findings await the results of ongoing, prospective, blinded clinical trials.

Two studies are used to illustrate the reason for this current enthusiasm. McGeer et al. (1990) reviewed 7,490 charts of patients treated with NSAIDs and who suffered from AD. The overall rate of AD was 6 to 12 times lower in NSAID patients than would have been predicted in this population. Tang et al. (1996) followed a large cohort of elderly females prospectively (5 years) to assess the role of estrogen replacement therapy (ERT) in delaying/ameliorating AD. Estrogen demonstrated significant effects in both domains.

Catecholamine Enhancement in Alzheimer's Disease

Several groups have investigated the other neurotransmitter abnormalities associated with AD, particularly the catecholamines. Although less compelling than the marked reductions in cholinergic neurotransmission, levels of norepinephrine and serotonin, but not dopamine, are diminished in postmortem studies of AD patients. With a few exceptions, most treatment strategies have studied the inhibition of monoamine oxidase (MAO), a major catecholaminergic (monoaminergic) degradative enzyme. Monoamine oxidase B inhibitors have been investigated on the assumption that (a) monoaminergic systems are directly involved in the pathophysiology of AD, (b) that intact monoaminergic systems facilitate the effects of cholinergic medications in AD, and (c) they may effect the deposition of amyloid in patients with AD. Most published reports show clear improvements in agitation and depression, along with many measures of cognition (Table 5.9). While enthusiasm among clinicians has been dampened by concerns about side effects and the requirement that patients remain on a tyramine-free diet while on MAO inhibitors. The final story will have to await results of ongoing clinical trials.

Neuropeptide-Based Treatment Strategies

Animal studies have shown that neuropeptide treatments enhance performance on a wide variety of experimental tasks. Based on these findings, several neuropeptides have been investigated as potential treatments for AD. The most extensively studied of these are naloxone (Table 5.10), vasopressin (Table 5.11), adrenocorticotropic hormone (ACTH), and somatostatin (for review of ACTH and somatostatin, see Thal, 1994). Naloxone has been shown to have direct facilitatory effects on memory performance in animals. Unfortunately, most investigations with either naloxone (administered intravenously) or naltrexone, a long-acting, orally active opiate antagonist, have not shown any benefit for AD patients. In addition to animal data showing improvements in maze learning and amnesia induced by electroconvulsive therapy (ECT), postmortem samples from AD patients have revealed small decreases in hippocampal vasopressin levels. Most clinical studies, including one Type 1 multicenter trial, failed to demonstrate significant improvements in AD.

Novel Treatment Strategies

Acetyl-L-Carnitine/Membrane Stabilizing Agents

One of the more interesting new treatment strategies involves the use of acetyl-L-carnitine hydrochloride and other membrane "stabilizing" agents (e.g., phosphatidyl serine) as primary prevention strategy to slow the disease progression (Table 5.12 and Table 5.13). Alzheimer's disease has been associated with disturbances in membrane phospholipid turnover (Pettegrew, 1989) and membrane oxidative metabolism. Animal studies show that carnitine acts as a carrier of fatty acids from the cytosol into the mitochondrial matrix, in which they can be subjected to beta oxidation. Carnitine increases the activity of acetyl-CoA and choline acetyltransferase and in this way may have cholinomimetic effects. It also normalizes alterations in membrane and energy metabolism and increases both the levels and utilization of nerve growth factor (NGF) in the CNS.

Several open clinical trials (Type 2 studies without placebo controls) have been conducted. Of the 22 trials reviewed in Calvani et al. (1992), clinical improvement was found in 7 trials compared to the placebo, and 4 of 7 trials showed substantial improvement. Recently, Thal et al. (1996), in a double-blind, randomized, placebo-controlled trial (Type 1), parallel design study found significant clinical improve-

ments on disability, attention, and apraxia over a 1-year period. They found that a subgroup of younger AD patients might benefit from this therapy, while older patients actually did poorer. Overall, there was little difference between the AD patients and the placebo controls. Both Type 1 studies of phosphatidyl serine, as well as two of four Type 2 studies, and one of two Type 3 studies, found modest positive effects.

Estrogen Replacement

The second of the antiamyloid strategies, based on (a) the preclinical observation that estrogen administration influences cholinergic function and increases binding sites of hypothalamic nicotinic acetylcholine receptors in rats and (b) recent data suggesting that estrogen has a clear role in diminishing amyloid deposition, estrogen replacement strategies have recently gained attention. Estrogen administration has been associated with modest improvements in measures of attention, memory, and concentration in pre-and post-menopausal women. Several small open trials (Fillit et al., 1986; Honjo et al., 1989; Ohkura et al., 1995) have found that estrogen replacement therapy improves psychometric test performance, as well as cortical cerebral blood flow and electroencephalogram (EEG) activity in patients with AD. Table 5.14 presents estrogen data to date.

Several recent studies have found this treatment strategy encouraging. In addition to Tang et al. (1996; see above discussion of cholinergic augmentation strategies), Schneider et al. (1996) recently reported on a 30-week, randomized, double-blind, placebo-controlled multicenter investigation of 343 female patients with AD. Women receiving estrogen replacement therapy (ERT) in addition to tacrine showed significantly greater improvement in AD symptoms than did patients receiving a placebo or tacrine alone. This suggests that prior, or continuing, treatment with estrogen may enhance response to tacrine in AD patients.

Other Treatment Strategies

A vast array of interventions have been tried for AD patients. Most strategies have been unconvincing, either because of limitations in study design or because the rationale was weak. They are summarized in Table 5.15. These unsuccessful strategies have included car-

TABLE 5.6 Lecithin and Tacrine[a]

Authors	Drug	Type	Design	N	Outcome Measures	Length of Study	Measure Results
Maltby et al. (1994)	Tacrine & lecithin	2	DB, PC, random parallel group	41	MMSE, V&V SRT, WNA, LPRS, IADL	35 weeks	No significant difference between groups
Minthon et al. (1993)	Tacrine & lecithin	2	DB, PC, random cross-over	17	VOCT, KBD, VL, DS, RT, CFF, EEG, rCBF	26 weeks	6 patients classified as responders
Gustafson (1993)[b]	Physostigmine, tacrine, & lecithin	2	DB, PC, random cross-over	10 & 17	rCBF, EEG, OBS-DS, OBS-CS, CGI, RR	2-hr IV (P), 26 weeks (T&L)	No significant improvement compared with placebo
Weinstein et al. (1991)[b]	Tacrine & lecithin	2	DB, PC, random parallel group	12	CAMCOG, IDDD	12 weeks	No significant difference between groups
Lampe et al. (1990)	TRH and lecithin	2	DB, PC, random cross-over	8	VFT, TMT, BSRT, BVRT	2 weeks	Significant improvement on part of BSRT
Chatellier & Lacomblez[b] (1990)	Tacrine & lecithin	2	DB, PC, random cross-over	67	MMSE, SCRS, MDS, LC, PVAS	8 weeks	Significant improvement on PVAS
Fitten et al. (1990)[b]	Tacrine & lecithin	2	DB, PC, random cross-over	10 & 6	MMSE, FOM, DS, TMT, NLT, OT, ADL, IADL, NOSIE, GDS, COWGT, GERRI, ADAS	3 weeks & 10 weeks	3 weeks, no significant improvement; 10 weeks, mild improvement in some
Gauthier et al. (1990)[b]	Tacrine & lecithin	2	DB, PC, random cross-over	52	MMSE, RDRS-II, HDS	20 weeks	Significant improvement on MMSE
Heyman et al. (1987)	Lecithin	2	DB, PC, random parallel group	37	MMSE, AST, VFT, BSRT, VSRT, SMT	6 months	No significant improvement
Jenike et al. (1986)[c]	Lecithin & ergoloid mesylates	2	DB, PC, random cross-over	7	DRS, DRST	10 weeks	No significant improvement
Schwartz & Kohlstaedt (1986)	Physostigmine & lecithin	2	DB, PC, random cross-over, & replication	11	BSRT	Acute injections	No significant improvement
Little et al. (1985)	Lecithin	2	DB, PC, random parallel group	51	PWT, VFT, OR, KT, IL, CA, DCT	6 months	No significant improvement

102

Study	Treatment		Design	N	Tests	Duration	Outcome
Smith et al. (1984)[d]	Lecithin & piracetam plus lecithin	2	DB, PC, random crossover	11 & 11	BSRT, AST, DRS, PMSE	10 months & 6 months	No significant improvement on lecithin; improvement on BSRT in 8/11 Piracetam + Lecithin
Weintraub et al. (1983)	Lecithin	2	DB, PC, random crossover	13	DRS	6 months	No significant improvement
Brinkman et al. (1989)	Lecithin	2	DB, PC, random crossover	10	BSRT	6 weeks	No significant improvement
Sullivan et al. (1982)	Lecithin	2	DB, PC, random crossover	18	VPAL-NVPAL, BPDP, VRMT	16 weeks	No significant improvement
Hyman, Esslinger, & Damasio (1982)	Lecithin	2	DB, PC, random crossover	18	MMSE, DS, VFT, AST	8 weeks	No significant improvement
Pomara et al. (1982)	Lecithin	2	DB, PC, random crossover	5	BSRT	4 weeks	No significant improvement
Dysken et al. (1982)	Lecithin	2	DB, PC, random crossover	10	WRT, WLL, PALT	4 weeks	No significant improvement
Vroulis et al. (1981)	Lecithin	2	DB, PC, random crossover	18	BSRT, AST, DRS, IMCI	4 to 16 weeks	No significant improvement; slight improvement in 8/15
Peters & Levin (1979)[b]	Physostigmine & lecithin	2	DB, PC, random crossover	5	BSRT	Acute subQ injection	No significant improvement compared with baseline
Etienne et al. (1981)	Lecithin	2	DB, PC, crossover	11	WMS, FRT	3 months	No significant improvement
Thal et al. (1983)[b]	Physostigmine & lecithin	3	Open label and DB, PC, crossover	8	BSRT	6 days for each	Significant improvement in 6 of 8
Wettstein (1983)[b]	Physostigmine & lecithin	3	DB, PC, rand X-over	8	Self-designed test battery	12 weeks	No significant improvement
Kaye et al. (1982)[c]	Tacrine & lecithin	3	PC, random crossover	10	SLT, BSRT, FR; subjects diagnosed with PDD	Acute 3 doses	No significant improvement

[a]Refer to "List of Acronyms," pp. 116–118, for definition of abbreviations.

[b]See also Table 5.3.

[c]See also Table 5.1.

[d]See also Table 5.2.

TABLE 5.7 Muscarinic/Cholinergic Agonists[a]

Authors	Drug	Type	Design	N	Measures	Length of Study	Measure Results
Harbaugh et al. (1989)	Bethanechol chloride muscarinic agonist	1	DB, PC, random cross-over	49	DS, DSY, BDT, WMS, TMT, BSRT, VFT, BNT, MMSE	24 weeks	Significant improvement on MMSE only
Wilson et al. (1995)	Nicotine patches	2	DB, PC, random cross-over	6	DMTS, DRS, RAT	3 weeks	Significant improvement on RAT
Soncrant et al. (1993)	Arecoline muscarinic/cholinergic agonist	2	Open label & DB, PC, random crossover	9	BSRT, COWGT, VFT, DS, BVRT, VCRMT, VBCRMT, SCWTT, TT, ERDT, CALC	Approximately 2 weeks for each	Significant improvement on part of BSRT; 6/9 were responders on BSRT
Raffaele, Berardi, Asthana, et al. (1991)	Arecoline muscarinic/cholinergic agonist	2	Open label & DB, PC, random crossover	8	BSRT	Approximately 2 weeks for each	Significant improvement in open label but not on double blind
Penn et al. (1988)	Bethanechol chloride muscarinic agonist	2	DB, PC, random cross-over, & escalating dose	10 & 8	MMSE, COWGT, BSDL, BSRT	24 weeks	No significant improvement in either study
Tariot et al. (1988)	Arecoline muscarinic/cholinergic agonist	2	DB, PC, random parallel group	12	PRT, VFT, BSRT	Acute 2-hour infusions	No significant difference between groups
Mouradian et al. (1988)	RS-86 muscarinic agonist	2	DB, PC, random cross-over	7	DS, PMT, VFDT, RF, DL, WLL, RT, LMT, SM	2 weeks	No significant improvement
Davis et al. (1987)	Oxo-tremorine	2	DB, PC, random cross-over	7	WRT	Acute	No significant improvement
Hollander et al. (1987)	RS-86 muscarinic agonist	2	DB, PC, random cross-over	12	ADAS	3 weeks	6/12 had >10% improvement on ADAS
Bruno et al. (1986)	RS-86 muscarinic agonist	2	DB, PC, random cross-over	8	IMPP, PMT, VFDT, RF, DL, WLL, RT	3 weeks	No significant improvement

Study	Drug		Design	N	Tests	Duration	Results
Wettstein & Spiegel (1984)	RS-86 muscarinic agonist	2	DB, PC, random crossover, & parallel group	6 & 17	MMSE, WRT, PRT, WLL, VT, CP	12 & 18 weeks	Significant improvement on VT in Study 1; No significant results in Study 2
Thal et al. (1981)	Choline chloride	2	DB, PC, random crossover	7	WLL, CP, VFT, CR, PB	12 weeks	No significant improvement
Caamano et al. (1994)	CDP-choline	3	Open label	20	MMSE, BCRS, FAST, TCD	4 weeks	Significant improvement in MMSE of EOAD subset
Jones et al. (1992)	Nicotine	3	SB, PC, crossover	70 (24 AD)	RVIP, DRMLO, CFF, FTT, DS	Acute injection	Significant improvement on parts of RVIP, DRMLO, CFF
Raffaele, Berardi, Morris, et al. (1991)	Arecoline muscarinic/cholinergic agonist	3	Open label	15	BSRT, ERDT	Acute 30-min injection	No significant improvement
Sahakian et al. (1989)	Nicotine	3	SB, PC, crossover	21	DS, FTT, CFF	Acute 7 day	Significant improvement on FTT, CFF
Newhouse et al. (1988)	Nicotine	3	SB, PC, crossover	6	COWGT, WLL	Acute 4 day	Significant decrease in intrusions
Harbaugh et al. (1984)	Bethanechol chloride muscarinic agonist	3	SB, PC, X-over pilot study	4	Subjective family response	8 months	Subjective improvement only during drug periods
Christie et al. (1981)[b]	Physostigmine & arecoline	3	DB, PC, random crossover	11 & 7	SPT	Acute 30-min iv	Significant improvement in both groups
Renvoize & Jerram (1979)	Choline chloride	3	DB, PC, parallel group	18	BRS	2 months	No significant improvement
Ferris et al. (1979)	Choline chloride	3	Open label	14	26 cognitive tests	4 weeks	No significant improvement
C. M. Smith et al. (1978)	Choline bitartate salt	3	DB, PC, crossover	10	RPMT, DS	1 month	No significant improvement

[a]Refer to "List of Acronyms," pp. 116–118, for definitions of abbreviations.
[b]See also Table 5.4.

TABLE 5.8 Nonsteroidal Anti-Inflammatory Drugs[a]

Authors	Drug	Type	Design	N	Outcome Measures	Length of Study	Measure Results
Rogers et al. (1993)	Indomethicin	2	DB, PC, random parallel group	28	MMSE, ADAS, BNT, TT	6 months	Significant differences across all measures
Rich et al. (1995)	NSAIDs	3	Chart review of Alzheimer's Disease Research Center	210	Duration of illness, MMSE, VFT, BNT, TT, BVRT, BDT, RNT, DRST, GIFT, PGDRS	1 year	Less decline on VFT, DRST, orientation subscale of PGDRS
Andersen et al. (1995)	NSAIDs	3	Chart review of dementia study	6,258	Relative risk for Alzheimer's disease	NA	RR .38 for NSAID users
Breitner et al. (1994)	NSAIDs, steroid/ACTH, or aspirin	3	Co-twin control	50 pairs	Age of onset of Alzheimer's disease	NA	Odds ratios for all drugs were below 1. Best for steroid/ACTH
Canadian Study of Health and Aging (1994)	NSAIDs and arthritis	3	Chart review of dementia study	793	Odds ratios of risk factors for Alzheimer's disease	NA	OR for NSAID and arthritis groups significant below 1

[a]Refer to "List of Acronyms," pp. 116–118, for definitions of abbreviations.

106

TABLE 5.9 Monoamine Oxidase Inhibitors[a]

Authors	Drug	Type	Design	N	Outcome Measures	Length of Study	Measure Results
Dysken et al. (1992)	Milacemide	1	DB, PC, random parallel group	228	CGI, WMS, VS, IADL, VFT	9 weeks	No significant improvement
Mangoni et al. (1991)	L-Deprenyl	1	DB, PC, random parallel group	119	BRS, DS, SS, VFT, DT, TPAT	3 months	Significant improvement on BRS, DS, SS, VFT, DT, TPAT
Marin et al. (1995)	L-Deprenyl & Physostigmine	2	DB, PC, random cross-over	17	DS, VFT, WLL, CP, WR, WRT	8 weeks	No significant improvement
Burke et al. (1993)	L-Deprenyl	2	DB, PC, random parallel group	39	CDR, MMSE, BRS, GERRI	First 2 months of 15-month trial	No significant improvement over first 2 months of study
Schneider et al. (1993)[b]	L-Deprenyl & tacrine or physostigmine	2	DB, PC, random cross-over	10	ADAS-Cog, MMSE	8 weeks	Sig. imp. on ADAS-Cog in those receiving drug first
Finali et al. (1991)	L-Deprenyl	2	DB, PC, random cross-over	19	WLL, R-AVL	6 months	Significant improvement on some R-AVL parameters
Piccinin, Finali, & Piccirilli (1990)	L-Deprenyl	2	DB, PC, random cross-over	20	TT, VFT, DS, AVLT, 7/24 Test, LC, TMT, PCT	6 months	Significant improvement on VFT, DS, LC, part of 7/24 test
Tariot, Cohen, et al. (1987)	L-Deprenyl	2	DB, PC, serial treatment	17	BPRS, BSRT, VFT, CPT, VT	8 weeks	Significant improvement on BPRS, BSRT on 10-mg dose
Tariot, Sunderland, et al. (1987)	L-Deprenyl	2	DB, PC, serial treatment	17	BSRT, VT, VFT, CPT	12 weeks	Significant improvement on free recall on BSRT
Goad et al. (1991)	Selegiline	3	Open label	8	MMSE	8 weeks	Clinically significant improvement recall and orientation
Schneider et al. (1991)	L-Deprenyl	3	Open label	14	MMSE, BSRT, COWGT, DS, NC	4 weeks	Significant improvement on BSRT
Falsaperla, Preti, & Olani (1990)	Selegiline & oxiracetam	3	SB, random parallel group	40	BRS, RMT, DS, SR, VFT, GS	90 days	Significant improvement on all tests with selegiline
Campi, Todeschini, & Scarzella (1990)	Selegiline & acetyl-L-carnitine	3	SB, random parallel group	40	BRS, RMT, DS, SR, VFT, GS	90 days	Significant improvement on all tests with selegiline
Monteverde et al. (1990)	Selegiline & phosphatidylserine	3	SB, PC, random cross-over	40	BRS, RMT, DS, SR, VFT, GS	90 days	Significant improvement on all tests with selegiline

[a]Refer to "List of Acronyms," pp. 116–118, for definitions of abbreviations.
[b]See also Tables 5.3 and 5.4.

107

TABLE 5.10 Naloxone/Naltrexone[a]

Authors	Drug	Type	Design	N	Outcome Measures	Length of Study	Measure Results
Henderson et al. (1989)	Naloxone	2	DB, PC, random crossover	54	MMSE, DS, FTT, VRT, VMT, VFT, BNT, modified TT, DSY	Acute injections	Significant improvement on intrusions in VMT
Tariot et al. (1986)	Naloxone	2	DB, PC, random crossover	12	COWGT, DS, BSRT, FTT, DSY, DYN, VT	Acute 3 day	No significant improvement
Hyman et al. (1985)	Naltrexone	2	DB, PC, random crossover	17	OR, DS, COWGT, VL, VMT, NC	6 weeks	No significant improvement
Pomara et al. (1985)	Naltrexone	2	DB, PC, random crossover	10	DS, TT, VFT, FTT, WLL, CNFN	Acute 4 injections	Significant improvement on TT
Tennant (1987)	Naltrexone	3	Open label and DB, PC, random crossover	6 & 3	MMSE, BRS	6 weeks	Significant improvement on MMSE, BRS
Knopman & Hartman (1986)	Naltrexone	3	Open label	10	AVLT, VFT, SD, WMS	6 weeks	Significant improvement on AVLT
Serby et al. (1986)	Naltrexone	3	Open label and DB for responders	9 & 2	BSRT, PMT, NYUMT	2 weeks each	No significant improvement
Steiger et al. (1985)	Naloxone	3	DB, PC, random crossover	16	BCRS	2 months	No significant improvement
Panella & Blass (1984)	Naloxone	3	DB, PC, random crossover	12	MMSE, MSQ, DS, BRS	Acute injections	No significant improvement
Reisberg et al. (1983a)	Naloxone	3	DB, PC, random crossover	7	BCRS, DSY, FTT, VFT, DS, PS	Acute injections	Significant improvement in all but VFT and PS
Reisberg et al. (1983b)	Naloxone	3	Open label	5	BCRS, DSY, FTT, VFT, DS, PS	Acute injections	Clinical improvement in 3/5

[a]Refer to "List of Acronyms," pp. 116–118, for definitions of abbreviations.

108

TABLE 5.11 Vasopressin[a]

Authors	Drug	Type	Design	N	Outcome Measures	Length of Study	Measure Results
Wolters et al. (1990)	Deglycin amide-arginine-vasopressin	1	DB, PC, random parallel group	115	SCAGS, BCRS, IADL, GAS, SLT, COC, VFT, MPM, SR, VR, MCGBRS	84 days	No significant improvement
Peabody, Davis et al. (1986)	Desamino-D-arginine-vasopressin	2	DB, PC, random parallel group	14	BSRT, LM, SV	4 weeks	No significant improvement on cognitive scales
Peabody et al. (1985)	Deglycin amide-arginine-vasopressin	2	DB, PC, random parallel group	17	BSRT, WLL	1 week	Significant improvement on parts of BSRT
Chase et al. (1982)	Lysine vasopressin	2	DB, PC, random parallel group	16	RT, TR, MPP, WLL, PMT, RF	10 days	Significant improvement on RT
Durso et al. (1982)	Lysine vasopressin	2	DB, PC, random parallel group	17	WLL, BSRT, PWT, SR, PMT, RT, RF, TR	10 days	Significant improvement on RT
Tinklenberg et al. (1982)	Deglycin amide-arginine-vasopressin	3	SB, PC, parallel group	11	BSRT, WLL	10 days	No significant improvement
Kaye et al. (1982)[b]	Desamino-D-arginine-vasopressin	3	SB, PC, crossover	7	WMS, BSRT, WLL, VFT	1 month	Significant improvement on VFT
Tinklenberg, Pfefferbaum, & Berger (1981)	Desamino-D-arginine-vasopressin	3	DB, PC, random parallel group	7	BSRT, PWT	1 to 2 weeks	No significant improvement
Weingartner et al. (1981)	Desamino-D-arginine-vasopressin	3	DB, PC, random crossover	7	VFT, WLL	Acute	Significant improvement on VFT

[a]Refer to "List to Acronyms," pp. 116–118, for definitions of abbreviations.
[b]See also Tables 5.3 and 5.6.

TABLE 5.12 Acetyl-L-Carnitine[a]

Authors	Drug	Type	Design	N	Outcome Measures	Length of Study	Measure Results
Spagnoli et al. (1991)	Acetyl-L-carnitine	1	DB, PC, random parallel group	130	SBI, BRS, BICMT, RPMT, VJMCT, VSMD, PRMT, SVL, BTT, TT, WAT, IBAT, GCAT, FAT	1 year	Significant decrease in deterioration on BRS, RPM, BSMD, IBAT
Pettegrew et al. (1995)	Acetyl-L-carnitine	2	DB, PC, parallel groups (3)	33	MMSE, ADAS	1 year	Significantly less deterioration on MMSE
Sano et al. (1992)	Acetyl-L-carnitine	2	DB, PC, random parallel group	30	BSRT, mMMSE, WMS, BVRT, VFT, cancellations	6 months	Significant difference on VFT, DS, cancellations
Passeri et al. (1990)	Acetyl-L-carnitine	2	DB, PC, random parallel group	60	MMSE, BRS, RCFT, VFT, CT, TPBT	3 months	Significant improvement on BRS, RCFT, CT, VFT, TPBT
Rai et al. (1990)	Acetyl-L-carnitine	2	DB, PC, random parallel group	20	KOL, DCT, NLT, VFT	24 weeks	No significant difference
Urakami et al. (1993)	Nebracetam fumarate	3		9	MMSE, GBS, HWDS	8 weeks	Significant improvement on GBS, HWDS
Sinforiani et al. (1990)	Acetyl-L-carnitine & piracetam	3	SB, open label	12 & 12	DS, DSY, BTT, GS, VFT, WLL	2-week iv & 90-day oral	Significant improvement on DSY, GS for ALC
Campi et al. (1990)	Acetyl-L-carnitine & selegiline	3	SB, random parallel group	40	BRS, RMT, DS, SR, VFT, GS	90 days	Significant improvement for selegiline on all measures
Bellagamba et al. (1990)	Acetyl-L-carnitine	3	DB, PC, random parallel group	35	DSY, RCFT, RPMT, and others	3 months	Significant improvement on DSY, RCFT, RPMT

[a]Refer to "List of Acronyms," pp. 116–118, for definitions of abbreviation.
[b]See also Table 5.4.

TABLE 5.13 "Membrane Stabilizing Agents"[a]

Authors	Drug	Type	Design	N	Outcome Measures	Length of Study	Measure Results
Crook et al. (1991)	Phosphatidylserine	1	DB, PC, random parallel group	149	FRT, NFA, TNR, MOR	12 weeks	Significant improvement on FRT, NFA
Amaducci & the SMID Group (1988)	Phosphatidylserine	1	DB, PC, random parallel group	142	DRS, RMT, SR, DS, BTT, TT, ST, CASE	3 months with 21-month follow-up	Significant improvement on ST, BTT, and BDS subscale
Flicker et al. (1994)	Ganglioside GM$_1$	2	DB, PC, random crossover	12	DS, TNR, DSY, BDT, FTT, ORT, SLT, MMSE, JLO	15 weeks	No significant improvement
Crook, Petrie, et al. (1994)	Phosphatidylserine	2	DB, PC, random parallel group	51	CGI, CRS, MAC-P	12 weeks	Significant difference on 2 CGI variables, 3 CRS variables
Ala et al. (1990)	Ganglioside GM$_1$	2	DB, PC, random parallel group	46	MMSE, BCRS, VFT, PB, LC, DSY, BSRT, RCFT, CD	12 weeks	No significant improvement
Delwaide et al. (1986)	Phosphatidylserine	2	DB, PC, random parallel group	35	CS, PRS	6 weeks	Significant improvement on PRS
Heiss et al. (1994)	Phosphatidylserine, pyritinol, cognitive training	3	Open label 4 parallel group combination of three "drugs"	70	MMSE, FTT, PMT, VMT, VFT, TT, RT, OT, IPT, QEEG, PET	6 months	No significant difference among the 4 groups
Monteverde et al. (1990)	Phosphatidylserine & selegiline	3	SB, PC, random crossover	40	BRS, RMT, DS, SR, VFT, GS	90 days	Significant improvement on subscales of BRS & RMT for P-serine

[a]Refer to "List of Acronyms," pp. 116–118, for definitions of abbreviations.

TABLE 5.14 Estrogen[a]

Authors	Drug	Type	Design	N	Outcome Measures	Length of Study	Measure Results
Hagino et al. (1995)	Estrogen replacement therapy	3	Open label	15 & 7	MMSE, HWDS, GBS	6 weeks & 5–28 months	Significant improvement on MMSE, HDS, GBS in Study 1 & in some subjects in Study 2
Ohkura et al. (1995)	Estrogen replacement therapy	3	Open label, case study	7	MMSE, HWDS, GBS	5–45 months	Nonsignificant improvement on MMSE and HDS in 4 cases
Weiss (1987)	Estrogen & nalmefene	3	Open label	5	GDS, MMSE, BSRT, TMT, VFT, BCRS	4 weeks	No significant improvement
Brenner et al. (1994)	Estrogen replacement therapy	2	Population-based case control	107 AD, 120 cntr.	Adjusted odds ratios of estrogen replacement therapy and AD	Followed for 6 years	No association between ERT and AD
Henderson et al. (1994)	Estrogen replacement therapy	3	Population-based case control	143 AD, 92 cntr.	Likelihood of developing AD in controls and comparison of MMSE scores	NA	Significant difference in risk and MMSE scores favoring ERT
Barrett-Conner & Kritz-Silverstein (1993)	Estrogen replacement therapy	1	Population-based case control	800	Adjusted odds ratio of ERT and cognitive function (BSRT, WMS, MMSE, BRS, TMT, VFT)	Followed for 15 years	No significant effect of estrogen on cognitive function
Honjo et al. (1989)	Estrogen replacement therapy	3	Open label, parallel group	7	JST, HWDS	6 weeks	Significant improvement on JST
Fillit et al. (1986)	Estrogen replacement therapy	3	Open label	7	GDS, BRS, WAIS, MMSE, RMT, DRS	6 weeks	Significant improvement in three subjects

[a]Refer to "List of Acronyms," pp. 116–118, for definitions of abbreviations.

TABLE 5.15 Other Interventions[a]

Authors	Drug	Type	Design	N	Outcome Measures	Length of Study	Measure Results
Scherder et al. (1995)	Trans-Q electrical nerve stimulation	2	DB, PC, random parallel group	16	DS, VMS, VFT, EWT, FRT, PRT	6 weeks	Significant effect on recognition in EWT and on FRT, PRT
Saletu et al. (1992)	Denbufylline in AD and MID	2	DB, PC, random parallel group	45 & 51	EEG mapping, CGI, MMSE, DSY, TMT, DS, SCAGS	12 weeks	Significant improvement on CGI, MMSE, DSY, SGAGS
Tollefson (1990)	Nimodepine	1	DB, PC, random parallel group	227	BSRT, VFT, FT, CGI, ADL, RAGS, SRT, SDMT, FLNT	12 weeks	Significant improvement on parts of the BSRT
Saletu et al. (1994)	Nicergoline in SDAT & Multi-infarct dementia	1	DB, PC, random parallel group	112	CGI, MMSE, SCAGS	8 weeks	Significant improvement on CGI & MMSE for both SDAT & MID
Battaglia et al. (1989)	Nicergoline	1	DB, PC, random parallel group	315	SCAGS	6 months	Significant improvement on SCAGS
Nicergoline Study Group (1990)	Nicergoline & ergoloid mesylates	3	SB placebo followed by DB, parallel group	73 & 73	SCAGS, PP	7 months	Significant improvement on SCAGS, PP for both groups
Miller, Fong, & Tinklenberg (1993)	ORG 2766 ACTH 4-9 analog	2	DB, PC, random parallel group	40	BSRT, MMSE, DSY, ADAS, GDS, RT, PTT	16 weeks	Significant improvement on RT
Kragh-Sorensen et al. (1986)	ORG 2766 ACTH 4-9 analog	2	DB, PC, random parallel group	156	SCAGS, GAGS, LPRS, BRS	4 weeks	Significant improvement on SCAGS, LPRS & GAGS at varied doses
Soininen et al. (1985)	ORG 2766 ACTH 4-9 analog	2	DB, PC, random parallel group	77	SCAGS, GPIE, LPRS, GAS	6 months	No significant improvement
Ferris et al. (1982)	L-Dopa	3	DB, PC, random crossover	56	BSRT	16 weeks	No significant improvement
Branconnier et al. (1979)	ACTH 4-10	2	DB, PC, random crossover	18	SPPT, BGT, RT, WMS	Acute injection	No significant improvement
Davidson et al. (1988)	4-Aminopyridine	2	DB, PC, random crossover	14	ADAS	4 weeks	No significant improvement
D. F. Smith et al. (1984)	Tryptophan	2	DB, PC, random crossover	28	PGRS, GRS	4 weeks	No significant improvement
Cutler et al. (1985)	Zimeldine	2	DB, PC, random crossover	4	RT, OM, WLL	23 weeks	No significant improvement
Dehlin et al. (1985)	Alaproclate	2	DB, PC, random parallel group	40	GBS, CGI, CPRS	8 weeks	Significant improvement on subtest of GBS

(continued)

TABLE 5.15 (continued)

Authors	Drug	Type	Design	N	Outcome Measures	Length of Study	Measure Results
Meador et al. (1993)	Thiamine 1 DB & 1 SB experiment	2 & 3	DB & SB, PC, random crossover	18 & 28	ADAS, MMSE, CGI	8 weeks	Significant improvement on ADAS in 13 DB subjects
Nolan et al. (1991)	Thiamine	2	DB, PC, random parallel group	15	BNT, MMSE, WLL	1 year	No significant improvement
Blass et al. (1988)	Thiamine	2	DB, PC, random crossover	16	MMSE	6 months	Significant improvement on MMSE
Adolfsson et al. (1982)	Levodopa	2	DB, PC, random parallel group	37	DS, SIM, FOM, BGT, RT, FTT	10 weeks	No significant improvement
Lebowitz & Crook (1991)	Guanfacine	1 & 2	DB, SB, PC, random parallel group	160 & 40	MAC-S, MAC-CGI, MAC-P, LM, BVRT, PAT	4 weeks	No significant improvement
Crook, Wilner, et al. (1992)	Guanfacine	2	DB, PC, random parallel group	29	CGI, CRS, MAC-F, ALT, LMT, BVRT	13 weeks	No significant improvement
Schlegel et al. (1989)	Guanfacine	2	DB, PC, random crossover	5	PMT, SM, VFT, DS, BVRT	4 weeks	No significant improvement
Mouradian et al. (1991)	Somatostatin (Octreotide)	2	DB, PC, random crossover	14	ADAS, BSRT, DS, SM, VFT, RVL, LMT	Acute injections and iv	No significant improvement
McLachlan et al. (1991)	Desferri-oxamine	2	DB, PC, random parallel group	48	ADL, VHB	24 months	Significant decrease in rate of decline of ADL
Mellow et al. (1989)	Thyrotropin-releasing hormone	2	DB, PC, random crossover	10	VT, VFT, PRT, BSRT	Acute 3 day	No significant improvement on cognition
Lampe TH et al. (1990)	TRH and lecithin	2	DB, PC, random crossover	8	VFT, TMT, BSRT, BVRT	2 weeks	Significant improvement on part of BSRT
Peabody et al. (1986)	Thyrotropin-releasing hormone	3	DB, PC, crossover	4	DS, BSRT, TET, ZVT	Acute injection	No significant improvement
Imagawa (1990)	Coenzyme Q₁₀, vitamin B₆, and iron	3	Open label	27	HWDS	8 weeks	Significant improvement on HWDS
Mohr et al. (1986)	THIP	2	DB, PC, random crossover	6	SR, VFDT, WLL, PMT, RT, RF	2 weeks	No significant improvement
Mohr et al. (1989)	Clonidine	2	DB, PC, random crossover	8	SM, VFT, DS, OP, VL	~4 weeks	No significant improvement
Ihl, Perisic, & Dierkes (1989)	Tenilsetam	3	Open label	12	RT, SLT, CGI, FJT(?)	3 months	Significant improvement on FJT & RT
Fleischhacker, Buchgeher, & Schubert (1986)	Memantine	3	SB, PC, random parallel group	20	FPB, PGRS, SCAGS, CGI, SKT	5 weeks	No significant improvement

[a]Refer to the "List of Acronyms," pp. 116–118, for definitions of abbreviations.

114

bon dioxide, carbonic anhydrous inhibitors, tocopherol (vitamin E; to date, though many well-controlled, large-scale clinical trials are under way, and early results suggest a role in primary prevention), hyperbolic oxygen, and vasodilators (papaverine, cyclandelate, isosuprine, cinnizarine).

Summary for the
Treating Clinician

Despite their long and mixed history, the most promising, symptomatic treatments for AD subjects remain the AChEs. Tacrine, in doses greater than 80 mg/day (for the small percentage of patients who are able to tolerate the medication and can reliably take the medication four times a day), has now demonstrated "real-world" outcomes: (a) consistent cognitive improvement, (b) improvement in behavioral symptoms of AD, and (c) the promise of substantial delays in nursing home placement (with attendant decreases in health care costs). The next generation of AChEs, with simpler dosing, minimal side effects, and negligible hepatotoxicity, will most likely bring these medications to a much larger percentage of patients. Donepezil has recently been approved for use in mild-to-moderate AD patients. It has been shown to be effective in doses of 5–10 mg/day. Others of this newer generation are soon to follow.

The recent report by Schneider et al. (1996) is likely to point the way to future intervention strategies. Combinations of NSAIDs and/or estrogen replacement with AChEs are now under way. While these combinations are now not approved interventions, these trials are likely to soon change this recommendation.

DEMENTIA ASSOCIATED WITH
PARKINSON'S DISEASE

Dementia is common in Parkinson's disease, but the exact pathophysiology, especially the relationship among Alzheimer's disease, Parkinson's dementia, and Lewy body dementia, has yet to be fully understood. Dementia is common in Parkinson's disease, affecting approximately 30% of all PD patients (Koller & Megaffin, 1994; Pollack & Hornabrook, 1988). Age and duration of illness appear to be significant risk factors in the development of dementia. Mayeux et al. (1990) found that the incidence rate of dementia was 69/1,000 population per years of follow-up, and that the risk of dementia as a function of age in this group reached 65% by age 85 (Koller & Megaffin, 1994). This resulted in an age-specific prevalence of 21% in patients whose other PD symptoms occurred after age 70. This dementia may be genetically determined. Marder et al. (1990) found that the risk of dementia among first-degree relatives of demented patients with PD was sixfold greater than in relatives of nondemented PD patients.

Table 5.16 summarizes a limited experience with treatments for the dementia associated with PD. Both piracetam and phosphatidylserine have been tried in Type 1 studies without success. Two Type 3 studies—open clinical trials with a small number of subjects—have both proposed that the coadministration of lecithin with sinemet resulted in improved performance in measures of cognitive performance. One encouraging note is that many of the ongoing trials mentioned above for AD subjects have now been extended to patients with Lewy body dementia and dementia associated with Parkinson's disease.

TABLE 5.16 Dementia in Parkinson's Disease[a]

Authors	Drug	Type	Design	N	Measures	Length of Study	Measure Results
Sano et al. (1990)	Piracetam	2	DB, PC, random crossover	20	mMMSE, BSRT, VFT, RT, CPT	24 weeks	No significant improvement
Garcia et al. (1982)	Lecithin	2	DB, PC, random parallel group	16	VOCT, BDT, RPMT, DSY, VFT, OR	9 weeks	No significant differences between groups
Barbeau (1980)	Lecithin	3	Open label	10	KBD	3 months	Improvement in KBD

[a]Refer to "List of Acronyms," pp. 116–118, for definitions of abbreviations.

List of Acronyms

AB	Aphasia Battery
ACPT	Auditory Continuous Performance Test
ACTH	adrenocorticotropic hormone
AD	Alzheimer's disease
ADAS	Alzheimer's Disease Assessment Scale
ADAS-Cog	Alzheimer's Disease Assessment Scale—Cognitive Scale
ADAS-NCog	Alzheimer's Disease Assessment Scale—Noncognitive Scale
ADL	activities of daily living
AF	Attentional Focusing
AMTS	Abbreviated Mental Test Score
ASMC	automatic speech and mental control
AST	Aphasia Screening Test
AVLT	Auditory Verbal Learning Test
BCRS	Brief Cognitive Rating Scale
BDT	Block Design subtest of the Wechsler Adult Intelligence Test
BGT	Bender-Gestalt Test
BI	Barthal Index
BICMT	Blessed Information-Concentration-Memory Test
BNT	Boston Naming Test
BPDP	Brown-Peterson Distractor Paradigm
BPRS	Brief Psychiatric Rating Scale
BRS	Blessed-Roth Scale
BS	Block Span
BSDL	Benton Serial Digit Learning
BSRT	Buschke Selective Reminding Task
BTT	Block Tapping Task
BVRT	Benton Visual Retention Test
BWLLT	Buschke Word List Learning Test
CA	Cube Analysis
CALC	calculations
CAMCOG	Cambridge Cognitive Examination
CANTAB	Cambridge Neuropsychological Test Automated Battery
CASE	Clifton Assessment Scale for the Elderly
CCSE	Cognitive Capacity Screening Examination
CD	Clock Drawing
CDR	Clinical Dementia Rating Scale
CFF	Critical Flicker Fusion
CFT	Complex Figure Test
CG-CGIC	Caregiver-Rated Clinical Global Impression of Change
CGI	Clinical Global Impression
CGIC	Clinical Global Impression—Change
CGII	Clinical Global Impression of Improvement

CIBC	Clinician Interview-Based Impression
CL-CGIC	Clinician-Rated Clinical Global Impression of Change
CN	Color Naming
CNFN	Confrontation Naming
COC	Cross-Out Concentration
COWGT	Controlled Oral Word Generation Test
CP	Constructional Praxis
CPRS	Comprehensive Psychopathological Rating Scale
CPT	Continuous Performance Task
CR	Category Recognition
CRTT	Choice Reaction Time Task
CS	Crichton Scale
CSCL	Clinical Status Checklist
CST	Color Slide Test
CT	Corsi's Test
CWAT	Controlled Word Association Test
DAT	dementia of the Alzheimer type
DB	double blind
DCT	Digit Copy Test
DL	Dichotic Listening
DMTS	Delayed Matching to Sample
DRMLO	Delayed Response Matching to Location Order
DRS	Dementia Rating Scale
DRST	Delayed Recognition Span Test
DS	Digit Span subtest of the Wechsler Adult Intelligence Test
DSY	Digit Symbol subtest of the Wechser Adult Intelligence Test
DYN	dynometry
EEG	electroencephalogram
EOAD	early onset Alzheimer's disease
ERDT	Extended Range Drawing Test
ERT	estrogen replacement therapy
EWT	Eight Word Test
FAST	Functional Assessment Stages
FAT	Finger Agnosia Test
FCCA	Final Comprehensive Consensus Assessment
FFT	Famous Faces Test
FLNT	First and Last Names Test
FLS	Functional Life Scale
FOM	Fuld Object Memory
FPB	Funktionspsychose-Skala-B
FR	Free Recall of Random and Related Words
FRT	Facial Recognition Test
FTT	Finger Tapping Task
GAS	Global Assessment Scale
GBS	Gottfries, Brane, and Steen Scale Test
GCAT	Geometrical Constructive Apraxia Test

GDS	Global Deterioration Scale	MSQ	Mental Status Questionnaire
GERRI	Geriatric Evaluations by Relatives Rating Instrument	NC	Number Cancellation
		NFA	Name Face Association
GIFT	Gollin Incomplete Figures Test	NLT	Name Learning Test
GPIE	General Psychiatric Impression— Elderly	NOSIE	Nurse's Observation Scale for In-Patients
GRS	Gerentopsychiatric Rating Scale	NSAID	nonsteroidal anti-inflammatory drug
GS	Gibson Spiral	NVPAL	Nonverbal Paired-Associate Learning
HDS	Hierarchic Dementia Scale	NYUMT	New York University Memory Task
HP	Hand Positions	OBS-CS	Organic Brain Syndrome—Confusion Scale
HVR	Halton's Visual Reproductions		
HWDS	Hasegawa's Dementia Scale	OBS-DS	OBS Disorientation Scale
IADL	instrumental activities of daily living	OM	Object Memory
IBAT	Ideomotor and Buccal-facial Apraxia Test	OP	Object Placement
		OR	Orientation
IDDD	Interview for Deterioration in Daily life in Dementia	ORT	Object Recognition Task
		OT	Orientation Test
IL	Incomplete Letters	PALT	Paired Associates Learning Test
IMCI	Information-Memory-Concentration Instrument	PB	Pegboard
		PC	placebo controlled
IMPP	Immediate Memory for Prose Passages	PCT	Picture Cancellation Task
IPSCE	Inventory of Psychic and Somatic Complaints in the Elderly	PDD	primary degenerative dementia
		PDS	Progressive Deterioration Scale
IPT	Incomplete Picture Task	PET	positron-emission tomography
IWRT	Immediate Word Recognition Task	PGDRS	Psychogeriatric Dependency Rating Scales
JLO	Judgment of Line Orientation		
JST	Japanese Screening Test	PGRS	Plutchik Geriatric Rating Scale
KBD	Koh's Block Design	PMSE	Pfeifer Mental Status Exam
KOL	Kendrick Object Learning	PMT	Picture Memory Task
KT	Kew Tests	PNRS	Plutchnik Nurse's Rating Scale
LAS	Luria Alternating Series	PP	Polarity Profile
LC	Letter Cancellation	PRMT	Prose Memory Test
LM	Letter Matching	PRS	Peri Scale
LMT	Logical Memory Test of the Wechsler Adult Intelligence Test	PRT	Picture Recognition Task
		PS	Perceptual Speed
LPRS	London Psychogeriatric Rating Scale	PSMS	Physical Self-Maintenance Scale
LS	Lawton Scale	PTT	Pursuit Tracking Task
LT	Labyrinth Test	PVAS	Physician Visual Analogue Scale
MAC-CGI	Memory Assessment Clinics Clinical Global Improvement Scale	PWT	Paired Words Test
		QEEG	Quantitative EEG
MAC-P	Memory Assessment Clinics Psychiatric Rating Scale	RAGS	Relative's Assessment of Global Symptomology
MAC-S	Memory Assessment Clinics Self-Rating Scale	RAT	Repeated Aquisition Task
		RAVL	Rey Auditory Verbal Learning Test
MC	Mental Control	rCBF	Regional Cerebral Blood Flow
MCGBRS	Modified Crighton Geriatric Behavior Rating Scale	RCFT	Rey Complex Figure Test
		RCGM	regional cerebral glucose metabolism
MDS	Mattis Dementia Scale	RDRS-II	Rapid Disability Rating Scale II
mMMSE	Modified Mini-Mental State Exam	RDT	Rosen Drawing Test
MMSE	Mini-Mental State Exam	RF	Recurring Figures
MOR	Misplaced Object Recall	RMPT	Roadmap Test
MPM	Modified Progressive Matricies	RMT	Randt Memory Test
MPP	Memory for Prose Passages	RNCP	Rosen Noncognitive Portion
MSCL	Mental Status Checklist	RNT	Responsive Naming Test

RPMT   Raven's Progressive Matricies Test
RR   Relative Reports
RT   Reaction Time
RVIP   Raid Visual Information Processing
SB   single blind
SBI   Spontaneous Behavior Interview
SCAGS Sandoz Clinical Assessment–Geriatric Scale
SCWIT Stroop Color Word Interference Test
SDAT   senile dementia of the Alzheimer's type
SDMT   Symbol Digit Modality Test
SGRS   Stockton Geriatric Rating Scale
SIM   Similarities subtest of the Wechsler Adult Intelligence Test
SKT   Syndrom-Kurztest
SLT   Shopping List Task
SM   Sentence Memory
SMT   Spatial Memory Test
SPECT single-photon emission computed tomography
SPPT   Sperling's Perceptual Trace
SPT   Shepard Picture Test
SR   Story Recall
SRT   Standardized Roadmap Test
SS   Short Story
ST   Set Test
SV   Sentence Verification
SVL   Supra Span Verbal Learning
SVT   Serial Visuographic Task
T & L Tacrine and Lecithin
TCD   transcranial Doppler ultrasonography
TET   Time Estimation Task
TG   Trigrams
THIP   4,5,6,7-tetrahydroisozalolo(5,4-c)-pyridin-3-ol
TMT   Trail Making Test
TNR   Telephone Number Recall
TPBT   Toulouse-Pieron Barrage Test
TR   Tachistoscopic Recognition
TRH   thyrotropin-releasing hormone
TT   Token Test
V&V SRT Visual and Verbal Selective Reminding Tasks
VCPT   Visual Continuous Performance Test
VCRMT Visual Continuous Recognition Memory Task
VFDT   Visual Form Discrimination Test
VFT   Verbal Fluency Test
VJ   Verbal Judgment
VL   Verbal Learning
VMS   Visual Memory Span from WMS
VMT   Visual Memory Task
VOCT   Vocabulary Test
VPAL   Verbal Paired-Associate Learning

VPM   Visual Pattern Matching
VR   Visual Recognition
VRMT   Verbal Recognition Memory Test
VRT   Verbal Reproduction Task
VSMD   Visual Search on Matrices of Digits
VSRT   Verbal Selective Reminding Task
VST   Visuomotor Task
VT   Vigilance Task
VVLT   Visuo-Verbal Learning Test
WAIS-R Wechsler Adult Intelligence Scale— Revised
WAT   Word Association Test
WLL   Word List Learning
WMS   Wechsler Memory Scale
WNA   Walsh Neuropsychological Approach
WR   Word Recall
WRT   Word Recognition Task
ZVT   Zahlen Verbindungs Test

References

Adolfsson, R., Brane, G., et al. (1982). A double-blind study with levodopa in dementia of Alzheimer type. In S. Corkin et al., *Alzheimer's disease: A report of progress in research*, Vol. 19. New York: Raven Press.

Ala, T., Remero, S, et al. (1990). GM-1 treatment of Alzheimer's disease: A pilot study of safety and efficacy. *Archives of Neurology, 47*, 1126–1130.

Alhainen, K., & Riekkinen, P. J. (1993). Discrimination of Alzheimer's patients responding to cholinesterase inhibitors. *Acta Neurologica Scandinavica, 149*, 16–21.

Amaducci, L., & the SMID Group. (1988). Phosphatylserine in the treatment of Alzheimer's disease: Results of a multicenter study. *Psychopharmacology Bulletin, 24*(1), 130–134.

American Psychiatric Association. (1994). *Diagnostic and statistical manual of mental disorders* (4th ed.). Washington, D.C.: Author.

Andersen, K., Launer, L. J., et al. (1995). Do nonsteroidal anti-inflammatory drugs decrease the risk for Alzheimer's disease. *Neurology, 45*, 1441–1445.

Antuona, P. G. (1995). Effectiveness and safety of velnacrine for the treatment of Alzheimer's disease: A double-blind, placebo controlled study. *Archives of Internal Medicine, 155*, 1766–1772.

Asthana, S., Raffaele, K. C., Bernardi, A., et al. (1996). Treatment of Alzheimer's Disease by continuous influsion of physostigmine. *Alzheimer's Disease & Associated Disorders, 9*(4), 223–232.

Ashford, J. W., Soldinger, S, et al. (1981). Physostigmine and its effect on six patients with dementia. *American Journal of Psychiatry, 138*(6), 829–830.

Banen, D. M. (1972). An ergot preparation (Hydergine)

for relief of symptoms of cerebrovascular insufficiency. *Journal of the American Geriatric Society, 24*, 22–24.

Barbeau, A. (1980). Lecithin in Parkinson's disease. *Journal of Neural Transmission, 16*(Suppl.), 187–193.

Barrett-Conner, E., & Kritz-Silverstein, D. (1993). Estrogen Replacement therapy and cognition in older women. *Journal of the American Medical Association, 269*(20), 2637–2641.

Battaglia, A., Bruni, G., et al. (1989). Nicergoline in mild to moderate dementia: A multicenter, double-blind, placebo-controlled study. *JAGS, 37*, 295–302.

Bellagamba, G., Postacchini, D., et al. (1990). Acetyl-L-carnitine activity in senile dementia Alzheimer type. *Neurobiology of Aging, 11*, 345.

Beller, S. A., Overall, J. E., et al. (1988). Long-term outpatient treatment of senile dementia with oral physostigmine. *Journal of Clinical Psychiatry, 49*(10), 400–404.

Beller, S. A., Overall, J. E., & Swann, A. C. (1985) Efficacy of oral physostigmine in primary degenerative dementia: A double-blind study of response to different dose levels. *Psychopharmacology, 87*, 147–151.

Bierer, L. M., Aisen, P. S., et al. (1994). A pilot study of clonidine plus physostigmine in Alzheimer's disease. *Dementia, 5*, 243–246.

Blass, J. P., Gleason, P., et al. (1988). Thiamine and Alzheimer's disease: A pilot study. *Archives of Neurology, 45*, 833–835.

Bottini, G., Vallar, G., et al. (1992). Oxiracetam in dementia: A double-blind, placebo-controlled study. *ACTA Neurologica Scandinavica, 86*, 237–241.

Branconnier, R. J., Cole, J. O., et al. (1983). The therapeutic efficacy of pramiracetam in Alzheimer's disease: Preliminary observations. *Psychopharmacology Bulletin, 19*(4), 726–730.

Branconnier, R. J., Cole, J. O., & Gardos, G. (1979). ACTH 4-10 in the amelioration of neuropsychological symptomatology associated with senile organic brain syndrome. *Psychopharmacology, 61*, 161–165.

Breitner, J. C. S. (1996). Inflammatory processes and anti-inflammatory drugs in Alzheimer's Disease: A current appraisal. *Neurobiology of Aging, 17*, 789–794.

Breitner, J. C. S., Gau, B. A., et al. (1994). Inverse association of anti-inflammatory treatments and Alzheimer's disease: Initial results of a co-twin control Study. *Neurology, 44*, 227–232.

Brenner, D. E., Kukull, W. A., et al. (1994). Postmenopausal estrogen replacement therapy and the risk of Alzheimer's disease: A population-based case-control study. *American Journal of Epidemiolgy, 140*(3), 262–267.

Brinkman, S. D., Pomara, N., et al. (1992) A dose-ranging study of lecithin in the treatment of primary degenerative dementia (Alzheimer disease). *Journal of Clinical Pharmacology, 2*(4), 281–285.

Bruno, G., Mohr, E., et al. (1986). Muscarinic agonist therapy of Alzheimer's disease: A clinical trial of RS-86. *Archives of Neurology, 43*, 659–661.

Burke, W. J., Ranno, A. K., et al. (1993). L-Deprenyl in the treatment of mild dementia of the Alzheimer type: Preliminary results. *Journal of the American Geriatric Society, 41*, 367–370.

Caamano, J., Gomez, M. J., et al. (1994) Effects of CDP-choline on cognition and cerebral hemodynamics in patients with Alzheimer's disease. *Meth. Find, Exp. Clin. Pharmacol., 16*(3), 211–218.

Calvani, M., Carta, A., et al. (1992). Action of acetyl-L-carnitine in neurodegeneration and Alzheimer's disease. *Annals of the N.Y. Academy of Sciences, 663*, 483–486.

Campi, N., Todeschini, G. P., & Scarzella, L. (1990) Seleginine versus L-acetylcarntine in the treatment of Alzheimer-type dementia. *Clinical Therapeutics, 12*(4), 306–314.

Canadian Study of Health and Aging. (1994). *The Canadian Study of Health and Aging: Risk factors for Alzheimer's disease in Canada. Neurology, 44*, 2073–2080.

Chase, T. N., Durso, R., et al. (1982). Vasopressin treatment of cognitive deficits in Alzheimer's disease. In S. Corkin et al., *Alzheimer's disease: A report of progress in research*, Vol. 19. New York: Raven Press.

Chatellier, G., & Lacomblez, L. (1990). Tacrine (tetrahydroaminoacridine: THA) and lecithin in senile dementia of the Alzheimer type: A multicenter trial. *British Medical Journal, 300*, 495–499.

Christie, J. E., Shering, A., et al. (1981). Physostigmine and arecoline: Effects of intravenous infusions in Alzheimer presenile dementia. *British Journal of Psychiatry, 138*, 46–50.

Clauss, J. J., Ludwig, C., et al. (1991). Nootropic drugs in Alzheimer's disease: Symptomatic treatment with pramiracetam. *Neurology, 41*, 570–574.

Croisile, B., Trillet, M., et al. (1993). Long-term and high-dose piracetam treatment of Alzheimer's disease. *Neurology, 43*, 301–305.

Crook, T., Petrie, W., et al. (1992). Effects of phosphatidylserine in Alzheimer's disease. *Psychopharmacology Bulletin, 28*(1), 61–66.

Crook, T., Wilner, E., et al. (1992). Noradrenergic intervention in Alzheimer's disease. *Psychopharmacology Bulletin, 28*(1), 67–70.

Crook, T. H., Tinklenberg, J., et al. (1991). Effects of phosphatidylserine on age-associated memory impairment. *Neurology, 41*, 644–649.

Cutler, N. R., Haxby, J., et al. (1985). Evaluation of zimeldine in Alzheimer's disease: Cognitive and biochemical measures. *Archives of Neurology, 42*, 744–748.

Dal-Bianco, P., Maly, J., et al. (1991). Galanthamine

treatment in Alzheimer's disease. *Journal of Neural Transmission, 33*(Suppl.), 59–63.

Davidson, M., Zemishlany, Z., et al. (1988). 4-Aminopyridine in the treatment of Alzheimer's disease. *Biological Psychiatry, 23,* 485–490.

Davis, K. L., Hollander, E., et al. (1987). Induction of depression with oxotremorine in patients with Alzheimer's disease. *American Journal of Psychiatry, 144*(4), 468–471.

Davis, K. L., & Mohs, R. C. (1982). Enhancement of memory processes in Alzheimer's disease with multiple-dose intravenous physostigmine. *American Journal of Psychiatry, 139*(11), 1421–1424.

Davis, K. L., Thal, L. J., et al. (1992). A double-blind, placebo-controlled multicenter study of tacrine for Alzheimer's disease. *New England Journal of Medicine, 327*(18), 1253–1259.

Dehlin, O., Hedenrud, B., et al. (1985). A double-blind comparison of alaproclate and placebo in the treatment of patients with senile dementia. *Acta Psychiatrica Scandinavica, 71,* 190–196.

Delwaide, P. J., Devoitille, & Ylieff, M. (1980). Acute effects of drugs on memory of patients with senile dementia. *Acta Psychiat. Belg., 80,* 748–754.

Delwaide, P. J., Gyselynck-Mambourg, A. M., et al. (1986). Double-blind randomized controlled study of phosphatidylserine in senile demented patients. *Acta Neurologica Scand., 73,* 136–140.

Durso, R., Fedio, P., et al. (1982). Lysine vasopressin in Alzheimer disease. *Neurology, 32,* 674–677.

Dysken, M. W., Fovall, P., et al. (1982). Lecithin administration in Alzheimer dementia. *Neurology, 32,* 1203–1204.

Dysken, M. W., Mendels, J., et al. (1992). Milacemide: A placebo-controlled study in senile dementia of the Alzheimer type. *Journal of the American Geriatric Society, 40,* 503–506.

Eagger, S. A., et al. (1991). Tacrine in Alzheimer's disease. *Lancet, 337,* 989–992.

Eagger, S. A., et al. (1992) Tacrine in Alzheimer's disease—Time course of changes in cognitive function and practice effects. *British Journal of Psychiatry, 16,* 36–40.

Eagger, S. A., Levy, R., & Sahakain, B. J. (1992). Tacrine in Alzheimer's disease. *ACTA Neurologica Scandinavica, 139*(Suppl.), 75–80.

Ebmeier, K. P., Hunter, R., et al. (1992) Effects of a single dose of the acetylcholinesterase inhibitor velnacrine on recognition memory and regional cerebral blood flow in Alzheimer's disease. *Psychopharmacology, 108,* 103–109.

Etienne, P., Dastoor, D., et al. (1981) Alzheimer's disease: Lack of effect of lecithin treatment for 3 months. *Neurology, 31,* 1552–1554.

Falsaperla, A., Preti, P. A. M., & Oliani, C. (1990) Selegiline versus oxiracetam in patients with Alzheimer-type dementia. *Clinical Therapuetics, 12*(5), 376–384.

Farlow, M., Gracon, S. I., et al. (1992). A controlled trial of tacrine in Alzheimer's disease. *Journal of the American Medical Association, 268*(18), 2523–2529.

Ferris, S., Mann, J. J., Stanley, M., et al. (1981). Central amine metabolism in Alzheimer's Disease: In vivo relationship to cognitive performance. *Neurobiology of Aging, 2,* 57–60.

Ferris, S. H., Sathananthan, G., et al. (1979). Long-term choline treatment of memory-impaired elderly patients. *Science, 205,* 1039–1040.

Fillit, H., Weinreb, H., et al. (1986). Observations in a preliminary open trial of estradiol therapy for senile dementia–Alzheimer's type. *Psychoneuroendochrinology, 11*(3), 337–345.

Finali, G., Piccirilli, M., et al. (1991). L-Deprenyl therapy improves verbal memory in amnesic Alzheimer's patients. *Clinical Neuropharmacology, 14*(6), 523–536.

Fitten, L. J., Perryman, K. M., et al. (1990) Treatment of Alzheimer's disease with short and long-term oral THA and lecithin: A double blind study. *American Journal of Psychiatry, 147*(2), 239–242.

Fleischhacker, W. W., Buchgeher, A., & Schubert, H. (1986). Memantine in the treatment of senile dementia of the Alzheimer type. *Progress in Neuro-Psychopharmacology & Biological Psychiatry, 10,* 87–693.

Garcia, C. A., Tweedy, J. R., et al. (1982). Lecithin and Parkinsonian dementia. In S. Corkin et al., *Alzheimer's disease: A report of progress in research,* Vol. 19. New York: Raven Press.

Gauthier, S., Bouchard, R., et al. (1990) Tetrahydroaminoacridine-lecithin combination treatment in patients with intermediate stage Alzheimer's disease. *New England Journal of Medicine, 322*(18), 1272–1276.

Goad, D. L., Davis, C. M., et al. (1991). The use of selegline in Alzheimer's patients with behavior problems. *Journal of Clinical Psychiatry, 52*(8), 342–345.

Green, R. C., Goldstein, F. C., et al. (1992). Treatment trial of oxiracetam in Alzheimer's disease. *Archives of Neurology, 49,* 1135–1136.

Growden, J. H., Corkin, S., et al. (1986). Piracetam combined with lecithin in the treatment of Alzheimer's disease. *Neurobiology of Aging, 7,* 296–276.

Gustafson, L. (1993). Physostigmine and tetrahydroaminoacridine treatment of Alzheimer's disease. *ACTA Neurologica Scandinavica, 149,* 39–41.

Gustafson, L., Edvinson, L., et al. (1987). Intravenous physostigmine treatment of Alzheimer's disease evaluated by psychometric testing, regional cerebral blood flow (rCBF) measurement, and EEG. *Psychopharmacology, 93,* 31–35.

Hagino, N., Ohkura, T., et al. (1995). Estrogen in clinical trials for dementia of Alzheimer type. In I. Hanin et al., *Alzheimer's and Parkinson's diseases*. New York: Plenum Press.

Harbaugh, R. E., Reeder, T. M., et al. (1989). Intracerebroventricular bethanechol chloride infusion in Alzheimer's disease: Results of a collaborative double-blind study. *Journal of Neurosurgery, 71,* 481–486.

Harbaugh, R. E., Roberts, D. W., et al. (1984). Preliminary report: Intracranial cholinergic drug infusion in patients with Alzheimer's disease. *Neurosurgery, 15*(4): 514–518.

Harrell, L. E., Callaway, R., et al. (1990). The effect of long-term physostigmine administration in Alzheimer's disease. *Neurology, 40,* 1350–1354.

Harrell, L. E., Jope, R. S., et al. (1990). Biological and neuropsychological characterization of physostigmine responders and nonresponders in Alzheimer's disease. *Journal of the American Geriatric Society, 38,* 113–122.

Heiss, W. D., Hebold, I., et al. (1988). Effect of piracetam on cerebral glucose metabolism in Alzheimer's disease as measured by positron emission tomography. *Journal of Cerebral Blood Flow and Metabolism, 8,* 613–617.

Heiss, W. D., Kessler, J., et al. (1994). Long-term effects of phosphatidylserine, pyritinol, and cognitive training in Alzheimer's disease: A neuropsychological, EEG, and PET investigation. *Dementia, 5,* 88–98.

Henderson, V. W., Paganini-Hill, A., et al. (1994) Estrogen replacement therapy in older women: Comparisons between Alzheimer's disease cases and nondemented control subjects. *Archives of Neurology, 51* 896–900.

Henderson, V. W., Roberts, E., et al. (1989). Multicenter trial of naloxone in Alzheimer's disease. *Annals of Neurology, 25,* 404–406.

Heyman, A., Schmechel, D., et al. (1987). Failure of long term high-dose lecithin to retard progression of early-onset Alzheimer's disease. *Journal of Neural Transmission, 24*(Suppl.), 279–286.

Hollander, E., Davidson, M., et al. (1987). RS 86 in the treatment of Alzheimer's disease: Cognitive and biological effects. *Biological Psychiatry, 22,* 1067–1078.

Hollingsworth, S. W. (1980). Response of geriatric patients from the satellite nursing homes of Maricopa County to Hydergine therapy: A double-blind study. *Current Therapeutic Research, 27*(3), 401–410.

Hollister, L. E., & Yesavage, J. (1984). Ergoloid mesylates for senile dementias: Unanswered questions. *Annals of Internal Medicine, 100,* 894–898.

Honjo, H., Ogino, Y., et al. (1989). In vivo effects by estrone sulfate on the central nervous system—Senile dementia (Alzheimer's type). *Journal of Steroid Biochemistry, 34*(1–6), 521–525.

Hyman, B., Esllinger, P. J., & Damasio, A. R. (1982). Effect of naltrexone on senile dementia of the Alzheimer type. *Journal of Neurology, Neurosurgery, and Psychiatry, 49,* 1321–1322.

Ihl, R., Perisic, I., & Dierks, T. (1989). Effects of 3 months of treatment with tenilsetam in patients suffering from dementia of the Alzheimer type (DAT). *Journal of Neural Transmission, 1*(Sec. P-D), 84–85.

Imagawa, M. (1992). Coenzyme Q, iron, and vitamin B-6 in genetically confirmed Alzheimer's Disease. *Lancet, 340* (8820), 671.

Imagawa, M. (1990). Therapy with a combination of coenzyme Q10, vitamin B6 and iron for Alzheimer's disease and senile dementia of the Alzheimer type. In K. Iqbal, D. R. C. McLachlan, et al. (Eds.), *Alzheimer's disease: Basic mechanisms, diagnosis and therapeutic strategies*. New York: John Wiley & Sons.

Jenicke, M. A., Albert, M. S., et al. (1986). Combination therapy with lecithin and ergoloid mesylates for Alzheimer's disease. *Journal of Clinical Psychiatry, 47*(5), 249–251.

———. (1990). Oral physostigmine treatment for patients with presenile and senile dementia of the Alzheimer type: A double-blind placebo-controlled trial. *Journal of Clinical Psychiatry, 51*(1), 3–7.

Jennings, W. G. (1972). An ergot alkaloid preparation (Hydergine) versus placebo for treatment of symptoms of cerebrovascular insufficiency: Double-blind study. *Journal of the American Geriatric Society, 20*(8), 407–412.

Jones, G. M. M., Sahakian, B. J., et al. (1992). Effects of acute subcutaneous nicotine on attention, information processing and short-term memory in Alzheimer's disease. *Psychopharmacology, 108,* 485–494.

Jotkowitz, S. (1983). Lack of clinical efficacy of chronic oral physostigmine in Alzheimer's disease. *Annals of Neurology, 14,* 690–691.

Kaufer, D. I., Cummings, J., Christine, D. (1996). Effect of tacrine on behavioral symptoms in Alzheimer's Disease: An open label study. *Journal of Geriatric Psychiatry and Neurology, 9,* 1–6.

Kaye, W. H., Weingartner, H., et al. (1982) Cognitive effects of cholinergic and vasopressinlike agents in patients with primary degenerative dementia. In S. Corkin et al., *Alzheimer's disease: A report of progress in research*, Vol. 19. New York: Raven Press.

Knapp, M. J., Knopman, D. S., et al. (1994) A 30-week randomized controlled trial of high-dose tacrine in patients with Alzheimer's disease. *Journal of the American Medical Association, 271*(13), 985–991.

Knopman, D. S., & Hartman, M. (1986). Cognitive effects of high-dose naltrexone in patients with probable Alzheimer's disease. *Journal of Neurology, Neurosurgery, and Psychiatry, 49,* 1321–1322.

Knopman, D., Schneider, L., Davis, K., et al. (1996). Long term tacrine (Cognex) treatment: Effects on nursing home placement and mortality, Tacrine Study Group. *Neurology, 47*(1), 166–177.

Koller, W., & Megaffin, (1994). Parkinson's Disease and Parkinsonism. In Coffey, C. E., & Cummings, J. L. (Eds)., *Textbook of geriatric neuropsychiatry* (pp. 433–456), Washington, D.C.: American Psychiatric Press.

Kragh-Sorensen, P., Olsen, R. B., et al. (1986) Neuropeptides: ACTH-peptides in dementia. *Progress in Neuro-Psychopharmacology & Biological Psychiatry, 10,* 479–492.

Lampe, T. H., Norris, J., et al. (1990). Therapeutic potential of thyrotropin-releasing hormone and lecithin coadministration in Alzheimer's disease. In K. Iqbal, D. R. C. McLachlan, et al. (Eds.), *Alzheimer's disease: Basic mechanisms, diagnosis and ...nerapeutic strategies.* New York: John Wiley & Sons.

Lampe, T. H., Norris, S. C., Risse, E., et al. (1991). Therapeutic potential of thyrotropin-releasing hormone and lecithin coadministration in Alzheimer's Disease. In Equable, K., McLachlan, D. R. C., Winblad, B., & Wisniewski, H. M. (Eds). *Alzheimer's Disease: Basic mechanisms, diagnosis, and therapeutic stragies.* New York: John Wiley and Sons.

Lebowitz, B., & Crook, T. (1991). Treatment of adult-onset cognitive disorders: Results of multicenter trials. *Psychopharmacology Bulletin, 27*(1), 41–46.

Little, A., Levy, R., et al. (1985). A double-blind, placebo-controlled trial of high-dose lecithin in Alzheimer's disease. *Journal of Neurology, Neurosurgery, and Psychiatry, 48,* 736–742.

Maltby, N., Broe, G. A., et al. (1994) Efficacy of tacrine and lecithin in mild to moderate Alzheimer's disease: Double blind trial. *British Medical Journal, 308,* 879–883.

Mangoni, A., Grassi, M. P., et al. (1991). Effects of a MAO-B inhibitor in the treatment of Alzheimer's disease. *European Neurology, 31,* 100–107.

Marder, K., Flood, P., and Cote, L. (1990). A pilot study of risk factors for dementia in Parkinson's Disease. *Movement Disorders, 5,* 156–161.

Marin, D. B., Bierer, L. M., et al. (1995). L-Deprenyl and physostigmine for the treatment of Alzheimer's disease. *Psychiatry Research, 58,* 181–189.

Matejcek, M., Knor, K., et al. (1979). Electroencephalographic and clinical changes in geriatric patients treated 3 months with and alkaloid preparation. *Journal of the American Geriatric Society, 27,* 198–202.

Mayeux, R., Chen, J., Mirabello, E. (1990). An estimate of the incidence of dementia in idiopathic Parkinson's Disease. *Neurology, 40,* 1513–1517.

McConnachie, R. W. (1973). A clinical trial comparing "Hydergine" with placebo in the treatment of cerebro-vascular insufficiency in elderly patients. *Current Medical Research and Opinion, 1*(8), 463–468.

McGeer, P. L., McGeer, E., Rodgers, J., et al. (1990). Anti-inflammatory drugs and Alzheimer's Disease. *Lancet, 335,* 1037.

McLachlan, D. R. C., Dalton, A. J., et al. (1991) Intramuscular desferrioxamine in patients with Alzheimer's disease. *Lancet, 337,* 1304–1308.

Meador, K., Loring, D., et al. (1993). Preliminary findings of high-dose thiamine in dementia of the Alzheimer type. *Journal of Geriatric Psychiatry and Neurology, 6,* 222–229.

Mellow, A. M., Stephen, M. A., et al. (1993). A peptide enhancement strategy in Alzheimer's disease: Pilot study with TRH-physostigmine infusions. *Biological Psychiatry, 34,* 271–271.

Mellow, A. M., Sunderland, T., et al. (1989). Acute effects of high-dose thyrotropin releasing hormone infusions in Alzheimer's disease. *Psychopharmacology, 98,* 403–407.

Miller, T. P., Fong, K., & Tinklenberg, J. R. (1993). An ACTH 4-9 analog (ORG 2766) and cognitive performance: High-dose efficacy and safety in dementia of the Alzheimer's type. *Biological Psychiatry, 33,* 307–309.

Minthon, L., Gustafson, L., et al. (1993). Oral tetrahydroaminoacridine treatment of Alzheimer's disease evaluated clinically by regional cerebral blood flow and EEG. *Dementia, 4,* 32–42.

Mohr, E., Bruno, G., et al. (1986) GABA-agonist therapy for Alzheimer's disease. *Clinical Neuropharmacology, 9*(3), 257–263.

Mohr, E., Schlegel, J., et al. (1989). Clonidine treatment of Alzheimer's disease. *Archives of Neurology, 46,* 376–378.

Mohs, R. C., Davis, B. M., et al. (1985) Oral physostigmine treatment of patients with Alzheimer's disease. *American Journal of Psychiatry, 142*(1), 28–33.

Molloy, D. W., Guyatt, G. H., et al. (1991). Effect of tetrahydroaminoacridine on cognition, function and behavior in Alzheimer's disease. *Canadian Medical Association Journal, 144*(1), 29–34.

Monteverde, A., Gnemmi, P., et al. (1990). Selegiline in the treatment of mild to moderate Alzheimer-type dementia. *Clinical Therapeutics, 12*(4), 315–322.

Mortimer, J. A., Ebbitt, B., et al. (1992) Predictors of cognitive and functional progression in patients with probable Alzheimer's disease. *Neurology, 42*(9), 1689–1696.

Mouradian, M. M., Thin, J., et al. (1991). Somatostatin replacement therapy for Alzheimer disease. *Annals of Neurology, 30,* 610–613.

Mouradian, M. M., Mohr, E., et al. (1988). No response to high-dose muscarinic agonist therapy in Alzheimer's disease. *Neurology, 38,* 606–608.

Muramoto, O., Sugishia, M., et al. (1979). Effect of physo-stigmine on constructional and memory tasks in Alzhei-mer's disease. *Archives of Neurology, 36*, 501–503.

Muramoto, O., Sugishia, M., & Ando, K. (1984). Cholin-ergic System and Constructional Praxis: A Further Study of Physostigmine in Alzheimer's Disease. *Jour-nal of Neurology, Neurosurgery, and Psychiatry, 47*, 485–491.

Murphy, M. F., Hardiman, S. T., et al. (1991). Evaluation of HP 029 (velnacrine maleate) in Alzheimer's dis-ease. *Annals of the N.Y. Academy of Sciences, 640*, 253–62.

Newhouse, P. A., Sunderland, T., et al. (1988). Intrave-nous nicotine in Alzheimer's disease: A pilot study. *Psychopharmacology, 95*, 171–175.

Nicergoline Study Group. (1990). A double-blind ran-domized study of two ergot derivatives in mild to moderate dementia. *Current Therapeutic Research, 48*(4), 597–612.

Nolan, K. A., Black, R. S., et al. (1991). A trial of thiamine in Alzheimer's disease. *Archives of Neurology, 48*, 81–83.

Novo, F. P., Ryan, R. P., & Frazier, E. L. (1978). Dihy-droergotexine mesylate in the treatment of symptoms of idiopathic cerebral dysfunction in geriatric patients. *Clinical Therapeutics, 1*(5), 359–369.

Ohkura, T., Isse, K., et al. (1995). Long-term estrogen replacement therapy in female patients with dementia of the Alzheimer type: Seven case reports. *Dementia, 6*, 99–107.

Panella, J. J., & Blass, J. P. (1984). Lack of clinical benefit for naloxone in a dementia day hospital. *Annals of Neurology, 15*(3), 306–307.

Passeri, M., Cucinotta, D., et al. (1990). Acetyl-L-carni-tine in the treatment of mildly demented elderly pa-tients. *International Journal of Clinical Pharmacology Research, 10*(1/2), 75–79.

Peabody, C. A., Davis, H., et al. (1986). Desamino-D-arginine-vasopressin (DDAVP) in Alzheimer's dis-ease. *Neurobiology of Aging, 7*, 301–303.

Peabody, C. A., Deblois, T. E., & Tinklenberg, J. R. (1986). Thyrotropin-releasing hormone (TRH) and Alzheimer's disease. *American Journal of Psychiatry, 143*(2), 262–263.

Peabody, C. A., Thiemann, O., et al. (1985). Desglycina-mide-9-arginine-8-vasopressin (DGAVP, Organon 5667) in patients with dementia. *Neurobiology of Aging, 6*, 95–100.

Penn, R. D., Martin, E. M., et al. (1988). Intraventricular bethanechol infusion for Alzheimer's disease: Results of double-blind and escalating-dose trials. *Neurology, 38*, 219–222.

Perryman, K. M., & Fitten, L. J. (1993). Delayed match-ing-to-sample performance during a double-blind trial of tacrine (THA) and lecithin in patients with Alzhei-mer's disease. *Life Sciences, 53*, 479–486.

Peters, B. H., & Levin, H. S. (1979). Effects of physostig-mine and lecithin on memory in Alzheimer's disease. *Annals of Neurology, 6*, 219–221.

Pettegrew, J. W. (1989). Molecular insights into Alzhei-mer's disease. *Annals of the N.Y. Academy of Sciences, 568*, 5–28.

Pettegrew, J. W., Klunk, W. E., et al. (1995). Clinical and neurochemical effects of acetyl-L-carnitine in Alzheimer's disease. *Neurobiology of Aging, 16*(1), 1–4.

Piccinin, G. L., Finali, G., & Piccirilli, M. (1990). Neuro-psychological effects of L-deprenyl in Alzheimer's type dementia. *Clinical Neuropharmacology, 13*(2), 147–163.

Pollack, M., & Hornbook, R. W. (1968). The prevalence, natural history, and dementia of Parkinson's Disease. *Brain, 89*, 429–448.

Pomara, N., Goodnick, P. J., et al. (1982). A dose-response study of lecithin in the treatment of Alzheimer's disease. In S. Corkin et al., *Alzheimer's disease: A report of progress in research*, Vol. 19. New York: Raven Press.

Pomara, N., Roberts, R., et al. (1985). Multiple, single dose naltrexone administrations fail to effect overall cognitive functioning and plasma cortisol in individu-als with probable Alzheimer's disease. *Neurobiology of Aging, 6*(3), 233–236.

Raffaele, K. C., Berardi, A., Asthana, S., et al. (1991). Effects of long-term continuous infusion of the musca-rinic cholinergic agonist arecoline on verbal memory in dementia of the Alzheimer's type. *Psychopharma-cology, 27*(3), 315–319.

Raffaele, K. C., Berardi, A., Morris, P. P., et al. (1991). Effects of acute infusion of the muscarinic cholinergic agonist arecoline on verbal memory and visuo-spatial function in dementia of the Alzheimer's type. *Progress in Neuro-Psychopharmacology & Biological Psychia-try, 15*, 643–648.

Rai, G., Wright, G., et al. (1990) Double-blind, placebo controlled study of acetyl-L-carnitine in patients with Alzheimer's dementia. *Current Medical Research and Opinion, 11*(10), 638–647.

Rechman, S. A. (1973). Two trials comparing "Hyder-gine" with placebo in the treatment of patients suffer-ing from cerebrovascular insufficiency. *Current Medi-cal Research and Opinion, 1*(8), 456–462.

Reisberg, B., Ferris, S. H., et al. (1983a). Effects of nalox-one in senile dementia: A double-blind trial. *New England Journal of Medicine, 308*(12), 721–722.

———. (1983). Naloxone effects on Primary Degenera-tive Dementia (PDD). *Psychopharmacology Bulletin, 19*(1), 45–47.

Renvoize, E. B., & Jerram, T. (1979). Choline in Alzhei-mer's disease. *New England Journal of Medicine, 301*, 330.

Rich, J. B., Rasmusson, D. X., et al. (1995). Nonsteroidal

anti-inflammatory drugs in Alzheimer's disease. *Neurology, 45*, 51–55.

Rodgers, S., Friedhof, L., & the Donepezil Study Group. (1996). The efficacy and safety of donepezil in patients with Alzheimer's Disease: Results of a U.S. Multicenter, randomized, double-blind, placebo-controlled trial. *Dementia, 7*, 293–303.

Rogers, L., Kirby, L. C., et al. (1993). Clinical trial of indomethacin in Alzheimer's disease. *Neurology, 43*, 1609–1611.

Rouy, J. M., Douillon, A. M., et al. (1989). Ergoloid mesylates ("Hydergine") in the treatment of mental deterioration in the elderly: A 6-month double-blind, placebo-controlled trial. *Current Medical Research and Opinion, 11*(6), 380–389.

Ruther, E., Ritter, R., et al. (1994). Efficacy of the peptidic nootropic drug cerebrolysin in patients with senile dementia of the Alzheimer type (SDAT). *Pharmacopsychiatrist, 27*, 32–40.

Sahakian, B. J., & Coull, J. T. (1993). Tetrahydroaminoacridine (THA) in Alzheimer's disease: An assessment of attentional and mnemonic function using CANTAB. *ACTA Neurologica Scandinavica, 149*, 29–35.

Sahakian, B., Jones, G., et al. (1989). The effects of nicotine on attention, information processing, and short-term memory in patients with dementia of the Alzheimer type. *British Journal of Psychiatry, 154*, 797–800.

Saletu, B., Anderer, P., et al. (1992). EEG mapping and psychopharmacological studies with denbufylline in SDAT and MID. *Biological Psychiatry, 32*, 668–681.

Saletu, B., Paulus, E., et al. (1994). Nicergoline in senile dementia of Alzheimer type and multi-infarct dementia: A double-blind, placebo-controlled, clinical and EEG/ERP mapping study. *Psychopharmacology, 117*, 385–395.

Sano, M., Bell, K., et al. (1992). Double-blind parallel design pilot study of acetyl levocarnitine in patients with Alzheimer's disease. *Archives of Neurology, 49*, 1137–1141.

———. (1993). Safety and efficacy of oral physostigmine in the treatment of Alzheimer disease. *Clinical Neuropharmacology, 16*(1), 61–69.

Sano, M., Stern, Y., et al. (1990). A controlled trial of piracetam in intellectually impaired patients with Parkinson's Disease. *Movement Disorders, 5*(3), 230–234.

Scherder, E. J. A., Bouma, A., & Steen, A. M. (1995). Effects of short-term transcutaneous electrical nerve stimulation on memory and affective behaviour in patients with probable Alzheimer's disease. *Behavioural Brain Research, 67*, 211–219.

Schlegel, J., Mohr, E., et al. (1989). Guanfacine treatment of Alzheimer's disease. *Clinical Neuropharmacology, 12*(2), 124–128.

Schneider, L. S., Farlow, M. R., Henderson, V. W. (1996). Effects of estrogen replacement therapy on response to tacrine in patients with Alzheimer's Disease. *Neurology, 46*, 1580–1584.

Schneider L. S., & Olin, J. T. (1994). Overview of clinical trials of Hydergine in dementia. *Archives of Neurology, 51*, 787–798.

Schneider, L., Olin, J. T., Pawluczyk, S. (1993). A double blind crossover pilot study of *l*-deprenyl (selegiline) combined with cholinesterase inhibitor in Alzheimer's Disease. *American Journal of Psychiatry, 150*, 321–333.

Schneider, L. S., Pollock, V. E., et al. (1991). A pilot study of low-dose L-deprenyl in Alzheimer's disease. *Journal of Geriatric Psychiatry and Neurology, 4*, 143–148.

Schneider, L. S., & Tariot, P. N. (1994). Emerging drugs for Alzheimer's disease. *Medical Clinics of North America, 78*(4), 911–934.

Schwartz, A. S., & Kohlstaedt, E. V. (1986). Physostigmine in Alzheimer's disease: Relationship to dementia severity. *Life Sciences, 38*(11), 1021–1028.

Serby, M., Resnick, R., et al. (1986). Naltrexone and Alzheimer's disease. *Progress in Neuro-Psychopharmacology & Biological Psychiatry, 10*, 587–590.

Sevush, S., Guterman, A., & Villalon, A. V. (1991). Improved verbal learning after outpatient oral physostigmine therapy in patients with dementia of the Alzheimer type. *Journal of Clinical Psychiatry, 52*(7), 300–303.

Sigfried, K. R. (1993). Pharmacodynamic and early clinical trials with velnacrine. *ACTA Neurologica Scandinavica, 149*, 26–28.

Sinforiani, E., Iannuccelli, M., et al. (1990). Neuropsychological changes in demented patients treated with acetyl-L-carnitine. *International Journal of Clinical Pharmacology Research, 10*(1/2), 69–74.

Smith, C. M., Swase, M., et al. (1978). Choline therapy in Alzheimer's disease. *Lancet, 2*, 318.

Smith, D. E., Stromgren, E., et al. (1984). Lack of effect of tryptophan treatment in demented gerontopsychiatric patients. *ACTA Psychiatrica Scandinavica, 70*, 470–477.

Smith, R. C., Vroulis, G., et al. (1984). Comparison of therapeutic response to long-term treatment with lecithin versus piracetam plus lecithin in patients with Alzheimer's disease. *Psychopharmacology Bulletin, 20*(3), 542–545.

Soininen, H., Koskinen, T., et al. (1985). Treatment of Alzheimer's disease with a synthetic ACTH49 analog. *Neurology, 35*, 1348–1351.

Soncrant, T. T., Raffaele, K. C., et al. (1993). Memory improvement without toxicity during chronic, low dose intravenous arecoline in Alzheimer's disease. *Psychopharmacology, 112*, 421–427.

Soni, S. D., & Soni, S. S. (1975). Dihydrogenated alkaloids of ergotexine in non-hospitalised elderly patients. *Current Medical Research and Opinion*, 3(7), 464–468.

Sourander, L. B., Portin, R., et al. (1987). Senile dementia of the Alzheimer type treated with aniracetam: A new nootropic agent. *Psychopharmacology*, 91, 90–95.

Spagnoli, A., Lucca, U., et al. (1991). Long-term acetyl-L-carnitine treatment in Alzheimer's disease. *Neurology*, 41, 1726–1732.

Steiger, W. A., Mendelson, M., et al. (1985). Effects of naloxone in treatment of senile dementia. *Journal of the American Geriatric Society*, 33, 155.

Stern, Y., Sano, M., & Mayeux, R. (1987). Effects of oral physostigmine in Alzheimer's disease. *Annals of Neurology*, 22, 306–310.

———. (1988). Long term administration of oral physostigmine in Alzheimer's disease. *Neurology*, 38, 1837–1841.

Sullivan, E. V., Shedlack, K. J., et al. (1982). Physostigmine and lecithin in Alzheimer's disease. In S. Corkin et al., *Alzheimer's disease: A report of progress in research*, Vol. 19. New York: Raven Press.

Summers, W. K., Majovski, L. V., et al. (1986). Oral tetrahydroaminoacridine in long-term treatment of senile dementia, Alzheimer type. *New England Journal of Medicine*, 315(20), 1241–1245.

Summers, W. K., & Viesselman, J. O. (1981). Use of THA in treatment of Alzheimer-like dementia: pilot study in 12 patients. *Biological Psychiatry*, 16(2), 145–153.

Tang, M. X., Jacobs, D., Stern, Y., et al. (1996). Effect of estrogen during menopause on risk and age at onset of Alzheimer's Disease. *Lancet*, 348(9025), 429–432.

Tariot, P. N., Cohen, R. M., et al. (1987). L-Deprenyl in Alzheimer's disease: Preliminary evidence for behavioral change with monoamine oxidase B inhibitors. *Archives of General Psychiatry*, 44, 427–433.

———. (1988). Multiple-dose arecoline infusions in Alzheimer's disease. *Archives of General Psychiatry*, 45, 901–905.

Tariot, P. N., Sunderland, T., et al. (1986). Naloxone and Alzheimer's disease: Cognitive and behavioral effects of a range of doses. *Archives of General Psychiatry*, 43, 727–732.

———. (1987). Cognitive effects of L-deprenyl in Alzheimer's disease. *Psychopharmacology*, 91, 489–495.

Tennant, F. S. (1987). Preliminary observations on naltrexone for the treatment of Alzheimer's type dementia. *Journal of the American Geriatric Society*, 35(4), 369–370.

Thal, L. (1994). Future directions for research in Alzheimer's Disease. *Neurobiology of Aging*, 15(Suppl 2), S71–72.

Thal, L. J., Fuld, P. A., et al. (1983). Oral physostigmine and lecithin improve memory in Alzheimer's disease. *Annals of Neurology*, 13, 491–496.

Thal, L. J., Masur, D. M., et al. (1986). Acute and chronic effects of oral physostigmine and lecithin in Alzheimer's disease. *Progress in Neuro-Psychopharmacology & Biological Psychiatry*, 10, 627–636.

———. (1989). Chronic oral physostigmine without lecithin improves memory in Alzheimer's disease. *Journal of the American Geriatric Society*, 37, 42–48.

Thal, L. J., Rosen, W., et al. (1981). Choline chloride fails to improve cognition in Alzheimer's disease. *Neurobiology of Aging*, 2, 205–208.

Thal, L. J., Salmon, D. P., et al. (1989). The safety and lack of efficacy of vinpocetine in Alzheimer's disease. *Journal of the American Geriatric Society*, 37, 515–520.

Thibault, A. (1974). A double-blind evaluation of "Hydergine" and placebo in the treatment of patients with organic brain syndrome and cerebral arteriosclerosis in a nursing home. *Current Medical Research and Opinion*, 2(8), 482–487.

Thienhaus, O. J., Wheeler, B. G., et al. (1987). A controlled double-blind study of high-dose dihydroergotexine mesylate (Hydergine) in mild dementia. *Journal of the American Geriatric Society*, 35, 219–223.

Thompson, T. L., Filly, C. M., et al. (1990). Lack of efficacy of Hydergine in patients with Alzheimer's disease. *New England Journal of Medicine*, 323(7), 445–448.

Tinklenberg, J. R., Pfefferbaum, A., & Berger, P. A. (1981). 1-Desamino-D-arginine vasopressin (DDAVP) in cognitively impaired patients. *Psychopharmacology Bulletin*, 17(3), 206–207.

Tinklenberg, J. R., Pigache, R., et al. (1982). Desglycinamide-9-arginine-8-vasopressin (DGAVP, Organon 5667) in cognitively impaired patients. *Psychopharmacology Bulletin*, 18(4), 202–204.

Tollefson, G. D. (1990). Short-term effects of the calcium channel blocker nimodepine (Bay-e-9736) in the management of primary degenerative dementia. *Biological Psychiatry*, 27, 1133–1142.

Triboletti, F., & Ferri, H. (1969). Hydergine for treatment of symptoms of cerebrovascular insufficiency. *Current Therapeutic Research*, 11(10), 609–620.

Urakami, K., Shimomura, T., et al. (1993). Clinical effect of WEB 1881 (nebracetam fumarate) on patients with dementia of the Alzheimer type and study of its clinical pharmacology. *Clinical Neuropharmacology*, 16(4), 347–358.

van Loveren-Huyben, C. M. S., Engelaar, H. F. J. W., et al. (1984). Double-blind clinical and psychologic study of ergoloid mesylates (Hydergine) in subjects with senile mental deterioration. *Journal of the American Geriatric Society*, 32(8), 584–588.

Villardita, C., Parini, J., et al. (1987). Clinical and neuropsychological study with oxiracetam versus placebo in patients with mild to moderate dementia. *Journal of Neural Transmission*, 24(Suppl.), 293–298.

Vroulis, G. A., Smith, R. C., et al. (1981). The effects of lecithin on memory in patients with senile dementia of the Alzheimer's type. *Psychopharmacology Bulletin, 17*(1), 127–129.

Weingartner, H., Kaye, W., et al. (1981). Vasopressin treatment of cognitive dysfunction in progressive dementia. *Life Sciences, 29*(26), 2721–2726.

Weinstein, H. C., Teunisse, S., & van Gool, W. A. (1991). Tetrahydroaminoacridine and lecithin in the treatment of Alzheimer's disease. *Journal of Neurology, 238*, 34–38.

Weintraub, S., Mesulam, M. M., et al. Lecithin in the treatment of Alzheimer's disease. (1983). *Archives of Neurology, 40*, 527–528.

Weis, B. L. (1987). Failure of nalmefene and estrogen to improve memory in Alzheimer's disease. *American Journal of Psychiatry, 144*(3), 386–387.

Wettstein, A. (1983). No effect from double-blind trial of physostigmine and lecithin in Alzheimer's disease. *Annals of Neurology, 13*, 210–212.

Wettstein, A., & Spiegel, R. (1984). Clinical trials with the cholinergic drug RS 86 in Alzheimer's disease (AD) and senile dementia of the Alzheimer type (SDAT). *Psychopharmacology, 84*, 572–573.

Wilcock, G. K., Surmon, D. J., et al. (1993). An evaluation of the efficacy and safety of tetrahydroaminoacridine (THA) without lecithin in the treatment of Alzheimer's disease. *Age and Aging, 22*, 316–324.

Wilson, A. L., Langley, L. K., et al. Nicotine patches in Alzheimer's disease: Pilot study on learning, memory and safety. (1995). *Pharmacology, Biochemistry and Behavior, 51*(2/3), 509–514.

Wolters, E. C., Riekkinen, P., et al. (1990). DGAVP (Org 5667) in early Alzheimer's disease patients: An international double-blind, placebo-controlled multicenter trial. *Neurology, 40*, 1099–1101.

6

Psychopharmacological Treatments of Substance Use Disorders

Charles P. O'Brien
James R. McKay

The treatment of substance abuse with pharmacologic agents is well established, although most experts agree that to be successful medication interventions must be combined with psychosocial therapies. In the treatment of nicotine addiction, controlled trials have established the benefits of nicotine gum and the nicotine patch in assisting with smoking cessation. Preliminary evidence suggests that antidepressants may also be effective. No medications have yet proven useful in controlled trials of cocaine addiction, although biological models suggest that psychopharmacological interventions should continue to be studied. In the treatment of alcoholism, disulfiram has proven to have limited usefulness. Naltrexone, in contrast, is an established therapy based on controlled trials and Food and Drug Administration (FDA) approval for the treatment of alcohol abuse. The first step in opiate abuse treatment is generally detoxification, followed by maintenance therapy. Methadone treatment has proven to be an effective maintenance option, particularly when combined with therapy and counseling. There are also alternatives to methadone among the opiate agonist therapies that have proven successful in controlled trials. Naltrexone is also approved by the FDA for the maintenance treatment of opiate addiction, but there are a number of factors that have limited its impact.

Substance use disorders affect virtually every sector of society. As a group, they are among the most common of all mental disorders. Household surveys have found a lifetime prevalence rate of 15% to 18% and a 6-month prevalence rate of 6% to 7% (Myers et al., 1984; Robins et al., 1984) These rates do not include nicotine addiction, the most devastating and difficult to treat of all the addictive disorders. Many individuals have multiple addictions; for example, alcoholics are frequently addicted to both cocaine and nicotine. There is also a good deal of overlap with such other mental disorders as anxiety and affective disorders. While there are common properties among the disorders produced by the major drugs of abuse, there are also important differences, particularly in treatment approaches. Thus, a chapter on treatment of substance

use disorders needs to consist of four distinct reviews focusing on the major drugs or drug categories: nicotine, alcohol, stimulants (cocaine), and opioids (heroin). Other drugs such as cannabinoids, hallucinogens, and minor tranquilizers may also be abused, but they account for a small proportion of patients needing treatment, and there are no effective medications currently available.

The features that define substance use disorders include compulsive use of the substance in spite of interference with normal activities and adverse effects on health. Terminology in this area is confusing because the *Diagnostic and Statistical Manual of Mental Disorders* (4th ed.) (*DSM-IV*; American Psychiatric Association [APA], 1994) describes two kinds of *dependence*. The diagnosis of dependence is the overall label for the syndrome produced by compulsive drug use; it may or may not include "physiological dependence." There is no justification for distinguishing physiological from "not physiological" because in the absence of the signs of classic drug withdrawal (tremors, vomiting, etc.), we now recognize major changes in the brain that may be evident only in the patient's behavior. Tolerance and physiological dependence were emphasized in previous definitions of addiction, but modern research has shown that these are simply normal adaptive reactions to the use of many substances, including ordinary medications such as those used in the treatment of hypertension. Tolerance is simply a reduced effect with repeated use of a drug, and physiological dependence refers to a state demonstrated by the appearance of physiological rebound symptoms when a drug to which the body had become adapted is suddenly withdrawn. While tolerance and physiological dependence are often present and will influence the course of treatment, these are not essential features of addiction (dependence in the diagnostic sense).

SUCCESS OF TREATMENT

In this chapter, we define *successful treatment* as significant improvement in the ability to function according to one's societal role. Total abstinence from the addicting substance is the accepted goal of treatment, but this is not often achieved. Significant reduction in substance use, such that function in society is improved, can be measured as a partial treatment success. In the case of opiate addiction, transfer to a stable maintenance medication, albeit similar in some ways to heroin, is considered successful treatment provided the person is able to refrain from socially and personally harmful behavior. This definition of success is commonly utilized for other chronic disorders such as arthritis or diabetes. This definition of success is, therefore, a pragmatic and medically acceptable definition based on functional capacity.

DETOXIFICATION

Detoxification is simply the removal of a drug from the body. This usually occurs because of metabolism by the liver and excretion via the kidneys. If the intake of the drug is gradually lowered, detoxification can be accomplished with little risk or discomfort as the body adapts to the absence of the drug. Detoxification is often confused with treatment. In reality, detoxification is, at best, the first step in treatment. Detoxification from sedatives such as alcohol can be dangerous because of medical complications during withdrawal, but these are readily treated in any medical facility. Treatment of the addiction involves a process of rehabilitation to reduce the probabilities of relapse and lengthen the period of time that the person is no longer using the drug of abuse. There is no evidence that rapid detoxification under general anesthesia is any more effective in the long term than less heroic and expensive means. Although some interesting research has been done on novel ways to achieve detoxification, for the purposes of this chapter we emphasize long-term treatment.

PSYCHOACTIVE AGENTS IN THE TREATMENT OF ADDICTION

The purpose of this chapter is to review psychopharmacological treatment of substance use disorders. One might reasonably ask whether medications are ever justified in the treatment of a disorder that involves excessive use of drugs. While there is controversy about this on philosophical grounds, empirical studies clearly show the benefits of medications when they are indicated. In addition to treatment of the addictive disorder itself, psychoactive medications are often indicated for accompanying psychiatric disorders. One school of thought that had many proponents in the past was that addicts were all more or less alike and all had to be treated by "getting at the underlying problem" and insisting on strict freedom from all chemicals. In that earlier era, nicotine and caffeine were not usually thought of as chemicals, but all psychoactive medications prescribed by physicians were avoided. Subsequent data, however, have demonstrated that all addicts are not alike. Even within a single drug category such as alcohol, there are alcoholics with different needs requiring different kinds of treatment. The concept of patient-treatment matching has become popular despite a relative paucity of replicated, empirical findings.

NICOTINE DEPENDENCE

Cessation of smoking may be very difficult even for smokers who strongly desire to quit; subsequent resumption of smoking, despite long periods of abstinence, is common. Those who begin smoking prior to age 21 are less likely to succeed in smoking cessation programs. Most smokers are nicotine dependent and experience a variable withdrawal syndrome when regular administration of nicotine is stopped. The nicotine withdrawal syndrome consists of irritability, impatience, hostility, anxiety, dysphoric or depressed mood, difficulty concentrating, restlessness, decreased heart rate, and increased appetite or weight gain.

Nicotine administration, whether given intravenously, by absorption though the mucosal membranes of the mouth (chewing gum), or by absorption through the skin (patch), can block these withdrawal symptoms. However, the peak nicotine levels associated with the psychoactive effects of smoking are not achieved by chewing gum or by patch administration. The widespread availability of the nicotine patch and chewing gum as over-the-counter medications has enabled many smokers to give up tobacco as a source of nicotine and thus avoid the serious health risks of tobacco smoke. Most smokers can then gradually reduce their nicotine dependence over several days to several weeks. Craving for the psychoactive effects continues, however, and relapses to smoking over the ensuing months are common. Table 6.1 summarizes some significant studies and reviews showing stable, confirmed abstinence rates at 6 and 12 months.

The preponderance of controlled studies shows that, in addicted smokers who are motivated to quit and remain abstinent, the use of the nicotine patch or chewing gum significantly increases the abstinence rate. Current research involves efforts to enhance the success rate of these nicotine delivery systems using behavior therapy. Another approach that shows promising results involves combining the nicotine patch with the nicotine antagonist, mecamylamine (Rose et al., 1994). Two other medications have been tested in clinical trials, but the results so far are inconclusive. These are clonidine, an antihypertensive medication that reduces central noradrenergic activity by stimulation of alpha$_2$ adrenergic autoreceptors, and naltrexone, an opiate receptor antagonist discussed below as a treatment for alcoholism and for opiate dependence.

The association of smoking and depression has prompted the use of antidepressant medication in conjunction with nicotine replacement in programs for treatment of smoking addiction. Fluoxetine and other antidepressants are often recommended for depressed smokers and for those attempting to quit whose symptoms meet diagnostic criteria for depression. A recent placebo-controlled study (Ferry et al., 1994) of bupropion in nondepressed smokers showed that this antidepressant significantly improved abstinence rates. Additional studies of antidepressants are in progress.

ALCOHOL DEPENDENCE (ALCOHOLISM)

Medications that have been evaluated as treatments for alcoholism include antidipsotropic agents, serotonergic antidepressants and anxiolytic agents, and agents that purportedly block the reinforcing effects of alcohol at the neurotransmitter level (O'Brien, Eckardt, & Linnoila, 1995). Studies of these agents are described in Table 6.2.

Antidipsotropic Medications

Antidipsotropic medications are agents that produce an unpleasant reaction when alcohol is consumed, thereby acting as a deterrent to drinking (Fuller, 1995). The studies presented in Table 6.2 indicate that, overall, disulfiram provided orally or through implants is not more effective than a placebo in reducing drinking. However, there is evidence that disulfiram may reduce further drinking in older patients who have relapsed but have good motivation and at least moderate social stability. Disulfiram may also be more effective in preventing relapse when it is used in treatment interventions that include contracts that specify disulfiram ingestion will be monitored by a significant other (Azrin, Sisson, Meyers, & Godley, 1982; O'Farrell, Cutter, & Floyd, 1985). Since poor compliance is a major obstacle to the effectiveness of disulfiram treatment, this sort of behavioral contracting may be an important component of treatment with this agent. However, the side effects of disulfiram and potential danger of disulfiram-ethanol reactions contraindicate the use of disulfiram in patients with a wide array of medical and psychiatric conditions and in pregnant women (Fuller, 1995; Schuckit, 1996).

Serotonergic Agents

Serotonin appears to play an important neurochemical role in the modulation of mood and impulse control and may therefore influence the development and maintenance of alcohol use disorders (Kranzler & Anton, 1994). Because studies have suggested that

TABLE 6.1 Treatment of Nicotine Use Disorder: Nicotine Replacement

Authors	Study Class	N	Treatment Length	Follow-Up Length	Results: Double-Blind, Placebo-Controlled Trials	Comments
Fiore, Smith, Jorenby, & Baker (1994)	4	5,098 17 studies	4 weeks or longer	6 months	Abstinence Rates End of Treatment: 6 months Nicotine patch 27% 22% Placebo 13% 9%	Excellent review; counseling added modestly to nicotine patch results.
Imperial Cancer Fund General Practice Research Group (1993)	1	1,686	12 weeks	—	Cessation rates Nicotine patch 19.4% Placebo patch 11.7%	No additional effect of detailed written material.
Fiore, Kenford, et al., (1994)	1	Study 1 = 88 Study 2 = 112	8 weeks 6 weeks	6 months	Post-Treatment Nicotine Placebo 1.22-mg patch, 8 weeks 59% 40% 2.22-mg patch, 4 weeks 37% 20% 11-mg patch, 2 weeks 6-months Follow-Up Study 1 34% 21% Study 2 18% 7%	Higher dose patch for 8 weeks shows somewhat better results.
Richmond, Harris, & de Alameida Neta (1994)	1	313	5 weeks	6 months	Abstinence Rates 3 Months 6 Months Nicotine patch 48% 33% Placebo patch 21% 14%	

Nicotine Patch Plus Nicotine Gum

| Kornitzer, Boutsen, Dramaix, Thijs, & Gustausson (1995) | 1 | 374 | 12 weeks | 12 months | 1. Nicotine patch + nicotine gum
2. Nicotine patch + placebo gum
3. Placebo patch + nicotine gum | This study suggests that the flexibility of nicotine gum adds significantly to the results of the patch alone. |

Abstinence Rates

	12 Weeks	24 Weeks	52 Weeks
1.	34.2%	27.5%	18.1%
2.	22.7	15.5	12.7
3.	17.3	14.7	13.3

Nicotine Patch Plus Mecamylamine

| Rose et al. (1994) | 1 | 48 | 6–8 weeks | 12 months | Mecamylamine 2.5–5 mg, twice daily + nicotine patch compared with placebo + nicotine patch | The addition of the nicotine antagonist improves outcome, but the nicotine alone results are lower than those seen in most studies. |

Abstinence Rates

	7 Weeks	6 Months	12 Months
Mecamylamine & nicotine	58%	37.5%	37.5%
Placebo & nicotine	29%	12.5%	4.2%

131

TABLE 6.2 Medications for Alcohol Dependence

Authors	Study Class	N	Treatment Length	Follow-Up Length	Results	Comments
Antidipsotropic medications						
Oral disulfiram						
Baekland, Lundwall, Kissen, & Shanahan (1971)	2	232	26 weeks	—	Patients who had a better response to disulfiram were older, had longer histories of heavy drinking, were less likely to be depressed, and had higher motivation and AA contact.	Subjects were participants in an outpatient clinic.
Gerrein, Rosenberg, & Manohar (1973)	2	49	8 weeks	—	Better attendance and abstinence rates in supervised disulfiram group, compared with nonsupervised and no disulfiram groups.	Statistical significance of abstinence not provided.
Fuller & Roth (1979)	1	128	12 month	—	Continuous abstinence rates higher in disulfiram group than placebo (23% vs. 12%) group, but not statistically significant.	Outcomes similar for 1 mg and 250 mg disulfiram conditions.
Fuller et al. (1986)	1	605	12 months	—	No differences between disulfiram and placebo in total abstinence, time to first drink, psychosocial functioning.	Disulfiram was effective for patients who drank and completed all assessments.
Chick et al. (1992)	2	126	26 weeks	—	Supervised disulfiram (200 mg/day) produced better outcomes on most drinking measures than placebo.	Patients in control condition were told they were receiving placebo.
Implanted disulfiram						
Johnsen et al. (1987)	2	21	—	20 weeks	No differences between disulfiram placebo in self-reported drinking or liver function measures.	Wound complications in 30% of disulfiram implant group.
Johnsen & Morland (1991)	1	76	—	300 days	Disulfiram implants (1 g) did not produce better drinking outcomes than placebo implants, although improvements were observed in both conditions.	Subjects in both conditions were told they were receiving disulfiram.

Serotonergic agents
SSRIs

Study		N	Duration		Results	Comments
Naranjo et al. (1987)	1	39	12 weeks	—	Citalopram (40 mg/day) produced better drinking outcomes than 20 mg/day or placebo.	Subjects were non-treatment-seeking male heavy drinkers.
Naranjo et al. (1989)	1	29	7 weeks	—	Viqualine (200 mg/day) produced better drinking outcomes than placebo. 100 mg/day was ineffective.	Subjects were non-treatment-seeking male heavy drinkers.
Gorelick & Paredes (1992)	1	20	4 weeks	—	Small advantage to fluoxetine (80 mg/day) over placebo in first week, but not in Weeks 2–4.	Study conducted on an inpatient research ward where alcohol was available.
Naranjo, Kadler, Sanhueza, Woodley-Remus, & Sellers (1990)	1	29	4 weeks	—	Fluoxetine (60 mg/day) reduced number of drinks consumed, but not days abstinent. 40 mg/day was ineffective.	Subjects were non-treatment-seeking male heavy drinkers.
Naranjo, Poulos, Bremner, & Lanctot (1992)	1	16	4 weeks	—	Citalopram (40 mg/day) increased abstinent days and decreased number of drinks consumed compared with placebo.	Alcohol-dependent subjects.
Kranzler et al. (1995)	1	101	12 weeks	—	Fluoxetine (60 mg/day) was no better than placebo in reducing alcohol consumption.	Subjects were alcohol-dependent outpatients also receiving relapse prevention.
Buspirone						
Bruno (1989)	2	50	8 weeks	—	Buspirone (20 mg/day) produced better retention than placebo. Comparisons of drinking outcomes not done due to high dropout rate in placebo condition.	Subjects were outpatients with mild-to-moderate alcohol abuse.
Tollefson, Montague-Clouse, & Tollefson (1992)	1	51	24 weeks	—	Buspirone (30 or 60 mg/day) produced better drinking outcomes than the placebo on a subjective, global measure.	Standardized measures of drinking outcomes not included. Subjects were abstinent alcoholics with comorbid anxiety disorder.
Malcolm et al. (1992)	1	67	26 weeks	—	Buspirone (45–60 mg/day) did not produce better outcomes than the placebo on any drinking measures.	Subjects were anxious alcohol-dependent male veterans.

(continued)

133

TABLE 6.2 (continued)

Authors	Study Class	N	Treatment Length	Follow-Up Length	Results	Comments
Kranzler et al. (1994)	1	61	12 weeks	—	Buspirone (up to 52 mg/day) produced better drinking outcomes than the placebo.	Subjects were alcohol-dependent with comorbid anxiety disorder who were in outpatient treatment.
Acamprosate						
Lhuintre et al. (1985)	1	85	90 days	—	Acamprosate produced lower rate of relapse than placebo.	
Lhuintre et al. (1990)	1	365	90 days	—	Acamprosate condition had lower liver enzyme values during follow-up than placebo.	
Paille et al. (1995)	1	538	12 months	6 months	Drinking outcomes consistently best in high-dose acamprosate (2 g/day), followed by low dose (1.3 g/day) and placebo.	Subjects also received outpatient, supportive therapy as required.
Whitworth et al. (1996)	1	455	12 months	—	Complete abstinence rates and days of abstinence favored acamprosate over placebo.	
Sass, Soyka, Mann, & Zieglgansberger (1996)	1	272	48 weeks	48 weeks	Drinking outcomes consistently favored acamprosate over placebo. Effect of acamprosate persisted during the post-treatment follow-up period.	Subjects were also offered outpatient therapy with a behavioral orientation during the study period.

Opioid Antagonists
Naltrexone

Study		Duration		Results	Comments
Volpicelli et al. (1992)	1	12 weeks	—	Less craving, fewer days drinking, lower relapse rate in naltrexone (50 mg/day) group, compared with placebo. Subjects who drank at all were much less likely to progress to full relapse if they received naltrexone.	Subjects were male veterans in an intensive day hospital rehabilitation program.
O'Malley et al. (1992)	1	12 weeks	(See next study)	Fewer days drinking, longer time to first relapse in naltrexone (50 mg/day) group compared with placebo.	Subjects also received coping skills or supportive therapy.
O'Malley et al. (1996)	1	—	26 weeks	Naltrexone led to higher abstinence rates in Month 1 (but not 2–6), lower relapse rate over all 6 months, as compared with placebo.	Among subjects who drank at all, best outcomes were in naltrexone/coping skills group.
Volpicelli et al. (in press)	1	12 weeks	—	Rates of relapse and days drinking were not significantly different in naltrexone (50 mg/day) and placebo groups. However, liver enzyme results were better in naltrexone group, and all results favored naltrexone in more compliant patients.	Subjects also received outpatient counseling; 2 times/week in first month, 1 time/week in Months 2 and 3.
Nalmefene					
Mason et al. (1994)	1	12 weeks	—	Nalmefene (40 mg) led to lower rates of relapse and more abstinent days than nalmefene (10 mg) or placebo. Both nalmefene conditions led to reductions in drinks per drinking day.	Subjects were alcohol dependent with no other substance dependence or major psychiatric disorders. Psychosocial treatment was not provided.

individuals with alcohol use disorders may have low levels of serotonin (Gorelick, 1989; Kranzler & Anton, 1994; Roy, Virkkunen, & Linnoila, 1990), a number of serotonergic drugs have been evaluated as possible treatments for alcoholism. The agents that have received the greatest attention are selective serotonin reuptake inhibitors (SSRIs), such as fluoxetine, and buspirone, a serotonin 1A receptor partial agonist. Studies of SSRIs presented in Table 6.2 indicate that these agents may lead to short-term reductions in alcohol consumption in heavy drinkers. However, studies that have been done with alcoholics in psychosocial treatment programs have not generated positive findings (e.g., Gorelick & Paredes, 1992; Kranzler et al., 1995). On the other hand, it appears that buspirone may be an effective treatment for alcoholics who have comorbid anxiety disorders. Finally, several recent studies suggest that tricyclic antidepressants may reduce both depression and alcohol use in patients with major depression (Mason et al., 1996; McGrath et al., 1996).

Acamprosate

Calcium bisacetyl homotaurine (acamprosate) has shown initial promise in improving treatment retention and decreasing drinking in alcoholics following initial detoxification. All five studies of acamprosate presented in Table 6.2 have generated positive findings. Although the action of acamprosate is not entirely clear, it appears the drug functions as a GABA receptor agonist, and that it may also lower neuronal excitability by reducing the postsynaptic efficacy of excitatory amino acid (EAA) neurotransmitters.

Opioid Antagonists

Studies described in Table 6.2 have produced compelling evidence that naltrexone can reduce drinking in alcoholics and may be particularly effective in preventing full-blown relapses in alcoholics who have had a "slip" after achieving abstinence (O'Malley et al., 1992; Volpicelli, Alterman, Hayashida, & O'Brien, 1992). Another opiate antagonist, nalmefene, also led to better drinking outcomes than a placebo in a double-blind pilot study (Mason et al., 1994).

Other studies have generated additional information about the effects of naltrexone. First, it appears that the effectiveness of naltrexone may continue beyond the period in which the drug is taken. In a 6-month posttreatment follow-up of the sample from the O'Malley et al. (1992) study, patients who received naltrexone in the initial 12-week portion of the trial were less likely to have one or more heavy drinking days during follow-up (O'Malley, Jaffe, Chang, et al., 1996). However, the positive effects of naltrexone over placebo were significantly larger early in the follow-up than at the end. Second, it appears that naltrexone may be particularly effective for patients with high levels of alcohol craving at intake to treatment (O'Malley, 1995; Volpicelli et al., 1995a), those with poor learning ability (O'Malley, 1995), and those with a high degree of somatic symptoms (Volpicelli et al., 1995b). Third, the effectiveness of naltrexone, relative to the placebo, appears to be greater in more compliant patients (i.e., those who adhere to the treatment protocol and are compliant in taking medication) (Volpicelli et al., in press). Finally, initial studies of subjective response to alcohol following administration of naltrexone (King, Volpicelli, Frazer, & O'Brien, 1997; O'Malley, Jaffe, Rode, et al., 1996; Swift, Whelihan, Kuznetsov, Buongiorno, & Hsuing, 1994; Volpicelli et al., 1995b) indicate that naltrexone may reduce the positive reinforcing stimulant effects and augment the sedative and aversive effects of alcohol (Swift, 1995).

COCAINE DEPENDENCE

Most efforts to identify medications that would be effective in treating patients with cocaine use disorders have been directed toward finding agents that either correct alterations in neurochemical substrates brought on by chronic cocaine use or block the reinforcing effects of cocaine (Kleber, 1995). Although there have been a number of promising leads, no pharmacological agent has yet generated consistent evidence of effectiveness in reducing cocaine use. In this section, we will provide a brief overview of studies of the following medications: antidepressants, dopaminergic agents, and other agents that have been evaluated in at least several studies. Details of the studies are presented in Table 6.3.

Antidepressants

Cocaine abusers frequently report anhedonia following cessation of cocaine use, and dysphoria and/or depression may play a role in the onset and maintenance of cocaine use. These observations have raised the possibility that antidepressant medications may reduce cocaine use in cocaine-dependent patients. Studies of tricyclic antidepressants indicate that these agents do not improve retention but may lead to reduced cocaine use in some patients, particularly those with less severe cocaine abuse (Carroll et al., 1994a; Nunes et al., 1995). Initial studies of fluoxetine and gepirone found no evidence that these agents were more effective than a placebo in improving retention or reducing cocaine use.

Dopaminergic Agents

Several agents with dopamine agonist properties that appear to relatively quickly counteract alterations in the dopamine system caused by chronic use of cocaine have been evaluated as adjuncts to detoxification and aids in initial treatment (e.g., amantadine, bromocriptine, and methylphenidate). However, none of these agents has shown consistent evidence of effectiveness in reducing cocaine use. Another line of medications research has focused on identifying agents that block the dopamine-mediated reinforcing effects of cocaine. Unfortunately, most of these agents (e.g., neuroleptics) have serious side effects and are not likely to lead to high compliance on the part of cocaine abusers. However, there is preliminary evidence that flupenthixol, which has antidepressant effects at low doses and neuroleptic effects at high doses, may be effective in reducing cocaine use.

Other Agents

Buprenorphine, an opioid agonist/antagonist that has been shown in animal models to selectively reduce cocaine self-administration, has not been more effective than methadone in reducing cocaine use in patients who are dependent on both cocaine and opioids. Other studies of buprenorphine are in progress. Carbamazepine, an anticonvulsant agent, has been evaluated as a treatment for cocaine abuse because it reverses cocaine-induced kindling in an animal model and dopamine receptor supersensitivity that can result from long-term cocaine use (Kleber, 1995). Once again, double-blind studies have found no difference between carbamazepine and a placebo in treatment retention or cocaine use outcomes.

Summary and Future Directions

None of the studies summarized in this review has produced compelling evidence for the efficacy of medications in the treatment of cocaine dependence. However, a number of limitations in these studies have been noted by Kleber (1995) and others, including low statistical power, possible subtherapeutic doses of medications, and the failure to control for the amount and type of psychosocial services received. Studies with larger sample sizes, such as those by Carroll et al. (1994a) and Nunes et al. (1995), were able to identify patient by treatment-matching effects, which underscores the importance of having adequate statistical power to examine relationships between patient characteristics and differential response to a particular medication. Future research efforts should also continue to examine the joint impact of psychosocial and psychopharmacological interventions as there is evidence that psychosocial treatments can reduce cocaine use (Alterman et al., 1994; Carroll et al., 1994b; Higgins et al., 1993; McKay, Cacciola, McLellan, Alterman, & Wirtz, 1997).

Despite the apparent lack of efficacy of pharmacotherapy interventions for cocaine dependence, preclinical evidence has shown that there are persistent changes in brain reward systems after cessation of chronic cocaine use, which suggests that there are biological factors that continue after cessation of cocaine use and may increase the probability of relapse (Koob, 1992). Evidence of postcocaine conditioned responses has been demonstrated in human studies showing craving and autonomic nervous system arousal in response to cocaine related-cues (Childress, McLellan, Ehrman, & O'Brien, 1987; O'Brien et al., 1988). Recently, focal changes in limbic activity as measured by cerebral blood flow have been reported in abstinent former cocaine-dependent patients (Childress et al., 1995); this phenomenon has been used to screen new medications that might diminish this conditioned craving effect (Robbins, Ehrman, Childress, & O'Brien, 1992; Berger et al., 1996). It seems reasonable to hope that a medication will ultimately be found that can ameliorate these biological effects of cocaine use and augment the effects of psychosocial interventions.

OPIOID DEPENDENCE

While the history of opiate addiction in the United States goes back more than 100 years, most of the societal response has been legal rather than medical. Physicians are heavily restricted in their ability to deal

TABLE 6.3 Medications for Cocaine Dependence

Authors	Class	N	Treatment Length	Follow-Up Length	Results	Comments
Antidepressants						
Desipramine						
Gawin et al. (1989b)	1	72	6 weeks	—	Desipramine (2.5 mg/kg) produced better cocaine use outcomes and lower craving than lithium or a placebo.	Subjects were cocaine dependent and received weekly psychotherapy.
Levin & Lehman (1991)	4	200	12–168 days	—	Retention in treatment: desipramine no better than placebo. Reducing cocaine use during trial: desipramine better than placebo.	In meta-analysis, only 2 of 6 studies found an advantage to desipramine in reducing cocaine use.
Weddington et al. (1991)	2	54	12 weeks	—	Trend indicated desipramine (200 mg/day) was associated with higher early dropout rate than amantadine or a placebo. No group differences in cocaine use or craving.	Subjects in this single-blind study also received outpatient psychotherapy (2 times/week). Dosage of desipramine may have been subtherapeutic.
Arndt, Dorozynsky, Woody, McLellan, & O'Brien (1992)	1	59	12 weeks	26 weeks	Desipramine (250–300 mg/day) was associated with higher dropout rate and worse cocaine use outcomes at 3- and 6-month follow-up than the placebo. No group differences in cocaine use during the 12-week treatment phase.	Subjects were methadone-maintained male veterans who also met *DSM-III* criteria for cocaine abuse.
Kolar et al. (1992)	2	22	12 weeks	—	Desipramine (200 mg/day) produced better retention rates and higher abstinence rates at the end of the trial than amantadine or a placebo.	Subjects were methadone maintenance patients who also met *DMS-III-R* criteria for cocaine dependence.
Kosten, Morgan, Falcione, & Schottenfeld (1992)	1	94	12 weeks	—	Desipramine (150 mg/day) did not produce better retention or cocaine urine toxicology results than amantadine or a placebo, but was associated with greater reductions in money spent for cocaine in Weeks 2 and 4 than the placebo.	Subjects were methadone-maintenance patients who also met *DSM-III-R* criteria for cocaine dependence.

Study		N			Results	Comments
Carroll et al. (1994a)	1	139	12 weeks	(See next study)	Desipramine (300 mg/day) did not produce better retention than the placebo. Reductions in cocaine use at 6 weeks (but not 12 weeks) were greater for desipramine than the placebo. Patients with lower baseline severity of cocaine use also had better cocaine use outcomes on desipramine than on the placebo.	Subjects also received either relapse prevention or clinical management therapy in an individual session (1 time/wk).
Carroll et al. (1994b)	1	97	—	12 months	No differences in cocaine use between desipramine and placebo group during the 12-month follow-up from the above study.	Differences favoring relapse prevention over clinical management emerged in Months 6–12.
Rawson, Shoptaw, & Minsky (1994)	1	99	16 weeks	10 weeks	No differences between desipramine (200 mg/day) and a placebo on any outcome measures.	Subjects also received a 26-week outpatient treatment package.
Imipramine Nunes et al. (1995)	1	113	12 weeks	—	Imipramine (150–300 mg/day) produced greater reductions in craving, cocaine euphoria, and depression, and also a trend ($p < .09$) toward higher rates of 3 consecutive cocaine-free weeks than the placebo. Imipramine effect was greater among nasal users.	Subjects also received weekly individual counseling.
Fluoxetine Grabowski et al. (1995)	1	155	12 weeks	—	Retention was lowest in high-dose fluoxetine (40 mg/day) group, followed by the low-dose (20 mg) group, and placebo group. No group differences in cocaine use outcomes.	Subjects also received one hour of behaviorally oriented therapy per week and visited the clinic at least one other time per week.
	1	21	8 weeks	—	Fluoxetine (20 mg/day) produced better cocaine outcomes than the placebo in Weeks 3 and 4, but not in the other 6 weeks.	Subjects were methadone-maintenance patients who were also cocaine dependent.

(continued)

TABLE 6.3 (continued)

Authors	Class	N	Treatment Length	Follow-Up Length	Results	Comments
Gepirone						
Jenkins et al. (1992)	1	41	12 weeks	—	No differences were found between gepirone (16 mg/day) and placebo on any outcome measures.	Subjects all received one week of inpatient treatment at start of study, followed by outpatient therapy.
Dopamanergic agents: agonists						
Amantadine						
Tennant & Sagherian (1987)	1	14	10 days	—	Amantadine (100 mg/day) led to greater retention and lower withdrawal scores during detoxification than bromocriptine.	Subjects were cocaine dependent and participating in an outpatient detoxification program.
Gawin et al. (1989c)	2	10	1 day	—	Amantadine (300 mg) did not result in reduced craving compared with placebo.	Subjects were severe cocaine abusers in outpatient treatment.
Giannini, Folts, Feather, & Sullivan (1989)	1	30	30 days	—	Amantadine (100 mg q 6 hr) led to lower ratings of psychiatric symptoms than the placebo early in withdrawal.	No measures of cocaine use were included in the study.
Weddington et al. (1991)	2	54	12 weeks	—	Amantadine (400 mg/day) did not produce better outcomes (retention, cocaine use) than the placebo.	Subjects in this single-blind study also received outpatient psychotherapy (2 times/week).
Kolar et al. (1992)	2	22	12 weeks	—	Amantadine (200 mg/day) did not produce better outcomes (retention, cocaine use) than the placebo.	Described on p. 138.
Kosten et al. (1992)	1	94	12 weeks	—	Amantadine (300 mg/day) did not produce better retention or cocaine urine toxicology results than the placebo but was associated with greater reductions in money spent for cocaine in Weeks 2 and 4.	Described on p. 138.
Alterman et al. (1992)	1	42	10.5 days	2 weeks	Amantadine (200 mg/day) produced higher rates of cocaine-free urines at 2 and 4 weeks postbaseline	Subjects were cocaine-dependent male veterans in a day hospital program.

		N	Duration		Results	Subjects
Bromocriptine						
Moscovitz, Brookoff, & Nelson (1993)	2	29	2 weeks	—	Bromocriptine (3.75 mg/day) produced a higher rate of cocaine-negative urine screens than the placebo, but statistical analyses were not performed.	Subjects were male veterans who were frequent cocaine users and presented for minor medical complaints at a hospital.
Methylphenidate						
Gawin, Riordan, & Kleber (1985)	3	5	2–5 weeks	—	Methylphenidate (up to 100 mg/day) appeared to increase cocaine use.	Patients did not have attention deficit disorder.
Dopamanergic agents: antagonists						
Flupenthixol						
Gawin et al. (1989a)	3	10	Not specified	Up to 62 weeks	Flupenthixol decanoate (10 or 20 mg every 2 to 4 weeks) appeared to enhance retention and abstinence rates.	Subjects in this open trial were poor-prognosis crack smokers who were cocaine dependent.
Khalsa, Jatlow, & Gawin (1994)	1	63	6 weeks	—	Flupenthixol and desipramine were both superior to the placebo in retention, cocaine use, cocaine craving. No comparisons of the two active drugs were provided.	Patients in this preliminary report were crack cocaine users receiving minimal psychotherapy.
Other agents						
Buprenorphine						
Strain, Stitzer, Liebson, & Bigelow (1994b)	1	164	26 weeks	—	Buprenorphine (8 mg/day) and methadone did not differ on rates of cocaine-positive urines.	Patients were new admissions to an opioid treatment program.
Strain, Stitzer, Liebson, & Bigelow (1994a)	1	51	26 weeks	—	Buprenorphine (11 mg/day) and methadone did not differ on rates of cocaine-positive urines.	Patients were new admissions to an opioid treatment program who were using cocaine prior to admission.
Carbamazepine						
Cornish et al. (1995)	1	82	10 weeks	—	Carbamazepine (200 mg) and the placebo did not differ on retention, rates of cocaine-positive urines, or craving.	Patients were male cocaine-dependent, new admissions to a Veteran's Administration outpatient program.
Montoya, Levin, Fudala, & Gorelick (1995)	1	62	8 weeks	—	Carbmazepine (600 mg) and placebo did not differ on retention or rates of cocaine-positive urines.	Patients were cocaine dependent and also received individual counseling 2 times a week.

with opiate addiction as a medical problem. Most treatment consists of detoxification, that is, removal of the drug from the body by metabolism while withdrawal symptoms are being treated by another medication. Detoxification is simply a first step in a long-term relapse prevention program. Two medical approaches to aid in detoxification are available. One is the use of an opioid agonist in gradually decreasing doses over 5–10 days. This permits a smooth, comfortable detoxification for most patients. A long-acting medication such as methadone is preferable because it permits a smooth transition to the drug-free state. A second option is the use of a drug, such as clonidine or lofexidine, that blocks certain aspects of the withdrawal syndrome.

Methadone

While some opioid addicts are able to detoxify and remain drug free, the majority relapse, even after intensive psychotherapy. More important, many heroin addicts will not even consider a drug-free treatment approach or entry into a therapeutic community. Maintenance treatment using methadone was developed in the 1960s and consists of transferring the patient from heroin, a short-acting opiate that must be taken by injection two to four times daily, to methadone, a long-acting opioid that need be taken only once daily by mouth. The changes produced by transfer to a long-acting opioid are significant. The treatment requires relatively little effort on the part of the patient, giving it wide appeal. This appeal is important from a public health perspective as infections such as HIV and resistant tuberculosis threaten the general public, as well as substance abusers.

Initially, most heroin addicts have poor motivation for changing their lives. When first introduced to methadone treatment, they still want to get "high" and mix other drugs with prescribed medication. With appropriate counseling in a structured program, the patient can make the transition from thinking as a street addict to behaving as a productive citizen. Methadone substitutes for heroin, reduces drug-seeking behavior, and blocks opiate withdrawal symptoms. It stabilizes physiological systems because of its long duration of action, in contrast to the short action of heroin, which produces ups and downs (Kreek, 1992). Typically, patients continue to use some heroin during the first few weeks or months on methadone. Methadone does not block the effects of heroin, but it produces cross-tolerance to heroin and all similar drugs. Thus, the effects of usual doses of heroin are diminished, and over time the typical patient decreases heroin use further and then stops. The evidence shows that the improvement in all areas of function shown by methadone patients is produced by a combination of medication (methadone) and psychosocial intervention. When the methadone dose is held constant at a level adequate for most patients (60 mg), there is an orderly relationship between the "dose" of psychotherapy and the outcome of treatment (McLellan, Arndt, Metzger, Woody, & O'Brien, 1993). Some improvement is seen with methadone alone, but with increments in psychosocial interventions, there is significantly greater improvement as measured by illicit drug use, psychiatric symptoms, family problems, and employment. Other studies have demonstrated that patients on methadone become healthier and have lower rates of exposure to infections, including HIV (Metzger et al., 1993).

The physiological stability produced by methadone is demonstrated in several ways. Patients report fewer sleep problems and less depression. Males report improved sexual performance. While on heroin, they were in and out of withdrawal; when they found time for sex, they frequently experienced premature ejaculations. On methadone, while sexual arousal and orgasm were reported to be slowed, the patients reported that sex was more satisfying (Mintz, O'Brien, & Goldschmidt, 1974). Women report irregular menses while on heroin, but on methadone there is at first a suppression of menstruation and then, after about 6–12 months, a resumption of regular cycling. A similar stabilization is noted in the hypothalamic-pituitary-adrenal axis. Women can conceive while on methadone, and the babies are born physically dependent on the opioid. While on methadone, expectant mothers can receive good prenatal care, and the withdrawal syndrome in newborns is readily treated. While it would be preferable to have women drug free during pregnancy, babies born to methadone-treated mothers are significantly healthier than babies born of mothers using street heroin.

Length of Methadone Treatment

Brief maintenance (extended detoxification) as defined by federal methadone regulations is up to 180 days of methadone treatment. This is enough time to give some patients a stable period during which they can organize their lives and become engaged in psychotherapy. Six months is too short for most patients, however, and the duration of methadone treatment should be determined by the patient's needs and not by an arbitrary time limit. Some patients require several years of stable methadone maintenance before they can be gradually detoxified by decreasing the dose of methadone. Many others require indefinite maintenance on this medication. For these patients, methadone should be considered as a hormone replacement therapy analogous to thyroxine for patients with hypothyroidism or prednisone for patients with Addison's disease.

The endogenous opioid system is so complicated that a simple diagnostic test has not yet been devised that could demonstrate a primary or secondary deficiency state, if one existed. Some data measuring spinal fluid or plasma endogenous opioids from addicts do exist, however, but they are limited to individual peptides and do not give a clear picture of the overall system (O'Brien, 1993). There are also data from nonaddict populations showing that the system can be congenitally hyperactive, resulting in babies born with stupor and respiratory depression that is reversed by opiate antagonists such as naloxone or naltrexone (Myer, Morris, Brase, Dewey, & Zimmerman, 1990). It is theoretically possible, therefore, that other individuals could be born with congenitally *low* endogenous opioids, possibly giving them a lower threshold for pain and making them more vulnerable to becoming opioid addicts. It is also possible, but not clearly demonstrated, that years of taking exogenous opiates such as heroin could suppress the production of endogenous opioids and create a need for lifetime methadone as "hormone replacement." This would explain why many former opioid addicts are unable to remain free of exogenous opioids despite apparently good motivation.

A hypothetical derangement of the endogenous opioid system would also be consistent with data demonstrating a protracted opioid withdrawal syndrome (Martin & Jasinski, 1969). While the acute opioid withdrawal syndrome diminishes in a matter of 5–10 days whether or not treatment is received, a more subtle withdrawal syndrome lasting 6 months has been described under controlled inpatient conditions. Symptoms consist of sleep disturbance and dysphoria with accompanying disturbances in appetite, blood pressure, and cortisol rhythms. These symptoms would be expected to increase the probability of heroin use if the patient were in an environment in which opiates were available.

Methadone Controversies

Despite overwhelming evidence demonstrating efficacy (Table 6.4), methadone remains a controversial treatment (Institute of Medicine Report, 1990). Methadone produces clear functional improvement, but not a cure. The patient remains physically dependent on a synthetic replacement medication and is capable of functioning normally. The general public expects methadone patients to be stuporous, but this is not the case for a properly regulated methadone patient. Tolerance develops to the sedating effects of opioids, and patients receiving methadone are quite alert (Zacny, 1995) and capable of operating motor vehicles and performing complex tasks such as teaching school or practicing law or medicine.

Approximately 120,000 patients in the United States at present are receiving methadone as treatment for heroin addiction. Good programs, as defined by having adequate counseling staff and using adequate doses of methadone, have success rates of 60–70% as defined by significant improvement in functional status. This is remarkable considering that the typical patient arrives with little motivation for change and numerous problems. Unfortunately, methadone programs are generally underfunded, and some programs do little more than dispense methadone. While this can be of some benefit, the full impact of methadone treatment requires a structured counseling/psychotherapy program. Eventually, frequent counseling sessions become unnecessary, and patients can be trusted to take methadone at home. Legal requirements permit only limited doses to be prescribed for use at home, even for patients who have demonstrated their trustworthiness. An exception is "medical maintenance" that requires only monthly visits, but this is available in only a few experimental programs (Novick, Pascarelli, & Joseph, 1988).

Recently, heroin in the United States has become cheaper, with historically high purity. Thus, the average street heroin addict is likely to have a higher level of physiological dependence. This has necessitated higher doses of methadone in order to prevent withdrawal and to produce sufficient cross-tolerance to counter the effects of very potent heroin. Although very few treatment outcome studies have been done under these new circumstances, there is anecdotal

TABLE 6.4 Medications for Heroin Dependence: Methadone

Authors	Study Class	N	Treatment Length	Follow-Up Length	Results	Comments
Dole et al. (1969)	2	32	12 months	12 months	18 of 20 nonmethadone heroin users were reincarcerated versus only 3 of 12 in methadone group. Use of heroin mainly limited to first 3 months on methadone.	Earliest methadone controlled trial randomized but not blinded.
Gunne & Gronbladh (1984)	2	34	24 months	5 years	At follow-up, 12 of 17 patients assigned to methadone were no longer using illegal drugs, while only 1 of 17 in control groups was doing well at follow-up.	Random assignment but not blinded.
Stimmel, Goldeberg, Rotkopf, & Cohen (1977)	3	335	Variable	6 years	At follow-up after detoxification from methadone, 83% of those who completed treatment were narcotic free. Including all patients, 35% were narcotic-free.	This study shows high abstinence rates for patients judged ready to detoxify from methadone.
Anglin, Speckart, Booth, & Ryan (1989)	3	99	—	2 years	Former patients followed after closing of methadone program; 54% returned to addiction, and incarceration rate was double that of comparison group.	This was not a typical outcome study, but it documented the social and economic loss when methadone treatment is cut off.
Newman & Whitehill (1978)	1	100	2.5 years	2.5 years	60% of maintenance patients remained in treatment for 2.5 years. Only 20% of detoxified patients remained in treatment for 60 days, and none for entire study.	Study was a controlled randomized trial, but drug-placebo differences were so great that patients all knew their assignment.

evidence that methadone treatment may be less effective, or at least more difficult, in the era of cheap and potent heroin.

Other Medications for Opioid Dependence

Levo-alpha-acetylmethadol (LAAM) (Table 6.5) is a long-acting opioid that was studied extensively in clinical trials prior to its approval by the Food and Drug Administration (FDA) in 1993. It is similar to methadone but its long half-life and even longer acting metabolites produce opiate effects for about 72 hours after a single daily ingestion. This makes LAAM very convenient because it requires dosing only three times per week and still provides physiological stability; this is in contrast to methadone, which must be taken daily.

Buprenorphine (Table 6.6) belongs to another class of medications called partial agonists. It is currently approved for the treatment of pain, and it has shown good efficacy as a maintenance drug in several clinical trials among heroin addicts. As a partial μ opiate agonist, buprenorphine activates opiate receptors, producing effects similar to heroin and methadone, but there is a "ceiling" such that higher doses produce no greater effect. In studies so far, overdose from buprenorphine has not been seen, and if heroin or other opioids are taken, their effects are attenuated or blocked by the presence of buprenorphine. This medication is expected to receive FDA approval, joining methadone and LAAM as a third option for maintenance in the treatment of heroin addicts. Based on experience from clinical trials, there are some heroin addicts who prefer methadone, others who prefer LAAM, and still others who feel that they are the most stable and alert on buprenorphine. As with other classes of medications, it is helpful for the clinician to have a selection of medications from which to choose.

Opioid Antagonist Treatment

The discovery of specific opiate receptor antagonists in the early 1970s gave rise to hopes for the "perfect" medication for the treatment of heroin addiction. Naltrexone (Table 6.7) seemed to be the answer because it specifically blocks μ opiate receptors and, to a lesser extent, k receptors (Raynor et al., 1994), but it has little or no direct or agonist effects of its own. Naltrexone and its short-acting analog naloxone have high

affinity for opiate receptors and will displace drugs like morphine or methadone, resulting in the sudden onset of withdrawal symptoms when given to people who are opioid dependent. If the heroin addict is first detoxified so that opiate receptors are gradually evacuated, naltrexone will bind to the receptors and prevent subsequent injections of heroin from having an effect. Numerous clinical trials showed that naltrexone was effective in blocking opiate receptors and was safe; thus, it was approved by the FDA in 1983. Unfortunately, naltrexone is a very underutilized medication in the treatment of heroin addiction. Unlike methadone, it has no positive psychoactive effects. Few street heroin addicts show any interest in this type of treatment, and few programs encourage patients to try it. Opioid antagonists are more complicated to prescribe than methadone, and most physicians have not been trained in their use. Opioid-dependent health care workers such as physicians, pharmacists, and nurses often do well on naltrexone because it enables them to return to work with no risk of relapse even though they work in areas with high drug availability. There is also evidence that naltrexone is helpful in preventing relapse in probationers who have a conditional release from prison after drug-related crimes (Brahen, Henderson, Copone, & Kordal, 1984; Cornish et al., 1997, in press).

Experience with naltrexone demonstrates that blocking opiate receptors does not impair normal function for most people. Studies in animals have implicated opiate receptors in a wide variety of functions, such as control of appetite, sexual behavior, and, of course, pain perception. Occasionally, normal volunteers given naltrexone report dysphoria or depression, but most former heroin addicts have few symptoms related to the antagonist. Some have remained on naltrexone for up to 10 years with no apparent change in appetite or pain perception and no impairment of ability to experience pleasure from sources such as sex or music.

CONCLUSIONS

The studies reviewed in this chapter indicate that, at this time, there are medications with at least some degree of efficacy in the treatment of nicotine, alcohol, and opiate use disorders. One the other hand, no medication has proved efficacious in the treatment of cocaine dependence. Long-term psychosocial inter-

TABLE 6.5 Medications for Heroin Dependence: Levo-Alpha-Acetylmethadol (LAAM)

Authors	Study Class	N	Treatment Length	Follow-Up Length	Results	Comments
Freedman & Czertko (1981)	2	48	4 months plus	—	Single blind to dose, not to medication; mean dose 26 mg methadone, after 16 weeks switches to LAAM, mean 24.1 mg. LAAM patients had significantly lower positive urines than methadone patients, longer retention, more satisfaction.	Results favorable to LAAM, but study was conducted in low-purity heroin era and may not be currently relevant.
Judson & Goldstein (1979)	3	179	5-week induction study	—	92 patients were slowly inducted to LAAM; 87 were inducted rapidly, with no significant difference in outcome.	Induction to LAAM is not difficult for most parts.
Herbert et al. (1995)	3	623	64 weeks	—	Labeling assessment study required by FDA; few side effects, results similar to earlier studies	Demonstrated usefulness of LAAM in the "real world."
Ling, Charuvastra, Kaim, & Klett (1976)	1	430	40 weeks	—	Random assignment among methadone 100 mg, methadone 50 mg, and LAAM 80 mg. LAAM and methadone 100 were superior in several respects to methadone 50 mg.	This is the pivotal efficacy study for LAAM.
Ling, Klett, & Gillis (1978)	3	636	40 weeks	—	Random assignment, open trial. No safety problems for either drug. No difference in patient acceptance or treatment outcome. Dropouts were higher for the LAAM group.	
Marcovici et al. (1981)	2	130	40 weeks	—	Patients were randomly assigned to LAAM or methadone. There were no significant differences in treatment retention or in drug-positive urines.	The study was not double blind, but did give a good, prospective comparison of the two medications.

TABLE 6.6 Medications for Heroin Dependence: Buprenorphine

Authors	Study Class	N	Treatment Length	Follow-Up Length	Results	Comments
Mello & Mendelson (1980)	1	10	14 days	—	This inpatient experiment showed that buprenorphine 8 mg daily suppressed heroin self-administration 69–98%.	Buprenorphine suppresses heroin use.
Bickel et al. (1988)	1	45	90 days	—	Detoxification, methadone versus buprenorphine; methadone was more effective in blocking opiate effects in lab, but use of street opiates was not different.	No clinical difference between methadone and buprenorphine.
Johnson et al. (1991)	1	162	6 months	—	Buprenorphine 8 mg was compared to methadone 20 mg and methadone 60 mg. Low dose methadone had lower retention rates than the other two groups. There was a trend for buprenorphine groups to have a higher percentage of opiate-free urines. There were no differences in urines positive for cocaine metabolites.	
Bickel & Amass (1995)	5	n/a	—	—	This is an excellent up-to-date review describing pros and cons of buprenorphine medication for opiate addiction.	
Ling et al. (1997)	1	736	16 weeks	—	Double-blind comparison of 1, 4, 8, 16 mg buprenorphine. 8 and 16 mg were significantly better than 1 mg.	8 to 16 mg appear to be optimal doses, but higher doses may be necessary in era of potent heroin.

TABLE 6.7 Medications for Heroin Dependence: Naltrexone

Authors	Study Class	N	Treatment Length	Follow-Up Length	Results	Comments
Gerra, Marcato, Caccavar, et al. (1995)	1	152	3 months	6 months	Double-blind, placebo-controlled, 3 month study of daily medication: clonidine only, clonidine and naltrexone, clonidine and naloxone; and placebos. Better results with a longer duration of naltrexone treatment.	Consistent with prior studies showing high dropout rate, but good results for patients who remain longer.
Shufman et al. (1994)	2	32		3 months	Fewer heroin-positive urine tests, more drug-free patients, more improvement in psychological parameters in naltrexone group.	Small sample size.
Azatian, Papiasvilli, & Joseph (1994)	6	68		7 weeks	Open study; only 3 of 44 inpatient detoxification subjects succeeded in entering maintenance phase. A total of 27 of 68 entered maintenance, and all discontinued by 50 days.	No control group; high early dropout rate.
Lerner, Sigal, Bacalul, et al. (1992)	1	31		2 months	Craving reduced in naltrexone group; reports of euphoria blocked when opiates used, but no evidence of reduced drug use as compared with a placebo.	
Greenstein, Arndt, McLellan, O'Brien, & Evans (1984)	3	327	6 months or longer	6 months	Few side effects, multiple treatment episodes, no evidence of increased nonopiate use, 1/3 of patients opiate free at 6 months follow-up.	

Study		N	Length	Follow-up	Results	Comments
Washton, Pottash, & Gold (1984)	3	114	6 months	12–18 months	All patients successfully detoxified and began naltrexone; 61% completed 6-month treatment; at 12–18-month follow-up, 64% still opiate free.	Shows excellent results with middle-class opiate addicts.
Ling & Wesson (1984)	3	60	6 months	Variable	Physicians and other health professionals. Average duration of naltrexone 6 months. All patients rated as much or moderately improved at 6 months.	Excellent results for health care workers.
Tennant, Rawson, Cohen, et al. (1984)	3	160	51 days (mean)		Mean treatment length: 51 days. 29.5% dropped out in first week. Better results with those completely detoxified before starting naltrexone.	
Judson, Carney, & Goldstein (1981)	2	119	12 months	End of treatment	60 mg versus 120 mg, thrice weekly. No difference between the two groups. Dramatic decrease in craving by end of first week.	Double-blind, two-dose comparison. No placebo group.
Hollister (1978)	1	192	9 months		Very high dropout rates in both groups. No significant differences.	Multiclinic trial
Cornish et al. (1997, in press)	1	51	6 months	6 months	All participants volunteers from federal probation. Those randomized to control group received equivalent counseling, but not placebo. 52% completion in naltrexone groups versus 33% for controls. Opioid use 8% in naltrexone groups versus 30% for controls. Only 26% of naltrexone groups were reincarcerated versus 56% for controls.	Demonstrates potential usefulness of naltrexone in a paroled population.

ventions should generally be used in conjunction with pharmacotherapy when treating substance use disorders to facilitate retention and compliance and to address the myriad psychological and social problems that often accompany addiction (O'Brien, 1996). It is also important to treat comorbid psychiatric disorders, particularly when they are either pre-existing or independent of the substance use disorder. Additional studies are needed to examine issues such as the long-term efficacy and effectiveness of existing and new medications, matching subgroups of patients to particular medications, and potential dangers associated with severe relapse while on medications (Schuckit, 1996).

References

Alterman, A. I., Droba, M., Antelo, R. E., Cornish, J. W., Sweeney, K. K., Parikh, G. A., & O'Brien, C. P. (1992). Amantadine may facilitate detoxification of cocaine addicts. *Drug and Alcohol Dependence, 31*, 19–29.

Alterman, A. I., O'Brien, C. P., McLellan, A. T., August, D. S., Snider, E. C., Droba., M., Cornish, J. W., Hall, C. P., Raphaelson, A. H., & Schrade, F. X. (1994). Effectiveness and costs of inpatient versus day hospital cocaine rehabilitations. *Journal of Nervous and Mental Disease, 182*(3), 157–163.

American Psychiatric Association. (1994). *Diagnostic and statistical manual of mental disorders* (4th ed.). Washington, D.C.: Author.

Anglin, M. D., Speckart, G. R., Booth, M. W., & Ryan, T. M. (1989). Consequences and costs of shutting off methadone. *Addictive Medicine, 14*, 307–326.

Arndt, I. O., Dorozynsky, L., Woody, G. E., McLellan, A. T., O'Brien, & C. P. (1992). Desipramine treatment of cocaine dependence in methadone-maintained patients. *Archives of General Psychiatry, 49*, 888–893.

Azatian, A., Papiasvilli, A., & Joseph, H. (1994). A study of the use of clonidine and naltrexone in the treatment of opioid addiction in former USSR. *Journal of Addictive Disease, 13*(1), 35–52.

Azrin, N. H., Sisson, R. W., Meyers, R., & Godley, M. (1982). Alcoholism treatment by disulfiram and community reinforcement therapy. *Journal of Behavioral Therapy and Experimental Psychiatry, 13*, 105–112.

Baekeland, F., Lundwalll, L., Kissen, B., & Shanahan, T. (1971). Correlates of outcome in disulfiram treatment of alcoholism. *Journal of Nervous and Mental Disease, 153*, 1–9.

Berger, S. P., Hall, S., Michalian, J. D., Reid, M. S., Crawford, C. A., Delucchi, K., Carr, K., & Hall, S. (1996). Haloperidol antagonism of cue-elicited cocaine craving. *Lancet, 347*, 504–508.

Bickel, W. K., & Amass, L. (1995). Buprenorphine treatment of opioid dependence: A review. *Experimental and Clinical Psychopharmacology, 3*(4), 477–489.

Bickel, W. K., Stitzer, M. L., Bigelow, G. E., Liebson, I. A., Jasinski, D. R., & Johnson, D. E. (1988). A clinical trial with buprenorphine: Comparison with methadone in the detoxification of heroin addicts. *Clinical Pharmacology and Therapeutics, 43*, 72–78.

Brahen, L. S., Henderson, R. K., Copone, T., & Kordal, N. (1984). Naltrexone treatment in a jail work-release program. *Journal of Clinical Psychiatry, 45*, 49–52.

Bruno, F. (1989). Buspirone in the treatment of alcoholic patients. *Psychopathology, 22*(Suppl. 1), 49–59.

Carroll, K. M., Rounsaville, B. J., Gordon, L. T., Nich, C., Jatlaw, P., Bisignini, R. M., & Gawin, F. H. (1994a). Psychotherapy and pharmacotherapy for ambulatory cocaine abusers. *Archives of General Psychiatry, 51*, 177–187.

Carroll, K. M., Rounsaville, B. J., Nich, C., Gordon, L. T., Wirtz, P. W., & Gawin, F. H. (1994b). One year follow-up of psychotherapy and pharmacotherapy for cocaine dependence: Delayed emergence of psychotherapy effects. *Archives of General Psychiatry, 51*(12), 989–997.

Chick, J., Gough, K., Falkowski, W., Kershaw, P., Hore, B., Mehta, B., Ritson, B., Roopner, R., & Torley, D. (1992). Disulfiram treatment of alcoholism. *British Journal of Psychiatry, 161*, 84–89.

Childress, A. R., McLellan, A. T., Ehrman, R., & O'Brien, C. P. (1987). Extinction of conditioned responses in abstinent cocaine or opioid users [Monograph]. *Problems of Drug Dependence, 76*, 189–195.

Childress, A. R., Mozley, D., Fitzgerald, J., Reivich, M., Jaggi, J., & O'Brien, C.P. (1995). Limbic activation during cue-induced cocaine craving. *25th Annual Meeting of Society for Neuroscience, 767.1*, 1956.

Cornish, J. W., Maany, I., Fudala, P. J., Neal, S., Poole, S. A., Volpicelli, P., & O'Brien, C. P. (1995). Carbamazepine treatment for cocaine dependence [Monograph]. *Drug and Alcohol Dependence, 38*, 221–227.

Cornish, J. W., Metzger, D., Woody, G. E., Wilson, D., McLellan, A. T., Vandergrift, B., & O'Brien, C. P. (1997). Naltrexone pharmacotherapy for opioid dependent federal probationers. *Journal of Substance Abuse Treatment* (in press).

Dole, V. P., Robinson, J. W., Orraca, J., Towns, E., Searcy, P., & Caine, E. (1969). Methadone treatment of randomly selected criminal addicts. *New England Journal of Medicine, 280*(25), 1372–1375.

Ferry, L. H., & Burchette, R. J. (1994). Evaluation of bupropion versus placebo for treatment of nicotine dependence. *147th Annual Meeting of the American Psychiatric Association,* 199–200.

Fiore, M. C., Kenford, S. L., Jorenby, D. E., Wetter, D. W., Smith S. S., & Baker, T. B. (1994). Two studies of the clinical effectivness of the nicotine patch with different counseling treatments. *Chest, 105*(2), 524–533.

Fiore, M. C., Smith, S. S., Jorenby, D. E., & Baker, T. B. (1994). The effectiveness of the nicotine patch for smoking cessation. A meta-analysis. *Journal of the American Medical Association, 271*(24), 1940–1947.

Freedman, R. R., & Czeretko, G. (1981). A comparison of thrice weekly LAAM and daily methadone in employed heroin addicts. *Drug and Alcohol Dependence, 8*(3), 215–222.

Fuller, R. K. (1995). Antidipsotropic medications. In R. K. Hester & W. R. Miller (Eds.), *Handbook of alcoholism treatment approaches: Effective alternatives* (2nd ed., pp. 123–133). Needham Heights, Mass.: Allyn & Bacon.

Fuller, R. K., Branchey, L., Brightwell, D. R., Derman, R. M., Emrick, C. D., Iber, F. L., James, K. E., Lacoursiere, R. B., Lee, K. K., Lowenstam, I., Maany, I., Neiderheiser, D., Nocks, J. J., & Shaw, S. (1986). Disulfiram treatment of alcoholism: A Veterans Administration cooperative study. *Journal of the American Medical Association, 256,* 1449–1455.

Fuller, R. K., & Roth, H. P. (1979). Disulfiram for the treatment of alcoholism: An evaluation in 128 men. *Annals of Internal Medicine, 90,* 901–904.

Gawin, F. H., Allen, D., & Humblestone, B. (1989a). Outpatient treatment of "crack" cocaine smoking with flupenthixol decanoate. *Archives of General Psychiatry, 46,* 322–325.

Gawin, F. H., Kleber, H. D., Byck, R., Rounsaville, B. J., Kosten, T. R., Jatlow, P. I., & Morgan, C. (1989b). Desipramine facilitation of initial cocaine abstinence. *Archives of General Psychiatry, 46,* 117–121.

Gawin, F. H., Morgan, C., Kosten, T. R., & Kleber, H. D. (1989c). Double-blind evaluation of the effect of acute amantadine on cocaine craving. *Psychopharmacology, 97,* 402–403

Gawin, F. H., Riordan, C., & Kleber, H. (1985). Methylphenidate treatment of cocaine abusers without attention deficit disorder: A negative report. *American Journal of Drug and Alcohol Abuse, 11,* 193–197.

Gerra, G., Marcato, A., Caccavar, R., et al. (1995). Clonidine and opiate receptor antagonists in the treatment of heroin addiction. *Journal of Substance Abuse Treatment, 12*(1), 35–41.

Gerrein, J. R., Rosenberg, C. M., & Manohar, V. (1973). Disulfiram maintenance in outpatient treatment of alcoholism. *Archives of General Psychiatry, 29,* 798–802.

Giannini, A. J., Folts, D. J., Feather, J. N. & Sullivan, B. S. (1989). Bromocriptine and amantadine in cocaine detoxification. *Psychiatry Research, 29,* 11–16.

Gorelick, D. A. (1989). Serotonin reuptake blockers and the treatment of alcoholism. In M. Galanter (Ed.), *Recent developments in alcoholism* (pp. 267–281). New York: Plenum Press.

Gorelick, D. A., & Paredes, A. (1992). Effect of fluoxetine on alcohol consumption in male alcoholics. *Alcoholism: Clinical and Experimental Research, 16,* 261–265.

Grabowski, J., Rhoades, H., Elk, R., Schmitz, J., Davis, C., Creson, D., & Kirby, K. (1995). Fluoxetine is ineffective for treatment of cocaine dependence or concurrent opiate and cocaine dependence: Two placebo-controlled, double blind trials. *Journal of Clinical Psychopharmacology, 15,* 163–174.

Greenstein, R. A., Arndt, I. C., McLellan, A. T., O'Brien, C. P., and Evans, B. (1984). Naltrexone: A clinical perspective. *Journal of Clinical Psychiatry, 45*(9, Sec. 2), 25–28.

Gunne, L., & Gronbladh, L. (1984). The Swedish methadone maintenance program. In G. Servan (Ed.), *Social and medical aspects of drug abuse* (pp. 205–213). Jamaica, N.J.: Spectrum Publications.

Herbert, S., Montgomery, A., Fudala, P., Vocci, F., Gampel, J., Mojsiak, J., Hill, J., & Walsh, R. (1995). LAAM labeling assessment study: Retention, dosing, and side effects in a 64-week study [Monograph]. *Problems of Drug Dependence, 153,* 259.

Higgins, S. T., Budney, A. J., Bickel, W. K., Hughes, J. R., Goerg, F., & Badger, G. (1993). Achieving cocaine abstinence with a behavioral approach. *American Journal of Psychiatry, 150,* 763–769.

Hollister, L. (1978). Clinical evaluation of naltrexone treatment for opiate-dependent individuals. *Archives of General Psychiatry, 35,* 335–340.

Imperial Cancer Fund General Practice Research Group. (1993). Effectiveness of a nicotine patch in helping people stop smoking: Results of a randomized trial in general practice. *British Medical Journal, 306*(6888), 1304–1308.

Institute of Medicine Report. (1990). The effectiveness of treatment. In D. R. Gerstein & H. J. Harwood (Eds.), *Treating drug problems* (pp. 132–199). Washington, D.C.: National Academy Press.

Jenkins, S. W., Warfield, N. A., Blaine, J. D., Cornish, J., Ling, W., Rosen, M. I., Urschel, H., Wesson, D., & Ziedonis, D. (1992). A pilot study of gepirone v. placebo in the treatment of cocaine dependency. *Psychopharmacology Bulletin, 28,* 21–26.

Johnsen, J., & Morland, J. (1991). Disulfiram implant: A double-blind placebo controlled follow-up on treatment outcome. *Alcoholism: Clinical and Experimental Research, 15,* 532–536.

Johnsen, J., Stowell, A., Bache-Wiig, J. E., Stendsrud, T., Ripel, A., & Morland, J. (1987). A double-blind placebo controlled study of male alcoholics given a subcutaneous disulfiram implantation. *British Journal of Addiction, 82*, 607–613.

Johnson, R. E., Jaffe, J. H., & Fudala, P. J. (1991). A controlled trial of buprenorphine treatment for opioid dependence. *Journal of the American Medical Association, 267*, 2750–2755.

Judson, B. A., Carney, T. M., & Goldstein, A. (1981). Naltrexone treatment of heroin addiction: Efficacy and safety in a double-blind dosage comparison. *Drug Alcohol Dependence, 7*(4), 325–346.

Judson, B. A., & Goldstein, A. (1979). Leva-alpha-acetyl-methadol (LAAM) in the treatment of heroin addicts. I. Dosage schedule for induction and stabilization. *Drug and Alcohol Dependence, 4*, 461–466.

Khalsa, E., Jatlow, P., & Gawin, F.(1994). Flupenthixol and desipramine treatment of crack users: double-blind results. *NIDA Research Monograph 141*, NIH Publication Number 94–3794, p. 438.

King, A. C., Volpicelli, J. R., Frazer, A., & O'Brien, C. P. (1997). Effect of naltrexone on subjective alcohol response in subjects at high and low risk for future alcohol dependence. *Psychopharmacology, 129*, 15–22.

Kleber, H. D. (1995). Pharmacotherapy, current and potential, for the treatment of cocaine dependence. *Clinical Neuropharmacology, 18*(Suppl. 1), S96–S109.

Kolar, A. F., Brown, B. S., Weddington, W. W., Haertzen, C. C., Michaelson, B. S., & Jaffe, J. H. (1992). Treatment of cocaine dependence in methadone maintenance clients: A pilot study comparing the efficacy of desipramine and amantadine. *International Journal of the Addictions, 27*, 849–868.

Koob, G. F. (1992). Neurobiological mechanisms in cocaine and opiate dependence. In C. P. O'Brien & J. Jaffe (Eds.), *Addictive states* (pp. 79–92). New York: Raven Press.

Kornitzer, M., Boutsen, M., Dramaix, M., Thijs, J., & Gustavsson, G. (1995). Combined used of nicotine patch and gum in smoking cessation: A placebo-controlled clinical trial. *Preventive Medicine, 24*(1), 41–47.

Kosten, T. R., Morgan, C. M., Falcione, J., & Schottenfeld, R. S. (1992). Pharmacotherapy for cocaine-abusing methadone-maintained patients using amantadine or desipramine. *Archives of General Psychiatry, 49*, 894–898.

Kranzler, H. R., & Anton, R. F. (1994). Implications of recent neuropsychopharmacologic research for understanding the etiology and development of alcoholism. *Journal of Consulting and Clinical Psychology, 62*, 1116–1126.

Kranzler, H. R., Burleson, J. A., Del Boca, F. K., Babor, T. F., Korner, P., Brown, J., & Bohn, M. J. (1994). Buspirone treatment of anxious alcoholics: A placebo-controlled trial. *Archives of General Psychiatry, 51*, 720–731.

Kranzler, H. R., Burleson, J. A., Korner, P., Del Boca, F. K., Bohn, M. J., Brown, J., & Liebowitz, N. (1995). Placebo-controlled trial of fluoxetine as an adjunct to relapse prevention in alcoholics. *American Journal of Psychiatry, 152*, 391–397.

Kreek, M. J. (1992). Rationale for maintenance pharmacotherapy of opiate dependence. In C. P. O'Brien & J. H. Jaffe (Eds.), *Addictive states* (pp. 205–330). New York: Raven Press.

Lerner, A., Sigal, M., Bacalul, E., et al. (1992). A naltrexone double blind placebo controlled study in Israel. *Israel Journal of Psychiatry & Related Sciences, 29*(1), 36–43.

Levin, F. R., and Lehman, A. F. (1991). Meta-analysis of desipramine as an adjunct in the treatment of cocaine addiction. *Journal of Clinical Psychopharmacology, 11*, 374–378.

Lhuintre, J. P., Moore, N. D., Saligaut, C., Boismare, F., Daoust, M., Chretien, P., Tran, G., & Hillemand, B. (1985). Ability of calcium bis acetyl homotaurinate, a GABA agonist, to prevent relapse in weaned alcoholics. *Lancet, 1*(8436), 1014–1016.

Lhuintre, J. P., Moore, N. D., Tran, G., Steru, L., Lancrenon, S., Daoust, M., Parot, P., Ladure, P., Libert, C., Boismare, F., & Hillemand, B. (1990). Acamprosate appears to decrease alcohol intake in weaned alcoholics. *Alcohol and Alcoholism, 25*, 613–622.

Ling, W., Charuvastra, C., Collins, J. F., Batki, S., Brown, L. S., Kintaudi, P., Wesson, D. R., McNicholas, L., Tusel, D. J., Malkerneker, U., Renner, J. A., Santos, E., Casadonte, P., Fye, C., Stine, S., Wang, R. I. H., & Segal, D. (1997). Buprenorphine maintenance treatment of opiate dependence: A multicenter, randomized clinical trial. *Addiction* (submitted for publication).

Ling, W., Charuvastra, C., Kaim, S. C., & Klett, J. (1976). Methadyl acetate and methadone as maintenance treatments for heroin addicts. *Archives of General Psychiatry, 33*, 709–720.

Ling, W., Klett, J., & Gillis, R. D. (1978). A cooperative clinical study of methadyl acetate. *Archives of General Psychiatry, 35*, 345–353.

Ling, W., & Wesson, D. R. (1984). Naltrexone treatment for addicted health-care professionals: A collaborative private practice. *Journal of Clinical Psychiatry, 34*(9, Sec. 2), 46–52.

Malcolm, R., Anton, R. F., Randall, C. L., Johnston, A., Brady, K., & Thevos, A. (1992). A placebo-controlled trial of buspirone in anxious inpatient alcoholics.

Alcoholism: Clinical and Experimental Research, 16, 1007–1013.

Marcovici, M., O'Brien, C. P., McLellan, A. T., & Kacio, J. (1981). A clinical, controlled study of l-α-acetylmethadol in the treatment of narcotic addiction. *American Journal of Psychiatry, 138,* 234–236.

Martin, W. R., & Jasinski, D. (1969). Psychological parameters of morphine in man tolerance, early abstinence, protracted abstinence. *Journal of Psychiatry Research, 7,* 9–16.

Mason, B. J., Kocsis, J. H., Ritvo, E. C., & Cutler, R. B. (1996). A double-blind, placebo controlled trial of desipramine for primary alcohol dependence stratified on the presence or absence of major depression. *Journal of the American Medical Association, 275,* 803–804.

Mason, B. J., Ritvo, E. C., Morgan, R. O., Salvato, F. R., Goldberg, G., Welch, B., & Mantero-Antienza, E. (1994). A double-blind, placebo-controlled pilot study to evaluate the efficacy and safety of oral nalmefene HCl for alcohol dependence. *Alcoholism: Clinical and Experimental Research, 18,* 1162–1167.

McGrath, P. J., Nunes, E. V., Stewart, J. W., Goldman, D., Agosti, V., Ocepek-Welikson, K., and Quitkin, F. M. (1996). Imipramine treatment of alcoholics with primary depression: A placebo-controlled clinical trial. *Archives of General Psychiatry, 53,* 232–240.

McKay, J. R., Cacciola, J., McLellan, A. T., Alterman, A. I., & Wirtz, P. W. (1997). An initial evaluation of the psychosocial dimensions of the ASAM criteria for inpatient and day hospital substance abuse rehabilitation. *Journal of Studies on Alcohol, 58,* 239–252.

McLellan, A. T., Arndt, I. O., Metzger, D., Woody, G., & O'Brien, C. P. (1993). The effects of psychosocial services in substance abuse treatment. *Journal of the American Medical Association, 269(15),* 1959–1993.

Mello, N. K., & Mendelson, J. H. (1980). Buprenorphine suppresses heroin use by heroin addicts. *Science, 207,* 657–659.

Metzger, D. S., Woody, G. E., McLellan, A. T., O'Brien, C. P., Druley, P., Navaline, H., DePhilippis, D., Stolley, P., & Abrutyn, E. (1993). Human immunodeficiency virus seroconversion along in- and out-of-treatment drugs users: An 18 month prospective follow-up. *Journal of Acquired Immune Deficiency Syndromes, 6,* 1049–1056.

Mintz, J., O'Brien, C. P., & Goldschmidt, J. (1974). Sexual problems of heroin addicts when drug free, on heroin, and on methadone. *Archives of General Psychiatry, 31,* 700–703.

Montoya, I. D., Levin, F. R., Fudala, P. J., & Gorelick, D. A. (1995). Double-blind comparison of carbamazepine and placebo for treatment of cocaine dependence [Monograph]. *Drug and Alcohol Dependence, 38,* 213–219.

Moscovitz, H., Brookoff, D., & Nelson, L. (1993). A randomized trial of bromocriptine for cocaine users presenting to the emergency department. *Journal of General Internal Medicine, 8,* 1–4.

Myer, E. C., Morris, D. L., Brase, D. A., Dewey, W. L., & Zimmerman, A. W. (1990). Naltrexone therapy of apnea in children with elevated cerebrospinal fluid b-endorphin. *Annals of Neurology, 27,* 75–80.

Myers, J. K., Weissman, M. M., Tischler, G. L., Holzer, C. E., Leaf, P. J., Orvaschel, H., Anthony, J. C., Boyd, J. H., Burke, J. D., Kramer, M. & Stoltzman, R. (1984). Six month prevalence of psychiatric disorders in three communities 1980–1982. *Archives of General Psychiatry, 41,* 959–967.

Naranjo, C. A., Kadlec, K. E., Sanhueza, P., Woodley-Remus, D. V., & Sellers, E. M. (1990). Fluoxetine differentially alters alcohol intake and other consumatory behaviors in problem drinkers. *Clinical Pharmacology and Therapeutics, 47,* 490–498.

Naranjo, C. A., Poulos, C. X., Bremner, K. E., & Lanctot, K. L. (1992). Citalopram decreases desirability, liking, and consumption of alcohol in alcohol-dependent drinkers. *Clinical Pharmacology and Therapeutics, 51,* 729–739.

Naranjo, C. A., Sellers, E. M., Sullivan, J. T., Woodley, D. V., Kadlec, K., & Sykora, J. (1987). The serotonin uptake inhibitor citalopram attenuates ethanol intake. *Clinical Pharmacology and Therapeutics, 41,* 266–274.

Naranjo, C. A., Sullivan, J. T., Kadlec, K. E., Woodley-Remus, D. V., Kennedy, G., & Sellers, E. M. (1989). Differential effects of viqualine on alcohol intake and other consumatory behaviors. *Clinical Pharmacology and Therapeutics, 41,* 266–274.

Newman, R. G., & Whitehill, W. G. (1978). Double-blind comparison of methadone and placebo maintenance treatment of narcotic addicts in Hong Kong. *Lancet, 8141,* 485–488.

Novick, D. M., Pascarelli, E. F., & Joseph, H. (1988). Methadone maintenance patients in general medical practice: A preliminary report. *Journal of the American Medical Association, 259,* 3299–3302.

Nunes, E. V., McGrath, P. J., Quitkin, F. M., Ocepek-Welikson, K., Stewart, J., Koenig, T., Wager, S., & Klein, D. F. (1995). Imipramine treatment of cocaine abuse: Possible boundaries of efficacy. *Drug and Alcohol Dependence, 39,* 185–195.

O'Brien, C. P. (1993). Opioid addiction. In A. Herz (Ed.), *Handbook of experimental pharmacology,* Vol. 104 (63, pp. 803–823). Berlin: Springer-Verlag.

———. (1996). Recent developments in the pharmacotherapy of substance abuse. *Journal of Consulting and Clinical Psychology, 64,* 677–686.

O'Brien, C. P., Childress, A. R., Arndt., I. O., McLellan, A. T., Woody, G. E., & Maany, I. (1988). Pharmacological and behavioral treatments of cocaine dependence: Controlled studies. *Journal of Clinical Psychiatry*, 49(2), 17–22.

O'Brien, C. P., Eckardt, M. J., & Linnoila, V. M. (1995). Pharmacotherapy of alcoholism. In F. E. Bloom & D. J. Kupfer (Eds.), *Psychopharmacology: The fourth generation of progress* (pp. 1745–1755). New York: Raven Press.

O'Farrell, J. J., Cutter, H. S. G., and Floyd, F. J. (1985). Evaluating behavioral marital therapy for male alcoholics: Effects on marital adjustment and communication from before to after therapy. *Behavior Therapy*, 16, 147–167.

O'Malley, S. S. (1995). Integration of opioid antagonists and psychosocial therapy in the treatment of narcotic and alcohol dependence. *Journal of Clinical Psychiatry*, 56(Suppl. 7), 30–38.

O'Malley, S. S., Jaffe, A. J., Chang, G., Rode, S., Schottenfeld, R. S., Meyer, R. E., & Rounsaville, B. J. (1996). Six month follow-up of naltrexone and psychotherapy for alcohol dependence. *Archives of General Psychiatry*, 53, 217–224.

O'Malley, S. S., Jaffe, A. J., Chang, G., Schottenfeld, R. S., Meyer, R. E., & Rounsaville, B. J. (1992). Naltrexone and coping skills therapy for alcohol dependence. *Archives of General Psychiatry*, 49, 881–887.

O'Malley, S. S., Jaffe, A. J., Rode, S., & Rounsaville, B. J. (1996). The experience of a "slip" among alcoholics on naltrexone versus placebo. *American Journal of Psychiatry*, 153, 281–283.

Paille, F. M., Guelfi, J. D., Perkins, A. C., Royer, R. J., Steru, L., & Parot, P. (1995). Double-blind randomized multicentre trial of acamprosate in maintaining abstinence from alcohol. *Alcohol and Alcoholism*, 30, 239–247.

Rawson, R. A., Shoptaw, M. J., & Minsky, S. (1994). Effectiveness of desipramine in treating cocaine dependence. *NIDA Research Monograph 153*, p. 494.

Raynor, K., Kong, H., Chen, Y., Yasuda, K., Yu, L., Bell, G. I., & Reisine, T., (1994). Pharmacological characterization of the cloned k-, d- and m-opioid receptors. *Molecular Pharmacology*, 45(2), 330–334.

Richmond, R. L., Harris, K., & de Almeida Neta, A. (1994). The transdermal nicotine patch: Results of a randomized placebo-controlled trial. *Medical Journal of Australia*, 161(2), 130–135.

Robbins, S., Ehrman, R., Childress, A. R., and O'Brien, C. P. (1992). Using cue reactivity to screen medications for cocaine abuse: Amantadine hydrochloride. *Addictive Behaviors*, 17, 491–499.

Robins, L. N., Helzer, J. E., Weissman, M. M., Orvaschel, H., Gruenberg, E., Burke, J. D., & Regier, D. A. (1984). Lifetime prevalence of specific psychiatric disorders in three sites. *Archives of General Psychiatry*, 41, 949–958.

Rose, J. E., Behm, F. M., Westman, E. C., Levin, E. D., Stein, R. M., & Ripka, G. V. (1994). Mecamylamine combined with nicotine skin patch facilitates smoking cessation beyond nicotine patch treatment alone. *Clinical Pharmacology and Therapeutics*, 56(1), 86–99.

Roy, A., Virkkunen, M., & Linnoila, M. (1990). Serotonin in suicide, violence, and alcoholism. In E. F. Coccaro, & D. L. Murphy (Eds.), *Serotonin in Major Psychiatric Disorders* (pp. 187–208). Washington, D.C.: American Psychiatric Press.

Sass, H., Soyka, M., Mann, K., & Zieglgansberger, W. (1996). Relapse prevention by acamprosate: Results from a placebo controlled study in alcohol dependence. *Archives of General Psychiatry*, 53, 673–680.

Schuckit, M. A. (1996). Recent developments in the pharmacotherapy of alcohol dependence. *Journal of Consulting and Clinical Psychology*, 64, 669–676.

Shufman, E. N., Porat, S., Witztum, E., Gandacu, D., Bar-Hamburger, R., & Ginath, U. (1994). The efficacy of naltrexone in preventing reabuse of heroin after detoxification. *Biological Psychiatry*, 35, 935–945.

Stimmel, B., Goldeberg, J., Rotkopf, E., & Cohen, M. (1977). Ability to remain abstinent after detoxification—a six year study. *Journal of the American Medical Association*, 237(12), 1216–1220.

Strain, E. C., Stitzer, M. L., Liebson, I. A., & Bigelow, G. E. (1994a). Buprenorphine versus methadone in the treatment of opioid-dependent cocaine users. *Psychopharmacology*, 116, 401–406.

———. (1994b). Comparison of buprenorphine and methadone in the treatment of opioid dependence. *American Journal of Psychiatry*, 151, 1025–1030.

Swift, R. M. (1995). Effect of naltrexone on human alcohol consumption. *Journal of Clinical Psychiatry*, 56(Suppl. 7), 24–29.

Swift, R. M., Whelihan, W., Kuznetsov, O., Buongiorno, G., & Hsuing, H. (1994). Naltrexone-induced alterations in human ethanol intoxication. *American Journal of Psychiatry*, 151, 1463–1467.

Tennant, F. S., Rawson, R. A., Cohen, A. J., et al. (1984). Clinical experience with naltrexone in suburban opioid addicts. *Journal of Clinical Psychiatry*, 34(9, Sec. 2), 42–45.

Tennant, F. S., & Sagherian, A. A. (1987). Double-blind comparison of amantadine and bromocriptine for ambulatory withdrawal from cocaine dependence. *Archives of Internal Medicine*, 147, 109–112.

Tollefson, G. D., Montague-Clouse, J., & Tollefson, S. L. (1992). Treatment of comorbid generalized anxiety in a recently detoxified alcohol population with a selective serotonergic drug (buspirone). *Journal of Clinical Psychopharmacology, 12,* 19–26.

Volpicelli, J. R., Alterman, A. I., Hayashida, M., & O'Brien, C. P. (1992). Naltrexone in the treatment of alcohol dependence. *Archives of General Psychiatry, 49,* 876–880.

Volpicelli, J. R., Clay, K. L., Rhines, J. S., Volpicelli, L. A., Alterman, A. I., and O'Brien, C. P. (in press). Naltrexone and alcohol dependence: Role of subject compliance. *Archives of General Psychiatry.*

Volpicelli, J. R., Clay, K. L., Watson, N. T., & O'Brien, C. P. (1995a). Naltrexone in the treatment of alcoholism: Predicting response to naltrexone. *Journal of Clinical Psychiatry, 56*(Suppl. 7), 39–44.

Volpicelli, J. R., Watson, N. T., King, A. C., Sherman, C. E., and O'Brien, C. P. (1995b). Effect of naltrexone on alcohol "high" in alcoholics. *American Journal of Psychiatry, 152,* 613–615.

Washton, A. M., Pottash, A. C., and Gold, M. S. (1984). Naltrexone in addicted business executives and physicians. *Journal of Clinical Psychiatry, 34*(9, Sec. 2), 39–41.

Weddington, W. W., Brown, B. S., Haertzen, C. A., Hess, J. M., Mahaffey, J. R., Kolar, A. F., and Jaffe, J. H. (1991). Comparison of amantadine and desipramine combined with psychotherapy for treatment of cocaine dependence. *American Journal of Drug and Alcohol Abuse, 17,* 137–152.

Whitworth, A. B., Fischer, F., Lesch, O. M., Nimmerichter, A., Oberbauer, H., Platz, T., Potgeiter, A., Walter, H., & Fleischhacker, W. W. (1996). Comparison of acamprosate and placebo in long-term treatment of alcohol dependence. *Lancet, 347,* 1438–1442.

Zacny, J. C. (1995). A review of the effects of opioids on psychomotor and cognitive functioning in humans. *Experimental and Clinical Psychopharmacology, 3*(4), 432–466.

7

Psychosocial Treatments for Alcohol Use Disorders

John W. Finney
Rudolf H. Moos

Of 15 psychosocial treatments examined in 3 or more studies each (mostly of the Type 1 and Type 2 variety), those with the most evidence of effectiveness helped patients shape and adapt to their life circumstances. Among the most promising of these cognitive-behavioral treatments include social skills training, community reinforcement, and behavioral marital therapy. Two recent multisite evaluations, not included in previous reviews, suggest that 12-step treatment is as effective as cognitive-behavioral treatment.

With regard to patient-treatment matching, interpersonally-oriented treatment appears more effective for patients who are functioning better, whereas cognitive-behavioral approaches seem to work better for more impaired patients. However, more research on patient-treatment matching is needed.

In general, patients of therapists who are more interpersonally skilled, less confrontational, and/or more empathic experience better outcomes.

On the issue of duration and amount of treatment, an effective strategy for many patients may be to provide lower intensity treatment for a longer duration—that is, treatment sessions spread at a lower rate over a longer period.

With respect to treatment setting, there is little or no difference in the outcome of inpatient versus outpatient treatment for patients who are clinically eligible for treatment in either setting. Patients who are more severely impaired and/or less socially stable may experience better outcomes following treatment in inpatient or residential settings.

Regier et al. (1993) estimated that 7.4% of the U.S. population 18 and older meet diagnostic criteria for alcohol abuse or dependence. Another substantial segment of the population has less severe forms of alcohol use disorders, that is, heavy drinking associated with adverse effects on health, work, social relationships, or psychological state that do not meet diagnostic criteria. The heavy toll exacted by alcohol use disorders has prompted an increase in the availability of treatment services. Weisner, Greenfield, and Room (1995) reported that the number of persons with alcohol use disorders using treatment services on a given day in the United States rose from 293,000 to 563,000 during the 1980s.

A large number of studies have been undertaken to evaluate the effects of different forms of treatment for alcohol use disorders. Several reviews of this research literature have been published in recent years (e.g., Finney & Monahan, 1996; Holder, Longabaugh, Miller, & Rubonis, 1991; Miller et al., 1995). Almost all of the prior studies have assumed that the outcome of treatment is a function of patients' characteristics at intake, especially the severity and chronicity of alcohol abuse and other aspects of psychosocial functioning (for an overview, see Institute of Medicine, 1989), and the treatment itself. From a broader perspective, however, treatment outcome is also influenced by life context factors prior to intake and those that occur during the treatment and posttreatment intervals (Moos, Finney, & Cronkite, 1990). We consider the relevant research evidence here in terms of the modality of treatment, therapists' characteristics, the duration and amount of treatment, and the treatment setting. We conclude that the most effective treatments are those that help patients shape and adapt to their life circumstances.

PSYCHOSOCIAL TREATMENT MODALITIES

In this section we consider the effectiveness of psychosocial treatment modalities that have been the focus of three recent reviews. We also review evidence on matching patients with psychosocial treatment modalities.

Effectiveness of Treatment Modalities

Table 7.1 provides the rankings for 15 psychosocial modalities that each had 3 or more studies addressing their effectiveness in the reviews by Holder et al. (1991), Miller et al. (1995), and Finney and Monahan (1996). Also included in Table 7.1 is the estimated cost of each modality as provided by Holder et al. (1991) but adjusted to 1995 dollars. There is no relationship between cost and Finney and Monahan's (1996) or Miller et al.'s (1995) modality effectiveness rankings. The Holder et al. (1991) rankings suggest that less-effective modalities are more costly, although the correlation ($r = -.46$) is not statistically significant at the .05 level (see all three reviews for additional data on the relationship between cost and broader arrays of treatment modalities).

For the most part, the modalities that have high effectiveness rankings across these reviews fall into the general category of cognitive-behavioral interventions, which focus primarily on enhancing patients' skills in coping with everyday life circumstances (including relapse-inducing situations) and on improving the match between patients' abilities and environmental demands. The relevant studies typically met the crite-

ria for either a Type 1 study (e.g., random assignment to treatment conditions, state-of-the art diagnostic procedures, adequate statistical power, appropriate statistical analyses, etc.) or, more frequently, Type 2 studies (those that were missing one or more of the criteria of a Type 1 study but not of poor methodological quality overall). Two modalities that were consistently found to be effective (that is, to be superior to at least one control or, more commonly, an alternative treatment condition against which they were compared on at least one drinking-related outcome variable at one or more follow-up points) are social skills training and the community reinforcement approach (CRA).

Social skills training focuses on developing assertion and communication skills. After an initial assessment to identify skill deficits, patients learn how to initiate social interactions, express their thoughts and feelings, respond appropriately to criticism from others, and so on. Treatment is usually in a group format so that patients can role-play, receive feedback, and model the behavior of others. There is some evidence (Smith & McCrady, 1991) that patients with neuropsychological impairment may benefit less from skills training because of their greater difficulty in learning and recalling skills.

The CRA has been somewhat of a moving target. It initially consisted of interventions to assist with family, job-related, and legal problems, as well as a club where the former patients could go to enjoy social activities without alcohol being present. In a later version, the social club was dropped, and a buddy system, mailed daily reports to identify problems that might lead to relapse, group counseling (as opposed to the previously used individual counseling), and a component to encourage patients to take Antabuse at a specific time and place and in the presence of another person were added to CRA. Still later, in an outpatient sample, the time devoted to CRA was reduced and the buddy system and early warning component were dropped. Despite this variation, CRA has retained a core, broad-spectrum focus on patients' drinking behaviors and their family-and job-related problems. Four studies have supported the effectiveness of CRA, but three were conducted by the same research group. Accordingly, studies by other investigators are needed to determine the generalizability of the findings.

With respect to patient-CRA matching, unmarried patients were found in one study (Azrin, Sisson, Meyers, & Godley, 1982) to benefit more from broad-

TABLE 7.1 Rankings by Effectiveness Indices of Psychosocial Treatment Modalities

Modality	Holder et al. (1991)	Miller et al. (1995)	Finney & Monahan (1996)	Cost[a] (1995 Dollars)
Social skills training	1	1	2	362
Self-control training	2	8	10	141
Brief motivational counseling	3	2	7	62
Marital therapy, behavioral	4	7	3	688
Community reinforcement	5.5	3	1	660
Stress management training	5.5	12	5	161
Aversion, covert sensitization	7	6	8.5	440
Marital therapy, other	8	9	4	688
Cognitive therapy	9.5	5	11	433
Hypnosis	9.5	11	15	738
Aversion, electric shock	11	10	8.5	410
Aversion, nausea	12	4	6	1380
Confrontational interventions	13	13	13	375
Educational lectures/films	14	15	12	135
General counseling	15	14	14	738

Note: Based on 15 psychosocial treatment modalities each having 3 or more studies in Finney and Monahan (1996), Holder et al. (1991), and Miller et al. (1995).

[a]The cost data are drawn from Miller et al. (1995) based on data collected by Holder et al. (1991) and were adjusted from 1987 to 1995 dollars using a Consumer Price Index weighting factor.

spectrum CRA treatment, perhaps because it provided an essential source of support for these individuals with fewer social resources. For married patients, most of whom had some family support, the Antabuse assurance component alone was as effective as more intensive CRA treatment.

Behavioral marital therapy (BMT; O'Farrell, Choquette, Cutter, Brown, & McCourt, 1993) is another psychosocial treatment approach that consistently has been shown to be effective (see Table 7.1). This therapy begins with a thorough assessment of the alcoholic patient's drinking behavior and of the marital relationship. Interventions to address drinking include behavioral contracts and Antabuse contracts. Marital interventions focus on improving the relationship, and resolving marital conflicts and problems, using such procedures as increasing caring behaviors, planning joint recreational activities, enhancing communication skills, and developing behavioral change agreements. Beyond the obvious condition of being in a relatively stable relationship, research has not addressed which types of patients benefit differentially from BMT versus other treatment modalities.

Other treatments with evidence of effectiveness in some of the reviews include motivational counseling (see the section below on brief interventions), behavioral contracting, stress management training, relapse

prevention training, and aversion conditioning. Again, most of these treatments tend to focus on enhancing patients' real-life coping skills, altering reinforcement contingencies in their natural environments, or both.

A noteworthy feature of Table 7.1 is the low effectiveness rankings of many of the prevalent treatment approaches in the United States—educational films, confrontational interventions, and general alcoholism counseling—a pattern that has been highlighted previously in reviews by Miller and his colleagues (e.g., Miller et al., 1995). However, it is difficult to think of education as a complete treatment in itself rather than a component of a multimodal approach. Confrontational interventions consistently fare poorly, perhaps because many individuals react negatively to pervasive criticism. General alcoholism counseling has little research support, but counseling sessions have often served as "control" conditions and may have been poorly implemented. In addition, these treatments may not focus as explicitly or intensively on helping patients cope with their life circumstances outside the treatment situation.

Table 7.1 also does not include the 12-step approach of Alcoholics Anonymous (AA). Although there is correlational evidence that links greater involvement in AA with more positive outcomes (for a review, see Emrick, Tonigan, Montgomery, & Little,

1993), AA was not found to be more effective than alternatives in the one or two studies included in each of the reviews included in Table 7.1. In each trial, AA attendance was compulsory rather than voluntary.

Two recent studies, not included in the reviews summarized in Table 7.1, provide support for the efficacy and effectiveness of 12-step treatment approaches. One is Project MATCH (Project MATCH Research Group, 1993), a randomized, multisite trial that examined the relative efficacy of a 12-step facilitation treatment along with that of cognitive-behavioral treatment and motivational enhancement therapy. Over 900 patients received one of these three treatments as outpatient "aftercare" following inpatient or day hospital treatment; the other arm of the study focused on over 700 individuals who had presented at outpatient clinics or had been recruited through advertisements. No overall main effect of treatment conditions was found in either arm on two primary drinking-related outcome variables over a 12-month follow-up period (Project MATCH Research Group, 1997). However, 12-step facilitation patients were functioning somewhat better with respect to several secondary outcome variables.

A naturalistic, multisite evaluation focused on over 3,000 Department of Veterans Affairs inpatients who received traditional 12-step, cognitive-behavioral, or mixed 12-step and cognitive-behavioral treatments under "normal" conditions of treatment delivery. At a 1-year follow-up, there were no differences among the three groups on 9 of 11 outcome criteria (Ouimette, Finney, & Moos, 1997). Patients in 12-step programs were significantly more likely than cognitive-behavioral patients to abstain from alcohol and other drugs in the 3 months prior to follow-up, and mixed-program patients were more likely to be unemployed than patients in the other two groups. Because of the prior empirical support for cognitive-behavioral treatment, the fact that 12-step patients fared as well as or better than those receiving cognitive-behavioral treatment in two large-scale evaluations is important new evidence supporting the efficacy/effectiveness of 12-step approaches.

Matching Patients to Effective Treatment Modalities

Mattson et al. (1994) recently reviewed studies addressing patient-treatment matching. They summarized the findings with respect to two general types of treatment: cognitive-behavioral approaches that teach coping and communication skills and interpersonal or relationship-oriented therapies. Overall, they concluded that relationship-oriented treatment is more effective for patients who are functioning better, that is, those with weaker urges to drink, good role-playing skills, and less sociopathy and psychiatric problem severity. Patients with antisocial personality disorders do better in cognitive-behavioral treatment than in relationship-oriented treatment. In general, the more-structured cognitive-behavioral approaches seem to work better for more-impaired patients. Thus, programs to teach coping skills are more effective for patients who have severe psychiatric disorders or who are sociopathic. Communication skills training is particularly effective for patients who have less education, are more anxious, and have stronger urges to drink. More anxious patients fare better when given communication skills training than mood management training, perhaps because such patients find the new interpersonal abilities they develop in communication skills training to be especially helpful in initiating and sustaining social interactions that were previously avoided.

In contrast, Project MATCH thus far has yielded almost no evidence of patient-treatment matching effects. Selected on the basis of prior research evidence and theoretical support, 16 *a priori* hypotheses were examined with respect to two primary drinking outcome variables in each of the two arms of the studies (64 contrasts overall). However, only one contrast was statistically significant. Contrary to expectation, there was little difference in outcome by treatment condition among outpatients with greater psychiatric impairment. Among those lower in psychiatric problem severity, however, 12-step facilitation patients experienced better outcomes than did patients in cognitive-behavioral treatment and motivational enhancement therapy (Project MATCH Research Group, 1997).

The lack of more evidence of patient-treatment interaction effects in the methodologically rigorous Project MATCH raises new questions about the possibility of matching patients to psychosocial treatment modalities. However, Project MATCH focused on three specific interventions provided to patients in individual sessions. Matching effects have been found when other psychosocial interventions were applied under other conditions such as group treatment (Mattson et al., 1994), but there have been few attempts to replicate findings. Overall, patient-treatment matching is a complex process (see Finney & Moos, 1986). Consequently, although future research may provide better guidance, patient-treatment matching is likely to remain a combination of art and science at the level of clinical practice.

THERAPIST CHARACTERISTICS

Therapist characteristics may have a stronger impact on treatment outcome than the type of treatment applied. Supporting this assertion, Najavits and Weiss (1994) reviewed seven studies that found substantial differences in either patient retention or outcome for different therapists. Therapist differences were not attributable to variation in the characteristics of patients being treated or to therapists' training, treatment orientation, or experience. A few studies have attempted to determine why patient outcomes differ across therapists (for a review, see Najavits & Weiss, 1994); most have focused on therapists' relational styles with patients. In general, patients of therapists who are more interpersonally skilled, less confrontational, more empathic, or all of these experience better outcomes.

Not all patients will respond in the same way to the same therapist. For example, consistent with the evidence on patient-treatment matching described above, McLachlan (1972) found less-directive and less-structured therapists were more successful with patients who had higher, more abstract levels of conceptual functioning; for patients at lower conceptual levels, more-directive therapists had better outcomes. Hser (1995) notes that the nature of patient-therapist interactions may vary with differences in substance abuse program characteristics. For example, Hser hypothesizes that therapist characteristics have more impact on patient outcomes in programs that are less highly structured.

DURATION AND AMOUNT
OF TREATMENT

In this section, we consider the effectiveness of brief interventions, longer versus shorter stays in inpatient/residential treatment, and aftercare participation.

Brief Interventions

Two reviews of predominantly Type 1 and Type 2 studies have reported considerable support for the effectiveness of brief interventions. Bien, Miller, and Tonigan (1993) concluded that brief interventions were more effective than no intervention and, in many cases, as effective as more extensive interventions. Among 43 treatment approaches considered by Miller et al. (1995), brief interventions had the highest score on the authors' effectiveness criterion. Project MATCH (Project MATCH Research Group, 1997) also found four planned sessions of motivational enhancement treatment to be as effective as cognitive-behavioral and 12-step facilitation treatments offered over 12 sessions. Several points should be kept in mind when considering this evidence, however.

First, Bien et al. (1993) reported that the average study effect size favoring brief interventions over a control condition was .38. This effect size falls in between what Cohen (1988) termed *small* and *medium* effects. However, each study's effect size was calculated for a single drinking-related outcome. The usual practice in a meta-analysis is to calculate an average effect size for all drinking-related outcomes or for different classes of drinking-related outcomes at each follow-up point (see Mattick & Jarvis, 1994). Such an approach might have yielded a smaller effect for brief intervention versus no intervention.

Second, Jonson, Hermansson, Ronnberg, Gyllen-Hammar, & Forsberg (1995) note that the brief interventions in some of the studies reviewed by Bien et al. (1993) were considered to be more extended interventions in other studies. As one example, Monahan and Finney (1996) calculated that the average patient in the single-session "advice" condition in the well-known study by Edwards et al. (1977) actually received more than 30 hours of assessment and treatment during the year that other participants were receiving extended "treatment." Typically, 30 hours would be classified as extended treatment.

In Project MATCH (Project MATCH Research Group, 1997), patients, on average, attended proportionately more of the four planned sessions of motivational enhancement therapy than they did of the 12 planned sessions of 12-step facilitation and cognitive-behavioral treatments. In addition, all patients received 8 hours of assessment prior to treatment and five follow-up contacts at 3-month intervals, all of which may have had a therapeutic impact. Overall, the difference in treatment intensity between the motivational enhancement condition and the other two conditions was not as large as it might at first appear.

Finally, in Miller et al.'s (1995) review, a brief intervention that was not significantly inferior to a more extensive intervention was considered "effective"—it received an effectiveness score of +1 (the more extensive comparison intervention received a score of −2). Thus, studies finding no difference in treatment outcome constituted "positive evidence" for the effectiveness of brief interventions. This aspect of Miller et al.'s (1995) box-scoring system combines cost and effectiveness. We believe these two dimensions should remain separate so that their relationship can be determined from independent data.

Even with these caveats in mind, the evidence supporting the effectiveness of low-cost brief interventions is impressive. Miller and Sanchez (1993) offered the acronym FRAMES to identify the six "active ingredients" of brief interventions they believe contribute to change in drinking behavior: feedback of personal risk or impairment, emphasis on personal responsibility for change, clear advice to change, a menu of alternative change options, therapeutic empathy, and enhancement of patients' self-efficacy or optimism. Bien et al. (1993) also note that many brief interventions have included ongoing follow-through contacts with patients. Overall, the FRAMES elements may help patients enhance their motivation to change their drinking behavior; ongoing contacts may supply the support needed by some individuals to maintain such change.

Studies of brief interventions have been conducted most often with clients of low-to-moderate severity in terms of their alcohol use disorders. Research is needed to examine the effectiveness of brief interventions among patient populations that vary more substantially in severity. At present, however, low-to-moderate alcohol severity patients with positive life contexts and without severe skills deficits appear to be the best candidates for brief interventions. There also is some indication that brief interventions may be less effective for persons who have failed to respond to previous advice to reduce their alcohol consumption (Bien et al., 1993).

Length of Stay in
Inpatient/Residential Treatment

Miller and Hester (1986) and Mattick and Jarvis (1994) reviewed several randomized Type 1 and Type 2 trials that compared different lengths of inpatient or residential treatment for alcohol abuse. The consistent finding was that there was no difference in outcome. In contrast, many correlational studies have found longer stays in treatment to be associated with better outcomes. In addition, Monahan and Finney (1996) found that amount of treatment, indexed by treatment in inpatient, residential, and day hospital settings, versus outpatient settings, was related to treatment group abstinence rates across 150 treatment groups included in 100 studies. They speculated that one reason for their finding was the difference in amount of treatment received in the high-and low-treatment groups. On average, patients in the high-intensity treatment groups received 148 hours of treatment compared with 14 hours for patients in the low-intensity groups. A 10 : 1 differential at these levels of treatment intensity has not been represented in many randomized trials of treatment duration.

It may be that beneficial effects of longer stays in inpatient/residential treatment apply only to more-impaired patients with fewer social resources. For example, Welte, Hynes and Sokolow (1981) found no relationship between length of stay (LOS) and outcome for patients with higher social stability; in contrast, for patients with lower social stability, those with longer stays had better outcomes. This finding is conceptually comparable to the finding that broad-spectrum CRA treatment may be more effective for unmarried patients.

Outpatient Care Following
Inpatient Treatment

Most clinicians recommend additional outpatient treatment to maintain or enhance the therapeutic gains achieved during inpatient/residential or intensive outpatient (e.g., day hospital) treatments. Outpatient treatment attempts to provide the ongoing support needed to continue a course of sobriety or to limit the course of a relapse. Ito and Donovan's (1986) review suggests a link between such aftercare participation and positive outcomes. A more recent randomized trial (O'Farrell et al., 1993) also linked aftercare involvement to positive outcomes. With respect to patient-treatment matching, Ito and Donovan point to evidence that aftercare is particularly beneficial for patients experiencing their first treatment episode. Most of the other evidence on patient-aftercare matching concerns the type of aftercare offered (i.e., the modality).

On a practical level, Ito and Donovan (1986) describe interventions and other, nonpatient factors that can increase aftercare participation, such as reminder telephone calls, orientation lectures, and behavior contracts. Also, patients are more likely to attend aftercare when it is offered at the same facility at which they received initial treatment or at locations closer to their residences.

Summary

These reviews indicate that an effective strategy may be to provide lower intensity treatment for a longer duration—that is, treatment sessions received at a lower rate over a longer period. The effectiveness of this strategy is suggested by the positive findings for outpatient care following inpatient treatment and for brief interventions that incorporate extended contacts with patients. More-extended treatment may improve patient outcomes because it provides patients with ongoing support and the potential to discuss and resolve problems prior to the occurrence of a full-blown relapse. In this vein, brief interventions may be most effective for relatively healthy patients who have intact community support systems. Patients who have severe alcohol dependence, concomitant psychiatric disorders, deficient social resources, or combinations of these appear to be appropriate candidates for longer (and more intensive) treatment to address their multiple disorders.

TREATMENT SETTING

Choosing the setting of treatment is an important decision for treatment providers and patients given the extent to which treatment setting drives treatment cost. Prompted by the cost differential between inpatient and outpatient treatment for alcohol abuse, three reviews of the literature on the relative effectiveness of treatment in these two types of settings were published in the 1980s (Annis, 1986; Miller & Hester, 1986; Saxe et al., 1983). After examining controlled studies employing either random assignment to treatment setting or matching inpatients and outpatients on pretreatment variables, each of these reviews concluded there was no evidence for the overall superiority of inpatient over outpatient treatment, although more severely impaired patients might be treated more effectively in inpatient or residential settings.

More recently, in a review of 14 relevant studies of the Type 1 and Type 2 varieties, Finney, Hahn, and Moos (1996) noted that 5 found inpatient treatment significantly superior to outpatient treatment on at least one drinking-related outcome variable, and 2 found day hospital treatment superior to inpatient treatment. In all but one instance in which a significant effect emerged, patients in the "superior" setting received more-intensive treatment. A subsequent analysis of effect sizes across studies yielded an average positive effect of inpatient treatment that was significant although small at 3-month follow-ups but no longer significant at 6- and 12-month follow-ups (Finney & Moos, 1996; cf. Mattick & Jarvis, 1994). Many of the studies focused primarily on patients considered eligible for treatment in outpatient settings.

Some aspects of hypothesized matches of patients and treatment settings have been captured in the American Society of Addiction Medicine (ASAM) Placement Criteria (American Society of Addiction Medicine, 1997). The criteria attempt to match patients to four levels of care: (a) outpatient treatment, (b) intensive outpatient/partial hospitalization treatment, (c) residential inpatient treatment, and (d) medically managed intensive inpatient treatment. Placement decisions are based on a patient's standing on six dimensions: (a) acute intoxication and/or withdrawal potential, (b) biomedical conditions and complications, (c) emotional/behavioral conditions or complications, (d) treatment acceptance/resistance, (e) relapse/continued use potential, and (f) recovery/living environment.

Although the rationales for matches of patients and treatment settings are generally compelling, few of them have been subjected to research (but see McKay, Cacciola, McLellan, Alterman, & Wirtz, 1997). For example, researchers have not yet examined the hypothesis that persons from environments that promote excessive drinking benefit more from a residential stay that provides a respite from that environment. However, some suggestive evidence (see Finney, Hahn, & Moos, 1996; Miller & Hester, 1986) indicates that patients with psychiatric impairment and those with few social resources may benefit more from inpatient or residential treatment, which, of course, is typically followed by outpatient care.

Overall, we believe that the best approaches for treatment providers now are those recommended in previous reviews: (a) provide outpatient treatment for most individuals with sufficient social resources and no serious medical/psychiatric impairment, (b) use less costly intensive outpatient treatment options for patients who have failed with brief interventions or for whom a more intensive intervention seems warranted but who do not need the structured environment of a residential setting, and (c) retain residential options for those with few social resources and/or environments that are serious impediments to recovery and retain inpatient treatment options for individuals with serious medical/psychiatric conditions.

Although it is very important from a cost perspective, the setting of treatment for alcohol abuse is a distal variable in relation to patients' posttreatment functioning. Other treatment variables, such as the treatment modality, therapists' characteristics, and the amount and duration of treatment, should have a more direct impact on patient posttreatment functioning. Treatment setting can affect duration and amount of treatment (Finney et al., 1996), however, and residential settings may attract some patients (e.g., homeless individuals) who would not present for outpatient treatment.

DISCUSSION

The reviews we have considered point to the effectiveness of cognitive-behavioral interventions. Many of the treatment modalities with evidence of effectiveness (e.g., the community reinforcement approach, behavioral marital therapy, and social skills training) address not only drinking behavior, but also life contexts and the ability to cope with life contexts. This broad-spectrum approach may be necessary to achieve positive outcomes with many patients whose alcohol abuse has produced, and is perpetuated by, deficits in coping skills and problems in multiple life areas. Likewise, 12-step interventions, which have been shown to be as effective as cognitive-behavioral treatment in two recent multisite evaluations, provide coping skills (Snow, Prochaska, & Rossi, 1994), social support over time in the form of 12-step groups and sponsors, and a general (spiritual) orientation toward life.

Regardless of the treatment applied, therapists are likely to have a significant impact on patients' posttreatment functioning. The few studies of therapist effects suggest that therapists who are interpersonally skilled, empathic, and less confrontational produce better patient outcomes, presumably because they establish better therapeutic alliances with their patients.

On the issue of duration and amount of treatment, an effective strategy for many patients may be to provide lower intensity treatment for a longer duration — that is, treatment sessions occurring at a lower rate over a longer period. Although more research is needed, it seems wise at this point to restrict brief interventions to less severely impaired patients. Longer term interventions, in some cases in an inpatient or residential setting, should be reserved for patients with more severe, treatment-resistant alcohol use disorders, fewer social resources, and more concomitant disorders and problems. Finally, reviews indicate that the setting in which treatment is provided exerts little average effect, but patients who have serious medical/psychiatric comorbidities and those who have few social resources may be better treated in inpatient and residential settings, respectively.

Although the research reviews we have summarized are valuable syntheses, they have limitations in terms of providing information to guide alcohol treatment practices. For the most part, the reviews have been of the box-score type. Box-score reviews use the proportion of relevant studies that have found a particular treatment approach to be significantly better than some alternative as the index of treatment effectiveness. This box-score method of summarizing research has significant problems.

For example, studies with low statistical power (due primarily to small patient samples) may yield nonsignificant effects even though the magnitude of difference among treatment conditions is comparable to that in studies finding significant effects. Morley, Finney, Monahan, & Floyd (1996) calculated the average statistical power of comparative alcohol treatment studies reported between 1980 and 1992 to be .54. In other words, studies had just over a 50–50 chance of detecting a medium-size difference between treatment conditions at a statistically significant level. Another methodological problem is that many studies examine multiple drinking-related outcome variables assessed at multiple follow-up points for multiple treatment conditions. There typically is no correction in box-score reviews for the number of tests for treatment effects that were conducted in studies (but see Finney & Monahan, 1996).

Box-score reviews of the alcohol treatment research literature also suffer from the fact that most studies are comparisons of alternative treatments, not of treatment and no-treatment control conditions. Consequently, the strength of the competition against which different modalities are pitted varies from study to study. If two highly effective modalities were consistently pitted against only each other in studies, each would be found to be "ineffective" in a box-score review. Finney and Monahan (1996) adjusted their box-score effectiveness ratings for the strength of the competition, but those competition ratings, themselves, were box-score indices. Overall, these methodological problems make the results of box-score reviews tenuous.

A desirable alternative to box-score reviews is research syntheses based on effect sizes. Effect sizes index the *magnitude* of treatment effects. Syntheses based on effect sizes are less likely than box-score approaches to be distorted by low power and multiple tests. Thus, different conclusions regarding treatment effectiveness may emerge in box-score and effect size reviews of the same set of studies.

Although an effect size synthesis is the more desirable approach, only a few reviews have used effect sizes as the index of alcohol treatment effectiveness (e.g., Bien et al., 1993; Finney & Moos, 1996). These reviews have focused on specific pairs of treatment conditions (e.g., brief versus extended treatment; inpatient versus outpatient treatment). The reason that comprehensive reviews using effect sizes are lacking is that there is no standard comparison group to make differences in effect sizes meaningful across studies of a number of treatment modalities (cf. Mattick & Jarvis, 1993). Less than one third of the comparative alcohol treatment evaluations reported between 1980 and 1992 employed a no- or minimal-treatment comparison group (Floyd, Monahan, Finney & Morley, 1996). Most studies compare alternative treatment conditions, none of which is common across a large number of studies. Effect sizes for a study comparing Treatment A and Treatment B and another study comparing Treatment C and Treatment D provide no information about the relative effectiveness of, say, Treatment A versus Treatment D.

Even with their limitations, box-score reviews of the results of a large number of studies can reveal important general patterns. However, because of the small number of studies of individual treatment modalities, patterns of findings across studies can change over time as more studies are considered. Moreover, quantitative syntheses can obscure important differences across studies, such as variation in treatment implementation (therapist characteristics, duration and amount of treatment, and treatment setting) and in patient characteristics, that should be considered in evaluating overall effectiveness.

Evaluating the effectiveness of alcohol treatment using study-level findings is best carried out, as are primary treatment evaluations, using a mixture of quantitative and qualitative (that is, examining individual studies) analyses. We have attempted to provide some general guidance to treatment providers regarding effective interventions, as well as to highlight some of the issues that they need to keep in mind as they attempt to make sense of research findings and to gauge how individual studies and research syntheses should be used to shape their clinical practice.

ACKNOWLEDGMENTS   Preparation of this manuscript was supported in part by the Department of Veterans Affairs Mental Health Strategic Health Group and Health Services Research and Development Service and by NIAAA Grants AA08689 and AA06699. We thank Courtney Ahrens, Paige Ouimette, Keith Humphreys, and two reviewers for their helpful comments on an earlier draft of this chapter.

References

American Society of Addiction Medicine. (1996). *Patient placement criteria for the treatment of substance-related disorders* (2nd edition): *ASAM PPC-2.* Chevy Chase, MD: American Society of Addiction Medicine.

Annis, H. M. (1986). Is inpatient rehabilitation cost effective? Con position. *Advances in Alcohol and Substance Abuse, 5,* 175–190.

Azrin, N. H., Sisson, R. W., Meyers, R., & Godley, M. (1982). Alcoholism treatment by disulfiram and community reinforcement therapy. *Journal of Behavior Therapy and Experimental Psychiatry, 13,* 105–112.

Bien, T. H., Miller, W. R., & Tonigan, J. S. (1993). Brief interventions for alcohol problems: A review. *Addiction, 88,* 315–336.

Cohen, J. (1988). *Statistical power analysis for the behavioral sciences* (2nd ed.). Hillsdale, N.J.: Lawrence Erlbaum.

Edwards, G., Orford, J., Egert, S., Guthrie, S., Hawker, A., Hensman, C., Mitcheson, M., Oppenheimer, E., & Taylor, C. (1977). Alcoholism: A controlled trial of "treatment" and "advice." *Journal of Studies on Alcohol, 38,* 1004–1031.

Emrick, C. D., Tonigan, J. S., Montgomery, H., & Little, L. (1993). Alcoholics Anonymous: What is currently known? In B. S. McCrady & W. R. Miller (Eds.),

Research on Alcoholics Anonymous: Opportunities and alternatives (pp. 41–76). New Brunswick, N.J.: Alcohol Research Documentation, Rutgers Center of Alcohol Studies.

Finney, J. W., Hahn, A. C., & Moos, R. H. (1996). The effectiveness of inpatient and outpatient treatment for alcohol abuse: The need to focus on mediators and moderators of setting effects. *Addiction, 91,* 1773–1796.

Finney, J. W., & Monahan, S. C. (1996). The cost effectiveness of treatment for alcoholism: A second approximation. *Journal of Studies on Alcohol, 57,* 229–243.

Finney, J. W., & Moos, R. H. (1986). Matching patients with treatments: Conceptual and methodological issues. *Journal of Studies on Alcohol, 47,* 122–134.

———. (1996). The effectiveness of inpatient and outpatient treatment for alcohol abuse: Effect sizes, research design issues, and explanatory mechanisms. *Addiction, 91,* 1813–1820.

Floyd, A. S., Monahan, S. C., Finney, J. W., & Morley, J. A. (1996). Alcoholism treatment outcome studies, 1980–1992: The nature of the research. *Addictive Behaviors, 21,* 413–428.

Holder, H., Longabaugh, R., Miller, W. R., & Rubonis, A. V. (1991). The cost effectiveness of treatment for alcoholism: A first approximation. *Journal of Studies on Alcohol, 52,* 517–540.

Hser, Y. (1995). Drug treatment counselor practices and effectiveness. *Evaluation Review, 19,* 389–408.

Institute of Medicine. (1989). *Prevention and treatment of alcohol problems: Opportunities for research: Report of a study.* Washington, D.C.: National Academy Press.

Ito, J., & Donovan, D. M. (1986). Aftercare in alcoholism treatment: A review. In W. R. Miller & N. Heather (Eds.), *Treating addictive behaviors: Processes of change* (pp. 435–452). New York: Plenum.

Jonson, H., Hermansson, U., Ronnberg, S., Gyllen-Hammar, C., & Forsberg, L. (1995). Comments on brief intervention of alcohol problems: A review of a review. *Addiction, 90,* 1118–1120.

Mattick, R. P., & Jarvis, T. J. (1993). *An outline for the management of alcohol problems: Quality assurance in the treatment of drug abuse project.* Kensington, Australia: National Drug and Alcohol Research Centre. University of New South Wales.

———. (1994). In-patient setting and long duration for the treatment of alcohol dependence? Out-patient care is as good. *Drug and Alcohol Review, 13,* 127–135.

Mattson, M. E., Allen, J. P., Longabaugh, R., Nickless, C. J., Connors, G. J., & Kadden, R. M. (1994). A chronological review of empirical studies of matching alcoholic clients to treatment. *Journal of Studies on Alcohol,* (Suppl. 12), 16–29.

McKay, J. R., Cacciola, J. S., McLellan, A. T., Alterman, A. I., & Wirtz, P. W. (1997). An initial evaluation of the psychosocial dimensions of the American Society of Addiction Medicine criteria for inpatient versus intensive outpatient substance abuse rehabilitation. *Journal of Studies on Alcohol, 58,* 239–252.

McLachlan, J. F. C. (1972). Benefit from group therapy as a function of patient-therapist match on conceptual level. *Psychotherapy: Theory, Research and Practice, 9,* 317–323.

Miller, W. R., Brown, J. M., Simpson, T. L., Handmaker, N. S., Bien, T. H., Luckie, L. F., Montgomery, H. A., Hester, R. K., & Tonigan, J. S. (1995). What works? A methodological analysis of the alcohol treatment outcome literature. In R. K. Hester & W. R. Miller (Eds.), *Handbook of alcoholism treatment approaches: Effective alternatives* (pp. 12–44). Boston, Mass.: Allyn and Bacon.

Miller, W. R., & Hester, R. K. (1986). Inpatient alcoholism treatment: Who benefits? *American Psychologist, 41,* 794–805.

Miller, W. R., & Sanchez, V. C. (1993). Motivating young adults for treatment and lifestyle change. In G. Howard (Ed.), *Issues in alcohol use and misuse by young adults.* Notre Dame, Ind.: University of Notre Dame Press.

Monahan, S. C., & Finney, J. W. (1996). Explaining abstinence rates following treatment for alcohol abuse: A quantitative synthesis of patient, research design, and treatment effects. *Addiction, 91,* 787–805.

Moos, R. H., & Finney, J. W., & Cronkite, R. C. (1990). *Alcoholism treatment: Context, process, and outcome.* New York: Oxford University Press.

Morley, J. A., Finney, J. W., Monahan, S. C., & Floyd, A. S. (1996). Alcoholism treatment outcome studies, 1980–1992: Methodological characteristics and quality. *Addictive Behaviors, 21,* 429–443.

Najavits, L. M., & Weiss, R. D. (1994). Variations in therapist effectiveness in the treatment of patients with substance use disorders: An empirical review. *Addiction, 89,* 679–688.

O'Farrell, T. J., Choquette, K. A., Cutter, H. S. G., Brown, E. D., & McCourt, W. F. (1993). Behavioral Marital Therapy with and without additional couples relapse prevention sessions for alcoholics and their wives. *Journal of Studies on Alcohol, 54,* 652–666.

Ouimette, P. C., Finney, J. W., & Moos, R. H. (1997). Twelve-step and cognitive-behavioral treatment for substance abuse: A comparison of treatment effectiveness. *Journal of Consulting and Clinical Psychology, 65,* 230–240.

Project MATCH Research Group. (1993). Project MATCH: Rationale and methods for a multisite clinical trial matching alcoholic patients to treatment.

Alcoholism: Clinical and Experimental Research, 17, 1130–1145.

———. (1997). Matching alcoholism treatments to client heterogeneity: Project MATCH posttreatment drinking outcomes. *Journal of Studies on Alcohol, 58,* 7–29.

Regier, D. A., Narrow, W. E., Rae, D. S., Manderscheid, R. W., Locke, B. Z., & Goodwin, F. K. (1993). The de facto U.S. mental and addictive disorders service system. *Archives of General Psychiatry, 50,* 85–93.

Saxe, L., et al. (1983). *The effectiveness and costs of alcoholism treatment.* Washington, D.C.: Office of Technology Assessment.

Smith, D. E., & McCrady, B. S. (1991). Cognitive impairment among alcoholics: Impact on drink refusal skill acquisition and treatment outcome. *Addictive Behaviors, 16,* 265–274.

Snow, M. G., Prochaska, J. O., & Rossi, J. (1994). Processes of change in Alcoholics Anonymous: Maintenance factors in long-term sobriety. *Journal of Studies on Alcohol, 55,* 362–371.

Weisner, C., Greenfield, T., & Room, R. (1995). Trends in the treatment of alcohol problems in the U.S. general population, 1979 through 1990. *American Journal of Public Health, 85,* 55–60.

Welte, J., Hynes, G., & Sokolow, L. (1981). Effect of length of stay in inpatient alcoholism treatment on outcome. *Journal of Studies on Alcohol, 42,* 483–499.

8

Pharmacological Treatments
of Schizophrenia

Brian B. Sheitman

Bruce J. Kinon

Beth A. Ridgway

Jeffrey A. Lieberman

More than 100 controlled trials have documented the efficacy of conventional antipsychotic medications in the treatment of schizophrenia. Moreover, these medications have been shown to significantly reduce the risk of symptomatic relapse and rehospitalization when taken on a maintenance basis. However, serious neurological side effects, including dystonia, parkinsonism, akathisia, and tardive dyskinesia, have made these drugs difficult to tolerate for patients with schizophrenia. More recently, a group of "atypical" antipsychotic drugs has been introduced that work at least as well, and in some cases better, than the conventional drugs with significantly less risk of neurological adverse events. Three such drugs are now Food and Drug Administration (FDA) approved (clozapine, risperidone, and olanzapine) and two are in late stages of development (sertindole and quetiapine). These drugs may also be more effective than conventional medications for the treatment of the negative symptoms associated with schizophrenia. Other medications have been studied for schizophrenia, including benzodiazepines, antidepressants, mood stabilizers, and dopamine agonists, although there is limited evidence that these are helpful except in certain specific situations (e.g., antidepressants for "postpsychotic" depression).

Schizophrenia is a chronic psychiatric disorder with a lifetime prevalence rate of approximately 1%. The diagnosis is dependent on the presence of specific symptoms (e.g., delusions, hallucinations, formal thought disorder, and unusual behavior) lasting for at least one month, with persistence in variable intensity or association with significant social and occupational deterioration prior to or subsequent to the psychotic symptoms. Schizophrenic psychopathology has been characterized into two, and possibly three, symptom clusters: positive symptoms comprised of delusions, hallucinations, and formal thought disorder; negative symptoms comprised of deficits in emotional and ver-bal expression and in motivation; and disorganization symptoms reflected by disordered thought processes, bizarre behavior, and inappropriate affect (Liddle, Carpenter, & Crow, 1994). In addition, patients with schizophrenia frequently exhibit affective symptoms during both the psychotic and residual phases of the illness.

Treatment strategies need to target both the acute psychotic phases of the disorder, as well as the chronic debilitating residual symptoms. Inherent in the long-term management of schizophrenia is the prophylaxis against symptom exacerbation and relapse. The illness course and outcome are variable among individuals, although complete symptom remission and return to premorbid status are not common. Progressive deterioration over time characterizes the course of a significant minority of patients, particularly in the early phase of the illness.

Beginning with the introduction of chlorpromazine in 1954 through the introduction of clozapine and risperidone and the novel compounds that have followed in their wake, antipsychotic drugs have come to be classified as conventional (chlorpromazine like) and atypical (clozapine like). Although there is no consensual definition of atypical antipsychotic drugs, the criteria that define them are generally felt to include decreased extrapyramidal side effects (EPS) and tardive dyskinesia (TD), some measure of increased efficacy (in refractory patients, against negative symptoms), and only limited prolactin elevation.

Antipsychotic medications have been incontrovertibly demonstrated to be effective and safe treatment for both the acute and chronic phases of treatment management. Conventional antipsychotic drugs have been thoroughly studied regarding efficacy and propensity to produce both acute and chronic side effects. Newer, atypical antipsychotic drugs are eagerly sought by clinicians as these agents hold out the promise for increased therapeutic efficacy with significantly less risk of extrapyramidal and neurocognitive adverse effects (Kinon and Lieberman, 1996). Clozapine has demonstrated superior efficacy in reducing symptoms in 30% of rigorously defined treatment-resistant patients when directly compared with the typical antipsychotic drug chlorpromazine (Kane, Honigfeld, Singer, & Meltzer, 1988). Risperidone (Marder & Meibach, 1994) and olanzapine (Beasly et al., 1996) have been reported to be more effective than the typical agent haloperidol in reducing negative symptoms and causing less motor side effects, while compounds in the last stages of development (sertindole, quetiapine) have been found to produce little or no acute EPS at therapeutic doses. Concomitant medications such as benzodiazepines, lithium, carbamazepine (CBZ), valproic acid (VPA), and dopamine agonists have been used individually and as adjuncts to antipsychotic treatment regimens in order to improve efficacy, although clear demonstration of effectiveness is lacking. Moreover, antidepressants have been extensively used to treat the affective symptoms associated with schizophrenia.

ACUTE TREATMENT EFFECTS

Typical Antipsychotics

The introduction of the prototypic conventional or typical antipsychotic drug chlorpromazine in the 1950s, with the subsequent development of other neuroleptic agents with similar pharmacological activity, led to a revolution in the treatment of schizophrenia. These drugs are credited with providing the first effective medical management strategy for schizophrenia and constitute one of the great medical advances of the 20th century. Early claims critical of the inherent efficacy of these compounds led to the design of rigorous clinical trial methodology, such as the placebo-controlled, double-blind study with thoughtful subject inclusion and exclusion criteria; random treatment assignment; and the use of standardized rating instruments to prove the value of these drugs.

Over 100 placebo-controlled trials have conclusively demonstrated the effectiveness of antipsychotic drugs (Davis, Barter, & Kane, 1989). Due to the volume and consistency of findings in these studies, it is not necessary to review each of them. A representative sample of methodologically rigorous acute treatment trials that demonstrate the superior efficacy of conventional antipsychotic drugs commonly used and currently available in the United States and compared with a placebo is listed in Table 8.1. Placebo-controlled studies in which antipsychotic efficacy could not be demonstrated are generally restricted to poorly designed early studies that involved doses of chlorpromazine that were less than 300 mg daily (Klein and Davis, 1969).

In general, these studies found that approximately 60% of antipsychotic-drug-treated subjects, as compared with 20% of placebo-treated subjects, demonstrated a nearly complete resolution of acute positive symptoms within a 6-week trial. Only 8% of medication-treated subjects showed no improvement or worsening, whereas nearly half of placebo-treated subjects did not improve or worsened (National Institute of Mental Health–Psychopharmacology Service Center [NIMH-PSC] Collaborative Study Group, 1964). All symptoms associated with schizophrenia improved on antipsychotic drugs, although the positive symptoms, as compared with negative symptoms, seem to respond to the greatest degree and most consistently. Although symptomatic improvement is clinically important and

TABLE 8.1 Relative Antipsychotic Drug Efficacy (versus Chlorpromazine and/or Haloperidol)

Drug	Number of Studies	Reference
Typical Antipsychotic Drugs		
Chlorpromazine	8	Clark et al. (1968)
		Hollister, Erickson, & Motzenbecker (1960)
		Casey et al. (1960a)
		Kurland, Hanlon, Tatom, Ota, & Simopoulos (1961)
		NIMH-PSC Collaborative Study Group (1964)
		Schiele, Vestre, & Stein (1961)
		Adelson & Epstein (1962)
Fluphenazine	2	NIMH-PSC Collaborative Study Group (1964)
Haloperidol	9	Vestre, Hall, & Schiele (1962)
		Garry & Leonard (1962)
		Azima, Durost, & Arthurs (1960)
		Samuels (1961)
		Chouinard et al. (1993)
		Brandrup & Kristjansen (1961)
		Beasley et al. (1996)
		Marder & Meibach (1994)
		Okasha & Twefik (1964)
		Reese & Davies (1965)
Loxapine	3	Simpson & Cuculic (1976)
		van der Velde & Kiltie (1975)
		Clark, Huber, Sullivan, Wood, & Costiloe (1972)
Mesoridazine	2	McIndoo (1971)
		Ritter & Tatum (1972)
Molindone	2	Gallant & Bishop (1968)
		Clarke et al. (1972)
Perphenazine	3	Kurland et al. (1961)
		Adelson & Epstein (1962)
Trifluoperazine	3	Casey et al. (1960)
		Hollister et al. (1960)
		Adelson & Epstein (1962)
Thiothixene	4	Wolpert, Sheppard, & Merlis (1968)
		Huang, Gerhardstein, Kim, & Hollister (1987)
		Yillmaz (1971)
		Gallant, Bishop, Timmons, & Gould (1966)
Thioridazine	2	NIMH-PSC Collaborative Study Group (1964)
Atypical Antipsychotic Drugs		
Clozapine	2	Shopsin, Klein, Aaronson, & Collora (1979)
		Pickar et al. (1992)
Risperidone	2	Marder & Meibach (1994)
		Chouinard et al. (1993)
Olanzapine	1	Beasley et al. (1996)

responsible for the deinstitutionalization of the treatment of schizophrenia, patient functioning and social reintegration have not consistently improved with the use of typical antipsychotic drugs. This disappointing observation was made soon after the introduction of these drugs into clinical practice (Schooler, Goldberg, Boothe, & Cole, 1967).

Despite the dozens of typical antipsychotic drugs that have become available to clinicians in the United States since 1954, these drugs, which share much the same mechanism of action, fail to distinguish among themselves with superior efficacy. Table 8.2 lists the efficacy as demonstrated in methodologically rigorous controlled clinical trials of a representative sample of

TABLE 8.2 Relative Antipsychotic Drug Efficacy (versus Chlorpromazine and/or Haloperidol)

Drug	Number of Studies				Reference
	Superior to CPZ	Equal to CPZ	Superior to HAL	Equal to HAL	
Typical Antipsychotic Drugs					
Fluphenazine		3			Cole et al. (1964)
					NIMH-PSC Collaborative Study Group (1964)
					Laskey et al. (1962)
					Hanlon, Michaux, Ota, Shaffer, & Kurland (1965)
Haloperidol	2				Pratt, Bishop, & Gallant (1964)
					Fox, Gobble, Clos, & Denison (1964)
		1			Serafetinides, Willis, & Clark (1972)
Loxapine	1				Tuason, Escobar, Garvey, & Schiele (1984)
		1			Rifkin, Rieder, Sarantakos, Saraf, & Kane (1984)
				2	Fruensgaard, Korsgaard, Jorgensen, & Jensen (1977)
					Tuason (1986)
Mesoridazine		1			Freeman, Oktem, & Oktem (1969)
Molindone				2	Binder, Glick, & Rice (1981)
					Escobar et al. (1985)
Perphenazine		4			Adelson & Epstein (1962)
					Hanlon et al. (1965)
					Kurland et al. (1961)
					Casey et al. (1960b)
Trifluoperazine		4			Adelson & Epstein (1962)
					Schiele et al. (1961)
					Hanlon et al. (1965)
					Hollister et al. (1960)
Thiothixene		1			Rickels et al. (1978)
Thioridazine		3			Schiele et al. (1961)
					Cole et al. (1964)
					NIMH-PSC Collaborative Study Group (1964)
					Laskey et al. (1962)
Atypical Antipsychotic Drugs					
Clozapine		1			Gelenberg & Doller (1979)
	4				Leon (1979)
					Shopsin et al. (1979)
					Kane et al. (1988)
					Claghorn et al. (1987)
				1	Klieser, Strauss, & Lemmer (1994)
Risperidone				4	Peuskens (1995)
					Ceskova & Svestka (1993)
					Min, Rhee, Kim, & Kang (1993)
					Borison et al. (1992)
			4		Chouinard et al. (1993)
					Marder & Meibach (1994)
					Claus et al. (1992)
					Muller-Spahn (1992)
Olanzapine			1		Beasley et al. (1996)

CPZ = chlorpromazine; HAL = haloperidol.

antipsychotic drugs compared with the reference drugs chlorpromazine or haloperidol.

The onset of the therapeutic effect of antipsychotic drugs during the treatment of an acute episode of schizophrenia usually is manifested within the first 1 to 3 weeks; most gains are noted within 6 to 8 weeks (Davis et al., 1989). Some patients, including first-episode patients (Lieberman, 1993), may require several months to achieve their full clinical response and symptom remission. Clinicians generally employ maneuvers such as dosage increase, switching to another typical antipsychotic, or maintaining the initial treatment for an extended trial when patients fail to respond to a standard course of treatment. Little evidence from controlled clinical trials supports the efficacy of any of these strategies (Kinon et al., 1993; Levinson et al., 1990; Rifkin, Doddi, Karajgi, Borenstein, & Wachspress, 1991; Van Putten, Marder, & Mintz, 1990; Volavka et al., 1992), although an individual patient may show a better response to one particular drug compared with another (Gardos, 1974). In addition, there is little data to support the usefulness of doses beyond the range of 400 to 1000 mg daily of chlorpromazine or an equivalent dose of other antipsychotics; megadoses of 2,000 mg daily of chlorpromazine or its equivalent are not generally associated with greater efficacy (Bjorndal et al., 1980; Ericksen, Hurt, & Chang, 1978; McCreadie and MacDonald, 1977; Neborsky, Janowsky, Munson, & Depry, 1981; Quitkin, Rifkin, & Klein, 1975) and can lead to a greater incidence of side effects. The practice of administering large parenteral doses of high-potency neuroleptics within a 24-hour period ("rapid neuroleptization") has not demonstrated any further gains in efficacy compared with the standard treatment and has largely been discontinued as a therapeutic strategy.

Atypical Antipsychotics

The introduction of atypical antipsychotics has offered hope for enhanced efficacy in the treatment of schizophrenic psychopathology, particularly in reducing negative symptoms, with a reduced burden of extrapyramidal motor dysfunction. Atypical agents currently approved by the Food and Drug Administration (FDA) include clozapine, risperidone, and olanzapine, while sertindole and quetiapine await formal approval.

Clozapine

Baldessarini and Frankenburg (1991) reviewed 14 double-blind studies from 1971 through 1988 that compared the efficacy of clozapine to that of a conventional neuroleptic in the treatment of schizophrenic psychopathology. Overall, these authors reported that 9% more subjects improved and mean ratings were 13% better in the clozapine-treated patients, though these differences were not statistically significant. Rates of EPS, however, were markedly lower in clozapine-treated patients. In one of these studies, Kane et al. (1988) entered 268 treatment-resistant schizophrenia patients into a double-blind comparison of clozapine and chlorpromazine. *Treatment-resistant patients* were defined as having previously failed to respond to at least three prior neuroleptics and to have been without any period of good functioning in the past 5 years, then not responding to a single-blind, 6-week haloperidol lead-in trial. At 6 weeks, 30% of the clozapine-treated group and only 4% of the chlorpromazine-treated group met the a priori response criteria of a reduction greater than 20% from the baseline in the Brief Psychiatric Rating Scale (BPRS) total score plus either a posttreatment Clinical Global Impression (CGI) score of 3 (mild) or lower or a posttreatment BPRS total score of 35 or lower.

Interestingly, there has been only one additional double-blind study examining the efficacy of clozapine published since the report of Kane et al. in 1988. Pickar et al. (1992) studied 21 neuroleptic, treatment-resistant, or intolerant schizophrenia patients in a crossover, placebo-controlled design of long-term typical neuroleptic (mean = 46 days) and clozapine (mean duration: moderate doses = 52 days, optimal doses = 107 days) treatment, with clozapine significantly reducing positive and negative symptoms in comparison to fluphenazine and a placebo. However, only 8 of 21 patients (38%) improved. Consistent with the above response rates, Zito et al. (1993), in a field trial of 227 treatment-resistant schizophrenia patients hospitalized in a state-operated public psychiatric system, found 29% and 33% of the patients were improved at 12 weeks and 1 year of clozapine treatment, respectively.

An incidence rate of 1% for clozapine-induced agranulocytosis was reported (Alvir, Lieberman, Safferman, Schwimmer, & Schaaf, 1993) and has resulted in clozapine use being limited to refractory patients. In addition to the agranulocytosis, frequent side effects of clozapine include sedation, weight gain, hypotension, tachycardia, and a dose-dependent risk for seizures. Nevertheless, the demonstrated efficacy of clozapine among a subgroup of refractory patients, with no acute EPS and the absence of risk for tardive dyskinesia, was a landmark achievement in psychopharmacology. Furthermore, the success of clozapine was the impetus for an enormous research effort that resulted in the development of other atypical antipsychotic drugs.

Risperidone

A number of double-blind studies, some placebo controlled, have been published that compared the efficacy of risperidone with a conventional antipsychotic. Muller-Spahn (1992), in an international, multicenter, 8-week study, reported that risperidone at doses of 4, 8, or 12 mg was superior to haloperidol in symptom reduction, while a dose of 16 mg was equally efficacious.

Claus et al. (1992), in a study of 44 chronic schizophrenia patients treated with risperidone (mean dose = 12 mg) or haloperidol (mean dose = 10 mg) in a 12-week parallel group trial, found a statistically significant greater improvement in overall psychopathology and significantly reduced need for antiparkinsonian medication in the risperidone-treated group.

Ceskova and Svestka (1993), in an 8-week double-blind comparison of risperidone (2–20 mg) and haloperidol (2–20 mg) in 62 schizophrenia and schizoaffective patients, found no differences between groups in total BPRS scores.

Chouinard et al. (1993) performed a multicenter placebo-controlled study of 135 chronic schizophrenia patients treated with 2, 6, 10, or 16 mg of risperidone, 20 mg of haloperidol, or a placebo. After a single-blind washout period, Chouinard et al. found risperidone at 6 mg superior to haloperidol on the total Positive and Negative Syndrome Scale (PANSS) and the PANSS general psychopathology subscale. Haloperidol treatment resulted in a statistically significant increase in EPS compared with doses of 2, 6, and 16 mg of risperidone; however, 10 mg of risperidone resulted in equal amounts of EPS.

Hoyberg et al. (1993) conducted a multicenter study of 107 chronic schizophrenia patients in an acute exacerbation. The patients were treated with risperidone (5–15 mg) or perphenazine (16–48 mg) for 8 weeks, and the Hoyberg group found no significant differences in total PANSS scores at the end point of the study. However, the number of patients with predominantly negative symptoms that had a 20% drop in total PANSS scores was significantly greater in the risperidone-treated group. Side-effect vulnerability was approximately equal between groups.

Marder and Meibach (1994) conducted a multi-center study of 388 schizophrenia patients treated with one of four doses of risperidone (2, 6, 10, or 16 mg), 20 mg of haloperidol, or a placebo. Marder and Meibach reported statistically significant differences in overall clinical improvement from 6, 10, and 16 mg of risperidone versus the placebo and from 6 and 16 mg risperidone versus haloperidol as assessed by the PANSS. Both negative and positive symptom scores were significantly reduced for the 6 and 16 mg of risperidone versus the placebo, while only positive symptoms were reduced significantly by haloperidol compared to the placebo. There were no significant differences found in the reduction of negative symptoms when any of the 4 doses of risperidone was directly compared with haloperidol. Both 16 mg of risperidone and 20 mg of haloperidol resulted in significant increases in parkinsonian side effects compared with the placebo, though not when compared with other risperidone doses.

Peuskens (1995) performed a multicenter, parallel-group, double-blind, 8-week study of 1,362 patients with schizophrenia. These patients were treated with 1, 4, 8, 12, or 16 mg of risperidone or 10 mg of haloperidol. Peuskens found no significant advantage for any dose of risperidone compared with haloperidol on PANSS and CGI assessments. However, 1, 4, 8, and 12 mg of risperidone had significantly lower incidence rates of EPS than haloperidol.

The trials described above that compared multiple doses of risperidone with one dose of haloperidol have been criticized as potentially biasing the results toward a more favorable response from risperidone. Nevertheless, the evidence suggests that risperidone is at least equal to conventional neuroleptics in the treatment of schizophrenic psychopathology, with a lower incidence rate of EPS at the lower dose ranges. Enhanced efficacy for risperidone compared with conventional neuroleptics for the treatment of negative symptoms or in treatment-refractory populations has not yet been established.

Olanzapine

Olanzapine has recently been approved by the FDA for the treatment of schizophrenia; one double-blind study has been published. Beasley et al. (1996) reported on the efficacy of olanzapine in a 6-week study of 3 dose ranges of olanzapine (5 ± 2.5, 10 ± 2.5, 15 ± 2.5 mg/day) compared with one dose range of haloperidol (15 ± 5mg/day) and a placebo in 335 schizophrenia patients. In overall symptomatology and positive symptom improvement, as assessed by the BPRS, the middle and higher doses of olanzapine, as well as haloperidol, were significantly superior to the placebo. In negative symptom improvement as assessed by the Scale for the Assessment of Negative Symptoms (SANS), only the low and high doses of olanzapine were superior to the placebo, while the higher dose of olanzapine was found superior to haloperidol. Despite the lack of statistically significant differences between olanzapine- and haloperidol-treated patients on measures of BPRS total and CGI scores at the end point of the study, there was a significant difference between the high-dose olanzapine group versus haloperidol in the number of patients that demonstrated at least an 80% improvement from the baseline. In addition, no acute dystonia was observed with olanzapine, and rates of parkinsonism and akathisia at the high dose of olanzapine were approximately 1/3 and 1/2 less than those observed in the haloperidol group, respectively.

Olanzapine appears to be a promising new drug, at least equal in efficacy to the conventional neuroleptics and with fewer EPS. Whether olanzapine will be superior to conventional neuroleptics in the treatment of negative symptoms and refractory populations and result in less tardive dyskinesia remains to be established.

Sertindole

Sertindole has been recommended by the FDA for approval but is not yet available in the marketplace. McEvoy et al. (1993), in a pilot, double-blind, placebo-controlled, 7-week study (dosing left to clinical judgment) of 38 schizophrenia and schizoaffective patients, found sertindole significantly superior to a placebo in reducing total and positive BPRS scores. In a 40-day, randomized, placebo-controlled study that treated 205 neuroleptic-responsive schizophrenia patients with the sertindole dose range of 8, 12, or 20 mg, Van Kamman et al. (1996) found a statistically significant difference between 20 mg of sertindole and the placebo on total PANSS, BPRS, and CGI scales.

The above studies report similar EPS rates for sertindole- and placebo-treated patients. A concern about sertindole causing a dose-related lengthening in the QT interval has been raised due to a number of unexplained sudden deaths during treatment. However, there has been no evidence that the lengthening in the QT interval was associated with any clinically significant symptoms (i.e., arrhythmias).

Sertindole treatment appears superior to the placebo for the treatment of schizophrenic psychopathology with comparable rates of acute EPS. However, the data available to date are too limited to draw any definitive conclusions about its overall efficacy as compared with conventional neuroleptics.

Quetiapine

Quetiapine has not yet been approved by the FDA; however, the efficacy of quetiapine has been evaluated in four controlled clinical trials. Hirsch et al. (1996) performed two 6-week, double-blind, placebo-controlled studies that enrolled 109 and 286 patients, respectively. The first study used a mean dose of quetiapine of 307 mg, while the second study used both a low-dose (mean = 209 mg) and a high-dose group (mean = 407 mg). There was evidence of benefit for the quetiapine-treated groups, with significant reductions in BPRS total scores, CGI scores, BPRS activation and thought disturbance subscores, and the SANS total score.

In a randomized, double-blind, 6-week study (Hirsch et al., 1996) of 201 patients that compared the efficacy of quetiapine to chlorpromazine, with doses up to 750 mg for each, no significant differences were found between groups on BPRS total or factor scores and on CGI or SANS scores.

In a 6-week, double-blind trial that compared the efficacy of five fixed doses of quetiapine (75, 150, 300, 600, or 750 mg/day) to haloperidol 12 mg and a placebo in 361 schizophrenia patients, Borison et al. (1996) reported that all doses of quetiapine, as well as haloperidol, were superior to the placebo in reducing total and positive symptom BPRS scores, while only 300 mg of quetiapine was superior to the placebo at reducing SANS total scores.

Quetiapine did not cause EPS at greater rates than the placebo in the 3 placebo-controlled studies. In the direct comparison with chlorpromazine, neither medication was associated with EPS.

Quetiapine may be a promising new medication. However, with the limited data available, claims of enhanced efficacy beyond what is obtained from conventional neuroleptics are premature.

Factors That Influence Antipsychotic Response

A significant effort is under way to understand factors that may be associated with antipsychotic treatment refractoriness as preventive measures may offer hope in lieu of the availability of newer drugs. For example, a delay in the antipsychotic drug treatment of the onset of first-episode schizophrenia (Loebel et al., 1992) and in the treatment of acute exacerbations (May et al., 1981a; Wyatt, 1991) may be associated with a poorer clinical outcome.

Extrapyramidal Side Effects (EPS)

Neuroleptic-induced EPS occur both acutely and after long-term treatment. Therapeutic doses of typical antipsychotics induce EPS at high rates, while the atypical drugs either result in no EPS (clozapine, sertindole, quetiapine) or substantially fewer EPS (risperidone, olanzapine). Commonly occurring acute EPS include akathisia, dystonia, and parkinsonism, with each having a characteristic time of onset subsequent to neuroleptic administration. Akathisia typically is witnessed in a few hours to days, dystonia within the first 96 hours, and parkinsonism from a few days to weeks (Casey, 1993). Neuroleptic malignant syndrome (NMS), another type of acute EPS, is characterized by rigidity, hyperthermia, and autonomic instability and may be fatal if untreated; fortunately, NMS occurs infrequently.

The treatment of acute EPS depends on the specific side effect (Casey, 1993). Dystonia can be quickly and successfully treated with either an intramuscular injection of an anticholinergic or an antihistaminic agent. The initial treatment for parkinsonian side effects is lowering the dose of neuroleptic. If an adequate response is not achieved, adding an anticholinergic or antihistaminic drug is usually efficacious. If symptoms persist, switching to a class of antipsychotic that produces fewer EPS is indicated.

Eliminating akathisia is more difficult, and lowering the neuroleptic dose followed by individual trials of beta-adrenergic blockers, antiparkinsonian agents, and benzodiazepines is a reasonable treatment algorithm (Casey, 1993). Controlled trials comparing the efficacy of the various treatments are not available.

Tardive dyskinesia (TD) is a hyperkinetic involuntary movement disorder induced by sustained exposure to neuroleptic medication; it occurs at the rate of 4% per year in the adult nongeriatric population (Glazer, Morgenstern, & Doucette, 1993; Kane, Woerner, & Lieberman, 1985; Morgenstern & Glazer, 1993). In addition to the more frequently observed orofacial and choreoathetoid signs of TD, tardive dystonias and tardive akathisia have also been described. Treatment of TD has largely been unsuccessful, though there are some data from controlled trials (Adler et al., 1993) suggesting that the antioxidant vitamin E may be useful in less-chronic patients. Tardive dyskinesia does not result from clozapine use; however, the other atypical antipsychotics have not been in use long enough to make a determination regarding similar effects.

Maintenance Treatment Effects

Numerous studies have demonstrated that schizophrenic patients who have successfully responded to antipsychotic medication will experience a clinical worsening, measured by either symptom worsening or an increased rate of rehospitalization, when their treatment is discontinued (Davis, 1975; Kane and Lieberman, 1987). Controlled clinical trials of drug discontinuation demonstrate that after 1 year of maintenance treatment, 30% of patients will relapse on medication compared with a rate of 65% of patients who have undergone placebo substitution. Even those patients who have been successfully maintained in the community for 2–3 years on antipsychotic drugs will demonstrate a reversion to a relapse rate of 66% by 1 year after their treatment is discontinued (Hogarty, Ulrich, Mussare, & Aristigneta, 1976). First-episode patients show a comparable drug effect, although at lower relapse rates. During the year following their initial recovery, a relapse rate of 40% of those on a placebo, compared to none while on medication, has been reported (Kane, Rifkin, Quitkin, Nayak, & Ramos-Lorenzi, 1982).

The benefits of maintenance antipsychotic drug treatment are tempered by the inherent risk to the patient of long-term side effects such as the development of tardive dyskinesia. Limiting antipsychotic drug exposure has intuitive appeal for the minimalization of side-effect risk. Maintenance studies of the dose-response relationship for up to one year of continuous antipsychotic drug treatment indicate that standard drug doses (fluphenazine decanoate 12.5–50 mg biweekly; haloperidol decanoate 50–200 mg monthly) provide significantly greater prophylaxis against relapse than do doses of one half to one tenth as much (Hogarty et al., 1988; Johnson, Ludlow, Street, & Taylor, 1987; Kane et al., 1983, 1993; Kane, Woerner, & Sarantakos, 1986; Marder et al., 1987; Schooler, Keith, Severe, & Mathews, 1993), although the lower doses may be associated with better social adjustment and less-adverse effects usually related to acute extrapyramidal side effects rather than tardive dyskinesia. A targeted approach that involves slowly titrating patients off maintenance medication with reintroduction of the medication rapidly during presumptive incipient relapsing has not been found to be more effective than the continuous administration of maintenance medication and is associated with risks of symptom exacerbation and relapse (Carpenter et al., 1990; Gaebel et al., 1993; Herz et al., 1991; Jolley, Hirsch, Morrison, McRink, & Wilson, 1990; Schooler et al., 1993).

Controlled maintenance treatment studies involving atypical antipsychotic drugs have not been done. Clozapine's efficacy in the maintenance phase of treatment is supported by 3 open-label studies. Meltzer, Burnett, Bastani, and Ramirez (1990) reported that the rehospitalization rate among treatment-resistant schizophrenia patients after 1 year of clozapine treatment was reduced by 83% in comparison with the year prior to clozapine treatment. Miller, Perry, Cadoret, and Andreasen (1992) found that patients treated with clozapine for 2½ years had fewer hospitalizations and the hospitalizations were of shorter durations compared with the previous 2½ years. Brier, Buchanan, Irish, and Carpenter (1993) also reported that a year of clozapine treatment was superior to the previous year of conventional neuroleptics, with fewer exacerbations of illness and fewer hospitalizations. An open mirror-image clinical study found that during 1 year of risperidone treatment the number of days of hospitalization was reduced compared with the preceding reference period (Addington et al., 1993). Long-term trials with atypical antipsychotic drugs will hopefully demonstrate that greater efficacy, as measured in reduced rates of relapse, more global symptom remission, and improved social reintegration, accompanied by a significantly decreased risk of tardive dyskinesia, can yet be realized in the maintenance treatment of schizophrenia.

Summary of Antipsychotic Drug Effects

Most studies of antipsychotic drugs have focused on positive symptom psychopathology and demonstrated that both conventional and atypical drugs clearly are effective both acutely and prophylactically. However, the response of patients beyond positive symptoms has been less well studied and antipsychotic drug efficacy much less well demonstrated.

OTHER PHARMACOLOGICAL TREATMENTS

Due to the limitations in the efficacy of antipsychotic medication in resolving the full range of schizophrenic psychopathology and the frequently occurring comorbid symptoms (e.g., anxiety, depression, mood lability, and motor unrest) that occur over the course of the illness, adjunctive treatments are often utilized in order to reduce morbidity. The following section reviews controlled trials of pharmacological agents not classified as antipsychotics that have been used to treat schizophrenia patients. We report on the efficacy of these drugs, for treatment of both schizophrenic psychopathology and comorbid conditions, when used either in combination with an antipsychotic drug or as a lone treatment. The classes of medication described are antianxiety/hypnotics, antidepressants, mood stabilizers, and dopamine agonists. In addition, we briefly review the efficacy of electroconvulsive therapy (ECT) as a treatment for schizophrenic psychopathology.

The use of adjunctive pharmacological treatments in schizophrenia patients has been the subject of numerous reviews (Christison, Kirch, & Wyatt, 1991; Donaldson, Gelenberg, & Baldessarini, 1983; Farmer & Blewett, 1993; Johns & Thompson, 1995; Lindenmayer, 1995; Meltzer, 1992; Meltzer, Sdommers, & Luchins, 1986; Rifkin, 1993; Siris, 1993; Wolkowitz, 1993). Due to space limitations and the large number of studies involved, recent review articles are summarized if applicable and updated with reports of subsequently published, methodologically rigorous studies.

Antianxiety/Hypnotics

Benzodiazepines have been used to treat patients with schizophrenia since the early 1960s. This specific topic has been extensively reviewed by Wolkowitz and Pickar (1991). These authors reported on 14 double-blind studies published from 1961 to 1982 in which benzodiazepines alone were used to treat schizophrenic psychopathology. Of the 14 studies, 9, including all those since 1975, reported some positive effects; however, in almost all studies there was variability in response, with some patients doing well while others did poorly. The authors noted that, due to methodologic limitations, conclusions that may be drawn from the data are limited, though there is some support for benzodiazepines alone having been efficacious as an antipsychotic for at least some patients.

These authors (Wolkowitz & Pickar, 1991) also reviewed the efficacy of benzodiazepines when used as adjunctive agents to neuroleptics. Of 16 double-blind studies published from 1966 to 1989, 11 indicated some positive results, again with the authors stating that in nearly all studies some individual patients responded well and others poorly. In one of the larger studies (Csernansky, Riney, Lombrozo, Overall, & Hollister, 1988), a double-blind comparison of alprazolam, diazepam, and a placebo for the treatment of negative symptoms in outpatients with schizophrenia that had been maintained on neuroleptics, there was no sustained significant effect on negative symptoms in those patients that received a benzodiazepine.

Wolkowitz and Pickar (1991) sought to determine if there were factors that would be predictive of a clinical response to the benzodiazepines. They examined if there was a differential efficacy among the benzodiazepines, if the onset of the response would predict the duration of the response, and whether there was a relationship between response and dose or plasma level. The only association noted was that higher doses of benzodiazepines and higher plasma levels were associated with a more favorable clinical response, though the authors noted that none of the studies specifically investigated dose-response relationships.

There have been two controlled studies published since the above review. Salzman et al. (1991) conducted a double-blind study that compared the efficacy of 2 mg of intramuscular lorazepam to 5 mg of intramuscular haloperidol administered to 60 psychotic inpatients (26 schizophrenic). At 2, 24, and 48 hours after the injection, lorazepam and haloperidol both reduced aggression, agitation, and assaultive behavior, with a significant difference in favor of lorazepam at 2 hours in the number of patients who had a decrease in aggression. Barbee, Mancuso, Freed, and Todorov (1992) compared the efficacy of haloperidol with either alprazolam or a placebo over a 72-hour period in 28 acutely psychotic schizophrenia patients. The Barbee study reported that both groups improved significantly, though the combination of haloperidol and alprazolam was more effective in controlling agitation than haloperidol alone, particularly in the first 48 hours, with lower doses of medication needed in the combination-treated group. This study supported the notion that benzodiazepine augmentation may be useful in limiting the quantity of neuroleptics used for the treatment of schizophrenia (Bodkin, 1992). Table 8.3 summarizes the studies of Wolkowitz and Pickar (1991), Salzman et al., and Barbee et al.

There are few studies in the literature that have specifically addressed in a double-blind fashion the use of benzodiazepines to treat the comorbid conditions that often afflict schizophrenia patients independent of psychosis. Nevertheless, there is some evidence from less methodologically rigorous studies to suggest that schizophrenia patients with anxiety, depression, hostility, irritability, and motor unrest may benefit from benzodiazepines (Wolkowitz & Pickar, 1991). In a well-designed small study that looked at benzodiazepine response among 6 anxious schizophrenia patients under double-blind conditions that lasted 12 weeks with multiple crossovers (Kellner et al., 1975), it was concluded that some patients from this subgroup may benefit from adjunctive benzodiazepine use with a reduction of anxiety. Though benzodiazepines are frequently used as hypnotic agents in clinical practice, there have been no controlled studies that have established their efficacy with schizophrenia patients.

Despite the evidence for a role for benzodiazepines in the treatment of at least some schizophrenia patients, there has been markedly little systematic research over the past 5 years. This may be due to the introduction of atypical antipsychotics, the potential for dependency, and the reluctance to prescribe these agents to patients with comorbid substance abuse disorders. In addition, there are reports that benzodiazepines may result in a "disinhibiting" (Karson, Weinberger, Bigelow, & Wyatt, 1982) or worsening of psychopathology in some patients (Wolkowitz & Pickar, 1991). Nevertheless, at a minimum the benzodiazepines appear to be a useful adjunct to neuroleptics in the treatment of agitated or anxious schizophrenia patients.

Antidepressants

The efficacy of antidepressant medication, either used alone or as adjuncts to neuroleptics, for the treatment of schizophrenic psychopathology was first comprehensively reviewed by Siris, Van Kammen, and Docherty (1978) by the analysis of the results of double-

TABLE 8.3 Benzodiazepines

Author	Study Design (Double Blind)	Number of Patients	Results
Wolkowitz & Pickar (1991) (review article)	Benzodiazepines versus placebo	14 studies 576 patients	9 studies reported positive results
	Benzodiazepines and neuroleptics versus neuroleptics	16 studies 644 patients	11 studies reported positive results
Salzman et al. (1991)	2 mg im lorazepam versus 5 mg im haloperidol administered to acutely psychotic patients	60	Greater number of subjects had a decrease in aggression with lorazepam
Barbee et al. (1992)	Acutely psychotic patients received either alprazolam and haloperidol or haloperidol alone	28	Combination of alprazolam and haloperidol superior to haloperidol alone in reducing aggression

blind controlled studies. When antidepressants were used alone, only 1 of 14 studies demonstrated clearly positive findings, while 2 of 12 studies that compared a combination of a tricyclic antidepressant with a neuroleptic to a neuroleptic alone found a superior response from the combination. Poor results were also observed when a combination of a monoamine oxidase (MAO) inhibitor and a neuroleptic were compared to a neuroleptic alone, with only 1 of 12 studies demonstrating a clear superiority for the combination. The authors acknowledged that antidepressants do not appear indicated as a sole treatment for schizophrenia; however, they cautioned that the overwhelming preponderance of negative findings may have resulted from weaknesses in study design, in particular, inadequate antidepressant dosages. In addition, the authors recommended that future research efforts be targeted to specific depressive syndromes afflicting a significant percentage of patients over the course of their illness (McGlashan & Carpenter, 1976).

The subsequent recognition and acceptance of a secondary or postpsychotic depression occurring among schizophrenia patients (Siris, 1991) led to additional research interest in adjunctive antidepressant usage, the efficacy of which was reviewed by analysis of double-blind studies (Plasky, 1991). Of six placebo-controlled studies using tricyclic antidepressants in addition to a neuroleptic, two demonstrated a significant reduction in depression. The author noted that these two studies were of patients whose acute psychosis was under control and suggested that adjunctive antidepressant treatment may be successful for the treatment of depression only when the acute psychotic

episode has stabilized. Furthermore, Plasky (1991) noted that, in two studies of acutely psychotic patients, the antidepressants appeared to have resulted in a worsening of the psychosis and cautioned about premature use of antidepressant medication.

Since the above reviews, there have been only a small number of double-blind studies that have continued to examine the efficacy of antidepressants as an adjunctive medication to neuroleptics. Siris et al. (1991) studied the therapeutic efficacy of adjunctive imipramine when added to fluphenazine decanoate and benzotropine. Among 27 well-stabilized, negative-symptom schizophrenia and schizoaffective disordered patients who also met criteria for a postpsychotic depression, Siris et al. found that the imipramine-treated group had superior global and negative symptom ratings at 6–9 weeks. The authors explain their positive findings in this subgroup of patients as further support for a syndromal overlap of postpsychotic depression and negative symptoms (Siris et al., 1988). In an additional double-blind, placebo-controlled study that examined the efficacy of antidepressants as an adjunctive treatment for negative symptoms among 30 schizophrenia patients, fluvoxamine was found superior to a placebo (Silver & Nassar, 1992). The authors noted that neither depression nor extrapyramidal symptoms improved, leading them to conclude that fluvoxamine's benefit was to the "primary" negative symptoms.

Two other studies also lend support for the efficacy of adjunctive antidepressant use in the treatment of schizophrenia patients. In a randomized, double-blind protocol (Siris, Bermanzohn, Mason, & Shuwall,

1994) that examined 24 schizophrenic or schizoaffective patients who had been successfully treated with imipramine, fluphenazine decanoate, and benzotropine for 6 months and were then either continued or tapered off the imipramine and followed for 1 year, continuous imipramine treatment prevented relapse into both depression and psychosis. Hogarty et al. (1995) reported on a 12-week, double-blind, placebo-controlled study of 33 depressed, stable schizophrenia patients maintained on antipsychotics who had undergone prior double-blind dose reduction and treatment with antiparkinsonian medication. Hogarty et al. found that desipramine was significantly superior to a placebo in reducing depression. These authors, consistent with others (Plasky, 1991), concluded that the chronic depression, in contrast to the acute episodic forms, found in schizophrenia patients is responsive to antidepressant medication.

Definitive conclusions to be drawn about antidepressant use for schizophrenia patients are limited by the paucity of methodologically rigorous studies available. However, the data do appear to suggest that adjunctive antidepressant treatment is warranted when a patient reports persistent symptoms of depression when not in an acute episode of their illness. See Table 8.4 for a summary of these studies on antidepressants.

Mood Stabilizers

Lithium

Lithium salts have been used both alone and as an adjunct to neuroleptics in the treatment of schizophrenia patients (Atre-Vaidya & Taylor, 1989; Christison et al., 1991). The double-blind studies suggest that neuroleptics are superior to lithium as a treatment for acutely psychotic schizophrenia patients, although some individual patients may improve on lithium alone. Atre-Vaidya and Taylor reported on three studies (Carmen et al., 1981; Growe et al., 1979; Small, Kellams, Milstein, & Moore, 1975) that examined lithium as an adjunct to neuroleptics for treatment-refractory patients. The three studies included 48 patients, 17 of them with a diagnosis of schizoaffective disorder. Small et al. reported the most impressive results, with 10 of 20 completers improved with adjunctive lithium treatment compared to the neuroleptic alone; however, these authors were unable to discern any predictors of response. The other two studies reported more modest positive findings, with Carmen

et al. reporting a correlation of response with affective symptom psychosis.

Wilson (1993), in a study of 21 treatment-resistant schizophrenia patients that compared haloperidol alone with the combination of haloperidol plus lithium in an 8-week trial, also reported no advantage for the combination. Terao et al. (1995), in a study of 21 treatment-resistant schizophrenia patients treated in an 8-week crossover design with lithium or a placebo in addition to a neuroleptic, reported that lithium patients had significantly lower anxiety and depression scores but no benefit for negative symptoms. Hogarty et al. (1995), as part of a larger study, compared adjunctive lithium to a placebo among 29 anxious, stable schizophrenia patients and found at 12 weeks an advantage for lithium in reducing anxiety and depression. This benefit was limited to the female patients.

The efficacy of lithium as an adjunctive agent to neuroleptics for schizophrenia patients, as determined by a review of double-blind studies, is not convincing. However, due to reports of a benefit in some treatment-refractory patients, a trial should be considered if the patient has not adequately responded or was unable to tolerate an atypical agent (e.g., clozapine). The concern of a potentially toxic interaction between a neuroleptic and lithium (Cohen & Cohen, 1974) appears not to be supported by the vast majority of the published literature (Rifkin, 1993).

Carbamazepine

Christison et al. (1991) reviewed five double-blind studies published through 1989 in which either carbamazepine (CBZ) or a placebo was added to a stable neuroleptic regimen. The results of these studies were mixed, with modest positive results seen in three (Klein et al., 1984; Neppe, 1983; Okuma et al., 1989). The study by Okuma et al. included 162 patients, of whom 127 met criteria for DSM-III (Diagnostic and Statistical Manual of Mental Disorders; American Psychiatric Association, 1980) schizophrenia and 35 had schizoaffective disorder, was larger than the other four studies combined. All patients were described as treatment resistant with "excited psychotic states." The CBZ augmentation was found superior to a neuroleptic alone in patients with "violence, aggression, and paranoia"; however, the authors acknowledged that the overall differences among groups were small.

Two additional double-blind placebo studies (Meszaros et al., 1991; Kunovac et al., 1991) examined the

TABLE 8.4 Antidepressants

Author	Study Design (Double Blind)	Number of Patients	Results
Siris et al. (1978) (review article)	MAO inhibitor versus placebo	6 studies 467 patients	All reported no improvement from the MAO inhibitor
	Tricyclic antidepressants versus placebo	8 studies 618 patients	1 study reported positive results
	Tricyclic antidepressant and neuroleptic versus neuroleptic alone	12 studies 1,724 patients	2 studies reported positive results
	MAO inhibitor and neuroleptic versus neuroleptic alone	12 studies 1,013 patients	1 study reported positive results
Siris et al. (1991)	Imipramine, benztropine, and fluphenazine decanoate versus benztropine and fluphenazine decanoate. 6-week study of negative symptom/depressed patients	27	Imipramine-treated group had superior global and negative symptom ratings at study termination
Silver & Nassar (1992)	Fluvoxamine, neuroleptic, and benzotropine versus neuroleptics and benzotropine. 7-week study	30	Fluvoxamine augmentation significantly reduced negative symptoms
Siris et al. (1994)	Stable patients on fluphenazine, benzotropine, and imipramine either continued or tapered off imipramine and followed for 1 year	24	Continuous imipramine treatment prevented relapse into both depression and psychosis
Hogarty et al. (1995)	Desipramine given to stable patients maintained on neuroleptics and antiparkinson medication	33	Desipramine superior to placebo in reducing depression

MAO = monoamine oxidase.

efficacy of CBZ when added to a neuroleptic for 24 and 20 stable schizophrenia patients, respectively; both studies reported a modest improvement in the magnitude of negative symptoms. For another study (Nachshoni, Levin, Levy, Kritz, & Neumann, 1994) of 28 predominantly negative-symptom patients, no difference was reported.

Carpenter et al. (1991), in a different type of study design, compared the efficacy of CBZ with that of a placebo after 27 patients had been withdrawn from stable neuroleptic doses; Carpenter et al. found that CBZ offered no advantage over the placebo, with both groups having high relapse rates when off the neuroleptics.

Overall, there is some evidence to support CBZ as an adjunctive agent to neuroleptics in the treatment of schizophrenia, particularly in a subpopulation of aggressive, agitated patients. Due to CBZ's ability to induce hepatic enzymes, plasma neuroleptic levels should be monitored regularly when CBZ is used (Christison, 1991).

Valproic Acid

Valproic acid (VPA) as an adjunct to neuroleptics has been the focus of only two controlled studies. Linnoila et al. (1976), performed a double-blind crossover study of 32 chronic psychiatric patients with dyskinesias; each phase of the study lasted 14 days. Linnoila et al. found that the combination of VPA with a neuroleptic was superior to a neuroleptic alone in reducing global psychopathology in 14 of the 32 patients. Ko et al.

(1985) also compared adjunctive VPA to a placebo in a 4-week study of 6 schizophrenia patients and found no significant differences between groups. Definitive conclusions on the efficacy of VPA for the treatment of schizophrenia patients are premature based on the limited data available.

Table 8.5 summarizes studies of the mood stabilizers.

Dopamine Agonists

Dopamine agonists are associated with an exacerbation of psychotic symptoms in 40–60% of schizophrenia patients; however, these agents have also been used as a treatment for patients with prominent negative symptoms. This strategy is consistent with the hypothesis of a hypodopaminergic state responsible for the negative symptoms of the illness (Davis, 1991). The efficacy of L-dopa has been assessed in three double-blind treatment studies (Christison et al., 1991), two of which used it as an adjunct to neuroleptics (Gerlach & Luhdorf, 1975; Inanaga et al., 1975). In a study of 18 schizophrenia patients with prominent negative symptoms, Gerlach and Luhdorf reported significant activation in some patients, though the overall change in level of functioning was small. In a study of 104 schizophrenia inpatients with negative symptoms, Inanaga et al. reported that there were significantly more excellent responders among the L-dopa-treated patients, although there was no difference in the number considered good or fair. Brambilla et al. (1979) studied 6 patients with chronic illness with both positive and negative symptoms. The study was a crossover design with a placebo and 4 weeks for each phase; Brambilla et al. found 2 of the patients much improved.

We could find only two other double-blind studies that assessed the efficacy of dopamine agonists in chronic schizophrenia patients. Gattaz et al. (1989), in a study of 30 schizophrenia patients that received either haloperidol plus bromocriptine or haloperidol alone, reported a nonsignificant improvement in overall functioning at 24 hours for the bromocriptine-treated group, though by 21 days there were no differences observed. Goldberg, Weinberger, Daniel, and Kleinman (1991) administered a single dose of dextroamphetamine to 21 patients with chronic schizophrenia who had been stabilized on haloperidol; Goldberg's group found improvement for the dextro-amphetamine-treated patients on a number of variables that assessed affect and cognition. Dopamine

agonists have been the subject of too few controlled studies to draw definitive conclusions. However, based on the above studies, they may represent an underutilized class of medication, particularly for the treatment of negative symptoms. The hesitancy on the part of clinicians to use these agents due to a concern about exacerbating psychotic symptoms may not be warranted if patients are maintained on neuroleptics (Persovich, Lieberman, Fleischhacker, & Alvir, 1989). Table 8.6 presents a summary of the studies of dopamine agonists.

Electroconvulsive Therapy

Electroconvulsive therapy (ECT), which had been an acceptable treatment option for schizophrenia prior to the introduction of neuroleptic medication, has been the subject of few controlled studies. Information gathered from open trials holds that ECT works best for schizophrenia patients in the early stages of their illness, those with catatonic or affective symptoms, and in conjunction with a neuroleptic (Salzman, 1980). Electroconvulsive therapy is rarely used in the treatment of schizophrenia patients today except in the most refractory cases.

Three double-blind controlled studies of schizophrenia patients maintained on neuroleptics that received either ECT or sham ECT have produced consistent results. Taylor and Fleminget (1980), in a study of 20 patients (not all schizophrenic), found that the ECT group improved much more rapidly than the sham group, but the differences dissipated by 16 weeks posttreatment. Brandon et al. (1985), in a study of 19 schizophrenia patients, found ECT superior at 2 and 4 weeks but by 12 weeks there was no clear difference. Abraham and Kulhara (1987), in a study of 22 patients, found ECT augmentation beneficial in the first 8 weeks, but there was no difference between the groups by 12 weeks. Interestingly, May et al. (1981b) reported on a 5-year prospective study of 228 first-episode schizophrenia patients who received one of five treatments (neuroleptics, ECT, psychotherapy, psychotherapy plus neuropleptic, milieu) by random assignment; May et al. found that the outcome in all groups was poor but that the ECT-treated group fared best. Table 8.7 provides a summary of the ECT studies.

Overall, based on the early reports of the efficacy of ECT and the few controlled studies that show a benefit (at least early in the course of treatment), ECT

TABLE 8.5 Mood Stabilizers

Authors	Study Design (Double Blind)	Number of Patients	Results
Atre-Vaidya & Taylor (1989) (Review article)	Lithium and neuroleptic versus neuroleptic alone	3 studies 48 patients	Positive findings reported in all 3 studies
Wilson (1993)	Lithium plus haloperidol versus haloperidol in treatment-resistant patients. 8-week trial	21	No advantage for the combination
Terao et al. (1995)	Lithium plus neuroleptic versus neuroleptic alone. 8-week crossover design	21	No benefit for lithium on negative symptoms, though anxiety and depression improved
Hogerty et al. (1995)	Lithium plus neuroleptic versus neuroleptic alone. 12-week trial for anxious, stable patients	29	Lithium beneficial in reducing anxiety in female patients only
Christison et al. (1991) (review article)	CBZ and neuroleptic versus neuroleptic alone	5 studies 251 patients	3 of 5 studies reported some positive results. CBZ augmentation found superior to neuroleptic in patients with "violence, aggression and paranoia" in the largest ($n = 162$ patients) study
Meszaros et al. (1991)	CBZ and neuroleptic versus neuroleptic alone	24	Modest improvement in negative symptoms from CBZ treatment
Kunovac et al. (1991)	CBZ and neuroleptic versus neuroleptic alone	20	Modest improvement in negative symptoms from CBZ treatment
Nachsoni et al. (1994)	CBZ and neuroleptic versus neuroleptic in predominantly negative symptom patients. 7-week trial	28	No difference between CBZ or placebo found
Carpenter et al. (1991)	Patients withdrawn from stable neuroleptic regimen for 95 days and placed on CBZ or placebo	27	Both groups had a high rate of relapse
Linnoila et al. (1976)	VPA and neuroleptic versus neuroleptic in 2-week (each phase) cross-over design	32	14 of 32 VPA-treated patients had an improvement in global psychopathology
Ko et al. (1985)	VPA and neuroleptic vs. neuroleptic alone in 4 week (each phase) crossover design	6	No significant differences between groups

CBZ = carbamazepine; VPA = valproic acid

TABLE 8.6 Dopamine Agonists

Author	Study Design (Double Blind)	Number of Patients	Results
Gerlach & Luhdorf (1975)	L-dopa versus placebo added to neuroleptic in 12-week (each phase) crossover design	18	Significant "activation" in some patients, though no difference in global ratings
Inanaga et al. (1975)	L-dopa plus neuroleptic versus neuroleptic alone	104	Significantly more L-dopa-treated patients rated as "excellent" responders
Brambilla et al. (1979)	L-dopa versus placebo in 4-week (each phase) crossover design	6	2 patients much improved
Gattaz et al. (1989)	Bromocriptine plus haloperidol versus haloperidol alone. 3-week study	30	Nonsignificant improvement at 24 hours that dissipated by 21 days
Goldberg et al. (1991)	Dextroamphetamine administered in a single dose to haloperidol-treated patients	21	Improvement on measures of affect and cognition

should remain a viable adjunctive treatment option among refractory patients.

CONCLUSIONS

Pharmacological treatment has had a profoundly positive impact on the course of schizophrenia, with the vast majority of patients no longer requiring chronic institutionalization. Nevertheless, schizophrenia remains a major public health problem, with patients over the course of their illness displaying varying degrees of social and vocational disability and remaining susceptible to psychotic exacerbations even when compliant with medication. The relatively recent introduction of atypical agents has been promising, with a reduction of negative symptomatology, reduced motor side effects, and enhanced efficacy in some refractory patients. It is hoped that the future will bring atypical agents that can specifically target desired receptors to both enhance efficacy and further limit side effects.

The difficulties in the pharmacological management of schizophrenia patients are compounded by an enhanced susceptibility to other psychiatric symptoms compared with the general population. The use of

TABLE 8.7 Electroconvulsive Therapy

Author	Study Design (Double Blind)	Number of Patients	Results
Taylor & Fleming (1980)	ECT versus sham ECT. 8–12 treatments. All patients on neuroleptics	20	Improvement was rapid with ECT; no difference at 16 weeks
Brandon et al. (1985)	ECT versus sham ECT. 8 treatments. Most maintained on neuroleptics	22	ECT superior at 2 and 4 weeks; no difference by 12 weeks
Abraham & Kulhara (1987)	ECT versus sham ECT. 8 treatments. All patients maintained on neuroleptics	22	ECT superior at 8 weeks; no difference by 12 weeks

ECT = electroconvulsive therapy

adjunctive medications to treat comorbid conditions has been the subject of limited numbers of methodologically rigorous studies, though targeted treatment trials with antidepressants for postpsychotic depression and benzodiazepines for anxiety and agitation may offer an opportunity to limit morbidity. Early identification of schizophrenia/schizophreniform disorder and aggressive treatment with antipsychotic medication to prevent the deterioration witnessed in some patients should be of the highest priority since the overall efficacy of pharmacological treatments remains limited.

References

Abraham, K. R., & Kulhara, P. (1987). The efficacy of electroconvulsive therapy in the treatment of schizophrenia. *British Journal of Psychiatry, 151,* 152–155.

Addington, D. E., Jones, B., Bloom, D., Chouinard, G., Remington, G., & Albright, P. (1993). Reduction of hospital days in chronic schizophrenic patients treated with risperidone: A retrospective study. *Clinical Therapeutics, 15*(5), 917–926.

Adelson, D., & Epstein, L. J. (1962) A study of phenothiazines with male and female chronically ill schizophrenic patients. *Journal of Nervous and Mental Disease, 134,* 543–554.

Adler, L. A., Peselow, E., Rotrosen, J., Duncan, E., Lee, M., Rosenthal, M., & Angrist, B. (1993). Vitamin E treatment of tardive dyskinesia. *American Journal of Psychiatry, 150*(9), 1405–1407.

Alvir, J. M., Lieberman, J. A., Safferman, A. Z., Schwimmer, J. L., & Schaaf, J. A. (1993). Clozapine-induced agranulocytosis. Incidence and risk factors in the United States. *New England Journal of Medicine, 329*(3), 162–167.

American Psychiatric Association. (1980). *Diagnostic and statistical manual of mental disorders* (3rd ed.). Washington, D.C.: Author.

Atre-Vaidya, N., & Taylor, M. A. (1989). Effectiveness of lithium in schizophrenia: Do we really have an answer? *Journal of Clinical Psychiatry, 50,* 170–173.

Azima, H., Durost, H., & Arthurs, D. (1960). The effect of R1625 (haloperidol) in mental syndromes; a multiblind study. *American Journal of Psychiatry, 117,* 546–547.

Baldessarini, R. J., & Franenburg, F. R. (1991). Clozapine, a novel antipsychotic agent. *New England Journal of Medicine, 324,* 746–754.

Barbee, J. G., Mancuso, D. M., Freed, C. R., & Todorov, A. A. (1992). Alprazolam as a neuroleptic adjunct in the emergency treatment of schizophrenia. *American Journal of Psychiatry, 149,* 4, 506–510.

Beasley, C. M., Tollefson, G., Tran, P., Satterlee, W., Sanger, T., & Hamilton, S., The Olanzapine HGAD Study Group (1996). Olanzapine versus placebo and haloperidol: Acute phase results of the North American double-blind olanzapine trial. *Neuropsychopharmacology, 14,* 111–123.

Binder, R., Glick, I., & Rice, M. (1981). A comparative study of parenteral molindone and haloperidol in the acutely psychotic patient. *Journal of Clinical Psychiatry, 42*(5), 203–206.

Bjorndal, N., Bjerre, M., Gerlach, J., Kristjansen, P., Magelund, G., Oestrich, I. H., & Waehrens, J. (1980). High dosage haloperidol therapy in chronic schizophrenic patients: A double-blind study of clinical response, side effects, serum haloperidol, and serum prolactin. *Psychopharmacology (Berlin), 67*(1), 17–23.

Bodkin, J. A. (1992). Emerging uses for high-potency benzodiazepines in psychotic disorders. *Journal of Clinical Psychiatry, 51*(5), 41–46.

Borison, R. L., Arvanitis, L. A., & Miller, B. G. (1996). ICI 204,636, an atypical antipsychotic: Efficacy and safety in a multicenter, placebo-controlled trial in patients with schizophrenia. *Journal of Clinical Psychopharmacology, 16,* 158–169.

Brambilla, F., Scarone, S., Ponzano, M., Maffei, C., Noble, P., Rovere, C., & Guastalla, A. (1979). Catecholaminergic drugs in chronic schizophrenia. *Neuropsychobiology, 5,* 185–200.

Brandon, S., Cowley, P., McDonald, C., Neville, P., Palmer, R., & Wellstood-Eason, S. (1985). Leicester ECT Trial: Results in schizophrenia. *British Journal of Psychiatry, 146,* 177–183.

Brandrup, E., & Kristjansen, P. (1961). A controlled clinical test of a new psycholeptic drug (haloperidol). *Journal of Mental Science, 107,* 778–782.

Breier, A., Buchanan, R. W., Irish, D., & Carpenter, W. T., Jr. (1993). Clozapine treatment of outpatients with schizophrenia: outcome and long-term response patterns. *Hosp Community Psychiatry, 44*(12), 1145–1149.

Carpenter, W. T., Kurg, R., Kirkpatrick, B., Hanlon, T. E., Summerfelt, T., Buchanan, R. W., Waltrip, R. W., & Breier, A. S. (1991). Carbamazepine maintenance treatment in outpatient schizophrenics. *Archives of General Psychiatry, 48,* 69–72.

Carpenter, W. T., Jr., Hanlon, T. E., Heinrichs, D. W., Summerfelt, A. T., Kirkpatrick, B., Levine, J., & Buchanan, R. W. (1990). Continuous versus targeted medication in schizophrenic outpatients: outcome results. *American Journal of Psychiatry, 147*(9), 1138–1148.

Casey, D. E. (1993). Neuroleptic-induced acute extrapyramidal syndromes and tardive dyskinesia. *Psychiatric Clinics of North America, 16*(3), 589–610.

Casey, J. F., Bennett, I. F., Lindley, C. J., Hollister, L. E., Gordon, M. H., & Springer, N. N. (1960a). Drug therapy in schizophrenia. A controlled study of the relative effectiveness of chlorpromazine, promazine, phenobarbital, and placebo. *Archives of General Psychiatry, 2,* 210–220.

Casey, J. F., Lasky, J. J., Klett, C. J., & Hollister, L. E. (1960b). Treatment of schizophrenic reactions with phenothiazine derivatives. A comparative study of chlorpromazine, triflupromazine, mepazine, prochloperazine, perphenazine and phenobarbital. *American Journal of Psychiatry, 117,* 97–105.

Ceskova, E., & Svestka, J. (1993). Double-blind comparison of risperidone and haloperidol in schizophrenic and schizoaffective psychoses. *Pharmacopsychiatry, 26*(4), 121–124.

Chouinard, G., Jones, B., Remington, G., Bloom, D., Addington, D., MacEwan, G. W., Labelle, A., Beauclair, L., & Arnott, W. (1993). A Canadian multicenter placebo-controlled study of fixed doses of risperidone and haloperidol in the treatment of chronic schizophrenic patients. *Journal of Clinical Psychopharmacology, 13*(1), 25–40.

Christison, G. W., Kirch, D. G., & Wyatt, R. J. (1991). When symptoms persist: Choosing among alternatives somatic treatments for schizophrenia. *Schizophrenia Bulletin, 17*(2), 217–245.

Claghorn, J., Honigfeld, G., Abuzzahab, F. S., Sr., Wang, R., Steinbook, R., Tuason, V., & Klerman, G. (1987). The risks and benefits of clozapine versus chlorpromazine. *Journal of Clinical Psychopharmacology, 7*(6), 377–384.

Clark, M. L., Huber, W. K., Kyriakopoulos, A. A., Ray, T. S., Colmore, J. P., & Ramsey, H. R. (1968). Evaluation of trifluperidol in chronic schizophrenia. *Psychopharmacologia, 12*(3), 193–203.

Clark, M. L., Huber, W. K., Sakata, K., Fowles, D. C., & Serafetinides, E. A. (1970). Molindone in chronic schizophrenia. *Clinical Pharmacology & Therapeutics, 11*(5), 680–688.

Clark, M. L., Huber, W. K., Sullivan, J., Wood, F., & Costiloe, J. P. (1972). Evaluation of loxapine succinate in chronic schizophrenia. *Diseases of the Nervous System, 33*(12), 783–791.

Claus, A., Bollen, J., De Cuyper, H., Eneman, M., Malfroid, M., Peuskens, J., Heylen, S. (1992). Risperidone versus haloperidol in the treatment of chronic schizophrenic inpatients: A multicentre double-blind comparative study. *Acta Psychiatrica Scandinavica, 85*(4), 295–305.

Cohen, W. J., & Cohen, N. H. (1974). Lithium carbonate, haloperidol and irreversible brain damage. *Journal of the American Medical Association, 230,* 1283–1287.

Cole, J. O., Goldberg, S. C., & Klerman, G. L. (1964). Phenothiazine treatment in acute schizophrenia. *Archives of General Psychiatry, 10,* 246–261.

Csernansky, J. G., Riney, S. J., Lombrozo, L., Overall, J. E., & Hollister, L. E. (1988). Double-blind comparison of alprazolam, diazepam, and placebo for the treatment of negative schizophrenic symptoms. *Archives of General Psychiatry, 45,* 655–659.

Davis, J. M. (1975). Overview: Maintenance therapy in psychiatry: I. Schizophrenia. *American Journal of Psychiatry, 132*(12), 1237–1245.

Davis, J. M., Barter, J. T., & Kane, J. M. (1989). Antipsychotic drugs. In H. I. Kaplan & B. J. Sadock (Eds.), *Comprehensive textbook of psychiatry* (5th ed., pp. 1591–1627). Baltimore, Md.: Williams & Wilkins.

Davis, K. L., Kahn, R. S., Ko, G., & Davidson, M. (1991). Dopamine in schizophrenia: A review and reconceptualization. *American Journal of Psychiatry, 148,* 1474–1486.

Donaldson, S. R., Gelenberg, A. J., & Baldessarini, R. J. (1983). The pharmacologic treatment of schizophrenia: A progress report. *Schizophrenia Bulletin, 9*(4), 504–527.

Ericksen, S. E., Hurt, S. W., & Chang, S. (1978). Haloperidol dose, plasma levels, and clinical response: A double-blind study. *Psychopharmacology Bulletin, 14*(2), 15–16.

Escobar, J. I., Mann, J. J., Keller, J., Wilkins, J., Mason, B., & Mills, M. J. (1985). Comparison of injectable molindone and haloperidol followed by oral dosage forms in acutely ill schizophrenics. *Journal of Clinical Psychiatry, 46*(8, Pt. 2), 15–19.

Farmer, A. E., & Blewett, A. (1993). Drug treatment of resistant schizophrenia: Limitations and recommendations. *Drugs, 45,* 374–383.

Fox, W., Gobble, I. F., Clos, M., & Denison, E. (1964). A clinical comparison of trifluperidol, haloperidol, and chlorpromazine. *Current Therapeutic Research Clinical and Experimental, 6,* 409–415.

Freeman, H., Oktem, M. R., & Oktem, N. (1969). A double-blind comparison of the therapeutic efficacy of mesoridazine versus chlorpromazine. *Current Therapeutic Research Clinical and Experimental, 11*(5), 263–270.

Fruensgaard, K., Korsgaard, S., Jorgensen, H., & Jensen, K. (1977). Loxapine versus haloperidol parenterally in acute psychosis with agitation. A double-blind study. *Acta Psychiatrica Scandinavica, 56*(4), 256–264.

Gaebel, W., Frick, U., Kopcke, W., Linden, M., Muller, P., Muller-Spahn, F., Pietzcker, A., & Tegeler, J. (1993, September). Early neuroleptic intervention in schizophrenia: are prodromal symptoms valid predictors of relapse? *British Journal of Psychiatry* Supplement, (21), 8–12.

Gallant, D. M., & Bishop, M. P. (1968). Molindone: A controlled evaluation in chronic schizophrenic patients. *Current Therapeutic Research Clinical and Experimental, 10*(9), 441–447.

Gallant, D. M., Bishop, M. P., Bishop, G., & Steele, C. A. (1968). Thiothixene: A controlled evaluation of the intramuscular antipsychotic preparation. *Current Therapeutic Research Clinical and Experimental, 10*(11), 561–565.

Gardos, G. (1974). Are antipsychotic drugs interchangeable? *Journal of Nervous and Mental Disease, 159*(5), 343–348.

Garry, J. W., & Leonard, T. J. (1962). A controlled trial in chronic schizophrenia. *Journal of Mental Science, 108*, 105–107.

Gattaz, W. F., Rost, W., Hubner, C. K., & Bauer, K. (1989). Acute and subchronic effects of low dose bromocriptine in haloperidol treated schizophrenics. *Biological Psychiatry, 25*, 247–255.

Gelenberg, A. J., & Doller, J. C. (1979). Clozapine versus chlorpromazine for the treatment of schizophrenia: Preliminary results from a double-blind study. *Journal of Clinical Psychiatry, 40*(5), 238–240.

Gerlach, J., & Luhdorf, K. (1975). The effect of L-dopa on young patients with simple schizophrenia, treated with neuroleptic drugs: A double-blind cross-over trial with madopar and placebo. *Psychopharmacologic, 44*, 105–110.

Glazer, W. M., Morgenstern, H., & Doucette, J. T. (1993). Predicting the long-term risk of tardive dyskinesia in outpatients maintained on neuroleptic medications. *Journal of Clinical Psychiatry, 54*(4), 133–139.

Goldberg, T. E., Bigelow, L. B., Weinberger, D. R., Daniel, D. G., & Kleinman, J. E. (1991). Cognitive and behavioral effects of the coadministration of dextroamphetamine and haloperidol in schizophrenia. *American Journal of Psychiatry, 148*(1), 78–84.

Growe, G. A., Crayton, J. W., Klass, D. B., Evans, H., & Strizich, M. (1979). Lithium in chronic schizophrenia. *American Journal of Psychiatry, 136*, 454–455.

Hanlon, T. E., Michaux, M. H., Ota, K. Y., Shaffer, J. W., & Kurland, A. A. (1965). The comparative effectiveness of eight phenothiazines. *Psychopharmacologia (Berlin), 7*, 89–106.

Herz, M. I., Glazer, W. M., Mostert, M. A., Sheard, M. A., Szymanski, H. V., Hafez, H., Mirza, M., & Vana, J. (1991). Intermittent versus maintenance medication in schizophrenia. Two-year results. *Archives of General Psychiatry, 48*(4), 333–339.

Hirsch, S. R., Link, C. G. G., Goldstein, J. M., & Arvanitis, L. A. (1996). ICI 204,636: A new atypical antipsychotic drug. *British Journal of Psychiatry, 168*(suppl. 29), 45–56.

Hogarty, G. E., McEvoy, J. P., Munetz, M., DiBarry, A. L., Bartone, P., Cather, R., Cooley, S. J., Ulrich, R. F., Carter, M., & Madonia, M. J. (1988). Dose of fluphenazine, familial expressed emotion, and outcome in schizophrenia. Results of a two-year controlled study. *Archives of General Psychiatry, 45*(9), 797–805.

Hogarty, G. E., McEvoy, J. P., Ulrich, R. F., DiBarry, A. L., Bartone, P., Cooley, S., Hammill, K., Carter, M., Munetz, M. R., & Perel, J. (1995). Pharmacotherapy of impaired affect in recovering schizophrenic patients. *Archives of General Psychiatry, 52*, 29–41.

Hogarty, G. E., Ulrich, R. F., Mussare, F., & Aristigueta, N. (1976). Drug discontinuation among long term, successfully maintained schizophrenic outpatients. *Diseases of the Nervous System, 37*(9), 494–500.

Hollister, L. E., Erickson, G. V., & Motzenbecker, F. P. (1960). Trifluoperazine in chronic psychiatric patients. *Journal of Clinical and Experimental Psychopathology, 21*, 15–24.

Hoyberg, O. J., Fensbo, C., Remvig, J., Lingjaerde, O., Sloth-Nielsen, M., & Salvesen, I. (1993). Risperidone versus perhenazine in the treatment of chronic schizophrenic patients with acute exacerbations. *Acta Psychiatrica Scandinavica, 88*(6), 395–402.

Huang, C. C., Gerhardstein, R. P., Kim, D. Y., & Hollister, L. (1987). Treatment-resistant schizophrenia: Controlled study of moderate- and high-dose thiothixene. *International Clinical Psychopharmacology, 2*(1), 69–75.

Inanaga, K., Nakazawa, Y., Inoue, K., Tachibana, H., Oshima, M., & Kotorii, T. (1975). Double-blind controlled study of L-dopa therapy in schizophrenia. *Japonica, 29*(2), 123–143.

Johns, C. A., & Thompson, J. W. (1995). Adjunctive treatments in schizophrenia: Pharmacotherapies and electoconvulsive therapy. *Schizophrenia Bulletin, 21*(4), 607–619.

Johnson, D. A., Ludlow, J. M., Street, K., & Taylor, R. D. (1987). Double-blind comparison of half-dose and standard-dose flupenthixol decanoate in the maintenance treatment of stabilised out-patients with schizophrenia. *British Journal of Psychiatry, 151*, 634–638.

Jolley, A. G., Hirsch, S. R., Morrison, E., McRink, A., & Wilson, L. (1990). Trial of brief intermittent neuroleptic prophylaxis for selected schizophrenic outpatients: clinical and social outcome at two years. *British Medical Journal, 301*(6756), 837–842.

Kane, J., Honigfeld, G., Singer, J., & Meltzer, H. (1988). Clozapine for the treatment-resistant schizophrenic. A double-blind comparison with chlorpromazine. *Archives of General Psychiatry, 45*(9), 789–796.

Kane, J. M., Davis, J. M., Schooler, N. R., Marder, S. R., Brauzer, B., & Casey, D. E. (1993). A one-year comparison of four dosages of haloperidol decanoate [Abstract]. *Schizophrenia Research, 9,* 239–240.

Kane, J. M., & Lieberman, J. M. (1987). Maintenance pharmacotherapy in schizophrenia. In H. Y. Meltzer (Ed.), *Psychopharmacology: The third generation of progress* (pp. 1103–1109). New York: Raven Press.

Kane, J. M., Rifkin, A., Quitkin, F., Nayak, D., & Ramos-Lorenzi, J. (1982, January). Fluphenazine versus placebo in patients with remitted, acute first episode schizophrenia. *Archives of General Psychiatry,* 70–73.

Kane, J. M., Rifkin, A., Woerner, M., Reardon, G., Sarantakos, S., Schiebel, D., & Ramos-Lorenzi, J. (1983). Low-dose neuroleptic treatment of outpatient schizophrenics. I. Preliminary results for relapse rates. *Archives of General Psychiatry, 40*(8), 893–896.

Kane, J. M., Woerner, M., & Lieberman, J. (1985). Tardive dyskinesia: prevalence, incidence, and risk factors. *Psychopharmacology, 2*(Suppl.), 72–78.

Kane, J. M., Woerner, M., & Sarantakos, S. (1986). Depot neuroleptics: A comparative review of standard, intermediate, and low-dose regimens. *Journal of Clinical Psychiatry, 47*(Suppl.), 30–33.

Karson, C. N., Weinberger, D. R., Bigelow, L., & Wyatt, R. J. (1982). Clonazepam treatment of chronic schizophrenia: Negative results in a double-blind, placebo-controlled trial. *American Journal of Psychiatry, 139*(12), 1627–1628.

Kellner, R., Wilson, R. M., Muldawer, M. D., & Pathak, D. (1975). Anxiety in schizophrenia: The responses to chlordiazepoxide in an intensive study design. *Archives of General Psychiatry, 32,* 1246–1254.

Kinon, B. J., Kane, J. M., Johns, C., Perovich, R., Ismi, M., Koreen, A., & Weiden, P. (1993). Treatment of neuroleptic-resistant schizophrenic relapse. *Psychopharmacology Bulletin, 29*(2), 309–314.

Kinon, B. J., & Lieberman, J. A. (1996). Mechanisms of action of atypical antipsychotic drugs: A critical analysis. *Psychopharmacology, 124,* 2–34.

Klein, D. F., & Davis, J. M. (1969). Review of the antipsychotic drug literature. In D. F. Klein & J. M. David (Eds.), *Diagnosis and drug treatment of psychiatric disorders* (pp. 52–138). Baltimore, Md.: Williams and Wilkins.

Klein, E., Bental, E., Lerer, B., & Belmaker, R. H. (1984). Carbamazepine and haloperidol v. placebo and haloperidol in excited psychoses. *Archives of General Psychiatry, 41,* 165–170.

Klieser, E., Strauss, W. H., & Lemmer, W. (1994). The tolerability and efficacy of the atypical neuroleptic remoxipride compared with clozapine and haloperidol in acute schizophrenia. *Acta Psychiatrica Scandinavica, 380*(Suppl.), 68–73.

Ko, G. N., Korpi, E. R., Freed, W. J., Zalcman, S. J., & Bigelow, L. B. (1985). Effect of valproic acid on behavior and plasma amino acid concentrations in chronic schizophrenic patients. *Biological Psychiatry, 20,* 209–214.

Kunovac, J., Leposavic, L. J., Jasovic-Gasic, M., & Paunovic, V. R. (1991). Efficacy of carbamazepine as an adjuvant therapy in the treatment of positive and negative symptoms in schizophrenia. *Biological Psychiatry, 29,* 395–402.

Kurland, A. A., Hanlon, T. E., Tatom, M. H., Ota, K. Y., & Simopoulos, A. M. (1961). The comparative effectiveness of six phenothiazine compounds, phenobarbital and inert placebo in the treatment of acutely ill patients: Global measures of severity of illness. *Journal of Nervous and Mental Disease, 133,* 1–18.

Laskey, J. J., Klett, C. J., Caffey, E. M., Bennett, J. L., Rosenblum, M. D., & Hollister, L. E. (1962). Drug treatment of schizophrenic patients. *Diseases of the Nervous System, 23,* 698–706.

Leon, C. A. (1979). Therapeutic effects of clozapine. A 4-year follow-up of a controlled clinical trial. *Acta Psychiatrica Scandinavica, 59*(5), 471–480.

Levinson, D. F., Simpson, G. M., Singh, H., Yadalam, K., Jain, A., Stephanos, M. J., & Silver, P. (1990). Fluphenazine dose, clinical response, and extrapyramidal symptoms during acute treatment. *Archives of General Psychiatry, 47*(8), 761–768.

Liddle, P., Carpenter, W. T., & Crow, T. (1994). Syndromes of schizophrenia. *British Journal of Psychiatry, 165*(6), 721–727.

Lieberman, J. A. (1993). Prediction of outcome in first-episode schizophrenia. *Journal of Clinical Psychiatry, 54*(Suppl.), 13–17.

Lindenmayer, J. P. New pharmacotherapeutic modalities for negative symptoms in psychosis. *Acta Psychiatrica Scandinavica, 91*(388), 15–19.

Linnoila, M., Viukari, M., & Hietala, O. (1976). Effect of sodium valproate on tardive dyskinesia. *British Journal of Psychiatry, 129,* 114–119.

Loebel, A. D., Lieberman, J. A., Alvir, J. M., Mayerhoff, D. I., Geisler, S. H., & Szymanski, S. R. (1992). Duration of psychosis and outcome in first-episode schizophrenia. *American Journal of Psychiatry, 149*(9), 1183–1188.

Marder, S. R., & Meibach, R. C. (1994). Risperidone in the treatment of schizophrenia. *American Journal of Psychiatry, 151*(6), 825–835.

Marder, S. R., Van Putten, T., Mintz, J., Lebell, M., McKenzie, J., & May, P. R. (1987). Low and conventional-dose maintenance therapy with fluphenazine decanoate. Two year outcome. *Archives of General Psychiatry, 44*(6), 518–521.

May, P. R., Tuma, A. H., Yale, C., Potepan, P., & Dixon,

W. J. (1981a, April). Schizophrenia—A follow-up study of results of treatment. *Archives of General Psychiatry, 33*(4), 481–486.

May, P. R., Tuma, A. H., Yale, C., et al. (1981b). Schizophrenia—A follow up study of results of treatment, II. Hospital stay over 2 to 5 years. *Archives of General Psychiatry, 33*, 487–491.

McCreadie, R. G., & MacDonald, I. M. (1977). High dosage haloperidol in chronic schizophrenia. *British Journal of Psychiatry, 131*, 310–316.

McEvoy, J. P., Borison, R., Small, J., Van Kammen, D. P., Melzer, H., Hammer, M., Morris, D., Shu, V., Sebree, T. B., Grebb, J., & Kashkin, K. (1993). The efficacy and tolerability of sertindole in schizophrenic patients: A pilot, double blind, placebo controlled, dose ranging study. *Schizophrenia Research, 9*, 244–254.

McGlashan, T. H., & Carpenter, W. T. (1976). Postpsychotic depression in schizophrenia. *Archives of General Psychiatry, 33*, 231–239.

McIndoo, M. V. (1971). A controlled study of mesoridazine: an effective treatment for schizophrenia. *Southern Medical Journal, 64*(5), 592–596.

Meltzer, H. Y. (1992). Treatment of the neuroleptic-nonresponsive schizophrenic patient. *Schizophrenia Bulletin, 18*(3), 515–541.

Meltzer, H. Y., Burnett, S., Bastani, B., & Ramirez, L. F. (1990). Effects of six months of clozapine treatment on the quality of life of chronic schizophrenic patients. *Hospital and Community Psychiatry, 41*(8), 892–897.

Meltzer, H. Y., Sommers, A. A., & Luchins, D. J. (1986). The effect of neuroleptics and other psychotropic drugs on negative symptoms in schizophrenia. *Journal of Clinical Psychopharmacology, 6*(6), 329–338.

Meszaros, K., Simhandl, C., Liechtenstein, A., Denk, E., Topitz, A., & Thau, K. (1991). Clinical efficacy of adjunctive carbamazepine in chronic schizophrenia. *Biological Psychiatry, 29*, 386–394.

Miller, D. D., Perry, P. J., Cadoret, R., & Andreasen, N. C. (1992). A two and one-half year follow-up of treatment-refractory schizophrenics treated with clozapine. *Biological Psychiatry, 31*(Suppl.), 85A.

Min, S. K., Rhee, C. S., Kim, C. E., & Kang, D. Y. (1993). Risperidone versus haloperidol in the treatment of chronic schizophrenic patients: A parallel group double-blind comparative trial. *Yonsei Medical Journal, 34*(2), 179–190.

Morgenstern, H., & Glazer, W. M. (1993). Identifying risk factors for tardive dyskinesia among long-term outpatients maintained with neuroleptic medications. Results of the Yale Tardive Dyskinesia Study. *Archives of General Psychiatry, 50*(9), 723–733.

Muller-Spahn, F. (1992). Risperidone in the treatment of chronic schizophrenic patients: An international double-blind parallel-group study versus haloperidol. The International Risperidone Research Group. *Clinical Neuropharmacology, 15*(Suppl. 1, Pt. A), 90A–91A.

Nachshoni, T., Levin, Y., Levy, A., Kritz, A., & Neumann, M. (1994). A double-blind trial of carbamazepine in negative symptom schizophrenia. *Biological Psychiatry, 35*, 22–26.

National Institute of Mental Health-Psychopharmacology Service Center Collaborative Study Group. (1964). Phenothiazine treatment in acute schizophrenia. *Archives of General Psychiatry, 10*, 246–261.

Neborsky, R., Janowsky, D., Munson, E., & Depry, D. (1981). Rapid treatment of acute psychotic symptoms with high- and low-dose haloperidol. Behavioral considerations. *Archives of General Psychiatry, 38*(2), 195–199.

Neppe, V. M. (1983). Carbamazide as adjunctive treatment in nonepileptic chronic inpatients with EEG temporal lobe abnormalities. *Journal of Clinical Psychiatry, 44*, 326–331.

Okasha, A., & Twefik, G. A controlled clinical trial in chronic disturbed psychotic patients. *British Journal of Psychiatry, 110*, 56–60.

Okuma, T., Yamashita, I., Takahashi, R., Itoh, H., Otsuki, S., Watanabe, S., Sarai, K., Hazasma, H., & Inanaga, K. (1989). A double-blind study of adjunctive carbamazepine versus placebo on excited states of schizophrenic and schizoaffective disorders. *Acta Psychiatrica Scandinavica, 80*, 250–259.

Persovich, R. M., Lieberman, J. A., Fleischhacker, W. W., & Alvir, J. (1989). The behavior toxicity of bromocriptine in patients with psychiatric illness. *Journal of Clinical Psychopharmacology, 9*(6), 417–422.

Peuskens, J. (1995). Risperidone in the treatment of patients with chronic schizophrenia: A multi-national, multi-centre, double-blind, parallel-group study versus haloperidol. Risperidone Study Group. *British Journal of Psychiatry, 166*(6), 712–726.

Pickar, D., Owen, R. R., Litman, R. E., Konicki, E., Gutierrez, R., & Rapaport, M. H. (1992). Clinical and biologic response to clozapine in patients with schizophrenia. Crossover comparison with fluphenazine. *Archives of General Psychiatry, 49*(5), 345–353.

Plasky, P. (1991). Antidepressant usage in schizophrenia. *Schizophrenia Bulletin, 17*(4), 649–657.

Pratt, J. P., Bishop, M. P., & Gallant, D. M. (1964). Comparison of haloperidol, trifluperidol, and chlorpromazine in acute schizophrenic patients. *Current Therapeutic Research Clinical and Experimental, 6*, 562–571.

Quitkin, F., Rifkin, A., & Klein, D. F. (1975). Very high dosage versus standard dosage fluphenazine in schizophrenia. A double-blind study of nonchronic treatment-refractory patients. *Archives of General Psychiatry*, 32(10), 1276–1281.

Reese, L., & Davies, B. (1965). A study of the value of haloperidol in the management and treatment of schizophrenic and manic patients. *International Journal of Neuropsychiatry*, 1, 263–265.

Rickels, K., Byrdy, H., Valentine, J., Postel, W., Norstad, N., & Downing, R. (1978). Double-blind trial of thiothixene and chlorpromazine in acute schizophrenia. *International Pharmacopsychiatry*, 13(1), 50–57.

Rifkin, A. (1993). Pharmacologic strategies in the treatment of schizophrenia. *Psychiatric Clinics of North America*, 16(2), 351–363.

Rifkin, A., Doddi, S., Karajgi, B., Borenstein, M., & Wachspress, M. (1991). Dosage of haloperidol for schizophrenia. *Archives of General Psychiatry*, 48(2), 166–170.

Rifkin, A., Rieder, E., Sarantakos, S., Saraf, K., & Kane, J. (1984). Is loxapine more effective than chlorpromazine in paranoid schizophrenia? *American Journal of Psychiatry*, 141(11), 1411–1413.

Ritter, R. M., & Tatum, P. A. (1972). Two studies of the effects of mesoridazine. *Journal of Clinical Pharmacology and New Drugs*, 12(8), 349–355.

Salzman, C. (1980). The use of ECT in the treatment of schizophrenia. *American Journal of Psychiatry*, 137(9), 1032–1041.

Salzman, C., Solomon, D., Miyawaki, E., Glassman, R., Rood, L., Flowers, E., & Thayer, S. (1991). Parenteral lorazepam versus parenteral haloperidol for the control of psychotic disruptive behavior. *Journal of Clinical Psychiatry*, 52, 177–180.

Samuels, A. S. (1961). A controlled study of haloperidol; the effects of small dosages. *American Journal of Psychiatry*, 118, 253–260.

Schiele, B. C., Vestre, N. D., & Stein, K. E. (1961). A comparison of thioridazine, trifuoperazine, chlorpromazine, and placebo: A double-blind controlled study on the treatment of chronic, hospitalized, schizophrenic patients. *Journal of Clinical and Experimental Psychopathology*, 22, 151–162.

Schooler, N. R., Goldberg, S. C., Boothe, H., & Cole, J. O. (1967). One year after discharge: Community adjustment of schizophrenic patients. *American Journal of Psychiatry*, 123, 986–995.

Schooler, N. R., Keith, S. J., Severe, J. B., & Mathews, S. M. Treatment strategies in schizophrenia. Effects of dosage reduction and family management outcome [Abstract]. *Schizophrenia Research*, 9, 260.

Serafetinides, E. A., Willis, D., & Clark, M. L. (1972). Haloperidol, clopenthixol, and chlorpromazine in chronic schizophrenia. *Journal of Nervous and Mental Disease*, 155(5), 366–369.

Shopsin, B., Klein, H., Aaronson, M., & Collora, M. (1979). Clozapine, chlorpromazine, and placebo in newly hospitalized, acutely schizophrenic patients: A controlled, double-blind comparison. *Archives of General Psychiatry*, 36(6), 657–664.

Silver, H., & Nassar, A. Fluvoxamine improves negative symptoms in treated chronic schizophrenia: An add-on double-blind, placebo-controlled study. *Biological Psychiatry*, 31, 698–704.

Simpson, G. M., & Cuculic, Z. (1976). A double-blind comparison of loxapine succinate and trifluoperazine in newly admitted schizophrenic patients. *Journal of Clinical Pharmacology*, 16(1), 60–65.

Siris, S. (1993). Adjunctive medication in the maintenance treatment of schizophrenia and its conceptual implications. *British Journal of Psychiatry*, 163, 66–78.

Siris, S. G. (1991). Diagnosis of secondary depression in schizophrenia: Implications for *DSM-IV*. *Schizophrenia Bulletin*, 17(1), 75–97.

Siris, S. G., Adam, F., Cohen, M., Mandeli, J., Aronson, A., & Casey, E. (1988). Postpsychotic depression and negative symptoms: An investigation of syndrome overlap. *American Journal of Psychiatry*, 145(12), 1532–1537.

Siris, S. G., Bermanzohn, P. C., Gonzaslez, A., Mason, S. E., White, C. V., & Shuwall, M. A. (1991). The use of antidepressants for negative symptoms in a subset of schizophrenic patients. *Psychopharmacology Bulletin*, 27(3), 331–335.

Siris, S. G., Bermanzohn, P. C., Mason, S. E., & Shuwall, M. A. (1994). Maintenance imipramine therapy for secondary depression in schizophrenia. *Archives of General Psychiatry*, 51, 109–115.

Siris, S. G., Van Kammen, D. P., & Docherty, J. P. (1978). Use of antidepressant drugs in schizophrenia. *Archives of General Psychiatry*, 35, 1368–1377.

Small, J. G., Kellams, J. J., Milstein, V., & Moore, J. (1975). A placebo-controlled study of lithium combined with neuroleptics in chronic schizophrenic patients. *American Journal of Psychiatry*, 132, 1315–1317.

Taylor, P., & Fleminget, J. J. (1980). ECT for schizophrenia. *Lancet*, 1380–1382.

Terao, T., Oga, T., Nozaki, S., Ohta, A., Ohtsubo, Y., Yamamoto, S., Zammi, M., & Okada, M. (1995). Lithium addition to neuroleptic treatment in chronic schizophrenia: a randomized, double-blind, placebo-controlled, cross-over study. *Acta Psychiatrica Scandinavica*, 92, 220–224.

Tuason, V. B. (1986). A comparison of parenteral loxapine and haloperidol in hostile and aggressive acutely schizophrenic patients. *Journal of Clinical Psychiatry*, 47(3), 126–129.

Tuason, V. B., Escobar, J. I., Garvey, M., & Schiele, B. (1984). Loxapine versus chlorpromazine in paranoid schizophrenia: a double-blind study. *Journal of Clinical Psychiatry, 45*(4), 158–163.

van der Velde, C. D., & Kiltie, H. (1975). Effectiveness of loxapine succinate in acute schizophrenia: A comparative study with thiothixene. *Current Therapeutic Research Clinical and Experimental, 17*(1), 1–12.

Van Kammen, D. P., McEvoy, J. P., Targun, S. D., Kardatzke, D., & Sebree, T. B. (1996). A randomized, controlled, dose ranging trial of sertindole in patients with schizophrenia. *Psychopharmacology, 124,* 168–175.

Van Putten, T., Marder, S. R., & Mintz, J. (1990). A controlled dose comparison of haloperidol in newly admitted schizophrenic patients. *Archives of General Psychiatry, 47*(8), 754–758.

Vestre, N. D., Hall, W. B., & Schiele, B. C. (1962). A comparison of fluphenazine, triflupromazine and phenobarbital in the treatment of chronic schizophrenic patients: A double-blind controlled study. *Journal of Clinical Psychopathology, 23,* 149–159.

Volavka, J., Cooper, T., Czobor, P., Bitter, I., Meisner, M., Laska, E., Gastanaga, P., Krakowski, M., Chou, J. C., Crowner, M., et al. (1992). Haloperidol blood levels and clinical effects. *Archives of General Psychiatry, 49*(5), 354–61.

Wilson, W. H. (1993). Addition of lithium to haloperidol in non-affective, antipsychotic non-responsive schizophrenia: A double-blind, placebo controlled, parallel design clinical trial. *Psychopharmacology, 111,* 359–366.

Wolpert, A., Sheppard, C., & Merlis, S. (1968). Thiothixene, thioridazine, and placebo in male chronic schizophrenic patients. *Clinical Pharmacology & Therapeutics, 9*(4), 456–464.

Wolkowitz, O. M. (1993). Rational polypharmacy in schizophrenia. *Annals of Clinical Psychiatry, 5,* 79–90.

Wolkowitz, O. M., & Pickar, D. (1991). Benzodizapines in the treatment of schizophrenia: A review and reappraisal. *American Journal of Psychiatry, 148*(6), 714–726.

Wyatt, R. J. (1991). Neuroleptics and the natural course of schizophrenia. *Schizophrenia Bulletin, 17,* 325–351.

Yilmaz, A. H. (1971). Thiothixene in chronic schizophrenia. A clinical trial. *Hawaiian Medical Journal, 30*(3), 178–181.

Zito, J. M., Volavka, J., Craig, T. J., Czobor, P., Banks, S., & Vitrai, J. (1993). Pharmacoepidemiology of clozapine in 202 inpatients with schizophrenia. *Annals of Pharmacotherapy, 27,* 1262–1269.

9

Psychosocial Treatments for Schizophrenia

Alex Kopelowicz
Robert Paul Liberman

Stressors like major life events and high expressed emotion in family and residential settings can adversely affect the course of schizophrenia when individuals vulnerable to the disorder are exposed to the stressors without the protection of medication, psychosocial treatment, and natural coping ability and social support. This being so, it is not surprising that the empirical data on treatment outcomes support a biopsychosocial view of treatment for schizophrenia, including medication, psychosocial treatments, and social support.

Five Type 1 and literally hundreds of Type 3 studies of behavior therapy and social learning/token economy programs support the value of treatments that structure, support, and reinforce prosocial behaviors in treatment-refractory persons with schizophrenia.

Several Type 1 randomized clinical trials (RCTs) using structured, educational family interventions have shown the superiority of adding family intervention to medication and customary case management for persons with schizophrenia.

More than 40 Type 1 or Type 2 RCTs support the efficacy of social skills training to enable persons with schizophrenia to acquire instrumental and affiliative skills to improve functioning in their communities.

OVERVIEW OF SCHIZOPHRENIA

Diagnosis

Schizophrenia, the most disabling of the major mental disorders, is characterized by two or more of the following: (a) delusions, (b) hallucinations, (c) disorganized speech, (d) grossly disorganized or catatonic behavior, and (e) negative symptoms. These symptoms must impair social and occupational functioning and be continuously present for at least 6 months. Since other disorders, some with known etiologies, can mimic schizophrenia, before making the diagnosis it is necessary to exclude psychoses resulting from substance abuse, medical conditions that affect the brain (e.g., tumors, Cushing's disease), pervasive developmental disorders, and mood disorders (e.g., bipolar disorder or psychotic depression). In this chapter reviewing the psychological and behavioral treatments for schizophrenia, we include schizoaffective disorder with schizophrenia since the two have very similar clinical features, prognoses, and responses to treatments. Because schizophrenia spectrum disorders are almost always treated with antipsychotic drugs, an inventory, evaluation, and interpretation of the literature on psychological and behavioral treatments must view the treatments as biobehavioral, that is, multidimensional therapies with pharmacological and psychosocial components.

Etiology and Course of Illness

While there is no definitive evidence identifying one or more causal factors in the etiology of schizophrenia, most authorities would view the extraordinary heterogeneity in psychopathology, psychosocial functioning, and course of illness in this disorder as indicating that our current ignorance of central nervous system functioning masks the likelihood that there is more than one etiology in what we see as the final common pathway of psychosis. There is sufficient data from family and adoptive studies to suggest that genetic factors may account for approximately 60% of the etiology of schizophrenia and that schizotypal personality traits may be the genetically determined phenotype (Raine, Lencz, & Mednick, 1995). Strong evidence also supports the role of socioenvironmental factors in influencing the course of the disorder. In particular, early identification and diagnosis followed by appropriate and continuous biopsychosocial treatment has been shown to improve the long-term outcomes of persons with schizophrenia (Wyatt, 1991, 1995).

The onset of schizophrenia typically occurs during adolescence and early adulthood; however, a tiny minority of cases begin during childhood. The disorder affects males and females equally, but males are disproportionately represented in treatment facilities, presumably because their illness-linked behavior and functioning become more visible and intolerable to families and society. The onset of the disorder is about 5 years later for females (late 20s) than males (early 20s), most likely because female hormones serve a protective function against abnormalities in neurotransmitter systems (Seeman, 1982).

The long-term course of the disorder can be divided into three groupings, although accessibility to and use of comprehensive, high-quality, continuous treatment will determine the proportion of individuals with schizophrenia in each group. One type of course is marked by one or more psychotic episodes with relatively rapid return to premorbid functioning and good prospects for recovery. The second and most common course followed by schizophrenic patients is characterized by many years of intercurrent acute psychotic relapses or exacerbations, with periods of full or partial remission and varying degrees of residual impairments in functioning. A final group of about 15% of individuals with schizophrenia fail to respond to currently available treatments and demonstrate the third form of the disorder, with prolonged and persistent psychotic symptoms with moderate-to-severe personal and social disabilities. The proportion of individuals with treatment-refractory schizophrenia is gradually diminishing with the advent of such novel, atypical antipsychotic drugs as clozapine.

Evidence from several countries documents that over 50% of individuals with well-diagnosed and severe forms of schizophrenia can achieve good states of remission and psychosocial functioning 20–30 years after their initial periods of illness (Harding, Zubin, & Strauss, 1992). A key element in recovery requires the patient and practitioner(s) to forge an informed partnership in which the patient is not a passive recipient of treatment but is an active participant in managing symptoms, preventing or containing relapses, and pursuing long-term social, personal, and occupational goals with abundant social support and training of skills (Liberman et al., 1993).

The course of schizophrenia can be complicated and adversely affected by concurrent abuse of alcohol, stimulant drugs (cocaine, amphetamines), or marijuana. These agents are all well documented as stressors in the exacerbation of psychosis in individuals vulnerable to schizophrenia. The financial cost to a family with a relative who has severe mental illness (e.g., schizophrenia) and concurrent substance abuse is significantly greater than the costs to families of a relative with mental illness alone; the annual costs were $13,891 per family versus $3,547 per family, respectively (Clark, 1994).

It is often difficult to diagnose a dually diagnosed person as having schizophrenia until the presence of the offending substance has cleared the body. Even then, as in amphetamine psychosis, recurrent psychotic symptoms may be manifested many months after the last use of the amphetamine. The prevailing view of comorbid substance abuse in schizophrenia that patients are attempting to self-medicate their depression or positive or negative symptoms is not borne out by the facts. Substances of abuse exacerbate, rather than ameliorate, psychiatric symptoms (Shaner et al., 1995). Treatment of comorbid schizophrenia and substance abuse requires a coordinated and integrated approach, adapting methods from the substance abuse field (e.g., urine checks, self-help groups) so they will properly fit the schizophrenic individual. It is widely believed that it is essential to integrate all components of treatment of the dually diagnosed substance-abusing person with schizophrenia "under the same roof," with the psychiatric treatment team offering and coordinating the array of modalities aimed at the psychosis and the substance abuse (Roberts, Shaner, Eckman, Tucker, & Vacarro, 1992).

Other factors complicating the treatment and outcome of schizophrenia are comorbidity with developmental disabilities (e.g., schizophrenic symptoms developing in adolescence in an individual who has had autism since birth), comorbidity with depression (commonly present and a risk factor for suicidality), and homelessness (which presents a challenge to engaging and maintaining the individual in treatment).

Environments that are high in stress—either through hostility or criticism of the person with schizophrenia or emotional overinvolvement ("high expressed emotion")—have been shown in replicated, international studies to carry a significantly higher risk of relapse in individuals with schizophrenia. Since the source of stressful social environments comes from caregivers' lack of education about the nature and proper treatment of schizophrenia, combined with the challenging and burdensome symptoms and disability exhibited by the person with schizophrenia, treatment techniques (see below, "Structured Family Interventions") have been designed and validated to improve the emotional climate in relationships that the patient has with significant others in his or her living environment. Improvements in the family emotional climate have resulted in reduced relapse rates.

Consensus among authorities in the field supports an explanatory and heuristic model of the etiology, course, and outcome of schizophrenia that incorporates *vulnerability, stress,* and *protective factors* (Nuechterlein et al., 1994). Vulnerability factors (e.g., genes, neurodevelopmental anomalies, abnormalities in brain neural networks and neurotransmitter systems) are relatively enduring abnormalities of individuals at risk for schizophrenia that are present before, during, and after psychotic episodes. Stressors include role expectations, daily hassles, and major life events that demand adaptive changes from the individual, challenge the individual's coping abilities, and sometimes serve as triggers for psychotic episodes (e.g., drugs of abuse, high stress in the patient's living environment, major life events, and even toxic side effects of antipsychotic medications). Personal and environmental protective factors (e.g., social skills, family sup-

port, judicious types and doses of antipsychotic medication embedded in comprehensive and continuous treatment services) allow a vulnerable individual to buffer the deleterious effects of stressors superimposed on vulnerability and avoid or mitigate relapse.

Prevalence and Cost

Based on epidemiological studies, there are 2 million persons in the United States afflicted with schizophrenia or schizoaffective disorder, representing 1.1% of the population (Regier, Farmer, Lock, Keith, & Rae, 1993). There are over 300,000 acute episodes of schizophrenia annually in the United States, and the economic cost of this disorder to the nation, in terms of treatment and lost income, is more than $30 billion per year (National Institute of Mental Health [NIMH], 1995). The lifetime loss of income for a male diagnosed as having schizophrenia late in adolescence has been calculated to be $1,027,000 (Wyatt & Clark, 1987). An estimated 100,000 hospital beds on any given day are used by persons having schizophrenia (Talbott, Goldman, & Ross, 1987).

An additional cost to society comes from the involvement of the law enforcement and correctional systems in providing crisis intervention and long-term institutionalization for persons with schizophrenia who commit criminal offenses. The lifetime prevalence of schizophrenia among prisoners in correctional facilities is 6.2% (Regier et al., 1990), and few of these prisoners receive appropriate treatment. In California, it costs over $20,000 per year to maintain each of its 25,000 mentally ill prisoners with only custodial services. State psychiatric hospitals can spend over $100,000 per year on services for a person with schizophrenia.

Schizophrenia not only carries the risk of substantial morbidity, it also has a risk of mortality. Approximately 25% of persons with schizophrenia attempt suicide and 10% succeed (Roy, 1992). Suicidality in schizophrenia is associated with being male, having fallen from a much higher premorbid level of functioning, and experiencing depression (Caldwell & Gottesman, 1990). There is a high level of comorbidity of depression with schizophrenia (Green, Nuechterlein, Ventura, & Mintz, 1990; Kessler et al., 1994).

Approximately one third of the homeless population in the United States suffers from schizophrenia, and many of these people also have a substance abuse disorder (Koegel, Burnam, & Farr, 1988). The number of persons with schizophrenia and other serious mental disorders joining the ranks of the disabled with Social Security pensions has risen dramatically, by 66.4%, since 1986 (Manderscheid & Sonnenschein, 1992); few of the mentally disabled ever return to work and achieve functional independence. Thus, they are a burden to society and to their families for their lifetimes.

HISTORICAL PERSPECTIVE AND SCOPE OF LITERATURE

Empirical studies of psychological and behavioral treatments for schizophrenia were first conducted in the late 1950s and early 1960s by former students of B. F. Skinner who obtained positions in psychiatric hospitals. Lindsley, Ferster, Ayllon, and Azrin published single-case controlled studies and laboratory analogues of treatment, showing clearly that environmental antecedents and consequences could powerfully influence psychotic behaviors (Liberman, 1976). These investigators documented that presentation of reinforcement produced increases in desirable, adaptive behavior and withdrawal of reinforcement produced decreases in that behavior. By the mid-1960s, Ayllon and Azrin had established the first token economy, the application of reinforcement principles to an entire ward of patients (Ayllon & Azrin, 1965). A book reviewing the first 10 years of behavior modification includes work done with mute and withdrawn psychotics, autistic children, the developmentally disabled, and patients with bizarre behaviors (Ullman & Krasner, 1975).

The original studies were carried out with "hopeless" and treatment-refractory patients who had failed to respond to antipsychotic medications. The back wards of psychiatric hospitals were hospitable to the pioneers of behavior therapy for schizophrenia because resistance was not as strong as in treatment settings in which clinicians had vested interests in more traditional therapies such as psychodynamic approaches. From 1968 to 1975, there was an exponential increase in publications devoted to the token economy and other behavior therapy approaches to individuals with chronic forms of schizophrenia (Liberman, 1976). Behavioral approaches were conducive to the growing scientific norm in psychiatry, fertilized

by the empiricism of psychopharmacology. Adherents of both behavior therapy and psychopharmacology relied on empiricism to document the value of their interventions; in addition, for patients who did not respond optimally to psychopharmacology, behavior therapy offered both symptomatic and rehabilitative treatments (Liberman, Kopelowicz, & Young, 1994). These studies were Type 3, using the criteria of this book, pinpointing and measuring specific, molecular, and aberrant behaviors to modify and utilizing A-B or case control designs. They were heuristic, however, in stimulating further work that would become more rigorous and methodologically substantial.

In the early 1970s, the second generation of behaviorally oriented clinicians and researchers began to publish the results of their work with persons having schizophrenia (Fichter, Wallace, & Liberman 1976; Liberman, King, & DeRisi, 1976; Liberman, Teigen, Patterson, & Baker, 1973; Paul & Lentz, 1977). The second-generation studies focused more on strengthening prosocial behaviors rather than eliminating or weakening bizarre behaviors. Some of the most disastrous effects of long-term institutionalization of persons with schizophrenia were the constriction of interpersonal responses and withdrawal from social interaction. The "good" patient in a custodial setting was quiet and unobtrusive. Enhancing the social repertoires of such patients was vital to their becoming capable of leaving the hospital and adjusting to life in the community. Competence in carrying on conversations, asking for directions, obtaining necessities, and, in general, navigating the social pathways were prerequisites for successful re-entry and tenure in the community. The investigators who carried out the studies of the 1970s also recognized the limitations of generalization of treatment when the treatment was conducted solely in hospitals without planning for the "transfer of training" into the community (Liberman, McCann, & Wallace, 1976).

In their landmark controlled study comparing behavior therapy with milieu and custodial therapies, Paul and Lentz (1977) prepared patients for community life by having case managers visit the cities and towns to which the improved patients would be discharged to create opportunities and encouragement for the patients to continue to utilize their treatment gains by using "natural reinforcers" and caregivers. Not only did patients, who were randomly assigned to the social learning program, show greater clinical improvement in all areas measured, but they also had a 98% discharge rate and significantly longer tenure in the community after discharge.

The use of social skills training, developed and validated by Liberman and his colleagues (Liberman, DeRisi, & Mueser, 1989; Liberman, King, DeRisi, & McCann, 1975; Wallace & Liberman, 1985), also was a step in the direction of improved generalization (Benton & Schroeder, 1990). Social skills training utilizes the full array of social learning and behavioral principles to bring about better verbal and nonverbal social interaction. Because social skills training can be performed in any treatment setting—including naturalistic community locales—it has become a treatment of choice in the 1990s for persons with schizophrenia. Skills training fits into the "vulnerability-stress-protective factors" model of schizophrenia, which has become the most favored explanation of the etiology and course of schizophrenia. Skills training has been effective in reducing relapse rates (Falloon et al., 1985; Hogarty et al., 1986; 1991), improving social functioning (Liberman, Mueser, & Wallace, 1986; Marder et al., 1996), and enhancing quality of life (Marder et al., 1996).

The literature on the treatment and rehabilitation of persons with schizophrenia is enormous, appearing in literally hundreds of journals devoted to psychiatry, clinical psychology, behavior therapy, psychosocial rehabilitation, vocational rehabilitation, as well as journals dedicated to this disorder (*Schizophrenia Bulletin*, *Schizophrenia Research*). Books devoted to schizophrenia could fill a moderate-size library. Rather than aim for an exhaustive review of the entire literature of the past decade, which would be an undertaking well beyond the scope of this chapter, we have drawn from review articles, selected books, and issues of the *Schizophrenia Bulletin*.

STATUS OF TREATMENTS

The prevailing "stress-vulnerability-protective factors" model of schizophrenia helps the clinician understand the etiology, course, and treatment of this lifelong disorder. Stressors, such as major life events and high expressed emotion in family and residential settings (Snyder, Wallace, Moe, & Liberman, 1994), can adversely affect the course of the disorder when individuals with vulnerability to the characteristic

symptoms and associated disabilities of the disorder (Liberman, Wallace, Vaughn, Snyder, & Rust, 1980) are exposed to the stressors without the protection of medication, psychosocial treatment, and natural coping ability and social support (Kopelowicz & Liberman, 1995). For veteran practitioners who have long considered only biological treatments as effective in protecting schizophrenic individuals from stress-induced relapse and disability, this chapter and the evidence that supports the protective value of psychosocial treatments (Wunderlich, Wiedemann, & Buchkremer, 1996) may serve as an antidote to the insidious biological reductionism that often characterizes the field of schizophrenia research and treatment. On the other hand, it is essential to view treatments of schizophrenia in their biopsychosocial matrix—leaving out any of the three components (bio, psycho, social) will diminish the impact and efficacy of treatment.

In this review of the extant treatments for schizophrenia, we use a multilevel and multidimensional set of criteria in rating the evidence that supports each of the treatments. While few studies incorporate a multilevel approach, the field is moving rapidly to an appreciation of the value of a comprehensive assessment of outcome, measuring changes in (a) symptoms, bizarre and intolerable behaviors, and relapse rates (psychopathology); (b) deficits in activities of community living, social competence, and social adjustment (social and instrumental role functioning); (c) self-management of illness, including medication adherence, avoiding drugs of abuse, identifying prodromal signs of relapse, and coping with persistent symptoms (illness self-management); (d) burden of the disorder on the family or other caregivers in daily contact with the patient (care burden); and (e) subjective quality of life in areas of finances, medical and psychiatric care, recreational and social activities, family life, spiritual life, work or school, and overall perceived quality of life. A multidimensional approach to the evaluation of outcome in the psychosocial or behavioral treatment of persons with schizophrenia and other disabling mental disorders is much "easier said than done" and is plagued with methodological complications. For example, multiple employment measures may be required in studying vocational rehabilitation for persons with mental disorders to properly capture the degree of independent and instrumental role functioning in a job (sheltered v. volunteer v. transitional v. supported v. competitive) and the duration, mobility, salary level, and satisfaction of the consumer and employer with the job performed (Bond & Boyer, 1988).

Similarly, multiple measures offer advantages in assessing the comprehensiveness of behavior that comprises the construct of social skills (Liberman, 1982). The efficacy of supported education or supported employment services may be reflected by changes in self-concept, subsequent vocational attainment, as well as educational accomplishments. Because schizophrenia is a lifelong disorder requiring lifelong services, it is not possible in a time-limited study to identify longitudinal outcomes that may be sequentially linked to a particular treatment; for instance, improvement in social skills at Time A may not have evident impact on the individual's social and community functioning at Time B because opportunities, encouragement, and reinforcement for using the learned skills only emerge in the person's environment at Time C many months or years later—well after the study's assessment has been completed.

There are methodological challenges to the use of a multidimensional approach to measuring change wrought by behavioral and psychosocial treatments as well. For example, since assessment measures do not typically include ethnically based response sets, differences in language, linguistic nuances, and translation of items from standardized assessments may create aberrant response patterns (Sue & Sue, 1987). Certain goals for minority clients may not be isomorphic with the rehabilitation goals of the majority population; for example, independent living status may have less relevance to clients from backgrounds of poverty (who cannot afford independent housing) or from backgrounds with extended kin networks and co-residence traditions (Cook & Pickett, 1994). Moreover, rehabilitation services may be delivered to minorities by practitioners from different racial and ethnic backgrounds who do not fully understand or positively relate with the client. Outcomes from a poor client-practitioner match may be suboptimal.

In any evaluative review of psychosocial treatment of schizophrenia, therefore, it is difficult to know whether good or poor outcomes derive from problems in measurement, the nature of the treatment itself, the failure of the treatment to hew faithfully to the proper model of service delivery, the failure to provide sufficient amounts of the treatment, or the fact that the client did not receive the proper combination of services linked to their phase or stage of illness. In summary, "the field of psychiatric treatment and rehabilitation of schizophrenia may have outstripped its evaluation counterpart, so that the growth of multidimensional models has occurred without accompanying ways to measure their effectiveness" (Cook, 1995, p. 4).

In addition to the importance of a multidimensional approach to validating the efficacy of treatments, it is also desirable to ensure that a particular treatment is, in fact, appropriate for the phase or stage of an individual's disorder. For example, higher doses of antipsychotic medication may be required for the acute, florid phase of illness, but lower doses usually provide a higher benefit/risk ratio for those in the maintenance or recovery phases. Similarly, while social skills training is utilitarian and of tangible benefit to persons in the reconstituting, maintenance, and recovery phases, patients in the acute stage of schizophrenia may not have the cognitive capacity to learn social skills—their distractibility and overarousal may, in fact, be adversely affected by the demands of a classroom-type learning environment. The multidimensional approach to treatment evaluation, the complex cube of psychiatric rehabilitation, is depicted in Figure 9.1.

While a multidimensional approach to evaluating the efficacy of treatments is only beginning to influence the work of treatment researchers, we endeavor to rate each treatment for schizophrenia in terms of those dimensions that have been shown to improve with the respective treatment. It is also necessary to place modalities of treatment—whether they are pharmacological or psychosocial—in the context of a system of mental health delivery. The various modalities that have been documented as efficacious in schizophrenia need to be organized, financed, and delivered by an agency or group of mental health practitioners that serve as a fixed point of responsibility. The treatments must be appropriately linked to the phase or stage of a person's disorder and must be coordinated, comprehensive, continuous, and integrated. Very few persons with schizophrenia can be adequately treated in an outpatient office practice by a single practitioner.

Thus, the pervasive deficits and requirements for linkage to multiple human service agencies require a team approach, which is best exemplified by the model of assertive community treatment developed and disseminated by Stein and Test and their col-

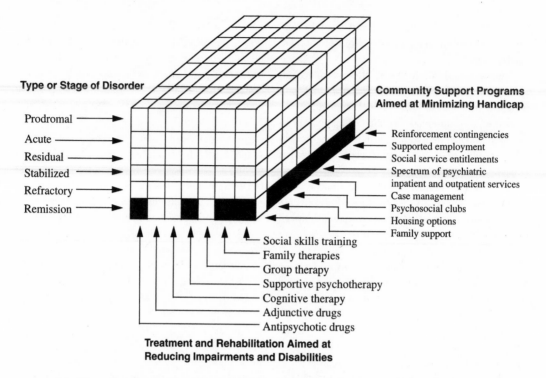

Type or Stage of Disorder

Prodromal ⟶

Acute ⟶

Residual ⟶

Stabilized ⟶

Refractory ⟶

Remission ⟶

Community Support Programs Aimed at Minimizing Handicap

Reinforcement contingencies
Supported employment
Social service entitlements
Spectrum of psychiatric
inpatient and outpatient services
Case management
Psychosocial clubs
Housing options
Family support

Social skills training
Family therapies
Group therapy
Supportive psychotherapy
Cognitive therapy
Adjunctive drugs
Antipsychotic drugs

Treatment and Rehabilitation Aimed at Reducing Impairments and Disabilities

FIGURE 9.1. The complex cube of psychiatric rehabilitation reflects the three major dimensions of treatment planning and implementation. The specific modalities of assessment and intervention are displayed along the horizontal axis and keyed to the phase or stage of the individual's disorder. Whatever the array of specific treatment modalities indicated for an individual, a treatment delivery system and social support program (e.g., housing, case management, entitlements and benefits) must be available if the treatments are to make an impact. In the particular graphic shown, an individual with schizophrenia that is in clinical remission is receiving maintenance antipsychotic medication, supportive psychotherapy (e.g., from a case manager), family intervention, and social skills training. A large number of social support services are concurrently being provided to this individual, as shown in the axis moving into the background of the figure.

leagues in Madison, Wisconsin (Stein & Test, 1985; Test, 1992). Thus, after the relatively demarcated treatment modalities for schizophrenia are rated, we include a section on the system of mental health delivery, focusing on models of agency-based treatment teams and case management.

Almost all of the available treatment research literature is about "efficacy," not "effectiveness." That is, efficacy is evaluated in highly controlled clinical research studies that are conducted in specialized research settings, supervised by academic personnel, and often working with the aid of grant support. There are precious few studies of effectiveness, in which the treatments under evaluation are being carried out in ordinary clinical service systems by practitioners who may or may not demonstrate fidelity to the treatment

parameters. Effectiveness is evaluated in mental health services research for which the use of carefully diagnosed populations and inflexible treatment manuals derived from clinical research is not always possible or desirable (Fensterheim & Raw, 1996).

One example of this is in the use of antipsychotic drugs. Clinical research demonstrates clearly the lack of efficacy of polypharmacy and the hazards of using high doses. When examining the practice of prescribing neuroleptic drugs in ordinary hospital and community settings, one discovers widespread polypharmacy and higher doses than desirable. Mental health services research is only in its infancy; thus, we rate treatments primarily in terms of their documented efficacy, not their effectiveness. When effectiveness evidence is available, we document it in our ratings.

Individual and Group Therapy

Traditional psychodynamically oriented individual and group psychotherapy have not been shown to be efficacious in schizophrenia; in fact, there is evidence that suggests an adverse effect of this form of psychotherapy on some persons with schizophrenia, presumably those with limited information-processing capacities (Mueser & Berenbaum, 1990). However, the supportive qualities inherent in treatment relationships of all types (e.g., with prescribing psychiatrist, nursing staff on an inpatient unit, case manager) are a necessary but not sufficient basis for delivering all types of treatments and for therapeutic change (Frank & Gunderson, 1990). In the past few decades, individual and group therapies for persons with schizophrenia have evolved from being informed by psychoanalytic theories and techniques to being inseminated by more supportive, practical, active, and personally reciprocal qualities. These qualities of the therapeutic alliance are delineated next in the supportive therapy treatment category.

Supportive Therapy

Supportive therapy—individual, family, and group— is characterized by

- A positive, therapeutic alliance and relationship
- A focus on reality issues, solving problems in everyday life, and practical advice
- An active, directive role by the therapist, who uses his or her own life experiences and self-disclosure as a role model for the patient
- Encouragement and education of the patient and family for proper use of antipsychotic medication.

While supportive forms of individual therapy have been broadly applied by practitioners in the course of delivering pharmacotherapy or more specific psychosocial services to persons with schizophrenia, there are only three Type 1 studies attesting to its efficacy. All of these studies were well controlled, with random assignment and comparison treatments. However, the evidence for the efficacy of supportive individual therapy was ambiguous, and, in one of the studies, extraordinarily high attrition limits the generality of the findings. In one study, individual supportive therapy led to worse outcomes at the 6-month point, but for those who survived past the first year and continued in supportive therapy, their relapse rates and social functioning were significantly better at the 2-year follow-up point (Hogarty, Goldberg, & Schooler, 1974). In a second study, reality-adapted supportive therapy was no better than exploratory insight-oriented therapy on most measures but did result in reduced rates of rehospitalization and improved role functioning (Gunderson et al., 1984). A third study found supportive group therapy significantly inferior to social skills training in terms of social functioning and subjective quality of life (Marder et al., 1996).

Supportive group therapy is also widely used, especially with outpatients. The same principles of supportive therapy are used in these groups, which may vary in emphasis from medication education to setting realistic goals, encouraging coping efforts, and socialization. There are a half dozen Type 2 empirical trials of supportive group therapy, most of which found this modality superior to other treatments (Malm, 1982).

Behavior Therapy and Social Learning Programs

Since the initial empirical demonstrations in the 1960s of the utility of laboratory-generated principles of learning for persons with schizophrenia (Ayllon & Azrin, 1968), behavior therapy has been used to manage the full spectrum of symptoms, deficits, and disturbing behaviors found in this disorder (Brenner, Hodel, & Roder, 1990; Wong, Massel, Mosk, & Liberman, 1986). The majority of the hundreds of Type 3 empirical studies documenting the efficacy of reinforcement schedules, stimulus control, social modeling, shaping, and fading have used subjects longitudinally as their own controls. The designs have featured baseline periods followed by intervention, withdrawal of intervention, and return to intervention, as well as multiple baselines for which each of 3 or 4 subjects have differing durations on baseline conditions before receiving the intervention. While these experimental designs lack the generality of randomized clinical trials with groups of subjects receiving different treatments, they do possess one methodological advantage, namely, capitalizing on and controlling for the vast interindividual differences in schizophrenia.

Since practitioners often have difficulty applying research results generated by standardized protocols that require all patients—no matter how different—to receive the same treatment, studies that use subjects as their own controls permit "fine tuning" the intervention until it shows clear-cut effects. Furthermore, intervention effects in these individualized protocols must be dramatically enough different from baseline rates of the targeted clinical problem so that the treatment effects can be "eyeballed" with little need for statistical significance. How often do we find results in the literature for which the differences between treatment and control groups are statistically significant but lack clinical significance?

There have been five Type 1 studies of behavior therapy and social learning programs (token economy) for treatment-refractory patients participating in hospital or day hospital programs in which social and tangible reinforcers were given to patients contingent on their engaging in prosocial behavior and activities (Baker, Hall, Hutchison, & Bridge, 1977; Fullerton, Cayner, & McLaughlin-Reidel, 1978; Kazdin, 1982; Menditto, Valdes, & Beck, 1994; Paul & Lentz, 1977; Schwartz & Bellack, 1975; Spiegler & Agigian, 1976). Typically, the token economy, supplemented with structured learning of self-care, recreational, and social skills, helps to organize and focus the staff-patient interactions around appropriate and functional behaviors. This contrasts with the inevitable attention given by staff in unstructured milieus to maladaptive and dangerous behaviors, thereby inadvertently reinforcing the very problems that brought the patient to the hospital in the first place.

The results of these studies have uniformly shown the efficacy of the token economy; however, because the delivery of contingent social reinforcement is a key element in the token economy, component analyses should "deconstruct" the multifaceted nature of this ward-wide, 24-hour-per-day modality. One such study found that day hospital patients were motivated to improve their behavior by the social reinforcement accompanying the contingent tokens rather than by the tangible rewards associated with the token exchanges (Liberman, Wallace, Vaughn, Snyder, & Rust, 1977). Generalization of improved behavior from a highly structured token economy to the more randomly programmed "real world" requires graded levels of reinforcement schedules and contingencies; hence, regressed patients who enter a token economy will require frequent reinforcement and shaping of their deficient behavior, while those whose functioning has improved to the point of discharge readiness will benefit from a "credit card" level in which they

have free and continuous access to privileges and rewards as long as they meet criteria for maintaining their performance at a high level.

The most rigorous and well-controlled study of the token economy randomly assigned treatment-refractory patients to a social learning program, milieu therapy, or customary, custodial care (Paul & Lentz, 1977). On all measures of outcome—symptoms, activities of daily living, social behavior, discharge, tenure in the community, and cost effectiveness—the patients in the social learning–token economy program fared significantly better. However, this study was conducted prior to the introduction of the *Diagnostic and Statistical Manual of Mental Disorders* (DSM-III; American Psychiatric Association, 1980) and may have included some individuals who would not meet current criteria for schizophrenia.

Cognitive Therapy

While cognitive therapy has been well documented for efficacy in depressive and anxiety disorders, it has only recently been used for persons who have schizophrenia. There are several different approaches to cognitive therapy, each based on the assumption that changing an individual's thoughts, attitudes, perceptions, self-efficacy, and information processing can have favorable effects on symptoms and personal functioning.

These approaches can be demarcated by the cognitive level targeted for therapy. The most "molecular" approach, termed *cognitive remediation*, focuses on improving or normalizing the most elementary cognitive functions—signal detection, sustained attention, verbal learning, and memory—each of which is abnormal in a large proportion of persons with schizophrenia (Green, 1993). The rationale fueling cognitive remediation holds that by improving elementary cognitive functions, an individual will improve in learning broader-based, and more clinically relevant, functions, such as work and social skills (Liberman & Green, 1992). Cognitive remediation does appear to improve basic cognitive functions, but there is no scientific evidence to date to support its spreading to influence clinical or social variables (Liberman & Green, 1992).

The most "molar" approach involves the consistent involvement of the patient in social skills training in which the patient is repeatedly taught to accurately perceive the social situation and its expectancies and to process the alternative responses that might be made for successfully dealing with that situation. There is limited evidence that this "top-down" method actually results in more salutary brain functioning (Storzbach & Corrigan, 1996).

In between the molecular and molar approaches are 15 studies that utilize methods for uncovering and changing irrational, automatic thoughts; negative self-appraisals; delusions; social schemas; and coping with persistent symptoms of the disorder (Kingdon & Turkington, 1994; Tarrier, Beckett, & Harwood, 1993). Here, the evidence is scanty, with only one Type 2 study extant that revealed promising, but not definitive, results (Garety et al., 1994; Tarrier, Beckett & Harwood, 1993). Five studies using subjects as their own controls—Type 3 studies—also found promising results for cognitive restructuring of delusions. However, many studies of this genre have used questionable methods of diagnosis, and it is possible that some subjects have delusional disorders, less serious illnesses than schizophrenia (Bouchard, Vallieres, Roy, & Maziade, 1996). The approach that has received the most empirical evaluation, termed *integrated psychological therapy*, consists of a sequential hierarchy of training procedures, starting with basic functions such as attention and progressing through problem solving to social skills training (Brenner et al., 1994). Results from studies of integrated psychological therapy must be viewed as tentative because of methodological limitations.

Structured, Educational Family Interventions

With the growing number of international replications of the family emotional climate as one of the most powerful predictors of relapse in schizophrenia (Bertrando et al., 1992; Jenkins & Karno, 1992; Kuipers & Bebbington, 1988), interventions have been designed and empirically validated that are aimed at engaging families as active participants in the treatment and rehabilitation process while improving their coping capacities and those of their mentally ill members. A variety of terms have been coined to describe these interventions, including *family psychoeducation, behavioral family management, behavioral family therapy, family-aided assertive community treatment,* and *multiple family therapy* (Mueser, Glynn, & Liberman, 1994).

These methods have substantial elements in common, including structured and clear expectations for participation by family members and patient; outreach and other efforts to connect with the family and provide them support; practical education about the nature of schizophrenia, and how to cope with it; assisting the family to effectively utilize available treatments and community resources; teaching stress management techniques; encouraging family members to pursue their own goals and well-being without becoming emotionally overinvolved with each other; and teaching the family better means of communicating and problem solving (Strachan, 1992).

Several Type 1 clinical trials have been conducted using structured, educational family interventions, all of them showing the superiority of adding family intervention to medication and customary case management (Falloon et al., 1985; Goldstein, Rodnick, Evans, May, & Steinberg, 1978; Hogarty et al., 1986; Leff et al., 1989; Leff, Kuipers, Berkowitz, Eberlein-Vries, & Sturgeon, 1982; Liberman, Falloon, & Aitchison, 1984; MacFarlane, Stastny & Deakins, 1992; Randolph et al., 1994). One key feature of efficacious family interventions is their duration—a minimum of 9 months or a year of weekly and biweekly family sessions appears necessary for therapeutic impact.

The outcomes assessed in these studies have included relapse rates, family attitudes and emotions, social functioning, quality of life, family burden, and cost effectiveness. In terms of relapse rates, converging evidence suggests that these structured family interventions reduce relapse by one half over that achieved with medication and case management alone. An multihospital study sponsored by the National Institute of Mental Health [NIMH] of family interventions found approximately the same relapse rates in a large sample of patients as reported in smaller, single-site, controlled studies; however, this multisite study did not show an advantage for more intensive behavioral family management over monthly, supportive, and educational family sessions (Schooler, 1996).

Because the multisite study used family clinicians who were second-generation users of these methods and were not identified with the individuals who developed the techniques, one might consider the results as evidence of effectiveness from a services research perspective. Unfortunately, this study did not use a control group receiving no family intervention, making it difficult to interpret the significance of the results. Moreover, assessment of families' problem-solving skills in the intensive form of intervention revealed no change from beginning to end of treatment, suggesting that the treatment failed to achieve its goal of improving family communication skills.

Social Skills Training

Social skills training is defined by behavioral techniques or learning activities that enable persons with schizophrenia and other disabling mental disorders to acquire instrumental and affiliative skills for improved functioning in their communities (Liberman, DeRisi, & Mueser, 1989). Training can be done with standardized curricula, or modules, that cover knowledge and skills that most persons with schizophrenia need for improved life functioning and management of their illness (e.g., use of antipsychotic medication, communication with mental health professionals, recognizing prodromal signs of relapse, developing a relapse prevention plan, coping with persistent psychotic symptoms, avoiding street drugs and alcohol, developing leisure skills, conversation skills). Alternatively, skills training can be individualized, with goals for improving personal effectiveness derived from each person's long-term and personalized aspirations for role functioning.

Sessions are typically conducted one to three times per week, with groups of 4–10 patients in office, community mental health center, day hospital, or hospital settings. Skills training requires that patients be reasonably well stabilized on their medications, be able to follow instructions and pay attention to the training process, and be able to tolerate sessions lasting 45–90 minutes. Thus, social skills training is generally used with outpatients who are living in the community in which their skills can be applied. Because of the attentional requirements of the training, this modality is not suitable for floridly and acutely symptomatic patients nor for those with persistent high levels of thought disorder and distractibility unless specially designed for these populations (Massel, Corrigan, Liberman, & Milan, 1991; Mueser, Wallace, & Liberman, 1995).

Trainers draw on behavioral learning principles and techniques such as behavioral rehearsal (role playing), social modeling, abundant positive reinforcement for incremental improvements in social skill, active coaching and prompting, in vivo exercises, and homework assignments (Corrigan, Schade, & Liberman, 1992). Skills training techniques also are components of other structured learning modalities, such as family interventions and vocational rehabilitation (Liberman, Vaccaro, & Corrigan, 1995).

Evidence for the efficacy of social skills training addresses the following outcome dimensions: acquisition, durability, and utilization of the skills in real life; improvements in social functioning; reductions in relapse rates and rehospitalization; and enhanced quality of life. There are more than 40 Type 1 or Type 2 studies and two meta-analyses that have addressed one or more of these areas of outcome (Benton & Schroeder, 1990; Corrigan, 1991). Overall, there is excellent and well-replicated evidence for the efficacy of social skills training in the acquisition of the skills taught, with durability extending for at least 1 year. Generalization of the skills to real-life use, social functioning, reductions in relapse rates, and enhanced quality of life has been studied less frequently, but the limited data are positive, especially when training extends for 1 year or longer.

In two Type 1 studies, the therapeutic impact of social skills training was well documented on several dimensions of outcome. With outpatients who were all receiving maintenance doses of depot antipsychotic medication, 1 year of weekly social skills training sessions reduced relapse by one half compared with those receiving medication alone (Hogarty et al., 1986). The reduction in relapse rate was the same as achieved by structured, educational family intervention plus maintenance medication. Patients receiving social skills training also evinced significant improvements in social adjustment. When social skills training and family intervention were combined, 1-year relapse was zero.

In the second Type 1 study (Eckman et al., 1992), stable outpatients with chronic schizophrenia were randomly assigned to twice weekly supportive group therapy or social skills training for which the training included medication and symptom self-management, social problem solving, and individualized personal effectiveness. While all patients received low-dose depot maintenance medication, those who experienced prodromal symptoms were randomized to receive time-limited oral antipsychotic drug or a placebo during the prodrome.

Results indicated that the patients receiving social skills training, but not those getting supportive group therapy, significantly improved their skill levels, which were durable over a 1-year period and were found to be utilized in their real-life settings. Moreover, even patients with relatively high levels of persisting symptoms (but not severe thought disorder) learned the skills as well as those with minimal symptoms. In addition, the patients who learned social skills showed significantly better social functioning and quality of life over the 2-year period of the study. Skills training also reduced relapse rates in the subgroup of patients who received a placebo, but not time-limited oral medication, during prodromal periods, suggesting that supplemental antipsychotic medication at times of prodromes or social skills training conferred similar degrees of protection against relapse to this population (Marder et al., 1996).

Vocational Rehabilitation

Lifelong unemployment, as well as disability pensions from the Social Security Administration, have contributed to the profound stigmatization of persons with schizophrenia as having a poor quality of life and of being a burden on their families and society. Until the past decade, most efforts at vocational rehabilitation were carried out in sheltered workshops or psychosocial rehabilitation clubhouses in which individuals with mental disorders had little opportunity to learn marketable skills for community employment. In addition, state-run vocational rehabilitation agencies gave short shrift to the mentally ill and infrequently coordinated their services in functional and effective ways with mental health professionals who were responsible for all other psychiatric services. Fragmentation led to futility and nihilism by rehabilitation specialists, as well as psychiatric practitioners.

There was one notable exception to this pattern, namely, the Fairweather Lodge program. In the 1960s and 1970s, George Fairweather and his colleagues designed a rehabilitation program at the Menlo Park (California) Veterans Administration Medical Center that brought together into cohorts groups of interpersonally compatible patients with serious mental disorders; trained them to offer cohesion and social support to each other; organized the cohorts so the skills, interests, and deficits of the group were complementary; and then gradually brought the group into the community as a "lodge." The emphasis was on work and independent living skills. Staff taught work and community living skills, first in the hospital and then in the community lodge, and then gradually faded their involvement and level of supervision so that the group was finally functioning autonomously.

The results were highly encouraging, with every dimension of outcome (e.g., work, rehospitalization) showing substantially and statistically significantly greater benefits for the lodge cohorts compared to randomly assigned controls (Fairweather, 1980; Fairweather, Sanders, Maynard, Cressler, & Bleck, 1969). Moreover, the lodge program was successfully disseminated to more than 100 institutions around the United States, indicating the robust nature of its multifaceted approach to rehabilitation. Its multifaceted nature was also a methodological problem, however, since the components of the lodge service system were never disassembled and studied analytically.

Because of the successful demonstrations of competitive employment for the mentally retarded, the Americans With Disabilities Act, the consumer advocacy movement, and community support programs that assumed responsibility for broader and better integrated services, vocational rehabilitation for the mentally disabled is rapidly shifting to a "place, then train" model of supported employment (Bond, 1992). Supported employment is based on the following principles:

1. Vocational rehabilitation is an integral, not separate, component of psychiatric treatment and requires a team approach with specialists in job development and placement.
2. The goal of supported employment is to place an individual in competitive employment in the community, with vocational assessment and training taking place on the job. Jobs are selected and support services are provided according to the preferences and choices of the consumer.
3. Job coaching and supports from mental health and rehabilitation professionals, including ready access to psychiatric, pharmacological, and crisis services, are provided indefinitely—consistent with the long-term, stress-related nature of schizophrenia and other disabling disorders.

The development of supported employment is so new that little empirical work has been published on this innovation. However, even more disabled and cognitively compromised mentally retarded clients have been repeatedly shown to benefit from supported employment (Wehman & Hill, 1989; Wehman & Moon, 1987). Data-based studies have reported 65% to 80% employment rates and 66% and 33% job retention rates at 6 months and 1 year, respectively, following placement.

Surveys of state vocational rehabilitation agencies have found a growing number of mentally disabled persons enrolled in supported employment programs, and research is slowly following practice. A Type 1 study of an approximation to supported employment (accelerated transitional employment) found that seriously mentally ill clients who made the transition more rapidly into real jobs had almost three times more success in attaining competitive employment 15 months later than a comparison group who made a gradual transition (Bond & Dincin, 1986). In addition, a series of three Type 3 studies of supported employment integrated with assertive case management teams have shown this model to result in twice the rate of competitive employment compared with more traditional rehabilitation services that offer extended periods of prevocational training and work adjustment (Drake & Becker, 1996).

One other method of vocational rehabilitation, the job-finding club, deserves mention. This approach assumes that a client is ready for work but requires training and structured support in the job search process. Individuals set goals for the types of jobs for which they are qualified and participate in a 1–2-week program that offers training in creating a resume, finding job leads, telephoning and interacting with employers to follow up leads, going through a job interview, and maintaining motivation for a job search that may require full-time effort for many weeks.

No controlled studies with mentally ill clients have been conducted for the job-finding club, but Type 3 empirical evaluations of this approach have indicated that 19% to 61% of mentally ill clients obtain competitive employment, usually after an average of 25 days of participating in the club (Eisenberg & Cole, 1986; Jacobs, 1988; Jacobs, Collier, & Wissusik, 1992; Jacobs, Kardashian, Kreinbring, Ponder, & Simpson, 1984). The wide variation in outcomes appears to be a function of the population studied, with psychotic individuals faring much worse than those with less-impairing disorders.

One approach to vocational rehabilitation that has become widely popular during the past 50 years is the psychosocial rehabilitation center or clubhouse. This model includes programs that are based on Fountain House in New York (Beard, Propst, & Malumud, 1982; Dincin, 1975). These programs provide an accepting peer-oriented clubhouse that deemphasizes

the patient's role and stresses the individual's own responsibility for rehabilitation. The program typically offers a continuum of vocational opportunities ranging from prevocational work crews, usually unpaid work opportunities within the center, to transitional employment, which consists of temporary community jobs employing patients under an arrangement between the program and a community employer. Although the long history of the clubhouse approach suggests that it has survived a trial-and-error process, empirical studies supporting its utility and efficacy are lacking (Bond, 1992).

Case Management and Treatment Teams

During the past two decades, well-controlled research has documented the improved outcomes and lower costs associated with brief hospitalization for acute psychotic episodes and the use of community-based alternatives to hospitalization, such as partial hospitals and intensive case management built into continuous, outpatient treatment teams (Goldman, 1996; Herz, 1996). For example, 11 days of hospitalization followed by day hospital and outpatient treatment produced better symptom outcomes than 60 days of hospitalization with outpatient follow-up. Social functioning 1 and 2 years later also was better for the patients who were hospitalized briefly and then returned to their natural social and family support networks (Herz, Endicott, & Spitzer, 1977).

Thus, patients with schizophrenia and other disabling mental disorders should be discharged when the specific indications for hospitalization are no longer present (e.g., assaultiveness, florid and disabling psychotic symptoms). In addition, clinicians should attempt to ensure that appropriate continuity of care, social and family supports, and housing are available before the patient is discharged to avoid the "revolving door" phenomenon of hospitalization-discharge-rehospitalization and the tragic but all too common homelessness that afflicts so many thousand of the seriously mentally ill today.

Case management, and the treatment teams in which it is embedded, are the "glue" that holds together and coordinates the array of biopsychosocial services described above. In addition, case management provides the mechanism for assuring that patients or clients obtain those services appropriate for their phase of illness, tailored to the individual's symptoms, psychosocial functioning, personal goals, and environmental resources. At a minimum, case managers function as monitors of the quality of services they broker and coordinate with various agencies and practitioners to fulfill the goals of their severely mentally ill clients. In theory, each case manager is a focal point of accessibility and accountability who maximizes the effectiveness and efficiency of services (Intagliata, 1982; Baker & Intagliata, 1992).

Three main forms of case management have evolved, distinguished by the level of training and quality and amount of direct clinical services delivered to the client: brokerage case management, clinical case management, and Training in Community Living. The brokerage model of case management has been found to be relatively ineffective in fulfilling the needs of severely mentally ill individuals. For example, one Type 3 study evaluated the effects of this brokerage model of case management on 417 severely mentally ill individuals, all of whom had been hospitalized at least twice (Franklin, Solovitz, Mason, Clemons, & Miller, 1987). Franklin's group found that the costs and use of services increased after case management was introduced into the mental health agency, but there was no corresponding improvement in functioning or reduction in the rates and durations of subsequent hospitalizations.

In contrast, the polar opposite model of case management—the Training in Community Living (TCL) program developed 20 years ago by Stein and Test and their colleagues—has been shown to be effective in several Type 1 studies (Stein & Test, 1985; Test, 1992). The TCL model organizes the service delivery system into multidisciplinary clinical treatment teams that "serve as fixed points of responsibility for assisting patients in meeting all of their needs from the day that they enter the program to a time extending many years into the future" (Test, 1992, p. 158). Each member of the interdisciplinary team serves case management functions, with a ratio of 1 : 20 or less of staff to clients.

Services are delivered in individuals' own environments and include direct assistance with managing their illnesses (e.g., medication, 24-hour crisis availability), modifying the environment to enhance its supportiveness (e.g., facilitating entitlements, family education, development of social networks), direct assistance with the tasks of community living (e.g., rehabilitation services, including home visits), and supported employment supervised by a vocational specialist on the TCL team. The full array of comprehensive and continuous services, keyed to each individual's changing needs, is provided by the team, avoiding the frequent fragmentation and occasional internecine "warfare" among service providers who are contracted through "brokerage" to deliver different types of services.

The effects of TCL have been favorable, with the qualification that services may need to extend for an indefinite period of time with a frequency and intensity that match the changing needs, interests, motivation, and priorities of the patient. The originators of TCL found that 14 months of TCL services resulted in lowered rates of hospitalization, more time in independent living, and improvements in role functioning (Stein & Test, 1980). Replications of the TCL model (Hoult, 1986; Mulder, 1982; Test, 1992) confirmed these results, particularly for lowered rates of hospitalization. It has been determined that for role functioning (e.g., friendships, employment) to improve, the TCL team must invest the time and effort of specialists on the team for teaching social and vocational skills and creating opportunities to use the skills in real-life situations.

From an early study of TCL that found that erosion of the gains achieved by 14 months in TCL occurred when patients were referred to customary care in the community (Test, Knoedler, & Allness, 1985), it was realized that TCL must be available indefinitely to ensure maintenance and extension of the clinical gains (Test, 1992). The TCL model is costly and labor intensive, but does have the capability to facilitate individuals' movements through the acute, stabilizing, stable, and recovery stages.

An intermediate model is clinical case management, for which the case manager has clinical training and skills, functions as a primary therapist (versus paraprofessional "enablers") and can provide interventions that improve individuals' clinical states, role functioning, and environmental supports. While this model attempts to provide comprehensive and continuous services to clients and has been found to result in improvements in subjective quality of life and satisfaction with case management (Huxley & Warner, 1992), the clinical case manager can easily become overburdened with responsibilities and is subject to "burnout" (Bachrach, 1992; Bond et al., 1991). Two other Type 2 studies of clinical case management have found empirical support for its efficacy, although one study was flawed by its use of historical controls and a lack of randomization (Goering, Wasylenki,

Farkas, Lancee, & Ballantyne, 1988; Modrcin, Rapp, & Poertner, 1988).

Figure 9.2 depicts the tripartite model of clinical case management in the shape of a triangle. At the base of the triangle are the basic clinical skills required to form and maintain a therapeutic alliance. The left limb of the triangle comprises a clinician's technical skills in assessment and treatment. The right limb of the triangle includes consultative, advocacy, coordinating, and liaison skills required to open community-based resources, such as housing and social service entitlements, for the client. In employing demonstrably efficacious and cost-effective methods of intensive or assertive clinical case management (Olfson, 1990; Weisbrod, Test, & Stein, 1980), it is important for practitioners to utilize the treatment methods with fidelity to the key features of the innovative model. For example, agencies that have implemented assertive community treatment, or PACT (Program for Assertive Community Treatment), with caseloads that are significantly greater than 1 to 20 per case manager or treatment team member, have not been successful in achieving good outcomes (McGrew, Bond, Dietzen, & Salyers, 1994).

Similarly, schizophrenia and substance abuse, which are often comorbidly present in high propor-

tions of urban populations, present special challenges to the treatment team and case manager in diagnosis, substance-specific interactions, psychosocial treatments, and psychopharmacology. In most settings, substance abuse and schizophrenia are treated by totally different agencies, resulting in fragmented and often incompatible approaches. Even when continuity of care is assured by a fixed point of clinical accountability for the dually diagnosed individual, poor treatment outcomes can ensue from overemphasizing the treatment of either disorder rather than providing a synchronous, seamless approach that leads to abstinence from substance abuse and remission of psychotic symptoms (Drake, Noordsy, & Ackerson, 1995).

FUTURE DIRECTIONS

It should come as no surprise that the efficacy of psychosocial treatments, requiring as they do a functional brain capable of assimilating and retaining information and skills, is attenuated by cognitive impairments that are enduring traits in most individuals with schizophrenia (Nuechterlein et al., 1994). Studies carried out in a variety of laboratories have documented the adverse influence of deficits in memory, sustained

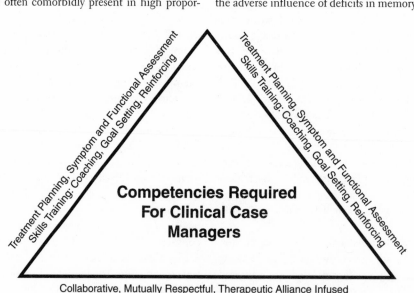

FIGURE 9.2. Competencies of clinical case managers can be organized into three major domains: (a) the bottom limb of the triangle represents relationship and personal engagement skills; (b) the left limb of the triangle represents technical, biobehavioral assessment, and treatment skills; and (c) the right limb of the triangle represents consultation-liaison and advocacy skills.

attention, and verbal learning on the capacity of individuals with schizophrenia to benefit from psychosocial interventions (Bowen et al., 1994; Corrigan, Wallace, Schade, & Green, 1994; Kern, Green, & Satz, 1992; Mueser, Bellack, Douglas, & Wade, 1991). These findings have generated interest in (a) determining the differential "rehabilitation readiness" of individuals with schizophrenia and (b) feasibility studies of cognitive remediation to improve information processing in the brain (Green, 1993; Liberman & Green, 1992).

Current methods for remediating cognitive impairments in schizophrenia have utilized rather conventional behavioral techniques such as monetary reinforcement and instructions. These techniques have not resulted in impressive durability or generalizability of treatment; hence, new strategies for remediation will undoubtedly be developed in the coming decade. For example, one study recently completed used "errorless learning" to promote durability of effects in teaching schizophrenic individuals greater cognitive flexibility in the Wisconsin Card Sorting Task. Not only did this method of training result in normalization of the responses by the persons with schizophrenia, but it also showed greater durability than the more conventional techniques (Kern, Wallace, Hellman, Womack, & Green, 1996).

Since verbal memory and verbal learning are serious impediments to psychiatric rehabilitation among persons with schizophrenia, techniques to compensate or overcome these deficits will need to be developed. One approach is to capitalize on the implicit or procedural learning capacity of individuals with schizophrenia. Implicit learning involves those psychomotor actions that are repetitive, overlearned, and can be employed "without thinking" or conscious awareness. Examples are riding a bicycle, catching a ball, saying nighttime prayers, or hitting a nail with a hammer. At the Clinical Research Center for Schizophrenia and Psychiatric Rehabilitation at UCLA, procedural learning was shown to be unimpaired in schizophrenia (Kern, Green, Wallace, & Goldstein, 1996).

Similarly, spatial visual learning is not as impaired in schizophrenia and can be utilized to overcome obstacles posed by verbal learning; for example, pictures of a concept, event, or interpersonal skill could be used to teach more flexible use of social skills than is currently available. Plans are being made to craft pictures that will delineate naturalistic situations in which certain "rules governing social behavior" will be taught. Generalization of the learning to everyday life interactions will be assessed.

Assessment Guiding Treatment

Given the factors that influence social and instrumental role functioning, there is a pressing need to develop better means of evaluating these functional domains. Moreover, evaluation methods must be linked to treatment planning and treatment monitoring and evaluation and not exist as a separate entity. Assuming that the goal of psychiatric treatment and rehabilitation is to assist individuals to reduce their symptoms and relapses, improve their functioning, enhance their quality of life, and attain their personalized goals, better methods of assessing roles, individuals, environments, and treatment effects (including both medication and psychosocial treatments) would foster research—both clinical and services research—and yield research that was more relevant to the needs of consumers and practitioners.

Clinicians could allocate scarce treatment resources based on information about the complexities of the specific role(s) to which an individual aspires, the skills in the individual's current behavioral repertoire, the degree and predictability of environmental supports and rewards, and obstacles (e.g., symptoms, bizarre behaviors) that stand in the way of goal attainment in role functioning. This allocation could be the result of an algorithm that prescribes the balance of skills training and environmental modifications that maximizes the probability of improving an individual's functioning. The algorithm could itself be developed based on research investigating the process of "expert" clinicians' decision making, yielding a system that could be modeled on a computer and available to all clinicians regardless of experience and discipline. The CD-ROM and virtual reality modalities will create learning opportunities for clinicians and consumers that are more cost effective, requiring minimal staff time.

Curricula for social skills training and family intervention can be refined, standardized, and distributed in a format that allows them to be easily accessed and efficiently delivered. Developing training curricula is extremely time consuming, and clinicians may achieve better outcomes by focusing their efforts on delivering training rather than producing it. Especially in the current era of cost containment and managed care, the use of reliable, validated, and standardized treatment programs that can be adapted to the individual will be in much demand. Current technology, such as computer-based, interactive training, may provide an efficiently delivered format that allows a relatively high degree of individuation. Furthermore, the current efforts to improve an individual's persistent cognitive deficits with "cognitive rehabilitation" techniques may also help them to participate more efficiently in skills training.

Social System Interventions

Developing techniques to explicitly increase environmental support could be helpful. Currently, the technology for this approach to rehabilitation emphasizes low-key and permissive "psychosocial clubhouses" and "consumer-run" rehabilitation services. The Social Security Administration has established "work incentives" for disabled individuals, such as the Program for Achieving Self-Support. Qualified individuals can continue to receive their SSI (supplemental security income) or SSDI (social security disability income) payments for up to 2 years while they earn money in jobs to pursue independent living or educational experiences that will enable them to become more independent and job ready. In the future, more of these work incentives will become available as empirical data reveal the harmful effects of prolonged disability status (Liberman & Mintz, 1990; Shaner et al., 1995). As the emphasis in our society moves more toward competitive employment, techniques that will more reliably assure job placement and training on the job are going to receive more interest from the federal, state, and local governments. Not only will welfare recipients be the focal point of interest, but individuals on Social Security disability will also gain priority for conversion into productive citizens. Training programs for employment specialists, mental health team members, consumers, family members, and employers will become increasingly focused, structured, and empirically based. The job-finding club is one example of an approach that can be "modularized" and fit into existing programs with a trainer's manual, participant's workbook, and demonstration video. Another example is the Workplace Fundamentals Module, which incorporates the job club into a broader approach to job placement and job maintenance (Wallace, 1996). In keeping with the Americans With Disabilities Act, these techniques could be used to accommodate individuals with varying levels of skills or to provide variations in support as an individual's skills increased with training and experience.

Dissemination and Adoption of Innovation

Empirical documentation of a treatment's efficacy rarely is sufficient to promote its dissemination and adoption by clinicians (Backer, Liberman, & Kuehnel, 1986). Even with new medications, which require only a physician's change in prescription-writing behavior, pharmaceutical firms use small armies of representatives to "teach" physicians about and introduce them to how to use the new medication. The utilization of a psychosocial innovation—such as social skills training—is much more difficult to bring about.

There have been some lessons learned about the basic principles that can be used to overcome inertia in practitioner's behavior, for example, personal influence (e.g., demonstrating the new treatment technique and offering mentoring and apprenticeships), administrative mandates and support, congruence of the innovation with previous practices, and "user friendliness" of the innovation. The social skills training modules in the University of California at Los Angeles Social and Independent Living Skills Program reflects user friendliness insofar as they are prestructured and well-organized curricula that can be readily used by most professionals and paraprofessionals who are comfortable working with the seriously mentally ill.

Large-scale field trials in many different settings suggest that the modules are indeed user friendly and widely adopted by clinicians (Eckman, Liberman, Phipps, & Blair, 1990). In fact, within a brief period of 10 years, the modules have been translated into more than 12 languages and have shown efficacy in controlled studies in Finland; Norway; Poland; Bulgaria; Korea; Quebec, Canada; and Japan.

References

American Psychiatric Association. (1980). *Diagnostic and statistical manual of mental disorders* (3rd ed.). Washington, D.C.: Author.

Ayllon, T., & Azrin, N. H. (1965). The measurement and reinforcement of behavior of psychotics. *Journal of the Experimental Analysis of Behavior, 8*, 357–383.

————. (1968). Reinforcer sampling: A technique for

increasing the behavior of mental patients. *Journal of Applied Behavior Analysis, 1,* 13–20.

Bachrach, L. L. (1992). Case management revisited. *Hospital and Community Psychiatry, 43,* 209–210.

Backer, T. E., Liberman, R. P., & Kuehnel, T. G. (1986). Dissemination and adoption of innovative psychosocial interventions. *Journal of Consulting and Clinical Psychology, 54,* 111–118.

Baker, F., & Intagliata, J. (1992). Case management. In R. P. Liberman (Ed.), *Handbook of psychiatric rehabilitation,* (pp. 213–243). New York: Macmillan.

Baker, R., Hall, J. N., Hutchison, K., & Bridge, G. (1977). Symptom changes in chronic schizophrenic patients on a token economy: A controlled experiment. *British Journal of Psychiatry, 131,* 381–393.

Beard, J. H., Propst, R. N., & Malumud, T. J. (1982). The Fountain House model of rehabilitation. *Psychosocial Rehabilitation Journal, 5,* 47–53.

Benton, M. K., & Schroeder, H. E. (1990). Social skills training with schizophrenics: A meta-analytic evaluation. *Journal of Consulting and Clinical Psychology, 58,* 741–747.

Bertrando, P., Beltz, J., Bressi, C., Clerici, M., et al. (1992). Expressed emotion and schizophrenia in Italy: A study of an urban population. *British Journal of Psychiatry, 161,* 223–229.

Bond, G. (1992). Vocational rehabilitation. In R. P. Liberman (Ed.), *Handbook of psychiatric rehabilitation* (pp. 244–275). New York: Macmillan.

Bond, G., & Boyer, S. L. (1988). Rehabilitation programs and outcomes. In J. A. Ciardiello & M. D. Bell (Eds.), *Vocational rehabilitation of persons with prolonged mental illness* (pp. 231–263). Baltimore, Md.: Johns Hopkins University Press.

Bond, G. R., & Dincin, J. (1986). Accelerating entry into transitional employment in a psychosocial rehabilitation agency. *Rehabilitation Psychology, 31,* 143–155.

Bond, G. R., Pensec, M., Dietzen, L., McCafferty, D., et al. (1991). Intensive case management for frequent users of psychiatric hospitals in a large city: A comparison of team and individual caseloads. *Psychosocial Rehabilitation Journal, 15,* 90–98.

Bouchard, S., Vallieres, A., Roy, M. A., & Maziade, M. (1996). Cognitive restructuring in the treatment of psychotic symptoms in schizophrenia. *Behavior Therapy, 27,* 257–278.

Bowen, L., Wallace, C. J., Glynn, S. M., Nuechterlein, K. H., Lutzger, J. R., & Kuehnel, T. G. (1994). Schizophrenics' cognitive functioning and performance in interpersonal interactions and skills training procedures. *Journal of Psychiatric Research, 28,* 289–301.

Brenner, H., Hodel, B., & Roder, V. (1990). Integrated cognitive and behavioral interventions in treatment of schizophrenia. *Psychosocial Rehabilitation Journal, 13,* 41–43.

Brenner, H. D., Roder, V., Hodel, B., Kienzle, N., Reed, D., & Liberman, R. P. (1994). *Integrated psychological therapy for schizophrenic patients.* Toronto: Hogrefe & Huber.

Caldwell, C., & Gottesman, I. (1990). Schizophrenics kill themselves too: A review of risk factors for suicide. *Schizophrenia Bulletin, 16,* 571–589.

Clark, R. E. (1994). Family costs associated with mental illness and substance use. *Hospital and Community Psychiatry, 45,* 808–813.

Cook, J. A. (1995). Research on psychosocial rehabilitation services for persons with psychiatric disabilities. *Psychotherapy and Rehabilitation Research Bulletin, 4,* 3–5.

Cook, J. A., & Pickett, S. A. (1994). Recent trends in vocational rehabilitation for persons with psychiatric disability. *American Rehabilitation, 20,* 2–12.

Corrigan, P., Schade, M., & Liberman, R. P. Social skills training. In R. P. Liberman (Ed.), *Handbook of psychiatric rehabilitation* (pp. 95–126). New York: Macmillan.

Corrigan, P. W. (1991). Social skills training in adult psychiatric populations: A meta-analysis. *Journal of Behavior Therapy and Experimental Psychiatry, 22,* 203–210.

Corrigan, P. W., Wallace, C. J., Schade, M. L., & Green, M. F. (1994). Learning medication self-management skills in schizophrenia: Relationships with cognitive deficits and psychiatric symptoms. *Behavior Therapy, 25,* 5–15.

Dincin, J. (1975). Psychiatric rehabilitation. *Schizophrenia Bulletin, 1,* 131–148.

Drake, R. E., & Becker, D. R. (1996). The Individual Placement and Support Model of supported employment. *Psychiatric Services, 47,* 473–475.

Drake, R. E., Noordsy, D. L., & Ackerson, T. (1995). Integrating mental health and substance abuse treatments for persons with chronic mental disorders. In A. F. Lehman & L. B. Dixon (Eds.), *Double jeopardy: Chronic mental illness and substance use disorders* (pp. 251–264). Chur, Switzerland: Harwood.

Eckman, T. A., Liberman, R. P., Phipps, C. C., & Blair, K. (1990). Teaching medication management skills to schizophrenic patients. *Journal of Clinical Psychopharmacology, 10,* 33–38.

Eckman, T. A., Wirshing, W. C., Marder, S. R., Liberman, R. P., et al. (1992). Technique for training schizophrenic patients in illness self-management: A controlled trial. *American Journal of Psychiatry, 149,* 1549–1555.

Eisenberg, M. G., & Cole, H. W. (1986, April–June). A behavioral approach to job seeking for psychiatrically impaired persons. *Journal of Rehabilitation*, 46–49.

Fairweather, G. W. (1980). The prototype lodge society. In G. Fairweather (Ed.), *The Fairweather Lodge: A 25 year retrospective* (pp. 13–32). San Francisco, Ca.: Jossey-Bass.

Fairweather, G. W., Sanders, D. H., Maynard, H., Cressler, D. L., & Bleck, D. S. (1969). *Community life for the mentally ill: An alternative to institutional care.* Chicago: Aldine.

Falloon, I. R. H., Boyd, J. L., McGill, C. W., et al. (1985). Family management in the prevention of morbidity of schizophrenia. *Archives of General Psychiatry, 42,* 887–896.

Fensterheim, H., & Raw, S. D. (1996). Psychotherapy research is not psychotherapy practice. *Clinical Psychological Scientist-Practitioner, 3,* 168–171.

Fichter, M., Wallace, C. J., & Liberman, R. P. (1976). Improving social interaction in a chronic psychotic using discriminated avoidance. *Journal of Applied Behavioral Analysis, 9,* 377–386.

Frank, A. K., & Gunderson, J. G. (1990). The role of the therapeutic alliance in the treatment of schizophrenia: Relationship to course and outcome. *Archives of General Psychiatry, 47,* 228–236.

Franklin, J. L., Solovitz, B., Mason, M., Clemons, J. R., & Miller, G. E. (1987). An evaluation of case management. *American Journal of Public Health, 77,* 675–678.

Fullerton, D. T., Cayner, J. J., & McLaughlin-Reidel, T. (1978). Results of a token economy. *Archives of General Psychiatry, 35,* 1451–1453.

Garety, P. A., Kuipers, L., Fowler, D., Chamberlain, F., et al. (1994). Cognitive behavioural therapy for drug-resistant psychosis. *British Journal of Medical Psychology, 67,* 259–271.

Goering, P. N., Wasylenki, D. A., Farkas, M., Lancee, W. J., & Ballantyne, R. (1988). What difference does case management make? *Hospital and Community Psychiatry, 39,* 272–276.

Goldman, H. H. (1996). Using cost-effectiveness data in benefit design. *Psychiatric Annals, 26,* 528–530.

Goldstein, M. J., Rodnick, E. H., Evans, J. R., May, P. R. A., & Steinberg, M. R. (1978). Drug and family therapy in the aftercare treatment of acute schizophrenia. *Archives of General Psychiatry, 35,* 169–177.

Green, M. F. (1993). Cognitive remediation in schizophrenia, *American Journal of Psychiatry, 150,* 178–187.

Green, M. F., Nuechterlein, K. H., Ventura, J., & Mintz, J. (1990). The temporal relationship between depressive and psychotic symptoms in recent-onset schizophrenia. *American Journal of Psychiatry, 147,* 179–182.

Gunderson, J. G., et al. (1984). Effects of psychotherapy in schizophrenia: II. Comparative outcome of two forms of treatment. *Schizophrenia Bulletin, 10,* 564–598.

Harding, C. M., Zubin, J., & Strauss, J. S. (1992). Chronicity in schizophrenia revisited. *British Journal of Psychiatry, 161,* 27–37.

Herz, M. I. (1996). Psychosocial treatment. *Psychiatric Annals, 26,* 531–535.

Herz, M. I., Endicott, J., & Spitzer, R. L. (1977). Brief hospitalization: A two year follow-up. *American Journal of Psychiatry, 134,* 502–507.

Hogarty, G. E., Anderson, C. M., Reiss, D. J., et al. (1986). Family education, social skills training and maintenance chemotherapy in aftercare treatment of schizophrenia. *Archives of General Psychiatry, 43,* 633–642.

Hogarty, G. E., Anderson, C. M., Reiss, D. J., Kornblith, S. J., Greenwald, D. P., Ulrich, R. F., & Carter, M. (1991). Family psychoeducation, social skills training, and maintenance chemotherapy in the aftercare treatment of schizophrenia. II. Two-year effects of a controlled study on relapse and adjustment. *Archives of General Psychiatry, 48,* 340–347.

Hogarty, G. E., Goldberg, S. C., & Schooler, N. (1974). Drug and sociotherapy in the aftercare of schizophrenic patients. III. Adjustment of non-relapsed patients. *Archives of General Psychiatry, 31,* 609–618.

Hoult, J. (1986). Community care of the acutely mentally ill. *British Journal of Psychiatry, 149,* 137–144.

Huxley, P., & Warner, R. (1992). Case management, quality of life, and satisfaction with services of long-term psychiatric patients. *Hospital and Community Psychiatry, 43,* 799–802.

Intagliata, J. (1982). Improving the quality of community care for the clinically mentally disabled: The role of case management. *Schizophrenia Bulletin, 8,* 655–674.

Jacobs, H. (1988). Vocational rehabilitation. In R. P. Liberman (Ed.), *Psychiatric rehabilitation of chronic mental patients* (pp. 245–284). Washington, D.C.: American Psychiatric Press.

Jacobs, H. E., Collier, R., & Wissusik, D. The Job-Finding Module: Training skills for seeking competitive community employment. In R. P. Liberman (Ed.), *Effective psychiatric rehabilitation. New directions for mental health services* (Number 53, pp. 105–115). San Francisco, Ca.: Jossey-Bass.

Jacobs, H. E., Kardashian, S., Kreinbring, R. K., Ponder, R., & Simpson, A. S. (1984). A skills-oriented model for facilitating employment among psychiatrically disabled persons. *Rehabilitation Counseling Bulletin, 28,* 87–96.

Jenkins, J. H., & Karno, M. (1992). The meaning of expressed emotion: Theoretical issues raised by cross-cultural research. *American Journal of Psychiatry, 149,* 9–21.

Kazdin, A. E. (1982). The token economy: A decade later. *Journal of Applied Behavior Analysis, 15,* 431–445.

Kern, R. S., Green, M. F., & Satz, P. (1992). Neuropsychological predictors of skills training for chronic psychiatric patients. *Psychiatry Research, 43,* 223–230.

Kern, R. S., Green, M. F., Wallace, C. J., & Goldstein, M. J. (1996). Verbal versus procedural learning in chronic schizophrenic inpatients. *Cognitive Neuropsychiatry, 2,* 16–22.

Kern, R. S., Wallace, C. J., Hellman, S. G., Womack, L. M., & Green, M. F. (1996). A training procedure for remediating WCST deficits in chronic psychotic patients: An adaptation of errorless learning principles. *Journal of Psychiatric Research, 30,* 283–294.

Kessler, R. C., McGonagle, K. A., Zhao, S., Nelson, C. B., et al. (1994). Lifetime and 12-month prevalence of *DSM-III-R* psychiatric disorders in the United States: Results from the National Comorbidity Study. *Archives of General Psychiatry, 51,* 8–19.

Kingdon, D. G., & Turkington, D. (1994). *Cognitive-behavioral therapy of schizophrenia.* New York: Guilford Press.

Koegel, P., Burnam, A. M., & Farr, R. K. (1988). The prevalence of specific psychiatric disorders among homeless individuals in the inner city of Los Angeles. *Archives of General Psychiatry, 45,* 1085–1092.

Kopelowicz, A., & Liberman, R. P. (1995). Biobehavioral treatment and rehabilitation of schizophrenia. *Harvard Review of Psychiatry, 3,* 55–64.

Kuipers, L., & Bebbington, P. (1988). Expressed emotion research in schizophrenia: Theoretical and clinical implications. *Psychological Medicine, 18,* 893–909.

Leff, J., Berkowitz, R., Shavit, N., Strachan, A., Glass, I., & Vaughn, C. (1989). A trial of family therapy versus a relatives' group for schizophrenia. *British Journal of Psychiatry, 154,* 58–66.

Leff, J., Kuipers, L., Berkowitz, R., Eberlein-Vries, R., & Sturgeon, D. (1982). A controlled trial of social intervention in the families of schizophrenic patients: Two-year follow-up. *British Journal of Psychiatry, 146,* 594–600.

Liberman, R. P. (1982). Assessment of social skills. *Schizophrenia Bulletin, 8,* 62–83.

———. (1976). Behavior therapy for schizophrenia. In L. J. West & D. Flinn (Eds.), *Treatment of schizophrenia* (pp. 142–169). New York: Grune and Stratton.

Liberman, R. P., DeRisi, W. J., & Mueser, K. T. (1989). *Social skills training for psychiatric patients.* Elmsford, N.Y.: Pergamon Press.

Liberman, R. P., Falloon, I. R. H., & Aitchison, R. A. (1984). Multiple family therapy for schizophrenia: A behavioral, problem-solving approach. *Psychosocial Rehabilitation Journal, 7,* 60–77.

Liberman, R. P., Fearn, C. H., DeRisi, W. J., Roberts, J., & Carmona, M. (1977). The credit incentive system: Motivating the participation of patients in a day hospital. *British Journal of Social and Clinical Psychology, 16,* 85–94.

Liberman, R. P., & Green, M. F. (1992). Whither cognitive therapy for schizophrenia? *Schizophrenia Bulletin, 18,* 27–35.

Liberman, R. P., King, L. W., & DeRisi, W. J. (1976). Behavior analysis and therapy in community mental health. In H. Leitaiberg (Ed.), *Handbook of behavior analysis and modification* (pp. 47–68). Englewood Cliffs, N.J.: Prentice-Hall.

Liberman, R. P., King, L. W., DeRisi, W. J., & McCann, M. (1975). *Personal effectiveness: Guiding people to assert themselves and improve their social skills.* Champaign, Ill.: Research Press, 1975.

Liberman, R. P., Kopelowicz, A., & Young, A. S. (1994). Biobehavioral treatment and rehabilitation of schizophrenia. *Behavior Therapy, 25,* 89–107.

Liberman, R. P., McCann, M. J., & Wallace, C. J. (1976). Generalization of behaviour therapy with psychotics. *British Journal of Psychiatry, 129,* 490–496.

Liberman, R. P., & Mintz, J. (1990). Psychiatric symptoms and the functional capacity for work. *Final report to the Social Security Administration on research grant to study psychiatric disability and employment outcomes.* Los Angeles: UCLA Clinical Research Center.

Liberman, R. P., Mueser, K. T., & Wallace, C. J. (1986). Social skills training for schizophrenic individuals at risk for relapse. *American Journal of Psychiatry, 143,* 523–526.

Liberman, R. P., Teigen, J., Patterson, R., & Baker, V. (1973). Reducing delusional speech in chronic paranoid schizophrenics. *Journal of Applied Behavior Analysis, 6,* 57–64.

Liberman, R. P., Vaccaro, J. V., & Corrigan, P. W. (1995). Psychiatric rehabilitation. In H. I. Kaplan & B. J. Sadock (Eds.), *Comprehensive textbook of psychiatry* (pp. 2125–2146). Baltimore, Md.: Williams & Wilkins.

Liberman, R. P., Wallace, C. J., Blackwell, G., Eckman, T., Vaccaro, J. V., & Kuehnel, T. G. (1993). Innovations in skills training for the seriously mentally ill. *Innovations and Research, 2,* 43–60.

Liberman, R. P., Wallace, C. J., Vaughn, C. E., Snyder, K. S., & Rust, C. (1980). Social and family factors in the course of schizophrenia: Toward an interpersonal problem-solving therapy for schizophrenics and their relatives. In J. Strauss, J. Fleck, & M. Bowers (Eds.), *Psychotherapy of schizophrenia: Current status and future directions* (pp. 21–54). New York: Plenum.

MacFarlane, W. R., Stastny, P., & Deakins, S. (1992). Family-aided assertive community treatment. In R. P. Liberman (Ed.), *Effective psychiatric rehabilitation: New directions for mental health services*. San Francisco, Ca.: Jossey Bass.

Malm, U. (1982). The influence of group therapy on schizophrenia. *Acta Psychiatrica Scandanavica, 65* (Suppl.), 65–73.

Manderscheid, R. W., & Sonnenschein, M. A. (1992). *Mental health in the United States: 1992*. Rockville, Md.: U.S. Department of Health and Human Services.

Marder, S. R., Wirshing, W. C., Mintz, J., McKenzie, J., Johnston-Cronk, K., Eckman, T. A., Lebell, M., & Liberman, R. P. (1996). Two-year outcome of social skills training and group psychotherapy for outpatients with schizophrenia. *American Journal of Psychiatry, 153*, 1585–1592.

Massel, H. K., Corrigan, P. W., Liberman, R. P., & Milan, M. (1991). Conversation skills training in thought-disordered schizophrenics through attention focusing. *Psychiatry Research, 38*, 51–61.

McGrew, J., Bond, G., Dietzen, L., & Salyers, M. (1994). Measuring the fidelity of implementation of a mental health program model. *Journal of Consulting and Clinical Psychology, 62*, 670–678.

Menditto, A. A., Valdes, L. A., & Beck, N. C. (1994). Implementing a comprehensive social-learning program within the forensic psychiatric service of Fulton State Hospital. In P. W. Corrigan & R. P. Liberman (Eds.), *Behavior therapy in psychiatric hospitals* (pp. 61–78). New York: Springer.

Modrcin, M., Rapp, C. A., & Poertner, J. (1988). The evaluation of case management services with the chronically mentally ill. *Evaluation and Program Planning, 11*, 307–314.

Mueser, K. T., Bellack, A. S., Douglas, M. S., & Wade, J. H. (1991). Predictions of social skill acquisition in schizophrenic and major affective disorder patients from memory and symptomatology. *Psychiatry Research, 37*, 281–296.

Mueser, K. T., & Berenbaum, H. (1990). Psychodynamic treatment of schizophrenia: Is there a future? *Psychological Medicine, 20*, 253–62.

Mueser, K. T., Glynn, S. M., & Liberman, R. P. (1994). Behavior family management for serious psychiatric illness. In A. B. Hatfield (Ed.), *Family interventions for the mentally ill relatives: New directions for mental health services*. San Francisco, Ca.: Jossey Bass.

Mueser, K. T., Wallace, C. J., & Liberman, R. P. (1995). New developments in social skills training. *Behaviour Change, 12*, 31–40.

Mulder, R. (1982). *Final evaluation of the Harbinger Program as a demonstration project*. Unpublished manuscript.

National Institute of Mental Health. (1995). *1995 Budget Estimate*. Rockville, Md.: U.S. Department of Health and Human Services.

Nuechterlein, K. H., Dawson, M. E., Ventura, J., Gitlin, M., Subotnik, K. L., Snyder, K. S., Mintz, J., & Bartzokis, G. (1994). The vulnerability/stress model of schizophrenic relapse. *Acta Psychiatrica Scandanavica, 89*, 58–64.

Olfson, M. (1990). Assertive community treatment: An evaluation of the experimental evidence. *Hospital and Community Psychiatry, 41*, 634–641.

Paul, G. L., & Lentz, R. J. (1977). *Psychosocial treatment of chronic mental patients: Milieu versus social-learning programs*. Cambridge, Mass.: Harvard University Press.

Raine, A., Lencz, T., & Mednick, S. A. (Eds.). (1995). *Schizotypal personality*. New York: Cambridge University Press.

Randolph, E., Eth, S., Glynn, S., Paz, G., Van Vort, W., Shaner, A., et al. (1994). Efficacy of behavioral family management in reducing relapse in veteran schizophrenics. *British Journal of Psychiatry, 164*, 501–506.

Regier, D. A., Farmer, M. E., Lock, B. Z., Keith, S. J., & Rae, D. S. (1993). The de facto U.S. mental and addictive disorders service system. *Archives of General Psychiatry, 51*, 492–499.

Regier, D. A., Farmer, M. E., Rae, D. S., Locke, B. Z., Keith, S. J., Judd, L. L., & Goodwin, F. K. (1990). Comorbidity of mental disorders with alcohol and other drug abuse. *Journal of the American Medical Association, 264*, 2511–2518.

Roberts, L. J., Shaner, A., Eckman, T. A., Tucker, D. E., & Vacarro, J. V. (1992). Effectively treating stimulant-abusing schizophrenics: Mission impossible? In R. P. Liberman (Ed.), *Effective psychiatric rehabilitation: New directions for psychiatric services* (Number 53, pp. 55–66). San Francisco, Ca.: Jossey-Bass.

Roy, A. (1992). Suicide in schizophrenia. *International Review of Psychiatry, 4*, 205–209.

Schooler, N. (1996). Advances in maintenance treatment. *Psychiatric Annals, 26*, 519–522.

Schwartz, J., & Bellack, A. S. (1975). A comparison of a token economy with standard inpatient treatment. *Journal of Consulting and Clinical Psychology, 43*, 107–108.

Seeman, M. V. (1982). Gender differences in schizophrenia. *Canadian Journal of Psychiatry, 27*, 107–111.

Shaner, A., Eckman, T. A., Roberts, L. J., Wilkins, J. N., et al. (1995). Disability income, cocaine use and repeated hospitalization among schizophrenic cocaine abusers: A government-sponsored revolving door. *New England Journal of Medicine, 333*, 777–783.

Snyder, K. S., Wallace, C. J., Moe, K., & Liberman, R. P. (1994). Expressed emotion by residential care operators and schizophrenic residents' symptoms and quality of life. *Hospital and Community Psychiatry, 45,* 1141–1143.

Spiegler, M. D., & Agigian, H. (1976). *An educational-behavioral-social systems model for rehabilitating psychiatric patients.* New York: Brunner/Mazel.

Stein, L. I., & Test, M. A. (1980). Alternative to mental hospital treatment, I. Conceptual model, treatment program, and clinical evaluation. *Archives of General Psychiatry, 37,* 392–397.

———. (1985). *The Training in Community Living Model: A decade of experience. New Directions for Mental Health Services* (Number 26). San Francisco, Ca.: Jossey-Bass.

Storzbach, D. M., & Corrigan, P. W. (1996). Cognitive rehabilitation for schizophrenia. In P. W. Corrigan & S. C. Yudofsky (Eds.), *Cognitive rehabilitation for neuropsychiatric disorders* (pp. 311–327). Washington, D.C.: American Psychiatric Press.

Strachan, A. (1992). Family management. In R. P. Liberman (Ed.), *Handbook of psychiatric rehabilitation* (pp. 183–212). New York: Macmillan.

Sue, S., & Sue, D. (1987). Cultural factors in the clinical assessment of Asian Americans. *Journal of Consulting and Clinical Psychology, 55,* 479–487.

Talbott, J. A., Goldman, H. H., & Ross, L. (1987). Schizophrenia: An economic perspective. *Psychiatric Annals, 17,* 577–579.

Tarrier, N., Beckett, R., & Harwood, S. (1993). A trial of two cognitive-behavioral methods of treating drug-resistant residual psychotic symptoms in schizophrenia. *British Journal of Psychiatry, 162,* 524–532.

Test, M. A. (1992). Training in community living. In R. P. Liberman (Ed.), *Handbook of psychiatric rehabilitation* (pp. 153–170). New York: Macmillan.

Test, M. A., Knoedler, W. H., & Allness, D. J. (1985). The long-term treatment of schizophrenics in a community suppport program. In L. I. Stein & M. A. Test (Eds.), *The Training in Community Living Model: A decade of experience. New directions for mental health*

services (Number 26, pp. 17–27). San Francisco, Ca.: Jossey-Bass.

Ullman, L. P., & Krasner, L. (1975). *A psychological approach to abnormal behavior* (2nd ed.). Englewood Cliffs, N.J.: Prentice-Hall.

Wallace, C. J. (1996). *Workplace fundamentals module.* Camarillo, Ca.: Psychiatric Rehabilitation Consultants.

Wallace, C. J., & Liberman, R. P. (1985). Social skills training for patients with schizophrenia: A controlled clinical trial. *Psychiatry Research, 15,* 239–247.

Wehman, P., & Hill, M. L. (1989). Competitive employment for persons with mental retardation: A benefit-cost analysis of outcomes. In W. E. Kiernan & R. L. Schalock (Eds.), *Economics, industry, and disability: A look ahead* (pp. 287–298). Baltimore, Md.: Paul E. Brookes.

Wehman, P. H., & Moon, M. S. (1987). Critical values in employment programs for persons with developmental disabilities: A position paper. *Journal of Applied Rehabilitation Counseling, 18,* 12–16.

Weisbrod, B., Test, M. A., & Stein, L. (1980). Alternatives to mental hospital treatment. II. Economic benefit-cost analysis. *Archives of General Psychiatry, 37,* 400–402.

Wong, S. E., Massel, H. K., Mosk, M. D., & Liberman, R. P. (1986). Behavioral approaches to the treatment of schizophrenia. In G. D. Burrows, T. R. Norman, & G. Rubinstein (Eds.), *Handbook of studies on schizophrenia* (pp. 79–100). Amsterdam: Elsevier Science.

Wunderlich, U., Wiedemann, G., & Buchkremer, G. (1996). Are psychosocial methods of intervention effective in schizophrenic patients? A meta-analysis. *Verhaltenstherapie, 6,* 4–13.

Wyatt, R. J. (1991). Neuroleptics and the natural course of schizophrenia. *Schizophrenia Bulletin, 17,* 325–351.

———. (1995). Early intervention for schizophrenia: Can the course of the illness be altered? *Biological Psychiatry, 38,* 1–3.

Wyatt, R. J., & Clark, K. P. (1987). Calculating the cost of schizophrenia. *Psychiatric Annals, 17,* 586–591.

10

Pharmacological Treatment of Unipolar Depression

Charles B. Nemeroff
Alan F. Schatzberg

The treatment of unipolar major depression with antidepressant medication is well established on the basis of scores of randomized placebo-controlled trials involving thousands of patients. Tricyclic antidepressants (TCAs) were the first to be studied extensively; meta-analyses of placebo-controlled trials show them to be consistently and substantially significantly more efficacious than a placebo. Because of a narrow safety margin and significant drug-induced adverse side effect problems, TCAs have now largely been replaced as the first-line treatment of depression by selective serotonin reuptake inhibitors (SSRIs)—fluoxetine, sertraline, and paroxetine—and other new compounds, including venlafaxine, bupropion, and nefazodone. Each of these agents has been shown to be superior to a placebo and equally effective as comparator TCAs in controlled trials. Clinical trials consistently show them to be better tolerated than TCAs, and they clearly have a wider margin of safety. However, there is a controversy concerning whether TCAs and venlafaxine are more effective than SSRIs for the treatment of the most severely ill depressed patients. Monoamine oxidase inhibitors (MAOIs), while also more effective than a placebo, are generally reserved for treatment-refractory patients. It is now generally recognized that patients with recurrent major depression benefit from continued antidepressant treatment, and there is evidence that TCAs and SSRIs are effective for the long-term management of recurrent major depression. An important issue in evaluating the antidepressant literature is to distinguish between response rated as a reduction in the level of symptoms on a rating scale and response rated as true remission from illness.

The efficacy of antidepressant medications has been well established in myriad controlled clinical trials, and in general the response of patients with unipolar depression is comparable to the success rates of treatment of major medical disorders such as coronary artery disease (by angioplasty), hypertension, and diabetes. Meta-analyses of the vast database of double-blind, placebo-controlled clinical trials have revealed a highly statistically significant effect of all of the currently available antidepressants approved by the Food and Drug Administration (FDA) for the acute management of unipolar depression. No other mental illness has received this much scrutiny. Because the FDA requires comparison to both a placebo and an already approved antidepressant, usually a tricyclic, large numbers of patients, literally thousands, have been involved in these trials.

The antidepressants currently available in the United States are usually classified by their purported neurochemical mechanism of action (e.g., see Table 10.1). Not only have all of the listed antidepressants been demonstrated to be effective in treating major

TABLE 10.1 Tricyclic and Tetracyclic Agents: Pharmacological Effects

	Reuptake Blockade		Receptor Blockade		
Drug	NE	5-HT	ACh	H1	α1
Imipramine	+	+	++	+	++
Desipramine	+++	0	+	0	+
Amitriptyline	±	++	++++	++++	+++
Nortriptyline	++	±	++	+	+
Doxepin	++	+	++	+++	++
Trimipramine	+	0	++	+++	++
Protriptyline	++	0	+++	+	+
Clomipramine	+	+++	++	+	++
Maprotiline	++	0	+	++	+
Amoxapine	++	0	0	±	++

Source: Based on Porter, Manji, & Rudorfer (1995). Reprinted with permission.

NE = norepinephrine; 5HT = serotonin; ACh = acetylcholine; H1 = histamine-1; α1 = alpha-1; + = mild effect; ++++ = marked effect.

depression, but no single antidepressant has conclusively ever been demonstrated to be more effective than any other antidepressant (Nemeroff, 1994). However, there is some controversy (see below) as to whether certain antidepressants such as venlafaxine and tricyclic antidepressants (TCAs) might be more effective than the others for severe or treatment-refractory depression.

One of the important issues to discuss in this chapter is, of course, the definition of response in an antidepressant drug trial. A 50% decline in a dimensional measure of depression severity such as the Hamilton Depression Rating Scale (HAM-D) or the Montgomery-Asberg Depression Rating Scale (MADRS) is the generally accepted definition of a responder. However, many patients with severe depression (HAM-D scores of, for example, greater than 28) can exhibit a 50% improvement in depression severity and therefore can be considered responders, but may have considerable residual depressive symptoms (e.g., a HAM-D score of 13). Thus, patients included as responders may, in fact, be partial responders and clearly not euthymic. More stringent definitions of response include HAM-D scores of less than 7 or some other measure of euthymia. Use of the more stringent definitions of response may reveal differences in antidepressant efficacy.

Another poorly understood issue is the response of depressed patients to a placebo, which can occur in surprisingly high rates, in clinical trials comparing a placebo and an antidepressant. This is no trivial issue because novel antidepressants must be shown to be statistically superior to a placebo and as efficacious as an already approved antidepressant, usually a TCA, in order to receive FDA approval. This subject has previously been discussed in considerable detail, but the major point to be made to the reader who is not familiar with clinical psychopharmacology trials in depression is that placebo treatment is not identical with no treatment. Patients taking part in clinical trials spend considerable periods of time with the staff (research nurses, research assistants), as well as with the trial physicians. The quantity of time spent by patients in clinical trials far exceeds the time spent by a patient treated by a mental health professional in a "standard" fee-for-service setting and certainly is greater than the time spent by those in managed care settings. The contact with the research team, frequently lasting 3–6 hours per visit, clearly has effects on the patient's clinical state. Because of the availability of treatments, both psychotherapeutic and psychopharmacological with documented efficacy, a "no treatment" arm, theoretically an appropriate comparison group to a novel antidepressant, would not be approved by institutional review boards reviewing such an experimental design. This is a reasonable stance in view of the morbidity and mortality (secondary to suicide and increased risk of cardiovascular and cerebrovascular disease) in untreated depressed patients.

Another issue that has received considerable attention is the rapidity of response to antidepressants. It is generally acknowledged that antidepressants require 3 to 5 weeks before their therapeutic response is clinically evident, likely due to neurochemical effects on receptor regulation and/or gene expression. A "holy grail" in psychopharmacological research has been the search for antidepressants that work more rapidly.

This is a very complex issue and space constraints preclude a comprehensive discussion of this controversial topic. However, it is important to note that the so-called lag time in antidepressant drug response in clinical trials is, of course, a mean of patients who respond relatively quickly, patients who respond after a few weeks, and patients who are nonresponders. In addition, the definition of response (given above) obviously has a major impact here; few patients show complete euthymia after 1 week. It has often been stated that if patients do not respond to antidepressants after 4 to 6 weeks, they should be treated for an additional 4 to 6 weeks. However, two recent studies (Boyer & Feigner, 1994; Nierenberg et al., 1995) have revealed that if the patient has not responded to paroxetine by 3 weeks of treatment or fluoxetine by 4 weeks of treatment, there is little likelihood that additional treatment, at that dose, will be successful.

Unfortunately, a generation of studies attempting to identify biological markers that predict treatment response to one or another antidepressant has provided no such valid predictors of either response or nonresponse to any antidepressant drug class. However, the use of positron-emission tomography (PET) to label neurotransmitter transporters and receptors in vivo may provide for the first time the ability to determine whether a given patient shows, for example, a deficit in serotonin transporter binding, which might predict response to one of the selective serotonin reuptake inhibitors (SSRIs).

Other critical areas that the reader might wish to consider are issues of age, gender, and comorbid medical disorders. There is a dearth of studies of antidepressant use in children and adolescents, and what is available does little to convince one of the antidepressants' efficacy. There is widespread belief among clinicians that antidepressants are effective in this age group, but few controlled studies have demonstrated such efficacy (see DeVane & Sallee, 1996, and Fisher & Fisher, 1996, for a review). Clearly, further studies are needed in this important area.

Similarly, there are reports of differences in efficacy of classes of antidepressant in the elderly. This controversy is described below, but surely further studies are needed in this area.

The exclusion of women of childbearing potential from clinical trials because of fears of potential teratogenic effects of antidepressants has resulted in an embarrassing lack of knowledge of pharmacokinetics and clinical efficacy in a population that has the highest prevalence rate of unipolar depression. Further studies with a focus on antidepressant-gonadal steroid interactions are advisable.

Finally, and of paramount importance, is the documentation of antidepressant efficacy and tolerability in patients with comorbid medical disorders. Prevalence rates of unipolar depression in patients with medical disorders such as cancer, diabetes, myocardial infarction, Parkinson's disease, multiple sclerosis, and Alzheimer's disease is remarkably high (25–50%), and relatively few controlled treatment trials have been conducted in these populations (see Boswell, Anfinson, & Nemeroff, 1997, for a review). However, such studies are now even more vitally important to conduct because there is increasing evidence that depression is associated with an increased risk of death after myocardial infarction (Frasure-Smith, Lesperance, & Talajic, 1993, 1995) and stroke. Similarly, depression has been suggested to have a profound negative impact on patients with cancer (McDaniel, Musselman, Porter, Reed, & Nemeroff, 1995). Virtually all of the controlled treatment trials of antidepressants in patients with comorbid medical disorders, including patients with depression and comorbid stroke, cancer, Parkinson's disease, chronic obstructive pulmonary disease, multiple sclerosis, or diabetes, have clearly documented efficacy of the antidepressant.

However, because the majority of patients with medical disorders is also prescribed a variety of other medications, it is of paramount importance to prescribe antidepressant medications that are safe and, in particular, have no untoward drug-drug interactions with other prescribed medications. This is not a trivial issue because most antidepressants are bound to plasma proteins and therefore can displace other commonly prescribed drugs, such as coumadin, from their protein binding site, increasing plasma coumadin concentrations and increasing bleeding times with potentially adverse consequences. Moreover, in recent years it has become evident that many antidepressants inhibit the activity of certain hepatic cytochrome P450 isoenzymes, which are responsible for metabolizing a wide variety of other commonly prescribed medications. Such drug-drug interactions, if not acknowledged, could lead to increases in plasma concentrations of drugs such as terfenadine and astemizole, two commonly prescribed antihistamines, that at high levels can exert toxic effects on the heart. These data have recently been comprehensively reviewed (DeVane, 1994; Ereshefsky, 1996; Nemeroff, DeVane, & Pollack, 1996).

A final area of crucial importance is that of maintenance treatment of depression and assessment of its efficacy compared with placebo treatment. It is generally recommended that, after a single episode of depression, patients should be treated for 6 months. If a patient has suffered more than one episode of depression, or if the first episode was particularly severe (e.g., with a serious suicide attempt), particularly difficult to treat, or the patient has a very strong family history, then long-term treatment should be considered. All of the studies that have evaluated treatment with antidepressants for 1 year or longer compared with a placebo have found highly significant beneficial effects of antidepressant treatment. Such studies have included TCAs, SSRIs, and venlafaxine. These data have recently been reviewed (Blacker, 1996; Hirschfeld & Schatzberg, 1994; Thase & Sullivan, 1995).

A final point should be made about the use of more than one medication to treat depression. For many years, the prevailing opinion in psychiatry has been that monotherapy for depression is highly desirable and conversely that polypharmacy is to be avoided. This is certainly not the case in other branches of medicine, in which polypharmacy is virtually the rule. Failure of a single agent to provide adequate control of hypertension, diabetes, or a neoplasm invariably leads to the use of two or three pharmacological agents. If the goal is to return the patient to complete euthymia, combination therapy of more than one psychotropic agent, as well as combination psychopharmacology and psychotherapy, may be necessary.

TRICYCLIC ANTIDEPRESSANTS

Tricyclic antidepressants were for many years the treatments of choice for major depression. They were originally introduced into the United States in the 1960s. In this country, seven TCAs are approved for treatment of major depression and one additional compound— clomipramine—is approved for obsessive compulsive disorder (OCD) but is viewed throughout the world as an efficacious antidepressant. Two other compounds (maprotiline and amoxapine) have four-ringed structures and are variants of the tricyclic class. Amoxapine is related to the antipsychotic agent loxapine.

There is a large amount of literature demonstrating efficacy for the TCAs (Potter et al., 1995). In the United States, some of the original randomized clinical trials (RCTs) in psychiatry included imipramine or amitriptyline and showed these agents to be effective in what we now term major depression. Efficacy of the TCAs has been revisited in SSRI comparator trials, and the TCAs still appear to be more effective than a placebo and to be of comparable efficacy to the SSRIs. Janicak and colleagues (1993) have performed meta-analyses of the TCA RCTs literature and reported these antidepressants to be overwhelmingly more effective than a placebo. For example, the 50 studies that have compared imipramine with a placebo have reported an aggregate response rate to the TCA of 68%, compared to a 40% response rate to the placebo, a difference significant at the $p < 10^{-40}$ level.

Imipramine was used in a comparator treatment against cognitive behavior therapy in the National Institute of Mental Health (NIMH) collaborative treatment study of outpatients with major depression. That study suggested that more severely depressed patients responded better to the TCA than they did to the psychosocial treatment (Elkin et al., 1989), although other studies have not borne this out (Hollon et al., 1992).

Some investigators have argued that the TCAs are more effective than the SSRIs in the treatment of more severely depressed or melancholic inpatients in that they are more likely to induce remission within 4 to 6 weeks. In a study by the Danish University Antidepressant Group (DUAG) (1990), clomipramine produced significantly higher rates of remission than did paroxetine. In another report on inpatients by this group (DUAG, 1986), clomipramine was also significantly more effective than citalopram, an SSRI available in Europe but not in the United States. More recently, Roose et al. (1994) reported that nortriptyline was more effective than fluoxetine in hospitalized cardiac patients with melancholia. Other studies have not borne out such differences (see below), although the perception of superior efficacy continues among some investigators.

The tricyclic antidepressants alone are less effective in major depression with psychotic features (delusional depression) or in those with so-called atypical features. In the former, TCA monotherapy has been found to be effective in only 35% of patients, in contrast to a 65% response rate in their nondelusional counterparts, a difference that is highly statistically significant (Chan et al., 1987). In delusional depressives, TCAs in combination with antipsychotics have been reported to be significantly more effective than TCAs alone (Schatzberg & Rothschild, 1992). For such patients, clinical practice now calls for combining TCAs or other antidepressants with antipsychotic agents. The presence of atypical features (hypersomnia, hyperphagia, prominent anxiety, reverse diurnal mood variation) predicts poorer responses to imipramine than to monoamine oxidase inhibitors (MAOIs) according to some RCTs (see below).

The TCAs as a class are potent inhibitors of the reuptake of norepinephrine into presynaptic neurons; they exert fewer effects on serotonin reuptake (Table 10.1). The one major exception is clomipramine, which is a potent serotonin reuptake blocker with a demethylated metabolite that is a potent norepinephrine reuptake blocker. Norepinephrine reuptake blocking effects probably account for some patients becoming activated (increased anxiety or agitation) on these agents. Generally, such effects are dose related and can be minimized by conservative dosing. Over time, TCAs are frequently anxiolytic in their effects.

The TCAs all have some affinity with muscarinic cholinergic receptors as antagonists (Table 10.1) and produce dry mouth, blurred vision, constipation, urinary hesitancy, memory disturbance, and tachycardia. Agents within the class vary in the degree to which they produce these side effects, with the so-called secondary tricyclics, which represent demethylated metabolites of parent tertiary TCAs, exerting more limited anticholinergic effects than their parents. Examples are nortriptyline (the metabolite of amitriptyline) and desipramine (the metabolite of imipramine).

The TCAs are also antihistaminic, with amitriptyline and doxepin being most potent at this site (Table 10.1) and being most likely to produce sedation and weight gain. These agents also block α_1 adrenergic receptors and produce orthostatic hypotension. Here, too, these side effects are mainly dose related and can be minimized by using lower doses of drugs, particularly when initiating treatment. Some patients may, however, not be able to tolerate even the most minimal doses of these agents.

Because of their α_1 adrenergic and anticholinergic effects, the TCAs are potentially cardiotoxic in overdose and have relatively narrow safety margins (low therapeutic index). They can result in death when taken in overdose and are the number one cause of overdose death among prescription drugs in the United States. Generally, clinicians initiating treatment with a TCA begin at low doses (e.g., 50 mg of amitriptyline, imipramine, or desipramine or 25 mg of nortriptyline) to avoid side effects as much as possible and to maximize compliance. Over 7 to 10 days, doses are increased gradually to 150 mg per day of amitriptyline, imipramine, or desipramine or to 75 mg per day of nortriptyline. After 2 weeks of these doses, further gradual dosage increments can be undertaken to achieve the maximum recommended doses. Therapeutic dosage ranges are summarized in Table 10.2.

There is a relatively rich literature on the relationship of TCA plasma levels to clinical response. Generally, such relationships have been demonstrated in studies of more severely depressed patients. Glassman et al. (1977) reported a so-called sigmoidal relationship between imipramine plasma concentrations and clinical response, with maximum response rates observed at plasma levels greater than or equal to 200 ng/ml of imipramine plus desipramine. A relationship between imipramine plasma level and clinical response has not been observed for milder depressives. For nortriptyline, a so-called therapeutic window has been described, with nortriptyline blood levels less than approximately 50 ng/ml and greater than 150 ng/ml being associated with poorer response than is seen at levels between 50 and 150 ng/ml (Asberg et al., 1971). Virtually identical data are available for protriptyline. Similarly, amitriptyline is also thought to have a therapeutic window of approximately 95–200 ng/ml (amitriptyline and nortriptyline). Some have argued that desipramine also has a therapeutic window, but data here are more limited.

Maintenance therapy with the TCAs has been the focus of two major studies. In one, Prien et al. (1984) reported relatively low efficacy for maintenance imipramine therapy; however, in that study patients were often maintained at relatively low doses. This reflected the common practice of the day. In the more recent study of Frank et al. (1990), imipramine was clearly demonstrated to be more effective than a placebo in 3-year maintenance therapy of recurrent unipolar depression (20% recurrence on imipramine v. approximately 90% on the placebo). This study maintained patients at the doses to which they had responded. Moreover, lower dose versus full-dose maintenance

TABLE 10.2 Typical Therapeutic Dosage Ranges of Tricyclic and Tetracyclic Antidepressant Drugs (Adult Patients)

Drug		Therapeutic Dose
Generic Name	Trade Name	Range (mg/day)
Imipramine	Tofranil	150–300
Desipramine	Norpramin	150–300
Amitriptyline	Elavil	150–300
Nortriptyline	Pamelor, Aventyl	50–150
Doxepin	Sinequan	150–300
Trimipramine	Surmontil	150–200
Clomipramine	Anafranil	75–200
Maprotiline	Ludiomil	75–200
Amoxapine	Asendin	200–400

strategies were tested in a subset of subjects (Frank et al., 1993). Full doses were significantly more effective than half doses (30% recurrence v. 70% recurrence, respectively). Thus, maintenance therapy with TCAs appears to require continuing patients on the doses effective during acute treatment. This has now become standard practice.

MONOAMINE OXIDASE INHIBITORS

The development of the MAOIs is one of the most interesting chapters in the history of psychopharmacology. When tuberculosis was ravaging civilizations and patients infected with the tubercular bacillus were admitted to sanitoriums for long-term care, new antitubercular drugs were tested for efficacy in these settings. One such antitubercular drug, iproniazid, was noted to produce mood elevation in many patients. This led to the development of the three MAOIs currently available in the United States: phenelzine, tranylcypromine, and isocarboxizid. The last drug was unavailable for some time, but is now once again available.

These are all irreversible, nonselective MAOIs and, compared to newer antidepressants (see below), have a less-favorable side-effect profile. Although selective and reversible MAOIs with a more favorable side-effect profile have been developed (e.g., moclobemide), they are not available for clinical use in the United States.

The MAOIs are believed to produce their therapeutic effects by preventing the degradation of monoamines, particularly serotonin, norepinephrine, and dopamine (DA), all posited to be reduced in availability in patients with unipolar depression. All of the available MAOIs have been shown to be effective in the treatment of unipolar depression and, in particular, atypical depression characterized by hypersomnia and hyperphagia (Krishnan, 1995). Table 10.3 lists the currently available MAOIs and their usual dose ranges. In addition to unipolar depression, MAOIs are also effective, like SSRIs and certain TCAs, in the treatment of panic disorder. They are also effective in the treatment of bipolar depression.

Some disadvantages of MAOIs include the necessity of dosing multiple times per day, associated with

TABLE 10.3 Monoamine Oxidase Inhibitors

Drug		Dose Range
Generic Name	Trade Name	(mg/day
Phenelzine	Nardil	45–90
Tranylcypromine	Parnate	10–30
Isocarboxizid	Marplan	10–30

considerably poorer compliance when compared to once a day dosing, and the necessity for dietary constraints.

Certain foods that contain high concentrations of tyramine, an endogenous amine, such as aged meats and cheeses, chocolate, Chianti wine, as well as over-the-counter cold medications (e.g., pseudoephedrine), are absolute contraindications in patients prescribed MAOIs because of the so-called cheese reaction, characterized by severe hypertension and possible medical sequelae such as stroke. Symptoms of this syndrome include severe headache, flushing, palpitations and nausea.

Although not practical, the proper manner to prescribe MAOIs is to first measure baseline platelet MAO activity, begin treatment with a MAOI, and repeat the platelet MAO activity measurement after 3–4 weeks of treatment. The best treatment responses are associated with 80–90% inhibition of platelet MAO activity. Because patients vary widely as to their MAO activity, it is impossible to predict what the ideal dose of a MAOI will be for any given patient.

In addition to the drug-drug and drug-food interactions noted above, MAOIs also have a number of other untoward side effects, including orthostatic hypotension, sexual dysfunction, dizziness, insomnia, tachycardia, palpitations, and edema.

The MAOIs are not generally considered first-line treatments for depression because of their unfavorable side-effect profile, dietary restrictions, need for dosing multiple times per day, and the general unavailability of platelet MAO activity measurements. There is also some evidence to suggest that MAOIs may be somewhat less efficacious than TCAs, SSRIs, and some of the newer antidepressants.

SELECTIVE SEROTONIN REUPTAKE INHIBITORS

The selective serotonin reuptake inhibitors (SSRIs) have become first-line treatments (Rush et al., 1994) for most patients with major depression (Table 10.4). The first of these agents, fluoxetine, was introduced in the United States in 1988. Since then, three others have been released in the U.S. market: sertraline, paroxetine, and fluvoxamine. Of these, fluvoxamine is only approved for use in the United States for OCD, but is used as an antidepressant in many other countries. In this chapter, we emphasize the SSRIs approved for use in major depression in this country.

These agents work primarily by blocking the reuptake of serotonin into presynaptic neurons. They have virtually no effect to date on blocking norepinephrine reuptake, and they also do not interfere with various ligands binding to muscarinic cholinergic, α_1 adrenergic, or histamine H_1 receptors. Thus, they produce little—if any—dry mouth, constipation, or urinary hesitance (anticholinergic effects), orthostatic hypotension (α_1 adrenergic blockade), or sedation and weight gain (H_1 blockade). Paroxetine is an exception in that it has weak anticholinergic potential and does produce some dry mouth, albeit less than is seen with the TCAs. It is also mildly sedating in some patients.

The side effects associated with increased serotonin availability and commonly seen with the SSRIs include nausea, diarrhea, insomnia, nervousness, and sexual dysfunction. The first four of these are commonly dose dependent, such that more conservative dosing frequently avoids their occurrence. Sexual dysfunction is less clearly dose related and can be seen even at low doses.

TABLE 10.4 Typical Antidepressant Therapeutic Dosage Ranges of Selective Serotonin Reuptake Inhibitors (Adult Patients)

Drug		Therapeutic Dose
Generic Name	Trade Name	Range (mg/day)
Fluoxetine	Prozac	20–80
Paroxetine	Paxil	20–50
Sertraline	Zoloft	50–200
Fluvoxamine	Fluvoxamine	100–300

The initial trials failed to report high rates of sexual dysfunction (e.g., delayed ejaculation in men and anorgasmia in women) with SSRI therapy. These side effects have become apparent with wider spread, long-term usage. It is probable that many depressed patients are not aware of or are not bothered by sexual dysfunction in the initial weeks of treatment but do become troubled by this annoying side effect over time as they resume their normal activities. In the initial trials of fluoxetine, sexual dysfunction was noted in some 4% of subjects. Currently, estimates are that at least 30% of patients on SSRIs experience it.

Because these drugs have limited anticholinergic and noradrenergic effects, they are not cardiotoxic and are thus safe in overdoses. This represented a major step forward in treatment over the TCAs, which have a narrow safety margin (discussed above in the TCA section).

The SSRIs can be coadministered with the TCAs, but this needs to be done cautiously because as a class these agents can inhibit P_{450} isoenzymes in the liver that metabolize TCAs and result in higher blood levels and increased side effects (Devane, 1994; Nemeroff et al., 1996). The coprescription of SSRIs with MAOIs is contraindicated because of a risk of the serotonergic syndrome—characterized by myoclonic jerks, hyperpyrexia, and coma.

The efficacy of the SSRIs has been clearly demonstrated in numerous RCTs; these data have been reviewed elsewhere (Nemeroff, 1994). Published data are most extensive for fluoxetine and paroxetine, with both drugs having been studied in several thousand patients. Data on sertraline are somewhat more limited.

Of the eight RCTs published before the release of fluoxetine that formed the basis of the FDA submission, fluoxetine was significantly more effective than the placebo in the four placebo-controlled studies and was generally comparable to TCA in the six comparison trials (Schatzberg, 1995a). In the majority of studies, the dropout rate was lower (often significantly) for fluoxetine than for the TCA or placebo. Subsequent to the FDA submission, over 3,000 papers on the drug have appeared in the archival literature. Studies have continued to show significantly greater efficacy for fluoxetine over the placebo in patients of all age groups with major depression. A recent RCT of fluoxetine in children and adolescents with major depression has found the drug to be significantly more effective than the placebo in that age group. More than 25 million patients have been treated with fluoxetine since its introduction.

Efficacy studies of paroxetine have also been reviewed in detail by our group and others (DeBattista & Schatzberg, 1995). We reviewed nearly 30 RCTs of paroxetine for major depression. Paroxetine was significantly more effective than the placebo in 8 of 11 comparison studies. Paroxetine was comparable in efficacy to the TCA in all but 5 studies, which found either the TCA or paroxetine to be more effective. Overall, dropout rates for paroxetine due to adverse events were lower in patients on paroxetine than on TCAs. An early inpatient study in Denmark reported greater efficacy with clomipramine than paroxetine, and this study has been cited in the debate on SSRI efficacy in more severely depressed patients. This study used a relatively low dose of paroxetine (30 mg/day).

Efficacy data for sertraline have also been reviewed in detail elsewhere (Janicak et al., 1993; Mendels, 1995). Sertraline has been reported to be more effective than a placebo in two large-scale clinical trials ($N = 545$) and to be of comparable efficacy to standard TCAs in two studies ($N = 320$). Sertraline has also been reported to be effective in the treatment of postpartum depression (Stowe, Casarella, Landry, & Nemeroff, 1995).

As indicated above, there is an ongoing debate regarding whether the SSRIs, particularly fluoxetine, are as effective as the TCAs in the treatment of severely depressed patients, particularly in the geriatric age group. These data have been reviewed in detail elsewhere (Schatzberg, 1996). While there are occasional reports in the literature that an SSRI is less effective in these subjects, the overall data from RCTs do not bear out this conclusion. In one study, we compared desipramine and fluoxetine in a group of moderate-to-severely depressed patients (Bowden et al., 1993). The two drugs were of comparable efficacy; however, fluoxetine had a far more benign side-effect profile. In a small-scale study of more severely depressed inpatients, Clerc et al. (1994) reported that venlafaxine (a mixed uptake blocker) was significantly more effective at 4–6 weeks than fluoxetine. Thus, the debate is likely to continue for some time, although to date the data overall do not support the impression of lower efficacy.

Because fluoxetine was reported in the early trials to be "activating," some clinicians and investigators advised against using it in depressed patients with prominent anxiety. Analyses of the comparative clinical trials have revealed that the drug is as effective in anxious depressives as it is in major depressives without anxiety (Schatzberg, 1995b; Tollefson, Holman, & Sayler, 1994). Some patients may, however, require starting at a lower dose (e.g., 10 mg/day of fluoxetine). Significant SSRI efficacy in purely anxious patients (e.g., panic disorder) has been revealed in RCTs as well. Thus, the SSRIs (including fluoxetine) appear effective in both depressed and anxious patients or in those who demonstrate mixed symptoms.

All three SSRIs have been reported to be significantly more effective than a placebo in preventing relapse or recurrence for up to 1 year of treatment. Of patients treated with fluoxetine for 1 year, 26% experienced a relapse or recurrence, in contrast to 57% on a placebo (Montgomery et al., 1988). Similarly, 14% of patients treated with paroxetine relapsed or recurred versus 30% on a placebo (Montgomery & Dunbar, 1993). Last, the sertraline relapse rate over 44 weeks of continuation treatment was 13%, in contrast to 46% for a placebo (Doogan & Caillard, 1992). These data are all remarkably similar and point to the efficacy of the SSRIs during continuation and maintenance treatment. Of note is that, in these longer term studies, new side effects of the SSRIs have not emerged. Thus, the relative safety of this class of agents appears to be maintained after long-term treatment.

The three SSRIs all have half-lives of at least 24 hours and can be given in a once-a-day dose. The long half-life of norfluoxetine (7–14 days), an active metabolite of fluoxetine, suggests the drug can be given 1 or 2 times a week; there are some data to suggest ongoing efficacy using such strategies during continuation or maintenance phases of treatment. Such data are not available for paroxetine or sertraline. Paroxetine has no active metabolites and is unlikely to be effective when prescribed on a weekly or twice weekly basis. Sertraline's demethylated metabolite has a half-life (3 days) that is much shorter than norfluoxetine and is formed in relatively lower concentrations. This drug is also not a likely candidate for less-frequent prescription.

Therapeutic antidepressant dosage ranges for the SSRIs are summarized in Table 10.4. The standard starting dose for fluoxetine and paroxetine is 20 mg/day; for sertraline, it is 50 mg/day. For most patients, 20 mg/day of fluoxetine is the therapeutic dose, with 40 mg/day the next most common dose. Some patients

require higher doses (e.g., 60–100 mg/day) to respond, while others derive benefit from 10 mg/day. In double-blind studies, 20 mg/day and 40 mg/day appeared to be the most effective doses, but a 5 mg/day dose also was more effective than a placebo. (For review of dosage issues, see Schatzberg, 1995a.) Paroxetine is generally effective at doses of 20–30 mg/day, with a maximum recommended dose in major depression of 50 mg/day. The usual starting dose is 20 mg/day. Sertraline may be effective at 50 mg/day, but many studies report average doses of 100–150 mg/day. The starting dose is typically 50 mg/day. The recommended maximum dose is 200 mg/day. In elderly patients or for those with prominent anxiety or agitation, the recommended starting doses for SSRIs are 50% lower. To date, there are no available data that correlate antidepressant responses to SSRI plasma levels.

VENLAFAXINE (EFFEXOR)

Venlafaxine (Effexor) is a dual 5HT/NE serotonin/norepinephrine reuptake inhibitor approved for the treatment of depression; recently, its pharmacological and clinical properties were reviewed (Andrews, Ninan, & Nemeroff, 1996). Because there is evidence that reduced availability of both NE and 5HT occurs in patients with depression and, moreover, because of evidence that both NE and 5HT reuptake blockade is associated with therapeutic efficacy in depression, an uptake blocker of both monoamines was considered of interest, especially if such a drug lacked the adverse side-effect profile of the TCAs. Venlafaxine is indeed such an agent and can be conceptualized as a TCA without the anticholinergic, antiadrenergic, and antihistaminergic effects of the TCAs. It therefore should have all of the efficacy and none of the unfavorable side effects of the TCAs.

There is indeed evidence that this is the case. Unlike TCAs, venlafaxine produces no orthostatic hypotension, is not lethal in overdose, and produces no dry mouth, constipation, blurry vision, or sedation. Its side-effect profile resembles exactly what one would predict from its postulated mechanism of action, namely, the combination of SSRIs' side effects (nausea, headache, sexual dysfunction, and insomnia) and NE reuptake blockers' side effects (hypertension, tachycardia, sweating). In our clinical experience, using lower than recommended doses initially, such as

TABLE 10.5 Atypical Antidepressants

Drug		Dose Range
Generic Name	Trade Name	(mg/day)
Trazadone	Desyrel	400–600
Nefazadone	Serzone	300–600
Bupropion	Wellbutrin	150–450
Venlafaxine	Effexor	75–375
Mirtazapine	Remeron	30–45

12.5 or 25.0 mg twice daily and gradually increasing the dose every 3 to 5 days depending on emergent side effects, allows the attainment of a therapeutic dose with minimal side effects. Although 75 mg is an effective dose in many patients, others require doses up to 375 mg per day (Table 10.5). Another major advantage of venlafaxine is its lack of inhibition of any of the cytochrome P450 hepatic isoenzymes responsible for drug-drug interactions with certain of the SSRIs (see the introductory section of this chapter). This allows for the combination of venlafaxine with TCAs and other medications in nonresponsive patients without concerns about increases in TCA plasma levels and associated toxicity.

One disadvantage of venlafaxine at the current time is the necessity for divided day dosing because of its short half-life, but the imminent introduction of a sustained-release form of the drug, expected within a year or so, will likely obviate this problem.

In contradistinction to the apparently less-optimal side-effect profile of venlafaxine compared with the SSRIs is its reputation for superb efficacy in the treatment of unipolar depression, particularly in treatment-refractory patients. There is little doubt among most psychopharmacologists that venlafaxine is successful in treating a sizable proportion of patients who have failed trials with other antidepressants, including SSRIs; this has been reported in an open study (Nierenberg et al., 1994). We have approximately 25 patients who failed trials with other antidepressants and electroconvulsive therapy (ECT) who were venlafaxine responders. Less clear is whether venlafaxine acts more rapidly than other antidepressants, an active avenue of investigation. Because of its short half-life, venlafaxine attains steady-state plasma levels very rapidly compared with other antidepressants.

In addition to its acknowledged efficacy in treatment-refractory depression is the evidence that venlafaxine is more effective than the SSRIs in severe depression (frequently defined as the melancholic subtype or the endogenous subtype) or in hospitalized depressed patients. Two double-blind controlled studies have evaluated the efficacy of venlafaxine for severe depression. In one (Guelfi et al., 1995), venlafaxine was shown to be effective for severe depression when compared with a placebo; most impressive was the lack of any effect of the placebo in this population. In a second study (Clerc et al., 1994), fluoxetine and venlafaxine were compared in depressed inpatients; both drugs were effective, but venlafaxine was more effective than fluoxetine and the antidepressant effect had a more rapid onset of action.

BUPROPION (WELLBUTRIN)

Bupropion (Wellbutrin) is an amino ketone that has little effect on either 5HT or NE reuptake, but is a blocker, albeit a weak one, of dopamine (DA) uptake. It has been demonstrated to be effective for major depression. Whether it exerts its therapeutic effects via this effect on DA systems or not remains unclear.

Like the other antidepressants, the efficacy of bupropion in the treatment of major depression is comparable to that of TCAs, as well as fluoxetine and trazodone. Because of its short half-life, bupropion must be administered twice per day; for that reason, as well as a propensity for high doses of the drug to produce seizures, a slow-release form of the drug has been developed, studied in clinical trials, and recently released. This preparation has the advantage of once-a-day dosing and a risk of seizures no greater than that observed with other antidepressants.

Bupropion has certain advantages when compared to TCAs, including a lack of orthostatic hypertension, few cardiovascular effects, and no anticholinergic effects. Bupropion produces no sedation or cognitive impairment and, most importantly, in contrast to the SSRIs, produces no sexual dysfunction. In contrast to the TCAs, which are well known to produce weight gain, many patients treated with bupropion exhibit weight loss, which can in certain clinical circumstances be problematic.

Bupropion has also been shown in two studies to be effective in the treatment of bipolar depression, with little propensity to cause a switch into mania, though this was not confirmed in a subsequent study. Whether bupropion is effective in the treatment of refractory depression remains unknown.

TRAZODONE (DESYREL)

Trazodone was the first antidepressant introduced in the United States that was not lethal when taken in overdose. A triazolopyridine derivative, it is structurally unrelated to the tricyclics, but is related to nefazodone (discussed in the next section). Trazodone is believed to act as an antidepressant primarily by virtue of its effects as a serotonin type 2 ($5HT_2$) receptor antagonist. Trazodone has a short half-life of 3–9 hours, but it can be administered once per day. In addition to antagonism of the 5HT2 receptor, trazodone is also known to be a weak inhibitor of serotonin reuptake, far less potent than any of the marketed SSRIs. Several trials revealed that trazodone is as effective as TCAs and fluoxetine in the treatment of major depression, though many clinicians have the impression that it is not effective in moderate-to-severe depression.

The major side effects include sedation, which can often limit its clinical usefulness, though frequently trazodone is combined with SSRIs to reverse SSRI-induced insomnia. Trazodone clearly has fewer anticholinergic side effects when compared with TCAs, but its major drawback, particularly in the elderly, is orthostatic hypotension, thought to be due to α_1 adrenergic receptor blockade. Another potentially serious adverse side effect of trazodone is the fact that a small percentage of men will develop priapism after trazodone use, and in a small percentage of those individuals, surgical intervention is necessary. It is also important to point out that trazodone has been associated with arrhythmias in patients with preexisting cardiac disease.

In terms of dosing, trazodone is usually begun at a dose of 100–150 mg per day, and patients are increased to doses of 400–600 mg per day. Although such doses can be administered once per day, they are often administered in divided doses, particularly when the dose exceeds 300 mg per day.

NEFAZODONE (SERZONE)

The antidepressant nefazodone (Serzone), structurally related to trazodone, is a potent 5HT2 antagonist, as well as an inhibitor of both 5HT and NE reuptake (Owens, Ieni, Knight, Winders, & Nemeroff, 1995; Taylor et al., 1995). It is an effective antidepressant and has the advantages of producing no sexual dysfunction, a major advantage compared with the SSRIs, and also preserves normal sleep architecture. Like the SSRIs, nefazodone has also been shown to be effective in reducing the anxiety associated with major depression as assessed with the Covi scale.

The major disadvantages of this drug include the necessity for twice daily dosing due to its short half-life and the necessity to titrate the dose. Although the manufacturer recommends a dose of 100 mg twice per day as the starting dose, many clinicians recommend a starting dose of 50 mg twice a day due to the sedation commonly observed with this drug. Nefazodone must be administered in a dose range of 300 to 600 mg per day to achieve maximal efficacy.

Nefazodone is a potent inhibitor of cytochrome P450 3A4 and as such is absolutely contraindicated in patients treated with terfenadine and astemizole, two commonly used antihistamines that are metabolized by this enzyme, because of toxic cardiac events that can ensue with such drug combinations. Moreover, caution must be used when using benzodiazepines such as alprazolam, triazolam, or midazolam in combination with nefazodone because these drugs are also metabolized by cytochrome P450 3A4 and exhibit markedly elevated plasma concentrations when coadministered with nefazodone.

MIRTAZAPINE (REMERON)

Mirtazapine (Remeron) is a novel antidepressant that is the newest entry into the antidepressant market in the United States. This tetracyclic is believed to act primarily as an α_2 antagonist at auto-and heteroreceptors and is also a 5HT2A and 5HT₃ receptor antagonist as well. Its net effect is the increase of 5HT and NE neurotransmission (DeBoer, 1996). Because of its recent introduction, most clinicians have had little clinical experience with this agent.

Its major advantages include a single daily dose, the lack of sexual dysfunction, and safety in overdose and sedating properties, which is particularly helpful in depressed patients with profound insomnia. Its major side effects include marked daytime somnolence, to which patients eventually become tolerant, as well as increased appetite, weight gain, and dizziness. Of 2,796 patients in clinical trials, 2 developed agranulocytosis and 1 developed severe neutropenia. Its efficacy in patients with treatment-refractory depression is unknown.

DISCUSSION

For all classes of antidepressants available in the United States, efficacy has been demonstrated in RCTs. The differences among these classes of agents revolve primarily around their side effects and safety. The first-generation TCAs and MAOIs are less well tolerated and are more dangerous in overdose than are the newer agents. For this reason alone, the SSRIs and other newer agents represent important steps forward in the treatment of major depression. Moreover, the TCAs are largely noradrenergic in their reuptake blocking effects, exerting little effect on serotonin reuptake (clomipramine is a notable exception). The difference in monoamine reuptake blockade most likely accounts for a wider range of efficacy for the SSRIs (e.g., panic, OCD, bulimia, premenstrual syndrome, etc.), as well as their demonstrated effects in milder forms of depression, such as dysthymia.

Although the various classes enjoy efficacy for major depression, a number of issues about their relative efficacy for specific subgroups or subtypes of depression remain in debate. For example, as indicated above, some argue that the TCAs are more efficacious antidepressants and are more likely to induce remission in melancholic depressives than the SSRIs. These data and the venlafaxine findings suggest the need in treating severely ill patients to have drugs that exert potent noradrenergic effects. Another issue is whether the MAOIs (and perhaps the SSRIs) are more effective in atypical depressives than are the TCAs. These areas require further prospective study.

The relatively high placebo response rates in outpatient studies are of concern in some studies, with both known and investigational antidepressants failing to separate from the placebo. Research and clinical experience suggest more severely ill patients show less in the way of placebo response, but they also show less in the way of drug response. Thus, just including more severely ill patients is not a panacea. As indicated above in the introduction, we need to clarify what placebo treatment in a study actually represents and what it should include. Certainly, a great deal of supportive handholding and patient contact do not reflect a no treatment condition but instead constitute powerful interventions. This area requires further study so that we can design better protocols to test drug efficacy.

Of related importance is that the Food and Drug Administration may approve a drug that has been shown to separate from the placebo in two studies, but that also has several so-called failed trials in which efficacy was not demonstrated. The result can be to cloud a new agent in some doubt and to undercut confidence in the drug. Thus, there is also a need to think through how much and in what types of patients efficacy should be required before approval. Although many issues remain regarding the range of efficacy for antidepressants, these drugs are certainly effective in patients with major depression, and their prescription and use have had a tremendous impact on the lives of many depressed patients.

ACKNOWLEDGMENTS   The authors are supported by NIH MH-40524, MH-39415, MH-42088, MH-51761, DA-09492 and an established investigator award from NARSAD (CBN), and NIH MH50604 and MH 47573 (AFS).

References

Andrews, J. M., Ninan, P. T., & Nemeroff, C. B. (1996). Venlafaxine: A novel antidepressant that has a dual mechanism of action. *Depression, 4*, 48–56.

Asberg, M., Cronholm, B., Sjoqvist, F., et al. (1971). Relationship between plasma level and therapeutic effect of nortriptyline. *British Medical Journal, 3*, 331–334.

Blacker, D. (1996). Maintenance treatment of major depression: A review of the literature. *Harvard Review of Psychiatry, 4*, 1–9.

Boswell, E. G., Anfinson, T. J., & Nemeroff, C. B. (1997). Depression associated with endocrine disorders. In M. Robertson & C. Katona (Eds.), *Depression and physical illness* (pp. 255–292). Sussex, U.K.: John Wiley & Sons.

Bowden, C. L., Schatzberg, A. F., Rosenbaum, A., et al. (1993). Fluoxetine and desipramine in major depressive disorder. *Journal of Clinical Psychopharmacology*, 13, 305–311.

Boyer, W. F., & Feigner, J. P. (1994). Clinical significance of early non-response in depressed patients. *Depression*, 2, 32–35.

Chan, C. H., Janicak, P. G., Davis, J. M., et al. (1987). Response of psychotic and nonpsychotic depressed patients to tricyclic antidepressants. *Journal of Clinical Psychiatry*, 48, 197–200.

Clerc, G. E., Ruimy, P., Verdeau-Pailles, J., et al. (1994). A double-blind comparison of venlafaxine and fluoxetine in patients hospitalized for major depression and melancholia. *International Clinical Psychopharmacology*, 9, 139–143.

Danish University Antidepressant Group (DUAG). (1986). Citalopram: Clinical effect profile in comparison with clomipramine: A controlled multicenter study. *Psychopharmacology*, 90, 131–138.

———. (1990). Paroxetine: A selective serotonin reuptake inhibitor showing better tolerance, but weaker antidepressant effect than clomipramine in a controlled multicenter study. *Journal of Affective Disorders*, 18, 289–299.

DeBattista, C., & Schatzberg, A. F. (1995). Paroxetine. In H. I. Kaplan & B. J. Sadock (Eds.), *Comprehensive textbook of psychiatry*, Vol. 2 (6th ed., pp. 2063–2069). Baltimore, Md.: Williams & Wilkins.

de Boer, T. (1996). The pharmacologic profile of mirtazapine. *Journal of Clinical Psychiatry*, 57(Suppl. 4), 19–25.

DeVane, L. (1994). Pharmacokinetics of the newer antidepressants: clinical relevance. *American Journal of Medicine*, 97(Suppl. 6A), 13–22.

DeVane, C. L., & Sallee, F. R. (1996). Serotonin selective reuptake inhibitors in child and adolescent psychopharmacology: A review of published experience. *Journal of Clinical Psychiatry*, 57, 55–65.

Doogan, D. P., & Caillard, V. (1992). Sertraline in the prevention of depression. *British Journal of Psychiatry*, 160, 217–222.

Elkin, I., Sheat, T., Watkins, J., et al. (1989). NIMH Treatment of Depression Collaborative Research Program, I: General effectiveness of treatments. *Archives of General Psychiatry*, 46, 971–982.

Ereshefsky, L. (1996). Drug interactions of antidepressants. *Psychiatric Annals*, 26, 342–350.

Fisher, R. L., & Fisher, S. (1996). Antidepressants for children: Is scientific support necessary? *Journal of Nervous and Mental Disease*, 184, 99–108.

Frank, E., Kupfer, D. J., Perel, J. M., et al. (1990). Three-year outcomes for maintenance therapies in recurrent depression. *Archives of General Psychiatry*, 47, 1093–1099.

———. (1993). Comparison of full-dose versus half-dose pharmacotherapy in the maintenance treatment of recurrent depression. *Journal of Affective Disorders*, 27, 139–145.

Frasure-Smith, N., Lesperance, F., & Talajic, M. (1993). Depression following myocardial infarction: Impact on 6 month survival. *Journal of the American Medical Association*, 270, 1819–1861.

———. (1995). Depression and 18 month prognosis after myocardial infarction. *Circulation*, 91, 999–1005.

Glassman, A. H., Perel, J. M., Shostak, M., et al. (1977). Clinical implications of imipramine plasma levels for depressive illness. *Archives of General Psychiatry*, 34, 197–204.

Guelfi, J. D., White, C., Hackett, D., et al. (1995). Effectiveness of venlafaxine in patients hospitalized for major depression and melancholia. *Journal of Clinical Psychiatry*, 56, 450–458.

Hirschfeld, R. M. A., & Schatzberg, A. F. (1994). Long-term management of depression. *American Journal of Medicine*, 97(Suppl. 6A), 33–38.

Hollon, S. D., DeRubeis, R., Evans, M. D., et al. (1992). Cognitive therapy and pharmacotherapy for depression: Singly and in combination. *Archives of General Psychiatry*, 49, 774–781.

Janicak, P. G., Davis, J. M., Preskorn, S. H., & Ayd, F. J. (1993). *Principles and practice of psychopharmacology*. Baltimore: Williams and Wilkins.

Krishnan, K. R. R. (1995). Monoamine oxidase inhibitors. In A. F. Schatzberg & C. B. Nemeroff CB (Eds.), *Textbook of psychopharmacology* (pp. 183–193). Washington, D.C.: American Psychiatric Association Press.

McDaniel, J. S., Musselman, D. L., Porter, M. R., Reed, D. A., & Nemeroff, C. B. (1995). Depression in patients with cancer: Diagnosis, biology and treatment. *Archives of General Psychiatry*, 52, 89–99.

Mendels, J. (1995). Sertraline. In H. I. Kaplan & B. J. Sadock (Eds.), *Comprehensive textbook of psychiatry*, Vol. 2 (6th ed., pp. 2069–2073). Baltimore, Md.: Williams & Wilkins.

Montgomery, S. A., & Dunbar, G. (1993). Paroxetine is better than placebo in relapse prevention and the prophylaxis of recurrent depression. *International Clinical Psychopharmacology*, 8, 189–195.

Montgomery, S. A., Dufour, H., Brion, S., et al. (1988). The prophylactic efficacy of fluoxetine in unipolar depression. *British Journal of Psychiatry*, 153(Suppl. 3), 69–76.

Nemeroff, C. B. (1994). Evolutionary trends in the pharmacotherapeutic management of depression. *Journal of Clinical Psychiatry*, 55, 3–15.

Nemeroff, C. B., DeVane, C. L., & Pollack, B. G. (1996). Newer antidepressants and the cytochrome P450 system. *American Journal of Psychiatry, 153*, 311–320.

Nierenberg, A. A., Feighner, J. P., Rudolph, R., et al. (1994). Venlafaxine for treatment-resistant depression. *Journal of Clinical Psychopharmacology, 14*, 419–423.

Nierenberg, A. A., McLean, N. E., Alpert, J. E., et al. (1995). Early nonresponse to fluoxetine as a predictor of poor 8-week outcome. *American Journal of Psychiatry, 152*, 1500–1503.

Owens, M. J., Ieni, J. R., Knight, D. L., Winders, K., & Nemeroff, C. B. (1995). The serotonergic antidepressant nefazodone inhibits the serotonin transporter: in vivo and ex vivo studies. *Life Sciences, 57*, 373–380.

Potter, W. Z., Manji, A. K., & Rudorfer, M. V. (1995). Tricyclics and tetracyclics. In A. F. Schatzberg & C. B. Nemeroff (Eds.), *Textbook of psychopharmacology* (pp. 141–160). Washington, D.C.: American Psychiatric Press.

Prien, R. F., Kupfer, D. J., Mansky, P. A., et al. (1984). Drug therapy in the prevention of recurrences in unipolar and bipolar affective disorders: A report of the NIMH Collaborative Study Group comparing lithium carbonate, imipramine, and a lithium carbonate-imipramine combination. *Archives of General Psychiatry, 41*, 1096–1104.

Roose, S. P., Glassman, A. H., Attia, E., et al. (1994). Comparative efficacy of selective serotonin reuptake inhibitors and tricyclics in the treatment of melancholia. *American Journal of Psychiatry, 151*, 1735–1739.

Rush, J. A., & the Depression Guideline Panel of the Agency for Health Care Policy and Research. (1994). Synopsis of the clinical practice guidelines for diagnosis and treatment of depression in primary care. *Archives of Family Medicine, 3*, 85–92.

Schatzberg, A. F. (1995a). Fluoxetine. In H. I. Kaplan & R. J. Sadock (Eds.), *Comprehensive textbook of psychiatry*, Vol. 2 (6th ed., pp. 2056–2063). Baltimore, Md.: Williams & Wilkins.

————. (1995b). Fluoxetine in the treatment of comorbid anxiety and depression [Monograph]. *Journal of Clinical Psychiatry, 13*(2), 2–12.

————. (1996). Treatment of severe depression with the selective serotonin reuptake inhibitors. *Depression, 4*, 182–189.

Schatzberg, A. F., & Rothschild, A. J. (1992). Psychotic (delusional) major depression: Should it be included as a distinct syndrome in *DSM-IV? American Journal of Psychiatry, 149*, 733–745.

Stowe, Z. N., Casarella, J., Landry, J., & Nemeroff, C. B. (1995). Sertraline in the treatment of women with post-partum major depression. *Depression, 3*, 49–55.

Taylor, D. P., Carter, R. B., Eison, A. S., et al. (1995). Pharmacology and neurochemistry of nefazodone, a novel antidepressant drug. *Journal of Clinical Psychiatry, 6*(Suppl.), 3–11.

Thase, M. E., & Sullivan, L. R. (1995). Relapse and recurrence of depression: A practical approach for prevention. *CNS Drugs, 4*, 261–277.

Tollefson, G. D., Holman, S. L., & Sayler, M. E. (1994). Fluoxetine, placebo, and tricyclic antidepressants in major depression with and without anxious features. *Journal of Clinical Psychiatry, 55*, 50–59.

11

Psychosocial Treatments for Major Depressive Disorder

W. Edward Craighead

Linda Wilcoxon Craighead

Stephen S. Ilardi

Behavior therapy (BT), cognitive-behavior therapy (CBT), and interpersonal psychotherapy (IPT) have each been shown by at least two Type 1 or Type 2 RCTs, as well as by two major meta-analytic reports of the literature, to be effective psychosocial interventions for patients meeting criteria for a major depressive disorder (MDD). All three psychosocial treatments have yielded substantial reductions in scores on the two major depression rating scales, the Beck Depression Inventory and the Hamilton Rating Scale for Depression, significant decreases in percentage of patients meeting the criteria for MDD posttreatment, and substantial maintenance of effect well after treatment has ended.

While the data on outcomes of psychosocial and pharmacological interventions for major depressive episodes suggest that the two treatment modes are comparable, there is some question about whether antidepressant medications, either alone or in combination with a psychosocial intervention, are superior to psychosocial interventions in the treatment of severely depressed patients.

A major depressive disorder (MDD) is the most commonly diagnosed psychiatric disorder among adults, with U.S. lifetime prevalence rates of 20–25% for women and 9–12% for men; point prevalence rates are about 6% and 3% for women and men, respectively (American Psychiatric Association [APA], 1994; Kessler et al., 1994; Regier, Kaelber, Roper, Rae, & Sartorius, 1994). These prevalence rates and gender differences are relatively constant across the adult life span. Depression engenders not only extraordinary personal and family suffering, but also significant societal burdens, such as an increased use of social and medical services (Johnson, Weissman, & Klerman, 1992), enormous financial costs for treatment, and lost productivity due to absenteeism from work (Greenberg, Stiglin, Finkelstein, & Berndt, 1993; Wells et al., 1989).

In order to receive a diagnosis of *major depressive disorder*, a person must experience marked distress and a decrease in level of functioning. In addition, the 2 weeks before examination must be characterized by the almost daily occurrence of a dysphoric mood (sad, empty, or tearful) or a loss of interest or pleasure in almost all activities (APA, 1994). The individual must also experience at least four (only three if both dysphoric mood and loss of interest or pleasure are present) of the following seven symptoms (with the second through sixth occurring nearly every day):

1. Significant weight loss (while not trying to lose weight) or a change in appetite
2. Insomnia or hypersomnia
3. Psychomotor agitation or retardation

4. Fatigue or loss of energy
5. Feelings of worthlessness or excessive or inappropriate guilt
6. Decreased concentration or indecisiveness
7. Suicidal ideation, plan, or attempt

Substantial advances have been made over the past three decades in the successful treatment of depression. Treatments of choice now include not only somatic interventions (antidepressant medications and electroconvulsive shock) but also a number of psychosocial interventions—behavior therapy (BT) (including marital therapy), cognitive-behavior therapy (CBT), and interpersonal psychotherapy (IPT). This chapter reviews the evidence regarding the efficacy of these specific psychosocial treatments (including their combinations with somatic treatments), discusses the possible mechanisms of change in these therapies, and addresses numerous issues regarding the appropriate use of psychosocial treatments. This review includes only those studies that obtained information for diagnosis via a structured interview such as the Structured Clinical Interview for *DSM-III-R* (SCID) (Spitzer et al., 1992) and employed a formal, defined system such as the Research Diagnostic Criteria (Spitzer, Endicott, & Robins, 1978) or *Diagnostic and Statistical Manual* for diagnostic purposes. Further, included studies must have employed cutoff scores on standard depression severity measures, such as clinical rating scales or self-report measures, as a criterion for admission to the study.[1] In other words, by virtue of the severity, frequency, and duration of their observed symptoms, the participants in these studies are typical of those who might seek and receive treatment by a mental health professional for an MDD. Within this book, these studies would all be considered Type 1 studies. Finally, only those therapeutic modalities that have been studied in at least two comparative Type 1 outcome trials with patients between the ages of 18 and 65 years have been included in this review.

BEHAVIOR THERAPY

Description

The first behavioral treatment program of significance was developed by Lewinsohn (1974), who built on previous behavioral formulations of depression (Ferster, 1973; Skinner, 1953). Refinements have subsequently been made by Lewinsohn and his colleagues,

as well as by Bellack, Hersen, and Himmelhoch, by Rehm, and by McLean and Hakstian as detailed below. Behavior therapy for depression has focused largely on improving social and communication skills, increasing adaptive behaviors such as positive and negative assertion, increasing response-contingent positive reinforcement for adaptive behaviors, and decreasing negative life experiences.

Empirical Evidence

In a randomized clinical trial (RCT), Lewinsohn and his group demonstrated that, relative to various control groups, behavior therapy increased pleasant experiences and reduced aversive experiences, which produced concomitant decreases in depression severity (see Lewinsohn & Gotlib, 1995, for a summary of Lewinsohn's contributions). This work was extended by Bellack, Hersen, and Himmelhoch (1981, 1983) and Hersen, Bellack, Himmelhoch, and Thase (1984), who demonstrated that behavior therapy was as effective as the antidepressant amitriptyline (AMI) in reducing depression over a 12-week treatment period; these effects were maintained with 6–8 booster sessions over a 6-month follow-up period. Consistent with Rehm's (1977) suggestions, McLean and Hakstian (1979) added problem-solving and self-control procedures to the behavior therapy treatment package, and they conducted a substantial 10-week clinical trial comparing this expanded treatment package to relaxation therapy, insight-oriented psychotherapy, and amitriptyline. The behavior therapy program was equal or superior to all treatment conditions; although questions have been raised regarding the adequacy of the medication dosage, the results for amitriptyline were generally comparable to those obtained in other drug studies. Furthermore, these results were maintained at a 27-month follow-up, at which time the behavior therapy subjects were more socially active and productive than participants in all the other treatment conditions (McLean & Hakstian, 1990).

Rehm's self-control therapy (1977) has been found to be superior to nonspecific psychosocial treatments and no-treatment controls (Rehm, 1990), but it has not been compared to standard antidepressant treatment. It is worth noting that the apparently essential ingredient (and perhaps the most important contribution) of this self-control therapy is the *self-monitoring* of thoughts and behaviors (Rehm, 1990), a component that is included in most other empirically supported psychosocial depression treatment protocols.

The only recent evaluation of BT occurred in a study designed to test the hypothesized theory of change of Beck's CBT for depression. In this study, Jacobson and his colleagues (1996) used as one comparison group a treatment labeled "behavioral activation" (BA), which consisted only of the behavioral components that occur early in CBT. In BA, the therapists focused only on the procedures designed to change overt behaviors: monitoring daily activities, assessment of pleasure and mastery of activities, assignment of increasingly difficult activities, imaging of behaviors to be performed, discussion of specific problems and identification of behavioral solutions to those problems, and interventions to ameliorate social skills deficits. This BA treatment is quite similar to the behavioral interventions previously reviewed, but the investigation included multiple assessment methods and process measures of adherence and competence, which reflect the advances made in research methodology over the past 10–15 years. The major finding of this study was that the BA treatment was equally effective to the entire CBT treatment protocol, even when both treatments were competently conducted by therapists who had a clear bias favoring CBT. This is the only direct comparison of BT and CBT.

Behavior Marital Therapy

Another development in behavioral approaches to the treatment of depression has been the employment of behavior marital therapy (BMT) with individuals who are concurrently suffering from an MDD and in a discordant marriage. Both O'Leary and colleague's and Jacobson and colleague's standard BMT (Beach, Sandeen, & O'Leary, 1990; Jacobson, Dobson, Fruzetti, Schmaling, & Salusky, 1991; O'Leary & Beach, 1990) have been demonstrated to be equal to individual CBT for the alleviation of depression among individuals with both MDD and marital discord; these research studies also found BMT to have the added advantage of being superior to individual CBT in the reduction of marital discord, a finding that argues for the use of BMT with depressed patients who also are experiencing marital discord. None of these studies employed adequate follow-up procedures to permit a determination of whether BMT confers greater prophylactic effects than individual CBT for the prevention of relapse of an MDD following successful treat-

ment. However, given that "marital disputes" is the most frequently discussed topic among depressed patients in maintenance therapy (Weissman & Klerman, 1973) and that marital friction is an enduring problem among formerly depressed patients even when asymptomatic (Bothwell & Weissman, 1977), it seems likely that successful BMT will reduce the rate of relapse among successfully treated MDD patients in discordant marriages. Unfortunately, BMT has not been evaluated with adequate numbers of severely depressed patients in discordant marriages to know if these findings will be applicable to such patients or whether the presence of severe depression will necessitate treatment with antidepressants administered either alone or in tandem with BMT.

Conclusions

Although these consistent findings support the efficacy of BT for depression, they have been overshadowed by subsequent outcome studies that have focused on cognitive-behavior therapy and interpersonal psychotherapy as psychosocial interventions for an MDD; as a result, BT is rarely mentioned among lists of empirically validated treatments for an MDD. However, given the applicability of BT to depressed patients of all age groups (see Lewinsohn & Gotlib, 1995) and the relative efficacy, efficiency, and endurance of behavioral interventions, as well as the recent results for both BA and BMT, it seems that this was an unwarranted and premature turn of events. From a historical perspective, it appears to have been due primarily to the sociology of science and to no small extent the exclusion of behavior therapy from the well-publicized National Institute of Mental Health (NIMH) clinical trial (Elkin, Parloff, Hadley, & Autry, 1985), rather than to the relative scientific merit and empirical outcomes of the then-available comparative treatment studies.

COGNITIVE-BEHAVIOR THERAPY

Description

The most extensively evaluated psychosocial treatment for an MDD is Beck's cognitive-behavior therapy (CBT) (Beck, Rush, Shaw, & Emery, 1979), alternatively referred to simply as cognitive therapy. Cognitive-behavior therapy is a short-term (16–20 sessions over a period of 12–16 weeks), directive therapy designed to change the depressed patient's negative view of the self, world, and future. The therapy begins with the presentation of the rationale, which is designed to inform the client of the therapy model and the process of therapeutic change. Following this, early CBT sessions consist of the implementation of strategies designed to increase active behavioral performance. The purpose of such an increase is to allow the monitoring of behaviors and their associated thoughts and feelings; behavioral changes are not posited to be directly responsible for the desired changes in depression. During the third week, expanded self-monitoring techniques are introduced in order to demonstrate the relationship between thoughts and feelings; patients are taught to evaluate their thoughts for logical errors, which include arbitrary inference, selective abstraction, overgeneralization, magnification and minimalization, personalization, and dichotomous thinking (Beck, 1976). In about the middle of therapy (around session 8 or 9), the concept of *schema*, or beliefs underlying negative and positive thoughts, is introduced, and therapy begins to focus on changing those negative schemas that have been activated and are posited to have resulted in the MDD. Toward the end of therapy (sessions 14–16), the focus shifts to termination and the use of cognitive strategies to prevent relapse or a future recurrence of depression.

Empirical Evidence

A number of studies have compared the effectiveness of CBT to several tricyclic antidepressant medications (Elkin et al., 1989; Hollon et al., 1992; Rush, Beck, Kovacs, & Hollon, 1977; Simons, Murphy, Levine, & Wetzel, 1986).[2] With the possible exception of the NIMH Treatment of Depression Collaborative Research Program (TDCRP; Elkin et al., 1989), the essential finding in all these studies is that CBT is equally effective to antidepressant medication in alleviating MDD among outpatients (see Tables 11.1 and 11.2). Typically, 50–70% of MDD patients who complete a course of CBT no longer meet the criteria for MDD at posttreatment, with pre-post changes from the high 20s to single digits for the Beck Depression Inventory (BDI) scores and changes from the high teens/low 20s to single digits for the Hamilton Rating Scale of Depression (HRSD) scores (see Tables 11.1 and 11.2). Furthermore, among the samples studied, CBT appeared to confer some enduring prophylactic

effects inasmuch as only 20–30% of those successfully treated relapsed during the first year following treatment. Indeed, 16 weeks of CBT produced a maintained one-year success rate that equals or slightly exceeds that achieved by a full year of antidepressant treatment (Evans et al., 1992), and CBT's maintenance effects are clearly superior to short-term (16 weeks) antidepressant treatment (16 weeks is not preferred but it is, unfortunately, longer than the actual average length of completed medication treatment in current clinical practice (Klein & Davis, 1969)).

Because the TDCRP study (Elkin et al., 1989) has received so much attention, including its significant role in the development of guidelines (not standards) for treatment of outpatients suffering from an MDD (Agency for Health Care Policy and Research [AHCPR], 1993; APA, 1993), it is worthy of special note. This study included 250 outpatients who were randomly assigned to one of four 16-week treatment conditions: CBT, IPT, imipramine hydrochloride plus clinical management (IMP-CM), or pill-placebo plus clinical management (PLA-CM). It is important to note that the PLA-CM was not the pure pill-placebo condition that Klein (1996) has insisted must be a control condition in all psychotherapy-versus-antidepressant comparison studies. Both the IMP-CM and the PLA-CM conditions included a "clinical management" component (20 minutes per week talking with an experienced psychiatrist), the effects of which simply are not known.

The results of the TDCRP for those patients who completed treatment generally support the equality of the three presumed active treatments in ameliorating depression at posttreatment (as measured by a Hamilton Depression Rating Scale score of 6 or less) (CBT 36%, IPT 43%, and IMP-CM 42%); however, only IPT and IMP-CM produced significantly greater reductions in depression than PLA-CM (21%) over the course of treatment, and only then for a few of the outcome measures. Apparently, the CM component added some treatment effectiveness to the PLA component of the treatment and perhaps also to the superior effects of IMI plus CM in this trial. Even these acute treatment effects were not maintained at the 18-month follow-up as the percentages of patients remaining nondepressed and not receiving treatment for depression were quite low (CBT 28%, IPT 17%, IMP plus CM 15%, and PLA plus CM 18%), so that none of the active treatments was superior to the PLA-CM condition at the 18-month follow-up (Shea,

TABLE 11.1 Hamilton Rating Scale of Depression Scores and Percentages "Recovered" for Major Random Clinical Trials Reviewed in This Chapter

	CBT							IPT			BT		BMT							Medications		
Study	1	2	3	4	5	9	10	6	3	7	8	5	9	10	1	2	3	4	5	6	7	8
N	15	19	37	16	44	12	20	17[a]	47	25	42	47	12	8	14	16	37	32[b]	—	20	14	—
Pre	21.2	18.5	19.2	24.8	18.6	—	20.0	17.3	18.9	22.2	—	17.3	—	23.4	22.4	19.7	19.2	24.0	—	16.8	25.5	—
Post	5.8	6.4	7.6	8.8	6.8	—	4.5	10.2	6.9	7.0	—	6.5	—	7.2	9.3	7.0	7.0	8.4	—	10.0	8.2	—
Percentage recovered	—	63[c]	51[d]	50[d]	—	—	—	—	55[d]	64[e]	—	—	—	—	—	50[a]	57[b]	53[b]	—	—	43[c]	—

List of studies: 1. Rush et al. (1977); 2. Murphy et al. (1984); 3. Elkin et al. (1989); 4. Hollon et al. (1992); 5. Jacobson et al. (1996); 6. DiMascio et al. (1979); 7. Bellack et al. (1981); 8. McLean & Hakstian (1979); 9. O'Leary & Beach (1990); 10. Jacobson et al. (1991).

BDI = Beck Depression Inventory; BMT = behavior marital therapy; BT = behavior therapy; CBT = cognitive-behavior therapy; HRSD = Hamilton Rating Scale of Depression; IPT = interpersonal psychotherapy.

[a] Data are only available for all patients who entered and completed at least one week of treatment.

[b] N = 31 for post.

[c] HRSD ≤ 7.

[d] HRSD ≤ 6.

[e] HRSD and BDI ≤ 10.

TABLE 11.2 Beck Depression Inventory Scores and Percentages "Recovered" for Major Random Clinical Trials Reviewed in This Chapter

	CBT							IPT			BT		BMT						Medications			
Study	1	2	3	4	5	9	10[a]	6	3	7	8	5	9[b]	10[b]	1	2	3	4	5	6	7	8
N	18	19	37	16	44	12	20	17	47	25	42[c]	48	12	8	14	16	36	32	—	17	14	49[c]
Pre	30.3	29.7	26.8	30.4	28.9	26	26.3	—	25.5	27.1	26.8	29.3	22	26.4	30.8	29.3	27.1	31.1	—	—	29.6	27.2
Post	5.9	9.5	10.2	7.9	9.7	6	6.5	—	7.7	7.4	9.7	8.5	5	7.0	13.0	8.9	6.5	10.5	—	—	12.8	14.2
Percentage recovered	83[d]	53[d]	65[e]	62[e]	57[c]	—	80[e]	—	70[e]	64[f]	50[g]	50[g]	—	88[e]	36[d]	56[d]	69[e]	56[e]	—	—	43[f]	25

List of studies: 1. Rush et al. (1977); 2. Murphy et al. (1984); 3. Elkin et al. (1989); 4. Hollon et al. (1992); 5. Jacobson et al. (1996); 6. DiMascio et al. (1979); 7. Bellack et al. (1981); 8. McLean & Hakstian (1979); 9. O'Leary & Beach (1990); 10. Jacobson et al. (1991).

BDI = Beck Depression Inventory; BMT = behavior marital therapy; BT = behavior therapy; CBT = cognitive-behavioral therapy; HRSD = Hamilton Rating Scale of Depression; IPT = interpersonal psychotherapy; MDD = major depressive disorder.

[a] Data are only for completers who met criteria for MDD and either presence or absence of marital discord.
[b] Data are only for completers who met criteria for comorbid MDD and marital discord; BMT was less effective for MDD and no marital discord.
[c] Data are only available for all patients who entered treatment.
[d] BDI ≤ 10.
[e] BDI ≤ 9.
[f] BDI and HRSD ≤ 10.
[g] BDI ≤ 7.

Elkin, et al., 1992). These follow-up outcomes indicate that all treatments in this study had considerably weaker effects than had typically been reported in other long-term follow-up studies of these same psychotherapies. Of course, as Klein (1996) has noted, such short-term treatment (16 weeks) with antidepressant medication would not be expected to produce sustained effectiveness. It is unfortunate that this is the only clinical trial of CBT in which a pill-placebo (albeit an embellished one) was employed; given the general discrepancies among the outcomes of this study and the other major studies demonstrating the equal effectiveness of CBT and antidepressants, it is essential that additional clinical trials, which include a pure pill-placebo control condition, be conducted.

Based on the original report of the TDCRP data at conferences and in print, it has been noted (Craighead, Evans, & Robins, 1992; Hollon, Shelton, & Loosen, 1991), and sustained by recent reanalyses of the original data tape (Jacobson & Hollon, 1996a), that the lack of unequivocal findings (coupled with the uniqueness of some of the exploratory findings) assures that any interpretation of the TDCRP data is likely to be controversial. One of the major problems described in the original report of the TDCRP was "consistently significant treatment-by-site interactions for the more severely depressed and functionally impaired patients" (Elkin et al., 1989, p. 980). Even though this conclusion has been somewhat attenuated with the use of more sophisticated reanalysis of the data (Elkin et al., 1996; Elkin, Gibbons, Shea, & Shaw, 1995), the general pattern for a treatment-by-site-by-severity interaction is still acknowledged, and the authors conclude: "In regard to the general efficacy of CBT in the treatment of severely depressed (and functionally impaired) outpatients, . . . we believe . . . that the answer is not yet in" (Elkin et al., 1996, p. 101).

In their reanalysis of the TDCRP data on this issue, Jacobson and Hollon (1996a) underscore the importance of this site-by-treatment-by-severity interaction. They present data illustrating that at one site CBT did as well as IMP-CM and better than PLA-CM with severely depressed patients (probably not coincidentally, this was also the site at which CBT was rated as having been done the best; see Elkin et al., 1996). At a second site, the data favored either IPT or IMP-CM over both CBT and PLA-CM, with the last two groups not significantly different from one another. At the third site, there were not enough

subjects to warrant a comparison. In fact, it is ironic that so much has been made of the findings among the severely depressed patients since even across three sites there were 15 or fewer severely depressed patients per condition, and "severity" was not taken into account in the random assignment procedure except for the minimal cutoff criterion of 14 on the HRSD.

The essential point here is that the findings regarding the appropriateness of CBT alone for severely depressed patients are inconclusive from the TDCRP data; clearly, it is essential that this question be addressed in new randomized clinical trials. Finally, although little has been made of it, there was also a treatment by marital status confound (compounded by differential treatment effects for single and married patients), making interpretation of the data even more difficult (see Jarrett, Eaves, Grannemann, & Rush, 1991; Sotsky et al., 1991).

Consistent with general principles of good science, including the necessity of replication, definitive conclusions cannot be drawn from one study of treatments of depression. The warning of Rush, Beck, and colleagues (1977) that unwarranted conclusions about the superior efficacy of CBT over tricyclics could not be drawn from one study is now equally applicable (in the reverse direction) to the TDCRP, a point well recognized by the study's investigators (Elkin et al., 1989, 1996) but not well heeded by those employing the data to create treatment guidelines of the AHCPR (1993; Depression Guideline Panel, 1993) and the APA (1993). To the extent that the TDCPR findings were the only scientific data used to formulate the guidelines' recommendation that CBT is not a treatment of choice for severe depression in the outpatient setting, the conclusion was premature, unwarranted, and unjustified; to the extent that the guidelines were based on clinical experience (as the developers of both guidelines claim—see Merriam & Karasu, 1996, and Rush, 1996), then the TDCRP data were irrelevant.

Conclusion

Given the substantial number of studies supporting the effectiveness and efficacy of CBT with patients diagnosed with an MDD, it is concluded that CBT is a viable treatment of choice for patients with an MDD. It remains to be determined whether or not it must be combined with antidepressants in order to be effective with severely depressed outpatients. Given the widely varying outcomes across studies, the apparent differential competence with which the therapy was delivered across sites in a multisite study, and the superior effectiveness of CBT performed in Beck's clinic, it is particularly important that therapists delivering CBT be well trained before they undertake the therapy with patients. Thus, in contrast to the view that CBT is simply a "power of positive thinking" therapy that any psychotherapist can easily do, these data suggest that it is complicated to deliver in a competent fashion and that it is essential that the CBT therapist, as any other psychotherapist, be well trained.

INTERPERSONAL PSYCHOTHERAPY

Description

Interpersonal psychotherapy was originally developed as a time-limited (12–16 weeks), weekly intervention for unipolar, nonpsychotic depression (Klerman, Weissman, Rounsaville, & Chevron, 1984). The IPT model is derived in large part from Sullivan's interpersonal theory (1953) and the psychobiological theory of Meyer (1957), with its emphasis on the reciprocal relationship between biological and psychosocial facets of psychopathology. Although the IPT model "makes no assumptions about the causes of depression" (Klerman & Weissman, 1993, p. 6), it does suggest that the patient's interpersonal relations may play a significant role in both the onset and maintenance of an MDD. Accordingly, the IPT intervention focuses on the identification and amelioration of the patient's difficulties in interpersonal functioning associated with the current MDD; the primary problem areas include unresolved grief, interpersonal disputes, role transitions, and interpersonal deficits (e.g., social isolation).

Empirical Evidence

As shown in Tables 11.1 and 11.2, there have been only two reported RCTs of IPT for the acute treatment of an MDE. Both of these studies included long-term follow-up assessments designed to evaluate the prophylactic effects of acute IPT treatment. In addition, there are two separate controlled studies of "maintenance" IPT following remission of the MDD.

The first RCT of IPT was conducted by the treatment's originators, Weissman and Klerman and their colleagues (DiMascio et al., 1979; Weissman et al.,

1979). They randomly assigned 81 patients to receive 16 weeks of IPT, AMI, combined IPT and AMI, or a "nonscheduled" (i.e., therapy on request, up to one session per month) supportive psychotherapy control. The study's method of data analysis renders a comparison of the specific treatments with the control group difficult. However, a survival analysis indicated that all three treatments were superior to the nonscheduled control condition, and that the combination of IPT and AMI was slightly more effective than either condition alone (this last finding was only marginally significant, with $p < .10$). Although the sample was selected from actual patients in medical school clinics, participants in this study were slightly less depressed than those from other major RCTs (see Table 11.1). Posttreatment HRSD scores were comparable to those in other studies, with the treated groups' mean scores ranging from 5.9 to 10.2.

The second and most important RCT of IPT is the NIMH multisite clinical trial noted above, the TDCRP (Elkin et al., 1989). As noted, the principal significant finding concerned the clinical rating of depression as measured by the HRSD. All groups began with a pretreatment mean of about 19 and, using the criterion of a posttest score of 6 or less, both IPT (43%) and IMI-CM (42%) had a significantly greater proportion of patients who achieved the recovery criterion than observed in the PLA-CM (21%) condition (as noted, CBT had a recovery rate of 36%, which was not significantly different from the other treatment conditions). In a secondary data analysis (Elkin et al., 1995), IPT and IMI-CM were also found to be of comparable efficacy among the subset of patients rated severely depressed (based on pretreatment HRSD scores of 20 or greater). However, as noted above, the presence in this investigation of either a strong trend or a significant treatment-by-site-by-severity interaction (depending on the analysis) precludes the drawing of definitive conclusions from this finding (Elkin et al., 1996; Jacobson & Hollon, 1996b).

After the completion of treatment, patients in both the Weissman et al. (Weissman, Klerman, Prusoff, Sholomskas, & Padian, 1981) and the TDCRP (Elkin et al., 1989) studies were evaluated longitudinally for several months in a naturalistic follow-up design as a means of examining possible prophylactic effects associated with the acute therapeutic interventions. In the first study, there was no prophylactic effect associated with IPT versus AMI based on a 12-month follow-up (Weissman et al., 1981); however, the authors noted significantly more adaptive social functioning among IPT patients. The TDCRP study also found no relative prophylactic effects for IPT. Among patients who recovered during acute treatment, the percentages of patients who neither relapsed nor sought treatment during the year following treatment were as follows: IPT (43%), CBT (59%), IMI-CM (39%), and PLA-CM (60%). Primarily because of the small number of subjects and corresponding lack of statistical power, none of these differences was statistically significant; therefore, none of the acute treatment differences was maintained over the follow-up, and none of the treatments was superior even to PLA-CM. It is essential that additional trials be undertaken to evaluate the follow-up prophylactic effects of IPT and CBT in comparison with antidepressant medications (as typically administered), as well as with a pure pill-placebo condition. Not only is it important to determine if the treatments are equal or if one or the other is superior with respect to short-term outcome, but it is equally significant, from both personal and public health standpoints, to know how they fare on a comparative basis in the long term.

The IPT protocol has also been employed as an ongoing maintenance therapy following recovery from an MDD. Klerman, DiMascio, Weissman, Prusoff, and Paykel (1974) found a nearly equivalent prophylactic benefit associated with weekly maintenance IPT or AMI over an 8-month follow-up period, with relapse rates of only 17% and 12%, respectively. Among a group of chronic and treatment-resistant depressed patients, Frank and her colleagues (1990) reported a significant decrease in relapse probability associated with monthly IPT maintenance sessions over a 36-month follow-up period. This study, however, found a substantially larger prophylactic benefit for this particular type of depressed patient associated with maintenance IMI, with a 36-month relapse rate of only 18% in the IMI group compared with 46% for the IPT group.

Conclusions

The data regarding IPT as a treatment alone and in combination with antidepressants for an MDD are very favorable. The IPT appears to be an effective and efficacious treatment both for acute treatment of an MDD and as a maintenance treatment (especially when combined with antidepressant medication) for chronic and treatment-resistant depressions.

PATIENT CHARACTERISTICS THAT MODERATE TREATMENT RESPONSE

Behavior Therapy

Although sorely needed, there has been little research on patient characteristics that may moderate treatment response to BT for an MDE. In one of the few relevant investigations, patients who endorsed "existential" reasons for their depression (i.e., attributed the depression to their feeling that life was meaningless) were found to respond less favorably to BT than to CBT (Addis & Jacobson, 1996).

Cognitive-Behavior Therapy

The amelioration of depressive cognitive schemata is the sine qua non of CBT; accordingly, one might expect those MDD patients who enter treatment with high levels of depressotypic cognitions to be especially likely to benefit from CBT. However, the very opposite appears to be the case: patients who score low on pretreatment measures of depressotypic cognitions respond best to CBT (see Rude & Rehm, 1991, for a review). Furthermore, it appears that MDD patients who report low levels of depressotypic cognitions actually respond preferentially to CBT compared with IPT and PLA-CM (Sotsky et al., 1991). This finding is consistent with the notion that effective therapies frequently capitalize on patients' preexisting strengths rather than compensate for presenting weaknesses (Cronbach & Snow, 1977).

Although comorbid Axis II personality disorders have been frequently documented as a predictor of poor response to various antidepressant interventions (Ilardi & Craighead, 1994/1995; Shea, Widiger, & Klein, 1992), there does not appear to be an association between personality pathology and unfavorable outcome in CBT (Shea et al., 1990; Simons & Thase, 1990). In fact, TDCRP patients with comorbid Axis II pathology responded more poorly than non-Axis II patients in every treatment modality except CBT (Shea et al., 1990). If replicated, this suggests CBT as a treatment of choice (alone or in combination with antidepressants) for the large subset of MDD patients with comorbid personality disorders.

Patient characteristics associated with poor outcome in CBT include high pretreatment depression severity (Elkin et al., 1995; Whisman, 1993), single or divorced status (Jarrett et al., 1991; Sotsky et al., 1991), dysfunctional social relationships (Sotsky et al., 1991), and low learned resourcefulness (Simons, Lustman, Wetzel, & Murphy, 1985).

Interpersonal Psychotherapy

In keeping with the aforementioned capitalization hypothesis (Cronbach & Snow, 1977), the TDCRP found that patients with low levels rather than high levels of social dysfunction responded more favorably to IPT than to other treatment interventions (Sotsky et al., 1991). Among other variables linked to an unfavorable response to IPT are Axis II comorbidity (Pilkonis & Frank, 1988; Shea et al., 1990), trait neuroticism (Frank, Kupfer, Jacob, & Jarrett, 1987), and cognitive dysfunction (Blatt, Quinlan, Pilkonis, & Shea, 1995; Sotsky et al., 1991).

CONCLUSIONS

Although additional research regarding the effectiveness of psychosocial interventions for MDDs is still needed, based on the current literature[3] adequate data exist to justify the following conclusions. For outpatients presenting with MDD, BT, CBT, and IPT are effective psychosocial interventions. This conclusion is consistent with the major meta-analytic reports of psychosocial treatments for MDDs (Nietzel, Russell, Hemmings, & Gretter, 1987; Robinson, Berman, & Neimeyer, 1990). It remains to be determined whether antidepressant medications (either alone or in combination with a psychosocial intervention) are superior to psychosocial interventions in the treatment of severely depressed outpatients; initial findings on this topic must be replicated before a firm conclusion is warranted. It seems clear that about one third of MDD patients do not respond to the first treatment offered, whether it be somatic intervention or psychosocial therapy. These treatment "failures" seem to be primarily composed of depressed bipolar patients (who have not yet had a manic episode), patients with comorbid Axis II diagnoses (with frequently associated histories of abuse), and patients with severe biological dysregulation (Craighead, 1990).

Finally, it is suggested that it will be heuristic in future research regarding psychosocial interventions for MDDs to plan, develop, and evaluate treatments that simultaneously affect MDD and comorbid disorders (e.g., marital discord, Axis II personality disorders, substance abuse, physical illness). This approach has been successfully employed in the study of comorbid MDD and marital discord, and preliminary data suggest the effectiveness of BMT for the subgroup of MDD patients who are also in discordant marriages. Except for the identification of a biological diathesis for MDDs (which may be somewhat correlated with severity, but is unlikely to be isomorphic to it), this approach to outcome treatment research is likely to have a greater payoff than the identification of subtypes based solely on variations in depressive symptomatology.

Notes

1. Additional comparative outcome trials of CBT have been conducted in other countries with different diagnostic systems; most notable of these studies are those by Blackburn, Bishop, Glen, Whalley, and Christie, 1981; Blackburn, Eunson, and Bishop, 1986; Wilson, Goldin, and Charbonneau-Powis, 1983; and Teasdale, Fennell, Hibbert, and Amies, 1984.

2. It must be remembered that the MDD patients who are suffering from psychotic features or are imminently suicidal have been excluded from all these evaluation studies comparing the effectiveness of antidepressant medications and psychosocial treatments; these patients typically are hospitalized and treated with some combination of somatic (e.g., antidepressants, neuroleptics, and electroconvulsive therapy) and psychosocial interventions.

3. Although space limitations preclude discussion, there are two topics that warrant brief mention: treatment of the elderly and treatment in inpatient settings. Several studies by Thompson and colleagues (Thompson & Gallagher, 1984; Thompson, Gallagher, & Breckenridge, 1987) and one by Steuer and colleagues (1984) have demonstrated that CBT is as effective as antidepressant medication for the treatment of depression among the elderly. Thompson and colleagues (1987) also found that short-term psychodynamic psychotherapy was equally effective as CBT and antidepressant medications for depression among the elderly. There is modest evidence that the presence of Axis II personality disorders predicts poor outcome among these patients (Thompson, Gallagher, & Czirr, 1988). In a study of IPT (a shortened version), Sloane, Staples, and Schneider (1985) compared the efficacy of 6 weeks of treatment with either IPT or nortrip-

tyline (NOR) in a small sample ($N = 43$) of elderly depressed patients. By the end of treatment, there was a nonsignificant trend for a superior response to IPT; however, this trend was largely due to patients' poor tolerance of medication side effects, and a corresponding high rate of attrition, in the NOR group. Although this study is frequently cited to support the relative effectiveness of IPT, the absence of details on dependent measures and data analytic techniques severely limit the contribution of this investigation.

There are three systematic studies of CBT of inpatients with MDDs. In a stringent test of the intervention, Thase and his colleagues (Thase, 1994; Thase, Bowler, & Harden, 1991) treated unmedicated MDD inpatients for up to 4 weeks with daily CBT. Although a large percentage of these patients responded well to CBT, not surprisingly the outcome was poorer for those inpatients whose HRSD scale scores were 25 or higher or who had hypercortisolemia. The other studies (Bowers, 1990; Miller, Norman, Keitner, Bishop, & Dow, 1989) have combined CBT with antidepressant medications, and this combination seems to reduce relapse among such patients if booster sessions of CBT are maintained following hospital discharge.

References

Addis, M. E., & Jacobson, N. S. (1996). Reasons for depression and the process and outcome of cognitive-behavioral psychotherapies. *Journal of Consulting and Clinical Psychology, 64,* 1417–1424.

Agency for Health Care Policy and Research (AHCPR) of the Department of Human Services. (1993). New federal guidelines seek to help primary care providers recognize and treat depression. *Hospital and Community Psychiatry, 44,* 598.

American Psychiatric Association. (1980) *Diagnostic and statistical manual of mental disorders* (3rd ed.). Washington, D.C.: Author.

———. (1993). Practice guidelines for major depressive disorder in adults. *American Journal of Psychiatry, 150*(Suppl.4), 1–26.

———. (1994). *Diagnostic and statistical manual of mental disorders* (4th ed.). Washington, D.C.: Author.

Beach, S. R. H., Sandeen, E. E., & O'Leary, K. D. (1990). *Depression in marriage: A model for etiology and treatment.* New York: Guilford.

Beck, A. T. (1976). *Cognitive therapy and the emotional disorders.* New York: International Universities Press.

Beck, A. T., Rush, A. J., Shaw, B. F., & Emery, G. (1979). *Cognitive therapy of depression: A treatment manual.* New York: Guilford.

Bellack, A. S., Hersen, M., & Himmelhoch, J. (1981).

Social skills training compared with pharmacotherapy and psychotherapy in the treatment of unipolar depression. *American Journal of Psychiatry, 138,* 1562–1566.

———. (1983). A comparison of social skills training, pharmacotherapy and psychotherapy for depression. *Behaviour Research and Therapy, 21,* 101–107.

Blackburn, I. M., Bishop, S., Glen, A. I. M., Whalley, L. J., & Christie, J. E. (1981). The efficacy of cognitive therapy in depression: A treatment trial using cognitive therapy and pharmacotherapy, each alone and in combination. *British Journal of Psychiatry, 139,* 181–189.

Blackburn, I. M., Eunson, K. M., & Bishop, S. (1986). A two-year naturalistic follow-up of depressed patients treated with cognitive therapy, pharmacotherapy and a combination of both. *Journal of Affective Disorders, 10,* 67–75.

Blatt, S. J., Quinlan, D. M., Pilkonis, P. A., & Shea, M. T. (1995). Impact of perfectionism and need for approval on the brief treatment of depression: The National Institute of Mental Health Treatment of Depression Collaborative Research Program revisited. *Journal of Consulting and Clinical Psychology, 63,* 125–132.

Bothwell, S., & Weissman, M. M. (1977). Social impairments four years after an acute depressive episode. *American Journal of Orthopsychiatry, 47,* 231–237.

Bowers, W. A. (1990). Treatment of depressed in-patients: Cognitive therapy plus medication, relaxation plus medication, and medication alone. *British Journal of Psychiatry, 156,* 73–78.

Craighead, W. E. (1990). There's a place for us: All of us. *Behavior Therapy, 21,* 3–23.

Craighead, W. E., Evans, D. D., & Robins, C. J. (1992). Unipolar depression. In S. M. Turner, K. S. Calhoun, & H. E. Adams (Eds.), *Handbook of clinical behavior therapy* (2nd ed., pp. 99–116). New York: John Wiley.

Cronbach, L. J., & Snow, R. E. (1977). *Aptitudes and instructional methods.* New York: Irvington.

Depression Guideline Panel. (1993). *Clinical Practice Guideline Number 5: Depression in Primary Care, 2: Treatment of Major Depression.* Rockville, MD: US Dept. of Health and Human Services, Agency for Health Care Policy and Research. AHCPR publication 93-0551.

DiMascio, A., Weissman, M. M., Prusoff, B. A., Neu, C., Zwilling, M., & Klerman, G. L. (1979). Differential symptom reduction by drugs and psychotherapy in acute depression. *Archives of General Psychiatry, 36,* 1450–1456.

Elkin, I., Gibbons, R. D., Shea, M. T., & Shaw, B. F. (1996). Science is not a trial (but it can sometimes be a tribulation). *Journal of Consulting and Clinical Psychology, 64,* 92–103.

Elkin, I., Gibbons, R. D., Shea, M. T., Sotsky, S. M., Watkins, J. T., Pilkonis, P. A., & Hedeker, D. (1995). Initial severity and differential treatment outcome in the National Institute of Mental Health Treatment of Depression Collaborative Research Program. *Journal of Consulting and Clinical Psychology, 63,* 841–847.

Elkin, I., Parloff, M. B., Hadley, S. W., & Autry, J. H. (1985). NIMH treatment of depression collaborative research program: Background and research plan. *Archives of General Psychiatry, 42,* 305–316.

Elkin, I., Shea, M. T., Watkins, J. T., Imber, S. D., Sotsky, S. M., Collins, J. F., Glass, D. R., Pilkonis, P. A., Leber, W. R., Docherty, J. P., Fiester, S. J., & Parloff, M. B. (1989). National Institute of Mental Health Treatment of Depression Collaborative Research Program: General effectiveness of treatments. *Archives of General Psychiatry, 46,* 971–982.

Evans, M. D., Hollon, S. D., DeRubeis, R. J., Piasecki, J. M., Grove, W. M., Garvey, M. J., & Tuason, V. B. (1992). Differential relapse following cognitive therapy and pharmacotherapy for depression. *Archives of General Psychiatry, 49,* 802–808.

Ferster, C. B. (1973). A functional analysis of depression. *American Psychologist, 28,* 857–870.

Frank, E., Kupfer, D. J., Jacob, M., & Jarrett, D. (1987). Personality features and response to acute treatment in recurrent depression. *Journal of Personality Disorders, 1,* 14–26.

Frank, E., Kupfer, D. J., Perel, T. M., Cornes, C. L., Jarrett, D. J., Mallinger, A., Thase, M. E., McEachran, A. B., & Grochocinski, V. J. (1990). Three-year outcomes for maintenance therapies in recurrent depression. *Archives of General Psychiatry, 47,* 1093–1099.

Greenberg, P. E., Stiglin, L. E., Finkelstein, S. N., & Berndt, E. R. (1993). The economic burden of depression in 1990. *Journal of Clinical Psychiatry, 54,* 405–418.

Hersen, M., Bellack, A. S., Himmelhoch, J. M., & Thase, M. E. (1984). Effects of social skill training, amitriptyline, and psychotherapy in unipolar depressed women. *Behavior Therapy, 15,* 21–40.

Hollon, S. D., DeRubeis, R. J., Evans, M. D., Wiemer, M. J., Garvey, M. J., Grove, W. M., & Tuason, V. B. (1992). Cognitive therapy and pharmacotherapy for depression: Singly and in combination. *Archives of General Psychiatry, 49,* 774–781.

Hollon, S. D., Shelton, R. C., & Loosen, P. T. (1991). Cognitive therapy and pharmacotherapy for depression. *Journal of Consulting and Clinical Psychology, 59,* 88–99.

Ilardi, S. S., & Craighead, W. E. (1994/1995). Personality

pathology and response to somatic treatments for major depression: A critical review. *Depression, 2,* 200–217.

Jacobson, N. S., Dobson, K. S., Fruzetti, A. E., Schmaling, K. B., & Salusky, S. (1991). Marital therapy as a treatment for depression. *Journal of Consulting and Clinical Psychology, 59,* 547–557.

Jacobson, N. S., Dobson, K. S., Truax, P. A., Addis, M. E., Koerner, K., Gollan, J. K., Gortner, E., & Prince, S. E. (1996). A component analysis of cognitive-behavioral treatment for depression. *Journal of Consulting and Clinical Psychology, 64,* 295–304.

Jacobson, N. S., & Hollon, S. D. (1996a). Cognitive-behavior therapy versus pharmacotherapy: Now that the jury's returned its verdict, it's time to present the rest of the evidence. *Journal of Consulting and Clinical Psychology, 64,* 74–80.

———. (1996b). Prospects for future comparisons between drugs and psychotherapy: Lessons from the CBT-versus-pharmacotherapy exchange. *Journal of Consulting and Clinical Psychology, 64,* 104–108.

Jarrett, R. B., Eaves, G. G., Grannemann, B. D., & Rush, A. J. (1991). Clinical, cognitive, and demographic predictors of response to cognitive therapy for depression: A preliminary report. *Psychiatry Research, 37,* 245–260.

Johnson, J., Weissman, M. M., & Klerman, G. L. (1992). Service utilization and social morbidity associated with depressive symptoms in the community. *Journal of the American Medical Association, 267* (11), 1478–1483.

Kessler, R., McGonagle, K., Zhao, S., Nelson, C., Hughes, M., Eshelman, S., Wittchen, H., & Kendler, K. (1994). Lifetime and 12-month prevalence of DSM-III-R psychiatric disorders in the United States. *Archives of General Psychiatry, 51,* 8–19.

Klein, D. F. (1996). Preventing hung juries about therapy studies. *Journal of Consulting and Clinical Psychology, 64,* 80–87.

Klein, D. F., & Davis, J. M. (1969). *Diagnosis and drug treatment of psychiatric disorders.* Baltimore, Md.: Williams & Wilkins, 1969.

Klerman, G. L., DiMascio, A., Weissman, M., Prusoff, B., & Paykel, E. S. (1974). Treatment of depression by drugs and psychotherapy. *American Journal of Psychiatry, 131,* 186–190.

Klerman, G. L., & Weissman, M. M. (1993). Interpersonal psychotherapy for depression: Background and concepts. In G. L. Klerman & M. M. Weissman (Eds.), *New applications of interpersonal psychotherapy* (pp. 3–26). Washington, D.C.: American Psychiatric Press.

Klerman, G. L., Weissman, M. M., Rounsaville, B. J., & Chevron, E. S. (1984). *Interpersonal psychotherapy of depression.* New York: Basic Books.

Lewinsohn, P. M. (1974). A behavioral approach to depression. In R. J. Friedman & M. M. Katz (Eds.), *The psychology of depression: Contemporary theory and research* (pp. 157–178). New York: John Wiley & Sons.

Lewinsohn, P. M., & Gotlib, I. H. (1995). Behavioral theory and treatment of depression. In E. E. Becker & W. R. Leber (Eds.), *Handbook of depression* (pp. 352–375). New York: Guilford Press.

McLean, P. D., & Hakstian, A. R. (1979). Clinical depression: Comparative efficacy of outpatient treatments. *Journal of Consulting and Clinical Psychology, 47,* 818–836.

———. (1990). Relative endurance of unipolar depression treatment effects: Longitudinal follow-up. *Journal of Consulting and Clinical Psychology, 58* (4), 482–488.

Merriam, A. E., & Karasu, T. B. (1996). The role of psychotherapy in the treatment of depression: Review of two practice guidelines. *Archives of General Psychiatry, 53,* 301–302.

Meyer, A. (1957). *Psychobiology: A science of man.* Springfield, Ill.: Charles C Thomas.

Miller, I. W., Norman, W. H., Keitner, G. I., Bishop, S. B., & Dow, M. G. (1989). Cognitive-behavioral treatment of depressed inpatients. *Behavior Therapy, 20,* 25–47.

Murphy, G. E., Simons, A. D., Wetzel, R. D., & Lustman, P. J. (1984). Cognitive therapy and pharmacotherapy: Singly and together in the treatment of depression. *Archives of General Psychiatry, 41,* 33–41.

Nietzel, M. T., Russell, R. L., Hemmings, K. A., & Gretter, M. L. (1987). Clinical significance of psychotherapy for unipolar depression: A meta-analytic approach to social comparison. *Journal of Consulting and Clinical Psychology, 55,* 156–161.

O'Leary, K. D., & Beach, S. R. H. (1990). Marital therapy: A viable treatment for depression and marital discord. *American Journal of Psychiatry, 147,* 183–186.

Pilkonis, P. A., & Frank, E. (1988). Personality pathology in recurrent depression: Nature, prevalence, and relationship to treatment response. *American Journal of Psychiatry, 145,* 435–441.

Regier, D. A., Kaelber, C. T., Roper, M. T., Rae, D.S., & Sartorius, N. (1994). The ICD-10 clinical field trial for mental and behavioral disorders: Results in Canada and the United States. *American Journal of Psychiatry, 151,* 1340–1350.

Rehm, L. P. (1977). A self-control model of depression. *Behavior Therapy, 8,* 787–804.

———. (1990). Cognitive and behavioral theories. In B. B. Wolman, & G. Stricker, (Eds.), *Depressive disorders: Facts, theories, and treatment methods* (pp. 64–91). New York: John Wiley & Sons.

Robinson, L. A., Berman, J. S., Neimeyer, R. A. (1990).

Psychotherapy for the treatment of depression: A comprehensive review of controlled outcome research. *Psychological Bulletin, 108,* 30–49.

Rude, S. S., & Rehm, L. P. (1991). Response to treatments for depression: The role of initial status on targeted cognitive and behavioral skills. *Clinical Psychology Review, 11,* 493–514.

Rush, A. J. (1996). The role of psychotherapy in the treatment of depression: Review of two practice guidelines. *Archives of General Psychiatry, 53,* 298–300.

Rush, A. J., Beck, A. T., Kovacs, M., & Hollon, S. D. (1977). Comparative efficacy of cognitive therapy in the treatment of depressed outpatients. *Cognitive Therapy and Research, 1,* 17–36.

Shea, M. T., Elkin, I., Imber, S. D., Sotsky, S. M., Watkins, J. T., Collins, J. F., Pilkonis, P. A., Beckham, E., Glass, D. R., Dolan, R. T., & Parloff, M. B. (1992). Course of depressive symptoms over follow-up: Findings from the National Institute of Mental Health Treatment of Depression Collaborative Research Program. *Archives of General Psychiatry, 49,* 782–787.

Shea, M. T., Pilkonis, P. A., Beckham, E., Collins, J. F., Elkin, I., Sotsky, S. M., & Docherty, J. P. (1990). Personality disorders and treatment outcome in the NIMH Treatment of Depression Collaborative Research Program. *American Journal of Psychiatry, 147,* 711–718.

Shea, M. T., Widiger, T. A., & Klein, M. H. (1992). Comorbidity of personality disorders and depression: Implications for treatment. *Journal of Consulting and Clinical Psychology, 60,* 857–868.

Simons, A. D., Lustman, P. J., Wetzel, R. D., & Murphy, G. E. (1985). Predicting response to cognitive therapy of depression: The role of learned resourcefulness. *Cognitive Therapy and Research, 9,* 79–89.

Simons, A. D., Murphy, G. E., Levine, J. L., & Wetzel, R. D. (1986). Cognitive therapy and pharmacotherapy for depression. *Archives of General Psychiatry, 43,* 43–48.

Simons, A. D., & Thase, M. E. (1990). Mood disorders. In M. E. Thase, B. A. Edelstein, & M. Hersen (Eds.), *Handbook of outpatient treatment of adults: Nonpsychotic mental disorders* (pp. 91–138). New York: Plenum.

Skinner, B. F. (1953). *Science and human behavior.* New York: Free Press.

Sloane, R. B., Staples, F. R., & Schneider, L. S. (1985). Interpersonal therapy versus nortriptyline for depression in the elderly. In G. Burrows, T. R. Norman, & L. Dennerstein (Eds.), *Clinical and pharmacological studies in psychiatric disorders* (pp. 344–346). London: John Libbey.

Sotsky, S. M., Glass, D. R., Shea, M. T., Pilkonis, P. A., Collins, J. F., Elkin, I., Watkins, J. T., Imber, S. D., Leber, W. R., Moyer, J., & Oliveri, M. E. (1991).

Patient predictors of response to psychotherapy and pharmacotherapy: Findings in the NIMH Treatment of Depression Collaborative Research Program. *American Journal of Psychiatry, 148,* 997–1008.

Spitzer, R. L., Endicott, J., & Robins, E. (1978). Research Diagnostic Criteria: Rationale and reliability. *Archives of General Psychiatry, 35,* 773–782.

Spitzer, R. L., Williams, J. B. W., Gibbon, M., & First, M. (1992). The structured clinical interview for DSM-III-R (SCID): I. History, rationale, and description. *Archives of General Psychiatry, 49,* 624–636.

Steuer, J. L, Mintz, J., Hammen, C. L., Hill, M. A., Jarvik, L. F., McCarley, T., Motoike, P., & Rosen, R. (1984). Cognitive-behavioral and psychodynamic group psychotherapy in treatment of geriatric depression. *Journal of Consulting and Clinical Psychology, 52,* 180–189.

Sullivan, H. S. (1953). *The interpersonal theory of psychiatry.* New York: Norton.

Teasdale, J. D., Fennell, M. J., Hibbert, G. A., & Amies, P. L. (1984). Cognitive therapy for major depressive disorder in primary care. *British Journal of Psychiatry, 144,* 400–406.

Thase, M. E. (1994). Cognitive behavior therapy of severe unipolar depression. In L. Grauhaus & J. F. Greden (Eds.), *Severe depressive disorders* (pp. 269–296). Washington, D.C.: American Psychiatric Press.

Thase, M. E., Bowler, K., & Harden, T. (1991). Cognitive behavior therapy of endogenous depression: II. Preliminary findings in 16 unmedicated inpatients. *Behavior Therapy, 22,* 469–477.

Thompson, L. W., & Gallagher, D. (1984). Efficacy of psychotherapy in the treatment of late-life depression. Special Issue: Psychological treatment of unipolar depression. *Advances in Behaviour Research and Therapy, 6,* 127–139.

Thompson, L. W., Gallagher, D., & Breckenridge, J. S. (1987). Comparative effectiveness of psychotherapies for depressed elders. *Journal of Consulting and Clinical Psychology, 55,* 385–390.

Thompson, L. W., Gallagher, D., & Czirr, R. (1988). Personality disorder and outcome in the treatment of late-life depression. *Journal of Geriatric Psychiatry, 21,* 133–146.

Weissman, M. M., & Klerman, G. L. (1973). Psychotherapy with depressed women: An empirical study of content themes and reflection. *British Journal of Psychiatry, 123,* 55–61.

Weissman, M. M., Klerman, G. L., Prusoff, B. A., Sholomskas, D., & Padian, N. (1981). Depressed outpatients: Results 1 year after treatment with drugs and/or interpersonal psychotherapy. *Archives of General Psychiatry, 38,* 51–55.

Weissman, M. M., Prusoff, B. A., DiMascio, A., Neu, C., Goklaney, M., & Klerman, G. L. (1979). The efficacy of drugs and psychotherapy in the treatment of acute depressive episodes. *American Journal of Psychiatry, 136*(4B), 555–558.

Wells, K. B., Stewart, A., Hays, R. D., Bumam, A., Rogers, W., Daniels, M., Berry, S., Greenfield, S., & Ware, J. (1989). The functioning and well-being of depressed patients: Results from the medical outcomes study. *Journal of the American Medical Association, 262,* 914–919.

Whisman, M. A. (1993). Mediators and moderators of change in cognitive therapy of depression. *Psychological Bulletin, 114,* 248–265.

Wilson, P. H., Goldin, J. C., & Charbonneau-Powis, M. (1983). Comparative efficacy of behavioral and cognitive treatments of depression. *Cognitive Therapy and Research, 7,* 111–124.

12

Psychosocial Treatments for Bipolar Disorder

W. Edward Craighead

David J. Miklowitz

Fiona C. Vajk

Ellen Frank

Although pharmacological interventions are the primary treatments for bipolar disorder, psychosocial treatments have been designed to increase adherence to medication regimens, decrease hospitalizations and relapses, improve quality of life, and enhance mechanisms for coping with stress.

Several Type 2 and Type 3 studies have established that psychoeducation, designed to provide information to bipolar patients and their families about the disorder, its pharmacological treatment, and the treatments' side effects, leads to greater adherence to pharmacological treatments among bipolar patients.

Only one Type 1 study has evaluated an individual psychotherapy—cognitive-behavior therapy—as an ancillary treatment for bipolar disorder. Designed to alter specific cognitions and behaviors hypothesized to interfere with medication adherence, the intervention led to significantly better medication adherence and significantly fewer hospitalizations.

Five large-scale, Type 1 random clinical trials (RCTs) designed to evaluate the effectiveness of individual and family therapy are currently under way.

Approximately 1% of the adult population experiences bipolar disorder (Robins, Helzer, & Weissman, 1984; Weissman & Myers, 1978), and for over 90% of those patients the disorder is characterized by a recurrent course of mood fluctuation over the lifetime (American Psychiatric Association [APA], 1994). Bipolar disorder has a strong impact on patients' work and social functioning. Approximately one of every three patients shows deficits in work functioning 2 years after hospitalization (Coryell, Andreasen, Endicott, & Keller, 1987), and only 20% work at expected levels of employment during the 6 months after an episode (Dion, Tohen, Anthony, & Waternaux, 1988). Rates of marital distress and family discord are higher than those of the general population (Goodwin & Jamison, 1990;

Targum, Dibble, Davenport, & Gershon, 1981). The risk of suicide in bipolar patients is 10–15% (APA, 1994). Unfortunately, despite recent advances in the treatment of this debilitating disorder, it is estimated that fewer than one third of bipolar patients receive treatment—a lower percentage than that of any other major psychiatric disorder (Goodwin & Jamison, 1990).

One leading view of the etiology of bipolar disorder is that it results from biological dysregulations (with a major genetic component) that are either activated or maintained by psychosocial stressors such as negative family environments or stressful life events. Because of the biological dysregulations associated with bipolar disorder, pharmacological treatments are the primary line of intervention. In particular, the introduction of lithium carbonate has dramatically improved both acute and prophylactic treatments (Baastrup & Schou, 1967; Goodwin & Ebert, 1973). In more recent years, anticonvulsant agents have also been successfully used to treat bipolar disorder (Keck & McElroy, 1996). Thus, with either lithium or anticonvulsants, the majority of patients can now experience some level of mood stabilization with continued use of medication.

Ironically, although patients can now benefit more from psychosocial interventions due to the mood stabilization available through pharmacotherapy, adjunctive psychosocial treatments are utilized less frequently than they were before the introduction of lithium (Zaretsky & Segal, 1994–1995). Because biological treatments are relied on so exclusively, the National Institute of Mental Health (NIMH) consensus conference on bipolar disorders concluded that "perhaps the most underdeveloped area in the treatment of bipolar disorder . . . is the use of adjunct psychosocial therapies" (Potter & Prien, 1989).

Within the context of pharmacological interventions as the primary treatment for bipolar disorder, psychosocial interventions have been designed to increase adherence to medication regimens, decrease hospitalizations and relapses, and improve the patients' quality of life. The major possible components of a multifaceted psychosocial treatment program include psychoeducation, attention to medication adherence, individual cognitive-behavioral or interpersonal therapy, and marital or family therapy. In this chapter, we review the empirical outcome data for each of these treatment components; these data, while promising, are meager, so we also summarize the relevant major ongoing Type 1 clinical trials that we know to be in progress.

PSYCHOEDUCATION AND MEDICATION ADHERENCE

Bipolar patients frequently express resentment at how little information they receive about their disorder or their medications (Goodwin & Jamison, 1990). Yet, the few studies that do exist show a positive effect of psychoeducation for both patients and their families.

The primary focus of psychoeducation is the provision of information regarding the multifaceted nature of the disorder and its successful treatment. The issue of medication adherence is a particularly salient aspect of the education and treatment of bipolar disorder. Despite the high risk of relapse due to nonadherence, 18% to 53% of patients on long-term lithium maintenance do not adhere to their prescribed medication (Goodwin & Jamison, 1990). It remains to be determined if the situation will differ for the anticonvulsants.

In a naturalistic, 18-month prospective study of 37 adolescents whose bipolar disorder had been stabilized with lithium carbonate during inpatient hospitalization, the relapse rate among patients who discontinued medication was 92.3%, compared with 37.5% for patients who continued lithium prophylaxis without interruption (Strober, Morrell, Lampert, & Burroughs, 1990). Not only is the risk of relapse greatly increased by medication nonadherence, there is also a possibility of discontinuation-induced refractoriness to further lithium treatment (Post, 1993). Therefore, enhancing medication adherence is one of the most important goals of ancillary psychosocial treatments.

Seltzer, Roncari, and Garfinkel (1980) evaluated the effects of psychoeducation on medication adherence among 67 psychiatric patients (44 schizophrenic, 16 bipolar, and 7 unipolar affective) who were treated with neuroleptic, lithium, or tricyclic antidepressant drugs. Within each diagnostic group, patients were divided into control and experimental groups. Patients in the experimental group were given a series of nine lectures about the nature of their disorder and its pharmacological management. "Educated" patients tended to adhere better to medication regimes at the outpatient follow-up 5 months later, and they were less fearful of medication side effects and addiction. Medication adherence was negatively related to fear of side effects and positively related to education and the resulting knowledge about the disorder and its treatment.

Peet and Harvey (1991) evaluated a more minimal psychoeducational intervention—a 12-minute videotape lecture and written handout containing factual information about lithium. Of consecutive patients attending a lithium clinic, 60 were randomly assigned to one of two groups: one group (N = 30) received the educational program immediately, and the other group of 30 served as a wait-list control group and were not given the program until 6 weeks later. After the wait-list control group had also received the educational program, the preintervention and postintervention data were also analyzed for all 60 patients. The educational program resulted in significant increases in patient knowledge about lithium; for example, their knowledge increased from a baseline comparable to that of social workers to a level similar to that of community psychiatric nurses. Patients' attitudes toward lithium also became more favorable after education. For all 60 patients, medication adherence improved, as measured by either self-reported tablet omissions or plasma lithium levels (Harvey & Peet, 1991). Thus, it appears that even a very minimal psychoeducational component can improve both patient attitudes and medication adherence. Unfortunately, this study did not include a long-term follow-up, so it is not possible to determine whether these gains were maintained over time or whether this intervention led to lower relapse rates following symptom remission.

Only one study (van Gent & Zwart, 1991) has examined the effects of educating the partners of bipolar patients. The subjects in this study were 26 manic bipolar patients and their partners: 14 partners attended psychoeducation sessions without the partners being present, while the partners of 12 remaining patients served as controls. At postintervention and at a 6-month follow-up, partners who attended psychoeducational sessions demonstrated a greater knowledge of the disorder, medications, social support, and coping strategies. However, patients' medication adherence did not change over the 12-month follow-up compared with either the preintervention or the control group.

In a descriptive Type 3 study, 15 bipolar patients were followed as they received Yalom's (1975) long-term interactional group therapy in addition to maintenance lithium therapy (Shakir, Volkmar, Bacon, & Pfefferbaum, 1979; Volkmar, Bacon, Shakir, & Pfefferbaum, 1981). During the 2 years following entry into the group treatment, patients had a lower mean length of hospitalization and increased medication adherence when compared with their 2 years' pretreatment. Unfortunately, the lack of a control group limits the ability to draw conclusions about the effects of the intervention. Nonetheless, if positive results were to be shown in future efficacy studies, group treatments for bipolar patients might prove to be a simple and cost-effective adjunct to pharmacotherapeutic prophylaxis.

It is possible that patient education leads only to changes in medication adherence; however, there may be additional effects of the enhanced social support gained from education of the patient's family or spouse, such as lower rates of relapse or improved quality of life. Because of the limited size, scope, and design of the existing studies, all of which are Type 2 as defined in this book, the long-term effects of either patient or family psychoeducation are not yet known.

INDIVIDUAL COGNITIVE-BEHAVIOR INTERVENTION

To date, there has been only one completed Type 1 outcome study that has evaluated an individual psychotherapy as an ancillary treatment for bipolar disorder. This single study provides promising data for the employment of psychosocial interventions as adjunctive treatments to pharmacological interventions.

In this study of individual therapy as an ancillary psychosocial treatment for bipolar disorder, one half of 28 newly admitted lithium-treated outpatients were randomly assigned to receive only lithium, while the other 14 received lithium and an additional preventive compliance intervention based on principles of cognitive-behavior therapy (Cochran, 1984). The therapeutic program was designed to alter specific cognitions and behaviors that were hypothesized to interfere with medication adherence. The intervention consisted of six weekly individual 1-hour therapy sessions. At both posttreatment and 6-month follow-up, patients who received the intervention had significantly better medication adherence. Also, over the 6-month follow-up period, the intervention group had significantly fewer hospitalizations (2 v. 8). Although the groups did not differ significantly in total number of relapses (9 v. 14), patients in the intervention group had significantly fewer mood disorder episodes (5 episodes experienced by 3 intervention patients v. 11 episodes experienced by 8 standard-treatment patients) judged to be precipitated by medication nonadherence.

Marital and Family Interventions

Bipolar disorder occurs and is maintained within a family context that both affects and is affected by the disorder. Difficulties in marital and family relationships may increase the likelihood of bipolar relapse. In addition, just as the patient needs to understand the disorder and its treatment, the family or spouse needs to be educated about the disorder in order to cope with its effects on interpersonal interactions. Finally, more successful psychosocial treatment may be offered within the context of the marriage or the family.

Marital and Family Difficulties

The marital interactions of bipolar patients are often problematic, both during patients' episodes and during well intervals. In a study of marital interactional patterns (McKnight, Nelson-Gray, & Gullick, 1989), bipolar patients' interactions during manic episodes were highly active (including interruptions and conversational dominance by the manic partner); when the patients were in remission, there was a reduced interactional level, but it was not replaced by positive communication (such as generating positive solutions to problems). These findings indicate a need for problem-solving and communication training among this group of patients.

Stressful family environments are also predictive of the course of bipolar disorder. Specifically, if an episodic bipolar patient returns to a "high expressed emotion" (high EE) family, in which one or both key relatives (parents or spouse) show critical, hostile, or emotionally overinvolved attitudes, the patient has a greater risk of relapse in the next 9–12 months than a patient who returns to a "low EE" family, that is, a less critical and normally involved family (Miklowitz, Goldstein, Nuechterlein, Snyder, & Mintz, 1988; Miklowitz, Simoneau, Sachs-Ericsson, Warner, & Suddath, 1996; O'Connell, Mayo, Flatow, Cuthbertson, & O'Brien, 1991; Priebe, Wildgrube, & Müller-Oerlinghausen, 1989). Two studies also suggest that negative patient-relative verbal interactional patterns predict poor symptomatic and social functioning in 1-year community follow-ups (Miklowitz et al., 1988; O'Connell et al., 1991).

Treatment Efficacy Studies

A group at the Cornell University Medical College (Clarkin et al., 1990; Clarkin, Hass, & Glick, 1988; Glick, Clarkin, Haas, Spencer, & Chen, 1991; Haas et al., 1988; Spencer et al., 1988) has developed and tested an inpatient family intervention (IFI) for families of hospitalized psychiatric (including bipolar) patients. The IFI is brief—an average of nine weekly or twice weekly sessions involving both patients and key relatives—and focuses on helping participants to cope with the hospitalization and make plans for a positive postdischarge adjustment. Similar to an outpatient,

crisis-oriented family program developed by Goldstein and his colleagues (Goldstein, Rodnick, Evans, May, & Steinberg, 1978) for schizophrenic patients, IFI encourages patients and family members to (1) accept that the disorder is real and probably chronic, and that medical and psychosocial treatments will be necessary after hospital discharge; (2) identify stressors both within and outside of the family (e.g., aversive family interaction patterns or stressful events) that may precipitate episodes of psychiatric disorder; and (3) learn ways to modify these family patterns and cope with future stressors (Glick et al., 1991).

In a Type 2, controlled clinical trial ($N = 186$) with hospitalized patients with major affective, schizophrenic, and other DSM-III (Diagnostic and Statistical Manual of Mental Disorders, third edition; APA, 1980) Axis I disorders, IFI was combined with standard hospital treatment (including pharmacotherapy) and compared to hospital treatment alone. At hospital discharge, the treatment effects were mostly evident in female patients with affective (including bipolar) disorders. However, the treatment effects were broader at 6-month and 18-month posthospital follow-ups: female patients with major affective and schizophrenic disorders performed better in the global functioning and symptomatic domains if they had received IFI than if they had received the comparison treatment. Finally, among female patients from the affective and schizophrenic groups, family treatment was associated with improvements at 6 and 18 months in certain measures of family attitudes, including feelings of rejection held by family members toward the patient and perceptions of family burden (Clarkin et al., 1990; Glick et al., 1991; Spencer et al., 1988).

Of the 50 affective disorder patients, 21 met criteria for bipolar disorder (Clarkin et al., 1990). When the treatment effects for bipolar patients were graphed separately by gender, treatment effects were only seen among the 14 female bipolar patients; thus, the sample size is too small to allow firm conclusions about the treatment's effects on this population. Furthermore, the obtained effect seems to have been due largely to the poor showing for standardized treatment for the female bipolar patients rather than a strong improvement among the IFI female bipolar patients. Perhaps due to lack of statistical power, the effect of treatment on global functioning for bipolar patients alone was only marginally significant at 6 months, and it was nonsignificant at 18 months. For role functioning (e.g., work performance), the effect of treatment was not significant at 6 months, but it was significant at 18 months. The trend for improved family attitudes toward the patient at 6 months was not apparent at 18 months. In short, while psychoeducational family treatment for bipolar patients may be a useful adjunctive therapy, the results from this encouraging study are equivocal and difficult to interpret.

Miller, Keitner, Bishop, and Ryan (1991) at Brown University Medical Center have studied the families of 24 manic bipolar patients. They found that patients whose families were rated as dysfunctional during the acute period of the manic episode had twice the rate of rehospitalization over a 5-year follow-up when compared with the other manic patients in this study. This led them to conduct a small, Type 3, pilot study comparing standard treatment (including medications) with standard treatment (including medications) plus family therapy. In the study, 14 patients were randomly assigned to one of the two treatments ($N = 7$ per condition), which began during hospitalization and continued for 18 weeks after discharge, with each patient in the combined standard treatment/family therapy group receiving 8–12 sessions of family therapy in addition to the standard treatment. At a 2-year follow-up, there was improved family functioning among the families of those patients who received the family therapy component. Recovery, as measured by two continuous months of absence of manic or depressive symptoms, was significantly greater for the standard treatment/family therapy regimen, and rehospitalization rates were one half those of the patients who only received standard treatment. Although the study was small and needs to be replicated in a large clinical trial, it points toward family discord as a major aspect of bipolar disorder and its amelioration as a primary goal of adjunctive psychosocial treatments.

Type 1 Clinical Trials in Progress

Based on the promising previous research on individual and family therapies as ancillary psychosocial treatments for bipolar disorder, there are now five controlled clinical trials under way to evaluate the effectiveness of individual and family therapy. Although these trials are not completed, the above-noted relevant findings and the promising preliminary data from these trials warrant a description of the treatments and a brief summary of the reported preliminary outcome data.

The following paragraphs describe treatments that are being evaluated in ongoing clinical trials at the University of Pittsburgh (Frank & Kupfer), University of Colorado (Miklowitz), and the University of California at Los Angeles (Goldstein & Miklowitz). Two other trials, one at Cornell Medical Center (Clarkin & Glick) and one at Brown University School of Medicine (Miller & Keitner), are evaluating similarly conceptualized marital and family interventions.

The individual therapy undergoing evaluation is interpersonal and social rhythm therapy (IPSRT), developed by Frank and her colleagues (Frank, 1995; Frank, Kupfer, Ehlers, & Monk, 1994). Although the social and interpersonal context is an important factor in bipolar disorder, some patients prefer an individual to a family treatment format. Furthermore, not all bipolar patients reside with families or have spouses. Because it focuses on interpersonal interactions and relationships, as well as rhythmic cycling, IPSRT psychotherapy may be particularly well suited as an ancillary treatment for bipolar disorder. It is an outpatient psychotherapy for bipolar disorder based on interpersonal psychotherapy (IPT) for depression (Klerman, Weissman, Rounsaville, & Chevron, 1984) and strongly influenced by the social rhythm stability hypothesis (Ehlers, Frank, & Kupfer, 1988).

There are two goals for IPSRT: (a) to help patients to understand and renegotiate the social context associated with mood disorder symptoms; and (b) to encourage patients to recognize the impact of interpersonal events on their social and circadian rhythms and to regularize these rhythms in order to gain control over their mood cycling.

Because bipolar disorder usually is a lifelong condition and may well require long-term prophylactic treatment, IPSRT does not have a specified length. In the clinical trial of Frank and colleagues, it is conducted weekly during a preliminary phase, then titrated to biweekly, and, if a symptomatic remission continues, is extended to monthly sessions for periods up to 2 years. The first stages of IPSRT involve assessments, including (a) taking a thorough history of the disorder, (b) conducting an "interpersonal inventory" in which the number and quality of relationships in the patient's social and familial network are identified, and (c) identifying a core interpersonal problem area. For unipolar and bipolar patients, these usually fall into one of several categories: grief over losses, interpersonal disputes (persistent conflicts with significant others), role transitions (disruptions in a person's work and social venues), and interpersonal deficits (deficits or disturbances in social skills). Furthermore, its originators (Frank et al., 1994) argue that patients with bipolar disorder also "grieve over their lost healthy selves," meaning that they experience intense sadness over the loss of their hopes, dreams, and aspirations brought about by their repeated episodes of mania or depression. Frank and her colleagues believe that this grieving is often at the root of medication nonadherence in that patients often discontinue their medications to "retrieve" the lost healthy self.

In the initial and continuing stages of treatment, the patient tracks his or her social routines and sleep-wake habits through a daily self-report measure, the Social Rhythm Metric (Monk, Flaherty, Frank, Hoskinson, & Kupfer, 1990; Monk, Kupfer, Frank, & Ritenour, 1991). In so doing, the patient begins to see how changes in daily routines affect his or her moods and identify those life events that trigger disruptions in daily routines (e.g., beginning a new job). The clinician strongly encourages the patient to stabilize and regularize these daily routines. The goal is to bring about an optimal balance in the patient's daily patterns of social activities, patterns of social stimulation, and sleep cycles, a balance that leads to the stabilization of mood states.

The majority of the IPSRT sessions conducted during the stabilization and maintenance phases of the disorder concern encouraging the patient to identify problematic interpersonal patterns and gain insight into the ways that their core problems in social and familial relationships (of the type reviewed above) have affected, and been affected by, mood disorder episodes. The clinician uses exploratory, clarifying, and interpretive interventions to guide patients toward better means of resolving these and other interpersonal problems in the future. For example, the clinician may explore and clarify the patient's grief over his or her lost hopes and aspirations and encourage the individual to set new life goals within the context of having a chronic illness requiring long-term drug treatment.

Interpersonal and social rhythm therapy is currently being evaluated in a Type 1, controlled efficacy trial by Frank and her colleagues. In this study, patients are randomly assigned (once during a preliminary treatment phase and again during a long-term maintenance phase) either to IPSRT with medications or to a comparison condition entitled "clinical status and symptom review treatment" (CSSRT), also with medi-

cations. Although this study is still in progress, the investigations have already shown a positive effect of IPSRT on social and circadian rhythm stability. Patients' daily rhythms became progressively more stable over 52 weeks if assigned to IPSRT, whereas patients in CSSRT—who also tracked their rhythms on a daily basis but did not receive IPSRT—did not regularize their daily routines over this same period (Frank, 1995). Results of this continuing clinical trial will determine whether IPSRT leads to delays in bipolar recurrences, perhaps as a function of the degree of regularity introduced into patients' daily routines. Nonetheless, one must remain cautious in drawing conclusions without the follow-up efficacy data.

Two other Type 1 trials currently in progress are evaluating the combined effectiveness of medication and outpatient family-focused treatment (FFT) (Miklowitz & Goldstein, 1990). This psychoeducational program is designed for patients who have been recently hospitalized or treated on an outpatient basis for a manic or depressive episode, and it is delivered in 21 outpatient sessions titrated over 9 months. The model is similar to Falloon, Boyd, and McGill's (1984) behavioral family management for schizophrenic disorders, but it is adapted to the needs of bipolar patients and their families.

The treatment model consists of five stages. First, there is a connecting and joining phase during which family clinicians explain the purposes of the program to patients and family members, learn the history and development of the most recent episode, and begin to develop a therapeutic alliance with the family. Second, during a functional assessment phase, clinicians conduct a series of evaluations of the family members' attitudes toward each other (EE) and the family's problem-solving styles and interactional behaviors. The third phase is primarily psychoeducational. In this module, participants are acquainted with facts about bipolar disorder: its nature and symptoms, the likely psychosocial precipitants of the patient's most recent episode, and avenues for preventing or at least minimizing the negative consequences of future episodes. There is a particular emphasis during psychoeducation, and throughout FFT, on exploring and confronting a patient's nonadherence to the prescribed medication regimen, a high-risk behavior that can often be linked to dynamics within the family.

As the patient begins to remit from the index manic or depressive episode and enters a postepisode maintenance phase, the individual and the family participate in skill-training exercises designed to decrease family stressors and increase the protective efforts of the family milieu. In the fourth treatment phase, communication enhancement training, participants learn to use basic communication skills (listening, delivering positive or negative feedback, or making requests for change in other family members' behaviors) through role-playing and behavioral rehearsal exercises. Finally, participants learn problem-solving techniques, including defining problems, generating problem solutions, evaluating various solutions, and solving core family conflicts usually related to the disorder (for example, the patient's medication nonadherence or difficulty resuming work or a social life).

In an initial, Type 2, pilot study (Miklowitz & Goldstein, 1990), nine manic patients received the 9-month FFT protocol with standard, aggressively delivered medications. In a 9-month follow-up, only one patient had relapsed (11%), a rate that favorably compares with a 61% rate among 23 patients followed naturalistically, with similar medication regimens. Lithium levels were not monitored or controlled, so one cannot be certain that both groups received adequately administered pharmacotherapy. The sample size was also relatively small. Therefore, determining the efficacy of FFT awaits the results of the ongoing Type 1 clinical trials.

CONCLUSIONS

Completed studies of the psychosocial treatment of bipolar disorder are scant. Those studies that are complete suggest an advantage in the domains of medication compliance and symptomatic outcome for patients treated with both psychotherapy and medication over those treated with medication alone. These studies, however, have often employed small sample sizes, and the treatments have not been fully articulated or written into exportable manuals. Thus, there is a pressing need for more controlled research in this area, which is made even more evident by the promising outcomes of the relevant (but limited) prior empirical studies.

A key, but unanswered, question concerns the stages at which psychotherapy will be most effective with bipolar patients. Should psychotherapy begin during the acute episode and continue throughout the stabilization and maintenance phases? Alternatively, will patients who are first stabilized pharmacologically be more receptive to psychosocial treatments? What types of interventions will be most effective when patients are symptomatic versus remitted? Likewise, at what stage of the disorder will family members be most receptive to interventions targeting the family environment?

Furthermore, the subpopulations that will most likely benefit from various forms of individual, family, or group therapy need to be specified. Must bipolar patients achieve and maintain a certain level of cognitive and psychosocial functioning before they will benefit from psychosocial interventions? What interventions are most appropriate for bipolar I versus bipolar II patients, for rapid-cycling patients, or for those with and without psychotic features? Will psychosocial interventions most likely benefit the first-episode patient, or are they equally applicable to recurrent, chronic patients?

Answering these questions requires controlled Type 1 clinical trials of specific, manualized treatments, including documentation of treatment integrity (adherence to the treatment protocol and competence of the therapy delivered). Such studies will require careful selection and assessment of the domains of outcome that different psychosocial interventions presume to influence (e.g., symptoms, social-occupational functioning, and family functioning). The successful investigation of these questions may broaden prevailing views of the treatment of bipolar disorder beyond purely pharmacological approaches to integrative models that provide the patient with more powerful protection against relapses and recurrences of the disorder.

References

American Psychiatric Association. (1980). *Diagnostic and statistical manual of mental disorders* (3rd ed.). Washington, D.C.: Author.

———. (1994). *Diagnostic and statistical manual of mental disorders* (4th ed.). Washington, D.C.: Author.

Baastrup, P. C., & Schou, M. (1967). Lithium as a prophylactic agent. *Archives of General Psychiatry, 16*, 162–172.

Clarkin, J. F., Glick, I. D., Haas, G. L., Spencer, J. H., Lewis, A. B., Peyser, J., DeMane, N., Good-Ellis, M., Harris, E., & Lestelle, V. (1990). A randomized clinical trial of inpatient family intervention: V. Results for affective disorders. *Journal of Affective Disorders, 18*, 17–28.

Clarkin, J. F., Haas, G. L., & Glick, I. D. (Eds.). (1988). *Affective disorders and the family: Assessment and treatment*. New York: Guilford.

Cochran, S. D. (1984). Preventing medical noncompliance in the outpatient treatment of bipolar affective disorders. *Journal of Consulting and Clinical Psychology, 52,* 873–878.

Coryell, W., Andreasen, N. C., Endicott, J., & Keller, M. (1987). The significance of past mania or hypomania in the course and outcome of major depression. *American Journal of Psychiatry, 144,* 309–315.

Dion, G. L., Tohen, M., Anthony, W. A., & Waternaux, C. S. (1988). Symptoms and functioning of patients with bipolar disorder six months after hospitalization. *Hospital & Community Psychiatry, 39,* 652–657.

Ehlers, C. L., Frank, E., & Kupfer, D. J. (1988). Social zeitgebers and biological rhythms: A unified approach to understanding the etiology of depression. *Archives of General Psychiatry, 45,* 948–952.

Falloon, I. R. H., Boyd, J. L., & McGill, C. W. (1984). *Family Care of schizophrenia: A problem-solving approach to the treatment of mental illness.* New York: Guilford.

Frank, E. (1995). *Regularizing social routines in patients with bipolar I disorder.* Paper presented at the 34th Annual Meeting of the American College of Neuropsychopharmacology, San Juan, Puerto Rico.

Frank, E., Kupfer, D. J., Ehlers, C. L., & Monk, T. H. (1994). Interpersonal and social rhythm therapy for bipolar disorder: Integrating interpersonal and behavioral approaches. *Behavior Therapist, 17,* 143.

Glick, I. D., Clarkin, J. F., Haas, G. L., Spencer, J. H., & Chen, C. L. (1991). A randomized clinical trial of inpatient family intervention: VI. Mediating variables and outcome. *Family Process, 30,* 85–99.

Goldstein, M. J., Rodnick, E. H., Evans, J. R., May, P. R. A., & Steinberg, M. R. (1978). Drug and family therapy in the aftercare of acute schizophrenics. *Archives of General Psychiatry, 35,* 1169–1177.

Goodwin, F. K., & Ebert, M. (1973). Lithium in mania: Clinical trials and controlled studies. In S. Gershon & B. Shopsin (Eds.), *Lithium: Its role in psychiatric research and treatment* (pp. 237–252). New York: Plenum Press.

Goodwin, F. K., & Jamison, K. R. (1990). *Manic-depressive illness.* New York: Oxford University Press.

Haas, G. L., Glick, I. D., Clarkin, J. F., Spencer, J. H., Lewis, A. B., Peyser, J., DeMane, N., Good-Ellis, M., Harris, E., & Lestelle, V. (1988). Inpatient family intervention: A randomized clinical trial: II. Results at hospital discharge. *Archives of General Psychiatry, 45,* 217–224.

Harvey, N. S., & Peet, M. (1991). Lithium maintenance: II. Effects of personality and attitude on health information acquisition and compliance. *British Journal of Psychiatry, 158,* 200–204.

Keck, P. E., & McElroy, S. L. (1996). Outcome in the pharmacological treatment of bipolar disorder. *Journal of Clinical Psychopharmacology, 16*(Suppl. 1), 15–23.

Klerman, G. L., Weissman, M. M., Rounsaville, B. J., & Chevron, E. S. (1984). *Interpersonal psychotherapy of depression.* New York: Basic Books.

McKnight, D. L., Nelson-Gray, R. O., & Gullick, E. (1989). Interactional patterns of bipolar patients and their spouses. *Journal of Psychopathology and Behavioral Assessment, 11,* 269–289.

Miklowitz, D. J., & Goldstein, M. J. (1990). Behavioral family treatment for patients with bipolar affective disorder. Special issue: Recent developments in the behavioral treatment of chronic psychiatric illness. *Behavior Modification, 14,* 457–489.

Miklowitz, D. J., Goldstein, M. J., Nuechterlein, K. H., Snyder, K. S., & Mintz, J. (1988). Family factors and the course of bipolar affective disorder. *Archives of General Psychiatry, 45,* 225–231.

Miklowitz, D. J., Simoneau, T. L., Sachs-Ericsson, N., Warner, R., & Suddath, R. (1996). Family risk indicators in the course of bipolar affective disorder. In E. Mundt et. al., *Interpersonal factors in the origin and course of affective disorders* (pp. 204–217). London: Gaskell Press.

Miller, I. W., Keitner, G. I., Bishop, D. S., & Ryan, C. E. (1991, November). *Families of bipolar patients: Dysfunction, course of illness, and pilot treatment study.* Paper presented at the meetings of the Association for the Advancement of Behavior Therapy, New York.

Monk, T. K., Flaherty, J. F., Frank, E., Hoskinson, K., & Kupfer, D. J. (1990). The Social Rhythm Metric: An instrument to quantify the daily rhythms of life. *Journal of Nervous & Mental Disease, 178,* 120–126.

Monk, T. H., Kupfer, D. J., Frank, E., & Ritenour, A. M. (1991). The Social Rhythm Metric (SRM): Measuring daily social rhythms over 12 weeks. *Psychiatry Research, 36,* 195–207.

O'Connell, R. A., Mayo, J. A., Flatow, L., Cuthbertson, B., & O'Brien, B. E. (1991). Outcome of bipolar disorder on long-term treatment with lithium. *British Journal of Psychiatry, 159,* 123–129.

Peet, M., & Harvey, N. S. (1991). Lithium maintenance: I. A standard education programme for patients. *British Journal of Psychiatry, 158,* 197–200.

Post, R. M. (1993). Issues in the long-term management of bipolar affective illness. *Psychiatric Annals, 23,* 86–93.

Potter, W. Z., & Prien, R. F. (1989). *Report on the NIMH Workshop on the Treatment of Bipolar Disorder.* Unpublished manuscript available from R. F. Prien, National Institute of Mental Health, Parklawn Building, 5600 Fishers Lane, Rockville, MD, 20857.

Priebe, S., Wildgrube, C., & Müller-Oerlinghausen, B. (1989). Lithium prophylaxis and expressed emotion. *British Journal of Psychiatry, 154,* 396–399.

Robins, L. N., Helzer, J. E., Weissman, M. M., Orvaschel, H., Gruenberg, E., Burke, J. D., & Regier, D. A. (1984). Lifetime prevalence of specific psychiatric disorders in three sites. *Archives of General Psychiatry, 41,* 949–958.

Seltzer, A., Roncari, I., & Garfinkel, P. E. (1980). Effect of patient education on medication compliance. *Canadian Journal of Psychiatry, 25,* 638–645.

Shakir, S. A., Volkmar, F. R., Bacon, S., & Pfefferbaum, A. (1979). Group psychotherapy as an adjunct to lithium maintenance. *American Journal of Psychiatry, 136,* 455–456.

Spencer, J. H., Glick, I. D., Haas, G. L., Clarkin, J. F., Lewis, A. B., Peyser, J., DeMane, N., Good-Ellis, M., Harris, E., & Lestelle, V. (1988). A randomized clinical trial of inpatient family intervention: III. Effects at 6-month and 18-month follow-ups. *American Journal of Psychiatry, 145,* 1115–1121.

Strober, M., Morrell, W., Lampert, C., & Burroughs, J.

(1990). Relapse following discontinuation of lithium maintenance therapy in adolescents with bipolar I illness: A naturalistic study. *American Journal of Psychiatry, 147,* 457–461.

Targum, S. D., Dibble, E. D., Davenport, Y. B., & Gershon, E. S. (1981). The Family Attitudes Questionnaire: Patients' and spouses' views of bipolar illness. *Archives of General Psychiatry, 38,* 562–568.

van Gent, E. M., & Zwart, F. M. (1991). Psychoeducation of partners of bipolar-manic patients. *Journal of Affective Disorders, 21,* 15–18.

Volkmar, F. R., Bacon, S., Shakir, S. A., & Pfefferbaum, A. (1981). Group therapy in the management of manic-depressive illness. *American Journal of Psychotherapy, 35,* 226–234.

Weissman, M. M., & Myers, J. K. (1978). Affective disorders in a U.S. urban community: The use of Research Diagnostic Criteria in an epidemiological survey. *Archives of General Psychiatry, 35,* 1304–1311.

Yalom, I. D. (1975). *The theory and practice of group psychotherapy.* New York: Basic Books.

Zaretsky, A. E., & Segal, Z. V. (1994–1995). Psychosocial interventions in bipolar disorder. *Depression, 2,* 179–188.

13

Pharmacological Treatment of Bipolar Disorders

Paul E. Keck, Jr.

Susan L. McElroy

Most pharmacological studies focus on treatment of bipolar I disorder. In general, studies have looked at both the treatment of acute mania and the use of medications as stabilizing agents to prevent recurrences of both the manic and depressed states. Lithium was first approved for the treatment of bipolar disorder in the United States in 1970 and remains an important medication. Five studies have demonstrated that lithium is superior to a placebo for the treatment of acute mania, although there are methodologic issues surrounding these studies. In seven controlled trials, lithium has also been compared to antipsychotic drug treatment for acute mania. These indicate that lithium is superior to antipsychotics in normalizing affective symptoms but has a slower onset of action compared to antipsychotics. Valproate and its divalproex formulation are also now approved for the treatment of acute mania, with six controlled trials supporting their efficacy. At least 5 double-blind controlled trials support the effectiveness of carbamazepine for the treatment of acute mania. A number of agents, including benzodiazepines, typical antipsychotics, and atypical antipsychotics, have also been studied for the treatment of acute mania. For the maintenance therapy of bipolar I disorder, 10 double-blind, placebo-controlled studies involving 514 patients have demonstrated that lithium is superior to a placebo in preventing recurrent affective episodes. However, a significant proportion of patients does not respond adequately to lithium maintenance therapy. Six controlled studies, one against a placebo and five against lithium, have assessed the efficacy of carbamazepine in the maintenance treatment of bipolar disorder. These studies are generally inconclusive as carbamazepine's effects appear to be incomplete for most patients. There are no published controlled trials of valproate maintenance treatment for bipolar disorder to date, although a 1-year maintenance study comparing valproate, lithium, and a placebo is nearing completion. Retrospective and prospective case series and open trials suggest that valproate may be an effective agent for maintenance therapy of bipolar I disorder.

Bipolar disorder (manic-depressive illness) is a severe psychiatric illness and a major public health problem. Estimates of the lifetime prevalence of bipolar disorder from two major surveys of the general population in the United States indicate that 1.0–1.6% of the adult population and 1.2% of children and adolescents (ages 9–17 years) are affected by this illness (1,2). Bipolar disorder is a recurrent illness. At least 80% of patients who have an initial episode of mania will have one or more subsequent episodes (3). Moreover, full functional recovery between episodes often lags behind symptomatic recovery (4), and in long-term outcome studies extending up to 4 years, less than half of patients followed after an initial manic episode had sustained a good response to treatment (5). In addition, recurrent affective episodes may cause progressive deterioration in functioning between episodes (6), and the number of episodes may affect subsequent treatment response and prognosis (7).

Thus, morbidity due to the illness is not limited to the acute affective episodes but may linger and lead to prolonged deficits in psychosocial and vocational functioning. For example, a study sponsored by the U.S. Public Health Service of the long-term impact of bipolar disorder estimated that, without adequate treatment, an average woman experiencing the onset of bipolar disorder at age 25 can expect a 9-year reduction in life expectancy, 14 years of cumulative loss of productivity (vocational, scholastic, and parental), and 12 years of overt illness (8).

Bipolar disorder is also a lethal illness. Suicide attempts are made by at least 25% of patients (9), and up to one half of patients with mixed mania are suicidal at the time of presentation for treatment (10).

Genetic studies reveal that bipolar disorder is a highly heritable illness (11). Concordance rates for monozygotic twins in bipolar illness are approximately 65–70%, whereas concordance rates for dizygotic twins are approximately 14% (11). In family studies, the risks for bipolar and unipolar illness among first-degree relatives of bipolar patients are clearly increased compared to risks for these disorders in first-degree relatives of people without psychiatric illnesses (11).

The *Diagnostic and Statistical Manual of Mental Disorders* (*DSM-IV*) describes four types of bipolar disorders: bipolar I disorder, bipolar II disorder, cyclothymic disorder, and bipolar disorder not otherwise specified (12). The *DSM-IV* criteria for manic, hypomanic, depressive, and mixed episodes are summarized in Table 13.1.

The criteria for bipolar I disorder require the presence of at least one manic or mixed episode; the manic or mixed episode is not better accounted for by schizoaffective disorder; is not superimposed on schizophrenia, schizophreniform disorder, delusional disorder, or psychotic disorder not otherwise specified; and is not due to a general medical condition or a substance-induced disorder. The criteria for bipolar II disorder require the presence of one or more major depressive episodes and at least one hypomanic episode, but without the occurrence of a manic or mixed episode. The criteria for cyclothymic disorder require,

for at least 2 years (in children and adolescents, for at least 1 year), the presence of numerous periods of hypomanic and depressive symptoms during the 2-year period; the person has not been without hypomanic or depressive symptoms for more than 2 months at a time; and no major depressive, manic, or mixed episode has been present during the first 2 years of the disturbance. The bipolar disorder not otherwise specified category includes disorders with bipolar features that do not meet criteria for any specific bipolar disorder. For example, patients with ultrarapid cycling, who experience rapid alternation (over days) between manic and depressive symptoms that do not meet the duration criteria for a manic or depressive episode, would fall into this diagnostic category.

The vast majority of psychopharmacological treatment research has focused on patients with bipolar I disorder. Thus, this chapter reviews treatment of bipolar I disorder. Since the pharmacological management of bipolar I disorder involves the acute treatment of manic and depressive episodes and maintenance treatment to prevent cycling and recurrent affective episodes, we review below studies of both acute and maintenance treatment. Finally, because studies of the pharmacological treatment of bipolar disorder vary in design, we attempt to make careful distinction between conclusions based on randomized, controlled trials as compared to case reports, case series, or open trials. (See reference coding system at the end of the chapter.)

PHARMACOLOGICAL TREATMENTS FOR ACUTE MANIA

Lithium

Lithium was the first modern antimanic agent and has been the pharmacologic cornerstone of treatment for patients with bipolar disorder in the United States since its approval by the Food and Drug Administration (FDA) in 1970 (13). Five studies have demonstrated that lithium is superior to a placebo for the treatment of acute mania (14–18). However, several methodologic limitations should be considered in interpreting these studies. First, only one study (18) employed a parallel design; the earlier four studies were crossover trials of varying duration (14–17). Second, two studies utilized nonrandom assignment to lithium or placebo (16,17). Third, the diagnostic criteria used

TABLE 13.1 Summary of *DSM-IV* Criteria for Mood Episodes Occurring in Bipolar Disorders

1. Manic Episode
   A. A distinctive period of abnormally and persistently elevated, expansive, or irritable mood, lasting at least 1 week (or any duration if hospitalization is necessary).
   B. During the period of mood disturbance three (or more) of the following symptoms have persisted (four if the mood is only irritable) and have been present to a significant degree:
      1) inflated self-esteem or grandiosity
      2) decreased need for sleep
      3) more talkative than usual or pressure to keep talking
      4) flight of ideas or subjective experience of racing thoughts
      5) distractibility
      6) increase in goal-directed activity or psychomotor agitation
      7) excessive involvement in pleasurable activities that have a high potential for painful consequences
   C. The symptoms do not meet criteria for a mixed episode.
   D. The mood disturbance is sufficiently severe to cause marked impairment in occupational functioning or in usual social activities or relationships with others, or to necessitate hospitalization to prevent harm to self or others, or there are psychotic features.
   E. The symptoms are not due to the direct physiological effects of a substance or general medical condition.
2. Major Depressive Episode
   A. Five (or more) of the following symptoms present during the same 2-week period and represent a change from previous functioning; at least one of the symptoms is either (1) depressed mood or (2) loss of interest or pleasure.
      1) depressed mood most of the day, nearly every day, as indicated by either subjective report or observation by others (note: in children and adolescents, can be irritable mood).
      2) markedly diminished interest or pleasure in all, or almost all, activities most of the day, nearly every day.
      3) significant weight loss when not dieting or weight gain, or decrease or increase in appetite nearly every day (note: in children, consider failure to make expected weight gains).
      4) insomnia or hypersomnia nearly every day.
      5) psychomotor agitation or retardation nearly every day.
      6) fatigue or loss of energy nearly every day.
      7) feelings of worthlessness or excessive or inappropriate guilt nearly every day.
      8) diminished ability to think or concentrate, or indecisiveness, nearly every day.
      9) recurrent thoughts of death, suicidal ideation, or a suicide attempt or a specific plan.
   B. The symptoms do not meet criteria for a mixed episode.
   C. The symptoms cause clinically significant distress or impairment in social, occupational or other important areas of functioning.
   D. The symptoms are not due to the direct physiological effects of a substance or a general medical condition.
   E. The symptoms are not better accounted for by bereavement.
3. Mixed Episode
   A. The criteria are met both for a Manic Episode and for a Major Depressive Episode nearly every day for at least 1 week.
   B. The mood disturbance is sufficiently severe to cause marked impairment in occupational functioning or in usual social activities or relationships with others, or to necessitate hospitalization to prevent harm to self or others, or there are psychotic features.
   C. The symptoms are not due to the direct physiological effects of a substance or a general medical condition.
4. Hypomanic Episode
   A. A distinct period of persistently elevated, expansive, or irritable mood, lasting throughout at least 4 days, that is clearly different from the usual nondepressed mood.
   B. During the period of mood disturbance, three (or more) of the following symptoms have persisted (four if the mood is only irritable) and have been present to a significant degree:
      1) inflated self-esteem or grandiosity
      2) decreased need for sleep
      3) more talkative than usual or pressure to keep talking
      4) flight of ideas or subjective experience of racing thoughts
      5) distractibility
      6) increase in goal-directed activity or psychomotor agitation
      7) excessive involvement in pleasurable activities that have a high potential for painful consequences
   C. The episode is associated with an unequivocal change in functioning that is uncharacteristic of the person when not symptomatic.
   D. The disturbance in mood and the change in functioning are observable by others.
   E. The episode is not severe enough to cause marked impairment in social or occupational functioning, or to necessitate hospitalization, and there are no psychotic features.
   F. The symptoms are not due to the direct physiological effects of a substance or a general medical condition.

(American Psychiatric Association, *DSM-IV*, 1994, pp. 327, 332, 335, 338) to define bipolar disorder in the early lithium studies (14–17) were not necessarily comparable to those of *DSM-III-R* (19) or *DSM-IV*.

In the first placebo-controlled, crossover study, Schou and colleagues (14) reported a definite response based on a global impression of improvement in 12 (40%) and a probable response in 15 (50%) of 30 patients with typical bipolar disorder. Response was less robust in 8 patients with atypical features (which implied a schizoaffective diagnosis), with 2 (25%) displaying a definite response and 3 (38%) displaying a probable response. In the first study to use formal rating scales (i.e., the Wittenborn scale) and to analyze data statistically, Maggs (15) found lithium superior to a placebo in 28 patients randomly assigned to lithium or a placebo in a crossover trial. In the first U.S. study, Goodwin, Murphy, and Bunney (16) studied the longitudinal efficacy of lithium versus a placebo in 12 patients with mania and 18 with depression. Of the manic patients, 8 (67%) displayed a complete response and 1 (8%) a partial response. In the fourth study, Stokes et al. (17) used a crossover design with alternating 7–10-day periods on lithium or a placebo in 38 patients. The brief 7–10-day trial periods may have limited the opportunity for patients to display a more robust lithium response, while the equally brief placebo period may have been confounded by residual lithium effects. With these caveats in mind, Stokes et al. reported a 75% response rate (partial and full) on lithium as compared to 40% on the placebo. The only randomized, placebo-controlled, double-blind, parallel design trial of lithium utilized lithium as an active control in a study designed primarily to assess the efficacy of divalproex for acute mania (18). In this study, 17 (49%) of 35 patients receiving lithium displayed at least 50% improvement on the Mania Rating Scale (MRS) derived from the Schedule for Affective Disorders and Schizophrenia (SADS-C) as compared to 18 (25%) of 73 patients receiving the placebo. Pooled response rates from these five placebo-controlled studies (14–18) show that 87 (70%) of 124 acutely manic patients experienced at least partial improvement on lithium. Thus, although patients who responded to lithium may still have been displaying some symptoms of mania, it is important to consider that this response was attributable to lithium alone. When adjunctive treatment with antipsychotics or benzodiazepines is provided clinically, further improvement would be expected.

Lithium has also been compared with antipsychotic agents in seven controlled trials in patients with acute mania (20–26). Interpretation of the results of these studies is limited, in part due to the inclusion of manic patients with schizoaffective disorder, as well as bipolar disorder, and because of the possibility of a Type II error (failure to find a significant difference between treatments because of a small sample size) in most studies (20–23,25). In addition, although Takahaski et al. (26) compared the efficacy of lithium and chlorpromazine in 71 acutely manic patients, the low lithium doses used in this trial may have contributed to the finding of superior efficacy for chlorpromazine.

In the largest and most rigorous study comparing lithium and an antipsychotic, Prien, Caffey, and Klett (24) assessed the efficacy of lithium as compared to chlorpromazine in 255 acutely manic (both schizoaffective and bipolar) patients. Prien and colleagues assessed response according to degree of psychomotor agitation by demarcating patients into "highly active" or "mildly active" groups. In the mildly active group, both medications produced comparable and significant improvement on the Brief Psychiatric Rating Scale (BPRS), Inpatient Multidimensional Psychiatric Scale (IMPS), and Psychotic Inpatient Profile (PIP). However, side effects were more frequent and severe among the chlorpromazine-treated patients. On the other hand, in the highly active group, chlorpromazine produced more rapid reduction in measures of agitation, excitement, grandiosity, hostility, and psychotic disorganization than lithium during the first week of treatment. In addition, due in part to a rapid lithium titration schedule, dropouts of the lithium-treated patients were higher (38%) than in the chlorpromazine-treated group (8%). Nevertheless, by 3 weeks of treatment, both drugs were significantly and comparably effective. Prien et al. concluded that chlorpromazine was superior to lithium in ameliorating the symptoms of agitation in highly active patients. This finding was supported by the results of all but one (22) other study. Conversely, all studies found lithium superior to antipsychotics in normalization of affective symptoms. Finally, in the only study comparing lithium with an antipsychotic other than chlorpromazine, Shopsin et al. (25) found that haloperidol produced a more rapid reduction in symptoms of agitation than chlorpromazine or lithium. It is also important to note that, in all studies in which improvement in psychotic symptoms was measured (15–18), lithium produced significant improvement in these symptoms, as well as in affective symptoms.

In summary, data from the controlled trials reviewed above indicate that lithium is superior in efficacy to a placebo and is relatively slow in onset of action, usually requiring a 2–3-week trial at therapeutic levels to reach maximum effect. These data also suggest that lithium is superior to antipsychotics for the normalization of affective symptoms and exerts antipsychotic effects in its own right, but that antipsychotics have a more rapid onset of action and therefore, may be more effective initially and in the acutely agitated patient.

Valproate

Valproate and its divalproex formulation have been shown to be effective for the treatment of acute mania in six controlled trials (18,27–31). Two of these trials led to the recent approval by the FDA of divalproex for the treatment of acute mania in bipolar disorder (18,28). These studies include comparisons of valproate versus placebo in crossover trials without concomitant psychotropics (29,31), against placebo in a parallel group trial of lithium-refractory or intolerant patients (28), against lithium in a parallel group trial (27), and against placebo and lithium in a parallel group trial (18). The last three studies (18,27,28), which enrolled the largest patient samples, allowed as needed lorazepam at low dosages only during the initial week of 3-week trials.

In the first parallel-group, double-blind, placebo-controlled study (28), Pope et al. studied 36 patients with bipolar disorder, manic phase (*DSM-III-R*), who were either lithium refractory or lithium intolerant and randomly assigned to divalproex (N = 17) or to a placebo (N = 19). Compared with the placebo-treated patients, the divalproex-treated patients displayed statistically significant improvement on all three measures used to assess response: the Young Mania Rating Scale (YMRS), BPRS, and the Global Assessment of Functioning Scale (GAF). Of 17 patients receiving divalproex, 9 (53%) displayed a greater than 50% reduction on the YMRS compared with 2 (10%) of 19 patients receiving the placebo. Patients receiving divalproex required significantly less lorazepam, and there was no statistically significant difference in the frequency of side effects between the two groups. Fur-

ther, in responders the onset of antimanic response to divalproex appeared rapid, with significant improvement evident within the first week of treatment despite a gradual titration schedule.

In the second parallel-group, double-blind controlled study, Freeman et al. (27) compared valproic acid with lithium in 27 patients with bipolar disorder, manic or mixed phase (*DSM-III-R*). Both drugs produced significant and comparable improvement as measured by the MRS of the SADS-C, BPRS, and GAF. Patients with mixed mania were more likely to respond to valproic acid than to lithium.

In the largest parallel-group, double-blind, placebo-controlled pharmacological study performed to date in acute mania, Bowden et al. (18) compared the efficacy of divalproex (N = 68), lithium (N = 35), and a placebo (N = 73) in a 3-week trial in patients meeting criteria for manic disorder (Research Diagnostic Criteria) (32). The proportion of patients improving at least 50% on the MRS of the SADS-C was comparable for divalproex (48%) and lithium (49%) and superior to the placebo (25%). Among divalproex responders, significant improvement was evident by Day 5 of treatment; a gradual titration schedule was used, beginning at an initial dose of 750 mg/day. All patients with rapid cycling (N = 8) were randomly assigned to divalproex; four (50%) displayed at least 50% improvement on the MRS, which was comparable to the response rate of the overall divalproex-treated group. This response rate, though limited by the small number of patients, is notable since rapid cycling is associated with poor lithium response (33). Divalproex has also been reported to be effective in two open trials in patients with rapid cycling (34,35). Finally, significantly more lithium-treated patients dropped out of this study due to side effects than patients receiving divalproex or placebo.

In summary, pooled response rates to divalproex or valproic acid from these three parallel-design, double-blind, controlled studies (18,27,28) revealed significant improvement (i.e., at least partial response or greater than 50% reduction in manic symptoms) in 54% of patients, superior efficacy compared with a placebo (18,28), and comparable efficacy compared with lithium (18,27). As with studies of lithium for acute mania, it is important to remember that the response rates from these studies were attributable to valproate monotherapy and would be expected to be more pronounced clinically with the use of adjunctive agents.

Divalproex has been compared with antipsychotic agents in patients with acute mania in one study (36). Drawing on open data from two studies (37,38) that reported rapid (1–3 days) onset of antimanic activity when divalproex was administered via an oral loading strategy of 20 mg/kg/day (which produces serum valproate concentrations of approximately 85 mg/L within 24 hours), this study compared the antimanic activity of divalproex (20 mg/kg/day) versus haloperidol (0.2 mg/kg/day) over a 6-day trial. Haloperidol was chosen as the comparison antipsychotic since it was found to produce the most rapid antimanic effects in the study by Shopsin et al. (25). Divalproex ($N = 21$) and haloperidol ($N = 16$) were equally effective in reducing manic symptoms, as measured by the YMRS, and in reducing psychotic symptoms, as measured by the Scale for the Assessment of Positive Symptoms (SAPS), over the acute 6-day study period. Also, similar proportions of divalproex- and haloperidol-treated patients were considered to be acute responders (48% for divalproex and 33% for haloperidol). The greatest rate of improvement for both drug regimens occurred over the first three full days of treatment, and side effects were infrequent and minor for both agents. It is possible that response rates to either drug may have been higher with a longer treatment trial and that significant differences between the drugs may have emerged with a larger sample. However, as with studies of lithium, in this and other studies in which improvement in psychotic symptoms was assessed (18,27,28), divalproex exerted improvement in both affective and psychotic symptoms.

Carbamazepine

In at least 14 double-blind controlled studies reported to date, carbamazepine has been shown to be effective in the treatment of acute mania (39). However, only five of these studies are not confounded by the administration of carbamazepine with antipsychotics and/or lithium (40–44). This is an important limitation because the combination of carbamazepine and lithium has been reported to be synergistic when patients failed to respond to either drug alone (45,46) and because the use of antipsychotics or lithium in combination with carbamazepine, although understandable clinically, makes delineation of the contribution of carbamazepine to therapeutic outcome virtually impossible. Of the remaining five studies, only one was placebo controlled (41), two compared carbamaze-

pine to lithium (42,43), and two compared carbamazepine to chlorpromazine (40,44).

In the only placebo-controlled study ($N = 19$), which utilized a crossover design, Ballenger and Post (41) reported that 63% of patients receiving carbamazepine (from 11 to 56 days) displayed significant improvement on global nursing staff measures of depression, mania, anxiety, anger, and psychosis and on the BPRS. Patients typically experienced a relapse on the placebo.

In studies comparing carbamazepine with lithium, Lerer et al. (42) found a trend toward greater improvement on the majority of BPRS items in the lithium-treated group, a trend that may have become significant with a larger sample ($N = 28$). In addition, only 4 (29%) of 14 patients receiving carbamazepine were evaluated as having a good response, compared with 11 (79%) of 14 patients receiving lithium.

In the second lithium comparison study (43), 70% of patients randomly assigned to lithium or carbamazepine dropped out by 8 weeks of treatment because of lack of efficacy. Of the remaining patients, 36% of carbamazepine-treated patients were rated as improved (at least partial remission of symptoms), compared with 37% of lithium-treated patients.

Carbamazepine has also been compared with chlorpromazine in two studies (40–44). Okuma et al. (40) compared the two drugs in 60 acutely manic patients in a 6-week trial and reported a 66% overall rate of improvement for the carbamazepine group compared with 54% improvement in the chlorpromazine group. In addition, carbamazepine was much better tolerated than chlorpromazine. Grossi, Sacchetti, and Vita (44) reported similar results in a 3-week study ($N = 37$), with 55% of carbamazepine-treated and 68% of chlorpromazine-treated patients demonstrating at least partial improvement.

Pooled data from these five randomized, controlled trials of carbamazepine in acute mania revealed an overall response rate for carbamazepine of 50%, compared with 56% for lithium-treated control groups and 61% for chlorpromazine-treated control groups (differences not significant).

Combination Mood Stabilizer Therapy

There have been no controlled studies comparing the use of combinations of mood stabilizers (lithium, valproate, carbamazepine) with single mood stabilizer treatment. Recently, Small et al. (47) compared lithium combined with carbamazepine versus lithium combined with haloperidol in 33 acutely manic patients over an 8-week trial. At Week 8, the lithium-carbamazepine group had a 56% improvement on the MRS compared with 55% for the lithium-haloperidol group. In addition, both regimens exerted comparable improvement in psychotic symptoms. A number of other reports indicate that treatment with combinations of mood stabilizers is necessary for many patients to achieve full remission of symptoms (45,47–50). These reports suggest that combinations of lithium and carbamazepine (44,45), lithium and valproate (47), and valproate and carbamazepine (49,50) are effective in patients who have only a partial response to one agent.

Antipsychotics

Prior to the introduction of lithium, antipsychotic medications were one of few available classes of pharmacological agents for the treatment of acute mania and as maintenance treatment for patients with bipolar disorder (51). However, the arrival of lithium, valproate, and carbamazepine has limited the role of antipsychotics in bipolar disorder to the acute treatment of psychotic mania or psychotic depression and as maintenance treatment in patients refractory to monotherapy or combination therapy with the three primary antimanic/mood-stabilizing agents (lithium, valproate, carbamazepine) (52). Despite the availability of antimanic/mood-stabilizing agents without the liabilities of antipsychotic side effects, antipsychotics remain the most commonly used adjunctive treatments for psychotic mania (53). However, since no study has prospectively examined the response of acute mania to antipsychotics, mood stabilizers, or their combination according to the presence or absence of psychotic symptoms, it is unknown whether or not psychotic mania truly requires adjunctive antipsychotics for optimal response more often than nonpsychotic mania.

No placebo-controlled study of any antipsychotic drug for the treatment of acutely manic bipolar patients has been reported to our knowledge. Most controlled studies of standard antipsychotics, primarily chlorpromazine, were conducted in comparison to lithium and were reviewed above (20–26). Janicak, Newman, and Davis (54), in a meta-analysis of five of these studies, found significantly superior efficacy for lithium (89% responders; 11% nonresponders)

compared with antipsychotics (54% responders; 46% nonresponders; chi-square = 13.1; $dF = 1$; $p < .001$). Three other controlled studies found comparable efficacy when antipsychotics were compared with carbamazepine (39,43) or divalproex (36).

Data from a number of open trials suggest that clozapine may have acute and long-term mood-stabilizing effects (as well as antipsychotic properties) in bipolar disorder, including patients with mixed mania and/or rapid cycling with psychotic features refractory to treatment with mood stabilizers, electroconvulsive therapy, and standard antipsychotics (55,56). Clozapine has also been reported to reduce manic symptoms, mixed affective symptoms, and rapid cycling in bipolar patients without psychosis (55). No controlled, double-blind study of clozapine for the treatment of patients with bipolar disorder has been published to date.

Zarate, Tohen, and Baldessarini (55) recently reviewed 30 studies of clozapine for the treatment of patients with bipolar and schizoaffective disorder. Use of clozapine for acute mania (typically in patients with treatment-refractory bipolar illness) was reported in two open-label studies (57,58). In the first study, Cole et al. (57) rated 13 (87%) of 15 patients with acute mania, who had failed to respond to a minimum 6-week trial of 500 mg/day of chlorpromazine-equivalent antipsychotic treatment in conjunction with lithium (mean plasma level 0.8 mEq/L), as much or very much improved. In the second study, Kimmel et al. (58) found clozapine to produce substantial improvement in mood and psychotic symptoms in 10 (53%) of 19 patients who had failed to respond to or tolerate previous trials of lithium, valproate, and carbamazepine. These intriguing preliminary findings require careful confirmation in controlled studies.

A small number of open trials and case reports have described the use of risperidone for the treatment of acute mania (59–65). Singh and Catalan (59) described the successful treatment with risperidone (2–4 mg/day) of four patients with maniclike psychoses due to HIV encephalopathy. Goodnick (60) reported improvement in manic symptoms in two patients with bipolar disorder treated with risperidone (3 mg/day and 10 mg/day, respectively) who had not responded to lithium. In an open-label trial, Tohen et al. (61) administered risperidone (2–6 mg/day) to the ongoing mood stabilizer/benzodiazepine (and in some cases other antipsychotic) regimens of 12 bipolar patients with acute psychotic mania. Of the 12 patients, 7 (60%)

displayed greater than 50% improvement on the BPRS, and 10 (83%) displayed greater than 50% improvement on the YMRS.

Recently, Keck et al. (62) reviewed the records of 144 state hospital patients (91% of whom were treatment refractory) with schizophrenia ($N = 49$), schizoaffective disorder ($N = 81$), bipolar disorder ($N = 11$; 7 manic, 2 mixed, 2 depressed), or major depression with psychotic features ($N = 3$) who were treated with open-label risperidone for at least 2 weeks. Favorable response to risperidone was associated with the diagnoses of bipolar disorder, schizoaffective disorder (depressive subtype), and psychotic depression. However, all bipolar patients were receiving concomitant mood stabilizers.

Other data from small case series, however, suggest that risperidone may exacerbate manic symptoms, especially when administered in higher doses and without concomitant mood stabilizers (63–65). These preliminary findings require confirmation in randomized controlled trials.

Benzodiazepines

Three recent surveys (66–68) have reported that 37% (66) to 95% (67) of bipolar manic patients started on antipsychotics while hospitalized remained on these medications 6 months after discharge. These findings are potentially troublesome since patients with bipolar disorder are at greater risk for developing tardive dyskinesia than patients with schizophrenia (69–71), and most naturalistic long-term outcome studies suggest that maintenance antipsychotic treatment may increase the likelihood of depressive episodes (72–74). With the recognition that the three primary antimanic/mood stabilizers themselves exert antipsychotic effects in psychotic mania, several recent studies have examined the use of benzodiazepines as alternatives to antipsychotics as adjunctive treatments for acute mania (75–79). Lenox et al. (75) found lorazepam (mean dose 9 mg/day) and haloperidol (mean dose 13 mg/day) comparable in efficacy when used as an adjunctive treatment to lithium in 20 acutely manic bipolar patients over a 14-day trial. Bradwejn et al. (76) conducted a 14-day double-blind comparison of lorazepam (mean dose 13 mg/day at Day 14) and clonazepam (mean dose 14 mg/day at Day 14) monotherapy in 24 acutely manic patients. Treatment with lorazepam produced marked improvement of symptoms, while clonazepam failed to produce a significant

therapeutic response. The investigators hypothesized that the beneficial effects observed in the lorazepam group may have been due to its more rapid onset of action and greater bioavailability as compared to clonazepam.

Clonazepam has been studied in three other controlled trials in patients with acute mania (77–79). Two controlled trials (77,78), one comparing clonazepam with lithium in a crossover design (77) and one parallel-group study comparing it with a placebo (78), found superior efficacy for clonazepam. However, in both studies antipsychotics (haloperidol [76] and chlorpromazine [78]) were used in each treatment group, undermining the certainty with which the response could be attributed to clonazepam. Finally, Chouinard (79) has also reported preliminary results of a 1-week, double-blind, parallel-group study of clonazepam versus haloperidol. The findings of this study, as described by the investigator, suggested comparable efficacy for both drugs by 1 week.

In summary, it is important to note that all of these studies were limited by small sample sizes, short durations of treatment, and difficulties in distinguishing the putative specific antimanic effects from the nonspecific sedative effects of these drugs. Thus, although benzodiazepines have a useful role as adjuncts to the primary antimanic/mood stabilizers, there are no persuasive data that they have specific mood-stabilizing properties.

Other Pharmacologic Treatments

Calcium Channel Blockers

Eight controlled trials of calcium channel blockers for the treatment of patients with acute mania have been reported to date (80–87). Unfortunately, the majority of these studies are limited by the use of concomitant antimanic medications (lithium or antipsychotics), unclear descriptions of the phase of bipolar disorder the patients were displaying, small sample sizes, absence of quantitative measures of improvement, and the use of a crossover design (53).

The best available evidence for the use of verapamil in acute mania is limited to two small studies (80,82). In the first study, Dubovsky et al. (80) reported that five (71%) of seven patients displayed a marked reduction in manic symptoms in response to verapamil compared with relapse of symptoms on a placebo in a crossover study. In the other study, Dose et al. (82) reported at least moderate improvement of symptoms in seven (88%) of eight patients treated with verapamil, with five exhibiting signs of relapse when switched to a placebo. However, three patients received either a concomitant antipsychotic ($N = 2$) or lithium ($N = 1$). Recently, Pazzaglia et al. (87) reported moderate or marked reduction in manic and depressive symptoms in five (56%) of nine patients with ultrarapid cycling bipolar disorder treated with nimodipine as compared to a placebo in a crossover trial.

Given the limitations inherent in the available studies, further randomized, controlled, parallel-design trials with sufficient sample sizes are required to clarify the efficacy of verapamil, nimodipine, and other calcium channel blockers for the treatment of acute mania.

Thyroid Augmentation

Bauer and Whybrow (88) reported significant reductions in both manic and depressive symptoms in 11 patients with rapid-cycling bipolar disorder treated with high doses of levothyroxine added to ongoing mood stabilizers (lithium and carbamazepine). Baumgartner, Bauer, and Hellweg (89) recently reported the successful treatment of six patients with treatment-refractory non-rapid-cycling bipolar disorder with high-dose thyroxine. These preliminary findings require confirmation in controlled trials.

PHARMACOLOGICAL TREATMENT FOR ACUTE DEPRESSION

Lithium and Antidepressants

In contrast to the available research regarding the pharmacological treatment of acute mania, there are few controlled studies of the pharmacological treatment of acute bipolar depression. Of 17 controlled pharmacological trials investigating the treatment of acute bipolar depression, 9 evaluated the efficacy of lithium in comparison to a placebo or tricyclic antidepressants (16,17,90–96). All placebo-controlled studies of lithium utilized a crossover design with short time intervals, ranging from 1 to 28 days, of lithium or placebo treatments (97). These short time intervals limit the interpretation of the studies because of the potential confounding effects of lingering lithium ac-

tivity during the placebo period and because optimal lithium response for some patients may have required a longer trial (97). Furthermore, abrupt discontinuation of lithium may have contributed to a more rapid rate of episode recurrence than that attributable to the natural course of the illness (98). With these limitations in mind, pooled results from five studies that provided sufficient data to assess degree of response revealed that 29 (36%) of 80 patients with bipolar depression displayed an unequivocal antidepressant response to lithium, while overall 63 (79%) of 80 patients displayed at least partial improvement in depressive symptoms (97).

Two controlled studies assessed the efficacy of lithium against tricyclic antidepressants (90,99). Watanabe, Ishino, and Otsuki (99) found comparable efficacy for lithium and imipramine in a 5-week, parallel-group study of 5 patients. However, lithium plasma concentrations were low (0.3–0.6 mEq/L) in this trial. In the second study, Fieve, Platman, and Plutchik (90) compared lithium, imipramine, and a placebo in a 3-week parallel-group trial in 29 patients. Although both lithium and imipramine were superior to the placebo, the mean decrease in depression scores for the imipramine-treated patients (58%) was significantly better than for the lithium-treated patients (32%).

The remaining controlled studies examined the efficacy of tricyclic antidepressants in comparison to other antidepressants (100–107). In the most methodologically rigorous of these studies, Himmelhoch et al. (100) found tranylcypromine significantly better than imipramine in 56 patients (bipolar I, $N = 24$; bipolar II, $N = 32$) treated for 4 weeks without concomitant lithium. In this study, 21 (81%) of 26 tranylcypromine-treated patients displayed a significant antidepressant response compared with 10 (48%) of 21 imipramine-treated patients. Response rates did not differ between bipolar I and bipolar II patients. Furthermore, in a follow-up crossover study (107) of initial nonresponders, 9 (75%) of 12 patients who had not responded to imipramine responded to tranylcypromine, whereas only 1 (25%) of 4 patients who had not responded to tranylcypromine responded to imipramine. In a second study of a monoamine oxidase inhibitor (MAOI), Baumhackl et al. (101) found comparable efficacy for moclobemide and imipramine (without concomitant lithium) in a 4-week trial of 32 patients with bipolar depression. A greater than 50% reduction in depressive symptoms was observed in 9

(53%) of 17 patients receiving moclobemide and 9 (60%) of 15 patients receiving imipramine.

Two controlled studies (102,103) comparing serotonin reuptake inhibitor (SRI) antidepressants with tricyclics have significant methodologic limitations. In the first study (102), a double-blind, randomized comparison of fluoxetine and imipramine to a placebo, only 64 (72%) of 89 patients remained in the trial after 3 weeks, and only 44 (49%) completed the 6-week trial because of side effects or lack of efficacy. Furthermore, seven (16%) subjects completing the study received lithium, whereas the remainder did not. By counting treatment dropouts as treatment failures, the response rates in this study were not statistically different for fluoxetine (60%) and imipramine (40%), and both were superior to the placebo (17%) (97). In the second SRI comparison trial, Asberg-Wistedt (103) studied four patients randomly assigned to zimelidine or desipramine in a crossover design for 4 weeks each, but the small sample size makes this study inconclusive.

Of the three remaining controlled trials of antidepressants for the treatment of bipolar depression, one study compared maprotiline versus imipramine in 14 patients treated for 6 weeks (104). In this study, six (67%) of nine patients in the maprotiline group responded, and two (40%) of five patients treated with imipramine responded (differences not significant). In the second study, Sachs et al.(105) conducted a randomized controlled trial to assess the efficacy and rate of treatment-emergent mood elevation in depressed bipolar patients (DSM-III-R) (N = 19) when bupropion or desipramine were added to ongoing therapeutic regimens of mood stabilizers. Although both drugs produced comparable response rates, patients treated with desipramine were significantly more likely to switch into hypomania or mania (5 of 10 patients) as compared to patients treated with bupropion (1 of 9 patients). These preliminary findings require confirmation in a larger study. Finally, Levine et al. (106) recently reported no significant difference between inositol (12 g/day) and a placebo in a double-blind parallel group trial in six patients with bipolar depression (DSM-III-R). However, inositol was significantly superior to placebo in a larger (N = 22) group of patients with unipolar major depression treated during the same trial. Significant differences between inositol- and placebo-treated bipolar depressed patients may have emerged with a larger sample.

Antidepressant-induced hypomania/mania or cycle acceleration is an important risk of antidepressant treatment in patients with bipolar depression. Unfortunately, this phenomenon has not been systematically evaluated in most of the studies described above. Two recent studies have examined the risk of antidepressant-induced mania and cycle acceleration (108,109) Altshuler et al. (108) using life-chart methodology in 51 patients with treatment-refractory bipolar disorder, found that 35% of patients had a manic episode rated as likely to have been antidepressant induced. Acceleration of cycling was also found to be associated with antidepressant treatment in 26% of patients. Stoll and colleagues (109) compared antidepressant-associated mania (N = 49) with spontaneous mania (N = 49) in a case control study. Antidepressant-associated mania was milder in severity and briefer in duration than spontaneous mania. Among antidepressants, MAOIs and bupropion were associated with the induction of milder manic states than either tricyclics or fluoxetine. These findings are in agreement with the study of Sachs et al. (l05), who found a lower switch rate associated with bupropion than desipramine in patients also on mood stabilizers, and with the results of Himmelhoch et al. (100), who found that 21% of tranylcypromine-treated patients developed euphoric hypomania not typically requiring hospitalization, whereas 25% of imipramine-treated patients became manic, 18% with mixed mania and 11% requiring hospitalization. Interestingly, in a recent meta-analysis of the rate of treatment-emergent switch into mania, with data derived from clinical trials comparing SRIs (fluoxetine, fluvoxamine, paroxetine and sertraline), tricyclics, or a placebo in 415 patients with bipolar depression, Peet (110) reported that manic switch occurred significantly more frequently with tricyclics (11%) than with SRIs (4%) or a placebo (4%).

Carbamazepine and Valproate

Three controlled studies (46,111,112) have evaluated the efficacy of carbamazepine in the treatment of patients with unipolar and bipolar depression. Data from these studies indicate that, like lithium, carbamazepine may be less effective for the treatment of acute depression than for acute mania. In the first of these studies, a placebo-controlled crossover study (median 45 days per treatment interval), Post et al. (111) reported marked improvement in 12 (34%) of 35 patients (24 bipolar, 11 unipolar) with treatment-resistant depression. A trend toward greater improvement in patients with bipolar compared with unipolar depression was observed, and the switch to the placebo was associated with deterioration in carbamazepine responders. Although the finding of a 34% marked response rate is comparable with placebo response rates in parallel-design studies, this response rate is, nevertheless, impressive given the treatment-refractory nature of the cohort. In the second study, Small (112) described the results of an interim analysis of an ongoing study comparing the response of 28 patients (4 bipolar, 24 unipolar) with treatment-resistant unipolar and bipolar depression in a 4-week trial of lithium, carbamazepine, or their combination. All patients were then treated with both drugs for an additional 4 weeks. Of patients receiving carbamazepine or the combination, 32% displayed moderate or marked improvement compared with 13% of lithium-treated patients. These results are consistent with those of Post et al. (111), although the cohort studied by Small had significantly fewer bipolar patients. Finally, Kramlinger and Post (46) evaluated the antidepressant effect of lithium versus placebo augmentation of carbamazepine and found that 6 (46%) of 13 patients who had not responded to carbamazepine alone responded to lithium augmentation.

To date, there are no controlled studies of valproate in the treatment of acute bipolar depression. In three of four open studies (34,35,48,113), valproate appeared to be more effective for the treatment of acute mania than for depression.

Maintenance Treatment

Lithium

During the late 1960s and 1970s, 10 double-blind, placebo-controlled studies involving 514 bipolar patients demonstrated that lithium was superior to placebo in preventing recurrent affective episodes (13). The average relapse rate over 1 year was 34% for lithium-treated patients compared with 81% for those receiving the placebo. These data also revealed that lithium exerted greater efficacy in preventing manic than depressive episodes (13). However, more recent data from five naturalistic long-term follow-up studies of patients maintained on lithium for greater than 1 year indicate that a substantial number of patients do not respond adequately to lithium prophylaxis (114–118).

For example, in a study conducted by the National Institute of Mental Health (NIMH) from 1972 to 1982, only one third of lithium-treated patients remained episode free over an 18- to 24-month follow-up period (114). In a second naturalistic outcome study of 43 patients initially hospitalized for acute mania and followed for up to 1.7 years, those receiving lithium did not have a better outcome than those not receiving lithium (115). In a third study, Maj, Pirozzi, and Kemali (116) followed for 5 years, 50 patients with bipolar disorder who had remained in remission on lithium for an initial 2-year period. At the end of the 5-year follow-up, only 36% of these patients who had initially responded well to lithium maintenance treatment were still successfully treated. Maj and colleagues concluded that "the impact of lithium carbonate prophylaxis on the long-term course of bipolar disorder in ordinary clinical conditions is less dramatic than currently believed."

O'Connell and colleagues (117) followed for 1 year 248 bipolar patients receiving lithium. Although 56% of patients had no affective episodes during the year, when outcome was measured by GAF scores, the outcome of 40% of patients was good, 41% fair, and 19% poor.

Most recently, Peselow et al. (118) assessed the efficacy of lithium maintenance treatment using lifetable analysis in 305 bipolar patients who had been in remission for 6 months and then followed over 5 years. Lithium maintenance treatment yielded an average 83% probability against relapse after 1 year, 52% after 3 years, and 37% after 5 years. These probabilities would likely have been lower if patients who had relapsed within the first 6 months of treatment had been included. However, the 37% probability of remaining in remission on lithium after 5 years is similar to the 36% of patients who remained well in the study by Maj et al. (116).

In contrast, the risks of discontinuing successful lithium treatment appear to be substantial. For example, in a meta-analysis by Suppes et al. (98) of 14 studies involving a total of 257 bipolar patients who discontinued lithium, the risk of recurrent affective episodes was approximately 28 times higher per month without medication than with medication. More than 50% of patients who discontinued successful lithium maintenance treatment experienced a relapse (more often of mania than depression) within 6 months. In addition to the risk of relapse, Post et al. (119) have also identified a second risk of lithium discontinuation—the phenomenon of subsequent refractoriness to reinstitution of previously successful lithium treatment.

The optimal maintenance serum concentration is also directly relevant to successful lithium maintenance treatment. Gelenberg et al. (120) found that the risk of relapse was 2.6 times higher in bipolar patients randomly selected for low (0.4–0.6 mEq/L) serum concentrations compared with standard (0.8–1.0 mEq/L) serum concentrations. However, patients treated with standard concentrations experienced significantly more side effects. In a second analysis of data from this study, Keller et al. (121) reported that patients randomly assigned to the lower range of lithium levels were more likely to experience subsyndromal symptoms and that their symptoms were more likely to worsen at any time than were symptoms of patients in the standard level group. Furthermore, the first occurrence of subsyndromal symptoms increased the risk of full-episode relapse fourfold. These findings suggest that the optimal longitudinal management of bipolar disorder requires titration of mood stabilizer therapy to eradicate subsyndromal symptoms in order to minimize the risk of their escalation into full-syndromic relapse.

From the studies reviewed above, it is clear that a significant proportion of patients with bipolar disorder does not respond adequately to lithium maintenance treatment. In addition, patients display a wide variation of responses to lithium, ranging from remission, partial remission with varying degrees of attenuation of length and/or severity of episodes, suppression of one phase of illness but not another, no response, and, finally, relapse after initial good response (13). A number of studies have identified clinical features associated with lithium response. Findings from these studies indicate that a family history of bipolar disorder and a previous episode sequence of mania-depression-euthymia are associated with favorable lithium response (122,123). Conversely, patients with rapid cycling (33), mixed mania (124), episode sequence of depression-mania-euthymia (123), multiple prior affective episodes (125), comorbid substance or alcohol abuse or dependence (13,117), and familial negative affective style (117,126) are less likely to respond well to lithium maintenance treatment.

Carbamazepine

Six controlled studies have assessed the efficacy of carbamazepine for the maintenance treatment of patients with bipolar disorder (127–132). Okuma et al. (127), in the only placebo-controlled study, reported a 60% response rate after carbamazepine treatment for 1 year compared with 22% for patients on a placebo.

In five other controlled studies (128–132), carbamazepine was compared with lithium maintenance treatment. In the most recent study, Coxhead, Silverstone, and Cookson (132) found comparable response rates (50% of lithium-treated patients without relapse; 49% of carbamazepine-treated patients without relapse) over 1 year in 32 patients maintained on each mood stabilizer alone. In the other studies (128–131), adjunctive treatment with antipsychotics, hypnotics, and antidepressants was permitted for breakthrough episodes. A majority of patients in these studies required adjunctive treatment, although specific percentages were not provided. Thus, although all five studies reported the efficacy of carbamazepine in the reduction of affective episodes and prolongation of euthymic periods, this effect was incomplete for most patients.

Murphy, Gannon, and McGennis (133) have suggested that the methodologic limitations inherent in the comparison studies of carbamazepine versus lithium leave open the question of the efficacy of carbamazepine as a maintenance treatment, at least in comparison to lithium. This is underscored by the findings from two recent naturalistic outcome studies. For example, Frankenburg et al. (134), in a retrospective survey of 34 patients with bipolar disorder treated with carbamazepine for 3–4 years, found that only 6 (18%) remained stable on carbamazepine alone. Similarly, in a 4-year follow-up study of 24 patients with treatment-refractory affective disorders, Post et al. (135) found that one half of patients followed had relapsed after 4 years. In addition, the majority of patients required treatment with lithium and other agents.

The optimal carbamazepine plasma concentration required to minimize relapse of bipolar disorder is not known. Even in the treatment of acute mania, there is only a weak correlation between carbamazepine concentrations and response (136). Recently, Simhandl, Denk, and Thou (137) compared the efficacy of low (15–25 mmol/L) and high (28–40 mmol/L) carbamazepine plasma concentrations and lithium plasma concentrations (0.6–0.8 mEq/L, the range not studied by Gelenberg et al. [120]) for the maintenance treatment of 84 patients with bipolar disorder ($N = 52$) and recurrent unipolar major depression ($N = 32$) over a 2-year period. Unfortunately, 31% of patients dropped out and were not included in the statistical analysis. Of those bipolar patients completing the 2-year observation period, there were no statistically significant differences in the relapse rates among the three treatment groups. However, the overall sample size remaining in the three treatment arms at the end of the study was small, leaving open the possibility that significant differences may have been apparent with a larger sample size.

In contrast to the available data for lithium, there have been few studies of the clinical factors associated with response to carbamazepine maintenance treatment. In two recent studies (138,139), carbamazepine response was greater in nonrapid-cycling patients than in rapid-cycling patients. Okuma (138) reported that, in a study of 215 bipolar patients followed for 2 years, patients whose course of illness had been dominated by manic episodes with nonrapid cycling, had onset of illness before 30 years of age, and who were characterized by atypical symptoms tended to respond well to carbamazepine. Nevertheless, 53% of rapid-cycling patients had a favorable outcome on carbamazepine in this cohort—a response rate substantially higher than the 20% response rate to lithium in rapid-cycling patients (33).

Valproate

There are no controlled studies of valproate maintenance treatment of bipolar disorder published to date. However, a 1-year maintenance treatment study comparing divalproex, lithium, and a placebo is near completion and should provide important data bearing on this issue. Thus, evidence supporting the efficacy of valproate as a maintenance treatment for bipolar disorder is based on retrospective and prospective case series and open trials (35,48,113,140). Taken together, these studies suggest that valproate may reduce the frequency and severity of affective episodes over time, including for patients with rapid cycling (34,35) and mixed mania (18,124). These studies also suggest that valproate, like lithium, may be more effective in the prevention of manic and mixed episodes than depres-

sive episodes. Clinical features associated with response to valproate maintenance treatment in these studies included mixed mania, nonpsychotic mania, and absence of comorbid personality disorder (141).

Antipsychotics

As discussed above, despite the risks of neurologic side effects associated with antipsychotics and the possibility that they may increase the likelihood of depressive episodes when used for maintenance treatment, antipsychotics continue to be widely used in the long-term treatment of patients with bipolar disorder (66–68). For example, in a survey of 257 patients (215 with bipolar disorder), Sachs reported that 37% were receiving maintenance antipsychotics, usually in combination with lithium (66). In a second survey, Sernyak et al. (67) reported that 38 (95%) of 40 patients who received antipsychotics at discharge from a hospital continued to receive them at 6-month follow-up. Recently, Keck et al. (68) reported that 52 (68%) of 77 patients with bipolar disorder who were followed up 6 months after hospitalization for a manic episode continued to receive antipsychotics. Maintenance treatment at 6-month follow-up was associated with being male, medication noncompliance in the month prior to hospitalization, severity of manic symptoms at admission, and prescription of antipsychotic medication at time of discharge (68).

Surprisingly, no prospective, double-blind, randomized, parallel-design trial comparing antipsychotics and mood stabilizers for the maintenance treatment of patients with bipolar disorder has been reported. Five open studies have investigated the efficacy of depot antipsychotics alone or in conjunction with lithium and/or carbamazepine (74,142–145). All studies found significant reductions in the number of manic episodes and overall time affectively ill when compared with prior treatment intervals when depot antipsychotics had not been administered.

Two open, prospective, comparative maintenance studies of depot flupenthixol in patients with bipolar disorder have also been reported. In the first study, Ahlfors et al. (146) compared flupenthixol with lithium maintenance treatment for up to 3 years in 42 patients, but found that neither treatment significantly reduced the frequency of affective episodes compared with the pretreatment course of illness. These investigators also described a second group of 162 patients with bipolar disorder who were refractory to or intolerant of lithium who received open flupenthixol decanoate for up to 3 years (146). This last group displayed significant reductions in the frequency of manic episodes and percentage of time ill due to mania but also displayed significant increases in the frequency of depressive episodes and percentage of time ill due to depression. In the second comparison trial, Esparon et al. (73) compared the addition of depot flupenthixol or placebo to ongoing lithium treatment in a double-blind, crossover 2-year study of 15 patients, most of whom had responded poorly to lithium. No significant difference was found between flupenthixol and the placebo.

In summary, although open trials of depot antipsychotics suggest efficacy for these agents as maintenance treatments for patients with bipolar disorder (74,142–145), the only two prospective comparison studies, both involving flupenthixol decanoate, failed to find a significant therapeutic benefit (73,146). In addition, the apparent greater efficacy of depot antipsychotics compared with prior treatments in open trials may be attributable to noncompliance with the earlier treatment followed by more certain drug delivery inherent in injected medications (68).

In an analysis of 30 open studies of clozapine for the treatment of severe mood disorders, Zarate, Tohen, and Baldessarini (55) identified 10 reports that addressed the efficacy of clozapine maintenance treatment for a total of 94 patients with bipolar disorder. Despite the fact that at least one third of the patients had not responded adequately to or did not tolerate previous treatment with lithium, valproate, carbamazepine, and standard antipsychotics, alone or in combination, 71% of patients displayed clinically significant improvement with clozapine treatment and were successfully maintained on clozapine therapy alone or with other treatments for follow-up periods averaging 20 months. As in acute mania, these studies, although preliminary and in need of replication in controlled trials, suggest that clozapine may be a useful maintenance treatment for patients refractory to or intolerant of standard mood stabilizers.

Benzodiazepines

To date, of the benzodiazepines, only clonazepam has been studied as a maintenance treatment for bipolar disorder (147,148). The only controlled study of clonazepam in the prophylaxis management of bipolar

disorder examined clonazepam in combination with lithium. In this study, Sachs, Weilburg, and Rosenbaum (147) randomly assigned bipolar patients requiring combined treatment with lithium and haloperidol to maintenance treatment with lithium and haloperidol or lithium and clonazepam. Analysis of the first 12 patients (6 receiving lithium and haloperidol, 6 receiving lithium and clonazepam) completing 12 weeks of treatment revealed no significant differences in rate of relapse between the two groups. However, three of six patients in the clonazepam group continued to require concomitant haloperidol. In the only study that attempted to assess the efficacy of clonazepam alone as a maintenance treatment, Aronson, Shukla, and Hirschowitz (148) prematurely terminated an open trial after the first five patients relapsed within the first 2 to 15 weeks of treatment. Thus, there are no compelling data to suggest that clonazepam is a viable alternative for the maintenance treatment of bipolar disorder.

FUTURE RESEARCH AND CONCLUSIONS

Major advances have been made in the pharmacological treatment of bipolar disorder. Evidence from studies reviewed in this chapter supports the efficacy of lithium, valproate, and carbamazepine in the treatment of acute mania. However, many patients have only partial responses to these agents, and some patients respond poorly to all three. Thus, the need for alternative agents and for studies of alternative strategies with these agents remains. For example, the efficacy of combinations of these agents as compared to treatment with a single agent, or to the combination of an antipsychotic and a single mood stabilizer, has not been studied in controlled trials.

Two other anticonvulsants, oxcarbazepine and gabapentin, may also have potential as antimanic agents. Oxcarbazepine, the 10-keto analogue of carbamazepine, has already been studied in four small controlled trials (149–151), but these studies are inconclusive because of methodologic limitations (39). Preliminary anecdotal experience with gabapentin has been promising enough to suggest further pilot studies of this drug in patients with acute mania.

Although several studies have suggested that benzodiazepines may be as effective, but potentially safer, alternatives to antipsychotics as adjunctive agents in acute mania, this strategy has not been definitively examined in a controlled trial of sufficient size or duration. Promising preliminary data from open trials of clozapine in patients with treatment-refractory acute mania are also in need of confirmation in controlled studies.

Risperidone may also have a role as an adjunctive treatment in acute mania, but concerns about its possible antidepressant rather than mood-stabilizing effects require clarification in controlled trials.

Four new atypical antipsychotics, olanzapine, seroquel, sertindole, and ziprasidone, which may be available for clinical use within the next several years, may also have a role as adjunctive treatments in acute mania. Preliminary studies that suggest the possible efficacy of calcium channel antagonists (e.g., verapamil, nimodipine) and thyroid hormone (thyroxine) augmentation are in need of confirmation in randomized, controlled trials.

Many fundamental questions regarding the treatment of bipolar depression remain unanswered. The available evidence suggests that the three mood-stabilizing agents, lithium, valproate, and carbamazepine, possess greater activity as antimanic agents than as antidepressant agents. Thus, many patients with acute bipolar depression require combination treatment with a mood stabilizer and an antidepressant. Although a variety of new antidepressants with novel mechanisms of action and better side-effect profiles (e.g., SSRIs, bupropion, venlafaxine, nefazodone) than older agents (e.g., tricyclics, MAOIs) are now available, these drugs have been virtually unstudied in patients with bipolar depression. Whether one or more of these antidepressants may have greater efficacy or a lower risk of treatment-associated switching into hypomania or mania than other agents remains to be studied. Similarly, the optimal dose and duration of adjunctive antidepressant treatment in bipolar depression are poorly understood.

With these unaddressed issues in mind, an important niche exists for a drug with mood-stabilizing and substantial antidepressant effects for the treatment of bipolar disorder. The anticonvulsant lamotrigine has recently been studied in an open-label pilot trial as a potential antidepressant/mood-stabilizing agent (152). In the trial, 50 patients received lamotrigine as adjunctive treatment to ongoing medication regimens, and 17 received lamotrigine as monotherapy. In this study, 9 (23%) of 39 patients who received lamotrigine for acute bipolar depression exhibited moderate improvement (25–49% decrease in HDRS scores) and 18 (46%) displayed marked improvement (greater than 50% decrease in HDRS scores). Of the 25 patients who received lamotrigine while manic (N = 9), hypomanic (N = 7), or mixed (N = 9), the baseline SADS-C mania ratings decreased significantly from 21 ± 8 to 8 ± 10. Four (16%) patients displayed moderate improvement and 15 (60%) marked improvement. These preliminary findings require further study.

For the maintenance treatment of bipolar disorder, optimal lithium treatment has been shown to substantially reduce the risk of recurrent affective episodes for many patients, but many also suffer breakthrough episodes or are not able to endure lithium's side effects. Maintenance studies of carbamazepine suggest that it also possesses efficacy but that it may be less effective than lithium. A placebo-controlled comparison trial of divalproex and lithium maintenance treatment is near completion, but thus far only open data are available. These data do, however, suggest that valproate is also effective as a maintenance treatment.

As in the treatment of acute mania, the important question of whether maintenance treatment with combinations of mood stabilizers may be more effective than monotherapy has not been addressed in controlled trials. Similarly, although data from open-label, long-term follow-up studies of patients with treatment-refractory bipolar disorder suggest that clozapine is an effective maintenance treatment for such patients (exerting mood-stabilizing, as well as antipsychotic, effects), these findings are in need of replication in controlled trials.

The emergence of other atypical antipsychotics with pharmacological activity similar to clozapine raises the possibility that these medications may be useful as maintenance treatment alternatives for patients refractory to or intolerant of lithium, valproate, carbamazepine, or their combinations.

References

The following coding system, with codes given at the end of each reference entry, indicates the nature of the supporting evidence from each citation:

(1) Randomized, prospective, clinical trial. A study must include comparison groups with random assignment, blinded assessments, clear presentation of inclusion and exclusion criteria, state-of-the-art diagnostic methods, adequate sample size

to provide statistical power, and clearly described statistical methods.

(2) Clinical trial. A study in which an intervention is made but some aspect of the Type 1 study criteria is missing.

(3) Clinical study. A study that has clear methodologic limitations. These studies include open treatment studies designed to obtain pilot data, naturalistic, and case control studies.

(4) A review with secondary data analysis (e.g., meta-analysis of comparably designed clinical trials).

(5) A review without secondary data analysis designed to convey an impression of the available literature.

(6) Textbook, reference manual, case reports, small case series, essays, and opinion papers.

1. Robins, L. N., & Regier, D. A. (Eds.). (1991). *Psychiatric disorders in America: The epidemiologic catchment area study.* New York: Free Press. (6)

2. Kessler, R. C., McGonagle, K. A., Zhao, S., et al. (1994). Lifetime and 12-month prevalence of *DSM-III-R* psychiatric disorders in the United States. *Archives of General Psychiatry, 51*, 8–19. (1)

3. Winokur, G., Clayton, P. J., & Reich, T. (1969). *Manic depressive illness.* St, Louis, Mo.: C. V. Mosby. (6)

4. Dion, G. L., Tohen, M., Anthony, W. A., et al. (1988). Symptoms and functioning of patients with bipolar disorder 6 months after hospitalization. *Hospital and Community Psychiatry, 39*, 652–657. (3)

5. Tohen, M., Waternaux, C. S., & Tsuang, M. T. (1990). Outcome in mania. A 4-year prospective follow-up on 75 patients utilizing survival analysis. *Archives of General Psychiatry, 47*, 1106–1111. (3)

6. Prien, R. F., & Gelenberg, A. J. (1989). Alternatives to lithium for preventative treatment of bipolar disorder. *American Journal of Psychiatry, 146*, 840–848. (5)

7. Post, R. M. (1992). Transduction of psychosocial stress into the neurobiology of recurrent affective disorder. *American Journal of Psychiatry, 149*, 999–1010. (5)

8. Department of Health, Education, and Welfare Medical Practice Project. (1979). *A state-of-the science report for the Office of the Assistant Secretary for the U.S. Department of Health, Education, and Welfare.* Baltimore, Md.: Policy Research. (5)

9. Hopkins, H. S., & Gelenberg, A. J. (1994). Treatment of bipolar disorder: How far have we come? *Psychopharmacology Bulletin, 30*, 27–37. (5)

10. Dilsaver, S. C., Chen, Y.-W., Swann, A. C., et al. (1994). Suicidality in patients with pure and depressive mania. *American Journal of Psychiatry, 151*, 1312–1315. (4)

11. Gurling, H. (1995). Linkage findings in bipolar disorder. *Nat Genet, 10*, 8–9. (4)

12. American Psychiatric Association. (1994). *Diagnostic and statistical manual of mental disorders* (4th ed.). Washington, D.C.: Author. (6)

13. Goodwin, F. K., & Jamison, K. R. (1990). *Manic-depressive illness.* New York: Oxford University Press. (6)

14. Schou, M., Juel-Nielson, N., Stromgren, E., et al. (1954). The treatment of manic psychoses by administration of lithium salts. *Journal of Neurological and Neurosurgical Psychiatry, 17*, 250–260. (2)

15. Maggs, R. (1963). Treatment of manic illness with lithium carbonate. *British Journal of Psychiatry, 109*, 56–65. (2)

16. Goodwin, F. K., Murphy, D. L., & Bunney, W. F., Jr. (1969). Lithium carbonate treatment in depression and mania: A longitudinal double-blind study. *Archives of General Psychiatry, 21*, 486–496. (2)

17. Stokes, P. E., Sharnoian, C. A., Stoll, P. M., et al. (1971). Efficacy of lithium as acute treatment of manic-depressive illness. *Lancet, 1*, 1319–1325. (2)

18. Bowden, C. L., Brugger, A. M., Swann, A. C., et al. (1994). Efficacy of divalproex versus lithium and placebo in the treatment of mania. *Journal of the American Medical Association, 271*, 918–924. (1)

19. American Psychiatric Association. (1987). *Diagnostic and statistical manual of mental disorders* (3rd ed., revised). Washington, D.C.: Author. (6)

20. Johnson, G., Gershon, S., & Hekiman, L. J. (1968). Controlled evaluation of lithium and chlorpromazine in the treatment of manic states: An interim report. *Comprehensive Psychiatry, 9*, 563–573. (2)

21. Johnson, G., Gerson, S., Burdock, E. I., et al. (1971). Comparative effects of lithium and chlorpromazine in the treatment of acute manic states. *British Journal of Psychiatry, 119*, 267–276. (2)

22. Spring, G., Schweid, D., Gray, C., et al. (1970). A double-blind comparison of lithium and chlorpromazine in the treatment of manic states. *American Journal of Psychiatry, 126*, 1306–1310. (2)

23. Platman, S. R. (1970). A comparison of lithium carbonate and chlorpromazine in mania. *American Journal of Psychiatry, 127*, 351–353. (2)

24. Prien, R. F., Caffey, E. M., Jr., & Klett, C. J. (1972). Comparison of lithium carbonate and chlorpromazine in the treatment of mania: Report of the Veterans Administration and National Institute of Mental Health Collaborative Study Group. *Archives of General Psychiatry, 26*, 146–153. (1)

25. Shopsin, B., Gerson, S., Thompson, H., et al. (1975). Psychoactive drugs in mania: A controlled comparison of lithium carbonate, chlorpromazine,

and haloperidol. *Archives of General Psychiatry, 32,* 34–42. (2)

26. Takahaski, R., Sakuma, A., Itoh, K., et al. (1975). Comparison of efficacy of lithium carbonate and chlorpromazine in mania: Report of collaborative study group on treatment of mania in Japan. *Archives of General Psychiatry, 32,* 1310–1318. (2)

27. Freeman, T. W., Clothier, J. L., Pazzaglia, P., et al. (1992). A double-blind comparison of valproic acid and lithium in the treatment of acute mania. *American Journal of Psychiatry, 149,* 247–250. (2)

28. Pope, H. G., Jr., McElroy, S. L., Keck, P. E., Jr., et al. (1991). Valproate in the treatment of acute mania: A placebo-controlled study. *Archives of General Psychiatry, 48,* 62–68. (1)

29. Emrich, H. M., Von Zerssen, D., & Kissling, W. (1981). On a possible role of GABA in mania: Therapeutic efficacy of sodium valproate. In E. Costa, G. Dicharia, & G. L. Gessa (Eds.), *GABA and benzodiazepine receptors* (pp. 287–296). New York: Raven Press. (2)

30. Brennan, M. I. W., Sandyk, R., & Borsook, D. (1994). Use of sodium valproate in the management of affective disorders: Basic and clinical aspects. In H. M. Emrich, T. Okuma, & A. A. Muller (Eds.), *Anticonvulsants in affective disorders* (pp. 56–65).. Amsterdam: Exerpta Medica. (2)

31. Post, R. M., Berretini, W., Uhde, T. W., et al. (1984). Selective response to the anticonvulsant carbamazepine in manic depressive illness: A case study. *Journal of Clinical Psychopharmacology, 4,* 178–185. (6)

32. Spitzer, R. L., Endicott, J., & Robbins, E. (1975). *Research Diagnostic Criteria (RDC) for a selected group of functional disorders* (2nd ed.). New York: New York State Psychiatric Institute. (6)

33. Dunner, D. L., & Fieve, R. R. (1974). Clinical factors in lithium carbonate prophylaxis failure. *Archives of General Psychiatry, 30,* 229–233. (3)

34. Calabrese, J. R., Markovitz, P. J., Kimmel, S. E., et al. (1992). Spectrum of efficacy of valproate in 78 rapid-cycling bipolar patients. *Journal of Clinical Psychopharmacology, 12*(Suppl.), 53–56. (3)

35. McElroy, S. L., Keck, P. E., Jr., Pope, H. G., Jr., et al. (1988). Valproate in the treatment of rapid cycling bipolar disorder. *Journal of Clinical Psychopharmacology, 8,* 275–279. (3)

36. McElroy, S. L., Keck, P. E., Jr., Stanton, S. P., et al. (1996). A randomized comparison of divalproex oral loading versus haloperidol in the initial treatment of acute psychotic mania. *Journal of Clinical Psychiatry, 59,* 142–146. (2)

37. Keck, P. E., Jr., McElroy, S. L., Tugrul, K. C., et al. (1993). Valproate oral loading in the treatment of acute mania. *Journal of Clinical Psychiatry, 54,* 305–308. (3)

38. McElroy, S. L., Keck, P. E., Jr., Tugrul, K. C., et al. (1993). Valproate as a loading treatment in acute mania. *Neuropsychobiology, 27,* 146–149. (3)

39. Keck, P. E., Jr., McElroy, S. L., & Nemeroff, C. B. (1992). Anticonvulsants in the treatment of bipolar disorder. *Journal of Neuropsychiatry and Clinical Neuroscience, 4,* 595–405. (4)

40. Okuma, T., Inanga, K., Otsuki, S., et al. (1979). Comparison of the antimanic efficacy of carbamazepine and chlorpromazine. *Psychopharmacology, 66,* 211–217. (2)

41. Ballenger, J. C., & Post, R. M. (1978). Therapeutic effects of carbamazepine in affective illness: A preliminary report. *Communications in Psychopharmacology, 2,* 159–175. (2)

42. Lerer, B., Moore, N., Meyendorff, E., et al. (1987). Carbamazepine versus lithium in mania: A double-blind study. *Journal of Clinical Psychiatry, 48,* 89–93. (2)

43. Small, J. G., Klapper, M. H., Miktein, V., et al. (1991). Carbamazepine compared with lithium in the treatment of mania. *Archives of General Psychiatry, 48,* 915–921. (2)

44. Grossi, E., Sacchetti, E., & Vita, A. (1984). Carbamazepine versus chlorpromazine in mania: A double blind trial. In H. M. Emrich, T. Okuma, & A. A. Muller (Eds.), *Anticonvulsants in affective disorders* (pp. 177–187). Amsterdam: Excerpta Medica. (2)

45. Lipinski, J. F., & Pope, H. G., Jr. (1982). Possible synergistic action between carbamazepine and lithium carbonate in the treatment of three acutely manic patients. *American Journal of Psychiatry, 139,* 948–949. (6)

46. Kramlinger, K. G., & Post, R. M. (1989). The addition of lithium to carbamazepine. *Archives of General Psychiatry, 46,* 794–800. (3)

47. Small, J. G., Klapper, M. H., Marhenke, J. D., et al. (1995). Lithium combined with carbamazepine or haloperidol in the treatment of mania. *Psychopharmacology Bulletin, 31,* 265–272. (2)

48. McElroy, S. L., Pope, H. G., Jr., Keck, P. E., Jr., et al. (1988). Treatment of psychiatric disorders with valproate: A series of 73 cases. *Psychiatrie Psychobiologie, 3,* 81–85. (3)

49. Keck, P. E., Jr., McElroy, S. L., Vuckovic, A., et al. (1992). Combined valproate and carbamazepine treatment of bipolar disorder. *Journal of Neuropsychiatry and Clinical Neuroscience, 4,* 319–322. (6)

50. Ketter, T. A., Pazzaglia, P. J., Post, R. M., et al. (1992). Synergy of carbamazepine and valproate in affective illness: Case report and literature review.

Journal of Clinical Psychopharmacology, 12, 276–281. (6)

51. Baldessarini, R. J. (1985). *Chemotherapy in psychiatry.* Cambridge, Mass.: Harvard University Press. (6)

52. Hirschfeld, F. M. A., Clayton, P. J., Cohen, I., et al. (1994). Practice guidelines for the treatment of patients with bipolar disorders. *American Journal of Psychiatry, 151*(Suppl.), 1–31. (6)

53. Janicak, P. G., Davis, J. M., Preskorn, S. H., et al. (1993). *Principles and practice of psychopharmacotherapy.* Baltimore, Md.: Williams & Wilkins. (6)

54. Janicak, P. G., Newman, R. H., & Davis, J. M. (1992). Advances in the treatment of manic and related disorders: A reappraisal. *Psychiatric Annals, 22,* 94. (4)

55. Zarate, C. A., Jr., Tohen, M., & Baldessarini, R. J. (1995). Clozapine in severe mood disorders. *Journal of Clinical Psychiatry, 56,* 411–417. (4)

56. McElroy, S. L., Dessain, E. C., Pope, H. G., Jr., et al. (1991). Clozapine in the treatment of psychotic mood disorders, schizoaffective disorder, and schizophrenia. *Journal of Clinical Psychiatry, 52,* 411–414. (3)

57. Cole, J. O., Banov, M. D., Green, A., et al. (1993, May 26). Clozapine in the treatment of refractory acute mania. In *New Research Program and Abstracts of the 146th Annual Meeting of the American Psychiatric Association,* San Francisco, Ca. [Abstract NR 455: 174]. (3)

58. Kimmel, S. E., Calabrese, J. R., Woyshville, M. J., et al. (1994). Clozapine in treatment-refractory mood disorders. *Journal of Clinical Psychiatry, 55*(Suppl.), 91–93. (3)

59. Singh, A. N., & Catalan, J. (1994). Risperidone in HIV-related manic psychosis. *Lancet, 344,* 1029–1030. (6)

60. Goodnick, P. J. (1995). Risperidone treatment of refractory acute mania. *Journal of Clinical Psychiatry, 56,* 446–447. (6)

61. Tohen, M., Zarate, C. A., Jr., Centorrino, F., et al. (1994, December). *Risperidone in the treatment of mania.* Paper presented at the 33rd Annual Meeting of the American College of Neuropsychopharmacology, San Juan, Puerto Rico. (3)

62. Keck, P. E., Jr., Wilson, D. R., Strakowski, S. M., et al. (1995). Clinical predictors of acute risperidone response in schizophrenia, schizoaffective disorder, and psychotic mood disorders. *Journal of Clinical Psychiatry, 56,* 466–470. (3)

63. Dwight, M. M., Keck, P. E., Jr., Stanton, S. P., et al. (1994). Antidepressant activity and mania associated with risperidone treatment of schizoaffective disorder. *Lancet, 344,* 554–555. (6)

64. Byerly, M. T., Greer, R. A., & Evans, D. L. (1995). Behavioral stimulation associated with risperidone initiation. *American Journal of Psychiatry, 152,* 1096–1097. (6)

65. Sajatovic, M. (1995, June 1). A pilot study evaluating the efficacy of risperidone in treatment refractory, acute bipolar and schizoaffective mania. In *New Research Abstracts of the 35th Annual Meeting of the New Clinical Drug Evaluation Unit (NCDEU),* Orlando, Fla., Poster No. 19. (6)

66. Sachs, G. S. (1990). Use of clonazepam for bipolar affective disorder. *Journal of Clinical Psychiatry,* (Suppl.), 31–34. (5)

67. Sernyak, M. J., Griffin, R. A., Johnson, R. M., et al. (1994). Neuroleptic exposure following inpatient treatment of acute mania with lithium and neuroleptic. *American Journal of Psychiatry, 151,* 133–135. (3)

68. Keck, P. E., Jr., McElroy, S. L., Strakowski, S. M., et al. (1996). Factors associated with maintenance antipsychotic treatment of patients with bipolar disorder. *Journal of Clinical Psychiatry, 57,* 147–151. (3)

69. Kane, J. M., & Smith, J. M. (1982). Tardive dyskinesia: Prevalence and risk factors. *Archives of General Psychiatry, 39,* 473–481. (3)

70. Wegner, J. T., Catalano, F., Gibralter, J., et al. (1985). Schizophrenics with tardive dyskinesia. *Archives of General Psychiatry, 42,* 860–865. (3)

71. Mukherjee, S., Rose, A. M., Caracci, G., et al. (1986). Persistent tardive dyskinesia in bipolar patients. *Archives of General Psychiatry, 43,* 342–346. (3)

72. Kukopulos, A., Reginaldi, D., Laddomada, P., et al. (1980). Course of manic-depressive cycle and changes caused by treatments. *Pharmacopsychiatry, 13,* 156–157. (3)

73. Esparon, J., Kollaori, J., Naylor, G. J., et al. (1986). Comparison of the prophylactic action of flupenthixol with placebo in lithium treated manic-depressive patients. *British Journal of Psychiatry, 148,* 723–725. (2)

74. White, E., Cheung, T., & Silverstone, T. (1993). Depot antipsychotics in bipolar affective disorder. *International Clinical Psychopharmacology, 8,* 119–122. (3)

75. Lenox, R. X., Newhouse, P. A., Creelman, W. L., et al. (1992). Adjunctive treatment of manic agitation with lorazepam versus haloperidol: A double-blind study. *Journal of Clinical Psychiatry, 53,* 47–52. (2)

76. Bradwejn, J., Shrinqui, C., Koszycki, D., et al. (1990). Double-blind comparison of the effects of clonazepam and lorazepam in mania. *Journal of Clinical Psychopharmacology, 10,* 403–408. (2)

77. Chouinard, G., Young, S. N., & Annable, L. (1983).

Antimanic effect of clonazepam. *Biol Psychiatr, 18,* 451–456. (2)

78. Edwards, R., Stephenson, U., & Flewett, T. (1991). Clonazepam in acute mania: A double blind trial. *Australian and New Zealand Journal of Psychiatry, 25,* 238–242. (2)

79. Chouinard, G. (1987). Clonazepam in acute and maintenance treatment of bipolar affective disorder. *Journal of Clinical Psychiatry, 48*(Suppl.), 29–36. (2)

80. Dubovsky, S. L., Franks, R. D., Allen, S., et al. (1986). Calcium antagonists in mania: A double-blind study of verapamil. *Psychiatry Research, 18,* 309–320. (2)

81. Giannini, A. J., Houser, W. L., Loiselle, R. H., et al. (1984). Antimanic effects of verapamil. *American Journal of Psychiatry, 141,* 1602–1603. (2)

82. Dose, M., Emrich, H. M., Cording-Tommel, C., et al. (1986). Use of calcium antagonists in mania. *Psychoneuroendocrinology, 11,* 241–243. (2)

83. Garza-Trevino, E. S., Overall, J. E., & Hollister, L. E. (1992). Verapamil versus lithium in acute mania. *American Journal of Psychiatry, 149,* 121–122. (2)

84. Arkonac, O., Kantarci, E., Eradamlar, N., et al. (1991). Verapamil versus lithium in acute mania. *Biological Psychiatry, 29,* 376S. (2)

85. Hoschl, C., & Kozeny, J. (1989). Verapamil in affective disorders: A controlled, double-blind study. *Biological Psychiatry, 25,* 128–140. (2)

86. Giannini, A. J., Loiselle, R. H., Pric, W. A., et al. (1985). Comparison of antimanic efficacy of clonidine and verapamil. *Journal of Clinical Pharmacology, 25,* 307–308. (2)

87. Pazzaglia, P. J., Post, R. M., Kelter, T. A., et al. (1993). Preliminary controlled trial of nimodipine in ultra-rapid cycling affective dysregulation. *Psychiatry Research, 49,* 257–272. (2)

88. Bauer, M. S., & Whybrow, P. C. (1990). Rapid cycling bipolar affective disorder II. Treatment of refractory rapid cycling with high-dose levothyroxine: A preliminary study. *Archives of General Psychiatry, 47,* 435–440. (3)

89. Baumgartner, A., Bauer, M., & Hellweg, R. (1994). Treatment of intractable non-rapid cycling bipolar affective disorder with high-dose thyroxine: An open clinical trial. *Neuropsychopharmacology, 10,* 183–189. (3)

90. Fieve, R. R., Platman, S. R., & Plutchik, R. R. (1968). The use of lithium in affective disorders I. Acute endogenous depression. *American Journal of Psychiatry, 125,* 79–83. (2)

91. Greenspan, K., Schildkraut, J. J., Gordon, E. K., et al. (1970). Catecholamine metabolism in affective disorders-III. *Journal of Psychiatry Research, 7,* 171–182. (2)

92. Goodwin, F. K., Murphy, D. L., Dunner, D. L., et al. (1972). Lithium response in unipolar versus bipolar depression. *American Journal of Psychiatry, 129,* 76–79. (2)

93. Noyes, R., Dempsey, G. M., Blum, A., et al. (1974). Lithium treatment of depression. *Comprehensive Psychiatry, 15,* 187–193. (2)

94. Mendels, J. (1976). Lithium in the treatment of depression. *American Journal of Psychiatry, 4,* 373–378. (2)

95. Baron, M., Gershon, E. S., Rudy, V., et al. (1975). Lithium carbonate response in depression. *Archives of General Psychiatry, 32,* 1107–1111. (2)

96. Donnelly, E. F., Goodwin, F. K., Waldman, I. N., et al. (1978). Prediction of antidepressant responses to lithium. *American Journal of Psychiatry, 135,* 552–556. (2)

97. Zornberg, G. L., & Pope, H. G., Jr. (1993). Treatment of depression in bipolar disorder: New directions for research. *Journal of Clinical Psychopharmacology, 13,* 397–408. (4)

98. Suppes, T., Baldessarini, R. J., Faedda, G. L. X., et al. (1991). Risk of recurrence following discontinuation of lithium in bipolar disorder. *Archives of General Psychiatry, 48,* 1082–1088. (4)

99. Watanabe, S., Ishino, H., & Otsuki, S. (1975). Double-blind comparison of lithium and imipramine in treatment of depression. *Archives of General Psychiatry, 32,* 659–668. (2)

100. Himmelhoch, J. M., Those, M. E., Mallinger, A. G., et al. (1991). Tranylcypromine versus imipramine in anergic bipolar depression. *American Journal of Psychiatry, 148,* 910–915. (1)

101. Baumhackl, U., Biziere, K., Fischback, G., et al. (1989). Efficacy and tolerability of moclobemide compared with imipramine in depressive disorder (*DSM-III*): An Austrian double-blind, multicentre study. *British Journal of Psychiatry, 155*(Suppl.), 78–83. (2)

102. Cohn, J. B., Collins, G., Ashbrook, E., et al. (1980). A comparison of fluoxetine, imipramine and placebo in patients with bipolar depressive disorder. *International Clinical Psychopharmacology, 4,* 313–322. (2)

103. Ashberg-Wistedt, A. (1982). Comparison between zimelidine and desipramine in endogenous depression. *Acta Psychiatrica Scandinavica, 66,* 129–138. (2)

104. Kessell, A., & Holt, F. (1975). A controlled study of tetracyclic antidepressant-maprotiline (Ludiomil). *Medical Journal of Australia, 1,* 773–776. (2)

105. Sach, G. S., Lafer, B., Stoll, A., et al. (1994). A double-blind trial of bupropion versus desipramine for bipolar depression. *Journal of Clinical Psychiatry, 55,* 391–393. (2)

106. Levine, J., Barak, Y., Gonzalves, M., et al. (1995). Double-blind, controlled trial of inasitol treatment of depression. *American Journal of Psychiatry, 152*, 792–794. (2)

107. Thase, M. E., Mallinger, A. G., McKnight, D., et al. (1992). Treatment of imipramine-resistant recurrent depression IV: A double-blind crossover study of tranylcypromine for anergic bipolar depression. *American Journal of Psychiatry, 149*, 195–198. (2)

108. Altshuler, L. L., Post, R. M., Leverich, G. S., et al. (1995). Antidepressant-induced mania and cycle acceleration: A controversy revisited. *American Journal of Psychiatry, 152*, 1130–1138. (3)

109. Stoll, A. L., Mayer, P. V., Kolbrener, M., et al. (1994). Antidepressant-associated mania: A controlled comparison with spontaneous mania. *American Journal of Psychiatry, 151*, 1642–1645. (3)

110. Peet, M. (1994). Induction of mania with selective serotonin re-uptake inhibitors and tricyclic antidepressants. *British Journal of Psychiatry, 164*, 549–550. (4)

111. Post, R. M., Uhde, T. W., Roy-Byrne, P. P., et al. (1986). Antidepressant effects of carbamazepine. *American Journal of Psychiatry, 143*, 29–34. (2)

112. Small, J. G. (1990). Anticonvulsants in affective disorders. *Psychopharmacology Bulletin, 26*, 25–36. (2)

113. Lambert, P.-A. (1984). Acute and prophylactic therapies of patients with affective disorders using valpromide (Dipropylacetamide). In H. M. Emrich, T. Okuma, & A. A. Muller (Eds.), *Anticonvulsants in affective disorders* (pp. 33–44). Amsterdam: Excerpta Medica. (3)

114. Prien, R. F., & Potter, W. Z. (1990). NIMH workshop on treatment of bipolar disorder. *Psychopharmacology Bulletin, 26*, 409–427. (4)

115. Harrow, M., Goldberg, J. F., Grossman, L. S., et al. (1990). Outcome in manic disorders: A naturalistic follow-up study. *Archives of General Psychiatry, 47*, 665–671. (2)

116. Maj, M., Pirozzi, R., & Kemali, D. (1991). Long-term outcome of lithium prophylaxis in bipolar patients. *Archives of General Psychiatry, 48*, 772. (3)

117. O'Connell, R. A., Mayo, J. A., Flatow, L., et al. (1991). Outcome of bipolar disorder on long-term treatment with lithium. *British Journal of Psychiatry, 159*, 123–129. (3)

118. Peselow, E. D., Fieve, R. R., Difaglia, C., et al. (1994). Lithium prophylaxis of bipolar illness. The value of combination treatment. *British Journal of Psychiatry, 164*, 208–214. (3)

119. Post, R. M., Leverich, G. S., Altshuler, L., et al. (1992). Lithium-discontinuation-induced refractoriness: Preliminary observations. *American Journal of Psychiatry, 149*, 1727–1729. (6)

120. Gelenberg, A. J., Kane, J. M., Keller, M. B., et al. (1989). Comparison of standard and low serum levels of lithium for maintenance treatment of bipolar disorder. *New England Journal of Medicine, 321*, 1489–1493. (1)

121. Keller, M. B., Lavori, P. W., Kane, J. M., et al. (1992). Subsyndromal symptoms in bipolar disorder. A comparison of standard and low serum levels of lithium. *Archives of General Psychiatry, 49*, 371–376. (4)

122. Maj, M. (1992). Clinical prediction of response to lithium prophylaxis in bipolar patients: A critical update. *Lithium, 3*, 15–21. (4)

123. Faedda, G. L., Baldessarini, R. J., Tohen, M., et al. (1991). Episode sequence in bipolar disorder and response to lithium treatment. *American Journal of Psychiatry, 148*, 1237–1239. (4)

124. McElroy, S. L., Keck, P. E., Jr., Pope, H. G., Jr., et al. (1992). Clinical and research implications of the diagnosis of dysphoric or mixed mania or hypomania. *American Journal of Psychiatry, 149*, 1633–1644. (4)

125. Solomon, D. A., Keitner, G. I., Miller, I. W., et al. (1995). Course of illness and maintenance treatments for patients with bipolar disorder. *Journal of Clinical Psychiatry, 56*, 5–13. (4)

126. Miklowitz, D. J., Goldstein, M. J., Nauechterlein, K. H., et al. (1988). Family factors and the course of bipolar affective disorder. *Archives of General Psychiatry, 45*, 225–231. (3)

127. Okuma, T., Inanaga, K., Otsuki, S., et al. (1981). A preliminary double-blind study on the efficacy of carbamazepine prophylaxis of manic depressive illness. *Psychopharmacology, 73*, 95–96. (1)

128. Placidi, G. F., Lenzi, A., Lazzerini, F., et al. (1986). The comparative efficacy and safety of carbamazepine versus lithium: A randomized, double-blind 3-year trial in 83 patients. *Journal of Clinical Psychiatry, 47*, 490–494. (2)

129. Watkins, S. E., Callender, K., & Thomas, D. R. (1987). The effect of carbamazepine and lithium on remission from affective illness. *British Journal of Psychiatry, 150*, 180–182. (2)

130. Bellaire, W., Demish, K., Stoll, K.-D., et al. (1988). Carbamazepine versus lithium in prophylaxis of recurrent affective disorders. *Psychopharmacology, 96*(Suppl.), 287. (2)

131. Lusznat, R. M., Murphy, D. P., & Nunn, C. M. H. (1988). Carbamazepine versus lithium in the treatment and prophylaxis of mania. *British Journal of Psychiatry, 153*, 198–204. (2)

132. Coxhead, N., Silverstone, T., & Cookson, J. (1992). Carbamazepine versus lithium in the prophylaxis

of bipolar affective disorder. *Acta Psychiatrica Scandinavica, 85,* 114–118. (2)

133. Murphy, D. J., Gannon, M. A., & McGennis, A. (1989). Carbamazepine in bipolar affective disorder. *Lancet, 2,* 1151–1152. (5)

134. Frankenburg, F. R., Tohen, M., Cohen, B. M., et al. (1988). Long-term response to carbamazepine. A retrospective study. *Journal of Clinical Psychopharmacology, 8,* 130–132. (3)

135. Post, R. M., Leverich, G. S., Rosuff, A. S., et al. (1990). Carbamazepine prophylaxis in refractory affective disorders: A focus on long-term follow-up. *Journal of Clinical Psychopharmacology, 10,* 318–327. (3)

136. Post, R. M. (1994). Anticonvulsants in refractory mood disorders. In W. A. Nolen, J. Rohar, & S. P. Roose (Eds.), *Refractory depression: Current strategies and future directions* (pp. 97–114). Chichester, U.K.: John Wiley & Sons. (4)

137. Simhandl, C., Denk, E., & Thou, K. (1993). The comparative efficacy of carbamazepine low and high serum level and lithium carbonate in the prophylaxis of affective disorders. *Journal of Affective Disorders, 28,* 221–231. (2)

138. Okuma, T. (1993). Effects of carbamazepine and lithium on affective disorders. *Neuropsychobiology, 27,* 138–145. (4)

139. Denicoff, K. D., Smith-Jackson, E., Disney, E., et al. (1994). *Outcome in bipolar patients randomized to lithium or carbamazepine prophylaxis and crossed over in Year 2.* Paper presented at the First International Conference on Bipolar Disorder, Pittsburgh, Pa., p. 2. (2)

140. Puzynski, S., & Klosiewicz, L. (1984). Valproic acid amide as a prophylactic agent in affective and schizoaffective disorders. *Psychopharmacology Bulletin, 20,* 151–159. (3)

141. Calabrese, J. R., Woyshville, M. J., Kimmel, S., et al. (1993). Predictors of valproate response in bipolar rapid cycling. *Journal of Clinical Psychopharmcology, 13,* 280–283. (4)

142. Naylor, G. J., & Scott, C. R. (1980). Depot injections for affective disorders. *British Journal of Psychiatry, 136,* 105. (3)

143. Lowe, M. R., & Batchelor, D. H. (1986). Depot neuroleptics and manic depressive psychosis. *International Clinical Psychopharmacology, 1*(Suppl.), 53–62. (3)

144. Lowe, M. R., & Batchelor, D. H. (1990). Lithium and neuroleptics in the management of manic depressive psychosis. *Human Psychopharmacology, 5,* 267–274. (3)

145. Littlejohn, R., Leslie, F., & Cookson, J. (1994). Depot antipsychotics in the prophylaxis of bipolar affective disorder. *British Journal of Psychiatry, 165,* 827–829. (3)

146. Ahlfors, U. G., Baastrup, P. C., Dencker, S. J., et al. (1981). Flupenthixol decanoate in recurrent manic depressive illness. *Acta Psychiatrica Scandinavica, 64,* 226–237. (2)

147. Sachs, G. S., Weilburg, J. B., & Rosenbaum, J. F. (1990). Clonazepam versus neuroleptics as adjunct to lithium maintenance. *Psychopharmacology Bulletin, 26,* 137–143. (2)

148. Aronson, T. A., Shukla, S., & Hirschowitz, J. (1989). Clonazepam treatment of five lithium refractory patients with bipolar disorder. *American Journal of Psychiatry, 146,* 77–80. (3)

149. Emrich, H. M., Dose, M., & von Zerssen, D. (1985). The use of sodium valproate, carbamazepine, and oxcarbazepine in patients with affective disorders. *Journal of Affective Disorders, 8,* 243–250. (2)

150. Emrich, H. M. (1990). Studies with oxcarbazepine (Trileptal) in acute mania. *International Clinical Psychopharmacology, 5*(Suppl.), 83–88. (2)

151. Muller, A. A., & Stoll, K.-D. (1984). Carbamazepine and oxcarbazepine in the treatment of manic syndromes: Studies in Germany. In H. M. Emrich, T. Okuma, & A. A. Muller (Eds.), *Anticonvulsants in affective disorders* (pp. 134–147). Amsterdam, The Netherlands: Excerpta Medica. (2)

152. Calabrese, J. R., Woyshville, M. H., McElroy, S. L., et al. (1995, September 4–8). *"Spectrum of efficacy" of lamotrigine in treatment-refractory manic depression.* Paper presented at the Second International Conference on Affective Disorders, Jerusalem, Israel. (23)

14

Treatments for Depression and Anxiety in the Aged

George Niederehe

Lon S. Schneider

A large number of Type 1 randomized clinical trials (RCTs) have established the efficacy of antidepressant medications, electroconvulsive therapy, and selected psychosocial interventions (including cognitive-behavioral therapy and brief psychodynamic treatment) for depression in the elderly. The relative efficacy of pharmacotherapy and psychosocial treatment for depression in the elderly has not been determined; in clinical practice, the combination of psychosocial and pharmacological treatment ought to be considered a standard of care.

Controlled clinical trials of treatments for late-life anxiety disorders are lacking. Recommendations about treatment, therefore, are generally extrapolated from studies with younger patients or nonsymptomatic elderly volunteer subjects or are simply based on clinical experience. Accordingly, recommended pharmacological treatment of anxiety in the elderly involves benzodiazepine medications; psychosocial treatment methods include relaxation methods, rational-emotive training, and anxiety management training.

Depression and anxiety disorders in late life are serious public health concerns—not expectable outcomes of normal aging—that represent significant sources of disability, increased dependency, and premature death. In discussing depression, we refer to the *DSM-IV* (*Diagnostic and Statistical Manual of Mental Disorders*, fourth edition; American Psychiatric Association [APA], 1994) categories of major depressive disorder and dysthymic disorder (sometimes termed *minor depression*). The spectrum of anxiety disorders in the aged includes generalized anxiety disorder (GAD), agoraphobia with and without panic, panic disorder, specific phobia, and obsessive compulsive disorder. Though all of these disorders are diagnosed the same in older as in younger patients, clinical observers often note that, while the elderly have increased rates of depressive symptoms, many symptomatic older adults fail to meet criteria for major depressive disorder, perhaps suggesting a need for distinctive diagnostic criteria. Because of the high prevalence of physical illnesses among the elderly, these syndromes can be diagnosed best on a simply descriptive basis without attempting to make etiological judgments, such as whether they are secondary to physical conditions (Reynolds, Alexopoulos, Katz, & Mulsant, 1997), and psychological symptoms may be particularly distinguishing diagnostic features. However, depressed older adults may not experience or acknowledge sadness or guilt to the same extent as others (Busse & Pfeiffer, 1977; Rabins, 1996), and other symptoms may more frequently predominate, such as lack of interest in normal pursuits, deterioration in self-care, and actual or perceived problems with memory and attention.

Although most older Americans lead healthy, fulfilling lives, approximately 15% of community residents over 65 years of age (about 5 million persons) experience serious and persistent depressive symptoms (National Institutes of Health [NIH] Consensus Development Panel, 1992). Whereas the prevalence of major depression among the elderly in the community is usually estimated at less than 3%, rates for major or minor depression among elderly people range from 5% in primary care clinics to 15–25% in nursing homes.

Anxiety disorders are also common among the aged. In the Epidemiological Catchment Area studies, the combined 1-month prevalence of phobia, panic, and obsessive compulsive disorders among persons 65 years of age or older was 5.5% (Flint, 1994; Regier et al., 1988). Among these disorders, phobias are the most common (Blazer, George, & Hughes, 1991). Pervasive anxiety symptoms (GAD) are probably the next most common form of anxiety disorder in late life; the prevalence of GAD among the aged has not been reliably estimated. Cumulatively, clinically significant symptoms of anxiety may be found in as many as 20% of the elderly (Sheikh, 1992). As in younger patients, there tends to be a considerable overlap between anxiety and depressive disorders in the aged (Alexopoulos, 1991; Gurian & Miner, 1991).

Both depression and anxiety disorders in late life are frequently chronic and recurring. Naturalistic research suggests that a quarter to a third of depressed older adults may fail to achieve a complete recovery, and the risk of relapse among those who recover following initial treatment increases over time (Murphy, 1994).

Age at first onset of the disorder is a significant source of clinical and neurobiological heterogeneity in late-life depression and anxiety, with major implications for treatment. For example, late-onset depressions appear to be linked more frequently than average with the presence of structural brain pathology, cognitive impairment, and medical comorbidity (Alexopoulos, 1994). Anxiety may represent a lifelong disorder in some elders and a late-onset one in others. At the same time, the elderly are typically subjected to an increasing number of real-life stressors known to be related to depression and anxiety (Hassan & Pollard, 1994). Depression in older adults may reflect caregiving burdens, mourning, or other chronic situational stress that may not be amenable to alleviation via ordinary treatment approaches (Becker & Morrissey, 1988). For example, those who care for patients with dementia (often elderly spouses or siblings of the pa-

tients) are at high risk for depression (prevalence reaches 50% or more in some caregiver studies). Worries that may often act as precursors to diagnosable anxiety disorders may more frequently reflect realistic, situationally based concerns among the aged than is true in younger adults (Person & Borkovec, 1995).

In older persons, mental disorders may be intertwined in various ways with medical illness or other comorbid conditions. Depression and anxiety may represent symptoms of a physical disorder (e.g., effects of a neurological disease on brain neurotransmitters), psychological reactions to physical problems and their functional or social consequences, or side effects of treatments for the physical condition (Reynolds et al., 1997). However, in the presence of medical illness, the symptoms of anxiety and depression are frequently overlooked (Turnbull, 1989). The elderly may more commonly focus on the somatic symptoms and consequences of their depression or chronic anxiety (Hersen & van Hasselt, 1992; Sheikh, 1992).

The elderly have the highest suicide rates of any age group, with the rate for those aged 80–85 double the overall U.S. rate. Most suicides occur in persons with at least one diagnosable mental or substance abuse disorder; among elderly as opposed to younger individuals, this disorder is most commonly uncomplicated major depression, often a first episode—the most treatable variety (Conwell, 1994). Up to 70% of the completed suicides had seen their primary care physicians in the month prior to the death, but generally their depression went unrecognized and untreated. Some data also suggest that depression increases the risk of death, independent of suicide or concomitant physical illness, among the elderly (Murphy, Smith, Lindesay, & Slattery, 1988; Rovner, German, Brant, Clark, Burton, & Folstein, 1991).

USUAL TREATMENT FOR THE AGED

For all patients, the treatment of depression and anxiety disorders must be differentiated into acute, continuation, and maintenance phases, which vary in treatment goals. In the acute treatment phase, the primary goal is to achieve symptom remission. Once the patient has improved symptomatically, continuation phase treatment attempts to prevent relapse into the same episode. The principal goals of maintenance treatment involve sustaining recovery and preventing recurrences of the disorder. Related treatment objectives with elderly patients include improving longevity and quality of life, enhancing functional capacity, and improving general medical health status. All of these issues, along with information about the costs of care, must be considered in selecting treatments and evaluating their outcomes.

Older adults who manifest diagnosable depression or anxiety warrant professional attention and vigorous treatment, particularly when symptoms begin to interfere with everyday functioning. Research has tended to confirm that standard treatment approaches with proven efficacy in younger populations are likely to be successful when extended to the elderly, and that old age in itself should not be considered a counterindication to employing them. However, even though safe and effective treatments are available, ageist attitudes on the part of professionals and negative attitudes of the elderly themselves about mental health treatment form barriers to accessing such services.

Coexisting factors that frequently accompany advanced age—in particular, comorbid medical and neurological illness and/or cognitive impairment—are probably greater influences than age itself on the efficacy of antidepressant and antianxiety treatments in elderly patients. For example, such comorbidities may interfere with the modes of action of specific treatments or may be markers for distinctive forms of the disorder with less treatable etiologies. Treatments for depression can affect the outcomes of medical treatments and rehabilitation efforts for physical illness in the elderly and even influence survival (for depression is a risk factor for mortality). Whether through neurobiological changes or by affecting health-promoting behavior, depression can cause physical illness or complicate its treatment (e.g., by leading to poor adherence to medical regimens). Thus, there may be serious risks of not treating depression in physically ill elders (Reynolds et al., 1997).

Use of psychoactive medications rises with age, even though the elderly are at increased risk for the negative side effects of many drugs and interactions among their multiple medications (Lamy, Salzman, & Nevis-Olesen, 1992). Most frequently used are the benzodiazepines, often on a long-term basis, even though this is not a generally recommended practice (e.g., Morgan, Dallosso, Ebrahim, Arie, & Fentem, 1988; Skoog, Nilsson, Landahl, & Steen, 1993). The benzodiazepines tend to be habituating, and prolonged use leads to a discontinuation syndrome, management of which tends to be a necessary element in clinical care for the many patients with anxiety disorders who use anxiolytic and sedative-hypnotic benzodiazepines.

Much of the treatment of depression and anxiety in the aged occurs within the primary medical health care context, if it occurs at all. Geriatric mental health services must be organized to operate effectively in conjunction with that context of care. Moreover, family members, typically spouses or daughters, provide the bulk of care for older patients with mental disorders, often experiencing considerable stress in the process. A comprehensive approach to treating mental disorders in the elderly should include services that support family members in their caregiving role and alleviate the associated stress.

TREATMENTS OF CHOICE FOR DEPRESSION

Antidepressant medications, electroconvulsive therapy (ECT), and selected psychosocial interventions have all been shown to be efficacious treatment approaches for depression in the elderly (Schneider, Reynolds, Lebowitz, & Friedhoff, 1994). Most studies have used drug and psychotherapy protocols specifically tailored for use with older patients. In evaluating the efficacy evidence, we have emphasized randomized clinical trials (RCTs) with elderly samples in which depression or anxiety has been objectively characterized. Corresponding to Type 1 studies as defined elsewhere in this volume, such trials employ parallel group (comparative treatment or placebo control) designs, clearly defined and operationalized treatment approaches, and quantitative outcome measures. In addition, among drug studies, we emphasize those incorporating placebo control groups as providing the most rigorous form of evidence. When evidence from such studies is lacking, findings from methodologically problematic (Type 2) trials or uncontrolled, open-treatment (Type 3) trials are cited as the next most reliable categories of information. For more detailed reviews, the reader is referred to other sources (e.g., Reynolds et al., 1997; Salzman, 1992, 1994; Schneider, 1996b; Schneider & Olin, 1995; Shamoian, 1992).

Psychopharmacological Treatment

Approximately 30 Type 1 RCTs using placebo-controlled designs support the efficacy of antidepressant medications in the acute-phase treatment of late-life depression (Schneider, 1995). The primary classes of medications for which strong evidence exists are the tricyclic antidepressants (TCAs) and heterocyclic antidepressants, selective serotonin reuptake inhibitors (SSRIs), and monoamine oxidase inhibitors (MAOIs).

Most of these antidepressants are thought to be roughly comparable in efficacy. In clinical trials, typically about 60% of elderly patients have shown improvement over 4–12 weeks of treatment. This was the rate of response to two different antidepressants in a study by Georgotas and colleagues (Georgotas et al., 1986), whereas only 13% of patients treated with placebo improved. However, even with improvement, many patients retain significant residual symptoms. Also, regardless of the specific medication, 25–30% of elderly patients treated with antidepressant medications have tended to drop out of these trials prior to completing treatment. Dropouts may be due to various factors, such as intercurrent medical episodes, but often are related to the experience of medication side effects that are poorly tolerated or pose unacceptable health risks.

Elderly patients often respond to treatment more slowly than younger patients. For example, extending treatment by 2 weeks produced an added benefit for those receiving either of two different medications (Georgotas & McCue, 1989). In the Type 3, open-trial, acute treatment phase of a current maintenance study, the median time to symptom remission for older depressed patients treated with a combination of medication and psychotherapy has been 12 weeks (Reynolds et al., 1992). Achieving a therapeutic response thus depends on continuing treatment for a sufficient length of time, as well as using appropriate doses that produce adequate blood levels. For the latter, medication compliance is especially important but is often fraught with difficulties in elderly patients, and the measurement of plasma levels assumes increased importance.

Given their equivalent efficacy, choices among antidepressants are often determined by variations in their side-effect profiles. In general, aging-related changes in pharmacokinetics and pharmacodynamics leave the elderly more vulnerable to adverse side effects. At least 18 published pharmacodynamic studies document that various antidepressant medications can impair attention and concentration, memory, and other aspects of cognitive function, mostly due to elderly patients' heightened sensitivity to these drugs'

anticholinergic properties. Successful pharmacotherapy in the aged requires selecting a medication that can reduce symptoms while also minimizing a negative impact on cognition and daily function and avoiding interactions with the patient's health conditions and other medications.

Tricyclic Antidepressants

About two dozen Type 1 RCTs provide evidence of efficacy for TCAs in late-life depression. Advantages of these medications include generally predictable kinetics and, with nortriptyline (Pamelor, Aventyl) and desipramine (Norpramin), the ability to monitor therapeutic blood levels. Achieving steady-state therapeutic levels may be associated with a wide range of oral doses. According to some clinical opinions, TCAs may also demonstrate efficacy somewhat superior to other classes of antidepressants for treating severe depression in hospitalized inpatients and depressions with melancholia. However, patient acceptance of TCAs tends to be highly variable due to bothersome side effects (e.g., dry mouth, constipation, increased heart rate, persisting psychomotor and cognitive impairments), and TCAs may introduce serious medical complications, including orthostatic hypotension and cardiotoxic effects (e.g., conduction delay, arrhythmias). The tertiary amine TCAs imipramine (Tofranil) and amitriptyline (Elavil) are generally not recommended for elderly patients, particularly due to the drugs' hypotensive actions.

Other than for these older medications, which have been used as reference drugs in various studies, nortriptyline has been the most intensively studied TCA in the aged. As indicated in Table 14.1, at least six placebo-controlled Type 1 clinical trials provide clear evidence of nortriptyline's efficacy in treating depression in elders, including frail elders with concomitant medical illness (Katz, Simpson, Curlik, Parmelee, & Muhly, 1990). With elderly patients, nortriptyline and desipramine are the most commonly used TCAs.

Among the related heterocyclic (but nontricyclic) antidepressants, bupropion (Wellbutrin) has been evaluated in two RCTs, and trazedone (Desyrel) has been examined in several short-term studies involving elderly patients. Compared with TCAs, these medications appear to have equivalent efficacy in treating major depression but produce fewer adverse side effects and are less frequently associated with cognitive impairment or sedation. However, the efficacy of bu-

TABLE 14.1 Summary of Placebo-Controlled Clinical Trials with Nortriptyline in Depressed Elderly Patients

Study	Comparison Conditions	Sample Size	Age (Years)	Gender (Percentage Female)	Duration (Weeks)	Dose (mg)	Baseline Hamilton	d, Effect Size
Georgotas et al. (1986)	Phenelzine	53	65	39	7	79	23	1.07
Katz et al. (1990)	—	23	84	93	7	65	23	0.67
Kernohan, Chambers, Wilson, & Daugherty (1967)	—	84	70	61	12	62	NA	0.27
Lipsey, Robinson, Pearlson, Rao, & Price (1984)	—	39	61	35	5	60	15	0.88
Nair et al. (1995)	Moclobemide	109	70	71	7	75	23	0.78
Sloane et al. (1985)	IPT	24	64	53	6	92	26	0.51

NA = not available; Age = approximate mean or median age; Dose = approximate daily dose of nortriptyline, estimated when mean or median is not provided; IPT = interpersonal psychotherapy.

propion in treating depression in medically ill patients has not been established.

Selective Serotonin Reuptake Inhibitors

To date, there have been about 20 published Type 1 clinical trials of SSRIs as treatments for depressed elderly patients—9 studies of fluoxetine (Prozac), 8 of paroxetene (Paxil), and 3 multicenter trials of sertraline (Zoloft). These RCTs (cumulatively involving over 1500 elderly outpatients) have generally compared the SSRIs with older, more established medications, rather than with each other or with a placebo. The only placebo-controlled trial suggested somewhat lower than expected efficacy rates for fluoxetine (Tollefson et al., 1995). Over 5–12 week study lengths, the various SSRIs (though directly compared in only one RCT) have appeared not to be differentially efficacious in treating older patients but were equivalent in efficacy to TCAs. One Type 2 study with elderly inpatients, however, has suggested a lesser efficacy for fluoxetine as compared with nortriptyline (Roose, Glassman, Attia, & Woodring, 1994).

The SSRIs may have advantages over TCAs in treating elderly patients, however, because of a more tolerable side-effect profile (Katona & Judge, 1996; Schneider, 1996b); in particular, they do not cause orthostasis or cognitive impairment and, based on clinical experience, appear to have fewer anticholinergic and cardiovascular side effects (though nausea tends to be a particular problem, and in RCTs their tolerability has appeared to be only marginally superior to that of TCAs). The SSRIs do not appear to differ substantially among themselves in side effects.

Monoamine Oxidase Inhibitors

Although the research evidence suggests that MAOIs, compared with TCAs and SSRIs, are comparably safe and efficacious, they are not widely used in the United States. At least 13 Type 1 RCTs support the efficacy of MAOIs for depression in the elderly. These include two studies with phenelzine (Nardil), nine with moclobemide (Aurorix, not marketed in the United States; two of the studies were placebo controlled), and one each with brofaromine (not marketed in the United States) and selegiline (Eldeprel). Typical of the results, phenelzine was demonstrated to be equivalent to nortriptyline in both short-term and longer term efficacy (Georgotas et al., 1986).

Like TCAs, MAOIs are associated with side effects that may limit their use. In general, they also present certain inconveniences in clinical management because of the need to avoid their potentially lethal interactions with other medications and foods.

Atypical Antidepressants

Newer mixed-action medications such as nefazodone (Serzone) and venlafaxine (Effexor), which selectively inhibits both norepinephrine and serotonin uptake, have not yet been well studied in the aged.

Special Populations

Most treatment studies have been done with depressed older adults who are physically healthy and residing in community settings, and few have focused on depressed elders who are very old (80+), medically ill or fragile, in nursing homes, or suffering from coexisting dementia. Thus, many treatment recommendations are extrapolated from experience with patients who are either younger or do not share similar clinical characteristics.

Current evidence is contradictory concerning whether concurrent medical illness has an adverse effect on response. In three of the studies cited above, TCA drugs have proven efficacious in elderly, medically ill patients; for example, depressed, very elderly nursing home residents responded well to standard doses of nortriptyline, but their medical fragility led to treatment-limiting side effects in one third (Katz et al., 1990). Thus, pharmacological treatments in such patients must be used carefully since medical comorbidity appears to increase vulnerability to side effects.

Three Type 1 RCTs have tested antidepressant medications in older adults with dementia who were also depressed. One trial found no difference between imipramine and a placebo (Reifler et al., 1989), though both groups improved. Clearer benefits were shown in trials with the MAOI moclobemide (Hebensreit et al., 1991) and the SSRI citalopram (Nyth & Gottfries, 1990), neither of which is marketed in the United States. Based on the limited data available, elders with depressions considered secondary to known brain lesions should be treated according to standard guidelines and doses and can be expected to respond as well as patients with primary depressions. Treatment and dosing must be judicious, however, because of potential cognitive impairment as a side effect of TCAs such as imipramine (Teri et al., 1991).

Antidepressant medications alone are generally not effective in the treatment of late-life depression with delusions. These psychotic depressions tend to be severe, recur in successive episodes, and carry a high risk for suicide. In these circumstances, the treatments of choice are combinations of TCAs with neuroleptic medications or electroconvulsive therapy (ECT). The pharmacological approach typically consists of combining nortriptyline or desipramine with high doses of neuroleptics (e.g., perphenazine) (Meyers, 1995). Research has not yet established whether SSRIs may be used as effectively as TCAs in delusional depression or how effective combinations of antidepressants and neuroleptics are as continuation/maintenance treatments for preventing relapses and recurrences (Martinez, Mulsant, Meyers, & Lebowitz, 1996).

Maintenance Treatment

Given that depressive symptoms can usually be improved with short-term treatments, a central challenge remains the development of interventions that will keep recovered patients healthy over time. Although few clinical trials have been conducted on this topic, according to current consensus the most effective pharmacological strategy for preventing recurrence of depression entails maintaining the dose of the antidepressant medication used during the acute phase of treatment for a longer time (Frank, 1994). Expert clinical opinion recommends maintaining the patient's medication at the same dose and plasma level that was effective in the acute treatment phase for 6 months after remission and for 12 months or longer after a second or third episode (Reynolds et al., 1997).

Electroconvulsive Therapy

Despite little research focusing exclusively on the aged, evidence for the efficacy of ECT in treating late-life depression has been derived primarily from two sources: (a) studies of mixed-age samples in which significant portions of the patients have been elderly and (b) findings that age does not predict therapeutic outcomes and that older patients appear to respond equivalently to younger patients. About one third of patients treated with ECT are elderly, and 16% of older inpatients hospitalized with affective disorders receive ECT (Thompson & Blaine, 1987). Patients older than 60 constitute the age group most likely to receive ECT as a treatment for depression because they tend to manifest more of the characteristics that, in general, are considered indications for the use of this treatment. These include a history of poor response to or intolerance of other antidepressant treatments, situations in which the risks of other treatments outweigh those of ECT, or a history of good ECT response in previous episodes (Sackeim, 1994). In practice, ECT is not used as a first-line treatment but is reserved for particular clinical situations. Evidence of its short-term efficacy appears to be particularly strong in severe and psychotic depressions.

Much of the controlled research on the general efficacy of ECT, conducted from the 1950s through 1970s, antedates modern methodological standards (e.g., random assignment, blinded ratings) and represents at best Type 2 studies (about half are retrospective/Type 3 in method) (Abrams, 1992). However, ECT demonstrated an antidepressant efficacy superior to TCAs in 3 Type 1 RCTs and superiority to sham ECT in 5 of 6 rigorous RCTs (Abrams, 1992; American Psychiatric Association Task Force, 1990).[1] In various other RCTs (mostly earlier and Type 2), ECT proved equal to or more effective than TCAs (10 studies) and MAOIs (6 studies). In addition, its efficacy is supported by several meta-analyses (e.g., Janicak et al., 1985) and has never been shown inferior to alternative treatments in short-term management of depression (*Electroconvulsive Therapy*, 1985). There have also been at least seven Type 3 open trials in which depressed patients responded favorably to ECT after documented drug therapy failure.

Consistently positive findings for the short-term efficacy of ECT in specifically treating late-life depression have been reported in 15 Type 3 studies (3 prospective open trials, 12 retrospective chart surveys) involving over 1000 elderly patients treated with ECT. Good outcomes were observed in 51–100% of the cases, with less than 40% of outcomes evaluated as "poor" (Mulsant, Rosen, Thornton, & Zubenko, 1991). Generally, ECT has been shown to be safe and sometimes safer than TCAs (e.g., for severely depressed or suicidal geriatric patients with clinical characteristics that make the use of psychoactive medications hazardous). However, the risks must be carefully weighed, particularly for older adults with cardiovascular illness, certain concomitant medications, and preexisting cognitive impairment. For more detailed reviews of this literature, see Kellner (1991) and Sackeim (1994).

As usually employed, ECT is a short-term treatment, and adjunctive strategies are needed for longer range maintenance of treatment gains. As with younger patients, relapse is frequent in elderly patients following ECT. Among the possibilities to be considered are maintenance ECT and use of antidepressants post-ECT, but these require further study. There are various case reports, but no controlled studies, that support the use of ECT on an outpatient basis as a continuation and maintenance treatment with the aged. Based mainly on clinical experience, it is generally held that medications that failed to produce a therapeutic response prior to ECT are not effective as post-ECT maintenance treatments (Reynolds et al., 1997).

Psychosocial Interventions

At least eight RCTs (seven Type 1, one Type 2) indicate that psychosocial interventions are efficacious in treating major depressive disorder in the aged (see Table 14.2). Other controlled studies (seven Type 1, three Type 2) demonstrate the utility of psychosocial approaches in elderly samples featuring mixes of depression subtypes, including less-severe forms of depression. The treatments studied include cognitive-behavioral, brief psychodynamic, interpersonal, reminiscence/life review,[2] and psychoeducational modalities. For extensive reviews, see other sources (Gallagher-Thompson & Thompson, 1994; Niederehe, 1994, 1996; Teri, Curtis, Gallagher-Thompson, & Thompson, 1994; Teri & McCurry, 1994).

Across several Type 1 RCTs, efficacy has appeared comparable for CBT and brief psychodynamic treatments. In one comparative study, 70% of elderly depressed patients (Gallagher-Thompson, Hanley-Peterson, & Thompson, 1990; Thompson, Gallagher, & Breckenridge, 1987) receiving cognitive, behavioral, and psychodynamic (insight/relational) treatments showed significantly reduced depression over 6 weeks, relative to a delayed-treatment control condition, and all the treatment groups improved equivalently by the end of therapy. At 1- and 2-year follow-ups, 58% and 70%, respectively, of the sample remained not depressed without significant differences among the treatment conditions. Interpersonal psychotherapy has not been directly compared with other psychosocial approaches but has proved equivalent to nortriptyline in the treatment of major depression in the aged (Sloane, Staples, & Schneider, 1985).

In two Type 1 RCTs, reminiscence therapy has been associated with clinical improvement in both older adults with mixed depressive states (Fry, 1983) and those with a major depressive disorder (Arean et al., 1993), but in the Arean et al. study was not as effective as CBT (problem-solving therapy), either

TABLE 14.2 Summary of Controlled Clinical Trials Using Psychosocial Interventions with Elderly Patients with Major Depressive Disorder

Study	Comparison Conditions	Sample Size	Age (Years)	Gender (Percentage Female)	Duration (Weeks)	Sessions	Baseline Hamilton	d, Effect Size
Arean et al. (1993)	Problem solving Reminiscence Wait list	75	66	75	12	12	24	0.94 0.45
Beutler et al. (1987)	CBT + pill placebo CBT + alprazolam Pill placebo Alprazolam	56	71	55	20	20	21	0.99
Brand & Clingempeel (1992)	Behavioral therapy + standard hospital program Standard hospital program	53	72	89	2	8	24	1.80
Gallagher & Thompson (1982)	Behavioral Cognitive Psychodynamic	30	68	77	12	16	18	NA
Sloane et al. (1985)	IPT Nortriptyline Pill placebo	24	64	53	16	16	26	0.25
Steuer et al. (1984)	CBT Psychodynamic	33	66	79	36	46	20	0.31[a] 0.12[a]
Thompson et al. (1987)	Behavioral Cognitive Psychodynamic Wait list	91	67	67	12–16	16–20	19	0.87 0.65 0.56
Thompson et al. (1991)	CBT Desipramine CBT + desipramine	102	67	67	12–16	16–20	19	NA

Age = approximate mean or median age; CBT = cognitive-behavioral therapy; NA = not available; IPT = interpersonal psychotherapy.
[a]Calculated relative to placebo condition in separate but linked drug study of Jarvik, Mintz, Steuer, & Gerner (1982).

after 12 weeks of treatment or at a 3-month follow-up. Four other RCTs yielding mixed results regarding a reminiscence effect on depressive mood are adequate methodologically in other respects but of limited relevance for present purposes because they did not operationally characterize their samples as depressed at baseline. Cumulatively, the evidence suggests that reminiscence interventions may be useful in mild-to-moderate depression, but appear not to be an optimal treatment approach with more severe or clinically complicated depressions.

Likewise, in at least five studies (four Type 1, one Type 2), psychoeducational interventions showed efficacy in reducing depressive symptoms and dysphoric affect in elders with subclinical (or possibly dysthymic)

forms of depression. Though such programs may help in preventing the development of a more serious disorder, their efficacy in treating older adults who already manifest clinically diagnosable depression has not been adequately studied or established.

Special Populations

At least seven studies (two Type 1, four Type 2, one Type 3) have examined psychosocial treatments with depressed older adults, such as nursing home residents, who had concomitant medical illness or physical impairments. These studies most commonly focused on variants of CBT (Rybarczyk et al., 1992) or IPT (Mossey, Knott, Higgins, & Talerico, 1996). Such approaches have generally shown some antidepressant efficacy, but often limitations in the power or duration of the benefit have also been noted. For example, in a 12-week Type 3 open trial of CBT, depressed older adults with chronic, disabling physical illnesses derived equivalent benefits compared with physically healthy patients, but only the nondisabled group continued to improve over the 6 months following treatment (Kemp, Corgiat, & Gill, 1991–1992).

A behavior therapy approach for treating depression in dementia patients entails training family caregivers in depression management skills (Teri & Uomoto, 1991). Preliminary findings have suggested that both this approach and caregiver problem-solving interventions significantly reduce depression in Alzheimer's disease patients relative to a wait-list condition, with superior results for those receiving the targeted behavioral therapy (Teri, Logsdon, Wagner, & Uomoto, 1995; Teri & McCurry, 1994).

Support groups, with various forms of leadership, have been the modal psychosocial intervention for the family caregivers of demented elderly individuals. However, only seven controlled treatment studies (five Type 1, two Type 2) out of the considerable body of research on caregiver support have been directed specifically to treatment of depression in samples that were at least largely elderly; the findings were mixed regarding efficacy in reducing depression. The greatest efficacy appears to derive from pychoeducational groups employing behavior therapy and CBT approaches specifically targeted toward management of caregivers' depressive symptoms (Lovett & Gallagher, 1988). In one study, 71% of clinically depressed caregivers achieved symptom remission, with no overall difference between CBT and brief psychodynamic therapy; however, those who had become caregivers relatively recently improved more with psychodynamic treatment, whereas caregivers for a longer duration (3½ years or more) benefited more with CBT (Gallagher-Thompson & Steffen, 1994). In a randomized longitudinal study, spouses of Alzheimer's disease patients who participated in a psychosocial intervention program involving individual and family counseling in addition to support groups remained stable over time whereas untreated control caregivers became increasingly (and by the eighth month, significantly more) depressed (Mittelman et al., 1995). Seemingly, effective intervention with depressed elderly caregivers must extend powerfully across multiple modalities, be sustained over time, and involve families in the support process.

Continuation and Maintenance Forms of Treatment

To the extent that findings with middle-aged adults (Frank et al., 1990) can be extrapolated to the elderly, longer durations of treatment with psychosocial therapies may be of preventive benefit for depressed older adults, but few empirical data are currently available. In one small continuation phase study (Type 1), a support group incorporating both psychodynamic and problem-solving techniques effectively reduced rehospitalization among elderly depressed patients after discharge from inpatient treatment (Ong, Martineau, Lloyd, & Robbins, 1987).

Cumulative Findings

In summary, various forms of psychotherapy (particularly cognitive-behavioral, psychodynamic, and interpersonal approaches) have demonstrated efficacy in decreasing depression in older adults to a degree that clearly exceeds spontaneous change over time. Treatment gains have been maintained well at follow-up. In comparative treatment trials, the various psychotherapies studied have generally proven equivalent in both their acute and longer range treatment impact.

These findings have been reaffirmed by a meta-analysis of 17 published studies of psychosocial treatments for depressed elderly patients, including cognitive, psychodynamic, reminiscence, and eclectic approaches (Scogin & McElreath, 1994). The analysis showed that these treatments were reliably more effective than no-treatment conditions in reducing depression, yielding an overall effect size of .78. This compares favorably with the effect sizes shown for psychosocial treatments of adults of younger ages and suggests that older patients benefit just as much as others from these treatments. The data did not indicate any clear advantage for group versus individual treatment formats or for any particular treatment approach. In general, the findings regarding treatment outcomes (and also about the factors that contribute to them) are comparable to those found in psychotherapy research with younger adults.

COMPARISONS OF PSYCHOTHERAPY AND PHARMACOTHERAPY

Though considerably more studies have been conducted on pharmacotherapies than on psychotherapies (as also is the case in research with younger patients), on a study-by-study basis the efficacy findings do not clearly favor either treatment approach in the elderly. For late-life depression, the authors calculated the effect size for ten psychosocial treatments based on six of the parallel group clinical trials shown in Table 14.2 (five Type 1, one Type 2) in which it was possible to compare each psychological intervention with a no-treatment (drug placebo or wait-list) control condition. These clinical trials involved 219 patients who were assigned to or had completed psychotherapy and 104 patients who were assigned to control conditions; the study durations for the data analyzed ranged from 2 to 26 weeks. All but one of these trials involved outpatients or depressed community-dwelling volunteers. The mean effect size from these studies, $d = .74$, is similar to the mean effect sizes ($d = .60$ and .62) calculated in a meta-analysis of studies of imipramine and nortriptyline, respectively, as psychopharmacological treatments for late-life depression (Schneider, 1994), suggesting that the effect of the psychotherapeutic treatments studied was comparable in magnitude to that of typical psychopharmacological treatments.

Though such results may seem to suggest that these treatments are equivalent, there is insufficient evidence on the outcomes of psychosocial interventions or medications (separately or in combination) in treating elderly depressives enrolled in the same study to reach any clear-cut conclusion at this time about their comparative efficacy. To date, only three RCTs have directly compared psychotherapeutic and pharmacological approaches in the treatment of late-life major depression. In one trial, IPT and nortriptyline showed equivalent efficacy after 6 and 16 weeks of acute treatment; IPT was associated with lower dropout rates (Sloane et al., 1985). In another RCT over 3 months of treatment, combining desipramine and CBT aided patients' recovery (relative to the results of either treatment individually), whereas CBT alone was superior to desipramine alone. Over a longer range (4–5 months of continuation/maintenance treatment and subsequent 6- and 12-month follow-ups), the combination failed to confer a significant advantage over treatment with CBT alone. No medication-only group

was continued past the acute phase in this research (personal communication, L. W. Thompson, January, 1996; Thompson, Gallagher-Thompson, Hanser, Gantz, & Steffen, 1991). In a third study of depressed older adults treated pharmacologically with alprazolam (Xanax) or a placebo, either alone or in combination with cognitive group therapy, all the treatment groups showed equivalent symptomatic improvement (Beutler et al., 1987). The cognitive therapy groups displayed more improvement on a measure of sleep efficiency and had fewer dropouts. These results are difficult to interpret, both because of the equivalent degree of change observed in the placebo-only group (all subjects also participated in medication/support groups) and because of questions about the use of alprazolam, an antianxiety benzodiazepine medication, in treating depression.

There has been much discussion about whether choice of treatment should be guided by the severity of depression since several reports suggested that, unlike antidepressant medications, psychotherapeutic approaches may be limited in utility primarily to cases of mild-to-moderate depression (Agency for Health Care Policy and Research, 1993; NIH Consensus Development Panel, 1992). This suggestion largely reflects existing patterns of care, and its fundamental accuracy is difficult to ascertain on a scientific basis. The few studies directly comparing psychopharmacological and psychosocial treatments in the elderly involved depressions treatable on an outpatient basis rather than the severe or clinically complicated depressions that require hospitalization. In general, drug studies are conducted almost exclusively with patients diagnosed with major depressive disorders, whereas many psychotherapy studies have encompassed mixes of major depression and milder and subclinical forms of depressive disorder (Schneider, 1995). Accordingly, the existing research data leave questions unanswered not only about the efficacy of psychotherapy with severely depressed, hospitalized patients but also about the benefits of psychopharmacological treatments for elderly persons with milder and subclinical forms of depression. Largely overlooked in this debate are factors affecting the delivery of either form of treatment in a high-quality fashion in various settings. Such considerations as the availability and relative cost of personnel qualified to deliver various treatments will often be critical in deciding between treatments of equivalent intrinsic efficacy.

In clinical practice, the combination of pharmacotherapy with psychosocial interventions (e.g., "clinical management" or nonspecific "supportive therapy") is very common and, rather than taking an either/or approach, such combined treatment might be considered a standard of care. Psychosocial elements clearly operate in the delivery of pharmacotherapies and should be more clearly specified (Niederehe, 1994). One recent study showed an incremental benefit of adding behavior therapy to the first several weeks of standard hospital treatment, including psychotropic medications, of newly admitted depressed geriatric inpatients (Brand & Clingempeel, 1992). Compared to patients who did not receive the added treatment, two to three times more patients in the behavior therapy group reached full remission of depressive symptoms, suggesting an acceleration of their overall treatment response.

Though the findings in the general adult population are equivocal (Antonuccio, Danton, & DeNelsky, 1995), combined treatments may have synergistic effects surpassing those of either approach taken alone. In an ongoing maintenance treatment study, elderly depressed patients treated openly during the acute treatment phase with the combination of interpersonal therapy and nortriptyline appear to show response rates higher than are typical in most studies of individual medications or psychotherapies, with 79% of the first 61 patients to complete 16 weeks in treatment achieving a full clinical remission (Reynolds et al., 1992). Moreover, for 30 patients with recurrent episodes who received the combined treatment during two consecutive depression episodes, 27 patients achieved stable symptom remission in both episodes, and for 22 the time to remission was briefer in the second episode (Reynolds et al., 1994). These open-trial results parallel those observed for middle-aged patients in a prior study (Kupfer, Frank, & Perel, 1989), suggesting that, with a combined approach, even recurrently depressed elderly patients are responsive to treatment to a degree equivalent to younger adults.

TREATMENTS OF CHOICE
FOR ANXIETY

Controlled clinical trials of treatments for late-life anxiety disorders are, for the most part, lacking, and the methodology of the available studies was often less rigorous than expected according to current standards. Recommendations about treatment, therefore, are generally extrapolated from studies with younger patients or nonsymptomatic elderly volunteer subjects or are simply based on clinical experience (Salzman, 1991). At the same time, it should be noted that anxiety has fairly often been assessed as an outcome dimension in studies of late-life depression (albeit as a symptom rather than as a primary diagnosis) and generally has been found to respond, along with other symptoms, to treatments for depression.

Pharmacological Treatments

As in younger patients, pharmacological treatment of anxiety in the elderly is generally with benzodiazepine medications. Only 11 clinical outcome studies have been conducted comparing benzodiazepine treatment of anxious elderly patients to other active or placebo treatments (3 studies of chlordiazepoxide or Librium, 3 of diazepam or Valium, and 5 of oxazepam or Serax). These are generally seriously flawed Type 2 RCTs, only 6 of which incorporated placebo controls (1 diazepam and 5 oxazepam) (Salzman, 1991). In general, these studies support the efficacy of benzodiazepines in alleviating anxiety symptoms in elderly individuals and do not indicate a superiority for any particular benzodiazepine. However, a number of the studies were concerned with the control of agitated behavior in dementia or chronic schizophrenic patients, and for this purpose several found benzodiazepines generally noneffective and inferior to neuroleptics.[3]

A large number of pharmacodynamic studies indicate that benzodiazepine medications are generally associated with at least some degree of cognitive impairment, even in younger subjects, and that the elderly are at increased risk for these negative effects (e.g., Pomara, Deptula, Singh, & Monroy, 1991). The memory and learning impairments may persist even after discontinuation of the medication (Davis, Morse, & Ivnik, 1993).

One Type 1 RCT (Böhm et al., 1990) and four Type 3 open trials support the efficacy of the nonbenzodiazepine medication buspirone (BuSpar) as an anxiolytic treatment in the aged and suggest that it causes less sedation as a side effect than do benzodiazepines. Several subanalyses of the elderly included in a large open trial suggest that elderly patients (even those age 80+) tend to benefit equivalently to younger adults.

However, clinical experience in the use of buspirone with elderly patients is sparse (Salzman, 1991).

No specific controlled research has been conducted on other possible treatments for anxiety disorders in the elderly (e.g., beta blockers, antidepressants). However, based on clinical experience and extrapolation from studies with younger patients, antidepressant medications are recommended as the treatments of choice for mixed depression and anxiety, panic disorders, and obsessive compulsive disorders in the elderly (Schneider, 1995, 1996a).

Psychosocial Interventions

Numerous clinical case reports (Gorenstein & Papp, 1995; Hersen & Van Hasselt, 1992; Johnson, 1991; McCarthy, Katz, & Foa, 1991), but only one controlled study, support the efficacy of psychotherapeutic treatment of elderly patients with diagnosed anxiety disorders. The empirical information is thus very limited about the extent and durability of the treatment effects that can be anticipated in more seriously disturbed, anxious elderly patients.

The one available Type 1 RCT compared CBT and supportive psychotherapy in treating older patients with generalized anxiety disorder (Stanley & Beck, 1995). The patients were all 55 years of age or older, had a mean duration of GAD of 35 years, and were not involved in any other treatment. Overall, the two treatments were equivalently efficacious in reducing anxiety and depression in these patients; CBT conferred some apparent advantage in alleviating specific fears.

At least nine other controlled studies (five Type 1, four Type 2) support the efficacy of psychosocial interventions in ameliorating anxiety symptoms in symptomatic but undiagnosed elderly subjects. The techniques studied include relaxation methods, rational-emotive training, and anxiety management training (DeBerry, 1981–1982, 1982; DeBerry, Davis, & Reinhard, 1989; Harp Scates, Randolph, Gutsch, & Knight, 1986; Keller, Croake, & Brooking, 1975; Sallis, Lichstein, Clarkson, Stalgaitis, & Campbell, 1983; Scogin, Rickard, Keith, Wilson, & McElreath, 1992; Welden & Yesavage, 1982; Yesavage, 1984). For example, both progressive relaxation and imaginal relaxation techniques were shown to be efficacious in reducing symptoms of subjective anxiety in community-dwelling elderly adults relative to waiting-list controls (Scogin et al., 1992), and treatment gains were

well maintained at follow-up (Rickard, Scogin, & Keith, 1995).

FUTURE DIRECTIONS IN TREATMENT AND TREATMENT RESEARCH

Over the next decade, the knowledge base on treatment of depression and anxiety in elderly adults will undoubtedly expand significantly. In particular, based partly on research efforts already under way, rigorous clinical trial data will accumulate on newer treatments (e.g., SSRIs), combined treatment approaches, and emerging approaches to long-term treatment and prevention of recurrence. New medications with more selective actions and fewer side effects can be anticipated. Schedules and techniques will be developed for delivering maintenance versions of psychosocial treatments, as well as extending psychopharmacological treatments over longer time periods. More will be known about additional interventions for which at present no data are available, such as the effects of aerobic exercise and bright light therapy on late-life depression. In the case of treatments for anxiety disorders, any additions to empirically based information cannot help being major advances.

One advance is likely to be the development of comprehensive treatment "packages" (e.g., depression and anxiety management programs), integrating both psychological and biological components. Such approaches entail more than simply having the patient see both a physician for medications and someone else for psychotherapy or counseling. For example, psychosocial techniques may be used to enhance compliance with medication regimens, and psychopharmacological medications may be used as techniques for creating the emotional state necessary for engaging in problem solving and implementing behavioral or situational changes rather than as a treatment sufficient in itself for recovery. An integration of psychosocial and psychopharmacological aspects of treatment in a complementary fashion requires interdisciplinary collaboration, adaptation to working within a primary care setting, and inclusion of family members as key players in the overall treatment strategy.

Treatment data will also be generated for a broader spectrum of the elderly population and for specific comorbidity factors about which we currently have very limited treatment efficacy information. In particular, more data will be generated about the treatment of depression in very old patients (age 80+) and in ethnic minority elders and about the effects of comorbid physical illnesses, cognitive impairment, and residency in long-term care settings on treatment response. We hope that considerably expanded research information will also be forthcoming on the treatment of elderly persons manifesting dysthymia or dysphoria syndromes that, though symptomatically less severe than major depressive disorders, tend also to be more chronic and less likely to respond to psychopharmacological intervention or remit spontaneously.

Various changes are needed in the ways in which treatment studies are conducted. Future research will be increasingly pointed in the following directions:

1. *Broadened outcome assessments.* More studies will evaluate interventions not only as regards their efficacy in reducing depressive symptoms, but also in terms of the achievement of other treatment goals, such as improvements in physical health, social integration, work performance, and everyday function, enhancement of coping skills, reduction in the (mis)use of primary health care services, and changes in overall quality of life. This is particularly important in comparing disparate treatments or studying combination treatments, for which differing components of the treatment package may influence quite distinct aspects of the overall outcome.

2. *More information on cost effectiveness.* In order to provide information that is practically useful to consumers, third-party insurers, and policy makers, studies will have to relate outcomes to input variables such as the cost, time, and effort, and other resources required to achieve them, and to look at these relationships over a longer time frame.

3. *More information on how to match patients to optimal treatments.* In order to optimize outcomes, treatments must be matched to patients' characteristics and tailored to their situations. Patients' attitudes and preferences regarding treatments and their expectations regarding which forms of assistance are likely to be helpful with their problems are key elements to be considered but need to be more carefully researched. Contrary to what is commonly assumed, many older persons prefer psychosocial to pharmacological treatments (Rokke & Scogin, 1995). Recent biological research suggests that matching of patients to the medications most apt to be effective for them might be facilitated by tests that can subtype patients who will metabolize drugs differently. In the aged, the patient's cognitive capacities and flexibility and

the availability of family or other social support are also critical influences on such critical treatment phenomena as compliance, problem solving, and new learning. Furthermore, the availability of treatment personnel who are well trained in aging, as well as in the treatment technique, and sensitized to the special features and needs of the older individual must be considered when determining which form of treatment can best be delivered in specific situations.

4. *More information on modes of treatment delivery.* It will be particularly important for researchers to determine the relative efficacy of individual versus group treatment formats, and to clarify what treatment personnel variables (e.g., levels of training, types of supervision) are essential for assuring optimum (or acceptable) outcomes. These service delivery issues pose critical questions relative to making treatment more accessible to the aged, and the answers may vary by type of treatment.

Notes

1. Much recent ECT research, while using randomization and blinding, has investigated variations in ECT techniques. For present purposes, these studies represent Type 3 open trials because comparisons to non-ECT treatment conditions have not been part of their designs.

2. Reminiscence and life review therapies, relatively specific to the elderly, emphasize the recall and recounting of past life experiences, sometimes with reinterpretation of their meanings or reworking of issues previously left unresolved (Lewis & Butler, 1974).

3. Such studies are peripheral to the present focus on anxiety disorders and more germane to treatment of behavioral symptoms in dementia (see chapter 5, this volume). Neuroleptic medications are generally not recommended as treatments for mood and anxiety disorders in elderly individuals.

References

Abrams, R. (1992). *Electroconvulsive therapy* (2nd ed.). New York: Oxford University Press.

Agency for Health Care Policy and Research. (1993). *Clinical practice guideline, No. 5, Depression in primary care: Vol. 2, Treatment of major depression.* (AHCPR Publication No. 93–0551). Rockville, Md.: Author.

Alexopoulos, G. S. (1994). Biological correlates of late-life depression. In L. S. Schneider, C. F. Reynolds, B. D. Lebowitz, & A. Friedhoff (Eds.), *Diagnosis and treatment of depression in late life: Results of the NIH*

Consensus Development Conference (pp. 101–116). Washington, D.C.: American Psychiatric Press.

Alexopoulos, G. S. (1991). Anxiety and depression in the elderly. In C. Salzman & B. D. Lebowitz (Eds.), *Anxiety in the elderly: Treatment and research* (pp. 63–77). New York: Springer.

American Psychiatric Association. (1994). *Diagnostic and statistical manual of mental disorders* (4th ed.). Washington, D.C.: Author.

American Psychiatric Association Task Force on Electroconvulsive Therapy. (1990). *The practice of electroconvulsive therapy: Recommendations for treatment, training and privileging.* Washington, D.C.: American Psychiatric Press.

Antonuccio, D. O., Danton, W. G., & DeNelsky, G. Y. (1995). Psychotherapy versus medication for depression: Challenging the conventional wisdom with data. *Professional Psychology: Research and Practice, 26,* 574–585.

Arean, P. A., Perri, M. G., Nezu, A. M., Schein, R. L., Christopher, F., & Joseph, T. X. (1993). Comparative effectiveness of social problem-solving therapy and reminiscence therapy as treatments for depression in older adults. *Journal of Consulting and Clinical Psychology, 61,* 1003–1010.

Becker, J., & Morrissey, E. (1988). Difficulties in assessing depressive-like reactions to chronic severe external stress as exemplified by spouse caregivers of Alzheimer patients. *Psychology and Aging, 3,* 300–306.

Beutler, L. E., Scogin, F., Kirkish, P., Schretlen, D., Corbishley, A., Hamblin, D., Meredith, K., Potter, R., Barnford, C. R., & Levinson, A. I. (1987). Group cognitive therapy and alprazolam in the treatment of depression in older adults. *Journal of Consulting and Clinical Psychology, 55,* 550–556.

Blazer, D., George, L. K., & Hughes, D. (1991). The epidemiology of anxiety disorders: An age comparison. In C. Salzman & B. D. Lebowitz (Eds.), *Anxiety in the elderly: Treatment and Research* (pp. 17–30). New York: Springer.

Böhm, C., Robinson, D. S., Gammans, R. E., Shrotriya, R. C., Alms, D. R., Leroy, A., & Placchi, M. (1990). Buspirone therapy in anxious elderly patients: A controlled clinical trial. *Journal of Clinical Psychopharmacology, 10*(3, Suppl.), 47S–51S.

Brand, E., & Clingempeel, W. G. (1992). Group behavioral therapy with depressed geriatric inpatients: An assessment of incremental efficacy. *Behavior Therapy, 23,* 475–482.

Busse, E. W., & Pfeiffer, E. (1977). Functional psychiatric disorders in old age. In E. W. Busse & E. Pfeiffer (Eds.), *Behavior and adaptation in late life* (2nd ed., pp. 158–211). Boston: Little, Brown.

Conwell, Y. (1994). Suicide in elderly patients. In L. S. Schneider, C. F. Reynolds, B. D. Lebowitz, & A. Friedhoff (Eds.), *Diagnosis and treatment of depression in late life: Results of the NIH Consensus Development Conference* (pp. 397–418). Washington, D.C.: American Psychiatric Press.

Davis, L. J., Morse, R. M., & Ivnik, R. J. (1993). Learning and memory impairment in older, detoxified, benzodiazepine-dependent patients. *Mayo Clinic Proceedings, 68,* 731–737.

DeBerry, S. (1981–1982). An evaluation of progressive muscle relaxation on stress related symptoms in a geriatric population. *International Journal of Aging and Human Development, 14,* 255–269.

———. (1982). The effects of meditation-relaxation on anxiety and depression in a geriatric population. *Psychotherapy: Theory, Research, and Practice, 19,* 512–521.

DeBerry, S., Davis, S., & Reinhard, K. E. (1989). A comparison of meditation-relaxation and cognitive/behavioral techniques for reducing anxiety and depression in a geriatric population. *Journal of Geriatric Psychiatry, 22,* 231–247.

Electroconvulsive therapy. (1985, June). NIH Consensus Development Conference Statement, *5*(11).

Flint, A. J. (1994). Epidemiology and comorbidity of anxiety disorders in the elderly. *American Journal of Psychiatry, 151,* 640–649.

Frank, E. (1994). Long-term prevention of recurrences in elderly patients. In L. S. Schneider, C. F. Reynolds, B. D. Lebowitz, and A. J. Friedhoff (Eds.), *Diagnosis and treatment of depression in late life: Results of the NIH Consensus Development Conference* (pp. 317–329). Washington, D.C.: American Psychiatric Press.

Frank, E., Kupfer, D. J., Perel, J. M., Cornes, C., Jarett, D., Mallinger, A. G., Thase, M. E., McEachran, A. B., & Grochocinski, V. J. (1990). Three-year outcomes for maintenance therapies in recurrent depression. *Archives of General Psychiatry, 47,* 1093–1099.

Fry, P. S. (1983). Structured and unstructured reminiscence training and depression among the elderly. *Clinical Gerontologist, 1*(3), 15–37.

Gallagher, D. E., & Thompson, L. W. (1982). Treatment of major depressive disorder in older adult outpatients with brief psychotherapies. *Psychotherapy: Theory, Research and Practice, 19,* 482–490.

Gallagher-Thompson, D., Hanley-Peterson, P., & Thompson, L. W. (1990). Maintenance of gains versus relapse following brief psychotherapy for depression. *Journal of Consulting and Clinical Psychology, 58,* 371–374.

Gallagher-Thompson, D., & Steffen, A. M. (1994). Comparative effects of cognitive-behavioral and brief psychodynamic psychotherapies for depressed family caregivers. *Journal of Consulting and Clinical Psychology, 62,* 543–549.

Gallagher-Thompson, D., & Thompson, L. W. (1994). Psychotherapy with older adults in theory and practice. In B. Bongor & L. Beutler (Eds.), *Foundations of psychotherapy: Theory, research, and practice* (pp. 359–379). New York: Oxford University Press.

Georgotas, A, & McCue, R. E. (1989). The additional benefit of extending an antidepressant trial past seven weeks in the depressed elderly. *International Journal of Geriatric Psychiatry, 4*(4), 191–195.

Georgotas, A., McCue, R. E., Hapworth, W., Friedman, E., Kim, O. H., Welkowitz, J., Chang, I., & Cooper, T. B. (1986). Comparative efficacy and safety of MAOIs versus TCAs in treating depression in the elderly. *Biological Psychiatry, 21*, 1155–1166.

Gorenstein, E. E., & Papp, L. A. (1995, August). *Cognitive-behavioral treatment of late-life anxiety disorders.* Paper presented at 103rd Annual Convention of the American Psychological Association, New York.

Gurian, B. S., & Miner, J. H. (1991). Clinical presentation of anxiety in the elderly. In C. Salzman & B. D. Lebowitz (Eds.), *Anxiety in the elderly: Treatment and research* (pp. 31–44). New York: Springer.

Harp Scates, S. K., Randolph, D. L., Gutsch, K. U., & Knight, H. V. (1986). Effects of cognitive-behavioral, reminiscence, and activity treatments on life satisfaction and anxiety in the elderly. *International Journal of Aging and Human Development, 22*, 141–146.

Hassan, R., & Pollard, A. (1994). Late-life onset panic disorder: Clinical and demographic characteristics of a patient sample. *Journal of Geriatric Psychiatry and Neurology, 7*, 86–90.

Hebenstreit, G. F., Baumhackl, U., Chan-Palay, V., Gruner, E., Kasas, A., Katsching, H., Krebs, E., Kummer, J., Martucci, N., Radmayr, E., Rieder, L., Saletu, M., Schlegel, S., & Lorscheid, T. (1991, August). *The treatment of depression in geriatric depressed and demented patients by moclobemide: Results from the international multicenter double blind placebo controlled trial.* Paper presented at Fifth Congress of the International Psychogeriatric Association, Rome, Italy.

Hersen, M., & Van Hasselt, V. B. (1992). Behavioral assessment and treatment of anxiety in the elderly. *Clinical Psychology Review, 12*, 619–640.

Janicak, P. G., Davis, J. M., Gibbons, R. D., Ericksen, S., Chang, S., & Gallagher, P. (1985). Efficacy of ECT: A meta-analysis. *American Journal of Psychiatry, 142*, 297–302.

Jarvik, L. F., Mintz, J., Steuer, J., & Gerner, R. (1982). Treating geriatric depression: A 26-week interim analysis. *Journal of the American Geriatrics Society, 30*, 713–717.

Johnson, F. A. (1991). Psychotherapy of the elderly anxious patient. In C. Salzman & B. D. Lebowitz (Eds.), *Anxiety in the elderly: Treatment and reserach* (pp. 215–248). New York: Springer.

Katona, C., & Judge, R. (1996). Antidepressants for elderly people: Should selective serotonin reuptake inhibitors (SSRIs) be the first-line choice? *Primary Care Psychiatry, 2*, 123–130.

Katz, I.R., Simpson, G. M., Curlik, S. M., Parmelee, P. A., & Muhly, C. (1990). Pharmacologic treatment of major depression for elderly patients in residential care settings. *Journal of Clinical Psychiatry, 51* (Suppl.), 41–48.

Keller, J. F., Croake, J. W., & Brooking, J. Y. (1975). Effects of a program in rational thinking on anxieties in older persons. *Journal of Counseling Psychology, 22*, 54–57.

Kellner, C. H. (Ed.) (1991). Electroconvulsive therapy. *Psychiatric Clinics of North America, 14*, 793–1020.

Kemp, B. J., Corgiat, M., & Gill, C. (1991–1992). Effects of brief cognitive-behavioral group psychotherapy on older persons with and without disabling illness. *Behavior, Health, and Aging, 2*(1), 21–28.

Kernohan, W. J., Chambers, J. L., Wilson, W. T., & Daugherty, J. F. (1967). Effects of nortriptyline on the mental and social adjustment of geriatric patients in a mental hospital. *Journal of the American Geriatrics Society, 15*, 196–202.

Kupfer, D. J., Frank, E., & Perel, M. J. (1989). The advantage of early treatment intervention in recurrent depression. *Archives of General Psychiatry, 46*, 771–775.

Lamy, P. P., Salzman, C., & Nevis-Olesen, J. (1992). Drug prescribing patterns, risks, and compliance guidelines. In C. Salzman (Ed.), *Clinical geriatric psychopharmacology* (2nd ed.). Baltimore: Williams & Wilkins.

Lewis, M. I., & Butler, R. N. (1974). Life review therapy: Putting memories to work in individual and group psychotherapy. *Geriatrics, 29*, 165–173.

Lipsey, J. R., Robinson, R. G., Pearlson, G. D., Rao, K., & Price, T. R. (1984). Nortriptyline treatment of post-stroke depression: A double-blind study. *Lancet, 1*, 297–300.

Lovett, S., & Gallagher, D. (1988). Psychoeducational interventions of family caregivers: Preliminary efficacy data. *Behavior Therapy, 19*, 321–330.

Martinez, R. A., Mulsant, B. H., Meyers, B. S., & Lebowitz, B. D. (1996). Delusional and psychotic depression in late life: Clinical research needs. *American Journal of Geriatric Psychiatry, 4*, 77–84.

McCarthy, P. R., Katz, I. R., & Foa, E. B. (1991). Cognitive-behavioral treatment of anxiety in the elderly: A proposed model. In C. Salzman & B. D. Lebowitz (Eds.), *Anxiety in the elderly: Treatment and research* (pp. 197–214). New York: Springer.

Meyers, B. S. (1995). Late-life delusional depression: Acute and long-term treatment. *International Psychogeriatrics, 7*(Suppl.), 113–124.

Mittelman, M. S., Ferris, S. H., Shulman, E., Steinberg, G., Ambinder, A., Mackell, J. A., & Cohen, J. (1995). A comprehensive support program: Effect on depression in spouse-caregivers of AD patients. *The Gerontologist, 35*, 792–802.

Morgan, K., Dallosso, H., Ebrahim, S., Arie, T., & Fentem, P. H. (1988). Prevalence, frequency, and duration of hypnotic drug use among the elderly living at home. *British Medical Journal, 296*, 601–602.

Mossey, J. M., Knott, K. A., Higgins, M., & Talerico, K. (1996). Effectiveness of a psychosocial intervention, interpersonal counseling, for subdysthymic depression in medically ill elderly. *Journal of Gerontology: Medical Sciences, 51A*, M172–M178.

Mulsant, B. H., Rosen, J., Thornton, J. E., & Zubenko, G. S. (1991). A naturalistic prospective study of electroconvulsive therapy in late-life depression. *Journal of Geriatric Psychiatry and Neurology, 4*, 3–13.

Murphy, E. (1994). The course and outcome of depression in late life. In L. S. Schneider, C. F. Reynolds, B. D. Lebowitz, & A. Friedhoff (Eds.), *Diagnosis and treatment of depression in late life: Results of the NIH Consensus Development Conference* (pp. 81–97). Washington, D.C.: American Psychiatric Press.

Murphy, E., Smith, E. R., Lindesay, J. E. B., & Slattery, J. (1988). Increased mortality rates in late-life depression. *British Journal of Psychiatry, 152*, 347–353.

Nair, N. P. V., Amin, M., Holm, P., Katona, C., Klitgaard, N., Ng Ying Kin, N. M. K., Kragh-Sorensen, P., Kuhn, H., Leek, C. A., & Stage, K. B. (1995). Moclobemide and nortriptyline in elderly depressed patients: A randomized, multicentre trial against placebo. *Journal of Affective Disorders, 33*, 1–9.

National Institutes of Health Consensus Development Panel on Depression in Late Life. (1992). Diagnosis and treatment of depression in late life. *Journal of the American Medical Association, 268*, 1018–1024.

Niederehe, G. (1994). Psychosocial therapies with depressed older adults. In L. S. Schneider, C. F. Reynolds, B. D. Lebowitz, & A. J. Friedhoff (Eds.), *Diagnosis and treatment of depression in late life: Results of the NIH Consensus Development Conference* (pp. 293–315). Washington, D.C.: American Psychiatric Press.

———. (1996). Psychosocial treatments with depressed older adults: A research update. *American Journal of Geriatric Psychiatry, 4*(Suppl. 1), 566–578.

Nyth, A. L., & Gottfries, C. G. (1990). The clinical efficacy of citalopram in treatment of emotional disturbances in dementia disorders: A Nordic multicentre study. *British Journal of Psychiatry, 157*, 894.

Ong, Y.-L., Martineau, F., Lloyd, C., & Robbins, I. (1987). A support group for the depressed elderly. *International Journal of Geriatric Psychiatry, 2*, 119–123.

Person, D. C., & Borkovec, T. D. (1995, August). *Anxiety disorders among the elderly: Patterns and issues.* Paper presented at the 103rd Annual Convention of the American Psychological Association, New York.

Pomara, N., Deptula, D., Singh, R., & Monroy, C. A. (1991). Cognitive toxicity of benzodiazepines in the elderly. In C. Salzman & B. D. Lebowitz (Eds.), *Anxiety in the elderly: Treatment and research* (pp. 175–196). New York: Springer.

Rabins, P. V. (1996). Barriers to diagnosing and treating depression in the elderly. *American Journal of Geriatric Psychiatry, 4*(Suppl. 1), 579–583.

Regier, D. A., Boyd, J. H., Burke, J. D., Rae, D. S., Myers, J. K., Kramer, M., Robins, L. N., George, L. K., Karno, M., & Locke, B. Z. (1988). One-month prevalence of mental disorders in the United States: Based on five epidemiologic catchment area sites. *Archives of General Psychiatry, 45*, 977–986.

Reifler, B. V., Teri, L., Raskind, M., Veith, R., Barnes, R., White, E., & McLean, P. (1989). Double-blind trial of imipramine in Alzheimer's disease in patients with and without depression. *American Journal of Psychiatry, 146*, 45–49.

Reynolds, C. F., Alexopoulos, G., Katz, I., & Mulsant, B. H. (1997). Treatment of geriatric mood disorders. *Current Review of Mood Disorders, 1*, 189–202.

Reynolds, C. F., Frank, E., Perel, J. M., Imber, S. D., Cornes, C., Morycz, R. K., Mazumdar, S., Miller, M. D., Pollock, B. G., Rifai, A. H., Stack, J. A., George, C. J., Houck, P. R., & Kupfer, D. J. (1992). Combined pharmacotherapy and psychotherapy in the acute and continuation treatment of elderly patients with recurrent major depression: A preliminary report. *American Journal of Psychiatry, 149*, 1687–1692.

Reynolds, C. F., Frank, E., Perel, J. M., Miller, M. D., Cornes, C., Rifai, A. H., Pollock, B. G., Mazumdar, S., George, C. J., Houck, P. R., & Kupfer, D. J. (1994). Treatment of consecutive episodes of major depression in the elderly. *American Journal of Psychiatry, 151*, 1740–1743.

Rickard, H. C., Scogin, F., & Keith, S. (1995). A one-year follow-up of relaxation training for elders with subjective anxiety. *The Gerontologist, 34*, 121–122.

Rokke P. D., & Scogin, F. (1995). Depression treatment preferences in younger and older adults. *Journal of Clinical Geropsychology, 1*, 243–257.

Roose, S. P., Glassman, A. H., Attia, E., & Woodring, S. (1994). Comparative efficacy of selective serotonin reuptake inhibitors and tricyclics in the treatment of melancholia. *American Journal of Psychiatry, 151*, 1735–1739.

Rovner, B. W., German, P. S., Brant, L. J., Burton, L., & Folstein, M. F. (1991). Depression and mortality in nursing homes. *Journal of the American Medical Association, 265*, 993–996.

Rybarczyk, B., Gallagher-Thompson, D., Rodman, J., Zeiss, A., Gantz, F. E., & Yesavage, J. (1992). Applying cognitive-behavioral psychotherapy to the chronically ill elderly: Treatment issues and case illustration. *International Psychogeriatrics, 4,* 127–140.

Sackeim, H. A. (1994). The use of electroconvulsive therapy in late life depression. In L. S. Schneider, C. F. Reynolds, B. D. Lebowitz, & A. Friedhoff (Eds.), *Diagnosis and treatment of depression in late life: Results of the NIH Consensus Development Conference* (pp. 259–277). Washington, D.C.: American Psychiatric Press.

Sallis, J. F., Lichstein, K. L., Clarkson, A. D., Stalgaitis, S., & Campbell, M. (1983). Anxiety and depression management for the elderly. *International Journal of Behavioral Geriatrics, 1*(4), 3–12.

Salzman, C. (1991). Pharmacologic treatment of the anxious elderly patient. In C. Salzman, & B. D. Lebowitz (Eds.), *Anxiety in the elderly* (pp. 149–173). New York: Springer.

———. (Ed.) (1992). *Clinical geriatric psychopharmacology,* 2nd ed. Baltimore: Williams & Wilkins.

———. (1994). Pharmacological treatment of depression in the elderly. In L. S. Schneider, C. F. Reynolds, B. D. Lebowitz, & A. Friedhoff (Eds.), *Diagnosis and treatment of depression in late life: Results of the NIH Consensus Development Conference* (pp. 181–244). Washington, D.C.: American Psychiatric Press.

Schneider, L. S. (1994). Comments on metaanalysis from a clinician's perspective. In L. S. Schneider, C. F. Reynolds, B. D. Lebowitz, & A. Friedhoff (Eds.), *Diagnosis and treatment of depression in late life* (pp. 361–373). Washington, D.C.: American Psychiatric Press.

———. (1995). Efficacy of clinical treatment for mental disorders among older persons. In M. Gatz (Ed.), *Emerging issues in mental health and aging* (pp. 19–65). Washington, D.C.: American Psychological Association.

———. (1996a). Overview of generalized anxiety disorder in the elderly. *Journal of Clinical Psychiatry, 57* (Suppl. 7), 34–45.

———. (1996b). Pharmacologic considerations in the treatment of late-life depression. *American Journal of Geriatric Psychiatry, 4*(Suppl. 1), 551–565.

Schneider, L. S., & Olin, J. T. (1995). Efficacy of acute treatment for geriatric depression. *International Psychogeriatrics, 7*(Suppl.), 7–25.

Schneider, L. S., Reynolds, C. F., Lebowitz, B. D., & Friedhoff, A. (Eds.). (1994). *Diagnosis and treatment of depression in late life: Results of the NIH Consensus Development Conference.* Washington, D.C.: American Psychiatric Press.

Scogin, F., & McElreath, L. (1994). Efficacy of psychoso-cial treatments for geriatric depression: A quantitative review. *Journal of Consulting and Clinical Psychology, 62,* 69–74.

Scogin, F., Rickard, H. C., Keith, S., Wilson, J., & McElreath, L. (1992). Progressive and imaginal relaxation training for elderly persons with subjective anxiety. *Psychology and Aging, 7,* 419–424.

Shamoian, C. A. (Ed.) (1992). *Psychopharmacological treatment complications in the elderly.* Washington, D.C.: American Psychiatric Press.

Sheikh, J. I. (1992). Anxiety disorders and their treatment. *Clinics of Geriatric Medicine, 8,* 411–426.

Skoog, I., Nilsson, L., Lahdahl, S., & Steen, B. (1993). Mental disorders and the use of psychotropic drugs in an 85-year-old urban population. *International Psychogeriatrics, 5,* 33–48.

Sloane, R. B., Staples, F. R., & Schneider, L. S. (1985). Interpersonal therapy versus nortriptyline for depression in the elderly. In G. D. Burrows, T. R. Norman, & L. Dennerstein (Eds.), *Clinical and pharmacological studies in psychiatric disorders* (pp. 344–346). London: John Libby.

Stanley, M. A., & Beck, J. G. (1995, August). *Cognitive-behavioral versus supportive treatments for GAD in the elderly.* Paper presented at the 103rd Annual Convention of the American Psychological Association, New York.

Steuer, J. L., Mintz, J., Hammen, C. L., Hill, M. A., Jarvik, L. F., McCarley, T., Motoike, P., & Rosen, R. (1984). Cognitive-behavioral and psychodynamic group psychotherapy in treatment of geriatric depression. *Journal of Consulting and Clinical Psychology, 52,* 180–189.

Teri, L., Curtis, J., Gallagher-Thompson, D., & Thompson, L. W. (1994). Cognitive-behavior therapy with depressed older adults. In L. S. Schneider, C. F. Reynolds, B. D. Lebowitz, & A. J. Friedhoff (Eds.), *Diagnosis and treatment of depression in late life: Results of the NIH Consensus Development Conference* (pp. 279–291). Washington, D.C.: American Psychiatric Press.

Teri, L., Logsdon, R., Wagner, A., & Uomoto, J. (1995). The caregiver role in behavioral treatment of depression in dementia patients. In E. Light, G. Niederehe, & B. D. Lebowitz (Eds.), *Stress effects in Alzheimer's disease caregivers: Future directions for research and treatment* (pp. 185–204). New York: Springer.

Teri, L., & McCurry, S. M. (1994). Psychosocial therapies. In C. E. Coffey & J. L. Cummings (Eds.), *Textbook of geriatric neuropsychiatry* (pp. 661–682). Washington, D.C.: American Psychiatric Press.

Teri, L., Reifler, B. V., Veith, R., Barnes, R., White, E., McLean, P., & Raskind, M. (1991). Imipramine in the treatment of depressed Alzheimer's patients: Impact on cognition. *Journal of Gerontology: Psychological Sciences, 46,* P372–P377.

Teri, L., & Uomoto, J. (1991). Reducing excess disability in dementia patients: Training caregivers to manage patient depression. *Clinical Gerontologist, 10,* 49–63.

Thompson, J. W., & Blaine, J. D. (1987). Use of ECT in the United States in 1975 and 1980. *American Journal of Psychiatry, 144,* 557–562.

Thompson, L. W., Gallagher, D., & Breckenridge, J. S. (1987). Comparative effectiveness of psychotherapies for depressed elders. *Journal of Consulting and Clinical Psychology, 55,* 385–390.

Thompson, L. W., Gallagher-Thompson, D., Hanser, S., Gantz, F., & Steffen, A. (1991, August). *Treatment of late-life depression with cognitive/behavioral therapy or desipramine.* Paper presented at the 99th Annual Convention of the American Psychological Association, San Francisco, Calif.

Tollefson, G. D., Bosomworth, J. C., Heiligenstein, J. H., Potvin, J. H., Holmin, S., & the Fluoxetine Collaborative Study Group. (1995). A double-blind, placebo-controlled clinical trial of fluoxetine in geriatric patients with major depression. *International Psychogeriatrics, 7,* 89–104.

Turnbull, J. M. (1989). Anxiety and physical illness in the elderly. *Journal of Clinical Psychiatry, 50,* 40–45.

Welden, S., & Yesavage, J. A. (1982). Behavioral improvement with relaxation training in senile dementia. *Clinical Gerontologist, 1,* 45–49.

Yesavage, J. A. (1984). Relaxation and memory training in 39 elderly patients. *American Journal of Psychiatry, 141,* 778–781.

15

Psychosocial Treatments for Panic Disorders, Phobias, and Generalized Anxiety Disorder

David H. Barlow

Jeanne Lawton Esler

Amy E. Vitali

A substantial number of excellent studies, largely Type 1, have established the clinical efficacy of situational in vivo exposure for patients with panic disorder with agoraphobia. The results of a single Type 1 study have suggested that adding cognitive therapy to graded situational in vivo exposure for these patients yields even better outcomes.

A substantial number of Type 1 studies have established the efficacy of cognitive-behavioral treatments for persons with panic disorder; these treatments focus on education about the nature of anxiety and panic, cognitive therapy, and some form of exposure and coping skills acquisition. Included among these treatments are traditional cognitive therapy and panic control treatment (PCT), which exposes the patient to interoceptive sensations similar to physiological panic sensations and breathing retraining, as well as a cognitive restructuring component. While some research has been conducted that explores the effectiveness of combined psychosocial and pharmacological treatment of panic disorder, much additional work remains to be done before the incremental value of these combined treatments can be determined.

The treatment of choice for specific phobias is exposure-based procedures, particularly in vivo exposure; this consensus reflects a very large number of Type 1 studies of these procedures with patients with specific phobias.

The most common treatment approaches to social phobia include social skills training (SST), relaxation techniques, exposure-based methods, and multicomponent cognitive-behavioral treatments; however, exposure-based procedures are the only treatments for social phobia that have attained the highest level of treatment efficacy in Type 1 studies.

In general, different treatment conditions for patients with generalized anxiety disorder (GAD) have not led to differential improvement rates, although most studies have shown that active treatments are superior to nondirective approaches and uniformly superior to no treatment. Recently, however, a few studies have suggested that the most successful psychosocial treatments for GAD combine relaxation exercises and cognitive therapy with the goal of bringing the worry process itself under the patient's control.

The development of empirically supported psychosocial treatments has been, perhaps, most evident in the appearance of effective new treatments for anxiety disorders, particularly during the last decade. Prior to 1970, anxiety disorders were a highly prevalent, but ill-defined group of problems subsumed under the general headings of "anxiety neuroses" or "phobic neuroses." Treatment of neurosis was most often carried out in the context of long-term psychotherapy, with little or no evidence available on the efficacy of this approach (Barlow, 1988; Barlow, Hayes, & Nelson, 1984b). During the late 1960s and into the 1970s, clinical trials began to establish the efficacy of exposure-based treatments for phobic disorders, specifically agoraphobia and specific phobias. In addition, early experimental analyses began to appear suggesting the efficacy of specific psychosocial treatments for obsessive compulsive disorder (e.g., Mills, Agras, Barlow, & Mills, 1973; Rachman & Hodgson, 1980).

The successful delineation of specific anxiety disorders with the appearance of the *Diagnostic and Statistical Manual of Mental Disorders*, third edition (*DSM-III*) in 1980 (American Psychiatric Association [APA], 1980) led to the development of more structured and targeted psychosocial and drug treatments. From the period 1985 through 1995, effective and empirically supported psychosocial treatments were developed for panic disorder, generalized anxiety disorder, and social phobia, as well as post traumatic stress disorder (Barlow, 1994; Barlow & Lehman, 1996). In addition, substantial improvements were made in the treatment of panic disorder with agoraphobia and certain varieties of specific phobia as our knowledge of the psychopathology and pathophysiology of these conditions deepened.

In this chapter, we review systematically the current status of the evidence regarding efficacious empirically supported treatments for panic disorder with and without agoraphobia, specific phobia, social phobia, and generalized anxiety disorder. This is followed by a brief concluding section on future directions in treatment development and research for these disorders.

In this chapter, empirical studies are evaluated according to a template recently created by the American Psychological Association to guide the development of practice guidelines (American Psychological Association Task Force on Intervention Guidelines, 1995). This template evaluates studies along two axes, one that examines the treatments' efficacy (internal validity) and a second that examines the clinical utility (external validity) of the treatments being researched. This template is included in Table 15.1. In addition, the studies reviewed in this chapter are also examined according to the classification system outlined in the initial chapter of this book. The studies held to the

most rigorous research standards are classified as Type 1 studies, while those that fall short of this standard of excellence are classified as Type 2 studies. Research studies conducted with even greater methodological limitations are classified as Type 3 through Type 6 studies.

PANIC DISORDER WITH AGORAPHOBIA

Though panic attacks have been discussed in the literature over the centuries (e.g., Freud 1895/1961), they were largely ignored by the diagnostic system until the last few decades. The two diagnoses of panic disorder and agoraphobia with panic attacks were not included in the diagnostic system until the publication of *DSM-III* in 1980 (APA, 1980). The most recent version of this diagnostic system, *DSM-IV* (APA, 1994), includes the related diagnoses of panic disorder without agoraphobia, panic disorder with agoraphobia, and agoraphobia without history of panic disorder.

Individuals diagnosed with panic disorder report experiencing recurrent unexpected panic attacks that consist of physical symptoms such as racing heart, shortness of breath, dizziness, sweating, and trembling or shaking. Moreover, they experience continued anxiety focused on experiencing future panic attacks and worry about consequences of the panic attacks or changes in their behavior due to the panic attacks. In addition, those with agoraphobia avoid situations that trigger panic attacks and for which escape would be difficult in the event of a panic attack, such as crowded shopping malls, restaurants, or movie theaters. Finally, individuals are diagnosed with agoraphobia without history of panic disorder when they experience agoraphobic avoidance due to anxiety focused on specific somatic symptoms, some of which may be defining symptoms of a panic attack, yet they have never met criteria for a full, unexpected panic attack. It should be noted that, clinically, patients presenting with agoraphobia without history of panic disorder can be treated with protocols intended for patients with panic disorder with agoraphobia, and they will usually benefit from such treatment (Craske & Barlow, 1993).

Reports on the prevalence of panic disorder, panic disorder with agoraphobia, and agoraphobia without history of panic disorder vary somewhat. The most recent epidemiological study, the National Comorbidity Survey (NCS), conducted in the United States cited a lifetime prevalence for panic disorder with or without agoraphobia at 3.5% of the population (Kes-

TABLE 15.1 Overview of Template for Constructing Psychological Intervention Guidelines

Internal Validity (Efficacy)	Clinical Utility (External Validity)

1. Better than alternative therapy
2. Better than nonspecific therapy (RCTs)
3. Better than no therapy (RCTs)
4. Quantified clinical observations
5. Strongly positive clinical consensus
6. Mixed clinical consensus
7. Strongly negative clinical consensus
8. Contradictory evidence
 	
Note: Confidence in treatment efficacy is based on both (a) the absolute and relative efficacy of the treatment and (b) the quality of the studies on which the judgment is made, as well as their replicability. Confidence in efficacy increases from item 8 (lowest) to item 1 (highest).
	1. Feasibility
	  a. patient acceptability (cost, pain, duration, side effects, etc.)
	  b. Patient choice in face of relatively equal efficacy
	  c. Probability of compliance
	  d. Ease of disseminability (e.g., number of practitioners with competence, requirements for training, opportunities for training, need for costly technologies or additional support personnel, etc.)
	2. Generalizability
	  a. Patient characteristics: cultural background issues, gender issues, developmental issues, other relevant patient characteristics
	  b. Therapist characteristics
	  c. Issues of robustness when applied in practice settings with different time frames and the like
	  d. Contextual factors regarding setting in which treatment is delivered
	3. Costs and benefits
	  a. Costs of delivering intervention to individual and society
	  b. Costs of withholding effective intervention from individual and society
	
	Note: Confidence in clinical utility as reflected on these three dimensions should be based on systematic and objective methods and strategies for assessing these characteristics of treatment as they are applied in actual practice. In some cases, randomized clinical trials will exist. More often, data will be in the form of quantified clinical observations (clinical replication series) or other strategies such as health economic calculations.

RCT = randomized clinical trials.

sler et al., 1994). This same report noted the lifetime prevalence of agoraphobia without history of panic disorder to be 5.3% of the population. Differences between these figures and earlier epidemiological reports may be due to different geographic areas sampled, different age ranges surveyed, and the utilization of different research methods. Kessler et al. utilized a more-advanced methodology than previous surveys had; consequently, the results of the National Comorbidity Survey are considered to be more credible than other epidemiological data currently available.

Finally, it seems that many more women than men experience these disorders. A recent meta-analysis found that fully three fourths of the participants in research studies on the treatment of the panic disorders are women (Gould, Otto, & Pollack, 1995). In addition, the National Comorbidity Survey found the lifetime prevalences of panic disorder and agoraphobia without history of panic disorder for women to be at least twice those listed for men (5.0% and 7.0% versus 2.0% and 3.5%, respectively) (Kessler et al.,

1994). These findings replicate the sex ratio in earlier reports (e.g., Myers et al., 1984; Thorpe & Burns, 1983). The most common explanation for this marked difference in prevalence among men and women involves cultural factors. In most cultures around the world, it is more acceptable for women to report fear and to avoid various situations due to this fear. Men, however, are expected to minimize their fears and overcome avoidant tendencies regardless of the cost. Many men seem to turn to alcohol to self-medicate their anxiety and panic (Barlow, 1988).

Most individuals with panic disorder can clearly recall life stressors that occurred when they experienced the onset of their panic attacks. One recent study noted that 72% of patients with panic disorder reported life stress existing when their panic attacks began (Craske, Miller, Rotunda, & Barlow, 1990). Moreover, patients with panic disorder often experience other Axis I disorders concurrent with their panic disorder (Sanderson, DiNardo, Rapee, & Barlow, 1990), and studies have noted that between 25% and

75% of patients with panic disorder meet criteria for an Axis II personality disorder, most often avoidant or dependent personality disorders (Chambless & Renneberg, 1988; Reich, Noyes, & Troughton, 1987).

Most models of etiology, although not entirely well developed, posit a nonspecific biological predisposition to experience anxiety and possibly panic attacks. This biological predisposition, combined with early development of a sense of uncontrollability over potentially threatening life events, creates a diathesis. The later experience of life stress then triggers an unexpected panic attack and, in those with the specific biological and psychological vulnerabilities (the diathesis), anxiety becomes focused on the next possible panic attack, and panic disorder subsequently develops. Agoraphobia may then follow as a complication of panic disorder in a large proportion of these individuals, mostly women (Barlow, 1988; Barlow, Chorpita, & Turovsky, in 1996).

In this section, we first review the development and evaluation of in vivo exposure strategies for treating agoraphobia, followed by a description of the development and evaluation of psychosocial treatments that target panic attacks directly. We conclude with a discussion of the current status of psychosocial treatment of panic disorder with agoraphobia, as well as our view of future directions in treatment development and assessment for this disorder.

Treatment of Agoraphobia

Treatment of agoraphobia has evolved considerably over the last several decades. Initial treatments, conducted in the 1960s and 1970s, for agoraphobic avoidance consisted of systematic desensitization. This procedure involved imaginal exposure to feared situations coupled with muscle relaxation. Systematic desensitization was used at that time since it was believed that actual exposure to feared situations (situational in vivo exposure) might be too intense and would have deleterious effects. Studies conducted to examine the efficacy of systematic desensitization consistently found this approach to be largely ineffectual (Gelder & Marks, 1966; Marks, 1971). During this same era, researchers began to treat patients with agoraphobia successfully by conducting graduated in vivo exposure exercises (Agras, Leitenberg, & Barlow, 1968). In this procedure, patients, under the supervision of a clinician, were expected to engage in exposure practices by which they systematically ventured away

from safe places and into the situations they had been avoiding.

Situational In Vivo Exposure

During the next several years, situational in vivo exposure continued to be evaluated and was found to be more effective than no treatment or attentional control procedures (Barlow, 1988; Jansson & Ost, 1982; Mavissakalian & Barlow, 1981). Situational in vivo exposure treatment routinely begins with the patients creating a hierarchy of feared situations or activities that have been consistently avoided. Examples of such items include driving out of a safety zone (which may be either several blocks or several miles from the home), shopping in a crowded mall alone, and going out to dinner in a restaurant or seeing a movie in a theater. Patients are then encouraged to repeatedly enter and remain in these feared situations, utilizing therapeutic coping procedures learned during sessions, until their anxiety diminishes. While patients with more severe agoraphobia may require the presence of their therapist during the initial exposures, most patients are able to conduct these exercises either alone or with a friend or family member who acts as a supportive coach (Barlow, 1988).

Throughout the past few decades researchers have examined the clinical efficacy of situational in vivo exposure utilizing the highest methodological standards. Nearly all of these studies fall into the top two categories of the internal validity axis (Axis 1) of the APA template; moreover, the vast majority of these studies also can be characterized as Type 1 studies according to the classification system of this volume. These studies have consistently shown evidence of the efficacy of situational in vivo exposure; the current consensus among researchers is that situational in vivo exposure is a highly effective treatment for many patients with panic disorder with agoraphobia.

Several reviews and meta-analyses conducted in the 1980s found that 60% to 75% of patients who completed situational in vivo exposure treatments show evidence of clinical improvement (Barlow, 1988; Jacobson, Wilson, & Tupper, 1988; Jansson & Ost, 1982; Munby & Johnston, 1980; Trull, Nietzel, & Main, 1988). Yet, relatively few of these patients were "cured" or completely symptom free at the conclusion of their exposure treatment. However, clinical gains that were achieved from this approach were maintained at long-term follow-up. For example, Jansson,

Jerremalm, and Ost (1986) reported maintenance of gains and some continued improvement at a 15-month follow-up. Burns, Thorpe, and Cavallaro (1986) also noted continuation of gains up to 8 years following treatment, albeit punctuated by brief setbacks.

Fava, Zielezny, Savron, and Grandi (1995) have also published long-term follow-up results of their research on exposure-based treatments for agoraphobia conducted in Bologna, Italy. This study falls into the Type 2 category due to the lack of a comparison group in the study design. However, since the efficacy of situational in vivo exposure has been proven extensively in the past, many researchers currently studying situational in vivo exposure do not view a comparison treatment group as a necessary treatment component in this type of research. Fava and his colleagues treated over 90 patients with 12 sessions of self-paced, graduated, exposure-based treatment. These 30-minute sessions were administered bi-weekly over a 6-month period. At the end of treatment, 87% of the patients were panic free and considered to be much improved on the global clinical measures. These patients were then followed for up to 7 years after treatment, with 67% still in remission at that point in time.

Using survival analysis to estimate the probability that the patients would remain in remission after they successfully completed exposure treatment, results indicated that 96% of the patients remained in remission throughout the first 2 years after treatment. In addition, 77% of the patients remained in remission throughout the first 5 years after treatment and 67% for the first 7 years after the completion of exposure treatment. Study results indicated that residual agoraphobia and the presence of a personality disorder were the most significant predictors of relapse for the patients in the study.

Strategies to Improve the Effectiveness of Exposure-Based Procedures

In the last decade, researchers have focused on improving the effectiveness of situational, in vivo, exposure-based treatments. For example, a number of studies attempted to determine whether adding relaxation training to situational in vivo exposure would improve the clinical efficacy of the situational in vivo exposure. In most of these studies, the combined treatments were no more effective than situational in vivo exposure alone (Michelson, Mavissakalian, & Marchione, 1988; Ost, Hellstrom, & Westling, 1989; Ost, Jerrem-

alm, & Jansson, 1984). In addition, researchers have attempted to improve the efficacy of situational in vivo exposure by adding cognitive therapy components such as paradoxical intention or Beck and Emery's (1985) cognitive therapy to exposure protocols. Again, the combined treatments were most often found to be no more effective than situational in vivo exposure alone (Emmelkamp, Brilman, Kuiper, & Mersch, 1986; Emmelkamp & Mersch, 1982; Michelson et al., 1988; Ost et al., 1989; Williams & Rappaport, 1983). Finally, two controlled studies examining the effectiveness of situational in vivo exposure and breathing retraining found the combined treatment to be no more effective than situational in vivo exposure alone (Bonn, Readhead, & Timmons, 1984; De Ruiter, Rijken, Garssen, & Kraaimaat, 1989).

More recently, Michelson, Marchione, and Greenwald (1989) reported on a study comparing the effectiveness of three different treatment conditions— graded situational in vivo exposure alone, graded situational in vivo exposure plus cognitive therapy, and graded situational in vivo exposure plus relaxation training. This Type 1 study produced notable results; they found the treatment condition consisting of situational in vivo exposure and cognitive therapy to be the most effective of the three conditions. At posttreatment assessment, 86% of the patients receiving situational in vivo exposure plus cognitive therapy achieved high end-state functioning as compared to 73% of the situational in vivo exposure plus relaxation training group and 65% of the situational in vivo exposure alone group. In addition, follow-up comparisons continued to underscore the effectiveness of the combined situational in vivo exposure plus cognitive therapy treatment condition. Of the situational in vivo exposure plus cognitive therapy patients, 87% were considered to have achieved high end-state functioning at the 1-year follow-up assessment, while 65% of the situational in vivo exposure alone patients and 47% of the situational in vivo exposure plus relaxation training patients had achieved this same clinical status.

Many researchers have manipulated the pace of situational in vivo exposure treatment in order to show evidence of maximum therapeutic gains. Massed and intensive exposure sessions have been repeatedly compared with spaced and graduated exposure sessions. Barlow (1988) discussed several advantages to spaced and graduated situation in vivo exposure. Advantages include lower attrition rates, as well as lower relapse rates (Hafner & Marks, 1976; Jansson & Ost, 1982).

In addition, gradual changes in agoraphobic avoidance are believed to be less stressful to the interpersonal system of the patient (Barlow, 1988).

Yet, the empirical literature does not entirely support this perspective since other studies have not found spaced and graduated situational in vivo exposures to hold such distinct advantages. For example, Chambless (1990) treated patients with agoraphobia and patients with specific phobias with either spaced exposures (conducted weekly) or massed exposures (conducted daily). The two conditions were found to be equally effective at both the posttreatment and 6-month follow-up assessments. Moreover, no differential dropout rates between the two conditions were found.

Perhaps the most striking finding regarding the effectiveness of massed, ungraded situational in vivo exposure was found in Germany. Feigenbaum (1988) treated a large number of severely agoraphobic persons with intensive, massed situational in vivo exposure. This innovative treatment consisted of massed exposures conducted throughout 4 to 10 days, during which individuals were expected to experience the situations they feared for several hours every day. Often, treatment began with therapist-assisted exposure exercises that were then followed by self-directed exposure. These patients were expected to engage in exposures such as using public transportation in a metropolitan area, taking an overnight train to a foreign city, and riding a cable car high above the Alps during the course of their intensive treatment. The progress of these patients was compared to the progress of patients who experienced more graded exposure exercises, gradually working up their hierarchy of feared situations.

While the two conditions proved to be equally effective at both the posttreatment assessment and the 8-month follow-up assessment, massed, ungraded, situational in vivo exposure proved to be superior at the 5-year follow-up assessment point. These results were later replicated with a much larger sample size (Feigenbaum, 1988). Feigenbaum and his colleagues treated over 120 patients, and over 75% were found to be symptom free at the 5-year follow-up assessment. Replication of this treatment has not yet occurred outside Germany.

Researchers have also focused their attention during treatment on the interpersonal support systems of persons with agoraphobia as a means of further improving treatment outcome. Since panic disorder with agoraphobia, at its more severe levels, produces a great deal of dependency, researchers theorized that the incorporation of spouses or partners in treatment might facilitate the treatment process. Barlow, O'Brien, and Last (1984a) found that spousal involvement significantly improved treatment effectiveness for a number of women with agoraphobia. In their study, two groups of women were offered identical exposure-based treatments, but one group was asked to have their spouses accompany them to treatment sessions. While the patients in both groups showed evidence of clinical improvements, a significantly greater percentage of patients in the spouse-accompanied group was treatment responders at the posttreatment assessment (86% versus 43%, respectively). In addition, follow-up results of these same patients determined that the gap in treatment efficacy between the two groups increased during the first and second years after treatment (Cerny, Barlow, Craske, & Himadi, 1987).

Finally, Arnow, Taylor, Agras, and Telch (1985) examined the effectiveness of communication skills training with spouses or partners by adding it to a situational in vivo exposure protocol. The combined communication skills training and situational in vivo exposure treatment was found to show evidence of greater clinical improvement at both the posttreatment and the 8-month follow-up assessment. In contrast, Cobb, Mathews, Childs-Clarke, and Blowers (1984) found no additional benefit from including spouses in their treatment protocol, although procedural differences in the treatment administration might account for this finding (see Cerny et al., 1987).

Briefer Cost-Effective Modifications to Exposure-Based Procedures

Researchers have also been studying the effectiveness of more self-directed treatment protocols for agoraphobic avoidance. These studies explore the questions raised on the second axis of the APA template mentioned above; they examine the clinical utility or external validity of these treatments. For example, Ghosh and Marks (1987) conducted a study that explored the effectiveness of a 10-week self-directed exposure treatment administered in three different conditions (therapist instructed, computer instructed, and book instructed). They enlisted a select group of patients to enter this study; patients with severe personality disorders or severe depression were not eligible for the protocol treatment. Patients in all three treatment conditions received the same initial introduction to treatment, which consisted of a review of the self-directed exposure program explained by a trained clinician.

After the initial assessment, the patients in the book-instructed condition (bibliotherapy) received no additional clinical appointments during the 10-week course of treatment, though they were contacted on three occasions to determine if they were engaged in the self-directed treatment program. In contrast, the patients in the computer-instructed condition had weekly 30-minute computer sessions. These were preceded by a brief 10-minute appointment with a clinician during which the doctor merely assessed the patient's mental status. The patients in the therapist-instructed condition had weekly sessions with their psychiatrist that lasted on average 40 minutes per session.

Ghosh and Marks found that patients in all three treatment conditions were significantly improved after the 10-week treatment. They found no differences among the three treatment conditions, suggesting that self-directed bibliotherapy can be both a clinically effective and cost-effective treatment for agoraphobic avoidance, at least in the cases treated in this study. In contrast, Holden, O'Brien, Barlow, Stetson, and Infantino (1983) found bibliotherapy ineffective with patients with more severe levels of agoraphobia; these patients required the intervention of a therapist.

More recently, Swinson, Fergus, Cox, and Wickwire (1995) studied the efficacy of telephone-administered self-exposure instructions. This research explored the viability of a more cost effective administration of situational in vivo exposure. They examined whether self-directed exposure would be an effective treatment modality for patients unable to attend more-traditional therapy sessions conducted in person. Most of the patients enrolled in the study (over 70%) suffered from moderate or severe levels of agoraphobic avoidance. In addition, the patients had suffered from panic disorder and agoraphobia for a mean duration of approximately 13 years. The patients were offered a 10-week course of treatment that included eight telephone sessions with the therapist; the results were compared with those of patients in a wait-list control group.

The telephone-administered exposure instructions were found to be effective in reducing the agoraphobic avoidance at posttreatment in comparison to the wait-list control group; moreover, the 3- and 6-month follow-up assessments showed evidence of continued treatment gains. Finally, the clinical improvements were comparable to gains made by patients treated in the more-traditional venue of individual face-to-face treatment sessions.

Treatment of Panic

Psychosocial treatments focusing on the unexpected and uncued panic attacks experienced by individuals with panic disorder were developed relatively recently. Since the publication of *DSM-III* (APA, 1980), several psychosocial treatments aimed at targeting panic attacks directly have been developed, and numerous research trials have been conducted to test their efficacy. The majority of these are cognitive-behavioral treatments, and they share many commonalities. They focus on education about the nature of anxiety and panic, cognitive therapy, and some form of exposure and coping skills acquisition. Typically, different aspects of treatment are emphasized in the various protocols. A selection of the more widely utilized treatments is reviewed here. The studies reviewed in this discussion are categorized as Type 1 research since they were all conducted utilizing the highest methodological standards.

Panic Control Treatment

Barlow and Craske (1994) developed a psychosocial treatment protocol for panic attacks, now known as the panic control treatment (PCT). This treatment focuses on exposing the patient to interoceptive sensations similar to physiological panic sensations. In addition to these systematized exposures, PCT includes a cognitive restructuring component directed at misconceptions about anxiety and panic, as well as "automatic" cognitions that focus on the overestimations of threat and danger associated with panic attacks. Finally, breathing retraining is incorporated into PCT; it serves to correct tendencies to hyperventilate in some panic patients and also provides a meditational calming exercise that can be effectively utilized by most patients. Panic control training has been extensively studied throughout the past several years, with good results.

In the first controlled study of PCT (Barlow, Craske, Cerny, & Klosko, 1989), three treatment conditions (PCT alone, relaxation alone, and PCT combined with relaxation) were compared to a wait-list control condition. The relaxation component consisted of progressive muscle relaxation training along with instructions to apply this relaxation when in anxiety-provoking situations. At posttreatment, all three treatment conditions proved to be more effective than the wait-list control condition. Of the patients, 60% in the relaxation condition and 87% in the PCT alone and PCT combined with relaxation conditions achieved panic-free status by the conclusion of the 15-week treatment.

Craske, Brown, and Barlow (1991) reported on a two year follow-up of this study. These follow-up data revealed that 81% of the patients in the PCT alone condition were panic free 2 years after acute treatment, compared to only 43% of the patients in the PCT combined with relaxation condition and 36% of the patients in the relaxation alone condition. It is believed that the patients in the PCT combined with relaxation condition were not able to show evidence of greater therapeutic gains due to the abbreviated nature of treatment; that is, neither the PCT nor relaxation therapy were presented as thoroughly in the combined treatment condition as compared with the two other treatment conditions.

In another study, Klosko, Barlow, Tassinari, and Cerny (1990) compared the efficacy of PCT and alprazolam to a drug placebo condition and a wait-list control condition. In this study, posttreatment assessment results showed that 87% of the patients in the PCT condition had achieved panic-free status compared to 50% of the patients in the alprazolam condition, 36% of the patients in the placebo drug condition, and 33% of the patients in the wait-list control condition. The PCT was found to be significantly more effective than all the other three conditions (Barlow & Brown, 1995).

In yet another study, Telch et al. (1993) found PCT to be effective when administered in a group treatment format. Patients were given 8 weeks of group PCT, and their progress was compared to patients in a wait-list control condition. At the conclusion of treatment, 85% of the patients who had received PCT had achieved panic-free status as compared with 30% of the patients in the wait-list control condition. In addition, when a more stringent composite outcome measure (considering panic attack frequency, as well as levels of general anxiety and avoidance behavior) was utilized, 63% of the patients in the PCT condition were considered improved compared with 9% of the

patients in the wait-list control condition. At the 6-month follow-up, 79% of the patients who had received PCT had remained panic free and 63% were still considered to be clinically improved according to the composite outcome measure.

Cognitive Therapy

In a controlled trial of more-traditional cognitive therapy, Beck, Sokol, Clark, Berchick, and Wright (1992) compared the efficacy of 12 weeks of cognitive therapy with 8 weeks of brief supportive therapy. After 8 weeks of treatment, 71% of the patients who received cognitive therapy were panic free as compared with 25% of the patients who received supportive therapy. Moreover, at posttreatment 94% of the patients in the cognitive therapy condition were panic free, and at the 1-year follow-up assessment, 87% of these patients continued to be panic free.

Clark and his colleagues have also developed a psychosocial treatment for panic disorder consisting of a unique variation of cognitive therapy (Clark, 1989; Salkovskis & Clark, 1991). This treatment also attempts to change patients' appraisals of bodily sensations and is similar to the PCT discussed above. However, Clark's approach places a greater emphasis on the cognitive therapy component of the treatment protocol.

Clark et al. (1994) conducted a randomized controlled trial comparing the effectiveness of three active treatments (cognitive therapy, applied relaxation [AR], and imipramine) to a wait-list control condition. Patients randomly assigned to one of the three active treatment conditions met weekly with a clinician throughout the first 3 months of the study; furthermore, they continued to meet with their therapist for a monthly booster session throughout the 3 months following the acute treatment phase of the study. Posttreatment results conducted after 6 months showed that all three active treatments were significantly more effective than the wait-list control condition. In fact, the cognitive therapy treatment was superior to the wait-list control condition on all panic and anxiety treatment outcome measures, while the AR condition and the imipramine treatment condition were superior to the wait-list control condition on just over half and fewer than half of the treatment outcome measures, respectively.

At posttreatment, 75% of the patients in the cognitive therapy condition were panic free compared with 70% of the patients in the imipramine condition and 40% of the patients in the AR condition. Moreover, the 9-month follow-up results that followed the discontinuation of the imipramine treatment showed that the patients in the cognitive therapy condition largely maintained their treatment gains. Of the patients who received cognitive therapy, 85% remained panic free, while 60% of the patients who received imipramine and 47% of the patients who were treated with AR were panic free.

Also, during the time between the posttreatment and 9-month follow-up, 40% of the patients in the imipramine treatment condition had sought further treatment compared with 25% of the patients in the AR condition and 5% of the patients in the cognitive therapy condition. At the final assessment point, the cognitive therapy condition was found to be significantly more effective than either the AR or the imipramine conditions.

Alternative Treatments

A recent study conducted by Ost and Westling (1995) reports positive results with AR treatment. In this study, patients were randomly assigned to 12 sessions of either an AR treatment or cognitive therapy treatment. Results showed that both treatments were equally effective. At posttreatment, 65% of the patients in the AR condition and 74% of patients in the cognitive therapy condition were panic free. At the 1-year follow-up, 82% of the patients who had received AR treatment and 89% of the patients who had received cognitive therapy treatment were panic free. It is interesting to note that, for the patients treated in this study, no relapses occurred during the 1-year post-acute treatment; in fact, many of the patients who had been experiencing panic attacks at the posttreatment assessment had achieved panic-free status by the 1-year follow-up. Thus, although not as effective in studies conducted by Clark et al. (1994) or Barlow et al. (1989), AR may deserve some further consideration and evaluation.

In addition, Shear, Pilkonis, Cloitre, and Leon (1994) recently developed a new approach called emotion focused therapy (EFT) that focuses on interpersonal triggers for panic attacks rather than interoceptive cues. Although attrition was high in this first study, preliminary results from this study suggest that

further evaluation of this therapy process could be fruitful.

Brief Cost-Effective Treatments

Recently, attention has turned toward exploring the effectiveness for panic attacks of cognitive behavioral treatment when it is administered in a more cost-effective manner, such as with limited therapist contact. These studies explore the questions raised on the second axis of the APA template; they examine the clinical utility or external validity of these treatments. Cote, Gauthier, Laberge, Cormier, and Plamondon (1994) conducted a study in which patients were randomly assigned to receive cognitive behavioral treatment with either a standard amount of therapist contact (weekly hour-long sessions) or reduced therapist contact (bi-monthly hour-long sessions with bi-monthly 10-minute telephone contacts). Results of this study demonstrated that both treatment modalities were equally effective; over 73% of the patients in both groups were both panic free and clinically improved at the 6-month follow-up assessment. It should be noted that therapist time in the reduced therapist contact condition was still considerable, amounting to approximately 10 hours of contact, as compared with approximately 20 hours of contact in the standard condition.

Lidren et al. (1994) examined the effectiveness of self-directed treatment utilizing a manual (bibliotherapy) for panic attacks. They found bibliotherapy to be as effective as cognitive behavioral therapy administered in a group therapy setting. Patients in both conditions were treated for 8 weeks and were compared with patients in a wait-list control condition. The patients in both of the active treatment conditions showed evidence of significant clinical improvement at posttreatment assessments, while the patients in the wait-list control condition did not. Moreover, patients in the bibliotherapy and group therapy conditions maintained their treatment gains at the 3- and 6-month follow-up assessments. In addition, an attrition rate of zero was reported for this study, pointing to the desirability of these interventions for patients suffering from panic attacks.

Craske, Maidenberg, and Bystritsky (1995) also examined the effectiveness of brief cognitive behavioral treatment. A four-session PCT protocol was compared to a four-session nondirective supportive therapy protocol. The brief PCT was found to be significantly more effective than the nondirective supportive therapy; the patients' clinical statuses were assessed by noting the frequency of their panic attacks, their degree of worry about panic attacks, and their level of phobic fear.

Current Status

Table 15.2 summarizes the results of studies of psychosocial treatment for panic disorder. Nearly all of these studies are classified as Type 1; the study by Ost, Westling, and Hellstrom (1993) falls into the Type 2 category due to an absence of comparison groups. Most studies demonstrate the effectiveness of PCT or similar cognitive behavioral approaches for patients with panic disorder with no more than mild agoraphobia (compared with either no treatment or credible psychotherapeutic alternatives).

Table 15.3 summarizes the results of a recent comprehensive meta-analysis of treatment outcome for panic disorder with all levels of agoraphobic avoidance (Gould et al., 1995). Included in the meta-analysis were 43 controlled studies. As can be seen in the table, the cognitive-behavioral treatments yielded the greatest effect size and the smallest rates of patient attrition when compared with either pharmacological treatment or treatments that combined both psychosocial and pharmacological treatments. Moreover, the subset of cognitive-behavioral treatments that utilized

TABLE 15.2 Clinical Trials of Cognitive-Behavioral Treatments for Panic Disorder: Intent-to-Treat Analysis

Study	Length of Follow-Up (Months)	Treatment (N)	Percentage Panic Free	Significant Comparison (Percentage Panic Free) Other Treatments (Yes/No)	Wait List (Yes/No)
Craske et al. (1991)[a]	24	PCT (N = 15)	81	Yes: AR = 36% Yes: PCT & AR = 43%	
Klosko et al. (1990)	PT	PCT (N = 15)	87	No: AL = 50% Yes: PL = 36%	Yes: 33%
Newman et al. (1990)	12	CTM (N = 24) CTNM (N = 19)	87 87	—	
Côte, Gauthier, Laberge, Cormier, & Plamon-don (1992)	12	CBTM (N = 13) CBTNM (N = 8)	92 100	—	
Beck et al. (1992)	PT	CT (N = 17)	94	Yes: ST = 25%[b]	
Black et al. (1993)	PT	CT (N = 25)	32	Yes: FL = 68% No: PL = 20%	
Margraf & Schneider (1991)	4 weeks	CT (N = 22)	91		Yes: 5%
Öst et al. (1993)	12	CT (N = 19)	89[c]	No: AR = 74%[c]	
Telch et al. (1993)	PT	PCT (N = 34)	85		Yes: 30%
Clark et al. (1995)	12	CT (N = 17)	76[c]	Yes: AR = 43%[c] Yes: IMI = 49%[c]	
Craske et al. (1995)	PT	CBT (N = 16)	53	Yes: NPT = 8%	
Shear et al. (1994)	6	CBT (N = 23)	45	No: NPT = 45%	

AL = alprazolam; AR = applied relaxation; CBT = cognitive-behavioral therapy; CBTM = cognitive-behavioral therapy and medication; CBTNM = cognitive-behavioral therapy without medication; CT = cognitive therapy; CTM = cognitive therapy and medication; CTNM = cognitive therapy without medication; FL = fluvoxamine; IMI = imipramine; NPT = nonprescriptive treatment; PL = pill placebo; PCT = exposure and cognitive restructuring; PT = posttreatment; ST = supportive therapy.

[a]Follow-up study of Barlow et al. (1989).

[b]At 8 weeks, which was the end of supportive therapy. At this time, 71% of CT patients were panic free.

[c]Percentage of patients panic free at follow-up who had received no additional treatment during the follow-up period.

Source: Reprinted with permission from Barlow and Lehman (1996), © 1996 American Medical Association.

TABLE 15.3 Meta-Analysis of 43 Controlled Studies of Treatment of Panic Disorder with Agoraphobia

	Cognitive-Behavioral Therapy	Cognitive Therapy and Interoceptive Exposure	Pharmacological Treatment	Combination Treatment
Effect size	.68	.88	.47	.56
Dropouts	5.6%		19.8%	22%

Source: Data from Gould et al. (1995).

interoceptive exposure yielded an even greater effect size, although most of these studies included patients with no more than mild agoraphobic avoidance.

Future Directions

Though the past decades have produced a number of empirically supported psychosocial treatment protocols for the treatment of panic disorder with and without agoraphobia, much work still lies ahead. There is a need to continue to explore the effectiveness of abbreviated treatment protocols for the panic disorders, noting which patients seem to benefit most from such treatments.

In addition, there is a need to consider and explore innovative treatment modalities. For example, the great majority of the work done during the past several years with psychosocial treatments artificially separates individuals with panic disorder into two categories— those with no more than mild agoraphobic avoidance and those with moderate-to-severe agoraphobia. Cognitive behavioral treatments such as PCT have been devised and utilized for the former group, while treatment for the latter group has primarily consisted of situational in vivo exposure. This demarcation is merely an artifact of the development of research studies in this area. Initially, agoraphobic avoidance was addressed by psychosocial researchers studying panic disorder with agoraphobia; a number of years later, psychosocial treatments focusing directly on panic attacks were introduced. Since pharmacological treatments focus almost exclusively on controlling panic attacks and anxiety related to these attacks, this demarcation does not exist in most pharmacological research protocols. Clinical investigators have recently begun to attempt to reintegrate these two approaches (e.g., Barlow & Craske, 1994; Craske & Barlow, 1993), and this trend should continue.

While some research has been conducted to explore the effectiveness of combined psychosocial and pharmacological treatment of panic disorder, much work remains to be done in this area also. Research conducted during the last decade has focused primarily on combining pharmacotherapy with exposure-based treatments for patients with moderate-to-severe levels of agoraphobia. Studies that have examined the effectiveness of tricyclic antidepressives such as imipramine and exposure-based procedures compared with exposure alone have, for the most part, shown evidence of superior posttreatment results for the combined treatment (Mavissakalian, 1996; Mavissakalian & Perel, 1985; Telch, Agras, Taylor, Roth, & Gallen, 1985). However, these results generally are not maintained at follow-up assessments due to the high incidence of relapse experienced by patients in the combined treatment condition after imipramine discontinuation had occurred (e.g., Mavissakalian & Michelson, 1986). These results underscore the need to study effective maintenance strategies.

Marks et al. (1993) found that a combined treatment consisting of alprazolam, a high-potency benzodiazepine, and exposure therapy was similar in its effectiveness to either alprazolam or exposure therapy administered alone. While this result was found at the posttreatment evaluation, the effectiveness of the combined treatment did not remain at the 6-month follow-up assessment. Those patients who had received the combination treatment had experienced a high relapse rate after the discontinuation of the alprazolam; thus, overall gains were reduced below the point of those receiving exposure alone. Of more concern are recent reports that high-potency benzodiazepines may interfere with and detract from CBT treatment gains (Brown & Barlow, 1995; Otto, Pollack, & Sabatino, 1995).

Clinical investigators have also begun to explore the possible facilitatory effect of combining psychosocial treatments with pharmacological treatments for patients with panic disorder with no more than mild agoraphobia. For example, a large multisite study is currently under way comparing four different treatment conditions (PCT plus imipramine, PCT plus placebo, PCT alone, and imipramine alone) to a placebo control group. Preliminary results indicate an advantage to the PCT plus imipramine treatment modality compared with either PCT or imipramine treatment administered individually at posttreatment. Although results are preliminary, continued work exploring the use of both psychosocial and pharmacological treatments in combination will provide much needed information about the most-effective treatments for panic disorder with agoraphobia.

In a recent innovation, psychosocial treatments such as modifications of PCT have also been utilized to help patients discontinue benzodiazepines. For example, Otto et al. (1993) conducted a study in which patients using alprazolam experienced either a slow taper of the drug or a slow taper in conjunction with 10 weeks of PCT. Results indicated that over 75% of the patients in the combined PCT-taper condition were able to discontinue their alprazolam usage, while only 25% of the slow taper alone condition were able to do so.

Spiegel, Bruce, Gregg, and Nuzzarello (1994) conducted a similar study. Patients were discontinued very gradually and flexibly from alprazolam. One treatment condition included 12 weekly sessions of individual PCT during the taper, while the other treatment condition involved routine supportive medical management. Nearly all patients were able to discontinue their medication usage (80% of the patients in the taper plus supportive medical management condition and 90% of the patients in the taper plus PCT condition). At the 6-month follow-up, fully half of the patients in the taper plus supportive medical management condition relapsed and had begun using alprazolam again, while no patients in the taper plus PCT condition had done so. Results from a 3-year follow-up revealed that 33% of the patients in the PCT condition had experienced a relapse between 6 and 18 months after their treatment was discontinued. Moreover, 70% of the patients in the supportive medical management condition had experienced a relapse and required additional treatment during the 3-year follow-up period (Spiegel, Bruce, Gregg, & Nuzzarello, 1995). These data suggest an innovative combination treatment, in which high-potency benzodiazepines are administered initially to those who need immediate relief or otherwise desire medication treatment, followed by psychosocial treatment such as PCT, may be quite effective for patients with panic disorder.

In addition, clinical investigators have begun to examine the effectiveness of psychosocial treatments for patients who were previous nonresponders to pharmacological treatment. For example, Pollack, Otto, Kaspi, Hammerness, and Rosenbaum (1994) found that 12 weeks of group cognitive-behavioral therapy helped patients who had shown evidence of an incomplete response to previous pharmacotherapy. While these patients had not shown evidence of improvement while using medication, they experienced significant improvement in global functioning, as well as panic attack frequency, after the 12-week cognitive-behavioral treatment. These results suggest that there might be a select group of patients with panic disorder who may not benefit from medication treatment, but then are able to show evidence of improvement when effective psychosocial treatments are administered. Of course, reversing the sequence for those who initially fail with cognitive-behavioral treatments by subsequently administering an effective pharmacological treatment might produce similar results.

Finally, we now know that even those individuals doing well at follow-ups of a year or more with cognitive-behavioral approaches often experience "setbacks" or other exacerbations of symptoms that occasionally progress to a full relapse (e.g., Burns et al., 1986). Often, these episodes are associated with emergent life stress or other difficulties (Brown, Antony, & Barlow, 1995). Thus, a finding that 75% of all patients treated responded to treatment at posttreatment, and 65% at a 2-year follow-up, may mask the fact that a number of these patients may have experienced significant setbacks in the months between the assessments. In view of the chronicity of panic disorder with agoraphobia, there is a need to investigate strategies to prevent exacerbations of symptoms, as well as full relapse. Based on preliminary studies demonstrating the possible value of maintenance strategies (e.g., Jansson et al., 1986; Ost, 1989b) efforts are now under way to develop more comprehensive and effective maintenance strategies for the purpose of preventing exacerbations or full relapses.

SPECIFIC PHOBIAS

The *DSM-IV* diagnosis of specific phobia replaces the diagnosis of simple phobia listed in *DSM-III-R* (APA, 1987). In *DSM-IV*, a specific phobia is defined as a marked and persistent fear cued by the presence or anticipation of an object or situation. The fear must be considered to be excessive or unreasonable and must be associated with functional impairment or subjective distress (APA, 1994).

Five subtypes of specific phobias are included in *DSM-IV*: animal, natural-environmental, blood-injection-injury, situational, and other. The "other" type serves as a catchall category for specific phobias such as choking or vomiting that do not readily fall into any of the first four subtypes. These subtypes were devised by the *DSM-IV* Anxiety Disorders Work Group as more information was gained about the heterogeneity among the specific phobias along a variety of dimensions (APA, 1996). These dimensions include age of onset, gender composition, and type of physiological reaction to the phobic situation, as well as other important variables such as natural course and type of treatment indicated. For example, the mean age of onset for animal, blood, storm, and water phobias tends to be in early childhood, while the mean age of onset for height phobia is in adolescence (Curtis, Hill, & Lewis, 1990; Marks & Gelder, 1966; Ost, 1987).

The *DSM-IV* diagnosis of specific phobia, when considered overall, is highly prevalent (Antony & Barlow, 1996a). Yet, when specific phobias are given as primary diagnoses, the clinician is not likely to observe an additional clinical diagnosis. In other words, principal diagnoses of specific phobias tend to have lower rates of comorbidity than principal diagnoses of most other Axis I disorders (Moras, DiNardo, Brown, & Barlow, 1994).

According to the NCS, approximately 11% of the population experience a specific phobia during his or her lifetime (Kessler et al., 1994). Gender differences are marked, with a lifetime prevalence for women noted to be 15.7% of the population compared with 6.7% for men. Interestingly, this gender difference in prevalence is most pronounced for the animal type of specific phobia and least apparent for height and blood-injury-injection phobias (Antony & Barlow, 1996b).

Treatments for Specific Phobias

A consensus has developed that the treatment of choice for specific phobias is exposure-based procedures, particularly in vivo exposure. Exposure has been shown to be effective for a wide spectrum of specific phobias. While imaginal exposure has been shown to produce fear reduction (Baker, Cohen, & Saunders, 1973) and should be used if situational in vivo exposure treatment is not feasible, in vivo exposure is generally accepted as the most powerful treatment for specific phobias (APA, 1994; Barlow, 1988; Marks, 1987).

In vivo exposure treatment often appears deceptively simple, yet there are many facets to the procedure (Antony & Barlow, 1996b). Therapists usually initiate exposure treatment with a few office visits. During these initial sessions, the therapist gathers more specific information about the patient's feelings, thoughts, and behaviors concerning the phobic object or situation. The patient is informed that systematic, repeated in vivo exposure will allow the patient to become desensitized to the phobic object or situation. The clinician also lets patients know that all in vivo exposures will be predictable and under their control and teaches patients a variety of adaptive coping strategies to utilize throughout treatment. Finally, the clinician and patient create a hierarchy of feared situations concerning the phobic object or situation and formulate a treatment plan consisting of in vivo exposure practices.

Extensive literature exists demonstrating the effectiveness of in vivo exposure treatments for specific phobias. Over the past few decades, in vivo exposure has been successfully utilized to treat most types of specific phobia (Antony & Barlow, in press-b). For example, clinical investigators have demonstrated the effectiveness of in vivo exposure to treat phobias of animals (e.g. Ost, 1989b; Ost, Salkovskis, & Hellstrom, 1991), heights (e.g. Bourque & Ladouceur, 1980), and flying (Howard, Murphy, & Clarke, 1983; Solyom, Shugar, Bryntwick & Solyom, 1973). In addition, in vivo exposure has been utilized to treat fear of dentists (Jerremalm, Jansson, & Ost, 1986b; Liddell, Ning, Blackwood, & Ackerman, 1991), as well as choking phobia (McNally, 1986, 1994) with good results. In addition, blood-injury-injection phobias also have been successfully treated with in vivo exposure, although these phobias and their treatments are unique and are described below (Ost, 1989b; Ost & Sterner, 1987).

Though exposure-based treatments for specific phobias are considered to be fairly straightforward, they are composed of many factors that may have an impact on the clinical results of treatment. These factors include the duration and temporal spacing of exposure sessions, the level of therapist involvement, and the incorporation of additional treatment components into exposure sessions. The following discussion reviews the available empirical evidence regarding these factors.

In general, it appears that massed exposure sessions result in the most robust clinical improvement (Marks, 1987). In fact, in as little as one session of therapist-guided exposure, 90% of persons with animal or injection phobias were found to be much improved or completely recovered (Ost, 1989b). Ost treated over 20 patients with a specific phobia for a particular animal or injections with in vivo exposure and therapist modeling. He completed each of these sessions in less than 3 hours, with a mean session length of approximately 2 hours. Of the patients, 90% showed evidence of immediate clinical improvement, and their clinically significant improvement was retained at follow-up assessments conducted up to 4 years posttreatment.

The degree of therapist involvement in exposure treatment is also considered to be an important component of the treatment. Though relatively few studies have directly examined the influence of the therapist's presence, most empirical findings point to the importance of therapist involvement during exposure treatment. For example, Ost et al. (1991) found that while 71% of persons with spider phobia improved with therapist-assisted exposure treatment, only 6% of persons who engaged in self-directed exposures evidenced clinical improvement. In addition, O'Brien and Kelley (1980) found that patients who engaged in therapist-directed exposure sessions for snake phobia showed evidence of significantly greater improvement than the patients who engaged in self-directed exposure sessions. Finally, while Bourque and Ladouceur (1980) found no differences in treatment outcome when they varied the degree of therapist involvement in the exposure sessions, their results might be due to the methodological limitations of their study. In their study design, even the patients in the self-directed exposure condition were presented with the exposure rationale by their therapist prior to engaging in the self-directed exposure. Moreover, they received verbal reinforcement from their therapist immediately after they completed their self-directed exposures.

Other empirical studies have shown that certain types of specific phobias require adaptation of exposure-based procedures that incorporate additional treatment components. For example, individuals with blood-injury-injection phobia tend to have a physio-logical reaction that can often inspire a fainting response. This physiological reaction, known as a vasovagal syncope, consists of an immediate increase in both heart rate and blood pressure when the person encounters the phobic stimulus, followed by a significant decrease in both the heart rate and blood pressure. It is this immediate decrease in both heart rate and blood pressure that so often induces fainting in these individuals. A physical strategy that prevents the fainting response has been developed and added to exposure treatment for these individuals. This coping strategy, known as applied tension, serves to temporarily sustain the patient's blood pressure and heart rate at an increased level, thereby eliminating the possibility of fainting.

The applied tension technique consists of completely tensing all the large muscle groups of the body (arms, torso, and legs) for 15 seconds and subsequently releasing the tensing for a similar time period. Patients are expected to begin the applied tension technique before the injection procedure is begun (completing at least five cycles), and they are to continue the applied tension technique both during and after the injection procedure to maintain an adequate blood pressure and heart rate. This applied tension technique has been empirically validated as an additional component of exposure treatment (Ost & Sterner, 1987).

Recently, a comprehensive treatment manual for the specific phobias has been developed by researchers at the Phobia and Anxiety Disorders Clinic in Albany, New York. This treatment manual presents general information regarding the nature and treatment of specific phobias, as well as detailed treatment information for several of the most common specific phobias (Antony, Craske, & Barlow, 1995). In addition, the treatments presented in this manual incorporate additional treatment strategies to be utilized in conjunction with in vivo exposure treatments. For example, cognitive strategies used to combat cognitive distortions and anxious thought patterns and interoceptive exposure utilized to desensitize patients to the physical sensations they associate with the phobic object or situation are included as additional treatment components. Interested readers are referred to *Mastery of Your Specific Phobia* (Antony, Craske, & Barlow, 1995).

Future Directions

Though a great deal of treatment outcome research exists for specific phobias, much remains to be learned. For example, researchers have only just begun to examine differences among the specific phobia subtypes. Little is known about different characteristics of the five subtypes, and additional information in this area could improve treatments for specific phobias. Just as patients with blood-injury-injection phobias benefit from the utilization of applied tension coupled with exposure therapy, many patients with other specific phobia subtypes might respond more robustly to exposure treatments tailored specifically to their phobic object or situation.

It is interesting to note that while a therapist's guidance seems necessary for patients with specific phobias to show evidence of improvement, self-directed bibliotherapy seems effective in treating panic disorder with agoraphobia (e.g., Ghosh & Marks, 1987). If subsequent research supports this finding, factors that might be relevant include differences in the disorders, as well as the differing natures of exposure treatments appropriate for each of them. For example, patients with specific phobias may have a more severe fear of their phobic object. Consequently, they may need a therapist's assistance to come into initial contact with the phobic object. Also, due to the unique nature of many specific phobias, patients may need the therapist's guidance to create a diversity of in vivo exposure experiences of adequate duration and difficulty. In contrast, patients with panic disorder and agoraphobia often fear having panic attacks in many common situations; they rarely believe that there is something inherently dangerous about the situation itself. With merely the assistance of a manual, motivated patients suffering from panic disorder with agoraphobia may be able to create their own fear and avoidance hierarchy of common situations and conduct effective self-directed in vivo exposures. Of course, these hypotheses are merely speculative at this time, given the limited empirical evidence regarding the effectiveness of self-directed exposure treatment for patients with either specific phobias or panic disorder with agoraphobia.

Moreover, in this era of managed care when cost effectiveness is considered to be of utmost importance, further research should be conducted to determine which of the many specific phobias can be treated in just one therapist-assisted in vivo exposure session. Though information has been gained regarding such intensive treatments for patients with certain animal and injection phobias, as well as blood phobias (Hellstrom, Fellenius, & Ost, 1996; Ost, 1989b), it has yet to be determined if other common specific phobias (e.g., height) and, in particular, situational phobias such as flying or claustrophobia would respond as well to such a treatment modality.

Ost (1989b) has suggested that specific phobias such as phobias of heights, elevators, and darkness, might respond very well to therapist-assisted, one-session exposure treatment. However, Ost speculates that flying phobia might require additional therapist-assisted sessions to incorporate substantial patient education regarding the flying process. In addition, Ost wonders whether or not claustrophobia would respond well to a one-session treatment since usually it is not circumscribed but instead encompasses many different situations. Since situational phobias are thought to be on a continuum with panic disorder with agoraphobia, there is reason to suspect the applicability of single-session treatments. While some studies are currently under way to examine the possible effectiveness of therapist-assisted, single-session exposure treatment, this is an area of research that could benefit from even further attention.

SOCIAL PHOBIA

Social phobia has recently been estimated as the most prevalent of all anxiety disorders, with a lifetime prevalence of 13.3% and a 12-month prevalence of 7.9% (Kessler et al., 1994). Moreover, social phobia is the third most prevalent of all mental disorders, exceeded only by major depressive disorder and alcohol dependence. This finding is truly remarkable, especially since social phobia was not included as a separate diagnostic category until DSM-III (APA, 1980).

According to DSM-IV (APA, 1994), individuals with social phobia fear a number of social and performance situations because of concerns that they will act in a way that will be humiliating or embarrassing or that they will visibly manifest anxiety symptoms (e.g. sweating, shaking, or blushing). For patients with social phobia, the fear and avoidance of people typically results in several areas of impairment, including occupational, academic, and social functioning (cf. Hope & Heimberg, 1993). The mean age of onset of social phobia is estimated to be 15.5 years, and onset after the age of 25 is relatively uncommon (Schneier, Johnson, Hornig, Liebowitz, & Weissman, 1992). Moreover, 69% of 361 individuals with social phobia in the large ECA (Epidemiological Catchment Area) study (Myers et al., 1984) also experienced lifetime major comorbid Axis I disorders such as specific phobia (59.0%), agoraphobia (44.9%), alcohol abuse (18.8%), major depression (16.6%), drug abuse (13.0%), dysthymia (12.5%), and obsessive compulsive disorder (11.1%) (Schneier et al., 1992). There is also recent evidence that from 22.1% to 70% of individuals with social phobia also meet criteria for avoidant personality disorder (cf. Hope & Heimberg, 1993).

Little is known about the etiology of social phobia, but numerous studies have examined the following possible factors: behavioral inhibition, genetics, biological mechanisms, developmental factors, conditioning, and cognitive models (Herbert, 1995). Barlow (1988; Barlow, Chorpita & Turovsky, 1996b) hypothesizes that one must be biologically and psychologically vulnerable to anxious apprehension to develop social phobia. For reasons of evolutionary significance, we are biologically vulnerable to anger, criticism, and other means of social disapproval. In addition, research suggests that at least some patients with social phobia are predisposed to focus anxious apprehension on events involving social evaluation. Social anxiety or stress from social evaluative situations involving performance forms the basis from which a false alarm develops in specific social situations. Of course, in some cases, individuals may have direct experience with a traumatic form of social rejection or humiliation, resulting in a true alarm. Another pathway to the acquisition of social phobia occurs when socially anxious individuals occasionally experience some performance deficits, even without an encounter with an alarm. Subsequent anxious apprehension in the future may lead to performance deficits, which sets off the vicious cycle of anxious apprehension (Barlow, 1988). Although the pathways of acquisition may vary, they all have biological vulnerability, stress/trauma, and psychological vulnerability in common.

There is also evidence that genetics plays a role in social phobia. By interviewing 2163 female twins, Kendler, Neale, Kessler, Heath, and Eaves (1992) found that probandwise concordance for social phobia was greater in monozygotic (24.4%) than dizygotic (15.3%) twin pairs. In another study examining the role of genetics in social phobia, first-degree relatives of social phobia probands ($n = 83$) had a significantly increased risk (16% v. 5%, relative risk = 3.12) for social phobia, as compared with first-degree relatives of never mentally ill controls ($n = 231$; Fyer, Mannuzza, Chapman, Liebowitz, & Klein, 1993).

Treatment of Social Phobia

Research on cognitive-behavioral treatments for social phobia has dramatically increased in recent years. The most common treatment approaches include social skills training (SST), relaxation techniques, exposure-based methods, and multicomponent cognitive-behavioral treatments (Heimberg & Juster, 1995). In this section, as above, empirical studies are evaluated according to a template recently created by the American Psychological Association to guide the development of practice guidelines (American Psychological Association, 1995; Barlow & Barlow, 1995). Effective treatments in this section are organized into one of the following three categories of increasing confidence in treatment efficacy: (a) better than no therapy (randomized clinical trials, RCTs), (b) better than nonspecific therapy (RCTs), and (c) better than alternative therapy (RCTs). All studies individually reviewed are Type 1 studies unless otherwise noted.

A comprehensive description of all the treatment outcome studies published to date is beyond the scope of this chapter. However, several excellent papers have been published recently that provide current information on this topic (Donohue, Van Hasselt, & Hersen, 1994; Heimberg & Juster, 1995; Herbert, 1995).

Social Skills Training

The rationale of SST is based on the concept that people with social phobias are deficient in verbal and nonverbal social skills. Heimberg and Juster (1995) point out that, although social skills deficits are inferred from poor social behavior, the term is often confused with performance deficits. They also conclude that although nine studies have used SST as a treatment condition, with some resulting in significant improvement, all but one failed to include appropriate control groups. Therefore, it is not possible to conclude that training in social skills was the component that led to positive outcomes (Heimberg & Juster, 1995). Similarly, Donohoe et al. (1994) also conclude that the heterogeneity of the samples and the paucity of controlled comparisons do not permit definitive conclusions on SST efficacy. Due to the recognized cognitive contributions in the maintenance of social phobia, as well as the fact that most individuals with social phobia have adequate social skills, therapy in recent years has targeted cognitive and behavioral interventions for the treatment of social phobia. Therefore, SST has been investigated less in recent years (Mersch, 1995).

Referring to the aforementioned template of treatment efficacy, we cannot definitively state at this time that SST is superior to even a wait-list control because of methodological limitations. This conclusion gains credence given that the only controlled study of SST completed two decades ago found that 15 weeks of SST did not result in better clinical outcomes than a wait-list control group (Marzillier, Lambert & Kelley, 1976).

Although SST by itself does not appear to be efficacious, there is some indication that combined SST and exposure appears to hold some promise (Turner, Beidel, Cooley, Woody, & Messer, 1994a). In this pilot study of a comprehensive multicomponent treatment (which was a Type 3 study), 13 patients with severe (generalized) social phobia demonstrated significant improvements posttreatment. The authors report that 84% of those completing treatment (four dropped out) showed moderate-to-high end-state functioning, although pretreatment status could not be calculated because there were no pretreatment Clinical Global Impression (CGI) ratings. Moreover, there was no control group. These preliminary findings suggest the importance of controlled clinical trials for this combined treatment. Furthermore, dismantling studies need to be conducted to explore whether the SST component itself leads to additional improvement above and beyond the gains made from the other components.

Relaxation Treatments

The effectiveness of relaxation training and other strategies targeting arousal reduction for social phobia has not yet been adequately evaluated (Heimberg & Juster, 1995). Two groups of investigators have concluded that progressive muscle relaxation alone is not an effective treatment (Al-Kubaisy et al., 1992; Alstrom, Nordlund, Persson, Harding, & Ljunqvist, 1984). There has been some indication by Ost, Jerremalm, and Johansson (1981) and Jerremalm, Jansson, and Ost (1986a) that AR, including application training in which relaxation skills are used during anxiety-producing role-plays (cf. Heimberg & Juster, 1995), is an effective treatment for social phobia (cf. Heimberg & Juster, 1995). Of the three controlled clinical trials

conducted in this area (Alstrom et al., 1984; Jerremalm et al., 1986a; Ost et al., 1981), AR was inferior to self-instruction training, exposure, and supportive counseling and was no better than SST (Donohue et al., 1994). At this time, there is no strong body of literature to support relaxation procedures alone as an effective treatment for social phobia.

Exposure and Cognitive Therapy

There is a growing body of literature in support of a combination treatment for social phobia based on exposure to feared social situations and cognitive therapy (Barlow & Lehman, 1996). Social phobia is partially maintained by the avoidance of anxiety-producing situations and the negative reinforcement that occurs as a result (Donohue et al., 1994). Barlow (1988) views some form of exposure as a central part of any psychosocial treatment for social phobia, and many others would agree. The essential part of exposure is to have a patient repeatedly confront the situation they fear until their anxiety response habituates. The exposures can be conducted in vivo, with the stimulus encountered in the natural environment, or through imaginal exercises. Many treatment programs involve simulated social interactions in which the therapist (and confederates, if necessary) will role-play the anxiety-producing social situation. The cognitive component of treatment addresses the role of fear of negative evaluation by identifying and modifying maladaptive cognitions that occur in these situations (Donohue et al., 1994).

In an early study examining combination treatments, Butler, Cullington, Munby, Amies, and Gelder (1984) randomly assigned 45 socially phobic outpatients to one of the three following conditions: in vivo exposure plus anxiety management (AM), in vivo plus a nonspecific filler, and wait list. The AM program consisted of distraction, relaxation, and rational self-talk. At posttreatment, both active treatment groups were superior to the wait-list controls. However, at 6-month follow-up, patients who received the combination treatment were more improved than the in vivo exposure alone group.

Mattick and Peters (1988) found that cognitive restructuring exercises may enhance the effects of exposure therapy for people with social phobia. In their study, 26 patients were randomly assigned to guided exposure, while 25 patients received guided exposure and cognitive restructuring. There were improvements in both groups at follow-up, and patients in the combined condition fared better at the 3-month follow-up.

In a subsequent study, Mattick, Peters, and Clarke (1989) randomly assigned 43 patients with social phobia to guided exposure alone, cognitive restructuring alone, guided exposure and cognitive restructuring, or a wait list. All active treatment conditions were significantly better than the wait list on a behavioral avoidance test (BAT), as well as self-report measures of negative evaluation and irrational beliefs. Patients in the combined condition evidenced the most improvement on the BAT. The authors conclude that the exposure therapy combined with cognitive restructuring was the most effective intervention overall.

Heimberg et al. (1990) compared a treatment package called cognitive behavioral group treatment (CBGT) consisting primarily of in-session exposure exercises, cognitive restructuring, and homework exercises to a credible placebo condition. This placebo condition, called educational supportive group therapy (ES), was a nondirective supportive group treatment that also consisted of psychoeducation about social phobia. Both groups improved significantly at posttreatment, but CBGT patients were more improved on some key measures at both posttreatment and 6-month follow-up. Moreover, a 5-year follow-up on a portion of the patients from the original study indicated that individuals who received CBGT were more likely to be improved and to maintain their gains relative to the ES group (Heimberg, Salzman, Holt, & Blendell, 1993). This investigation provides further support for combination treatments involving both exposure and cognitive restructuring.

To date, only a few projects have compared effective pharmacotherapy treatments to effective psychosocial treatments. In the first published study of this nature, 65 patients with social phobia were assigned randomly to one of the four following conditions: cognitive-behavioral group treatment, alprazolam with instructions for self-directed exposure (EXP), phenelzine with EXP, or placebo with EXP (Gelernter et al., 1991). All treatments, including the combination of a placebo plus self-exposure instructions, were associated with substantial improvements in severe and chronic social phobia, although the results failed to demonstrate definitively the superiority of one treatment over another.

Turner, Beidel, and Jacob (1994b) assigned 72 patients with social phobia randomly to receive either behavior therapy (flooding), atenolol, or a placebo. On composite and improvement indices, the behavior therapy patients were significantly more improved and demonstrated superior end-state functioning. However, although beta blockers such as atenolol may minimize the somatic symptoms associated with social phobia, such as trembling (Barlow, 1988), these drugs seem incapable of reducing other difficulties associated with this disorder (Turner et al., 1994b). Other research has suggested that atenolol is not the most-effective drug treatment for social phobia (Heimberg & Juster, 1995).

Phase 1 of an important multisite (the State University of New York at Albany Center for Stress and Anxiety Disorders and the New York State Psychiatric Institute) collaborative project directed by Richard Heimberg and Michael Liebowitz has just reached completion (Heimberg et al., 1994). In this study, 133 individuals with social phobia were placed randomly into one of the following four treatment conditions: CBGT, phenelzine, a psychosocial placebo (ES), and a pill placebo. Results indicate the following:

1. CBGT and phenelzine were equally effective after 12 weeks of treatment, with approximately 75% of patients in each group showing substantial improvement. Both were superior to ES and pill placebo, which produced improvement rates of approximately 35% and 40%, respectively.
2. After 12 weeks, phenelzine was more effective than CBGT on some measures.
3. During untreated follow-up, a number of phenelzine patients deteriorated, while CBGT patients maintained their gains (Heimberg & Juster, 1995).

An extension of this project, which is currently under way, will examine the combination of CBGT and phenelzine compared to CBGT alone, phenelzine alone, or a pill placebo. Based on the empirical research, we can conclude that combined exposure and cognitive therapy treatments are superior to wait-list, nonspecific therapy, and, in some cases, alternative therapies.

Psychological Intervention Guidelines

If we return to the psychological intervention guidelines template mentioned above, exposure-based procedures are the only treatment for social phobia that attain the highest level of treatment efficacy, "better than alternative therapy." Heimberg and Juster (1995) maintain that every study demonstrates significant reductions in social phobia, compared with various control groups, with this approach. Moreover, there is some evidence to support the idea that combining exposure with cognitive restructuring is even more effective that exposure alone (Butler et al., 1984; Mattick & Peters, 1988; Mattick, Peters, & Clarke, 1989).

Table 15.4 (Barlow and Lehman, 1996) indicates that combined treatments are more effective than exposure or educational supportive group psychotherapy in all but one case. In this study (Hope, Heimberg, & Bruch, 1990), CBGT and exposure alone were equally effective, and both were superior to wait-list control. Two studies with medications did not demonstrate the superiority of combined treatments over drug treatments. Gelernter et al. (1991) found that all treatments (CBGT, alprazolam and exposure, phenelzine and exposure, placebo and exposure) were associated with substantial improvements, although the superiority of one treatment over another was not definitively demonstrated. Heimberg et al. (1994) found that CBGT and phenelzine treatments were equally effective and superior to a placebo and educational supportive treatments.

Looking at other treatment approaches, at this time we cannot definitively state that social skills training or relaxation are better than no therapy. This is partially due to the methodological limitations of these studies. However, AR, which includes exposure, appears promising.

Future Directions

Clearly, more research needs to be done to evaluate the effectiveness of certain treatments compared to wait-list controls, nonspecific treatment, and alternative therapies. Given the favorable outcomes of the combined cognitive and exposure treatments, it is imperative that we, as researchers, disseminate this treatment to clinicians for widespread use. Barlow and Lehman (1996) state that few attempts have been made to make these treatments more "user friendly" and present them for use by clinicians. To date, little work has been done to evaluate specific treatments beyond their original settings. Moreover, many research studies have exclusion criteria that eliminate "messy" subjects and may threaten the treatment's generalizability beyond academic clinical settings (Herbert, 1995). We do not yet know how effectively these combined treatments can be used outside experi-

TABLE 15.4 Controlled Trials of Psychosocial Treatments for Social Phobia

Study	Length of Follow-Up (Months)	Treatment (N)	Percentage Clinical Improvement of Completers (If Available)	Significant Comparison (Percentage Clinical Improvement)	
				Other Treatments (Yes/No)	Wait List (Yes/No)
Butler et al. (1984)	6	AMT & E (N = 15)		Yes: E	Yes
Mattick & Peters (1988)	3	E & CR (N = 11)	86	Yes: E = 52%	Yes
Mattick et al. (1989)	3	E & CR (N = 25)		Yes: E	Yes
Heimberg et al. (1990)	6	CBGT (N = 20)	81	Yes: ES = 47%	
Heimberg et al. (1993)[a]	54–75	CBGT (N = 10)		Yes: ES (most measures)	
Hope et al. (1990)	6	CBGT (N = 13)		No: E	Yes
Gelernter et al. (1991)	2	CBGT (N = 20)		No: PH, AL, PL	
Lucas & Telch (1993)	PT	CBGT (N = 18)	61	Yes: ES = 24%	
		CBTI	50		
Heimberg et al. (1994)	PT	CBGT (N = 28)	75	No: PH = 77%	
				Yes: PL = 41%	
				Yes: ES = 35%	

AL = alprazolam; AMT = anxiety management therapy; CBGT = cognitive-behavioral group treatment; CBTI = cognitive-behavioral treatment—individual; CR = cognitive restructuring; E = exposure; ES = educational supportive group psychotherapy (placebo treatment); PL = pill placebo; PH = phenelzine; PT = posttreatment.

[a]Follow-up study of Heimberg et al. (1990).

Source: Reprinted with permission from Barlow and Lehman (1996), © 1996 American Medical Association.

generally assumed that those
...fficacy studies are systematically
...ose who are excluded (Barlow, in
...a recent study on the generalizability
...avioral group treatment for social pho-
...ients in a highly controlled efficacy
...ho refused random assignment (and
...a drug condition) or were excluded
...& Engelberg, 1995). Although the
...ded clients differed systematically
...ed clients on a variety of variables,
...s of social support and socioeconomic
...ients showed evidence of comparable
...n from the treatment under evaluation.
...nust continue to create and evaluate effec-
...ients for social phobia while simultaneously
...nating them to practitioners and evaluating
...eir effectiveness "in the field."

GENERALIZED ANXIETY DISORDER

The diagnostic criteria for generalized anxiety disorder (GAD) have undergone substantial modification over the past 15 years (Brown, O'Leary, & Barlow, 1993). In the past, the diagnostic category of GAD, first formulated in 1980 (APA, 1980), resulted in enormous confusion (Barlow, 1988; Barlow & Wincze, in press). This was partially due to its residual status, which meant that the diagnosis of GAD could not be assigned if a person met criteria for any other mental disorder (Brown et al., 1993). This convention was based on the notion that generalized anxiety was an integral part of many disorders and therefore could not be easily separated from the general clinical presentation. In *DSM-III-R* (APA, 1987), for the first time key defining features (e.g., excessive worry and persistent somatic concerns) were presented that elevated GAD beyond a strictly residual category (Brown et al., 1993). These criteria were further delineated and sharpened by *DSM-IV* (APA, 1994). The recently published NCS study (Kessler et al., 1994) estimates the lifetime prevalence of GAD to be 5.1% and the 12-month prevalence to be 3.1% according to *DSM-III-R* criteria (APA, 1987).

As a result of changes in the diagnostic criteria and new data on prevalence, research on important characteristics of GAD, as well as empirical treatment outcome studies, has increased in the past decade. However, given the fact that GAD may be the "basic"

anxiety disorder, in the sense that generalized anxiety is a consistent component of other anxiety disorders with the possible exception of specific phobia, treatments for GAD have still received surprisingly little attention (Barlow, 1988; Brown et al., 1993; Rapee, 1991).

Barlow's (1988) model of the etiology of GAD suggests that biological and psychological vulnerabilities, combined with negative life events, trigger stress-related neurobiological reactions. Reactions to these events are accompanied by physiological arousal associated with stress-related neurobiological reactions and the sense that events are proceeding in an uncontrollable and unpredictable way, which results in negative affect. The focus of attention is shifted from the task at hand to a maladaptive self-evaluative mode, which further increases arousal. This results in increased vigilance and the narrowing of attention to the focus of worry or concern. This arousal-driven cognitive process continues to escalate in a negative feedback loop, resulting in excessive and intense worry, an inability to control the worry, and even performance disruption (Barlow, 1988; Barlow, Chorpita, & Turovsky, in 1996b).

Treatment of Generalized Anxiety Disorder

Until recently, clinical outcome studies have demonstrated only modest treatment gains in GAD symptomatology. These minimal treatment gains have been hypothesized to result from, among other things, high rates of comorbidity found in patients with GAD. In fact, studies have found GAD to be the most frequently assigned additional diagnosis for patients that meet criteria for another anxiety or mood disorder (cf. Brown et al., 1993). The modest treatment gains seen in patients with GAD in early studies may also have resulted from the fact that GAD tends to be chronic in nature, with patients often recalling a lifelong history of the disorder (Brown et al., 1993).

In general, different treatment conditions have not led to differential improvement rates. Given the vagueness of earlier criteria, initial studies on the treatment of GAD utilized nonspecific treatment approaches, such as relaxation or biofeedback, in contrast to specific treatment components directed at key features of other anxiety disorders, such as panic disorder. With the successive refinements of GAD criteria in *DSM-III-R* and *DSM-IV*, researchers now have more information regarding the key features to target in treatment. It has only been in the last decade that more rigorous controlled trials of treatment for GAD have been conducted, utilizing more specific treatment techniques, aimed at targeting the key features of the disorder, such as cognitive therapy, behavior therapy, and combinations of several treatment components.

To properly evaluate the question of treatment choice, one must consider both the efficacy of the treatment, as well as the clinical utility of that technique. In this section, as above, the treatment techniques reviewed focus on treatment efficacy. However, because there are fewer treatment outcome studies for GAD (relative to other disorders), they are organized in three categories of increasing confidence in treatment efficacy: (a) better than no therapy (randomized clinical trials, RCTs), (b) better than nonspecific therapy (RCTs), and (c) better than alternative therapy (RCTs).

Better Than No Therapy

In an early Type 2 investigation, five patients meeting *DSM-III* (APA, 1980) criteria for GAD received a treatment package consisting of EMG (electromyographic) biofeedback, relaxation, and cognitive treatment; they were compared to four GAD patients assigned to a wait list (Barlow et al., 1984). Those receiving active treatment had 18 sessions over a 14-week period. Compared to controls, the patients receiving the active treatment demonstrated a generalized improvement at posttreatment and 3-month follow-up on a variety of measures, including physiological reactivity, self-report questionnaires, and clinician ratings.

Another early controlled clinical trial for the treatment of GAD was conducted to investigate the efficacy of anxiety management (AM), a multicomponent treatment package in the form of a self-help booklet that was utilized in conjunction with therapist-conducted treatment sessions (Butler, Cullington, Hibbert, Klimes & Gelder, 1987). In this study, 45 patients meeting Research Diagnostic Criteria (RDC) for GAD were randomly assigned to either the AM ($n = 22$) or wait-list (WL) ($n = 23$) condition.

The treatment components included psychoeducation about anxiety, relaxation, distraction, cognitive restructuring, and exposure through graded practice. In addition, patients were encouraged to identify their strong points and engage in rewarding and pleasurable

activities. Patients could stop treatment after a minimum of four sessions if they were no longer experiencing the symptoms of anxiety, their anxiety ratings were stable for two weeks, and their therapist agreed that the patient could control his or her symptoms. The average length of treatment was 8.7 sessions.

Patients were actively involved in their treatment by establishing goals and creating homework assignments, as well as scheduling more pleasurable activities and noting areas in their life in which things were going well. Some of the exercises were first practiced with the therapist in session and in addition at home. Furthermore, patients were encouraged to reduce their medication intake. During booster sessions at the end of treatment, the treatment components were reviewed, as well as relapse prevention strategies.

At the end of treatment, the patients receiving AM improved significantly, as compared to the wait-list controls, on every measure, including the State-Trait Anxiety Inventory, the Hamilton rating scales for anxiety and depression, and problem ratings of severity and interference. In addition, these gains were maintained or improved at a 6-month follow-up. Although these results are extremely encouraging, it should be noted that patients were excluded if they had suffered from anxiety for 2 years or more, thus eliminating the patients with more chronic levels of anxiety.

Other studies have added a "placebo" therapy condition to examine whether improvements are caused by specific anxiety treatment techniques or merely general therapy effects. Referring to our template of increasing treatment efficacy, we would have greater confidence in the efficacy of a certain treatment if it was shown to be superior to a nonspecific or placebo therapy. Two investigations that used both wait-list controls and a nondirective treatment condition were unable to demonstrate differential effectiveness between the active therapies and the nondirective treatments, although all treatments were superior to wait-list control groups (Blowers, Cobb & Mathews, 1987; White & Keenan, 1992).

In one such investigation (Blowers et al., 1987), 66 patients meeting *DSM-III* criteria for GAD were assigned to one of three groups: anxiety management training (AMT), nondirective counseling (NDC), or wait-list (WL) control. All patients were assessed pretreatment, posttreatment, and at a 6-month follow-up. The AMT package involved relaxation exercises and a cognitive component based on an abbreviated version of Beck and Emery's cognitive therapy (1985). Patients in the NDC condition were offered the rationale that they could be helped by understanding and becoming aware of their thoughts and feelings and would find the symptoms of anxiety to be less distressing as a result. There were few significant differences in the active treatment conditions, but both were superior to the wait-list controls according to self-report measures and clinician ratings.

Other researchers have also encountered the finding that different active treatments have not led to differential efficacy (Barlow, Rapee & Brown, 1992; Borkovec & Mathews, 1988; Durham & Turvey, 1987). In a study conducted in our Center for Stress and Anxiety Disorders (Barlow et al., 1992), 65 patients meeting DSM-III-R criteria as established by the ADIS-R (Anxiety Disorders Interview Schedule-Revised) (DiNardo & Barlow, 1988) were randomized to one of four treatment groups: applied progressive muscle relaxation (REL), cognitive restructuring (COG), a combination of relaxation and cognitive restructuring (COM), or a wait list (WL). All patients in the active treatment conditions received 15 hour-long sessions conducted by senior doctoral students and staff psychologists.

Treated patients were significantly better compared to those in the wait-list control group. However, as stated above, differential efficacy was not found among active treatment components. Moreover, differential dropout rates were encountered among the active treatments (8% in the COM group to 38% in the REL group).

The two additional studies mentioned above also did not find a difference among treatment conditions, although they did not assign a wait-list control group. Durham and Turvey (1987) randomly assigned 41 patients to either behavior therapy or Beck's cognitive therapy and found that there were no significant differences posttreatment. At 6-month follow-up, however, there was a trend for those receiving cognitive therapy to continue to improve or maintain their gains more frequently than those patients receiving behavior therapy. In another investigation, Borkovec and Mathews (1988) randomly assigned 30 patients to one of three groups: progressive muscle relaxation (PMR) with nondirective therapy, PMR with coping desensitization, or PMR with cognitive therapy. All patients had significant improvement, but they did not differ from each other.

Better Than Nonspecific Therapy

More recently, a few controlled clinical trials have found that a certain type of treatment is better than nondirective treatment (Borkovec et al., 1987; Borkovec & Costello, 1993). In the earlier study (Borkovec et al., 1987), 30 patients who met DSM-III criteria according to the ADIS (Anxiety Disorders Interview Schedule) (DiNardo, O'Brien, Barlow, Waddell, & Blanchard, 1983) were randomly assigned to one of two groups: progressive muscle relaxation (PMR) with cognitive therapy (CT) or PMR with nondirective therapy (ND). Overall, all patients improved substantially at the end of treatment and also at the 6-to-12-month follow-up, as shown by clinician ratings, self-report questionnaires, and daily self-monitoring. However, the PMR and CT group was superior to the PMR and ND group on all but one posttreatment outcome measure. In addition, patients receiving cognitive therapy attributed more of their improvement to the cognitive component of treatment than patients receiving nondirective therapy did to the general psychotherapy they received. The authors conclude that cognitive therapy contains an active ingredient above and beyond the nonspecific psychotherapy treatment factors.

Better Than Alternative Therapy

A final group of studies has been conducted that compares at least two efficacious psychotherapy treatments to each other. According to the template, demonstrated efficacy in this category results in the highest level of confidence in a given treatment. Although most investigations of this type have not resulted in significant differences emerging among active treatments (Barlow et al., 1992; Blowers et al., 1987; Borkovec & Mathews, 1988; Durham & Turvey, 1987; White & Keenan, 1992), a few empirical studies have demonstrated the superiority of one active treatment over another (Butler, Fennell, Robson, & Gelder, 1991; Durham, Murphy, Allan, Richard, Treliving & Fenton, 1994).

In an empirical investigation, 57 patients meeting DSM-III-R criteria for GAD were randomly assigned to one of three treatment groups: cognitive-behavioral treatment (CBT), behavior therapy (BT), or a wait list control group (Butler, Fennell, Robson, & Gelder, 1991). In this controlled clinical trial, independent assessments were conducted pretreatment, posttreatment, at 6-month follow-up, and at 18-month follow-up. Treatment lasted for up to 12 sessions; patients could stop treatment after 4 sessions if they no longer experienced significant symptoms of anxiety, their anxiety ratings were stable for at least 2 weeks, and their therapist agreed with the patient that the patient could control anxiety symptoms effectively.

The BT package consisted of progressive muscle relaxation, reducing avoidance through graduated exposure, and building confidence by reinitiating pleasurable activities. The rationale for BT was that anxiety is maintained by avoidance of anxiety-producing situations, the person's reaction to the symptoms, and loss of confidence. The CBT package consisted of cognitive therapy as described by Beck and Emery (1985), as well as behavioral assignments. The rationale of CBT treatment was that anxiety is maintained by anxious thoughts and lack of self-confidence, which can be controlled by recognizing anxious thoughts, seeking helpful alternatives, and taking action to test these alternatives.

Results showed a superiority of CBT over BT, as demonstrated through measures of anxiety, depression, and cognition. However, the patients in the BT group improved significantly on all but one measure of anxiety and maintained their gains 6 months later. The authors (Butler et al., 1991) note that theirs is one of the few studies in which CBT is shown to be superior to BT, and they offer several possible explanations:

1. BT could not adequately address additional problems such as depression or social anxiety.
2. Cognitive techniques can be effectively applied to treatment reservations and low motivation.
3. CBT deals with worry, as well as somatic symptoms.
4. This study employed unusually rigorous methods of double-checking the integrity of treatment to reduce error variance and overlap between CBT and BT.

In a more recent investigation mentioned above, Borkovec and Costello (1993) compared the efficacy of CBT, AR, and ND in a sample of 55 patients that met DSM-III-R criteria for GAD. For this study, patients in the ND condition were told that the goals of treatment were to enhance self-understanding and to discover things they could do differently to affect how they feel. All three treatments were equal in

length and were reported to be highly credible to the patients. The AR and CBT treatment conditions did not differ significantly from each other but were both superior to ND at posttreatment. However, during a 1-year follow-up, 57.9% of patients receiving CBT met a high end-state functioning criterion (meaning they were close to "cured"), which was significantly better than the 33.3% of patients receiving AR that met this criterion and the 22.2% of patients receiving ND therapy that met this criterion. In addition, significantly fewer patients receiving CBT or AR requested additional treatment (15.8% and 16.7%, respectively) as compared to ND (61.1%).

In another recent controlled clinical trial, 110 patients who met DSM-III-R criteria for GAD were randomly assigned to receive one of the following treatments over a 6-month period: 16–20 sessions of cognitive therapy, 8–10 sessions of cognitive therapy, 16–20 sessions of psychodynamic psychotherapy, 8–10 sessions of psychodynamic psychotherapy, or 8–10 sessions of behaviorally based anxiety management training (Durham et al., 1994). Experienced therapists conducted the cognitive therapy and psychodynamic therapy sessions, and the anxiety management sessions were conducted by registrars in psychiatry after a brief period of training.

Although all treatments resulted in substantial improvements, cognitive therapy was significantly more effective than analytic therapy, with about 50% of cognitive therapy patients "considerably" better at follow-up. There was no significant effect for level of contact. Although the authors make the point that significant improvements in symptoms can be made after only brief therapist training, it remains unclear whether there is a significant advantage for the experienced therapist because experienced and inexperienced therapists were conducting different types of treatment. Due to the fact that therapist experience differed according to treatment type, this is considered to be a Type 2 study.

Cognitive-behavioral therapy has also been shown to be superior to benzodiazepine medication in several controlled clinical trials (Lindsay, Gamsu, McLaughlin, Hood & Espie, 1987; Power et al., 1990; Power, Jerrom, Simpson, Mitchell & Swanson, 1989). In one study (Power et al., 1990), 101 patients meeting DSM-III criteria for GAD were randomly assigned to one of the following 10-week treatment conditions: CBT, diazepam (DZ), placebo, CBT and DZ, or CBT and placebo. Posttreatment and 6-month follow-up measures indicated a superiority of all CBT treatments, especially CBT alone and the CBT/DZ combination. For more information on psychopharmacological treatments of GAD, please refer to chapter 16.

Future Directions

The more we learn about the nature of GAD, the more we should be able to improve our psychotherapeutic treatments. Additional dismantling studies should assist in determining the specific mechanisms of action in successful therapy. At this time, the most successful psychosocial treatments combine relaxation exercises and cognitive therapy with the goal of bringing the worry process itself under the patient's control (Barlow & Lehman, in press). The results of 12 studies comparing cognitive therapy or cognitive-behavioral therapy to other treatments or a wait list are summarized in Table 15.5 (Barlow & Lehman, 1996). Until recently, most studies have not demonstrated differential rates of efficacy for active treatment techniques, although most studies have shown that active treatments are superior to nondirective approaches and uniformly superior to no treatment. Although more research in this area is still warranted, we have made substantial progress in the past decade.

TABLE 15.5 Controlled Trials of Cognitive-Behavioral Treatments for Generalized Anxiety Disorder

Study	Length of Follow-Up (Months)	Treatment (N)	Percentage Clinical Improvement of Completers (If Available)	Significant Comparison (Percentage Clinical Improvement)	
				Other Treatments (Yes/No)	Wait List (Yes/No)
Barlow et al. (1984c)	6	CBT (N = 5)			Yes
Blowers et al. (1987)	6	CBT (N = 20)		Yes: ND (some measures)	Yes
Borkovec et al. (1987)	6–12	CT + PR (N = 16)		Yes: ND + PR (some measures)	
Butler et al. (1987)	6	CBT (N = 22)	58.5		Yes (0%)
Borkovec & Mathews (1988)	12	CT + PR (N = 6)		No: SCD + PR	No: ND + PR
Power et al. (1989)	PT	CBT (N = 10)		Yes: PL (one central measure) No: DZ (one central measure)	
Power et al. (1990)	PT	CBT (N = 21)	61.9	No: CBT + DZ 69.8% No: CBT + PL = 55.6% Yes: DZ = 30.3% Yes: PL = 17.5%	
Butler et al. (1991)	6	CBT (N = 18)	42	Yes: BT = 5%	Yes
Barlow et al. (1992)	24	CBT (N = 29)	55		Yes (0%)
White & Keenan (1992)	6	CBT (N = 26)		No: BT, CT	Yes Yes: APL
Borkovec & Costello (1993)	12	CBT (N = 18)	57.9	Yes: ND = 26.7% Yes: AR = 37.5%	
Durham et al. (1994)[a]	6	CT (N = 40)	>60	Yes: AP < 31% Yes: AMT < 37%	

AMT = anxiety management training; AP = analytic psychotherapy; APL = attention placebo; AR = applied relaxation; BT = behavior therapy; CBT = cognitive-behavioral therapy; CT = cognitive therapy; DZ = diazepam; FU = follow-up; ND = nondirective therapy; PL = pill placebo; PR = progressive relaxation; PT = posttreatment; SCD = self-control desensitization

[a]Intent-to-treat.

Source: Reprinted with permission from Barlow and Lehman (1996), © 1996 American Medical Association. Adapted from Borkovec & Whisman (1996).

Although one of the clinical trials (Butler et al., 1987) eliminated people who reported having anxiety for more than 2 years, the essence of GAD is that it seems to be characterological, with most people reporting that they have been worriers all of their lives. Thus, it is imperative that we study this population as Butler et al. (1991) did in a later project.

If efficacious treatments can be found for the most resistant and chronically anxious patients, then treatments should also benefit those who are on the less-severe end of the anxiety continuum. Perhaps as many as 30–40% of the population may experience anxiety severe enough to warrant some clinical intervention (cf. Barlow, 1988). In a recent survey, 33% of over 6000 patients completing an up-to-date screening instrument in the offices of 75 physicians in a large health maintenance organization (HMO) reported elevated symptoms of anxiety and/or anxiety disorders (Fifer et al., 1994).

Additional surveys also suggest that people with anxiety difficulties are prevalent in primary care settings (Barlow, Lerner & Esler, 1996). In the era of rising costs of health care, developing brief, cost-effective, and perhaps self-directed treatments with proven efficacy for the treatment of anxiety in primary care offices will be an important step, particularly since individuals with anxious symptoms, even if not fully syndromal, are impaired and at risk for the development of more severe disorders (Barlow, Lerner, & Esler, 1996; Barlow & Lehman, 1996).

CONCLUSIONS

We have reviewed the development of effective psychosocial treatments for a variety of anxiety disorders, but it is fair to say that we have only reached the first plateau of the development of these procedures. Although we now have treatments that are clearly more effective than credible alternative psychosocial interventions for most disorders, we know little about the generality of the effectiveness of these procedures. In addition to questions about the generality of effectiveness across patients, settings, and therapists of differing skills and abilities, questions have also been raised about the feasibility of these treatments, as well as their cost-effectiveness. Many of these issues are outlined succinctly in the template for psychological intervention guidelines referred to above (American Psychological Association, 1995), which provides a roadmap for future research. Some research along

these lines is beginning to appear, suggesting, in an encouraging way, that many of these procedures are just as effective or more effective when applied in a variety of practice settings as they are in the clinical research settings in which they were developed (Barlow, 1996; Barlow & Barlow, 1995). But, most of this research lies ahead of us.

Equally important will be improving efforts to disseminate these treatments to the variety of practice settings in which they should prove useful, many of them primary care settings, in order to meet the demands of many patients with these disorders desiring brief, effective treatments. Evidence indicates that effective psychological treatments are rarely available and much less readily available than pharmacological treatments in most settings (Barlow, 1996). Thus, it is not enough simply to develop these treatments and report on their effectiveness. Rather, it is the responsibility of those involved in treatment development to make these treatments as user friendly as possible and to evaluate alternative methods of training and dissemination that would ensure that these approaches reach the greatest number of people who need them.

References

Agras, W. S., Leitenberg, H., & Barlow, D. H. (1968). Social reinforcement in the modification of agoraphobia. *Archives of General Psychiatry, 19,* 423–427.

Al-Kubaisy, T., Marks, I. M., Logsdail, S., Marks, M.P., Lovell, K., Sungur, M., & Araya, R. (1992). Role of exposure homework in phobia reduction: A controlled study. *Behavior Therapy, 23,* 599–621.

Alstrom, J. E., Nordlund, C. L., Persson, G., Harding, M. & Ljungqvist, C. (1984). Effects of four treatment methods on social phobic patients not suitable for insight-oriented psychotherapy. *Acta Psychiatrica Scandinavica, 70,* 97–110.

American Psychiatric Association. (1980). *Diagnostic and statistical manual of mental disorders* (3rd ed.). Washington, D.C.: Author.

———. (1987). *Diagnostic and statistical manual of mental disorders* (3rd ed., rev.). Washington, D.C.: Author.

———. (1994). *Diagnostic and statistical manual of mental disorders* (4th ed.). Washington, D.C.: Author.

———. (1996). *DSM-IV sourcebook,* Vol. 2. Washington, D.C.: Author.

American Psychological Association Task Force on Psychological Intervention Guidelines. (1995, February). *Template for developing guidelines: Interventions for mental disorders and psychosocial aspects of physical disorders.* Washington, D.C.: American Psychological Association.

Antony, M. M., & Barlow, D. H. (1996a). Social and specific phobias. In D. H. Taylor & A. Tasman (Eds.), *Psychiatry*. Philadelphia: W. B. Saunders.

———. (1996b). Specific phobia. In V. E. Caballo & R. M. Turner (Eds.), *International handbook of cognitive/behavioral treatment of psychiatric disorders*. Madrid, Spain: Siglio XXI.

Antony, M. M., Craske, M. G., & Barlow, D. H. (1995). *Mastery of your specific phobia*. Albany, N.Y.: Graywind Publications.

Arnow, B. A., Taylor, C. B., Agras, W. S., & Telch, M. J. (1985). Enhancing agoraphobia treatment outcome by changing couple communication patterns. *Behavior Therapy*, 16, 452–467.

Baker, B. L., Cohen, D. C., & Saunders, J. T. (1973). Self-directed desensitization for acrophobia. *Behaviour Research and Therapy*, 11, 79–89.

Barlow, D. H. (1988). *Anxiety and its disorders: The nature and treatment of anxiety and panic*. New York: Guilford Press.

———. (1994). Effectiveness of behavior treatment for panic disorder with and without agoraphobia. In B. E. Wolfe & J. D. Maser (Eds.), *Treatment of anxiety disorder: A consensus development conference* (pp. 105–120). Washington, D.C.: American Psychiatric Press.

———. (1996). The effectiveness of psychotherapy: Science and policy. *Clinical Psychology: Science and Practice*, 3, 236–240.

Barlow, D. H. & Barlow, D. G. (1995). Practice guidelines and empirically validated psychosocial treatments: Ships passing in the night? *Behavioral Healthcare Tomorrow, May–June*, 25–29, 76.

Barlow, D. H., & Brown, T. A. (1995). Correction to Klosko et al. (1990). *Journal of Consulting and Clinical Psychology*, 63, 830.

———. (1996). Panic disorder and panic disorder with agoraphobia: Psychological treatments. In M. Mavissakalian & R. Prien (Eds.), *Long-term treatments of anxiety disorders* (pp. 221–240). Washington, D.C.: American Psychiatric Press.

Barlow, D. H., Chorpita, B. F., & Turovsky, J. (1996b). Fear, panic, anxiety, and disorders of emotion. In D. A. Hope (Ed.), *Nebraska symposium on motivation: Perspectives on anxiety, panic, and fear* (Vol. 43) (251–328). Lincoln, Neb.: University of Nebraska Press.

Barlow, D. H., Cohen, A. S., Waddell, M. T., Vermilyea, B. B., Klosko, J. S., Blanchard, E. B., & DiNardo, P. A. (1984c). Panic and generalized anxiety disorders: Nature and treatment. *Behavior Therapy*, 15, 431–449.

Barlow, D. H., & Craske, M. G. (1989). *Mastery of your anxiety and panic*. Albany, N.Y.: Graywind Publications.

———. (1994). *Mastery of your anxiety and panic (MAP II)*. Albany, N.Y.: Graywind Publications.

Barlow, D. H., Craske, M. G., Cerny, J. A., & Klosko, J. S. (1989). Behavioral treatment of panic disorder. *Behavior Therapy*, 20, 261–282.

Barlow, D. H., Hayes, S. C., & Nelson, R. O. (1984b). *The scientist practitioner: Research and accountability in clinical and educational setting*. New York: Pergamon.

Barlow, D. H., & Lehman, C. (1996). Advances in the psychosocial treatment of anxiety disorders: Implications for national health care. *Archives of General Psychiatry*, 53, 727–735.

Barlow, D. H., Lerner, J. A., & Esler, J. K. L. (1996a). Behavioral health care in primary care settings: Recognition and treatment of anxiety disorders. In R. J. Resnick and R. H. Rozensky (Eds), *Health psychology through the life span: Practice and research opportunities* (pp. 133–148). Washington, DC: American Psychological Association Press.

Barlow, D. H., O'Brien, G. T., & Last, C. G. (1984a). Couples treatment of agoraphobia. *Behavior Therapy*, 15, 41–58.

Barlow, D. H., Rapee, R. M., & Brown, T. A. (1992). Behavioral treatment of generalized anxiety disorder. *Behavior Therapy*, 23, 551–570.

Barlow, D. H., & Wincze, J. (in press). DSM-IV and beyond: What is generalized anxiety disorder? *Acta Psychiatric Scandinavia*.

Beck, A. T., & Emery, G. (1985). *Anxiety disorders and phobias: A cognitive perspective*. New York: Basic Books.

Beck, A. T., Sokol, L., Clark, D. A., Berchick, R., & Wright, F. (1992). A crossover study of focused cognitive therapy for panic disorder. *American Journal of Psychiatry*, 149, 778–783.

Black, D. W., Wesner, R., Bowers, W., & Gabel, J. (1993). A comparison of fluvoxamine, cognitive therapy, and placebo in the treatment of panic disorder. *Archives of General Psychiatry*, 50, 44–50.

Blowers, C., Cobb, J., & Mathews, A. (1987). Generalised anxiety: A controlled treatment study. *Behavior Research and Therapy*, 25(6), 493–502.

Bonn, J. A., Readhead, C. P. A., & Timmons, B. H. (1984). Enhanced adaptive behavioral response in agoraphobic patients pretreated with breathing retraining. *Lancet*, 2, 665–669.

Borkovec, T. D., & Costello, E. (1993). Efficacy of applied relaxation and cognitive-behavioral therapy in the treatment of generalized anxiety disorder. *Journal of Consulting and Clinical Psychology*, 61(4), 611–619.

Borkovec, T. D., & Mathews, A. M. (1988). Treatment of nonphobic anxiety disorders: A comparison of nondirective, cognitive, and coping desensitization therapy. *Journal of Consulting and Clinical Psychology*, 56(6), 877–884.

Borkovec, T. D., Mathews, A. M., Chambers, A., Ebrahimi, S., Lytle, R., & Nelson, R. (1987). The effects of relaxation training with cognitive or nondirective therapy and the role of relaxation-induced anxiety in the treatment of generalized anxiety. *Journal of Consulting and Clinical Psychology, 55*(6), 883–333.

Borkovec, T. D., & Whisman, M. A. (1996). Psychosocial treatment for generalized anxiety disorder. In M. Mavissakalian & R. Prien (Eds.), *Long-term treatments of anxiety disorders* (pp. 171–199). Washington, D.C.: American Psychiatric Press.

Bourque, P., & Ladouceur, R. (1980). An investigation of various performance-based treatments with acrophobics. *Behaviour Research and Therapy, 18,* 161–170.

Brown, T. A., Antony, M. M., & Barlow, D. H. (1995). Diagnostic comorbidity in panic disorder: Effect on treatment outcome and course of comorbid diagnoses following treatment. *Journal of Consulting and Clinical Psychology, 63,* 408–418.

Brown, T. A., & Barlow, D. H. (1995). Long-term outcome in cognitive-behavioral treatment of panic disorder: Clinical predictors and alternative strategies for assessment. *Journal of Consulting and Clinical Psychology, 63,* 754–765.

Brown, T. A., O'Leary, T. A., & Barlow, D. H. (1993). Cognitive-behavioral treatment of generalized anxiety disorder. In: D. H. Barlow (Ed.), *Clinical handbook of psychological disorders* (2nd ed.). New York: Guilford Publications.

Burns, L. E., Thorpe, G. L., & Cavallaro, L. A. (1986). Agoraphobia 8 years after behavioral treatment: A follow-up study with interview, self-report, and behavioral data. *Behavioral Therapy, 17,* 580–591.

Butler, G., Cullington, A., Hibbert, G., Klimes, I., & Gelder, M. (1987). Anxiety management for persistent generalised anxiety. *British Journal of Psychiatry, 151,* 535–542.

Butler, G., Cullington, A., Munby, M., Amies, P., & Gelder, M. (1984). Exposure and anxiety management in the treatment of social phobia. *Journal of Consulting and Clinical Psychology, 52,* 642–650.

Butler, G., Fennell, M., Robson, P., & Gelder, M. (1991). Comparison of behavior therapy and cognitive behavior therapy in the treatment of generalized anxiety disorder. *Journal of Consulting and Clinical Psychology, 59*(1), 167–175.

Cerny, J. A., Barlow, D. H., Craske, M. G., & Himadi, W. G. (1987). Couples treatment of agoraphobia: A two-year follow-up. *Behavior Therapy, 18,* 401–415.

Chambless, D. L. (1990). Spacing of exposure sessions in treatment of agoraphobia and simple phobia. *Behavior Therapy, 21,* 217–229.

Chambless, D. L., & Renneberg, B. (1988, September). *Personality disorders of agoraphobics.* Paper presented at World Congress of Behavior Therapy, Edinburgh, Scotland.

Clark, D. M. (1989). Anxiety states: Panic and generalized anxiety. In K. Hawton, P. Salkovskis, J. Kirk, & D. M. Clark. (Eds.), *Cognitive behavior therapy for psychiatric problems: A practical guide.* Oxford, U.K.: Oxford University Press.

Clark, D. M., Salkovskis, P. M., Hackmann, A., Middleton, H., Anastasiades, P., & Gelder, M. (1994). A comparison of cognitive therapy, applied relaxation, and imipramine in the treatment of panic disorder. *British Journal of Psychiatry, 164,* 759–769.

Cobb, J. P., Mathews, A. M., Childs-Clarke, A., & Blowers, C. M. (1984). The spouse as co-therapist in the treatment of agoraphobia. *British Journal of Psychiatry, 144,* 282–287.

Côté, G., Gauthier, J. G., Laberge, B., Cormier, H. J., & Plamondon, J. (1994). Reduced therapist contact in the cognitive behavioral treatment of panic disorder. *Behavior Therapy, 25,* 123–145.

Craske, M. G., & Barlow, D. H. (1993). Panic disorder and agoraphobia. In D. H. Barlow (Ed.), *Clinical handbook of psychological disorders* (pp. 1–47). New York: Guilford Press.

Craske, M. G., Brown, T. A., & Barlow, D. H. (1991). Behavioral treatment of panic disorder: A two-year follow-up. *Behavior Therapy, 22,* 289–304.

Craske, M. G., Maidenberg, E., & Bystritsky, A. (1995). Brief cognitive-behavioral versus non directive therapy for panic disorder. *Journal of Behavior Therapy and Experimental Psychiatry, 26,* 113–120.

Craske, M. G., Miller, P. P., Rotunda, R., & Barlow, D. H. (1990). A descriptive report of features of initial unexpected panic attacks in minimal and extensive avoiders. *Behaviour Research and Therapy, 28,* 395–400.

Curtis, G. C., Hill, E. M., & Lewis, J. A. (1990). *Heterogeneity of DSM-III-R simple phobia and the simple phobia/agorpahobia boundary: Evidence from the ECA study.* Report to the *DSM-IV* Anxiety Disorders Work Group. Ann Arbor, Mich.: University of Michigan.

De Ruiter, C., Rijken, H., Garssen, B., & Kraaimaat, F. (1989). Breathing retraining, exposure, and a combination of both in the treatment of panic disorder with agoraphobia. *Behaviour Research and Therapy, 27,* 663–672.

DiNardo, P. A., & Barlow, D. H. (1988). *Anxiety Disorders Interview Schedule-Revised (ADIS-R).* Albany, N.Y.: Phobia and Anxiety Disorders Clinic, State University of New York at Albany.

DiNardo, P. A., O'Brien, G. T., Barlow, D. H., Waddell, M. T., & Blanchard, E. (1983). Reliability of *DSM-III* anxiety disorder categories using a new structured interview. *Archives of General Psychiatry, 40,* 1070–1078.

Donohue, B. C., Van Hasselt, V. B., & Hersen, M. (1994). Behavioral assessment and treatment of social phobia. *Behavior Modification, 18*(3), 262–288.

Durham, R. C., Murphy, T., Allan, T., Richard, K.,

Treliving, L. R., & Fenton, G. W. (1994). Cognitive therapy, analytic psychotherapy and anxiety management training for generalized anxiety disorder. *British Journal of Psychiatry*, 165, 315–323.

Durham, R. C., & Turvey, A. A. (1987). Cognitive therapy versus Behavior therapy in the treatment of chronic general anxiety. *Behavior Research and Therapy*, 25(3), 229–234.

Emmelkamp, P. M. G., Brilman, E., Kuiper, H., & Mersch, P. P. (1986). The treatment of agoraphobia: A comparison of self-instructional training, rational emotive therapy, and exposure in vivo. *Behavior Modification*, 10, 37–53.

Emmelkamp, P. M. G., & Mersch, P. P. (1982). Cognition and exposure in vivo in the treatment of agoraphobia: Short-term and delayed effects. *Cognitive Therapy and Research*, 6, 77–90.

Fava, G. A., Zielezny, M., Savron, G., & Grandi, S. (1995). Long-term effects of behavioural treatment for panic disorder with agoraphobia. *British Journal of Psychiatry*, 166, 87–92.

Feigenbaum, W. (1988). Long-term efficacy of ungraded versus graded massed exposure in agoraphobics. In I. Hand & H. Wittchen (Eds.), *Panic and phobias: Treatments and variables affecting course and outcome* (pp. 83–88). Berlin: Springer-Verlag.

Fifer, S. K., Mathias, S. D., Patrick, D. L., Majonson, P. D., Lubeck, D. P., & Buesching, D. P., (1994). Untreated anxiety among adult primary care patients in a health maintenance organization. *Archives of General Psychiatry*, 51, 740–750.

Freud, S. (1961). On the grounds for detaching a particular syndrome from neurasthenia under the description of anxiety neurosis. In J. Strachey (Ed. & Trans.), *The standard edition of the complete psychological works of Sigmund Freud*, Vol. 3 (pp. 85–116). London: Hogarth Press. (Original work published 1895)

Fyer, A. J., Mannuzza, S., Chapman, T. F., Liebowitz, M. R., & Klein, D. F. (1993). A direct interview family study of social phobia. *Archives of General Psychiatry*, 50, 286–293.

Gelder, M. G., & Marks, I. M. (1966). Severe agoraphobia: A controlled prospective trial of behavioral therapy. *British Journal of Psychiatry*, 112, 309–319.

Gelernter, C. S., Uhde, T. W., Cimbolic, P., Arnkoff, C. B., Vittone, B. J., Tancer, M. E., & Bartko, J. J. (1991). Cognitive-behavioral and pharmacological treatments for social phobia: A controlled study. *Archives of General Psychiatry*, 48, 938–945.

Ghosh, A., & Marks, I. M. (1987). Self-treatment of agoraphobia by exposure. *Behavior Therapy*, 18, 3–16.

Gould, R. A., Otto, M. W., & Pollack, M. H. (1995). A meta-analysis of treatment outcome for panic disorder. *Clinical Psychology Review*, 15, 819–844.

Hafner, J., & Marks, I. M. (1976). Exposure in vivo of agoraphobics: Contributions of diazepam, group exposure, and anxiety evocation. *Psychological Medicine*, 6, 71–88.

Heimberg, R. G., Dodge, C. S., Hope, D. A., Kennedy, C. R., Zollo, L., & Becker, R. E. (1990). Cognitive-behavioral group treatment for social phobia: Comparison to a credible placebo control. *Cognitive Therapy and Research*, 14, 1–23.

Heimberg, R. G., & Juster, H. P. (1995). Cognitive-behavioral treatments: Literature review. In R. G. Heimberg, M. R. Liebowitz, D. A. Hope, & F. R. Schneier (Eds.), *Social phobia: Diagnosis, assessment and treatment*. New York: Guilford Press.

Heimberg, R. G., Juster, H. R., Brown, E. J., Holle, C., Makris, G. S., Leung, A. W., Schneier, F. R., Gitow, A., & Liebowitz, M. R. (1994, November). *Cognitive-behavioral versus pharmacological treatment of social phobia: Posttreatment and follow-up effects.* Paper presented at the annual meeting of the Association for Advancement of Behavior Therapy, San Diego, Calif.

Heimberg, R. G., Salzman, D. G., Holt, C. S., & Blendell, K. A. (1993). Cognitive-behavioral group treatment for social phobia: Effectiveness at five-year followup. *Cognitive Therapy and Research*, 17, 325–339.

Hellstrom, K., Fellenius, J., & Ost, L.-G. (1996). One versus five sessions of applied tension in the treatment of blood phobia. *Behaviour Research and Therapy*, 34, 101–112.

Herbert, J. D. (1995). An overview of the current status of social phobia. *Applied and Preventive Psychology*, 4, 39–51.

Holden, A. E., Jr., O'Brien, G. T., Barlow, D. H., Stetson, D., & Infantino, A. (1983). Self-help manual for agoraphobia: A preliminary report of effectiveness. *Behavioral Therapy*, 14, 545–556.

Hope, D. A., & Heimberg, R. G. (1993). Social phobia and social anxiety. In: Barlow, D. H., (Ed.) *Clinical handbook of psychological disorders* (2nd ed.). New York: Guilford Publications.

Hope, D. A., Heimberg, R. G., & Bruch, M. A. (1990, March). *The importance of cognitive intervention in behavioral group therapy for social phobia.* Paper presented at the 10th National Conference on Phobias and Related Anxiety Disorders, Bethesda, Md.

Howard, W. A., Murphy, S. M., & Clarke, J. C. (1983). The nature and treatment of fear of flying: A controlled investigation. *Behavior Therapy*, 14, 557–567.

Jacobson, N. S., Wilson, L., & Tupper, C. (1988). The clinical significance of treatment gains resulting from exposure-based interventions for agoraphobia: A reanalysis of outcome data. *Behavior Therapy*, 19, 539–554.

Jansson, L., Jerremalm, A., & Ost, L. G. (1986). Follow-up of agoraphobic patients treated with exposure in vivo or applied relaxation. *British Journal of Psychiatry, 149,* 486–490.

Jansson, L., & Ost, L. G. (1982). Behavioral treatments for agoraphobia: An evaluative review. *Clinical Psychology Review, 2,* 311–336.

Jerremalm, A., Jansson, L., & Ost, L. G. (1986a). Cognitive and physiological reactivity and the effects of different behavioral methods in the treatment of social phobia. *Behaviour Research and Therapy, 24,* 171–180.

———. (1986b). Individual response patterns and the effects of different behavioral methods in the treatment of dental phobia. *Behaviour Research and Therapy, 24,* 587–596.

Juster, H. R., Heimberg, R. G., & Engelberg, B. (1995). Self selection and sample selection in a treatment study of social phobia. *Behaviour Research and Therapy, 33,* 321–324.

Kendler, K. S., Neale, M. C., Kessler, R. C., Heath, A. C., & Eaves, L. J. (1992). The genetic epidemiology of phobias in women: The interrelationship of agoraphobia, social phobia, situational phobia, and simple phobia. *Archives of General Psychiatry, 49,* 273–281.

Kessler, R. C., McGonagle, K. A., Zhao, S., Nelson, C. B., Hughes, M., Eshleman, S., Wittchen, H. U., & Kendler, K. S. (1994). Lifetime and 12-month prevalence of *DSM-III-R* psychiatric disorders in the United States: Results form the national comorbidity survey. *Archives of General Psychiatry, 51,* 8–19.

Klosko, J. S., Barlow, D. H., Tassinari, R., & Cerny, J. A. (1990). A comparison of alprazolam and behavior therapy in treatment of panic disorder. *Journal of Consulting and Clinical Psychology, 58,* 77–84.

Liddell, A., Ning, L, Blackwood, J., & Ackerman, J. D. (1991, November). *Long-term follow-up of dental phobics who completed a brief exposure based behavioral treatment program.* Paper presented at the annual convention of the Association for Advancement of Behavior Therapy, New York.

Lidren, D. M., Watkins, P. L., Gould, R. A., Clum, G. A., Asterino, M., & Tulloch, H. L. (1994). A comparison of bibliotherapy and group therapy in the treatment of panic disorder. *Journal of Consulting and Clinical Psychology, 62,* 865–869.

Lindsay, W. R., Gamsu, C. V., McLaughlin, E., Hood, E., & Espie, C. A. (1987). A controlled trial of treatment for generalized anxiety. *British Journal of Clinical Psychology, 26,* 3–15.

Lucas, R. A., & Telch, M. J. (1993, November). *Group versus individual treatment of social phobia.* Paper presented at the annual meeting of the Association for Advancement of Behavior Therapy, Atlanta, Ga.

Magraf, J. & Schneider, S. (1991). *Outcome and active ingredients of cognitive-behavioral treatment for panic disorder.* Presented at the annual meeting of the Association for Advancement of Behavior Therapy, New York, NY.

Marks, I. M. (1971). Phobic disorders four years after treatment: A prospective follow-up. *British Journal of Psychiatry, 129,* 362–371.

———. (1987). *Fears, phobias, and rituals.* New York: Oxford University Press.

Marks, I. M., & Gelder, M. G. (1966). Different ages of onset in varieties of phobia. *American Journal of Psychiatry, 123,* 218–221.

Marks, I. M., Swinson, R. P., Basoglu, M., Kuch, K., Noshirvani, H., O'Sullivan, G., Lelliott, P. T., Kirby, M., McNamee, G., Sengun, S., & Wickwire, K. (1993). Alprazolam and exposure alone and combined in panic disorder with agoraphobia: A controlled study in London and Toronto. *British Journal of Psychiatry, 162,* 776–787.

Marzillier, J. S., Lambert, C., & Kelley, J. (1976). A controlled evaluation of systematic desensitization and social skills training for socially inadequate psychiatric patients. *Behaviour Research and Therapy, 14,* 225–238.

Mattick, R. P., & Peters, L. (1988). Treatment of severe social phobia: Effects of guided exposure with and without cognitive restructuring. *Journal of Consulting and Clinical Psychology, 56,* 251–260.

Mattick, R. P., Peters, L., & Clarke, J. C. (1989). Exposure and cognitive restructuring for social phobia: A controlled study. *Behavior Therapy, 20,* 3–23.

Mavissakalian, M. R. (1996). Antidepressant medications for panic disorder. In M. Mavissakalian & R. Prien (Eds.), *Anxiety disorders: Psychological and pharmacological treatments* (pp. 265–284). Washington, D.C.: American Psychiatric Press.

Mavissakalian, M., & Barlow, D. H. (Eds.). (1981). *Phobia: Psychological and pharmacological treatment.* New York: Guilford Press.

Mavissakalian, M., & Michelson, L. (1986). Two-year follow-up of exposure and imipramine treatment of agoraphobia. *American Journal of Psychiatry, 143,* 1106–1112.

Mavissakalian, M., & Perel, J. (1985). Imipramine in the treatment of agoraphobia: Dose-response relationships. *American Journal of Psychiatry, 142,* 1032–1036.

McNally, R. J. (1986). Behavioral treatment of choking phobia. *Journal of Behavior Therapy and Experimental Psychiatry, 17,* 185–188.

———. (1994). Choking phobia: A review of the literature. *Comprehensive Psychiatry, 35,* 83–89.

Mersch, P. P. A. (1995). The treatment of social phobia: The differential effectiveness of exposure in vivo and an integration of exposure in vivo, rational emotive therapy and social skills training. *Behaviour Research and Therapy, 33*(3), 259–269.

Michelson, L., Marchione, K., & Greenwald, M. (1989, November). *Cognitive-behavioral treatments of agoraphobia.* Paper presented at the annual meeting of the Association for the Advancement of Behavior Therapy, Washington, D.C.

Michelson, L., Mavissakalian, M., & Marchione, K. (1988). Cognitive, behavioral, and psychophysiological treatments of agoraphobia: A comparative outcome investigation. *Behavior Therapy, 19,* 97–120.

Mills, H. L., Agras, W. S., Barlow, D. H., & Mills, J. R. (1973). Compulsive rituals treated by response prevention. *Archives of General Psychiatry, 28,* 524–529.

Moras, K., DiNardo, P. A., Brown, T. A., & Barlow, D. H. (1994). *Comorbidity, functional impairment, and depression among the DSM-III-R anxiety disorders.* Manuscript submitted for publication.

Munby, J., & Johnston, D. W. (1980). Agoraphobia: The long-term follow-up of behavioral treatment. *British Journal of Psychiatry, 137,* 418–427.

Myers, J. K., Weissman, M. M., Tischler, G. L., Holzer, C. E., III, Leaf, P. J., Orvaschel, H., Anthony, J. D., Boyd, J. H., Burke, J. D., Jr., Kramer, M., & Stolzman, R. (1984). Six-month prevalence of psychiatric disorders in three communities. *Archives of General Psychiatry, 41,* 959–967.

Newman, C. F., Beck, J. S., & Beck, A. T. (1990). *Efficacy of cognitive therapy in reducing panic attacks and medication.* Presented at the annual meeting of the Association for Advancement of Behavior Therapy, San Francisco.

O'Brien, T. P., & Kelley, J. E. (1980). A comparison of self-directed and therapist-directed practice for fear reduction. *Behaviour Research and Therapy, 18,* 573–579.

Ost, L. G. (1987). Age of onset of different phobias. *Journal of Abnormal Psychology, 96,* 223–229.

———. (1989a). A maintenance program for behavioral treatment of anxiety disorders. *Behaviour Research and Therapy, 27,* 123–130.

———. (1989b). One-session treatment for specific phobias. *Behaviour Research and Therapy, 27,* 1–7.

Ost, L. G., Hellstrom, K., & Westling, B. E. (1989, November). *Applied relaxation, exposure in vivo, and cognitive methods in the treatment of agoraphobia.* Paper presented at the meeting of the Association for the Advancement of Behavior Therapy, Washington, D.C.

Ost, L. G., Jerremalm, A., & Jansson, L. (1984). Individual response patterns and the effects of different behavioral methods in the treatment of agoraphobia. *Behaviour Research and Therapy, 22,* 697–707.

Ost, L. G., Jerremalm, A., & Johansson, J. (1981). Individual response patterns and the effects of different be-

havioral methods in the treatment of social phobia. *Behaviour Research and Therapy, 19,* 1–16.

Ost, L. G., Salkovskis, P. M., & Hellstrom, K. (1991). One-session therapist directed exposure versus self-exposure in the treatment of spider phobia. *Behavior Therapy, 22,* 407–422.

Ost, L. G., & Sterner, U. (1987). Applied tension: A specific behavioral method for treatment of blood phobia. *Behaviour Research and Therapy, 25,* 25–29.

Ost, L. G., & Westling, B. E. (1995). Applied relaxation versus cognitive behavior therapy in the treatment of panic disorder. *Behaviour Research and Therapy, 33,* 145–158.

Ost, L. G., Westling, B. E., & Hellstrom, K. (1993). Applied relaxation, exposure in vivo and cognitive methods in the treatment of panic disorder with agoraphobia. *Behaviour Research and Therapy, 31,* 383–395.

Otto, M. W., Pollack, M. H., & Sabatino, S. A. (1995). *Maintenance of remission following CBT for panic disorder: Possible deleterious effects for concurrent medication treatment.* Paper presented at the World Congress of Behavioural and Cognitive Therapies, Copenhagen, Denmark.

Otto, M. W., Pollack, M. H., Sachs, G. S., Teiter, S. R., Meltzer-Brody, S., & Rosenbaum, J. F. (1993). Discontinuation of benzodiazepine treatment: Efficacy of cognitive-behavioral therapy for patients with panic disorder. *American Journal of Psychiatry, 150,* 1485–1490.

Pollack, M. H., Otto, M. W., Kaspi, S. P., Hammerness, P. G., & Rosenbaum, J. F. (1994). Cognitive behavior therapy for treatment-refractory panic disorder. *Journal of Clinical Psychiatry, 55,* 200–205.

Power, K. G., Jerrom, D. W. A., Simpson, R. J., Mitchell, M. J., & Swanson, V. (1989). A controlled comparison of cognitive-behaviour therapy, Diazepam, and placebo in the management of generalized anxiety. *Behavioural Psychotherapy, 17,* 1–14.

Power, K. G., Simpson, R. J., Swanson, V., Wallace, L. A., Feistner, A. T. C., & Sharp, D. (1990). A controlled comparison of cognitive-behaviour therapy, diazepam, and placebo, alone and in combination, for the treatment of generalised anxiety disorder. *Journal of Anxiety Disorders, 4,* 267–292.

Rachman, S. J., & Hodson, R. S. (1980). *Obsessions and compulsions.* Englewood Cliffs, N.J.: Prentice-Hall.

Rapee, R. M. (1991). Generalized anxiety disorder: A review of clinical features and theoretical concepts. *Clinical Psychology Review, 11,* 419–440.

Reich, J., Noyes, R., & Troughton, E. (1987). Dependent personality disorder associated with phobic avoidance in patients with panic disorder. *American Journal of Psychiatry, 144,* 323–326.

Salkovskis, P. M., & Clark, D. M. (1991). Cognitive therapy for panic disorder. *Journal of Cognitive Psychotherapy, 5*, 215–226.

Sanderson, W. S., DiNardo, P. A., Rapee, R. M., & Barlow, D. H. (1990). Syndrome comorbidity in patients diagnosed with a DSM-III-R anxiety disorder. *Journal of Abnormal Psychology, 99*, 308–312.

Schneier, F. R., Johnson, J., Hornig, C. D., Liebowitz, M R., & Weissman, M. M. (1992). Social phobia: Comorbidity and morbidity in an epidemiologic sample. *Archives of General Psychiatry, 48*, 282–288.

Shear, M. K., Pilkonis, P. A., Cloitre, M., & Leon, A. C. (1994). Cognitive behavioral treatment compared with nonprescriptive treatment of panic disorder. *Archives of General Psychiatry, 51*, 395–401.

Solyom, L., Shugar, R., Bryntwick, S., & Solyom, C. (1973). Treatment of fear of flying. *American Journal of Psychiatry, 130*, 423–427.

Spiegel, D. A., Bruce, T. J., Gregg, S. F., & Nuzzarello, A. (1994). Does cognitive behavior therapy assist slow-taper alprazolam discontinuation in panic disorder? *American Journal of Psychiatry, 151*, 876–881.

———. (1995). *Alprazolam discontinuation with and without cognitive behavior therapy in panic disorder: Clinical outcome and predictors of success.* Paper presented at the World Congress of Behavioral and Cognitive Therapies in Copenhagen, Denmark.

Swinson, R. P., Fergus, K. D., Cox, B. J., & Wickwire, K. (1995). Efficacy of telephone-administered behavioral therapy for panic disorder with agoraphobia. *Behaviour Research and Therapy, 33*, 465–469.

Telch, M. J., Agras, W. S., Taylor, C. B., Roth, W. T., & Gallen, C. (1985). Combined pharmacological and behavioral treatment for agoraphobia. *Behaviour Research and Therapy, 23*, 325–335.

Telch, M. J., Lucas, J. A., Schmidt, N. B., Hanna, H. H., Jaimez, T. S., & Lucas, R. A. (1993). Group cognitive-behavioral treatmetn of panic disorder. *Behaviour Research and Therapy, 31*, 279–287.

Thorpe, G. L., & Burns, L. E. (1983). *The agoraphobic syndrome.* New York: Wiley Press.

Trull, T. J., Nietzel, M. T., & Main, A. (1988). The use of meta-analysis to assess the clinical significance of behavior therapy for agoraphobia. *Behavior Therapy, 19*, 527–538.

Turner, S. M., Beidel, D. C., Cooley, M. R., Woody, S. R., & Messer, S. C. (1994a). A multicomponent behavioral treatment for social phobia: Social Effectiveness Therapy. *Behaviour Research and Therapy, 32*, 381–390.

Turner, S. M., Beidel, D. C., & Jacob, R. G. (1994b). Social phobia: A comparison of behavior therapy and atenolol. *Journal of Consulting and Clinical Psychology, 62*, 350–358.

White, J., & Keenan, M. (1992). Stress control: A controlled comparative investigation of large group therapy for generalized anxiety disorder. *Behavioral Psychotherapy, 20*, 97–114.

Williams, S. L., & Rappaport, A. (1983). Cognitive treatment in the natural environment for agoraphobics. *Behavior Therapy, 14*, 299–313.

16

Pharmacological Treatment of Panic, Generalized Anxiety, and Phobic Disorders

Peter P. Roy-Byrne

Deborah S. Cowley

Medication therapies for three types of anxiety disorder—panic disorder, generalized anxiety disorder, and phobic disorders—are reviewed. Of 12 placebo-controlled studies, 9 have conclusively shown that imipramine is effective for treating panic disorder. Other heterocycles are less well studied, although three placebo-controlled trials have shown efficacy for chlomipramine. The benzodiazepine alprazolam has been shown effective for panic disorder in 8 placebo-controlled studies. There are also controlled data indicating efficacy for other benzodiazepines, including clonazepam, lorazepam, and diazepam. Placebo-controlled trials have shown the efficacy of the selective serotonin reuptake inhibitors (SSRIs) paroxetine (3 studies), sertraline (2 studies), and fluvoxamine (4 studies) for panic disorder. There is also anecdotal evidence for the efficacy of the SSRI fluoxetine. Numerous double-blind, controlled trials have examined the efficacy of benzodiazepines for the treatment of generalized anxiety disorder. Benzodiazepines have been found superior to a placebo in most of the recent studies. All benzodiazepines appear equally effective. Buspirone, pharmacologically unrelated to benzodiazepines, has been shown in several double-blind studies to be comparable to benzodiazepines in the treatment of generalized anxiety disorder. Three controlled trials have also shown efficacy for tricyclic antidepressants (TCAs) in generalized anxiety disorder. The phobic disorders include specific and social phobias, but no pharmacological intervention has been shown to be effective for specific phobia. Three double-blind, randomized trials have supported the efficacy of the monoamine oxidase inhibitor phenelzine in the treatment of social phobia. One controlled trial found efficacy in social phobia for the benzodiazepine clonazepam, and two controlled trials suggest that SSRIs (fluvoxamine and sertraline) may be helpful for social phobia.

Panic attacks, "generalized" or free-floating anxiety, and context-dependent fears (phobias) are the modern syndromes previously known as "neurotic anxiety" and thought at that time (before *DSM-III*; American Psychiatric Association [APA], 1980) to be poorly responsive to pharmacotherapy. However, the last 15 years, beginning with the introduction of *DSM-III*, have seen a growing appreciation of the important role of pharmacotherapy in the treatment of these syndromes and an accumulating body of evidence documenting the efficacy of specific classes of medication for specific anxiety disorders. This chapter reviews the clinical characteristics and pharmacotherapy of the three major anxiety disorders: panic disorder (with or without agoraphobia), generalized anxiety disorder, and phobic disorders (principally social phobia).

PANIC DISORDER

Panic attacks are sudden, unexpected bursts of extreme anxiety accompanied by at least four physical or cognitive symptoms that include palpitations; chest discomfort; shortness of breath; dizziness; sweating; numbness or tingling; hot or cold flashes; abdominal discomfort; nausea or diarrhea; depersonalization or derealization; and fear of dying, going crazy, or losing control. Panic disorder is characterized by the presence of recurrent spontaneous (i.e., unexpected) panic attacks followed by a month of persistent anxiety about having attacks, concern about the implications of attacks (often marked by hypochondriacal preoccupations), or avoidance of situations that the individual feels will bring on attacks (agoraphobia). Although as many as one third to one half of the population will experience a panic attack in their lifetimes (Norton, Cox, & Malan, 1992), only about 1 in 10 of these people will develop the recurrent attacks and accompanying chronic anxiety, bodily/illness preoccupation, or phobia avoidance that characterize panic disorder.

Panic disorder is a chronic illness with a 1-month prevalence in the general population of 1.5% and a lifetime prevalence of about 3.5% (Eaton, Kessler, Wittchen, & Magee, 1994). Twice as many women as men are affected, with peak age of onset typically in the late teens and early twenties (Eaton et al., 1994). Although there is an increased rate of the disorder in family members and greater concordance in monozygotic versus dizygotic twins, the results of genetic linkage studies thus far have been negative. Pathophysiologic theories have focused on dysregulation of brainstem respiratory control centers and nearby noradrenergic and serotonergic nuclei that project to subcortical and limbic sites known to modulate emotion and its autonomic nervous system components (Papp, Coplan, & Gorman, 1992). However, stressful life events occur at an increased rate around the time of panic onset (Roy-Byrne, Geraci, & Uhde, 1986), and panic patients have an increased tendency to amplify body sensations and an anxious experience via catastrophic and other cognitive distortions (Beck, 1988). Hence, the disorder is likely to involve a heritable biological vulnerability and a series of stressful triggers modulated perhaps by a cognitive style that may have both innate and learned origins.

Despite demonstration of the antipanic efficacy of imipramine in the early 1960s, these findings were not integrated into clinical practice in the 1960s and 1970s. Hence, treatment in the community was generally ineffective (Doctor, 1982) as inadequate doses of benzodiazepines and various forms of nonbehavioral psychotherapy were used with disappointing results. This trend continued to a lesser degree in the 1980s, with one report documenting a surprisingly high utilization rate of nonspecific psychotherapy and low-dose benzodiazepines and surprisingly low rates (<15%) of behavioral and antidepressant treatment (Taylor et al., 1989).

The mainstays of pharmacological treatment of panic disorder have been, in order of historic and chronologic development, tricyclic antidepressants and monoamine oxidase (MAO) inhibitors in the 1960s and 1970s, high-potency benzodiazepines in the 1980s, and, more recently, in the 1990's, selective serotonin reuptake inhibitors (SSRIs). It should be noted that only alprazolam has Food and Drug Administration (FDA) approval for panic, and that there is, in general, poor concordance between established efficacy and approved indication for panic, as well as other anxiety, disorders. This review of antipanic treatments includes agoraphobia under the rubric of panic disorder since virtually all clinical medication trials have included patients with panic disorder complicated by phobic avoidance. In fact, because there is no evidence that agoraphobia exists in the absence of a history of panic attacks, DSM-IV (APA, 1994) precludes the diagnosis of agoraphobia in the absence of a history of panic attacks.

Tricyclic (Heterocyclic) Antidepressants

Extensive evidence supports the efficacy of tricyclic antidepressants (TCAs) in panic disorder. The initial demonstration of reduction in panic attacks, but more variable and sometimes less robust effects on anticipatory anxiety and phobic avoidance, with imipramine compared to a placebo (Klein, 1964, 1967) has been replicated many times over in the last three decades. Designs have varied in duration (6 weeks to 8 months), dosage of imipramine (i.e., whether minimally effective doses of 150 mg have been used), breadth of symptoms measured (panic, phobia, disability), sample size, proportion of sample with comorbid phobia and depression, and use of additional behavioral therapies. Of placebo-controlled trials, 9 of 12 have conclusively shown that imipramine is superior to a placebo for reduction of panic attacks (Cross National Collaborative Treatment Study, 1992; Mavissakalian and

Michelson, 1986; Mavissakalian and Perel, 1995; Schweizer, Rickels, Weiss, & Zavodnick, 1993; Sheehan, Ballenger, & Jacobsen, 1980; Taylor et al., 1990; Uhlenhuth, Matuzas, Glass, & Easton, 1989; Zitrin, Klein, & Woerner, 1978, 1983), and most that measured phobic avoidance showed similar efficacy. Three negative studies have been compromised by inadequate dosage (Evans, Kenardy, Schneider, & Hoey, 1986; Marks et al., 1983) and small sample size (Evans et al., 1986; Telch, Agras, Taylor, Roth, & Gallen, 1985). Studies using higher doses were more likely to show beneficial effects, and some studies also showed a clear dose response relationship, with doses of 150 mg or greater yielding beneficial effects. More recent data (Mavissakalian & Perel, 1995) have suggested that therapeutic plasma levels are lower for phobia than for panic, explaining the occasionally observed dissociation between effects on these two different measures and further documenting the need for approximately 1.5 to 2.0 mg/kg of imipramine for phobia and 2.0 to 2.5 mg/kg for panic.

Time course of effect can only be estimated from reported mean values, which are the average of numerous, somewhat variable, individual time course profiles. Nonetheless, most studies do not show drug placebo response differences until week 4, with maximal responses continuing for many measures to the trial's end (usually week 8). One of the earlier studies (Zitrin et al., 1983) actually showed significant continuing improvement in phobic avoidance between weeks 14 and 26, reinforcing Klein's original hypothesis that panic improves before phobia. Experts reviewing open trial data maintain that peak effects on panic, phobia, and anxiety measures may be delayed until 10–12 weeks in many patients (Lydiard & Ballenger, 1987) and controlled studies with SSRIs clearly show responses in some patients occur between weeks 9 and 12 (Oehrberg et al., 1995). In general, antipanic effects of TCAs may, in some patients, take as long, if not longer, than traditionally reported antidepressant effects.

Many studies show that TCAs are less well tolerated than, for example, benzodiazepines, with many patients dropping out of clinical trials both early (30% in the large Cross National Study; over 50% in some smaller studies) and late (i.e., during maintenance treatment). Although these trials do not provide clear indications of the reasons, open studies (Noyes, Garvey, Cook, & Samuelson, 1989) suggest that the most common reason for early discontinuation is overstimu-

lation/jitteriness, while for later discontinuation it is weight gain. Low initial doses, slower titration, and use of adjunctive benzodiazepines or beta blockers may attenuate early overstimulation. Elevated heart rate and blood pressure with imipramine (Taylor et al., 1990) may be a problem in older patients or those with cardiac conditions.

Few other heterocyclic agents have been studied. Desipramine was superior to a placebo for anxiety and phobia but not panic attack frequency reduction at a mean dose of 177± mg/day in the only study of this agent performed (Lydiard et al., 1993). Open trials have also supported the efficacy of desipramine (Kalus et al., 1991), as well as nortriptyline (Munjack et al., 1988), with estimated rates of response between 60% and 80% depending on design and sample composition. Nortriptyline's lower rate of postural hypotension and anticholinergic effects compared to imipramine may improve tolerability in some patients. Of other antidepressants in this class, lesser efficacy is suggested for trazodone (compared with imipramine and alprazolam) (Charney et al., 1986) and maprotiline (compared with fluvoxamine) (Den Boer and Westenberg, 1988). Unfortunately, these two studies were not placebo controlled.

Benzodiazepines

The availability of high-potency benzodiazepines with the introduction of alprazolam in the mid-1980s reversed a prior tendency to view this class of medications as ineffective for panic disorder. Eight placebo-controlled, double-blind trials (Ballenger et al, 1988; Chouinard, Annable, Fontaine, & Solyom, 1982; Cross National Collaborative Treatment Study, 1992; Lydiard et al., 1992; Munjack et al., 1989; Schweizer et al., 1993; Sheehan, Raj, Harnett-Sheehan, Soto, & Knapp, 1993; Uhlenhuth et al., 1989) have found alprazolam to be superior to placebo in the treatment of panic attacks, with 55% to 75% of patients free of attacks at the end point of the study. Completer analyses showed less striking and sometimes only nonsignificant differences because of the high placebo dropout rate. Alprazolam showed similar robust effects on phobic avoidance (six of seven studies), disability (five of five studies), anticipatory anxiety (three of three studies), and generalized anxiety (seven of eight studies). Although daily mean doses of 5–6 mg were used in these studies, two studies of lower, 2-mg fixed doses (Lydiard et al., 1992; Uhlenhuth et al., 1989) also showed superiority to a placebo, although panic-free rates were lower than those seen with higher doses (25–50% v. 55–75%).

The time course of effect with alprazolam is much more rapid than with tricyclic antidepressants. In general, superiority to a placebo was evident in the first week or two of treatment. While some experts suggest a superiority of these agents for phobia and anticipatory anxiety (Lydiard & Ballenger, 1987), panic attacks still appear to improve before phobia with this class of medication as well. While patients with significant primary major depression were excluded in most trials, patients meeting criteria for major depression judged secondary to panic disorder were included in some studies (mean Hamilton Depression Rating Scale [HAM-D] around 15) and in general fared as well as those without a major depression diagnosis (Ballenger et al., 1988).

The tolerability of alprazolam was in general superior to imipramine, with greater retention in studies looking at head-to-head comparisons (Cross National Collaborative Treatment Study, 1992; Schweizer et al., 1993; Uhlenhuth et al., 1989). The most common adverse effects of alprazolam were sedation or drowsiness, reported in 38% to 75%, and memory impairment, reported in up to 15% patients. The frequent lack of patient awareness of memory effects suggests caution prescribing these agents in older patients or those needing to perform complex cognitive tasks.

Placebo-controlled trials have also supported the efficacy of clonazepam (Tesar et al., 1991), and diazepam (Dunner, Ishiki, Avery, Wilson, & Hyde, 1986) for panic disorder and head-to-head comparisons with alprazolam in other non-placebo-controlled studies (Charney & Woods, 1989; Schweizer et al., 1988) have shown uniform equivalence with lorazepam. The common clinical practice of using adjunctive alprazolam with imipramine early in treatment has been studied using a placebo control only once (Woods et al., 1992). Although adjunctive alprazolam produced no advantage in decreasing imipramine dropouts (in fact, probably because of a rapid taper after 4 weeks of imipramine treatment, patients in this group actually did worse), this trial did not mirror the usual clinical practice of tapering alprazolam slowly over months.

The major public health concern regarding benzodiazepines has focused on their abuse potential, despite the fact (Nagy et al., 1989) that panic patients on long-term treatment do not escalate their doses over time (in fact, their doses go down) and that abuse of these drugs does not occur in patients without comorbid alcohol or substance abuse (Garvey & Tollefson, 1986). There is also no evidence of tolerance to the therapeutic effects of benzodiazepines in the several long-term studies that have been done. However, virtually all studies show that discontinuation of alprazolam and other benzodiazepines in panic disorder patients is associated with withdrawal symptoms, recurrent panic attacks, and failure to complete the taper in 25–50% of patients after as little as 6–8 weeks of treatment (Pecknold et al., 1988; Roy-Byrne, Dager, Cowley, Vitaliano, & Dunner, 1989). The use of a fairly rapid taper (several weeks) in all these studies fails to mirror the current clinical practice of a long, gradual taper, shown to reduce the incidence of withdrawal in one series to 7% (Pecknold, 1990). Direct comparisons with imipramine (Fyer, Liebowitz, & Gorman, 1989; Rickels et al., 1993b) indicate greater taper difficulty and symptom recrudescence over the short term (1 month). However, studies showing that relapse rates after imipramine discontinuation gradually increase over 6 months (Mavissakalian & Perel, 1992b) suggest that this difference in short-term (1-month) relapse rates may merely reflect the mirror image of the time course in initial response (i.e., alprazolam more rapid, 1–2 weeks, and imipramine more slowly, 1–3 months). This suggests that much "withdrawal" may in fact be symptom reemergence/relapse, although this relapse is perhaps fueled by bona fide withdrawal reactions.

Monoamine Oxidase Inhibitors

In six double-blind, placebo-controlled studies, MAO inhibitors (phenelzine, $n = 5$; iproniazid, $n = 1$) have been shown to be superior to a placebo for overall syndrome improvement (panic, anxiety, and phobia) (Lipsedge et al., 1973; Mountjoy, Roth, Garside, & Leitch, 1977; Sheehan et al., 1980; Solyom et al., 1973; Solyom, Solyom, La Pierre, Pecknold, & Morton, 1981; Tyrer, Candy, & Kelly, 1973). Unfortunately, in these older pre-DSM-III studies patients were not selected to meet diagnostic criteria for panic, there were no separate measures of panic frequency obtained, and measures of phobic avoidance or anxiety employed were different from those used in later panic studies. Of the studies, three of the six employed adjunctive exposure treatment or supportive psychotherapy and one employed adjunctive diazepam. All these studies employed relatively low doses (usually 45 mg phenelzine). Although higher doses are now recommended by most experts, there are few data to support this. The one study comparing phenelzine to imipramine suggested that phenelzine was superior for phobic avoidance (Sheehan et al., 1980), providing the only empirical evidence to support the impression of many clinicians that this class of medications may have special efficacy for treatment of resistant patients.

The time course of effect is more difficult to estimate precisely from these older studies. Delayed effects are suggested by superior effects at 8 weeks compared with 4 weeks. Of the two studies that lasted 12 weeks, one showed greater efficacy at 12 weeks versus 6 weeks (Sheehan et al., 1980). In general, the time course of effect is likely comparable to that seen for other antidepressants.

These medications are well tolerated in the short term due to the absence of early overstimulation effects. However, weight gain, insomnia with paradoxical daytime sedation, sexual dysfunction, and the need to follow a special low monoamine diet limit their acceptability for some patients. A recent placebo-controlled study has shown that the selective and reversible MAO inhibitor brofaromine, which does not require a diet, is effective for panic, with a 70% response rate (Van Vliet, Westenberg, & Den-Boer, 1993), confirming both open trials (Garcia Borreguero et al., 1992) and a blind comparative trial showing equivalence to clomipramine (Bakish, Saxena, Bowen, & D'Souza, 1993).

Serotonin Reuptake Inhibitors (Including Selective Serotonin Reuptake Inhibitors)

The efficacy of the TCA clomipramine in panic disorder has been supported in three double-blind, placebo-controlled studies (Fahy, O'Rourke, Brophy, Scharzmann, & Sciascia, 1992; Johnston, Troyer, & Whitsett, 1988; Modigh, Westberg, & Eriksson, 1992), with one study actually showing superiority to imipramine at 12 weeks (Modigh et al., 1992). Another open study suggested that a dose of 75 mg, lower than the 150–200 mg tricyclic doses usually required for antipanic efficacy, may be effective (Gloger et al., 1989). Two of the four currently available selective SRIs are either approved (paroxetine) or pending approval (sertraline) by the FDA for treatment of panic. Three double-blind, placebo-controlled studies support paroxetine's efficacy (Lecrubier et al., 1994;

Oehrberg et al., 1995; Steiner et al., 1995) and two double-blind, placebo-controlled trials support sertraline's efficacy (Gorman & Wolkow, 1994; DuBoff et al., 1995) in the acute treatment of panic disorder. At least four double-blind, placebo-controlled studies demonstrate fluvoxamine's efficacy (Black et al., 1993b; deBeurs, van Balkom, Lange, Koele, & van Dyck, 1995; Den Boer and Westenberg, 1990; Hoehn-Saric, McLeod, & Hipsley, 1993) but FDA approval for treatment of panic has not been pursued. Fluoxetine's efficacy is supported by open case series (Louie, Lewis, & Lannon, 1993; Schneier et al., 1990). These studies have shown effects on panic frequency, generalized anxiety, disability, and phobic avoidance, although no study measured all of these components.

A number of studies (deBeurs et al., 1995; Oehrberg et al., 1995) have shown that this class of medication is superior to a placebo when both are added to some form of cognitive-behavioral therapy (CBT); this contradicts other panic treatment studies, which have seemed to show drug-psychotherapy equivalence (Klosko, Barlow, Tassinari, & Cerny, 1990). Sample composition (i.e., severity of illness), study design (patients are sometimes rated after drugs are tapered), as well as integrity of cognitive-behavioral therapy techniques doubtless explain some of these differences. One interesting meta-analysis showed a greater effect size for serotonin antidepressants compared with both tricyclics and benzodiazepines (Boyer, 1995), with the effect reduced but still maintained when only studies using high-dose imipramine or alprazolam were compared. Single studies using direct comparisons have also shown superiority to noradrenergic heterocyclics (fluvoxamine v. maprotiline [Den Boer & Westenberg, 1990] and zimeledine v. imipramine [Evans et al., 1986]). These findings suggest, but do not conclusively demonstrate, that serotonergic antidepressants may have an advantage as antipanic agents.

Studies have shown that doses of 100–200 mg fluvoxamine, 40 mg paroxetine, 100–200 mg sertraline, and 5–20 mg fluoxetine have been effective. Early overstimulation has been especially noted with fluoxetine in open reports (Schneier et al., 1990), prompting recommendations for low (5 mg) starting doses. Such effects have not been noted with paroxetine or fluvoxamine. Furthermore, the side-effect burden with this class of medication has been much less severe, with much higher percentages of patients completing treatment (80–90%) than in studies of tricyclics (50–60%). However, abrupt withdrawal of SRIs has been associated with a withdrawal syndrome marked by irritability, nausea, dizziness, and headache in the case of both fluvoxamine (Black et al., 1993a) and paroxetine (Oehrberg et al., 1995), probably due to their relatively shorter half-life compared with fluoxetine and sertraline.

The time course of effect has been shown to be delayed as it is with tricyclics and MAO inhibitor antidepressants. Of the various studies, superiority to placebo has emerged, depending on the effect and study, as early as 3 weeks and as late as 8–10 weeks.

Other Agents

Although treatment-resistant panic disorder occurs, it is relatively uncommon when adequate doses of the above medication classes have been tried in conjunction with skilled cognitive-behavioral therapy. Few additional classes of medication are effective. Anticonvulsants have been reportedly effective in open trials using both valproate (Keck, Taylor, Tugrul, McElroy, & Bennett, 1993; Woodman & Noyes, 1994) and carbamazepine (Klein, Uhde, & Post, 1986), although the only existing placebo-controlled trial (with carbamazepine) (Uhde, Stein, & Post, 1988) failed to show drug efficacy greater than that of a placebo. One case series showed valproate combined with clonazepam effectively treated resistant panic in four patients (Ontiveros & Fontaine, 1992). Other reports indicate that patients with electroencephalogram (EEG) abnormalities might preferentially respond to anticonvulsants (McNamera & Fogel, 1990). One small placebo-controlled trial showed that the calcium channel blocker verapamil was an effective antipanic agent (Klein & Uhde, 1988), although curiously no other open reports have followed up on this preliminary finding. Another report documents the efficacy of inositol (Benjamin et al., 1995), a precursor of a key second messenger for signal transduction in certain G-protein-linked receptors. Clonidine has not been found to be effective (Uhde et al., 1989), nor has propranolol (Munjack et al., 1989), bupropion (Sheehan et al., 1983), or buspirone (Sheehan, Raj, Sheehan, & Soto, 1990). A recent study testing the addition of buspirone versus a placebo to cognitive therapy did show effects on generalized anxiety but not panic frequency or phobic avoidance (Cottraux et al., 1995) suggesting perhaps a role for buspirone as an adjunctive agent.

Combined augmentation treatment using multiple agents has never been studied. Anecdotal reports support combined benzodiazepine-antidepressant treatment (Ries & Wittkowsky, 1986), as well as SSRI and tricyclic combinations (Tiffon, Coplan, Papp, & Gorman, 1994). Consistent with this last combination of serotonin and norepinephrine reuptake blockers, one recent report describes the efficacy of the combined reuptake blocker venlafaxine in four cases of panic disorder (Geracioti, 1995) and a recently completed placebo-controlled study also supports venlafaxine efficacy for panic (Pollack et al., 1996).

Future agents that may emerge for treatment of panic include a variety of benzodiazepine partial agonists with a unique profile of activating select subreceptor families (Johnson & Lydiard, 1993). Such agents might effect symptoms without producing problems on withdrawal (i.e., discontinuation emergent symptoms). However, at this date no agents of this kind are close to FDA approval despite years of interest and work in this area.

Predictors of Response

Although the result of both controlled and open trials are inconsistent, the presence and severity of both depression (Maddock et al., 1993) and phobic avoidance (Slaap et al., 1995) sometime predict relatively poorer acute treatment response. This is consistent with naturalistic outcome studies (Roy-Byrne & Cowley, 1995), suggesting that these factors are associated with poorer long-term outcome.

Duration of Treatment/Chronic Treatment

All classes of agents described have been shown to retain their effectiveness over 8–12 months (Schweizer et al., 1993; Dager et al., 1992; Burnham et al., 1995). However, questions remain about the optimal duration of treatment following remission of panic attacks, as well as the need for continuing full doses of medication during the maintenance phase of treatment (prior to discontinuation). For tricyclics, one study suggests that after 6 months the dose can be cut in half without symptom exacerbation over the next year (Mavissakalian & Perel, 1992a). Nonexperimental studies with alprazolam and other benzodiazepines clearly show that patients, over time, reduce their doses by one third to one half without loss of clinical effect (Nagy et al., 1989). Suggestions that long-term benzodiazepine treatment, for anxious patients in general, is associated with cognitive deterioration have not been borne out by studies showing similar memory function in anxious patients off long-term benzodiazepines (Lucki et al., 1986).

Only one study (Mavissakalian & Perel, 1992b) has examined the effect of varying treatment durations on relapse, showing that imipramine discontinuation after 18 versus 6 months of treatment is associated with significantly reduced relapse rates in the next 6 months (25% v. 83%, respectively). Many naturalistic studies have shown relapse rates between 30% and 90% following medication discontinuation after 6–12 months of treatment (reviewed in Roy-Byrne & Cowley, 1995). Relapse in these studies appears strongly related to illness characteristics, specifically Axis I (depression and phobic avoidance) and Axis II comorbidity.

GENERALIZED ANXIETY DISORDER

Generalized anxiety disorder (GAD) is characterized by excessive worry about a number of different areas. The worry is difficult to control, occurs most of the time for at least 6 months, and is accompanied by significant distress or functional impairment, as well as by at least three of the following six symptoms: restlessness or feeling on edge, ease of fatigue, concentration difficulties, irritability, muscle tension, or sleep disturbance. Since its original definition in 1980, GAD has been a problematic diagnosis with poor interrater reliability (DiNardo, Moras, Barlow, Rapee, & Brown, 1993) and high rates of psychiatric comorbidity (Brawman-Mintzer et al., 1993; Breslau & Davis, 1985). There has been an ongoing debate as to whether GAD exists as a valid, distinct disorder or is instead a prodromal, residual, or subthreshold form of other Axis I disorders or a characterological condition predisposing patients to a variety of Axis I diagnoses (e.g., Breslau & Davis, 1985; Brown, Barlow, & Liebowitz, 1994). However, it is evident that there exists a group of patients with primary or isolated, severe, generalized anxiety associated with significant functional impairment.

Generalized anxiety disorder usually begins in the teens or early adulthood and is twice as common in women as in men. Data from the National Comorbidity Survey suggest that GAD has a current prevalence (in the past month) of 1.6% and a lifetime prevalence of 5.1% in the general population of the United States between the ages of 15 and 45 (Wittchen, Zhao, Kessler, & Eaton, 1994). Up to 90% of patients with GAD have a lifetime history and 60% a current history of at least one other Axis I disorder, with the most common being social phobia, specific phobias, depression, dysthymia, panic disorder, and substance abuse or dependence (Brawman-Mintzer et al., 1993). As defined in *DSM-III-R* (APA, 1987), GAD appears distinct from panic disorder in its familial transmission (Noyes et al., 1992) and shows heritability of about 30% in a study of female twins (Kendler, Neale, Kessler, Heath, & Eaves, 1992b).

The pathophysiology of GAD is unclear, although findings of increased muscle tension as assessed by direct measurement of muscle fiber activity using electromyogram (EMG) and of decreased "autonomic flexibility," with diminished autonomic responsivity and delayed recovery after a variety of laboratory stressors, are intriguing (Cowley & Roy-Byrne, 1991). The efficacy of benzodiazepines in treating anxiety and animal studies implicating the gamma-aminobutyric acid–benzodiazepine receptor in anxiety states suggest that this receptor system may be involved in the pathophysiology of human anxiety (Ninan, Insel, Cohen, Skolnick, & Paul, 1982). Indeed, human studies indicate that patients with GAD (Cowley et al., 1991b) or high in "neuroticism" (Glue et al., 1995), a personality trait strongly associated with pathological anxiety, may be less sensitive to the effects of benzodiazepine challenge testing.

Historically, generalized anxiety has been treated with barbiturates, methaqualone, or, since the 1960s and 1970s, benzodiazepines. Within the past decade, alternative medication treatments, including buspirone and antidepressants, have been used for GAD. It should also be noted that cognitive-behavioral therapy approaches specific for GAD have now been developed and appear quite effective.

Benzodiazepines

Numerous double-blind controlled trials have examined the efficacy of benzodiazepines in the treatment of generalized anxiety. For example, in 1978 Solomon and Hart reviewed 78 double-blind studies, concluding that benzodiazepines had not been shown to be superior to a placebo in the treatment of "neurotic anxiety."

Barlow (1988) reviewed eight double-blind, 2–6 week trials performed between 1978 and 1983 and, using the Hamilton anxiety rating scale as the outcome measure, found 22–62% reductions in score in benzodiazepine-treated patients with generalized anxiety versus 18–48% decreases in placebo groups. He concluded that the effects of benzodiazepines were marginal. However, dropout rates were substantially higher in placebo groups in five of six studies supplying this information, perhaps reflecting lack of efficacy.

Two studies performed in the early 1980s suggested that patients with *DSM-III* GAD seen in primary care settings responded equally well to diazepam and a placebo after the first week or two of treatment (Catalan et al., 1984; Shapiro et al., 1983). However, diazepam was superior to a placebo for those with the most severe anxiety (Shapiro et al., 1983).

All of these studies are difficult to interpret because treatment populations were very heterogeneous and, even since 1980, the definition of GAD has changed. As defined in *DSM-III*, for example, GAD included very mild and short-lived bouts of anxiety lasting only 1 month. More recently, with GAD requiring both persistent, hard to control worrying and a 6-month duration, benzodiazepines have been found superior to a placebo in acute (4–6-week) double-blind treatment of GAD in most (e.g., Borison, Albrecht, & Diamond, 1990; Boyer & Feighner, 1993; Cutler et al., 1993; Enkelmann, 1991; Rickels et al., 1988; Rickels et al., 1993a) but not all (e.g., Pecknold et al., 1989; Ross & Matas, 1987) studies. All benzodiazepines appear equally effective (Shader & Greenblatt, 1993). About two thirds of patients experience moderate-to-marked improvement of anxiety symptoms (usually assessed using Hamilton anxiety and Clinical Global Impression [CGI] ratings) with these medications, with therapeutic effects evident within the first 1 to 2 weeks. Doses are lower by approximately half than those used in treating panic disorder (usually the equivalent of 10–25 mg/day of diazepam). Benzodiazepines appear particularly effective for somatic anxiety symptoms (Rickels et al., 1982), while patients with minor depressive symptoms respond more poorly to most of these agents (Rickels et al., 1993a) with the possible exception of alprazolam.

Side effects of benzodiazepines in GAD are similar to those in panic disorder and include sedation, psychomotor impairment, anterograde amnesia (Lucki, Rickels, & Geller, 1986), and tolerance and withdrawal symptoms. However, a recent study suggests that GAD patients may be less vulnerable than panic patients to withdrawal symptoms (Klein, Stolk, & Lenox, 1994). Of note, as with panic, dose escalation is rare in GAD patients without a history of substance abuse. For example, no dosage increases were observed in 119 anxious patients taking benzodiazepines for an average of 8 years (Rickels et al., 1986).

Azapirones

Buspirone, an azapirone anxiolytic and 5HT-1A receptor partial agonist, has been shown in several double-blind studies to be comparable to benzodiazepines, including diazepam, lorazepam, clorazepate, oxazepam, and alprazolam, for the acute treatment of GAD (Ansseau, Papart, G'erard, von Frenckell, & Franck, 1990–1991; Cohn, Bowden, Fisher, & Rodos, 1986; Enkelmann, 1991; Feighner, Meredity, & Hendrickson, 1982; Petracca et al., 1990; Rickels et al., 1982, 1988; Strand et al., 1990), yielding 30–50% reductions in Hamilton anxiety scale scores in 2–6-week trials. Another azapirone, ipsapirone, has also proven effective in placebo-controlled, double-blind trials (Borison et al., 1990; Boyer & Feighner, 1993; Cutler et al., 1993), but is not yet available in the United States.

In comparison with benzodiazepines, buspirone has a delayed (2–4 week) onset of action, may affect cognitive anxiety symptoms to a greater extent than physical symptoms (Feighner & Cohn, 1989; Rickels et al., 1982), and has the advantage of being nonsedating and without evidence of tolerance or withdrawal symptoms. Common side effects of buspirone include nausea, dizziness, and headaches. Average therapeutic doses are 20–45 mg/day, although doses of up to 60 mg/day may be necessary. Buspirone displays antidepressant effects in patients with comorbid depression, usually at higher doses of 45–60 mg/day (Gammans et al., 1992).

In general, patients on chronic benzodiazepine treatment do not respond well when switched to buspirone (Lader & Olajide, 1987). A recent double-blind study (Delle Chiaie et al., 1995) of 44 GAD patients switched to buspirone versus a placebo after 5 weeks of lorazepam treatment, with lorazepam tapered during the first 2 weeks of buspirone versus placebo treatment, showed that buspirone was superior to a placebo and comparable to lorazepam in anxiolytic effects. There was no evidence of benzodiazepine withdrawal symptoms. Whether these promising results with a gradual taper of the benzodiazepine after initiation of buspirone are generalizable to patients maintained on long-term benzodiazepine treatment remains to be seen.

Antidepressants

Three double-blind trials have shown that sedating antidepressants are effective in treating GAD (Hoehn-Saric, McLeod, & Zimmerli, 1988; Kahn et al., 1986; Rickels et al., 1993a). In addition, one case series supports the use of clomipramine for this disorder (Wingerson, Nguyen, & Roy-Byrne, 1992). Kahn et al. (1986) reported that imipramine performed better than chlordiazepoxide in the treatment of nondepressed outpatients retrospectively diagnosed as having GAD. In a study by Hoehn-Saric et al. (1988) of nondepressed patients with GAD, imipramine was comparable to alprazolam after the first 2 weeks of treatment. Imipramine was more effective in reducing psychic anxiety symptoms such as obsessionality, dysphoria, negative anticipatory thinking, and interpersonal sensitivity, while alprazolam was superior in alleviating cardiovascular and autonomic symptoms.

Rickels et al. (1993a) compared imipramine (mean dose 143 mg/day), trazodone (mean dose 255 mg/day), diazepam (mean dose 26 mg/day), and a placebo in 230 patients with GAD treated for 8 weeks. Although all active treatments were superior to the placebo, diazepam yielded the most improvement in anxiety ratings for the first 2 weeks, and imipramine was the most effective treatment thereafter, with 73% of patients moderately or markedly improved compared with 69% on trazodone, 66% on diazepam, and 47% on the placebo. Once more, antidepressants reduced cognitive anxiety symptoms to a greater extent than did diazepam. Patients on antidepressants also reported more side effects.

These studies suggest that antidepressants are promising treatments for GAD. The optimal dosage of these agents and the efficacy of nonsedating antidepressants have not been established.

Other Medications

Studies performed prior to 1980 showed no efficacy of beta blockers for the treatment of generalized anxiety (Hayes & Schulz, 1987). The one double-blind, placebo-controlled trial conducted more recently is more promising (Meibach, Mullane, & Binstok, 1987). This 3-week, multicenter study of propranolol (average maximum dose 189 mg/day) versus chlordiazepoxide (average dose 50 mg/day) versus a placebo in 417 outpatients with "anxiety sufficiently severe to warrant treatment with an anxiolytic agent" showed the superiority of both active drugs but fewer side effects with propranolol than with chlordiazepoxide. Surprisingly, propranolol was particularly effective in reducing psychic symptoms of anxiety. Nevertheless, most experts continue to feel that beta blockers are not an effective primary treatment for GAD but instead should be reserved for use as an adjunct, particularly in patients with prominent autonomic symptoms.

A multicenter, double-blind, 4-week trial of hydroxyzine 50 mg/day versus a placebo in 133 GAD patients displayed significantly greater reductions in anxiety in the hydroxyzine group, although side effects were more common than in the placebo group (Ferreri, Hantouche, & Billardon, 1994). Newer treatments under investigation include the cholecystokinin receptor antagonists and benzodiazepine receptor partial agonists with anxiolytic properties but without the risks of sedation and withdrawal symptoms accompanying currently available benzodiazepines.

Long-Term Treatment and Outcome

Although there is extensive literature regarding acute treatment of generalized anxiety, there is less information available regarding long-term efficacy or optimal duration of treatment.

Few studies have examined results of benzodiazepine treatment beyond the first 6 weeks. Cutler et al. (1993) found lorazepam more effective than a placebo after 6 weeks, but not after 8 weeks, of treatment, primarily due to continued improvement in the placebo group. Both alprazolam and lorazepam remained superior to a placebo after 16 weeks in another study (Cohn & Wilcox, 1984). In a study of 101 GAD patients treated with cognitive-behavioral treatment, a placebo, or diazepam for 10 weeks, the greatest improvement was seen in patients receiving a combination of CBT and diazepam, and diazepam alone was more effective than a placebo alone (Power, Simpson, Swanson, & Wallace, 1990). Rickels et al. (1988) showed the continued efficacy of clorazepate over a 6-month trial, with no tolerance to anxiolytic effects, but there was no placebo comparison.

Thus, benzodiazepines seem to have continued anxiolytic effects for up to 6 months, but the paucity of studies leaves the question of whether benzodiazepines are superior to a placebo after the initial phase of treatment without a clear answer. Buspirone has been shown to yield continued efficacy over a treatment period of 3–6 months (Feighner, 1987; Rickels et al., 1988).

Two studies have addressed the issue of optimal duration of treatment. Rickels et al. (1983) found that 50% of patients treated with diazepam for 6 weeks had relapsed 3 months later, and 63% had relapsed after 1 year. In another trial performed by the same group (Rickels, Schweizer, & Canalosi, 1988), 45 patients with GAD who responded to 6 months of treatment with clorazepate or buspirone were then followed up 6 and 40 months after the end of the study. At 6 months, 55% of clorazepate-treated patients and 38% of those treated with buspirone reported moderate-to-marked anxiety. At 40 months, 34 patients were contacted and 57% of clorazepate-treated versus 25% of buspirone-treated subjects reported moderate-to-severe anxiety. This suggests that for many people GAD is a chronic illness requiring treatment for longer than 6 months. The apparently better outcome with initial buspirone treatment is interesting but may be attributable to the higher dropout rate in the buspirone group during the initial treatment period, with only the most treatment-responsive patients remaining in the study.

PHOBIC DISORDERS

The phobic disorders include specific (formerly "simple") phobias and social phobia. Specific or simple phobias are fears and avoidance of discrete objects or situations such as spiders, heights, and so on. The treatment of choice for specific phobias is behavior therapy, specifically, systematic desensitization. Pharmacological treatments have not proven effective for specific phobias. For this reason, the phobic disorder on which we focus in this chapter is social phobia.

Social phobia is defined as a fear of social or performance situations in which the person fears scrutiny by others and acting in a humiliating or embarrassing way. Feared social situations are avoided or endured with distress, and social anxiety causes significant functional impairment. Social phobia has been subdivided into a "specific" form limited to one or a few situations (most commonly, public speaking) and a "generalized" form involving fear and avoidance of multiple social situations. Some authors have argued that generalized social phobia is indistinguishable from avoidant personality disorder (see Widiger, 1992).

Social phobia is common. In the Epidemiological Catchment Area (ECA) study, the 1-month prevalence was 1.3%, and the lifetime prevalence was 2.8% (Regier et al., 1990). More recently, the National Comorbidity Survey of over 8000 people in the United States found a 12-month prevalence of 7.9% and a lifetime prevalence of 13.3% (Kessler et al., 1994). Social phobia has an early age of onset, with a peak in childhood and the teenage years (Schneier et al., 1992b), and is more common in women than in men (Bourdon et al., 1988). It is associated with significant disability, with 22% of those with uncomplicated social phobia in the ECA study receiving public assistance and more than 50% of social phobics reporting at least moderate functional impairment due to social anxiety (Schneier et al., 1994). In up to 70% of cases, social phobia is accompanied by, and commonly precedes, other significant comorbid psychiatric disorders, such as depression, other anxiety disorders, and alcohol abuse and dependence (Schneier et al., 1992b).

A number of studies have failed to show distinctive baseline biological abnormalities in social phobia with anxiogenic challenges or in response to public speaking. However, behavioral inhibition, with autonomic arousal in response to novelty starting in infancy and shyness and introversion as a toddler, is strongly associated with later social phobia, suggesting an underlying inborn vulnerability in many individuals (Rosenbaum et al., 1991). In addition, family and twin studies suggest that social phobia is familial and has a heritable component of about 30% (Fyer et al., 1988; Kendler et al., 1992a).

Social phobia has been until recently a relatively neglected disorder. Although behavioral and cognitive-behavioral techniques have been proven effective, few studies have examined psychopharmacological treatment of this condition. Liebowitz et al. (1986, 1992) published the first open and then controlled trials of medication treatment for patients with social phobia. These trials used the beta blocker atenolol, based on prior reports of the utility of beta blockers in treating performance anxiety, and the MAO inhibitor phenelzine, based on the efficacy of this medication in treating mixed agoraphobia and social phobia and its success in treating atypical depression, which shares with social phobia the prominent symptom of interpersonal sensitivity. Since these early trials, there have been several studies using both reversible and irreversible MAO inhibitors, benzodiazepines, serotonin reuptake inhibitors, and beta blockers to treat social phobia.

Monoamine Oxidase Inhibitors

In 1986, Liebowitz et al. reported that 7 of 11 patients with *DSM-III* social phobia showed a "marked" response to phenelzine, while the other 4 had "moderate" improvement. Since then, three double-blind, randomized trials have supported the efficacy of phenelzine for social phobia. Liebowitz et al. (1992) treated 74 patients with social phobia with phenelzine ($n = 25$; mean dose, 75.7 mg/day), atenolol ($n = 23$; mean dose, 97.6 mg/day), and a placebo ($n = 26$). By week 8, "response" rates (much or very much improved as assessed by an independent rater) were 64% for phenelzine, 30% for atenolol, and 23% for the placebo. The superiority of phenelzine persisted at week 16, with a 52% response rate versus 19% for the placebo. Patients with generalized social phobia responded better to phenelzine than to the other treatments. However, the number of patients with specific social phobias was too small to analyze the differential efficacy of atenolol versus phenelzine.

Gelernter et al. (1991), in a study of 65 social phobics given phenelzine, alprazolam, a placebo, or group cognitive-behavioral therapy, found that all groups improved, perhaps because all patients were encouraged to expose themselves to feared situations. Nevertheless, patients taking phenelzine were more likely than those in the other groups to display functional improvement and to fall below the mean score for the general population on the social phobia subscale of the Fear Questionnaire at the end of 12 weeks. Finally, Versiani et al. (1992) completed a double-blind trial of phenelzine ($n = 26$; mean dose, 67.5 mg/day), the reversible MAO inhibitor moclobemide ($n = 26$; mean dose, 580.7 mg/day), and a placebo ($n = 26$). After 8 weeks, phenelzine and moclobemide were both significantly more effective than the placebo, and these gains were maintained for a further 8 weeks. Responders were then maintained on active medication or changed to a placebo. Those switched to the placebo demonstrated significant increases in symptomatology that persisted for at least 5 weeks, suggesting a high rate of relapse.

Thus, double-blind trials to date support the efficacy of phenelzine in the treatment of social phobia. Although it has been suggested that generalized social phobia may be more responsive to MAO inhibitors than is specific social phobia, this has not yet been demonstrated. Furthermore, the fact that 74% of subjects in Gelernter et al.'s (1991) study had specific social phobia would indicate that phenelzine is effective in this group. Interestingly, isolated case reports suggest that phenelzine may also be effective in the treatment of conditions related to social phobia, such as elective mutism (Golwyn & Weinstock, 1990) and social phobia secondary to physical disfigurement (Oberlander, Schneier, & Liebowitz, 1994). Other irreversible MAO inhibitors have not been studied in double-blind trials. However, an open trial of tranylcypromine (Versiani, Mundim, & Nardi, 1988) yielded 20 "marked responders" from 29 subjects.

Irreversible MAO inhibitors such as phenelzine have significant side effects, most notably hypertensive crisis, insomnia, weight gain, and sexual dysfunction. Reversible MAO inhibitors such as moclobemide and brofaramine bind reversibly, are selective for the A isoenzyme of monoamine oxidase, and have fewer side effects, including a much lower rate of hypertensive crisis. The efficacy of reversible MAO inhibitors in social phobia has been demonstrated in two double-blind, placebo-controlled trials of brofaramine (Fahlen, Nilsson, Borg, Humber, & Pauli, 1995; van Vliet et al., 1993) and the trial of moclobemide, phenelzine, and a placebo (Versiani et al., 1992) noted above. In this last study, by 16 weeks side effects were significantly more common in patients taking phenelzine (in 95%) than in those taking moclobemide (12%) or the placebo (29%). Unfortunately, despite the promise of reversible MAO inhibitors for social phobia, the development of these medications has been discontinued in the United States.

Beta Blockers

Despite an early, promising open study of atenolol for social phobia (Gorman et al., 1985) and several studies demonstrating the efficacy of single doses of beta blockers for treating performance anxiety in nonclinical groups such as musicians and public speakers (see Jefferson, 1995, for a review), beta blockers have not been proven effective in double-blind trials with patients with social phobia. In the study by Liebowitz et al. (1992) mentioned above, atenolol was not significantly more effective than a placebo.

Behavior therapy, primarily flooding, was superior to both a placebo and atenolol in one study (Turner,

Beidel, & Jacob, 1994), while propranolol showed no advantage over a placebo in another trial in which subjects also received social skills training (Falloon, Lloyd, & Harpin, 1981).

The suggestion that beta blockers may be particularly useful for patients with discrete or specific social phobia (Liebowitz et al., 1992) has not been tested rigorously. Thus, at present beta blockers may be useful for treating performance anxiety or discrete social phobia accompanied by prominent palpitations, tachycardia, or sweating. However, there as yet is no evidence to support their use as a primary treatment for social phobia.

Benzodiazepines

In open trials, both alprazolam, at doses of 3–8 mg/day, and clonazepam, 1–6 mg/day, have been effective in the treatment of social phobia (see Davidson, Tupper, & Potts, 1994, for a review). The only double-blind, placebo-controlled trial of alprazolam was that of Gelernter et al. (1991). Although alprazolam (mean dose, 4.2 mg/day) was not superior to a placebo, this study was complicated by the inclusion of self-directed exposure in all treatment groups. Clonazepam, at an average dose of 2.4 mg/day, decreased social anxiety, interpersonal sensitivity, phobic avoidance, and disability in a 10-week, double-blind study of 75 patients with social phobia (Davidson et al., 1993). Response rates were 78.3% for clonazepam and 20% for a placebo.

Use of benzodiazepines for social phobia is complicated both by their side effects (see above) and by the high rate of comorbid alcohol abuse or dependence (Schneier et al., 1992b), which may put patients at an increased risk for benzodiazepine abuse and dependence.

Serotonin Reuptake Inhibitors

Case reports and open trials suggest that serotonin reuptake inhibitors, including fluoxetine (Ameringen, Mancini, & Streiner, 1993; Black, White, & Taylor, 1992; Schneier et al, 1992a; Sternbach, 1990), paroxetine (Ringold, 1994), sertraline (Ameringen, Mancini, & Streiner, 1994), citalopram (Lepola, Koponen, & Leinonen, 1994), and fluvoxamine (Hoehn-Saric et al., 1993), are useful in the treatment of social phobia. There are two published double-blind, placebo-controlled trials of serotonin reuptake inhibitors

for social phobia. Van Vliet, den Boer, and Westernberg (1994) demonstrated that fluvoxamine, 150 mg/day, was superior to a placebo in reducing social and generalized anxiety after 12 weeks. Differences in phobic avoidance did not reach statistical significance, and substantial improvement was seen in 46% of patients on fluvoxamine versus 7% of those on the placebo. Similarly, in a double-blind, crossover study of sertraline, 50–200 mg/day (mean dose 133.5 mg/day), versus a placebo in 12 patients with social phobia, sertraline yielded significantly greater reductions in social anxiety and increases in social functioning than did the placebo (Katzelnick et al., 1995).

These studies are promising, although direct comparisons with MAO inhibitors are necessary to assess further the efficacy of serotonin reuptake inhibitors. In clinical practice, the much lower rate of side effects and lack of dietary restrictions with these agents make them preferable to MAO inhibitors as a first-line treatment despite the relative paucity of rigorous, controlled trials.

Other Medications

Surprisingly, there have been no controlled trials of tricyclic antidepressants for patients with social phobia. Although isolated case reports suggest that they may be effective (Benca, Matuzas, & Al-Sadir, 1986), other anecdotal evidence has been cited suggesting that tricyclics are inferior to MAO inhibitors (e.g., Liebowitz et al., 1986; Versiani et al., 1988). Open trials of buspirone appear promising, particularly when doses exceed 45 mg/day (Munjack, Brun, & Baltazar, 1991; Schneier et al., 1993). However, the only double-blind trial using buspirone showed no significant improvement with doses averaging 32 mg/day in musicians seeking treatment for performance anxiety (Clark & Agras, 1991). Successful treatment of social phobia with bupropion (Emmanuel, Lydiard, & Ballenger, 1991) and clonidine (Goldstein, 1987) has also been reported.

Long-Term Treatment

There is scant information available regarding long-term pharmacological treatment of social phobia. However, this is frequently a chronic illness (Reich, Goldenberg, Vasile, Goisman, & Keller, 1994) requiring long-term treatment. In 26 patients with social phobia treated with clonazepam for an average of

11.3 months (range 1–29 months) by Davidson et al. (1991a), clonazepam was well tolerated, 20 patients were able to reduce their dose, and 5 discontinued their medication. A recent trial comparing a placebo and brofaromine (Fahlen et al., 1995) followed responders for 9 months. Those on brofaromine (*n* = 22) showed further symptomatic improvement over this period. On the placebo, 6 of 10 relapsed, versus none of 22 maintained on brofaromine.

SUMMARY

Over the past 15 years, a number of pharmacological treatments have been shown effective for panic disorder, GAD, and social phobia. Despite the relative paucity of controlled trials of SRIs for panic disorder, these medications are now considered by most experts to be the first-line pharmacological treatment for this condition based on their low rate of side effects, lack of dietary restrictions, and absence of tolerance and withdrawal symptoms. Similarly, SRIs are an attractive first-line treatment for social phobia. The pharmacological treatment of choice for GAD is currently buspirone, with sedating antidepressants providing a promising alternative to benzodiazepines. Benzodiazepines, although effective for all of these disorders, carry with them the risk of physiological dependence and withdrawal symptoms and ineffectiveness for comorbid depression. Their greatest utility at present seems to be as an initial or adjunct medication for patients with disabling symptoms requiring rapid relief and for those unable to tolerate other medications. Chronic treatment with benzodiazepines is safe and effective but should probably be reserved for patients who are nonresponsive or intolerant to other agents.

The major challenges in acute treatment of all three of these disorders are to determine the most effective and also cost-effective initial combination of pharmacological and nonpharmacological treatments and to develop new anxiolytic agents with a rapid onset of action but without the risks of tolerance and withdrawal. For existing agents, particular subtypes of these disorders or types of comorbidity may respond better to some agents than to others, and studies of combination treatments may enhance efficacy, especially in patients unresponsive to or only minimally improved with single agents.

At this point, little is known regarding optimal duration of treatment or long-term outcome of these disorders. However, it appears that all three conditions begin early in life, often in childhood or adolescence, and may be chronic in many people. Thus, further study of treatment of anxiety disorders in children and of long-term management of panic disorder, GAD, and social phobia is very important.

References

American Psychiatric Association. (1980). *Diagnostic and statistical manual of mental disorders* (3rd ed.). Washington, D.C.: Author.

———. (1987). *Diagnostic and statistical manual of mental disorders* (3rd ed., revised). Washington, D.C.: Author.

———. (1994). *Diagnostic and statistical manual of mental disorders* (4th ed.). Washington, D.C.: Author.

Ameringen, M. V., Mancini, C., & Streiner, D. L. (1993). Fluoxetine efficacy in social phobia. *Journal of Clinical Psychiatry, 54*, 27–32.

Ameringen, M. V., Mancini, C., & Streiner, D. (1994). Sertraline in social phobia. *Journal of Affective Disorders, 31*, 141–145.

Ansseau, M., Papart, P., G'erard, M. A., von Frenckell, R., & Franck, G. (1990–1991). Controlled comparison of buspirone and oxazepam in generalized anxiety. *Neuropsychobiology, 24*, 74–78.

Bakish, D., Saxena, B. M., Bowen, R., & D'Souza, J. (1993). Reversible monoamine oxidase-A inhibitors in panic disorder. *Clinical Neuropharmacology, 16*(Suppl. 2), S77–S82.

Ballenger, J. C., Burrows, G. D., DuPont, R. L., et al. (1988). Alprazolam in panic disorder and agoraphobia: Results from a multicenter trial. *Archives of General Psychiatry, 45*, 413–422.

Barlow, D. H. (1988). *Anxiety and its disorders.* New York: Guilford Press.

Beck, A. T. (1988). Cognitive approaches to panic disorder: Theory and therapy. In S. Rachman & J. D. Maser (Eds.), *Panic: Psychological perspectives* (pp. 91–109). Hillsdale, N.J.: Lawrence Erlbaum Associates.

Benca, R., Matuzas, W., & Al-Sadir, J. (1986). Social phobia, MVP, and response to imipramine. *Journal of Clinical Psychopharmacology, 6*, 50–51.

Benjamin, J., Levine, J., Fux, M., Aviv, A, Levy, D., & Belmaker, R. H. (1995, July). Double-blind, placebo-controlled crossover trial of inositol treatment for panic disorder. *American Journal of Psychiatry, 152*(7), 1084–1086.

Black, B., Uhde, T. W., & Taylor, M. E. (1992). Fluoxetine for the treatment of social phobia. *Journal of Clinical Psychopharmacology, 12*, 293–295.

Black, D. W., Wesner, R., & Gabel, J. (1993a). The abrupt discontinuation of fluvoxamine in patients with panic disorder. *Journal of Clinical Psychology, 54*(4), 146–149.

Black, D. W., Wessner, R., Bowers, W., & Gabel, J. (1993b). A comparison of fluvoxamine, cognitive therapy and placebo in the treatment of panic disorder. *Archives of General Psychiatry, 50*, 44–50.

Borison, R. L., Albrecht, J. W., & Diamond, B. I. (1990). Efficacy and safety of a putative anxiolytic agent: ipsapirone. *Psychopharmacology Bulletin, 26*, 207–210.

Bourdon, K. H., Boyd, J. H., Rae, D. S., Burns, B. J., Thompson, J. W., & Locke, B. Z. (1988). Gender differences in phobias: Results of the ECA community survey. *Journal of Anxiety Disorders, 2*, 227–241.

Boyer, W. (1995). Serotonin uptake inhibitors are superior to imipramine and alprazolam in alleviating panic attacks: A meta-analysis. *International Clinical Psychopharmacology, 10*, 45–49.

Boyer, W. F., & Feighner, J. P. (1993). A placebo-controlled double-blind multicenter trial of two doses of ipsapirone versus diazepam in generalized anxiety disorder. *International Clinical Psychopharmacology, 8*, 173–176.

Brawman-Mintzer, O., Lydiard, R. B., Emmanuel, N., Payeur, R., Johnson, M., Roberts, J., Jarrell, M. P., & Ballenger, J. C. (1993). Psychiatric comorbidity in patients with generalized anxiety disorder. *American Journal of Psychiatry, 150*, 1216–1218.

Breslau, N., & Davis, G. C. (1985). *DSM-III* generalized anxiety disorder: an empirical investigation of more stringent criteria. *Psychiatry Research, 15*, 231–238.

Brown, T. A., Barlow, D. H., & Liebowitz, M. R. (1994). The empirical basis of generalized anxiety disorder. *American Journal of Psychiatry, 151*, 1272–1280.

Burnham, D. B., Steiner, M. X., Gergel, I. P., et al. (1995). Paroxetine long-term and efficacy in panic disorder and prevention of relapse: A double-blind study. Paper presented at the 33rd annual meeting of the American College of Neuropsychopharmacology, San Juan, Puerto Rico.

Catalan, J., Gath, D., Edmonds, G., et al. (1984). The effects of non-prescribing of anxiolytics in general practice, I: Controlled evaluation of psychiatric and social outcome. *British Journal of Psychiatry, 144*, 593–602.

Charney, D. S., & Woods, S. W. L. (1989). Benzodiazepine treatment of panic disorder: a comparison of alprazolam and lorazepam. *Journal of Clinical Psychiatry, 50*, 418–423.

Charney, D. S., Woods, S. W., Goodman, W. K. et al. (1986). Drug treatment of panic disorder: The comparative efficacy of imipramine, alprazolam and trazodone. *Journal of Clinical Psychiatry, 47*, 580–586.

Chouinard, G., Annable, L., Fontaine, R., & Solyom, L. (1982). Alprazolam in the treatment of generalized anxiety and panic disorders: A double-blind placebo-controlled study. *Psychopharmacology Berlin, 77*, 229–233.

Clark, D. B., & Agras, W. S. (1991). The assessment and treatment of performance anxiety in musicians. *American Journal of Psychiatry, 148*, 598–605.

Cohn, J. B., Bowden, C. L., Fisher, J. G., & Rodos, J. J. (1986). Double-blind comparison of buspirone and clorazepate in anxious outpatients. *American Journal of Medicine, 80*, 10–16.

Cohn, J. B., & Wilcox, C. S. (1984). Long-term comparison of alprazolam, lorazepam and placebo in patients with an anxiety disorder. *Pharmacotherapy, 4*, 93–98.

Cottraux, J., Note, I. D., Cungi, C., Legeron, P., et al. (1995). A controlled study of cognitive behaviour therapy with buspirone or placebo in panic disorder with agoraphobia. *British Journal of Psychiatry, 167*, 635–641.

Cowley, D. S., & Roy-Byrne, P. P. (1991). The biology of generalized anxiety disorder and chronic anxiety. In R. M. Rapee & D. H. Barlow (Eds.), *Chronic anxiety* (pp. 52–75). New York: Guilford Press.

Cowley, D. S., Roy-Byrne, P. P., Hommer, D., Greenblatt, D. J., Nemeroff, C., & Ritchie, J. (1991). Benzodiazepine sensitivity in anxiety disorders. *Biological Psychiatry, 29*, 57A.

Cross National Collaborative Treatment Study. (1992). Drug treatment of panic disorder. Comparative efficacy of alprazolam, imipramine, and placebo. *British Journal of Psychiatry, 160*, 191–202.

Cutler, N. R., Sramek, J. J., Hesselink, J. M. K., Krol, A., Roeschen, J., Rickels, K., & Schweizer, E. (1993). A double-blind, placebo-controlled study comparing the efficacy and safety of ipsapirone versus lorazepam in patients with generalized anxiety disorder: A prospective multicenter trial. *Journal of Clinical Psychopharmacology, 13*, 429–437.

Dager, S. R., Roy-Byrne, P., Hendrickson, H., Cowley, D. S., et al. (1992). Long-term outcome of panic states during double-blind treatment and after withdrawal of alprazolam and placebo. *Annals of Clinical Psychiatry, 4*, 251–258.

Davidson, J. R. T., Ford, S. M., Smith, R., et al. (1991b). Long-term treatment of avoidant personality disorder. *Comprehensive Psychiatry, 30*, 498–504.

Davidson, J. R. T., Ford, S. M., Smith, R. D., & Potts, N. L. S. (1991a). Long-term treatment of social phobia with clonazepam. *Journal of Clinical Psychiatry, 52*(Suppl. 11), 16–20.

Davidson, J. R. T., Potts, N., Richichi, E., Krishnan, R., et al. (1993). Treatment of social phobia with clonazepam and placebo. *Journal of Clinical Psychopharmacology, 13*, 423–428.

Davidson, J. R. T., Tupler, L. A., & Potts, N. L. S. (1994). Treatment of social phobia with benzodiazepines. *Journal of Clinical Psychiatry, 55*(Suppl. 6), 28–32.

deBeurs, E., van Balkom, A. J., Lange, A., Koele, P., & van Dyck, R. (1995, May). Treatment of panic disorder with agoraphobia: Comparison of fluvoxamine, placebo, and psychological panic management combined with exposure and of exposure in vivo alone. *American Journal of Psychiatry, 152*(5), 683–691.

Delle Chiaie, R., Pancheri, P., Casacchia, M., Stratta, P., et al. (1995). Assessment of the efficacy of buspirone in patients affected by generalized anxiety disorder, shifting to buspirone from prior treatment with lorazepam: A placebo-controlled, double-blind study. *Journal of Clinical Psychopharmacology, 15*, 12–19.

Den-Boer, J. A., & Westenberg, H. G. (1988). Effect of a serotonin and noradrenaline uptake inhibitor in panic disorder: a double-blind comparative study with fluvoxamine and maprotiline. *International Clinical Psychopharmacology, 3*, 59–74.

———. (1990). Serotonin function in panic disorder: A double blind placebo controlled study with fluvoxamine and ritanserin. *Psychopharmacology (Berlin), 102*, 85–94.

Di Nardo, P. A., Moras, K., Barlow, D. H., Rapee, R. M., & Brown, T. A. (1993). Reliability of *DSM-III-R* anxiety disorder categories. *Archives of General Psychiatry, 50*, 251–256.

Doctor, R. M. (1982). Major results of a large-scale pretreatment survey of agoraphobics. In R. L. DuPont (Ed.), *Phobia: A comprehensive summary of modern treatments* (pp. 203–214). New York: Brunner/Mazel.

DuBoff, E., England, D., Ferguson, J. M., et al. (1995). Sertraline in the treatment of panic disorder. Paper presented at the VIIIth Congress of the European College of Neuropsychopharmacology, Venice, Italy.

Dunner, D. L., Ishiki, D., Avery, D. H., Wilson, L. G., & Hyde, T. S. (1986). Effect of alprazolam and diazepam on anxiety and panic attacks in panic disorder: A controlled study. *Journal of Clinical Psychiatry, 47*, 458–460.

Eaton, W. W., Kessler, R. C., Wittchen, H. U., & Magee, W. J. (1994, March). Panic and panic disorder in the United States. *American Journal of Psychiatry, 151*(3), 413–420.

Emmanuel, N. P., Lydiard, R. B., & Ballenger, J. C. (1991). Treatment of social phobia with bupropion. *Journal of Clinical Psychopharmacology, 11*, 276–277.

Enkelmann, R. (1991). Alprazolam versus buspirone in the treatment of outpatients with generalized anxiety disorder. *Psychopharmacology (Berlin), 105*, 428–432.

Evans, L., Kenardy, J., Schneider, P., & Hoey, H. (1986). Effect of a selective serotonin uptake inhibitor in agoraphobia with panic attacks. *Acta Psychiatrica Scandinavica, 73*, 49–53.

Fahlen, T., Nilsson, H. L., Borg, K., Humber, M., & Pauli, U. (1995). Social phobia: The clinical efficacy of tolerability of the monoamine oxidase-A and serotonin uptake inhibitor brofaromine: A double-blind placebo-controlled study. *Acta Psychiatrica Scandinavica, 92*, 351–358.

Fahy, T. J., O'Rourke, D., Brophy, J., Schazmann, W., & Sciascia, S. (1992). The Galway study of panic disorder I: Clomipramine and lofepramine in *DSM III-R*: A placebo controlled trial. *Journal of Affective Disorders, 25*, 63–76.

Falloon, I. R. H., Lloyd, G. G., & Harpin, R. E. (1981). The treatment of social phobia: Real-life rehearsal with non-professional therapists. *Journal of Nervous Mental Disease, 169*, 180–184.

Feighner, J. P. (1987). Buspirone in the long-term treatment of generalized anxiety disorder. *Journal of Clinical Psychiatry, 48*, 3–6.

Feighner, J. P., & Cohn, J. B. (1989). Analysis of individual symptoms in generalized anxiety—a pooled, multistudy, double-blind evaluation of buspirone. *Neuropsychobiology, 21*, 124–130.

Feighner, J. P., Merideth, C. H., & Hendrickson, G. A. (1982). A double-blind comparison of buspirone and diazepam in outpatients with generalized anxiety disorder. *Journal of Clinical Psychiatry, 43*, 103–108.

Ferreri, M., Hantouche, E. G., & Billardon, M. (1994). Advantages of hydroxyzine in generalized anxiety disorder: A double blind controlled versus placebo study. *L'Encephale, 20*, 785–791.

Fyer, A. J., Liebowitz, M. R., & Gorman, J. M. (1989, December 11–16). *Comparative discontinuation of alprazolam and imipramine in panic patients.* Paper presented at the 27th Annual Meeting of the American College of Neuropsychopharmacology, San Juan, Puerto Rico.

Fyer, A. J., Mannuzza, S., Chapman, T. F., et al. (1988). A direct interview family study of social phobia. *Archives of General Psychiatry, 29*, 72–75.

Gammans, R. E., Stringfellow, J. C., Hvizdos, A. J., Seidehamel, R. J., et al. (1992). Use of buspirone in patients with generalized anxiety disorder and co-existing depressive symptoms: A meta-analysis of eight randomized controlled studies. *Neuropsychobiology, 25*, 193–201.

Garcia-Borreguero, D., Lauer, C. J., Ozdagler, A., Wiedemann, K., Holsboer, F., & Krieg, J. C. (1992, November). Brofaromine in panic disorder: A pilot study with a new reversible inhibitor of monoamine oxidase-A. *Pharmacopsychiatry, 25*(6), 261–64.

Garvey, M. J., & Tollefson, G. D. (1986). Prevalence of misuse of prescribed benzodiazepines in patients with primary anxiety disorder or major depression. *American Journal of Psychiatry, 143*, 1601–1603.

Gelernter, C. S., Uhde, T. W., Cimbolic, P., et al. (1991). Cognitive-behavioral and pharmacological treatments of social phobia: A controlled study. *Archives of General Psychiatry, 48*, 938–945.

Geracioti, T. D., Jr. (1995, September). Venlafaxine treatment of panic disorder: A case series. *Journal of Clinical Psychiatry, 56*, 408–410.

Gloger, S., Grunhaus, L., Gladic, D., O'Ryan, F., Cohen, L., & Codner, S. (1989, February). Panic attacks and agoraphobia: Low dose clomipramine treatment. *Journal of Clinical Psychopharmacology, 9*(1), 28–32.

Glue, P., Wilson, S., Corpland, N., Ball, D., & Nutt, D. (1995). The relationship between benzodiazepine receptor sensitivity and neuroticism. *Journal of Anxiety Disorders, 9*, 33–45.

Goldstein, S. (1987). Treatment of social phobia with clonidine. *Biological Psychiatry, 22*, 369–372.

Golwyn, D. H., & Weinstock, R. C. (1990). Phenelzine treatment of elective mutism: A case report. *Journal of Clinical Psychiatry, 51*, 384–385.

Gorman, J. M., Liebowitz, M. R., Fyer, A. J., et al. (1985). Treatment of social phobia with atenolol. *Journal of Clinical Psychopharmacology, 5*, 298–301.

Gorman, J. M. & Wolkow, R. (1994). Sertraline as a treatment for panic disorder. *Neuropsychopharmacology, 10*, 35–39.

Hayes, P. E., & Schulz, S. C. (1987). Beta-blockers in anxiety disorders. *Journal of Affective Disorders, 13*, 119–130.

Hoehn-Saric, R., McLeod, D. R., & Hipsley, P. A. (1993). Effect of fluvoxamine on panic disorder. *Journal of Clinical Psychopharmacology, 13*, 321–326.

Hoehn-Saric, R., McLeod, D. R., & Zimmerli, W. D. (1988). Differential effects of alprazolam and imipramine in generalized anxiety disorder: Somatic versus psychic symptoms. *Journal of Clinical Psychiatry, 49*, 293–301.

Jefferson, J. W. (1995). Social phobia: A pharmacologic treatment overview. *Journal of Clinical Psychiatry, 56*(Suppl. 5), 18–24.

Johnson, M. R., & Lydiard, R. B. (1993). Future trends in the psychopharmacology of anxiety disorders. In D. L. Dunner (Ed.), *Current psychiatric therapies* (pp. 539–544). Philadelphia, Penn.: W. B. Saunders.

Johnston, D. G., Troyer, I. E., & Whitsett, S. F. (1988). Clomipramine treatment of agoraphobic women. *Archives of General Psychiatry, 45*, 453–459.

Kahn, R. J., McNair, D. M., Lipman, R. S., Covi, L., Rickels, K., Downing, R., Fisher, S., & Frankenthalar, L. M. (1986). Imipramine and chlordiazepoxide in depressive and anxiety disorders. II. Efficacy in anxious outpatients. *Archives of General Psychiatry, 43*, 79–85.

Kalus, O., Asnis, G. M., Rubinson, E., et al. (1991). Desipramine treatment in panic disorder. *Journal of Affective Disorders, 21*(4), 239–244.

Katzelnick, D. J., Kobak, K. A., Greist, J. H., Jefferson, J. W., Mantle, J. M., & Serlin, R. C. (1955). Sertraline for social phobia: A double-blind, placebo-controlled crossover study. *American Journal of Psychiatry, 152*, 1368–1371.

Keck, P. E., Jr., Taylor, V. E., Tugrul, K. C., McElroy, S. L., & Bennett, J. A. (1993, April). Valproate treatment of panic disorder and lactate-induced panic attacks. *Biological Psychiatry, 33*(7), 542–46.

Kendler, K. S., Neale, M. C., Kessler, R. C., et al. (1992a). The genetic epidemiology of phobias in women. *Archives of General Psychiatry, 49*, 273–281.

Kendler, K. S., Neale, M. C., Kessler, R. C., Heath, A. C., & Eaves, L. J. (1992b). Generalized anxiety disorder in women: A population-based twin study. *Archives of General Psychiatry, 49*, 267–272.

Kessler, R. C., McGonagle, K. A., Zhao, S., et al. (1994). Lifetime and 12-month prevalence of *DSM-III-R* psychiatric disorders in the United States: results from the National Comorbidity Survey. *Archives of General Psychiatry, 51*, 8–19.

Klein, D. F. (1964). Delineation of two drug-responsive anxiety syndromes. *Psychopharmacologia, 5*, 397–408.

———. (1967). Importance of psychiatric diagnosis in prediction of clinical drug effects. *Archives of General Psychiatry, 16*, 118–126.

Klein, E., Colin, V., Stolk, J., & Lenox, R. H. (1994). Alprazolam withdrawal in patients with panic disorder and generalized anxiety disorder: Vulnerability and effect of carbamazepine. *American Journal of Psychiatry, 151*, 1760–1766.

Klein, E., & Uhde, T. W. (1988). Controlled study of verapamil for treatment of panic disorder. *American Journal of Psychiatry, 145*, 431–434.

Klein, E., Uhde, T. W., & Post, R. M. (1986). Preliminary evidence for the utility of carbamazepine in alprazolam withdrawal. *American Journal of Psychiatry, 143*, 235–236.

Klosko, J. S., Barlow, D. H., Tassinari, R., & Cerny, J. A. (1990). A comparison of alprazolam and behavior therapy in treatment of panic disorder. *Journal of Consulting and Clinical Psychology, 58*, 77–84.

Lader, M., & Olajide, D. (1987). A comparison of buspirone and placebo in relieving benzodiazepine withdrawal symptoms. *Journal of Clinical Psychopharmacology, 7*, 11–15.

Lecrubier, V., on behalf of the Panic Disorder Study Group. (1994). A double-blind, placebo-controlled study of paroxetine and clomipramine in the treatment of panic disorder. Paper presented at the 7th Congress of the Association of European Psychiatrists, Copenhagen, Denmark.

Lepola, U., Koponen, H., & Leinonen, E. (1994). Citalopram in the treatment of social phobia: A report of three cases. *Pharmacopsychiatry, 27,* 186–188.

Liebowitz, M. R., Fyer, A. J., Gorman, J. M., et al. (1986). Phenelzine in social phobia. *Journal of Clinical Psychopharmacology, 6,* 93–98.

Liebowitz, M. R., Schneier, F., Campeas, R., Hollander, E., Hatterer, J., Fyer, A., Gorman, J., Papp, L., Davies, S., Gully, R., & Klein, D. F. (1992). Phenelzine versus atenolol in social phobia: A placebo-controlled comparison. *Archives of General Psychiatry, 49,* 290–300.

Lipsedge, J. S., Hajjoff, J., Huggins, P., et al. (1973). The management of severe agoraphobia: A comparison of iproniazid and systematic desensitization. *Psychopharmacology, 32,* 67–80.

Louie, A. K., Lewis, T. B., & Lannon, R. A. (1993, November). Use of low-dose fluoxetine in major depression and panic disorder. *Journal of Clinical Psychiatry, 54*(11), 435–438.

Lucki, I., Rickels, K., & Geller, A. M. (1986). Chronic use of benzodiazepines and psychomotor and cognitive test performance. *Psychopharmacology, 88,* 426–433.

Lydiard, R. B., & Ballenger, J. C. (1987). Antidepressants in panic disorder and agoraphobia. *Journal of Affective Disorders, 13,* 153–168.

Lydiard, R. B., Lesser, L. M., Bellenger, J. C., Rubin, R. T., Laraia, M., & DuPont, R. (1992). A fixed-dose study of alprazolam 2 mg, alprazolam 6 mg, and placebo in panic disorder. *Journal of Clinical Psychopharmacology, 12,* 96–103.

Lydiard, R. B., Morton, W. A., Emmanuel, N. P., et al. (1993). Preliminary report: Placebo-controlled, double-blind study of the clinical and metabolic effects of desipramine in panic disorder. *Psychopharmacology Bulletin, 29*(2), 183–188.

Maddock, R., Carter, C., Blacker, K., et al. (1993). Relationship of past depressive episodes to symptom severity and treatment response in panic disorder with agoraphobia. *Journal of Clinical Psychiatry, 54,* 88–95.

Marks, I. M., Gray, S., Cohen, D., Hill, R., Mawson, D., Ramm, E., & Stern, R. (1983). Imipramine and brief therapist-aided exposure in agoraphobics having self-exposure homework. *Archives of General Psychiatry, 40,* 153–162.

Mavissakalian, M., & Michelson, L. (1986). Agoraphobia: Relative and combined effectiveness of therapist-assisted in vivo exposure and imipramine. *Journal of Clinical Psychiatry, 47,* 117–122.

Mavissakalian, M., & Perel, J. M. (1992a, April). Clinical experiments in maintenance and discontinuation of imipramine therapy in panic disorder with agoraphobia. *Archives of General Psychiatry, 49*(4), 318–323.

———. (1992b, August). Protective effects of imipramine maintenance treatment in panic disorder with agoraphobia. *American Journal of Psychiatry, 149*(8), 1053–1057.

———. (1995). Imipramine treatment of panic disorder with agoraphobia: dose ranging and plasma level-response relationships. *American Journal of Psychiatry, 152*(5), 673–682.

McNamara, M. E., & Fogel, B. S. (1990). Anticonvulsant-responsive panic attacks with temporal lobe EEG abnormalities. *Journal of Neuropsychiatry and Clinical Neurosciences, 2*(2), 193–196.

Meibach, R. C., Mullane, J. F., & Binstok, G. (1987). A placebo-controlled multicenter trial of propranolol and chlordiazepoxide in the treatment of anxiety. *Current Therapeutic Research, 41,* 65–76.

Modigh, K., Westberg, P., & Eriksson, E. (1992). Superiority of clomipramine over imipramine in the treatment of panic disorder. *Journal of Clinical Psychopharmacology, 12,* 251–261.

Mountjoy, C. Q., Roth, M., Garside, R. F., & Leitch, I. M. (1977). A clinical trial of phenelzine in anxiety, depressive and phobic neuroses. *British Journal of Psychiatry, 31,* 486–492.

Munjack, D. J., Brun, J., & Baltazar, P. L. (1991). A pilot study of buspirone in the treatment of social phobia. *Journal of Anxiety Disorders, 5,* 87–88.

Munjack, D. J., Crocker, B., Cabe, D., et al. (1989). Alprazolam, propranolol, and placebo in the treatment of panic disorder and agoraphobia with panic attacks. *Journal of Clinical Psychopharmacology, 9,* 22–27.

Munjack, D. J., Usigli, R., Zulueta, A., et al. (1988). Nortriptyline in the treatment of panic disorder and agoraphobia with panic attacks. *Journal of Clinical Psychopharmacology, 8*(3), 204–207.

Nagy, L. M., Krystal, J. H., Woods, S. W., et al. (1989). Clinical and medication outcome after short-term alprazolam and behavioral group treatment in panic disorder. *Archives of General Psychiatry, 46,* 993–999.

Ninan, P., Insel, T. R., Cohen, R. M., Skolnick, P., & Paul, S. M. (1982). A benzodiazepine receptor mediated model of anxiety. *Science, 218,* 1332–1334.

Norton, G. R., Cox, B. J., & Malan, J. (1992). Nonclinical panickers: A critical review. *Clinical Psychology Review, 12,* 121–139.

Noyes, R., Jr., Garvey, M. J., Cook, B. L., & Samuelson, L. (1989, May). Problems with tricyclic antidepressant use in patients with panic disorder or agoraphobia: Results of a naturalistic follow-up study. *Journal of Clinical Psychiatry, 50*(5), 163–169.

Noyes, R., Woodman, C., Garvey, J. M., Cook, B. L., Suelzer, M., Clancy, J., & Anderson, D. J. (1992). Generalized anxiety disorder versus panic disorder:

distinguishing characteristics and patterns of comorbidity. *Journal of Nervous and Mental Disease, 180,* 369–379.

Oberlander, E. L., Schneier, F. R., & Liebowitz, M. R. (1994). Physical disability and social phobia. *Journal of Clinical Psychopharmcology, 14,* 136–143.

Oehrberg, S., Christiansen, P. E., Behnke, K., et al. (1995). Paroxetine in the treatment of panic disorder, a randomised, double-blind, placebo-controlled study. *British Journal of Psychiatry, 167,* 374–379.

Ontiveros, A., & Fontaine, R. (1992). Sodium valproate and clonazepam for treatment-resistant panic disorder. *Journal of Psychiatric Neurosciences, 17*(2), 78–80.

Papp, L. A., Coplan, J., & Gorman, J. M. (1992). Neurobiology of anxiety. In A. Tasman & M. B. Riba (Eds.), *Review of psychiatry* Vol. 11 (pp. 307–322). Washington, D.C.: American Psychiatric Press.

Pecknold, J. C. (1990, June 19–22). *Discontinuation studies: Short-term and long-term.* Paper presented at Panic and Anxiety: A Decade of Progress, Geneva, Switzerland.

Pecknold, J. C., Matas, M., Howarth, B. G., Ross, C., Swinson, R., Vezeau, C., & Ungar, W. (1989). Evaluation of buspirone as an antianxiety agent: buspirone and diazepam versus placebo. *Canadian Journal of Psychiatry, 34,* 766–771.

Pecknold, J. C., Swinson, R. P., Kuch, K., et al. (1989). Alprazolam in panic disorder and agoraphobia: Discontinuation effects. *Archives of General Psychiatry, 45,* 429–436.

Petracca, A., Nisita, C., McNair, D., Melis, G., Guerani, G., & Cassano, G. B. (1990). Treatment of generalized anxiety disorder: Preliminary clinical experience with buspirone. *Journal of Clinical Psychiatry, 51,* 31–39.

Pollack, M. H., Worthington, J. J., Otto, M. W., et al. (1996). Venlafaxine for panic disorder: Results from a double-blind, placebo-controlled study. *Psychopharmacology Bulletin, 32,* 667–670.

Power, K. G., Simpson, R. J., Swanson, V., & Wallace, L. A. (1990). Controlled comparison of pharmacological and psychological treatment of generalized anxiety disorder in primary care. *British Journal of General Practice, 40,* 289–294.

Regier, D. A., Farmer, M. E., Rae, D. S., Locke, B. Z., Keigh, S. J., Judd, L. L., & Goodwin, F. K. (1990). Comorbidity of mental disorders with alcohol and other drug abuse: Results from the epidemiological catchment area (ECA) study. *Journal of the American Medical Association, 264,* 2511–2518.

Reich, J., Goldenberg, I., Vasile, R., Goisman, R., & Keller, M. (1993). A prospective follow-along study of the course of social phobia. *Psychiatry Research, 54,* 249–258.

Rickels, K., Case, W. G., Downing, R. W., et al. (1983). Long-term diazepam therapy and clinical outcome. *Journal of the American Medical Association, 250,* 767–771.

Rickels, K., Case, W. G., Schweizer, E., et al. (1986). Low-dose dependence in chronic benzodiazepine users: A preliminary report on 119 patients. *Psychopharmacology Bulletin, 22,* 407–415.

Rickels, K., Downing, R., Schweizer, E., & Hassman, H. (1993a). Antidepressants for the treatment of generalized anxiety disorder: A placebo-controlled comparison of imipramine, trazodone, and diazepam. *Archives of General Psychiatry, 50,* 884–895.

Rickels, K., & Schweizer, E. (1990). The clinical course and long-term management of generalized anxiety disorder. *Journal of Clinical Psychopharmacology, 10,* 101S–110S.

Rickels, K., Schweizer, E., Canalosi, I., et al. (1988). Long-term treatment of anxiety and risk of withdrawal: Prospective comparison of clorazepate and buspirone. *Archives of General Psychiatry, 45,* 444–450.

Rickels, K., Schweizer, E., Weiss, S., & Zavodnick, S. (1993b). Maintenance drug treatment for panic disorder, II. Short- and long-term outcome after drug taper. *Archives of General Psychiatry, 50,* 61–68.

Rickels, K., Weisman, K., Norstad, N., Singer, M., Stoltz, K., Brown, A., & Danton, J. (1982). Buspirone and diazepam in anxiety: A controlled study. *Journal of Clinical Psychiatry, 43,* 81–86.

Ries, R. K., & Wittkowsky, A. K. (1986). Synergistic action of alprazolam with tranylcypromine in drug-resistant atypical depression with panic attacks. *Biological Psychiatry, 21,* 522–526.

Ringold, A. L. (1994). Paroxetine efficacy in social phobia. *Journal of Clinical Psychiatry, 55,* 363–364.

Rosenbaum, J. F., Biederman, J., Hirshfield, D. R., et al. (1991). Further evidence of an association between behavioral inhibition and anxiety disorders: Results from a family study of children from a nonclinical sample. *Journal of Psychiatry Research, 25,* 49–65.

Ross, C. A., & Matas, M. (1987). A clinical trial of buspirone and diazepam in the treatment of generalized anxiety disorder. *Canadian Journal of Psychiatry, 32,* 351–355.

Roy-Byrne, P. P., & Cowley, D. S. (1995). Course and outcome in panic disorder: a review of recent follow-up studies. *Anxiety, 1,* 151–160.

Roy-Byrne, P. P., Dager, S. R., Cowley, D. S., Vitaliano, P., & Dunner, D. L. (1989). Relapse and rebound following discontinuation of benzodiazepine treatment of panic attacks: Alprazolam versus diazepam. *American Journal of Psychiatry, 146,* 860–865.

Roy-Byrne, P. P., Geraci, M., & Uhde, T. W. (1986).

Life events and the onset of panic disorder. *American Journal of Psychiatry, 143*, 1424–1427.

Schneier, F. R., Chin, S. J., Hollander, G., et al. (1992a). Fluoxetine in social phobia. *Journal of Clinical Psychopharmacology, 12*, 61–64.

Schneier, F. R., Heckelman, L. R., Garfinkel, R., Campeas, R., et al. (1994). Functional impairment in social phobia. *Journal of Clinical Psychiatry, 55*, 322–331.

Schneier, F. R., Johnson, J., Hornig, C. D., et al. (1992b). Social phobia: Comorbidity and morbidity in an epidemiological sample. *Archives of General Psychiatry, 49*, 282–288.

Schneier, F. R., Liebowitz, M. R., Davies, S. O., et al. (1990). Fluoxetine in panic disorder. *Journal of Clinical Psychopharmacology, 10*(2), 119–121.

Schneier, F. R., Saoud, J. B., Campeas, R., Fallon, B. A., et al. (1993). Buspirone in social phobia. *Journal of Clinical Psychopharmacology, 13*, 251–256.

Schweizer, E., Fox, I., Case, G., & Rickels, K. (1988). Lorazepam versus alprazolam in the treatment of panic disorder. *Psychopharmacology Bulletin, 24*, 224–227.

Schweizer, E., Rickels, K., Weiss, S., & Zavodnick, S. (1993). Maintenance drug treatment of panic disorder, I. Results of a prospective, placebo-controlled comparison of alprazolam and imipramine. *Archives of General Psychiatry, 50*, 51–60.

Shader, R. I., & Greenblatt, D. J. (1993). Use of benzodiazepines in anxiety disorders. *New England Journal of Medicine, 328*, 1398–1405.

Shapiro, A. K., Struening, E. L., Shapiro, E., et al. (1983). Diazepam: How much better than placebo? *Journal of Psychiatry Research, 17*, 51–53.

Sheehan, D. V., Ballenger, J., & Jacobsen, G. (1980). Treatment of endogenous anxiety with phobic, hysterical, and hypocondrical symptoms. *Archives of General Psychiatry, 37*, 51–59.

Sheehan, D. V., Davidson, J., Manschreck, T., et al. (1983). Lack of efficacy of a new antidepressant (bupropion) in the treatment of panic disorder with phobias. *Journal of Clinical Psychopharmacology, 3*, 28–31.

Sheehan, D. V., Raj, A. B., Harnett-Sheehan, K., Soto, S., & Knapp, E. (1993). The relative efficacy of high-dose buspirone and alprazolam in the treatment of panic disorder: A double-blind placebo-controlled study. *Acta Psychiatrica Scandinavica, 88*, 1–11.

Sheehan, D. V., Raj, A. B., Sheehan, K. H., & Soto, S. (1990). Is buspirone effective for panic disorder? *Journal of Clinical Psychopharmacology, 10*(1), 3–11.

Slaap, B. R., van Vliet, I. M., Westenberg, H. G., & den-Boer, J. A. (1995, January). Phobic symptoms as predictors of nonresponse to drug therapy in panic

disorder patients (a preliminary report). *Journal of Affective Disorders, 33*(1), 31–8.

Soloman, K., & Hart, R. (1978). Pitfalls and prospects in clinical research on antianxiety drugs: benzodiazepines and placebos. *Journal of Clinical Psychiatry, 39*, 823–831.

Solyom, C., Solyom, L., LaPierre, Y., Pecknold, J. C., & Morton, L. (1981). Phenelzine and exposure in the treatment of phobias. *Biological Psychiatry, 16*, 239–247.

Solyom, L., Heseltine, G. F. D., McClure, D. J., Solyom, C., Ledgwidge, B., & Steinburg, G. (1973). Behaviour therapy versus drug therapy in the treatment of phobic neurosis. *Canadian Psychiatric Association Journal, 18*, 25–31.

Steiner, M., Oakes, R., Gergel, I. D., et al. (1995). A fixed dose study of paroxetine and placebo in the treatment of panic disorder. Paper presented at the 148th Annual Meeting of the American Psychiatric Association, Miami, FLorida.

Sternbach, H. (1990). Fluoxetine treatment of social phobia. *Journal of Clinical Psychopharmacology, 10*, 230.

Strand, M., Hetta, J., Rosen, A., Sorensen, S., et al. (1990). A double-blind, controlled trial in primary care patients with generalized anxiety: A comparison between buspirone and oxazepam. *Journal of Clinical Psychiatry, 51*, 40–50.

Taylor, C. B., Hayward, C., King, R., et al. (1990). Cardiovascular and symptomatic reduction effects of alprazolam and imipramine in patients with panic disorder: Results of a double-blind, placebo-controlled trial. *Journal of Clinical Psychopharmacology, 10*(2), 112–118.

Taylor, C. B., King, R., Margraf, J., et al. (1989, November). Use of medication and in vivo exposure in volunteers for panic disorder research. *American Journal of Psychiatry, 146*(11), 1423–1426.

Telch, M. J., Agras, S., Taylor, C. B., Roth, W. T., & Gallen, C. (1985). Combined pharmacological and behavioural treatment for agoraphobia. *Behaviour Research & Therapy, 23*, 325–335.

Tesar, G. E., Rosenaum, J. F., Pollack, M. H., et al. (1991). Double-blind, placebo-controlled comparison of clonazepam and alprazolam for panic disorder. *Journal of Clinical Psychiatry, 52*, 69–76.

Tiffon, L., Coplan, J. D., Papp, L. A., & Gorman, J. M. (1994, February). Augmentation strategies with tricyclic or fluoxetine treatment in seven partially responsive panic disorder patients. *Journal of Clinical Psychiatry, 55*(2), 66–69.

Turner, S. M., Beidel, D. C., & Jacob, R. G. (1994). Social phobia: A comparison of behavior therapy and atenolol. *Journal of Consulting & Clinical Psychology, 62*, 350–358.

Tyrer, P., Candy, J., & Kelly, D. A. (1973). A study of the clinical effects of phenelzine and placebo in the treatment of phobic anxiety. *Psychopharmacology, 32*, 237–254.

Uhde, T. W., Stein, M. B., & Post, R. M. (1988). Lack of efficacy of carbamazepine in the treatment of panic disorder. *American Journal of Psychiatry, 145*, 1104–1109.

Uhde, T. W., Stein, M. B., Vittone, B. J., et al. (1989). Behavioral and psychologic effects of short-term and long-term administration of clonidine in panic disorder. *Archives of General Psychiatry, 46*(2), 170–177.

Uhlenhuth, E. H., Matuzas, A. W., Glass, R. M., & Easton, C. (1989, November–December). Response of panic disorder to fixed doses of alprazolam or imipramine. *Journal of Affective Disorders, 17*(3), 261–270.

van Vliet, I. M., den Boer, J. A., & Westernberg, H. G. M. (1994). Psychopharmacological treatment of social phobia: a double blind placebo controlled study with fluvoxamine. *Psychopharmacology, 115*, 128–134.

van Vliet, I. M., Westenberg, H. G., & Den-Boer, J. A. (1993). MAO inhibitors in panic disorder: Clinical effects of treatment with brofaromine. A double-bond placebo controlled study. *Psychopharmacology Berlin, 112*(4), 483–489.

Versiani, M., Mundim, F. D., & Nardi, A. E. (1988). Tranylcypromine in social phobia. *Journal of Clinical Psychopharmacology, 8*, 279–283.

Versiani, M., Nardi, A. E., Mundim, F. D., Alves, A. B., Liebowitz, M. R., & Amrein, R. (1992). Pharmacotherapy of social phobia: A controlled study with moclobemide and phenelzine. *British Journal of Psychiatry, 161*, 353–360.

Widiger, T. A. (1992). Generalized social phobia versus avoidant personality disorder: A commentary on three studies. *Journal of Abnormal Psychology, 101*, 340–343.

Wingerson, D., Nguyen, C., & Roy-Byrne, P. P. (1992). Clomipramine treatment for generalized anxiety disorder. *Journal of Clinical Psychopharmacology, 12*, 214–215.

Wittchen, H. U., Zhao, S., Kessler, R. C., & Eaton, W. (1994). *DSM-III-R* generalized anxiety disorder in the national comorbidity survey. *Archives of General Psychiatry, 51*, 355–364.

Woodman, C. L., & Noyes, R., Jr. (1994). Panic disorder: Treatment with valproate. *Journal of Clinical Psychiatry, 55*(4), 134–136.

Woods, S. W., Nagy, L. M., Koleszer, A. S., et al. (1992). Controlled trial of alprazolam supplements during imipramine treatment of panic disorder. *Journal of Clinical Psychopharmacology, 12*, 32–38.

Zitran, C. M., Klein, D. F., Woerner, M. G., & Ross, D. S. (1983). Treatment of phobias. I. Comparison of imipramine hydrochloride and placebo. *Archives of General Psychiatry, 40*, 125–138.

Zitrin, C. M., Klein, D. F., & Woerner, M. G. (1980). Treatment of agoraphobia with group exposure in vivo and imipramine. *Archives of General Psychiatry, 37*, 63–73.

———. (1978). Behavior therapy, supportive psychotherapy, imipramine, and phobias. *Archives of General Psychiatry, 35*, 307–316.

17

Cognitive-Behavioral Treatments for Obsessive Compulsive Disorder

Martin E. Franklin
Edna B. Foa

A very substantial number of Type 1 and Type 2 studies, as well as several meta-analytic studies and literature reviews, have established the efficacy of cognitive-behavioral therapy involving exposure and ritual prevention (EX/RP) methods to treat the obsessions and behavioral and mental rituals of OCD. Recent efforts brought on by the desire to increase efficiency and limit costs have led to reducing the number of EX/RP sessions, spacing and shortening them, and relying on instructions for self-exposure and ritual prevention. These modifications appear to have resulted in diminished treatment efficacy.

Methodological and conceptual shortcomings of relevant research to date have prevented a definitive answer to the question of whether adding cognitive procedures enhances the efficacy of EX/RP. Similarly, methodological problems have rendered the vast majority of direct comparisons of the relative efficacy of EX/RP and pharmacotherapy with serotonin reuptake inhibitors (the pharmacological treatment of choice for OCD) uninterpretable. Preliminary results from a single well-controlled study suggest the superiority of intensive EX/RP over clomipramine.

The symptoms that characterize what we now call obsessive compulsive disorder (OCD) have been recognized for centuries in many cultures (for a review, see Pitman, 1994). However, it was only in the last three decades that effective psychosocial and pharmacological therapies for OCD were developed and studied. We briefly discuss diagnostic and theoretical issues, then review the literature about available treatments. In this chapter, we focus primarily on the outcome of cognitive-behavioral therapy (CBT) by exposure and ritual prevention (EX/RP) (originally referred to as "response prevention") because most experts consider it to be the treatment of choice for OCD.

DEFINITION OF OBSESSIVE COMPULSIVE DISORDER

According to the *DSM-IV* (*Diagnostic and Statistical Manual of Mental Disorders*, 4th ed.; American Psychiatric Association [APA], 1994), OCD is characterized by recurrent obsessions and/or compulsions that interfere considerably with daily functioning. Obsessions are "persistent ideas, thoughts, impulses, or images that are experienced as intrusive and inappropriate and cause marked anxiety or distress" (p. 418). Compulsions are "repetitive behaviors . . . or mental acts . . . the goal of which is to prevent or reduce anxiety or distress" (p. 418).

The updated *DSM-IV* definition of OCD is on the whole similar to the conceptualization posed in *DSM-III-R* (APA, 1987), but includes several noteworthy changes based on recent thinking about the disorder. The view that obsessions and compulsions are functionally related, that is, compulsions are performed in order to decrease distress associated with obsessions (Foa & Tillmanns, 1980), became more prominent in the *DSM-IV* definition of OCD because of strong empirical support for this view. In the recently completed *DSM-IV* field study on OCD, 90% of participants reported that their compulsions aim to either prevent harm associated with their obsessions or reduce obsessional distress; only 10% perceived their compulsions as unrelated to obsessions (Foa et al., 1995). Accordingly, obsessions are defined in *DSM-IV* as thoughts, images, or impulses that cause marked anxiety or distress, and compulsions are defined as overt (behavioral) or covert (mental) actions that are performed in an attempt to reduce the distress brought on by obsessions or according to rigid rules.

Data from the *DSM-IV* field study also indicated that the vast majority (over 90%) of obsessive compulsives manifest both obsessions and behavioral rituals. When mental rituals are included, only 2% of the sample reported obsessions only (Foa et al., 1995). Behavioral rituals are equivalent to mental rituals (such as silently repeating prayers) in their functional relationship to obsessions: both serve to reduce obsessional distress, prevent feared harm, or restore safety. Thus, the traditional view that obsessions are mental events and compulsions are behavioral events is not valid: while all obsessions are indeed mental events, compulsions are either mental or behavioral.

It has been argued that a continuum of "insight" or "strength of belief" more accurately represents the clinical picture of OCD than the previously prevailing view that *all* obsessive compulsives recognize the senselessness of their obsessions and compulsions (Kozak & Foa, 1994). The growing consensus about this issue (Foa et al., 1995; Insel & Akiskal, 1986; Lelliott, Noshirvani, Basoglu, Marks, & Monteiro, 1988) led to an important revision of the *DSM-IV* definition of OCD. Individuals who show evidence of obsessions and compulsions but do not recognize their senselessness now receive the diagnosis of OCD "with poor insight."

PREVALENCE AND COURSE

Once thought to be a rare disorder, OCD is now estimated to occur in about 2.5% of the adult population in the United States (Karno, Golding, Sorenson, & Burnam, 1988). Recent epidemiological studies with children and adolescents suggest similar lifetime prevalence rates in these samples (e.g., Flament et al., 1988; Valleni-Basile et al., 1994). Slightly more than half of the adults suffering from OCD are female (Rasmussen & Tsuang, 1986), whereas a 2 : 1 male-to-female ratio has been observed in several pediatric clinical samples (e.g., Hanna, 1995; Swedo, Rapoport, Leonard, Lenane, & Cheslow, 1989). Age of onset of the disorder typically ranges from early adolescence to young adulthood, with earlier onset in males; modal onset in males is 13–15 years old and in females 20–24 years old (Rasmussen & Eisen, 1990). However, cases of OCD have been documented in children as young as age 2 (Rapoport, Swedo, & Leonard, 1992). Development of the disorder is usually gradual, but acute onset has been reported in some cases.

While chronic waxing and waning of symptoms is typical, episodic and deteriorating courses have been observed in about 10% of patients (Rasmussen & Eisen, 1989). OCD is frequently associated with impairments in general functioning, such as disruption of gainful employment (Leon, Portera, & Weissman, 1995), and with marital and other interpersonal relationship difficulties (Emmelkamp, de Haan, & Hoogduin, 1990; Riggs, Hiss, & Foa, 1992). Adolescents identified as having OCD (Flament et al., 1988) reported in a subsequent follow-up study that they had withdrawn socially to prevent contamination and to conserve energy for obsessive compulsive behaviors (Flament et al., 1990).

ETIOLOGY AND MAINTENANCE OF OBSESSIVE COMPULSIVE DISORDER

There are several theoretical accounts of the etiology and maintenance of OCD. Mowrer's (1939, 1960) two-stage theory for the acquisition and maintenance of fear and avoidance behavior was invoked by Dollard and Miller (1950) to explain OCD. Accordingly, a neutral event comes to elicit fear after being experienced along with an event that by its nature causes distress. Distress can be conditioned to mental events (e.g., thoughts), as well as to physical events (e.g., floors, bathrooms). Once fear is acquired, escape or avoidance patterns (i.e., compulsions) develop to reduce fear and are maintained by the negative reinforcement of fear reduction. While Mowrer's theory does adequately account for fear acquisition (Rachman & Wilson, 1980), it is consistent with observations about the maintenance of compulsive rituals: obsessions give rise to anxiety/distress, and compulsions reduce it (e.g., Roper & Rachman, 1976; Roper, Rachman, & Hodgson, 1973).

Cognitive theorists have argued that OCD is founded in ideas of exaggerated negative consequences (Carr, 1974; McFall & Wollersheim, 1979). However, clinical observations suggest that mistaken evaluation of danger and the idea that self-worth is connected with being perfect are typical of *all* anxiety disorders. These theories do not address the characteristics that distinguish OCD from other disorders.

Salkovskis (1985) offered a more thorough cognitive analysis of OCD. He proposed that five assumptions are specifically characteristic of OCD:

1. Thinking of an action is analogous to its performance.
2. Failing to prevent (or failing to try to prevent) harm to self or others is morally equivalent to causing the harm.
3. Responsibility for harm is not diminished by extenuating circumstances.
4. Failing to ritualize in response to an idea about harm constitutes an intention to harm.
5. One should exercise control over one's thoughts (Salkovskis, 1985, p. 579).

An interesting implication of this theory is that whereas the obsessive intrusions may be seen by the patient as unacceptable, the mental and overt rituals that they prompt will be acceptable. Foa and Kozak (1985) hypothesized that obsessive compulsives often conclude that a situation is dangerous based on the absence of evidence for safety and fail to make inductive leaps about safety from information about the absence of danger. For example, in order to feel safe, an OCD sufferer requires a guarantee that the toilet seat is safe before sitting on it, whereas a person without OCD would sit on the toilet seat unless there was something particular about it indicating danger, such as visible brown spots on the seat. Consequently, rituals that are performed to reduce the likelihood of harm can never really provide safety and must be repeated.

The prevailing biological account of OCD hypothesizes that abnormal serotonin metabolism is expressed as OCD symptoms. The efficacy of serotonin reuptake inhibitors (SRIs) for OCD as compared with nonserotonergic compounds and to a pill placebo (PBO) has provided a compelling argument for this hypothesis (Zohar & Insel, 1987). Significant correlations between clomipramine (CMI) plasma levels and improvement in OCD have led researchers to suggest that serotonin function mediates obsessive compulsive symptoms, thus lending further support to the serotonin hypothesis (Insel et al., 1983; Stern, Marks, Wright, & Luscombe, 1980). However, the studies that directly investigated serotonin functioning in obsessive compulsive individuals are inconclusive (Joffe & Swinson, 1991). For example, serotonin platelet uptake studies have failed to differentiate obsessive compulsive individuals from control subjects (Insel, Mueller, Alterman, Linnoila, & Murphy, 1985; Weizman et al., 1986). Also inconsistent with the serotonin hypothesis is the finding that clomipramine, a nonselective serotonergic medication, appears to produce greater OCD symptom reduction than selective serotonin reuptake inhibitors such as fluoxetine, fluvoxamine, and sertraline (Greist, Jefferson, Kobak, Katzelnick, & Serlin, 1995).

EARLY TREATMENTS FOR OBSESSIVE COMPULSIVE DISORDER

Until the middle of the 1960s, OCD was considered to be a refractory psychiatric condition. Neither psychodynamic psychotherapy nor a wide variety of pharmacological treatments had been proven successful in ameliorating OCD symptoms. Early case reports employing exposure procedures (e.g., systematic desensitization, paradoxical intention, imaginal flooding, satiation) also yielded generally unimpressive results, as did several operant-conditioning procedures aimed at blocking or punishing obsessions and compulsions (e.g., thought stopping, aversion therapy, covert sensitization). For a review see Foa, Steketee, and Ozarow (1985).

A dramatic shift occurred when Victor Meyer (1966) reported on two patients treated successfully with a behavioral program that included prolonged exposure to obsessional cues and strict prevention of rituals (EX/RP). This treatment program was subsequently found to be very successful in 10 of 15 cases and partly effective in the remainder; after 5 years, only 2 of 15 patients in this open clinical trial had relapsed (Meyer & Levy, 1973; Meyer, Levy, & Schnurer, 1974). Another shift occurred with the finding that the tricyclic clomipramine (Anafranil) was effective in reducing OCD symptoms (e.g., Fernandez-Cordoba & Lopez-Ibor Alino, 1967). Subsequent research efforts were aimed at developing these treatments further and determining their relative efficacy.

REVIEW OF OBSESSIVE COMPULSIVE DISORDER TREATMENT OUTCOME LITERATURE

In the three decades following these initial reports, the efficacy of two treatments has been established: cognitive-behavioral therapy by EX/RP and pharmacotherapy with SRIs. We begin by discussing review papers and examining results from several meta-analytic studies. We then evaluate results emerging from controlled studies of EX/RP employing a set of criteria that we label the "gold standard" for treatment outcome studies.

Meta-analytic Studies and Literature Reviews

By 1981, there were numerous uncontrolled investigations of EX/RP's efficacy but only three well-controlled studies had been reported (Marks, Hodgson, & Rachman, 1975; Marks, Stern, Mawson, Cobb, & McDonald, 1980; Roper, Rachman, & Marks, 1975); more than 200 OCD patients had been treated in available studies (Marks, 1981). Marks concluded that EX/RP treatment produces lasting improvements for up to 3 years and was the treatment of choice for compulsive ritualizers. He also recommended that treatment include therapist-assisted exposure in vivo, self-exposure homework, and the use of prolonged continuous exposure rather than brief interrupted exposures.

A few years later, Foa et al. (1985) reexamined the literature on EX/RP following the publication of two studies investigating the relative effects of exposure and ritual prevention and one study investigating the additive effect of imaginal exposure (Foa, Steketee, Grayson, Turner, & Latimer, 1984; Foa, Steketee, & Milby, 1980a; Steketee, Foa, & Grayson, 1982). Consistent with Marks's opinion, Foa et al. concluded that across many controlled and uncontrolled investigations, about 75% of patients treated with EX/RP improved significantly and stayed so at follow-up. The importance of ritual prevention in the treatment of OCD was emphasized, and the additive role of imaginal exposure to enhance long-term outcome was also discussed.

Investigation of the efficacy of EX/RP and serotonergic medications continued throughout the 1980s, but by 1987 there were only two publications reporting on direct comparison between the two treatment modalities (Marks et al., 1980; Solyom & Sookman, 1977). Moreover, methodological problems in both studies precluded definitive conclusions about their relative efficacy. Meta-analytic techniques were therefore utilized to integrate this research literature. Calculating effect sizes for 71 studies published during the period 1961–1984, Christensen, Hadzi-Pavlovic, Andrews, and Mattick (1987) found that in those studies for which precise effect-size estimates could be calculated, effect sizes for exposure-based therapy ($n = 13$; $M = 1.22$; 95% confidence limits = 0.84–1.60) and antidepressant medications, primarily clomipramine ($n = 10$; $M = 1.40$; 95% confidence limits = 0.84–1.60), were significantly superior to nonspecific treatment programs ($n = 5$; $M = 0.21$; 95% confidence limits = 0.10–0.52) and thought stopping ($n = 2$; $M = 0.43$; 95% confidence limits = 0.15–0.69) but did not differ from one another.

A second meta-analysis was conducted by Cox, Swinson, Morrison, and Lee (1993) to examine the relative efficacy of serotonin reuptake inhibitors and behavioral treatments. Results indicated that fluoxetine, clomipramine, and exposure therapy were highly effective for ameliorating OCD symptoms, with effect sizes of 3.45, 3.25, and 2.56, respectively. Again, no differences among these treatments emerged. Only 25 treatment studies conducted between 1975 and 1991 were considered appropriate for this analysis, of which just 9 included an exposure-based behavior therapy (BT) condition. Studies were excluded if they were case studies, reported only percentages of improved patients, or if it was determined that there was insufficient information (e.g., no reporting of means and standard deviations) to calculate Cohen's d for conversion to Z scores. Notably, many seminal studies of EX/RP (e.g., Foa & Goldstein, 1978; Marks et al., 1975) were excluded from this analysis.

In a third meta-analysis, studies on the efficacy of antidepressants, exposure-based behavior therapy, cognitive therapy (CT), and the combination of these methods were included (van Balkom et al., 1994). The literature search for this analysis yielded 86 studies published between 1970 and 1993 that provided sufficient information to calculate effect sizes; a total of 2569 patients were available for posttest following a 13% dropout rate across studies. Serotonergic antidepressants, behavior therapy, cognitive therapy, and the combination of antidepressants plus behavior therapy and a placebo plus behavior therapy were associated with large effect sizes (1.63, 1.47, 1.04, 1.99, and 1.85, respectively) for improvements in assessor-rated OCD symptoms of depression, general anxiety, and social adjustment; behavior therapy alone and in combination with serotonergic antidepressants were significantly superior to a PBO. Moreover, on some measures of OCD, behavior therapy yielded a superior outcome to that of SRIs. The authors noted the lack of data on long-term efficacy.

Using a less-sophisticated method, Foa and Kozak (1996) summarized both the short-term and long-term efficacies of EX/RP, focusing on rate of responding. Immediately after therapy, 83% of 330 OCD patients treated in 12 studies were identified as treatment responders. At follow-up ($M = 2.4$ years; range 3 months to 6 years), 76% of 376 OCD patients in 16 studies were responders. The 83% responder rate after CBT contrasts with the 61% rate for CMI found in the largest study of this medication (DeVeaugh-Geiss, Landau, & Katz, 1989). The contrast of the 76% follow-up responder rate for CBT compared with CMI is even more striking because of the high relapse rate (89%) on CMI discontinuation (Pato, Zohar-Kadouch, Zohar, & Murphy, 1988).

Several methodological drawbacks of the meta-analytic studies described above render their results inconclusive. First, results from uncontrolled and controlled studies were given equal weight, thereby potentially inflating the effects of EX/RP by including nonspecific treatment effects. Second, meta-analysis of EX/RP treatments is particularly problematic because studies varied greatly in how this treatment was implemented. Specifically, studies varied with respect to the setting in which treatment was conducted (inpatient v. outpatient), length and frequency of treatment sessions, extent of therapist involvement in exposure

exercises, strictness of ritual prevention rules, extent and nature of homework assignments, and inclusion of imaginal exposure. Several of these parameters have been shown to influence outcome substantially (e.g., Foa et al., 1984; Rabavilas, Boulougouris, & Stefanis, 1976), accentuating the inherent problem of collapsing across disparate procedures.

Gold Standard Obsessive Compulsive Disorder Treatment Outcome Studies

Given the problems with the existing meta-analytical studies, we move on now to a review of EX/RP studies. The following study selection criteria were used:

1. The sample comprised OCD patients.
2. There was at least one comparison group.
3. There were at least eight patients per experimental cell.

The validity of each study's results was evaluated by considering the set of criteria that defines our "ideal" treatment outcome study. These include

1. Clearly defined inclusion/exclusion criteria.
2. Reliable and valid diagnostic methods.
3. Random assignment to treatment condition.
4. Blind assessments by trained assessors using reliable and valid outcome measures.
5. Manualized treatments.
6. Measures of treatment adherence.
7. Adequate sample size for statistical power.
8. Appropriate statistical analyses.
9. Exposure and ritual prevention that meets acceptable clinical practice standards as suggested by expert consensus (see Kozak & Foa, 1996).

Adequate planned systematic exposure was defined as involving confrontation of obsession-evoking stimuli of sufficient duration (typically 90 minutes or longer), frequency (15–20 sessions), and spacing (initially at least once/week, but often more frequently). Adequate ritual prevention should occur immediately after exposure and include patients' voluntary compliance with instructions to refrain from ritualizing and procedures to help the patient achieve the greatest reduction in rituals possible. Exposure and ritual prevention should also be exercised between sessions.

We review these studies by topic in order to provide a sense of which issues in OCD treatment outcome have already been addressed adequately, as well as to acknowledge those areas that need to be addressed.

The Separate Effects of Exposure In Vivo, Imaginal Exposure, and Ritual Prevention

In early studies of the efficacy of EX/RP for OCD (e.g., Foa & Goldstein, 1978; Meyer et al., 1974), exposure and ritual prevention were implemented concurrently, thus making it impossible to determine the contribution of each procedure alone to outcome. To address this issue, Foa et al. (1984) assigned patients with washing rituals to treatment by exposure only, ritual prevention only, or their combination. Each treatment was conducted intensively (15 daily 2-hour sessions conducted over 3 weeks) and was followed by a home visit. Blind assessors evaluated patients' symptoms at pretreatment, posttreatment, and follow-up; patients also completed self-report measures at each assessment. All treatments were effective, and gains were maintained at follow-up (M = 12 months, range 3 to 24 months). Assessor ratings of obsessions were reduced at posttreatment by 36% for EX, 28% for RP, and 63% for EX/RP; at follow-up, reductions from pretreatment ratings of 25% for EX, 29% for RP, and 48% for EX/RP were observed. On assessor ratings of ritual severity, the following reductions were observed: 50% for EX, 45% for RP, and 63% for EX/RP at posttreatment and 15% for EX, 26% for RP, and 63% for EX/RP at follow-up. The combined treatment was superior to the single-component treatments on almost every symptom measure at both posttreatment and follow-up. In comparing the single-component treatments to one another, EX patients had lower ratings of anxiety than RP patients on confrontation with feared contaminants in a posttreatment exposure test, and RP patients reported greater decreases in the urge to ritualize than did EX patients, suggesting that the two components affect OC symptoms differently.

Patients were allocated to groups by a serial assignment procedure to balance for level of depression, gender, and therapist. In studies with small samples (cell sizes ranged from 9 to 12), this procedure is advantageous compared to random assignment because it ensures across-group equality on outcome-related factors. Inclusion/exclusion criteria were clearly described, and blind assessors rated patients' symptoms using reliable and valid outcome measures. Treatments were described in detail although they were not manualized and treatment integrity was not assessed. Statistical analyses were generally appropriate, although setting a more conservative alpha level or correcting for the large number of tests may have been advisable.

In the Foa and Goldstein (1978) open clinical trial, EX/RP was accompanied by imaginal exposure (I/EX). To examine the additive effect of imaginal exposure, patients with checking rituals were treated with either ten 2-hour sessions of EX/RP delivered over 2 weeks or ten sessions of EX/RP plus I/EX (Foa, Steketee, Turner, & Fischer, 1980b). Sessions were 2 hours long and consisted of either 90-minute I/EX and 30-minute in vivo EX or 2 hours of in vivo EX only. Immediately after treatment, the mean symptom reduction in the EX/RP group was 66% for obsessions and 75% for compulsions; the EX/RP plus I/EX group showed evidence of reductions of 63% for obsessions and 70% for compulsions. No posttreatment group differences were detected on six OC symptom outcome measures. However, group differences did emerge at follow-up (M follow-up = 11 months, range 3 months to 2.5 years): on four out of six measures, the group receiving I/EX was less symptomatic compared with pretreatment. Specifically, mean reductions in obsessions and compulsions at follow-up were 43% and 53%, respectively, for EX/RP alone and 72% and 74% for EX/RP plus I/EX. Thus, imaginal exposure seems to contribute to maintenance of treatment gains. The results of this study underscore the importance of obtaining follow-up data; in the absence of these data, the effects of I/EX would not have been detected.

The Foa et al. study (1980b) specified inclusion/exclusion criteria, treatments were described clearly and implemented in accordance with accepted clinical practice standards, blind assessors rated symptom severity, and statistical analyses were conducted appropriately. While the design met some of our gold standard criteria, several methodological problems should be noted. Patients were assigned to a condition according to order of applying for treatment rather than randomly, diagnostic methods were not described, measures of treatment adherence were not included, and sample size (15) was marginal.

To further examine whether the addition of I/EX to EX/RP enhances treatment efficacy, de Araujo, Ito, Marks, and Deale (1995) replicated the Foa et al. (1980b) design, but the treatment program and the patient population differ across the two studies. Patients in this study had a range of rituals, and treatment included a mean of 9 weekly 90-minute sessions of either in vivo EX or 30-minute I/EX and 60 minutes in vivo EX. At posttreatment, both groups showed evidence of reductions on measures of OC symptoms including the Yale-Brown Obsessive Compulsive Scale (Y-BOCS) (46% reduction in Y-BOCS total for EX/RP group, 48% for EX/RP plus I/EX), as well as on measures of depression and disability. No group differences were found either at posttreatment or at 6-month follow-up (42% reduction in Y-BOCS total for EX/RP group, 49% for EX/RP plus I/EX), suggesting no augmentive effect for imaginal exposure.

The de Arauja et al. (1995) study had several strengths, including utilization of random assignment to condition, blind assessors, clearly stated inclusion/exclusion criteria, adequate sample size for completer data ($n = 23$ per cell), appropriate outcome measures (Y-BOCS, Hamilton Depression Rating Scale [HAM-D]), and clearly described treatments. However, assessor training was not described, diagnostic methods were not explicated ("patients who met *DSM-III-R* criteria for OCD . . . "), and treatment adherence was not measured. Moreover, because in the Foa et al. (1980b) study the effects of imaginal exposure were not detected until an average of 11 months posttreatment, the length of follow-up (6 months) in the de Araujo et al. (1995) study may have been insufficient to detect such effects. Also, the treatment procedure and patient samples of the two studies differ in important ways that were likely to produce different results. Specifically, treatment was conducted daily in the Foa et al. study, sessions were of 2-hour duration, and imaginal exposure was 90-minutes long; in the de Araujo et al. study, treatment was conducted weekly, sessions were 90 minutes in duration, and imaginal exposure was conducted over 30 minutes only. These procedural differences are troublesome because they reflect a general tendency in treatment research. Namely, researchers who intend to examine the replicability of a previous result do not always adhere to the procedure of the treatment they choose to examine, and therefore resultant differences in outcome are uninterpretable.

Does the Addition of Cognitive Procedures Enhance Efficacy of Exposure and Ritual Prevention?

The increased interest in cognitive therapy (e.g., Beck, 1976; Ellis, 1962) has prompted researchers to examine the efficacy of cognitive procedures for OCD. The impetus for this originated from growing dissatisfaction with existing formulations of pathological anxiety and its treatment as mediated by automatic processes such as extinction (Stampfl & Levis, 1967) or habituation (Watts, 1973). In the first study that explores cognitive therapy for OCD, Emmelkamp, van der Helm, van Zanten, and Plochg (1980) compared a combination of self-instructional training (SIT) (Meichenbaum, 1974) plus EX/RP to EX/RP alone. Treatment was conducted twice weekly, and sessions were of 2-hour duration. Following three sessions of information gathering, all patients received two sessions of progressive relaxation training. In the EX/PE only condition, 10 treatment sessions began with 30 minutes of relaxation followed by 90 minutes of exposure in vivo; in the combined treatment, 30 minutes of relaxation and self-instructional training were followed by 90 minutes of exposure in vivo. Both groups improved on all outcome measures; a mean posttreatment reduction of 56% in anxiety and 57% in avoidance associated with the main compulsive problem was observed on assessor ratings of all patients. Data for each treatment group were not presented separately. On assessor-rated avoidance associated with the main compulsion, a superiority of EX/RP alone emerged. Thus, self-instructional training seemed to have hindered outcome.

The Emmelkamp et al. (1980) study meets some of our outcome trial standards, but a number of procedural and methodological difficulties remain. Patients were allocated to groups randomly, and outcome was evaluated by a blind assessor on standard measures of OC symptoms (e.g., avoidance, anxiety) at pre-and posttreatment; however, at follow-up, therapist and patient ratings were substituted for blind assessor ratings, introducing possible biases. Also, assessor training, diagnostic methods, and inclusion/exclusion criteria were not described. The treatment was described clearly, was conducted by graduate students, and was supervised by the first author; however, treatment adherence data were not reported. Statistical analyses were described clearly, but the small cell sizes (eight in EX/RP; seven in SIT plus EX/RP) may have obscured group differences. Moreover, the choice to collapse across the treatment group in presenting results makes it impossible for readers to examine these data to determine for themselves the influence of power on the failure to find a group effect.

The failure of self-instructional training to affect OCD symptoms more than EX/RP did led Emmelkamp, Visser, and Hoekstra (1988) to examine the efficacy of another cognitive approach, rational emotive therapy (RET). Emmelkamp et al. randomly assigned patients to one of two treatments, EX/RP or RET. Treatment consisted of 10 sessions (60 minutes each) conducted over 8 weeks; patients in both conditions were also given homework assignments. Outcome was assessed by self-report measures and by pooled ratings of OC symptom severity by therapists and patients. Both groups were improved at posttreatment: on the pooled OC symptom ratings, the RET group showed evidence of an average posttreatment improvement of 40%, and the EX/RP showed improvement of 51%. Two thirds of patients in both groups received additional treatment during follow-up, thus precluding conclusions about long-term maintenance of gains.

Emmelkamp et al.'s (1988) study included random assignment, treatment manuals, and a thorough discussion of treatment integrity. But, several limitations should be noted: inclusion/exclusion criteria and diagnostic methods were not described adequately, and assessment was not blind to treatment conditions, instead relying on therapists' and patients' ratings. A primary difficulty lies in the treatment procedure itself: sessions were only 60 minutes in length, held approximately once per week, did not include therapist-assisted exposure, included only two homework assignments per week, and seems to have employed a more gradual response prevention than is typically recommended. This truncated treatment program may have been responsible for the inferior outcome of EX/RP compared with that shown in other studies (e.g., Foa, Kozak, Steketee, & McCarthy, 1992).

In a further comparison of cognitive therapy with EX/RP, Emmelkamp and Beens (1991) compared a program that included 6 sessions of RET alone followed by 6 sessions of RET plus self-controlled EX/RP to a program that included 12 sessions of self-controlled EX/RP. In both programs, the first 6 sessions were followed by 4 weeks of no treatment, after which the additional 6 sessions were delivered. As in Emmelkamp et al.'s (1988) study, treatment sessions were conducted approximately once per week and lasted for 60 minutes each. The EX/RP sessions did not include therapist-assisted exposure, and patients were assigned twice-weekly exposure homework exercises. The RET program was equivalent to that employed in the Emmelkamp et al. (1988) study; when self-controlled EX/RP was introduced following the first 6 RET-only sessions, the cognitive procedures focused on irrational thoughts that occurred in response

to exposure homework exercises. Assessments were conducted at seven points over 44 weeks and involved patient, therapist, and assessor ratings of five OCD targets, as well as self-report measures (e.g., Maudsley Obsessional-Compulsive Inventory [MOCI]; Hodgson & Rachman, 1977). Immediately following the completion of six sessions of cognitive therapy without exposure and EX/RP (Week 9), mean reduction of anxiety associated with the main OC problem was only 25% for RET and 23% for EX/RP. Following six more sessions (RET plus EX/RP in one condition and EX/RP only in the other), both groups improved on most measures over time, and no significant group differences emerged. The authors interpreted the absence of group differences to indicate that cognitive therapy is as effective as EX/RP for OCD. This interpretation is somewhat confusing because it appeared that EX/RP was more effective on mean reduction in assessor-rated anxiety associated with the main OC problem (59% for EX/RP v. 36% for RET) yet less effective on patient-rated anxiety associated with the main OC problem (26% for EX/RP v. 53% for RET). Insufficient power to compare active treatments may have obscured between-group differences. Final follow-up data are uninterpretable because most patients received additional treatments after the first follow-up.

Many of the same methodological strengths noted for Emmelkamp et al. (1988) were also evident in this study: random assignment to treatment, blind assessments, clear inclusion/exclusion criteria, use of treatment manuals, and considerable attention to treatment integrity despite the absence of formal adherence measures. Approximately 33% of the sample dropped out during treatment, which is higher than reported in several other studies and has a negative impact on the generalizability of findings. Again, the main criticism of this study was the use of an EX/RP treatment that did not meet acceptable practice standards. In both studies, cognitive therapy was compared to a truncated version of EX/RP that may not have served as a sufficiently powerful comparison.

In a further examination of the efficacy of cognitive therapy for OCD, van Oppen et al. (1995) compared the efficacy of self-controlled EX/RP and a version of cognitive therapy developed to correct specific cognitive distortions hypothesized by Salkovskis (1985) to underlie OCD. The study included a medication condition (fluvoxamine), but only data from the psychosocial treatments are presented. Patients were randomly assigned to receive 16 sessions of cognitive therapy or EX/RP. Behavioral experiments (exposures) were not introduced into the cognitive treatment until after Session 6. Conversely, in the first six EX/RP sessions care was taken by the therapist to specifically avoid any discussion of disastrous consequences. The authors regarded this procedure as measuring the effects of "purer" versions of cognitive therapy and EX/RP. Cognitive therapy focused primarily on themes of danger overestimation and inflated personal responsibility. The EX/RP included self-exposure, with patients determining the speed at which they worked through the fear hierarchy. Sessions in both treatment conditions lasted for 45 minutes. Results were similar to the studies of cognitive therapy reviewed above. After six sessions of cognitive therapy without behavioral experiments and EX/RP without discussion of disastrous consequences, Y-BOCS reductions of 20% and 23% were observed for cognitive therapy and EX/RP, respectively. At posttreatment, both groups improved on almost all measures, including the Y-BOCS and Beck Depression Inventory (BDI) (Beck, Ward, Mendeleson, Mock, & Erbaugh, 1961). However, inspection of the mean Y-BOCS scores for the EX/RP condition suggested that outcome at posttreatment (45% Y-BOCS reduction for CT, 32% for EX/RP) was inferior to that achieved in other studies (e.g., Foa et al., 1992). It also appeared that there was very little effect for adding discussion of disastrous outcomes in EX/RP at midtreatment (10% reduction from midtest to posttreatment). It should be noted that in many outcome studies a Y-BOCS score of 17, the posttreatment mean for the EX/RP group, is considered sufficiently severe to meet inclusion criteria.

Random assignment to treatments, reliable and valid diagnostic procedures, clear inclusion and exclusion criteria, use of treatment manuals, attention to treatment adherence, adequate sample size, and sophisticated statistical analyses all constitute strengths of van Oppen et al.'s (1995) preliminary report. In particular, the authors use state-of-the-art reliable change indices to examine the clinical relevance of their data. However, several methodological shortcomings should be noted. No mention is made of assessor blindness or training nor is data on treatment adherence provided. Most importantly, as noted above, the EX/RP version employed in this study was inadequate. First, the length of the session was relatively short (45 minutes), and sessions were held once per week instead of the more frequent schedule recommended. Second, it is unclear how much homework patients were asked to complete between sessions, how long their homework exposures were, and to what extent patients complied with homework assignments. Third, discussion of negative consequences in the first six sessions is an important component of EX/RP, and banning such discussion constitutes further diluting of this treatment and its rationale (see Foa & Kozak, 1996). As would be expected, the results of this truncated treatment were at best modest, with a mean 32% reduction of OCD symptoms at posttreatment.

Hiss, Foa, and Kozak (1994) conducted an investigation of whether adding a formal relapse prevention program following intensive EX/RP enhanced maintenance of therapeutic gains. In this study, all components typically included to address relapse prevention (e.g., discussion of lapse v. relapse, posttreatment exposure instructions, themes of guilt and personal responsibility) were removed from the 15 daily sessions of the intensive phase. All patients ($n = 20$) received the modified EX/RP followed by either a relapse prevention treatment or a psychosocial control treatment (associative therapy). All patients were responders (defined as 50% or greater reduction in OCD symptoms) to EX/RP at posttreatment. Nonparametric analyses of 6-month follow-up data indicated significantly less relapse in the relapse prevention group than in the associative therapy condition: 87% of patients in the relapse prevention condition remained improved (≥50% reduction from pretreatment), compared with 50% of the associative therapy group. On the Y-BOCS, the percentages of responders at follow-up were 75% in the relapse prevention condition and 33% in the associative therapy condition, respectively. Interestingly, the exclusion of discussion about cognitions related to themes of personal responsibility and guilt during EX/RP somewhat attenuated the efficacy of the core treatment at 6-month follow-up in the associative therapy group specifically. The posttreatment outcome for EX/RP (66% and 60% Y-BOCS reductions for relapse prevention and associative therapy conditions, respectively) was still far superior to that reported by van Oppen et al. (1995), who also excluded cognitive interventions during the first part of their EX/RP treatment. It seems, therefore, that the inferior outcome in the last study was due in the main to other factors, such as shorter sessions, the absence of therapist-assisted exposure, or the increased spacing of sessions.

The Hiss, Foa and Kozak (1994) study met most of the criteria delineated above. Inclusion/exclusion criteria, diagnostic methods, and treatments were described clearly, treatment assignment was random, trained assessors evaluated patients using reliable and valid measures, statistical analyses were appropriate, and treatment was implemented according to accepted standards of clinical practice. Although close supervision to promote treatment integrity was discussed, treatment integrity measures were not provided.

Exposure and Ritual Prevention versus Pharmacotherapy

The first study that compared EX/RP to medication (pharmacotherapy) was conducted by Marks et al. (1980); preliminary results from this same trial had been reported earlier by Rachman et al. (1979). Using a complex experimental design, 40 patients were randomly assigned to receive either clomipramine or a pill placebo (PBO) for 4 weeks. This was followed by 6 weeks of inpatient psychological treatment (daily 45-minute sessions). During the first three weeks of this phase, 10 patients from each medication condition received EX/RP, while the other 10 received relaxation. At Week 7, those patients who had received relaxation were switched to EX/RP, and the remaining patients continued to receive EX/RP. At the end of the 6-week psychosocial treatment period, patients were discharged from the hospital but remained on medication until Week 36, when a 4-week taper period commenced. Patients were followed for another year after drug discontinuation. Results suggested that, compared to a placebo, clomipramine produced significant improvements in mood and rituals only in those patients who were initially depressed. Compared to relaxation at Week 7, EX/RP was associated with greater reductions in rituals, but not with improvements in mood.

This study meets several of our gold standard criteria: patients were randomly assigned to treatment conditions, blind raters assessed patients' symptoms on psychometrically acceptable measures, reasonable exclusion criteria were used, sample size ($n = 40$; 10 per experimental cell) was sufficient to detect at least moderate-size group differences, statistical analyses were described clearly, and the treatments were described in sufficient detail. Several methodological issues, including an overly complex experimental design, made interpretation of their findings difficult: diagnostic methods were not described at all ("Patients were considered suitable . . . if they had handicapping

obsessional-compulsive rituals"); no reference was made to assessor training on the outcome measures; no treatment adherence measures were used; and the inpatient behavior therapy condition, consisting of 45-minute daily sessions for 3–6 weeks (depending on treatment condition), may have employed insufficiently strict response prevention instructions ("After exposure [in session], patients were asked not to carry out rituals for the rest of the session and to resist ritualizing for a specified time thereafter"). Length of treatment session may also have been problematic, as was the lack of information regarding what patients did on the inpatient unit for 6 weeks when they were not in session. Weaknesses in the experimental design led to underestimation of changes attributable to the behavioral treatment at Week 7 (EX/RP v. relaxation comparison), and the design did not allow for a direct comparison of clomipramine and exposure alone across the same time period. Moreover, the drug-only period was too short (4 weeks) to allow optimal assessment of the efficacy of clomipramine alone.

In a subsequent comparison of clomipramine and EX/RP in 49 obsessive compulsive individuals (Marks et al., 1988), patients were assigned randomly to one of four treatment conditions, three of which included CMI for approximately 6 months and one that included a pill placebo (PBO). One of the CMI groups received antiexposure instructions for 23 weeks, the second group had self-controlled exposure for 23 weeks, and the third group received self-controlled exposure for 8 weeks followed by therapist-aided exposure from Week 8 until Week 23; the PBO group also received self-controlled exposure for 8 weeks, followed by therapist-aided exposure from Week 8 until Week 23. Inspection of the means in the PBO group at the different treatment stages revealed clear superiority for therapist-aided exposure over self-exposure. The mean reductions after 8 weeks of self-exposure were 20% for rituals and 23% for OCD-related discomfort; the mean reductions after an additional nine sessions of therapist-aided exposure were 71% and 68% for rituals and OCD-related discomfort, respectively. However, in the absence of a placebo group that received therapist-aided exposure first, we cannot rule out the alternative hypothesis that order effect mediated the superiority of therapist-aided exposure. Because of confounds introduced by the complicated design, it is impossible to compare the effects of CMI with those of EX/RP.

Marks et al. (1988) provided a clear description of inclusion/exclusion criteria, employed random assignment, and utilized psychometrically acceptable outcome measures. A major problem with this study is the design adopted by the authors, which introduced major confounds. Thus, the two major questions of interest, the relative efficacy of CMI versus EX/RP and the relative efficacy of self-exposure versus therapist-aided exposure, cannot be answered with certainty. Several other problems complicate interpretation of the findings: diagnostic methods were not described, treatment adherence data were not provided, treatment descriptions were sparse, and time spent on exposure homework was not reported. The last point is especially important because of the authors' interest in the efficacy of self-exposure programs. An additional confound stems from the evaluators' ability to guess accurately 90% of the time whether patients received CMI or PBO, indicating an inadequate blinding procedure due to the evaluators' inquiry about medication side effects during assessment of OC symptoms.

With the growing interest in selective SRIs and the growing awareness of the severe side effects of CMI, Cottraux et al. (1990) compared the efficacy of another SRI, fluvoxamine (FLX), with that of EX/RP. Patients were assigned to one of three conditions: FLX with antiexposure instructions, FLX plus EX/RP, and pill placebo (PBO) with EX/RP. In the antiexposure condition, patients were specifically instructed to avoid feared situations or stimuli. Treatment continued for 24 weeks, after which EX/RP was stopped and medication was tapered over 4 weeks. The EX/RP treatment was provided in weekly sessions and consisted of two distinct treatment phases: self-controlled exposure between sessions and imaginal exposure during sessions for the first 8 weeks, followed by 16 weeks of therapist-guided exposure and ritual prevention. Other psychosocial interventions (e.g., couples' therapy, cognitive restructuring, assertiveness training) were also provided as deemed necessary. Assessment included ratings by blind evaluators and self-report measures. At posttreatment (Week 24), reductions in assessor-rated duration of rituals per day were FLX plus antiexposure 42%, FLX plus EX/RP 46%, and PBO plus EX/RP 25%. At 6-month follow-up, reductions in assessor-rated duration of rituals per day were FLX plus antiexposure 42%, FLX plus EX/RP 45%, and PBO plus EX/RP 35%. While FLX plus EX/RP produced slightly greater improvement in depression at posttreatment than did PBO plus EX/RP, the superiority of the combined treatment for depression was not evident at follow-up. Interestingly, the FLX plus

antiexposure group complied minimally with therapy instructions: most reported doing exposure on their own, thus invalidating the comparison between exposure and antiexposure with fluvoxamine.

Cottraux et al. (1990) randomly assigned patients to treatment conditions, used blind assessors, conducted appropriate nonparametric statistical analyses because of skewed distributions, provided estimates of power to detect differences on OC symptom measures, and used adequate inclusion/exclusion criteria. They did not, however, describe diagnostic methods adequately or provide treatment adherence ratings. The primary problem with this study lies in the implementation of EX/RP. The EX/RP treatment description was inadequate; it was described only as "flexible," included the use of myriad other techniques (e.g., couples' therapy, cognitive restructuring, assertion training) on an "as needed" basis, and ritual prevention instructions were not provided. Moreover, treatment sessions were conducted just once per week for an unspecified length of time.

To examine the validity of Marks et al.'s (1980) assertion that antidepressant medication reduces OCD symptoms only via reduction of depression, and the common observation that depression hinders the effects of EX/RP, Foa et al. (1992) divided OCD patients into highly depressed (BDI $\geq$ 21) and mildly depressed (BDI $\leq$ 20) groups. Patients in each group were randomly assigned to receive either 6 weeks of treatment by imipramine or a placebo (PBO). On completion of the pills-only phase, all patients received 3-week (15-session) intensive EX/RP followed by 12 weekly supportive sessions. Independent evaluators rated patients' OC and depressive symptoms at pretreatment, the end of the pills-only phase (Week 6), the end of intensive EX/RP (Week 10), the end of weekly supportive BT (Week 22), and at three follow-up periods. Contrary to the hypothesis, while imipramine reduced depression in the depressed patients, it did not significantly reduce OCD symptoms in either depressed or nondepressed patients at Week 6: mean reductions of 13% and 26% in assessor-rated fear were observed in depressed and nondepressed imipramine patients, respectively, as were reductions of 17% and 34% on assessor-rated compulsive behavior for depressed and nondepressed imipramine patients, respectively. Moreover, imipramine did not enhance immediate or long-term outcome of EX/RP in either group: OCD and depressive symptoms were both significantly reduced in each of the four groups following

EX/RP, even in the depressed group who initially received the placebo. Mean percentage reductions in assessor ratings of obsessions and compulsions at posttreatment (Week 10) were as follows: 58% and 82%, respectively, for the depressed imipramine group; 42% and 85%, respectively, for the depressed placebo group; 51% and 82%, respectively, for the nondepressed imipramine group; and 64% and 84%, respectively, for the nondepressed placebo group.

Foa et al.'s (1992) study met several gold standard criteria: random assignment to treatments, clearly described inclusion and exclusion criteria, blind assessments using reliable and valid outcome measures, clearly described treatments, adequate sample sizes (minimum nine per cell) with appropriate statistical analysis of completer data, and EX/RP meeting acceptable clinical practice standards. This study does not, however, describe the diagnostic methods, does not report use of a treatment manual, and does not provide treatment adherence data. Another problem is the report on completer data only, especially in light of the removal of seven patients from EX/RP conditions for treatment noncompliance and three from drug conditions because of side effects. Inclusion of these patients in an intent-to-treat analysis may have revealed different patterns from those found in completers.

As discussed above, previous comparisons of EX/RP and pharmacotherapy have utilized experimental designs that made direct comparisons of their relative efficacy uninterpretable (e.g., Marks et al., 1980, 1988) or examined the efficacy of antidepressant medications not known to have specific effects on OCD symptoms (e.g., Foa et al., 1992). A multicenter study is in progress at Allegheny University of the Health Sciences (formerly Medical College of Pennsylvania and Hahnemann University) and Columbia University, aiming at providing a clear comparison of the efficacy of CMI, intensive EX/RP, and their combination. In this study, an EX/RP program that includes an intensive phase (fifteen 2-hour sessions conducted over 3 weeks) and follow-up phase (six brief sessions delivered over 8 weeks) is compared to CMI, EX/RP plus CMI, and PBO. Preliminary analyses of completer data (61 subjects that completed the 3-month active treatment period) suggest that at 1 month (the end of intensive BT) and 3 months (the end of CMI), significant differences were obtained on the Y-BOCS. Mean percentage reductions on Y-BOCS at 1 month were as follows: EX/RP, 54%; CMI plus EX/RP, 58%;

CMI, 21%; and PBO, 2%. At 3 months, they were EX/RP, 47%; CMI plus BT, 55%; CMI, 32%; and PBO, 6%. Additional analyses were conducted to examine the percentage of respondents in each treatment, with responding defined as a score of much improved (2) or very much improved (1) on the 7-point Clinical Global Impression (CGI) Scale. Mean percentages of responders at 1 month were as follows: EX/RP, 92%; CMI plus EX/RP, 79%; CMI, 50%; and PBO, 6%. At 3 months, they were as follows: EX/RP, 85%; CMI plus BT, 71%; CMI, 18%; and PBO, 0%. Thus, it appears that EX/RP is more efficacious than CMI, and the combination of the two treatments is not superior to EX/RP alone. However, the design adopted in the Allegheny-Columbia study may not have been appropriate for promoting an additive effect because the EX/RP program was largely completed before the effects of CMI could be realized.

In the multicenter study still in progress, diagnostic status was determined by structured clinical interview, patients were randomly assigned to treatments, and assessments were conducted by trained blind evaluators. Treatments were manualized, measures of treatment adherence were included, OCD severity was assessed at pre- and posttreatment, and follow-up used reliable and valid measures (e.g., Y-BOCS). In addition, intent-to-treat analyses were conducted to examine treatment effects with dropouts included for each condition.

In summary, there is ample information about the efficacy of both pharmaceutical and EX/RP treatments, but information about their relative efficacy is scarce because most of the few studies that addressed this issue are plagued with design and procedural deficiencies. Interestingly, the results of all studies failed to find clear long-term superiority for treatments that combined pharmacotherapy and EX/RP. Despite this clear consensus, many experts advocate combined procedures as the treatment of choice for OCD (e.g., Greist, 1992).

Individual Versus Group Exposure and Ritual Prevention

Efficacy of group and individual behavior therapy was examined in a study by Fals-Stewart, Marks, and Schafer (1993). The OCD patients were randomly assigned to receive EX/RP conducted individually, group EX/RP treatment, or a psychosocial placebo (relaxation). Each of the active treatments was 12 weeks long, with sessions held twice weekly, and included daily exposure homework assignments. Results indicated significant reductions in OC symptoms at posttreatment only in the two active treatments: mean Y-BOCS reduction was 40% for individual EX/RP, 46% for group EX/RP, and 9% for attention control. Moreover, no differences between individual and group EX/RP were detected at posttreatment or at 6-month follow-up (mean Y-BOCS reduction at follow-up = 36% for individual EX/RP, 37% for group EX/RP), although profile analysis of Y-BOCS scores collected throughout treatment indicated a faster reduction in symptoms for patients receiving individual treatment. These results offer evidence for the efficacy of group treatment, considered by the authors to be especially important in light of efficiency and practicality of treatment delivery afforded by group approaches.

Fals-Stewart et al.'s (1993) study had several strengths. Diagnostic interviews were conducted by trained social workers, and outcome measures were acceptable (e.g., Y-BOCS). Sample size was more than sufficient (30–32 per cell), and there were only four dropouts from treatment following randomization. Statistical analyses were appropriate, and therapy was provided by trained social workers experienced with OCD treatment. Difficulties interpreting the study's results arise, however, from the inclusion/exclusion criteria and from the specific form of EX/RP used. Patients were excluded from the study if they were diagnosed with any personality disorder or with comorbid major depression with a BDI greater than 22. This exclusion criterion, together with the relatively low pretreatment Y-BOCS scores (range 19 to 22) and the fact that all 93 patients had never received previous treatment for OCD, render the sample atypical. This limits the generalizability of findings that group and individual treatments are equally effective.

Family Involvement Versus Standard Treatment

Influenced by findings that efficacy of exposure therapy for panic disorder with agoraphobia is enhanced by partner assistance, Emmelkamp et al. (1990) examined whether such assistance would also enhance the efficacy of EX/RP for OCD. Patients who were married or living with a romantic partner were randomly assigned to receive EX/RP either with or without partner involvement in treatment. Each treatment lasted 5 weeks and consisted of eight 45–60 minute sessions

with the therapist; exposures were not practiced in session. Patients and partners rated their symptoms at four assessment periods; independent evaluators rated patients only before and after treatment. Results indicated that OCD severity was significantly reduced immediately after treatment for both groups: a mean 33% reduction in assessor-rated anxiety-discomfort was observed for the sample as a whole. No group differences were detected, and initial marital distress did not predict outcome. It is important to note that, similar to the results from Emmelkamp and his colleagues described earlier, while the mean pre-post symptom reduction reached statistical significance, the modest reduction may not reflect clinically significant improvement.

In the Emmelkamp et al. (1990) study, eligible patients (those with partners) were randomly assigned to treatment. Blind assessors were used, but only at two assessment periods, and training on the measures was not discussed. Inclusion/exclusion criteria were clearly described, although diagnostic methods were not. Sample size (50) was more than adequate, and there were very few treatment dropouts. Statistical analyses were conducted appropriately, although in the tabular presentation of results the group condition was collapsed. Description of treatments did not include sufficient details regarding how ritual prevention was discussed with patients, and treatment adherence data were not provided. As with studies discussed above, no therapist-assisted exposure was included and between-session exposure homework was assigned only twice per week. These diluted procedures seem to have produced only modest symptom reductions.

Mehta (1990) also examined the adjunctive role of family involvement in EX/RP treatment in a study conducted in India. In order to adapt the treatment to serve the large numbers of young unmarried people seeking OCD treatment and the "joint family system" prevalent in India, a family-based rather than spouse-based treatment approach was utilized. Patients (n = 30) previously nonresponsive to pharmacotherapy were randomly assigned to receive treatment by systematic desensitization and EX/RP either with or without family assistance. Sessions in both conditions were held twice per week for 12 weeks; response prevention was "gradual . . . to reduce the frequency of the target behavior until they reached a desired level." In the family condition, a designated family member (parent, spouse, or adult child) assisted with homework assignments, supervised relaxation therapy, participated in response prevention, and was instructed to be supportive when patients became depressed and anxious. On the only measure of OCD symptoms, the MOCI, increased improvement was found for the family-based intervention at posttreatment and 6-month follow-up: MOCI reductions of 56% at posttreatment and 61% at follow-up were observed in the family treatment, compared to 39% at posttreatment and 29% at follow-up for individual treatment.

In Mehta's (1990) study, patients were randomly assigned to treatment, and sample size was satisfactory. However, OC symptoms were assessed exclusively by self-report (MOCI), introducing a possible bias. Inclusion/exclusion criteria and diagnostic methods were not specified in sufficient detail. While the number of treatment sessions was sufficient, treatment descriptions were sketchy (e.g., degree to which relaxation training was emphasized), and no treatment adherence data were provided. The statistical analyses consisted of between-subject t tests at each assessment occasion; a mixed-design analysis of variance (ANOVA) would have been more appropriate. Despite its shortcomings, the study does provide interesting information about the efficacy of EX/RP treatment within the context of a culture in which family relationships are thought to be especially important.

SUMMARY AND CONCLUSIONS

Since Victor Meyer introduced treatment by exposure and response prevention in 1966, the efficacy of this treatment for OCD has been established in numerous studies. It should be noted, however, that until the middle of the 1980s the treatment used in most outcome studies was intensive, with long therapist-assisted exposure sessions conducted daily (e.g., Foa & Goldstein, 1978; Marks et al., 1975). Rules for ritual prevention were explicit, and its implementation was either supervised by staff members for inpatients or by designated individuals at home for outpatients (e.g., Foa et al., 1984; Meyer et al., 1974). The results of studies using these intensive programs were extremely favorable. In the last 10 years, because of increasing concerns with managed care demands and treatment cost, exposure and ritual prevention programs have been attenuated by reducing the number of sessions, spacing and shortening them, and relying on instructions for self-exposure and ritual prevention. As is apparent from the above review, such attenuation resulted in

the decreasing of efficacy to the extent that degree of observed improvement, albeit statistically significant, often failed to reach clinical significance.

Another issue that deserves attention is the role of cognitive procedures in the treatment of OCD. Are they necessary? Are they useful? As noted above, the interest in cognitive therapy for anxiety disorders stemmed from dissatisfaction with theories that invoked automatic ("noncognitive") processes such as extinction or habituation to explain pathological anxiety and the mechanisms underlying treatments that have ensued from conditioning theory such as exposure therapy. Interestingly, learning theorists have reconceptualized conditioning phenomena within the information processing framework (e.g., Rescorla & Cunningham, 1977; Rescorla & Heth, 1975), invoking concepts of meaning to understand why a red light associated with shock comes to elicit fear. In contrast, behavior therapists remained committed to noncognitive accounts of the efficacy of exposure therapy. This view was expressed by Emmelkamp et al. (1980), who maintained that "treatment by exposure and response prevention focuses on a modification of both passive and active avoidance behavior . . . no attempt is made to alter the cognitions of obsessive-compulsive patients directly" (p. 61). Those dissatisfied with noncognitive accounts of OCD further argue that adequate treatment for OCD should modify pathological cognitions thought to underlie the disorder. Since exposure does not address these cognitions directly, cognitive therapy should be employed. This was indeed the rationale for the application of cognitive therapy for panic disorder (e.g., Clark, 1986) and for social phobia (Mattick & Peters, 1988).

A more unified approach was advanced by Foa and Kozak (1986) who, like modern learning theorists, invoked an information processing framework to explain pathological fear and its treatment. Specifically, they proposed that fear reduction involves emotional processing, which they defined as the modification of cognitive structures. They further suggested that exposure therapy is successful to the extent that it activates the fear structure and introduces information that is incompatible with its pathological elements and thereby modifies them. Thus, emotional processing theory views both exposure and cognitive therapy as targeting pathological cognitions.

Support for this view comes from two studies. With panic-disordered individuals, Margraf and Schneider

(1995) found that, after treatment, both cognitive therapy and exposure therapy were highly effective. As would be predicted by emotional theory, degree of improvement with both treatments was highly associated with change in the dysfunctional cognitions thought to be involved in the maintenance of panic disorder. At 2-year follow-up, improvement was still highly associated with change in cognition in both programs. Similar results were reported by Mattick, Peters, and Clarke (1989) for social phobics: improvement in social anxiety was related to change in socially relevant irrational beliefs regardless of whether patients received exposure or cognitive therapy.

On first sight, the absence of differences between EX/RP alone and cognitive therapy alone for OCD seem consistent with the findings mentioned above for panic disorder and social phobia. However, the OCD data are dissimilar on two accounts. First, in the case of panic disorder and social anxiety, both exposure and cognitive therapy treatments were highly effective, whereas both therapies, as reported in Emmelkamp and Beens (1991) and van Oppen et al. (1995), failed to induce a clinically significant reduction in OCD symptoms. Second, the specific irrational beliefs implicated in OCD were not measured, and therefore the effects of the two procedures on these cognitions cannot be ascertained.

Immersed in the theoretical debate about the relative role of extinction (habituation) versus cognitive modification in the amelioration of pathological anxiety, many experts on behavior therapy for anxiety disorders have downplayed the degree to which they have been employing cognitive procedures, albeit informally, during therapist-aided exposure exercises. Examples are typical discussions such as, "You have touched the floor many times during last week and you did not get sick. How do you explain this?" or, "During the last few days you have successfully stopped retracing your driving routes to check whether or not you've hit somebody. Do you think you have become a reckless driver?" Thus, while EX/RP strategies emphasize confrontation with fear-evoking material and the refraining from rituals, behavior therapists customarily facilitate cognitive changes by addressing the patient's dysfunctional beliefs via discussions and Socratic questioning. It is important to note that, just as exposure therapy typically involves cognitive procedures, so does the implementation of cognitive therapy often include exposure components in the form of behavioral experiments or instructions for in vivo exposure between sessions aimed at "testing" the patient's distorted cognition.

If the premises proposed above are valid, then the discourse should shift from theoretical to practical grounds. Accordingly, instead of debating whether habituation or cognitive modification underlies successful reduction of OCD symptoms, we should focus our attention on delineating which procedures are best suited for correcting identified pathological emotions or behaviors. Then, the questions of interest become: Is pathological meaning underlying circumscribed fear and avoidance better modified by exposure? Is irrational guilt more amenable to change by procedures that utilize verbal discussion? Research that addresses such questions is more likely to advance our knowledge than comparison among treatments that comprise overlapping components.

FUTURE DIRECTIONS

While a great deal is already known about the efficacy of EX/RP and pharmacotherapy for OCD, some issues await further research. Studies indicate that OCD patients who respond to SRIs are likely to relapse when the medication is withdrawn, suggesting the need for long-term administration of this treatment. Despite this drawback of psychopharmacology, a substantial number of OCD patients prefer this treatment over behavior therapy because they find the latter too frightening. Perhaps the optimal treatment for most patients should involve medication at the start, followed by behavior therapy implemented after medication has decreased the OCD symptoms and thereby increased the acceptability of EX/RP. Such a combined program has not been systematically studied yet.

As is apparent from the above review, many variants of EX/RP programs have been utilized in outcome studies, but the effects of the different parameters on treatment outcome have not been studied systematically. Studies comparing intensive versus weekly EX/RP protocols, both consisting of treatment components believed to be important (e.g., imaginal and in vivo exposure, strict ritual prevention, therapist-assisted exposure), will help determine the degree to which outcome is compromised simply by decreasing frequency of sessions. Similarly, we need more studies comparing therapist-aided exposure versus self-exposure before advocating reduction of therapist contact. Early investigations did address some of these issues, but their methodologies were flawed and the number of patients was too small to arrive at firm conclusions.

Researchers have already identified several factors that are associated with poor outcome of EX/RP and medication (e.g., presence of schizotypal personality disorder; Minichiello, Baer, & Jenike, 1987). Further investigation of predictors is needed as such information will help clinicians determine what type of treatment to offer the individual patient. The study of readiness for behavior change may also yield important findings relevant to clinical decision making, as readiness may prove as an important predictor of treatment outcome, as well as treatment acceptance. Approximately 25% of patients offered EX/RP refuse treatment; evaluation of patients' initial readiness to change OCD behaviors may allow researchers to identify variables that differentiate patients who are ready for EX/RP from those who are not. This research may also lead to the development of clinical interventions that increase readiness for the highly effective, but quite intimidating, EX/RP treatment.

Another important question is the influence of treatment choice on outcome. Most carefully executed outcome studies use random assignment to treatment conditions. Random assignment, however, may obscure important determinants of outcome. Specifically, such studies cannot elucidate the effects of treatment choice on outcome and what factors are involved in such a choice. We also do not know whether a patient who does not respond to his or her first choice is likely to respond to a different treatment modality. These questions are best addressed using this type of naturalistic design. Because patients treated outside expert clinical research settings many times end up choosing their treatment, studies that incorporate choice will inform us about the generalizability of findings from well-controlled treatment outcome studies to clinical settings.

ACKNOWLEDGMENT   This chapter was supported by grant #MH 45404, awarded to the second author.

References

American Psychiatric Association. (1987). *Diagnostic and statistical manual of mental disorders* (3rd ed., revised). Washington, D.C.: Author.

——. (1994). *Diagnostic and statistical manual of mental disorders* (4th ed.). Washington, D.C.: Author.

Beck, A. T. (1976). *Cognitive therapy and the emotional disorders*. New York: International Universities Press.

Beck, A. T., Ward, C. H., Mendeleson, M., Mock, J., & Erbaugh, J. (1961). An inventory for measuring depression. *Archives of General Psychiatry, 4*, 561–571.

Carr, A. T. (1974). Compulsive neurosis: A review of the literature. *Psychological Bulletin, 81*, 311–318.

Christensen, H., Hadzi-Pavlovic, D., Andrews, G., & Mattick, R. (1987). Behavior therapy and tricyclic medication in the treatment of obsessive-compulsive disorder: A quantitative review. *Journal of Consulting and Clinical Psychology, 55*(5), 701–711.

Clark, D. M. (1986). A cognitive approach to panic. *Behaviour Research and Therapy, 24*, 461–470.

Cottraux, J., Mollard, E., Bouvard, M., Marks, I., Sluys, M., Nury, A. M., Douge, R., & Ciadella, P. (1990). A controlled study of fluvoxamine and exposure in obsessive-compulsive disorder. *International Clinical Psychopharmacology, 5*, 17–30.

Cox, B. J., Swinson, R. P., Morrison, B., & Lee, P. S. (1993). Clomipramine, fluoxetine, and behavior therapy in the treatment of obsessive-compulsive disorder: A meta-analysis. *Journal of Behavior Therapy and Experimental Psychiatry, 24*(2), 149–153.

de Araujo, L. A., Ito, L. M., Marks, I. M., & Deale, A. (1995). Does imagined exposure to the consequences of not ritualising enhance live exposure for OCD? A controlled study. I. Main outcome. *British Journal of Psychiatry, 167*(1), 65–70.

DeVeaugh-Geiss, J., Landau, P., & Katz, R. (1989). Treatment of Obsessive Compulsive Disorder with clomipramine. *Psychiatric Annals, 19*(2), 97–101.

Dollard, J., & Miller, N. E. (1950). *Personality and psychotherapy: An analysis in terms of learning, thinking and culture*. New York: McGraw-Hill.

Ellis, A. (1962). *Reason and emotion in psychotherapy*. New York: Lyle Stuart Press.

Emmelkamp, P. M. G., & Beens, H. (1991). Cognitive therapy with obsessive-compulsive disorder: A comparative evaluation. *Behaviour Research and Therapy, 29*, 293–300.

Emmelkamp, P. M. G., de Haan, E., & Hoogduin, C. A. L. (1990). Marital adjustment and obsessive-compulsive disorder. *British Journal of Psychiatry, 156*, 55–60.

Emmelkamp, P. M. G., van der Helm, M., van Zanten, B. L., & Plochg, I. (1980). Treatment of obsessive-compulsive patients: The contribution of self-instructional training to the effectiveness of exposure. *Behaviour Research and Therapy, 18*, 61–66.

Emmelkamp, P. M. G., Visser, S., & Hoekstra, R. J. (1988). Cognitive therapy versus exposure in vivo in the treatment of obsessive-compulsives. *Cognitive Therapy and Research, 12*, 103–114.

Fals-Stewart, W., Marks, A. P., & Schafer, J. (1993). A comparison of behavioral group therapy and individual behavior therapy in treating obsessive-compulsive disorder. *Journal of Nervous and Mental Disease, 181*(3), 189–193.

Fernandez-Cordoba, E., & Lopez-Ibor Alino, J. (1967). Monochlorimipramine in mental patients resisting other forms of treatment. *Actas Luso-Espanolas de Neurologia y Psiquitria, 26*(2), 119–147.

Flament, M. F., Koby, E., Rapoport, J. L., Berg, C. J., Zahn, T., Cox, C., Denckla, M., & Lenane, M. (1990). Childhood obsessive-compulsive disorder: A prospective follow-up study. *Journal of Child Psychology and Psychiatry and Allied Disciplines, 31*(3), 363–380.

Flament, M. F., Whitaker, A., Rapoport, J. L., Davies, M., Zaremba, C., Kalikow, K., Sceery, W., & Shaffer, D. (1988). Obsessive compulsive disorder in adolescence: An epidemiological study. *Journal of the American Academy of Child and Adolescent Psychiatry, 27*(6), 764–771.

Foa, E., & Goldstein, A. (1978). Continuous exposure and complete response prevention in the treatment of obsessive-compulsive neurosis. *Behavior Therapy, 9,* 821–829.

Foa, E. B., & Kozak, M. J. (1985). Treatment of anxiety disorders: Implications for psychopathology. In A. H. Tuma & J. D. Maser (Eds.), *Anxiety and the anxiety disorders* (pp. 421–452). Hillsdale, N.Y.: Lawrence Erlbaum Associates.

———. (1986). Emotional processing of fear: Exposure to corrective information. *Psychological Bulletin, 99,* 20–35.

———. (1996). Psychological treatment for obsessive-compulsive disorder. In M. R. Mavissakalian & R. F. Prien (Eds.), *Long-term treatments of anxiety disorders* (pp. 285–309). Washington, D.C.: American Psychiatric Press.

Foa, E. B., Kozak, M. J., Goodman, W. K., Hollander, E., Jenike, M., & Rasmussen, S. (1995). *DSM-IV* field trial: Obsessive-compulsive disorder. *American Journal of Psychiatry, 152*(1), 90–94.

Foa, E. B., Kozak, M. J., Steketee, G. S., & McCarthy, P. R. (1992). Treatment of depressive and obsessive-compulsive symptoms in OCD by imipramine and behavior therapy. *British Journal of Clinical Psychology, 31*(3), 279–292.

Foa, E. B., Steketee, G., Grayson, J. B., Turner, R. M., & Latimer, P. (1984). Deliberate exposure and blocking of obsessive-compulsive rituals: Immediate and long-term effects. *Behavior Therapy, 15*(5), 450–472.

Foa, E. B., Steketee, G. S., & Milby, J. B. (1980a). Differential effects of exposure and response prevention in obsessive-compulsive washers. *Journal of Consulting and Clinical Psychology, 48,* 71–79.

Foa, E. B., Steketee, G. S., & Ozarow, B. J. (1985). Behavior therapy with obsessive-compulsives: From theory to treatment. In M. Mavissakalian (Ed.), *Obsessive-compulsive disorders: Psychological and pharmacological treatments* (pp. 49–129). New York: Plenum Press.

Foa, E. B., Steketee, G., Turner, R. M., & Fischer, S. C. (1980b). Effects of imaginal exposure to feared disasters in obsessive-compulsive checkers. *Behaviour Research and Therapy, 18,* 449–455.

Foa, E. B., & Tillmanns, A. (1980). The treatment of obsessive-compulsive neurosis. In A. Goldstein & E. B. Foa (Eds.), *Handbook of behavioral interventions: A clinical guide* (pp. 416–500). New York: Wiley.

Greist, J. H. (1992). An integrated approach to treatment of obsessive compulsive disorder. *Journal of Clinical Psychiatry, 53,* 38–41.

Greist, J. H., Jefferson, J. W., Kobak, K. A., Katzelnick, D. J., & Serlin, R. C. (1995). Efficacy and tolerability of serotonin transport inhibitors in obsessive-compulsive disorder: A meta-analysis. *Archives of General Psychiatry, 52*(1), 53–60.

Hanna, G. L. (1995). Demographic and clinical features of obsessive-compulsive disorder in children and adolescents. *Journal of the American Academy of Child and Adolescent Psychiatry, 34*(1), 19–27.

Hiss, H., Foa, E. B., & Kozak, M. J. (1994). Relapse prevention program for treatment of obsessive-compulsive disorder. *Journal of Consulting and Clinical Psychology, 62*(4), 801–808.

Hodgson, R., & Rachman, S. (1977). Obsessional compulsive complaints. *Behaviour Research and Therapy, 15,* 389–395.

Insel, T. R., & Akiskal, H. S. (1986). Obsessive-compulsive disorder with psychotic features: A phenomenologic analysis. *American Journal of Psychiatry, 143* (12), 1527–1533.

Insel, T. R., Mueller, E. A., Alterman, I., Linnoila, M., & Murphy, D. L. (1985). Obsessive-compulsive disorder and serotonin: Is there a connection? *Biological Psychiatry, 20*(11), 1174–1188.

Insel, T. R., Murphy, D. L., Cohen, R. M., Alterman, I. S., Kilts., C., & Linnoila, M. (1983). Obsessive-compulsive disorder: A double-blind trial of clomipramine and clorgyline. *Archives of General Psychiatry, 40,* 605–612.

Joffe, R. T., & Swinson, R. P. (1991). *Biological aspects of obsessive compulsive disorder.* Paper presented at the *DSM-IV* Committee on Obsessive Compulsive Disorder.

Karno, M., Golding, J. M., Sorenson, S. B., & Burnam, M. A. (1988). The epidemiology of obsessive-compulsive disorder in five U.S. communities. *Archives of General Psychiatry, 45*(12), 1094–1099.

Kozak, M. J., & Foa, E. B. (1994). Obsessions, overvalued ideas, and delusions in obsessive-compulsive disorder. *Behaviour Research and Therapy, 32*(3), 343–353.

———. (1996). Obsessive compulsive disorder. In V. B. V. Hasselt & M. Hersen (Eds.), *Sourcebook of psychological treatment manuals for adult disorders* (pp. 65–122). New York: Plenum Press.

Lelliott, P. T., Noshirvani, H. F., Basoglu, M., Marks, I. M., & Monteiro, W. O. (1988). Obsessive-compulsive beliefs and treatment outcome. *Psychological Medicine, 18*, 697–702.

Leon, A. C., Portera, L., & Weissman, M. M. (1995). The social costs of anxiety disorders. *British Journal of Psychiatry, 166*(Suppl. 27), 19–22.

Margraf, J., & Schneider, S. (1995). *Psychological treatment of panic: What works in the long run?* Paper presented at the World Congress of Behavioural and Cognitive Therapies, Copenhagen, Denmark.

Marks, I. M. (1981). Review of behavioral psychotherapy, I: Obsessive-compulsive disorders. *American Journal of Psychiatry, 138*, 584–592.

Marks, I., Hodgson, R., & Rachman, S. (1975). Treatment of chronic obsessive-compulsive neurosis by *in vivo* exposure. *British Journal of Psychiatry, 127*, 349–364.

Marks, I. M., Lelliott, P. T., Basoglu, M., Noshirvani, H., Monteiro, W., Cohen, D., & Kasvikis, Y. (1988). Clomipramine, self-exposure and therapist-aided exposure for obsessive-compulsive rituals. *British Journal of Psychiatry, 152*(April), 522–534.

Marks, I. M., Stern, R. S., Mawson, D., Cobb, J., & McDonald, R. (1980). Clomipramine and exposure for obsessive-compulsive rituals—I. *British Journal of Psychiatry, 136*, 1–25.

Mattick, R. P., & Peters, L. (1988). Treatment of severe social phobia: Effects of guided exposure with and without cognitive restructuring. *Journal of Consulting and Clinical Psychology, 56*, 251–260.

Mattick, R. P., Peters, L., & Clarke, J. C. (1989). Exposure and cognitive restructuring for social phobia: A controlled study. *Behavior Therapy, 20*, 3–23.

McFall, M. E., & Wollersheim, J. P. (1979). Obsessive-compulsive neurosis: A cognitive behavioral formulation and approach to treatment. *Cognitive Therapy and Research, 3*, 333–348.

Mehta, M. (1990). A comparative study of family-based and patients-based behavioural management in obsessive-compulsive disorder. *British Journal of Psychiatry, 157*, 133–135.

Meichenbaum, D. (1974). Self-instructional methods. In F. H. Kanfer & A. P. Goldstein (Eds.), *Helping people change*. New York: Pergamon Press.

Meyer, V. (1966). Modification of expectations in cases with obsessional rituals. *Behaviour Research and Therapy, 4*,, 273–280.

Meyer, V., & Levy, R. (1973). Modification of behavior in obsessive-compulsive disorders. In H. E. Adams & P. Unikel (Eds.), *Issues and trends in behavior therapy* (pp. 77–136). Springfield, Ill.: Charles C Thomas.

Meyer, V., Levy, R., & Schnurer, A. (1974). The behavioural treatment of obsessive-compulsive disorders. In H. R. Beech (Ed.), *Obsessional states* (pp. 233–258). London: Methuen.

Minichiello, W. E., Baer, L., & Jenike, M. A. (1987). Schizotypal personality disorder: A poor prognostic indicator for behavior therapy in the treatment of obsessive-compulsive disorder. *Journal of Anxiety Disorders, 1*(3), 273–276.

Mowrer, O. H. (1939). A stimulus-response analysis of anxiety and its role as a reinforcing agent. *Psychological Review, 46*, 553–565.

———. (1960). *Learning theory and behavior.* New York: Wiley.

Pato, M. T., Zohar-Kadouch, R., Zohar, J., & Murphy, D. L. (1988). Return of symptoms after discontinuation of clomipramine in patients with obsessive-compulsive disorder. *American Journal of Psychiatry, 145*(12), 1521–1525.

Pitman, R. (1994). Obsessive compulsive disorder in western history. In E. Hollander, J. Zohar, D. Marazziti, & B. Olivier (Eds.), *Current insights in obsessive compulsive disorder* (pp. 3–10). New York: Wiley.

Rabavilas, A. D., Boulougouris, J. C., & Stefanis, C. (1976). Duration of flooding sessions in the treatment of obsessive-compulsive patients. *Behaviour Research and Therapy, 14*, 349–355.

Rachman, S., Cobb, J., Grey, S., McDonald, B., Mawson, D., Sartory, G., & Stern, R. (1979). The behavioural treatment of obsessional-compulsive disorders, with and without clomipramine. *Behaviour Research and Therapy, 17*, 467–478.

Rachman, S. J., & Wilson, G. T. (1980). *The effects of psychological therapy.* Oxford: Pergamon Press.

Rapoport, J. L., Swedo, S. E., & Leonard, H. L. (1992). Childhood obsessive compulsive disorder. 144th Annual Meeting of the American Psychiatric Association: Obsessive compulsive disorder: Integrating theory and practice (1991, New Orleans, Louisiana). *Journal of Clinical Psychiatry, 53*(4, Suppl.), 11–16.

Rasmussen, S. A., & Eisen, J. L. (1989). Clinical features and phenomenology of Obsessive Compulsive Disorder. *Psychiatric Annals, 19*(2), 67–73.

———. (1990). Epidemiology of obsessive compulsive disorder. *Journal of Clinical Psychiatry, 51*(2, Suppl.), 10–13.

Rasmussen, S. A., & Tsuang, M. T. (1986). Clinical characteristics and family history in *DSM-III* obsessive-compulsive disorder. *American Journal of Psychiatry, 143*(3), 317–322.

Rescorla, R. A., & Cunningham, C. L. (1977). The erasure of reinstated fear. *Animal Learning & Behavior, 5,* 386–394.

Rescorla, R. A., & Heth, C. D. (1975). Reinstatement of fear to an extinguished conditioned stimulus. *Journal of Experimental Psychology: Animal Behavior Processes, 1,* 88–96.

Riggs, D. S., Hiss, H., & Foa, E. B. (1992). Marital distress and the treatment of obsessive compulsive disorder. *Behavior Therapy, 23*(4), 585–597.

Roper, G., & Rachman, S. (1976). Obsessional-compulsive checking: Experimental replication and development. *Behaviour Research and Therapy, 14,* 25–32.

Roper, G., Rachman, S., & Hodgson, R. (1973). An experiment of obsessional checking. *Behaviour Research and Therapy, 11,* 271–277.

Roper, G., Rachman, S., & Marks, I. (1975). Passive and participant modelling in exposure treatment of obsessive-compulsive neurotics. *Behaviour Research & Therapy, 13,* 271–279.

Salkovskis, P. M. (1985). Obsessional compulsive problems: A cognitive behavioral analysis. *Behaviour Research and Therapy, 23,* 571–583.

Solyom, L., & Sookman, D. (1977). A comparison of clomipramine hydrochloride (Anafranil) and behaviour therapy in the treatment of obsessive neurosis. *Journal of International Medical Research, 5*(Suppl. 5), 49–61.

Stampfl, T. G., & Levis, D. J. (1967). Essentials of implosive therapy: A learning-theory-based psychodynamic behavioral therapy. *Journal of Abnormal Psychology, 72*(6), 496–503.

Steketee, G. S., Foa, E. B., & Grayson, J. B. (1982). Recent advances in the treatment of obsessive-compulsives. *Archives of General Psychiatry, 39,* 1365–1371.

Stern, R. S., Marks, I. M., Wright, J., & Luscombe, D. K. (1980). Clomipramine: Plasma levels, side effects and outcome in obsessive-compulsive neurosis. *Post Graduate Medical Journal, 56,* 134–139.

Swedo, S. E., Rapoport, J. L., Leonard, H. L., Lenane, M., & Cheslow, D. (1989). Obsessive-compulsive disorder in children and adolescents: Clinical phenomenology of 70 consecutive cases. *Archives of General Psychiatry, 46*(4), 335–341.

Valleni-Basile, L. A., Garrison, C. Z., Jackson, K. L., Waller, J. L., McKeown, R. E., Addy, C. L., & Cuffe, S. P. (1994). Frequency of obsessive-compulsive disorder in a community sample of young adolescents. *Journal of the American Academy of Child and Adolescent Psychiatry, 33*(6), 782–791.

van Balkom, A. J. L. M., van Oppen, P., Vermeulen, A. W. A., van Dyck, R., Nauta, M. C. E., & Vorst, H. C. M. (1994). A meta-analysis on the treatment of obsessive compulsive disorder: A comparison of antidepressants, behavior, and cognitive therapy. *Clinical Psychology Review, 5,* 359–381.

Van Oppen, P., de Haan, E., Van Balkom, A. J. L. M., Spinhoven, P., Hoogduin, K., & van Dyck, R. (1995). Cognitive therapy and exposure in vivo in the treatment of obsessive compulsive disorder. *Behaviour Research and Therapy, 33*(4), 379–390.

Watts, F. N. (1973). Desensitization as an habituation phenomenon: II. Studies of interstimulus interval length. *Psychological Reports, 33,* 715–718.

Weizman, A., Carmi, M., Hermesh, H., Shahar, A., Apter, A., Tyano, S. & Rehavi, M. (1986). High-affinity imipramine binding and serotonin uptake in platelets of eight adolescent and ten adult obsessive-compulsive patients. *American Journal of Psychiatry, 143*(3), 335–339.

Zohar, J., & Insel, T. R. (1987). Drug treatment of obsessive-compulsive disorder. Special Issue: Drug treatment of anxiety disorders. *Journal of Affective Disorders, 13*(2), 193–202.

18

Pharmacological Treatment of Obsessive Compulsive Disorder

Scott L. Rauch

Michael A. Jenike

Multiple randomized, double-blind, placebo-controlled studies support the efficacy of medications that block the presynaptic reuptake of serotonin (serotonin reuptake inhibitors, SRIs) in the treatment of obsessive compulsive disorder. These medications include the tricyclic agent chlomipramine and the selective SRIs fluvoxamine, paroxetine, fluoxetine, and sertraline. Large-scale studies have generally shown that approximately 40% to 60% of patients respond to these medications, with mean improvement in the active treatment groups of approximately 20% to 40%. Numerous agents have been tried as augmentors in combinations with SRIs for patients who were unresponsive or only partially responsive to monotherapy, although few controlled trials of such strategies have been conducted. Numerous studies also show impressive efficacy for behavioral therapies, with exposure and response prevention constituting the main elements of the treatment. Other behavioral strategies that have undergone limited investigation but appear promising include imaginal flooding and "thought stopping." A recent controlled trial suggests that cognitive therapy can also be effective. Neurosurgical treatment is reserved for patients with severe and debilitating illness who have failed to respond to an array of other treatment options.

DIAGNOSTIC CRITERIA AND CLINICAL CHARACTERISTICS

Obsessive compulsive disorder (OCD) is a common condition, with lifetime prevalence estimates of approximately 2–3% in the United States and 0.5–5.5% worldwide (Angst, 1994; Karno, Golding, Sorenson, & Burnam, 1988; Rasmussen & Eisen, 1994). Classified among the anxiety disorders, the hallmark signs and symptoms of OCD include intrusive unwanted thoughts (i.e., obsessions) and repetitive behaviors (i.e., compulsions) (American Psychiatric Association [APA], 1994). Classic obsessions include violent, religious, or sexual themes, as well as preoccupations with contamination, pathological doubting or uncertainty,

concerns with symmetry, and a general sense that something bad will happen if a particular ritual is not performed in precisely the right manner. Classic compulsions include washing, cleaning, counting, checking, repeating, and arranging behaviors. For most, the disease manifests itself as multiple obsessions and multiple compulsions (Rasmussen & Eisen, 1994).

Experiencing occasional unwanted thoughts, performing repetitive or ritualistic behaviors, and having transient feelings of anxiety are all part of normal human experience; however, in order to meet the criteria for OCD the symptoms must be sufficiently intense or frequent to cause marked distress or impair functioning. In fact, people with OCD are often severely impaired by the symptoms of their disease. Unlike psychosis, OCD is characterized by intact insight; because people with OCD recognize that their thoughts and behaviors are extreme or nonsensical, they are often embarrassed or ashamed of their condition and frightened that they may be "going crazy." In severe cases of OCD, insight can become tenuous as obsessions progress to overvalued ideas, prompting the special diagnostic designation of "OCD with poor insight" (APA, 1994).

The differential diagnosis of OCD includes other psychiatric disorders that are characterized by repetitive thoughts or behaviors. For instance, the obsessions of OCD are to be distinguished from the ruminations of major depression, the racing thoughts of mania, the psychotic thoughts of schizophrenia, and the preoccupation with food and body image associated with eating disorders. Likewise, the compulsions of OCD are to be distinguished from the tics of Tourette syndrome (TS), the ritualized self-injurious behaviors of borderline personality disorder, the rhythmic movements that can be present in autism or mental retardation, and the stereotypes of complex partial seizures. By definition, the diagnosis of OCD should not be made if the symptoms can be attributed to another disorder or are the consequence of substance use (APA, 1994).

Although the current diagnostic scheme classifies OCD as an anxiety disorder, a variety of disorders from other categories within *DSM-IV* (*Diagnostic and Statistical Manual of Mental Disorders*, 4th ed.; APA, 1994) are also characterized by repetitive symptoms (Hollander, 1993; McElroy, Phillips, & Keck, 1994). The term *obsessive compulsive spectrum disorders* (OCSDs) has been coined to reflect the notion that a family of similar disorders may exist that shares some common phenomenological, etiological, and perhaps pathophysiological characteristics. Such OCSDs include TS (characterized by intrusive sensations and urges, as well as a drive to perform motor and vocal tics), trichotillomania (characterized by compulsive hair pulling), and body dysmorphic disorder (characterized by a preoccupation with certain aspects of one's own appearance). It remains to be seen whether the concept of OCSDs will prove clinically useful or neurobiologically valid, as well as which disorders can be meaningfully grouped together and by what criteria. Comorbidity with OCD is common; in addition to other OCSDs, frequently coexisting conditions include major affective disorders, other anxiety disor-

ders, and substance use disorders (Karno et al., 1988; Rasmussen & Eisen, 1994).

ETIOLOGY AND NEUROBIOLOGY

The cause of OCD remains unknown. However, family-genetic studies suggest that there may be multiple etiological subtypes (e.g., Pauls et al., 1995; Pauls & Leckman 1986). Specifically, family-genetic studies indicate that in some cases OCD seems to arise sporadically, whereas in others there exist an apparent familial relationship suggestive of an autosomal dominant mode of inheritance with incomplete penetrance. In cohorts in which a familial relationship is present, in some cases the affected members present with only OCD, whereas in other pedigrees the affected individuals have OCD or a tic disorder or both. The apparent phenomenological and familial overlap between OCD and TS extends to neurobiology as well.

Again, although the pathophysiology of these disorders is incompletely understood, for both OCD and TS contemporary neurobiological models implicate dysfunction in one or another of several segregated corticostriatal pathways (Baxter et al., 1990; Insel, 1992; Rapoport & Wise, 1988; Rauch & Jenike, 1993; Rauch & Jenike, in press). Obsessive compulsive disorder seems to involve subtle structural abnormalities in the caudate nucleus, as well as functional dysregulation of neural circuits of the orbitofrontal cortex, cingulate cortex, and the caudate. Similarly, TS seems to involve subtle structural abnormalities in the putamen. In this way, OCD can be conceptualized as a disease involving cognitive and paralimbic corticostriatal networks, while TS involves a sensorimotor corticostriatal network (see Rauch & Jenike, in press, for review).

Recent research suggests that autoimmune processes, precipitated in some cases by beta-hemolytic streptococcal infection, may cause damage to striatal neurons in occasional sporadic childhood-onset cases of OCD and TS (Allen, Leonard, & Swedo, 1995; Swedo, 1994; Swedo, Leonard, & Kiessling, 1994). Neurochemically, serotonergic systems have been implicated in OCD (e.g., Barr, Goodman, Price, McDougle, & Harney, 1992), whereas dopaminergic systems have been implicated in TS (e.g., Mallison et al., 1995). This reflects the neurochemistry of the projections to the relevant striatal territories and also parallels what has been observed regarding the effective pharmacotherapy for these disorders (see Rauch & Jenike, in press).

HISTORICAL PERSPECTIVE

Descriptions of probable OCD date to the 15th century, and through the 1700s the malady was conceptualized in religious or supernatural terms (Hunter & Macalpine, 1982; Pitman, 1994). Treatments such as exorcism not withstanding, clinical reports and attempts to characterize OCD medically or scientifically did not emerge until the late 1800s, when neurologists, including Georges Gilles de la Tourette, described OCD symptoms in the context of movement disorders (Gilles de la Tourette, 1885). In the early 1900s, other clinicians contributed eloquent phenomenological descriptions of obsessive compulsive symptoms (Janet, 1903; Meige & Feindel, 1907), but little progress was made toward effective treatment of OCD. Freud's case of the Rat man (1909/1924) introduced the application of psychodynamic principles in attempts both to understand and to relieve what he termed obsessional neurosis.

It was not until 1967 that the tricyclic antidepressant clomipramine (CMI), the first available serotonin reuptake inhibitor (SRI), emerged as an effective treatment for OCD (Fernandez & Lopez-Ibor, 1967). Contemporaneously, behavioral therapy for OCD was emerging as a viable treatment modality and the object of formal study (Rachman, Hodgson, & Marks, 1971). Interestingly, it was also in the 1960s that Ballantine and colleagues first began their pioneering efforts to systematically study the safety and efficacy of anterior cingulotomy, a neurosurgical treatment for severe treatment-refractory OCD and other psychiatric illnesses (Ballantine, Bouckoms, Thomas, & Giriunas, 1987).

The subsequent quarter century has seen great development in the assessment and treatment of OCD. Several educational and self-help books written for lay audiences (e.g., Baer, 1991; Rapoport, 1989), articles appearing in the general medical literature (Jenike, 1989), and the birth of an advocacy group (OC Foundation, Inc., P.O. Box 70, Milford, Conn. 06460–0070, (203) 878–5669) all contributed to a growing awareness of OCD. Whereas it had still been believed that OCD was a relatively rare disorder (~0.1% lifetime prevalence), publication of Epidemiological Catchment Area (ECA) study results (Karno et al., 1988) surprised much of the psychiatric and public health community by suggesting that OCD had a lifetime prevalence of 2.6%, ranking it as the fourth most common psychiatric illness in the United States. In 1989, a collaborative group of investigators from Yale (New Haven, Conn.) and Brown (Providence, R.I.) Universities published studies reporting on the validation of a scale for quantifying the severity of OCD symptoms (Goodman et al., 1989b, 1989c). The Yale-Brown Obsessive Compulsive Scale (Y-BOCS) has since become the gold standard measure for many of the clinical trials that followed.

During this same era, the pharmaceutical industry produced a new class of compounds known as selective serotonin reuptake inhibitors (SSRIs) that, like CMI, acted via blockade of serotonergic reuptake sites. Unlike CMI, however, these new SSRIs had much lower affinities for adrenergic and cholinergic receptors, presumably conferring on them a more favorable side-effect profile. Investigators in psychopharmacology proceeded systematically to study these new agents, as well as other novel compounds, while their psychotherapist counterparts conducted investigations of cognitive and behavioral treatments. During the past decade, there have been over 1500 reports published in medical sources about drug treatments and OCD. Moreover, during this decade of the brain, neuroscience advances have brought us closer to understanding the etiology and pathophysiology of OCD and related disorders.

CONTEMPORARY TREATMENT FOR OBSESSIVE COMPULSIVE DISORDER

Numerous reviews have been written in the last few years regarding treatment recommendations for OCD (e.g., Dominguez & Mestre, 1994; Goodman, McDougle, & Price, 1992; Jenike 1993a, 1993b, 1994; Montgomery 1994; Rauch & Jenike, 1994; see Table 18.1). There is broad agreement among experts in the field that first-line treatments for OCD include SRIs (CMI or SSRIs) and/or behavior therapy. When these first-line interventions fail, second-line pharmacological approaches include augmentation of SRIs with additional medications or trials of alternative medications as monotherapies in place of SRIs. Third-line treatments may include experimental treatments such as unproven augmentation therapies or intravenous

TABLE 18.1 Sample Treatment Recommendations for Obsessive Compulsive Disorder

Treatment	Dosage	Time Course
First line		
Behavior therapy		
Exposure and response prevention		≥20 hours
Medication: Serial SRI trials (consider at least 2 SSRI trials and one of CMI)		
CMI	150–250 mg/day	≥10 weeks
Fluoxetine	40–80 mg/day	≥10 weeks
Sertraline	50–200 mg/day	≥10 weeks
Fluvoxamine	200–300 mg/day	≥10 weeks
Paroxetine	40–60 mg	≥10 weeks
Second line		
Modifications to behavior therapy		
Consider inpatient sessions; home visits or other in situ sessions; or cognitive therapy		
Medication: SRI augmentation		
Clonazepam	0.5–5 mg/day	≥4 weeks
Buspirone	15–60 mg/day	≥8 weeks
Neuroleptics (if patient has comorbid tics)		
Pimozide	1–3 mg/day	≥4 weeks
Haloperidol	0.5–10 mg/day	≥4 weeks
Medication: Alternative monotherapies		
Clonazepam	0.5–5 mg/day	≥4 weeks
Phenelzine	60–90 mg/day	≥10 weeks
Buspirone	30–60 mg/day	≥6 weeks
Third line		
Low-risk experimental or insufficiently studied therapies		
Other augmentation strategies		
Intravenous CMI (if available via experimental protocol)		
ECT (if patient has comorbid major depression)		
Fourth line		
Consider neurosurgery		
(Only if OCD is long standing, severe, debilitating, and unresponsive to an exhaustive array of other treatments)		

CMI = clomipramine; SRI = serotonin reuptake inhibitor; SSRI = selective serotonin reuptake inhibitor.

CMI if available (Fallon et al., 1992; Warneke, 1989). Finally, other nonpharmacologic treatments, including neurosurgery and electroconvulsive therapy (ECT), have remained more controversial and are reserved for particular clinical situations or as treatments of last resort. In the following section, the scientific evidentiary basis for these various treatment recommendations are reviewed. Although the focus in this chapter is on psychopharmacology, the authors wish to emphasize explicitly that most experts view behavior therapy as a critical and effective first-line treatment for OCD, and that this brand of treatment is all too often overlooked or unavailable.

Measures of Symptom Severity and Treatment Response

Before reviewing the extensive database on clinical trials in OCD, it is worth considering the instruments available for measuring severity of symptoms and clinical improvement. The tools for quantifying the dependent variables in these studies, as well as the thresholds that are adopted to operationalize "treatment response," have a profound impact on the results and interpretations of clinical research.

As noted above, the gold standard instrument for quantifying OCD symptom severity is the Y-BOCS

(Goodman et al., 1989b, 1989c), a rater-administered scale scored from 0 to 40, with high values reflecting more severe symptoms. The Y-BOCS is composed of 10 elements, 5 elements about obsessions and 5 about compulsions (i.e., frequency/time consumed, interference, distress, resistance, and control over symptoms). Each element is rated from 0 to 4.

Alternative contemporary rater-administered instruments include unidimensional global scales (Pato, Eisen, & Pato, 1994). The National Institute of Mental Health Global Obsessive Compulsive Scale (NIMH-GOCS; Insel et al., 1983) is a 15-point scale that has been shown to correlate with the Y-BOCS, although the descriptive anchor points of the NIMH-GOCS tend to emphasize elements of interference and resistance. Clinical Global Impression (CGI; see Pato et al., 1994) scales represent another type of unidimensional rater-administered instruments commonly used in clinical trials, such as the 7-point CGI with anchor points including 1 = very much improved, 4 = no change, and 7 = very much worse. The rater-administered CGI has also been shown to correlate well with the Y-BOCS and NIMH-GOCS; modified versions of the CGI can be self-administered by patients. Other self-administered instruments include the Leyton Obsessional Inventory (LOI; Cooper 1970) and the Maudsley Obsessional Compulsive Inventory (MOCI; Rachman & Hodgson, 1980). As inventories, both consist of symptom-related and/or trait-related questions with binary response options (i.e., yes/no or true/false). Self-ratings can be particularly problematic in OCD, which, together with the fact that these scales are limited to specific symptom sets, make them suboptimal for characterizing symptom severity or gauging clinical improvement in treatment trials (see Kim, Dysken, & Kuskowski, 1990; Pato et al., 1994).

Typically, for studies that report a percentage of responders, criteria for response might include a decrease in Y-BOCS equal to or greater than 25% or 35% and/or a CGI of 1 or 2. Therefore, it is important to appreciate that a substantial proportion of "responders" in these studies remain symptomatic and meaningfully affected by their residual illness.

First-Line Pharmacotherapy: Serotonin Reuptake Inhibitors

There is overwhelming evidence from multiple randomized, double-blind, placebo-controlled studies supporting the efficacy of SRIs in the treatment of OCD (Table 18.2). Specifically, in adults, well-designed and well-controlled trials have demonstrated the relative efficacy of CMI versus a placebo, as well as the relative efficacy of SSRIs, including fluoxetine, sertraline, and fluvoxamine versus a placebo (analogous data are on file for the newest SSRI, paroxetine; however, the reports of these findings have not yet been published in peer-reviewed sources, e.g., Wheadon, Bushnell, & Steiner, 1995). Moreover, SRIs have been shown to be significantly more effective than non-SRI tricyclic antidepressants (TCAs) in placebo-controlled, as well as non-placebo-controlled, studies (Table 18.3). In the only randomized, double-blind, placebo-controlled study involving non-SRI TCAs, nortriptyline was not shown to be significantly more effective than a placebo (Thoren et al., 1980; Table 18.2), supporting the view that non-SRI TCAs are not an effective monotherapy for OCD.

Despite a wide range of observed SRI response rates, large-scale studies have generally yielded approximately 40–60% responders, with mean improvement in the active treatment group of approximately 20–40% (see Greist et al., 1995b). In terms of the relative efficacy among SRIs, the data are inadequate to draw firm conclusions. Three head-to-head, randomized, double-blind trials have been reported, one comparing CMI to fluoxetine (Pigott et al., 1990), and two comparing CMI to fluvoxamine (Den Boer et al., 1987; Freeman, Trimble, Deakin, Stokes, & Ashford, 1994). All failed to show any significant difference in efficacy; however, only the trial of Freeman et al. was not severely underpowered. A large-scale meta-analysis of multicenter trials of SRIs was performed by Greist and colleagues (1995b) in which CMI ($N = 520$), fluoxetine ($N = 355$), sertraline ($N = 325$), and fluvoxamine ($N = 320$) were all shown to be significantly superior to placebo. This meta-analysis further indicated that CMI might have superior efficacy over SSRIs. Although the meta-analysis of Greist et al. had many strengths, including that all studies used comparable parameters and were conducted at essentially the same centers, the results should be interpreted with caution. Since there was a serial progression to the availability of these agents and to the performance of these trials, CMI was studied in an SRI-naive population, whereas each successive agent was undoubtedly tried on a cohort composed of a larger subpopulation of patients with histories of past SRI unresponsiveness. Consequently, each successive trial might well have been conducted on a more treatment-

TABLE 18.2 Placebo-Controlled Trials of Serotonin Reuptake Inhibitor Therapy for Obsessive Compulsive Disorder (Adults)

Treatment Conditions	N	Comments	Study
CMI versus placebo	20	CMI significantly superior to placebo	Karabanow (1977)
CMI versus placebo crossover	14	CMI significantly superior to placebo	Montgomery (1980)
CMI versus nortriptyline versus placebo	24	CMI, but not nortriptyline, superior to placebo	Thoren et al. (1980)
CMI versus placebo	12	CMI significantly superior to placebo	Mavissakalian, Turner, Michelson, & Jacob (1985)
CMI versus placebo	27	CMI significantly superior to placebo	Jenike et al. (1985)[a]
CMI versus placebo	32	73% improved on CMI; 6% improved on placebo	Greist et al. (1990)[a]
CMI versus placebo	239	38% average decrease in symptoms with CMI 3% average decrease in symptoms with placebo	Clomipramine Collaborative Group (1991)
CMI versus placebo	281	44% average decrease in symptoms with CMI 5% average decrease in symptoms with placebo	Clomipramine Collaborative Group (1991)
Sertraline versus placebo	87	Sertraline significantly superior to placebo	Chouinard et al. (1990)
Sertraline versus placebo	19	Sertraline significantly superior to placebo	Jenike et al. (1990c)[b]
Sertraline versus placebo	325	Sertraline significantly superior to placebo	Greist et al. (1995a)
Fluvoxamine versus placebo	16	Fluvoxamine significantly superior to placebo	Perse et al. (1987)
Fluvoxamine versus placebo	42	Fluvoxamine significantly superior to placebo	Goodman et al. (1989a)
Fluvoxamine versus placebo	38	Fluvoxamine significantly superior to placebo	Jenike et al. (1990a)
Fluvoxamine versus placebo	320	Fluvoxamine significantly superior to placebo	Rasmussen et al. (in press)
Fluoxetine versus placebo	355	Fluoxetine significantly superior to placebo	Tollefson et al. (1994)

Source: Adapted from Jenike (1993b).

CMI = clomipramine.

[a]Included in Clomipramine Collaborative Group (1991) report.

[b]Included in Chouinard et al. report.

resistant population, biasing the efficacy in favor of agents studied in earlier years (i.e., CMI).

Data regarding duration of treatment, optimal dose, and side effects are also plentiful, but difficult to interpret with confidence because studies were often not designed to answer these questions specifically. The collective wisdom, purportedly supported by the data from the multicenter trials, as well as anecdotal clinical experience, has been that response to SRIs is typically delayed such that an adequate trial of an SRI requires at least 10 weeks. Indeed, a meaningful proportion of responders continues to emerge past the 8-week mark in these studies, as well as in anecdotal clinical experience. Experts also suggest that optimal

TABLE 18.3 Nonplacebo Controlled Trials of Drug Therapy for Obsessive Compulsive Disorder (Adults)

Treatment Conditions	N	Comments	Study
CMI versus amitriptyline	20	CMI significantly superior to amitriptyline	Ananth, Pecknold, van den Steen, & Engelsmann (1981)
CMI versus clorgyline	13	CMI effective; clorgyline ineffective	Insel et al. (1983)
CMI versus clorgyline	12	CMI superior to clorgyline	Zahn et al. (1984)
CMI versus imipramine	16	CMI superior to imipramine	Volavka, Neziroglu, & Yaryura-Tobias (1985)
CMI versus imipramine crossover	12	CMI superior to imipramine	Lei (1986)
CMI versus doxepin	32	78% markedly improved on CMI 36% markedly improved on doxepin	Cui (1986)
CMI versus fluvoxamine	6	Comparable efficacy	Den Boer et al. (1987)
CMI versus fluoxetine	11	Comparable efficacy	Pigott et al. (1990)
Fluvoxamine versus desipramine	40	Fluvoxamine superior to desipramine	Goodman et al. (1990)
CMI versus amitriptyline	39	95% improved on CMI 56% improved on amitriptyline	Zhao (1991)
CMI versus fluvoxamine	66	Comparable efficacy	Freeman et al. (1994)

Source: Adapted from Jenike (1993b).

CMI = clomipramine.

doses of SRIs for OCD may exceed those typically used for major depression (e.g., Montgomery et al., 1993), although the dose comparison studies of OCD have not always shown significant dose-dependent responses across the OCD study population (e.g., Greist et al., 1995a).

As to side effects, although the meta-analysis of Greist et al. (1995b) did not find any significant difference among medication groups regarding dropout rates due to side effects, this is a relatively insensitive measure of side-effect profile. Also, the aforementioned cohort effects apply for side effects as well; subjects participating in the early CMI trials may have viewed that agent as the only available course of treatment, whereas subjects in later SSRI trials may have been aware of the wider variety of available treatments, making them less willing to endure nuisance side effects. Clearly, as with other TCAs, the risks and side effects mediated by anticholinergic and antiadrenergic mechanisms (e.g., constipation, cardiac conduction disturbances, orthostatic hypotension) are more commonly associated with CMI than with SSRIs. Furthermore, CMI is believed to pose a significant risk with regard to lowering seizure threshold. All SRIs can pose risks (e.g., serotonergic syndrome) and produce a variety of side effects (e.g., nausea, sleep disturbances, sexual disturbances, etc.) attributable to their primary mechanism of action via serotonergic reuptake blockade (Grimsley & Jann, 1992). There is no substantive evidence that any SRI is significantly superior or inferior to any other with regard to serotonergically mediated side effects.

In addition to the above data regarding pharmacotherapy for OCD in adults, there are analogous studies in children and adolescents documenting the efficacy of CMI over non-SRI TCAs, as well as placebos (see Table 18.4). To date, there is only one placebo-controlled study of an SSRI for OCD in children, which likewise supports the efficacy of fluoxetine, although several open trials of SSRIs have produced findings paralleling those in adults.

Second-Line Pharmacotherapy: Serotonin Reuptake Inhibitor Augmentation and Alternative Monotherapies

For patients who do not derive satisfactory reduction of symptoms with SRI therapy, second-line pharmacological treatments include SRI augmentation and alternative monotherapies. It is important to appreciate that only a minority of patients with OCD do not respond favorably to SRIs and that this relatively treatment-resistant group may be quite heterogeneous, including with respect to underlying pathophysiology.

TABLE 18.4 Controlled Trials of Serotonin Reuptake Inhibitor Therapy for Obsessive Compulsive Disorder (Children and Adolescents)

Treatment Conditions	N	Comments	Study
CMI versus desipramine versus placebo crossover	8 adolescents	No significant differences	Rapoport et al. (1980)
CMI versus placebo crossover	14 children	CMI superior to placebo	Flament et al. (1985a, 1985b)
CMI versus desipramine	48	CMI superior to desipramine	Leonard et al. (1988)
CMI substituted with desipramine in half of subjects	26	89% receiving desipramine relapsed 18% remaining on CMI relapsed	Leonard et al. (1991)
CMI versus placebo	61	37% average decrease with CMI 8% average decrease with placebo	Devaugh-Geiss et al. (1992)
Fluoxetine versus placebo	14 children	Fluoxetine superior to placebo	Riddle et al. (1992)

Source: Adapted from Jenike (1993b).

CMI = clomipramine.

Therefore, specific subsequent treatments may be very effective for some subset of this population while having only modest mean efficacy for the overall cohort. Consequently, some second-line treatment trials have focused on the number or proportion of patients who meet responder criteria rather than the mean decrease in symptom severity over the entire study population. Moreover, in some instances attention has been focused on the clinical characteristics that might distinguish responders from nonresponders.

Augmentation of Serotonin Reuptake Inhibitors

Numerous agents have been tried as augmentors in combination with SRIs for patients who were unresponsive or only partially responsive to SRIs alone (see Jenike, 1993a); however, few controlled trials of such strategies have been conducted (see Table 18.5). Despite numerous case reports suggesting that lithium might be an effective augmentor in combination with various SRIs, the only two controlled trials of lithium, added to fluvoxamine (McDougle et al., 1991) and CMI (Pigott et al., 1991), speak against the efficacy of these combinations.

Similarly, the encouraging results from case series and uncontrolled trials of buspirone augmentation (see Jenike, 1993a) were followed by only marginal success in controlled trials. In Pigott and colleagues' study of buspirone plus CMI (1992a), despite a 29% responder rate, there was no significant improvement over the entire cohort with respect to OCD symptoms,

and 3 of 14 subjects suffered an exacerbation of greater than 25% on measures of depression for unclear reasons. In Grady and colleagues' (1993) double-blind crossover study of buspirone augmentation of fluoxetine, only 1 of 14 subjects showed improvement, which may have reflected the brief duration of treatment (only 4 weeks in each phase).

Contrary to a small case series reporting unimpressive results, the use of clonazepam as an augmentor with CMI or fluoxetine has been studied in a placebo-controlled fashion, suggesting significant antiobsessional efficacy, as well as a nonspecific decrease in anxiety measures (Pigott et al., 1992b; see Rauch & Jenike, 1994).

The most impressive augmentation data document the benefits of adding low doses of high-potency neuroleptics (i.e., pimozide or haloperidol) to fluvoxamine in patients with comorbid tic disorders (McDougle et al., 1990, 1994). Uncontrolled studies of augmentation with the atypical antipsychotic risperidone have also yielded encouraging preliminary results (Jacobsen, 1995; McDougle et al., 1995b) that await confirmation via controlled trials.

Pertinent negative findings include those from a controlled crossover trial of L-triiodothyronine added to CMI, which did not yield significant antiobsessional benefits (Pigott et al., 1991).

Numerous other agents have been tried in combination with SRIs, including clonidine, tryptophan, fenfluramine, and trazodone, as well as other antidepressants (see Jenike, 1993a, for review). The small number of subjects, lack of sufficient controls, and

TABLE 18.5 Serotonin Reuptake Inhibitor Augmentation Therapies for Obsessive Compulsive Disorder: Controlled Trials

Augmenting Agent	SRI	N	Trial	Results	Study
Lithium	Fluvoxamine	30	2 or 4-week double blind, placebo controlled	Very little improvement	McDougle et al. (1991)
Lithium	CMI	9	Double-blind crossover (with T3)	None	Pigott et al. (1991)
L-Triiodo-thyronine (T3)	CMI	9	Double-blind crossover (with lithium)	None	Pigott et al. (1991)
Buspirone	CMI	14	2-week placebo, then 10 weeks buspirone	4/14 (29%) improved ≥ an additional 25% on buspirone; 3/14 (21%) worsened > 25% on depression scores	Pigott et al. (1992a)
Buspirone	Fluoxetine	14	Double-blind crossover with placebo; 4 weeks per treatment condition	1/14 (7%) improved significantly more with buspirone	Grady et al. (1993)
Haloperidol	Fluvoxamine	34	Double blind, placebo controlled, with 17 per group; 4-week trial; after failing, fluvoxamine alone	11/17 (65%) responded to haloperidol; 0/17 to placebo; 8/8 with tics responded to haloperidol	McDougle et al. (1994)
Clonazepam	CMI or fluoxetine	16	Placebo controlled, crossover; 4-week trial; after 20 weeks; stable dose on CMI or fluoxetine	Significant improvement in OCD on 1/3 measures for clonazepam versus placebo; significant improvement in global anxiety as well	Pigott et al. (1992b) (see Rauch & Jenike, 1994)

CMI = clomipramine; OCD = obsessive compulsive disorder; SRI = serotonin reuptake inhibitor.

mixed results preclude drawing even preliminary conclusions as to the potential efficacy of such strategies. If an augmenting agent is indicated for treatment of some comorbid condition (e.g., lithium for bipolar disorder, trazodone for insomnia, or clonidine for TS) and no strong contraindication is present, then a trial of the agent in combination with an SRI is easily rationalized. Anecdotally, these strategies have appeared to be of tremendous benefit in some isolated cases. No studies have sought to establish the optimal dosage or duration of treatment for any of these augmentation strategies. Therefore, current guidelines reflect the parameters used in the reported successful trials, as well as anecdotal experience with OCD and other psychiatric disorders.

Alternative Monotherapies

For patients who fail to derive a satisfactory response from trials of SRIs alone, as well as augmentation strategies, the next recommended step is to consider alternative monotherapies in place of SRIs. In addition to uncontrolled data, positive controlled studies lend some support for trials of clonazepam, monoamine oxidase inhibitors (MAOIs), and buspirone (see Table 18.6).

In the case of clonazepam, both small case series (see Hewlett, 1993, for review) and one placebo-controlled study (Hewlett, Vinogradov, & Agras, 1992) support its efficacy in OCD. In light of the circumstantial evidence supporting its efficacy as an augmentor with SRIs for OCD and its well-established efficacy more generally as an anxiolytic, trials of clonazepam as an alternative monotherapy in treatment-resistant cases seem well justified. Recommendations in this context regarding dosage (i.e., 0.5 to 5 mg per day) and duration (i.e., ≥4 weeks) have no controlled empirical basis and are simply extrapolated from clinical experience with benzodiazepines for other anxiety disorders and these few reports of its use in OCD.

Non-placebo-controlled studies involving the MAOI clorgyline speak against its efficacy in OCD, showing no significant decrease in OCD severity (Insel et al., 1983) and inferior efficacy in comparison to SRIs (Insel et al., 1983; Zahn, Insel, & Murphy, 1984).

In contrast, small case series suggested beneficial results from the MAOI phenelzine in patients with comorbid OCD and panic disorder (Jenike et al., 1983). A non-placebo-controlled study of phenelzine versus CMI suggested significant clinical improvement in both groups and no significant difference in efficacy between the two agents (Vallejo, Olivares, Marcos, Bulbena, & Menchon, 1992). The results of Vallejo and colleagues must be interpreted with caution, however, since the study was underpowered to identify a difference between CMI and phenelzine, and suboptimal clinical measures of improvement were employed. Therefore, the efficacy of phenelzine as a monotherapy for OCD should be viewed as provisional pending a placebo-controlled study. Specific recommendations regarding dosage (i.e., phenelzine 60 to 90 mg per day) have little empirical basis, reflecting extrapolation from clinical practice with MAOIs for major depression and panic disorder; the duration of trials (i.e., ≥10 weeks) mirrors that of SRIs for OCD. In addition to the usual low-tyramine diet and other precautions typically indicated in the context of a MAOI trial, it is critical to be cautious regarding the transition from serotonergic medications to a MAOI due to the risks of dangerous interactions, including serotonergic crisis. Current guidelines are based primarily on the half-lives of the agents involved rather than direct empirical data related to adverse events per se. Conservative recommendations are washout periods of at least 2 weeks when transitioning from CMI or a short-half-life SSRI to an MAOI, at least 5 weeks when transitioning from fluoxetine to a MAOI, and at least 2 weeks when transitioning from phenelzine to an SRI.

Although one open trial of buspirone did not yield significant antiobsessional benefit (Jenike & Baer, 1988), a controlled trial of buspirone versus CMI suggested that both were comparably effective (Pato et al., 1991). The relatively short duration of the trial, the modest power for detecting a difference between treatments, and the absence of a placebo group mitigate against drawing firm conclusions from Pato and colleagues' study. Still, given the excellent tolerability of buspirone, other circumstantial evidence of possible efficacy as an augmentor, and its general efficacy as an anxiolytic, the clinical use of buspirone as an alternative monotherapy for cases of treatment-resistant OCD seems justified pending further information. Specific recommendations regarding dosage (i.e., up to 60 mg per day) and duration of trials (i.e., ≥6

TABLE 18.6 Alternative Medications as Monotherapies for Obsessive Compulsive Disorder: Controlled Trials

Treatment Conditions	N	Comments	Study
Clorgyline versus CMI	13	Clorgyline ineffective; CMI effective	Insel et al. (1983)
Clorgyline versus CMI	12	Clorgyline inferior to CMI	Zahn et al. (1984)
Phenelzine versus CMI	30	Both effective and comparable	Vallejo et al. (1992)
Clonazepam versus CMI versus clonidine versus active placebo crossover	25	35% average decrease with clonazepam; clonazepam comparable to CMI and superior to active placebo	Hewlett et al. (1992)
Buspirone versus CMI crossover	20	Both effective and comparable; > 20% improvement in >55% of both groups	Pato et al. (1991)

CMI = clomipramine.

weeks) have little empirical basis, simply reflecting the protocol adopted in Pato and colleagues' study.

Some pertinent negative findings are worthy of mention. In contrast to promising results with risperidone as an augmentor, an open trial of the atypical antipsychotic clozapine suggests its inefficacy as an antiobsessional monotherapy (McDougle et al., 1995a). Although one case report suggested antiobsessional benefit in a patient with OCD (Young, Bostic, & McDonald, 1994) and another described a marked reduction in OC symptoms for a patient with schizophrenia (LaPorta, 1994), several case reports suggest that clozapine can actually precipitate OC symptoms in patients with psychotic disorders (see McDougle et al., 1995a, for a review).

Nonpharmacological Therapies

Behavior Therapy

It is extremely challenging to design and conduct a controlled study of psychotherapy. Among other issues, the optimal analog to placebo treatment in medication trials is unclear. Perhaps consequently, much of the clinical research to date regarding behavior therapy for OCD has focused on determining salient elements of the therapy rather than comparing behavior therapy to other treatments or a placebo (see Baer & Minichiello, 1990).

The gold standard mode of behavior therapy for OCD is exposure and response prevention. This entails the patient actually being exposed to provocative stimuli (e.g., touching a "contaminated" object) and refraining from carrying out his or her usual compulsions (e.g., refraining from hand washing)—that is response prevention. It appears that in vivo exposure and response prevention represent the salient elements of effective behavior therapy regardless of setting, supervision, or addition of cognitive techniques (Emmelkamp & De Lange, 1983; Emmelkamp & Kraanen, 1977; Emmelkamp, Van Der Helm, Van Zanten, & Plochg, 1980).

One challenge or limitation of exposure and response prevention therapy relates to generalizability of results since gains are often specific to the symptoms explicitly addressed and sometimes limited to the settings in which the therapies are practiced (Rachman et al., 1971, 1979; Rachman & Hodgson, 1980). Although it is commonly believed that behavior therapy is more effective for compulsive rituals than obsessive thoughts, only one (Foa & Goldstein, 1978) of four

behavior therapy studies (Foa et al., 1984; Foa & Goldstein, 1978; Foa, Steketee, & Milby, 1980; Solyom & Sookman, 1977) addressing this issue found a significantly greater improvement in compulsions versus obsessions. In all four studies, significant gains were made in both obsessions and compulsions; however, patients with pure obsessions (e.g., intrusive thoughts of sex or violence without accompanying compulsions) tended to fare worse than patients with obsessions and compulsions (e.g., contamination with cleaning or doubting with checking) (Rachman & Hodgson, 1980).

There are numerous partially controlled trials of exposure and response prevention behavior therapy that have consistently shown impressive antiobsessional efficacy in less than 1 month (see Table 18.7). Dropout rates for these studies averaged approximately 20% (Rachman & Hodgson, 1980). Still, follow-up studies suggested that treatment gains were maintained for up to 1 to 5 years after discontinuation of active treatment, although these results were confounded by occasional "booster" sessions (Marks, 1981; Marks, Hodgson, & Rachman, 1975; Mawson, Marks, & Ramm, 1982). The study of Boulougouris (1977) stands as a notable exception in that patients who were treated with 11 sessions of behavior therapy maintained their gains over a 2-to-5 year follow-up period in the absence of any intercurrent therapy sessions. Furthermore, a meta-analysis (Christensen, Hadzi-Pavlovic, Andrews, & Mattick, 1987; Quality Assurance Project, 1985) based on data from 38 studies between 1961 and 1984 found comparable effect sizes for CMI (1.7) and behavior therapy (1.8) at the end of treatment; the benefits from exposure and response prevention persisted at a mean 80-week follow-up (effect size = 1.7), whereas no such follow-up data were available for CMI. In contrast, psychosurgery resulted in an effect size of 1.4, which dropped to 1.0 at 60-weeks follow-up. In a separate study, Pato and colleagues (1988) showed that almost 90% of patients who received CMI therapy for OCD relapsed after discontinuation of the medication. Thus, pending well-controlled, head-to-head studies, based on partially controlled data and the limited method of meta-analysis the implication is that, in comparison with CMI or psychosurgery, behavior therapy may produce the highest mean effect size and the most enduring gains following discontinuation of active treatment.

In practice, medication and behavior therapy are routinely used in concert, and experts in the field

TABLE 18.7 Summary of Partially Controlled Studies of Behavior Therapy for Obsessive Compulsive Disorder

Study	N	Sessions	Responders
Rachman et al. (1971)	10	40 minutes–1 hour × 15 (10–15 hrs) over 3 weeks; all inpatients	70%
Rachman, Marks, & Hodgson (1973)	5	40 minutes × 15 (10 hours) over 3 weeks; all inpatients	60%
Marks et al. (1975)	20	40 minutes–1 hour × 15 (10–15 hours) over 3 weeks; all inpatients	70%
Boulougouris (1977)	15	90 minutes × 11 (16.5 hours); all outpatients	60%
Foa et al. (1984)	32	2 hours × 15 (30 hours) over 3 weeks; 10 inpatients/22 outpatients	90%
Total (mean)	82		(70%)

Source: Adapted from Baer & Minichiello (1990) and Jenike (1993b).

have long recommended this as an optimal treatment approach (e.g., Baer & Minichiello, 1986; Rauch & Jenike, in press). The literature, however, reports only two studies directly comparing behavior therapy and CMI and only one testing the combination versus either treatment alone (Rachman et al., 1979). Rachman and colleagues (1979) found behavior therapy to outperform CMI significantly, as well as no significant incremental benefit from the two treatments in combination. This study is limited, however, in that the CMI condition entailed relatively low doses (mean = 164 mg/day and maximum = 225 mg/day), as well as inadequate duration of CMI treatment (6 weeks). In the other head-to-head comparison of behavior therapy and CMI, medication was found to be more effective for reducing obsessional doubt, whereas behavior therapy was more effective for reducing compulsive rituals (Solyom & Sookman, 1977). Currently, a large-scale, dual-site study is under way to address these questions more thoroughly (M. Leibowitz & E. B. Foa, personal communication, 1995).

Beyond exposure and response prevention, limited trials of alternative behavioral methods have supported the use of imaginal flooding for checkers (Steketee et al., 1982) and "thought stopping" for patients with pure obsessions (Rimm & Masters, 1974). Moreover, a recent controlled trial suggests that cognitive therapy can also be effective for OCD (Van Oppen et al., 1995). Finally, although controlled data are not currently available regarding cognitive-behavioral therapy for OCD in children and adolescents, preliminary findings of open trials and case reports suggest that, with age-appropriate modifications to the regimen, results can be comparable to those in adults (March, 1995; March, Mulle, & Herbel, 1994).

Neurosurgery

Despite a large body of uncontrolled data reporting antiobsessional benefits from a variety of neurosurgical procedures (see Cosgrove & Rauch, 1995, and Mindus et al., 1994, for reviews), thus far ethical factors and technical limitations have precluded the performance of sham-controlled studies to definitively establish the efficacy of these strategies. Neurosurgical treatment of OCD is reserved for patients with severe and debilitating illnesses who have failed an exhaustive array of other available treatment options and who provide informed consent or assent. Currently, the most commonly employed neurosurgical treatments for OCD include anterior cingulotomy, anterior capsulotomy, and limbic leukotomy. In recent prospective trials of cingulotomy and capsulotomy, approximately 45% of patients experienced symptom reduction of at least 35% (see Mindus et al., 1994).

Studies directly comparing the relative efficacy and safety among the different neurosurgical approaches are also lacking. Adverse effects, in the context of contemporary techniques, include seizures and transient headaches. Perhaps surprisingly, discernible adverse effects on cognition or personality are rare (see Corkin, 1980; Mindus et al., 1994).

With the advent of innovative surgical devices that allow functional neurosurgery without a craniotomy (e.g., by gamma knife or proton beam), the performance of ethical double-blind, sham-controlled trials of neurosurgery for OCD are now feasible. One such study, testing the efficacy of anterior capsulotomy, is currently being conducted by a collaborative research team involving investigators from Brown University and Massachusetts General Hospital (Boston, Mass.).

More definitive data are sorely needed to determine the efficacy of these treatments.

Electroconvulsive Therapy

There are no controlled data regarding the efficacy of ECT for OCD. Given the high comorbidity of major affective illness in OCD and the well-established efficacy of ECT for major depression, it is not surprising that some patients with OCD have reportedly shown clinical improvement with ECT. Several limited case series and anecdotal reports suggest that ECT may be useful in some circumstances, and such intervention would seem prudent in cases for which ECT is indicated based on the presence of comorbid severe affective illness (see Jenike & Rauch, 1994). Controlled data are needed, however, before meaningful conclusions can be drawn regarding the specific antiobsessional efficacy of ECT for OCD. In this regard, important considerations include the effects of ECT on patients with OCD in the absence of major depressive disorder, the careful clinical distinction between genuine OCD versus ruminations or intrusive thoughts due to a different diagnosis, and the use of clinical instruments to tease apart antidepressant effects versus antiobsessional effects versus global improvement. Currently available data do not provide compelling support for the use of ECT in OCD without comorbid ECT-responsive conditions.

New Horizons and Future Treatments for Obsessive Compulsive Disorder

Future OCD treatment research can be divided into two categories: (a) initiatives to assess and optimize the use of currently available treatments and (b) initiatives to develop new treatments. As documented by the above review, there is much work to be done in establishing the efficacy of various treatments, following up on preliminary data with well-controlled prospective trials. Moreover, optimal doses and durations for various treatments need to be determined empirically and in a scientifically rigorous fashion. Clinical subtyping may uncover important predictors of treatment response (Ackerman, Greenland, Bystritsky, Morgenstern, & Katz, 1994; Ravizza, Barzega, Bellino, Bogetto, & Maina, 1995), informing patients and clinicians which treatments should be tried first or avoided in particular cases.

Public policy issues regarding treatment access loom large for mental health care delivery in the United States. Education of health care consumers, as well as policy makers and clinicians, will be critical to high-quality care in the years ahead. Primary care physicians must be informed about OCD, and trends in training must be established to ensure an adequate supply of therapists with expertise in behavioral methods. Technological innovations such as telepsychiatry may help provide specialized assessment and treatment to remote regions and ultimately reduce the costs of care (Baer, 1991; Baer et al., 1995).

Truly novel treatments for OCD may emerge from advances in our understanding of its pathophysiology or serendipitously. As new compounds become available that interact with the serotonergic and dopaminergic systems via specific receptor subtypes (e.g., 5HT1D, 5HT1A, or 5HT3; Swerdlow, 1995), it is likely that several will be antiobsessional candidates. Beyond monoaminergic systems, agents that modulate neuropeptidergic transmission may represent the next wave of psychopharmacological agents to be tested for OCD and related disorders. For instance, we have proposed that, based on the neurochemistry of corticostriatal pathways, substance P antagonists might serve as potent antiobsessionals (Rauch & Jenike, in press). Such compounds are already available within the pharmaceutical industry, but currently are only being studied for other indications. The hypothalamic neuropeptide oxytocin is also the subject of intensive study because of its purported role in species-specific grooming behaviors (Leckman et al., 1994). Beyond neuropharmacology, research regarding autoimmune-mediated causes of OCD has prompted investigation of plasmapheresis to clear autoantibodies plus prophylactic antibiotic treatment to prevent subsequent infections and further damage (Allen et al., 1995; Swedo, 1994; Swedo et al., 1994).

Finally, recent neuroimaging studies have documented consistent brain activity changes following successful treatment with either SRIs or behavior therapy (Baxter et al., 1992; Schwartz et al., 1996). Such findings underscore the potential power of neuroimaging methods in searching for predictors of treatment responsiveness.

SUMMARY

In conclusion, the past 30 years have seen tremendous advances in the treatment and understanding of OCD, with an acceleration of progress during this most recent decade. It is now appreciated that OCD is a common disorder, and effective treatments including medication, behavior therapy, and neurosurgery have emerged. There is overwhelming evidence of the most rigorous type supporting the efficacy of SRIs for the treatment of OCD. Along with SRIs, behavior therapy must be considered a viable first-line therapy. The best available data suggest that behavior therapy is at least as effective as medication in some instances and may be superior with respect to risks, costs, and enduring benefits.

A variety of second-line medication treatments for OCD have been studied in a controlled or systematic fashion. Augmentation of SRIs with clonazepam or buspirone and with high-potency neuroleptics in cases of a comorbid tic disorder is provisionally recommended based on the marginal available data. Other augmentation strategies find very limited support at present. Alternative monotherapies, including buspirone, clonazepam, and phenelzine, have all been the subject of positive controlled or partially controlled studies; however, the quality of these data makes recommendations for these strategies tentative as well, pending additional information.

Beyond second-line treatments, the current database is inadequate for making difficult treatment decisions. There is now considerable clinical experience with neurosurgery for severe, debilitating, treatment-refractory OCD. The apparent modest success rates with neurosurgery and its relative safety based on open trials would seem to pose a reasonable option for a small number of cases. Still, controlled data on neurosurgery are sorely needed.

The future of OCD treatment will hopefully entail rigorous research to more clearly establish the efficacy and safety of preexisting treatment options, as well as a refined sense of which patients might respond preferentially to which interventions, at what dose, and after how long. Furthermore, we can look forward to emerging novel treatment strategies that might include modified cognitive-behavioral therapies; new compounds acting via serotonergic, dopaminergic, or neuropeptidergic systems; and interventions that counteract autoimmune processes.

ACKNOWLEDGMENTS Doctors Rauch and Jenike are supported in part by the David Judah Research Fund.

References

Ackerman, D. L., Greenland, S., Bystritsky, A., Morgenstern, H., & Katz, R. J. (1994). Predictors of treatment response in obsessive-compulsive disorder: Multivariate analyses from a multicenter trial of clomipramine. *Journal of Clinical Psychopharmacology, 14*, 247–254.

Allen, A. J., Leonard, H. L., & Swedo, S. E. (1995). Case study: A new infection-triggered, autoimmune subtype of pediatric OCD and Tourette's syndrome. *Journal of the American Academy of Child and Adolescent Psychiatry, 34*(3), 307–311.

American Psychiatric Association. (1994). *Diagnostic and statistical manual of mental disorders* (4th ed.). Washington, D.C.: Author.

Ananth, J., Pecknold, J. C., van den Steen, N., & Engelsmann, F. (1981). Double-blind comparative study of clomipramine and amitriptyline in obsessive neurosis. *Progressive Neuropsychopharmacology, 5*(3), 257–262.

Angst, J. (1994). The epidemiology of obsessive compulsive disorder. In E. Hollander, J. Zohar, D. Marazziti, & B. Olivier (Eds.), *Current insights in obsessive compulsive disorder* (pp. 93–104). Chichester, U.K.: John Wiley & Sons.

Baer, L. (1991). *Getting control.* Boston: Little Brown.

Baer, L., Cukor, P., Jenike, M. A., Leahy, L., O'Laughlin, J., & Coyle, J. T. (1995). Pilot study of telemedicine for patients with obsessive-compulsive disorder. *American Journal of Psychiatry, 152*, 1383–1385.

Baer, L., & Minichiello, W. E. (1986). Behavior therapy for obsessive-compulsive disorder. In M. A. Jenike, L. Baer, & W. E. Minichiello (Ed.), *Obsessive-compulsive disorders: Theory and management.* Littleton, Mass.: PSG Publishing.

———. (1990). Behavioral treatment for obsessive-compulsive disorder. In R. Noyes, Jr., M. Roth, & G.D. Burrows (Eds.), *Handbook of anxiety, Vol. 4, The treatment of anxiety* (pp. 363–387). New York: Elsevier Science Publishers.

Baer, L., Minichiello, W. E., Jenike, M. A., & Holland, A. (1989). Use of a portable computer program to assist behavioral treatment in a case of obsessive compulsive disorder. *Behavior Therapy & Psychiatry, 19*, 237–240.

Ballantine, H. T., Bouckoms, A. J., Thomas, E. L., & Giriunas, I. E. (1987). Treatment of psychiatric illness by stereotactic cingulotomy. *Biological Psychiatry, 22*, 807–819.

Barr, L. C., Goodman, W. K., Price, L. H., McDougle, C. J., & Charney, D. S. (1992). The serotonin hypothesis of obsessive compulsive disorder: Implications of pharmacologic challenge studies. *Journal of Clinical Psychiatry, 53*(Suppl. 4), 17–28.

Baxter, L. R., Schwartz, J. M., Guze, B. H., et al. (1990). Neuroimaging in obsessive-compulsive disorder: seeking the mediating neuroanatomy. In M. A. Jenike, L.

Baer, & W. E. Minichiello (Eds.), *Obsessive compulsive disorder: Theory and management* (2nd ed., pp. 167–188). Chicago, Ill.: Year Book Medical Publishers.

Baxter, L. R., Jr., Schwartz, J. M., Bergman, K. S., et al. (1992). Caudate glucose metabolic rate changes with both drug and behavior therapy for obsessive-compulsive disorder. *Archives of General Psychiatry, 49,* 681–689.

Boulougouris, J. C. (1977). Variables affecting the behavior modification of obsessive-compulsive patients treated by flooding. In J. C. Boulougouris & A. D. Rabavilas (Eds.), *The treatment of phobic and obsessive compulsive disorders* (pp. 73–84). Oxford: Pergamon Press.

Chouinard, G., Goodman, W., Greist, J., et al. (1990). Results of a double-blind placebo controlled trial using a new serotonin uptake inhibitor, sertraline, in obsessive-compulsive disorder. *Psychopharmacology Bulletin, 26,* 279–284.

Christensen, H., Hadzi-Pavlovic, D., Andrews, G., & Mattick, R. (1987). Behavior therapy and tricyclic medication in the treatment of obsessive-compulsive disorder: A quantitative review. *Journal of Consulting and Clinical Psychology, 55*(5), 701–711.

Clomipramine Collaborative Group. (1991). Clomipramine in the treatment of patients with obsessive-compulsive disorder. *Archives of General Psychiatry, 48,* 730–738.

Cooper, J. (1970). The Leyton obsessional inventory. *Psychiatric Medicine, 1,* 48.

Corkin, S. (1980). A prospective study of cingulotomy. In E. S. Vanenstein (Ed.), *The psychosurgery debate* (pp. 164–204). San Francisco, Calif.: W. H. Freeman.

Cosgrove, G. R., & Rauch, S. L. (1995). Psychosurgery. *Neurosurgical Clinics of North America, 6,* 167–176.

Cui, Y. E. (1986). A double-blind trial of chlorimipramine and doxepin in obsessive-compulsive disorder. *Chung Hua Shen Ching Shen Ko Tsa Chih, 19*(5), 279–281.

Den Boer, J. A., Westenberg, H. G. M., Kamerbeek, W. D. J., et al. (1987). Effect of serotonin uptake inhibitors in anxiety disorders: A double-blind comparison of clomipramine and fluvoxamine. *International Clinical Psychopharmacology, 2*(1), 21–32.

DeVeaugh-Geiss, J., Moroz, G., Biederman, J., et al. (1992). Clomipramine hydrochloride in childhood and adolescent obsessive-compulsive disorder—A multicenter trial. *Journal of the American Academy of Child and Adolescent Psychiatry, 31*(1), 45–49.

Dominguez, R. A., & Mestre, S. M. (1994). Management of treatment-refractory obsessive compulsive disorder patients. *Journal of Clinical Psychiatry, 55*(Suppl. 10), 86–92.

Emmelkamp, P. M. G., & De Lange, I. (1983). Spouse involvement in the treatment of obsessive-compulsive patients. *Behavior Research & Therapy, 21,* 341–346.

Emmelkamp, P. M. G., & Kraanen, J. (1977). Therapist-controlled exposure in vivo versus self-controlled exposure in vivo: A comparison with obsessive-compulsive patients. *Behavior Research & Therapy, 15,* 491–495.

Emmelkamp, P. M. G., Van Der Helm, M., Van Zanten, B. L., & Plochg, I. (1980). Treatment of obsessive-compulsive patients: The contribution of self-instructional training to the effectiveness of exposure. *Behavior Research & Therapy, 18,* 61–66.

Fallon, B. A., Campeas, R., Schneier, F. R., et al. (1992). Open trial of intravenous clomipramine in five treatment refractory patients with obsessive compulsive disorder. *Journal of Neuropsychiatry, 4,* 70–75.

Fernandez, C. E., & Lopez-Ibor, J. J. (1967). Monochlorimipramine in the treatment of psychiatric patients resistant to other therapies. *Actas Luso Esp Neurol Psiquiatr Cienc, 26,* 119.

Flament, M. F., Rapoport, J. L., Berg, C. J., et al. (1985a). Clomipramine treatment of childhood obsessive-compulsive disorder. *Archives of General Psychiatry, 42,* 977–983.

———. (1985b). A controlled trial of clomipramine in childhood obsessive-compulsive disorder. *Psychopharmacology Bulletin, 21*(1), 150–151.

Foa, E. B., & Goldstein, A. (1978). Continuous exposure and complete response prevention in the treatment of obsessive-compulsive neurosis. *Behavior Therapy, 9,* 821–829.

Foa, E. B., Steketee, G., Grayson, J. B., et al. (1984). Deliberate exposure and blocking of obsessive-compulsive rituals: Immediate and long term effects. *Behavior Therapy, 15,* 450–472.

Foa, E. B., Steketee, G., & Milby, J. B. (1980). Differential effects of exposure and response prevention in obsessive-compulsive washers. *Journal of Clinical and Consulting Psychology, 48*(1), 71–79.

Freeman, C. P. L., Trimble, M. R., Deakin, J. F. W., Stokes, T. M., & Ashford, J. J. (1994). Fluvoxamine versus clomipramine in the treatment of obsessive compulsive disorder: A multicenter, randomized, double-blind, parallel group comparison. *Journal of Clinical Psychiatry, 55*(7), 301–305.

Freud, S. (1924). Notes upon a case of obsessional neurosis. In *Collected papers,* Vol. 2 (pp. 122–132). London: Hogarth Press. (Original work published 1909)

Gilles de la Tourette, G. (1885). Etude sur une affection nerveuse caracterisee par de l'incoordination motrice accompagnee de echolalie et de coprolalie. *Archives of Neurology, 9,* 19–42, 158–200.

Goodman, W. K., McDougle, C. J., & Price, L. H. (1992). Pharmacotherapy of obsessive compulsive disorder. *Journal of Clinical Psychiatry, 53*(Suppl.), 29–37.

Goodman, W. K., Price, L. H., Delgado, P. L., et al. (1990). Specificity of serotonin reuptake inhibitors in the treatment of obsessive compulsive disorder. *Archives of General Psychiatry, 47, 47,* 577–585.

Goodman, W. K., Price, L. H., Rasmussen, S. A., et al. (1989a). Efficacy of fluvoxamine in obsessive-compulsive disorder: A double-blind comparison with placebo. *Archives of General Psychiatry, 46,* 36–44.

———. (1989b). The Yale-Brown Obsessive Compulsive Scale (Y-BOCS), part I: Development, use, and reliability. *Archives of General Psychiatry, 46,* 1006–1011.

———. (1989c). The Yale-Brown Obsessive Compulsive Scale (Y-BOCS), part II: Validity. *Archives of General Psychiatry, 46,* 1012–1016.

Grady, T. A., Pigott, T. A., L'Heureux, F., Hill, J. L., Bernstein, S. E., & Murphy, D. L. (1993). A double-blind study of adjuvant buspirone hydrochloride in fluoxetine treated patients with obsessive compulsive disorder. *American Journal of Psychiatry, 150,* 819–821.

Greist, J., Chouinard, G., DuBoff, E., et al. (1995a) Double-blind comparison of three doses of sertraline and placebo in the treatment of outpatients with obsessive compulsive disorder. *Archives of General Psychiatry, 52*(4), 289–295.

Greist, J. H., Jefferson, J. W., Kobak, K. A., Katzelnick, D. J., & Serlin, R. C. (1995b). Efficacy and tolerability of serotonin transport inhibitors in obsessive-compulsive disorder: A meta-analysis. *Archives of General Psychiatry, 52*(1), 53–60.

Greist, J. H., Jefferson, J. W., Rosenfeld, R., et al. (1990). Clomipramine and obsessive-compulsive disorder: A placebo-controlled double-blind study of 32 patients. *Journal of Clinical Psychiatry, 51*(7), 292–297.

Grimsley, S. R., & Jann, M. W. (1992). Paroxetine, sertraline, and fluvoxamine: New selective serotonin reuptake inhibitors. *Clinical Pharmacology, 11,* 930–957.

Hewlett, W. A. (1993). The use of benzodiazepines in obsessive compulsive disorder and Tourette's syndrome. *Psychiatric Annals, 23,* 309–316.

Hewlett, W., Vinogradov, S., & Agras, W. (1992). Clomipramine, clonazepam, and clonidine treatment of obsessive compulsive disorder. *Journal of Clinical Psychopharmacology, 12,* 420–430.

Hollander, E. (Ed.) (1993). Obsessive-compulsive spectrum disorders. *Psychiatric Annals, 23,* 355–407.

Hunter, R. & Macalpine, I. (1982). *Three hundred years of psychiatry 1535–1860: A history presented in selected English texts.* Hartsdale, NY: Carlisle.

Insel, T. R. (1992). Toward a neuroanatomy of obsessive-compulsive disorder. *Archives of General Psychiatry, 49,* 739–744.

Insel, T. R., Murphy, D. L., Cohen, R. M., et al. (1983). Obsessive-compulsive disorder: A double-blind trial of clomipramine and clorgyline. *Archives of General Psychiatry, 40,* 605–612.

Jacobsen, F. M. (1995). Risperidone in the treatment of severe affective illness and obsessive-compulsive disorder. *Journal of Clinical Psychiatry, 56*(9), 423–429.

Janet, P. (1903). *Les Obsessions et la Psychasthenie,* Vol. 1. Paris: Alcan.

Jenike, M. A. (1989). Obsessive compulsive and related disorders: A hidden epidemic. *New England Journal of Medicine, 321,* 539–541.

———. (1993a). Augmentation strategies for treatment-resistant obsessive-compulsive disorder. *Harvard Review of Psychiatry, 1,* 17–26.

———. (1993b). Obsessive-compulsive disorder: Efficacy of specific treatments as assessed by controlled trials. *Psychopharmacology Bulletin, 29,* 487–499.

Jenike, M. A., & Baer, L. (1988). Buspirone in obsessive-compulsive disorder: An open trial. *American Journal of Psychiatry, 145,* 1285–1286.

Jenike, M. A., Baer, L., & Minichiello, W. E. (Eds.). (1990b). *Obsessive-compulsive disorders: Theory and management* (2nd ed.). Chicago, Ill.: Year Book Medical Publishers.

Jenike, M. A., Baer, L., Summergrad, P., et al. (1989). Obsessive-compulsive disorder: A double-blind, placebo-controlled trial of clomipramine in 27 patients. *American Journal of Psychiatry, 146,* 1328–1330.

———. (1990c). Sertraline in obsessive-compulsive disorder: A double-blind comparison with placebo. *American Journal of Psychiatry, 147,* 923, 928.

Jenike, M. A., Hyman, S. E., Baer, L., et al. (1990a). A controlled trial of fluvoxamine for obsessive-compulsive disorder: Implications for a serotonergic theory. *American Journal Psychiatry, 147,* 1209–1215.

Jenike, M. A., & Rauch, S. L. (1994). Managing the patient with treatment resistant obsessive compulsive disorder: Current strategies. *Journal of Clinical Psychiatry, 55*(3, Suppl.), 11–17.

———. (1995). ECT for OCD. *Journal of Clinical Psychiatry, 56,* 81–82.

Jenike, M. A., Surman, O. S., Cassem, N. H., et al. (1983). Monoamine oxidase inhibitors in obsessive-compulsive disorder. *Journal of Clinical Psychiatry, 44,* 131–132.

Karabanow, O. (1977). Double-blind controlled study in phobias and obsessions. *Journal of International Medical Research, 5*(Suppl. 5), 42–48.

Karno, M., Golding, J. M., Sorenson, S. B., & Burnam, A. (1988). The epidemiology of obsessive-compulsive disorder in five U.S. communities. *Archives of General Psychiatry, 45,* 1094–1099.

Kim, S., Dysken, M., & Kuskowski, M. (1990). The Yale-Brown obsessive compulsive scale: A reliability and validity study. *Psychiatric Research, 34,* 94–106.

Kozak, M. J., Foa, E. B., & Steketee, G. (1988). Process and outcome of exposure treatment with obsessive-compulsive: Psychophysiological indicators of emotional processing. *Behavior Therapy, 19,* 157–169.

LaPorta, L. D. (1994). More on obsessive-compulsive symptoms and clozapine [Letter]. *Journal of Clinical Psychiatry, 55,* 312.

Leckman, J. F., Goodman, W. K., North, W. G., Chappell, P. B., Price, L. H., Pauls, D. L., Anderson, G. M., Riddle, M. A., McDougle, C. J., & Barr, L. C. (1994). The role of central oxytocin in obsessive-compulsive disorder and related normal behavior. *Psychoneuroendocrinology, 19*(8), 723–749.

Lei, B. S. (1986). A cross-over treatment of obsessive compulsive neurosis with imipramine and chlorimipramine. *Chung Hua Shen Ching Shen Ko Tsa Chih, 19*(5), 275–278.

Leonard, H. L., Swedo, S. E., Lenane, M. C., et al. (1991). A double-blind desipramine substitution during long-term clomipramine treatment in children and adolescents with obsessive-compulsive disorder. *Archives of General Psychiatry, 48,* 922–927.

Leonard, H. L., Swedo, S., Rapoport, J. L., et al. (1988). Treatment of childhood obsessive-compulsive disorder with clomipramine and desmethylimiparmine: A double-blind crossover comparison. *Psychopharmacology Bulletin, 24,* 93–95.

Mallison, R. T., McDougle, C. J., van Dyck, C. H., Scahill, L., Baldwin, R. M., Seibyl, J. P., et al. (1995). I-123-CIT SPECT imaging of striatal dopamine transporter binding in Tourette's disorder. *American Journal of Psychiatry, 152,* 1359–1361.

March, J. S. (1995). Cognitive-behavioral psychotherapy for children and adolescents with OCD: a review and recommendations for treatment. *Journal of the American Academy of Child and Adolescent Psychiatry, 34*(1), 7–18.

March, J. S., Mulle, K., & Herbel, B. (1994). Behavioral psychotherapy for children and adolescents with obsessive-compulsive disorder: An open trial of a new protocol driven treatment package. *Journal of the American Academy of Child and Adolescent Psychiatry, 33*(3), 333–341.

Marks, I. M. (1981). Review of behavioral psychotherapy, I: Obsessive-compulsive disorders. *American Journal of Psychiatry, 138,* 584–592.

Marks, I. M., Hodgson, R., & Rachman, S. (1975). Treatment of chronic obsessive-compulsive neurosis by in-vivo exposure: A two-year follow-up and issues in treatment. *British Journal of Psychiatry, 127,* 349–364.

Mavissakalian, M., Turner, S. M., Michelson, L., & Jacob, R. (1985). Tricyclic antidepressants in obsessive-compulsive disorder: Antiobsessional or antidepressant agents? *American Journal of Psychiatry, 142,* 572–576.

Mawson, D., Marks, I. M., & Ramm, L. (1982). Clomi-

pramine and exposure for chronic obsessive-compulsive rituals: III. Two year follow-up and further findings. *British Journal of Psychiatry, 140,* 11–18.

McDougle, C. J., Barr, L. C., Goodman, W. K., Pelton, G. H., Aronson, S. C., Anand, A., & Price, L. H. (1995a). Lack of efficacy of clozapine monotherapy in refractory obsessive-compulsive disorder. *American Journal of Psychiatry, 152*(12), 1812–1814.

McDougle, C. J., Fleischmann, R. L., Epperson, C. N., Wasylink, S., Leckman, J. F., & Price, L. H. (1995b). Risperidone addition in fluvoxamine-refractory obsessive-compulsive disorder: Three cases. *Journal of Clinical Psychiatry, 56*(11), 526–528.

McDougle, C. J., Goodman, W. K., Leckman, J. F., Lee, N. C., Heninger, G. R., & Price, L. H. (1994). Haloperidol addition in fluvoxamine-refractory obsessive-compulsive disorder: A double-blind, placebo-controlled study in patients with and without tics. *Archives of General Psychiatry, 51,* 302–308.

McDougle, C. J., Goodman, W. K., Price, L. H., et al. (1990). Neuroleptic addition in fluvoxamine refractory obsessive compulsive disorder. *American Journal of Psychiatry, 147,* 652–654.

McDougle, C. J., Price, L. H., Goodman, W. K., et al. (1991). A controlled trial of lithium augmentation in fluvoxamine-refractory obsessive compulsive disorder: Lack of efficacy. *Journal of Clinical Psychopharmacology, 11,* 175–184.

McElroy, S. L., Phillips, K. A., & Keck, P. E. (1994). Obsessive compulsive spectrum disorder. *Journal of Clinical Psychiatry, 55*(Suppl.), 15–32.

Meige, H., & Feindel, E. (1907). *Tics and their treatment* (S. A. K. Wilson, Trans.). New York: William Wood.

Mindus, P., Rauch, S. L., Nyman, H., Baer, L., Edman, G., & Jenike, M. A. (1994). Capsulotomy and cingulotomy as treatments for malignant obsessive compulsive disorder: An update. In E. Hollander, J. Zohar, D. Marazziti, & B. Olivier (Eds.), *Current insights in obsessive compulsive disorder* (pp. 245–276). Chichester, U.K.: John Wiley & Sons.

Montgomery, S. A. (1980). Clomipramine in obsessional neurosis: A placebo-controlled trial. *Pharmaceutical Medicine, 1*(2), 189–192.

———. (1994). Pharmacological treatment of obsessive compulsive disorder. In E. Hollander, J. Zohar, D. Marazziti, & B. Olivier (Eds.), *Current insights in obsessive compulsive disorder* (pp. 215–225). Chichester, U.K.: John Wiley & Sons.

Montgomery, S. A., McIntyre, A., Osterheider, M., et al. (1993). A double-blind placebo-controlled study of fluoxetine in patients with *DSM-III-R* obsessive-compulsive disorder. *European Neuropsychopharmacology, 3,* 143–152.

Pato, M. T., Eisen, J. L., & Pato, C. N. (1994). Rating scales for obsessive compulsive disorder. In E. Hollander, J. Zohar J, D. Marazziti, & B. Olivier (Eds.), *Current insights in obsessive compulsive disorder* (pp. 77–92). Chichester, U.K.: John Wiley & Sons.

Pato, M. T., Pigott, T. A., Hill, J. L., Grover, G. N., Bernstein, S., & Murphy, D. L. (1991). Controlled comparison of buspirone and clomipramine in obsessive-compulsive disorder. *American Journal of Psychiatry, 148,* 127–129.

Pato, M. T., Zohar-Kaduch, R., Zohar, J., et al. (1988). Return of symptoms after discontinuation of clomipramine in patients with obsessive compulsive disorder. *American Journal of Psychiatry, 145,* 1521–1525.

Pauls, D. L., Alsobrook, J. P., Goodman, W., et al. (1995). A family study of obsessive-compulsive disorder. *American Journal of Psychiatry, 152,* 76–84.

Pauls, D. L., & Leckman, J. F. (1986). The inheritance of Gilles de la Tourette's syndrome and associated behaviors: Evidence for autosomal dominant transmission. *New England Journal of Medicine, 315,* 993–997.

Perse, T. L., Greist, J. H., Jefferson, J. W., et al. (1987). Fluvoxamine treatment of obsessive-compulsive disorder. *American Journal of Psychiatry, 144,* 1543–1548.

Pigott, T. A., L'Heureux, F., Hill, J. L., Bihari, K., Bernstien, S. E., & Murphy, D. L. (1992a). A double-blind study of adjuvant buspirone hydrochloride in clomipramine-treated patients. *Journal of Clinical Psychopharmacology, 12,* 11–18.

Pigott, T. A., L'Heureux, F., Rubenstein, C. S., Hill, J. L., & Murphy, D. L. (1992b, May 2–7). *A controlled trial of clonazepam augmentation in OCD patients treated with clomipramine or fluoxetine.* Paper presented at the American Psychiatry Association Annual Meeting, Washington, D.C.

Pigott, T. A., Pato, M. T., Bernstein, S. E., et al. (1990). Controlled comparisons of clomipramine and fluoxetine in the treatment of obsessive-compulsive disorder. *Archives of General Psychiatry, 47,* 926–932.

Pigott, T. A., Pato, M. T., L'Heureux, F., et al. (1991). A controlled comparison of adjuvant lithium carbonate or thyroid hormone in clomipramine-treated patients with obsessive compulsive disorder. *Journal of Clinical Psychopharmacology, 11,* 242–248.

Pitman, R. K. (1994). Obsessive compulsive disorder in western history. In: Hollander E, Zohar J, Marazziti D, Olivier B, eds. Current Insights in Obsessive Compulsive Disorder (pp. 3–10). Chichester, U.K.: John Wiley & Sons.

Quality Assurance Project. (1985). Treatment outlines for the management of obsessive-compulsive disorders. *Austrian and New Zealand Journal of Psychiatry, 19,* 240–253.

Rachman, S., Cobb, J., Grey, S., et al. (1979). The behavioural treatment of obsessional-compulsive disorders, with and without clomipramine. *Behavior Research & Therapy, 17,* 467–478.

Rachman, S., Hodgson, R., & Marks, I. M. (1971). The treatment of chronic obsessive-compulsive neurosis. *Behavior Research & Therapy, 9,* 237–247.

Rachman, S., Marks, I. M., & Hodgson, R. (1973). The treatment of obsessive-compulsive neurotics by modeling and flooding in vivo. *Behavior Research & Therapy, 11,* 463–471.

Rachman, S. J., & Hodgson, R. J. (1980). *Obsessions and compulsions.* Englewood Cliffs, N.J.: Prentice-Hall.

Rapoport, J., Elkins, R., Mikkelsen, E., et al. (1980). Clinical controlled trial of chlorimipramine in adolescents with obsessive-compulsive disorder. *Psychopharmacology Bulletin, 16*(3), 61–63.

Rapoport, J. L. (1989). *The boy who couldn't stop washing.* New York: E. P. Dutton.

Rapoport, J. L., & Wise, S. P. (1988). Obsessive-compulsive disorder: is it a basal ganglia dysfunction. *Psychopharmacology Bulletin, 24,* 380–384.

Rasmussen, S. A., & Eisen, J. L. (1994). The epidemiology and differential diagnosis of obsessive compulsive disorder. *Journal of Clinical Psychiatry, 55*(Suppl.), 5–14.

Rasmussen, S., Goodman, W. K., Greist, J. H., Jenike, M. A., Kozak, M. J., Liebowitz, M., Robinson, D. G., & White, K. L. (in press). Fluvoxamine in the treatment of obsessive compulsive disorder: A multicenter, double-blind placebo-controlled study in outpatients. *American Journal of Psychiatry.*

Rauch, S. L., Baer, L., & Jenike, M. A. (in press). Management of treatment resistant obsessive compulsive disorder: Practical considerations and strategies. In M. H. Pollack, M. W. Otto, & J. F. Rosenbaum (Eds.), *Challenges in psychiatric treatment: Pharmacologic and psychosocial perspectives.* New York: Guilford.

Rauch, S. L., & Jenike, M. A. (1993). Neurobiological models of obsessive-compulsive disorder. *Psychosomatics, 34,* 20–32.

———. (1994). Management of treatment resistant obsessive-compulsive disorder: concepts and strategies. In B. Berend, E. Hollander, D. Marazitti, & J. Zohar (Eds.), *Current insights in obsessive-compulsive disorder* (pp. 227–244). Chichester, U.K.: John Wiley & Sons.

———. (1997). Neural mechanisms of obsessive-compulsive disorder. *Current Review of Mood Disorders, 1,* 84–94.

Ravizza, L., Barzega, G., Bellino, S., Bogetto, F., & Maina, G. (1995). Predictors of drug treatment response in obsessive-compulsive disorder. *Journal of Clinical Psychiatry, 56,* 368–373.

Remington, G., & Adams, M. (1994). Risperidone and obsessive-compulsive symptoms. *Journal of Clinical Psychopharmacology, 14*(5), 358–359.

Riddle, M. A., Scahill, L., King, R. A., et al. (1992). Fluoxetine in the treatment of obsessive-compulsive disorder in children and adolescents. *Journal of the American Academy of Child and Adolescent Psychiatry, 31*(3), 575.

Rimm, D. C., & Masters, J. C. (1974). *Behavior therapy: Techniques and empirical findings.* New York: Academic.

Schwartz, J. M., Stoessel, P. W., Baxter, L. R., et al. (1996). Systematic changes in cerebral glucose metabolic rate after successful behavior modification. *Archives of General Psychiatry, 53*, 109–113.

Solyom, L., & Sookman, D. (1977). A comparison of clomipramine hydrochloride (Anafranil) and behaviour therapy in the treatment of obsessive neurosis. *Journal of International Medical Research, 5*(Suppl. 5), 49–106.

Steketee, G., Foa, E., & Grayson, J. B. (1982). Recent advances in the behavioral treatment of obsessive-compulsives. *Archives of General Psychiatry, 39*, 1365–1371.

Swedo, S. E. (1994). Sydenham's chorea: A model for childhood autoimmune neuropsychiatric disorders. *Journal of the American Medical Association, 272*(22), 1788–1791.

Swedo, S. E., Leonard, H. L., & Kiessling, L. S. (1994). Speculations on antineuronal antibody-mediated neuropsychiatric disorders of childhood. *Pediatrics, 93*(2), 323–326.

Swerdlow, N. R. (1995). Serotonin, obsessive-compulsive disorder and the basal ganglia. *International Review of Psychiatry, 7*(1), 115–129.

Thoren, P., Åsberg, M., Cronholm, B., et al. (1980). Clomipramine treatment of obsessive compulsive disorder. I. A controlled clinical trial. *Archives of General Psychiatry, 37*, 1281–1285.

Tollefson, G. D., Rampey, A. H., Jr., Potvin, J. H., Jenike, M. A., Rush, A. J., Dominguez, R. A., Koran, L. M.,

Shear, M. K., Goodman, W., & Genduso, L. A. (1994). A multicenter investigation of fixed-dose fluoxetine in the treatment of obsessive-compulsive disorder. *Archives of General Psychiatry, 51*(7), 559–567.

Vallejo, J., Olivares, J., Marcos, T., Bulbena, A., & Menchon, J. (1992).Clomipramine versus phenelzine in obsessive-compulsive disorder: A controlled trial. *British Journal of Psychiatry, 161*, 665–670.

van Oppen, P., de Haan, E., van Balkom, A. J. L. M., Spinhoven, P., Hoogduin, K., & van Dyck, R. (1995). Cognitive therapy and exposure in vivo in the treatment of obsessive compulsive disorder. *Behavior Research Therapy, 33*, 379–390.

Volavka, J., Neziroglu, F., & Yaryura-Tobias, J. A. (1985). Clomipramine and imipramine in obsessive-compulsive disorder. *Psychiatry Research, 14*(1), 83–91.

Warneke, L. B. (1989). The use of intravenous chlorimipramine therapy in obsessive compulsive disorder. *Canadian Journal of Psychiatry, 34*, 853–859.

Wheadon, D. E., Bushnell, W. D., & Steiner, M. (1995). Paroxetine versus placebo in the treatment of obsessive-compulsive disorder. Manuscript submitted for publication.

Young, C. R., Bostic, J. Q., & McDonald, C. L. (1994). Clozapine and refractory obsessive compulsive disorder: A case report [Letter]. *Journal of Clinical Psychopharmacology, 14*, 209–211.

Zahn, T. P., Insel, T. R., & Murphy, D. L. (1984). Psychophysiological changes during pharmacological treatment of patients with obsessive-compulsive disorder. *British Journal of Psychiatry, 145*, 39–44.

Zhao, J. P. (1991). A controlled study of clomipramine and amitriptyline for treating obsessive-compulsive disorder. *Chung Hua Shen Ching Shen Ko Tsa Chih, 24*(2), 68–70.

19

Psychopharmacological Treatment of Post-Traumatic Stress Disorder

Rachel Yehuda

Randall Marshall

Earl L. Giller, Jr.

Psychosocial treatments were the first to be described for post-traumatic stress disorder (PTSD). Psychodynamic, behavioral, and cognitive approaches have been described in the literature. More recently, pharmacotherapy for this condition has been evaluated. Seven controlled medication trials have been performed for use in PTSD. A randomized placebo-controlled trial of the monoamine oxidase inhibitor (MAOI) phenelzine confirmed earlier reports of the drug's efficacy for treating PTSD and its superiority over the tricyclic imipramine. One small controlled trial did not confirm this finding. Three controlled trials indicated that tricyclics have a modest but clinically meaningful benefit, particularly for hyperarousal and intrusive symptoms. Six open trials have shown efficacy for selective serotonin reuptake inhibitors (SSRIs). One placebo-controlled trial of the SSRI fluoxetine also showed efficacy on some measures, although the 5-week trial length may have limited the ability to detect medication effects. Many other classes of medication have also been reported for use on PTSD patients, including reversible inhibitors of MAO-A, benzodiazepines, lithium, anticonvulsants, beta blockers, alpha-2 agonists, buspirone, cyproheptadine, and opioid antagonists. Pharmacotherapy of PTSD is at an early stage, although promising, and extensive controlled investigation is required.

BRIEF DESCRIPTION OF POST-TRAUMATIC STRESS DISORDER AS CURRENTLY DEFINED

The diagnosis of post-traumatic stress disorder (PTSD) first appeared in the *Diagnostic and Statistical Manual of Mental Disorders*, third edition (*DSM-III*), in 1980 with the intention of describing the characteristic symptoms that occur in individuals following exposure to extremely traumatic events (American Psychiatric Association [APA], 1980). Although classified as an anxiety disorder, PTSD also has features of mood, dissociative, and personality disorders.

Principal Diagnostic Criteria

The first diagnostic criterion (Criterion A) for PTSD is that a person must experience or witness an event that involves "actual or threatened physical harm" and have an immediate subjective response to this experience that involves "intense fear, helplessness or horror" (*DSM-IV*, APA, 1994).

The symptoms of PTSD are then classified into three discrete clusters that constitute diagnostic criteria B through D. Intrusive symptoms (Criterion B) include: (a) having recurrent and unwanted recollections of the event, (b) having distressing dreams of the event, and (c) acting and feeling as if the event were reoccurring (e.g., dissociative flashback). In addition, psychological and physiological distress following exposure to symbolic representations of the event may also occur. Avoidant symptoms (Criterion C) reflect both behaviors indicative of actively avoiding reminders of the trauma and symptoms of generalized emotional numbing. The former include (a) efforts to avoid thoughts, feelings, or talk of the trauma; (b) efforts to avoid reminders of the trauma; and (c) inability to recall important aspects of the trauma (e.g., psychogenic amnesia). The symptoms of generalized emotional numbing are (a) markedly diminished interest in normally significant activities, (b) feelings of detachment or estrangement from others, (c) restricted range of affect, and (d) sense of a foreshortened future. Hyperarousal symptoms (Criterion D) include (a) difficulty falling or staying asleep, (b) irritability or angry outbursts, (c) difficulties with concentration, (d) hypervigilance, and (e) exaggerated startle response. Meeting diagnostic criteria for PTSD requires the concurrent presence of one intrusive symptom, three avoidant symptoms, and two hyperarousal symptoms.

In addition to the above criteria, symptoms must be present for at least 1 month (Criterion E) and must be accompanied by clinically significant impairment in social, occupational, or other areas of functioning (Criterion F). If symptoms last for more than 3 months following the traumatic event, the diagnosis of chronic, rather than acute, PTSD is given. The diagnosis of delayed-onset PTSD is given if symptoms begin at least 6 months after the traumatic event. Post-traumatic stress disorder may be diagnosed in any person, adult or child, who meets the above diagnostic criteria, regardless of other preexisting or concurrent psychopathology.

Prevalence

Recent epidemiological studies have demonstrated that PTSD is a common psychiatric condition with an estimated lifetime prevalence of between 1% and 14% in the U.S. general population (Breslau, Davis, Andreski, & Peterson, 1991; Davidson, Hughes, Blazer, & George, 1991b; Helzer, Robin, & McEvoy, 1987; Shore, Vollmer, & Tatum, 1989). The high frequency of PTSD primarily reflects the extraordinarily high prevalence of interpersonal violence in this society. In a random sample of young adults living in urban Detroit, more than one third of the population had experienced life-threatening traumatic events such as rape, assault, and motor vehicle accidents (Breslau et al., 1991). Roughly one quarter of those exposed to traumatic events had lifetime PTSD.

In *DSM-IV*, estimates of the prevalence of PTSD among those exposed to Criterion A stressors range from 3% to 58% (APA, 1994). This wide range reflects the fact that some types of traumatic events are more likely to result in PTSD than others. Among those who have experienced torture, such as concentration camp survivors and prisoners of war (POWs), the prevalence of PTSD can be quite high, with estimates of 50–75% for PTSD in such samples (Goldstein, van Kammen, Shelly, Miller, & van Kammen, 1987; Kluznick, Speed, Van Valenburg, & Magraw, 1986). Among war veterans, estimates of lifetime PTSD are about 30%. However, in individuals who have been exposed to natural disasters such as earthquakes, volcanic eruptions, and bush fires, the prevalence of lifetime PTSD is lower, with estimates ranging from 3.5% to 16% (McFarlane, 1992; Shore, et al., 1989; Shore, Tatum, & Vollmer, 1986). Estimates of the prevalence of PTSD in trauma survivors may also vary depending on the amount of time that has elapsed between the traumatic event and assessment of PTSD. The few studies that have examined the longitudinal course of PTSD prospectively demonstrated that the frequency of PTSD following a specific traumatic event declines with time (McFarlane, 1989), with symptoms for the majority of trauma survivors resolving within 2 to 3 years (Green, in press). However, for the minority of individuals who remain symptomatic, not only do the symptoms of PTSD actually intensify over time, but there is an increased risk of developing secondary and chronic comorbid mood, anxiety, substance abuse, or personality disorders (Freedy, Shaw, & Jarrell, 1992; Friedman & Yehuda, 1995; Green, Lindy, Grace, & Leonard, 1992; Kulka et al., 1990; North, Smith, & Spitznagel, 1994).

Etiology

By definition, exposure to a traumatic event is a necessary requirement for the development of PTSD. However, as discussed above, not everyone who is exposed to a traumatic event develops PTSD. Therefore, there are other factors that influence the development or persistence of symptoms following trauma exposure (see Yehuda & McFarlane for review). Factors that have been associated with increased risk for the development of chronic PTSD include the severity of the trauma (Foy, Sipprelle, Rueger, & Carroll, 1984; March, 1993; Yehuda, Southwick, & Giller, 1992a); history of stress, abuse, or trauma (Bremner, Southwick, Johnson, Yehuda, & Charney, 1993; Zaidi & Foy, 1994); history of behavioral or psychological problems (Helzer et al., 1987); comorbid psychopathology (McFarlane, 1989); genetic factors (True et al., 1993); family history of psychopathology (Davidson, Swartz, Storck, Krishnan, & Hammett, 1985); and subsequent exposure to reactivating environmental events (Goldstein et al., 1987; Green, in press; Kluznick et al., 1986; McFarlane, 1990; Schnurr, Friedman, & Rosenberg, 1993; Solomon & Preager, 1992; Solomon & Smith, 1994; True et al., 1993; Yehuda et al., 1995). The acknowledgment of these risk factors may have significant implications for pharmacotherapy, as described in the next section.

BRIEF HISTORICAL PERSPECTIVE ON TREATMENT

Importance of Psychosocial Treatments

When first described in *DSM-III*, PTSD was conceptualized as defining the normal symptoms that occur following exposure to extremely stressful events. Because of the emphasis on both the environmental etiology of PTSD and the psychological nature of the response, earliest formulations of treatment were psychosocial in nature.

Psychodynamic theories emphasized that PTSD occurred when normal coping mechanisms were overwhelmed and interfered with the processing of the trauma (Horowitz, 1974; Schwartz, 1990). These theories postulated that the symptoms of PTSD would be relieved when the individual could integrate the traumatic event into his or her overall meaning structure. The best vehicle for achieving this integration was initially thought to be traditional psychotherapy. The aim of psychotherapy for trauma survivors was to modify the poor defenses and coping strategies used in the aftermath of the trauma by helping the patient understand why these responses were present. More recently, it has been suggested that these goals can also be successfully addressed using the modality of group psychotherapy (Herman, 1992).

Behavioral theorists explained PTSD as a conditioned fear response and postulated that effective treatments involved reexposing individuals to aspects of the traumatic event through systematic desensitization or the more extreme technique of "flooding" (Keane, Fairbank, Caddell, & Zimering, 1989). According to this approach, symptoms could be relieved by applying learning principles such as habituation or extinction, and monitoring the response to the exposed triggers, until patients became less fearful of reminders of the trauma (Cooper & Clum, 1989; Keane et al., 1989). More recent treatments have combined behavioral and cognitive principles (Foa, Steketee, & Olasov Rothbaum, 1989; Foa, Olasov Rothbaum, Riggs, & Murdock, 1991; Kilpatrick, Veronen, & Resick, 1982). These treatments utilize behavioral principles such as extinction and habituation but add anxiety reducing techniques such as relaxation training (Kilpatrick et al., 1982). An important goal of these treatments is to help the patients modify their misperceptions about the trauma (such as that they could have anticipated, avoided, or mitigated the event or its impact), as well as addressing the maladaptive behavioral responses. This combination of techniques appears to be particularly effective with trauma survivors such as rape victims who are treated relatively soon after a circumscribed traumatic event.

What all of these therapeutic approaches have in common is that they focus on the traumatic event as the direct cause of symptoms of PTSD and emphasize that the normative response to the traumatic event can be modified through further environmental intervention. All three psychosocial approaches are currently used in the treatment of PTSD and appear to be at least partially effective in reducing symptoms of this disorder (for review, see Solomon, Gerrity, & Muff, 1992). However, PTSD appears to involve factors in addition to exposure to a traumatic event. Furthermore, chronic PTSD in particular is associated with the presence of several other comorbid symptoms or disorders (Keane & Wolfe, 1990). Therefore, the treatment of PTSD may require interventions in addition to psychosocial treatments.

Role of Pharmacotherapy

Two conceptions of the role of pharmacotherapy in the treatment of PTSD have arisen in parallel. The first view posits that pharmacotherapy is best considered as an adjunct to trauma-focused psychotherapy (van der Kolk, 1987). In this conception, PTSD arises from impaired behavioral and cognitive responses to an abnormal event, and symptom improvement is addressed by changing the behaviors and cognitions associated with the trauma. The modalities that address these changes are predicated on exposing the individual to the traumatic material and producing abreaction that can then be monitored and systematically desensitized. However, it is difficult to titrate anxiety and affect precisely using these techniques, and many patients report overwhelming responses that actually interfere with recovery. Thus, pharmacotherapy can allow the individual to continue in psychosocial treatment modalities. An additional adjunctive role for pharmacotherapy is in treating comorbid conditions that are not thought to be directly related to the experience of trauma but may arise either as separate illnesses or as secondary consequences of the chronic state of PTSD. For example, pharmacotherapy may be useful in treating secondary panic attacks or depressive illness, which may result in overall global improvement (Marshall, Printz, Cardenas, Abbate, & Liebowitz, 1994).

A second conception views pharmacotherapy as directly relieving the maladaptive symptoms of the disorder (Davidson, 1992; Friedman, 1988). As it becomes clearer from epidemiological and longitudinal studies that PTSD describes a more complex process of debilitation that cannot solely be explained by the presence of a traumatic event, a question arises about whether specialized psychosocial treatments for PTSD can really address the full complement of problems present in symptomatic trauma survivors.

The increasing recognition of biological alterations in PTSD has strengthened this second view and has justified a more central role for psychopharmacology in the treatment of PTSD. Furthermore, the findings of catecholaminergic, serotonergic, hypothalamic-pituitary-adrenal axis, and opioid involvement in PTSD have provided a cogent argument for a rational pharmacotherapy that would directly address some of the biological abnormalities and reduce symptoms. This conception is also more traditional in that it seeks to reduce symptoms in PTSD using the same conceptions that are present in reducing similar symptoms in related disorders. Almost all clinicians agree that psychopharmacology is best supplemented by a supportive therapeutic milieu and/or individual psychotherapy (e.g., Davidson, 1992; Friedman, 1988; van der Kolk, 1987).

Past Treatment Choices

Prior to the official establishment of the diagnosis of PTSD, trauma survivors were often diagnosed as having some kind of anxiety, depressive, or psychotic disorder, depending on the predominant symptoms. Initial pharmacological approaches were based on determining the salient presenting symptoms and using a medication that would be most expected to target those symptoms. For example, flashbacks were treated with antipsychotics, and avoidant and hyperarousal symptoms were characterized more as being part of a depression or phobic response and were accordingly medicated with antidepressants and benzodiazepines. Clinical experience suggested that although antipsychotics could be used for behavioral control and severe arousal, they were not helpful for intrusive recollections and tended to worsen avoidance and numbing symptoms. Therefore, these medications are contraindicated for PTSD (Davidson, 1992; Friedman, 1988). On the other hand, at about the time that PTSD was formally recognized in *DSM-III* (APA, 1980), case reports appeared supporting the efficacy of antidepressants and, to a lesser extent, benzodiazepines in PTSD. The initial efficacy of these drugs helped formulate PTSD as a type of anxiety or mood disorder.

The efficacy of antidepressants in disorders with similar symptoms to PTSD provided a major rationale for pursuing clinical trials with these agents for PTSD. For example, monoamine oxidase inhibitors (MAOI) were considered for PTSD because investigators noted that in double-blind, placebo-controlled trials, phenelzine particularly improved symptoms of irritability, hyperactivity, increased emotionality, depression, phobic symptoms, and hysteria, as well as panic symptoms (Quitkin, Rifkin, & Klein, 1979). All these symptoms are present in PTSD patients. Tricyclic antidepressants were similarly considered because of their efficacy for panic disorder and depression. As selective serotonin reuptake inhibitors (SSRIs) became available for depression and anxiety disorders, including obsessive compulsive disorders, these agents were also tried for PTSD. As for most disorders, the rationale for employing medications for PTSD has not tended to occur as a result of an a priori knowledge about the specific pathophysiology of this disorder, but rather has been an empirical process based on the fundamental assumption of the similarities between PTSD and other mood and anxiety disorders.

Issues in Evaluating the Efficacy of Pharmacotherapy in Post-Traumatic Stress Disorder

It is possible to distinguish among the efficacy of medications in three separate domains: core PTSD symptoms, associated symptoms or disorders such as depression and anxiety, and global nonspecific improvement. Several issues arise in attempting to determine whether a medication has been effective in one or more of these domains. First, it is difficult to separate the nonspecific effects of a medication from effects on the intrusive, avoidant, and hyperarousal symptoms in patients who have chronic illness. Most published reports have examined the efficacy of medications in patients with lifetime or concurrent psychiatric disorder in addition to PTSD. A second issue is that the majority of studies have been performed on chronic PTSD patients who have often been unresponsive to prior treatments. Therefore, the response to a medication in a closed or open trial in a treatment-refractory group may not be generalizable to groups without such treatment histories. Indeed, the majority of treatment studies have been conducted with combat Vietnam veterans who have received chronic treatment in Veterans Administration facilities and are subject to the above-mentioned considerations. Furthermore, combat veterans are not likely to be representative of the prototypic trauma survivor in many other regards. Indeed, in a study that examined combat veterans and "civilians" in tandem, the combat veterans were less likely to respond to pharmacological intervention (e.g., van der Kolk et al., 1994).

Ideally, the efficacy of psychopharmacological agents should first be tested in individuals who have met diagnostic criteria for PTSD for several months or years (as opposed to decades), who are not involved in compensation or disability claims as a result of their traumatic experiences, who previously had a good socioeconomic level and good social and occupational functioning, and who are motivated to return to their previous level of functioning. The effect of concurrent nonpsychopharmacological treatments either before or during a drug trial should also carefully be considered. Follow-up studies should address issues related to relapse versus remission in successfully treated patients.

CURRENT TREATMENT CHOICES

Seven controlled clinical trials have been performed to date in PTSD (Braun, Greenberg, Dasberg, & Lerer, 1990; Davidson et al., 1990; Katz et al., 1995; Kosten, Frank, Dan, McDougle, & Giller, 1991; Reist et al., 1989; Shestatzky, Greenberg, & Lerer, 1988; van der Kolk et al., 1994). Only four of those trials can be correctly considered as Type 1 studies (Davidson et al., 1990; Katz et al., 1995; Kosten et al., 1991; van der Kolk et al., 1994). The rest of the literature consists of open trials, case reports, and retrospective chart reviews. Table 19.1 presents a summary of all medication trials for PTSD and ranks these studies according to the criteria specified in this book (i.e., Type 1, Type 2, etc.). Table 19.2 presents a summary of the results of case reports. The findings of efficacy for each class of medications are reviewed below.

Monoamine Oxidase Inhibitors

Monoamine oxidase inhibitors (MAOIs) were historically the first medications to be considered as a possible treatment for PTSD. The first published open trial reported dramatic global improvement, and an almost complete reduction of intrusive symptoms, with phenelzine in five extremely symptomatic combat veterans who had not responded to other medications (Hogben & Cornfield, 1981). In subsequent studies, phenelzine was also found to produce good global improvement, as well as a reduction in intrusive symptoms in two open trials of combat veterans with PTSD (Davidson, Walker, & Kilts, 1987; Milanes, Mack, Dennison, & Slater, 1984).

The results from the above-mentioned trials were confirmed by a randomized placebo-controlled study by Kosten et al. (1991; preliminary results reported in Frank, Kosten, Giller, & Dan, 1988), who found phenelzine superior to a placebo and imipramine. Phenelzine resulted in a 68% global improvement, compared with a 45% improvement with imipramine and a 28% improvement in the placebo group. Phenelzine was particularly helpful with core symptoms of intrusion and insomnia, with a trend toward an improvement in avoidance. Scores on the Impact of Event Scale improved 45% in the phenelzine group, 25% in the imipramine group, and 5% in the placebo group. Other hyperarousal symptoms were not re-

Class of Drug	Type	Study	Drug	Type study	Weeks	n	Population
MAOI	1	Kosten et al. (1991)	Phenelzine	PBO, random, DB	8	60	Combat veterans
	2	Shestatsky et al. (1988)	Phenelzine	PBO, crossover, DB	5	10	Combat and civilians
	3	Davidson et al. (1987)	Phenelzine	Open trial	6	11	Combat veterans
	3	Lerer et al. (1987)	Phenelzine	Open trial	4 to 18	25	Combat veterans
	3	Milanes et al. (1984)	Phenelzine	Open trial	8	6	Combat veterans
	4	Hogben & Cornfield (1981)	Phenelzine	Open trial	3+	5	Combat veterans
TCA	1	Davidson et al. (1990)	Amitriptyline	PBO, random, DB	8	46	Combat veterans
	1	Kosten et al. (1991)	Imipramine	PBO, random, DB	8	60	Combat veterans
	2	Reist et al. (1989)	Desipramine	PBO, crossover, DB	4	18	Combat veterans
	3	Burstein (1984)	Imipramine	Open trial	3	10	Motor vehicle accident
	3	Chen (1991)	Clomipramine	Open trial	2	7	Combat veterans
	3	Burdon et al. (1991)	Mixed	Open trial	52	158	Combat veterans
	4	Bleich et al. (1986)	Amitriptyline	Retrospective	7	14	Combat veterans
	4	Bleich et al. (1986)	Doxepin	Retrospective	7	7	Combat veterans
	4	Birkhimer et al. (1985)	Mixed	Retrospective, chart	Variable	15	Combat veterans
	4	Falcon et al. (1985)	Mixed	Retrospective	6 to 8	17	Combat veterans
SSRI	1	van der Kolk et al. (1994)	Fluoxetine	PBO, random, DB	5	64	Civilian, combat
	3	Davidson et al. (1991a)	Fluoxetine	Open trial	8 to 32	5	Mixed civilians
	3	McDougle et al. (1991)	Fluoxetine	Open trial	4 to 48	20	Combat veterans
	3	Nagy et al. (1993)	Fluoxetine	Open trial	10	19	Combat veterans
	3	Shay (1992)	Fluoxetine	Open trial	52–108	18	Combat veterans
	3	DeBoer et al. (1992)	Fluvoxamine	Open trial	12	24	Combat veterans
	3	Marshall et al. (in press)	Paroxetine	Open trial	12	17	Civilians
	3	Kline et al. (1994)	Sertraline	Open trial	12+	19	Combat veterans
MAOI/SSRI	1	Katz et al. (1995)	Brofaramine	PBO, random, DB	14	45	Primarily civilians
Benzodiazepine	2	Braun et al. (1990)	Alprazolam	PBO, random, DB	5	10	Civilians and veterans
	3	Dunner et al. (1985)	Alprazolam	Open trial			
	4	Lowenstein et al. (1988)	Clonazepam	Open trial		5	Early sex abuse

Comorbid Diagnosis	Concurrent Rx	No. of Responders	Global Improvement	PTSD Improvement
Dysthmia (n = 28)	Counseling	Not rated	Very good	Good for intrusion and sleep
Not assessed	Not specified	None	Same as placebo	Drug not more effective than placebo
Not assessed	Not specified	6 of 7	In depression and anxiety	Moderate to good for intrusive and less so for arousal
Depression, anxiety	Psychotherapy	4 of 25	Modest for depression and anxiety	Poor to moderate improvement, best for sleep
Depression	Not specified	4 of 6	Good to very good	Moderate, best for intrusion and arousal
Mood, anxiety	Psychotherapy	5 of 5	Very good for panic and depression	Excellent, curative for intrusion and arousal
Depression, anxiety, SA	Supportive	14 of 40 (8 weeks)	Moderate to good if no comorbidity	Modest improvement for PTSD
Dysthymia	Counseling	Not specifically rated	Very good	Good for intrusive symptoms
Depression, anxiety, SA	Inpatient milieu	5 drug, 3 placebo	Depression improved	Poor, not effective
None	Not specified	6 of 10	Reduced anxiety	Moderate, best for intrusive symptoms
Not assessed	Inpatient milieu	6 of 7	Very good for obsessions	Moderate for intrusion, good for obsessions
Depression	Milieu, clonazepam	Not reported	Good for depression	Moderate for depression, intrusion, arousal
Depression, anxiety	Psychotherapy	4 of 14	Improved psychosocial function	Good for arousal, mood, intrusion
Depression, anxiety	Psychotherapy	1 good, 3 moderate	Moderate	Moderate response
Many comorbid Axis I	Varied	Almost none	Poor	Patients did not improve
Panic, anxiety, SA	Varied	14 very good, 3 good	Good for anxiety	Overall symptom reduction, particularly intrusions
Depression	Supportive counseling	Not assessed	Very good	Good for civilians for numbing and arousal
Anxiety	Psychotherapy	5 of 5	Very good	Good for intrusion and avoidance
Depression	"Milieu" VA	13 of 20	Very good	Very good, best for avoidance
Depression, anxiety	Psychotherapy, meds	7 of 19	Very good	Good for avoidance, not good for intrusion, sleep problems
Depression	"Milieu" VA	13 of 18	Less anger, better mood states	Modest overall, good for explosiveness
Depression	None	9 of 15	Modest global effect	Modest, good for insomnia and intrusion
Depression, panic social phobia	None	11 of 17	Very good	Very good for all core symptoms and dissociative symptoms
Depression	Not specified	12 of 19	Improved dysphoria	Generally poor, improvement in sleep
None	Supportive counseling	12 of 22	Good	Good, but there was a high placebo response
Depression, anxiety	Supportive counseling	None	Modest	Poor for core PTSD symptoms
Multiple personality	Individual psychotherapy	5 of 5	Moderate	Moderate

(continued)

TABLE 19.1 *(continued)*

Class of Drug	Type	Study	Drug	Type study	Weeks	n	Population
Mood Stabilizers							
Lithium	4	van der Kolk (1983)	Lithium	Open trial	NR	14	Combat veterans
	3	Kitchner & Greenstein (1985)	Lithium	Open trial	NR	5	Combat veterans
Anticon-vulsants	3	Lipper et al. (1986)	Carbamazepine	Open trial	5	10	Combat veterans
	3	Wolf et al. (1988)	Carbamazepine	Open trial	NR	10	Combat veterans
	3	Fesler (1991)	Valproate	Open trial	8 to 52	16	Combat veterans
Antihypertensives							
Beta-blockers	3	Kolb et al. (1984)	Propranolol	Open trial	NR	9	Combat veterans
	2	Famularo et al. (1988)	Propranolol	A-B-A design	6	11	Abused children
Alpha2-agonists	3	Kolb et al. (1984)	Clonidine	Open trial	NR	9	Combat veterans
	3	Kinzie & Leung (1989)	Clonidine	Open trial	52	9	Torture victims
5-HT1A-agonist	3	Fitchner et al., (1994)	Buspirone	Open trial	16	12	Combat veterans
Opiate antago-nist	3	Glover (1992)	Nalmefene	Open trial	3+	18	Combat veterans

Type 1 studies: Rigorous, randomized, prospective, clinical trials with random group assignment, blinded assessments, appropriate exclusion and inclusion criteria, state-of-the-art diagnostic methods, adequate sample size to offer statistical power and appropriate statistical analyses. Type 2 studies: Clinical trials in which an intervention is made but some aspect of the Type 1 study requirement is missing, such as small subject number or the like. Type 3 studies: Good open trial studies or case control studies. Type 4 studies: Reviews with secondary data analysis.

DB = double blind; MAOI = monoamine oxidase inhibitor; NR = no recorded; PBO = placebo; SA = substance abuse; SSRI = selective serotonin reuptake inhibitor; TCA = tricyclic antidepressant; VA = Veterans Administration.

ported. This study was particularly well conducted for several reasons. Veterans were chosen from a Readjustment Veterans Outreach Center and not a VA hospital. Most of the veterans were employed, and none had comorbid substance abuse or major Axis I diagnoses. Subjects were selected from a pool of veterans who were already receiving supportive psychotherapy at the center. Therapeutic drug levels were monitored, and an adequate time of 8 weeks was used to assess efficacy. Thus, the study was able to determine the specific effect of the medication on symptom improvement.

The MAOIs may potentially augment norepinephrine, dopamine, and serotonin neurotransmission by blocking the degradation of these agents. The global effectiveness of phenelzine on these systems may in part reflect this "broad spectrum" psychotropic activity. On the other hand, it has also been suggested that phenelzine may improve PTSD symptoms by specifically downregulating adrenergic activity in the locus coeruleus (Davidson et al., 1987), which has been postulated as playing an important role in intrusive symptoms (Charney, Deutch, Krystal, Southwick, & Davis, 1993).

Two groups failed to note significant improvement with phenelzine in Israeli combat veterans with PTSD. Lerer et al. (1987) reported that phenelzine did not show a dramatic effect in an open prospective trial, although some symptoms, such as sleep disturbances and intrusive thoughts, were reduced in Israeli war veterans. In considering their findings, this group emphasized sociocultural differences between Israeli and American combat veterans (e.g., in the incidence of substance abuse and antisocial personality) and

Comorbid Diagnosis	Concurrent Rx	No. of Responders	Global Improvement	PTSD Improvement
	Psychotherapy	8 of 14	Good	Good reduction in hyperarousal and alcohol use
	therapy/ medications	4 of 5	Good	Good for explosiveness and arousal
Axis II, past SA, anxiety	None	7 of 10	Good	Moderate, best for intrusion and sleep
Depression/SA/ anxiety	Psychotherapy	8 of 10	Good	Good for impulse controls and explosiveness
Depression/thought dis/anxiety	Milieu	10 of 16	Good	Good for sleep and avoidance
Not specified	Not specified	9 of 9	Good, reduced anger	Reduced intrusive and hyperarousal symptoms
Mood and anxiety		8 of 11	Good	Good for intrusion and arousal symptoms
Not specified	Not specified	9 of 9	Good	Good for intrusion and hyperarousal symptoms
Depression	Group therapy, imipramine	Very good	Very good	Very good for intrusion and hyperarousal
Not assessed	Group, individual therapy	4 of 12	Good for those who improved	Good for hyperarousal and intrusion for only a minority
Anxiety, depressive disorders	Other medications	8 of 18	Increased access to feelings	Good for numbing, as well as intrusion and arousal

postulated that some of the differences in efficacy may be due to the fact that, overall, Israeli veterans were not as globally symptomatic. In a 5-week, randomized, crossover design, Shestatzky et al. (1988) also did not find phenelzine to be effective. However, only 10 subjects (a mix of Israeli war veterans and civilians) were studied. The small number of subjects and the limited time period makes this controlled trial a Type 2 study.

In summary, phenelzine (therapeutic dose range 45 to 90 mg) appears to be superior to imipramine for PTSD and effective for intrusive symptoms in particular. A limitation of this medication is that it did not appear to be particularly effective for avoidant symptoms. Yet, these symptoms are often quite disabling to the PTSD patient. Other disadvantages of MAOIs include the risk of hypertensive crisis from tyramine-containing foods and certain other medications. Phenelzine is also associated with many side effects. Side effects that contributed to dropout rates in the various studies included intensification of sleep disorder, dizziness, erectile failure, delayed ejaculation, delayed urination, constipation, dry mouth, blurred vision, drowsiness, behavioral inhibition, blackouts, perceptual changes, and hypomania (Davidson et al., 1987; Kosten et al., 1991).

Tricyclic Antidepressants

It has been harder to evaluate the efficacy of tricyclic antidepressants (TCAs) because no single medication has been used. The TCAs vary in their mechanisms and spectrum of action across neurotransmitter systems. Nonetheless, TCAs have been among the best-studied class of medications for PTSD, with three randomized clinical trials (Davidson et al., 1990; Kosten et al., 1991; Reist et al., 1989), three open trials (Burdon, Sutker, Foulks, Crane, & Thompson, 1991; Burstein, 1984; Chen, 1991), and several retrospective studies (Bleich, Siegel, Garb, & Lerer, 1986; Birkhimer, De Vane, & Muniz, 1985; Falcon, Ryan, Chamberlain, & Curtis, 1985) and case reports (Blake, 1986; Burstein et al., 1988; Shen & Park, 1983; Turchan, Holmes, & Wasserman, 1992). Generally, prospective open trials have shown moderate efficacy for intrusive and hyperarousal symptoms (Burdon et al.,

TABLE 19.2 Summary of Clinical Case Reports for Post-Traumatic Stress Disorder

Class	Study	Drug	Type of Trauma	Comments
MAOI	Shen & Park (1983)	Phenelzine	Combat	Improvement of intrusive symptoms; caused sexual failure
TCA	Marshall (1975)	Imipramine	ICU stay	Reduced nightmares and insomnia
		Imipramine	Injury	Reduced nightmares and hyperarousal
	Blake (1986)	Doxepine	Burn injury	Improved dysphoria, startle, insomnia
		Imipramine	Burn injury	Remission of anxiety, panic insomnia, nightmares
		Imipramine	Car accident	Improvement in nightmares, startle, depression
	Burstein et al. (1988)	TCA (unspecified)	Combat	Symptom improvement between crises
		TCA (unspecified)	Car accident	Reduced anxiety about being in cars
	Turchan et al. (1992)	Amitriptyline	Airplane crash	Prevented anxiety and depression in early PTSD
		Nortryptyline	Airplane crash	Improved sleep, resolved guilt, hopelessness, helplessness
	Pohl & Balon (1992)	Desipramine	Rape	Relieved panic, not PTSD symptoms
	Basoglu et al. (1992)	Amitriptyline	Torture	Depression and anxiety improved, but not PTSD symptoms
SSRI	Marshall & Klein (1995)	Paroxetine	Sexual abuse	Good for all PTSD symptoms
	March (1992)	Fluvoxamine	Combat	Good for all PTSD symptoms
Anticonvulsants	Stewart & Bartucci (1986)	Carbamazepine	Combat	Drug added to control seizures, but relieved PTSD symptoms
	Szymanski & Olympia (1991)	Divalproex	Combat	Reduced temper outbursts
		Divalproex + amitriptyline	Combat	Reduced irritability, improved mood
	Hargrave (1993)	Buspirone/ trazadone	Veteran (dementia)	Reduced intrusive symptoms and explosiveness
	Duffy (1992)	Buspirone	Combat	Reduced intrusive symptoms and hyperarousal
	LaPorta & Ware (1992)	Buspirone	Physical abuse	Reduction in insomnia, nightmares, anxiety
		Buspirone	Childhood abuse	Elimination of intrusive thoughts and nightmares
5-HT antagonist	Brophy (1991)	Cyproheptadine	Combat	Reduced nightmares
		Cyproheptadine	Combat	Reduced nightmares
		Cyproheptadine	Combat	Reduced nightmares

ICU = intensive care unit; MAOI = monoamine oxidase inhibitor; SSRI = selective serotonin reuptake inhibitor; TCA = tricyclic antidepressant.

1991; Burstein, 1984; Chen, 1991). Retrospective chart reviews have been more mixed, with some investigators reporting efficacy for TCAs (Bleich et al., 1986; Falcon et al., 1985), while other have not (Birkhimer et al., 1985; Bleich et al., 1986). In case reports, improvements in generalized anxiety, panic, and depressive symptoms have been particularly noted (Basoglu, Marks, & Sengün, 1992; Blake, 1986; Burstein et al., 1988; Pohl & Balon, 1992; Turchan et al., 1992). However, many also reported a direct reduction in sleep (Blake, 1986; Burstein et al., 1988; Turchan et al., 1992) and other intrusive or arousal symptoms.

The case reports are particularly noteworthy because the majority have reported on the efficacy of TCAs in noncombat populations such as rape victims (Pohl & Balon, 1992), motor vehicle accident victims (Blake, 1986; Burstein et al., 1988), torture survivors (Basoglu et al., 1992), survivors of plane crashes (Turchan et al., 1992), and burn victims (Blake, 1986) and have therefore provided at least some evidence for the generalizability of the effects of TCAs across populations of trauma survivors.

The two most definitive and methodologically sound studies examining the efficacy of TCA are Davidson et al.'s (1990) randomized trial comparing amitriptyline to a placebo in combat veterans and Kosten et al.'s (1991) randomized trial comparing imipramine to phenelzine and a placebo. In the first study, Davidson et al. reported modest efficacy for amitriptyline (dose range 150 to 300 mg) on some variables in those who completed at least 4 weeks of the study (40 out of 46). Overall improvement was particularly noted in veterans who did not meet diagnostic criteria for major depression. Kosten et al. showed that imipramine (dose range 150 to 300 mg) was more effective than a placebo (but less effective than phenelzine) in producing global symptom improvement and improvement in intrusive symptoms of combat veterans. Both these studies used standardized assessments for both diagnoses and symptom ratings and considered comorbidity in evaluating treatment outcome. The study by Davidson et al. also made an important contribution in comparing responses at 4 and 8 weeks and demonstrating that symptom reduction was not significant at the 4-week period. In contrast, Reist et al. (1989) did not find significant differences between desipramine (doses no greater than 200 mg per day) and a placebo in a 4-week crossover trial. In considering these findings, Davidson has suggested that insufficient dosing, shorter duration of treatment, and failure to evaluate the importance of comorbidity may have contributed to these negative results (Davidson, 1992).

Overall, the therapeutic effects of tricyclic drugs have been modest, but clinically meaningful, particularly for hyperarousal and intrusive symptoms. Although TCAs have not been directly compared in randomized clinical trials, it may be that their differential efficacy across trials in PTSD is related to slight variations in the neurotransmitter systems that are affected by these agents. Also of note in studies of TCAs is the lack of placebo response in the three controlled trials with veterans, which is consistent with a treatment refractory study population (Davidson, 1992). Although TCAs have been generally well tolerated in the above study groups, these medications have been associated with anticholinergic and cardiac side effects in patients with conduction defects. These medications appear to work best after at least 8 weeks in trauma survivors without significant comorbidity. However, it should be noted that TCAs are effective for reducing associated symptoms of mood and anxiety in subjects with PTSD.

Selective Serotonin Reuptake Inhibitors

As SSRIs became popular treatments for depression and anxiety, clinicians began to consider whether these drugs might be effective for PTSD. In all six open trial studies (Davidson, Roth, & Newman, 1991a; DeBoer et al., 1992; Kline, Dow, Brown, & Matloff, 1994; McDougle, Southwick, Charney, & St. James, 1991; Nagy, Morgan, Southwick, & Charney, 1993; Shay, 1992), SSRIs have been reported as very effective in reducing the symptoms of PTSD. The literature on SSRIs is qualitatively better than for MAOIs and TCAs, largely reflecting the growing knowledge about PTSD and the utilization of standardized clinical assessments. Several results from open trials were published concerning the use of fluoxetine, and all reported good efficacy. Davidson et al. (1991a) first suggested that fluoxetine may improve avoidant and intrusive symptoms but is less effective in relieving hyperarousal symptoms. This conclusion was based on a prospective report of five individuals with assorted types of traumatic events ranging from childhood incest to motor vehicle accidents as an adult. McDougle et al. (1991) studied 20 combat veterans for a variable length of time and reported significant symptom improvement for more than half the sample. This group also noted the particular effectiveness of fluoxetine on avoidance symptoms. The observation that fluoxetine was effective for avoidant symptoms was further confirmed by Nagy et al. (1993), but the number of responders and the magnitude of response was somewhat lower than in the other two reports. Shay (1992) studied 18 combat veterans who were concurrently engaged in milieu outpatient therapy for over a year. Of these, 13 responded and particularly improved in behavioral explosiveness. In a study using polypharmacy, Burdon et al. (1991) administered fluoxetine in combination with low-dose amitriptyline and clonazepam to 158 outpatient veterans in a PTSD clinic for 12 months. They reported that this combination of medications was good for hyperarousal, intrusive thoughts, and depression.

Other SSRIs have also been tried. Marshall et al. conducted a 12-week trial of paroxetine in 17 subjects with noncombat-related PTSD, hypothesizing that paroxetine's anxiety-reducing properties might be particularly beneficial for this disorder (submitted for publication). Sixty-five percent (11 out of 17) of subjects were rated significantly improved by an independent evaluator, and there were no dropouts due to adverse effects. There was improvement in all 3 symptom clusters, with reductions of 50% (intrusive symptoms), 50% (avoidance), and 43% (hyperarousal). A controlled trial is now underway. DeBoer et al. (1992) studied 24 World War II Dutch resistance veterans using fluvoxamine for 12 weeks. Fluvoxamine reduced intrusion and hyperarousal but did not reduce avoidant symptoms. This study was notably different from the other reports because subjects were not recruited from a treatment setting. Rather, they were community-dwelling individuals who were functioning well within the community. Thus, they were only moderately symptomatic at the beginning and likely did not have the characteristics typical of a clinical population. Kline et al. (1994) reported good preliminary results with sertraline. This open trial studied 19 treatment-refractory combat veterans for over 12 weeks. Of the 19, 12 showed good responses for symptoms of arousal, intrusion, and explosiveness. Sertraline also produced improvement in dysphoria and hopelessness.

The only randomized, double-blind, placebo-controlled trial to date using SSRIs was performed by van der Kolk et al. (1994). This was a 5-week study of fluoxetine (average dose 40 mg/day) in two groups of PTSD patients: 31 war veterans and 33 civilian patients in a trauma clinic. More than half of the patients also met criteria for major depression. About 25% did not complete the study. This study showed that, in the complete sample, fluoxetine was superior to placebo for overall PTSD symptoms, and also dramatically improved depressive symptoms. Fluoxetine also particularly improved numbing and hyperarousal, whereas other symptoms of avoidance and intrusive symptoms did not improve. This study was the first to demonstrate that veterans showed a worse outcome when directly compared with civilians. However, when each group was analyzed separately, fluoxetine was not more effective than placebo in reducing symp-

toms. Although this study did find that fluoxetine was effective for a group of civilians, a 5-week trial is probably not a long enough interval in which to assess the efficacy of a medication for PTSD (Southwick, et al., 1994). As such, it cannot be ruled out that the brevity of the treatment trial accounted for the failure of van der Kolk and his colleagues to observe symptom improvement in the combat veteran group.

The SSRIs are extremely promising medications for PTSD because they have come the closest to targeting the whole syndrome of PTSD and not just discrete symptom clusters. Side effects that have been reported for SSRIs are insomnia, sexual dysfunction, decreased libido, weight loss and decreased appetite, diarrhea, headaches, and sweating, but these vary based on the specific medication. As different SSRIs are associated with slightly different profiles of serotonergic activity, it will be important to conduct randomized clinical trials with a variety of different agents.

Benzodiazopines

Benzodiazepines were initially tried in PTSD because of their efficacy in relieving general symptoms of anxiety; they were found effective in a small number of open trials. Dunner et al. (1985) observed positive effects with alprazolam (therapeutic dose range 0.5 to 6 mg/day) in veterans with PTSD. Lowenstein et al. (1988) demonstrated improvement in five patients with multiple personality disorder and PTSD whose symptoms responded well to clonazepam (1 mg to 5 mg daily). Improvement was noted for nightmares, initial insomnia, intrusive recollections, panic attacks, severe anxiety, flashbacks, and overall well-being. In a randomized, placebo-controlled, double-blind study, alprazolam showed only modest benefits for anxiety symptoms and no benefit for core PTSD symptoms. However, this was only a 5-week trial with only 10 subjects (a mixed sample of veterans and civilians). In an interesting study, Shalev and Rogel-Fuchs failed to note improvements in the startle response in patients being successfully treated with clonazopam (1992).

Although benzodiazepines do show moderate efficacy for PTSD, they should be used with caution. In particular, in trauma survivors such as combat veterans who show a high comorbidity of PTSD and substance abuse, the use of benzodiazepines may be contraindicated because of the severe withdrawal symptoms that are associated with discontinuation of these agents

(Risse et al., 1990), as well as the high risk of perpetuating dependence or abuse of these drugs. It may be that benzodiazepines will be most useful at early stages of PTSD in individuals without histories of substance abuse.

Reversible Monoamine Oxidase Inhibitors

As discussed above, both serotonin uptake inhibition and monoamine oxidase A (MAO-A) inhibition appear to be helpful in PTSD. Brofaramine is an experimental drug that combines serotonin uptake inhibition with selective, reversible MAO-A inhibition. Furthermore, the MAO-A inhibiting properties of brofaramine are not associated with some of the safety or tolerability problems of phenelzine.

There has only been one study examining the efficacy of this agent in PTSD. However, this trial is noteworthy for representing the first multicenter, randomized, placebo-controlled, double-blind study in PTSD, which studied both men and women who had a history of a wide range of traumatic events. The study used stringent inclusion/exclusion criteria such that no subjects met criteria for primary Axis I disorders other than PTSD. Clinical assessments were performed using contemporary diagnostic instruments. Brofaramine was not superior to placebo in the total sample ($n = 64$) but was effective in the subgroup of patients symptomatic for at least 1 year. Although brofaramine did produce a significant improvement in PTSD, there was a high placebo response in this study. By the end of the study, over half of the brofaramine-treated patients no longer met the criteria for PTSD, whereas one quarter of those on the placebo did not meet the criteria for PTSD. Thus, brofaramine resulted in symptom reduction in twice as many individuals than did the placebo. Although the high placebo rate in this study is in contrast to the other six trials discussed above, this may be explained by the fact that this is the only study to evaluate a group of mostly civilians with a relatively recent exposure to trauma and few comorbid disorders. The findings therefore suggest that the symptoms that are present relatively soon after a trauma (e.g., months or years following an event as opposed to decades) may be more responsive to clinical intervention. It would be interesting to compare the efficacy of brofaramine in more treatment-refractory, chronic patients as this drug does appear promising. However, brofaramine is not commercially available or Food and Drug Administration (FDA) approved and is not being further tested for PTSD treatment.

Lithium

There is scant information about the efficacy of lithium carbonate for the treatment of PTSD, although two open trials can be found in the literature. The primary rationale for initially trying lithium in the treatment of PTSD was its mood-stabilizing properties. Van der Kolk performed an open trial of lithium carbonate (therapeutic dose 300–1500 mg/day) in 14 treatment-refractory combat veterans who reported feeling out of control, on the verge of exploding, emotionally cut off from their families, and preoccupied by feelings of guilt (1983). Of the 14 veterans, 8 showed good improvement with lithium carbonate, particularly for subjective feelings of control and improvement in hyperarousal. Kitchner and Greenstein (1985) reported similar results in an open trial with five combat veterans. These studies did not utilize structured scales to assess comorbid diagnoses or severity of PTSD symptoms. Scales were also not used to assess improvement for either global or PTSD symptoms. Information about dosing, duration of treatment, or side effects is also not available. Therefore, follow-up studies should be conducted to assess the true efficacy of these agents for reducing PTSD symptoms.

Anticonvulsants

The use of anticonvulsants such as carbamazepine and valproate in PTSD has stemmed from suggestions that the behavioral and neurobiological sensitization of trauma survivors might be relieved by raising the neuronal threshold for arousal in limbic areas (Keck, McElroy, & Friedman, 1992). Anticonvulsants act as mood stabilizers and enhance the stimulating activity of gamma-aminobutyric acid (GABA) by acting on $GABA_A$ (valproate) and $GABA_g$ (carbamazepine) receptors, thereby causing an increase in chloride conductance and a resultant neuronal hyperpolarization (stabilization).

Lipper et al. (1986) specifically hypothesized that the intrusive symptoms of PTSD would respond to anticonvulsants because these symptoms would most likely be considered "kindled" or paroxysmal experiences. Indeed, Lipper et al. found that carbamazepine (therapeutic dose 600–1000 mg/day) was moderately effective for intrusive recollections, sleep impairment, and hostility in 7 of 10 combat veterans who participated in a 5-week open trial. All the patients studied had comorbid personality disorder, and all had some history of substance abuse. None had comorbid mood disorder, and only one had a comorbid generalized anxiety disorder. Significant improvements were also noted in overall anxiety, somatization, hostility, psychoticism, and confusion bewilderment (as assessed by the Profile of Mood States).

Wolf, Alavi, and Mosnaim (1988) reported on the efficacy of carbamazepine in 10 veterans whose histories included poor impulse control, violent behavior, and angry outbursts. All veterans had comorbid substance abuse, and some had Axis II diagnoses. One of the patients had a history of partial complex seizures. All subjects had normal sleep and waking electroencephalograms (EEGs). By staff observation and patient self-report, carbamazepine was found to be helpful in improving impulse controls and angry outbursts.

A single case study also showed the efficacy of carbamazepine for treating PTSD symptoms in a patient with seizure disorder. In some subjects, carbamazepine produced side effects such as ataxia, headache, rash, mental confusion, and drowsiness (Davidson, 1992).

Fesler (1991) reported improvement in hyperarousal and avoidant symptoms in a group of 16 combat veterans following an open trial with divalproex (therapeutic dose range 750 to 1750 mg/day) over a period of several months. Most patients had histories of mood, anxiety, substance abuse, and thought disorders, and all but three were also being treated with one other medication (usually an antidepressant, anxiolytic, or neuroleptic). Of the veterans, 11 had significantly improved quality and length of sleep, whereas 9 had improved avoidant and numbing symptoms. No improvements were noted for intrusive symptoms. Only one patient dropped out of the study because of the adverse side effects of nausea and vomiting. Other side effects noted were vivid dreaming, sleepwalking, headache, impaired memory, slowed thinking, and vertigo. In two case reports, divalproex has been reported effective for reducing irritability, temper outbursts, and mood disturbance.

In summary, lithium and anticonvulsants can be helpful with impulsivity and explosiveness, whereas anticonvulsants appear to have more specific effects on intrusive symptoms and sleep. It should be noted that all observations of mood stabilizers have been made with treatment-refractory combat veterans who were specifically selected to be on these medications because of problems with impulsivity and explosiveness, and the results in this population may not be generalizable to the whole trauma-affected population.

Beta Blockers and Alpha-2 Agonists

Although beta blockers and alpha-2 agonists exert their actions differently, these agents are similar in their overall effect on catecholamines and in fact are both used as antihypertensives. Beta blockers such as propranolol are thought to exert a more peripheral attenuation of catecholaminergic neurotransmission, whereas clonidine suppresses locus coeruleus activity and reduces adrenergic tone.

These drugs have been used in the treatment of panic disorder (Ravaris, Friedman, Hauri, & McHugo, 1991; Tanna, Penningroth, & Woolson, 1977). However, the use of beta blockers and alpha-2 agonists began in direct response to scientific observations regarding the pathophysiology of PTSD. Following Kardiner's seminal depiction of "physioneurosis" in combat veterans and preliminary descriptions of increased sympathetic nervous system activation in war veterans (1941), Kolb, Burris, and Griffiths (1984) studied propranolol (dose range 120 to 160 mg per day) in 12 Vietnam combat veterans in an attempt to directly address sympathetic hyperarousal in PTSD. An improvement in explosiveness, nightmares, intrusive recollections, startle response, hyperalertness, impaired sleep, self-esteem, and psychosocial function was noted. Famularo, Kinscherff, and Fenton (1988) employed an A-B-A design (6 weeks off, 6 weeks on, 6 weeks off) to explore the effects of propranolol in physically or sexually abused children with acute PTSD. Propranolol treatment significantly reduced symptoms of intrusion and arousal in 8 of 11 children. Propranolol treatment is associated with several side effects, such as depression, fatigue, forgetfulness, sexual impairment, bradycardia, hypotension, and mental confusion.

In the same report as mentioned above, Kolb et al. (1984) also reported good results in alleviating flashbacks and hyperarousal using clonidine (dose range 0.1 mg to 0.4 mg per day). Kinzie and Leung (1989) added clonidine to imipramine in the treatment of nine Cambodian refugees and noted sleep improvement, reduction of nightmares, and partial improvement in startle response but no improvement of avoidant behavior.

To date, there have been no published reports of randomized, double-blind, placebo-controlled trials of clonidine. However, one such study is in progress (S. M. Southwick, personal communication, January, 1997). Future data may reveal that clonidine is effective for hyperarousal and reexperiencing symptoms such as nightmares and flashbacks in the subset of individuals who show evidence of increased catecholamine activity.

Although earlier studies described catecholamine alterations as possibly central to the pathophysiology of PTSD (Kosten et al., 1987; Perry, Southwick, Yehuda, & Giller, 1990; Yehuda, Southwick, Giller, Ma, & Mason, 1992b), recent studies suggest that catecholaminergic hyperactivity may be confined to a subset of trauma survivors with PTSD. Indeed, some investigators have failed to note increased catecholamines in PTSD subjects (Mellman, Kumar, Kulick-Bell, Kumar, & Nolan, 1995; Murburg, McFall, Lewis, & Beith, 1995). Dampening locus coeruleus activity for the individuals who do show evidence of noradrenergic hyperarousal may result in symptom improvement with propranolol or clonidine.

Other Medications

Serotonergic Drugs

There are some preliminary reports examining the serotonin 5HT1A partial agonist buspirone and the serotonin antagonist cyproheptadine. Buspirone is used as an anxiolytic and has been reported as effective in a case study describing three combat veterans (Wells et al., 1991). Buspirone (therapeutic dose range 35 to 60 mg) reduced associative symptoms of anxiety and depression, as well as insomnia and flashbacks. Avoidant symptoms were not improved with buspirone.

There are two case reports in which cyproheptadine was used for the treatment of traumatic nightmares (Brophy, 1991; Harsch, 1986). This drug (therapeutic dose 4–28 mg) appears to be effective in suppressing traumatic nightmares in combat veterans.

Opioid Antagonists

Many theorists have postulated that alterations in the opioid system may be relevant to PTSD (Charney et

al., 1993; Glover, 1992; van der Kolk, 1987). However, to date there is scant evidence for this. In one study, Pitman, van der Kolk, Orr, and Greenberg (1990) demonstrated a naloxone-reversible stress-induced analgesia in combat veterans who were exposed to trauma-related imagery. Nonetheless, the idea of treating PTSD with opiate antagonists such as nalmefedene is largely grounded in this theory. Glover reported improvement in numbing and other PTSD symptoms in 8 of 18 combat veterans after using nalmefedene (therapeutic dose 200–400 mg/day). Other subjects either worsened or showed no improvement (Glover, 1992).

FUTURE VISTAS

The pharmacologic literature for PTSD is a relatively small body, with only a few studies that can legitimately be considered Type 1 studies. Moreover, most studies were conducted in veteran populations. However, these studies have been important in demonstrating that medications can be quite effective in treating circumscribed symptoms of PTSD and can lead to an overall global improvement in symptomatic trauma survivors. As such, these studies have tended to confirm the results of open trials and clinical case reports. Future controlled trials are needed to examine other promising medications in different trauma populations.

One of the conclusions that can be drawn is that most medications that have been tried in PTSD do not seem to target the uniform syndrome but rather specific aspects of the disorder. The medications that appear to work best on intrusive symptoms are the MAOIs and TCAs. However, these agents, primarily the TCAs, do not seem to improve avoidant or hyperarousal symptoms, with the possible exception of sleep. There appears to be preliminary information from open trials and case reports that some SSRIs, such as clomipramine and buspirone, and other agents, such as carbamazepine and clonidine, may also be effective for intrusive symptoms. However, these observations need to be confirmed by controlled trials. Open and controlled trials taken together, the SSRIs may prove to be a class of medication effective for all 3 symptom clusters. The opiate antagonist nalmefedene has also been shown to reduce numbing, but again this observation must be at least replicated and then confirmed by controlled trials. Hyperarousal symptoms appear primarily to respond best to mood stabilizers such as lithium and anticonvulsants and adrenergic inhibitors such as clonidine and propranolol. However, these medications have little effectiveness for the other symptom clusters.

The fact that different medications target different core symptoms of PTSD has been interpreted as reflecting the complex pathophysiology of this disorder. It may be that medications with specific effects in some neurotransmitter systems may have particular effects on those symptoms that are primarily mediated by those systems. However, the fact that no one medication has yet been found to address the complex syndrome of PTSD also raises the question of whether all symptoms of PTSD should be addressed by pharmacotherapy. And, if so, should polypharmacy strategies be used to specifically target different types of symptoms in trauma survivors?

To date, it is unknown which of the core symptom clusters are most responsible for the functional impairment of PTSD. A recent study in a non-treatment-seeking group of Holocaust survivors showed that all survivors had intrusive, distressing thoughts about the Holocaust, whereas only a subset of these survivors showed impairment in social or occupational functioning and met diagnostic criteria for PTSD. Rather, overall impairment, and neurobiological dysregulation, was related to the presence of avoidant symptoms of Holocaust survivors (Yehuda et al., 1995). Thus, it is possible that individuals eventually learn to cope with some of the symptoms of PTSD through non-pharmacological strategies, whereas other symptoms lead more directly to impairment and require more direct pharmacological intervention.

The literature demonstrates that pharmacotherapy for PTSD results in a global improvement by relieving associated or comorbid symptoms such as depression, panic, anxiety, and impulsivity. This raises the question of whether medications for PTSD exert their effects by addressing comorbid conditions or associative features of PTSD. As many of the patients whose treatment is recounted in this literature have chronic PTSD and a current or past history of comorbid psychiatric disorder, future studies will need to examine the effect of comorbid symptoms and diagnoses on treatment responses to various medications.

The pharmacotherapy of PTSD is in its early stages, and more controlled trials need to be done with diverse groups of trauma survivors. One of the major difficulties with the literature is that it is difficult to determine whether one can use similar strategies for the treatment of individuals who may be at different stages of their illness. The majority of studies have tended to focus on chronically ill, treatment-refractory combat veterans with multiple presenting problems. Future studies will need to determine whether different pharmacological strategies are optimal for more acute conditions and whether other factors such as type of trauma and developmental stage at which one survived traumatic events are relevant to pharmacological intervention. Eventually, medication selection for PTSD may be guided by factors other than symptom presentation.

Future studies must also address the interaction of psychopharmacology and psychosocial treatments. Other questions concern the appropriate duration for pharmacotherapy. This is a difficult question because the natural history of PTSD is still unknown. The effects of discontinuing medications on PTSD symptoms must also be formally studied. Finally, future research should address the issue of whether medications can be used to prevent relapse of symptoms from one episode of PTSD and/or for prevention of a reoccurrence in response to a subsequent episode.

References

American Psychiatric Association. (1980). *Diagnostic and statistical manual of mental disorders* (3rd ed.). Washington, D.C.: Author.

————. (1994). *Diagnostic and statistical manual of mental disorders* (4th ed.). Washington, D.C.: Author.

Basoglu, M., Marks, I. M., & Sengun, S. (1992). Amitriptyline for PTSD in a torture survivor: A case study. *Journal of Traumatic Stress, 5,* 77–83.

Birkhimer, L. J., DeVane, C. L., & Muniz, C. E. (1985). Posttraumatic stress disorder: Characteristics and pharmacological response in the veteran population. *Comprehensive Psychiatry, 26,* 304–310.

Blake, D. (1986). Treatment of acute posttraumatic stress disorder with tricyclic antidepressants. *Southern Medical Journal, 79,* 201–204.

Bleich, A., Siegel, B., Garb, R., & Lerer, B. (1986). Posttraumatic stress disorder following combat exposure: Clinical features and psychopharmacological treatment. *British Journal of Psychiatry, 149,* 365–369.

Braun, P., Greenberg, D., Dasberg, H., & Lerer, B. (1990). Core symptoms of posttraumatic stress disorder unimproved by alprazolam treatment. *Journal of Clinical Psychiatry, 51*, 236–238.

Bremner, J. D., Southwick, S. M., Johnson, D. R., Yehuda, R., & Charney, D. S. (1993). Childhood physical abuse and combat-related posttraumatic stress disorder in Vietnam veterans. *American Journal of Psychiatry, 150*, 235–239.

Breslau, N., Davis, G. C., Andreski, P., & Peterson, E. (1991). Traumatic events and post-traumatic stress disorder in an urban population of young adults. *Archives of General Psychiatry, 48*, 216–220.

Brophy, M. H. (1991). Cyproheptadine for combat nightmares in post-traumatic stress disorder and dream anxiety disorder. *Military Medicine, 156*, 100–101.

Burdon, A. P., Sutker, P. B., Foulks, E. F., Crane, M. U., & Thompson, K. E. (1991). Pilot program of treatment for PTSD [Letter]. *American Journal of Psychiatry, 148*, 1269–1270.

Burstein, A. (1984). Treatment of post-traumatic stress disorder with imipramine. *Psychosomatics, 25*, 681–686.

Burstein, A., Ciccone, P. E., Greenstein, R. A., Daniels, N., Olsen, K., Mazarek, A., Decatur, R., & Johnson, N. (1988). Chronic Vietnam PTSD and acute civilian PTSD: A comparison of treatment experiences. *General Hospital Psychiatry, 10*, 245–249.

Charney, D. S., Deutch, A. Y., Krystal, J. H., Southwick, S. M., & Davis, M. (1993). Psychobiologic mechanisms of posttraumatic stress disorder. *Archives of General Psychiatry, 50*, 294–305.

Chen, C. J. (1991). The obsessive quality and clomipramine treatment in PTSD (letter). *American Journal of Psychiatry, 148*, 1087–1088.

Cooper, N. A., & Clum, B. A. (1989). Imaginal flooding as a supplementary treatment for PTSD in combat veterans: A controlled study. *Behavioral Therapy, 20*, 381–391.

Davidson, J. (1992). Drug therapy of post-traumatic stress disorder. *British Journal of Psychiatry, 160*, 309–314.

Davidson, J., Kudler, H., Smith, R., Mahorney, S. L., Lipper, S., Hammett, E., Saunders, W. B., & Cavenar, J. L., Jr. (1990). Treatment of posttraumatic stress disorder with amitriptyline and placebo. *Archives of General Psychiatry, 47*, 259–266.

Davidson, J., Roth, S., & Newman, E. (1991a). Fluoxetine in post-traumatic stress disorder. *Journal of Traumatic Stress, 4*, 419–423.

Davidson, J., & Smith, R. (1990). Traumatic experiences in psychiatric outpatients. *Journal of Traumatic Stress, 3*, 459–475.

Davidson, J., Swartz, M., Storck, M., Krishnan, R. R., & Hammett, E. (1985). A diagnostic and family study of posttraumatic stress disorder. *American Journal of Psychiatry, 142*, 90–93.

Davidson, J., Walker, J. I., & Kilts, C. (1987). A pilot study of phenelzine in the treatment of post-traumatic stress disorder. *British Journal of Psychiatry, 150*, 252–255.

Davidson, J. R. T., Hughes, D. L., Blazer, D. G., & George, L. K. (1991b). Post-traumatic stress disorder in the community: An epidemiological study. *Psychological Medicine, 21*, 713–721.

DeBoer, M., Op den Velde, W., Falger, P. J., Hovens, J. E., De Groen, J. H., & Van Duijn, H. (1992). Fluvoxamine treatment for chronic PTSD: A pilot study. *Psychother Psychosom, 57*, 158–163.

Duffy, J. (1992). Rapid response to buspirone in a case of posttraumatic stress disorder. *Annals of Clinical Psychiatry, 4*, 193–196.

Dunner, F. J., Edwards, W. P., Copeland, P. C. (1985). Clinical efficacy of alprazolam in PTSD patients. New Research, American Psychiatric Association, 138th Annual Meeting, Los Angeles, 1985.

Falcon, S., Ryan, C., Chamberlain, K., & Curtis, G. (1985). Tricyclics: Possible treatment for posttraumatic stress disorder. *Journal of Clinical Psychiatry, 46*, 385–388.

Famularo, R., Kinscherff, R., & Fenton, T. (1988). Propranolol treatment for childhood post-traumatic stress disorder, acute type: A pilot study. *Am J Dis Child, 142*, 1244–1247.

Fesler, F. A. (1991). Valproate in combat-related posttraumatic stress disorder. *Journal of Clinical Psychiatry, 52*, 361–364.

Fichtner, G., Arora, R. C., O'Connors, F. L., & Crayton, J. W. (1994). Platelet paroxetine binding and fluoxetine pharmacotherapy in posttraumatic stress disorder. *Life Science, 54*, 39–44.

Foa, E. B., Olasov Rothbaum, B., Riggs, D. S., & Murdock, T. B. (1991). Treatment of posttraumatic stress disorder in rape victims: A comparison between cognitive-behavioral procedures and counseling. *Journal of Consulting and Clinical Psychology, 59*, 714–723.

Foa, E. B., Steketee, G., & Olasov Rothbaum, B. (1989). Behavioral/cognitive conceptualizations of post-traumatic stress disorder. *Behavioral Therapy, 20*, 155–176.

Foy, D. W., Sipprelle, R. C., Rueger, D. B., & Carroll, E. M. (1984). Etiology of posttraumatic stress disorder in Vietnam veterans. *Journal of Consulting and Clinical Psychology, 40*, 1323–1328.

Frank, J. B., Kosten, T. R., Giller, E. L., & Dan, E. (1988). A randomized clinical trial of phenelzine and imipramine for post traumatic stress disorder. *American Journal of Psychiatry, 145*, 1289–1291.

Freedy, J. R., Shaw, D. L., & Jarrell, M. P. (1992). Towards an understanding of the psychological impact of natural disaster: An application of the conservation resources stress model. *Journal of Traumatic Stress, 5,* 441–454.

Friedman, M. J. (1988). Toward rational pharmacotherapy for posttraumatic stress disorder: An interim report. *American Journal of Psychiatry, 145,* 281–285.

Friedman, M. J., & Yehuda, R. (1995). Post-traumatic stress disorder and comorbidity: Psychobiological approaches to differential diagnosis. In M. J. Friedman, D. S. Charney, & A. Y. Deutch (Eds.), *Neurobiological and clinical consequences of stress: From normal adaptation to PTSD.* Philadelphia: Lippincott-Raven Publishers.

Glover, H. (1992). Emotional numbing: A possible endorphin-mediated phenomenon associated with posttraumatic stress disorder and other allied psychopathologic states. *Journal of Traumatic Stress, 5,* 643–675.

Goldstein, G., van Kammen, W., Shelly, C., Miller, D. J., & van Kammen, D. P. (1987). Survivors of imprisonment in the Pacific theater during World War II. *American Journal of Psychiatry, 144,* 1210–1213.

Gorman, J. M., Liebowitz, M. R., Fyer, A. J., Goetz, D., Campeas, R. B., Fyer, M. R., Davies, S. O., & Klein, D. F. (1987). An open trial of fluoxetine in the treatment of panic attacks. *Journal of Clinical Psychopharmacology, 7,* 329–332.

Green, B. L., Lindy, J. D., Grace, M. C., & Leonard, A. C. (1992). Chronic posttraumatic stress disorder and diagnostic comorbidity in a disaster sample. *Journal of Nervous and Mental Disease, 180,* 760–766.

Hargrave, R. (1992). Serotonic agents in the management of dementia and posttraumatic stress disorder. *Psychosomatics, 34,* 461–462.

Harsch, H. H. (1986). Cyproheptadine for recurrent nightmares. *American Journal of Psychiatry, 143,* 1491–1492.

Helzer, J. E., Robin, L. N., & McEvoy, L. (1987). Posttraumatic stress disorder in the general population: Findings from the Epidemiological Catchment Area Survey. *New England Journal of Medicine, 317,* 1630–1634.

Herman, J. L. (1992). *Trauma and recovery.* New York: Basic Books.

Hogben, G. L., & Cornfield, R. B. (1981). Treatment of traumatic war neurosis with phenelzine. *Archives of General Psychiatry, 38,* 440–445.

Horowitz, M. (1974). Stress response syndromes, character style, and dynamic psychotherapy. *Archives of General Psychiatry, 31,* 768–781.

Kardiner, A. (1941). *The traumatic neurosis of war.* New York: Paul Hoeber.

Katz, R. J., Lott, M. H., Arbus, P., Crocq, L., Lingjaerde, O., Lopez, G., Loughrey, G. C., MacFarlane, D. J., Nugent, D., Turner, S. W., Weisaeth, L., & Yule, W. (1995). Pharmacotherapy of post-traumatic stress disorder with a novel psychotropic. *Anxiety, 1,* 169–174.

Keane, T. M., Fairbank, J. A., Caddell, J. M., & Zimering, R. T. (1989). Implosive (flooding) therapy reduces symptoms of PTSD in Vietnam combat veterans. *Behavioral Therapy, 20,* 245–260.

Keane, T. M., & Wolfe, J. (1990). Comorbidity in posttraumatic stress disorder: An analysis of community and clinical studies [Special issue]. *Journal of Applied Social Psychology, 20,* 1776–1788.

Keck, P. E., McElroy, S. L., & Friedman, L. M. (1992). Valproate and carbamazepine in the treatment of panic and posttraumatic stress disorders, withdrawal states, and behavioral dyscontrol syndromes. *Journal of Clinical Psychopharmacology, 12*(Suppl.), 36S–41S.

Kilpatrick, D. G., Veronen, L. J., & Resick, P. A. (1982). Psychological sequelae to rape: assessment and treatment strategies. In D. M. Dolays & R. L. Meredith (Eds.), *Behavioral medicine: Assessment and treatment strategies* (pp. 473–497). New York: Plenum Press.

Kinzie, J. D., & Leung, P. (1989). Clonidine in Cambodian patients with posttraumatic stress disorder. *Journal of Nervous and Mental Disease, 1777,* 546–550.

Kitchner, I., & Greenstein, R. (1985). Low dose lithium carbonate in the treatment of post traumatic stress disorder: Brief communication. *Military Medicine, 150,* 378–381.

Kline, N. A., Dow, B. M., Brown, S. A., & Matloff, J. L. (1994). Sertraline efficacy in depressed combat veterans with posttraumatic stress disorder [Letter]. *American Journal of Psychiatry, 151,* 621.

Kluznick, J. C., Speed, N., Van Valenburg, C., & Magraw, R. (1986). Forty-year follow-up of United States prisoners of war. *American Journal of Psychiatry, 143,* 1443–1446.

Kolb, L. C., Burris, B. C., & Griffiths, S. (1984). Propranolol and clonidine in the treatment of posttraumatic stress disorders of war. In B. A. van der Kolk (Ed.), *Posttraumatic stress disorder: Psychological and biological sequelae* (pp. 98–105). Washington, D.C.: American Psychiatric Press.

Kosten, T. R., Frank, J. B., Dan, E., McDougle, C. J., & Giller, E. L. (1991). Pharmacotherapy for posttraumatic stress disorder using phenelzine or imipramine. *Journal of Nervous and Mental Disease, 179,* 366–370.

Kosten, T. R., Mason, J. W., Giller, E. L., et al. (1987). Sustained urinary norepinephrine and epinephrine elevation in posttraumatic stress disorder. *Psychoneuroendocrinology, 12,* 13–20.

Kulka, R. A., Schlenger, W. E., Fairbank, J. A., Hough, R. L., Jordan, B. K., Marmar, C. R., & Weiss, D. S.

(1990). *Trauma and the Vietnam War generation: Report of findings from the National Vietnam Veterans Readjustment Study.* New York: Brunner/Mazel.

LaPorta, L. D., & Ware, M. R. (1992). Busirone in the treatment of posttraumatic stress disorder [Letter]. *Journal of Clinical Psychopharmacology, 12,* 133–134.

Lerer, B., Bleich, A., Kotler, M., Garb, R., Hertzberg, M., & Levin, B. (1987). Posttraumatic stress disorder in Israeli combat veterans: Effect of phenelzine treatment. *Archives of General Psychiatry, 44,* 976–981.

Lipper, S., Davidson, J. R. T., Grady, T. A., Edinger, J. D., Hammett, E. B., Mahorney, S. L., & Cavenar, J. O. (1986). Preliminary study of carbamazopine in post-traumatic stress disorder. *Psychosomatics, 27,* 849–854.

Lowenstein, R. J., Hornstein, N., Farber, B. (1988). Open trial of clonazepam in the treatment of posttraumatic stress symptoms in multiple personality disorder. *Dissociation, 1,* 3–12.

March, J. S. (1992). Fluoxetine and fluvoxamine in PTSD [Letter]. *American Journal of Psychiatry, 149,* 413.

Marshall, J. R. (1975). The treatment of night terrors associated with the posttraumatic syndrome. *American Journal of Psychiatry, 132,* 293–295.

Marshall, R. D., & Klein, D. F. (1995). Pharmacotherapy in the treatment of posttraumatic stress disorder. *Psychiatry Annals. 25,* 588–597.

Marshall, R. D., Printz, D., Cardenas, D., Abbate, L., & Liebowitz, M. R. (1994). Adverse events in patients with PTSD and panic attacks on fluoxetine [Letter]. *American Journal of Psychiatry, 152,* 1238.

McDougle, C. J., Southwick, S. M., Charney, D. S., & St. James, R. L. (1991). An open trial of fluoxetine in the treatment of posttraumatic stress disorder [Letter]. *Journal of Clinical Psychopharmacology, 11,* 325–327.

McFarlane, A. C. (1989). The aetiology of post-traumatic morbidity: predisposing, precipitating, and perpetuating factors. *British Journal of Psychiatry, 154,* 221–228.

———. (1990). Vulnerability to posttraumatic stress disorder. In M. E. Wolf & A. D. Mosnaim (Eds.), *Posttraumatic stress disorder: Etiology, phenomenology and treatment* (pp. 2–20). Washington, D.C.: American Psychiatric Press.

———. (1992). Multiple diagnoses in posttraumatic stress disorder in the victims of a natural disaster. *Journal of Nervous and Mental Disease, 180,* 498–504.

Mellman, T. A., Kumar, A., Kulick-Bell, R., Kumar, M., & Nolan, B. (1995). Nocturnal/daytime urine noradrenergic measures and sleep in combat-related PTSD. *Biological Psychiatry, 38,* 174–179.

Milanes, F. J., Mack, C. N., Dennison, J., & Slater, V. L. (1984, June). Phenelzine treatment of post-Vietnam stress syndrome. *VA Practitioner,* 40–49.

Murburg, M. M., McFall, M. E., Lewis, N., & Beith, R. C. (1995). Plasma norepinephrine kinetics in patients with posttraumatic stress disorder. *Biological Psychiatry, 38,* 819–825.

Nagy, L. M., Morgan, C. A., III, Southwick, S. M., & Charney, D. S. (1993). Open prospective trial of fluoxetine for posttraumatic stress disorder. *Journal of Clinical Psychopharmacology, 13,* 107–113.

North, C. S., Smith, E. M., & Spitznagel, E. L. (1994). Posttraumatic stress disorder in survivors of a mass shooting. *American Journal of Psychiatry, 151,* 82–88.

Perry, B. D., Southwick, S. M., Yehuda, R., & Giller, E. L. (1990). Adrenergic receptor regulation in posttraumatic stress disorder. In E. L. Giller (Ed.), *Biological assessment and treatment of posttraumatic stress disorder* (pp. 87–114). Washington, D.C.: American Psychiatric Press.

Pitman, R. K., van der Kolk, V. A., Orr, S. P., & Greenberg, M. S. (1990). Naloxone-reversible analgesic response to combat-related stimuli in post traumatic stress disorder. *Archives of General Psychiatry, 47,* 541–544.

Pohl, R., & Balon, R. (1992). Antidepressants, panic disorder, and PTSD [Letter]. *American Journal of Psychiatry, 149,* 1752–1753.

Quitkin, R. F., Rifkin, A., & Klein, D. F. (1979). Monoamine oxidase inhibitors: A review of antidepressant effectiveness. *Archives of General Psychiatry, 36,* 749–760.

Ravaris, C. L., Friedman, M. J., Hauri, P. J., & McHugo, G. J. (1991). A controlled study of alprazolam and propranolol in panic-disordered and agoraphobic outpatients. *Journal of Clinical Psychopharmacology, 11,* 344–350.

Reaves, M. E., Hansen, T. E., & Whisenand, J. M. (1989, May). The psycho-pharmacology of PTSD. *VA Practitioner,* 65–72.

Reist, C., Kauffman, C. D., Haier, R. J., Sangdahl, C., DeMet, E. M., Chicz-DeMet, A., & Nelson, J. N. (1989). A controlled trial of desipramine in 18 men with posttraumatic stress disorder. *American Journal of Psychiatry, 146,* 513–516.

Risse, S. C., Whitters, A., Burke, J., Chen, S., Scurfield, R. M., & Raskind, M. A. (1990). Severe withdrawal symptoms after discontinuation of alprazolam in eight patients with combat-induced posttraumatic stress disorder. *Journal of Clinical Psychiatry, 51,* 206–209.

Rothbaum, B. O., Foa, E. B., Riggs, D. S., Murdock, T., & Walsh, W. (1992). A prospective examination of post-traumatic stress disorder in rape victims. *Journal of Traumatic Stress, 55,* 455–475.

Schnurr, P. P., Friedman, M. J., & Rosenberg, S. D. (1993). Premilitary MMPI scores as predictors of combat-related PTSD symptoms. *American Journal of Psychiatry, 150,* 479–483.

Schwartz, L. S. (1990). A biopsychosocial treatment approach to post-traumatic stress disorder. *Journal of Traumatic Stress, 3,* 221–238.

Shalev, A. Y., & Rogel-Fuchs, Y. (1992). Auditory startle reflex in post-traumatic stress disorder patients treated with clonazepam. *Israeli Journal of Psychiatry Related Sciences, 29,* 1–6.

Shay, J. (1992). Fluoxetine reduces explosiveness and elevates mood of Vietnam combat vets with PTSD. *Journal of Traumatic Stress, 5,* 97–101.

Shen, W. W., & Park, S. (1983). The use of monoamine oxidase inhibitors in the treatment of traumatic war neurosis: Case report. *Military Medicine, 148,* 430–431.

Shestatzky, M., Greenberg, D., & Lerer, B. (1988). A controlled trial of phenelzine in posttraumatic stress disorder. *Psychiatry Research, 24,* 149–155.

Shore, J. H., Tatum, E. L., & Vollmer, W. M. (1986). Psychiatric reactions to disaster: The Mount St. Helens experience. *American Journal of Psychiatry, 143,* 590–595.

Shore, J. H., Vollmer, W. M., & Tatum, E. L. (1989). Community patterns of post traumatic stress disorders. *Journal of Nervous and Mental Disease, 77,* 681–685.

Solomon, S., Gerrity, E. T., & Muff, A. M. (1992). Efficacy of treatments for posttraumatic stress disorder. *Journal of the American Medical Association, 268,* 633–638.

Solomon, S., & Smith, E. (1994). Social support and perceived controls as moderators of responses to dioxin and flood exposure. In R. J. Ursano, B. G. McCaughey, & C. S. Fullerton (Eds.), *Individual and community responses to trauma and disaster: The structure of human chaos.* New York: Cambridge University Press.

Solomon, Z., & Preager, E. (1992). Elderly Israeli Holocaust survivors during the Persian Gulf War: A study of psychological distress. *American Journal of Psychiatry, 149,* 1707–1710.

Southwick, S. M., & Yehuda, R. (1993). The interaction between pharmacotherapy and psychotherapy in the treatment of posttraumatic stress disorder. *American Journal of Psychotherapy, 47,* 404–411.

Southwick, S. M., Yehuda, R., Giller, E. L., & Charney, D. S. (1994). The effects of antidepressants in the treatment of posttraumatic stress disorder: A quantitative review. In M. M. Murburg (Ed.), *Catecholamines in post-traumatic stress disorder.* Washington, D.C.: American Psychiatric Press.

Stewart, J. T., & Bartucci, R. J. (1986). Posttraumatic stress disorder and partial complex seizures [Letter]. *American Journal of Psychiatry, 143,* 113–114.

Szymanski, H. V., & Olympia, J. (1991). Divalproex in posttraumatic stress disorder [Letter]. *American Journal of Psychiatry, 148,* 1086–1087.

Tanna, V. T., Penningroth, R. P., & Woolson, R. F. (1977). Propranolol in the treatment of anxiety neurosis. *Comprehensive Psychiatry, 18,* 319–326.

True, W. R., Rice, J., Eisen, S., Heath, A. C., Goldberg, J., Lyons, M., & Nowak, J. (1993). A twin study of genetic and environmental contributions to liability for posttraumatic stress symptoms. *Archives of General Psychiatry, 50,* 257–264.

Turchan, S. J., Holmes, V. F., & Wasserman, C. S. (1992). Do tricyclic antidepressants have a protective effect in post-traumatic stress disorder? *New York State Journal of Medicine, 92,* 400–402.

van der Kolk, B. A. (1987). The drug treatment of posttraumatic stress disorder. *Journal of Affective Disorders, 13,* 203–213.

———. (1983). Psychopharmacological issues in posttraumatic stress disorder. *Hospital and Community Psychiatry, 34,* 683–691.

van der Kolk, B. A., Dreyfuss, D., Michaels, M., Shera, D., Berkowitz, R., Fisler, R., & Saxe, G. (1994). Fluoxetine in posttraumatic stress disorder. *Journal of Clinical Psychiatry, 55,* 517–522.

Wells, G. B., Chu, C., Johnson, R., Nasdahl, C., Ayubi, M. A., Sewell, E., & Statham, P. (1991). Buspirone in the treatment of post-traumatic stress disorder and dream anxiety disorder. *Military Medicine, 11,* 340–343.

Wolf, M. E., Alavi, A., & Mosnaim, A. D. (1988). Posttraumatic stress disorder in Vietnam veterans clinical and EEG findings; possible therapeutic effects of carbamazepine. *Biological Psychiatry, 23,* 642–644.

Yehuda, R., Kahana, B., Schmeidler, J., Southwick, S. M., Wilson, S., & Giller, E. L. (1995). Impact of cumulative lifetime trauma and recent stress on current posttraumatic stress disorder symptoms in Holocaust survivors. *American Journal of Psychiatry, 152,* 1815–1818.

Yehuda, R., & McFarlane, A. C. (1995). Conflict between current knowledge about posttraumatic stress disorder and its original conceptual basis. *American Journal of Psychiatry, 152,* 1705–1713.

Yehuda, R., Schmeidler, J., Elkin, A., Houshmand, E., Siever, L., Binder-Brynes, K., Wainberg, M., Aferiot, D., Lehman, A., Guo, L. S., & Yang, R. K. (in press). Phenomenology and psychobiology of the intergenerational response to trauma. In Y. Danieli (Ed.), *Intergenerational handbook: Multigenerational legacies of trauma.* New York: Plenum Press.

Yehuda, R., Southwick, S. M., & Giller, E. L. (1992a). Exposure to atrocities and severity of chronic posttraumatic stress disorder in Vietnam combat veterans. *American Journal of Psychiatry, 149,* 333–336.

Yehuda, R., Southwick, S., Giller, E. L., Ma, X., & Mason, J. W. (1992b). Urinary catecholamine excre-

tion and severity of PTSD symptoms in Vietnam combat veterans. *Journal of Nervous and Mental Disease, 180,* 321–325.

Zaidi, L. Y., & Foy, D. W. (1994). Childhood abuse and combat-related PTSD. *Journal of Traumatic Stress, 7,* 33–42.

20

Psychological and Behavioral Treatments of Post-Traumatic Stress Disorder

Terence M. Keane

Several Type 1 and Type 2 random clinical trials (RCTs) have confirmed exposure therapy (including systematic desensitization, flooding, prolonged exposure, and implosive therapy) and, to a lesser extent, anxiety management techniques (using both cognitive and behavioral strategies) as the psychosocial treatments of choice for post-traumatic stress disorder (PTSD).

Eye-movement desensitization and reprocessing (EMDR), a recently introduced approach to the treatment of PTSD, has shown some promise, although its research base to date, consisting largely of open clinical trials, is inadequate.

PHENOMENOLOGY

When individuals are exposed to life-threatening events or other catastrophic stressors, some can develop a persistent and potentially debilitating syndrome known as post-traumatic stress disorder (PTSD). The syndrome is often characterized by high levels of anxiety and depression, but its distinctive symptomatology includes (a) reliving experiences such as intrusive thoughts, nightmares, dissociative flashbacks to elements of the original traumatic event, and psychophysiological reactivity to cues of the traumatic event and preoccupation with that event; (b) avoidance of thoughts, people, and places that resemble the traumatic event, emotional numbing that is tantamount to an absence of emotional attachments, and an inability to feel the range of positive emotions that contributes to the complete human experience; and (c) symptoms of hyperarousal, including heightened startle sensitivity, sleep problems, attentional difficulties, hypervigilance, and the presence of irritability, anger, or rage (cf.

Diagnostic and Statistical Manual of Mental Disorders, 4th ed. [*DSM-IV*], American Psychiatric Association [APA], 1994).

PREVALENCE

Post-traumatic stress disorder occurs in contemporary society at high rates. Recent epidemiological studies indicate that in the United States prevalence rates for exposure to traumatic stressors may be as high as 70% of the adult population (Norris, 1992; Resnick, Kilpatrick, Dansky, Saunders, & Best, 1993); corresponding rates for the development of PTSD indicate that at least 8% of the general population ultimately develops PTSD (Breslau, Davis, Andreski, & Peterson, 1991; Kessler, Sonnega, Bromet, Hughes, & Nelson, 1995). Such estimates conservatively yield 20 million cases of PTSD (current or lifetime) in the United States alone. Perhaps most important is the recognition that violence in the home and the community continues unabated in society, that almost daily we learn of newly occurring natural or technological disasters, and that the presence of armed conflicts across the world adversely affects the lives of many more individuals and their families.

General population statistics, of course, do not provide a comprehensive view of the nature of trauma exposure and PTSD. Inspection of special groups at elevated risk provides an important perspective on the depth of the problem. To do so, we must rely again on statistics from the United States since the strongest methodological studies have been completed there. Among American women, approximately 13% have experienced a completed rape; 31% of these women (for a total of about 4% of the general population) developed PTSD following the assault (Kilpatrick, Edmonds, & Seymour, 1992).

Similarly, in the most comprehensive study of the effects of war on its combatants, the National Vietnam Veterans Readjustment Study (NVVRS; Kulka et al., 1990) found a lifetime rate of PTSD of 30% and a current rate of PTSD of 15%. Moreover, in a national study of women, Resnick et al. (1993) estimated prevalence rates of current PTSD to be 5%, with lifetime rates of 12%.

Examination of the rates of trauma exposure and PTSD across studies does yield interesting gender differences. It seems that while men report higher rates of exposure to traumatic events, women report more PTSD. Many possible explanations exist for these observed differences. Women may be more susceptible to PTSD due to a possible link to factors associated with the gender differences in depression. Alternatively, the types of stressors to which women are differentially exposed (e.g., sexual assault) may be those most strongly related to the development of PTSD irrespective of gender. More research to illuminate further the underlying factors responsible for these observations is clearly needed.

ETIOLOGY

While the occurrence of a traumatic event that evokes feelings of terror, horror, or helplessness is essential for conferring the diagnosis of PTSD, it is clearly only one of the factors associated with the development of PTSD. Clearly, not everyone exposed to a potentially traumatic event develops PTSD. To explain this, psy-

chopathologists have evoked the concept of individual differences. The classic paradigm on the effects of life stressors, initially proposed by Dohrenwend and Dohrenwend (1981), indicates the relative importance of (a) the stimulus component of the stressor in affecting outcome, (b) the ongoing situational context within which the event occurs, and (c) the personal characteristics, including biological and psychological factors, exposure to previous traumatic events, and an individual's coping style in the development of PTSD.

King, King, Foy, and Gudanowski (1996) conducted supplementary analyses of the NVVRS data in an effort to understand more fully the etiological factors associated with the development of combat-related PTSD. These analyses identified wartime traumatic stressors as the primary contributor to PTSD, as predicted. They also found that prior exposure to traumatic events, age at the time of combat exposure, and premilitary family instability added significantly to their understanding of who develops PTSD, as did postmilitary factors such as social support, the presence of additional life stressors, and personal hardiness.

While many factors are involved in the etiology of PTSD, Sutker, Allain, and Johnson (1993) provided a brilliant example of the primary importance of trauma exposure in the development of PTSD. In a case study, two identical twins who were raised, educated, and trained together as aviator pilots, but who were discordant for combat exposure and prisoner-of-war status, were administered a comprehensive psychological and neuropsychological examination. The results indicated that the former POW reported symptoms of PTSD, several other psychiatric diagnoses, intellectual performance deficits, as well as significant cognitive defects. None of these was observed in his identical twin. The findings point directly to the pathogenic effects of war zone stress exposure.

Clearly, the etiology of PTSD is a complex phenomenon. To appreciate fully the factors involved in its development requires an understanding of the event itself, the context in which the event occurs in the life of the individual, the resources and deficits the individual brings to it, as well as the post-trauma environment. Advances in structural equation modeling have helped us to begin to understand how, in aggregate, traumatic events affect the lives of those exposed (Fontana & Rosenheck, 1993; King et al., 1996).

HISTORICAL PRECEDENTS
OF CURRENT
PSYCHOLOGICAL TREATMENTS

Historically, the works of Janet (1889) and Freud (1936) have most influenced the treatment of PTSD. The objectives of each approach share much in common with contemporary models of treatment, and thus current treatments owe a substantive debt to these pioneers. As presented by Fenichel (1945), there are two components to the psychoanalytic treatment of "traumatic neurosis": (a) attempts to quiet the high levels of anxiety and reactivity to the event and (b) attempts to reconstruct the details of the event with the accompanying emotional reactions to promote mastery over memories of the event.

Janet's (1889) contributions, reanalyzed and discussed frequently since the inclusion of PTSD in the DSM in 1980, focus on the idiographic phenomenology and the psychological symptoms often observed in traumatized patients. The inclusion of hypnosis as a viable treatment for traumatized people added a systematic and technical approach to achieving the psychoanalytic objective of reconstructing details of the event in order to achieve mastery.

In the aftermath of World War II, the use of sodium amytal interviews to recreate and to recall details of traumatic war events became increasingly widespread. Again, the objective of these interviews was to identify critical elements of traumatic war events that were not reported by the patients so that efforts to address the psychological sequelae of these events could begin. Typically, the events involved human devastation, atrocities, anxiety in the face of death and danger, and helplessness.

Today, the issue of traumatic memories has entered contemporary study of PTSD, with some denying the idea that memories of traumatic events have distinctive characteristics in comparison to memories of other life events, some challenging the nature of the constructs often invoked to explain traumatic memories (e.g., dissociation or repression), while others are vigorously holding to scientific standards recognizing that work in this area has only attained the scientific status of clinical observation. Despite the debate, which has at times reached vitriolic dimensions, it is clear that thousands of clinicians over the lengthy history of psychotherapy have noted that, during therapy, traumatized patients do indeed come to understand the nature and details of past traumatic events, whether these events occurred in childhood, as in the case of incest, or in adulthood, as with war veterans. Additional research directly on the issue of traumatic memory would contribute immeasurably to our understanding of developmental psychopathology and to the treatment of PTSD.

CURRENT TREATMENTS OF
CHOICE FOR POST-TRAUMATIC
STRESS DISORDER

Largely driven by the psychological and social problems of returning American Vietnam veterans, mental health practitioners established treatment programs to treat traumatic disorders (e.g., Keane & Kaloupek, 1982). Concomitantly, clinical researchers began to understand more fully the psychological consequences of exposure to sexual assault and rape (Burgess & Holmstrom, 1974; Kilpatrick, Veronen, & Resick, 1979) and to develop treatments for these problems.

At the outset, conceptual models of PTSD borrowed from Mowrer's (1960) two-factor learning theory (Fairbank & Keane, 1982; Keane, Zimering, & Caddell, 1985; Kilpatrick, Resick, & Veronen, 1981), which posits that fear and other aversive emotions are learned through association via classical conditioning mechanisms. This is the first factor in the acquisition of aversive emotions. The second factor is that individuals will do whatever is necessary to escape from and to avoid cues that stimulate these aversive emotions.

Recent theoretical models have grown to increasingly accommodate cognitive factors (Foa, Steketee, & Rothbaum, 1989; Lang, 1977; Litz & Keane, 1989), yet the treatments that evolved from the two-factor learning theory model remain among those most widely practiced and researched. Specifically, exposure therapy and anxiety management techniques have evolved as two of the most accepted treatments for PTSD patients. Although group therapies, both structured and unstructured, and psychodynamically informed psychotherapy are also widely used to treat PTSD, there are few studies in the literature that document the clinical efficacy of these approaches. However, the parallels between the objectives of psychoanalytic approaches as delineated above and those of anxiety management and exposure therapy are unmistakable (i.e., directly reducing anxiety to cues of the event and mastering the memory).

A more recent approach to treating PTSD is eye-movement desensitization and reprocessing (EMDR; Shapiro, 1989). This is essentially an atheoretical technique that was accidentally discovered to alter disturbing thoughts, feelings, and images (Shapiro, 1995). It has been applied to a broad range of psychological problems, but the only available research on its efficacy is with PTSD, so it is discussed in this chapter. Accordingly, the focus of this section of the chapter on psychological treatments of PTSD examines the data supporting the use of exposure therapies, anxiety management therapies, their combination, and EMDR.

Exposure Therapies

There is a long, rich tradition for treating anxiety disorders with one or another of the exposure therapies, whether it be systematic desensitization, flooding, prolonged exposure, implosive therapy, or the like (e.g., Barlow, 1988; Levis, 1980; Rachman, 1980). Keane and colleagues were among the first to apply exposure therapy to the treatment of PTSD. Initially, this application took the form of single-subject designed studies to document the effects of systematic exposure to memories of the traumatic events experienced by combat veteran patients (Black & Keane, 1982; Fairbank & Keane, 1982; Keane & Kaloupek, 1982). Significant reductions in anxiety and other related symptoms were noted as a function of these interventions. These Type 3 studies were instructive because they employed a consistent conceptual model of PTSD in the implementation of a treatment, utilized systematic diagnostic measures for case identification, and measured outcome in replicable, standardized ways.

This preliminary work led to the development of a randomized clinical trial (RCT; Type 1) that compared two active treatments (exposure therapy and anxiety management therapy) to a waiting list condition in the treatment of combat-related PTSD in Vietnam veterans. The results of this study were clear-cut. Compared to the wait-list condition, those patients receiving imagery-based exposure therapy showed reductions on standard psychometrics and on clinician ratings of symptoms at the posttreatment assessment. Changes on these measures were maintained at a 6-month follow-up evaluation. Interestingly, the less-intensive treatment (anxiety management) experienced so many treatment dropouts that insufficient data were available for analyses (Keane, Fairbank, Caddell, & Zimering, 1989).

In the Netherlands, Brom, Kleber, and Defares (1989) also conducted a Type 1 RCT comparing three active treatments for 112 patients who had experienced a traumatic event and were seeking psychotherapy. The treatments were exposure therapy (i.e., systematic desensitization), hypnotherapy, and psychodynamic treatment. Patients were evaluated before treatment, immediately after treatment, and at a 3-month follow-up using standardized psychometric instruments. The patients receiving exposure therapy showed a reduction in symptoms at posttest that was maintained at the 3-month follow-up. While comparable levels of change were noted in the other two active treatment groups, all three groups demonstrated greater change than the waiting list condition.

In possibly the most methodologically rigorous Type 1 RCT for PTSD, Foa, Rothbaum, Riggs, and Murdock (1991) examined exposure therapy, an anxiety management condition termed stress inoculation, supportive counseling, and a wait-list condition for the treatment of rape-induced PTSD. Measures included clinical ratings of symptoms and standardized psychometric inventories, all administered at pretreatment, posttreatment, and at a 3.5-month follow-up. The stress inoculation treatment was superior to the counseling and wait-list conditions at posttest. However, at the follow-up the patients receiving exposure therapy performed the best on measures of PTSD compared to all other conditions.

Two additional studies with combat veterans with PTSD also demonstrate the salutary effects of exposure therapy. Boudewyns and Hyer (1990) and Cooper and Clum (1989), in Type 1 RCTs, demonstrated that the addition of exposure therapy to available treatments of PTSD improved outcome for patients.

In what may ultimately prove to be the most instructive lesson for the treatment of individuals exposed to traumatic events, Foa, Hearst-Ikeda, and Perry (1995) examined the efficacy of a brief intervention to prevent the development of chronic PTSD. For women who had been recently raped, the authors developed a program based on that which worked so well in earlier trials with chronic PTSD (Foa et al., 1991). Exposure therapy figured prominently in the package of treatments assembled. This package also included elements of education, breathing retraining, and cognitive restructuring. Compared to a matched control group, this Type 2 study found that at 2 months postintervention only 10% of the treated group met criteria for PTSD, while 70% of the untreated comparison group did.

In another Type 2 study, Frank and Stewart (1983) reported the effects of systematic desensitization on women who had been raped and who developed significant psychological symptomatology. Compared to an untreated comparison group, those women treated with graduated exposure improved most on a range of anxiety and depression symptom measures.

Richards, Lovell, and Marks (1994; Type 2) compared imaginal and in vivo exposure in a randomized study of survivors of diverse traumatic events. At the 12-month follow-up, patients reported consistent reductions in PTSD symptoms and improved social adjustment. These data further substantiate the effectiveness of exposure therapy for some patients and also suggest that improvements in symptoms are also reflected in critical domains of life functioning.

In summary, the extant data support the use of exposure therapy in the treatment of PTSD. In a previous review of this literature (Type 5 study), Solomon, Gerrity, and Muff (1992) derived the same conclusion from data available at that time. Similar conclusions were drawn by Otto, Penava, Pollack, and Smoller (1996) in a more recent review (Type 5) of the literature.

As data continue to accrue on exposure therapy, there is a distinct need for studies to examine combinations of treatments, employ measures that assess social and occupational functioning, and employ a broader range of patient types (i.e., beyond combat and rape PTSD). At this time, samples examined in many of the studies have necessarily been small, so larger samples need to be treated.

Although definitive studies have not yet been conducted in this area, clearly the available efficacy studies demonstrate the value of extending exposure therapies to PTSD patients. With a rich tradition deeply rooted in experimental psychology and tested in the treatment of many anxiety disorders, exposure therapy in its many formats should be given priority by clinicians encountering patients with PTSD.

Anxiety Management Training

Typically, anxiety management training (AMT) involves teaching patients an assortment of behavioral and cognitive strategies to enhance their capacity to manage the emotions associated with PTSD. Such skills might be relaxation training, breathing retraining, trauma education, guided self-dialogue, cognitive restructuring, and communication skills training. Some programs for PTSD have emphasized the incorporation of anger management training as a part of the skills taught to patients (Chemtob, Novaco, Hamada, & Gross, 1997; Keane et al., 1989) given the saliency of this interpersonal problem among patients with PTSD.

Studies described above by Foa et al. (1991) and Keane et al. (1989) compared exposure therapy to AMT. In the Keane et al. study, therapists were instructed to explicitly avoid discussing or processing the traumatic events of the patients in an effort to minimize the amount of exposure provided in this treatment condition. Perhaps this severe restriction led to the high rate of dropouts in the AMT condition. While the treatment appeared to be face valid in its emphasis on treating the precise symptoms of PTSD, it evidently did not provide sufficient relief to the combat veterans enrolled in this trial. However, this treatment did result in significant reductions in symptoms for female rape victims in the Foa et al. (1991) study, as discussed above. The long-term effects were just not as strong as those found for exposure therapy.

Some studies primarily employed one form of AMT rather than a multifaceted treatment package. For example, Peniston (1986) conducted a Type 1 project examining the effects of biofeedback-assisted relaxation treatment for veterans with combat-related PTSD. This form of AMT did result in significant short-term positive effects for the experimental group.

Similarly, Chemtob et al. (1997) presented data on the treatment of anger and rage in PTSD veterans. Although the sample size of this Type 2 study was small, behavioral treatment employing an anger-focused version of AMT yielded impressive reductions on psychometric measures of anger and on laboratory measures (behavioral) of anger reactivity. Importantly, these changes were associated with reductions in reexperiencing symptoms of PTSD.

Clearly, there is evidence to suggest that a skills training approach such as AMT can have a favorable impact on symptoms of PTSD. While the data are neither as strong nor as consistent as those for exposure therapy, it seems reasonable to conclude that there is some empirical validation for the use of AMT in treating PTSD. Possibly the strongest potential application for treating PTSD is within a package combining exposure therapy with AMT. There are ample precedents in the mental health literature for combining techniques to yield stronger therapeutic effects (cf. Barlow, 1988).

Combinations of Exposure Therapy and Anxiety Management Training

Resick and Schnicke (1992) have proffered a multidimensional behavioral treatment package for women who have rape-related PTSD. This package, entitled cognitive processing therapy (CPT), combines elements of exposure therapy, AMT, and cognitive restructuring. In a Type 2 evaluation of CPT, the authors compared outcomes at pretreatment, posttreatment, 3 and 6 months for a treatment group, and a wait-list comparison group (no random assignment was used). On clinician ratings and psychometric inventories of PTSD, the patients receiving CPT improved markedly. At the posttreatment assessment, impressively, none of the treated patients met criteria for PTSD.

This form of psychological treatment combination promises to strengthen the resources available to clinicians to treat PTSD. Comparisons of CPT to exposure therapy are ongoing in this research laboratory and will evaluate the extent to which CPT leads to greater improvement than exposure therapy alone. Extensions of its use to other forms of PTSD will then be warranted.

Eye-Movement Desensitization and Reprocessing

Eye movement desensitization and reprocessing (EMDR) is a technique designed by Shapiro (1989, 1995) that has received considerable attention from practitioners and academics alike. Worldwide training institutes are well attended by clinicians seeking to learn about EMDR and its use in PTSD. While Shapiro (1995) alleges that this technique is helpful for treating a range of disorders, its use is often directly associated with PTSD.

Since the first publication described the technique (Shapiro, 1989), a series of single subject cases and open clinical trials has suggested that this approach to treating the psychological effects of trauma exposure may promote recovery. From an operational perspec-

tive, the essence of EMDR seems to be (a) the evocation of trauma-relevant images and memories, (b) the psychological evaluation of the aversive qualities of these images/memories, (c) the identification (with or without therapist assistance) of an alternative cognitive appraisal of the image/memory, (d) examination of physiological reactions to the image/memory, (e) focusing on the idiographically determined positive appraisal of the image/memory, and (f) repeated sets of lateral eye movements while the patient is focusing on elements of the traumatic response.

Examining the efficacy and effectiveness of EMDR is challenging. Its mechanism of action is not, realistically, based on any contemporary theories of human behavior, learning, or cognitive science, although some discussion of Pavlovian neurophysiology is provided across publications (Shapiro, 1989, 1995). For this reason, it has been seriously criticized in the scientific literature (Herbert & Mueser, 1992; Lohr, Kleinknecht, Tolin, & Barrett, 1995). Yet, the absence of theory or a conceptual foundation is not sufficient to dismiss totally the preliminary findings of the technique. If there is efficacy, then serious scholars can assume responsibility for identifying the precise mechanism responsible for any effects observed. The questions are, therefore, is there evidence for EMDR's efficacy? and, most importantly, is EMDR more effective or efficient than tested techniques?

Probably because EMDR is not based on any existing theoretical or treatment literature, there is a surprisingly large number of case studies in the literature. Reviewing this literature comprehensively is beyond the scope of this chapter. Rather, the focus is on those studies and reviews of the literature that provide the nexus for an evaluation. Only one of the existing studies meets criteria for a solid Type 1 designation (Carlson, Chemtob, Rusnak, Hedlund, & Muraoka, 1995). In that study, EMDR was compared to biofeedback-assisted relaxation training and routine clinical care. The authors reported that at the 180-day follow-up the group receiving EMDR showed greater clinical improvement than either of the two comparison groups on self-reported, psychometric, and clinician-rated measures of PTSD.

Wilson, Becker, and Tinker (1995; Type 2) reported on the treatment of traumatic memories in a heterogeneous sample of individuals recruited through newspaper advertisements and other means. Half of their subjects received EMDR, while the remaining half were placed on a waiting list. Of the 80 subjects in this study, less than half reached *DSM* criteria for PTSD. Following three sessions of EMDR, the treated group demonstrated a greater reduction on psychometric measures and clinician ratings of symptoms than did the wait-list subjects.

Other studies on EMDR's efficacy have been less encouraging. Projects by Boudewyns, Stwertka, Hyer, Albrecht, and Sperr (1993), Jensen (1994), and Vaughan et al. (1994) found only modest effects for EMDR. These studies all have significant methodological limitations (Type 2 studies), but they are comparable in quality and design to those projects providing the empirical support for this technique. One study by Renfrey and Spates (1994; Type 2) found no differences between a group receiving the eye movements compared to a similar group that did not, thus challenging the eye movements' role in the treatment.

In summary, much work needs to be done before research will firmly support the use of EMDR for the treatment of PTSD. Unlike exposure therapy, which has a long tradition of ameliorating a range of anxiety-mediated clinical problems and is embedded in the rich conceptual tradition of experimental psychology, EMDR falters seriously at the theoretical level and has limited scientific support. Needed are basic studies to examine the effects of eye movements (or other laterally alternating stimuli), small-scale, well-controlled efficacy studies that meet contemporary standards for treatment outcome research, and the formulation of a testable theory for the technique. Implicit in this last recommendation is the development of a conceptual model of PTSD and how EMDR attempts to correct either the deficits or excesses involved in this disabling psychological condition.

In concluding this review of EMDR, it may be valuable to delineate the possible strengths of this technique. First, EMDR does share some components of exposure therapy and cognitive therapy. These overlapping components should be identified and be made operational to promote our ability to study the approach more fully. Second, the technique builds assessment into the ongoing therapy process. Third, EMDR suggests that instructions to modify images and alter cognitive self-statements may be a reasonable treatment objective for PTSD patients. Fourth, the training programs established for technique dissemination and supervision are enviable. And, fifth, Shapiro and colleagues have always promoted the need

for empirical documentation to support their perspective on treating PTSD.

The primary weakness of EMDR stems from a distinct lack of integration with existing psychological models of psychopathology and psychotherapy. While existing models may have their own failings, it is incumbent on the proponents of EMDR to postulate how their view of the problems associated with PTSD differs from other views and how this technique can allay specific targeted symptoms of this multidimensional disorder.

Future Treatments of Choice

There is much to be learned about the treatment of PTSD. To be sure, there will be no simple answers for treating people who have experienced the most horrific events life offers. Undoubtedly, combinations of treatments as proposed by Keane (1995), Foa et al. (1991), and Resick and Schnicke (1992) may prove to be the most powerful interventions.

As these treatment packages are developed, there is a need for additional work from perspectives other than the cognitive-behavioral one. Interpersonal therapy (Klerman, Weissman, Rounsaville, & Chevron, 1984) and other short-term psychodynamically informed treatments need to be developed, evaluated, and then compared to existing behavioral and cognitive-behavioral treatments to determine which patients benefit most from these methods.

Similarly, there is a need to develop psychopharmacological interventions further so that they can be compared and contrasted with effective psychological methods, both individually and in combination. The PTSD research in this area is only in the nascent stages of development.

Finally, there is an assumption of uniformity of traumatic events that strings throughout this review. While it is reasonable to speculate fundamental similarities among patients who have experienced diverse traumatic events and then develop PTSD, whether these patients respond to clinical interventions in the same way is an empirical question that has yet to be addressed. Studies posing a question such as this would be a welcome addition to the clinical literature.

The problems associated with war, rape, violence, criminal assault, and disaster do not appear to be declining. As a result, sound public policy is needed to guide society's response to survivors of these experiences. Post-traumatic stress disorder in its most chronic form is a debilitating condition that affects individuals, their families, their communities, and the nation. Those who are the targets of violence may ultimately become perpetrators, thus contributing to the cycle of violence initially documented by Widom (1989). If this is so, then interventions need to be implemented to prevent the occurrence of violence (primary prevention) or to mitigate its effects once it occurs (secondary prevention). Reliance on sound empirical work to devise and implement these prevention efforts may ultimately be the best solution to the problems associated with PTSD.

References

American Psychiatric Association. (1994). *Diagnostic and statistical manual of mental disorders* (4th ed.). Washington, D.C.: Author.

Barlow, D. H. (1988). *Anxiety and its disorders*. New York: Guilford Press.

Black, J. L., & Keane, T. M. (1982). Implosive therapy in the treatment of combat related fears in a World War II veteran. *Journal of Behavior Therapy and Experimental Psychiatry, 13,* 163–165.

Boudewyns, P. A., & Hyer, L. (1990). Physiological response to combat memories and preliminary treatment outcome in Vietnam veteran PTSD patients treated with direct therapeutic exposure. *Behavior Therapy, 21*(1), 63–87.

Boudewyns, P. A., Stwertka, S. A., Hyer, L. A., Albrecht, J. W., & Sperr, E. V. (1993). Eye movement desensitization for PTSD of combat: A treatment outcome pilot study. *The Behavior Therapist, 16*(2), 42.

Breslau, N., Davis, G. C., Andreski, P., & Peterson, E. (1991). Traumatic events and posttraumatic stress disorder in an urban population of young adults. *Archives of General Psychiatry, 48,* 216–222.

Brom, D., Kleber, R. J., & Defares, P. B. (1989). Brief psychotherapy for posttraumatic stress disorders. *Journal of Consulting and Clinical Psychology, 57*(5), 607–612.

Burgess, A. W., & Holmstrom, L. L. (1974). Rape trauma syndrome. *American Journal of Psychiatry, 131*(9), 981–986.

Carlson, J. G., Chemtob, C. M., Rusnak, K., Hedlund, N. L., & Muraoka, M. Y. (1995). *Eye movement desensitization and reprocessing (EMDR) treatment for combat related posttraumatic stress disorder.* Paper presented at the International Society for Traumatic Stress Studies, Boston, Mass.

Chemtob, C. M., Novaco, R. W., Hamada, R. S., &

Gross, D. M. (1997). Cognitive behavioral treatment of severe anger in posttraumatic stress disorder. *Journal of Consulting and Clinical Psychology, 65,* 184–189.

Cooper, N. A., & Clum, G. A. (1989). Imaginal flooding as a supplementary treatment for PTSD in combat veterans: A controlled study. *Behavior Therapy, 20,* 381–391.

Dohrenwend, B. P., & Dohrenwend, B. S. (1981). Socioenvironmental factors, stress, and psychopathology. *American Journal of Community Psychology, 9*(2), 128–164.

Fairbank, J. A., & Keane, T. M. (1982). Flooding for combat-related stress disorders: Assessment of anxiety reduction across traumatic memories. *Behavior Therapy, 13,* 499–510.

Fenichel, O. (1945). *The psychoanalytic theory of neuroses.* New York: Wiley.

Foa, E. B., Hearst-Ikeda, D., & Perry, K. J. (1995). Evaluation of a brief cognitive-behavioral program for the prevention of chronic PTSD in recent assault victims. *Journal of Consulting and Clinical Psychology, 63,* 948–955.

Foa, E. B., Rothbaum, B. O., Riggs, D. S., & Murdock, T. B. (1991). Treatment of posttraumatic stress disorder in rape victims: A comparison between cognitive-behavioral procedures and counseling. *Journal of Consulting and Clinical Psychology, 59,* 715–723.

Foa, E. B., Steketee, G., & Rothbaum, B. (1989). Behavioral/cognitive conceptualizations of posttraumatic stress disorder. *Behavior Therapy, 20,* 155–176.

Fontana, A., & Rosenheck, R. (1993). A causal model of the etiology of war-related PTSD. *Journal of Traumatic Stress, 6,* 475–500.

Frank, E., & Stewart, B. D. (1983). Treating depression in victims of rape. *Clinical Psychologist, 36*(4), 95–98.

Freud, S. (1936). *The basic writings of Sigmund Freud.* New York: Random House.

Herbert, J. D., & Mueser, K. T. (1992). Eye movement desensitization: A critique of the evidence. *Journal of Behavior Therapy and Experimental Psychiatry, 23*(3), 169–174.

Janet, P. (1889). *L'automatisme psychologie.* Paris: Balliere.

Jensen, J. A. (1994). An investigation of eye movement desensitization and reprocessing (EMD/R) as a treatment for posttraumatic stress disorder symptoms of Vietnam combat veterans. *Behavior Therapy, 25*(2), 311–325.

Keane, T. M. (1995). The role of exposure therapy in the psychological treatment of PTSD. *National Center for PTSD Clinical Quarterly, 5*(4), 1–6.

Keane, T. M., Fairbank, J. A., Caddell, J. M., & Zimering, R. T. (1989). Implosive (flooding) therapy reduces symptoms of PTSD in Vietnam combat veterans. *Behavior Therapy, 20,* 245–260.

Keane, T. M., & Kaloupek, D. G. (1982). Imaginal flooding in the treatment of posttraumatic stress disorder. *Journal of Consulting and Clinical Psychology, 50*(1), 138–140.

Keane, T. M., Zimering, R. T., & Caddell, J. M. (1985). A behavioral formulation of posttraumatic stress disorder in Vietnam veterans. *Behavior Therapist, 8,* 9–12.

Kessler, R. C., Sonnega, A., Bromet, E., Hughes, M., & Nelson, C. B. (1995). Posttraumatic stress disorder in the National Comorbidity Survey. *Archives of General Psychiatry, 52*(12), 1048–1060.

Kilpatrick, D. G., Edmonds, C. N., & Seymour, A. K. (1992). *Rape in America: A report to the nation.* Arlington, Va.: National Victim Center.

Kilpatrick, D. G., Resick, P. A., & Veronen, L. J. (1981). Effects of a rape experience: A longitudinal study. *Journal of Social Issues, 37,* 105–122.

Kilpatrick, D. G., Veronen, L. J., & Resick, P. A. (1979). The aftermath of rape: Recent empirical findings. *American Journal of Orthopsychiatry, 49*(4), 658–669.

King, D. W., King, L. A., Foy, D. W., & Gudanowski, D. M. (1996). Prewar factors in combat-related posttraumatic stress disorder: Structural equation modeling with a national sample of female and male Vietnam veterans. *Journal of Consulting and Clinical Psychology, 64*(3), 520–531.

Klerman, G. L., Weissman, M. M., Rounsaville, B. J., & Chevron, E. S. (1984). *Interpersonal psychotherapy of depression.* New York: Basic Books.

Kulka, R. A., Schlenger, W. E., Fairbank, J. A., Hough, R. L., Jordan, B. K., Marmar, C. R., & Weiss, D. S. (1990). *Trauma in the Vietnam war generation: Report of findings from the National Vietnam Veterans Readjustment Study.* New York: Brunner/Mazel.

Lang, P. J. (1977). Imagery in therapy: An information processing analysis of fear. *Behavior Therapy, 8*(5), 862–886.

Levis, D. J. (1980). Implementing the technique of implosive therapy. In A. Goldstein, & E. B. Foa (Eds.), *Handbook of behavioral interventions: A clinical guide* (pp. 92–151). New York: Wiley & Sons.

Litz, B. T., & Keane, T. M. (1989). Information processing in anxiety disorders: Application to the understanding of posttraumatic stress disorder. *Clinical Psychology Review, 9,* 243–257.

Lohr, J. M., Kleinknecht, R. A., Tolin, D. F., & Barrett, R. H. (1995). The empirical status of the clinical application of eye movement desensitization and reprocessing. *Journal of Behavior Therapy and Experimental Psychiatry, 26*(4), 185–191.

Mowrer, O. H. (1960). *Learning theory and behavior.* New York: Wiley.

Norris, F. H. (1992). Epidemiology of trauma: Frequency and impact of different potentially traumatic events on different demographic groups. *Journal of Consulting and Clinical Psychology, 60*(3), 409–418.

Otto, M., Penava, S., Pollack, R., & Smoller, J. (1996). Cognitive-behavioral and pharmacologic perspectives on the treatment of posttraumatic stress disorder. In M. Pollack, M. Otto, & J. Rosenbaum (Eds.), *Challenges in clinical practice: Pharmacologic and psychosocial strategies* (pp. 219–260). New York: Guilford Press.

Peniston, E. G. (1986). EMG biofeedback-assisted desensitization treatment for Vietnam combat veterans' posttraumatic stress disorder. *Clinical Biofeedback and Health: An International Journal, 9*(1), 35–41.

Rachman, S. (1980). Emotional processing. *Behavior Research and Therapy, 18,* 51–60.

Renfrey, G., & Spates, R. C. (1994). Eye movement desensitization: A partial dismantling study. *Journal of Behavior Therapy and Experimental Psychiatry, 25*(3), 231–239.

Resick, P. A., & Schnicke, M. K. (1992). Cognitive processing therapy for sexual assault victims. *Journal of Consulting and Clinical Psychology, 60*(5), 748–756.

Resnick, H. S., Kilpatrick, D. G., Dansky, B. S., Saunders, B. E., & Best, C. L. (1993). Prevalence of civilian trauma and posttraumatic stress disorder in a representative national sample of women. *Journal of Consulting and Clinical Psychology, 61*(6), 984–991.

Richards, D. A., Lovell, K., & Marks, I. M. (1994). Posttraumatic stress disorder: Evaluation of a behavioral treatment program. *Journal of Traumatic Stress, 7,* 669–680.

Shapiro, F. (1989). Eye movement desensitization: A new treatment for posttraumatic stress disorder. *Journal of Behavior Therapy and Experimental Psychiatry, 20*(3), 211–217.

———. (1995). *Eye movement desensitization and reprocessing: Basic principles, protocols, and procedures.* New York: Guilford Press.

Solomon, S. D., Gerrity, E. T., & Muff, A. M. (1992). Efficacy of treatments for posttraumatic stress disorder. *Journal of the American Medical Association, 268,* 633–638.

Sutker, P. B., Allain, A. N., & Johnson, J. L. (1993). Clinical assessment of long-term cognitive and emotional sequelae to World War II prisoner-of-war confinement: Comparison of pilot twins. *Psychological Assessment, 5*(1), 3–10.

Vaughan, K., Armstrong, M. S., Gold, R., O'Connor, N., Jenneke, W., & Tarrier, N. (1994). A trial of eye movement desensitization compared to image habituation training and applied muscle relaxation in post-traumatic stress disorder. *Journal of Behavior Therapy and Experimental Psychiatry, 25*(4), 283–291.

Widom, C. S. (1989). The cycle of violence. *Science, 244*(4901), 160–166.

Wilson, S., Becker, L., & Tinker, R. (1995). Eye movement desensitization and reprocessing (EMDR) treatment for psychologically traumatized individuals. *Journal of Consulting and Clinical Psychology, 63*(6), 928–937.

21

Management of Somatoform and Factitious Disorders

Gregory E. Simon

Somatoform and factitious disorders are characterized by somatic symptoms or disease fears that are out of proportion to any identifiable somatic cause, including a heightened sensitivity to noxious physical stimuli, exaggerated or irrational disease fears, and adoption of a patient role. Effective management of these conditions requires special attention to establishing and maintaining a working treatment alliance. Treatments proven effective, in a large number of Type 1 and especially, Type 2 RCTs, are remarkably similar to those commonly used in the management of anxiety and affective disorders.

GENERAL PRINCIPLES OF TREATMENT

Treatment of patients with somatoform disorders raises several issues not often encountered in the management of other psychiatric disorders. While the most commonly applied clinical interventions (e.g., cognitive-behavioral psychotherapy, antidepressant medication) are widely used, establishment of a cooperative therapeutic relationship often requires special attention. During the initial phase of treatment, providers should consider each of the issues listed below.

Attend to the circumstances of referral. While some patients suffering from unexplained somatic symptoms or hypochondriacal worries may seek mental health care, referral by a medical provider is the most common entry into treatment. Some patients may respond to such a referral with relief, but many will be skeptical or reluctant. Referral to a mental health provider may be misinterpreted as rejection or dismissal (e.g., "The doctor must think it's all in my head.").

Identify the patient's primary concerns. While the presenting symptom may be straightforward, its meaning or importance should always be explored. For example, different patients presenting with medically unexplained chest pain may have quite different concerns. One may seek only pain relief and have no worries about the cause of the pain. Another may be preoccupied with fear of an impending heart attack. A third may recognize the pain as tension related and focus primarily on workplace stresses. Effectively addressing these different concerns will require quite different therapeutic approaches.

Clearly establish the position that all symptoms are "real." Patients (and many physicians) may falsely dichotomize somatic distress into the "real" symptoms and the "psychological" ones. Not only is such a dichotomy inconsistent with scientific knowledge, it creates major barriers to effective treatment. Accepting this dichotomous view means that any symptom amenable to psychiatric or psychological intervention was not real at the start. One could hardly imagine a scenario less conducive to effective symptom relief and rehabilitation.

Negotiate a mutually acceptable treatment goal. Because many patients with somatoform disorders enter treatment at the urging of physicians, employers, or disability insurers, clear establishment of a collaborative relationship is essential. Treatment will certainly fail if the patient perceives the mental health provider as a judge or adversary. If the therapist has clear obligations to some other party (employer, disability agency), the therapist should clearly disclose them. Negotiating a treatment goal should begin with a list of the patient's requests. Forming a working treatment alliance may require modifying unrealistic goals (e.g., complete freedom from pain, absolute certainty about medical diagnoses) into realistic ones (e.g., improved functioning and well-being despite some pain, tolerance of reasonable uncertainty about health).

Focus on symptom management, not diagnosis and cure. Patients with somatoform disorders often focus on a biomedical approach to somatic symptoms. Such an approach is based on a number of underlying assumptions about bodily distress (e.g., pain or discomfort signals the presence of a diagnosable disease; health is the absence of discomfort; medicine is an exact science; persistence of symptoms should prompt more vigorous diagnostic efforts). Effective treatment must shift the agenda from diagnosis and cure to symptom management and rehabilitation. Rehabilitative management is based on a very different set of assumptions about the meaning of somatic symptoms (e.g., physical symptoms are common and often have no specific medical cause; health is the ability to function and enjoy life despite bodily discomfort; persistence of symptoms is annoying and unfortunate, but doesn't imply an incorrect diagnosis). The rehabilitative approach takes a long-term view of treatment and recovery.

Coordination of care with medical and surgical providers is essential. In the management of somatoform disorders, the therapeutic relationship is rarely a dyadic one. At least one medical provider (and often several) will play as important a role in ongoing treatment as the mental health provider. For patients with more severe somatoform disorders, mental health treatment is episodic, while medical treatment is lifelong. While the mental health provider may sometimes assume a primary treatment role, the provider is more often a consultant to the patient and the patient's medical physician.

TREATMENT OF COMORBID DEPRESSIVE AND ANXIETY DISORDERS

Evaluation and management of somatoform disorders should focus first on the identification and treatment of comorbid anxiety and depressive disorders. Epidemiologic research in community (Simon & VonKorff, 1991) and primary care (Ustun & Sartorius, 1995) samples has demonstrated that many (if not most) somatoform disorders occur in the setting of anxiety or depressive disorders. Somatic symptoms and excessive worry about physical health appear to be core components of depression (Katon & Russo, 1989; Silver, 1987) and panic disorder (Fava, Grandi, Rafanelli, & Canestrari, 1992; Sheehan, Ballenger, & Jacobsen, 1980). Effective treatment of depression (Smith, 1992) and anxiety (Noyes, Reich, Clancy, & O'Gorman, 1986; Sheehan et al., 1980) reduces somatic distress and disease fears. As reviewed below, many of the interventions found effective in the management of somatoform disorders are widely used in the management of anxiety and depressive conditions.

SOMATIZATION DISORDER

Clinical Features

Somatization disorder is a lifelong condition characterized by multiple somatic symptoms without medical explanation. The *Diagnostic and Statistical Manual of Mental Disorders*, fourth edition (*DSM-IV*; American Psychiatric Association [APA], 1994) diagnostic criteria require the presence of four pain symptoms, two gastrointestinal symptoms, one sexual symptom, and one pseudoneurological symptom for a formal diagnosis. Typical symptoms may vary considerably across cultures. Somatization disorder begins early in adolescence or early adulthood and is usually chronic.

Specific somatic symptoms may vary over time, but affected individuals are rarely without some unexplained somatic symptoms. Community surveys have found prevalence rates of less than 0.5% in the general adult population, while medical clinic studies often find much higher rates. These differences may reflect differences in diagnostic methods (structured interview v. review of medical records).

Historical Perspective

Briquet's clinical description of somatization disorder (Briquet, 1859) predates even the early psychoanalytic descriptions of hysteria (Breuer & Freud, 1957). Work by Guze and colleagues (Guze, 1967) established Briquet's syndrome as a stable and well-defined diagnostic category. More recent descriptions (Katon et al., 1991; Simon & VonKorff, 1991) have viewed somatization disorder as the most extreme manifestation of somatization, a process characterized by heightened sensitivity to somatic distress and help-seeking behavior.

Treatment Alternatives

Expert recommendations on the management of somatization disorder have typically encouraged a conservative approach (Monson & Smith, 1983; Murphy, 1982; Quill, 1985). This approach emphasizes regular contact with a caring physician, acceptance of patients' somatic symptoms as valid, avoidance of unnecessary diagnostic testing, minimal use of new medications or therapies, and a stable level of contact regardless of symptomatic exacerbations. Such a program should lead to improved symptom tolerance, less unnecessary medical care, and less iatrogenic morbidity.

Smith and colleagues have evaluated one version of this approach in two randomized trials. In the first study (Smith, Monson, & Ray, 1986), patients with somatization disorder treated by community medical providers were randomly assigned to intervention and control groups. Physicians of patients in the intervention group received a consultation report describing somatization disorder and recommending the management plan described above. Compared to the control group, intervention patients showed significant decreases in health care utilization and no significant differences in measures of mental and physical health status. The second study (Rost, Kashner, & Smith, 1994) randomly assigned 59 primary care physicians (serving 73 patients with somatization disorder) to an intervention program similar to that described above or to a control condition. The psychiatric consultation intervention led to significant improvement in physical functioning and reduction in health care utilization compared to the comparison group.

Future Prospects

Recommendations regarding psychotherapeutic management of somatization disorder have changed little over the last 15 years. No specific pharmacological treatment appears likely to emerge. Consequently, no major changes in recommended treatment are anticipated.

UNDIFFERENTIATED SOMATOFORM DISORDER

Clinical Features

Undifferentiated somatoform disorder is characterized by one or more physical complaints that cannot be fully explained by a known medical condition. In any individual, the pattern of symptoms may be stable or changing over time. While any unexplained somatic symptom may merit this diagnosis, literature in this area has considered specific symptoms such as dizziness (Kroenke, 1993) and palpitations (Barsky, Cleary, Coeytaux, & Ruskin, 1994) or more generalized syndromes such as chronic fatigue (Kroenke, Wood, Mangelsdorff, Neier, & Powell, 1988); multiple chemical sensitivity (Simon, Daniell, Stockbridge, Claypole, & Rosenstock, 1993); and fibromyalgia (Goldenberg, 1987), a syndrome of diffuse muscular pain and tenderness. Some specific pain syndromes such as noncardiac chest pain (Cormier et al., 1988) and unexplained pelvic pain (Walker et al., 1988) are formally classified as somatoform pain disorders (see below) but are probably more similar to this group of conditions in mechanism and treatment response. Epidemiologic data suggest that this group of disorders is much more frequent than somatization disorder (Escobar, Burnam, Karno, Forsythe, & Golding, 1987; Katon et al., 1991) and accounts for the majority of somatoform disorders seen in medical practice.

While the term *somatization* is often used to describe this group of conditions, pathophysiologic mechanisms are probably heterogeneous. Potential mechanisms of somatization include exaggerated sensitivity to normal physiologic phenomenon, psychophysiologic hyperreactivity, and "masked" expression of typical anxiety and depressive symptoms. In several of these syndromes, the relative contributions of organic medical illness and psychologic distress are the focus of controversy and ongoing research.

Historical Perspective

Traditional views of somatization (strongly influenced by psychoanalysis) emphasized its defensive function (Adler, 1981). Somatic symptoms were viewed as masked expressions of psychological conflict or distress. Recent research supports a broader biopsychosocial model (Kirmayer & Robbins, 1991). Perception and reporting of somatic distress is determined by biological vulnerability, psychological characteristics, and social influence (i.e., relative reinforcement of somatic or emotional distress).

Treatment Alternatives

As mentioned above, this category of somatization symptoms and syndromes encompasses a range of possible pathophysiologic mechanisms. Treatment response may be similarly heterogeneous. While this discussion considers the general management of patients with unexplained somatic symptoms, treatment response in one syndrome may not necessarily generalize to others.

Several authors have described similar psychotherapeutic approaches toward the management of unexplained somatic symptoms (Ford & Long, 1977; Gask, Goldberg, Porter, & Creed, 1989; Goldberg, Gask, & O'Dowd, 1989; Sharpe, Peveler, & Mayou, 1992). Central elements of this approach include acceptance of somatic symptoms as real and distressing, emphasis on adaptation to somatic distress, and a gentle shift in attention from somatic symptoms themselves to life stresses or affective states that may provoke or exacerbate symptoms.

Such an approach can eventually lead to more conventional psychotherapeutic interventions such as problem solving or cognitive restructuring. Case series describe the success of such an approach delivered in either a group (Melson & Rynearson, 1986) or individual (Wilkinson & Mynors-Wallis, 1994) format. In two randomized trials, a similar group psychotherapeutic approach was found superior to an attention control condition for patients with a mixture of somatic symptoms (Hellman, Budd, Borysenko, McClelland, & Penson, 1990) or a more homogeneous group with unexplained oral symptoms (Bergdahl, An-

neroth, & Perris, 1995). In two randomized trials, individual cognitive-behavioral therapy was found superior to standard medical treatment for patients with irritable bowel syndrome (Payne & Blanchard, 1995) and for a heterogeneous group with unexplained somatic symptoms (Speckens et al., 1995). In a series of 77 patients with fibromyalgia receiving group meditation training (Kaplan, Goldenberg, & Galvin-Nadeau, 1993), 51% reported at least moderate improvement.

Fewer systematic data are available regarding the effectiveness of dynamic psychotherapy among patients with unexplained somatic symptoms. In one randomized trial among patients with irritable bowel syndrome (Guthrie, Creed, Dawson, & Tomenson, 1993), brief dynamic psychotherapy with relaxation was found superior to an attention control condition. A second case series (Nielsen, Barth, Brit, & Havik, 1988) describes improvement in 7 of 10 patients with unexplained somatic symptoms receiving brief dynamic psychotherapy.

Lipowski has described an intensive inpatient program for patients with more persistent or severe somatization syndromes (Lipowski, 1988). Components of the program include relaxation training, behavioral activation, and pharmacotherapy. In a case series of 92 patients (Shorter, Abbey, Gillies, Singh, & Lipowski, 1992), approximately one third were much improved and another third somewhat improved.

Smith and colleagues have extended the work on somatization disorder described above to the broader group of patients with unexplained somatic symptoms (Smith, Rost, & Kashner, 1995). Using a similar psychiatric consultation intervention, they report improved physical functioning and reduced general medical utilization.

Several case series and a few randomized trials have examined the use of antidepressant medication among patients with specific somatization syndromes. Two placebo-controlled randomized trials of low-dose amitriptyline for fibromyalgia (Carette, McCain, Bell, & Fam, 1986; Goldenberg, Felson, & Dinerman, 1986) report positive results, while one case series of 20 patients treated with moderate-dose imipramine (Wysenbeek, Mor, Lurie, & Weinberger, 1985) described high dropout rates and no apparent benefit. One randomized trial of fluoxetine for fibromyalgia (Wolfe, Cathey, & Hawley, 1994) found no advantage over a placebo. In a series of 138 patients with irritable bowel syndrome (Clouse, Lustman, Geisman, & Alpers, 1994) treated with various tricyclic antidepressants, 61% experienced remission and 89% were at least somewhat improved. In a series of 12 patients with globus pharyngis (Deary & Wilson, 1994) treated with amitriptyline, 9 discontinued treatment because of side effects. The authors concluded that anxiety and somatization may increase sensitivity to antidepressant side effects.

Future Prospects

Future work should help clarify treatment effectiveness in specific somatization syndromes. Because the "targets" of cognitive-behavioral therapy (symptom sensitivity, exaggerated disease fear) are central components of somatization, the psychotherapeutic approaches used above should be widely applicable. Because antidepressant medications may act through a variety of mechanisms (e.g., improvement in mood, direct pain relief, reduction of gastrointestinal motility), specific somatization syndromes may show differential response to antidepressants.

CONVERSION DISORDER

Clinical Features

Conversion symptoms are abnormalities or deficits in motor or sensory function that suggest a medical or neurologic illness. A diagnosis of conversion disorder should only be made after appropriate assessment has excluded a medical or neurologic cause. The presence of significant medical or neurologic illness does not exclude a diagnosis of conversion disorder if the conversion symptoms are not explained by medical illness. The DSM-IV diagnostic criteria require that the onset or exacerbation of symptoms be preceded by identifiable psychologic conflicts or stressors. Symptoms may be presented in dramatic or histrionic fashion or with a remarkable lack of concern ("la belle indifference"). Conversion symptoms are reported more commonly among women, among those from lower socioeconomic classes, and among those from less urbanized or Westernized areas. Conversion disorder may be an isolated condition or part of a more generalized somatization syndrome (e.g., somatization disorder).

Historical Perspective

Descriptions of hysterical conversion syndromes predate even the Hippocratic era (Ford & Folks, 1985). Theories of etiology have progressed from ancient Egyptian beliefs about the wandering uterus through early psychoanalytic descriptions of forbidden impulses to modern concepts of dissociation.

Treatment Alternatives

The literature on management of conversion symptoms includes only case reports and case series; no data from controlled studies are available. Clinical descriptions reflect the broad range of illness duration and psychiatric comorbidity seen in patients with conversion symptoms. In general, patients with a longer duration of symptoms and greater psychiatric comorbidity (anxiety, depressive, and somatoform disorders) require more intensive treatment and experience poorer outcomes (Brooksbank, 1984; Couprie, Wijdicks, Rooijmans, & vanGijn, 1995; Kent, Tomasson, & Coryell, 1995; Kotsopoulos & Snow, 1986; Krull & Schifferdecker, 1990; Turgay, 1990).

Acute and uncomplicated conversion reactions appear to respond favorably to a wide variety of supportive treatments. In a series of 100 consecutive Libyan patients with acute conversion reactions (Pu, Mohamed, Iman, & El-Roey, 1986), approximately half recovered rapidly with support, education, and suggestion, with most of the remainder improving after brief treatment with anxiolytic or antidepressant medication. Other case reports and small case series describe good response to a single sodium amytal interview (Steibel & Kirby, 1994), lorazepam combined with hypnosis (Stevens, 1990), or suggestion and supportive management (Brooksbank, 1984; Lazarus, 1990). While these reports vary in recommendations regarding somatic treatments (amytal, anxiolytics, physical therapy, etc.), they all describe a similar psychotherapeutic approach: emotional support regarding precipitating stresses, explanation that not all physical symptoms have a definite physical cause, expectation that symptoms will resolve rapidly, and reinforcement of any improvement. All sources also agree that convincing patients of links between physical symptoms and emotional stresses or conflicts is unnecessary and may be counterproductive.

Chronic or complicated conversion reactions (e.g., those occurring in the setting of somatization disorder) appear to require more intensive behavioral treatment. Several case reports (Klonoff & Moore, 1986; Mizes, 1985; Sullivan & Buchanan, 1989) describe successful inpatient treatments based on systematic reinforcement for symptom improvement. Rangaswami (1985) describes positive results in most of 30 Indian patients treated using reinforcement and aversive stimuli. One small case series (Teasell & Shapiro, 1994) describes poor response to behavioral treatment in three patients with chronic conversion symptoms. All responded to a combined behavioral and strategic inpatient program. These reports all suggest that more established symptoms will require a more organized and systematic behavioral approach. Inpatient management may be necessary.

Future Prospects

Recent reports do not suggest any significant changes in the management of conversion symptoms. It seems likely that the psychotherapeutic approaches described above will remain the recommended treatments for the foreseeable future. While some reports describe the use of anxiolytic or antidepressant medication, the literature does not suggest any specific pharmacological treatment. Controlled clinical trials in this area would be difficult to complete; acute conversion symptoms typically resolve rapidly, and persistent symptoms are relatively rare.

SOMATOFORM PAIN DISORDER

Clinical Features

Somatoform pain disorders are characterized by persistent pain that is distressing and/or disabling. The DSM-IV criteria for diagnosis require that psychological factors have an important role in the onset, severity, exacerbation, or maintenance of the pain. Intentionally produced or feigned pain symptoms are specifically excluded from this category. Pain symptoms such as headache, back pain, and abdominal pain are common causes of suffering, lost productivity, and health care utilization.

Historical Perspective

Traditional thinking has viewed pain symptoms as either "physical" (clearly attributed to a known bio-

medical process) or "psychogenic." The DSM-IV criteria reflect this dualistic view. More recent writing, however, suggests that all pain complaints are both physical and psychogenic (Coderre, Katz, Vaccarine, & Melzack, 1993). All pain symptoms are influenced by psychological factors and even the most psychogenic pain symptoms are probably associated with detectable pathologic changes in the central nervous system.

Treatment Alternatives

This review does not consider the wide range of somatic treatments used in the management of chronic pain (e.g., analgesics, nerve blocks). Nor does it specifically discuss the management of specific pain complaints (e.g., headache, orofacial pain, back pain). Instead, this summary reviews the general management of pain conditions, with emphasis on interventions familiar to mental health providers: psychotherapy and antidepressant medications.

Several randomized trials support the efficacy of cognitive and behavioral psychotherapy in reducing pain-related distress and disability. Group cognitive-behavioral interventions have been found superior to no-treatment control conditions for patients with chronic low back pain, (Turner, 1982), chronic temporomandibular pain (Dworkin et al., 1994), and two samples with a mix of chronic pain conditions (Moore & Chaney, 1985; Subramanian, 1991). Group cognitive-behavioral treatment has also been found superior to alternative "active" treatments: traditional group psychotherapy (Figueroa, 1982) and standard pain clinic treatment (Linton, Melin, & Stjernlof, 1985). In a study of school-age children with recurrent abdominal pain (Sanders, Sheperd, Cleghorn, & Woolford, 1994), cognitive-behavioral family therapy was found superior to standard pediatric care. One comparison of group and individual cognitive-behavioral treatment in patients with chronic upper extremity pain (Spence, 1989) found that both treatment groups fared better than wait-list controls, but the individual treatment was preferred by patients. Descriptions of these proven treatment programs typically include support and validation of pain as real, relaxation training, activity scheduling, reinforcement of non-pain behaviors, and cognitive restructuring. Most reports describe more robust effects on distress and disability than on actual pain intensity.

As noted in several recent reviews (Egbunike & Chaffee, 1990; Magni, 1991; Philipp & Fickinger,

1993; Stimmel & Escobar, 1986), over 50 placebo-controlled trials have examined the efficacy of antidepressant drugs for the management of chronic pain, and most have found pharmacotherapy superior to a placebo. These studies generally found that antidepressants do reduce pain intensity, that analgesic effect is delayed, and that pain relief is not necessarily dependent on improvement in mood. Analgesic effects are often noted at doses lower than typically recommended for treatment of depression (e.g., 50–75 mg per day of amitriptyline). While the analgesic effect of tricyclic antidepressants has been thoroughly studied, fewer data are available supporting the efficacy of serotonin reuptake inhibitor (SRI) antidepressants. Randomized trials of serotonin reuptake inhibitors in headache have reported mixed results (Langemark & Olesen, 1994; Saper, Silberstein, Lake, & Winters, 1994), and randomized trials in patients with neuropathic pain show that serotonin reuptake inhibitors may be slightly less effective than tricyclic drugs (Max et al., 1992; Sindrup, Gram, Brosen, Eshoj, & Mogensoen, 1990). Benefits of antidepressants may not be uniform across pain conditions; only weak evidence supports the benefit of antidepressants for back pain (Turner & Denny, 1993).

Two randomized trials have examined the combined effects of antidepressants and cognitive-behavioral psychotherapy. In a four-group factorial design, Pilowsky and colleagues (Pilowsky & Graham, 1990) found that amitriptyline increased activity level and reduced pain intensity, while psychotherapy increased perceived pain but improved productivity. In a follow-up study (Pilowsky, Spence, Rounsefell, & Forsten, 1995), addition of cognitive-behavioral therapy to amitriptyline treatment yielded only slight benefits.

Future Prospects

Given the number of randomized trials supporting the efficacy of cognitive-behavioral treatment and antidepressant medications, it seems unlikely that either of these treatments will be discredited. Instead, advances in treatment will probably focus on specificity of action. Proven cognitive-behavioral treatments include a variety of components (relaxation training, behavioral activation, cognitive restructuring), and future research may identify the specific effects of these various components. Future research on the analgesic effects of antidepressants should help to clarify which

pain conditions do and do not respond to antidepressant drugs and to determine which antidepressant drugs have the strongest analgesic action.

HYPOCHONDRIASIS

Clinical Features

The central feature of hypochondriasis is fear of or preoccupation with a medical illness. This fear often arises from misinterpretation of or exaggerated emphasis on a minor physical symptom or abnormality. Hypochondriacal patients are not reassured despite appropriate (and sometimes excessive) medical evaluation and reassurance. Disease worries may sometimes appear bizarre, but clearly delusional beliefs call for a separate diagnosis of paranoid disorder or other psychotic disorder. The presence of a diagnosed medical condition does not preclude a diagnosis of hypochondriasis if essential diagnostic features are present. Anxiety and depressive disorders are common comorbid conditions. Hypochondriacal patients vary in level of insight; some may recognize that medical worries are somewhat exaggerated, while others remain completely certain that fears are well founded. Depending on the measures used, the reported prevalence of hypochondriasis among general medical outpatients ranges from 4% to 9%. Onset is typically in early adulthood, and the course is often chronic or recurrent.

Historical Perspective

While the term *hypochondriasis* dates from early Greek medicine, its current usage (morbid preoccupation with health) dates from the 19th century (Kenyon, 1976). Early 20th century writings viewed hypochondriacal fears as defenses against awareness of unwanted affect, while more recent descriptions view hypochondriasis as a cognitive process characterized by morbid disease fear and exaggerated attention to bodily sensations (Barsky & Wyshak, 1989; Kellner, 1992).

Treatment Alternatives

Several case series and uncontrolled studies support the efficacy of cognitive-behavioral psychotherapy for hypochondriasis. Kellner (1982) described the essential features of a cognitive approach as correcting mis-information and exaggerated beliefs, as well as pointing out the cognitive processes (selective perception, misattribution, etc.) that maintain disease fears. He reported substantial improvement in a series of 36 patients treated with this approach. Barsky and colleagues (Barsky, Geringer, & Wool, 1988) describe a similar program delivered in a group format. Warwick (1989) described a behavioral treatment that included exposure to anxiety-provoking situations, prevention of checking behaviors, and prevention of reassurance seeking. In a series of seven patients with AIDS-focused illness phobias treated using this approach, all experienced substantial improvement (Logsdail, Lovell, Warwick, & Marks, 1991). Other case series describe a good response in the majority of patients treated with individual (Visser & Bouman, 1992) or group (Stern & Fernandez, 1991) cognitive-behavioral therapy.

Fewer data are available regarding the effectiveness of other psychotherapeutic approaches. Diamond (Diamond, 1987) describes the use of a self-psychology approach, but no systematic information on patient outcomes is available.

Two interesting papers discuss the benefits and risks of offering reassurance to patients with hypochondriacal fears. Starcevi'c (1991) discusses the therapeutic benefit of repeated and consistent reassurance in the framework of psychodynamic psychotherapy. In contrast, Salkovskis and Warwick (1986) view reassurance-seeking as an avoidance ritual that perpetuates disease fears. They describe two single-case experiments demonstrating the therapeutic benefits of a behavioral approach that restricts reassurance.

A growing body of literature supports the efficacy of antidepressant pharmacotherapy for the treatment of hypochondriasis. This work emphasizes similarities between hypochondriasis and obsessive compulsive disorder in both clinical presentation and treatment response. Two case series describe positive responses to clomipramine (Stone, 1993) and fluoxetine (Fallon, Javitch, Hollander, & Liebowitz, 1991). Building on that experience, Fallon (Fallon et al., 1993) reported an open trial of fluoxetine (40 to 80 mg/day) in 16 patients with hypochondriasis. Of these, 2 discontinued treatment, and 10 of the remaining 14 showed significant improvement. Wesner and Noyes (1991) described an open trial of imipramine (150 mg/day) in 10 patients with "illness phobia" (all met DSM-III-R [APA, 1987] criteria for hypochondriasis). Of these patients, 2 discontinued treatment because of side effects, and all of the remaining 8 were at least moderately improved.

Future Prospects

Reports from case series and uncontrolled treatment trials suggest that symptoms of hypochondriasis respond to psychotherapeutic and pharmacological treatments proven effective against phobic and obsessive compulsive disorders (cognitive-behavioral psychotherapy and serotonergic antidepressants). It seems likely that these suggestive findings will be confirmed by more rigorous clinical trials. Developments in the management of hypochondriasis will likely parallel those for the treatment of anxiety disorders. Clinicians treating hypochondriacal patients, however, must be mindful of specific issues raised by disease fears. Unlike many of the anxieties seen in phobias or obsessive compulsive disorder, illness fears can never be dismissed with complete certainty. In addition, the behavioral patterns of hypochondriasis usually include involvement of medical professionals and/or family members. Including these other participants in the design and practice of a behavioral treatment program is often necessary.

BODY DYSMORPHIC DISORDER

Clinical Features

Body dysmorphic disorder (BDD; previously known as dysmorphophobia) is defined by distressing preoccupation with an imagined defect in physical appearance or by an exaggerated or excessive concern with some physical feature. Complaints most often focus on the head or face (e.g., a "deformed" nose) but may involve any body part (e.g., asymmetry in breast size). Accurate estimates of prevalence are not available. Bodily preoccupations typically begin in adolescence and are often chronic. Concern about physical defects sometimes reaches delusional levels; available evidence does not clearly indicate whether delusional preoccupations represent a severe form of BDD or a distinct delusional disorder. These concerns are often presented to dermatologists or cosmetic surgeons. Medical or surgical treatment is invariably dissatisfying and may intensify symptoms. Common associated psychiatric disorders include depression, delusional disorder, social phobia, obsessive compulsive disorder, and eating disorder.

Historical Perspective

Body dysmorphic disorder (under the name dysmorphophobia) has been described in the European psychiatric literature for the last 100 years. Early psychoanalytic descriptions (such as Freud's Wolf-Man) emphasized the unconscious meaning of bodily preoccupations. Later descriptions viewed dysmorphophobia as a variant of hypochondriasis or obsessive compulsive disorder. Until the publication of *DSM-III-R*, BDD was not included in American psychiatric nomenclature.

Treatment Alternatives

The available evidence suggests that a focused form of cognitive-behavioral therapy is an effective treatment for BDD. Rosen and colleagues (Rosen, Reiter, & Orosan, 1995) described a group cognitive-behavioral program delivered in eight sessions. In a randomized trial design, patients assigned to the group program showed significant improvements in body image, self-esteem, and psychological distress when compared to a no-treatment control group. Several other case reports (Newell & Shrubb, 1994; Neziroglu & Yaryura, 1993; Schmidt & Harrington, 1995) describe a sustained benefit from individual cognitive-behavioral psychotherapy. Common elements of these psychotherapeutic treatments include identifying and challenging distorted body perceptions, interrupting self-critical thoughts, planned exposure to anxiety-provoking situations (e.g., wearing clothing that accentuates the perceived bodily defect), and response prevention (e.g., refraining from self-inspection). One report describes the effectiveness of psychodynamic psychotherapy (Bloch & Glue, 1988), but no systematic data on the efficacy of psychodynamic or other psychotherapeutic treatments are available.

Some data also support the efficacy of SRI antidepressants for the treatment of BDD and related conditions. Case series and case reports describe sustained therapeutic responses to clomipramine (Fernando, 1988; Hollander, Liebowitz, Winchel, Klumker, & Klein, 1989; Sondheimer, 1988), fluoxetine (Hollander et al., 1989), and fluvoxamine (Hollander et al., 1994). The SRI drugs were typically prescribed at doses recommended for management of obsessive compulsive disorder (e.g., 40–60 mg per day of fluoxetine). While none of these reports included control or comparison groups, the case reports suggest a low likelihood that reported benefits of pharmacotherapy represent a placebo response. Most patients had failed to respond to a variety of prior treatments. Several reports describe failure to respond to antidepressants without potent serotonin reuptake inhibition.

Future Prospects

The evidence summarized above suggests that BDD responds to treatments (cognitive-behavioral psychotherapy and serotonin reuptake inhibitor antidepressants) that act on obsessional thinking, phobic anxiety, and phobic avoidance. It seems likely that more rigorous study of pharmacotherapy will confirm the efficacy of SRI antidepressants. The relative efficacy of group or individual psychotherapeutic treatments also deserves attention. Group treatments may be especially helpful since realistic feedback about one's appearance from peers may be more powerful than feedback from a psychotherapist.

FACTITIOUS DISORDERS

Clinical Features

Factitious disorders are defined by the intentional production of signs or symptoms of disease. Symptoms may be either physical (abdominal pain, hematuria) or psychological (hallucinations, memory loss). The primary motivation for production of symptoms is a desire to assume the sick role. Because presenting symptoms represent a patient's beliefs about expected symptoms, presentations range from those clearly inconsistent with any known disease to sophisticated mimics of medical or psychiatric conditions. In factitious disorder by proxy, a caregiver intentionally produces symptoms or signs of illness in a child or dependent adult. Factitious disorder is distinct from malingering, in which the primary motivation is obtaining some concrete benefit (e.g., liability award, disability pension). Conversion disorder differs from factitious disorder in that conversion symptoms are neither intentionally nor consciously produced. No reliable data are available on the prevalence or demographic pattern of factitious disorders.

Historical Perspective

The prototypical factitious disorder, Munchausen's syndrome, was first described in 1951 (Asher, 1951). Subsequent work has broadened this category and clarified the place of factitious disorders among somatoform and dissociative disorders (Taylor & Hyler, 1993). While *DSM-IV* clearly provides for the diagnosis of factitious disorder with psychological symptoms, this category remains ill defined. As discussed by Rogers and colleagues (Rogers, Bagby & Rector, 1990), the core elements of factitious disorder are more difficult to establish in the domain of psychological symptoms. While the conscious production of somatic symptoms can sometimes be objectively demonstrated (e.g., detection of exogenous insulin in blood samples), production of psychological symptoms is much more complex. Motivations are typically complex, and it is difficult to determine whether the motivation for the behavior is to assume the sick role.

Treatment Alternatives

Most of the literature on factitious disorder discusses recognition and diagnosis. These case reports and case series describe the clinical presentation of factitious illness in specific medical areas (Folks, 1995; Schmaling, Rosenberg, Oppenheimer, & Moran, 1991; Sno, Storosum, & Wortel, 1991; Wallach, 1994). Clinical descriptions often mention associated affective, substance use, or personality disorders (Sutherland & Rodin, 1990). Diagnosis of factitious disorder necessarily distorts the traditional doctor-patient relationship. Uncovering a patient's deceptions often requires that treating physicians employ deception themselves. Recent literature has discussed one example of this ethical dilemma: covert videotaping for the detection of Munchausen's syndrome by proxy (Foreman & Farsides, 1993).

Systematic data on the treatment of factitious disorders are not available. The treatment literature consists entirely of case reports and small case series. These reports typically emphasize the difficulty of engaging patients with factitious disorders in any treatment plan; most abruptly discontinue treatment when discovered or confronted. While many case descriptions end with the patient's discharge against medical advice, several describe modest success (Earle & Folks, 1986; Guziec, Lazarus, & Harding, 1994; Plassman, 1994; Schwarz, Harding, Harrington, & Farr, 1993; Solyom & So-

lyom, 1990). These reports have typically described long-term psychotherapeutic treatment in which focus shifted from factitious somatic symptoms to associated personality disorder (Earle & Folks, 1986; Guziec et al., 1994; Plassman, 1994). Plassman describes a series of 24 patients with factitious disorders, 12 of whom were willing to enter psychotherapeutic treatment. Of the 12, 10 patients continued in psychodynamic psychotherapy (up to 4 years), and all were said to have "progressed favorably." Solyom and Solyom describe two patients who responded positively to a more behaviorally oriented inpatient treatment program designed to reduce reinforcement of the sick role while avoiding confrontation or "loss of face" (Solyom & Solyom, 1990). One case report (Earle & Folks, 1986) describes a positive response to antidepressant pharmacotherapy coupled with long-term psychotherapeutic treatment.

No clear guidance is available regarding the treatment of factitious disorder by proxy. Published reports emphasize that caregivers typically deny any responsibility for producing symptoms (Feldman, 1994) and that further fabrications of illness may persist for years (Bools, Beale, & Meadow, 1993).

Future Prospects

It seems unlikely that systematic studies of the management of factitious disorders will ever be conducted. Both the relative rarity of the condition (or rarity of its recognition) and the patient's resistance to treatment will preclude formal treatment trials. For the foreseeable future, treatment of patients with factitious disorders must rely on recommendations from earlier case reports filtered by clinical judgment. Future reports may help to guide treatment by clarifying the nature of associated or underlying psychiatric disorders.

SUMMARY

The evidence reviewed above suggests that distressing somatic symptoms often respond to appropriate clinical management. Treatments proven effective for the management of somatoform disorders are remarkably similar to those commonly used in the management of anxiety and affective disorders. As discussed above, however, establishing a working treatment alliance and maintaining treatment adherence does involve issues unique to this group of conditions.

While the discussion above is organized according to formal diagnostic categories, the evidence reviewed suggests an alternative organization according to specific target symptoms. Major symptoms common to several of the somatoform disorders include heightened sensitivity to somatic distress, exaggerated fear of disease, and adoption of a withdrawn or disabled role.

Heightened sensitivity to noxious sensations may manifest as pain complaints or as increased sensitivity to specific kinds of somatic distress (e.g., irritable bowel syndrome, fibromyalgia). The available evidence supports the effectiveness of both pharmacotherapy and appropriate psychotherapy. While antidepressants have not been proven effective in the management of all types of somatic distress, data support their use for irritable bowel syndrome, fibromyalgia, and several chronic pain syndromes. Most data supporting the efficacy of antidepressants concerns older tricyclic drugs. Several reports describe therapeutic effects at doses one third to one half those recommended for treatment of depression. Moderately strong evidence supports the effectiveness of behavioral techniques such as relaxation training in reducing symptom sensitivity. Psychotherapeutic treatments may be more effective in reducing distress and disability than in directly affecting symptom intensity.

Disease fear and disease conviction are maladaptive cognitive processes amenable to both pharmacological and psychotherapeutic treatments. Studies of hypochondriasis and body dysmorphic disorder, the two conditions most characterized by exaggerated disease fear, provide strong evidence for the effectiveness of cognitive-behavioral psychotherapy and moderate evidence for the effectiveness of antidepressant pharmacotherapy. The available evidence supports the use of serotonergic-type antidepressants. Given the apparent advantages of such drugs in the management of obsessions and compulsions, serotonergic drugs should probably be favored in the pharmacological management of hypochondriacal beliefs. Case series and case reports describe antidepressant doses similar to those used in management of obsessive compulsive disorder.

The adverse behavioral consequences of somatoform disorders often call for a behavioral approach. Withdrawal from usual activities and adoption of the sick role may occur in several of the above-described disorders and are especially prominent in conversion

disorders and factitious disorders. Moderate evidence supports the effectiveness of behavioral approaches for management of illness behaviors. Components of such an approach include reducing incentives for withdrawal, positively rewarding return to normal function, and developing specific plans for reactivation. More intractable illness behavior may require inpatient behavioral management.

Because patients typically present with a mixture of somatic, cognitive, and behavioral difficulties, effective treatment must integrate a variety of active ingredients. Treatment planning should identify the target symptoms (e.g., pain, disease fear, social isolation) that cause the most distress or interference with function. True collaboration in identifying treatment priorities is essential for therapeutic success.

References

Adler, G. (1981). The physician and the hypochondriacal patient. *New England Journal of Medicine, 304,* 1394–1396.

American Psychiatric Association. (1987). *Diagnostic and statistical manual of mental disorders,* 3rd ed., revised. Washington, D.C.: Author.

———. (1994). *Diagnostic and statistical manual of mental disorders,* 4th ed. Washington, D.C.: Author.

Asher, R. (1951). Munchausen's syndrome. *Lancet, 1,* 339–341.

Barsky, A., Cleary, P. D., Coeytaux, R. R., & Ruskin, J. N. (1994). Psychiatric disorders in medical outpatients complaining of palpitations. *Journal of General Internal Medicine, 9,* 306–313.

Barsky, A., Geringer, E., & Wool, C. A. (1988). A cognitive-educational treatment for hypochondriasis. *General Hospital Psychiatry, 10,* 322–327.

Barsky, A., & Wyshak, G. (1989). Hypochondriasis and related health attitudes. *Psychosomatics, 30,* 412–420.

Bergdahl, J., Anneroth, G., & Perris, H. (1995). Cognitive therapy in the treatment of patients with resistant burning mouth syndrome: A controlled study. *Journal of Oral Pathology & Medicine, 24,* 213–215.

Bloch, S., & Glue, P. (1988). Psychotherapy and dysmorphophobia: A case report. *British Journal of Psychiatry, 152,* 271–274.

Bools, C., Beale, B. A., & Meadow, S. R. (1993). Follow-up of victims of fabricated illness (Munchausen syndrome by proxy). *Archives of Disease in Childhood, 69,* 625–630.

Breuer, J., & Freud, S. (1957). *Studies on hysteria.* New York: Basic Books.

Briquet, P. (1859). *Traite de l'Hysterie.* Paris: Bailliere et Fils.

Brooksbank, D. (1984). Management of conversion reaction in five adolescent girls. *Journal of Adolescence, 7,* 359–376.

Carette, S., McCain, G. A., Bell, D. A., & Fam, A. G. (1986). Evaluation of amitriptyline in primary fibrositis. *Arthritis and Rheumatism, 29,* 655–659.

Clouse, R., Lustman, P. J., Geisman, R. A., & Alpers, D. H. (1994). Antidepressant therapy in 138 patients with irritable bowel syndrome: A five-year clinical experience. *Alimentary Pharmacology and Therapeutics, 8,* 409–416.

Coderre, T., Katz, J., Vaccarine, A. L., & Melzack, R. (1993). Contribution of central neuroplasticity to pathological pain: Review of clinical and experimental evidence. *Pain, 52,* 259–285.

Cormier, L. E., Katon, W., Russo, J., Hollifield, M., Hall, M. L., & Vitaliano, P. P. (1988). Chest pain with negative cardiac diagnostic studies: Relationship to psychiatric illness. *Journal of Nervous and Mental Disease, 176,* 351–358.

Couprie, W., Wijdicks, E. F., Rooijmans, H. G., & van-Gijn, J. (1995). Outcome in conversion disorder: A follow-up study. *Journal of Neurological and Neurosurgical Psychiatry, 58,* 750–752.

Deary, I., & Wilson, J. A. (1994). Problems in treating globus pharyngis. *Clinical Otolaryngology, 19,* 55–60.

Diamond, D. (1987). Psychotherapeutic approaches to the treatment of panic attacks, hypochondriasis, and agoraphobia. *British Journal of Medical Psychology, 60,* 79–84.

Dworkin, S., Turner, J. A., Wilson, L., Massoth, D., Whitney, C., Huggins, K. H., Burgess, J., Sommers, E., & Truelove, E. (1994). Brief group cognitive-behavioral intervention for temporomandibular disorders. *Pain, 59,* 175–187.

Earle, J., & Folks, D. G. (1986). Factitious disorder and coexisting depression: A report of successful psychiatric consultation and case management. *General Hospital Psychiatry, 8,* 448–450.

Egbunike, I., & Chaffee, B. J. (1990). Antidepressants in the management of chronic pain syndromes. *Pharmacotherapy, 10,* 262–270.

Escobar, J. I., Burnam, M. A., Karno, M., Forsythe, A., & Golding, J. M. (1987). Somatization in the community. *Archives of General Psychiatry, 44,* 713–718.

Fallon, B., Javitch, J. A., Hollander, E., & Liebowitz, M. R. (1991). Hypochondriasis and obsessive-compulsive disorder: Overlaps in diagnosis and treatment. *Journal of Clinical Psychiatry, 52,* 437–460.

Fallon, B., Liebowitz, M. R., Salman, E., Schieier, F. R., Jusino, C., Hollander, E., & Klein, D. F. (1993). Fluoxetine for hypochondriacal patients without major depression. *Journal of Clinical Psychopharmacology, 13,* 438–441.

Fava, G., Grandi, S., Rafanelli, C., & Canestrari, R. (1992). Prodromal symptoms in panic disorder with agoraphobia: A replication study. *Journal of Affective Disorders, 26,* 85–88.

Feldman, M. (1994). Denial in Munchausen syndrome by proxy: The consulting psychiatrist's dilemma. *International Journal of Psychiatric Medicine, 24,* 121–128.

Fernando, N. (1988). Monosymptomatic hypochondriasis treated with a tricyclic antidepressant. *British Journal of Psychiatry, 152,* 851–852.

Figueroa, J. (1982). Group treatment of chronic tension headaches: A comparative treatment study. *Behavior Modification, 6,* 229–239.

Folks, D. (1995). Munchausen's syndrome and other factitious disorders. *Neurology Clinics, 13,* 267–281.

Ford, C., & Folks, D. G. (1985). Conversion disorders: An overview. *Psychosomatics, 26,* 371–383.

Ford, C., & Long, K. D. (1977). Group psychotherapy of somatizing patients. *Psychotherapy and Psychosomatics, 28,* 294–304.

Foreman, D., & Farsides, C. (1993). Ethical use of covert videoing techniques in detecting Munchausen syndrome by proxy. *British Medical Journal, 307,* 611–613.

Gask, L., Goldberg, D., Porter, R., & Creed, F. (1989). The treatment of somatization: Evaluation of a teaching package with general practice trainees. *Journal of Psychosomatic Research, 33,* 697–703.

Goldberg, D., Gask, L., & O'Dowd, T. (1989). The treatment of somatization: Teaching techniques of reattribution. *Journal of Psychosomatic Research, 33,* 689–695.

Goldenberg, D. (1987). Fibromyalgia syndrome: An emerging but controversial condition. *Journal of the American Medical Association, 257,* 2782–2787.

Goldenberg, D., Felson, D. T., & Dinerman, H. (1986). A randomized, controlled trial of amitriptyline and naproxen in the treatment of patients with fibromyalgia. *Arthritis and Rheumatism, 29,* 1371–1377.

Guthrie, E., Creed, F., Dawson, D., & Tomenson, B. (1993). A randomised controlled trial of psychotherapy in patients with refractory irritable bowel syndrome. *British Journal of Psychiatry, 163,* 315–321.

Guze, S. (1967). The diagnosis of hysteria: What are we trying to do? *American Journal of Psychiatry, 124,* 491–498.

Guziec, J., Lazarus, A., & Harding, J. J. (1994). Case of a 29-year old nurse with factitious disorder. *General Hospital Psychiatry, 16,* 47–53.

Hellman, C., Budd, M., Borysenko, J., McClelland, D. C., & Benson, H. (1990). A study of the effectiveness of two group behavioral medicine interventions for patients with psychosomatic complaints. *Behavioral Medicine, 16,* 165–173.

Hollander, E., Cohen, L., Simeon, D., Rosen, J., Decaria, C., & Stein, D. J. (1994). Fluvoxamine treatment of body dysmorphic disorder. *Journal of Clinical Psychopharmacology, 14*, 75–77.

Hollander, E., Liebowitz, M. R., Winchel, R., Klumker, A., & Klein, D. F. (1989). Treatment of body dysmorphic disorder with serotonin reuptake inhibitors. *American Journal of Psychiatry, 146*, 768–770.

Kaplan, K., Goldenberg, D. L., & Galvin-Nadeau, M. (1993). The impact of a group meditation-based stress reduction program on fibromyalgia. *General Hospital Psychiatry, 15*, 284–289.

Katon, W., Lin, E., VonKorff, M., Russo, J., Lipscomb, P., & Bush, T. (1991). Somatization: A spectrum of severity. *American Journal of Psychiatry, 148*, 34–40.

Katon, W., & Russo, J. (1989). Somatic symptoms and depression. *Journal of Family Practice, 29*, 65–69.

Kellner, R. (1982). Psychotherapeutic strategies in hypochondriasis: A clinical study. *American Journal of Psychotherapy, 36*, 146–157.

———. (1992). Diagnosis and treatments of hypochondriacal syndromes. *Psychosomatics, 33*, 278–279.

Kent, D., Tomasson, K., & Coryell, W. (1995). Course and outcome of conversion and somatization disorders: A four-year follow-up. *Psychosomatics, 36*, 136–144.

Kenyon, F. (1976). Hypochondriacal states. *British Journal of Psychiatry, 129*, 1–14.

Kirmayer, L., & Robbins, J. M. (1991). *Current concepts of somatization: Research and clinical perspectives.* Washington, D.C.: American Psychiatric Press.

Klonoff, E., & Moore, D. J. (1986). "Conversion reactions" in adolescents: A biofeedback-based operant approach. *Journal of Behavior Therapy and Experimental Psychiatry, 17*, 179–184.

Kotsopoulos, S., & Snow, B. (1986). Conversion disorders in children: A study of clinical outcome. *Psychiatric Journal of the University of Ottowa, 11*, 134–139.

Kroenke, K., Lucas, C. A., Rosenberg, M. L., & Scherokman, B. J. (1993). Psychiatric disorders and functional impairment in patients with persistent dizziness. *Journal of General Internal Medicine, 8*, 530–535.

Kroenke, K., Wood, D. R., Mangelsdorff, A. D., Neier, N. J., & Powell, J. B. (1988). Chronic fatigue in primary care: Prevalence, patient characteristics, and outcome. *Journal of the American Medical Association, 260*, 929–934.

Krull, F., & Schifferdecker, M. (1990). Inpatient treatment of conversion disorder: A clinical investigation of outcome. *Psychotherapy and Psychosomatics, 53*, 161–165.

Langemark, M., & Olesen, J. (1994). Sulpiride and paroxetine in the treatment of chronic tension-type headache. An explanatory double-blind trial. *Headache, 34*, 20–24.

Lazarus, A. (1990). Somatic therapy for conversion disorder. *Psychosomatics, 31*, 357.

Linton, S., Melin, L., & Stjernlof, K. (1985). The effects of applied relaxation and operant activity training on chronic pain. *Behavioural Psychotherapy, 13*, 87–100.

Lipowski, Z. (1988). An inpatient programme for persistent somatizers. *Canadian Journal of Psychiatry, 33*, 275–278.

Logsdail, S., Lovell, K., Warwick, H., & Marks, I. (1991). Behavioural treatment of AIDS-focused illness phobias. *British Journal of Psychiatry, 159*, 422–425.

Magni, G. (1991). The use of antidepressants in the treatment of chronic pain. *Drugs, 42*, 730–748.

Max, M., Lynch, S. A., Muir, J., Shoaf, S. E., Smoller, B., & Dubner, R. (1992). Effects of desipramine, amitriptyline, and fluoxetine on pain in diabetic neuropathy. *New England Journal of Medicine, 326*, 1250–1256.

Melson, S., & Rynearson, E. K. (1986). Intensive group therapy for functional illness. *Psychiatric Annals, 16*, 687–692.

Mizes, J. (1985). The use of contingent reinforcement in the treatment of conversion disorder. *Journal of Behavior Therapy and Experimental Psychiatry, 16*, 341–345.

Monson, R., & Smith, G. R. (1983). Current concepts in psychiatry: Somatization disorder in primary care. *New England Journal of Medicine, 308*, 1464–1465.

Moore, J., & Chaney, E. F. (1985). Outpatient group treatment of chronic pain: Effects of spouse involvement. *Journal of Consulting and Clinical Psychology, 53*, 326–334.

Murphy, G. (1982). The clinical management of hysteria. *Journal of the American Medical Association, 247*, 2559–2564.

Newell, R., & Shrubb, S. (1994). Attitude change and behavior therapy in body dysmorphic disorder: Two case reports. *Behavioural and Cognitive Psychotherapy, 22*, 163–169.

Neziroglu, F., & Yaryura, T. J. A. (1993). Exposure, response prevention, and cognitive therapy in the treatment of body dysmorphic disorder. *Behavior Therapy, 24*, 431–438.

Nielsen, G., Barth, K., Brit, H., & Havik, O. (1988). Brief dynamic psychotherapy for patients presenting physical symptoms. *Psychotherapy and Psychosomatics, 50*, 35–41.

Noyes, R., Reich, J., Clancy, J., & O'Gorman, T. W. (1986). Reduction in hypochondriasis with treatment of panic disorder. *British Journal of Psychiatry, 149*, 631–635.

Payne, A., & Blanchard, E. B. (1995). A controlled comparison of cognitive therapy and self-help support groups in the treatment of irritable bowel syndrome. *Journal of Consulting and Clinical Psychology, 63*, 779–786.

Philipp, M., & Fickinger, M. (1993). Psychotropic drugs in the management of chronic pain syndromes. *Pharmacopsychiatry, 26*, 221–234.

Pilowsky, I., & Graham, B. C. (1990). A controlled study of psychotherapy and amitriptyline used individually and in combination in the treatment of chronic intractable "psychogenic" pain. *Pain, 40*, 3–19.

Pilowsky, I., Spence, N., Rounsefell, B., & Forsten, C. (1995). Outpatient cognitive-behavioral therapy with amitriptyline for chronic non-malignant pain: A comparative study with 6-month follow-up. *Pain, 60*, 49–54.

Plassman, R. (1994). Inpatient and outpatient long-term psychotherapy of patients suffering from factitious disorders. *Psychotherapy and Psychosomatics, 62*, 96–107.

Pu, T., Mohamed, E., Iman, K., & El-Roey, A. M. (1986). One hundred cases of hysteria in Eastern Libya: A sociodemographic study. *British Journal of Psychiatry, 148*, 606–609.

Quill, T. (1985). Somatization disorder: One of medicine's blind spots. *Journal of the American Medical Association, 254*, 3075–3079.

Rangaswami, K. (1985). Treatment of hysterical conditions by avoidance conditioning. *Dayalbagh Educational Institute Research Journal of Education, 3*, 53–56.

Rogers, R., Bagby, R. M., & Rector, N. (1990). Diagnostic legitimacy of factitious disorder with psychological symptoms. *American Journal of Psychiatry, 147*, 1312–1314.

Rosen, J., Reiter, P., & Orosan, P. (1995). Cognitive-behavioral body image therapy for body dysmorphic disorder. *Journal of Consulting and Clinical Psychology, 63*, 263–269.

Rost, K., Kashner, T. M., & Smith, G. R. (1994). Effectiveness of psychiatric intervention with somatization disorder patients: Improved outcomes at reduced costs. *General Hospital Psychiatry, 16*, 381–387.

Salkovskis, P., & Warwick, H. M. (1986). Morbid preoccupations, health anxiety, and reassurance: A cognitive-behavioural approach to hypochondriasis. *Behaviour Research and Therapy, 24*, 597–602.

Sanders, M., Sheperd, R. W., Cleghorn, G., & Woolford, H. (1994). The treatment of recurrent abdominal pain in children: A controlled comparison of cognitive-behavioral family intervention and standard pediatric care. *Journal of Consulting and Clinical Psychology, 62*, 306–314.

Saper, S., Silberstein, S. D., Lake, A. E., & Winters, M.

E. (1994). Double-blind trial of fluoxetine: Chronic daily headaches and migraine. *Headache, 34*, 497–502.

Schmaling, K., Rosenberg, S. J., Oppenheimer, J., & Moran, M. G. (1991). Factitious disorder with respiratory symptoms. *Psychosomatics, 32*, 457–459.

Schmidt, N., & Harrington, P. (1995). Cognitive-behavioral treatment of body dysmorphic disorder: a case report. *Journal of Behavior Therapy and Experimental Psychiatry, 26*, 161–167.

Schwarz, K., Harding, R., Harrington, D., & Farr, B. (1993). Hospital management of a patient with intractable factitious disorder. *Psychosomatics, 34*, 265–267.

Sharpe, M., Peveler, R., & Mayou, R. (1992). The psychological treatment of patients with functional somatic symptoms: A practical guide. *Journal of Psychosomatic Research, 36*, 515–529.

Sheehan, D., Ballenger, J., & Jacobsen, G. (1980). Treatment of endogenous anxiety with phobic, hysterical, an hypochondriacal symptoms. *Archives of General Psychiatry, 37*, 51–59.

Shorter, E., Abbey, S. E., Gillies, L. A., Singh, M., & Lipowski, Z. J. (1992). Inpatient treatment of persistent somatization. *Psychosomatics, 33*, 295–300.

Silver, H. (1987). Physical complaints are port of the core depressive syndrome: Evidence from a cross-cultural study in Israel. *Journal of Clinical Psychiatry, 48*, 140–142.

Simon, G., Daniell, W., Stockbridge, H., Claypoole, K., & Rosenstock, L. (1993). Immunologic, psychological, and neuropsychological factors in multiple chemical sensitivity. *Annals of Internal Medicine, 119*, 97–103.

Simon, G., & VonKorff, M. (1991). Somatization and psychiatric disorder in the NIMH Epidemiologic Catchment Area Study. *American Journal of Psychiatry, 148*(11), 1494–1500.

Sindrup, S., Gram, L. F., Brosen, K., Eshoj, O., & Mogensoen, E. F. (1990). The selective serotonin reuptake inhibitor paroxetine is effective in the treatment of diabetic neuropathy syndromes. *Pain, 42*, 135–144.

Smith, G. (1992). The epidemiology and treatment of depression when it coexists with somatoform disorders, somatization, or pain. *General Hospital Psychiatry, 14*, 265–272.

Smith, G., Monson, R. A., & Ray, D. C. (1986). Psychiatric consultation in somatization disorder. *New England Journal of Medicine, 314*, 1407–1413.

Smith, G., Rost, K., & Kashner, T. M. (1995). A trial of the effect of standardized psychiatric consultation on health outcomes and costs in somatizing patients. *Archives of General Psychiatry, 52*, 238–243.

Sno, H., Storosum, J. G., & Wortel, C. H. (1991). Psychogenic "HIV infection." *International Journal of Psychiatric Medicine, 21*, 93–98.

Solyom, C., & Solyom, L. (1990). A treatment program for functional paraplegia/Munchausen syndrome. *Journal of Behavior Therapy and Experimental Psychiatry, 21*, 225–230.

Sondheimer, A. (1988). Clomipramine treatment of delusional disorder—somatic subtype. *Journal of the American Academy of Child and Adolescent Psychiatry, 27*, 188–192.

Speckens, A., vanHemert, A. M., Spinhoven, P., Hawton, K. E., Holk, J. H., & Rooijmans, G. M. (1995). Cognitive behavioural therapy for medically unexplained physical symptoms: A randomised controlled trial. *British Medical Journal, 311*, 1328–1332.

Spence, S. (1989). Cognitive-behavior therapy in the management of chronic, occupational pain of the upper limbs. *Behaviour Research and Therapy, 27*, 435–446.

Starcevi'c, V. (1991). Reassurance and treatment of hypochondriasis. *General Hospital Psychiatry, 13*, 122–127.

Steibel, V., & Kirby, J. V. (1994). The amytal interview in the treatment of conversion disorder: Three case reports. *Military Medicine, 159*, 350–353.

Stern, R., & Fernandez, M. (1991). Group cognitive and behavioural treatment for hypochondriasis. *British Medical Journal, 303*, 1229–1231.

Stevens, C. (1990). Lorazepam in the treatment of acute conversion disorder. *Hospital and Community Psychiatry, 41*, 1255–1257.

Stimmel, G. L., & Escobar, J. I. (1986). Antidepressants in chronic pain: A review of efficacy. *Pharmacotherapy, 6*, 262–267.

Stone, A. (1993). Treatment of hypochondriasis with clomipramine. *Journal of Clinical Psychiatry, 54*, 200–201.

Subramanian, K. (1991). Structured group work for the management of chronic pain: An experimental investigation. *Research on Social Work Practices, 1*, 32–45.

Sullivan, M., & Buchanan, D. C. (1989). The treatment of conversion disorder in a rehabilitation setting. *Canadian Journal of Rehabilitation, 2*, 175–180.

Sutherland, A., & Rodin, G. M. (1990). Factitious disorder in a general hospital setting: clinical features and a review of the literature. *Psychosomatics, 31*, 392–399.

Taylor, S., & Hyler, S. E. (1993). Update on factitious disorders. *International Journal of Psychiatric Medicine, 23*, 81–94.

Teasell, R., & Shapiro, A. P. (1994). Strategic behavioral intervention in the treatment of chronic nonorganic motor disorders. *American Journal of Physical Medicine and Rehabilitation, 73*, 44–50.

Turgay, A. (1990). Treatment outcome for children and adolescents with conversion disorder. *Canadian Journal of Psychiatry, 35*, 585–588.

Turner, J. (1982). Comparison of group progressive-relaxation training and cognitive-behavioral group therapy for chronic low back pain. *Journal of Consulting and Clinical Psychology, 50*, 757–765.

Turner, J. A., & Denny, M. C. (1993). Do antidepressant medications relieve chronic low back pain? *Journal of Family Practice, 37*, 545–553.

Ustun, T., & Sartorius, N. (1995). *Mental illness in general health care: An international study.* London: John Wiley & Sons.

Visser, S., & Bouman, T. K. (1992). Cognitive-behavioural approaches in the treatment of hypochondriasis: Six single-case crossover studies. *Behaviour Research and Therapy, 30*, 301–306.

Walker, E., Katon, W., Harrop-Griffiths, G., Holm, L., Russo, J., & Hickok, L. R. (1988). Relationship of chronic pelvic pain to psychiatric diagnosis and childhood sexual abuse. *American Journal of Psychiatry, 145*, 75–80.

Wallach, J. (1994). Laboratory diagnosis of factitious disorder. *Archives of Internal Medicine, 154*, 1690–1696.

Warwick, H. (1989). A cognitive-behavioural approach to hypochondriasis and health anxiety. *Journal of Psychosomatic Research, 33*, 705–711.

Wesner, R., & Noyes, R. (1991). Imipramine an effective treatment for illness phobia. *Journal of Affective Disorders, 22*, 43–48.

Wilkinson, P., & Mynors-Wallis, L. (1994). Problem-solving therapy in the treatment of unexplained physical symptoms in primary care: A preliminary study. *Journal of Psychosomatic Research, 38*, 591–598.

Wolfe, F., Cathey, M. A., & Hawley, D. J. (1994). A double-blind placebo controlled trial of fluoxetine in fibromyalgia. *Scandinavian Journal of Rheumatology, 23*, 255–259.

Wysenbeek, A., Mor, J., Lurie, Y., & Weinberger, A. (1985). Imipramine for the treatment of fibrositis: A therapeutic trial. *Annals of the Rheumatic Diseases, 44*, 752–753.

22

Treatments for Dissociative Disorders

Jose R. Maldonado

Lisa D. Butler

David Spiegel

To date, no controlled studies have explored either psychosocial or psychopharmacological treatments for dissociative amnesia. Similarly, no controlled treatment studies of dissociative fugue have been reported. Clinicians have generally employed hypnosis and amytal narcosynthesis to facilitate memory recovery in both conditions. Psychodynamic psychotherapy designed to address the conflicts presumed to have precipitated the amnesia or fugue has also been widely utilized.

No controlled studies have yet addressed the treatment of dissociative identity disorder (DID; multiple personality disorder, MPD), although several longitudinal studies reporting on the treatment of substantial numbers of these patients have been published over the past 15 years. As with dissociative amnesia and dissociative fugue, hypnosis and psychodynamic psychotherapy appear to be treatments of choice, although some clinicians have also reported the successful use of family and group therapies to treat this condition.

Dissociative disorders can be understood as the pathological separation of aspects of mental functioning, including perception, memory, identity, and consciousness, that would normally be processed together. The lack of integration of memory results in dissociative amnesia; in identity and consciousness, dissociative fugue and dissociative identity disorder (DID); and in perception, depersonalization disorder. Dissociative symptoms often occur in the context of traumatic stressors and are components of the symptom patterns of acute and post-traumatic stress disorders. They should be understood as failures in integration or defects in control systems, rather than as the creation of multiple identities, memories, or perceptions. They are thought to help individuals maintain emotional equilibrium in the face of acute or chronic traumatic stressors, but result in distress and dysfunc-tion, including intrapsychic, vocational, and interpersonal disabilities.

THE DISSOCIATIVE DISORDERS: AN OVERVIEW

Dissociative Amnesia (Psychogenic Amnesia)

The hallmark of dissociative (psychogenic) amnesia is the inability to recall important personal information, usually of a traumatic or stressful nature; the inability is too extensive to be explained by ordinary forgetfulness (American Psychiatric Association [APA], 1994). It is considered the most common of all dissociative disorders (Putnam, 1985). Amnesia is not only a disorder by itself, but also a symptom found in a number of other dissociative and anxiety disorders. In fact, amnesia is one of the symptom criteria for the diagnoses of acute and post-traumatic stress disorders, somatization disorder, dissociative fugue, and dissociative identity disorder (APA, 1994). A higher incidence of dissociative amnesia has been described in the context of war and other natural and man-made disasters. Studies suggest a direct relationship between the severity of the exposure to trauma and the incidence of amnesia (Brown & Anderson, 1991; Chu & Dill, 1990; Kirshner, 1973; Putnam, 1985, 1993; Sargant & Slater, 1941).

Amnesic patients are usually aware of their memory loss. Dissociative amnesia can also be distinguished from amnesias of neurological origin because the capacity to learn new information is usually retained and cognition is intact. Occasionally, there may be a history of head trauma. If that is the case, usually the trauma is too slight to have physiological consequences. Because the amnesia involves primarily difficulties in retrieval rather than encoding or storage, the memory deficits exhibited are usually reversible. Once the amnesia has cleared, normal memory function is resumed (Schacter, Wang, Tulving, & Freedman, 1982).

Most cases can be divided into two clinical presentations: acute and generally severe amnesia and a more chronic and insidious form. It has been suggested that the acute cases are usually associated with traumatic circumstances. The second presentation includes patients who experienced a traumatic event years prior to their presentation. The amnesia usually involves difficulties with explicit or episodic memory (Schacter & Kihlstrom, 1989; Squire, 1987), that is, memory associated with autobiographical information. In most cases, implicit or semantic memory (memory for skills, facts, concepts, and vocabulary) is intact.

The epidemiology of this disorder is unknown. The lack of studies and data about the incidence and prevalence of this disorder has been noted (Putnam, 1985). Nevertheless, dissociative amnesia is considered to be the most common of all dissociative disorders (Putnam, 1985). The disorder may be especially difficult to diagnose in childhood, in which the symptoms may be obscured or mistaken for more common diagnoses such as attention deficit disorder, oppositional behavior, learning disability, mental retardation, or pervasive developmental disorder.

The etiology of amnesic disorders is presumed to be post-traumatic since they generally occur within the "context of severe psychosocial stress" (Kluft, 1988). Extensive review of clinical cases suggests that victims of intense trauma experience dissociative symptoms during the event and afterward. Such symptoms may buffer the full impact of the traumatic experience (Putnam, 1985; Spiegel, 1984, 1986, 1988, 1990; Spiegel, Hunt, Dondershine, 1988; van der Kolk & van der Hart, 1989).

At the time of overwhelming trauma, some victims experience a fragmentation of their experience. This is characterized by a polarization of their sense of self and a selective dissociation of affects and memories. Yet, even though dissociated memories may be unavailable to consciousness, there is evidence that they continue to influence conscious (and other unconscious) experiences and behavior (Hilgard, 1977; Kihlstrom, 1984). The fact that trauma victims cannot consciously recall these memories does not mean that they do not affect them: they are out of sight but not out of mind. In fact, many of the psychological and physiological symptoms experienced by trauma victims can be explained by the influence exerted by dissociated memories (Kihlstrom, 1984, 1990).

The duration of the disorder varies from a few days to a few years. Even though it is possible to experience a single episode of amnesia, many patients have experienced several episodes during their lifetime. This is more common if the stressors that caused the initial episode are not resolved. The spontaneous resolution of the symptoms is rather common. At times, the recovery is gradual as a more generalized presentation becomes progressively more narrow and localized. Sometimes, patients experience spontaneous recovery without treatment other than a protective environment. At other times, more systematic treatment is necessary.

It is necessary to rule out a number of physical and psychological conditions that may mimic the amnesic deficits. Any assessment of an acute onset amnesia, regardless of the presence or absence of psychosocial stressors, should include a battery of tests that explore possible medical and neurological disorders such as epilepsy, brain malignancy, head trauma, medication side effect (e.g., from benzodiazepines), drug abuse and acute intoxication, and cardiovascular and metabolic abnormalities. Other psychiatric diagnoses to consider include other dissociative disorders, an organic brain syndrome, a factitious disorder, and malingering.

Dissociative Fugue (Psychogenic Fugue)

Dissociative (psychogenic) fugue is characterized by "sudden, unexpected travel away from home or one's customary place of daily activities, with inability to recall some or all of one's past" (APA, 1994). Because of the degree of amnesia involved, patients develop a sense of confusion about personal identity or assume a new identity (Riether & Stoudemire, 1988). Patients suffering from this disorder appear "normal," usually exhibiting no signs of psychopathology or cognitive deficit. Often, patients suffering from fugue states take on an entirely new (and unrelated) identity and occupation. In contrast to patients suffering from dissociative identity disorder, in fugue states the old and new identities do not alternate. The underlying motivating factor appears to be a desire to withdraw from emotionally painful experiences.

Predisposing factors may include extreme psychosocial stress such as war or natural and man-made disasters, personal and/or financial pressures or losses, heavy alcohol use, or intense and overwhelming stress such as assault or rape. The most common stressors triggering fugue states include marital discord, financial and occupational difficulties, and war-related factors. Of interest, it has been reported that the onset of some fugue episodes may occur during sleep or be associated with sleep deprivation (Kluft, 1988). As in dissociative amnesia, there may be a history of head trauma associated with the onset of the condition.

Dissociative fugue patients usually wander away from home in a purposeful way, often far away and for days at a time. Fugue patients differ from those with dissociative amnesia in that the former are usually unaware of their amnesia. Only on resumption of their former identities do they recall past memories, at which time they usually become amnesic for experiences during the fugue episode. However, not all patients experiencing dissociative fugue states develop a new identity. If patients do adopt a new identity, it is usually quiet and somewhat reclusive, with the patient doing nothing to draw attention to him or herself (APA, 1994).

A prevalence rate of 0.2% has been described in the general population (APA, 1994). It is theorized that the prevalence of the disorder is higher during times of exposure to extreme stress, but actual data confirming this are not available. The incidence and sex ratio are not known (Kluft, 1988). Most available reports come from military personnel exposed to war and sectors of the population that have experienced major psychosocial stress or natural disasters (Putnam, 1985).

Similar to cases of acute dissociative amnesia, the onset of the disorder is usually associated with a traumatic or overwhelming event accompanied by strong emotions such as depression, grief, suicidal or aggressive impulses, or shame. Dissociative fugue is the least understood dissociative disorder. This may be due to the fact that most of these patients do not present for treatment. Usually, they do not come to the attention of medical personnel until they have recovered their identity and memory and have returned home. Typically, patients seek psychiatric attention once the fugue is over and they are seeking to recover their original identity or retrieve their memory for events that occurred during the fugue (Riether & Stoudemire, 1988). There is also only limited research into appropriate treatment modalities for this disorder.

Dissociative Identity Disorder (Multiple Personality Disorder)

Formerly known as multiple personality disorder (MPD), dissociative identity disorder (DID) is defined by the presence of two or more distinct identities or personality states that recurrently take control of behavior (APA, 1994). It represents the failure to integrate various aspects of identity, memory, and consciousness. Also characteristic of this disorder are memory disturbances and amnesia (Kluft, 1991, 1996). Patients commonly suffer from gaps in personal history affecting both recent and remote memory. The amnesia is usually asymmetrical, selectively involving different areas of autobiographical information, that is, "alters" (personality states or identities) differ in the degree of amnesia for the experiences of other alters.

Characteristically, there is a primary or host personality that carries the patient's given name. Usually, the primary personality is the one who pursues treatment. Commonly, the host is not completely aware of the presence of alters. Different personalities may have varying levels of awareness with respect to the existence of other personalities. On average, there are 2 to 4 personalities present at the time of diagnosis. Over the course of exploration and treatment, an average of 13 to 15 personalities may be discovered (Boon & Draijer, 1993; Coons, Bowman, & Milstein, 1988; Kluft, 1984b, 1991, 1996; Putnam, Guroff, Silberman, Barban, & Post, 1986; Ross, Norton, & Wozney, 1989).

The host personality may experience a number of symptoms that may cause the patients to seek treatment or make the families and spouses bring them to treatment. These symptoms include memory deficits, moodiness, erratic and unpredictable behavior, depression, self-mutilation, suicidal ideation or attempts, or the overt manifestation of an alternate personality. The transition from one personality to another is usually sudden and is commonly triggered by environmental factors. The alter identities may have different names, sexes, ages, and personal characteristics. The different personalities may reflect various attempts to cope with difficult issues and problems (Kluft, 1988). Personalities can either have a name or be named after their function or description, such as "the Angry One."

The factors that can lead to the development of dissociative identity disorder are quite varied. Most authors seem to agree that physical and sexual abuse during childhood is the most commonly found etiological factor in these patients. Chronic exposure to early childhood trauma has been linked to the development of a number of chronic forms of anxiety disorders like post-traumatic stress disorder (PTSD), as well as dissociative identity disorder (Coons, Bowman, & Pellow, 1989; Kluft, 1984b; Spiegel, 1984, 1986; Spiegel & Cardena, 1991). Indeed, it is very uncommon to see a patient suffering from DID who has not been exposed to intense trauma, usually physical (or sexual) abuse, to the point of also fulfilling Criterion A for the diagnosis of PTSD (APA, 1994).

Dissociative identity disorder may represent the end product of a number of traumatic experiences taking place during childhood. Among the multiple traumas associated with its development, most authors agree that DID represents the long-term sequelae of severe childhood physical or sexual abuse or neglect (Braun, 1990; Bryer, Nelson, Miller, & Krol, 1987; Coons et al., 1988; Finkelhor, 1984; Goodwin, 1982; Kluft, 1984b; Pribor & Dinwiddie, 1992; Putnam, 1988; Putnam et al., 1986; Ross, 1989; Russell, 1986; Spiegel, 1984). In fact, a history of sexual and/or physical abuse has been reported in 70% to 97% of patients suffering from dissociative identity disorder (Coons &

Milstein, 1992; Coons et al., 1988; Kluft, 1988; Putnam, 1988; Putnam et al., 1986; Ross, 1989; Ross et al., 1990a; Schultz, Braun, & Kluft, 1989). Incest is the most common form of sexual trauma (68%) reported (Putnam et al., 1986). Other forms of childhood trauma associated with later development of DID include physical abuse other than sexual abuse (75%), neglect, confinement, severe intimidation with physical harm, witnessing physical or sexual abuse of a sibling, witnessing the violent death of a relative or close friend, traumatic physical illness of self, and near-death experiences (Kluft, 1984b; Putnam et al., 1986). Several authors have described DID as a complex and chronic form of PTSD that is usually in response to childhood physical or sexual abuse (Kluft, 1987b, 1988; Spiegel, 1984).

Factors that may be involved in the development of DID as a defense against overwhelming trauma may include the age of the victim, the relationship between the perpetrator and the victim, the victim's natural hypnotic capacity (Bliss, 1986; Kluft, 1984b, 1984c, 1988; Morgan & Hilgard, 1973; Spiegel, 1984, 1986; Spiegel et al., 1988; Spiegel & Cardena, 1991), the effects of state-dependent memory (Bower, 1981), and the patient's developmental maturity at the time of trauma (Kluft, 1988; Watkins & Watkins, 1982).

The actual incidence and prevalence of this disorder are unclear. The initial systematic report on the epidemiology of dissociative identity disorder estimated a prevalence of DID in the general population of 0.01% (Coons, 1984). After this initial report, several other studies have looked at the prevalence of the disorder, but most of the studies have been conducted in selected populations or inpatient psychiatric settings. These results indicated a higher prevalence (0.5–10%), but because of the specialized nature of the populations from which the data were obtained, the estimates may be biased (Bliss & Jeppsen, 1985; Boon & Draijer, 1993; Kluft, 1996; Ross et al., 1991a, 1991b; Saxe et al., 1993). The average time from the appearance of symptoms to an accurate diagnosis is 6 years (APA, 1994; Putnam et al., 1986).

The findings in studies conducted in the general population are more limited but suggest a higher prevalence than initially reported by Coons (1984) but lower (about 1%) than described in psychiatric settings and specialized treatment units (Ross, 1991; Vanderlinden, Van Dyck, Vandereycken, & Vertommen, 1991). Recently, Loewenstein reported that the prevalence in North America is about 1%, compared to a prevalence of 10% for all dissociative disorders as a group (Loewenstein, 1994).

On the other hand, several authors (McHugh, 1995a, 1995b; Ganaway, 1989, 1995; Mayer-Gross, Slater, & Roth, 1969; Spanos, Weekes, & Bertrand, 1985; Spanos, Weekes, Menary, & Bertrand, 1986) have suggested that the symptoms associated with DID represent an artificial construct rather than a true psychiatric disorder and that recent public interest in the diagnosis has sparked the increase in the number of reported cases. Mayer-Gross et al. (1969) described dissociative identity disorder (multiple personality disorder) as an "artificial production, the product of the medical attention that they arouse." McHugh (1995a) describes DID as "a psychiatric artifact [created out of] behavioral efforts—conscious or unconscious—on the part of patients to capture medical attention and achieve the advantages offered by the sick role" (p. 164). Ganaway (1995) argues that the proposed models suggesting exogenous traumas as the etiological factors in DID are not sufficient explanation for the large number of cases recently reported. He suggests that a more likely explanation is that DID symptoms are generated as the result of unconscious conflicts and compromises in both patient and therapist transference within the therapeutic dyad. Spanos et al. (1985, 1986) have attempted to demonstrate the iatrogenic origin of DID by simulation studies with normal volunteers in the laboratory setting. While some authors insist that iatrogenesis is responsible for many cases of the disorder (Frankel, 1995; McHugh, 1995a, 1995b), this cannot account for the existence of all cases or for the fact that patients persist with dissociative symptoms despite influence from doctors who deny the existence of the disorder (Spiegel, 1995; Spiegel & McHugh, 1995).

Dissociative identity disorder has been described more commonly during adolescence and young adulthood. Nevertheless, the average age at diagnosis is 29 to 35 years (Bliss, 1980; Coons & Sterne, 1986; Horevitz & Braun, 1984; Kluft, 1984b, 1985b; Putnam et al., 1986). Recently, there has been increased awareness that the age of onset of the disorder occurs much earlier, during childhood. Limited data indicate that usually the appearance of the first alter personality occurs by age 12 (Fagan & McMahon, 1984; Hornstein & Putnam, 1992; Kluft, 1985a, 1986b, 1991; Peterson, 1990, 1991; Putnam, 1985, 1991; Riley &

Mead, 1988; Tyson, 1992). The youngest case described in the literature was 3 years old when diagnosed (Riley & Mead, 1988).

Dissociative identity disorder seems to be more common in women than men, at a ratio of 3 to 9 women to 1 man (APA, 1994; Allison, 1974; Bliss, 1980; Bliss & Jeppsen, 1985; Coons & Sterne, 1986; Horevitz & Braun, 1984; Kluft, 1984c, 1988; Putnam et al., 1983, 1986; Solomon, 1983; Stern, 1984). Likewise, females are reported to present more personalities (average of 15) than men (average of 8) (APA, 1994). Reports on contemporary case studies and samples indicate a total average of 13 to 15 personalities (Kluft, 1985b; Putnam et al., 1986; Ross et al., 1989c; Schultz et al., 1989). Likewise, there is a high incidence of first-degree relatives who have the disorder (Braun, 1985; Coons, 1985; Kluft, 1984a).

Patients suffering from dissociative identity disorder usually present with a number of associated psychiatric and medical syndromes. Among the psychiatric symptoms, depression is the most common (85–88%; Putnam et al., 1986; Ross & Norton, 1989), and it is the most likely reason for seeking psychiatric consultation (Bliss, 1984; Coons, 1984; Putnam et al., 1986). Other psychiatric symptoms include insomnia (Putnam et al., 1986); suicide attempts or gestures (Bliss, 1980, 1984; Coons, 1984; Putnam et al., 1986; Ross, 1989); self-destructive behaviors (Bliss, 1980, 1984; Coons, 1984; Greaves, 1980; Putnam et al., 1986); phobias, anxiety, and panic attacks (Bliss, 1984; Coons, 1984; Fraser & Lapierre, 1986; Putnam et al., 1986); substance abuse (Coons, 1984; Putnam et al., 1986; Rivera, 1991); auditory and visual hallucinations (Bliss, Larson, & Nakashima, 1983; Coons, 1984; Putnam et al., 1986; Ross et al., 1990a); somatization (Ross & Norton, 1989); and psychoticlike behavior (Coons, 1984; Ellason & Ross, 1995; Kluft, 1987a; Putnam et al., 1986; Ross, 1990b; Ross & Norton, 1988).

Dissociative identity disorder patients experience an unusually high incidence of dissociative symptoms common to other dissociative disorders. For example, amnesia has been described as the single most common dissociative symptom in DID patients, occurring in 85–98% of the cases (Bliss, 1984; Coons, 1984; Putnam et al., 1986). Fugue episodes are experienced by 55% of patients, feelings of depersonalization by 53%, and derealization by 54% (Bliss, 1984; Putnam et al., 1986).

Dissociative identity disorder has been identified across all major racial groups, socioeconomic classes, and cultures. Most cases have been described in the United States and among Caucasians (Carlson, 1981). Nevertheless, there are multiple reports of DID in almost all societies, making it a true cross-cultural diagnosis (Coons, Bowman, Kluft, & Milstein, 1991), although it is rare among dissociative disorders in some societies (Saxena & Prasad, 1989). Indeed, case reports have described DID among blacks (Coons & Sterns, 1986; Ludwig et al., 1972; Solomon, 1983; Stern, 1984), Asians (Putnam, 1989; Yap, 1960), Hispanics (Allison, 1978; Ronquillo, 1991; Solomon, 1983), Europeans (van der Hart, 1993), and inhabitants of Canada (Horen, Leichner, & Lawson, 1995; Ross et al., 1989, 1991a, 1991b; Vincent & Pickering, 1988), India (Adityanjee, Raju, & Khandelwal, 1989; Varma, Bouri, & Wis, 1981), Australia and New Zealand (Gelb, 1993; Price & Hess, 1979), the Netherlands (Boon & Draijer, 1993; Vanderlinden et al., 1991), and the Caribbean (Wittkower, 1970).

Depersonalization Disorder

Depersonalization is characterized by persistent or recurrent episodes of feelings of detachment or estrangement from one's self (APA, 1994). Commonly, individuals report feeling like an automaton or as if they are living a dream or a movie. Patients suffering this condition describe it being as if they were an outside observer of their own mental processes and actions. Different from delusional disorders and other psychotic processes, reality testing is intact (APA, 1994). The phenomena associated with depersonalization are not uncommon. In fact, depersonalization is seen in a number of psychiatric and neurological disorders (Pies, 1991; Putnam, 1985).

Some of the associated psychiatric conditions include agoraphobia and panic disorder (Ambrosino, 1973; Hollander, Fairbanks, Decaria, & Liebowitz, 1989; James, 1961; Roth, 1959), acute and post-traumatic stress disorders, schizophrenia (Bezzubova, 1991; Rosenfeld, 1947; Sedman & Kenna, 1963), other dissociative disorders, personality disorders (Hunter, 1966; Sedman & Reed, 1963; Torch, 1978), acute drug intoxication or withdrawal (Good, 1989; Guttmann & Maclay, 1936; Mathew, Wilson, Humphreys, Lowe, & Weithe, 1993; Melges, Tinklenberg, Hollister, & Gillespie, 1970; Moran, 1986; Szymanski, 1981; Waltzer, 1972), and psychotic mood disorders (Blank, 1954; Sedman & Reed, 1963; Tucker, Harrow, & Quinlan, 1973).

Depersonalization associated with neurological disorders includes epilepsy (Devinsky, Feldmann, Burrowes, & Bromfield, 1989; Harper & Roth, 1962; Kenna & Sedman, 1965), Meniere's disease (Grigsby & Johnson, 1989), sensory deprivation (Horowitz, 1964; Reed & Sedman, 1964), sleep deprivation (Bliss, Clark, & West, 1959), hyperventilation (Cohen, 1988), and migraine headaches. Depersonalization can even be transiently experienced by people with no psychiatric condition at all (Castillo, 1990; Edinger, 1985; Fewtrell, 1984; Kennedy, 1976; Signer, 1988; Wineburg & Straker, 1973). Because of this it is important that the diagnosis be applied only when the presence of symptoms causes severe impairment in functioning or marked distress (Criterion C, APA, 1994).

As in other dissociative disorders, the incidence and prevalence of this condition is unknown. The *symptom* of depersonalization has been described as being the third most common psychiatric symptom, after depression and anxiety (Cattell & Cattell, 1974). It is believed that under severe stress up to 50% of all adults have experienced at least one single brief episode of depersonalization. Likewise, about 12–46% of normal college students (Dixon, 1963; Myers & Grant, 1970; Trueman, 1984), nearly 30% of individuals exposed to life-threatening danger (Noyes & Kletti, 1971; Noyes, Hoenk, Kupperman, & Slymen, 1977), and up to 40% of hospitalized psychiatric patients have experienced transient episodes of depersonalization (APA, 1994; Brauer, Harrow, & Tucker, 1970; Noyes et al., 1977). Cases of depersonalization have been reported during childhood (Elliott, Rosenberg, & Wagner, 1984; Fast & Chethik, 1976) and adolescence (Meares & Grose, 1978; Meyer, 1961; Shimizu & Sakamoto, 1986).

The sex distribution is unknown. Several studies have described a greater incidence in women, ranging from 2 to 4 women for each man affected (Mayer-Gross, 1935; Roberts, 1960). However, other studies have contradicted such findings and have described no sex differences (Chee & Wong, 1990; Dixon, 1963; Sedman, 1966). There is no known familial pattern of inheritance described.

Theories of the etiology of this disorder range from the completely physiological, such as anatomical defects similar to those for epilepsy (Ackner, 1954; Sedman, 1970); to the purely psychological, such as a defense against painful and conflictual affects (Cattell & Cattell, 1974; Frances, Sacks, & Aronoff, 1977; Oberndorf, 1950; Shraberg, 1977; Stamm, 1962); or the split between observing and participating ego/self (Noyes & Kletti, 1971); to combinations, such as the result of a preformed functional response of the brain as an adaptation to overwhelming trauma (Mayer-Gross, 1935). In any event, exposure to traumatic experiences seems to be the common etiological factor in this disorder. The course of the illness is usually chronic, with exacerbations usually following exposure to real or perceived stress.

HISTORICAL PERSPECTIVE
ON TREATMENT

Dissociative Amnesia
(Psychogenic Amnesia)

Historically, the development of most treatments for dissociative (psychogenic) amnesia has occurred in wartime. Army psychiatrists recommended a treatment consisting of removing the soldier from the front line and supplying food and rest (Brown, 1918; Kardiner & Spiegel, 1947; Kubie, 1943). They also stressed the need to provide a therapeutic environment based on safety and support. In many instances, patients experienced spontaneous recovery of their memory on removal from stressful or threatening situations, when feeling physically and psychologically safe, and/or on exposure to cues from the past (i.e., family members) (Brown, 1918; Kardiner & Spiegel, 1947; Kubie, 1943; Loewenstein, 1991; Riether & Stoudemire, 1988). Psychiatric intervention was based on helping the patient sort through memories during the course of an extensive history, in the context of reassurance regarding current safety.

When additional help was necessary, pharmacologically facilitated questioning (called narcosynthesis or narcoanalysis; Grinker & Spiegel, 1945; Horsley, 1943; Kolb, 1985; Marcos & Trujillo, 1978; Perry & Jacobs, 1982; Ruedrich, Chu, & Wadle, 1985; Tureen & Stein, 1949) was used. Hypnosis, consisting primarily of permissive suggestions for memory recall or abreaction of the traumatic experience, was also a popular adjuvant for treatment (Brown, 1919; Fisher, 1945; Grinker & Spiegel, 1945).

Dissociative Fugue (Psychogenic Fugue)

As in the case of dissociative amnesia, the onset, and therefore the treatment, of dissociative (psychogenic) fugue is associated with traumatic experiences. The initial reports of treatment for dissociative amnesia are also associated with war experiences (Abeles & Schilder, 1935; Akhatar & Brenner, 1979; Berrington, Liddell, & Foulds, 1956; Fisher, 1945; Fisher & Joseph, 1949; Horsley, 1943; Kolb, 1985; Luparello, 1970; Marcos & Trujillo, 1978; Parfitt & Carlyle-Gall, 1944; Stengel, 1941, 1943). The treatment approach suggested by these studies and case reports is basically the same as outlined above for cases of dissociative amnesia. Unfortunately, most of these studies were poorly designed and consisted of case reports and collected cases. In addition, diagnostic criteria were not well developed at the time, and many reports did not distinguish well between cases of amnesia and fugue or even cases of dissociative identity disorders or dissociative disorders not otherwise specified (NOS) (Loewenstein, 1995).

No single treatment modality has been systematically studied in this patient population. Nevertheless, the literature proposes the use of permissive suggestions and psychodynamiclike approaches. Hypnosis, as described below, has been suggested to facilitate both the recovery of personal identity and traumatic factors triggering the fugue, as well as integration of these memories and the self. Except for the use of benzodiazepines and barbiturates for drug-facilitated interviews and to reduce the anxiety associated with the treatment process, no pharmacological treatment has been described as effective for this condition.

Dissociative Identity Disorder
(Multiple Personality Disorder)

Seen in historical context, the earliest patients described in the literature suffering from DID (multiple personality disorder) were believed to be possessed. Treatment at the time consisted of depossession rituals or exorcisms. As in the case of other dissociative disorders, not much information is available regarding early treatments. Most of what has been reported consists of elaborate descriptions of cases, but little description of treatment. The first reported case of DID dates to the time of Paracelsus (Bliss, 1980). Gmelin reported in 1791 a patient suffering from a case of "exchange personalities" whom he treated with hypnosis (Ellenberger, 1970). In North America, Rush is recognized as the first to present case reports on patients suffering from DID (Carlson, 1981). Detailed and well known are the descriptions of Felida X (Azam, 1887), Mary

Reynolds (Mitchell, 1888), Despine's case of Estelle and Janet's cases of Leonie and Lucie (Ellenberger, 1970), Christine Beauchamp (Prince, 1906), Doris Fisher (Prince, 1917), Eve (Thigpen & Cleckley, 1957), and Cornelia Wilbur's case of Sybil (Schreiber 1974).

The treatment in most of these cases consisted of the application of psychoanalytic techniques, the use of suggestion or formal hypnosis as an adjuvant in order to facilitate memory retrieval and abreaction, and an emphasis on integration. The most detailed descriptions of these therapeutic techniques are those of W. F. Prince's treatment of Doris (Prince, 1917) and Cornelia Wilbur's treatment of Sybil (Schreiber, 1974).

Depersonalization Disorder

Because depersonalization is rare and most cases tend to remit spontaneously, no controlled studies of therapeutic efficacy have been undertaken. The literature contains reports of a number of therapeutic modalities used for the treatment of this condition. Historical reports pertaining to the treatment of this condition are sparse and nonconclusive.

CURRENT TREATMENTS OF CHOICE

Dissociative Amnesia
(Psychogenic Amnesia)

To date, there are no controlled studies addressing the treatment of dissociative (psychogenic) amnesia. All the information available reflects the experience and case reports of clinicians and treatment centers. No single treatment modality has been systematically studied in this patient population. There are no established pharmacological treatments except for the use of benzodiazepines or barbiturates for drug-assisted interviews.

In general, most approaches to the treatment of these patients are similar to those for patients suffering from traumatic experiences (Loewenstein, 1995) and for the treatment of dissociative fugue (Loewenstein, 1991). Before treatment is started, it is necessary to establish that the amnesia or fugue state is of dissociative origin, particularly because of the commonality of fugue states in temporal lobe epilepsy (Akhatar & Brenner, 1979; Kapur, 1991; Lishman, 1987). Lishman (1987, described in Kapur, 1991) has noted that

psychogenic fugues, compared to epileptic fugues, tend to persist for relatively longer periods (days or weeks), involve more purposeful and well-integrated behavior, and show less disturbance in consciousness and fewer cognitive and physical abnormalities.

Loewenstein (1991) has distinguished between classic and nonclassic presentations of amnesia and fugue. In classic presentations, the dissociative symptomatology is overt and often dramatic. In the nonclassic cases, the primary complaint does not usually involve amnesia, and the condition may be described as a "covert" dissociative disorder. Instead, this group may seek treatment for a variety of conditions, including depression or mood swings; substance abuse sleep or eating problems; somatoform, anxiety, or panic symptoms; suicidal or self-mutilatory impulses or acts; violent outbursts; or interpersonal difficulties. The treatment is usually defined by the presentation. Those patients with an acute onset of amnesia are usually treated more directly and aggressively than patients presenting with chronic amnesia.

In cases of acute presentation, the initial step in the treatment is to provide a safe environment. On numerous occasions, simply removing the person from the threatening situation and providing security and protection has allowed the spontaneous recovery of memory (Abeles & Schilder, 1935; Grinker & Spiegel, 1945; Kennedy & Neville, 1957). At times, additional help may be needed to obtain the necessary biographical information or to facilitate the patient's recall. Among the adjuvants to treatment cited, hypnosis and barbiturate- or benzodiazepine-facilitated recall are the most popular and better described.

Almost every barbiturate has been used to facilitate pharmacologically mediated interviews. Probably the most popular are sodium pentobarbital and sodium amobarbital. Protocols for the administration of tranquilizers (i.e., barbiturates and benzodiazepines) for this purpose have been detailed elsewhere (Baron & Nagy, 1988; Naples & Hackett, 1978; Perry & Jacobs, 1982; Wettstein & Fauman, 1979). Depending on the agent used (i.e., half-life) and the length of the procedure, additional or continuous dosing may be required to maintain adequate disinhibition without overt sedation. The adjuvant use of caffeine (McCall, 1992) or methylphenidate (Hurwitz, 1988) has been reported in order to allow optimal disinhibition and patient cooperation while antagonizing oversedation.

As with the use of medication-facilitated interviews, no studies have addressed the efficacy of hypnosis for the treatment of dissociative amnesia. Nevertheless, most researchers in this area agree that hypnosis is a very useful tool for the recovery of repressed and dissociated memories. Once the amnesia has been reversed, treatment should be directed at restructuring the events and defining the factors that led to the development of the amnesia (Maldonado & Spiegel, in press). This is followed by the establishment of appropriate defenses and mechanisms to prevent a further need for dissociation. This is best done within the context of more extensive therapeutic work. From this point, therapy would be similar to the treatment of more chronic forms of amnesia, described next.

The covert form (chronic presentation) of amnesia is that experienced by patients who have memory gaps regarding substantial periods of time in the past. This is most commonly described in patients suffering from childhood sexual and physical abuse. In these cases, drug-facilitated recall is generally not recommended. Hypnosis can prove very useful and effective in recovering and working through traumatic memories. It has the advantage that it allows a controlled recovery of traumatic experience at a pace the patient can tolerate. Extensive abreaction is not necessary or recommended. The hypnotic process should be used to allow the patient to access the memories and to reframe the experience. In this sense, this work is similar to the working through of memories associated with PTSD (Maldonado & Spiegel, 1994; Spiegel, 1988). An extensive description of the uses of hypnosis is included under discussion of the treatment of dissociative identity disorder.

Loewenstein (1991) has suggested that longer term psychotherapy is indicated for patients with nonclassic, covert amnesia because of the complexity of the psychological response to the original traumatic event (which may have been childhood abuse, combat, or adult victimization). Therapy then aims to facilitate the recall and integration of dissociated material.

Dissociative Fugue (Psychogenic Fugue)

So far, there are no controlled studies addressing the treatment of dissociative (psychogenic) fugue. Current information is based on the experience of clinicians reporting on limited numbers of patients. They all suggest a treatment that involves provision of rest and assurances of safety, development of a trusting therapeutic relationship, recovery of personal identity, review of triggers or factors associated with the onset of the fugue, reprocessing of traumatic material, reintegration of traumatic memories into personal history, and returning the patient to his or her previous life.

Hypnosis and drug-facilitated interviews, as outlined above, have commonly been used during the stages of recovery of personal identity and memories associated with the onset of the fugue (Maldonado & Spiegel, in press). Except for the facilitation of memory retrieval (narcosynthesis) or diminution of anxiety related to the therapeutic process, no pharmacotherapeutic agents have been systematically studied for the treatment of this condition.

The treatments for acute dissociative amnesia and fugue states have been generally similar (reviewed in Loewenstein, 1991). Traditionally, hypnosis and amytal narcosynthesis were the treatments of choice for memory recovery in amnesia and fugue (Loewenstein, 1991; Riether & Stoudemire, 1988). In the case of fugue, it was urged that treatment be undertaken as quickly as possible while the repressed material was more readily accessible, before the memories had consolidated into a nucleus, thereby increasing the possibility of future flight episodes (Nemiah, 1989; Riether & Stoudemire, 1988). Patients may also experience spontaneous memory recovery on removal from the stressful situation, when exposed to cues from their past, or when they feel psychologically safe (Loewenstein, 1991; Riether & Stoudemire, 1988). In addition, psychodynamic psychotherapy may help to address the conflicts that precipitated the amnesia or fugue, thereby reducing subsequent dissociation under stress (Loewenstein, 1991; Nemiah, 1989; Riether & Stoudemire, 1988).

Dissociative Identity Disorder (Multiple Personality Disorder)

General Overview

Treatment for DID (multiple personality disorder) generally involves (a) development of a therapeutic relationship based on safety and trust, (b) negotiation with the patient about cooperation with treatment, (c) development of a contract against harm to self or others, (d) history taking and understanding personality structure, (e) abreaction and working through of traumatic experiences and, frequently, repressed or dissociated material, (f) negotiating and modulating "conflicts" among aspects of identity and personality states, (g) development of mature and more appropriate, nondissociative defenses, and (h) working toward integration of alters (Braun, 1990; Maldonado & Spiegel, in press; Spiegel, 1984; Kluft, 1984a, 1988). Techniques such as hypnosis can facilitate control over dissociative episodes and integration of traumatic memories. Efforts to develop a social network and support system are helpful. They may include working with the current family and/or the family of origin. Special efforts are often required to prevent further traumatization, and it is important to maintain appropriate protection and separation from abusive family members. Once integration has been achieved, further work is needed to deal with residual or renewed dissociative responses to external stress or internal conflicts and to integrate further with society.

Even Kluft, who has reported the best results in treatment outcomes described in the literature (1984c, 1986a, 1994) warns that "the treatment of MPD [DID] can be arduous, painful and prolonged. . . . The achievement of integration is usually considered desirable, but in some cases a reasonable degree of conflict-free collaboration among the personalities is all that can be achieved" (Kluft, 1988, p. 578).

In a survey of mental health workers involved in the treatment of dissociative disorder patients, Putnam (1993) discovered that the most common treatment modality used is individual psychotherapy facilitated by the use of hypnosis. The same study indicated that the average DID patient is seen twice a week for a period of about 4 years. The survey also mentions the use of several psychoactive drugs for the treatment of associated symptoms.

In the largest reported longitudinal study, Kluft (1985b) has clearly established that patients suffering from DID do not experience spontaneous remission of their illness if left untreated. Likewise, reports have suggested that the treatment of the many symptoms and associated diagnoses do not help in the resolution of the problem unless the dissociation is addressed directly (Kluft, 1985c; Putnam, 1986). Although there are a number of authors who have reported excellent therapeutic success, others, probably the majority of clinicians, have encountered more modest and limited results (Coons, 1986; Ross, 1989).

Comprehensive systematic research into the treatment of DID has yet to be conducted. Putnam (1986) has enumerated a number of factors that would make such research difficult:

1. It would require complex study designs with large numbers of patients because there is an extremely large number of variables to control, including both the usual research variables (demographics; concurrent medical, neurological, or other psychiatric pathology; amount and kind of current or past treatment), as well as variables unique to DID (such as patient type, presence or absence of specific types of alternate personalities, and age at the time of therapeutic intervention).
2. There are pragmatic difficulties of working with DID patients in a research setting, including complex transference and countertransference interactions, placebo responses, heightened sensitivity to medication side effects, and clinicians who may be wary about administering control or placebo interventions.
3. There is a lack of resources for such research.

To address many of these issues, Putnam proposed a large, multicenter collaborative study by which researchers could investigate a number of the issues described above in a series of coordinated, small-scale studies of carefully chosen overlapping questions. To our knowledge, such a program of research has yet to be initiated, a decade after Putnam's suggestion.

At that time, Putnam (1986) noted that "Our current knowledge of the diagnosis and treatment of MPD is based on pragmatic clinical experience" (p. 193). Apparently, his assessment still stands. To date, only three authors have published treatment outcome data on DID patients (Coons, 1986; Kluft, 1984c, 1986a, 1994; Ross, 1989), and none of these studies employed control groups. So, it is important to bear in mind that the question addressed by these studies is, Does therapy (broadly defined) work? rather than, What kind of therapy works best? Or, as Kluft (1993) has put it, What to do until the controlled studies come (p. 87).

Richard Kluft published the first report of MPD patient outcome following therapy (1984c). Of an initial pool of 171 MPD patients Kluft had interviewed in his practice and research or through referrals, 123 patients with clearly defined MPD had sought treatment and become subjects of follow-up study. At the time of the report, 40 patients (33% of the 123) had not achieved integration (20 patients were still in treatment, 10 had interrupted treatment, and 10 treatments were unsuccessful), while 83 (67%) were success-fully treated to fusion. Fusion was defined on the basis of:

> Three stable months of (1) continuity of contemporary memory, (2) absence of overt behavioral signs of multiplicity, (3) subjective sense of unity, (4) absence of alter personalities on hypnotic reexploration, (5) modification of transference phenomena consistent with the bringing together of personalities, and (6) clinical evidence that the unified patient's self-representation included acknowledgment of attitudes and awareness which were previously segregated in separate personalities. (Kluft, 1984c, p. 12)

(Meeting these criteria for three months is described by Kluft as apparent fusion.) Of this fusion group, 33 patients (27% of the entire treatment group) met the additional criterion of showing no signs of dissociation for a minimum of 27 months (which Kluft describes as stable fusion) and were available to undergo an extensive reassessment of the stability of their integration.

In this select sample, 32 of 33 patients reported and were independently assessed to have attained a better quality of life and global improvement. About a quarter of the sample had experienced relapse events, though only two patients (6%) were diagnosable with MPD at the time of follow-up. The average duration of treatment was 21.6 months. Kluft also noted a number of treatment trends in the group: individuals with fewer personalities required shorter periods of treatment and were less likely to relapse, male patients had fewer personalities and briefer treatments, and persons with borderline features were more difficult to treat to the point of stable fusion. More recently, Putnam (1986; reported in Kluft, 1993) offered a further examination of Kluft's (1984c) data. His analysis demonstrated that complexity (number of personalities) correlated positively with the time to reach integration, and this predicted that about 3 months of therapy was necessary per alter. However, this ratio only applied to those patients with 18 or fewer alters.

Kluft (1984c) emphasizes the need for continuity of treatment beyond initial fusion, noting that "treatment that ends at a point of apparent fusion is rarely complete or stable" (p. 24). From his overall results, Kluft concluded that "with appropriate treatment,

DID patients can achieve a stable remission of the symptoms that characterize the condition, and live stable and productive lives as unified individuals" (p. 19).

Since publication of the 1984 data, Kluft has issued further treatment outcome updates on the initial sample. Kluft re-reported (1986a) the 1984 results with the addition of 19 patients who had not, at the time of the original report, achieved integration of sufficient duration (i.e., 27 months) to be included or who had not been thoroughly reassessed at that time. In this enlarged group, patients were reassessed between 27 and 99 months after achieving integration. Although Kluft presents the data for the total sample (now 52, which includes the original 33), the overall findings appear virtually identical to those reported initially for the subset. Only 21% had relapse events, and of these only 3 patients (6%) had diagnosable DID. Overall, 94% showed clear evidence of improved function and progress in their lives. In a more recent article, a decade later, Kluft (1994) reports that 103 (84%) of the original 123 patients whose treatments were followed had achieved stable integration, and 6 remained in active treatment.

Subjects in a study by Coons (1986) were the first 20 DID patients (17 women, 3 men) the author encountered in a state psychiatric facility. All met DSM-III-R (APA, 1987) criteria for MPD and the additional requirement that they exhibit amnesia (thereby making this sample relatively comparable to those who would currently fulfill DSM-IV criteria). Hypnosis was not used to determine the diagnosis, and all patients had a history of dissociation before entering the study. On intake, a detailed psychiatric and collateral social history was gathered, along with neurological and psychological testing.

Of the original 20 patients, 18 were located for follow-up, and further data were gathered at that time through an interview with the patient and a questionnaire completed by the therapist. The data were collected 3 to 129 months after intake (mean 39 months). On follow-up, 10 of the 18 patients were still in outpatient treatment, and eight had terminated treatment. Of those who had terminated treatment, five (25% of the total sample) had achieved integration defined by five of Kluft's (1982) six criteria for integration (hypnotic reexploration was not conducted). In addition, two patients (10%) had achieved partial integration, and two (10%) others had achieved integration but had subsequently re-dissociated. Coons notes that the unintegrated patients had experienced emotional trauma during the course of therapy at approximately twice the rate of those patients who eventually became integrated. However, this difference was not statistically significant.

Most patients in the Coons (1984) study had been seen weekly (67%), with four patients (20%) receiving two to five sessions a week. Patients had received a wide variety of concurrent therapeutic interventions, including general modalities such as psychodynamic psychotherapy (95%), psychoeducation (40%), homogeneous group therapy (35%), marital therapy (35%); and specialized incest group therapy (15%); as well as specific techniques and interventions such as hypnosis (80%), audio/visual taping (75%), journal writing (55%), crisis intervention (35%), day care (20%), sodium amytal interviews (15%), and vocational therapy (15%). Coons reports that therapists rated the effectiveness of psychodynamic psychotherapy, hypnotherapy, and homogenous group therapy very highly. No data were reported on the success of the other interventions. Somatic treatments were also quite commonly employed, including antipsychotic medication (45%), antidepressant medication (40%), anxiolytic medication (15%), and electroconvulsive therapy (ECT) (10%). No improvement or worsening of condition was reported for the majority of patients prescribed antipsychotic medications and minor tranquilizers. Antidepressants were found to be effective in half of the cases in which they were used. No data were reported on the efficacy of ECT with the two patients for whom it was used.

Coons (1986) reports that almost all of the 20 patients showed an improvement in clinical status. Both patient and therapist reports suggest that about two thirds of patients were considered moderately to greatly improved and only one patient was definitely judged to be clinically worse at follow-up. In all cases (of those described by the 70% of therapists who returned the questionnaire), patients had accepted their diagnosis, and approximately three quarters of this sample had achieved coconsciousness.

Ross (1989) briefly describes the treatment outcomes of 22 patients who entered active specific treatment at his Dissociative Disorders Clinic in Winnipeg, Canada, or were treated by outside colleagues. Of these 22 patients, 6 (27%) had achieved integration, 5 (23%) were currently in treatment and expected

to integrate, and 1 (4.5%) had reached an unstable integration and had relapsed, but was expected to reach stable integration. Of the remaining sample, four patients (18%) were still in treatment, and their outcome was uncertain; two (9%) patients deemed treatable had left the area unintegrated; one patient (4.5%) had reached an unstable integration, had relapsed, and was now lost to follow-up; and three (14%) had dropped out unintegrated. (Interestingly, Ross reports that of the first 40 cases seen in the clinic, 27 (67.5%) met *DSM-III* criteria for borderline personality disorder; however, borderline features did not appear to be a predictor of poor outcome in those who were treated.)

Ross (1989) notes that 12 of the 22 patients (54%) had reached or were expected to reach integration, and he suggests that this may well be a conservative estimate of successful treatment outcome because this total does not include the 4 patients in treatment with uncertain outcomes and the 2 treatable (but relocated) patients who would likely reach integration with proper treatment. With the addition of these 6 patients, 18 of 22 patients might be expected to achieve integration, resulting in an 82% successful treatment rate. In consideration of these and Kluft's findings, Ross concludes that "MPD is a treatable disorder" (p. 203).

Clinical Research on Individual Modalities

"The scientific literature on the treatment of multiple personality [dissociative identity disorder] is largely descriptive and prescriptive" (Kluft, 1984c, p. 10), and as such, there has been no systematic research support for the following, which are based on case reports and the reflections of individual therapists experienced in working with DID. The virtue of these reports is that they represent the conclusions drawn by those practitioners who have led the field in the treatment of DID; their limitation is that they are based on limited samples, without proper controlled scientific scrutiny and comparison, and they may be subject to the expectations and biases of their reporters.

Homogeneous Group Therapy Although individual psychotherapy is widely considered the treatment of choice for DID, a number of experts have suggested that these patients may benefit from homogeneous group therapy as a supplemental or adjunctive intervention that may enhance overall therapeutic progress (Caul, 1984; Caul, Sacks, & Braun, 1986; Coons & Bradley, 1985). Caul and colleagues have observed "Multiple personality [DID] patients rarely have had the opportunity or ability to understand the concepts of self and self in the world. Group therapy presents an opportunity for the MPD patient to participate in a sense of togetherness with other humans in a social context. The group presents a potential to learn interaction, acceptance, tolerance, patience, compassion, sharing" (1986, p. 147). In Coons and Bradley's (1985) description of their 2½-year-long group, they found that the themes of trust, negative self-worth, and dependence were especially prominent, and that the group was particularly valuable for instilling feelings of hope and universality, offering support to members (once trust and a sense of cohesion were established), and stimulating change through peer pressure (although the authors caution against pressure to prematurely integrate). Virtually all experts seem to agree that DID patients should only be included in group therapy if they are in concomitant individual therapy (Benjamin & Benjamin, 1992; Caul, 1984; Caul et al., 1986; Coons & Bradley, 1985). As Caul and his colleagues have stated, "Group process is a supplement to individual therapy for MPD patients, not a modality that could or should be used alone" (1986, p. 149).

Family Treatments   Benjamin and Benjamin (1992) have observed that "It seems ironic to us that a family-based approach has been underutilized since this disorder is precisely about the failure of a healthy family process" (p. 236). Multiple authors (Benjamin and Benjamin, 1992, 1993, 1994a, 1994b; Chiappa, 1994; Panos, Panos, & Allred, 1990; Porter, Kelly, & Grame, 1993; Putnam, 1989; Sachs, 1986; Sachs, Frischholz, & Wood, 1988; Williams, 1991) have proposed that family interventions should be an integral part of an overall treatment plan for dissociative disorders that seeks to facilitate healthy relationships within the family in addition to enhancing the treatment of the identified DID patient. Generally, commentators propose such interventions for the current family of the patient rather than the family of origin (Benjamin & Benjamin, 1992; Chiappa, 1994), although some have reported on family treatments for the extended families of child DID patients (Sachs et al., 1988). In the last case, the authors assert that it is essential that the abuse in the family that precipitated dissociation in the MPD child has ceased, that the abuser be identified and be willing to admit to the abuse and to change, and that the cessation of the abuse cycle can be verified (Sachs, 1986; Sachs et al., 1988). "Any therapeutic attempt is useless unless the trauma is terminated" (Sachs et al., 1988, p. 253).

Hypnosis as a Treatment Tool   Many traumatic memories may be elicited during the course of psychotherapy without the utilization of techniques for memory enhancement. Nevertheless, the use of hypnosis can facilitate access to repressed memories that have not emerged using other methods (Maldonado & Spiegel, 1995; Spiegel, 1989). Many trauma victims respond to the traumatic event by using dissociative-like defenses during or after the trauma. In instances of repeated trauma, it is likely that victims "learn" how to trigger these dissociative responses (self-hypnosis-like defenses) in order to avoid further trauma. Most patients suffering from dissociative disorders are highly hypnotizable (Kluft, 1984a; Maldonado & Spiegel, 1994, 1995, 1996; Putnam, 1991; Spiegel, 1988, 1989; Spiegel et al., 1988; Spiegel, Detrick, & Frishholz, 1982; Stuntman & Bliss, 1985). If hypnotic-like states are used during traumatic experiences, it makes sense that the very entry into this same state could lead to the retrieval of memories and affects associated with the original trauma, as would be predicted by the theory of state-dependent memory (Bower, 1981).

What makes hypnosis one of the most helpful tools in the treatment of patients suffering from dissociative disorders is its ability to be used both as a diagnostic tool and as a powerful therapeutic technique. The hypnotic state can be seen as a controlled form of dissociation (Nemiah, 1989). Hypnosis allows the recovery and reprocessing of recovered memories at a pace the patient can tolerate (Fine, 1991; Kluft, 1989; Maldonado & Spiegel, 1995). Despite the fact that most clinicians and researchers in the treatment of dissociative disorders agree on the usefulness of hypnotic approaches in the treatment of these conditions, no systematic studies regarding their efficacy have been conducted. Properly done, this technique effectively facilitates symbolic restructuring of the traumatic experience under hypnosis. This can be coupled with the use of a grief work model (Lindemann, 1944; Spiegel, 1988). As an adaptation of the techniques used for the treatment of PTSD, hypnosis can be used to provide controlled access to the dissociated or repressed memories and then can help patients restructure their memories (Maldonado & Spiegel, 1995; Spiegel, 1996).

Psychopharmacology of Dissociative Identity Disorder   Little is known about the rational approach to the use of psychoactive substances for the treatment of DID. Putnam (1989) remarked that "until appropriate methodology [for the study of medications in DID] can be devised, the psychopharmacology of DID will remain a pragmatic art" (p. 253). He stressed that "there is no good evidence that medication of any type has a direct therapeutic effect on the dissociative process [manifested by DID patients]" (p.253). Loewenstein (1991) attempted to summarize the general consensus and knowledge regarding the psychopharmacological aspects of DID but finally arrived at the same conclusion: "There is no known definitive pharmacotherapy for the 'core' symptoms of [DID]" (p. 721). Furthermore, he reported that "most dissociative symptoms seem relatively impervious to pharmacologic intervention" (p. 721).

To date, there has been no double-blind controlled study of psychopharmacological agents in DID patients. The little data available are limited to case reports and small uncontrolled samples. Treatment has been limited to control of signs and symptoms afflicting DID patients. Because of the nature of the studies and their poor design (or lack thereof), it is impossible to know if the "success" of these medications was due to improvement of a comorbid diagnosis (different from DID) or to the direct effect on controlling symptoms directly associated with DID. To complicate matters even further, several authors (Barkin, Braun, & Kluft, 1986; Braun, 1983; Kluft, 1984a; Putnam, 1984, 1986) have suggested that there is variability in response to medication related to the predominance of different personality states. This has reportedly included the same dose having varying effects or different profiles of adverse reactions.

Antidepressant Medications.   Kluft (1984a, 1985b) described the need for maintenance of tricyclic antidepressants (TCAs) in the treatment and eventual integration of a small sample ($n = 6$) of DID patients suffering from major depression. In another study, Barkin et al. (1986) reported that polycyclic antidepressants should be used for the treatment of DID

patients only when the host and a large number of alters experience symptoms of major depression. In the same sample, the authors warn about the lack of consistent therapeutic results across the alters. The same study (Barkin et al., 1986) strongly discouraged the use of monoamine oxidase inhibitors (MAOIs) due to the high lethality associated with drug-drug interactions and the potential interaction with dietary tyramine. Newer, selective serotonin reuptake inhibitors are effective at reducing comorbid depressive symptoms and have the advantage of lessened lethality in overdose.

Neuroleptics.   Almost every author writing on the psychopharmacology of DID (Barkin et al., 1986; Kluft, 1984a, 1988; Putnam, 1989; Ross, 1989) has reported an extremely high incidence of adverse side effects with the use of neuroleptic medications. Complications include the creation of new alters in response to medication. The same authors recommend that it is preferable to try a nonpharmacological agent or other psychotropic agents before risking the use of neuroleptics. These medications may be useful, albeit rarely, for the control of extreme agitation or disorganization, but are not helpful for maintenance use. If misdiagnosed patients thought to be schizophrenic are treated, neuroleptics complicate the situation by flattening affective response while not affecting key symptoms of personality fragmentation and amnesia, thereby apparently confirming the misdiagnosis.

Benzodiazepines.   Barkin et al. (1986) suggested that the use of benzodiazepine agents should be limited to cases in which high levels of anxiety are experienced across all alters or anxiety interferes with therapeutic work. Loewenstein, Hornstein, and Farber (1988) described the only systematic study of pharmacotherapy of DID. In their study, they used clonazepam successfully to control PTSD-like symptoms in a small sample ($n = 5$) of DID patients. After treatment, patients exhibited improvement in sleep continuity and decreased flashbacks and nightmares.

Anticonvulsants.   Fichtner, Kuhlman, Gruenfeld, and Hughes (1990) described a single case of a 21-year-old woman with active suicidal ideation. Manic-depressive illness was limited to that single personality. The antiepileptic carbamazepine was used over the course of 8 months, during which the patient exhibited decreased violent behavior and improved control over dissociation (decreased switching). Mesulam (1981) and Schenk and Bear (1981) reported a decrease in dissociative symptomatology in DID patients who exhibited concurrent temporal lobe abnormalities on electroencephalogram (EEG). Unfortunately, no controlled studies have been done, and no follow-up of reported cases has been published. Devinsky, Putnam, Grafman, Bromfield, & Theodore (1988) suggested that unless there are clear EEG changes, anticonvulsants (in particular, carbamazepine) play no role in the treatment of DID and should be avoided due to the high incidence of serious side effects.

Beta Blockers. Braun (1990) proposed the use of clonidine and high-dose propranolol for the treatment of hyperarousal, anxiety, poor impulse control, disorganized thinking, and rapid or uncontrolled switching in DID patients. His open trials suggest "good outcomes" with these agents. However, no specific data about the patients or the drug trials were reported, such as the number of patients given either drug, actual success rate, comorbid diagnoses in the sample, or prevalence of adverse drug reactions.

Mood Stabilizers. Barkin and colleagues (1986) stated that not enough data are available regarding mood stabilizers, but concluded that the available data suggest that most DID patients do not respond to lithium.

Electroconvulsive Therapy Coons (1986) reported the use of ECT in 2 of his 20 patients. Unfortunately, no data were reported regarding the effects of ECT on their overall condition. More recently, though, Bowman and Coons (1992) reported that, in a prospective study of three dissociative disorder patients (one DID, two DDNOS, dissociative disorder, not otherwise specified) with severe treatment-resistant depression, ECT resulted in a 50% drop in depression scores and marked clinical improvement with gains maintained for at least 4 months. They caution, however, that ECT did not affect the dissociative condition and should only be used when depression is experienced by most of the active alters rather than just by one.

Eye-Movement Desensitization and Reprocessing The technique known as eye-movement desensitization and reprocessing (EMDR) was initially described by Shapiro (1995) and has been mostly applied to the treatment of traumatic memories, in particular PTSD

(Forbes, Creamer, & Rycroft, 1994; Shapiro, 1995; Shapiro, Vogelmann-Sine, & Sine, 1994; Silver, Brooks, & Obenchain, 1995; Young, 1995; Wilson, Becker, & Tinker, 1995). Nevertheless, a recent article has reported on the use of EMDR for the treatment of dissociative identity disorder patients (Young, 1994). Systematized or controlled studies are lacking. So far, most reports confirming its usefulness are anecdotal. Other studies present equivocal findings and do not confirm any specific effects (Oswalt, Anderson, Hagstrom, & Berkowitz, 1993). To date, Paulsen (1995) has written the only article specifically on the use of EMDR for the treatment of dissociative disorders providing theoretical guidelines for its application.

Finally, PTSD has been described as the most common comorbid disorder of DID patients, often requiring active treatment (Loewenstein, 1991). This is likely due to the traumatic origin of both diagnoses. Because of this, the discrete use of medications for the treatment of PTSD may sometimes assist in controlling some of the symptoms exhibited by DID patients. A detailed discussion of the pharmacological treatment of PTSD is beyond the scope of this chapter and can be found elsewhere (Braun, Greenberg, Dasberg, & Lerer, 1990; Davidson et al., 1990; Fesler, 1991; Frank, Kosten, Giller, & Dan, 1988; Friedman, 1988, 1991; Kitchner & Greenstein, 1985; Kolb, Burris, & Griffiths, 1984; Kosten, Mason, Giller, Ostroff, & Harkness, 1987; Lipper, 1988; Maldonado & Spiegel, 1994; Reist, Kauffman, & Haier, 1976; Shestatzky, Greenberg, & Lerer, 1988; van der Kolk 1983, 1987).

Depersonalization Disorder

To date, there are no controlled studies addressing the treatment of depersonalization disorder. All the available information regarding treatment options reflects the experience and case reports of clinicians and a few treatment centers. No single treatment modality has been systematically studied in this patient population.

Treatment modalities employed include paradoxical intention (Blue, 1979), record keeping and positive reward (Dollinger, 1983), flooding (Sookman & Solyom, 1978), psychodynamic psychotherapy (Lehman, 1974; Noyes & Kletti, 1971; Schilder, 1939; Shilony & Grossman, 1993; Torch, 1987), psychoeducation (Fewtrell, 1986; Torch, 1987), psychostimulants (Cattell & Cattell, 1974; Davison, 1964; Shorvon, 1946), antidepressants (Fichtner, Horevitz, & Braun, 1992; Hollander et al., 1989, 1990; Noyes, Kupperman, & Olson, 1987; Walsh, 1975), antipsychotics (Ambrosino, 1973; Nuller, 1982), anticonvulsants (Stein & Uhde, 1989), benzodiazepines (Ballenger et al., 1988; Nuller, 1982; Spier, Tesar, Rosenbaum, & Woods, 1986; Stein & Uhde, 1989), and ECT (Ambrosino, 1973; Davison, 1964; Roth, 1959; Shorvon, 1946). The use of hypnosis has been described in multiple case reports. Authors have described the role of suggestibility in the etiology of the disorder and recommend the use of hypnosis as a treatment modality (Kluft, 1988; Spiegel, 1988). All of these studies were inadequately designed, including the use of small samples, lack of double-blind procedures, and no use of controls. Most of them were case reports.

In considering somatic treatments for depersonalization, it is important to determine whether the complaint represents the primary condition or whether it is secondary to another disorder. In the latter case, the experiences of depersonalization may remit with successful treatment of the primary condition (Walsh, 1975). For example, depersonalization is a common complaint in depressive illnesses (Noyes et al., 1987) and anxiety conditions (Fichtner et al., 1992; Hollander et al., 1989, 1990; Shorvon, 1946; Steinberg, 1991). The most important aspect of the treatment of depersonalization disorder is careful assessment of possible psychiatric comorbidity and treatment of those conditions.

References

Abeles, M., & Schilder, P. (1935). Psychogenic loss of personal identity. *Archives of Neurology and Psychiatry, 34,* 587–604.

Ackner, B. (1954). Depersonalization, I: Aetiology and phenomenology. *Journal of Mental Science, 100,* 838–853.

Adityanjee, R. G. S. P., & Khandelwal, S. K. (1989). Current status of multiple personality disorder in India. *American Journal of Psychiatry, 146,* 1607–1610.

Akhatar, S., & Brenner, I. (1979). Differential diagnosis of fugue-like states. *Journal of Clinical Psychiatry, 40,* 381–385.

Allison, R. B. (1974). A new treatment approach for multiple personalities. *American Journal of Clinical Hypnosis, 17,* 15–32.

Ambrosino, S. V. (1973). Phobic anxiety-depersonalization syndrome. *New York State Journal of Medicine, 73,* 419–425.

American Psychiatric Association. (1980). *Diagnostic and statistical manual of mental disorders* (3rd ed.). Washington, D.C.: Author.

———. (1987). *Diagnostic and statistical manual of mental disorders* (3rd ed., revised). Washington, D.C.: Author.

———. (1994). *Diagnostic and statistical manual of mental disorders* (4th ed.). Washington, D.C.: Author.

Azam, E. E. (1887). *Hypnotisme, double conscience et alteration de la personnalite.* Paris: J. B. Balliere.

Ballenger, J. C., Burrows, G. D., Dupont, R. L., Lesser, I. M., et al. (1988). Alprazolam in panic disorder and agoraphobia; results from a multicenter trial, I: efficacy in short term treatment. *Archives of General Psychiatry, 45,* 413–422.

Barkin, R., Braun, B. G., & Kluft, R. P. (1986). The dilemma of drug therapy for multiple personality disorder. In B. G. Braun (Ed.), *Treatment of multiple personality disorder* (pp. 107–132). Washington, D.C.: American Psychiatric Press.

Baron, D. A., & Nagy, R. (1988). The amobarbital interview in a general hospital setting, friend or foe: A case report. *General Hospital Psychiatry, 10,* 220–222.

Benjamin, L. R., & Benjamin, R. (1992). An overview of family treatment in dissociative disorders. *Dissociation, 5*(4), 236–241.

———. (1993). Interventions with children in dissociative families: A family treatment model. *Dissociation, 6*(1), 54–65.

———. (1994a). A group for partners and parents of MPD clients. Part I: Process and format. *Dissociation, 7*(1), 35–43.

———. (1994b). A group for partners and parents of MPD clients. Part III: Marital types and dynamics. *Dissociation, 7*(3), 191–196.

Berrington, W. P., Liddell, D. W., & Foulds, G. A. (1956). A re-evaluation of the fugue. *Journal of Mental Science, 102,* 280–286.

Bezzubova, E. B. (1991). Clinical characteristics of vital depersonalization in schizophrenia. *Zhurnal Nevropatologii i Psikhiatrii Imeni, 91*(7), 83–86.

Blank, H. R. (1954). Depression, hypomania, and depersonalization. *Psychoanalytic Quarterly, 23,* 20–37.

Bliss, E., Clark, L., & West, C. (1959). Studies of sleep deprivation: relationship to schizophrenia. *Archives of Neurological Psychiatry, 81,* 348–359.

Bliss, E. L. (1980). Multiple personalities: A report of 14 cases with implications for schizophrenia and hysteria. *Archives of General Psychiatry, 37,* 1388–1397.

———. (1984). A symptom profile of patients with multiple personalities, including MMPI results. *Journal of Nervous and Mental Disease, 172,* 197–202.

———. (1986). *Multiple personality, allied disorders, and hypnosis.* New York: Oxford.

Bliss, E. L., & Jeppsen, E. A. (1985). Prevalence of multiple personality among inpatients and outpatients. *American Journal of Psychiatry, 142*, 250–251.

Bliss, E. L., Larson, E. M., & Nakashima, S. R. (1983). Auditory hallucinations and schizophrenia. *Journal of Nervous and Mental Disease, 171*, 30–33.

Blue, F. R. (1979). Use of directive therapy in the treatment of depersonalization neurosis. *Psychological Reports, 49*, 904–906.

Boon, S., & Draijer, N. (1993). *Multiple personality disorder in the Netherlands: A study on reliability and validity of the diagnosis.* Amsterdam: Swets & Zeitlinger.

Boon, S., & Draijer, N. (1993). Multiple personality disorder in The Netherlands: a clinical investigation of 71 patients. *American Journal of Psychiatry, 150*(3), 489–494.

Bower, G. H. (1981). Mood and memory. *American Psychology, 36*, 129–141.

Bowman, E. S., & Coons, P. M. (1992). The use of electroconvulsive therapy in patients with dissociative disorders. *Journal of Nervous and Mental Disease, 180*(8), 524–528.

Brauer, R., Harrow, M., & Tucker, G. J. (1970). Depersonalization phenomena in psychiatric patients. *British Journal of Psychiatry, 117*, 509–515.

Braun, B. G. (1983). Psychophysiologic phenomena in multiple personality and hypnosis. *American Journal of Clinical Hypnosis, 26*, 124–137.

———. (1985). The transgenerational incidence of dissociation and multiple personality disorder: A preliminary report. In R. P. Kluft (Ed.), *Childhood antecedents of multiple personality* (pp. 128–150). Washington D.C.: American Psychiatric Press.

———. (1990). Multiple personality disorder: An overview. *American Journal of Occupational Therapy, 44*, 971–976.

Braun, P., Greenberg, D., Dasberg, H., & Lerer, B. (1990). Core symptoms of posttraumatic stress disorder unimproved by alprazolam treatment. *Journal of Clinical Psychiatry, 51*, 236–238.

Brown, G. R., & Anderson, B. (1991). Psychiatric morbidity in adult inpatients with childhood histories of sexual and physical abuse. *American Journal of Psychiatry, 148*, 55–61.

Brown, W. (1918). The treatment of cases of shell shock in an advance neurological centre. *Lancet*, 197–200.

———. (1919). Hypnosis, suggestion and dissociation. *British Medical Journal, 191*, 734–736.

Bryer, J. B., Nelson, B. A., Miller, J. B., & Krol, P. A. (1987). Childhood sexual and physical abuse as factors in adult psychiatric illness. *American Journal of Psychiatry, 144*, 1426–1430.

Carlson, E. T. (1981). The history of multiple personality disorder in the United States. *American Journal of Psychiatry, 138*, 666–668.

Castillo, R. J. (1990). Depersonalization and meditation. *Psychiatry, 53*, 158–168.

Cattell, J. P., & Cattell, J. S. (1974). Depersonalization: Psychological and social perspectives. In S. Arieti (Ed.), *American handbook of psychiatry* (pp. 767–799). New York: Basic Books.

Caul, D. (1984). Group and videotape techniques for multiple personality. *Psychiatric Annals, 14*, 43–50.

Caul, D., Sachs, R. G., & Braun, B. G. (1986). Group psychotherapy in treatment of multiple personality disorder. In B. G. Braun (Eds.), *Treatment of multiple personality disorder* (pp. 145–156). Washington, D.C.: American Psychiatric Press.

Chee, K. T., & Wong, K. E. (1990). Depersonalization syndrome — A report of nine cases. *Singapore Medical Journal, 31*, 331–334.

Chiappa, F. (1994). Effective management of family and individual interventions in the treatment of dissociative disorders. *Dissociation, 7*, 185–190.

Chu, D. A., & Dill, D. L. (1990). Dissociative symptoms in relation to childhood physical and sexual abuse. *American Journal of Psychiatry, 147*, 887–892.

Cohen, S. (1988). The pathogenesis of depersonalization: A hypothesis. *British Journal of Psychiatry, 152*, 578.

Coons, P. M. (1984). The differential diagnosis of multiple personality: A comprehensive review. *Psychiatric Clinics of North America, 7*, 51–65.

———. (1985). Children of parents with multiple personality disorder. In R. P. Kluft (Ed.), *Childhood antecedents of multiple personality* (pp. 151–165). Washington, D.C.: American Psychiatric Press.

———. (1986). Treatment progress in 20 patients with multiple personality disorder. *Journal of Nervous and Mental Disease, 174*, 715–721.

Coons, P. M., Bowman, E. S., Kluft, R. P., & Milstein, V. (1991). The cross-cultural occurrence of MPD: Additional cases from a recent survey. *Dissociation, 4*, 124–128.

Coons, P. M., Bowman, E. S., & Milstein, V. (1988). Multiple personality disorder: A clinical investigation of 50 cases. *Journal of Nervous and Mental Disease, 17*, 519–527.

Coons, P. M., Bowman, E. S., & Pellow, T. A. (1989). Post-traumatic aspects of the treatment of victims of sexual abuse and incest. *Psychiatric Clinic of North America, 12*, 325–337.

Coons, P. M., & Bradley, K. (1985). Group psychotherapy with multiple personality disorder patients. *Journal of Nervous and Mental Disease, 173*(9), 515–521.

Coons, P. M., & Millstein, V. (1992). Psychogenic amnesia: A clinical investigation of 25 cases. *Dissociation, 5*(2), 73–79.

Coons, P. M., & Sterne, A. L. (1986). Initial and follow-up psychological testing on a group of patients with multiple personality disorder. *Psychological Reports*, 58, 43–49.

Davidson, J., Kudler, H., Smith, R., Mahorney, S. L., Lipper, S., Hammett, E., Saunders, W. B., & Cavenar, J. O. (1990). Treatment of posttraumatic stress disorder with amitriptyline and placebo. *Archives of General Psychiatry*, 47, 259–266.

Davison, K. (1964). Episodic depersonalization: Observations on seven patients. *British Journal of Psychiatry*, 110, 505–513.

Devinsky, O., Feldmann, O., Burrowes, K., & Bromfield, E. (1989). Autoscopic phenomena with seizures. *Archives of Neurology*, 46, 1080–1088.

Devinsky, O., Putnam, F. W., Grafman, J., Bromfield, E., & Theodore, W. H. (1988). Dissociative states and epilepsy. Unpublished manuscript.

Dixon, J. C. (1963). Depersonalization phenomena in a simple population of college students. *British Journal of Psychiatry*, 109, 371–375.

Dollinger, S. (1983). A case report of dissociative neurosis (depersonalization disorder) in an adolescent treated with family therapy and behavior modification. *Journal of Consultative Clinical Psychology*, 51, 479–484.

Edinger, J. D. (1985). Relaxation and depersonalization. *British Journal of Psychiatry*, 146, 103.

Ellason, J. W., & Ross, C. A. (1995). Positive and negative symptoms in dissociative identity disorder and schizophrenia: A comparative analysis. *Journal of Nervous and Mental Disease*, 183, 236–241.

Ellenberger, H. F. (1970). *The discovery of the unconscious: The history and evolution of dynamic psychiatry*. New York: Basic Books.

Elliott, G. C., Rosenberg, M., & Wagner, M. (1984). Transient depersonalization in youth. *Social Psychology Quarterly*, 47, 115–129.

Fagan, J., & McMahon, P. P. (1984). Incipient multiple personality disorder in children. *Journal of Nervous and Mental Disease*, 172, 26–36.

Fast, I., & Chethik, M. (1976). Aspects of depersonalization-derealization in the experience of children. *International Review of Psychoanalysis*, 3, 483–490.

Fesler, F. A. (1991). Valproate in combat-related posttraumatic stress disorder. *Journal of Clinical Psychiatry*, 52, 361–364.

Fewtrell, W. (1986). Depersonalization: A description and suggested strategies. *British Journal of Guidance and Counseling*, 14, 263–269.

Fewtrell, W. D. (1984). Relaxation and depersonalization. *British Journal of Psychiatry*, 145, 217.

Fichtner, C. G., Horevitz, R. P., & Braun, B. G. (1992). Fluoxetine in depersonalization disorder [Letter]. *American Journal of Psychiatry*, 149(2), 1750–1751.

Fichtner, C. G., Kuhlman, D. T., Gruenfeld, M. J., & Hughes, J. R. (1990). Decreased episodic violence and increased control of dissociation in a carbamazepine-treated case of multiple personality. *Biological Psychiatry*, 27, 1045–1052.

Fine, C. G. (1991). Treatment stabilization and crisis prevention: Pacing the therapy of the MPD and allied dissociative disorders. *Dissociation*, 2(2), 77–82.

Finkelhor, D. (1984). *Child sexual abuse: New theory and research*. New York: Free Press.

Fisher, C. (1945). Amnesic states in war neuroses: The psychogenesis of fugue. *Psychoanalytic Quarterly*, 14, 437–468.

Fisher, C., & Joseph, E. D. (1949). Fugue with awareness of loss of personal identity. *Psychoanalytic Quarterly*, 18, 480–493.

Forbes, D., Creamer, M., & Rycroft, P. (1994). Eye movement desensitization and reprocessing in posttraumatic stress disorder: A pilot study using assessment measures. *Journal of Behavior Therapy and Experimental Psychiatry*, 25, 113–120.

Frances, A., Sacks, M., & Aronoff, M. (1977). Depersonalization: A self relations perspective. *International Journal of Psychoanalysis*, 58, 325–331.

Frank, J. B., Kosten, T. R., Giller, E. L., & Dan, E. (1988). A randomized clinical trial of phenelzine and imipramine for posttraumatic stress disorder. *American Journal of Psychiatry*, 145, 1289–1291.

Frankel, F. H. (1995). Discovering new memories in psychotherapy—childhood revisited, fantasy, or both? *New England Journal of Medicine*, 333(9), 591–4.

Fraser, G. A., & Lapierre, Y. D. (1986). Lactate-induced panic attacks in dissociative states (multiple personalities). In B. G. Braun (Ed.), *Proceedings of the International Conference on Multiple Personality/Dissociative States* (p.124). Chicago: Rush-Presbyterian-St. Luke's Medical Center.

Friedman, M. (1988). Toward rational pharmacotherapy for post-traumatic stress disorder. *American Journal of Psychiatry*, 145, 281–285.

———. (1991). Biological approaches to the diagnosis and treatment of post-traumatic stress disorder. *Journal of Traumatic Stress*, 4, 67–91.

Ganaway, G. K. (1989). Historical versus narrative truth: Clarifying the role of exogenous trauma in the etiology of MPD and its variants. *Dissociation*, 2(4), 205–220.

———. (1995). Hypnosis, childhood trauma, and dissociative identity disorder. *International Journal of Clinical and Experimental Hypnosis*, 43, 127–144.

Gelb, J. L. (1993). Multiple personality disorder and satanic ritual abuse. *Australian & New Zealand Journal of Psychiatry*, 27, 701–708.

Good, M. (1989). Substance induced dissociative disorders and psychiatric nosology. *Journal of Clinical Psychopharmacology, 9,* 88–93.

Goodwin, J. (1982). *Sexual abuse: Incest victims and their families.* Boston: Wright/PSG.

Greaves, G. B. (1980). Multiple personality: 165 years after Mary Reynolds. *Journal of Nervous and Mental Disease, 168,* 577–596.

Grigsby, J. P., & Johnson, C. L. (1989). Depersonalization, vertigo and Meniere's disease. *Psychological Reports, 64,* 527–534.

Grinker, R. B., & Spiegel, J. P. (1945). *Men under stress.* Philadelphia: Blakiston.

Guttmann, E., & Maclay, W. S. (1936). Mescalin and depersonalization. *International Journal of Psychoanalysis, 41,* 193–212.

Harper, H., & Roth, M. (1962). Temporal lobe epilepsy and the phobic-anxiety-depersonalization syndrome: Part I: A comparative study. *Comprehensive Psychiatry, 3,* 129–151.

Hilgard, E. R. (1977). *Divided consciousness: Multiple controls in human thoughts and action.* New York: John Wiley.

Hollander, E., Fairbanks, J., Decaria, C., & Liebowitz, M. R. (1989). Pharmacological dissection of panic and depersonalization. *American Journal of Psychiatry, 146,* 402.

Hollander, E., Liebowitz, M. R., Decaria, C., Fairbanks, J., Fallon, B., & Klein, D. F. (1990). Treatment of depersonalization with serotonin reuptake blockers. *Journal of Clinical Psychopharmacology, 10,* 200–203.

Horen, S. A., Leichner, P. P., & Lawson, J. S. (1995). Prevalence of dissociative symptoms and disorders in an adult psychiatric inpatient population in Canada. *Canadian Journal of Psychiatry, 40,* 185–191.

Horevitz, R. P., & Braun, B. G. (1984). Are multiple personalities borderline? *Psychiatric Clinics of North America, 7,* 69–88.

Hornstein, N., & Putnam, F. W. (1992). Clinical phenomenology of child and adolescent dissociative disorders. *Journal of the Academy of Child and Adolescent Psychiatry, 31,* 1077–1085.

Horowitz, M. J. (1964). Depersonalization in spacemen and submarines. *Military Medicine,* 1058–1060.

Horsley, J. S. (1943). *Narcoanalysis.* New York: Oxford Medical Publications.

Hunter, R. C. A. (1966). The analysis of episodes of depersonalization in a borderline patient. *International Journal of Psychoanalysis, 47,* 32–41.

Hurwitz, T. A. (1988). Narcosuggestion in chronic conversion symptoms using combined intravenous amobarbital and methylphenidate. *Canadian Journal of Psychiatry, 33,* 147–152.

James, I. P. (1961). The phobic-anxiety-depersonalization syndrome. *American Journal of Psychiatry, 118,* 163–164.

Kapur, N. (1991). Amnesia in relation to fugue states—Distinguishing a neurological from a psychogenic basis. *British Journal of Psychiatry, 159,* 872–877.

Kardiner, A., & Spiegel, H. (1947). *War, stress and neurotic illness.* New York: Hoeber.

Kenna, J. C., & Sedman, G. (1965). Depersonalization in temporal lobe epilepsy and the organic psychoses. *British Journal of Psychiatry, 111,* 293–299.

Kennedy, R. B. (1976). Self-induced depersonalization syndrome. *American Journal of Psychiatry, 133,* 1321–1328.

Kennedy, R. B., & Neville, J. (1957). Sudden loss of memory. *British Journal of Medicine, 2,* 428–433.

Kihlstrom, J. F. (1984). Conscious, subconscious, unconscious: A cognitive perspective. In Bowers & Meichenbaum (Eds.), *The unconscious reconsidered* (pp. 149–211). New York: John Wiley.

Kihlstrom, J. F. (1990). Repression, dissociation and hypnosis. In J. L. Singer (Ed.), *Repression and dissociation* (pp. 180–208). Chicago: University of Chicago Press.

Kirshner, L. A. (1973). Dissociative reactions: An historical review and clinical study. *Acta Psychiatrica Scandinavica, 49,* 696–711.

Kitchner, L., & Greenstein, R. (1985). Low dose lithium carbonate in the treatment of post traumatic stress disorder. *Military Medicine, 150,* 378–381.

Kluft, R. P. (1982). Varieties of hypnotic interventions in the treatment of multiple personality. *American Journal of Clinical Hypnosis, 24,* 230–240.

———. (1984a). Aspects of the treatment of multiple personality disorder. *Psychiatric Annals, 14,* 51–55.

———. (1984b). An introduction to multiple personality disorder. *Psychiatric Annals, 14,* 19–24.

———. (1984c). Treatment of multiple personality disorder: A study of 33 cases. *Psychiatric Clinics of North America, 7,* 9–29.

———. (1985a). Childhood multiple personality disorder: Predictors, clinical findings, and treatment results. In R. P. Kluft (Ed.), *Childhood antecedents of multiple personality* (pp. 167–196). Washington, D.C.: American Psychiatric Press.

———. (1985b). The natural history of multiple personality disorder. In R. P. Kluft (Ed.), *Childhood antecedents of multiple personality* (pp. 197–238). Washington, D.C.: American Psychiatric Press.

———. (1985c). The treatment of multiple personality disorder (MPD): Current concepts. In F. F. Flach (Ed.), *Directions in psychiatry.* New York: Hatherleigh.

———. (1986a). Personality unification in multiple personality disorder: A follow-up study. In B. G. Braun (Ed.), *Treatment of multiple personality disorder* (pp.

31–60). Washington, D.C.: American Psychiatric Press.

———. (1986b). Treating children with multiple personality disorder. In B. G. Braun (Ed.), *Treatment of multiple personality disorder* (pp. 79–105). Washington, D.C.: American Psychiatric Press.

———. (1987a). First-rank symptoms as a diagnostic clue to multiple personality disorder. *American Journal of Psychiatry, 144,* 293–298.

———. (1987b). Multiple personality disorder: An update. *Hospital and Community Psychiatry, 38,* 363–373.

———. (1988). The dissociative disorders. In J. A. Talbot, R. E. Hales, & S. C. Yudofsky (Eds.), *Textbook of psychiatry* (pp. 557–585). Washington, D.C.: American Psychiatric Press, Washington, D.C.

———. (1989). Iatrogenic creation of new alter personalities. *Dissociation, 2,* 83–91.

———. (1991). Clinical presentations of multiple personality disorder. *Psychiatric Clinics of North America, 14,* 605–630.

———. (1993). The treatment of dissociative patients: An overview of discoveries, successes, and failures. *Dissociation, 6*(2–3), 87–101.

———. (1994). Treatment trajectories in multiple personality disorder. *Dissociation, 7*(1), 63–75.

———. (1996). Dissociative identity disorder. In L. K. Michelson & W. J. Ray (Eds.), *Handbook of dissociation: Theoretical, empirical and clinical perspectives* (pp. 337–366). New York: Plenum Press.

Kolb, L. C. (1985). The place of narcosynthesis in the treatment of chronic and delayed stress reactions of war. In S. M. Sonnenberg, A. S. Blank, & J. A. Talbott (Eds.), *The trauma of war.* Washington D.C.: American Psychiatric Press.

Kolb, L., Burris, B., & Griffiths, S. (1984). Propranolol and clonidine in the treatment of the chronic post traumatic stress disorder of war. In B. A. van der Kolk (Ed.), *Post-traumatic stress disorder: Psychological and biological sequelae.* Washington, D.C.: American Psychiatric Press.

Kosten, T. R., Mason, J. W., Giller, E. L., Ostroff, R. B., & Harkness, L. (1987). Sustained urinary norepinephrine and epinephrine elevation in post-traumatic stress disorder. *Psychoneuroendocrinology, 12,* 13–30.

Kubie, L. S. (1943). Manual of emergency treatment for acute war neuroses. *War Medicine, 4,* 582–598.

Lehmann, L. S. (1974). Depersonalization. *American Journal of Psychiatry, 131*(11), 1221–1224.

Lindemann, E. (1994). Symptomatology and management of acute grief. *American Journal of Psychiatry, 151,* 155–160.

Lipper, S. (1988). PTSD and carbamazepine. *American Journal of Psychiatry, 145,* 1322–1323.

Lishman, A. W. (1987). *Organic psychiatry* (2nd ed.). Oxford, UK: Blackwell Scientific Publications.

Loewenstein, R. J. (1991). Psychogenic amnesia and psychogenic fugue: A comprehensive review. In A. Tasman & S. M. Goldfinger (Eds.), *American Psychiatric Press Review of Psychiatry* (pp. 189–222). Washington, D.C.: American Psychiatric Press.

———. (1994). Diagnosis, epidemiology, clinical course, treatment, and cost effectiveness of treatment of dissociative disorders and MPD: Report submitted to the Clinton Administration Task Force on Health Care Financing Reform. *Dissociation, 7,* 3–11.

———. (1995). Dissociative amnesia and dissociative fugue. In G. O. Gabbard (Ed.), *Treatment of psychiatric disorders* (pp. 1570–1597). Washington, D.C.: American Psychiatric Press.

Loewenstein, R. J., Hornstein, N., & Farber, B. (1988). Open trial of clonazepam in the treatment of post-traumatic stress symptoms in MPD. *Dissociation, 1,* 3–12.

Ludwig, A. M., Brandsma, J. M., Wilbur, C. B., Bendfeldt, F., & Jameson, D.H. (1972). The objective study of a multiple personality. Or, are four heads better than one? *Archives of General Psychiatry, 26*(4), 298–310.

Luparello, T. J. (1970). Features of fugue: A unified hypothesis of regression. *Journal of the American Psychoanalytic Association, 18,* 379–398.

Maldonado, J. R., & Spiegel, D. (1994). Treatment of post traumatic stress disorder. In S. J. Lynn & R. Rhue (Eds.), *Dissociation: Clinical, theoretical and research perspectives* (pp. 215–241). New York: Guilford Press.

———. (1995). Using hypnosis. In C. Classen (Ed.), *Treating women molested in childhood* (pp. 163–186). San Francisco: Jossey-Bass Publishers.

———. (1996). Hypnosis. In A. Tashman, J. Kay & J. Lieberman (Eds.), *Psychiatry.* Philadelphia, PA.: W. B. Saunders Co.

Marcos, L. R., & Trujillo, M. (1978). The sodium amytal interview as a therapeutic modality. *Current Psychiatric Therapies, 18,* 129–136.

Mathew, R. J., Wilson, W. H., Humphreys, D., Lowe, J. V., & Weithe, K. E. (1993). Depersonalization after marijuana smoking. *Biological Psychiatry, 33,* 431–441.

Mayer-Gross, W. (1935). On depersonalization. *British Journal of Medical Psychology, 15,* 103–126.

Mayer-Gross, W., Slater, E., & Roth, M. (1969). *Clinical psychiatry* (3rd ed.). London: Bailliere, Tindal and Cassell.

McCall, W. V. (1992). The addition of intravenous caffeine during an amobarbital interview. *Journal of Psychiatry and Neuroscience, 17,* 195–197.

McHugh, P. (1995a). The pros and cons of dissociative

identity (multiple personality) disorder. *Journal of Practical Psychiatry and Behavioral Health*, 1, 158–166.

McHugh, P. R. (1995b). Witches, multiple personalities, and other psychiatric artifacts. *Nature Medicine*, 1(2), 110–114.

———. (1996). Hippocrates a la mode. *Nature Medicine*, 2(5), 507–509.

Meares, R., & Grose, D. (1978). On depersonalization in adolescence: A consideration from the view-points of habituation and "identity." *British Journal of Medical Psychology*, 51, 335–342.

Melges, F. T., Tinklenberg, J. R., Hollister, L. E., & Gillespie, H. K. (1970). Temporal disintegration and depersonalization during marijuana intoxication. *Archives of General Psychiatry*, 23, 204–210.

Mesulam, M. M. (1981). Dissociative states with abnormal temporal lobe EEG: Multiple personality and the illusion of possession. *Archives of Neurology*, 38, 178–181.

Meyer, J. E. (1961). Depersonalization in adolescence. *Psychiatry*, 24, 537–560.

Mitchell, S. W. (1888). Mary Reynolds: A case of double consciousness. *Transactions of the College of Physicians of Philadelphia*, 10, 366–389.

Moran, C. (1986). Depersonalization and agoraphobia associated with marijuana use. *British Journal of Medical Psychology*, 59, 187–196.

Morgan, A. H. & Hilgard, E. R. (1973). Age differences in susceptibility to hypnosis. *International Journal of Clinical and Experimental Hypnosis*, 21, 78–85.

Myers, D. H., & Grant, G. (1970). A study of depersonalization in students. *British Journal of Medical Psychology*, 121, 59–65.

Naples, M., & Hackett, T. (1978). The amytal interview: History and current uses. *Psychosomatics*, 19, 98–105.

Nemiah, J. C. (1989). Dissociative disorders (hysterical neuroses, dissociative type). In H. I. Kaplan & B. J. Sadock (Eds.), *Comprehensive textbook of psychiatry*, (pp. 1028–1044), 5th ed., Vol. I, Baltimore, Md.: Williams & Wilkins.

Noyes, R., Hoenk, P. R., Kupperman, B. A., & Slymen, D. J. (1977). Depersonalization in accident victims and psychiatric patients. *Journal of Nervous and Mental Disease*, 164, 401–407.

Noyes, R., & Kletti, R. (1971). Depersonalization in response to life-threatening danger. *Comprehensive Psychiatry*, 18, 375–384.

Noyes, R., Kupperman, S., & Olson, S. B. (1987). Desipramine: A possible treatment for depersonalization. *Canadian Journal of Psychiatry*, 32, 782–784.

Nuller, Y. L. (1982). Depersonalization—Symptoms, meaning, therapy. *Acta Psychiatrica Scandinavica*, 66, 451–458.

Oberndorf, C. (1950). Role of anxiety in depersonalization. *International Journal of Psychoanalysis*, 31, 1–5.

Oswalt, R., Anderson, M., Hagstrom, K., & Berkowitz, B. (1993). Evaluation of the one-session eye-movement desensitization reprocessing procedure for eliminating traumatic memories. *Psychological Reports*, 73, 99–104.

Panos, P. T., Panos, A., & Allred, G. H. (1990). The need for marriage therapy in the treatment of multiple personality disorder. *Dissociation*, 3(1), 10–14.

Parfitt, D. N., & Carlyle-Gall, C. M. (1944). Psychogenic amnesia: The refusal to remember. *Journal of Mental Science*, 379, 519–531.

Paulsen, S. (1995). Eye movement desensitization and reprocessing: Its cautious use in the dissociative disorders. *Dissociation*, 8, 32–44.

Perry, J. C., & Jacobs, D. (1982). Overview: Clinical applications of the amytal interview in psychiatric emergency settings. *American Journal of Psychiatry*, 139, 552–559.

Peterson, G. (1990). Diagnosis of childhood multiple personality disorder. *Dissociation*, 3, 3–9.

———. (1991). Children coping with trauma: Diagnosis of "dissociation identity disorder." *Dissociation*, 4, 152–164.

Pies, R. (1991). Depersonalization's many faces. *Psychiatric Times*, 8(4), 27–28.

Porter, S., Kelly, K. A., & Grame, C. J. (1993). Family treatment of spouses and children of patients with multiple personality disorder. *Bulletin of the Menninger Clinic*, 57(3), 371–379.

Pribor, E. F., & Dinwiddie, S. H. (1992). Psychiatric correlates of incest in childhood. *American Journal of Psychiatry*, 149, 52–56.

Price, J., Hess, N. C. (1979). Behaviour therapy as precipitant and treatment in a case of dual personality. *Australian and New Zealand Journal of Psychiatry*, 13(1), 63–66.

Prince, M. (1906). *Dissociation of a personality*. New York: Longman, Green.

Prince, W. F. (1917). The Doris case of quintuple personality. *Journal of Abnormal Psychology*, 11, 73–122.

Putnam, F. W. (1984). The psychophysiologic investigation of multiple personality disorder. *Psychiatric Clinics of North America*, 7, 31–40.

———. (1985). Dissociation as a response to extreme trauma. In R. P. Kluft (Ed.), *Childhood antecedents of multiple personality* (pp. 63–97). Washington, D.C.: American Psychiatric Press.

———. (1986). The treatment of multiple personality: State of the art. In B. G. Braun (Ed.), *The treatment of multiple personality disorder*. Washington, D.C.: American Psychiatric Press.

———. (1988). The disturbance of "self" in victims of

childhood sexual abuse. In R. P. Kluft (Ed.), *Incest-related syndromes of adult psychopathology*. Washington, D.C.: American Psychiatric Press.

Putnam, F. W. (1989). *Diagnosis and treatment of multiple personality disorder*. New York: Guilford Press.

Putnam, F. W. (1991). Dissociative disorders in children and adolescents: A developmental perspective. *Psychiatric Clinics of North America, 14*, 519–532.

Putnam, F. W. (1993). Dissociative disorders in children: Behavioral profiles and problems. *Child Abuse and Neglect, 17*, 39–45.

Putnam, F. W., Guroff, J. J., Silberman, E. K., Barban, L., & Post, R. (1986). The clinical phenomenology of multiple personality disorder: Review of 100 recent cases. *Journal of Clinical Psychiatry, 47*, 285–293.

Putnam, F. W., Post, R. M., Guroff, J. J., et al. (1983). *100 cases of multiple personality disorder* [New Research Abstract #77]. Presented at the American Psychiatric Association Annual Meeting, New York.

Reed, G. E., & Sedman, G. (1964). Personality and depersonalization under sensory deprivation conditions. *Perceptual and Motor Skills, 18*, 650–660.

Reist, C., Kauffman, C. D., & Haier, R. J. (1976). A controlled trial of desipramine in 18 men with post-traumatic stress disorder. *American Journal of Psychiatry, 146*, 513–516.

Riether, A. M., & Stoudemire, A. (1988). Psychogenic fugue states: A review. *Southern Medical Journal, 81*(5), 568–570.

Riley, R. L., & Mead, J. (1988). The development of symptoms of multiple personality disorder in a child of three. *Dissociation, 1*, 41–46.

Rivera, M. (1991). Multiple personality disorder and the social systems: 185 cases. *Dissociation, 4*, 79–82.

Roberts, W. W. (1960). Normal and abnormal depersonalization. *Journal of Mental Science, 106*, 478–493.

Ronquillo, E. B. (1991). The influence of "Espiritismo" on a case of multiple personality disorder. *Dissociation, 4*, 39–45.

Rosenfeld, H. (1947). Analysis of a schizophrenic state with depersonalization. *International Journal of Psychoanalysis, 28*, 130–139.

Ross, C. A. (1989). *Multiple personality disorder: Diagnosis, clinical features, and treatment*. New York: Wiley.

——. (1991). Epidemiology of multiple personality disorder and dissociation. *Psychiatric Clinics of North America, 14*, 503–518.

Ross, C. A., Anderson, G., Fleischer, W. P., & Norton, G. R. (1991b). The frequency of multiple personality disorder among psychiatric inpatients. *American Journal of Psychiatry, 148*, 1717–1720.

Ross, C. A., Joshi, S., & Currie, R. (1991a). Dissociative experiences in the general population: A factor analysis. *Hospital and Community Psychiatry, 42*, 297–301.

Ross, C. A., Miller, D. S., Reagor, P., Bjornson, L., Fraser, G. A., & Anderson, G. (1990a). Schneiderian symptoms in multiple personality disorder and schizophrenia. *Comprehensive Psychiatry, 31*, 111–118.

——. (1990b). Structured interview data on 102 cases of multiple personality disorder from four centers. *American Journal of Psychiatry, 147*, 596–601.

Ross, C. A., & Norton, G. R. (1988). Multiple personality disorder patients with a prior diagnosis of schizophrenia. *Dissociation, 1*, 39–42.

——. (1989). Suicide and parasuicide in multiple personality disorder. *Psychiatry, 52*, 365–371.

Ross, C. A., Norton, G. R., & Wozney, K. (1989). Multiple personality disorder: An analysis of 236 cases. *Canadian Journal of Psychiatry, 34*, 413–418.

Roth, M. (1959). The phobic-anxiety-depersonalization syndrome. *Proceedings of the Royal Society of Medicine, 52*, 587–595.

Ruedrich, S. L., Chu, C. C., & Wadle, C. V. (1985). The amytal interview in the treatment of psychogenic amnesia. *Hospital and Community Psychiatry, 36*, 1045–1046.

Russell, D. E. H. (1986). *The secret trauma: Incest in the lives of girls and women*. New York: Basic Books.

Sachs, R. G. (1986). The adjunctive role of social systems in the treatment of multiple personality disorder. In B. A. Braun (Ed.), *Treatment of multiple personality disorder*. Washington, D.C.: American Psychiatric Press.

Sachs, R. G., Frischholz, E. J., & Wood, J. I. (1988). Marital and family therapy in the treatment of multiple personality disorder. *Journal of Marital and Family Therapy, 14*(3), 249–259.

Sargant, W., & Slater, E. (1941). Amnestic syndromes in war. *Proceedings of the Royal Society of Medicine, 34*, 757–764.

Saxe, G. N., van der Kolk, B. A., Berkowitz, R., Chinman, G., Hall, K., Liegerg, G., & Schwartz, J. (1993). Dissociative disorders in psychiatric inpatients. *American Journal of Psychiatry, 150*, 1037–1042.

Saxena, S., & Prasad, K. (1989). *DSM-III* subclassification of Dissociative Disorders applied to psychiatric outpatients in India. *American Journal of Psychiatry, 146*, 261–62.

Schacter, D. L., & Kihlstrom, J. F. (1989). Functional amnesia. In F. Boller & J. Grafman (Eds.), *Handbook of neuropsychology* (pp. 209–231). Amsterdam: Elsevier Science.

Schacter, D. L., Wang, P. L., Tulving, E., & Freedman, M. (1982). Functional retrograde amnesia: A quantitative case study. *Neuropsychologia, 20*, 523–532.

Schenk, L., & Bear, D. (1981). Multiple personality and related dissociative phenomena in patients with temporal lobe epilepsy. *American Journal of Psychiatry, 138*, 1311–1315.

Schilder, P. (1939). The treatment of depersonalization. *Bulletin of the New York Academy of Science, 15,* 258–272.

Schreiber, F. R. (1974). *Sybil.* New York: Warner Paperbacks.

Schultz, R., Braun, B. G., & Kluft, R. P. (1989). Multiple personality disorder: Phenomenology of selected variables in comparison to major depression. *Dissociation, 2,* 45–51.

Sedman, G. (1966). Depersonalization in a group of normal subjects. *British Journal of Psychiatry, 112,* 907–912.

———. (1970). Theories of depersonalization: A reappraisal. *British Journal of Psychiatry, 117,* 1–14.

Sedman, G., & Kenna, J. C. (1963). Depersonalization and mood changes in schizophrenia. *British Journal of Psychiatry, 109,* 669–673.

Sedman, G., & Reed, G. F. (1963). Depersonalization phenomena in obsessional personalities and in depression. *British Journal of Psychiatry, 109,* 376–379.

Shapiro, F. (1995). *Eye movement desensitization and reprocessing: Basic principles, protocols, and procedures.* Guilford Press: New York.

Shapiro, F., Vogelmann-Sine, S., & Sine, L. F. (1994). Eye movement desensitization and reprocessing: Treating trauma and substance abuse. *Journal of Psychoactive Drugs, 26,* 379–391.

Shestatzky, M., Greenberg, D., & Lerer, B. (1988). A controlled trial of phenelzine in posttraumatic stress disorder. *Psychiatry Research, 24,* 149–155.

Shilony, E., & Grossman, F. K. (1993). Depersonalization as a defense mechanism in survivors of trauma. *Journal of Traumatic Stress, 6*(1), 119–128.

Shimizu M., & Sakamoto, S. (1986). Depersonalization in early adolescence. *Japanese Journal of Psychiatry, 40,* 603–608.

Shorvon, H. J. (1946). The depersonalization syndrome. *Proceedings of the Royal Society of Medicine, 39,* 779–785.

Shraberg, D. (1977). The phobic-anxiety-depersonalization syndrome. *Psychiatric Opinion, 14,* 35–40.

Signer, S. F. (1988), Mystical-ecstatic and trance states. *British Journal of Psychiatry, 152,* 296–297.

Silver, S. M., Brooks, A., & Obenchain, J. (1995). Treatment of Vietnam War veterans with PTSD: A comparison of eye movement desensitization and reprocessing, biofeedback, and relaxation training. *Journal of Traumatic Stress, 8*(2), 337–342.

Solomon, R. (1983). The use of the MMPI with multiple personality patients. *Psychological Reports, 53,* 1004–1006.

Sookman, D., & Solyom, L. (1978). Severe depersonalization treated with behavior therapy. *American Journal of Psychiatry, 135,* 1543–1545.

Spanos, N. P., Weekes, J. R., & Bertrand, L. D. (1985).

Multiple personality: A social psychological perspective. *Journal of Abnormal Psychology, 94,* 362–376.

Spanos, N. P., Weekes, J. R., Menary, E., & Bertrand, L. D. (1986). Hypnotic interview and age regression procedures in elicitation of multiple personality symptoms: A simulation study. *Psychiatry, 49,* 298–311.

Spiegel, D. (1984). Multiple personality as a post-traumatic stress disorder. *Psychiatric Clinics of North America, 7,* 101–110.

———. (1986). Dissociating damage. *American Journal of Clinical Hypnosis, 29,* 123–131.

———. (1988). Dissociation and hypnosis in posttraumatic stress disorder. *Journal of Traumatic Stress, 1,* 17–33.

———. (1989). Hypnosis in the treatment of victims of sexual abuse. *Psychiatric Clinics of North America, 12,* 295–305.

———. (1990). Hypnosis, dissociation and trauma: Hidden and overt observers. In J. L. Singer (Ed.), *Repression and dissociation* (pp. 121–142). Chicago: University of Chicago Press.

———. (1995). Psychiatry disabused [Letter]. *Nature Medicine, 1*(6), 490–491.

———. (1996). Hypnosis and suggestion. In D. Schacter (Ed.), *Memory distortion.* Cambridge, Mass.: Harvard University Press.

Spiegel, D., & Cardena, E. (1991). Disintegrated experience: The dissociative disorders revisited. *Journal of Abnormal Psychology, 100*(3), 366–378.

Spiegel, D., Detrick, D., & Frischholz, E. J. (1982). Hypnotizability and psychopathology. *American Journal of Psychiatry, 139,* 431–437.

Spiegel, D., Hunt, T., & Dondershine, H. E. (1988). Dissociation and hypnotizability in posttraumatic stress disorder. *American Journal of Psychiatry, 145,* 301–305.

Spiegel, D., & McHugh, P. (1995). The pros and cons of dissociative identity (multiple personality) disorder. *Journal of Practical Psychiatry and Behavioral Health, 1,* 158–166.

Spier, S. A., Tesar, G. E., Rosenbaum, J. F., & Woods, S. W. (1986). Treatment of panic disorder and agoraphobia with clonazepam. *Journal of Clinical Psychiatry, 47*(5), 238–242.

Squire, L. (1987). *Memory and brain.* New York: Oxford University Press.

Stamm, J. (1962). Altered ego states allied to depersonalization. *Journal of the American Psychoanalytic Association, 12,* 762–783.

Stein, M. B., & Uhde, T. W. (1989). Depersonalization disorder: Effects of caffeine and response to pharmacotherapy. *Biological Psychiatry, 26,* 315–320.

Steinberg, M. (1991). The spectrum of depersonalization: Assessment and treatment. In A. Tasman & S. M. Goldfinger (Eds.), *American Psychiatric Press review of psychiatry* (pp. 223–247). Washington, D.C.: American Psychiatric Press.

Stengel, E. (1941). On the aetiology of the fugue states. *Journal of Mental Science, 87,* 572–599.

———. (1943). Further studies on pathological wandering (fugues with the impulse to wander). *Journal of Mental Science, 89,* 224–241.

Stern, C. R. (1984). The etiology of multiple personalities. *Psychiatric Clinics of North America, 7,* 149–160.

Stuntman, R. K., & Bliss, E. L. (1985). Posttraumatic stress disorder, hypnotizability and imagery. *American Journal of Psychiatry, 142,* 741–743.

Szymanski, H. V. (1981). Prolonged depersonalization after marijuana use. *American Journal of Psychiatry, 138,* 231–233.

Thigpen, C. H., & Cleckley, H. (1957). A case of multiple personality. *Journal of Abnormal and Social Psychology, 49,* 135–151.

Torch, E. M. (1978). Review of the relationship between obsession and depersonalization. *Acta Psychiatrica Scandinavica, 58,* 191–198.

———. (1987). The psychotherapeutic treatment of depersonalization disorder. *Hillside Journal of Clinical Psychiatry, 9,* 133–143.

Trueman, D. (1984). Anxiety and depersonalization and derealization experiences. *Psychological Reports, 54,* 91–96.

Tucker, G. J., Harrow, M., & Quinlan, D. (1973). Depersonalization, dysphoria, and thought disturbance. *American Journal of Psychiatry, 130,* 702–706.

Tureen, L. L., & Stein, M. (1949). The base section psychiatric hospital. *Bulletin of the U.S. Army Medical Department, 9*(Suppl.), 105–137.

Tyson, G. M. (1992). Childhood MPD/dissociative identity disorder. *Dissociation, 5,* 20–27.

van der Hart, O. (1993). Multiple personality disorder in Europe: Impressions. *Dissociation, 6,* 102–118.

van der Kolk, B. A. (1983). Psychopharmacological issues in post-traumatic stress disorder. *Hospital and Community Psychiatry, 34,* 683–691.

van der Kolk, B. A. (1987). The drug treatment of post-traumatic stress disorder. *Journal of Affective Disorder, 13,* 203–213.

van der Kolk, B. A., & van der Hart, O. (1989). Pierre Janet and the breakdown of adaptation in psychological trauma. *American Journal of Psychiatry, 146,* 1530–1540.

Vanderlinden, J., Van Dyck, R., Vandereycken, W., & Vertommen, H. (1991). Dissociative experiences in the general population of the Netherlands and Belgium: A study with the Dissociative Questionnaire (DIS-Q). *Dissociation, 4,* 180–184.

Varma, V. K., Bouri, M., & Wig, N. N. (1981). Multiple personality in India: Comparison with hysterical possession state. *American Journal of Psychotherapy, 35,* 113–120.

Vincent, M., & Pickering, M. R. (1988). Multiple personality disorder in childhood. *Canadian Journal of Psychiatry, 33*(6), 524–529.

Walsh, R. N. (1975). Depersonalization: Definition and treatment. *American Journal of Psychiatry, 132,* 873.

Waltzer, H. (1972). Depersonalization and the use of LSD; A psychoanalytic study. *American Journal of Psychoanalysis, 32,* 45–52.

Watkins, J. G., & Watkins, H. H. (1982). Ego state therapy. In L. E. Abt & I. R. Stuart (Eds.), *Newer therapies: A source book.* New York: Van Nostrand Reinhold.

Wettstein, R. M., & Fauman, B. J. (1979). The amobarbital interview. *Jacep, 8,* 272–274.

Williams, M. B. (1991). Clinical work with families of MPD patients. *Dissociation, 4,* 92–98.

Wilson, S. A., Becker, L. A., & Tinker, R. H. (1995). Eye movement desensitization and reprocessing (EMDR) treatment for psychologically traumatized individuals. *Journal of Consulting and Clinical Psychology, 63,* 928–937.

Wineburg, E., & Straker, N. (1973). An episode of acute, self-limiting depersonalization following a first session of hypnosis. *American Journal of Psychiatry, 130,* 98–100.

Wittkower, E. D. (1970). Transcultural psychiatry in the Caribbean: Past, present and future. *American Journal of Psychiatry, 127,* 162–166.

Yap, P. M. (1960). The possession syndrome: A comparison of Hong Kong and French findings. *Journal of Mental Science, 106,* 114–137.

Young, W. C. (1994). EMDR treatment of phobic symptoms in multiple personality disorder. *Dissociation, 7,* 129–133.

———. (1995). Eye movement desensitization/reprocessing: Its use in resolving the trauma caused by the loss of a war buddy. *American Journal of Psychotherapy, 49*(2), 282–291.

23

Psychotherapy and Pharmacotherapy of Sexual Dysfunctions

R. Taylor Segraves

Stanley Althof

Historically, the treatment of sexual dysfunctions can be divided into five eras: psychoanalytic, early behavioral, Masters and Johnson, neo–Masters and Johnson, and psychobiological. Many methodologic problems have been pointed out concerning studies evaluating the effects of all of these forms of treatment. Some long-term follow-up studies have demonstrated the positive sustained effect of therapy on individuals' and couples' subjective senses of sexual satisfaction and self-acceptance. Treatments for the specific sexual disorders are reviewed: hypoactive sexual desire, erectile dysfunction, premature ejaculation, female orgasmic disorder, male orgasmic disorder, dyspareunia and vaginismus, and substance-induced sexual disorders. Controlled clinical trials meeting rigid research requirements are sparse, and more research has been done on male than female sexual dysfunction. In the next decade, there will be a pressing need to define the indications for specific types of psychotherapeutic and psychopharmacological interventions and when a combined approach is indicated.

HISTORICAL OVERVIEW OF THERAPY FOR SEXUAL PROBLEMS

Historically, the treatment of sexual dysfunctions can be divided into five eras:

1. Psychoanalytic
2. Early behavioral
3. Masters and Johnson
4. Neo–Masters and Johnson
5. The current psychobiological

Prior to 1970, psychoanalytic concepts guided clinicians in their understanding and treatment of sexual problems. Sexual symptomatology was linked to discrete, unresolved, unconscious conflicts that occurred during specific developmental periods. Sexual symptoms were traced to designated constellations of conflict occurring in early childhood (Meyer, 1976). Psychoanalytic notions were heterosexist and male centered, as was clearly evident in the construction of the controversial concept of penis envy and the psychological interpretation given to the classification of orgasm as either clitoral or vaginal.

In a classical analysis, patients were seen three to five times weekly over the course of several years. Freud's revolutionary method employed free association, dream analysis, interpretation of unconscious motives, and the recapitulation of significant emotional attachments through transference. Because of the focus on individual intrapsychic dynamics, couples treatment was rarely undertaken. The analytic literature was replete with elegant, richly detailed descriptions of individual case histories and analysis. By contemporary standards, these often-fascinating reports qualify only as untested case formulations.

In the late 1950s, behavioral therapists described promising results from treating sexual disorders by utilization of symptom-oriented direct treatment approaches (Brady, 1966; Cooper, 1969; Haslam, 1965; Lazarus, 1963; Wolpe, 1958). These interventions were loosely modeled on classical conditioning paradigms and assumed the dysfunction was a learned (conditioned) anxiety response. The guiding principle of behavior therapy (LoPicollo & LoPicollo, 1978; Marks, 1981; Obler, 1973) was to extinguish the anxiety or performance demands that interfered with normal sexual function. The most common behavioral technique, systematic desensitization, pairs relaxation with a series of carefully designed, hierarchical, anxiety-provoking sexual situations, in vivo or by imagery. Like psychoanalysis, however, behavior therapy concentrated on individual psychopathology and tended to ignore the dynamics of relationships. These studies, while more rigorously documented than the analytic reports, failed to dampen the prevailing enthusiasm for the treatment of sexual problems by analytic techniques.

In 1970, Masters and Johnson published their results of a study of 790 cases employing a quasi-residential blend of daily individual and couples psychotherapy under the auspices of a mixed sex cotherapy team. The ingredients of their treatment model consisted of physical examination, history taking, education, prescription of behavioral tasks, and counseling for intrapsychic or interpersonal issues that interfered with natural sexual function.

> Their treatment was based on three fundamental postulates: 1) a parallel, four stage sequence of physiological and subjective arousal in both genders; 2) the primacy of psychogenic factors, particularly learning deficits and performance anxiety in the etiology and maintenance of sexual dysfunctions and 3) the amenability of most sexual disorders to a brief, problem focused treatment approach. (Rosen & Leiblum, 1995)

Masters and Johnson's most important contribution was the emphasis given to the deleterious effects of performance anxiety and their prescription of sensate focus exercises to alleviate this troubling state. Performance anxiety, the fear of future sexual failure based on a previous failure, is a universal experience that appears in all sexual dysfunctions, including those of organic etiologies. Masters and Johnson provided clear descriptions of their treatment method and re-

ported initial and 5-year posttreatment "failure rates" for lifelong and acquired arousal, orgasm, and pain disorders. Their work revolutionized the treatment of sexual problems and generated great enthusiasm among clinicians for their novel short-term, directive treatment methods.

By present-day standards, their outcome data can be criticized for not (a) utilizing standardized, valid, and reliable assessment measures; (b) specifying the basis for classifying cases as successful or failed; (c) employing control, waiting list, or placebo groups; and (d) blinding the investigators to the experimental conditions. In addition, it was questionable whether their results were generalizable because of the atypical, affluent, well-educated and highly motivated patients studied. These vital concerns linger because 25 years later researchers have been unable to replicate the magnitude of the positive outcomes achieved (Heiman & LoPiccolo, 1983; Rosen & Beck, 1988; Wright, Perreault, & Mathieu, 1977; Zilbergeld & Evans, 1980). Nonetheless, their reports revolutionized the treatment of sexual problems and generated great enthusiasm among clinicians for their treatment method.

The neo–Masters and Johnson era was heralded by the publication of Helen Singer Kaplan's (1974) widely acclaimed book, *The New Sex Therapy*. As a discipline, sex therapy had come of age. Kaplan integrated modifications of Masters and Johnson's treatment methods with behavioral and analytic interventions. She treated couples by addressing both partners' intrapsychic and interpersonal contributions to the initiation and maintenance of the dysfunction. By distinguishing between the recent and remote etiological causations, she recommended direct treatment approaches for the former while reserving traditional psychodynamic methods for the latter. The more commonly seen recent etiological causes were relationship deterioration, performance anxiety, widowhood, health concerns, and aging. Examples of remote influences included preoedipal separation-individuation conflicts, unresolved Oedipal struggles, paraphiliac scripts, gender identity conflicts, and adolescent masturbatory guilt. Kaplan's prolific writings did not include outcome statistics on the follow-up of her suggested treatment interventions.

Treatments for sexual dysfunction proliferated and evolved into blends of psychodynamic, behavioral, and cognitive therapies utilizing individual, couples, and group formats (Althof, 1989; Gagnon, Rosen, & Leiblum, 1982; Leiblum & Rosen, 1989; Leiblum,

Rosen, & Pierce, 1976; Levine, 1992; McCarthy & McCarthy, 1984; Scharf, 1982; Zilbergeld, 1992). As the field matured, clinicians began to develop more sophisticated methodologies that included control groups, placebo treatments, randomization of experimental conditions, and standardized, valid, and reliable questionnaires. However, the majority of these research reports lacked long-term follow-up.

The middle 1980s ushered in the current psychobiological era. This epoch is distinguished by the medicalization (Tiefer, 1995) of treatment approaches, primarily for male sexual dysfunction. Sophisticated studies with adequate long-term follow-up describing the efficacy and psychological impact of intracavernosal injection, vacuum tumescence therapy, and treatment of rapid ejaculation by serotonin reuptake inhibitors began to appear in the literature (Althof, 1995a, 1995b; Althof et al., 1995; Assalian, 1988; Barada & McKimmy, 1994; Segraves, Saran, Segraves, & Maguire, 1993). These innovative discoveries turned the tide toward the blending of medical and psychological treatments for male sexual dysfunction. This medicalization has not had a significant impact on the treatment of female sexual dysfunction.

NOSOLOGY

Knowledge concerning the treatment of sexual dysfunction and interest in this area of psychobiology have grown significantly in the last 20–30 years. The recent emergence of this field can be appreciated by realizing that the first two *Diagnostic and Statistical Manuals of Mental Disorders* published by the American Psychiatric Association (APA) (*DSM-I, DSM-II*; APA, 1952, 1968) did not contain diagnostic terms for the sexual dysfunctions. The *DSM-III* (APA, 1980) provided a radical departure from the previous diagnostic manuals by including a section on sexual dysfunctions. These diagnoses and their criteria sets were based on the concept of a normal sexual response cycle for men and women (Schmidt, 1995) and were strongly influenced by the works of Masters and Johnson (1966) and Helen Singer Kaplan (1974). Changes in nomenclature for the psychosexual dysfunctions in the different versions of the *Diagnostic and Statistical Manuals* are listed in Table 23.1.

The current nomenclature was officially adopted by the American Psychiatric Association in 1994 (APA, 1994). Sexual dysfunctions listed in *DSM-IV* include hypoactive sexual desire disorder, sexual aversion disorder, female sexual arousal disorder, male erectile disorder, female orgasmic disorder, male orgasmic disorder, premature ejaculation, dyspareunia, and vaginismus. Two new diagnostic entities were included in *DSM-IV*: sexual dysfunction due to a general medical condition and substance-induced sexual dysfunction. The *DSM-IV* criteria sets do not specify a minimum duration or frequency of a disorder before it reaches diagnostic criteria. Instead, diagnosis is contingent on the disorder causing marked distress or interpersonal difficulty and depends to a large degree on clinical judgment. The diagnostic entities in *DSM-IV* are listed in Table 23.2 and the changes from *DSM-III-R* are listed in Table 23.3.

Although the diagnoses in *DSM-IV* are based primarily on disturbances in discrete phases of the sexual response cycle, there is some evidence that there is considerable overlap of diagnoses (Segraves & Segraves, 1990; Segraves & Segraves, 1991a, 1991b). For example, many individuals with hypoactive sexual desire disorder will also meet diagnostic criteria for arousal and orgasm disorders. In one multisite pharmaceutical study, diagnostic evaluations were available for 906 subjects, 532 females and 374 males. Approximately 40% of patients diagnosed as having hypoactive sexual desire disorder also met diagnostic criteria for arousal or orgasm disorders. In the same study, only 2% of women had a solitary diagnosis of female arousal disorder. Most patients diagnosed with a female arousal disorder also met criteria for hypoactive sexual desire disorder, as well as anorgasmia. This frequent overlap among diagnostic categories needs to be kept in mind when one reviews treatment outcome research as little of this research is based on patients with secondary, as well as primary, diagnoses.

Similarly, in the clinical situation, it can often be extremely difficult to decide which condition is primary. For example, if a patient presents for treatment with complaints of anorgasmia, as well as decreased libido, and it is unclear which problem came first, the choice of primary diagnosis may reflect the clinician's theoretical bias as much as it reflects the presented symptomatology.

EPIDEMIOLOGY

There are few studies of the prevalence and incidence of sexual disorders in community samples that might

TABLE 23.1 Modifications in Sexual Disorders Nomenclature in the *Diagnostic and Statistical Manuals* of the American Psychiatric Association

1. *DSM-I* was published in 1952 and did not contain diagnostic terms for the psychosexual dysfunctions (APA, 1952).

2. *DSM-II* was published in 1968. The only diagnostic entity pertaining to psychosexual disorders was *psychophysiological genitourinary disorders,* which referred to disorders of micturition, menstruation, and sexual function (APA, 1968).

3. *DSM-III* was published in 1980 (APA, 1980). It included diagnoses for the psychosexual disorders. The term *homosexuality* was deleted and the term *ego dystonic homosexuality* was added as a diagnostic entity. The term *inhibited sexual excitement* referred to both male erectile disorder, as well as female arousal disorder.

4. *DSM-III-R* was published in 1987 (APA, 1987). The term *sexual aversion disorder* was added. The term *ego dystonic homosexuality* was deleted. The use of the term *inhibited* in diagnostic entities was deleted. The term *inhibited sexual excitement* was changed to male erectile disorder and female arousal disorder.

5. *DSM-IV* was published in 1994 (APA, 1994). Subjective criteria were dropped from definitions of male erectile disorder and female arousal disorder. Sexual disorder secondary to a general medical condition and substance-induced sexual disorder terms were added.

DSM = Diagnostic and Statistical Manual.

TABLE 23.2 *DSM-IV* Psychosexual Disorders

1. *Hypoactive sexual desire disorder:* Persistently or recurrently deficient or absent sexual fantasies and desire for sexual activity.

2. *Sexual aversion disorder:* Persistent or recurrent extreme aversion to, and avoidance of, all, or almost all, sexual contact with a partner.

3. *Female sexual arousal disorder:* Persistent or recurrent inability to attain or to maintain until completion of the sexual activity, an adequate lubrication and swelling response of sexual excitement.

4. *Male erectile disorder:* Persistent or recurrent inability to obtain, or to maintain until completion of the sexual activity, an adequate erection.

5. *Female orgasmic disorder:* Persistent or recurrent delay in, or absence of, orgasm following a normal sexual excitement phase. This diagnosis is based on the clinician's judgment that the woman's orgasmic capacity is less than would be reasonable for her age, sexual experience, and the adequacy of sexual stimulation.

6. *Male orgasmic disorder:* Persistent or recurrent delay in, or absence of, orgasm following a normal excitement phase during sexual activity, with the clinician taking into account the person's age and judging the sexual stimulation to be adequate in focus, intensity, and duration.

7. *Premature ejaculation:* Persistent or recurrent ejaculation with minimal sexual stimulation, before, on, or shortly after penetration and before the person wishes it.

8. *Dyspareunia:* Recurrent or persistent genital pain associated with sexual intercourse not due exclusively to vaginismus or lack of lubrication.

9. *Vaginismus:* Recurrent or persistent involuntary spasm of the musculature of the outer third of the vagina that interferes with intercourse.

10. *Sexual dysfunction due to general medical condition:* Clinically significant sexual dysfunction that results in marked distress or interpersonal difficulty; the sexual dysfunction is fully explained by the physiological effects of a general medical condition.

11. *Substance-induced sexual dysfunction:* Clinically significant sexual dysfunction that is fully explained either by substance intoxication or by medication use.

Subtypes:
  Lifelong versus acquired
  Generalized versus situational
  Due to psychological factors versus due to combined factors

TABLE 23.3 Changes in *DSM-IV* from *DSM-III-R*

1. Requirements that each of the dysfunctions causes marked distress or interpersonal difficulty.
2. *Female sexual arousal disorder:* Requires that the diagnosis be based solely on lack of physiological arousal only.
3. *Male erectile disorder:* Requires that the diagnosis be made solely on the basis of lack of physiological arousal.
4. *Female orgasmic disorder:* Name has been changed from inhibited sexual orgasm.
5. *Male orgasmic disorder:* The name has been changed from inhibited male orgasm.
6. Sexual dysfunction due to general medical condition is a new entry.
7. Substance-induced sexual dysfunction is a new entry.

be safely used as reflections of the general population for epidemiology data. The surveys that do exist have employed different thresholds for diagnosing disorders and differing methodologies, making comparison among studies difficult. The changing nomenclature in this field also hampers generalization from the existing data.

There have been several reviews of the existing literature (Nathan, 1986; Spector & Carey, 1990). Spector and Carey concluded that the available evidence suggests a current prevalence of 5–10% for female orgasmic disorder, 4–9% for male erectile disorder, 4–10% for male orgasmic disorder, and 36–38% for premature ejaculation. They concluded that insufficient evidence exists for the determination of the prevalence of female arousal disorder, vaginismus, dyspareunia, and hypoactive sexual desire disorder.

Other recent surveys highlight the increased frequency of male erectile problems with age (especially after 50) and that methodological issues greatly influence outcome data. In a study of the frequency of sexual dysfunction in a representative sample of 51-year-old Danish men, Solstad and Hertoft (1993) found, in responses to a questionnaire, that only 4% of men reported erectile dysfunction. On interview, 26% reported some erectile problems. Lendorf, Juncker, and Rosenkilde (1994), in a questionnaire study of a representative sample of Danish men between 30 and 80 years of age, noted that approximately 25% reported some impaired erectile function, with the frequency of impairment increasing with age. They estimated that 10% of men ages 70–79 had impotence of a prob-

able organic etiology. In the 60–69-year-old group, they estimated that 8% had probable organogenic impotence. In a recent study of erectile problems in men 40–70 years old in 11 randomly selected cities and towns near Boston, Feldman, Goldstein, Hatzichristou, Krane, and McKunlay (1994) reported that approximately 15% of the males had complete impotence. A number of studies have demonstrated decreased sexual activity with aging in both sexes, although the etiology of these changes is unclear (Segraves & Segraves, 1995).

Some sexual dysfunctions may be associated with other Axis I disorders. For example, mood disorder may be associated with an increased prevalence of hypoactive sexual desire disorder and male erectile dysfunction (Howell et al., 1987; Thase et al., 1988), and euthymic patients with a current diagnosis of hypoactive sexual desire disorder have an increased lifetime prevalence of mood disorder (Schreiner-Engel & Schiavi, 1986). There are also reports of decreased libido and female orgasmic disorder being more common in patients with schizophrenia (Freidman & Harrison, 1984) and anorexia nervosa (Raboch & Faltus, 1991). However, most cases of sexual dysfunction do not have a clear relationship to another Axis I disorder. There also is minimal evidence of a relationship between sexual dysfunction and personality disorder or even specific personality traits (Segraves, 1989). Most clinicians assume that the immediate causes of sexual dysfunction involve anxiety about performance, a cycle of demand and negative expectancy, and self-defeating cognitions (Segraves, 1989b).

WHAT CONSTITUTES A SUCCESSFUL OUTCOME FOR SEXUAL THERAPY

Psychotherapy outcome studies are notoriously difficult to design and conduct. The challenge facing researchers is not only to design methodologically pure studies but to design studies that demonstrate regard for the complexity of the human condition. Thus, outcomes conceived solely in terms of women's facility in achieving coital orgasm, men's prowess at delaying ejaculation, the buckling force of an erection, the blood flow through the vagina, or the frequency with which partners bring their bodies to one another are far too narrow and mechanistic criteria for success. Sexuality outcome studies need to assess the complex interplay among the biological, emotional, psychological, and relational components of individual's and couples' lives. Thus, it is not solely how many orgasms individuals achieve but the degree of satisfaction, passion, and sense of psychological and relational well-being of two individuals.

There is also disagreement as to what constitutes success even when the solely mechanistic criteria are employed. For instance, in treating female anorgasmia, what defines success: simply achieving orgasm once, achieving orgasm from manual or oral stimulation on some arbitrary percentage basis, achieving coital orgasm with or without clitoral stimulation on some arbitrary percentage basis, or another criterion? And, what constitutes success in treating erectile dysfunction: the ability to consummate intercourse or the degree of penile rigidity?

The disagreements regarding success are further complicated by the primacy conferred on intercourse as the essential determinant of success. Is intercourse to be considered the sine qua non of outcome variables or simply one alternative sexual behavior in which couples may choose to engage? To date, this controversial issue has not been scientifically resolved, and success is defined through the eyes of the researcher.

METHODOLOGICAL PROBLEMS IN SEX THERAPY OUTCOME STUDIES

Spence (1991) criticizes sex therapy outcome studies' methodologies because they (a) employ small sample sizes; (b) do not use experimental control groups (waiting list, no treatment, attention placebo controls); (c) lack random allocation to conditions; (d) fail to offer clear-cut definitions of diagnostic criteria to permit replication; (e) generally do not include assessments of long-term outcome; and (f) do not adequately describe the therapy method utilized.

While anxiety is theoretically regarded as causing sexual dysfunction, scientific investigations supporting this important concept are sorely lacking. A number of studies have identified the role of cognitive distraction in sexual problems (Beck, Barlow, Sakheim, & Abrahamson, 1987; Cranston-Cuebas & Barlow, 1990; Palace & Gorzalka, 1992). Rosen and Leiblum (1995) suggest:

that the role of anxiety in sexual dysfunction needs to be reconceptualized. It appears that it is not anxiety per se that is responsible for initiating or maintaining sexual difficulties in most cases; rather it is the alternations in perceptual and attentional processes that occur in sexual dysfunction male and female patients.

The few studies that reported long-term follow-ups suffered from serious problems of sample attrition. Thus, the generalizations from these important studies are open to questions as to whether the results mirror the sample as a whole.

Other problems with sex therapy studies involve the contamination of study populations. This is most apparent in the early reports on erectile disorder in which men suffering from organic etiologies were incorrectly diagnosed as suffering from psychogenic dysfunction. In the Masters and Johnson era, knowledge regarding the pathophysiology of erectile function was lacking, as were more accurate diagnostic tests. Men who were not likely to benefit from a psychological intervention were inappropriately included in the population under study, and the outcome statistics were biased in a negative direction.

Finally, the evolution of psychiatry's diagnostic nomenclature was inconsistent regarding the categorization of and the criteria for sexual dysfunctions throughout the successive publications DSM-I through DSM-IV. This is most obvious in reviewing disorders of desire. Prior to DSM-III, desire disorders were diagnosed as either arousal or orgasmic dysfunctions. Thus, the early studies on arousal and orgasm disorders included individuals who today would be considered incorrectly diagnosed. Unfortunately, this diagnostic inconsistency hampers researchers' attempts to replicate the results of earlier studies.

PSYCHOLOGICAL TREATMENT OF SEXUAL DYSFUNCTIONS: GENERAL FORMULATIONS

Masters and Johnson's innovative format of employing mixed-sex cotherapy teams working with couples in a quasi-residential, daily combination of individual and conjoint treatment was an expensive, therapist-intensive, impractical model to reproduce. Modifications of Masters and Johnson's format were investigated to ascertain if similar results could be achieved with a more conservative, conventional outpatient treatment model. Investigators examined the impact of a single therapist versus a mixed-sex cotherapy team and weekly versus daily treatment sessions. The results indicated that couples did as well when treated on a weekly basis and by a single therapist (Clement & Schmidt, 1983; Crowe, Gillan, & Golombok, 1981; Hawton, 1995; Heiman & LoPiccolo, 1983). Two studies examined whether matching the gender of the therapist with the gender of the symptom bearer would result in improved outcome; no differences were found (Crowe et al., 1981; LoPiccolo, Heiman, Hogan, & Roberts, 1985).

Hawton (1995) cautions that not all patients with sexual complaints are suitable candidates for sex therapy. He has compiled five factors associated with positive sex therapy outcome:

1. The quality of the couple's general relationship, specifically, the female partner's pretreatment assessment of the relationship (Hawton & Catalan, 1986).
2. The motivation of the partners, particularly the male partner, for treatment (Hawton & Fagg, 1991; Whitehead & Mathews, 1986).
3. Absence of serious psychiatric disorder in either partner.
4. Physical attraction between the partners.
5. Early compliance with the treatment program (homework assignments).

Researchers also examined the efficacy of individual versus group treatment formats. Group formats were advantageous because they were less costly in terms of therapist time, provided patients with the knowledge that they were not alone in their suffering, offered peer support, and allowed patients to learn from the experiences of others. In addition, competition within the group motivated patients to change behaviors and desensitized patients to discussions of their private sexual lives (Spence, 1991). Conversely, group treatment is difficult to organize and institute because it requires the bringing together of several people's schedules and the fortuitous circumstance of several appropriate patients presenting with similar complaints at the same time. Group treatment also reduces the amount of time and attention any one patient can receive, increases patients' anxiety about confidentiality, and does not allow for patients proceeding at either an accelerated or delayed pace.

Spence (1991) reported that individual treatment was slightly more advantageous than group therapy for women with primary and secondary anorgasmia. Minimal differences between group and individual

therapy have been reported in the treatment of premature ejaculation (Perelman, 1977), total anorgasmia (Ersner-Hershfield & Kopel, 1979) and sexual anxiety (Nemetz, Craig, & Reith, 1978). Regardless of the efficacy of groups, it seems that the vast majority of patients are seen in individual or couples therapy.

Long-term follow-up studies demonstrated the positive sustained effect of therapy on individuals' and couples' subjective senses of sexual satisfaction and self-acceptance (DeAmicus, Goldberg, LoPiccolo, Friedman, & Davies, 1985). These studies also documented improved marital adjustment both immediately posttermination and over the course of follow-up. Most important, these findings also hold for patients who reported little change in sexual symptomatology posttreatment or who evidenced symptom relapse during follow-up. This may be interpreted to mean that individual's attitudes toward their sexual lives and the quality of couples' relationships tended to be enhanced through the process of therapy and tended to be sustained over time.

OUTCOME OF TREATMENTS FOR SPECIFIC SEXUAL DYSFUNCTIONS

Hypoactive Sexual Desire Disorders

Psychotherapy

Of men and women with disorders of sexual desire, 50% to 70% appear to achieve modest gains immediately following psychotherapy. However, a marked deterioration in function was noted at a 3-year follow-up (DeAmicus et al., 1985; Hawton, 1986, 1995) (see Table 23.4 for a summary of outcome studies for females). Half the individuals who reported success after treatment did not maintain heightened desire 3 years later. Paradoxically, couples reported improved and sustained levels of sexual satisfaction despite the regression in levels of sexual desire.

Pharmacotherapy

There is no pharmacotherapy with established efficacy for primary hypoactive sexual desire disorder. There is substantial evidence establishing that a certain minimal level of androgen is a necessary biological component of sexual desire (Davidson, Kwan, & Greenleaf, 1982) and the use of antiandrogenic drugs such as

TABLE 23.4 Psychotherapy Outcome Studies for Female Hypoactive Sexual Desire Disorders

Study	Type of Study	Results Posttherapy	Long-Term Follow-Up Results
DeAmicus et al. (1985)	Type 3	21/25 women self-reported improvement posttherapy.	11/25 women sustained improvement 3 years after termination of treatment. On average, the women continued to report sustained levels of sexual satisfaction in spite of regression in sexual desire.
Hawton, Catalan, Martin, & Fagg (1986), Hawton (1995)	Type 3	22/32 women self-reported improvement posttherapy.	11/32 women sustained improvement 1 to 6 years after termination of treatment.

cyproterone acetate has been demonstrated to diminish libido (Kellet, 1993). However, a relationship between individual endogenous androgen production within the normal range and sexual interest has not been demonstrated, and numerous studies have failed to demonstrate a beneficial effect of exogenous androgen in eugonadal men with erectile problems and diminished sexual desire (Segraves, 1988b). In a well-controlled study, O'Carroll and Bancroft (1984) reported that exogenous androgen administration increased the frequency of sexual thoughts but had no effect on sexual activity in eugonadal men. It is possible that androgen administration may have a subtle influence on libido in eugonadal men. There is no evidence to date that this effect is clinically significant.

There is suggestive evidence that endogenous androgen levels may be related to libido in the female (Bancroft, Sherwin, Alexander, Davidson, & Walker, 1991; Persky, Lief, & Strauss, 1978) and that exogenous androgen may increase libido (Waxenberg, Drellich, & Sutherland, 1959). However, a controlled study by Mathews, Whitehead, and Kellet (1983) failed to demonstrate the efficacy of sublingual testosterone for the treatment of women with desire disorders. Combined androgen-estrogen replacement may have a role in restoring libido in women who have had oophorectomies (Sherwin & Gelfand, 1987). A controlled study by Dow, Hart, and Forrest (1983) did not demonstrate a beneficial effect of exogenous androgen in postmenopausal women with complaints of low libido. It is possible that androgen therapy may be useful in women after an oophorectomy but not in women who have experienced a nonsurgical menopause (Welling, Anderson, & Johnson, 1990). Current evidence does not permit a clear statement of the indications for androgen therapy in female sexual disorders.

Female Arousal Disorders

Female arousal disorders are typically diagnosed in women who also report desire and orgasmic difficulties. The authors did not find any controlled studies on the treatment of arousal disorders in women independent of orgasmic or desire disorders. A recent laboratory study conducted by Palace (1995) evaluated the effects of heightened autonomic arousal and false feedback on genital and subjective responses in a large sample of dysfunctional women. She noted that general autonomic arousal (produced by exposure to a dangerous situation) significantly increased both physiological and subjective sexual arousal. These fascinating findings require further study regarding how heightened autonomic arousal can be achieved in a real-life sexual setting and whether the gains associated with this form of arousal are sustainable over time.

Erectile Dysfunction

Psychotherapy

Men with lifelong and acquired erectile dysfunctions achieved significant gains both initially and over the long term following participation in sex psychotherapy (see Table 23.5). Men with acquired disorders tended to fare better than those with lifelong problems. Masters and Johnson (1970) reported initial failure rates of 41% for primary impotence and 26% for secondary impotence. These failure rates were 41% and 31% for primary and secondary dysfunctions, respectively, 5

TABLE 23.5 Psychotherapy Outcome Studies for Male Erectile Disorder

Study	Type of Study	Results Posttherapy	Long-Term Follow-Up Results
Masters & Johnson (1970)	Type 3	Failure rate posttherapy was 41%.	At the 5-year follow-up, the failure rate for lifelong dysfunction was 41%.
Masters & Johnson (1970)	Type 3	For acquired dysfunction, failure rate was 26%.	The 5-year follow-up for acquired dysfunction failure rate was 31%.
Levine & Agle (1981)	Type 3	11/16 couples noted improvement in erectile function posttherapy.	One year later, only one couple was able to sustain the gains achieved in treatment.
Heiman & LoPiccolo (1983)	Type 3	Of 19 couples, 65–70% of men reported improvement posttherapy.	65–70% of men sustained their gains 3 months after therapy ended.
Goldberg, LoPiccolo, DeAmicus, et al. (1985)	Type 3	21/32 self-reported increased arousal and ability to achieve erection.	At the 3-year follow-up, 16/31 men self-reported sustained increased arousal and ability to achieve erection.
Hawton et al. (1986), Hawton (1995)	Type 3	14/18 men reported improvement at the termination of treatment.	For 1 to 6 years after therapy ended, 11/18 men sustained their improvement.
Kilman et al. (1987)	Type 2	13/16 (81%) men with acquired erectile dysfunction noted improvement posttherapy.	13/16 men (81%) with acquired erectile dysfunction sustained improvement at 3-month follow-up.

years later. There have been several other well-controlled investigations (DeAmicus et al., 1985; Hawton et al., 1992; Heiman & LoPiccolo, 1983; Kilmann et al., 1987; Reynolds, 1991) that have demonstrated the efficacy of psychological interventions for erectile dysfunctions, although none of these later studies have achieved the impressive results of Masters and Johnson's original study.

In an excellent review of the studies of treatment for erectile dysfunction, Mohr and Beutler (1990) wrote that:

[The] component parts of these treatments typically include behavioral, cognitive, systemic and interpersonal communications interventions. Averaging across studies, it appears that approximately two-thirds of the men suffering from erectile failure will be satisfied with their improvement at follow-up ranging from six weeks to six years.

These studies utilized either a couples or group format. The duration of couples therapy ranged between 4 and 20 weekly meetings. Group therapies met weekly for 10 to 20 meetings. All forms of intervention except biofeedback were equally effective in producing sustained change. There are few controlled reports on individual therapy for men, except for the report by Reynolds (1991), who highlighted the difficulties of treating men without partners.

All studies with long-term follow-up noted a tendency for men to suffer relapses. The most discouraging report came from Levine and Agle (1978), who treated 16 couples in a Masters and Johnson format. Posttherapy, 11 of the 16 men noted improvement in erectile function. At the 1-year follow-up, only one couple was able to sustain its gains. Hawton et al. (1992) suggest that positive treatment outcome is associated with better pretreatment communication and general sexual adjustment, especially the female's partner's interest and enjoyment of sex, absence of a psychiatric history in the woman, and the couple's willingness to complete homework.

Hawton (1986), in writing about the problem of relapse in treating all forms of sexual dysfunction, reported that:

Recurrence of, or continuing difficulty with the presenting sexual problem was commonly being reported by 75% of couples, this caused little to no concern for 34%. Patients indicated that they discussed the difficulty with the partner, practiced the techniques learned during therapy, accepted that difficulties were likely to recur and read books about sexuality.

These techniques proved to be effective coping strategies, in contrast to couples who stopped having sex or pretended that nothing was wrong.

Pharmacotherapy

Pharmacotherapy for erectile dysfunction consists of both oral medication and injection of vasoactive substances into the corpora cavernosa of the penis. Of the two approaches, there is greater evidence concerning the efficacy of corporal injection therapy. The parameters of such therapy, dose regimes, and side effects are well established. The efficacy for psychogenic erectile problems, as well as organic erectile problems, appears well established (Althof et al., 1991). There is much less research concerning the psychological benefits of this form of therapy. In other words, we know that we can use vasoactive agents to induce erections in a man with psychogenic erectile problems. We have minimal information concerning the effect of such therapy on hypothetical etiological factors such as marital discord or fear of intimacy.

The three most common agents used to induce erections are papaverine hydrochloride, phentolamine, and prostaglandin$_{E1}$. Although they are frequently combined, each agent can be used singly (Althof & Seftel, 1995). The advent of intracorporeal injection therapy for the treatment of erectile dysfunction was the result of astute clinical observation. Virag (1982), during a vascular surgical procedure, injected papaverine, an agent commonly used by vascular surgeons to attenuate vasospasm, into the hypogastric artery and observed that the patient had a rigid intraoperative penile erection. He subsequently employed direct intracorporeal injection of papaverine in men with erectile dysfunction (Virag, Frydman, Legman, & Virag, 1984). A number of subsequent clinical trials included men with psychogenic erectile problems (Gilbert & Gingell, 1991; Loman & Jarow, 1992). Most of theses studies were performed by urologists and consisted of a series of patients with varying etiologies. In most of these investigations, data for men with psychogenic impotence were not reported separately.

A year after Virag's discovery, Brindley (1986) first attempted self-injection of phentolamine or phenoxybenzamine. Both drugs are alpha-adrenergic blockers and induce erections by relaxation of the smooth muscle penile vasculature (Barada & McKimmy, 1994). Phenoxybenzamine has received minimal subsequent use, although phentolamine has been frequently employed in combination with papaverine. The effectiveness of this combination has been demonstrated in a double-blind, placebo-controlled study (Gasser, Roach, & Larsen, 1987). This combination has been employed in men with impotence of varying etiologies (Dhabuwala, Kerkar, & Bhutwala, 1990; Weiss, Ravalli, & Badlani, 1991). Again, most of these clinical series were reported by urologists, and minimal data concerning men with psychogenic problems were included.

Prostaglandin$_{E1}$ was also discovered by astute clinical observation. Ishii, Watanabe, and Irisawa (1989) observed that patients receiving intravenous prostaglandins reported improved erectile function. They subsequently injected this drug into the penile corpus cavernosum and found a good erectile response. Several double-blind studies have established this drug to be superior to papaverine-phentolamine in terms of quality of the erection produced (Kattan, Collins, & Mohr, 1991; Lee, Stevensen, & Szasz, 1989; Sarosy, Hudnall, & Erikson, 1989). This drug has also been utilized for impotence of varying etiologies, including psychogenic impotence (Schramek, Dorninger, & Waldhauser, 1990).

As one might expect, there have also been a number of reports and studies employing the triple therapy of papaverine, phentolamine, and prostaglandins (Barada & McKimmy, 1994). Triple therapy appears to have superior results compared to the use of papaverine-phentolamine combination therapy for some conditions, such as severe arteriogenic disease (McMahon, 1991). Triple therapy has also been used in patients with psychogenic impotence (Bennett, Carpenter, & Barada, 1991).

Papaverine and papaverine-phentolamine injection therapy have the disadvantages of delayed corporeal fibrosis, variable efficacy, systemic reactions, and the risk of prolonged erections (Levine et al., 1989). Prostaglandin has the advantages of having a reliable dose response curve, less risk for prolonged erection, less systemic side effects, and less delayed corporeal fibrosis. It has a major disadvantage of pain at the injection site. With all agents, a proper dose is established, and the patient is instructed in self-administration and given a "home kit." There have been recent attempts to find more acceptable routes of administration. Padma-Nathan et al. (1995) recently reported success using a transurethral delivery system of prostaglandin to induce an erection. Another novel approach has been the use of transdermal nitroglycerin and or transdermal nitroglycerin-minoxidil to induce erections (Baert, 1989; Cavallini, 1991; Owen et al., 1989). There is not enough data available on these new methods to judge their general applicability or efficacy.

Probably the best study of intracavernosal therapy for psychogenic male erectile disorder was conducted by the Althof group (Althof et al., 1989; Turner et al., 1989). In one of their studies, 15 men with psychogenic impotence (4 lifelong, 11 acquired; average age 49; average duration of impotence 12 years) were compared to 74 men with organic impotence and 42 men with impotence of mixed etiology. All patients completed an extensive psychometric battery that included the Case Western Reserve University Sexual Functioning Questionnaire, the Dyadic Adjustment Scale, the Beck Depression Inventory, the Spielberger State-Trait Anxiety Inventory, the Personal Evaluation Inventory, and a 40-item self-report scale. All patients were started on the same papaverine-phentolamine self-injection program and assessed at baseline and 1, 3, and 6 months. At the 6-month follow-up, the men with psychogenic impotence who were still participating in the self-injection program reported an average use of four times monthly and satisfactory erections after injection on 94% of the occasions. There was no evidence of psychological deterioration, no evidence of symptom substitution, and some evidence of improvement in anxiety measures. Unfortunately, only 6 of the 15 patients with psychogenic impotence completed the trial. However, the three groups did not differ in dropout rates; all groups experienced approximately a 60% dropout rate. The three major factors accounting for dropout were idea of self-injection, worry about side effects, and concern about artificiality. The available evidence does not suggest a harmful psychosocial effect of intracavernosal therapy for psychogenic erectile problems. However, these conclusions have to be tempered by the extremely small sample who completed treatment.

Clearly, the most acceptable pharmacotherapy for erectile dysfunction would be a medication taken orally. Major efforts to date have focused on drugs affecting the adrenergic, dopaminergic, and opiod systems (Segraves, 1989, 1994). Most efforts to find an adrenergic drug to treat male erectile function have focused on yohimbine, an alpha-2 adrenergic antagonist (Morales, Heaton, & Condra, 1994). There has been one double-blind study of yohimbine for the treatment of psychogenic erectile disorder (Reid et al., 1987), although there have been other double-blind studies of varying degrees of methodological sophistication demonstrating the efficacy of yohimbine for treatment of erectile dysfunction of uncertain etiology (Riley, Goodman, Kellet, & Orr, 1989; Sondra, Mazo, & Chancelor, 1990; Susset et al., 1989). One well-conducted double-blind study failed to demonstrate a significant effect of yohimbine for the treatment of organogenic impotence (Morales, Surridge, & Marshall, 1987).

Reid and coworkers (1987) assigned patients to psychogenic or organogenic categories by the use of an extensive evaluation that included nocturnal penile tumescence monitoring employing strict criteria. Men with psychogenic impotence entered a 10-week, double-blind, partial crossover study. The dose employed was 18 mg per day, and the trial included 48 subjects. Yohimbine was clearly superior to a placebo in this trial. Subject self-report was the dependent variable. The positive response in the control group was 16%, while the positive response in the experimental group was 62%. Clearly, other centers utilizing well-defined patient groups need to replicate this finding.

The mechanism by which yohimbine might influence erectile function is not known; central mechanisms are suspected. Direct injection of yohimbine into the corpora cavernosa of dogs does not induce erections (Sondra et al., 1990), and yohimbine does not affect the catecholamine levels of in vitro baths of corpus cavernous tissue (Steers, McConnell, & Benson, 1984). Intracerebral injection of yohimbine in the rat brain has been shown to decrease mount, intromission, and ejaculatory latency and intromission interval (Sala et al., 1990).

Yohimbine is a relatively safe drug with major side effects, including nervousness, induction of panic attacks in susceptible individuals, and increased blood pressure. The usual prescribing practice in the United States is to give 5.4 mg three times a day, although its half-life is 0–12 minutes, suggesting that an active metabolite may be responsible for its action. It is also possible that higher doses of this drug might be tolerated and increase its effectiveness.

There has recently been a trial combining yohimbine with trazodone (Montosi et al., 1994). In this combined trial, 63 men with psychogenic impotence established by accepted criteria either received 15 mg yohimbine plus 50 mg trazodone daily for 8 weeks or a placebo. Approximately 70% of the men had a restoration of function on the combination, and it was superior to the placebo condition.

Trazodone is a serotonergic antidepressant with considerable alpha-adrenergic blockade as a side effect. There have been case reports of trazodone being associated with clitoral priapism (Pescatori, Enhelman, Davis, & Goldstein, 1993), penile priapism (Scher et al., 1988) spontaneous orgasm (Purcell & Ghurye, 1995), increased libido (Gartrell, 1986), and improved erectile function (Lal, Rios, & Thavundayil, 1990). It is assumed that the enhanced erectile function associated with trazodone is related to its peripheral alpha-adrenergic blockade (Segraves, 1989a). To the authors' knowledge, no one has replicated the trial combining trazodone with yohimbine.

Another approach to the oral pharmacotherapy of male erectile disorder is the use of dopaminergic agents. Subcutaneous injection of apomorphine, a dopamine agonist, in the arm has been reported to elicit spontaneous erections in three separate double-blind studies involving either normal subjects or men with psychogenic erectile problems (Danjov, Alexandre, Warot, Combiez, & Pvech, 1988; Lal, Ackman, Thavundayil, Kieley, & Etienne, 1984; Segraves, Bari, Segraves, & Spirnak, 1991). In an open-label study, Lal et al. (1987) suggested that men demonstrating an erectile response to subcutaneous apomorphine were responsive to oral bromocriptine therapy for erectile dysfunction. This study has not been replicated. Benkert, Cronbach, & Kockott (1972), in a double-blind study of levodopa in male diabetics, found that it increased the frequency of early morning erections without restoring erectile function. In a double-blind study of levodopa in idiopathic erectile function, Pierini and Nusimovich (1981) reported restoration of function in the group receiving levodopa. However, this study did not include clear specification of outcome criteria.

To the authors' knowledge, there has been one double-blind study of the effect of naltrexone, an opioid antagonist, on erectile function in men with idiopathic erectile dysfunction. Fabbri et al. (1987) reported that 50 mg of oral naltrexone restored erectile function in 11 of 15 men. This was statistically different from a placebo.

Clearly, the use of intracavernosal injection of vasoactive agents can produce erections in most men with psychogenic erectile dysfunction. The small number of men adequately studied from a psychological viewpoint did not reveal any psychiatric contraindication to such therapy. The high dropout rates reported in the literature indicate that many men do find this approach unacceptable. The studies conducted using oral agents have yielded interesting leads for further research. To date, not enough men with psychogenic impotence have been treated by these methods to comment on their safety, acceptability, or advisability. It is of note that men with psychogenic impotence have responded to pharmacological treatment of erectile problems without evidence of increased marital discord or personal turmoil.

Vacuum Tumescence Devices

An alternative strategy for the man who is resistant to or has not benefited from psychotherapy and who finds the concept of self-injection of a substance into the penis somewhat aversive is the use of the external vacuum erection device. The vacuum device is placed over the penis, and a negative pressure facilitates blood flow into the penis, producing an erection. A tension ring (rubber band) is slipped from the base of the vacuum erection device to the base of the penis, maintaining the erection. Different studies utilizing diverse patient populations have reported that between 70% and 100% of men will achieve erections using this device (Althof & Seftel, 1995; Turner et al., 1991, 1992). Dropout rates are around 20%. Side effects are minimal, and there is no evidence of significant negative psychological effects from employing this device. To date, there is insufficient evidence for the clinician to know differentially when to employ the many interventions possible for erectile disorder.

Premature Ejaculation

Psychological Treatment

Since the early 1970s, an array of individual, conjoint, and group therapy approaches employing behavioral strategies such as stop-start (Masters & Johnson, 1970) or squeeze techniques (Semans, 1956) have evolved as the psychological treatments of choice for rapid ejaculation (Halvorsen & Metz, 1992; Kaplan, 1974, 1989; Levine, 1992; McCarthy, 1989; St. Lawrence & Madakasira, 1992). It is now known that the impressive initial posttreatment success rates, ranging from 60% to 95% (Hawton, 1986, 1988; Masters & Johnson,

1970), are not necessarily sustainable (see Table 23.6). Three years after treatment, success rates dwindled to 25% (Bancroft & Coles, 1976; DeAmicus et al., 1985; Hawton, 1988).

Men have resorted to wearing multiple condoms, applying desensitization ointment to the penis, repeatedly masturbating prior to intercourse, not allowing partners to stimulate them, or distracting themselves by performing complex mathematical computations while making love to overcome rapid ejaculation. These tactics, however creative, curtail the pleasures of lovemaking and are generally unsuccessful.

The prevailing opinions regarding the etiology of rapid ejaculation have typically assumed that the dysfunction is either psychological or learned, depending on the theorists' assumptions about how the mind operates. Some clinicians surmise that the lowered ejaculatory threshold stems from anxiety regarding unresolved fears of the vagina, hostility toward women, interpersonal conflicts with a particular partner, or conditioning patterned on early hurried sexual experiences with prostitutes or hasty lovemaking in the backseat of a car. Once established, performance anxiety was thought to maintain the rapid ejaculatory pattern. Recently, Strassberg, Kelly, Carroll, and Kircher (1987) and Godpodinoff (1989) independently speculated that a subgroup of rapid ejaculators may have a neurophysiological vulnerability and that this biological vulnerability explains some failures of psychological treatments. There is yet little evidence to support this most interesting notion.

Pharmacological Treatment

A large number of psychiatric drugs have been recognized as the cause of delayed ejaculation, and a number of clinicians have published case reports of successfully using a variety of pharmacological agents, including thioridazine, monoamine oxidase inhibitors, clomipramine, and lorazepam, to treat premature ejaculation (Segraves et al., 1993). Double-blind studies have established that clomipramine, paroxetine and sertraline can be used to treat premature ejaculation.

Segraves and coworkers (1993) reported on the double-blind comparison of clomipramine and a placebo on ejaculatory latency in 20 men complaining of premature ejaculation. Self-report of ejaculatory latency was utilized, with a partial check of validity supplied by a partner's report of ejaculatory latency in married subjects. Both 25 and 50 mg doses of clomipramine taken 6 hours prior to anticipated coitus increased ejaculatory latency significantly more than the placebo. Subjects also completed biweekly ratings of quality of libido, quality of ejaculation, satisfaction with ejaculatory timing, and overall sexual satisfaction. All indices improved in patients receiving clomipramine. Side effects were minimal and consisted of transient fatigue and nausea in a few subjects.

Althof et al. (1995) reported a double-blind, randomized, placebo-controlled study of clomipramine for the treatment of premature ejaculation. Both 25 and 50 mg doses were reported to treat premature

TABLE 23.6 Psychotherapy Outcome Studies for Premature Ejaculation

Study	Type of Study	Results Posttherapy	Long-Term Follow-Up Results
Masters & Johnson (1970)	Type 3	Of 186 men, a 2.2% posttreatment failure rate is reported.	At 5-year follow-up, a 2.7% failure rate is reported.
Heiman & LoPiccolo (1983)	Type 3	Of 21 couples, men lasted between 4 to 6 minutes more than pretreatment.	At 3-month follow-up, men lost 2 minutes of ejaculatory latency from the end of therapy but were still improved over the baseline.
DeAmicus et al. (1985)	Type 3	On self-report, 15/20 men reported improvement at the end of therapy. Improvement was also noted on questionnaires.	At the 3-year follow-up, by self-report 15/20 men sustained improvement. The questionnaire responses suggested a regression to pretherapy levels.
Hawton et al. (1986), Hawton (1995)	Type 3	6/8 men reported improvement following termination of therapy.	From 1 to 6 years after ending treatment, 2/8 men still reported improvement.

ejaculation successfully. A successful outcome was associated with improvement in sexual satisfaction of both partners. Psychometric indices of psychological well-being also demonstrated improvement of symptom relief. At a 2-month follow-up after drug discontinuation, all patients had again become symptomatic.

Waldinger, Heneveld, and Zwenderman (1994), in a double-blind, placebo-controlled trial, studied the effect of paroxetine on ejaculation in men with premature ejaculation. The dose of paroxetine was increased from 20 mg to 40 mg after the first week. Successful outcomes were noted in most patients, and side effects were minimal.

Mendels, Camera, and Sikes (1995) reported a study of the efficacy of sertraline to treat premature ejaculation and reported success with this serotonin reuptake inhibitor. In this placebo-controlled, double-blind study, doses were titrated to maximum efficacy, and 121 mg per day was the average daily dose used.

Sertraline, paroxetine, and clomipramine all appear successful for reversing premature ejaculation. Clomipramine may be the preferred drug as it can be taken on an as-needed basis. All three drugs have relatively benign side-effect profiles at the doses employed in these studies. A disadvantage of the pharmacological therapy of premature ejaculation is that it appears that treatment has to be lifelong. However, the studies to date have employed relatively brief treatment periods. It is possible that a longer period of pharmacotherapy might produce a permanent change in ejaculatory patterns.

Female Orgasmic Disorders

Spence (1991) offers a cogent summary of the dilemmas to be considered in assessing the efficacy of psychological therapy for women with orgasmic disorders. The major issue remains unresolved: Is success predicated solely on coital orgasm, or orgasm through any means, or by a subjective rating of increased satisfaction with the sexual relationship? Adding to our confusion is the media's constant reinforcement of unrealistic expectations from sexual encounters. Both men and women are led to believe that women can easily and regularly achieve intense multiple orgasms from intercourse alone.

Several studies (Kuriansky & Sharpe, 1981; Kuriansky, Sharpe, & O'Connor, 1982; McMullen & Rosen, 1979; Riley & Riley, 1978; Spence, 1991) have documented the success of masturbatory training programs in facilitating women who have never achieved orgasm to become orgasmic. Initial success rates range between 70% and 90%, with women being treated individually, in couples, or groups, or exposed to either videotapes or written material concerning masturbatory training programs. Kuriansky and Sharpe (1981) reported that 15% of their subjects were not able to sustain orgasmic achievement at a 2-year follow-up.

Whatever the success in achieving orgasm(s) via masturbatory training, it begins to diminish as the woman moves from self-induced orgasm, to partner-induced orgasm through manual or oral stimulation, to intercourse-induced orgasm without manual stimulation. Immediately posttherapy, Kuriansky reported 89% of women achieved orgasm by themselves, 21% within the "context of a partner encounter" and 16% with intercourse alone. Heiman and LoPiccolo (1983) reported a two- to threefold (35–40% success rate) increase in coital orgasm at a 3-month follow-up. See Table 23.7 for a summary of psychotherapy outcome studies.

The long-term results for female orgasmic dysfunction differ in two significant directions from treatments of other sexual disorders. First, over time women demonstrate an increased capacity to achieve orgasm in partner-related, as well as coital, encounters. Within 2 years, women achieved greater facility in achieving orgasm within the context of a partner encounter (47%) and via intercourse (26%). In addition, those women who dropped out of a treatment program also reported improved orgasmic functioning 2 years after beginning therapy. Second, the prognosis appears more positive for women with lifelong orgasmic dysfunction in comparison to women who acquire the dysfunction after a period of normal function. These fascinating findings can be explained by (a) practice, (b) reinforcement by success, (c) decreased inhibition, and (d) increased harmony with the body and willingness to generate pleasurable internal sensations that culminate in orgasm. The worse outcome for an acquired dysfunction rests on the belief that the psychological causes (i.e., relationship deterioration) for the appearance of the dysfunction generally were not addressed in masturbatory training programs.

Male Orgasmic Disorder

Male orgasmic dysfunction, often referred to as retarded ejaculation, delayed ejaculation, incompetent ejaculation (Masters & Johnson, 1970), partner anor-

TABLE 23.7 Psychotherapy Outcome Studies for Female Orgasmic Dysfunction

Study	Type of Study	Results Posttherapy	Long-Term Follow-Up Results
Masters & Johnson (1970)	Type 3	Of 193 women with lifelong and 149 with acquired dysfunction, 16.6% and 22.8% failure rates, respectively, were reported at termination.	Of 193 women with lifelong and 149 with acquired dysfunction, 17.6% and ??? failure rates, respectively, were reported 5 years after termination.
Riley & Riley (1979)	Type 3	90% of women with lifelong dysfunction were able to achieve orgasm posttherapy.	
Kuriansky et al. (1982)	Type 3	18/19 (95%) were able to achieve orgasm posttreatment.	16/19 women were able to maintain ability to achieve orgasm 2 years after treatment.
Heiman & LoPiccolo (1983)	Type 3	Posttherapy, of 25 women with lifelong and 16 with acquired dysfunction, 40% and 15%, respectively, reported improvement.	At 3-month follow-up, of 25 women with lifelong dysfunction all maintained gains and of the 16 with acquired dysfunction another 5% reported success.
DeAmicus et al. (1985)	Type 3	14/22 with lifelong and 16/21 with acquired dysfunction self-reported improvement.	At 3-year follow-up, 18/22 with lifelong and 17/21 with acquired dysfunction self-reported improvement.
Kilmann et al. (1986)	Type 2	Of 35 women with acquired dysfunction, 9 (25%) were significantly improved.	At 5-month follow-up, 11/30 (33%) with acquired dysfunction demonstrated significant improvement.

gasmia (Apfelbaum, 1989), or absent ejaculation, is found in only 3% to 8% of men (Hawton, 1982; Masters & Johnson, 1970; Spector & Carey, 1990). Surprisingly, while difficulty achieving orgasm is the most prevalent dysfunction among women, it is the most uncommon presentation among men. It is not clear why this dysfunction is so infrequent; one could speculate that up to some point delayed orgasm is a valued commodity, and only when it surpasses some subjective personal or partner threshold, or is typically absent, does it become problematic. Unlike erectile dysfunction or rapid ejaculation, it does not mechanically thwart intercourse, although it can detract from each partner's gratification.

There are no large-scale, long-term, controlled outcome studies of men in whom this is considered a purely psychogenic condition. There are two antithetical points of view for understanding this dysfunction: the inhibition model versus a desire deficit model. Treatment efforts are guided by the assumptions underlying these contrary models. When seen through the lens of the inhibition model, behaviorists assume that the man is not receiving sufficient stimulation to reach the orgasmic threshold. Dynamic clinicians

who adhere to the inhibition model assume that the symptom is a conscious or unconscious expression of the man's aggression—he is withholding or depriving his partner of something they desire. Treatment efforts therefore aim to increase excitement through prolonged, intense, rough stimulation or by interpreting the man's aggressive impulses. Masters and Johnson (1970) reported a failure rate of 17.6% using a combination of sensate focus, vigorous noncoital penile stimulation, and modifications in intercourse technique. Schnellen (1968) reported that 81% of men who prior to treatment were anorgasmic were successful in reaching orgasm through vibrator stimulation.

Apfelbaum (1989) presents an alternative model, suggesting that delayed ejaculation is a desire disorder disguised as a performance disorder. He criticizes those employing the inhibition model, stating that intense stimulation is a demanding coercive strategy that heightens performance anxiety. His treatment efforts are aimed at having the man acknowledge his lack of both desire to have intercourse and arousal during intercourse. This model mirrors the conventional therapy for female anorgasmia—decreasing demand and helping the woman to focus on heightening sensation. No outcome statistics for this intriguing model have been presented.

It is the authors' contention that one could bridge these two models by understanding the inhibition model as appropriate when the man presents with global anorgasmia and the desire deficit model as more suitable when he presents with partner anorgasmia.

Dyspareunia and Vaginismus

Dyspareunia, or painful intercourse, is a common sexual complaint among women, accounting for 10–15% of female respondents in community-based surveys (Rosen & Leiblum, 1995). Physical factors (hymenal scarring, infection, sexually transmitted diseases [STDs], estrogen deficiency, pelvic inflammatory disease, and vulvar vestibulitis) frequently underlie this condition; however, even if the etiology is entirely physical, there is likely to be a conditioned psychological response that may require subsequent psychological intervention (Sarrel & Sarrel, 1989; Schover, Youngs, & Canata, 1992). In addition, psychosocial factors alone, such as relationship discord and prior sexual abuse, have also been cited as etiological agents (Binik et al., 1995; Rosen & Leiblum, 1989, 1995).

Vaginismus, or the persistent and recurrent involuntary spasm of the musculature of the outer third of the vagina, has been characterized as a psychosomatic disorder, a phobia, a conditioned response, or a conversion reaction (Leiblum, Pevrin, & Campbel, 1988). A spectrum of etiological factors, such as specific trauma(s), interpersonal and intrapsychic conflict, penetration anxiety, and multiple organic pathologies, causes this dysfunction. Approximately 10–30% of the male partners of these women report erectile or ejaculatory dysfunctions (Levine, 1988, 1992).

Vaginismus is typically treated through a combination of (a) banning intercourse, (b) in vivo graduated self-insertion of dilators of increasing size, (c) systematic desensitization, (d) Kegel exercises, and (d) interpretation of resistance and psychodynamic fears. Masters and Johnson (1970) reported a 100% success rate in their treatment of 29 women. Similarly, Scholl (1988) reported that 83% of his sample successfully completed therapy and were having intercourse at the 1-year follow-up. Spence (1991) suggests that more treatment sessions are required when women have (a) experienced the dysfunction over extended periods of time, (b) undergone surgery, or (c) thoughts of anatomical abnormality and a negative attitude toward their genitals. The need for treatment sessions was related to a strong desire for pregnancy, presence of an assertive husband, and sexual knowledge on the woman's part.

Substance-Induced Sexual Disorders

The diagnostic entity of substance-induced sexual disorders, which refers to sexual disorders associated with drug intoxication and associated with the use of prescribed medication, was introduced in DSM-IV. A variety of chemical agents have been associated with sexual dysfunction. Most of the reports concern substances of abuse, antihypertensive agents, and psychiatric drugs.

Sexual dysfunction has been long assumed to be related to chronic alcohol abuse. In particular, it has been assumed that chronic alcohol abuse in males is associated with erectile dysfunction (Miller & Gold, 1988; Schiavi, 1990). Although less evidence is available concerning the effects of chronic alcohol abuse in females, most clinicians assume that chronic alcohol abuse may also be detrimental to female sexual function (Rosen, 1991). There is considerable evidence that chronic alcohol abuse may have deleterious effects on hypothalamic-pituitary and testicular function (Schiavi, Stimmel, Mandeli, & White, 1995). Chronic alcohol abuse is associated with damage to the central nervous system, as manifested by dementia and Wernicke-Korsakoff syndrome. Peripheral polyneuropathy is also associated with myelin and axon degeneration as a common neurological complication of chronic alcoholism. Thus, there are several mechanisms by which chronic alcohol abuse could cause sexual dysfunction.

In reality, the controlled evidence linking chronic alcohol abuse to sexual dysfunction is limited and only concerns male alcoholics. Much of the available evidence contains numerous methodological flaws. The major studies to date have either been retrospective (Lemere & Smith, 1973), lacked control groups (Fahner, 1987), or had other methodological flaws, such as including patients on disulfiram treatment (Jensen, 1984) or other pharmacological agents associated with sexual dysfunction (Whalley, 1978). Studies utilizing nocturnal penile tumescence as a measure of erectile function have reported decreased erectile capacity in patients with chronic alcoholism. These studies have methodological flaws, such as studying the patient shortly after detoxification (Snyder & Karacan, 1981a, 1981b). As disulfiram treatment has been shown to decrease erectile capacity (Tan, Johnson, Lambie, Vijayasenah, & Whiteside, 1984), it is important that studies clearly indicate whether or not patients received this treatment.

In a recent investigation, Schiavi et al. (1995) investigated sexual function and nocturnal penile tumescence and conducted various laboratory tests, including those for testosterone, luteinizing hormone, prolactin, and liver enzymes, in 20 healthy alcoholics with at least a 10-year history of problem drinking who had been abstinent for 2 months and were in a stable sexual relationship as compared to an age-matched nonalcoholic control group. Surprisingly, they found no significant differences between the two groups in sexual function, nocturnal penile tumescence, or hormone levels. These data suggest that a history of alcoholism in the absence of significant hepatic or gonadal failure and in a period of sobriety may be compatible with normal sexual function. It should be noted that this population may represent a particular subgroup of patients with chronic alcoholism in that they were disease free and capable of maintaining a stable sexual relationship.

Evidence concerning the effects of narcotics on sexual function has been uniform and convincing. The evidence consists of anecdotal reports, surveys, and clinical studies. All of the studies are uniform in finding a diminished libido while on narcotics (Abel, 1985). Retrospective studies suggest that normal libido returns during drug-free periods (Segraves, Madsen, Carver, & Davis, 1985). Cocaine and amphetamine use has been reported to cause increased libido and spontaneous erections (Abel, 1985). However, there is evidence that chronic abuse of these agents may lead to decreased libido and other sexual dysfunctions (Siegel, 1977). It is unclear whether sexuality returns to the baseline during abstinence from these agents.

A number of clinical series and case reports establish the likelihood of a high frequency of sexual disorders, including decreased libido, erectile dysfunction, and anorgasmia while on most antihypertensive agents (e.g., spironolactone, chlorthalidone, alpha methyldopa, reserpine, guanethidine, propranolol, clonidine, verapamil, and nifidipine) (Rosen & Leiblum, 1995; Segraves, 1988; Segraves et al., 1985). Unfortunately, most of these reports do not include control groups or utilize appropriate measures of sexual function. In one of the few properly controlled studies in this area of inquiry, Rosen and Kostis (1991) compared sexual function in men randomly assigned to propranolol or a placebo for 3 months. Propranolol therapy led to a significant decrease in the frequency of full erections.

Psychiatric drugs have also been reported to cause sexual problems. This is true of almost all classes of psychiatric drugs. Most of the evidence concerning the action of these drugs comes from clinical reports, and only a handful of controlled studies have been performed. Benzodiazepines have been frequently reported to cause delay in orgasm and/or no orgasm. This has been reported with chlordiazepoxide, lorazepam, diazepam, and alprazolam (Segraves, 1995a, 1995b). A double-blind controlled study by Riley and Riley (1988) demonstrated a dose response relationship between diazepam dose and orgasmic delay. There have been reports of antipsychotic agents such as thioridazine, chlorpromazine, trifluoperazine, and haloperidol being associated with either decreased libido or erectile problems. Ejaculatory problems have been reported with thioridazine, chlorpromazine, chlorprothixine, mesoridazine, perphenazine, trifluoperazine, and risperidone. The one double-blind controlled study in this area of inquiry utilized minimal drug dosages and is thus of little value for this review (Tennett, Bancroft, & Cass, 1972).

Of the psychiatric drugs, most has been written about the sexual side effects of antidepressant agents (Segraves, 1995b). Most of the antidepressant drugs available in the United States, with the possible exceptions of bupropion and nefazadone, have been reported to cause sexual problems, including loss of libido, erectile dysfunction, and orgasm or ejaculatory delay (Segraves, 1995a). It appears that orgasmic delay is especially common with the selective serotonin reuptake inhibitors. Fortunately, there have been a few controlled studies in this area of inquiry. In a double-blind controlled study of imipramine, phenelzine, and a placebo, Harrison et al. (1985) reported that both phenelzine and imipramine, as compared with the placebo, were associated with a higher incidence of decreased libido and ejaculatory problems. It was interesting that they did not find a significant association between imipramine use and erectile problems. In another double-blind study, Kowalski, Stanley, and Dennerstein (1985) found that both mianserin and amitriptyline decreased total nocturnal penile tumescence as compared to a placebo. It is of note that the normal volunteers in this study did not report problems in their usual sexual activities. Monteiro, Noshivani, Marks, and Lelliott (1987), in a controlled study of clomipramine in patients with obsessive compulsive disorder, reported that this drug significantly interfered with orgasm in all subjects who took a dose in excess of 100 mg. Many subjects experienced total anorgasmia.

FUTURE DEVELOPMENTS

A meaningful discussion of potential future developments in the treatment of sexual disorders requires an appreciation of the rudimentary level of our current knowledge, as well as the unevenness of our current database. Controlled inquiry concerning the treatment of human sexual disorders is a relatively recent phenomenon. Much more work has been published concerning the treatment of male than female disorders, and great advances have been made in biological interventions, often without research documenting how these interventions might be optimally employed in differing psychosocial contexts. Normal sexual function involves a complicated interactive sequencing of biological, social, relational, and individual psychological events, and effective interventions will require an appreciation of the potential complexity of these different interactive influences. This appreciation is not present in many clinical contexts.

Certain areas of advance appear almost certain to occur in the near future. These include the development of new pharmacological treatments for sexual disorders, refinement of our diagnostic assessment and psychosocial treatment of sexual dysfunction, and clarification of the differential and combined use of biological and psychological treatment strategies.

Pharmacotherapy will undoubtedly play an increasing role in the treatment of sexual disorders (Riley & Riley, 1993). A considerable database has accumulated concerning the biological substrate of various sexual behaviors in laboratory animals. The importance of the medial preoptic area of the ventral diencephalon and its interconnections with other areas in the diencephalon, limbic system, and cerebral cortex has been recognized, as well as the responsivity of the neurons in the medial preoptic area to gonadal hormones (Wilson, 1993). Neurochemical studies have identified dopaminergic, noradrenergic, and serotonergic inputs into this area, and psychopharmacological studies have begun to differentiate the effects

of stimulation of various monoaminergic receptor subtypes on sexual behavior (Foreman & Doherty, 1993).

Throughout history, humans have searched for substances that might augment sexual behavior. Today, such an effort can be based on a solid foundation of the neural mechanisms involved in the expression of sexual behavior in the laboratory animal. With an increased interest in sexual behavior by a wide variety of health care professionals, and with the increasing use of drugs with actions within the central nervous system, there is also the possibility of fortuitous discoveries of unanticipated actions of pharmacological agents, such as illustrated by the recent discovery of the use of serotonergic antidepressants to cure premature ejaculation.

The diagnostic system currently utilized for coding sexual disorders is based on the triphasic model of sexual responsivity proposed by Masters and Johnson (1966), which was modified to include desire phase disorders. This modification was based principally on the contributions of the work of Kaplan (1974). The nosology employed is based on uncontrolled clinical observation and often appears to involve arbitrary separation of interrelated aspects of sexual function (Foreman & Doherty, 1993). In certain contexts, the clinician will assess presenting symptomatology and begin treatment, with *DSM-IV* coding of the disorder being an afterthought rather than a guide to treatment. This stands in marked contrast to other areas of psychiatry, in which diagnostic considerations guide treatment decisions, and attests to the inadequacy of the current diagnostic system for sexual disorders. It is anticipated that future research will result in the adoption of operationalized criteria sets for the diagnoses of sexual disorders and the development of a more clinically relevant nosology.

In the next decade, there will be a pressing need to define the indications for specific types of psychotherapeutic and psychopharmacological interventions and when a combined psychotherapeutic and psychopharmacologic approach is indicated. For example, desire disorders are currently treated with a variety of individual and dyadic psychological interventions, and premature ejaculation and psychogenic erectile disorder can be treated either pharmacologically or psychotherapeutically. With current technology, rapidity of ejaculation can be tempered, and most men can have some form of erectile function restored. However, modern technology cannot predict which man successfully treated for premature ejaculation or erectile failure will resume coital activity, whether his partner will allow that event to occur, or whether either of them will find pleasure with the restored function. Clearly, future research will focus on identifying the most cost-effective, symptomatic interventions, as well as the indications for combined dyadic or individual psychotherapy in conjunction with pharmacotherapy. With contemporary concern about improving the quality of life, the patient's and his or her partner's subjective appreciation of the sexual experience must be considered, as must the return of normal physiological function. The authors anticipate that our knowledge concerning the treatment of sexual disorders will continue to grow at a rapid pace in the next century.

References

Abel, E. L. (1985). *Psychoactive drugs and sex*. New York: Plenum.

Ackerman, M. D., & Carey, M. P. (1995). Psychology's role in the assessment of erectile dysfunction: Historical precedents, current knowledge, and methods. *Journal of Consulting and Clinical Psychology, 63*, 862–876.

Althof, S. (1989). Psychogenic impotence: Treatment of men and couples. In R. C. Rosen & S. R. Leiblum (Eds.), *Principles and practice of sex therapy: Update for the 1990s* (pp. 237–268). New York: Guilford Press.

Althof, S. E. (1995a). Pharmacological treatment of rapid ejaculation. *Psychiatric Clinics of North America*, 85–94.

Althof, S. (1995b). Pharmacological treatment for rapid ejaculation: Preliminary strategies, concerns and questions [Leading Comments Section]. *Sex and Marital Therapy, 10*, 247–251.

Althof, S., Levine, S., Corty, E., Risen, C., Stern, E., & Kurit, D. (1995). Clomipramine as a treatment for rapid ejaculation: A double-blind crossover trial of 15 couples. *Journal of Clinical Psychiatry, 56*, 402–407.

Althof, S., Turner, L., Levine, S., Kursh, E., Bodner, D., & Resnick, M. (1989). Why do so many people drop out from auto injection therapy for impotence? *Journal of Sex and Marital Therapy, 15*, 121–129.

Althof, S., Turner, L., Levine, S., Risen, C., Bodner, D., Kursh, E., & Resnick, M. (1991). Long term use of intra cavernous therapy in the treatment of erectile dysfunction. *Journal of Sex and Marital Therapy, 17*(2), 101–112.

Althof, S. E., & Seftel, A. D. (1995). The evaluation and treatment of erectile dysfunction. *Psychiatric Clinics of North America*, 171–192.

American Psychiatric Association. (1952). *Diagnostic and statistical manual: Mental disorders*. Washington, D.C.: Author.

———. (1968). *Diagnostic and statistical manual of mental disorders* (2nd ed.). Washington, D.C.: Author.

———. (1980). *Diagnostic and statistical manual of mental disorders* (3rd ed.). Washington, D.C.: Author.

———. (1987). *Diagnostic and statistical manual of mental disorders* (3rd ed., revised). Washington, D.C.: Author.

———. (1994). *Diagnostic and statistical manual of mental disorders* (4th ed.). Washington, D.C.: Author.

Apfelbaum, B. (1989). Retarded ejaculation: A much misunderstood Syndrome. In R. C. Rosen & S. R. Leiblum (Eds.), *Principles and practice of sex therapy: Update for the 1990s* (pp. 168–206). New York: Guilford Press.

Assalian, P. (1988). Clomipramine in the treatment of premature ejaculation. *Journal of Sex Research, 24*, 231–215.

Baert, H. C. (1989). Transcutaneous nitroglycerin therapy in the treatment of impotence. *Urology International, 44*, 309–312.

Bancroft, J., & Coles, L. (1976). Three years experience in a sexual problems clinic. *British Medical Journal, 1*, 1575–1577.

Bancroft, J., Sherwin, B. B., Alexander, G. M., Davidson, D. W., & Walker, A. (1991). Oral contraceptives and the sexuality of young women. *Archives of Sexual Behavior, 20*, 121–136.

Barada, J. H., & McKimmy, R. M. (1994). Vasoactive pharmacotherapy. In A. H. Bennett (Ed.), *Impotence. Diagnosis and management of erectile dysfunction* (pp. 229–250). Philadelphia: Saunders.

Beck, J. G., Barlow, D. H., Sakheim, D. K., & Abrahamson, D. J. (1987). Shock threat and sexual arousal: The role of selective attention, thought content and affective states. *Psychophysiology, 24*, 165–172.

Benkert, O., Cronbach, G., & Kockott, G. (1972). Effect of L-dopa on sexually impotent patients. *Psychopharmacology, 23*, 91–95.

Bennett, A. H., Carpenter, A. J., & Barada, J. H. (1991). Improved vasoactive drug combination for pharmacological erection program. *Journal of Urology, 1*(146), 1564–1568.

Binik, Y. U., Meana, U., Khalife, S., Bergerer, S., Cohen, D., & Howe, D. (1995). *Painful intercourse: A controlled study*. Paper presented at the annual meeting of the Society for Sex Therapy and Research, New York.

Brady, J. P. (1966). Brevital-relaxation treatment of frigidity. *Behavior Research and Therapy, 4*, 171–177.

Brindley, G. S. (1986). Maintenance treatment of erectile impotence by cavernosal unstriated muscle relaxation injection. *British Journal of Psychiatry, 149,* 210–215.

Cavallini, G. (1991). Minoxidil versus nitroglycerin: a prospective double-blind controlled trial intranacutaneous erection facilitation for organic impotence. *Journal of Urology, 146,* 50–53.

Clement, U., & Schmidt, G. (1983). The outcome of couple therapy for sexual dysfunctions using three different formats. *Journal of Sex and Marital Therapy, 9,* 67–78.

Cranston-Cuebas, M. A., & Barlow, D. H. (1990). Cognitive and affective contributions to sexual functioning. *Annual Review of Sex Research, 1,* 119–161.

Cooper, A. J. (1969). Factors in male sexual inadequacy: A review. *Journal of Nervous Disease, 149,* 337–359.

Crowe, M. J., Gillan, P., & Golombok, S. (1981). Form and content in the conjoint treatment of sexual dysfunction: A controlled study. *Behavior Research and Therapy, 19,* 47–54.

Danjov, P., Alexandre, L., Warot, D., Combiez, L., & Pvech, A. J. (1988). Assessment of erectogenic properties of apomorphine and yohimbine in man. *British Journal of Clinical Pharmacology, 26,* 733–739.

Davidson, J. M., Kwan, M., & Greenleaf, W. (1982). Hormonal replacement and sexuality in men. *Clinics in Endocrinology and Metabolism, 11,* 599–623.

DeAmicus, L., Goldberg, D. C., LoPiccolo, J., Friedman, J., & Davies, L. (1985). Clinical follow-up of couples treated for sexual dysfunction. *Archives of Sexual Behavior, 14,* 467–489.

Dhabuwala, C. B., Kerkar, P., & Bhutwala, A. (1990). Intracavernosus papaverine in the management of psychogenic impotence. *Archives of Andrology, 124,* 185–191.

Dow, M. G. T., Hart, D. M., & Forrest, C. A. (1983). Hormonal treatment of sexual unresponsiveness in post-menopausal women: A comparative study. *British Journal of Obstetrics and Gynecology, 90,* 361–366.

Ersner-Hershfield, R., & Kopel, S. (1979). Group treatment of preorgasmic women: Evaluation of partner involvement and spacing of sessions. *Journal of Consulting and Clinical Psychology, 47,* 750–759.

Fabbri, A., Jannini, E. A., Gnessi, L. Moretti, C., Ulisse, S., Franzese, A., Lazzari, R., Fraoili, F., & Fahner, E. (1987). Sexual dysfunction in male addicts: Prevalence and treatment. *Archives of Sexual Behavior, 16,* 247–256.

Feldman, H. A., Goldstein, I., Hatzichristou, D. G., Krane, R. J., & McKunlay, J. B. (1994). Impotence and its medical and psychosocial correlates: Results of the Massachusetts Male Aging Study. *Journal of Urology, 151,* 54–61.

Foreman, M. M., & Doherty, P. C. (1993). Experimental approaches for the development of pharmacological

therapies for erectile dysfunction. In A. J. Riley, M. Peet, & C. Wilson (Eds.), *Sexual pharmacology* (pp. 97–113). Oxford, U.K.: Clarendon Press.

Friedman, S., & Harrison, G. (1984). Sexual histories, attitudes and behavior of schizophrenic and normal women. *Archives of Sexual Behavior, 13,* 555–567.

Gagnon, J., Rosen, R., & Leiblum, S. (1982). Cognitive and social aspects of sexual dysfunction: Sexual scripts in sex therapy. *Journal of Sex and Marital Therapy, 8*(1), 44–56.

Gartrell, N. (1986). Increased libido in women receiving trazodone. *American Journal of Psychiatry, 143,* 781–782.

Gasser, T. C., Roach, R. M., & Larsen, R. H. (1987). Intracavernous self-injection with phentolamine and papaverine for the treatment of impotence. *Journal of Urology, 137,* 678–680.

Gilbert, H. W., & Gingell, J. C. (1991). The results of an intra corporeal papaverine clinic. *Sex and Marital Therapy, 4,* 49–53.

Godpodinoff, J. L. (1989). Premature ejaculation: Clinical subgroups and etiology. *Journal of Sex and Marital Therapy, 15,* 130–134.

Halvorsen, J., & Metz, M. (1992). Sexual dysfunction, part II: Classification, etiology and pathogenesis. *Journal of the American Board of Family Practice, 5,* 177–192.

Harrison, W. M., Stewart, J., Ehrhardt, A. A., Rabkin, J., McGrath, P., Liebowitz, M., & Quitkin, F. M. (1985). A controlled study of the effects of antidepressants on sexual function. *Psychopharmacology Bulletin, 21,* 85–88.

Haslam, M. T. (1965). The treatment of psychogenic dyspareunia by reciprocal inhibition. *British Journal of Psychiatry, 111,* 280–282.

Hawton, K. (1982). The behavioral treatment of sexual dysfunction. *British Journal of Psychiatry, 140,* 94–101.

———. (1995). Treatment of sexual dysfunctions by sex therapy and other approaches. *British Journal of Psychiatry, 167,* 307–314.

Hawton, K., & Catalan, J. (1986). Prognostic factors in sex therapy. *Behavior Research & Therapy, 24,* 377–385.

Hawton, K., Catalan, J., & Fagg, J. (1992). Sex therapy for erectile dysfunction: Characteristics of couples, treatment outcome, and prognostic factors. *Archives of Sexual Behavior, 21,* 161–175.

Hawton, K., Catalan, J., Martin, P., & Fagg, J. (1986). Long-term outcome of sex therapy. *Behavior Research & Therapy, 24,* 665–675.

Hawton, K., & Fagg, J. (1991). Low sexual desire: Sex therapy results and prognostic factors. *Behaviour Research & Therapy, 29,* 217–224.

Heiman, J. R., & LoPiccolo, J. (1983). Clinical outcome

of sex therapy. *Archives of General Psychiatry, 40*, 443–449.

Howell, J. R., Reynolds, C. F., Thase, M. E., Frank, E., Jennings, R., Hock, P. R., Berman, S.,

Ishii, N., Watanabe, H., & Irisawa, C. (1989). Intracavernous injection of prostaglandin$_{E1}$ for the treatment of erectile impotence. *Journal of Urology, 141*, 423–425.

Jensen, S. B. (1984). Sexual function and dysfunction in younger married alcoholics. *Acta Psychiatric Scandinavica, 69*, 543–549.

Kaplan, H. S. (1974). *The new sex therapy: Active treatment of sexual dysfunctions.* New York: Brunner/Mazel.

———. (1989). *Overcoming premature ejaculation.* New York: Brunner Mazel.

Kattan, S., Collins, J. P., & Mohr, Z. D. (1991). Double-blind crossover study comparing prostaglandin$_{E1}$ and papaverine in patients with vasculogenic impotence. *Urology, 37*, 516–518.

Kellet, J. (1993). The nature of human sexual desire and its modification by drugs. In A. J. Riley, M. Peet, & C. Wilson (Eds.), *Sexual Pharmacology* (pp. 100–145). Oxford, U.K.: Clarendon Press.

Kilmann, P. R., Milan, R. J., Boland, J. P., Nankin, H. R., Davidson, E., West, M. O., Sabalis, R. F., Caid, C., & Devine, J. M. (1987). Group treatment of secondary erectile dysfunction. *Journal of Sex and Marital Therapy, 13*, 168–182.

Kilmann, P. R., Mills, K. H., Caid, C., Davidson, E., Bella, B., Milan, R., Drose, G., Boland, J., Follingstad, D., Montgomery, B., & Wanlass, R. (1986). Treatment of secondary orgasmic dysfunction: An outcome study. *Archives of Sexual Behavior, 15*, 211–229.

Kowalski, A., Stanley, R. O., & Dennerstein, L. (1985). The sexual side-effects of antidepressant medication: A double blind comparison of two antidepressants in a non-psychiatric population. *British Journal of Psychiatry, 147*, 413–418.

Kuriansky, J. B., & Sharpe, L. (1981). Clinical and research implications of the evaluation of women's group therapy for anorgasmia: A review. *Journal of Sex and Marital Therapy, 7*, 268–277.

Kuriansky, J. B., Sharpe, L., & O'Connor, D. (1982). The treatment of anorgasmia: Long-term effectiveness of a short-term behavioral group therapy. *Journal of Sex and Marital Therapy, 8*, 29–43.

Lal, S., Ackman, D., Thavundayil, J. X., Kieley, M. E., & Etienne, P. C. (1984). Effect of apomorphine, a dopamine receptor agonist on penile tumescence in normal subjects. *Progress in Neuropsychopharmacology, 8*, 695–699.

Lal, S., Laryea, E., Thavundayil, J. X., Nir, N. P., Negrete, J., Ackman, D., Blundell, P., & Gardiner, R. J. (1987). Apomorphine-induced penile tumescence in impotent patients: Preliminary findings. *Progress in Neuropsychopharmacology Biological Psychiatry, 11*, 235–242.

Lal, S., Rios, S., & Thavundayil, J. X. (1990). Treatment of impotence with trazodone. *Journal of Urology, 143*, 819–820.

Lazarus, A. A. (1963). The treatment of chronic frigidity by systematic desensitization. *Journal of Nervous and Mental Diseases, 136*, 272–278.

Lee, L. M., Stevensen, R. W., & Szasz, G. (1989). Prostaglandin$_{E1}$ versus phentolamine/papaverine for the treatment of erectile impotence: A double-blind comparison. *Journal of Urology, 141*, 551–553.

Leiblum, S. R., Pervin, L. A., & Campbel, H. C. (1988). The treatment of vaginismus. In S. R. Leiblum & R. C. Rosen (Eds.), *Principles and practice of sex therapy* (pp. 167–194). New York: Guilford Press.

Leiblum, S. R., & Rosen, R. C. (1989). *Principles and practice of sex therapy: Update for the 1990s.* New York: Guilford Press.

Leiblum, S. R., Rosen, R. C., & Pierce, D. (1976). Group treatment format: Mixed sexual dysfunctions. *Archives of Sexual Behavior, 5*, 313–322.

Lemere, F., & Smith, J. W. (1973). Alcohol-induced sexual impotence. *American Journal of Psychiatry, 130*, 212–213.

Lendorf, A., Juncker, L., & Rosenkilde, P. (1994). Frequency of erectile dysfunction in a Danish subpopulation. *Nordisk Sexologi, 12*, 118–124.

Levine, S. (1988). *Sex is not simple.* Columbus: Ohio Psychology Publishing Company.

Levine, S. B. (1992a). Intrapsychic and interpersonal aspects of impotence: Psychogenic erectile dysfunction. In R. C. Rosen & S. R. Leiblum (Eds.), *Erectile disorders: Assessment and treatment* (pp. 198–225). New York: Guilford Press.

Levine, S. (1992b). *Sexual life: A clinicians guide.* New York: Plenum.

Levine, S. B., & Agle, D. (1978). The effectiveness of sex therapy for chronic secondary psychological impotence. *Journal of Sex and Marital Therapy, 4*, 235–258.

Levine, S., Althof, S., Turner, L., Risen, C., Bodner, D., Kursh, E., & Resnick, M. (1989). Side effects of self-administration of intracavernosal papaverine and phentolamine for the treatment of impotence. *Journal of Urology, 141*, 54–57.

Lief, H. I. (1989). Introduction. In American Psychiatric Association Task Force on Treatments of Psychiatric Disorders (Ed.), *Treatment of psychiatric disorders*, Vol. 3 (pp. 2237–2238). Washington, D.C.: American Psychiatric Press.

Loman, G. M., & Jarow, J. P. (1992). Risk factors for papaverine-induced priapism. *Journal of Urology, 147*, 1280–1281.

LoPiccolo, J., Heiman, J., Hogan, D., & Roberts, C. (1985). Effectiveness of single therapists versus co-therapy teams in sex therapy. *Journal of Consulting and Clinical Psychology, 53*, 287–294.

LoPiccolo, J., & LoPiccolo, J. (1978). *Handbook of sex therapy*. New York: Plenum Publishers.

Marks, I. M. (1981). Review of behavioral psychotherapy, II: Sexual Disorders. *American Journal of Psychiatry, 138*, 750–756.

Masters, W., & Johnson, V. (1966). *Human sexual response*. London: Churchill, Livingstone.

———. (1970). *Human sexual inadequacy*. Boston: Little Brown.

Mathews, A., Whitehead, A., & Kellet, J. (1983). Psychological and hormonal factors in the treatment of female sexual dysfunctions. *Psychosomatic Medicine, 13*, 83–92.

McCarthy, B. (1990). Cognitive-behavioral strategies and techniques in the treatment of early ejaculation. In S. R. Leiblum & R. C. Rosen (Eds.), *Principles and practice of sex therapy: Update for the 90s* (pp. 141–167). New York: Guilford Press.

McCarthy, B., & McCarthy, E. (1984). *Sexual awareness: Sharing sexual pleasure*. New York: Carroll & Graff.

McMahon, C. G. (1991). A comparison of the response to the intracavernosal injection of a combination of papaverine and phentolamine, prostaglandin PG_{E1} and a combination of all three in the management of impotence. *International Journal of Impotence Research, 3*, 113–121.

McMullen, S., & Rosen, R. C. (1979). Self-administered masturbation training in the treatment of primary orgasmic dysfunction. *Journal of Consulting and Clinical Psychology, 47*, 912–918.

Mendels, J., Camera, A., & Sikes, C. (1995). Sertraline treatment for premature ejaculation. *Journal of Clinical Psychopharmacology, 15*, 341–346.

Meyer, J. K. (1976). Psychodynamic treatment of the individual with a sexual disorder. In J. K. Meyer (Ed.), *Clinical Management of Sexual Disorders*. Baltimore: Williams and Wilkins.

Miller, N. S., & Gold, M. S. (1988). The human sexual response and alcohol and drugs. *Journal of Substance Abuse Treatment, 5*, 171–177.

Mohr, D. C., & Beutler, L. E. (1990). Erectile Dysfunction: A review of diagnostic and treatment procedures. *Clinical Psychology Review, 10*, 123–150.

Monteiro, W. O., Noshivani, H. F., Marks, I. M., & Lelliott, P. T. (1987). Anorgasmia from clomipramine in obsessive-compulsive disorder: A controlled study. *British Journal of Psychiatry, 51*, 107–112.

Montosi, G., Strabi, L. Z. F., Guezzang, G., Gall, L., Barbieri, L., Rigatt, P., Pizini, G., & Mian, A. (1994).

Effect of yohimbine-trazodone on psychogenic impotence: A randomized, double-blind, placebo-controlled study. *Urology, 44*, 733–736.

Morales, A. (1989). Topical nitroglycerin: A potential treatment for impotence. *Journal of Urology, 141*, 546–648.

Morales, A., Heaton, J. W. P., & Condra, M. (1994). The pharmacology of impotence. In A. H. Bennett (Ed.), *Impotence. Diagnosis and management of erectile dysfunction* (pp. 145–155). Philadelphia: W. B. Saunders.

Morales, A., Surridge, D. H., & Marshall, P. G. (1987). Is yohimbine effect in the treatment of organic impotence? Results of a controlled trial. *Journal of Urology, 137*, 1168–1172.

Nathan, S. G. (1986). The epidemiology of the DSM-III psychosexual dysfunction. *Journal of Sex and Marital Therapy, 12*, 267–281.

Nemetz, G. H., Craig, K. D., & Reith, G. (1978). Treatment of female sexual dysfunction through symbolic modeling. *Journal of Consulting and Clinical Psychology, 46*, 62–73.

Obler, M. (1973). Systematic desensitization in sexual disorders. *Journal of Behavior Therapy and Experimental Psychiatry, 4*, 93–101.

O'Carroll, R. F., & Bancroft, J. (1984). Testosterone for low sexual desire and erectile dysfunction in men. *British Journal of Psychiatry, 145*, 146–151.

Owen, J. A., Saunders, F., Harris, C., Fenemore, J., Reid, J. Surridge, D., Condra, M., &

Padma-Nathan, H., Bennett, A., Gesundeit, N., Hellstrom, W., Henry, D., Lu, T., Moley, J.,

Palace, E. M. (1995). Modification of dysfunctional patterns of sexual response through autonomic arousal and false physiological feedback. *Journal of Consulting and Clinical Psychology, 63*, 604–615.

Palace, E. M., & Gorzalka, B. B. (1992). Differential patterns of arousal in sexually functional and dysfunctional women: Physiological and subjective components of sexual response. *Archives of Sexual Behavior, 21*, 135–159.

Perelman, M. (1980). Treatment of premature ejaculation. In S. R. Leiblum & L. A. Pervin (Eds.), *Principles and practice of sex therapy* (pp. 199–233). New York: Guilford Press.

Persky, H., Lief, H., & Strauss, D. (1978). Plasma testosterone level and sexual behavior in couples. *Archives of Sexual Behavior, 7*, 157–162.

Pescatori, E. S., Enhelman, J. C., Davis, G., & Goldstein, I. (1993). Priapism of the clitoris, *Journal of Urology, 149*, 1557–1559.

Peterson, C., Prendergast, J. P., Tam, P., Teresu, A., & Place, V. (1995). Treatment of erectile dysfunction by the medicated urethral system for erection (MUSE), *Proceedings of the American Urological Journal, 153*(Suppl. 472A).

Pierini, A. A., & Nusimovich, B. (1981). Male diabetic sexual impotence: Effect of dopaminergic agents. *Archives of Andrology, 6,* 347–350.

Purcell, P., & Ghuyre, R. (1995). Trazodone and spontaneous orgasm in an elderly postmenopausal women. *Journal of Clinical Psychopharmacology, 15,* 293–294.

Raboch, J., & Faltus, F. (1991). Sexuality of women with anorexia nervosa. *Acta Psychiatrica Scandinavica, 84,* 9–11.

Reid, K., Morales, A., Harris, C., Surridge, D. H. C., Condra, M., Owen, J., & Fenemore, J. (1987). Double-blind trial of yohimbine in the treatment of psychogenic impotence. *Lancet, 2,* 421–423.

Reynolds, B. (1991). Psychological treatment of erectile dysfunction in men without partners: Outcome results and a new direction. *Journal of Sex and Marital Therapy, 2,* 136–145.

Riley, A. J., Goodman, R. E., Kellet, J. M., & Orr, R. (1989). Double-blind trial of yohimbine hydrochloride in the treatment of erection inadequacy. *Sexual and Marital Therapy, 4,* 17–26.

Riley, A. J., & Riley, E. J. (1978). A controlled study to evaluate directed masturbation in the management of primary orgasmic failure in women. *British Journal of Psychiatry, 133,* 404–409.

———. (1988). The effect of single dose diazepam on female sexual response induced by masturbation. *Sexual and Marital Therapy, 1,* 49–53.

———. (1993). Pharmacotherapy for sexual dysfunction: Current status. In A. J. Riley, M. Peet, & C. Wilson (Eds.), *Sexual Pharmacology* (pp. 211–256). Oxford, U.K.: Clarendon Press.

Rosen, R. C. (1991). Alcohol and drug effects of sexual response: Human experiment and clinical studies. *Annual Review of Sex Research, 2,* 119–179.

Rosen, R. C., & Beck, J. G. (1988). *Patterns of sexual arousal: Psychophysiological processes and clinical applications.* New York: Guilford Press.

Rosen, K. C., & Kostis, J. B. (1991). *Sexual sequellae of antihypertensive drugs.* Paper presented at the 13th annual meeting of the Society of Behavioral Medicine, Washington, D.C.

Rosen, R. C., & Leiblum, S. R. (1989). Assessment and treatment of desire disorders. In R. C. Rosen & S. R. Leiblum (Eds.), *Principles and practice of sex therapy: Update for the 1990s* (pp. 1–18). New York: Guilford Press.

———. (1995). Treatment of sexual disorders in the 1990s: An integrated approach. *Journal of Clinical and Consulting Psychology, 63,* 877–890.

St. Lawrence, J., & Madakasira, S. (1992). Evaluation and treatment of premature ejaculation: A critical review. *International Journal of Psychiatry, 22,* 77–97.

Sala, M., Braida, D., Leone, M. P., Calcaterra, P., Monti, I., & Gor, E. (1990). Central effect of yohimbine on sexual behavior in the rat. *Physiology and Behavior, 47,* 166–173.

Sarosy, M. F., Hudnall, C. H., & Erikson, D. R. (1989). A prospective double-blind trial of intra corporeal papaverine versus prostaglandin$_{E1}$ in the treatment of impotence. *Journal of Urology, 141,* 551–553.

Sarrel, P., & Sarrel, L. (1989). Dyspareunia and vaginismus. In American Psychiatric Association Task Force on Treatments of Psychiatric Disorders (Ed.), *Treatment of psychiatric disorders,* Vol. 3 (pp. 2291–2298). Washington, D.C.: American Psychiatric Press.

Scharf, D. E. (1982). *The sexual relationship: An object relations view of the family.* London: Routledge, Kegan, Paul.

Scher, M., Krieger, J. N., & Juergensens, S. (1988). Trazodone and priapism. *American Journal of Psychiatry, 140,* 1362–1363.

Schiavi, R. C. (1990). Chronic alcoholism and male sexual function. *Journal of Sex and Marital Therapy, 16,* 23–33.

Schiavi, R. C., Stimmel, B. B., Mandeli, J., & White D. (1995). Chronic alcoholism and male sexual function. *American Journal of Psychiatry, 152,* 1045–1051.

Schmidt, C. W. (1995). Sexual psychopathology and DSM-IV. In J. M. Oldham & M. B. Riba (Eds.), *American Psychiatric Press review of psychiatry,* Vol. 14 (pp. 719–733). Washington, D.C.: American Psychiatric Press.

Schnellen, T. M. C. M. (1968). Introduction of ejaculation by electrovibration. *Fertility and Sterility, 19,* 566–569.

Scholl.

Schover, L. R., Youngs, D. D., & Canata, R. (1992). Psychosexual aspects of the evaluation and management of vulvar vestibulitis. *American Journal of Obstetrics and Gynecology, 167,* 630–638.

Schramek, P., Dorninger, R., & Waldhauser, M. (1990). Prostaglandin$_{E1}$ in erectile dysfunction. Efficacy and incidence of priapism. *British Journal of Urology, 65,* 68–71.

Schreiner-Engel, P., & Schiavi, R. C. (1986). Lifetime psychopathology in individuals with low sexual desire. *Journal of Nervous and Mental Disease, 174,* 646–651.

Segraves, R. T. (1978). Treatment of sexual dysfunction. *Comprehensive Therapy, 4,* 38–43.

———. (1988a). Drugs and sex. In S. R. Leiblum & R. C. Rosen (Eds.), *Sexual desire disorders* (pp. 313–347). New York: Guilford Press.

———. (1988b). Hormones and libido. In S. R. Leiblum & R. C. Rosen (Eds.), *Sexual desire disorders* (pp. 271–312). New York: Guilford Press.

———. (1989a). Effects of psychotropic drugs on human erection and ejaculation. *Archives of General Psychiatry, 46,* 275–284.

———. (1989b) Male erectile disorder. In American Psychiatric Association Task Force on Treatments of Psychiatric Disorders (Ed.), *Treatments of psychiatric disorders,* Vol. 3 (pp. 2218–2329). Washington, D.C.: American Psychiatric Press.

———. (1994). Pharmacological enhancement of human sexual behavior. *Journal of Sex Education and Therapy, 17,* 283–289.

———. (1995a). Antidepressant-induced orgasm disorder. *Journal of Sex and Marital Therapy, 21,* 192–201.

———. (1995b). Psychopharmacological influences on human sexual behavior. In J. M. Oldham & M. B. Riba (Eds.), *American Psychiatric Press review of psychiatry,* Vol. 14 (pp. 697–718). Washington, D.C.: American Psychiatric Press.

Segraves, R. T., Bari, M., Segraves, K. B., & Spirnak, P. (1991). Effect of apomorphine on penile tumescence in men with psychogenic impotence. *Journal of Urology, 145,* 1174–1175.

Segraves, R. T., Madsen, R., Carver, S. C., & Davis, J. M. (1985). Erectile dysfunction associated with pharmacological agents. In R. T. Segraves & H. W. Schoenberg (Ed.), *Diagnosis and treatment of erectile disturbances* (pp. 23–64). New York: Plenum.

Segraves, R. T., Saran, A., Segraves K., & Maguire, E. (1993). Clomipramine versus placebo in the treatment of premature ejaculation: A pilot study. *Journal of Sex and Marital Therapy, 19,* 198–200.

Segraves, R. T., & Segraves, K. B. (1990). Categorical and multi-axial diagnosis of male erectile disorder. *Journal of Sex and Marital Therapy, 16,* 208–213.

———. (1991a). Diagnosis of female arousal disorder. *Sex and Marital Therapy, 6,* 9–13.

———. (1991b). Hypoactive sexual desire disorder: Prevalence and comorbidity in 906 subjects. *Journal of Sex and Marital Therapy, 17,* 55–58.

———. (1991c). Multiple phase sexual dysfunction. *Journal of Sex Education and Therapy, 17,* 153–156.

———. (1993). Medical aspects of orgasm disorders, In W. O'Donohue & J. H. Geer (Eds.), *Handbook of sexual dysfunction: Assessment and treatment* (pp. 225–252). Boston: Allyn and Bacon.

———. (1995). Human sexuality and aging. *Journal of Sex Education and Therapy, 21,* 88–102.

Semans, J. H. (1956). Premature ejaculation: A new approach. *Southern Medical Journal, 49,* 353–357.

Sherwin, B. B., & Gelfand, M. M. (1987). The role of androgen in the maintenance of sexual functioning in oophorectomized women. *Psychosomatic Medicine, 49,* 397–409.

Siegel, R. K. (1982). Cocaine and sexual dysfunction. *Journal of Psychoactive Drugs, 14,* 71–74.

Snyder, S., & Karacan, I. (1981a). Disulfiram and nocturnal penile tumescence in the chronic alcoholic. *Biological Psychiatry, 16,* 399–406.

———. (1981b). Effects of chronic alcoholism on nocturnal penile tumescence. *Psychosomatic Medicine, 43,* 423–429.

Solstad, K., & Hertoft, P. (1993). Frequency of sexual problems and sexual dysfunction in middle-aged Danish men. *Archives of Sexual Behavior, 22,* 51–58.

Sondra, L. P., Mazo, R., & Chancelor, M. D. (1990). The role of yohimbine for the treatment of erectile impotence. *Journal of Sex and Marital Therapy, 16,* 15–21.

Spector, I. P., & Carey. (1990). Incidence and prevalence of the sexual dysfunction: A critical review of the literature. *Archives of Sexual Behavior, 9,* 389–408.

Spence, S. H. (1991). *Psychosexual therapy. A cognitive-behavioral approach.* London: Chapman and Hall.

Steers, W. D., McConnell, J., & Benson, G. S. (1984). Some pharmacological effects of yohimbine on human and rabbit penis. *Journal of Urology, 131,* 799–802.

Strassberg, D., Kelly, M., Carroll, C., & Kircher, J. (1987). The psychophysiological nature of premature ejaculation. *Archives of Sexual Behavior, 16,* 327–336.

Sussett, J. G., Tessier, C. D., Wincze, J., Banal, S., Malhtra, C., & Schwaba, M. G. (1989). Effect of yohimbine hydrochloride on erectile impotence: A double-blind study. *Journal of Urology, 141,* 1360–1363.

Tan, E. T. H., Johnson, R. A., Lambie, D. G., Vijayasenah, M. E., & Whiteside, E. A. (1984). Erectile impotence in chronic alcoholics. *Alcoholism: Clinical and Experimental Research, 8,* 297–301.

Tennett, G., Bancroft, J., & Cass, J. (1972). The control of deviant sexual behavior by drugs: A double-blind controlled study of benperidol, chlorpromazine and placebo. *Archives of Sexual Behavior, 3,* 216–271.

Thase, M. E., Reynolds, C. F., Jennings, R., Frank, E., Howell, J. R., Houch, P. R., Berman, S., & Kupfer, D. J. (1988). Nocturnal penile tumescence is diminished in depressed men. *Biological Psychiatry, 24,* 33–46.

Tiefer, L. (1995). *Sex is not a natural act and other essays.* Boulder, Colo.: Westview Press.

Turner, L., Althof, S., Levine, S., Bodner, D., Kursh, E., & Resnick, M. (1991). Long term use of vacuum pump devices in the treatment of erectile dysfunction. *Journal of Sex & Marital Therapy, 17*(2), 81–93.

————. (1992). A 12-month comparison of the effectiveness of two treatments for erectile dysfunction: Self-injection versus external vacuum devices. *Urology, 39,* 139–144.

Turner, L., Althof, S., Levine, S., Risen, C., Bodner, D., Kursh, E., & Resnick, M. (1989). Self injection of papaverine and phentolamine in the treatment of psychogenic impotence. *Journal of Sex & Marital Therapy, 15,* 163–176.

Virag, R. (1982). Intracavernous injection of papaverine for erectile failure. *Lancet, 2,* 935.

Virag, R., Frydman, D., Legman, M., & Virag, H. (1984). Intracavernous injection of papaverine as a diagnostic and therapeutic method in erectile failure. *Angiology, 35,* 79–87.

Waldinger, M. D., Heneveld, M. Z., & Zwenderman, A. H. (1994). Paroxetine treatment of premature ejaculation: A double-blind, randomized, placebo controlled study. *American Journal of Psychiatry, 151,* 1377–1379.

Waxenberg, S. E., Drellich, M. G., & Sutherland, A. M. (1959). The role of androgens in human behavior. Changes in female sexuality after adrenalectomy. *Journal of Clinical Endocrinology and Metabolism, 19,* 193–197.

Weiss, J. N., Ravalli, R., & Badlani, I. (1991). Intracavernous pharmacotherapy in psychogenic impotence. *Urology, 37,* 441–443.

Welling, M., Anderson, B. I., & Johnson, S. R. (1990). Hormonal replacement therapy for post menopausal women: A review of sexual outcomes and related gynecological effects. *Archives of Sexual Behavior, 19,* 119–137.

Whalley, L. J. (1978). Sexual adjustment of alcoholics. *Acta Psychiatrica Scandinavica, 58,* 281–298.

Whitehead, A., & Mathews, A. (1986). Factors related to successful outcome in the treatment of sexually unresponsive women. *Psychological Medicine, 16,* 373–378.

Wilson, C. A. (1993). Pharmacological targets for the control of male and female sexual behavior. In A. J. Riley, M. Peet, & C. Wilson (Ed.), *Sexual pharmacology* (pp. 1–58). Oxford, U.K.: Clarendon Press.

Wolpe, J. (1958). *Psychotherapy by reciprocal inhibition.* Stanford, Ca.: Stanford University Press.

Wright, J., Perreault, R., & Mathieu, M. (1977). The treatment of sexual dysfunction. *Archives of General Psychiatry, 34,* 881–890.

Zilbergeld, B. (1992). *The new male sexuality.* New York: Bantam Books.

Zilbergeld, B., & Evans, M. (1980). The inadequacy of Masters and Johnson. *Psychology Today,* 29–34.

24

The Paraphilias:
Research and Treatment

Barry M. Maletzky

The literature on paraphilias has been focused chiefly on theoretical, etiologic, and epidemiologic concerns rather than on issues of treatment. However, a trend toward treatment outcome studies is emerging. At present, there is a consensus that cognitive-behavioral therapies form the standard against which other approaches must be judged. Behavior therapies include various forms of aversive conditioning, social skills training, biofeedback, and sexual impulse control training, among others. Cognitive approaches include restructuring cognitive distortions, relapse prevention, and empathy training. Somatic treatments have also been reported, including the administration of medroxyprogesterone acetate (MPA) and cyproterone acetate (CPA). Both reduce circulating testosterone. Unfortunately, large outcome evaluations of any of these treatments are still lacking.

It is an irony of semantics that those disorders we call the paraphilias are most often loveless. One can sense that as much from the rhetoric of the *Diagnostic and Statistical Manual of Mental Disorders*, fourth edition (*DSM-IV*; American Psychiatric Association [APA], 1994) as from the decades of observation, treatment, and research and the countless clinical hours spent helping patients with these disorders. This chapter attempts to summarize our understanding of the nature and treatment of this diverse cluster of disorders, but, in doing so, it is recognized that far more detail will reward the inquisitive reader who consults sources in the reference list.

DEFINITIONS

Among all sexual disorders addressed in *DSM-IV*, just one subsection comprises the paraphilias. Proximate disorders, such as those of lowered sexual arousal; sexual aversions; orgasmic, erectile, and ejaculatory disorders; sexual pain disorders; and gender identity disorders are left to other authors. Typical paraphilias are listed in Table 24.1 along with their *DSM-IV* criteria, much condensed. The present scheme does not claim to be anything but one in a series of evolving concepts about these disorders that will undoubtedly be altered repeatedly in the future.

One overriding phenomenon of taxonomy seems particularly critical in classifying paraphilias: the sensitivity of human sexual response to the chances of environmental conditioning. Our sexual behavior is assuredly idiosyncratic, often unpredictable and resistant to classification schemes. In general, however, *DSM-IV* makes the reasonable demand that paraphilias conform to several fundamental criteria:

1. That they are characterized by recurrent, intense, sexually arousing fantasies, urges, or behaviors involving *inappropriate* objects.

TABLE 24.1 *DSM-IV* Paraphilias and Their Criteria

These must be of at least 6 months' duration, cause significant distress or impair social, occupational, or other important functions, and produce recurrent sexually arousing fantasies, urges, or behaviors involving

1. Nonhuman objects
2. Suffering or humiliation of oneself or one's partner
3. Children or other nonconsenting individuals

Exhibitionism 302.4
Fantasies, urges, or behaviors involving the exposure of one's genitals to a stranger.

Fetishism 302.81
Fantasies, urges, or behaviors involving the use of objects, not limited to articles of female clothing, used in cross-dressing (as in transvestic fetishism) or devices designed for genital stimulation (for example, a vibrator).

Frotteurism 302.89
Fantasies, urges, or behaviors involving touching or rubbing against a nonconsenting person.

Pedophilia 302.2
Fantasies, urges, or behaviors involving sexual activity with a prepubescent child by a person at least 16 years old and at least 5 years older.

Sexual masochism 302.83
Fantasies, urges, or behaviors involving the act of being humiliated, beaten, bound, or otherwise made to suffer.

Sexual sadism 302.84
Fantasies, urges, or behaviors involving acts in which the suffering of a victim is sexually exciting.

Transvestic fetishism 302.3
Fantasies, urges, or behaviors in a heterosexual male involving cross-dressing.

Voyeurism 302.82
Fantasies, urges, or behaviors involving observing unsuspecting persons who are nude, disrobing, or in sexual activity.

Sexual dysfunction not otherwise specified 302.70
Sexual dysfunctions that do not meet the above criteria.

Source: From American Psychiatric Association *Diagnostic and Statistical Manual of Mental Disorders* (4th ed.), American Psychiatric Association, Washington, D.C., 1994.

2. That they be of greater than 6 months' duration.
3. That they cause clinically significant distress or impair day-to-day function.

Such paraphilias commonly include exhibitionism, frottage, the pedophilias, sadomasochism, transvestic fetishism, and voyeurism. However, several rather common paraphilias are relegated to the category "paraphilias, not otherwise specified." No explanation is offered for this classification, which can include telephone scatologia and bestiality. A more serious problem occurs when an individual has combinations of these paraphilias, a not uncommon clinical presentation. Exhibitionism, voyeurism, and telephone scatology are more often combined than not (Freund & Watson, 1980); other combinations, such as heterosexual and homosexual pedophilia, are also not uncommon (Maletzky, 1991a, chap. 10). Most obvious by its absence is any mention of hebephilia: Many homosexual and heterosexual pedophiles prefer sexual activity with teenagers.

Even more serious problems occur in clinical practice inasmuch as most sexual offenders[1] do not readily admit all their deviant behavior (Abel et al., 1987). Such patients cannot be readily compared for epidemiologic purposes to patients with other psychiatric disorders that are more commonly ego dystonic. There are very few more damaging evils to admit than molesting a child or raping a woman. The best data available prompt the conclusion that treatment providers may never know the full extent of an offender's fantasies and actual deviant behaviors. Treatment in such cases is equivalent to treating major depressive disorder by guessing about thoughts, feelings, and even behaviors particular to that patient.

The *DSM-IV* implies that the paraphilic is often impaired in appropriate sexual and social activities. It is not unusual, however, to encounter a pedophile who, in most regards, is unimpaired in any other way, especially if his deviant behavior goes undetected. As another example, a man who rapes may use aggression in the service of sexual access but may not be aroused by it. There is often no impairment of appropriate reciprocal and affectionate relationships with adults, and, despite implications in *DSM-IV*, paraphilics most often do not have personality disorders (Marshall & Hall, 1995). The *DSM-IV* is in accord, however, with evidence that sexually abnormal behavior due to another disease process should not be included.

The largest proportion, between 55% and 90%, of offenders comprising most clinical outpatient samples is composed of situational pedophiles (Maletzky & Steinhauser, in press). Other classifications make a distinction between *incestuous* and *nonincestuous* offenders. Equally nonspecific and confusing are references to *child molesters*. More recently, the terms *paraphilic* (primarily attracted to deviant stimuli) and *nonparaphilic* (primarily attracted to adults) have appeared. Other artificial schemes have attempted to distinguish age differences between perpetrator and victim (over 16 years of age, 5 years' difference, etc.), which leaves unresolved the problem of adolescent offenders. Within this chaotic sea, the only safe harbor may lie in distinguishing between *situational* and *predatory* offenders. A situational offender is one who would not have offended had an enticing situation not arose. The term *predatory* refers to a behavioral pattern, whereas *preferential* implies a knowledge of motives (often hidden), while *paraphilic* implies a knowledge of arousal patterns, not always easily gleaned. Predatory behavior, more dangerous and treatment resistant (Maletzky, 1993), includes an active search for potential victims in the community, grooming victims (buying gifts, dating), offending against multiple victims, and, in many cases, preferring deviant sexual activity to normal sexual outlets. Table 24.2 highlights the distinctions among situational, preferential, and predatory offenders. It is the combination of preferential and predatory traits that characterizes the most dangerous sexual offenders.

EPIDEMIOLOGY

Since sexual offenders rarely report their crimes to authorities, data on incidence and prevalence lie mostly hidden in the offenders' memories and, unfortunately, in the memories of their victims. What data are available, however, indicate that reported sexual crimes are increasing. The figures continue to astonish: between 30% and 70% of college-age females have been victimized in some fashion (Russell, 1988). The majority of victims experience hands-on contact before the age of 16 (Wyatt, 1985); 50% of women report being victims of exhibitionism (Zverina, Lachman, Pondelickova, & Vanek, 1987). Of even more startling impact, 44% to 55% of college males say they would use force against a woman to obtain sexual gratification if they were guaranteed no consequences (Malamuth, Haber, & Feshbach, 1980).

We have insufficient data to identify exact prevalence rates in population samples. Our guesses stem largely from identified offenders. However, many researchers believe that over 90% of paraphilic acts go undetected, even for the closely scrutinized pedophilias (as reviewed in MacKinnon, 1985). If the modest figure of female molestation before the age of 18 is taken as 30%, and if there are four times the number of adults as children in North America, then approximately 5% of men have molested young girls, a finding depressingly similar to estimates derived through other means: A recent nationwide survey estimated that between 4% and 17% of males had molested children of one or both genders (Herman, 1980).

MODELS OF ETIOLOGY

Compared with the absence of data on the epidemiology of the paraphilias, there is a wealth of literature describing a variety of overlapping yet well-articulated theories of etiology, although most are difficult to test empirically. A review of these conceptual domains provides a background for understanding how treatment paradigms have evolved from the different ways of explaining the causes of these disorders.

Behavioral Learning Models

Some of the earliest and most influential studies of the paraphilias stressed the primacy of early conditioning in the development of sexual deviations (e.g., Kinsey, Pomeroy, & Martin, 1948; McGuire, Carlisle, & Young, 1965; VanWyk & Geist, 1984). These efforts created laboratory equivalents of the acquisition and maintenance of sexual behavior. From these studies, a number of general principles emerged:

1. Unconditioned stimuli can elicit sexual arousal and release (orgasm).

TABLE 24.2 Distinctions Among Situational, Preferential, and Predatory Pedophiles

Situational Pedophile	Preferential Pedophile	Predatory Pedophile
Living with victim	Not living with victim or, if living with victim, having at least one other victim in the community	Not living with victim
Well known to victim	May be well known to some victims	Not well known to at least some victims
Single victim	Usually multiple victims	Multiple victims
Single pedophilia, usually heterosexual	Single pedophilia, either hetero- or homosexual	Single or double pedophilia, hetero- or homosexual
Frequently married or living with a woman	May be married or living with a woman	Often not married or living with a woman

Note: These categories are not mutually exclusive.

2. Conditioned stimuli can become associated with unconditioned stimuli so they can also, eventually and with repeated pairings, produce sexual arousal and release.
3. Such sexual conditioning is robust given the physiological power of sexual release.
4. Actions increasing the probability of sexual release are highly reinforced and thus are likely to occur in the future.
5. Human sexual behavior consists of ordered sequences in a chain of behavior leading to sexual release.
6. Actions leading to aversive consequences, such as interruption of this chain, will be reduced in frequency.
7. Humans can become aroused through stimulus generalization to objects close to, but not the same as, those initially arousing.

In behavioral models, the offender is assumed to exhibit sexual arousal to deviant stimuli. While this is often true, over 30% of admitting offenders show no deviant arousal on plethysmograph tests (Maletzky, 1991a, chap. 10). However, the artificial circumstances of the plethysmograph may be blamed for its lack of sensitivity and its high rate of false negatives. One difficulty in analyzing these data stems from the inclusion of undetected offenders in "normal" comparison groups.

The behavioral model has been only partly displaced as newer theories have emerged to explain paraphilias. People's own sexual experiences and the manner in which behavioral principles have been able to predict outcomes (Maletzky, 1993) have kept alive the suspicion that life's experiences, particularly in childhood, somehow have influenced our own sexual preferences and behaviors.

Critical Stages Model

One way in which behavioral models have been augmented is through the addition of research about purported sensitivities in central nervous system development (Leitenberg, Greenwald, & Tarran, 1989). Children may go through critical stages of growth in which, during crucial intervals, various aspects of sexuality develop. Situations occurring before or after those periods (as yet not clearly defined) are weaker in influencing the development of sexual preferences. For example, a young boy caught in the act of undressing by a female relative may later in life obtain some sexual satisfaction in exposing his genitals to women. Unfortunately, no objective verification of critical stages has as yet been made.

Social Learning Models

More prevalent today, and perhaps more politically acceptable, social learning models include the culture in which offenders live as an important factor in increasing the likelihood of offending. Early studies (as reviewed in Stermac, Segal, & Gillis, 1990) pointed toward family background and the influence of behavioral modeling in shaping future sexual activity. More recent work has suggested that the lack of parental care, physical punishment, and frequent or aggressive sexual activity within the family may all predispose children to begin sexual offending in late childhood or adolescence and to use aggression to obtain gratification, to show impairment of social inhibitions against the use of force, and to act impulsively regardless of long-term consequences (Ward, Hudson, Marshall, & Siegert, 1995).

A number of recent surveys appear to lend credence to this model. Factors such as self-esteem (Marshall & Mazzucco, 1995), capacity for affection and empathy (Marshall & Barbaree, 1984), and ability to postpone gratification (Seidman, Marshall, Hudson, & Robertson, 1994) are reduced in some offender samples compared to nonoffender populations and even to nonsexual offenders. Marshall and Barbaree (1990a) have developed this model to its current position of prominence in the North American literature. In summary, they postulate that a deficiency in forming attachment bonds in childhood leads to low self-esteem and a lack of intimacy in adult relationships.

Proponents of social learning models have relied on the anthropological and sociological literature (e.g., Gibbens & Ahrenfeldt, 1966; Quinsey, 1984), which suggests that societies with high rates of aggressive sexual behavior show high rates of nonsexual violence, greater male dominance, and a negative attitude toward women. There has also been a greater acceptance of rape myths in societies in which sexual aggression has been prominent (Burt, 1980; Sanday, 1981; Tieger, 1981).

However, not all evidence supports these theories. Studies controlling for sexual, as well as nonsexual, violence find no causative specific sexual element (as reviewed in McConaghy, 1993, pp. 286–290). Confounding factors of family socioeconomic class, genetic heritage, availability of pornography, and influence of peers have not been adequately controlled. While there is no doubt that social and cultural factors partially influence adult sexual choice, there is as yet no comprehensive proposal of mechanisms leading inalterably from a troubled background to a lifetime of deviant sexual behavior.

Compensation Theories

Following closely on social learning models, many early workers proposed a theory, commonly embraced by many nonspecialists as well, in which an offender, deprived of normal social and sexual contacts, compensates by seeking gratification through deviant means (Groth, 1979). While attractive on common-sense grounds, studies providing an empirical basis for this

theory have not been forthcoming. Most pedophiles enjoy normal sexual relationships with adult female partners, as do many men who rape and those who expose (Marshall & Barbaree, 1990a). Work accomplished over the past decade fails to confirm this theory (Langevin & Lang, 1987) and leaves unexplained the presence in most exhibitionists of adequate social and sexual outlets (Maletzky, in press-a).

A Feminist Perspective

In its radical form, the feminist perspective model of sexual offending considers all men to be potential sexual aggressors. According to this perspective, rape, most certainly, and other sexual crimes, more probably, are driven by men's wishes to dominate women and, by extension, children as well (as reported in Herman, 1980). Proponents of these views believe that sexual crimes may not be sexually driven but may represent latent aggressive impulses that many men harbor toward women. One benefit of these notions has been the increasing awareness of sexual offending itself and the need for public education about its harmful effects.

However, extreme positions can convey an advantage to contrary views: Backlash to the victims' movement has been reported (Finkelhor, 1994). Sober reflection on the available data leads to conclusions that counter the belief that sexual offending is nonsexual in nature:

1. Virtually all sexual offenders in treatment report being sexually aroused by fantasies of their deviant activities and using these fantasies in masturbation.
2. Nonoffenders may share with sexual offenders an apparently endogenous predilection toward aggression and sexuality (as reviewed in McConaghy, 1993, pp. 343–346). Nonoffenders may differ only in keeping it more successfully hidden.
3. Most offenders display a single deviant behavioral pattern. The feminist model should lead to the finding of a broad range of sexual deviations within each patient.
4. Male sexual offenders display marked reductions in sexual arousal when their testosterone levels are artificially reduced with hormone therapy (Maletzky, 1991a).
5. Many men who rape are sexually aroused by the aggressive elements of sexuality. However, they are also aroused by normal sexual stimuli.

Only a handful of men who rape are aroused by aggression in the absence of sexual cues (Abel, Barlow, Blanchard, & Guild, 1977).

6. A number of more recent studies show no strong correlation between attitude and hostility in males and propensity to act in a sexually aggressive manner (as reviewed in Stermac et al., 1990).

Addiction Models

Often, the behavior of sexual offenders appears compulsive in nature. The addiction model, as summarized in Herman (1980), equates offenders with alcohol and drug addicts. Deviant sexual activity in this model acts as a drug substitute in filling some (unspecified) need that can be determined in therapy. Like other addicts, some offenders come from stormy backgrounds, manipulate relationships for their own advantage, and do not learn from prior negative consequences. The analogy is internally consistent, and a popular feature in discussions of sexual abuse in the media (Carnes, 1983).

However, like other common-sense notions of causative factors, addiction models have not received empirical support. Sexual offenders are noticeable more for their normality than for their deviancy. No single personality factor, based either on psychological testing or interviewing technique, is pathognomonic of sexual offending (Langevin & Lang, 1987; Maletzky, 1991a, chap. 10; Marshall & Hall, 1995). Unfortunately, offenders do not respond to 12-step programs as alcoholics do, and their deviations are much more responsive to cognitive and behavioral treatment approaches than are more standard addictions (Maletzky, 1991a, chap. 10).

The Offender as Victim

The harm of sexual abuse is most clearly reflected in the faces of its victims. Many believe that among these lurk future offenders bound to commit further abuse because they themselves were victimized. The predominant theme in this model suggests that offenders are revisiting and reliving their earlier traumas, perhaps to gain a greater measure of control over their fractured world (Groth, 1979). Others propose identification with the aggressor as a mechanism by which offenders can gain control (Justice & Justice, 1979). More recent studies have documented differences in offenders who were or were not victims as children

themselves (Dhawan & Marshall, 1996). However, the majority of retrospective, prospective, and well-controlled comparisons find that fewer than 30% of offenders were victims of sexual abuse before the age of 18 (Abel et al., 1987; Maletzky, 1993). It is unlikely the remaining 70% could not remember the abuse. The finding that these figures do not vary as a consequence of the type of offense is surprising. An exhibitionist is as likely to have been a victim as a rapist or pedophile.

Physiological Models

The Role of Sexual Hormones

Because many sexual offenders combine elements of aggression with sexual behavior, a search for a relationship between aggression and male sexual hormones has interested many researchers. A number of studies have revealed little difference in circulating testosterone among sexual offenders and both nonsexual offenders and nonoffenders (as reviewed in Hucker & Bain, 1990). Such studies, however, have typically included small numbers of subjects and been poorly controlled. Despite decades of interest, no replicated differences of hormone levels have yet been found between sexual offenders and nonsexual offenders. It remains possible that in utero hormonal levels may contribute to the nature and intensity of sexual drive later in life, but interest in this area is just awakening.

Central Nervous System Damage

Brain damage has been associated with changes in sexual behavior, typically in the expression of anomalous sexual responses previously unknown or suppressed. Studies in primates have demonstrated a possible uncovering of latent sexual aggression with destruction of portions of the temporal lobe (Kluver & Bucy, 1939) or stimulation of diencephalic structures (MacLean, 1973). Some authors have reported findings of central nervous system (CNS) damage in sexual offenders, although often these abnormalities were minor in extent (Flor-Henry & Lang, 1988). More recent and extensive testing, including the Halstead-Reitan Battery, has revealed no statistically significant differences when adequate controls were included (Langevin et al., 1985).

While clinicians have expressed the hope that modern techniques of neuroimaging will reveal subtle abnormalities in the brain structures of offenders, there are few studies addressing this issue. Of the new imaging techniques, only results of computerized tomography (CT) scanning have been reported thus far. These results revealed no structural changes in the majority of offenders (Langevin et al., 1985). Of interest, however, is a preliminary impression that single photon emission computed tomography (SPECT) (and perhaps positron-emission tomography [PET]) scans can show altered limbic activity when a subject is sexually aroused (Richard D. Watson, personal communication, January 12, 1995). Should costs be more readily controlled, further exploration of this intriguing impression is warranted. The common clinical opinion that CNS damage destroys control mechanisms that result in disinhibition and subsequent offending begs for further study.

Genetic Factors

Few studies have examined the possible role of genetic factors predisposing to abuse. However, chromosomal abnormalities have been implicated in the etiology of atypical sexual behaviors (Schiavi, Thielgaard, Owen, & White, 1988) and in those with gender dysphoria disorders (Money & Pollitt, 1964). The lack of any published research investigating the genetic heritage of sexual offending in the face of such ample research for other *DSM-IV* categories underscores not only the present bias against biological contributions, but the relative lack of medical researchers in this field.

Sociobiological Models

In human societies, incest is more likely with weak familial bonds and most likely with no such bond (Erickson, 1993). Among all cases of adult-child sexual contact, the overwhelming majority (between 70% and 90%) occur between males and young females whom these males did not raise from infancy (Maletzky, 1991a, chap. 10, 1993).

In addition, sexual "offending" is known among nonhuman primates, our closest living relatives (see Griffen & Cherfas, 1983, for a review). Examples of pedophilia, exhibitionism, and rape have been reported in many species (Maletzky, in press-b). When male gorillas are thwarted in attempts to mount an adult female, they will occasionally turn their attentions to an adolescent female. More often than not, female relatives of the adolescent drive off the sulking perpetrator. Quite commonly, a male chimpanzee will expose his erect penis as one of the initiating behaviors that culminate in coitus. Occasionally, female gorillas will be unsuccessful in warding off the sexual advances of powerful males who will grasp and forcefully hold them during intercourse.

A number of authors have speculated about evolutionary mechanisms gone awry as an explanation for sexual abuse (Quinsey & Lalumiere, 1995), while others have warned against this trend as overly facile, with more cachet than substance (Krause, 1994). Although we are probably well warned to not always see, in the pool of complex human behavior, the reflections of an ape, sociobiological models are important because they open a previously neglected area of thinking about sexual abuse. For example, most male nonhuman primates display erections before attempting to mount a female. Exhibitionism is the most commonly encountered human paraphilia. Primate juveniles may become attractive to some adults due to stimulus generalization and accessibility. While pedophilia is rare among apes, it is seen in nondominant males that lose females to competitors. Sexual aggression is common in apes, although it is not commonly successful. These observations suggest that the forerunners of misaligned passions may reside in phylogenetic templates for aggression in the service of sexual access.

ASSESSMENT

No single instrument, psychological, social, or physiological, has been proven to be definitive in the assessment of the sexual offender. Thus, combinations of techniques have become essential in distinguishing an offender's patterns that merit clinical concern. Problems in assessment have arisen because of the private nature of sexual activity, the hesitation some therapists show in inquiring about sex, and the sexual offender's frequent reluctance to divulge crucial information. In the treatment of depression, bipolar disorder, obsessive compulsive disorder (OCD), phobias, and the like, therapists and patients combine forces to defeat the identified symptoms because these arouse painful affects. However, a sexual offender may have reservations about full disclosure, in part due to legal consequences and in part due to ego preservation. Many offenders, even when presented with irrefutable evidence that they committed deviant acts, still cannot accept responsibility. Indeed, overcoming denial is believed by most therapists to be a crucial step in effective treatment.

More common than outright denial is minimization, by which offenders may claim no memory of events due to drug or alcohol abuse or camouflage the sexual intent of their actions, as, for example, by claiming sexual molestation was motivated by educational goals ("I was teaching her about sex") or that it occurred by accident ("my hand slipped"). Assessment techniques have thus aimed not only to recover information from reports by patients themselves, but from significant others, police reports, presentence investigations, and psychological and physiological measures in attempts to comprehend the breadth and variety of deviant sexual motivations and behaviors.

Part of any outpatient assessment is the determination of risk for the patient to be at large. Risk assessment has occupied a subindustry of evaluators concerned with the prevention of further harm to victims in the community. One large retrospective study (Maletzky, 1993) identified clusters of risk factors related to victim, offender, and offense characteristics and plethysmographic findings. A more recent effort (Proulx, Pellerin, Paradis, McKibben, & Aubut, in press) examined recidivism rates for offenders treated in a secure prison hospital facility. Both reports relied on quantitative analysis rather than clinical impression, and both agreed with suggestions in the literature and from general clinical experience that predatory, aggressive behavior in individuals with histories of unstable employment and relationships predicts heightened risk. Table 24.3 lists factors indicating the risk to be at large within the community. It is unfortunately not

TABLE 24.3 Risk Factors To Be at Large Within the Community

Multiple victims

Multiple paraphilias

Offender not living with the victim(s)

Offender not well known to the victim(s)

Predatory pattern such as victim search and grooming

Aggression used in the commission of the act(s)

Denial or marked minimization of the act(s)

Reluctance to enter treatment

Unstable employment history

Unstable history of relationships

uncommon to encounter many patients meeting these criteria who are released from institutions due to crowding and the perception that some offenders represent more of a nuisance than a risk.

While the determination of whether an individual has offended appears straightforward, diagnostic assessment does not end at that point. The clinician will need to determine the duration and extent of offending, against whom it has occurred, how the crime has been perpetrated, what meaning it may have for the offender, and, of even greater practical significance, how the offender might best be treated. The steps of comprehensive assessment form the foundation on which a treatment plan is then based.

Review of Materials

Every effort must be made to obtain information about the offender before the first interview. Materials often available include police reports, a presentence investigation, psychological and psychiatric evaluations, psychological testing, child protection agency reports, depositions, and any testimony recorded. As offenders often distort information about their sexual activities, reviewing these documents is an essential element in assessment. Records of the present offense are crucial, but information about any prior sexual or nonsexual crimes is also relevant. Of particular interest are histories of any drug or alcohol use and any prior psychiatric treatment.

The Clinical Interview

Clinicians are uncommonly skilled in eliciting information from patients, yet the simple values of clinical history taking and mental status evaluations are often underestimated. These skills are put to a challenge in obtaining histories from sexual offenders, not the most therapist friendly of clients. Frequently, early sessions are reserved for trust building and reflection rather than for insightful history taking. It often can take 5 to 10 nonconfrontive sessions before patients in either individual or group therapy feel comfortable sharing the sexual details of their offenses.

Although structured clinical interviews of psychiatric patients have appeared in the literature, none have focused on the sexual offender. Most clinicians favor unstructured interviews to elicit as much information as possible while enhancing the therapist-patient relationship. While information may be gained at various times during interviews, it should be organized into a concise, yet comprehensive, report.

In many cases, 2 or 3 hours of interviewing, perhaps separated into several sessions, should prove sufficient to gain and report an understanding of the offender's problem areas, sexual or nonsexual, and some indication of early treatment goals. Offenders come to these sessions at their lowest point, often defensive, isolated, and angry, with self-reproach and fears of financial loss. They deserve, and will appreciate, the therapist's support.

As part of a clinical interview, the mental status examination can be helpful as the therapist's organized report of behavioral observations. Particularly noteworthy in the examination of sexual offenders are issues of awareness and orientation, understanding and empathy toward the victim, acceptance of responsibility, and any signs of a psychiatric illness predisposing the offender to act impulsively or without consideration of others' emotions. Particularly, the clinician needs to know if the offender is aware that the behavior was wrong and why. Are there faulty assumptions and distortions? What does the offender think and feel about treatment? At this point, the therapist will gain more from nonjudgmental prompts than from vigorous probes.

Self-Reports

Aside from obtaining a history of the present offenses, the therapist can ask the patient to keep a record of covert deviant acts, such as sexual urges, fantasies, and dreams, and of actual deviant behavior, such as molesting or masturbating to fantasies of deviant sexual activity. Are these reports of any value, however, given the offender's predisposition to misreport data based on self-interest? An exhaustive review under strictly confidential conditions (Abel et al., 1987) revealed that authorities and therapists will learn about only a small percentage of the sexual crimes that these men have committed. In the present state of knowledge, it is best to collect such data and regard it with a critical eye.

Psychological Tests

Despite frequent attempts, both historical (Gebhard, Gargon, Pomeroy, & Christenson, 1965) and modern day (Schlank, 1995), to typify sexual offenders by results on standard and specialized psychological assess-

ment tools, no single instrument or combination of instruments has yielded a clearly defined set of characteristic responses for this group or for any subgroups within it. As a corollary, an evaluator is not yet justified in predicting the probability of future acts based on any combination of tests alone. The lack of strong correlations among test results, diagnoses, and prediction of treatment response may stem from a heterogeneity among sexual offenders in general.

A novel assessment technique, including a variety of noninvasive methods such as card sorts, ratings of interest in computer-driven slides of deviant sexual activity, and measurements of reaction times (without the client's awareness), has recently been described (Osborn, Abel, & Warberg, 1995) but will require further empirical assessment to determine validity and reliability when compared to the plethysmograph, described below. Summarizing a thorough review of the utility of psychological testing for sexual offenders, Marshall and Hall (1995) conclude that such instruments "however they are scored or represented, do not satisfactorily distinguish any type of sexual offender from various other groups of subjects, including, most particularly, nonoffenders" (pp. 216–217).

Corroborating Information

Since sexual offenders often distort information, a therapist would do well to seek the observations of partners, parents, and friends even though some of these individuals may be swayed by their own loyalties. It is vital to include a corrections official, usually a probation or parole officer, in observations and recommendations about treatment as well as dispositional planning as this officer plays a key role in many offenders' lives. Including the official in treatment decisions reduces manipulation and ensures more complete disclosure of pertinent facts to all interested parties. In addition, scrutiny of updated police files can be helpful, although not definitive, in determining whether an offender, during or following treatment, has reoffended. Since such records are open to the public, confidentiality has generally not been an issue.

Physiological Assessment

The Penile Plethysmograph

The most widely used measure of sexual preference, the penile plethysmograph has an extensive and varied history in its application to sexual offenders. Originally employed to test impotence, this device has become a standard for the assessment of the sexual offender. The first devices measured penile volume changes (Freund, 1963), but penile circumference is now preferred because the methodology is available, the technique feasible, its reliability reasonable (Proulx, 1989), and its validity now demonstrated (Quinsey & Laws, 1990).

Technical details in the application of the plethysmograph point toward a practitioner consensus, now codified in guidelines for its use in assessment and treatment of the sexual offender (Association for the Treatment of Sexual Abusers [ATSA], 1993). Briefly, in the standard technique, a mercury-in-rubber strain gauge, thin as a rubber band (but loose, not tight), is placed by the patient, in private, onto the midshaft of his penis, which can remain covered by clothing. He is next asked to view explicit material, such as slides, movies, and videotapes of deviant and normal sexuality, to listen to tapes describing such activity, and to create his own descriptions of sexual activity as well. Penile circumference changes are recorded, usually in terms of percentage of previously determined full erection, throughout this process. Changes less than 20% of full erection are considered too minor to be of clinical import. Testing can consume several hours.

Such testing is now the standard by which other assessment techniques are judged. Of constant surprise is the fact that, under such artificial laboratory conditions and under pressure to appear normal, a majority of offenders demonstrate deviant sexual arousal. Studies vouchsafing validity, reliability, and clinical relevance have appeared over the past two decades (as reviewed in Howes, 1995). To date, penile tumescence changes have been associated with sexual offending in predicted directions. Child molesters, for example, show increases in circumference in reaction to stimuli depicting sexual scenes involving children, and rapists generally show increased arousal to aggressive scenes of sexual activity.

However, limitations with circumference changes have become increasingly obvious:

1. Just over 30% of pedophiles and incest offenders show either normal plethysmographs or a "flat line," that is, no response to any stimulus. These figures jump to over 40% of rapists and exhibitionists, perhaps indicating greater heterogeneity in these populations (Maletzky, 1991a, chap. 2).

2. Cheating is possible and probably is the case with many offenders:
   a. An offender might not pay attention to the stimulus, but this can be prevented by a detection task, such as requiring the patient to report a randomly presented signal in part of the stimulus display or requiring the patient to describe what he sees.
   b. Cheating could also occur through cognitive control, such as engaging in a competing, nonsexual mental task. When instructed to produce this result, subjects have been shown to affect arousal. To combat this, some clinicians first present sexual stimuli to generate erections, then present deviant stimuli. It is generally more difficult for an offender to lose an erection than to block its occurrence.

3. Studies purporting to demonstrate validity and reliability often include a small number of subjects. Much larger populations should be studied, but in reality such research would be labor intensive and expensive. In an age of funding cutbacks, such research is unlikely in the near future.

4. The plethysmograph is insufficiently standardized. Different stimuli are used in different laboratories. Exposure times vary, as do numbers and types of stimuli used; different measures of sexual arousal are used as well. Most centers report data in terms of percentage of full erection, but other clinicians use actual millimeters of circumference change. It is as if electrocardiograms (EKGs) were conducted with electrode placement at the whim of the examiner.

5. The testing situation is highly intrusive. A small number of offenders refuse it outright, even when faced with legal consequences. Few therapists and fewer patients enjoy it. It also announces that we expect deceit.

6. The test requires the purchase of expensive equipment and is costly to administer.

7. Its use within a legal framework can be deceptive. It smacks of objectivity, and while it is one of the few physical tests that can be definitive in psychiatry, it cannot be used to prove or disprove whether an individual has or has not committed any particular act. In addition, it can only lend marginal weight to an assumption of guilt or innocence, thus bolstering or weakening any particular case. Admittedly, false negatives are common, but fortunately false positives are probably rare.

8. Results thus far have suffered from a sampling bias. We evaluate only those offenders who are caught.
9. Results correlate better with a history of pedophilia than with exhibitionism or rape (McConaghy, 1993, chap. 1), perhaps because these last offenses stem from a greater heterogeneity of causes. Other offenses, such as telephone scatologia and frotteurism, yield very low levels of any deviant arousal (Maletzky, 1993).
10. Some findings indicate that the test has greater validity in measuring type rather than strength of sexual interest.

In summary, the plethysmograph remains controversial in determining deviant sexual arousal in offenders, although most clinicians and researchers continue to employ it. Indeed, the greatest benefit of the plethysmograph may lie not in assessment but in treatment, as described below.

The Polygraph

If possible, even more controversy surrounds the use of the poorly named "lie detector." During a polygraph examination, an offender is asked, among a number of questions, about engaging in sexually deviant acts at critical periods based on the offending history, while recordings are made of pulse, blood pressure, EKG, and galvinic skin response (GSR). As with the plethysmograph, the offender is in an artificial and potentially hostile environment and is aware that the reason for this test is the suspicion of dishonesty. It is an intrusive test and one not accorded full validity in the scientific and popular literature (Abrams, 1991). However, polygraphy, a field with its own literature, has been accorded an increasing measure of respect, particularly due to its value in working with sexual offenders.

Despite some similarities, the test differs from the plethysmograph in important ways. The plethysmograph measures a physiologic change both more specific and more focused than the polygraph. Conclusions about the past, such as whether an individual did or did not commit a specific act, cannot be drawn from the plethysmograph, while such conclusions are frequently made based on polygraph results.

Experience with polygraph examinations of offenders is mixed. Some offenders fail the test and then admit culpability for some or all of their crimes. Many others pass, having conquered the machine and their own anxiety. Although it is commonly asserted that antisocial offenders often succeed on the test as they are adept at unimpassioned trickery, no definitive studies of sexual offenders are at hand.

However, in one attribute the plethysmograph and polygraph share an important similarity—they are equally important as devices for treatment:

A 20-year-old college student frequented a campus laundromat at odd hours. He was charged with exposing himself to several female students. He denied culpability and several plethysmograph evaluations failed to demonstrate any deviant arousal. Following a *no contest* plea to charges of indecent exposure, he entered an outpatient sexual abuse clinic that required regular polygraphs. Several weeks before his first examination, the therapist explained that the staff wanted him to succeed on the polygraph and, to help him do so, he needed to think very hard about his recent activities and tell the entire truth before undergoing the test. In a subsequent session, he confessed to several additional acts of exposing, peeking in dormitory windows, and rubbing against women on escalators and in campus activities.

In this case, the polygraph uncovered additional areas for inquiry and treatment. Overall, the polygraph has been useful in assessment and treatment. Whether bodily measures of general anxiety and arousal can be relied on to extricate truth from deception with scientific accuracy will, in all likelihood, continue to be debated into the foreseeable future.

TREATMENT

The foundation of treatment for the paraphilias rests on principles shared with all patient-therapist endeavors: trust and mutual respect. This is especially true given the often involuntary nature of this population. Most such patients are mandated into treatment; indeed, the majority of sexual offenders disclaim a need for treatment at all. As a consequence, many offenders view the therapist as an extension of a coercive system rather than as a professional trying to help. They recognize that their therapist may have to report progress or lack of it to authorities, creating an oppositional atmosphere. This is magnified by the inclusion in therapy of invasive testing techniques such as the plethysmograph and polygraph. However, although not an easy task, the development of a trusting relationship between therapist and patient can be built, even in the face of massive denial.

Institutional Versus Community-Based Treatment

While more aggressive sexual offenders, such as rapists, may receive long-term prison sentences, most men with paraphilias are not sent to prison, although they often spend short terms in jail (Knight & Prentky, 1990). Most sexual offenders are treated within the communities in which they committed their crimes. Often, "lesser" sexual offenses, such as exhibitionism or incest, result in lighter sentences. The decisions of disposition are usually made, often by the court and the corrections officer, before the offender is seen by a therapist. At times, however, a therapist may be asked to testify at a sentencing hearing about a person's dangerousness to be at large. Fortunately, some data have been presented that inform these choices (Maletzky, 1993).

The techniques described here can be employed within either an inpatient or an outpatient setting. Inpatient venues generally include prisons, jails, halfway houses, and state institutions. Only a handful of private inpatient resources exist nationwide. Typical outpatient settings include private subspecialty clinics and community mental health centers. Unfortunately, the latter are poorly funded, even within metropolitan counties. However, more psychiatrists are expressing interest in this field and contributing to the literature, once the exclusive domain of the nonmedical specialist.

Group Versus Individual Treatment

While much of therapy at present is delivered in a group format, sexual behavior is idiosyncratic, and approaches to its deviations are often best provided through individual therapy. Unfortunately, such decisions are often affected more by issues of finance than of efficacy. While groups are effective vehicles for delivering some of the techniques described below, often combining approaches offers the greatest efficacy. An orientation group to begin treatment can introduce offenders to concepts of therapy and serve as a better forum in which to challenge minimization and denial. A group may also be an efficient medium within which to review principles of cognitive therapy and relapse prevention. Certain behavioral techniques

can be introduced in this format as well, such as the use of the plethysmograph and the rationale behind aversive conditioning. However, offenders will benefit from individual sessions exploring specifics about deviant chains of behavior, antecedents, and consequences. In addition, most behavioral techniques, such as aversive conditioning, aversive behavior rehearsal, plethysmographic biofeedback, and orgasmic reconditioning, can be most intensively and successfully provided in individual therapy.

Nonetheless, group sessions can reduce the number of future and more costly individual sessions while providing easier and more rapid access to treatment. Several such groups have been described in recent literature (O'Donohue & Letourneau, 1993; Schlank & Shaw, 1996).

Cognitive-Behavioral Therapy

Literature on the paraphilias has been focused chiefly on theoretical, etiological, and epidemiological concerns rather than on issues of treatment. This disparity may reflect the present state of our science, more descriptive than curative. However, a trend toward treatment outcome studies is emerging (Marshall, Jones, Ward, Johnston, & Barbaree, 1991). While much of the treatment literature of the 1970s and 1980s consisted of case reports and retrospective analyses of outcomes, over the past half decade many researchers have constructed more closely controlled studies, including some prospective and well-conceived efforts isolating crucial treatment factors (Dwyer, in press; Marques, 1994). From these, a consensus has arisen that cognitive-behavioral therapies form the standard against which other approaches must be judged.

Behavioral Approaches

A flurry of activity in the 1960s and 1970s led to the application, at times exclusive, of treatment based on a strict rendering of behaviorism. With advances in research and experience, behavioral approaches today are employed as part of a comprehensive program utilizing a broad range of empirically and clinically tested techniques, including aversive conditioning, positive conditioning, and reconditioning.

Aversive Conditioning Techniques

Electroshock Aversive therapy based on classical conditioning paradigms attempts to pair an unconditioned aversive stimulus with a deviant response in order to reduce the likelihood of that response occurring in the future. It was hoped the reduction in sexual arousal produced in the treatment laboratory would generalize to cues in the patient's real-life experience. The earliest work employed shock as the aversive stimulus, usually at a level unpleasant but not harmful (MacCulloch, Waddington, & Sanbrook, 1978). Other aversive stimuli, such as foul odors or tastes, were also employed (Maletzky, 1991a, chap. 3). Criticisms of the application of a simple punishment model, however, were soon raised. McConaghy (1993, chap. 8), citing evidence from the 1970s and 1980s, criticized conclusions about shock aversion based on small numbers of subjects, retrospective uncontrolled data, and the use of questionable stimulus materials. In addition, electroshock is not well regarded by patients' families and the media. Moreover, its flexibility is limited as it can only be introduced for brief durations and cannot be used with stimuli that require longer intervals to build sexual arousal, such as slides and stories. As a result, electroshock aversion has not been cited in the literature extensively since the early 1980s, although nationwide surveys of current clinical practice give indications that it is still employed in combination with a variety of other techniques in outpatient programs (Knopp, Freeman-Longo, & Stevenson, 1992).

Covert Sensitization   By the mid-1970s, many therapists had devised aversive procedures that were less intrusive and easier to administer and did not alienate the sensitivity of patients' families and the public. One such technique, covert sensitization, emerged as a hopeful replacement for physically aversive procedures.

In this technique, the patient is first trained in relaxation and then, in a relaxed state, is asked to visualize scenes of deviant sexual activity followed by an aversive event. For example, a patient who typically exposed to schoolgirls from his car was asked to imagine driving by a group of girls on their way to school:

> As you see their young faces, you start to get hard. You feel your penis stiffen as you rub it. They notice you! You call the girls over to the car. They don't know what's waiting for them. As they approach the car, you take it out and begin to masturbate violently. The girls are shocked. They don't know what to do. They're just staring at it as you rub it, but suddenly there's a pain. You've got your

penis stuck in your pants' zipper. You try to yank it free, but it only catches more. It's starting to bleed and you go soft. The girls are laughing and a policeman is coming over.

In such scenes, an escape associated with nonoffending is usually added:

> You are able, finally, to get your penis back in your pants. You drive off, and, as you get away, you begin to relax and breathe easier.

Such scenes commonly contain three elements:

1. The build-up of deviant sexual arousal.
2. An aversive consequence.
3. An escape from aversion associated with turning away from the deviant stimulus.

Covert sensitization has won a place in almost all treatment programs (Knopp et al., 1992) because it is easy to implement, requires no expensive equipment, and enjoys the blessing of community approval. However, despite its multiple advantages, this technique has not produced as robust a response as desired. Some patients demonstrate reductions in deviant arousal but no actual behavior change. Others have modest responses and complain that the procedure lacks sufficient power (Maletzky, 1980).

Assisted Covert Sensitization   For just such patients, who are more difficult to treat, an augmented procedure was devised. After the buildup of sexual arousal in a deviant scene and at the point where aversive imagery begins, a foul odor is also introduced via an opened vial or an automated odor pump (Maletzky, 1991a, appendix D) and is continuously presented until the escape portion is reached:

> You pick up a young boy, 13 or 14, outside a videogame store. You offer to take him home and he accepts. As you park by his house, you put your arm around his shoulder and he doesn't resist. Pretty soon, you reach down to feel his crotch. You slowly unzip his fly, pull his penis out, and start stroking it back and forth. As you start to suck on his penis, suddenly there's a foul odor. It's like rotting flesh, putrid and nauseating. You glance down and see there's a sore on the underside of his penis, red and full of pus, and it's broken. Some of the blood and pus has gotten into your mouth

and down your throat. It's nauseating. You can feel the pus in the back of your throat, and you gag. Food comes up in your throat and your mouth. You're going to vomit. You vomit all over him and yourself. You've got to get out of there. You leave the car and get a rag to clean yourself off. As you get away from him, that smell goes away and you can deeply breathe the fresh air.

As can be seen, this procedure is not simply aversive olfactory conditioning because no real conditioned stimulus is employed; it is, rather, imagined, although the consequences of the unconditioned stimuli are real.

Although ammonia has often been suggested as the aversive stimulus (Maletzky & George, 1973), it may produce a painful response rather than a nauseous one. Rotting tissue has been more effective, perhaps because it travels via the first (olfactory) nerve to limbic areas thought to be important in the perception of sexual pleasure. A number of studies have demonstrated that the response of nausea is more powerful than that of pain for reducing harmful consummatory behaviors such as overeating (Kennedy & Foreyt, 1968), smoking (Lichtenstein & Kruetzer, 1969), and sexual response (Maletzky & George, 1973). While the covert stimuli can be modeled after real-life situations, this is a difficult task for the treatment of men who expose or rape as scenes of such activities may not trigger arousal in some men, especially in a laboratory setting (McConaghy, 1993, chap. 1). In addition, stimuli arousing to an exhibitionist, for example, may not be deviant at all, such as coming on an attractive woman at night in an isolated location. Despite these drawbacks, variations on this technique have been employed in the majority of cognitive-behavioral treatment programs in recent years (Knopp et al., 1992).

Minimal Arousal Conditioning   In a novel use of aversive conditioning principles, Jenson, Laws, and Wolfe (1994) and Gray (1995) found sexual arousal too powerful for deconditioning in some patients. These authors placed the aversive stimulus earlier in the response chain, when minimal arousal was present and before intense sexual pleasure was attained. This point could then be advanced in the sexual chain increasingly closer to sexual release. While this procedure has not enjoyed extensive use, it is promising for offenders whose arousal levels are too high to allow typical aversion paradigms.

Aversive Behavior Reversal   Sometimes inaccurately called *shame therapy* (Serber, 1970), this technique has enjoyed fame and notoriety as much for its reported efficacy as its apparent simplicity (Wickramaseekera, 1980). While reported to be markedly effective, its present-day use is considered insensitive and possibly unethical, although not absolutely contraindicated:

A 23-year-old graduate student could not stop his compulsive exposing to attractive coeds on campus. Arrested twice by campus police, he was threatened with expulsion from school unless he obtained therapy. He gave consent for a procedure in which he exposed to hospital staff for 3 minutes on each of three occasions. The staff was instructed to offer no response but merely to watch silently. Following the first session, he reported that he lost all urges to expose. He had not reexposed on 9-year follow-up.

Theoretically, this procedure is thought to produce such an aversive situation that it renders future exposing unlikely. Although attractive because of its reported efficacy, limitations include the difficulty of obtaining consent, the problems in soliciting staff members to participate, the possibility of adverse effects on staff, and, in the main, its terribly aversive nature. While submitting offenders to mental anguish might be considered by some as due reward, other, less aversive, yet equally effective, techniques exist. It would be difficult to condone its use, a paradox in that its major advances are also its unfortunate drawbacks.

Variations on this theme, however, can be employed as part of a comprehensive treatment program. A patient might be asked to expose to himself in a mirror and record his observations on tape. He might expose in front of a videotape camera, then view the tape in private or with staff or family. A pedophile might be asked to show, with a life-size doll, what the pedophile had done sexually to a child. This may also be videotaped for viewing. Faced with the reality of their own behaviors, some offenders may recoil at the images of their offenses.

Vicarious Sensitization   This novel technique, recently introduced for the treatment of a variety of sexual offenses, contains elements of cognitive restructuring, empathy training, and aversive conditioning. In this procedure, originally crafted for adolescent offenders (Weinrott & Riggan, 1996), an offender views a series of videotapes depicting adverse outcomes of deviant behaviors, both likely and improbable. Table 24.4 provides summaries of typical scenarios, depicted on screen by professional actresses and actors. Although it may appear that this technique is cerebral, a form of cognitive therapy, the effect on a viewer is often visceral. Many offenders complain of nausea while viewing these tapes. Although vicarious sensitization has been applied mainly to adolescents, its scenarios flow naturally from a variety of sexual crimes, and results in adult offenders are promising (Maletzky & McFarland, 1996).

Positive Conditioning Techniques   While therapists commonly employ the positive reinforcement of appropriate arousal as described in some of the techniques above, a variety of positive approaches stand on their own as important contributions to the treatment of offenders, including social skills training and alternative behavior completion.

Social Skills Training   Most therapists believe that the large array of techniques called social skills training forms a crucial element of an offender treatment program. McFall (1990) outlined an assessment procedure for social skills deficits and proposed an individualized treatment approach based on an information-processing analysis of social skills. A variety of such techniques has been helpful for offenders and nonoffenders alike. Female therapists may be particularly effective in applying these approaches to male offenders. Although not easily researched, methods such as cue-assisted learning, psychodrama, assertive training, and the use of in vivo relaxation techniques are important components in the therapeutic arsenals of most treatment programs.

Alternative Behavior Completion   Based on work with the treatment of compulsive gamblers, McConaghy (1993, chap. 8) outlined a procedure reported as helpful for a variety of offenders. A patient listens to descriptions of typical offending situations, including entry into the behavioral chain leading to offending. However, in the image, the patient successfully tolerates the stimuli causing urges to offend, completes the chain without doing so, then leaves the scene in a relaxed state:

> As you drive home one night, you notice an attractive woman driver on your right in a van. She can see into your car. You slow down and drive parallel with her as you begin to get aroused. You want to rub your penis and take it out to show her; the urge this time is weaker than before, and you drive past her quickly without exposing. You feel good about yourself for being able to stay in control.

This technique is similar to one that others have termed *success imagery* and is based on techniques of desensitization already shown to be effective in reducing social anxieties. If proven effective in larger trials, it may indicate that offending carries with it not only pleasurable feelings, but anxious ones as well.

Reconditioning Techniques   A number of techniques appear to stand midway between aversive conditioning and purely cognitive approaches, perhaps combining elements of both; these include plethysmographic biofeedback, masturbation techniques, and sexual impulse control.

Plethysmographic Biofeedback   While debate surrounds the use of the plethysmograph as an assessment

TABLE 24.4 Vicarious Sensitization Videotape Vignettes

An experienced inmate describes the brutal rape of a young male sexual offender in prison; the offender is chased across the prison yard.

Neighbors, outraged about an offender's sexual abuse of several girls in their community, chase and corner him, force him to undress, and subject him to cruel ridicule.

A victim describes the revenge she would like to extract from her offender while, on screen, scenes are shown of an actual surgical castration and phallectomy.

An adolescent offender is shunned by several groups of high school girls, who whisper about him, point, and make jokes; he complains to friends, who remain unsupportive, that he cannot get a date.

Several victims are shown in various states of psychological disarray due to their sexual abuse: a young girl cuts her wrists, an older woman requires electroconvulsive therapy after being raped.

---

technique, its use in treatment is both less controversial and less publicized. Several authors (Maletzky 1991a, chap. 4; McConaghy 1993, chap. 8) mention this potentially important and innovative approach. In this technique, the plethysmograph is automatically or manually connected to an external light or sound device to provide feedback to the patient about his arousal level. Commonly, a bank of colored vertical lights is employed (Maletzky, 1991a, appendix D), although an escalating sound can be used as well. Red lights can be used to denote higher levels of arousal, orange to denote intermediate levels, and green to denote low levels. The offender's task during any session might be to keep out of the red area when exposed to deviant stimuli or to keep in the red area with normal stimuli.

Masturbation Techniques   Many clinicians believe that pleasure in masturbation and climax are important reinforcers of sexual behavior. Pairing fantasies of deviant sexual imagery with these pleasures repeatedly reinforces deviant arousal. Admonitions to offenders to discontinue these pairings probably go unheeded. Additional techniques are needed to recondition the powerful arousal associated with offending: fantasy change and satiation.

In fantasy change (Maletzky, 1986), an offender is asked to masturbate to deviant fantasies until the point of ejaculatory inevitability, and at that moment to switch to nondeviant fantasies. As treatment progresses, the patient is asked to make that switch earlier and earlier in the masturbatory chain until he is masturbating exclusively to nondeviant fantasies. Many therapists request that the offender tape record these sessions in order to (partially) guarantee compliance.

In satiation (Laws & Marshall, 1991; Maletzky, 1986), the offender is asked to masturbate to ejaculation using only nondeviant fantasies. Following climax, he is asked to continue masturbating, this time to deviant fantasies, for periods of time varying from 30 to 60 minutes. Again, therapists request that tape recordings be made to ensure that this homework is completed. (Actual observation of masturbatory behavior is contraindicated as overly intrusive.) This technique pairs deviant imagery with the period of minimal sexual arousal. Having to masturbate following ejaculation may be an aversive practice. Some therapists believe that simple verbal satiation produces results equal to forced masturbation (Laws, 1995).

Boredom, fatigue, and deconditioning all may play some active role.

Sexual Impulse Control Training   Regardless of their origins, paraphilias represent the end of a journey of many steps. Constructing obstacles early in this chain may be more effective than designing interventions closer to the sexual pleasure of release. Under the rubric of sexual impulse control (Maletzky, 1991a, chap. 7), a loose band of techniques attempts to construct such obstacles.

For example, a pedophile might be asked to begin masturbating to pedophilic fantasies, then stop before ejaculation, or to read about and look at pictures of pedophilic situations, then abstain from masturbation or intercourse for at least 24 hours. Partial verification of completing these homework assignments can occur either by asking the offender to tape record masturbation sessions or by interviewing a partner (neither is proof positive). Some therapists have asked an offender to approach deviant situations, then smell a foul odor or chew a bitter tablet. Needless to say, these last methods are best used after verification that arousal has been reduced or that the patient is well advanced in a treatment program.

Cognitive Approaches

A diverse and varied collection of cognitive techniques is widely applied to offenders to reduce the likelihood of repeated deviant behavior. Since many of these methods appear to be at least somewhat effective (Marshall et al., 1991), Quinsey and Earls (1990) suggested that all of them may act in a general, rather than specific, fashion. At present, it appears unlikely that any such technique can be isolated and tested in a prospective double-blind study due to ethical concerns about withholding treatment.

While cognitive therapies are not easily categorized and broad overlap between categories exists, most therapists agree that within the cognitive approaches three domains can be identified: recognition and correction of cognitive distortions, relapse prevention, and empathy training.

Restructuring Cognitive Distortions   Based in part on the work of Yochelson and Samenow (1977) and unfortunately described as "thinking errors," a set of typical distortions (actually assumptions and justifications) has come to be widely recognized in many offenders; examples of frequently used distortions in several paraphilias are presented in Table 24.5. Identification of a distortion is only the first part of treatment. The next, and perhaps more difficult step, is skillfully presenting it as such to the offender. Many patients are reluctant to endorse a distortion once it is pointed out as, to most, it is patently false. In these tasks, question-and-answer techniques, psychodrama, illustration by example, and role reversal have all been helpful in treatment (Murphy, 1990).

Simply labeling these as errors rarely leads to significant behavioral change. Incorporating corrections of these distortions into a habit of thinking by frequent conscious repetition can, however, be helpful. In discussing these, a therapist encourages the offender to give self-corrective messages often enough for them to become innate, reflexive, and automatic responses.

Relapse Prevention   Based on a treatment approach for addictive behaviors (Marlatt & Gordon 1985), re-lapse prevention has been extended to include treatment for many sexual offenders (Pithers, 1990). Central to relapse prevention is the concept of behavioral chains and cycles. Offending is conceived as the culmination of a chain beginning with seemingly innocuous behavior, gathering momentum in a cascade of behaviors that result in the offending act. In chains ending with a pleasurable act, it is much more likely that interventions with optional choices will be successful early rather than late in the behavioral chain.

Relapse prevention begins with self-awareness and self-scrutiny. The offender is asked to keep a record of lapses and their triggers to be better able to identify dangerous situations. Next, stimulus control procedures can be put into place:

A young, married exhibitionist would often "forget" something in his office and return at night after supper to retrieve it. Often, when doing so, he would drive through parking lots and look for isolated women. As part of treatment, he was re-

TABLE 24.5   Examples of Distortions, Assumptions, and Justifications in Sexual Paraphilias

Category	Pedophilia	Exhibitionism	Rape
Misattributing blame	"She started it by being too cuddly." "She would always run around half dressed."	"She kept looking at me like she was expecting it." "The way she was dressed, she was asking for it."	"She was saying 'no' but her body said 'yes.'" "I was always drinking when I did it."
Minimizing or denying sexual intent	"I was just teaching her about sex . . . better from her father than someone else."	"I was just looking for a place to pee." "My pants just slipped down."	"I was just trying to teach her a lesson . . . she deserved it."
Debasing the victim	"She'd had sex before with her boyfriend." "She always lies."	"She was just a slut anyway."	"The way she came on to me at the party, she deserved it." "She never fought back . . . she must have liked it."
Minimizing consequences	"She's always been real friendly to me, even afterward." "She was messed up even before it happened."	"I never touched her so I couldn't have hurt her." "She smiled so she must have liked it."	"She'd had sex with hundreds of guys before. It was no big deal."
Deflecting censure	"This happened years ago . . . why can't everyone forget about it?"	"It's not like I raped anyone."	"I only did it once."
Justifying the cause	"If I wasn't molested as a kid, I'd never have done this."	"If I knew how to get dates, I wouldn't have to expose."	"If my girlfriend gave me what I want, I wouldn't be forced to rape."

quired always to notify his wife of his whereabouts. She would call him toward the end of the day to remind him to be sure to take any work he needed home with him.

A lapse, such as entering a dangerous situation, is not a defeat but an opportunity to learn which stimuli control which behaviors. A relapse is a failure, although that does not preclude learning from it as well. The patient and therapist need to review situations of heightened risk and problem solve alternative escape strategies, thus accumulating sufficient skills to avoid offending in the future. Several workbooks, complete with exercises and homework assignments, have proven of benefit for the offender in internalizing these concepts (Freeman-Longo & Bays, 1989).

Empathy Training   Although rarely conceptualized as a series of therapies, empathy training can be arbitrarily divided into five segments: (a) identification of the victim, (b) identification of the victimizing act, (c) identification of the harm, (d) role reversal, and (e) development of empathy.

Put into practice, these techniques can begin with identification of the victim and how she or he was selected. Even supposedly nuisance acts, such as obscene telephone calling or exhibitionism, are associated with long-term effects in victims (Cox & Maletzky, 1980). Psychodramatic techniques, such as role reversal, can be employed in identifying victimization. Videotapes of victims describing their experiences can be helpful in this regard. These techniques lead naturally to discussions of offending as a victimizing act, with lasting impressions. Offenders need to be able to identify the harm they have caused and its lasting effects. Guilt induction is not the goal; emotional, as opposed to intellectual, acceptance should occur. Employing role reversal, the offender can try to imagine how a victim might feel, not only during the offending act, but thereafter, as the residue of trauma persists. From such methods, the development of empathy can hopefully emerge.

The usefulness of these techniques has been reviewed by Murphy (1990). Almost all clinical programs currently include such techniques (Knopp et al., 1992); however, they do not lend themselves well to controlled research.

Biological Approaches

Based on work demonstrating some biological abnormalities in sexual offenders (Lang, Langevin, Bain,

Frenzel, & Wright, 1989), therapists have expressed the hope that somatic treatments might prove helpful. While surgical approaches are too drastic to be considered in America, several medications have been demonstrated to reduce sexual drive in males and hence to afford some protection against reoffending among offenders treated in a community setting. However, despite promising leads, no controlled study of the use of medications by sexual offenders has been published. Nonetheless, reawakening interest in this area offers hope of continuing advances.

Hormonal Treatment

Medroxyprogesterone acetate (MPA), also known as Depo-Provera, and cyproterone acetate (CPA) are the two medications most studied for the treatment of sexual offenders. Each may act at different points in hormonal function to reduce circulating testosterone by either increasing its metabolism in the liver (MPA) or by blocking cellular adhesion of normal circulating testosterone (CPA). In the United States, MPA is used, while CPA, not approved by the Food and Drug Administration (FDA) due to rare liver reactions, is used in Canada and the European continent. Both reduce circulating testosterone levels, but controversy exists about how to measure effective doses. While some physicians aim to reduce testosterone to prepubertal levels (less than 50 ng/dL), others aim for a reduction to 30% to 50% of pretreatment levels. Clinical studies find both criteria adequate in markedly reducing the risk of reoffense (as reviewed in Bradford, 1990).

Both substances can be administered in long-acting Depo form, especially necessary for offenders in mandated treatment. Intramuscular doses have ranged from 400 mg per week to 200 mg twice per month for MPA and 300 to 600 mg every 10 days to 3 weeks for CPA.

There is little doubt that both hormones reduce male sexual drive, as demonstrated by a reduction in frequency of erections, self-initiated sexual behaviors, and sexual fantasies, as well as a consequent decrease in frequency of masturbation and intercourse. Many offenders comment parenthetically that there is a concomitant reduction in aggression (Maletzky, 1991b). Side effects of both agents have included mild weight gain, headaches, muscle cramping, and, rarely, blood clots, particularly in leg veins.

As expected, most offenders treated with hormones

show a rapid return to deviant arousal following the discontinuance of medication (Berlin & Meinecke, 1981). The majority of treatment centers using hormones now combine hormonal treatment with cognitive and behavioral methods in a multimodal approach (McConaghy, 1993, chap. 8). In such programs, the hormone is tapered, then discontinued while the offender is still under supervision in order to monitor progress without the drug. An unusually high percentage of offenders subsequently treated hormonally had suffered central nervous system damage in the past and were felt to have impaired impulse control (Maletzky, 1991a, chap 8). Many had been diagnosed with a multitude of paraphilias and had a high rate of reoffending regardless of consequences, yet had been afforded reaccess to the community. One large outpatient clinic has reported the use of MPA in 1.9% of all treated offenders (Maletzky, 1993).

Psychotropic Medications

A number of other medications have been proposed for the treatment of sexual offenders. While neuroleptic medications, particularly thioridazine, have been employed in the past, newer serotonin reuptake inhibitors are most often mentioned for use in treatment-resistant paraphilias in the present day. The drug most discussed is fluoxetine (Kafka, 1995), although clomipramine was actually the first antidepressant used to reduce deviant sexual arousal (Casals-Ariet & Cullen, 1993). While these psychotropic medications reduce sexual drive, they can also produce side effects such as nausea and agitation.

Since both fluoxetine and clomipramine have been of some benefit in the treatment of obsessive compulsive disorder, and since sexual offending is often obsessive in thought and compulsive in deed, some clinicians have expressed the hope that such agents could reduce the pressure of deviant fantasies and preoccupations. However, at present it appears these medications simply reduce overall sexual drive rather than target only deviant fantasies. In addition, no psychotropic medication has been proven as powerful in clinical practice as the hormones MPA and CPA in reducing sexual drive. Currently, the use of these hormones is considered the first medical approach for treating offenders dangerous to be at large until, hopefully, cognitive and behavioral methods take hold.

EFFICACY OF TREATMENT TECHNIQUES

The literature on treatment outcome for the sexual offender contains a number of review articles. One widely quoted study reached the pessimistic conclusion that inadequate controls and variable rating instruments precluded any judgment about efficacy (Furby, Weinrott, & Blackshaw, 1989). A more recent report offered a different and more sanguine view— that newer and more sufficient documentation combined with clinical experience warrants a less gloomy outlook (Marshall & Barbaree, 1990b). Problems noted in such reviews include short duration of follow-up and varying exclusion criteria. The use of no-treatment control groups has been believed to be unethical. However, an ongoing outcome project in California (Marques, 1994) hopes to avoid this problem through the use of untreated institutionalized offender volunteers (Marshall & Barbaree, 1990b).

Outcome studies have often grouped various types of sexual offenders together, despite evidence that treatment results can be heavily influenced by taxonomy (Marshall & Barbaree, 1990b) and diagnosis (Maletzky, 1993). Early studies indicated that, in the absence of treatment, by 6 years following discovery 41% of offenders had reoffended, including 57% of repeat offenders in the original group (Frisbie & Dondis, 1965). High rates of recidivism, up to 67%, have been shown for exhibitionists using electroshock aversion alone (Rooth & Marks, 1974). Somewhat better rates were obtained for exhibitionists by Evans at 1 year (1967) and 3 years (1970) posttreatment: covert sensitization alone proved effective in the majority (61%) of patients. However, adding aversive odor to covert sensitization reduced relapse rates to just under 25%.

Among approaches attempting to treat offenders, medical treatment, at first ignored in the psychological literature, appears at once intriguing yet limited. The antiandrogens MPA and CPA have long been employed for sexual offenders deemed dangerous to be at large. Placebo-controlled studies have not been reported due to ethical concerns, but large case reports indicate a very low rate of recidivism among offenders taking these medications (Laschet & Laschet, 1975; Maletzky, 1991b). Unfortunately, relapse following termination of antiandrogens has been high (Berlin & Meinecke, 1981). These treatments might best be reserved for those at highest risk to reoffend and, in the main, used over a period of time during which behavioral and cognitive elements in treatment are beginning to exert some effect.

There have been no large outcome evaluations of a single treatment technique for offenders. Multifaceted approaches have been described, and retrospective reviews have been published. All have been Type 3 studies. These are open trials, following patients throughout treatment and follow-up, subjecting offenders to a combination of cognitive-behavioral techniques, and measuring changes over time in treatment with standardized instruments. Their strengths derive from their large numbers, clear presentation of inclusion criteria, rigid adherence to a commonly approved diagnostic scheme, sophisticated statistical methods, and, in many cases, their long follow-up periods. Weaknesses are apparent in their lack of double-blind techniques and, especially, their lack of comparison groups.

It should come as little surprise that there has been thus far an absence of Type 1 studies (double-blind, controlled trials) or even Type 2 studies (lacking but one element of a Type 1 study). It has been difficult to isolate single techniques and subject one group of offenders to them while substituting an active placebo treatment for a control group, especially in outpatient practice.

These practical problems are compounded by the lack of funding and interest in sexual offending in government and university based psychiatry and psychology programs. Hence, we must await improved circumstances to be able to state with scientific rigor which treatments work and which will likely fail.

Even with the data presently available, a major problem in evaluating treatment programs is the lack of a comparison group with an expected rate of recidivism. Such data have not been collected from the same populations as those under treatment. Outcome studies have typically combined a variety of populations, including those known to have widely differing prognoses, such as incest offenders and men who rape. Follow-up periods have been apparently adequate compared to outcome analyses in other *DSM-IV* categories, but sexual offending can have a lifetime potential and follow-ups under 2 years may be of practical insignificance (Marshall & Barbaree, 1990b). Finally, all the outcome studies to be further discussed have combined elements of cognitive and behavioral treatment rather than isolated single treatment factors.

Such combinations represent the standard treatment approach offered in the modern day; hence, a value in these studies is clinical relevance—they represent what one likely can expect the results of treatment to be. Unfortunately, they do not allow us to state definitely that any of the techniques employed, or their conjoint use, have without a shadow of a doubt led to the improvements reported.

Institutional Programs

Just three programs have reported treatment results in a sufficiently systematic form to regard them as well tested. The first of these reported on sexual offenders incarcerated in a penitentiary. Marshall and Williams (1975) studied, in one of the few comparison trials with a crossover design, child molesters and rapists in sufficient numbers (101) to reach meaningful statistical significance. They found a program combining early elements of cognitive and behavioral treatment significantly more effective than a traditional psychotherapy program. Of interest is the opportunity afforded by their colleagues (Davidson, 1979, 1984) to follow these men over a period of 9 years and compare data for untreated offenders in the same institution. Davidson used sophisticated methods of calculating recidivism, including the portion of those at risk to reoffend, and found that treated offenders reoffended at a rate of approximately 15% compared to over 50% for those treated with traditional psychotherapy. However, further analysis revealed better outcomes for incest offenders (8% recidivism) as opposed to men who molested girls (10.9%) or boys (13.3%) outside their families.

In a series of reports, Quinsey described the treatment outcome from a Canadian institution, a maximum security hospital (Quinsey, 1983; Quinsey, Chaplin, & Carrigan, 1980; Whitman & Quinsey, 1981). This mixed population of child molesters, pedophiles, and rapists was believed to be composed of refractory offenders. Data, obtained from official police records, indicated a 20% recidivism rate over a 6-year period. Unfortunately, these data are difficult to evaluate due to a lack of anticipated reoffense rates in a similar population, although many of these offenders were in high-risk categories, such as preferential pedophiles and men who rape.

In the United States, the Sexual Offender Unit at Oregon State Hospital has been described by Smith

(1984) and evaluated by Freeman-Longo (1984). This unit housed a variety of offenders deemed dangerous to be at large and in need of institutional treatment. However, it excluded any inmate who declined to enter a treatment program, perhaps eliminating offenders who were more difficult to treat. While outcome data were encouraging as no patient who successfully completed the program reoffended, just 20 such offenders successfully completed treatment in follow-up over 3 years. In addition, a significant proportion of these offenders failed to complete treatment and was returned to correctional facilities. Follow-up data on these offenders would have been instructive.

Table 24.6 provides an overview of institutional outcome research. It is apparent that shortcomings in methodology, particularly by contamination with mixed populations and lack of broad-based outcome measures, limit confidence in the application of these techniques. However, these programs were attempting to treat the most serious offenders, and a general trend can be detected in favor of treatment as opposed to no treatment, such that more extensive controlled studies would seem indicated in such populations.

Outpatient Programs

All six of the programs reporting outcome data on outpatient sexual offenders employed the same cognitive-behavioral techniques already described for the inpatient populations. While these studies suffered the same deficiencies as those of the inpatient programs described above, they generally included larger numbers of subjects, a broader base of diagnostic groups, and a wider range of assessment techniques.

Wolfe (1984) excluded physically violent offenders and those with nonsexual criminal histories, but did include most offenders commonly treated in outpatient settings. He reported results of treatment for 67 molesters of girls, 17 molesters of boys, 3 rapists, and 27 exhibitionists, scrutinizing probation records for 28 months after termination of treatment. Surprisingly, molesters of boys (not further defined as pedophilic) and rapists had no reoffenses, while molesters of girls reoffended at a 4.5% rate and exhibitionists at a 14.8% rate. Wolfe continues to collect data, and subsequent reports are expected.

In a review of another highly regarded clinic's outcome data, Abel, Mittelman, Becker, Rathner, and Rouleau (1988) report, among 98 molesters of boys or girls (not differentiating the two), a reoffense rate of 12.2%. Unfortunately, these data come only from self-report and are hence suspect. In fairness, Abel's group has gone to great lengths to insure confidentiality in data collection (Abel et al., 1987), and thus self-interest may have been minimized. Nonetheless, these data suffer from a lack of additional assessment techniques.

TABLE 24.6 Outcome Data for Inpatient Programs for Sexual Offenders

Program	Types (and Numbers) of Offenders[a]	Percentage Reoffending	Types of Assessment	Length of Follow-Up	
				Range	Mean
Kingston Sexual Behavior Clinic (Marshall & Barbaree, 1990b)	Incest (50) CMg (63) CMb (37)	8.0 17.5 13.5	Official police reports	1–9 years	2.5 years
Oak Ridge Mental Health Center, Ontario, Canada (Quinsey, 1983; Quinsey et al., 1980; Whitman & Quinsey, 1981)	Incest (76) CMg (59) CMb (40) Rapists (33)	11.8 16.9 22.5 27.2	Official police reports	1–6 years	3 years
Oregon State Hospital Sex Offender Unit (Freeman-Longo, 1984; Smith, 1984)	Incest (3) CMg (10) CMb (4) Rapists (3)	0 0 0 0	Official police records, Penile plethsymograph	6 months– 3 years	1.5 years

[a]CMg = men who molest nonfamilial girls; CMb = men who molest nonfamilial boys.

Marshall and Barbaree (1990b) have reported outcomes from their cognitive-behavioral-based treatment program in Ontario, Canada. Of note is their inclusion of a comparison among self-reports, official police records, and official childrens' agencies' reports. The last yielded the highest rates of recidivism, 2.4 times greater than the other methods, catching some offenders who were not detected by self-report or police records. These researchers treated 48 incest offenders, 49 molesters of girls, 29 molesters of boys, and 44 exhibitionists, with outcomes as detailed in Table 24.7. The table groups all outpatient outcome studies for ease of comparison. In a positive departure from the norm, Abel et al. included a no-treatment control group, although comparison is difficult as this group included offenders who simply chose to refuse treatment for a variety of reasons, hence biasing results in favor of treatment. Still, outcome was significantly better for treated offenders in all groups but one— the exhibitionists. Follow-ups ranged from 12 to 125 months.

In the largest group of patients yet reported (Maletzky, 1993), over 4,000 offenders were followed from 1973 through 1993, with average follow-up of 9 years. This clinic, employing the usual panoply of cognitive-behavioral techniques, has attempted to follow annually all offenders assessed and treated, employing a range of assessment techniques, including self-reports, reports of significant others, the penile plethysmograph, the polygraph, and official nationwide police

TABLE 24.7 Outcome Data for Outpatient Programs for Sexual Offenders

Program	Types (and Numbers) of Offenders[a]	Percentage Reoffending	Types of Assessment	Length of Follow-Up	
				Range	Mean
Northwest Treatment Associates (Wolfe, 1984)	CMg (67) CMb (17) E (27) Rapists (3)	4.5 0 0 14.8	Probation reports	6–28 months	13.5 months
New York State Institute (Abel et al., 1988)	CMgb (98)	12.2	Patient's self-reports	12–125 months	2 years
Kingston Sexual Behavior Clinic (Marshall & Barbaree, 1990b)	Incest (48) CMg (49) CMb (29) E (44)	8.0 17.9 13.3 47.8	Official police records, Children's Services Agencies' records		
The Sexual Abuse Clinic (Maletzky, 1993, and updated through 1996)	SPedg (3,012) SPedb (717) SPedg (864) PPedb (596) E (1,130) Rapists (543)	4.4 8.1 11.7 19.9 4.6 24.5	Self-reports, penile plethysmograph, official police records	1–23 years	9 years
Phillippe Pinel Institute, University of Montreal (Proulx et al., in press)	CMg (118) CMb (111) CMg&b (40) Rapists (113)	11.0 16.2 22.5 21.2	Psychologic testing, penile plethysmograph, official police records	6 months– 13 years	64.5 months
Program in Human Sexuality, University of Minnesota (Dwyer, in press)	CMg (27) CMb (11) PPed & PPedb (115)	8 18 5 2	Personal interview, anonymous questionnaire, official policy records	6 months– 17 years	3.5 years

[a]CMg = men who molest nonfamilial girls; CMb = men who molest nonfamilial boys; SPedg = situational offenders with girl victims; SPedb = situational offenders with boy victims; PPedg = predatory offenders with girls; PPedb = predatory offenders with boys; E = exhibitionists.

reports. Data are now (1996) available on over 7,000 offenders followed for at least 1 year and are presented in Table 24.8, along with the stringent requirements for any patient to be rated a success. Outcome varied based on initial diagnosis, ranging from an absence of reoffense for 95.6% of men who molested girls to 75.5% for men who raped. In contrast to Wolfe (1984), exhibitionists enjoyed among the highest success rates (95.4%), while in contrast to Marshall and Barbaree (1990b), men who molested boys did not do as well (although 80% did not reoffend). Strengths in this line of research include the large numbers of subjects, clinically relevant treatment techniques, stringent outcome criteria, and careful and extensive use of a variety

TABLE 24.8 Treatment Outcome for Paraphilias (N = 7,156)

Category	N	Percentage Meeting Criteria for Success[a]
Situational pedophilia, heterosexual	3,012	95.6
Predatory pedophilia, heterosexual	864	88.3
Situational pedophilia, homosexual	717	91.8
Predatory pedophilia, homosexual	596	80.1
Exhibitionism	1,130	95.4
Rape	543	75.5
Voyeurism	83	93.9
Public masturbation	77	94.8
Frotteurism	65	89.3
Fetishism	33	94.0
Transvestic fetishism	14	78.6
Telephone scatologia	29	93.1
Zoophilia	23	95.6

[a]A treatment success was defined as an offender who

1. Completed all treatment sessions.*
2. Reported no covert or overt deviant sexual behavior at the end of treatment or at any follow-up session.†
3. Demonstrated no deviant sexual arousal, defined as greater than 20% on the penile plethsymograph, at the end of treatment or at any follow-up session.†
4. Had no repeat legal charges for any sexual crime at the end of treatment or at any follow-up session.†

*Any offender who dropped out of treatment, even if the offender met other criteria for success, was counted as a treatment failure.
†Follow-up sessions occurred at 6, 12, 24, 36, 48, and 60 months after the end of active treatment.

of assessment techniques to cross-validate results. Because this research is so clinically based, however, it suffers from a lack of adequate comparison groups. It would be enlightening, yet in the opinion of many foolhardy as well, to allow an untreated control group to be at large in the community. One possible solution, although imperfect, would be to include as a comparison group men sentenced to an institution who did not undergo treatment.

Two more recent reports detail outcomes of cognitive-behavioral programs that attempt to address some deficiencies in earlier reports. Proulx et al. (in press) reported on 118 men who molested girls, 111 who molested boys, 40 who molested both, and 113 rapists. Proulx et al. utilized a variety of dynamic assessment techniques to provide an ongoing analysis of risk. These techniques include deviant sexual arousal on the plethysmograph and results of ongoing psychological assessment, as well as a review of police records. Treatment included the typical cognitive-behavioral package described above. Outcome measures detected recidivism for 13% of child molesters and 21.2% of rapists over an average follow-up period of over 5 years. These data are strengthened by stringent inclusion criteria and careful scrutiny of outcome measures.

Finally, Dwyer (in press) has reported on recidivism rates over a 17-year period of 180 offenders. Subjects were seen following completion of a cognitive-behavioral program at 6 months and then annually. Data consisted of a personal interview and an anonymous questionnaire, but self-reports were cross-validated with official records searches. Among these offenders, 64% were preferential pedophiles, 21% child molesters, and 15% exhibitionists. No rapists were included. Just 5% of pedophiles, 11% of child molesters, and 2% of exhibitionists reoffended. An overall recidivism rate of 9% was gleaned from the data, which matched that reported by Maletzky (1993) over the same time periods and with similar treatment techniques. While this research must be accorded clinical significance due to the large number of subjects and long follow-ups, criteria for inclusion as a Type 1 or Type 2 study are lacking, as is true for all six of the above outpatient studies and the three inpatient reports cited above as well.

In summary, only Type 3 studies (and some of these may be considered more nearly Type 5) have been accomplished to date regarding treatment outcomes employing cognitive-behavioral treatment techniques for the sexual offender. Nonetheless, it does appear that a combination of these approaches has markedly reduced the rate of reoffense (and, when measured, deviant sexual arousal) by most offenders. Unfortunately, the difficulty in conducting controlled trials combines with the lack of funding to pose significant obstacles to well-designed research in this field. However, double-blind studies do not have a monopoly on truth. It appears that combinations of the cognitive and behavioral therapies described above have been very successful in reducing the risk of reoffense.

FUTURE DIRECTIONS AND CONCLUSIONS

Estimates of the prevalence of sexual offending are so variable that epidemiological studies would be helpful to assess the scope of this problem. Of equal importance, we need to assess the occurrence of a variety of paraphilias to understand how each might be a part of, distinct from, or preparatory to, the other. In addition, special populations of offenders have not enjoyed much attention thus far in the scientific literature. Female exposers and molesters are known, and further reports would be welcome. Treatment programs specifically designed for adolescent offenders (Page, 1995) are just now being reported.

A variety of factors impedes our ability to generalize about treatment effectiveness. Inclusion criteria vary, yet are known to influence outcome. For example, exhibitionists with central nervous system damage have greater rates of reoffending, yet many programs exclude such patients. In addition, treatment refusals and high dropout rates are not uncommon. One report cites refusal rates of 67% for electrical aversion and 63% for aversive behavior rehearsal (Maletzky, 1991a, chap. 3). If a patient begins treatment, then drops out, his next victim may not be cheered by the fact that he is not counted among a clinic's failures.

Sometimes statistics tell just half the tale. Practical issues of treatment expense, refusal, dropout rates, sources of referral, program reputation, ease of access, and inclusion criteria all combine to contribute to patient outcome. If a comprehensive cognitive-behavioral treatment program directed by doctoral-level clinicians treats one offender for $3,000 and reports a success rate of 90%, is it to be preferred over a simpler program using a single treatment technique, costing $1,000, and yielding a 75% success rate? If 100 pedo-

philes are treated with a 75% success rate, at least 75 victims are saved. If 10 are treated with a 90% success rate, just nine victims are spared.

At present, assessment techniques are frankly inadequate. Physiologic measurement tools for the paraphilias are based on conjecture, not empirical studies of reliability and validity. Confidential surveys should not be a substitute for measurement, but our sole physiologic device, the plethysmograph, is faulty in several directions: it produces too many false negatives to be useful diagnostically and produces occasional but sufficient false positives to render it suspect for forensic purposes. Novel assessment measures, such as the Stroop Color Test (Greco, 1993) and the Hanson Sex Attitudes Questionnaire (Hanson, Gizzarelli, & Scott, 1994) are unlikely to offer robust validity. The Abel Screen II (Osborn et al., 1995) offers a promising venue for future research.

Physiologic reactions may in the future detect sexual intent. Finite chemical changes occur on arousal (George, 1995), although rapid and inexpensive detection is problematic. Perhaps patterns of central nervous system activity will in the future reveal sexual excitement. This is no longer far-fetched fantasy: several medical centers are at work on imagery techniques such as PET that are said to be able to detect a specific neural firing pattern on sexual arousal.

Due to financial and ethical constraints, it is unlikely that controlled double-blind studies of treatment outcome will occur soon. Large, clinically based studies, however, can be as valuable as those more tightly controlled studies and can point the way to improving technologies. In addition, making treatment affordable should be made a priority by teaching, encouraging, and exhorting governmental agencies to staff and maintain sexual offender treatment programs. Fewer than 10% of county and state community-based mental health treatment facilities now offer such programs (Damon, 1994). The majority of offenders will, in all likelihood, never be treated because of lack of funding even if their crimes are disclosed. Tragically, many may be incarcerated, then released, never to test how effective treatment might have been.

Clinicians and researchers also have both obligation and opportunity to provide education to a variety of audiences in order to reduce the damages caused by offending. Chief among these damages is the real trauma suffered by a victim, harm often regarded lightly, even in public discourse. In addition, we need to address the prevention of sexual offending as thoroughly as we advocate its treatment. While public education is not a panacea, it could inform potential offenders and victims of the harm such offending causes, document the number of otherwise law-abiding individuals who carry it out, and explain the potential of treatment to reduce its likelihood. Perhaps this will increase the motivation of some offenders to obtain treatment who would otherwise have been too afraid or too ashamed or who wished to stop offending but could not. With an increase in the numbers of sexual offenders entering treatment, we should be better able to understand the causes of such aggressive acts, the best ways to prevent them, and, perhaps, the very nature of these offenses, a veritable shopping list of mankind's darkest passions.

Note

1. Several semantic problems must be solved in any article about the paraphilias: (a) an *offender* may be different from a *patient*, but the commonly employed term *offender* is used here as it proves easier to access the literature employing that term; (b) over 95% of identified offenders have thus far been male. Use of the male pronoun is a convention widely tolerated in technical literature in this field. Female offenders are identified as such in the text.

References

Abel, G. G., Barlow, D. H., Blanchard, E. B., & Guild, D. (1977). The components of rapists' sexual arousal. *Archives of General Psychiatry, 34*, 895–903.

Abel, G. G., Becker, J. V., Mittelman, M. S., Cunningham-Rathner, J., Rouleau, J. L., & Murphy, W. D. (1987). Self-reported sex crimes of nonincarcerated paraphiliacs. *Journal of Interpersonal Violence, 2*, 3–25.

Abel, G. G., Mittelman, M. S., Becker, J. V., Rathner, J., & Rouleau, J. L. (1988). Predicting child molesters' response to treatment. *Annals of the New York Academy of Sciences, 528*, 223–234.

Abrams, S. (1991). The use of polygraphy with sex offenders. *Annals of Sex Research, 4*, 239–263.

American Psychiatric Association. (1994). *Diagnostic and statistical manual of mental disorders* (4th ed.). Washington, D.C.: Author.

Association for the Treatment of Sexual Abusers (ATSA). (1993). *The ATSA practitioners' handbook*. Portland, Ore.: Author.

Berlin, F. S., & Meinecke, C. F. (1981). Treatment of sex offenders with antiandrogenic medication: Conceptualization, review of treatment modalities and preliminary findings. *American Journal of Psychiatry, 138*, 601–607.

Bradford, J. M. W. (1990). The antiandrogen and hormonal treatment of sex offenders. In W. L. Marshall, D. R. Laws, & H. E. Barbaree (Eds.), *Handbook of sexual assault: Issues, theories, and treatment of the offender* (pp. 297–310). New York: Plenum.

Burt, M. R. (1980). Cultural myths and support for rape. *Journal of Personality and Social Psychology, 38*, 217–230.

Carnes, P. (1983). *The sexual addiction*. Minneapolis, Minn.: ComCare.

Casal-Ariet, C., & Cullen, K. (1993). Exhibitionism treated with clomipramine. *American Journal of Psychiatry, 150*, 1273–1274.

Colson, C. E. (1972). Olfactory aversion therapy for homosexual behavior. *Journal of Behavior Therapy and Experimental Psychiatry, 3*, 185–187.

Cox, D. J., & Maletzky, B. M. (1980). Victims of exhibitionism. In D. J. Cox & R. J. Daitzman (Eds.), *Exhibitionism: Description, assessment, and treatment* (pp. 289–293). New York: Garland Press.

Damon, P. P. (1994). *Tough issues, hard facts: The report of the National Council on Crime and Delinquency*. Washington, D.C.: U.S. Government Printing Office.

Davidson, P. (1979, May). *Recidivism in sexual aggressors: Who are the bad risks?* Paper presented at the National Conference on the Evaluation and Treatment of Sexual Aggressors, New York.

———. (1984, March). *Outcomes data for a penitentiary-based treatment program for sex offenders*. Paper presented at the Conference on the Assessment and Treatment of the Sex Offender, Kingston, Ontario, Canada.

Dhawan, S., & Marshall, W. L. (1996). Sexual abuse histories of sexual offenders. *Sexual Abuse: A Journal of Research and Treatment, 8*, 7–15.

Dwyer, S. M. (in press). Treatment outcome study: 17 years after sexual offender treatment. *Sexual Abuse: A Journal of Research and Treatment, 9*, 157–162.

Erickson, M. T. (1993). An evolutionary perspective of incest avoidance. *American Journal of Psychiatry, 150*, 411–416.

Evans, D. R. (1967). An exploratory study into the treatment of exhibitionism by means of emotive imagery and aversive conditioning. *Canadian Psychologist, 8*, 162.

Evans, D. R. (1970). Subjective variables and treatment effects in aversive therapy. *Behavior Research and Therapy, 8*, 141–152.

Finkelhor, D. (1994). The "backlash" and the future of child protection advocacy: Insights from the study of social issues. In J. E. B. Myer (Ed.), *The backlash: Child protection under fire* (pp. 113–137). Thousand Oaks, Ca.: Sage Press.

Flor-Henry, P., & Lang, R. (1988). Quantitative EEG analysis in genital exhibitionists. *Annals of Sex Research, 1,* 49–62.

Freeman-Longo, R. E. (1984). The Oregon State Hospital Sex Offender Unit: Treatment outcome. In F. H. Knopp (Ed.), *Retraining adult sex offenders: Methods and models* (pp. 185–209). Syracuse, N.Y.: Safer Society Press.

Freeman-Longo, R. E., & Bays, L. (1989). *Who am I and why am I in treatment?* Orwell, Vt.: Safer Society Press.

Freund, K. (1963). A laboratory method of diagnosing predominance of homo- or hetero-erotic interest in the male. *Behavior Research and Treatment, 12,* 355–359.

Freund, K., & Watson, R. (1980). Mapping the boundaries of courtship disorder. *Journal of Sex Research, 27,* 589–606.

Frisbie, L. U., & Dondis, E. H. (1965). *Recidivism among treated sex offenders.* California Mental Health Research Monograph No. 5. Sacramento, Ca.: Department of Mental Health.

Furby, L., Weinrott, M. R., & Blackshaw, L. (1989). Sex offender recidivism: A review. *Psychological Bulletin, 105,* 3–30.

Gebhard, P. H., Gargon, J. H., Pomeroy, W. B., & Christenson, C. V. (1965). *Sex offenders: An analysis of types.* New York: Harper and Row.

George, M. S. (1995). The clinical use of SPECT in depressive disorders. In M. A. Schuckit (Chairperson), Difficult differential diagnoses in psychiatry: The clinical use of SPECT (pp. 542–544). *Journal of Clinical Psychiatry, 56,* 539–546.

Gibbens, T. C. N., & Ahrenfeldt, R. H. (1966). *Cultural factors in delinquency.* London: Tavistock Press.

Gray, S. R. (1995). A comparison of verbal satiation and minimal arousal conditioning to reduce deviant arousal in the laboratory. *Sexual Abuse: A Journal of Research and Treatment, 7,* 143–153.

Greco, E. (1993). The emotional Stroop Test: A review of the literature. *Psichiatrica e Psicoterapia Analitica, 12,* 219–223.

Griffen, J., & Cherfas, J. (1983). *The monkey puzzle: Reshaping the evolutionary tree.* New York: Pantheon Press.

Groth, N. A. (1979). *Men who rape: The psychology of the offender.* New York: Plenum.

Hanson, R. K., Gizzarelli, R., & Scott, H. (1994). The attitudes of incest offenders: Sexual entitlement and acceptance of sex with children. *Criminal Justice and Behavior, 21,* 187–202.

Herman, J. L. (1980). Sex offenders: A feminist perspec-

tive. In W. L. Marshall, D. R. Laws, & H. E. Barbaree (Eds.), *Handbook of sexual assault: Issues, theories, and treatment of the offender* (pp. 177–193). New York: Plenum.

Heston, L. L., & Shields, J. (1968). Homosexuality in twins. *Archives of General Psychiatry, 18,* 149–160.

Howes, R. J. (1995). A survey of plethysmographic assessment in North America. *Sexual Abuse: A Journal of Research and Treatment, 7,* 9–24.

Hucker, S. J., & Bain, J. (1990). Androgenic hormones and sexual assault. In W. L. Marshall, D. R. Laws, & H. E. Barbaree (Eds.), *Handbook of sexual assault: Issues, theories, and treatment of the offender* (pp. 93–102). New York: Plenum.

Jensen, S., Laws, D. R., & Wolfe, R. (1994, November). *Reduction of sexual arousal: What to do and not to do.* Symposium presented at the annual conference of the Association for the Treatment of Sexual Abusers, San Francisco.

Justice, B., & Justice, R. (1979). *The broken taboo.* New York: Human Sciences Press.

Kafka, M. (1995, October). *Hypersexual desire in males: An operational definition and clinical implications for men with paraphilias and paraphilic-related disorders.* Paper presented at the annual conference of the Association for the Treatment of Sexual Abusers, New Orleans, La.

Kennedy, W. A., & Foreyt, J. (1968). Control of eating behaviors in obese patients by avoidance and conditioning. *Psychological Reports, 23,* 571–573.

Kinsey, A. C., Pomeroy, W. B., & Martin, C. E. (1948). *Sexual behavior in the human male.* Philadelphia: Saunders.

Kluver, H., & Bucy, P. E. (1939). Preliminary analysis of functions of the temporal lobe in monkeys. *Archives of Neurology and Psychiatry, 42,* 979–1000.

Knight, R. A., & Prentky, R. A. (1990). Classifying sexual offenders: The development and corroboration of taxonomic models. In W. L. Marshall, D. R. Laws, & H. E. Barbaree (Eds.), *Handbook of sexual assault: Issues, theories, and treatment of the offender.* New York: Plenum.

Knopp, F. H., Freeman-Longo, R. E., & Stevenson, W. F. (1992). *Nationwide survey of juvenile and adult sex offender treatment programs and models.* Orwell, Vt: Safer Society Press.

Krause, B. (1994). Rethinking Oepidus. *American Journal of Psychiatry, 151,* 296–297.

Lang, R. A., Langevin, R., Bain, J., Frenzel, R., & Wright, P. (1989). Sex hormones profiles in genital exhibitionists. *Annals of Sex Research, 2,* 67–75.

Langevin, R., Bain, J., Ben-Aron, M., Coulthard, R., Day, D., Handy, L., Heasman, G., Hucker, S. J., Purins, J. E., Roper, V., Russon, A., Webster, C. D., & Wortzman, G. (1985). Sexual aggression: Constructing a predictive equation. In R. Langevin (Ed.), *Erotic preference, gender identity, and aggression in men* (pp. 39–76). Hillsdale, N.J.: Lawrence Erlbaum.

Langevin, R., & Lang, R. A. (1987). The courtship disorders. In G. D. Wilson (Ed.), *Variant sexuality: Research and theory* (pp. 202–228). London: Croon Helm.

Laschet, V., & Laschet, L. (1975). Antiandrogens in the treatment of sexual deviations in men. *Journal of Steroid Biochemistry, 6,* 831–826.

Laws, D. R. (1995). Verbal satiation: Notes on procedure with speculations on its mechanism of effect. *Sexual Abuse: A Journal of Research and Treatment, 7,* 155–166.

Laws, D. R., & Marshall, W. L. (1991). Masturbatory reconditioning with sexual deviates: An evaluative review. *Advances in Behavior Research and Therapy, 13,* 13–25.

Laws, D. R., & Serber, M. (1975). Measurement and evaluation of assertive training with sexual offenders. In R. E. Hosford & C. S. Moss (Eds.), *The crumbling walls: Treatment and counseling of prisoners* (pp. 165–172). Champaign, Ill.: University of Illinois Press.

Leitenberg, H., Greenwald, E., & Tarran, M. J. (1989). The relation between sexual activity among children during preadolescence and/or early adolescence and sexual behavior and sexual adjustment in young adulthood. *Archives of Sexual Behavior, 18,* 199–243.

Lichtenstein, E., & Kruetzer, C. S. (1969). Investigation of diverse techniques to modify smoking: A follow-up report. *Behavior Research and Therapy, 7,* 139–140.

MacCulloch, M. J., Waddington, T. L., & Sanbrook, J. E. (1978). Avoidance latencies reliably reflect sexual attitude during aversion therapy for homosexuality. *Behavior Therapy, 9,* 562–577.

MacKinnon, C. A. (1985). Pornography, civil rights and speech. *Harvard Civil Rights—Civil Liberties Law Review, 20,* 1–70.

MacLean, P. D. (1973). New findings on brain function and sociosexual behavior. In J. Zubin & J. Money (Eds.), *Contemporary sexual behavior: Critical issues in the 1970s* (pp. 53–75). Baltimore, Md.: Johns Hopkins University Press.

Malamuth, N. W., Haber, S., & Feshbach, S. (1980). Testing hypotheses regarding rape: Exposure to sexual violence, sex differences and the "normality" of rapists. *Journal of Research in Personality, 14,* 121–137.

Maletzky, B. M. (1980). "Assisted" covert sensitization. In D. J. Cox & R. J. Daitzman (Eds.), *Exhibitionism: Description, assessment, and treatment* (pp. 187–251). New York: Garland Press.

———. (1986). Orgasmic reconditioning. In A. S. Bellack & M. Hersen (Eds.), *Dictionary of behavior ther-*

apy techniques (pp. 57–58). New York: Pergamon Press.

———. (1987, October). *Data generated by an outpatient sexual abuse clinic.* Paper presented at the annual conference of the Association for the Treatment of Sexual Abusers, Newport, Ore.

———. (1991a). *Treating the sexual offender.* Newbury Park, Ca.: Sage Publications.

———. (1991b). The use of medroxyprogesterone acetate to assist in the treatment of sexual offenders. *Annals of Sex Research, 4,* 117–129.

———. (1992, November). *Factors associated with success in a behavioral/cognitive outpatient treatment program for the sexual offender.* Paper presented at the annual conference of the Association for the Treatment of Sexual Abusers, Portland, Ore.

———. (1993). Factors associated with success and failure in the behavioral and cognitive treatment of sexual offenders. *Annals of Sex Research, 6,* 241–258.

———. (in press-a). Evolution, psychopathology and sexual offending: Aping our Ancestors. *Aggression and Violent Behavior: A Review Journal.*

———. (in press-b). Exhibitionism: Assessment and treatment. In D. R. Laws & W. O'Donohue (Eds.), *Handbook of sexual deviance.* New York: Guilford Publications.

Maletzky, B. M., & George, F. S. (1973). The treatment of homosexuality by "assisted" covert sensitization. *Behavior Research and Therapy, 11,* 655–657.

Maletzky, B. M., & McFarland, B. (1996). *Vicarious sensitization in the treatment of adult nonparaphlic sexual offenders: A pilot study.* Manuscript submitted for publication.

Maletzky, B. M., & Steinhauser, C. (in press). Community-based treatment programs for sexual offenders. In W. L. Marshall, S. M. Hudson, T. Ward, & Y. M. Fernandez (Eds.), *Sourcebook of treatment programs with sexual offenders.* New York: Plenum Press.

Marlatt, G. A., & Gordon, J. R. (Eds.) (1985). *Relapse prevention.* New York: Guilford Press.

Marques, J. U. (1994, November). *New outcome data from California's Sex Offender Treatment and Evaluation Project.* Paper presented at the annual conference of the Association for the Treatment of Sexual Abusers, San Francisco.

Marshall, W. L. (1989). Pornography and sexual offenders. In D. Zillman & J. Bryan (Eds.), *Pornography: Recent research, interpretations, and policy considerations* (pp. 185–214). Hillsdale, N.J.: Lawrence Erlbaum.

Marshall, W. L., & Barbaree, H. E. (1984). Disorders of personality, impulse, and adjustment. In S. M. Turner & M. Hersen (Eds.), *Adult psychopathology and diagnosis* (pp. 406–449). New York: Wiley.

————. (1990a). An integrated theory of the etiology of sexual offending. In W. L. Marshall, D. R. Laws, & H. E. Barbaree (Eds.), *Handbook of sexual assault: Issues, theories, and treatment of the offender* (pp. 257–275). New York: Plenum.

————. (1990b). Outcome of comprehensive cognitive/behavioral treatment programs. In W. L. Marshall, D. R. Laws, & H. E. Barbaree (Eds.), *Handbook of sexual assault: Issues, theories, and treatment of the offender* (pp. 363–385). New York: Plenum.

Marshall, W. L., & Hall, G. C. N. (1995). The value of the MMPI in deciding forensic issues in accused sexual offenders. *Sexual Abuse: A Journal of Research and Treatment, 7,* 205–219.

Marshall, W. L., Jones, R., Ward, T., Johnston, P. & Barbaree, H. G. (1991). Treatment outcome with sex offenders. *Clinical Psychology Review, 11,* 465–485.

Marshall, W. L., & Mazzucco, A. (1995). Self-esteem and parental attachments in sexual offenders. *Sexual Abuse: A Journal of Research and Treatment, 7,* 279–285.

Marshall, W. L., & Williams, D. (1975). A behavioral approach to the modification of rape. *Quarterly Bulletin of the British Association for Behavioral Psychotherapy, 4,* 78.

McConaghy, N. (1993). *Sexual behavior: Problems and management.* New York: Plenum.

McFall, R. M. (1990). The enhancement of social skills. In W. L. Marshall, D. R. Laws, & H. E. Barbaree (Eds.), *Handbook of sexual assault: Issues, theories, and treatment of the offender* (pp. 311–330). New York: Plenum.

McGuire, R. J., Carlisle, J. M., & Young, B. G. (1965). Sexual deviations as conditioned behavior: A hypothesis. *Behavior Research and Therapy, 2,* 185–190.

Money, J., & Pollitt, E. (1964). Cytogenic and psychosexual ambiguity. *Archives of General Psychiatry, 11,* 589–595.

Murphy, W. D. (1990). Assessment and modification of cognitive distortions in sex offenders. In W. L. Marshall, D. R. Laws, & H. E. Barbaree (Eds.), *Handbook of sexual assault: Issues, theories, and treatment of the offender* (pp. 331–342). New York: Plenum.

O'Donohue, W., & Letourneau, E. (1993). A brief group treatment for the modification of denial in child sexual abusers: Outcome and follow-up. *Child Abuse and Neglect, 17,* 297–304.

Osborn, C., Abel, G. G., & Warberg, B. W. (1995, October). *The Abel Assessment: Its comparison to plethysmography and resistance to falsification.* Paper presented at the annual conference of the Association for the Treatment of Sexual Abusers, New Orleans, La.

Page, J. (1995, October). *Development and adaptation of material for the adolescent sex offender.* Paper pre-

sented at the annual conference of the Association for the Treatment of Sexual Abusers, New Orleans, La.

Pithers, W. D. (1990). Relapse prevention with sexual aggressors. In W. L. Marshall, D. R. Laws, & H. E. Barbaree (Eds.), *Handbook of sexual assault: Issues, theories, and treatment of the offender* (pp. 343–361). New York: Plenum.

Proulx, J. (1989). Sexual preference assessment of sexual aggressors. *International Journal of Law and Psychiatry, 6,* 431–441.

Proulx, J., Pellerin, B., Paradis, Y., McKibben, A., & Aubut, J. (in press). Static and dynamic predictors of recidivism in sexual aggressors. *Sexual Abuse: A Journal of Research and Treatment.*

Quinsey, V. L. (1983). Prediction of recidivism and the evaluation of treatment programs for sex offenders. In S. N. Verdun-Jones & A. A. Keltner (Eds.), *Sexual aggression and the law* (pp. 27–40). Burnaby, B.C., Canada: Criminology Research Center Press.

————. (1984). Sexual aggression: Studies of offenders against women. In D. Weisstub (Ed.), *Law and mental health: International perspectives* Vol. 1 (pp. 84–121). New York: Pergamon Press.

Quinsey, V. L., Chaplin, T. C., & Carrigan, W. F. (1980). Biofeedback and signalled punishment in the modification of inappropriate age preferences. *Behavior Therapy, 11,* 567–576.

Quinsey, V. L., & Earls, C. M. (1990). The modification of sexual preferences. In W. L. Marshall, D. R. Laws, & H. E. Barbaree (Eds.), *Handbook of sexual assault: Issues, theories, and treatment of the offender* (pp. 279–295). New York: Plenum.

Quinsey, V. L., & Lalumiere, M. L. (1995). Evolutionary perspectives on sexual offending. *Sexual Abuse: A Journal of Research and Treatment, 7,* 301–315.

Quinsey, V. L., & Laws, D. R. (1990). Validity of physiological measures of pedophilic sexual arousal in a sexual offender population: A critique of Hall, Proctor and Nelson. *Journal of Consulting and Clinical Psychology, 58,* 886–889.

Rooth, G., & Marks, I. M. (1974). Persistent exhibitionism: Short-term response to aversion, self-regulation, and relaxation treatments. *Archives of Sexual Behavior, 8,* 227–248.

Russell, D. E. H. (1988). The incidence and prevalence of intrafamilial and extrafamilial sexual abuse of female children. In L. E. A. Walker (Ed.), *Handbook on sexual abuse of children* (pp. 19–36). New York: Springer.

Sanday, P. R. (1981). The socio-cultural context of rape: A cross-cultural study. *Journal of Social Issues, 37,* 5–27.

Schiavi, R. C., Thielgaard, A., Owen, D. R., & White,

D. (1988). Sex chromosome anomalies, hormones, and sexuality. *Archives of General Psychiatry, 45,* 19–24.

Schlank, A. M. (1995). The utility of the MMPI and the MSI in identifying a sexual offender typology. *Sexual Abuse: A Journal of Research and Treatment, 7,* 185–194.

Schlank, A. M., & Shaw, T. (1996). Treating sexual offenders who deny their guilt: A pilot study. *Sexual Abuse: A Journal of Research and Treatment, 8,* 21–29.

Seidman, B., Marshall, W. L., Hudson, S. M., & Robertson, R. J. (1994). An examination of intimacy and loneliness in sex offenders. *Journal of Interpersonal Violence, 9,* 518–534.

Serber, M. (1970). Shame aversion therapy. *Journal of Behavior Therapy and Experimental Psychiatry, 1,* 213–215.

Smith, R. (1984). The Oregon State Hospital Sex Offender Unit: Program description. In F. H. Knopp (Ed.), *Retraining adult sex offenders: Methods and models* (pp. 185–209). Syracuse, N.Y.: Safer Society Press.

Sternack, L. E., Segal, Z. V., & Gillis, R. (1990). Social and cultural factors in sexual assault. In W. L. Marshall, D. R. Laws, & H. E. Barbaree (Eds.), *Handbook of sexual assault: Issues, theories, and treatment of the offender* (pp. 143–159). New York: Plenum.

Tieger, T. (1981). Self-reported likelihood of raping and the social perception of rape. *Journal of Research in Personality, 15,* 147–158.

Van Wyk, P. H., & Geist, C. S. (1984). Psychosocial development of heterosexual, bisexual, and homosexual behavior. *Archives of Sexual Behavior, 13,* 505–544.

Ward, T., Hudson, S. M., Marshall, W. L., & Siegert, R. (1995). Attachment style and intimacy deficits in sexual offenders: A theoretical framework. *Sexual Abuse: A Journal of Research and Treatment, 7,* 317–335.

Weinrott, M. R., & Riggan, M. (1996). *Vicarious sensitization: A new method to reduce deviant arousal in adolescent offenders.* Manuscript submitted for publication.

Whitman, W. P., & Quinsey, V. L. (1981). Heterosocial skill training for institutionalized rapists and child molesters. *Canadian Journal of Behavioral Science, 13,* 105–114.

Wickramaseekera, I. (1980). Aversive behavioral rehearsal: A cognitive-behavioral procedure. In D. J. Cox and R. J. Daitzman (Eds.), *Exhibitionism: Description, assessment and treatment* (pp. 123–149). New York: Garland Press.

Wolfe, R. (1984). Northwest Treatment Associates: A comprehensive, community-based evaluation and treatment program for adult sex offenders. In F. H. Knopp (Ed.), *Retraining adult sex offenders: Methods and models* (pp. 85–101). Syracuse, N.Y.: Safer Society Press.

Wyatt, G. T. (1985). The sexual abuse of Afro-American and white American women in childhood. *Child Abuse and Neglect, 9,* 507–519.

Yochelson, S., & Samenow, S. E. (1977). *The criminal personality. Vol. 2: The change process.* New York: Jason Aronson.

Zverina, J., Lachman, M., Pondelickova, J., & Vanek, J. (1987). The occurrence of atypical sexual experience among various female patient groups. *Archives of Sexual Behavior, 16,* 325–326.

25

Treatments for Eating Disorders

G. Terence Wilson
Christopher G. Fairburn

The relative paucity of research on outcomes of treatment for anorexia nervosa (AN) contrasts sharply with the quantity and quality of research on outcomes of treatment for bulimia nervosa (BN). Because the literature on the treatment of AN contains a number of uncontrolled follow-up studies of various treatment programs, it is impossible to generalize from one clinical setting to another, to make comparisons among the studies, or to identify effective treatments.

A large number of good-to-excellent outcome studies (Type 1 and Type 2) suggest that several different classes of antidepressant drugs produce significantly greater reductions in the short term for binge eating and purging in BN patients than a placebo treatment; the long-term effects of antidepressant medication on BN remain untested. A very substantial number of well-designed studies (Type 1 and Type 2) have shown that manual-based cognitive-behavioral therapy (CBT) is currently the first-line treatment of choice for BN; roughly half of patients receiving CBT cease binge eating and purging. Well accepted by patients, CBT is the most effective means of eliminating the core features of the eating disorder and is often accompanied by improvement in comorbid psychological problems such as low self-esteem and depression; long-term maintenance of improvement is reasonably good. There is little evidence that combining CBT with antidepressant medication significantly enhances improvement in the core features of BN, although it may aid in treating comorbid depression.

While controlled studies of their long-term effectiveness are lacking, several different psychological treatments appear equally effective in reducing the frequency of binge eating in the short term in binge eating disorder (BED); these treatments include CBT, interpersonal therapy, and behavioral weight loss programs with or without an accompanying very low calorie diet (VLCD). There is currently little evidence that antidepressant medication is effective for treating binge eating in BED patients.

There are two generally recognized eating disorders, anorexia nervosa (AN) and bulimia nervosa (BN). In addition, many patients present with "atypical eating disorders." In the *Diagnostic and Statistical Manual of Mental Disorders* (DSM-IV), these disorders are placed together in the residual category of "eating disorder not otherwise specified" (American Psychiatric Association [APA], 1994). These atypical eating disorders may be classified into two broad groups: those resembling AN or BN but not quite meeting their diagnostic criteria and those with a qualitatively different clinical picture (Fairburn & Walsh, 1995). Among the latter, a specific group has recently received particular attention, namely, those with "binge eating disorder" (BED) (APA, 1994).

In this chapter, we review the research on the treatment of AN, BN, and BED, focusing on randomized, controlled treatment trials. The treatment of obesity is beyond the scope of the chapter since obesity is not an eating disorder, although it may coexist with one.

ANOREXIA NERVOSA

Anorexia nervosa (AN) is mainly seen among female adolescents and is characterized by a severe restriction of food intake. Body weight is very low, and physical health is correspondingly impaired. The patients are often described as having a "morbid fear of fatness" and a "relentless pursuit of thinness," and these extreme concerns about shape and weight appear to drive their avoidance of eating. Many also engage in other weight-control behaviors, including overexercising, self-induced vomiting, and the misuse of laxatives or diuretics. A minority of patients reports episodes of binge eating. The disorder varies markedly in severity and responsiveness to treatment. For some, it is brief and self-limiting, whereas for others it is unremitting and ends in premature death. In general, those cases with an early onset and short duration have the best prognosis (Hsu, 1990; Steinhausen, Rauss-Mason, & Seidel, 1991).

The goals of the treatment of AN are the restoration of healthy eating habits and a normal body weight, as well as the resolution of any intra- and interpersonal problems that may be maintaining the eating disorder. Most patients are treated exclusively on an outpatient basis, although they may be hospitalized for a variety of reasons, ranging from serious physical complications to the need to separate patients from their family (Fichter, 1995). When hospitalization is necessary, it is followed by outpatient treatment.

Inpatient Treatment

The literature contains a number of uncontrolled reports of the effects of various inpatient treatment programs. These reports cannot be used to identify effective treatments since patients in different clinical settings vary considerably in their characteristics and responsiveness to treatment. The findings of single-case experimental designs suggest that certain behavioral procedures facilitate weight gain when implemented within the broader context of an inpatient treatment program (Agras & Kraemer, 1984), and different elements of these programs have been manipulated to determine their effect on the rate of weight gain. For example, Touyz, Lennerts, Freeman, and Beaumont (1990) examined the effects of giving patients different amounts of feedback about their weight, and Solanto, Jacobson, Heller, Golden, and Hertz (1994) compared regimes that differed in their expected rates of weight gain. There is now evidence that traditional operant programs may be unnecessarily rigid and restrictive since satisfactory rates of weight gain can be achieved using simple and flexible behavioral regimes. For example, Touyz, Beumont, Glaun, Philips, and Cowie (1984) and Touyz, Beumont, and Dunn (1987) obtained mean daily weight gains of 0.16 kg and 0.20 kg using two versions of a straightforward "lenient" program. The use of medication does not appear to facilitate weight gain (Walsh, 1992).

Inpatient treatment is effective for restoring weight. The problem, however, is that this short-term improvement does not predict long-term outcome (Hsu, 1990). Patients frequently lose weight and relapse, often necessitating their readmission to a hospital.

Outpatient Treatment

There has been a small number of randomized, controlled studies of the outpatient treatment of AN. Channon, De Silva, Helmsley, and Perkins (1989) compared individual outpatient cognitive-behavioral treatment (CBT) with strictly behavioral treatment and a control treatment that was eclectic in nature and focused mainly on weight restoration and monitoring. Treatment consisted of 18 sessions. At 6- and 12-month follow-ups, all groups showed weight gain, enhanced sexual and social functioning, and improvement in depressed mood, but there were no significant differences among them. The small sample size of only eight patients per treatment militated against identifying group differences. Other methodological limitations included apparent differences among treatment groups at pretreatment on variables that have been linked to outcome (e.g., age of onset and previous hospitalization) and the administration of inadequately specified cognitive-behavioral and behavioral treatments by the same individual therapist who conducted the assessments of outcome.

The St. George's Studies

Two studies have been conducted by Crisp and his colleagues at St. George's Hospital in London (Crisp et al., 1991). In the first, Hall and Crisp (1987) assigned patients to either 12 outpatient sessions of dietary advice or joint individual and family psychotherapy. At 1-year follow-up, only the former was associated with statistically significant weight gain, although the latter group improved in sexual and social adjustment.

In the second, larger study, 90 patients were randomly assigned to one of the following four conditions (Crisp et al., 1991):

Group 1 ($n = 30$)—Inpatient treatment until normal weight was restored, followed by 12 sessions of individual outpatient therapy. Inpatient treatment was multifaceted, including weight restoration, individual therapy, family therapy, dietary counseling, and occupational therapy. The average length of hospitalization was 20 weeks.

Group 2 ($n = 20$)—12 sessions of outpatient individual and family psychotherapy.

Group 3 ($n = 20$)—10 sessions of outpatient group psychotherapy for patients and parents.

Group 4 ($n = 20$)—No treatment.

Groups 2 and 3 received dietary counseling during four sessions of their treatment. Of the 30 patients assigned to inpatient treatment, 18 (60%) accepted. Of the 20 assigned patients, 18 (90%) accepted outpatient individual treatment, and 17 (85%) of the 20 assigned patients accepted outpatient group treatment. Patients assigned to the "no treatment" condition were referred to their local physician. In practice, only 6 received no treatment of any kind. The others received either outpatient or inpatient treatment elsewhere during the course of the study.

Dropouts occurred in all treatment conditions, although the rates for each treatment were not specified, thereby complicating the interpretation of the results. Attrition was most marked in the outpatient group treatment (Group 3), for which the mean number of sessions attended was only 5, compared with 8.25 for the individual and family treatment (Group 2). Among those who completed treatment, the mean weight gains at follow-up 1 year after initial assessment were

9.6 kg, 9.0 kg, and 10.2 kg for the three active treatment conditions, respectively, all of which were significantly greater than for the control condition (Group 4). Patients in all four treatment conditions showed improved sexual adjustment and social functioning, with no clear evidence of between-group differences.

There are two striking findings from this study. First, brief outpatient treatment was as effective as much longer, intensive inpatient treatment. Second, all three treatments were associated with a clinically significant amount of weight gain at 1-year follow-up. Crisp et al. (1991) emphasized that their preferred clinical practice would have been to follow inpatient treatment with four times as many outpatient sessions over a period of 2 years. The added value of such intensive (and expensive) treatment remains to be demonstrated.

One of the methodological limitations of this study was that the two outpatient treatments were administered by different sets of therapists, a design that confounds therapist with therapy. A second limitation was the inadequate specification of the psychological treatments. The psychotherapy in this study is described elsewhere as mainly psychodynamic therapy with some cognitive-behavioral elements (Gowers, Norton, Halek, & Crisp, 1994). A third limitation was that assessment was conducted by a member of the research staff who was not blind to the treatment offered.

A 2-year follow-up of patients in Groups 2 and 4 of this study showed that those who had received outpatient individual and family therapy had gained significantly more weight and showed greater improvement in social and psychosexual functioning than those in the control condition (Gowers et al., 1994). The mean weight of patients in Group 2 was 94.5% of what would be normally expected, compared with 83% for those in the control group. The respective body mass indexes (BMIs) of patients in Groups 2 and 4 were 20.1 and 17.8. Before treatment, patients in both groups were at 75% of normal weight. Of the Group 2 patients, 12 were judged to have a good clinical outcome (i.e., within 15% of expected weight, menstruating regularly, and eating normally) versus 4 of the Group 4 patients. Improvement was positively correlated with attendance at treatment sessions.

It is of note that the response of these AN patients is surprisingly good as it is inconsistent with other clinical reports of longer term outcome. The failure to report the status of the other two treatment conditions is unfortunate and clouds the interpretation of the study. That the combined inpatient and outpatient treatment (Group 1) was less effective than an average of eight outpatient sessions is a finding in need of explanation and replication.

The Maudsley Studies

Treasure and her colleagues at the Maudsley Hospital in London evaluated the effects of two outpatient therapies for the treatment of older AN patients (mean age 25 years, range 18 to 39 years), who would be presumed to have a relatively poor prognosis (Treasure et al., 1995). The average age of onset of AN in these 30 patients was 20 years (range 12 to 30 years). The patients were randomly assigned to one of two therapies comprising 20 weekly individual sessions. One was labeled "educational behavioral treatment," in which patients monitored their daily food intake, set progressive eating and weight goals, and discussed weight and shape issues. The other treatment was called "cognitive analytical therapy," which, according to Treasure et al. (1995), "integrates psychodynamic factors with behavioural ones and focuses on interpersonal and transference issues" (p. 365). At 1-year posttreatment, 63% (19/30) were rated as having a good (within 15% of average body weight and normal menstrual cycles) or intermediate (within 15% of average weight but persistent amenorrhea) outcome. The two treatments did not differ except on one subjective measure of progress that favored the cognitive analytical therapy.

The methodological limitations of this pilot study, such as the use of inexperienced therapists to administer untested therapies in the absence of any control treatment, make it impossible to identify effective treatment strategies. Nonetheless, the results are noteworthy in that the success rate with these relatively poor prognosis patients is similar to that obtained in other studies with younger patients with an earlier onset. Given that these results were obtained with a truncated and simple form of behavior therapy (BT) consisting of only a few elements of a state-of-the-art cognitive-behavioral treatment, the added value of more sophisticated cognitive-behavioral treatments (e.g., Garner & Bemis, 1985; Pike, Loeb, & Vitousek, 1996) needs to be determined.

Dysfunctional family processes have been implicated in the development and maintenance of AN, and family therapy enjoys considerable clinical popularity (Vandereycken, Kog, & Vanderlinden, 1989).

A controlled outcome study of family therapy for AN (also from the Maudsley Hospital) compared this approach with individual supportive psychotherapy for 57 patients who had received inpatient therapy as the first phase of their treatment (Russell, Szmukler, Dare, & Eisler, 1987). Treatment lasted 1 year. For those patients with a young age of onset (under 19 years) and short duration of the disorder (less than 3 years), family therapy was significantly more effective than individual psychotherapy at both posttreatment and a 5-year follow-up. Of the 10 patients who received family therapy, 9 were rated as having a good ($n = 6$) or intermediate ($n = 3$) outcome compared with only 2 of 11 in the individual supportive psychotherapy condition. With patients with an older age of onset or longer duration of the condition, the two treatments were comparable. Outcomes for these patients were poor.

This study indicates that family therapy is an effective treatment for a subgroup of AN patients. Subsequent research by this group of investigators has focused on methods of implementing family therapy. It is widely assumed by family therapists that the family "system" is the problem, and the entire family needs to be the focus of therapy. To test this assumption, le Grange, Eisler, Dare, and Russell (1992) compared what they called conjoint family therapy, in which the whole family was treated together, with family counseling, in which parents were treated separately from their child. Both treatments were brief, with an average of nine sessions over a 6-month period. The patients were adolescents whose ages ranged from 12 to 17 years. At a 32-week reassessment, the two groups did not differ in their weight (which was in the normal range) or on psychosocial measures of improvement. These results must be interpreted cautiously, however, because of the small sample size ($n = 18$). It is reported that a subsequent study of 40 patients replicated these results (Dare & Eisler, 1995). Taken together, these findings suggest that brief therapy separately involving parents and their daughters can be effective, and they challenge long-standing assumptions about the practice of family therapy for AN (Dare & Eisler, 1995).

An American Outpatient Study

In the United States, Robin, Siegel, and Moye (1995) compared behavioral family systems therapy (BFST) with ego-oriented individual therapy (EOIT) in a sample of 22 adolescent girls who had developed AN within the previous 12 months. Such patients would be expected to have a good outcome. The patients were randomly assigned to the two treatments, which were conducted on an outpatient basis for a period of 12 to 18 months. (Five BFST and three EOIT patients were briefly hospitalized at the onset of the study to ensure that they were at 80% or more of target weight.)

The BFST consisted of parental control over eating, cognitive restructuring, problem solving, and communication training. The EOIT emphasized building ego strength, adolescent autonomy, and insight. Parents of patients in EOIT met separately with therapists on a bimonthly basis. Both treatments were manual based, and independent checks of representative sessions established that the therapists adhered to the treatment manuals.

Although both treatments resulted in significant increases in BMI, BFST was significantly superior to EOIT at both posttreatment and 1-year follow-up. At posttreatment, 55% of the BFST patients and 46% of the EOIT patients had achieved the target weights set by their pediatricians and had resumed menstruating. At follow-up, the figures were 82% and 50% for BFST and EOIT, respectively, although this difference did not reach statistical significance. Both therapies produced significant reductions in negative communication and parent-child conflict within the families.

Robin et al.'s (1995) finding that individual therapy produced significant change in family functioning supports le Grange et al.'s (1992) results in demonstrating that conjoint family therapy is not needed to modify interactions between the adolescent AN patient and family. It is not possible to tell from this well-controlled study whether the superiority of BFST in increasing BMI was due to its cognitive-behavioral approach or more generally to an advantage of family therapy over individual treatment.

Summary and Clinical Recommendations

The research on treatment outcome for AN contrasts sharply with the quantity and quality of studies of BN, discussed below. This unsatisfactory state of affairs is probably attributable in part to the low incidence of the disorder and in part to the clinical and methodological difficulties inherent in such research.

It is clear that inpatient treatment featuring nutritional counseling and behavioral elements can effectively restore body weight. Controlled studies of both antipsychotic medication and antidepressant drugs suggest that the addition of pharmacotherapy conveys

no added benefit in terms of weight gain (Vandereycken & Meerman, 1984; Walsh, 1992). Nor has cisapride (a gut motility stimulant) been shown to be more effective than a placebo for enhancing delayed gastric emptying (Szmukler, Young, Miller, Lichtenstein, & Binns, 1985). The challenge is to maintain restoration of weight once patients are discharged from the hospital. Kaye et al. (1997) reported a double-blind, placebo-controlled trial of fluoxetine as a means of preventing relapse in patients who had successfully completed an inpatient phase of treatment. Of patients followed for one year as outpatients, those who received fluoxetine ($n = 16$) responded significantly better than those ($n = 19$) administered a pill placebo. Fluoxetine was associated with significant weight gain and significant reduction in depression, anxiety, obsessions, and compulsions.

Strober, Freeman, DeAntonio, Lampert, and Diamond (1997) conducted a two-year, naturalistic follow-up of 33 patients with anorexia nervosa who had been treated in an intensive inpatient program. Fluoxetine was part of the continuing treatment they received as outpatients. Comparison of outcomes for these patients with those of matched historical controls who received identical inpatient and follow-up treatment without fluoxetine showed no significant effect of the drug. It is possible that the intensity and general effectiveness of the outpatient treatment made it difficult to detect an effect of fluoxetine. Additional studies of the value of fluoxetine as a means of preventing relapse are warranted.

Although inpatient treatment is often routine practice, patients may be managed exclusively on an outpatient basis. Both regimes have been tested in a handful of controlled outcome studies, and both have been associated with promising results. The evidence that brief outpatient treatment can be as effective as combined inpatient and outpatient treatment calls for additional research on what are optimal interventions for AN patients.

Research has corroborated clinical consensus about the value of involving family members in the treatment of young patients. Contrary to the assumptions of many family therapists, it seems that it is unnecessary to treat the whole family together or to modify directly the family's characteristic way of relating to each other.

The effectiveness of cognitive-behavioral therapy for AN, the psychological treatment that has proved effective with bulimia nervosa, has yet to be established. It would be expected to be of value given the similarities between the AN and bulimia nervosa and the overlap in the processes that are likely to be maintaining the two disorders (Fairburn, 1997a). Two studies of cognitive-behavioral therapy as an intervention for maintaining weight gain in patients following an inpatient phase of treatment are currently under way (K. Halmi, personal communication, January 1997; K. Pike, personal communication, April 1997).

BULIMIA NERVOSA

Bulimia nervosa (BN) mainly occurs among young adult women, although it is seen in adolescence and middle age. It is characterized by a severe disturbance of eating in which determined attempts to restrict food intake are punctuated by episodes of uncontrolled overeating. These binges are commonly followed by self-induced vomiting or the misuse of laxatives, although some patients do not "purge." The effects of these behaviors on body weight tend to cancel each other, with the result that most patients have a weight that is within the normal range. There are extreme concerns about shape and weight similar to those seen in AN, with self-worth being judged largely or even exclusively in terms of shape, weight, or both. There is also a high level of psychosocial impairment. Among cases that present for treatment, the disorder tends to run a chronic, unremitting course (Fairburn et al., 1995). For this reason, short-lived treatment effects are of limited clinical significance.

The aim of treatment is to establish healthy eating habits by removing both the overeating and undereating, the latter being thought to encourage the former (Fairburn, 1997a). Purging also needs to be addressed. Generally, the successful resolution of the eating disorder is associated with a marked decrease in associated psychosocial impairment. With most patients, these goals can be achieved on an outpatient basis.

Pharmacological Treatment

A number of different drugs have been used to treat BN. These drugs have included the anticonvulsant phenytoin, the opiate antagonist naltrexone, the appetite suppressant fenfluramine, and a wide range of antidepressant drugs, as well as lithium (Mitchell &

de Zwaan, 1993). The main focus has been on appetite suppressant and antidepressant medication.

Appetite Suppressant Medication

The effects of the appetite suppressant fenfluramine have been evaluated in two controlled trials. In the first study, Russell and his colleagues compared d-fenfluramine with a pill placebo in BN patients who also received supportive psychotherapy with some behavioral instructions regarding food intake (Russell, Checkley, Feldman, & Eisler, 1988). Fenfluramine was superior to the placebo in reducing binge eating and vomiting but not attitudes toward shape and weight. The dropout rate was high, 40%. Oddly, among patients who dropped out, those who had been receiving the active drug showed reduced frequencies of binge eating and purging, whereas those on the placebo had become more symptomatic. There were no differences between the completers in each condition.

In a second study, Fahy, Eisler, and Russell (1993) randomly assigned 43 BN patients to treatment with either d-fenfluramine (45 mg/day) or a placebo for an 8-week period. All patients also received outpatient CBT that was an abbreviated version of the Fairburn, Marcus, and Wilson (1993) program. The patients showed a clinically and statistically significant reduction in binge eating, purging, and attitudes toward body shape and weight at posttreatment and at 16-week and 1-year follow-ups. At no stage, however, was there was any difference between the d-fenfluramine and placebo conditions. The drug was well tolerated, with a dropout rate of only 9%.

The authors raise the possibility that the concurrent CBT might have prevented the detection of an effect of fenfluramine by creating a ceiling effect. This seems unlikely. At posttreatment, only 20% of the patients were asymptomatic and 46% still met diagnostic criteria for BN. The authors themselves concluded that d-fenfluramine is not an effective treatment for BN.

Antidepressant Medication

The most intensively studied and commonly used drugs for BN are antidepressants. The drugs have included tricyclic antidepressants, monoamine oxidase inhibitors, selective serotonin uptake inhibitors (SSRIs), and atypical antidepressants. The original rationale for treating BN with antidepressant drugs was that this eating disorder is a form of major depression (Pope, Hudson, Jonas, & Yurgelun-Todd, 1983). Although several lines of inquiry have discredited this view (Levy, Dixon, & Stern, 1989), the evidence is consistent in showing that antidepressant drugs produce significantly greater reductions in binge eating and purging than treatment with a placebo.

Previous reviews of the literature have followed the practice of providing a box score average of outcome based on studies available at the time (Craighead & Agras, 1991; Mitchell et al., 1990). To update these box score averages, we summarize the results of the 14 controlled outcome studies listed by Devlin and Walsh (1995) in their recent review of the effectiveness of antidepressant medication for BN (Agras, Dorian, Kirkley, Arnow, & Bachman, 1987; Alger et al., 1991; Barlow, Blouin, Blouin, & Perez, 1988; Blouin et al., 1988; Fluoxetine Bulimia Nervosa Collaborative Study Group, 1992; Horne et al., 1988; Hughes, Wells, Cunningham, & Ilstrup, 1986; Kennedy et al., 1988, 1993; Mitchell & Groat, 1984; Pope et al., 1983; Pope, Keck, McElroy, & Hudson, 1989; Walsh et al., 1988; Walsh, Hadigan, Devlin, Gladis, & Roose, 1991).[1]

These studies yielded a mean reduction in binge eating of 61.4% (range 31% to 91%), with an average remission rate of 22% (range 10% to 35%). The comparable figures for purging are a mean reduction of 58.9% (range 34% to 91%), with an average remission rate of 34% (range 23% to 44%). Several of the studies did not report remission rates. For example, only four studies reported remission rates for purging. In some instances, median reductions in binge eating and purging were reported, and in others we derived the reduction rates from examination of the graphs in the original articles. The average attrition rate was 27% (range 13% to 42%).

A major problem with all tallies of this nature is that averages compiled from studies differing widely in procedures, measurement, and methodological rigor can be misleading. The extreme variability in outcome among these studies is noteworthy. For example, one of the studies obtained a striking average reduction of 91% in purging, with a 68% remission rate after only 6 weeks of treatment with desipramine ($n = 13$), a rate virtually twice that of any other study using a tricyclic antidepressant (Hughes et al., 1986). Devlin and Walsh (1995) issue another caveat. Patients' response to a pill placebo has varied widely across the studies, indicating substantial differences in treatment responsiveness.

Several conclusions can be drawn from the antidepressant drug studies to date.

1. *Most antidepressant drugs are more effective than a pill placebo for reducing binge eating and purging.* Of the 14 published studies that have made this direct comparison (excluding Sabine, Yonace, Farrington, Barratt, & Wakeling's 1983 study—see note 1), 12 showed the statistically significant superiority of medication. An apparent exception concerns the SSRI fluvoxamine. In a well-conducted controlled trial in Britain, it was found to be no more effective than a pill placebo (P. Cooper, personal communication, April 1997; R. Palmer, personal communication, April 1997). Why fluvoxamine should be ineffective whereas the SSRI fluoxetine does have an effect is not clear, although it could be due to the two drugs' different effects on the 5-HT$_{2C}$ receptor since this receptor appears to have a role in the control of food intake and satiety (Cowen, Clifford, Williams, Walsh, & Fairburn, 1995; Spedding et al., 1996).[2]

2. *With one exception, there have been no systematic dose response studies.* The exception showed that 60 mg/day, but not 20 mg/day, of fluoxetine is more effective than a pill placebo (Fluoxetine Bulimia Nervosa Collaborative Study Group, 1992). Mitchell and de Zwaan (1993) concluded that there is no correlation between tricyclic serum levels and response, although there may be a relationship between fluoxetine levels and outcome (Ceccherini-Nelli & Guidi, 1993).

3. *Different classes of antidepressants seem to be equally effective.* The data for fluoxetine (Fluoxetine Bulimia Nervosa Collaborative Study Group, 1992) are comparable to those for tricyclic antidepressants. However, there have been no direct comparisons of different drugs within the same study. At present, fluoxetine (60 mg daily) would appear to be the drug of choice because of its relative freedom from adverse side effects.

4. *Patients who fail to respond to an initial antidepressant drug may respond to another.* This was found in two open-label, uncontrolled studies (Mitchell et al., 1989; Walsh et al., 1991). It has been replicated in a more recent study in which treatment with desipramine (for 8 weeks) was followed by treatment with fluoxetine (60 mg/day for 8 weeks) if the patient's binge frequency had not declined by at least 75% or the patient experienced intolerable side effects (Walsh et al., 1997). This two-stage regime was designed to approximate more closely actual clinical practice than conventional single-drug protocols. Of the patients

randomly selected for active medication, two thirds were sequentially administered the two drugs. Their average reduction in binge frequency was 69%, and 29% ceased binge eating. This compares with 47% and 13%, respectively, among patients treated with desipramine alone in an earlier placebo-controlled study conducted at the same center with a similar patient population (Walsh et al., 1991).

5. *The long-term effects of antidepressant medication remain largely untested.* Pope, Hudson, Jonas, and Yurgelun-Todd (1985) reported their experience over 2 years with 20 patients who were initially treated with imipramine. They found that most patients had to be kept on medication to maintain the initial treatment effects.

Walsh et al. (1991) required that patients in their study of desipramine versus a placebo show a minimum reduction of 50% in binge eating after 8 weeks in order to be entered into a 16-week maintenance phase. Only 41% (29 of 71 patients) met this criterion. Of these patients, 8 declined to participate in the maintenance phase because of lack of interest, intolerable side effects, or other problems. Therefore, just 21 patients entered the maintenance phase. Of these, 11 (52.4%) patients completed the 16 weeks, 6 (28.6%) of whom relapsed (i.e., binged more than 50% of their baseline binge frequency), 2 (9.5%) dropped out to seek treatment elsewhere, and 2 (9.5%) were discontinued due to intolerable side effects. Patients who completed the full 16 weeks of maintenance failed to show statistically significant improvement over this period. These results indicate that, even over this modest period of follow-up, the outcome is poor among those who remain on active medication. Similar results were obtained by Pyle et al. (1990), as described below.

The only other study of the longer term effects of antidepressant drugs was by Agras, Rossiter, et al. (1994), described below. They found that 6 months of treatment with desipramine produced lasting improvement even after the medication was withdrawn. In contrast, treatment with desipramine for only 4 months was associated with substantial relapse. This curious finding requires replication. The mechanism(s) by which 6 but not 4 months of treatment with desipramine reduces the probability of relapse is unclear.

6. *Few drug studies have evaluated the effects of antidepressant medication on aspects of BN other than binge eating and purging.* There is evidence that antidepressant drugs do not produce improvement in patients' eating between binge eating/purging episodes. One study found that desipramine actually increased rather than decreased dietary restriction between episodes of binge eating (Rossiter, Agras, Losch, & Telch, 1988). This failure to moderate the dieting of these patients may account for the poor maintenance of change with antidepressant medication since the extreme and rigid form of dieting seen in BN is thought to encourage binge eating (Polivy & Herman, 1993; Fairburn, 1997a). The finding that antidepressant drugs do not reduce dieting is difficult to reconcile with the evidence that both desipramine and fluoxetine can moderate concerns about body shape and weight (Goldbloom & Olmsted, 1993; Walsh et al., 1991). The explanation may lie in the measures of concern used since some measures of overconcern address mood-related concerns about shape and weight rather than the core cognitive disturbance (Cooper & Fairburn, 1993). One way of improving maintenance of change might be to combine antidepressant treatment with CBT with the hope that the overevaluation of shape and weight might lessen and with it dietary restraint. As discussed below, Agras, Rossiter, et al. (1994) found that combining CBT with 6 months of desipramine treatment reduced the relapse rate at 1-year follow-up. However, the combination of CBT and antidepressant drugs has little advantage over CBT alone (see below).

7. *Consistent predictors of a positive response to antidepressant medication have yet to be identified.* Pretreatment levels of depression appear not to be related to treatment outcome (Agras, Dorian, Kirkley, Arnow, & Bachman, 1987; Walsh et al., 1988, 1991).

8. *The mechanism(s) by which antidepressant medication exerts its effects is unknown.* Its effects cannot be mediated by reductions in depression since pretreatment levels of depression are unrelated to outcome. The apparent comparability of different classes of antidepressant drugs suggests some mechanism common to these agents. One possibility is that antidepressant medication attenuates hunger, thereby making it easier for BN patients to maintain their strict dieting (McCann & Agras, 1990; Rossiter et al., 1988). There is evidence that fluoxetine produces small but significant short-term reduction in weight in BN patients (Fichter et al., 1991; Fluoxetine Bulimia Nervosa Collaborative Study Group, 1992; Walsh et al., 1997).

Other Physical Treatments

There have been two controlled studies of light therapy based on the observation that there are seasonal variations in bulimic symptomatology. Both were short-term studies (2 weeks and 1 week). In the first, there was a reduction in the frequency of binge eating (Lam, Goldner, Solyom, & Remick, 1994), whereas in the second binge eating did not change (Blouin et al., 1996). In both studies, there was a decrease in the level of depressive symptoms. Given the potent and sustained influence of other treatments for bulimia nervosa (see below), there seems to be little to commend light therapy.

Psychological Treatments

Cognitive-Behavioral Therapy

By far the most intensively studied treatment for BN is cognitive-behavioral therapy (CBT). The use of CBT derives directly from Fairburn's first formulation of this approach in Oxford, England (Fairburn, 1981), and the publication of a detailed treatment manual in 1985 (Fairburn, 1985). A more recent, expanded version of this manual was published in 1993 (Fairburn, Marcus, & Wilson, 1993). Although there are differences in the ways in which cognitive-behavioral treatment has been implemented across different clinical and research settings, all are derived from the Oxford approach. It is the current Oxford manual that is the standard outpatient treatment for BN, and it is increasingly being adopted across all major clinical research centers (Wilson, Fairburn, & Agras, 1997).

The cognitive-behavioral treatment for BN is based on a model that emphasizes the critical role of both cognitive and behavioral factors in the maintenance of the disorder. It is described in detail by Fairburn (1997a). Figure 25.1 summarizes the model.

Of primary importance is the extreme personal value that is attached to an idealized body shape and low body weight. This results in an extreme and rigid restriction of food intake, which in turn makes patients physiologically and psychologically susceptible to periodic episodes of loss of control over eating (i.e., binge eating). The episodes are in part maintained by negative reinforcement since they temporarily reduce negative affect. Purging and other extreme forms of weight control are used in an attempt to compensate for the effects on weight of binge eating. Purging itself helps maintain binge eating by temporarily reducing the anxiety about potential weight gain and by disrupting the learned satiety that regulates food intake. In turn, binge eating and purging cause distress and lower self-esteem, thereby reciprocally fostering the conditions that will inevitably lead to more dietary restraint and binge eating.

It follows from this model that treatment must address more than the presenting behaviors of binge eating and purging. The extreme dietary restraint must be replaced with a more normal pattern of eating, and the dysfunctional thoughts and attitudes about body shape and weight must also be addressed. A key prediction of the model is that the severity of cognitive disturbance at the end of treatment will predict relapse. This was confirmed by Fairburn, Jones, Peveler, Hope, and O'Connor (1993): among patients who had recovered in behavioral terms, 9% of those with the least cognitive disturbance relapsed, compared with 29% and 75% among those with moderate and severe degrees, respectively, of cognitive disturbance. This important finding needs to be replicated.

To achieve these goals, the cognitive-behavioral treatment for BN uses an integrated sequence of cognitive and behavioral interventions. These are listed in Table 25.1.

The treatment is conducted on an outpatient basis and is suitable for all patients but the small minority (less than 5%) who require hospitalization. A detailed manual has been published (Fairburn, Marcus, & Wilson, 1993), together with a recent supplement in which certain aspects of its implementation are reviewed (Wilson et al., 1997).

As in the case of antidepressant drug treatment, box score averages of the effectiveness of CBT have been reported. For example, Craighead and Agras's (1991) summary of 10 studies yielded a mean reduction in purging of 79%, with a 57% remission figure. A tally of nine controlled studies of CBT published after their review yields estimates of a mean reduction in purging of 83.5%, with a 47.5% remission figure; the comparable estimates for binge eating are 79% and 62%, respectively (Agras et al., 1992; Fairburn et al., 1991; Freeman, Barry, Dunkel-Turnbull, & Henderson, 1988; Garner et al., 1993; Griffiths, Hadzi-Pavlovic, & Channon-Little, 1994; Laessle et al., 1991; Leitenberg et al., 1994; Thackray, Smith, Bodfish, & Meyers, 1993; Wilson, Nonas, & Rosenblum,

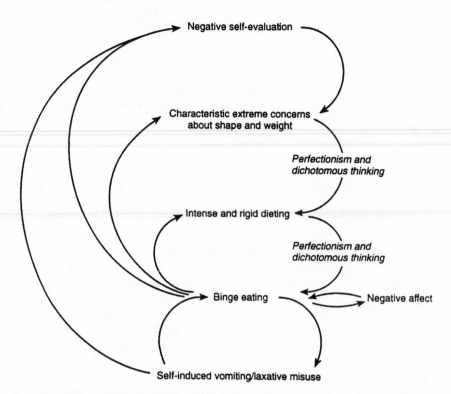

FIGURE 25.1. Cognitive model of bulimia nervosa. (From C. G. Fairburn, 1997a, Eating disorders, In D. M. Clark & C. G. Fairburn, Eds., *Science and Practice of Cognitive Behaviour Therapy*, Oxford, U.K.: Oxford University Press.)

TABLE 25.1 Main Elements of Cognitive-Behavioral Therapy for Bulimia Nervosa

1. Development of a good therapeutic relationship.
2. Self-monitoring.
3. Education about the cognitive model of the maintenance of BN and the need for both behavioral and cognitive change.
4. Establishment of regular weekly weighing.
5. Education about body weight regulation, the adverse effects of dieting, and the consequences of purging.
6. Prescription of a regular pattern of eating (three meals a day plus planned snacks).
7. Self-control strategies (e.g., stimulus control techniques).
8. Problem solving.
9. Modifying rigid dieting (e.g., consumption of previously avoided foods).
10. Cognitive restructuring for overcoming concerns about eating and body shape and weight.
11. Exposure methods for increasing acceptance of body weight and shape.
12. Relapse prevention training.

1993). Craighead and Agras (1991) reported an average attrition rate of 15.3% (range 0% to 29%). In the nine studies summarized here, the mean was 17.6%, with a range of 4.3% to 34.4%. Among the many differences across these diverse studies, treatment length varied from 8 to 20 sessions.

Comparisons of Cognitive-Behavioral Therapy with Delayed Treatment

Cognitive-behavioral therapy has been shown to be consistently superior to wait-list (WL) control groups, which show no improvement across a range of measures (Agras, Schneider, Aarnow, Raeburn, & Telch, 1989; Lee & Rush, 1986; Leitenberg, Rosen, Gross, Nudelman, & Vara, 1988; Freeman et al., 1988).

Comparisons of Cognitive-Behavioral Therapy with Antidepressant Medication

A more powerful approach to evaluating CBT is to compare its effects directly with alternative treatments within the same study. Since antidepressant medication is well established as having a significant short-term impact on BN, it provides a stringent standard of comparison for the effects of CBT or any other psychological treatment. Six studies have directly evaluated the relative and combined effectiveness of CBT and antidepressant drug treatment in controlled studies (Agras et al., 1992; Fichter et al., 1991; Leitenberg et al., 1994; Mitchell et al., 1990; Walsh et al., 1997).

In the first of these studies, Mitchell et al. (1990) found that medication (imipramine) alone was superior to a placebo but inferior to intensive group psychological treatment (mainly cognitive and behavioral in nature) combined with either the drug or placebo. The combinations of psychological treatment with drug and placebo respectively showed mean percentage reductions in binge eating of 89% and 92%; 51% of the patients were in remission during the last 2 weeks of treatment, and an additional 35% averaged one or fewer binges. Adding imipramine to the psychological treatment had no effect other than to produce greater reductions in symptoms of depression and anxiety. In this case, it is possible that the major improvement in frequency of binge eating and purging produced by the intensive psychological treatment precluded showing a medication effect because of a ceiling effect.

All patients who had responded to treatment (defined as no more than two binge-purge episodes during the final 2 weeks) were assigned to a 4-month maintenance program and were followed up at 6 months (Pyle et al., 1990). Only 9 of 54 patients (17%) who received drug treatment could be classified as responders. Of these 9, just 2 maintained their improvement at 6 months. The psychological treatment, in contrast, showed good maintenance of change at follow-up.

A second study, by Agras and colleagues (1992), produced similar results. The CBT alone and combined treatment were equally effective in reducing the frequency of binge eating and purging. Medication (desipramine) was administered for either 16 or 24 weeks. The combined treatment with medication for 24 weeks was superior to CBT alone on only a single self-report measure of hunger. This combined group, but not CBT alone, showed significantly greater reduction in binge eating and purging than the 16-week medication group at the 32-week assessment. Accordingly, this study is often taken as showing the superiority of combined treatment. A careful look at the data, however, suggests caution in drawing such a conclusion. The CBT alone was administered for only 15 weeks (with three additional "booster" sessions), so it is difficult to compare it with 24 weeks of combined treatment. Moreover, the data failed to show differences between CBT alone and either combined condition except for a composite measure of disinhibition and hunger from the Stunkard and Messick (1985) Eating Inventory. A 1-year follow-up showed the following remission rates from binge eating and purging: 18% of patients who had received 16 weeks of drug treatment, 67% of the 24-week drug treatment, 54% of the CBT group, and 78% of those in the combined CBT and 24-week medication treatment. As mentioned above, the finding that 24 weeks of desipramine treatment was substantially more effective than 16 weeks of desipramine treatment is difficult to explain.

In Germany, Fichter et al. (1991) compared a 35-day trial of fluoxetine (35 mg/day) with a placebo in 40 BN patients who were concurrently participating in an inpatient program of intensive behavioral therapy focused on the modification of abnormal eating and emotional expression and social skills training. There were no dropouts. Both the fluoxetine and placebo treatments were associated with statistically and clinically significant reductions in frequency of binge eating and attitudes toward eating. Similarly, both treatments resulted in significant improvement on self-rating scales of associated psychopathology, such as the SCL-90 (Derogatis, Rickels, & Rock, 1976) and the Hamilton Depression Rating Scale (Hamilton, 1967). On none of these measures was fluoxetine significantly more effective than the placebo. The only treatment-by-time interaction was for body weight, with fluoxetine producing greater weight loss.

A common interpretation of these findings is that the intensive behavioral treatment program produced a ceiling effect that made it impossible to show a treatment effect for fluoxetine (Fichter et al., 1991; Mitchell & de Zwaan, 1993). This seems implausible. Fichter et al.'s data show that fluoxetine resulted in a mean reduction in "binge attacks" of only 47% and in "urge to binge" of 46%, which would seem to leave ample room for a differential treatment effect to emerge.

The fourth study compared CBT, desipramine, and a combined CBT plus desipramine condition (Leitenberg et al., 1994). The study was terminated prematurely after only seven subjects had been treated in each condition because of the high dropout rate and poor response of the desipramine-only patients. The resulting small sample size makes the findings difficult to interpret. Of the seven subjects who received the drug-only treatment, four dropped out early, without showing any improvement, because of negative side effects. Two subjects in the combined treatment condition also dropped out because of side effects, and a third refused to continue to take medication after the 9th week of the 20-week program. Only one CBT subject dropped out. Five of the six CBT subjects and four of the five subjects in the combined treatment had ceased purging at posttreatment. These results were maintained at a 6-month follow-up.

The fifth study in this series randomly assigned patients either to antidepressant medication or a pill placebo (Walsh et al., 1997). Half the patients also received 20 individual sessions of CBT, and the other half a form of supportive psychotherapy (SPT) over a 16-week interval. Patients randomly assigned to receive active medication first received desipramine for 8 weeks. If the patient's binge frequency had not declined by at least 75% or if they experienced intolerable side effects, the desipramine was replaced by fluoxetine (60 mg/day) for the next 8 weeks. Patients randomly assigned to the placebo first received desipramine placebo and, following the same criteria, were then given fluoxetine placebo. As mentioned above,

this two-stage drug treatment was designed to approximate more closely actual clinical practice than do conventional single-drug protocols. The CBT was adapted from Fairburn's (1985) manual. The Eating Disorder Examination (EDE) (Fairburn & Cooper, 1993) was one of two main measures of outcome. The EDE is widely regarded as the best measure of eating disorder psychopathology (e.g., Garner, 1995).

Two main findings have emerged from the treatment phase of this study. Follow-up results are not yet available. The first was that, although medication was not statistically superior to a placebo in reducing binge eating as measured by the EDE (which assesses binge eating over 4 weeks), it was significantly more effective than the placebo in terms of patients' self-monitoring over the last 2 weeks of therapy. Differences between medication and placebo failed to reach statistically significant levels on either the EDE or self-monitoring measure of vomiting frequency. Effect sizes on the EDE for medication were $f = .15$ for binge eating and $f = .18$ for vomiting. Based on self-monitoring, effect sizes for medication were $f = .21$ for binge eating and $f = .20$ for vomiting. According to Stevens (1990), these are small effects. Medication also produced significantly greater reductions in depression and body weight (a mean of 3.5 versus 0.6 pounds).

The second main finding was that CBT was found to be significantly superior to SPT in reducing both 2-week self-monitoring and 4-week EDE measures of binge eating and vomiting. Effect sizes were $f = .38$ for binge eating and $f = .41$ for vomiting. Stevens (1990) rates an f greater than .40 as a large effect. There was no difference on depression, but CBT resulted in a slight but statistically significant increase in body weight (a mean of 1.24 versus 0.2 pounds). There were no statistically significant interactions between drug and psychological treatments. Two planned comparisons revealed that adding CBT to antidepressant medication produced a significantly greater improvement in vomiting frequency (and a trend in binge eating frequency) than medication only, whereas combining SPT with medication had no incremental benefit. Although the difference was not statistically significant, the drug plus CBT condition had a higher remission rate for binge eating and vomiting (50%) than the placebo plus CBT (24%).

The sixth study, from Toronto, compared 16 weeks of individual CBT with fluoxetine (60 mg) and a combined CBT/fluoxetine treatment (Goldbloom et al., in press). The combined treatment was significantly more effective than fluoxetine only in reducing frequency of binge eating and purging but did not differ from CBT only. Although these findings suggest that adding antidepressant medication to CBT has no significant incremental benefit, they must be interpreted cautiously. The attrition rate was unusually high. Of the 76 patients enrolled in the study, 33 (43%) failed to complete treatment. No follow-up was reported.

In a related study, Beaumont et al. (in press) compared intensive nutritional counseling combined with either fluoxetine (60 mg) or pill placebo for 8 weeks of individual treatment. The nutritional counseling used by this Australian group was a form of psychoeducational treatment that focused on correcting misconceptions about eating and body weight, and on replacing unhealthy dieting with normal eating. It shared some of the educational and behavioral features of CBT, such as self-monitoring and self-control techniques (e.g., stimulus control), but lacked the systematic cognitive focus and techniques of CBT. The two treatments showed equivalent, clinically significant reductions in binge eating and purging at the end of 8 weeks. The only advantage for the active drug was on the restraint and shape and weight concern subscales of the EDE. A three-month follow-up showed that the improvement in binge eating and purging was maintained, but that the fluoxetine was no longer superior to pill placebo on the EDE subscales.

The results of the five comparisons of CBT and antidepressant drugs suggest the following conclusions:

1. *CBT seems more acceptable to patients than antidepressant medication.* Patients with bulimia nervosa appear reluctant to take antidepressant medication and seem to prefer psychological treatment (Mitchell et al., 1990). Leitenberg et al. (1994) reported that 15% of potential subjects for their study rejected participation in the medication-only treatment condition.

2. *The dropout rate is lower with CBT than pharmacological treatments.* In the Mitchell et al. (1990) study, the dropout rates for imipramine with and without group psychological treatment were 25% and 42.6%, respectively. The comparable rates for patients who received the pill placebo with and without psychological treatment were 14.7% and 16.1%, respectively. Agras et al. (1992) had only one CBT patient drop out, a rate of 4.3%, compared with 17% for the desipramine patients. Leitenberg et al. (1994) reported

a 14% dropout rate in their CBT condition versus 57% in the desipramine-only treatment. Although not statistically significant, the rates in the Walsh et al. (1996) study were as follows: 36% for CBT plus placebo, 35% for CBT plus medication, 27% for both SPT plus medication and placebo, and 43% for antidepressant medication alone.

3. *CBT seems to be superior to treatment with a single antidepressant drug* (Agras et al., 1992; Leitenberg et al., 1994). It remains to be established whether or not CBT is superior to a two-stage drug intervention or longer duration pharmacotherapy than has typically been the case.

4. *Combining CBT with antidepressant medication is significantly more effective than using medication alone* (Agras et al., 1992; Goldbloom et al., (in press); Leitenberg et al., 1994; Mitchell et al., 1990; Walsh et al., 1997).

5. *Combining CBT and antidepressant medication produces few consistent benefits over CBT alone.* However, there is the isolated finding of Agras et al. (1992), which suggested that the combination might have a synergistic effect that could be superior to CBT alone on some measures.

6. *CBT plus medication has not been shown to be superior to CBT plus a pill placebo* (Fichter et al., 1991; Mitchell et al., 1990; Walsh et al., 1997).

7. *The combination of CBT and antidepressant medication may be more effective than CBT alone in reducing anxiety and depressive symptoms.* Mitchell et al. (1990) found that a combination of imipramine and intensive group psychological treatment, which was largely cognitive and behavioral in nature, was significantly superior to group therapy plus a pill placebo in reducing anxiety and depression. Similarly, Walsh et al. (1997) reported that antidepressant medication was significantly more effective than the placebo in reducing depressive symptoms, averaging above the CBT and supportive psychotherapy treatments in that study. The design did not permit a direct comparison between CBT plus antidepressant medication and CBT alone.

8. *Longer term maintenance of change appears to be better with CBT than antidepressant drugs.* Only two of these five comparative studies have reported longer term follow-up. As mentioned above, in the Pyle et al. (1990) follow-up of the Mitchell et al.(1990) study, there was poor maintenance of change among those who received drug treatment, whereas there was good maintenance among those who received psycho-

logical treatment. Similarly, Agras, Rossiter, et al. (1994) found that 4 months of desipramine was followed by a high relapse rate, but one that was prevented when the drug was combined with CBT. The findings of the comparative psychological treatment studies (see below) also suggest that maintenance of change is good with CBT.

The relative absence of sound data on the longer term effects of antidepressant drugs is a serious problem since short-lived treatment effects are of limited clinical significance given the tendency of BN to run a chronic course. As noted above, there are data indicating that patients relapse rapidly when antidepressant medication is discontinued (Mitchell & de Zwaan, 1993). In contrast, CBT has shown good medium- and long-term maintenance (Fairburn, Jones, et al., 1993; Fairburn et al., 1995). It is possible that combining CBT with medication might prevent the relapse associated with drug treatment (Agras, Rossiter, et al., 1994), although the combination has thus far been shown to have little advantage over CBT alone.

Comparisons of Cognitive-Behavioral Therapy with Alternative Psychological Treatments

"Nonspecific" Psychological Treatments Cognitive-behavioral therapy has also proved consistently superior to comparison treatments designed to control for the so-called nonspecifics of psychological treatment, such as the provision of a credible therapeutic rationale, the therapeutic relationship, and nondirective therapeutic exploration of intrapsychic issues. In the first of four studies in this category, Kirkley, Schneider, Agras, and Bachman (1985) reported that CBT administered in a group setting was superior to supportive psychotherapy with self-monitoring, although this difference was no longer present at 4-month follow-up. In the second study by the same group of investigators, CBT conducted on an individual basis was found to be more effective than supportive psychotherapy with self-monitoring, both at the end of treatment and at a 6-month follow-up (Agras et al., 1989).

A third study compared CBT with two alternative treatments. One was behavior therapy, a truncated form of CBT as discussed below. The other was what the authors called a nonspecific self-monitoring treatment, a nondirective intervention designed to serve as a face-valid comparison condition (Thackwray et

al., 1993). The CBT produced significantly greater improvement on binge eating and purging than the nonspecific self-monitoring condition at both post-treatment and a 6-month follow-up. A puzzling feature of this study is the remarkably high rate of success that was achieved. Following brief, individual treatment of only eight sessions, 92% of patients in CBT and 69% of the nonspecific self-monitoring condition patients had ceased binge eating and purging. No other study of CBT has produced such impressive success rates. The remission rates at 6-month follow-up were 69% and 15%, respectively, for the two conditions, indicating that the improvements obtained in the self-monitoring condition were short lived.

The fourth study (Walsh et al., 1997) has already been mentioned in the context of its antidepressant arm. It compared CBT with SPT for patients who concurrently received either antidepressant medication or a pill placebo. The SPT treatment was adapted from Fairburn, Kirk, O'Connor, and Cooper's (1986) focal psychotherapy condition, but differed in that it eliminated elements that overlapped with the putative active therapeutic ingredients of CBT, such as the self-monitoring of eating and the circumstances preceding binge eating. It was also less focal in nature, with the emphasis on patient self-exploration and understanding. The SPT was primarily designed to control for nonspecific therapeutic influences inherent in CBT. The strengths of this study include the fact that both treatments were manual based and closely supervised and the EDE was used as a primary outcome measure.

Posttreatment results showed that CBT was more effective than SPT, despite the fact that the two treatments created comparable expectations of improvement and resulted in equally favorable ratings of the therapeutic relationship. The CBT resulted in mean reductions of 84.7% and 84.6% in frequency of binge eating and vomiting, respectively, as measured by the EDE. The comparable results for SPT were 61.7% and 50.7%, respectively. On the self-monitoring measure, CBT resulted in reductions of 72% on binge eating and 69% on vomiting. The parallel numbers for SPT were 51.8% and 46.4%, respectively. The CBT was also significantly better on the EAT (Garner, Olmsted, Bohr, & Garfinkel, 1982), a self-report measure of eating disorder features. The findings at follow-up are not yet available.

Supportive-Expressive Psychotherapy Controlled studies have also compared CBT with other forms of psychotherapy. Garner and colleagues compared CBT with supportive-expressive psychotherapy (SET) (Garner et al., 1993). Both treatments produced substantial improvements by the end of treatment. The two treatments were equally effective in reducing binge eating, but CBT was significantly superior to SET in decreasing purging, lessening dietary restraint, and modifying dysfunctional attitudes to shape and weight. The CBT produced greater improvement in depression, self-esteem, and general psychological distress and also produced more rapid improvement than SET. No follow-up data have been reported.

Focal Interpersonal Psychotherapies   In the first of two related outcome studies, Fairburn et al. (1986) compared CBT with an adaptation of a form of brief focal psychotherapy (Rosen, 1979). The rationale for the latter treatment was that BN is maintained by a variety of ongoing problems (mostly of an interpersonal nature), and that to overcome the eating disorder these problems have to be identified and resolved. The focal psychotherapy included the self-monitoring of binge eating since binges are often triggered by interpersonal problems, and therefore they can serve as a useful marker of such problems (Fairburn, 1997b; Stunkard, 1980). Both treatments produced striking improvements in the core symptomatology of BN at posttreatment and over a 1-year closed follow-up. The CBT produced a 90% reduction in binge eating and a 93% reduction in purging at posttreatment. Beyond the specific eating disorder psychopathology, CBT was more effective than the focal psychotherapy in its effects on patients' social adjustment and overall clinical state.

The second study from the Oxford group (Fairburn et al., 1991, 1995) yielded several interesting and important findings. It is also one of the best controlled studies to date. In this study, CBT was compared with two alternative treatments; the first was behavior therapy (BT), comprising the CBT treatment minus cognitive restructuring and the behavioral and cognitive methods for modifying abnormal attitudes about weight and shape, and the second treatment was an adaptation of interpersonal psychotherapy (IPT) (described in more detail below). In the last treatment, little attention was paid to the eating disorder per se. All three treatments were manual based, and their implementation was closely monitored. For the first time in the field, the EDE was used as the main measure of outcome.

At posttreatment, the three therapies were equally effective in reducing binge eating. The mean reductions were 71% for CBT, 62% for BT, and 62% for IPT. However, CBT was significantly more effective than IPT in reducing purging, dietary restraint, and attitudes to shape and weight, and superior to BT on the last two variables despite equivalent ratings of suitability of treatment and expectations of outcome. This pattern of results shows that CBT had specific effects on different measures of outcome consistent with its theoretical rationale. As in the previous study by the Oxford group, treatment was followed by a 1-year closed follow-up (i.e., it was treatment free). It showed that the effects of CBT were well maintained and significantly superior to BT but equal to IPT, as discussed below (Fairburn, Jones, et al., 1993). Both binge eating and purging had ceased for 36% of CBT patients, 20% of BT patients, and 44% of IPT patients. The patients were followed up once more after an average of 5.8 (SD ± 2.0) years, thereby providing a unique perspective of the long-term impact of these three treatments. There was a clear difference among them, even after this long period of time. Those patients who had received CBT or IPT were doing equally well, with 63% and 72%, respectively, having no *DSM-IV* eating disorder, compared with 14% for those who had received BT (Fairburn et al., 1995).

Behavioral Treatments   Laessle et al. (1991) compared what they called a nutritional management (NM) treatment with stress management (SM). The former closely approximated the behavioral components of CBT; the latter included standard cognitive-behavioral strategies such as active coping and problem solving, but never focused directly on the modification of eating or attitudes about weight and shape. The results showed marginally significant but consistent differences in favor of NM at both posttreatment and 1-year follow-up. The NM produced significantly more rapid changes in eating behavior and purging than SM.

Using an abbreviated eight-session version of the Fairburn, Marcus, and Wilson (1993) manual, Griffiths et al. (1994) compared CBT with hypnobehavioral treatment. The first 4 weeks of this treatment were identical to that of CBT. The second half of treatment consisted of hypnosis designed to reinforce behavioral change and prevent relapse. The remission rates for binge eating in the week following treatment were 50% for CBT and 43% for the hypnobehavioral treatment. A weakness of this study was that a single therapist carried out both treatments. The rates for purging for CBT and the hypnobehavioral treatment were 40% and 33%, respectively. A 9-month closed follow-up showed no differences in remission rates between the two treatments and that the remission rate increased over time (Griffiths, 1996).

Other studies have dismantled CBT, comparing the complete treatment with its behavioral component. Unlike Fairburn, Jones, et al.'s (1993) manual-based CBT, the behavioral methods in these studies have not focused on modifying problematic thoughts about dieting and abnormal attitudes about body shape and weight. They also have not included the cognitive procedures of CBT, such as cognitive restructuring.

In the first of these studies, Freeman et al. (1988) compared CBT with behavior therapy (BT), group psychotherapy, and a wait-list control condition. There were no between-group differences among the three treatments, although all were superior to the wait-list control. No follow-up data were provided. A second study pitted a brief, eight-session CBT treatment against its behavioral component and a wait-list control (Wolf & Crowther 1992). Both treatments were administered on a group basis. The results showed that both treatments were comparably superior to the wait-list control. A 3-month follow-up indicated that the behavioral treatment was associated with better maintenance of reduction in binge eating than the CBT treatment. It must be noted that caution is warranted when interpreting the results of brief treatments like this and those in the Griffiths et al. (1994) and Thackwray et al. (1993) studies since it is highly unlikely that the cognitive components of the full Fairburn, Marcus, and Wilson (1993) manual can be effectively implemented in so abbreviated a program. The Wolf and Crowther (1992) study is also weakened by the fact that the same single therapist administered both treatments and conducted the posttreatment assessment.

The failure of the foregoing two studies to show that CBT was superior to BT contrasts markedly with the results from the Fairburn et al. (1991, 1993, 1995) study described above. In that study, CBT was more effective than BT at posttreatment on measures of dietary restraint and attitudes about body shape and weight. The superiority of CBT became even more evident at the 1- and 6-year follow-ups. Whereas CBT was associated with good maintenance of change, patients in the BT treatment fared poorly, with 48%

dropping out or being withdrawn from the study because of lack of improvement during the closed 1-year follow-up (Fairburn, Jones, et al., 1993). As mentioned, the outcome of the BT patients remained poor at the 6-year follow-up: Fairburn et al. (1995) argued that it was likely to reflect the natural outcome of clinic cases not exposed to an effective treatment.

The crucial importance of systematic follow-up is demonstrated by the findings of the Fairburn et al. study (1995), which revealed differential effects over time of the three treatments. Similar findings emerged from the study by Thackwray et al. (1993). At posttreatment, they found that CBT and BT were equally successful. At 6-month follow-up, however, CBT was superior to BT. Of patients who had received CBT, 69% remained abstinent from binge eating and purging compared with only 38% of those treated with BT.

A 6-to-12-month follow-up is essential when investigating the clinical value of treatments for BN. A well-designed study by Cooper and Steere (1995) compared a modified version of Fairburn, Marcus, and Wilson (1993) manual-based CBT with a more narrowly focused behavioral treatment that excluded the cognitive components of the treatment. In place of the emphasis on cognitive restructuring in Stage 2 of the manual, Cooper and Steere substituted eight sessions of exposure and response-prevention treatment based on Leitenberg and Rosen's (1985) behavioral treatment. This necessitated omitting from CBT measures designed to tackle dieting in order to minimize overlap between the treatments. Patients in both treatment conditions received the first eight sessions of CBT, as well as the final three sessions of relapse prevention. As such, this study provided the most searching test to date of the merits of CBT versus a more purely behavioral treatment.

Of the original 31 patients, 1 in each treatment dropped out, and 2 were withdrawn because of severe depression. The posttreatment analyses were conducted on the completers (CBT, $n = 13$; behavioral treatment, $n = 14$) with the EDE being the main measure of outcome. Both treatments produced clinically significant improvements with no between-group differences. The CBT produced a mean percentage reduction of 78% in binge eating and 82.8% in purging. The comparable figures for the behavioral treatment were 78.7% and 91.1%, respectively. The CBT resulted in remission rates of 46% and 54% in binge eating and purging, respectively. The comparable percentages for the behavioral treatment were 50% and 46%. Both treatments also resulted in significant improvements in dietary restraint and attitudes toward shape and weight. A 1-year follow-up of 25 of the patients (during which no patient received additional therapy) showed that, whereas patients who had been treated with CBT maintained their improvements, those who had received the behavioral treatment showed significant relapse. For example, of the 7 CBT patients who had ceased purging, only 1 relapsed. Of the 6 behavioral patients who had ceased purging, 5 relapsed. The CBT was significantly superior to the behavioral treatment on purging, with near significant trends on binge eating, dietary restraint, and scores on the EAT. These findings, taken together with those from the second Oxford trial, indicate that the cognitive component of CBT is needed if treatment effects are to persist.

Self-Help Cognitive-behavioral therapy was designed for use within specialist settings. It is time consuming (involving about 20 sessions over 5 months) and, to be executed optimally, training is required. Since there are unlikely ever to be sufficient specialist treatment resources for those with eating disorders, and BN in particular (it being much the more common of the two established eating disorders), there is a need to develop simpler and briefer forms of CBT suitable for widespread use (Carter & Fairburn, 1996). Attempts to do this are at an early stage. A brief form of CBT has been devised for use by nonspecialist therapists in primary care, and it seems promising (Waller, Fairburn, McPherson, Lee, & Nowell, 1996). In addition, two cognitive behavioral self-help books have been published (Cooper, 1995; Fairburn, 1995), both of which are designed to be used either by sufferers on their own (pure self-help) or with a limited amount of guidance from a nonspecialist therapist (guided self-help). In a large case series ($n = 82$), Cooper, Coker, and Fleming (1995) obtained good results with guided self-help, and Carter and Fairburn (in press) have obtained good preliminary results in a controlled trial comparing pure and guided self-help for the treatment of binge eating disorder (see below).

As yet, there has been just one controlled study of self-help for the treatment of BN. Treasure et al. (1994, 1996) compared CBT with a type of self-help treatment (based on an eclectic self-manual) supplemented, if necessary, with sessions of CBT. However, the findings are difficult to interpret for a number of rea-

sons, including the use of an unusual patient sample (cases of BN and "atypical BN" from a tertiary referral center), a complex staged design, and a poor response rate at follow-up. However, it is clear from their data that some patients obtained lasting benefits from the self-help condition, confirming that a subgroup of patients respond to minimal interventions of this type.

Conclusions Several conclusions can be drawn from these comparisons of CBT with alternative psychological treatments.

1. *CBT is more effective than credible comparison treatments that control for the nonspecifics of therapy.*

2. *CBT is superior to behavioral versions of the treatment that omit cognitive restructuring and the focus on modifying attitudes toward body shape and weight.*

3. *CBT is significantly more effective than, or at least as effective as, any form of psychotherapy with which it has been compared.*

4. *CBT produces a clinically significant degree of improvement.* One measure of the clinical importance of treatment-induced change is the extent to which patients engage in normative levels of behavior after treatment. Fairburn et al. (1995) reported that, at their 5.8-year follow-up, 74% of patients who had received CBT had global scores on the EDE within one standard deviation of the mean for young women in that community. Another study found that EDE scores of patients treated by CBT were lower (namely, less disturbed) than those of a comparison group of restrained eaters who neither binged nor purged (Wilson & Smith, 1989).

5. *CBT reliably produces changes across all four of the specific features of BN, namely, binge eating, purging, dietary restraint, and abnormal attitudes about body shape and weight* (Fairburn, Agras, & Wilson, 1992). The latter are key psychopathological features that are central to the cognitive-behavioral model of BN (Fairburn, 1996).

6. *CBT is comparatively fast acting.* It produces more rapid improvement than SET (Garner et al., 1993), stress management therapy (Laessle et al., 1991), and IPT (Fairburn et al., 1991). This rapidity of effect is consistent with data from CBT treatment of panic disorder (Clark et al., 1994) and depression (Ilardi & Craighead, 1994).

7. *CBT affects both the specific and general psychopathology of BN.* Most studies have shown significant improvements in depression, self-esteem, social func-

tioning, and measures of personality disturbance (e.g., Fairburn et al., 1986, 1992; Garner et al., 1993).

8. *CBT is associated with good maintenance of change at 6-month and 1-year follow-up* (e.g., Agras et al., 1989; Agras, Rossiter, et al., 1994; Fairburn, Jones, et al., 1993). The strongest findings have come from the Oxford group. After a 1-year follow-up, binge eating and purging (as assessed by the EDE) had declined by over 90%. Of the patients, 36% had ceased all binge eating and purging. Given that the follow-up was closed, this ensured that patients seeking additional or different treatment did not confound evaluation of maintenance of change (Fairburn, Jones, et al., 1993). The subsequent 6-year follow-up showed that the effects of CBT were maintained (an abstinence rate of 50%) (Fairburn et al., 1995). These findings contrast markedly with Keller, Herzog, Lavori, Bradburn, and Mahoney's (1992) conclusion, based on a naturalistic follow-up study, that patients with BN show "extraordinarily high rates of chronicity, relapse, recurrence, and psychosocial morbidity" (p. 1). The patients in their sample were not treated with manual-based CBT.

9. *A subgroup of patients appear to respond to brief and simplified forms of CBT.* Controlled evaluations of these simplified versions of manual-based CBT are a research priority.

10. *No reliable predictors of response to CBT have been identified.* A number of predictor variables have been proposed, but the treatment studies have yielded inconsistent results. Some studies have found that the lower the patients' previous low weight, the worse the outcome with CBT (Davis, Olmsted, & Rockert, 1992; Fahy & Russell, 1993; Wilson, Rossiter, Kleifield, & Lindholm, 1986). Agras et al. (1987) reported the same finding with imipramine treatment. Yet, Fairburn, Jones, et al. (1993) obtained no effect of previous low weight on the effects of CBT. Indeed, Blouin et al. (1994) found that patients with lower past and present weights showed greater reductions in vomiting frequency. At the other end of the weight spectrum, Fairburn et al. (1995) found that premorbid and paternal obesity were the only predictors of poor long-term treatment outcome for both CBT and IPT. The Oxford group found in both their studies that low self-esteem predicted a poor outcome (Fairburn et al. 1987, 1993).

The most consistent finding has been that comorbid personality disorders are a negative prognostic factor. This seems especially true of borderline person-

ality disorder (Coker, Vize, Wade, & Cooper, 1993; Johnson, Tobin, & Dennis, 1990; Rossiter, Agras, Telch, & Schneider, 1993). Fahy et al. (1993) found that BN patients with personality disorder responded poorly to CBT, but this association was no longer significant when BMI and depressed mood were controlled. Fairburn, Jones, et al. (1993) reported that patients who dropped out or were withdrawn from their study had more severe personality disturbance. Even here, however, contradictory findings exist. Davis et al. (1992) reported that a questionnaire measure of borderline personality was unrelated to outcome.

The Status of Other Psychological Treatments

Interpersonal Psychotherapy Other than CBT, the psychological treatment with the most support is interpersonal psychotherapy (IPT). It was originally devised by Klerman, Weissman, Rounsaville, & Chevron (1984) as a short-term treatment for depression. It is a focal psychotherapy, the main emphasis of which is to help patients identify and modify current interpersonal problems. The treatment is both nondirective and noninterpretative and, as adapted for BN (Fairburn, 1997), pays little attention to the patient's eating disorder. It is therefore very different from CBT. In the Fairburn et al. (1991) comparison of CBT and IPT, as noted above, IPT was as effective as CBT in reducing the frequency of binge eating (as assessed using the EDE), but it was inferior at posttreatment with respect to vomiting, dietary restraint, and attitudes toward body shape and weight. During the 1-year follow-up, however, patients who received IPT showed continuing improvement, to the point at which their outcomes were comparable to those who received CBT. Indeed, IPT was as effective as CBT on all measures by 8- and 12-month follow-ups. Of IPT patients, 44% were no longer binge eating or purging. The CBT and IPT showed an impressive 95% reduction in binge eating and a 91% reduction in vomiting. The differences between CBT and IPT in the temporal pattern of response suggests that, although the treatments were equivalent in their longer term outcome, each treatment had specific effects, probably through the operation of different mechanisms (Fairburn, Jones, et al., 1993).

Psychodynamic Therapy Controlled studies of the effectiveness of psychodynamic therapies are lacking.

The exception is Garner et al.'s (1993) comparison of CBT with supportive expressive psychotherapy (SET). Although equally effective in reducing binge eating, SET was inferior to CBT for other measures of BN, as well as for associated psychopathology. The absence of a no-treatment control group makes it difficult to interpret the binge eating result. The lack of follow-up data is another limitation of this study.

Despite the absence of data to support the use of psychodynamic psychotherapy for the treatment of BN, it remains very popular in the United States. For example, the American Psychiatric Association's *Practice Guidelines for Eating Disorders* state that "psychoanalytic therapies . . . may be particularly useful for long-term functioning" (APA, 1993, p. 218). Johnson et al. (1990) suggested that CBT is appropriate for patients with "simple" but not "complex" BN. So-called complex cases refer to the complicating presence of borderline personality disorder, which allegedly demands longer term psychodynamic therapy that focuses on distal, unconscious mediators of symptoms (Tobin, 1993). There is no evidence from BN or any other clinical disorder to show that CBT fares less well than an alternative psychodynamic approach for treating patients with comorbid borderline disorder. The best controlled study to date has shown that dialectical behavior therapy (a modified version of CBT) is significantly more effective than therapy as usual for the treatment of patients with borderline personality disorder (Linehan, Armstrong, Suarez, Allmon, & Heard, 1991). Johnson et al.'s (1990) own clinical report shows that BN patients with borderline personality disorder did significantly worse than their counterparts not so burdened despite 100 sessions or more of combined CBT and psychodynamic treatment.

Family Therapy A family approach to treating eating disorders has a long clinical tradition (Vandereycken et al., 1989). The American Psychiatric Association's practice guidelines assert that family-oriented therapies may be especially useful in the treatment of BN, yet only a single controlled study has evaluated the effectiveness of a family therapy approach (Russell et al., 1987). This study was marked by a high dropout rate (44%) and an unusually poor outcome (only a 9% abstinence rate), especially in adult patients. (It should be remembered that most patients with BN are adults.) However, since the patients in this study may have been a particularly recalcitrant group given

that they had been referred to a specialist treatment center, the generalizability of these findings could be questioned.

Summary and Clinical Recommendations

Manual-based CBT, as described by Fairburn, Marcus, and Wilson, (1993) and elaborated by Wilson et al. (1997), is currently the treatment of choice for BN. Well accepted by patients, it is the most effective means of eliminating the core features of the eating disorder and is usually accompanied by improvement in comorbid psychological problems such as low self-esteem and depression. Longer term maintenance of improvement appears to be good, although additional studies are needed.

Not every patient requires the full program of individual CBT (Fairburn & Carter, 1997). Some patients respond to briefer and simpler interventions, including cognitive-behavioral self-help manuals (Cooper, 1995; Fairburn, 1995), brief group psychoeducational programs (Olmsted et al., 1991), and a version of CBT designed for use by nonspecialists in primary care (Waller et al., 1996).

The chief limitation of CBT is that a significant proportion of patients does not make a full response. On average, roughly half of all patients cease binge eating and purging. Of the remainder, some show partial improvement, whereas others derive no benefit at all. Unfortunately, reliable predictors of outcome have yet to be identified. Comorbid personality disorder appears to be associated with a poorer response not only to CBT, but also drug and other psychological therapies.

Different options for improving on the success rate of CBT have been elaborated by Wilson (1996). One strategy would be to combine CBT with antidepressant medication. Combined treatment can be recommended for cases complicated by comorbid depression, but there is little evidence that the combination significantly enhances improvement with respect to the core features of BN. A second option would be to treat nonresponders with IPT, an alternative psychological therapy with the best available empirical support. In some patients, this can prove effective (Peveler & Fairburn, 1992). A third option would be to expand or intensify CBT. Whether or not these strategies would be effective for treating nonresponders to CBT is an empirical question. The possibility cannot be overlooked that a subset of patients will prove intractable regardless of the form of treatment used.

BINGE EATING DISORDER

Binge eating disorder (BED) is characterized by recurrent episodes of binge eating in the absence of the extreme methods of weight control seen in BN. Thus, there is no purging, overexercising, or extreme and rigid dieting. Rather, the binge eating occurs against a background of a general tendency to overeat. Not surprisingly, many patients with BED are overweight or frankly obese. The disorder is accompanied by concerns about shape and weight, but these are more understandable than those seen in BN given these patients' weight, and, unlike BN, self-evaluation tends not to be focused on shape and weight. Partly for this reason, Fairburn (1997a) has questioned the relevance to BED of the cognitive model of BN. Like BN, however, BED is associated with shame and self-recrimination and some degree of psychosocial impairment.

The distribution and prevalence of BED are not known. It appears to affect an older age group than BN, with many patients in their forties. Male cases are not uncommon. Also unlike BN, BED appears to run a phasic course, with extended periods (often lasting many months) when there is control over eating.

In BED, the aim of treatment is to establish healthy eating habits by helping patients avoid all forms of overeating. As in BN, the successful resolution of the eating disorder is generally associated with a marked decrease in associated psychosocial impairment. Weight loss does not always accompany a reduction in the frequency of binge eating, possibly because of the general tendency of these patients to overeat. Treatment is generally on an outpatient basis.

Pharmacological Treatment

Appetite Suppressant Medication

Appetite suppressants are a logical class of drug to evaluate for the treatment of BED given the obvious overeating and association with obesity. The only study of appetite suppressants involved an 8-week, double-blind, placebo-controlled evaluation of d-fenfluramine (Stunkard, Berkowitz, Tanrikut, Reiss, & Young,

1997). For the study, 50 obese patients with BED participated in a 4-week placebo washout phase; 22 patients improved to the point at which they no longer met criteria for BED. The remaining 28 were randomly assigned to d-fenfluramine (15 mg once a day during Week 1; 15 mg twice a day during Weeks 2–7; and 15 mg once a day during Week 8) or a placebo. Three patients dropped out of the drug treatment, one from the placebo group. Analyses of the data from the 12 patients in each group who completed the 8-week treatment showed that d-fenfluramine was significantly more effective than the placebo in reducing binge eating. Of the 10 patients with adequate plasma levels of the drug, 8 ceased binge eating. No other statistically significant differences were found on a variety of measures, including the Stunkard and Messick (1985) Eating Inventory, the Binge Eating Scale (Gormally, Black, Daston, & Rardin, 1982), and body weight.

Two findings from this study are of particular note. The first is the strong placebo response. Stunkard et al. (1997) also point out that Alger et al. (1991) reported a 68% decrease in binge eating of their placebo patients. The second finding is that d-fenfluramine reduced binge eating but not body weight. As such, it is inconsistent with other studies on the weight-reducing effect of the drug for obese patients (National Task Force on the Prevention and Treatment of Obesity, 1996). It is also at odds with the Fahy et al. (1993) study that found no effect of fenfluramine on binge eating in normal-weight patients with bulimia nervosa. Whether the last discrepancy indicates a difference in binge eating between bulimia nervosa and BED patients or the operation of other unidentified processes remains to be seen. The potential value of d-fenfluramine as a treatment for BED cannot be determined in the absence of long-term follow-up.

Antidepressant Medication

Given the short-term effectiveness of antidepressant medication for the treatment of BN, it is not surprising that researchers have been quick to apply these drugs to BED.

Using a 12-week, double-blind design, McCann and Agras (1990) evaluated the effectiveness of the tricyclic antidepressant desipramine versus a placebo in the absence of any counseling regarding nutrition, weight loss, or psychological concerns. The average dose of desipramine was 188 mg/day. The desipramine resulted in a mean reduction in binge eating of 63%, whereas there was a 16% increase in binge eating in the placebo condition. The remission rates were 60% and 15%, respectively, for desipramine and the placebo groups. The active drug was associated with a significant reduction in hunger ratings and increased dietary restraint, although there was no significant weight loss. Discontinuation of the drug after the 12-week treatment produced rapid relapse.

A second study by Agras and his colleagues evaluated the effects of a trial of desipramine (285 mg/day) during the last 6 months of a 9-month cognitive-behavioral treatment for binge eating and weight loss in obese BED patients (Agras, Telch, et al., 1994). The drug failed to improve either the reduction of binge eating or weight loss at posttreatment. Consistent with previous findings, desipramine significantly reduced disinhibition and hunger ratings as measured by the Stunkard and Messick (1985) Eating Inventory. A small, 8-week study by Alger et al. (1991) compared imipramine (200 mg/day) with a pill placebo for obese binge eaters whose weights were between 120% and 200% of desirable weight. Clinical samples of obese binge eaters overlap with the diagnosis of BED but may not meet all the diagnostic criteria. Imipramine was not significantly superior to the placebo in reducing the frequency of binge eating.

Selective Serotonin Reuptake Inhibitors

Two controlled studies have evaluated the effects of an SSRI. In the first, Marcus et al. (1990) evaluated the effectiveness over 52 weeks of fluoxetine (60 mg/day) versus a pill placebo in a double-blind study of obese binge eaters and non-binge eaters. The fluoxetine treatment resulted in significantly greater weight loss but did not reduce binge eating or depressed mood in the binge eaters.

The second study compared fluvoxamine (100 mg/day) with a pill placebo for BED patients who were concurrently treated with either CBT or dietary management (de Zwaan, Nutzinger, & Schoenbeck, 1992). There was no evidence of any effect of the fluvoxamine on binge eating. All treatment groups showed a modest and comparable weight loss during treatment, followed by weight regain at 1-year follow-up. The only evidence of the efficacy of fluvoxamine was a reduc-

tion in depression. It will be recalled that fluvoxamine appears to have no effect in BN.

Psychological Treatments

Cognitive-Behavioral Therapy

Given the success of CBT for BN, it is not surprising that this approach has been adapted for treating patients with BED. Four controlled studies have been carried out by Agras and his colleagues at Stanford. The first evaluated 10 weekly sessions of group CBT compared with a WL control group in patients who reported recurrent binge eating without purging (Telch, Agras, Rossiter, Wilfley, & Kenardy, 1990). The selection criteria closely resemble what *DSM-IV* subsequently designated as BED. The average BMI of these patients was 32.6, with a range of 22.2 to 42.6. At posttreatment, CBT patients who completed the treatment program showed a mean reduction in binge eating episodes of 94%, with a 79% remission rate over the last week of therapy. Replication of the same CBT treatment with the WL controls produced similar results, namely, a mean reduction of 85% and a remission rate of 73%. A 10-week follow-up revealed significant relapse in patients treated with CBT, although binge eating frequency was still below pretreatment levels. The CBT group did not differ from the WL group in posttreatment reductions in dietary restriction, food preoccupation, body weight, or depression.

A second study by this group compared CBT with IPT and a WL condition (Wilfley et al., 1993). Both treatments were administered in a group format over a 4-month period. The results, which are discussed more fully in the next section, showed that group CBT and IPT were significantly superior to the WL condition but did not differ from each other in outcome. The CBT produced a mean reduction in days binged of 48%, with a modest remission rate of 28%. A 1-year follow-up on a subgroup of patients revealed that, although there was reasonable maintenance of change in both groups, patients were still, on average, binge eating on 2 days a week.

The third Stanford study evaluated the effects of 12 weekly group sessions of CBT versus a wait-list condition for obese patients with BED (Agras et al., 1995). The treatment used in the Telch et al. (1990) study was modified to include a systematic exercise program plus education in choosing low-fat foods as a means of controlling weight. The CBT resulted in an 84% reduction in mean frequency of binge eating, with a 55% remission rate. The corresponding outcomes for the WL condition were 8% and 9%. Weight remained unchanged in the CBT group, but increased by 4.1 kg in the WL group.

The fourth Stanford study compared the short-term effects of CBT with a behavioral weight loss program (Agras, Telch, et al., 1994) and is summarized in the next section.

In the first study to apply BN research methodology to BED, Marcus, Wing, and Fairburn (1995) compared an adaptation of CBT for BN (Fairburn, Marcus, & Wilson, 1993) with a behavioral weight loss treatment (BT) and a delayed treatment (DT) condition. Both treatments lasted 6 months. In contrast to other studies of CBT for BED, both the BT and CBT treatments were administered on a one-to-one basis. Treatment outcome was assessed using the EDE. The results were striking. At posttreatment, both CBT and BT produced significantly greater reductions in days that binge eating occurred during the previous month than DT. The number of days binged over the 1-month period were 0.7 for CBT, 2.7 for BT, and 18.1 for DT. This represents an impressive 98% reduction in binge days for CBT. The overall attrition rate was 34%, with no differences among the three treatment conditions. However, BT had one major advantage over CBT in that it also resulted in substantial weight loss (mean = 21.6 pounds). A preliminary 1-year follow-up indicated that the improvements in binge eating had been maintained but that the patients in the BT condition had begun to regain weight.

As in the treatment of BN, a cognitive-behavioral self-help treatment may be a cost-effective alternative to full CBT. Carter and Fairburn (in press) compared a pure self-help (PSH) treatment, in which BED subjects were mailed a self-help book (Fairburn, 1995) and advised to follow its recommendations, with one in which they also received up to eight 25-minute supportive sessions from a therapist without clinical qualifications (guided self-help [GSH]). The therapist's role was to encourage the patients to follow the advice in the self-help book (which was a direct translation of full CBT). Treatment lasted 12 weeks. Both treatments were compared with a delayed treatment control condition. An intent-to-treat analysis revealed binge eating cessation rates (EDE based) of 56% for GSH, 34% for PSH, and 8% for the DT

condition, with percentage reductions in binge eating of 74%, 49%, and 29% respectively. A 3-month follow-up of the patients in the two active treatment conditions showed that these improvements were maintained. They were accompanied by a substantial and maintained decrease both in the overall level of eating disorder symptoms (as measured by the self-report version of the EDE; Fairburn & Beglin, 1995) and in the level of general psychiatric symptoms. Whether these benefits persist in the longer term remains to be determined. The findings suggest that, as in BN, cognitive behavioral self-help may be an effective intervention for a subgroup of those with BED.

Interpersonal Psychotherapy

Wilfley et al. (1993) evaluated the effectiveness of a group adaptation of the IPT treatment originally applied to BN by Fairburn et al. (1991). The comparison treatments were CBT, as noted above, and a waiting-list control condition. At the 16-week posttreatment assessment, IPT resulted in a 71% reduction in the number of days binged. The remission rate was 44%. As mentioned above, the comparable figures for CBT were 48% and 28%, respectively, and for the WL condition they were 10% and 0%, respectively. Both IPT and CBT were significantly more effective than the WL condition, but they did not differ from each other. The same pattern held true for disinhibited eating, as measured by the Stunkard and Messick (1985) Eating Inventory, and measures of self-esteem and depression. The IPT had an attrition rate of 11% compared with 33% for CBT, although this difference was not statistically significant. As noted above, while there was reasonable maintenance of change at 1-year follow-up, patients in both treatment conditions were still, on average, binge eating 2 days a week.

Group IPT was also evaluated as a treatment for those BED patients who failed to respond to CBT in the Agras et al. (1995) study. A 12-week trial failed to produce improvement on any measure.

Behavioral Weight Control Treatments

Behavioral weight control programs have also been used to treat binge eating in overweight BED patients. Some programs have emphasized moderate caloric reduction, others more severe low calorie diets.

Moderate Caloric Restriction　Using an additive experimental design, Agras, Telch, et al. (1994) compared a 9-month behavioral weight loss (BWL) program focused on moderate caloric restriction with two alternative treatments: one was an initial 3-month CBT treatment aimed at reducing binge eating, followed by the weight control program (CBT/BWL); the other was a combined CBT and behavioral weight loss program supplemented by the addition of desipramine over the last 6 months of treatment (CBT/BWL/D), as noted above. Although the CBT treatment produced a significantly greater reduction in binge eating at the 12-week stage, there were no significant differences among the three treatments at the end of 9 months on either binge eating frequency or weight loss. At posttreatment, 41% of the CBT/BWL/D treatment, 37% of the CBT/BWL treatment, and 19% of the BWL treatment had ceased binge eating. Weight losses for these three treatments were 6.0 kg, 1.6 kg, and 3.7 kg for CBT/BWL/D, CBT/BWL, and BWL, respectively. Although patients who ceased binge eating lost more weight than their counterparts who did not at the 3- and 6-month assessments, this difference had disappeared by the end of treatment. Smith, Marcus, and Kaye (1992) similarly found that obese binge eaters who stop binge eating lose more weight than those who do not.

A second study of obese binge eaters (who are likely to have met criteria for BED) compared a group CBT program designed to reduce binge eating with a standard group behavioral weight loss program (Porzelius, Houston, Smith, Arfken, & Fisher, 1995). Both treatments produced clinically significant but comparable reductions in severity of binge eating at posttreatment and 1-year follow-up. Similarly, as discussed above, the study by Marcus et al. (1995) showed that both a behavioral weight loss control treatment and CBT, administered on an individual basis, produced striking and equal improvement in binge eating in obese BED patients. Collectively, the results of these three studies indicate that a comprehensive behavioral weight loss program is the most effective treatment of BED.

Severe Caloric Restriction   It is well established that dieting is a proximal antecedent to the development of binge eating in most patients with BN (Polivy & Herman, 1993; Wilson, 1995). Accordingly, modification of dietary restraint is an important goal of CBT for BN (Fairburn, Marcus, & Wilson, 1993). Extrapolating from these findings, several clinical investigators have warned against using treatments involving either moderate or severe caloric restriction for obese BED patients on the grounds that they might encourage binge eating (e.g., Garner & Wooley, 1991). The findings from the three studies summarized in the preceding section fail to support this prediction as it applies to moderate caloric restriction. The research on the effects of very low calorie diets (VLCDs) similarly provides no support for this assertion.

Telch and Agras (1993) identified binge eating in a series of obese patients entering a combined VLCD and behavioral weight loss program. The patients are very likely to have met the criteria for BED. During the 3 months of the VLCD, the frequency of binge eating declined substantially. Over the course of a subsequent 9-month phase of refeeding and behavioral treatment, the frequency of binge eating began to return to its baseline level but was the same as its rate of occurrence in those obese patients who had not reported binge eating prior to treatment.

In a study of obese women with and without BED, Yanovski and Sebring (1994) similarly found that a VLCD treatment did not worsen the severity of binge eating in BED patients. In fact, the frequency and severity of binge eating had declined by the end of treatment. The probable explanation for these findings is that BED patients differ from those with BN. In BN, binge eating represents periodic breakdowns in otherwise excessive dietary control. The BED patients, however, show little dietary restriction between binge eating episodes (Yanovski & Sebring, 1994). Moreover, in marked contrast to BN, binge eating precedes dieting in over 50% of obese binge eaters (Mussell et al., 1995; Wilson et al., 1993).

Summary and Clinical Recommendations

The first point that must be emphasized is that the research on the treatment of BED is at an early stage. As mentioned above, the histories of these patients suggest that, unlike BN, it is a phasic condition with extended periods of remission. The disorder also appears vulnerable to "placebo effects" in that substantial improvement often occurs among those allocated to delayed treatment control conditions or a pill placebo. The implications of these observations for clinical practice and research have yet to be fully realized. They certainly suggest that studies need to include a long period of follow-up.

The treatment that shows the most promise is behavioral weight control treatment. Not only is it associated with a marked reduction in the frequency of binge eating, but there may also be weight loss, at least in the short term. Contrary to some suggestions, it has emerged that treatments that encourage dietary restraint do not promote binge eating among those with BED. Cognitive-behavioral therapy shows promise, but it appears to have no advantages over behavioral weight control programs and, as currently practiced, it does not result in weight loss. On the other hand, cognitive-behavioral self-help programs may prove to be effective for a subgroup of patients.

There are too few pharmacotherapy studies to draw firm conclusions about the use of drugs for the treatment of BED. Nevertheless, it should be noted that four of the five controlled studies of antidepressant medication showed no advantage of the drug over a placebo. This finding is very different from that for BN.

Overall, the results to date reinforce the differences between BED and BN. While there are superficial similarities between the disorders in terms of binge eating, the differences in treatment response mirror the differences in psychopathology and course. Much remains to be learned about BED.

ACKNOWLEDGMENTS We are grateful to Kelly Vitousek, Ph.D., Susan Yanovski, M.D., Tim Walsh, M.D., and Manfred Fichter, M.D., for their helpful input in the preparation of this chapter. C. G. Fairburn is grateful to the Wellcome Trust for their personal support.

Notes

1. We excluded the study by Sabine et al. (1983) on mianserin versus placebo because there was no change in binge eating or purging in either condition.

2. A study by Fichter et al. (1996) evaluated the effect of fluvoxamine in promoting maintenance of change following discharge from an intensive inpatient program. During the 15-week maintenance phase, the dropout rate for the fluvoxamine condition was a striking 51% compared with 14% for the placebo condition. The data were analyzed using an intention-to-treat approach in which each subject's last available data point was used. While this method usually results in a conservative test of the effects of treatment, in a maintenance design the converse is the case. Since there was substantial attrition in the drug condition but not in the placebo condition, this method of analysis introduced substantial bias in favor of finding a drug effect, thereby rendering the findings uninterpretable.

References

American Psychiatric Association (1993). Practice guideline for eating disorders. *American Journal of Psychiatry, 150,* 212–228.

Agras, W. S., Dorian, B., Kirkley, B. G., Arnow, B., & Bachman, J. (1987). Imipramine in the treatment of bulimia: A double-blind controlled study. *International Journal of Eating Disorders, 6,* 29–38.

Agras, W. S., & Kraemer, H. (1984). The treatment of anorexia nervosa: Do different treatments have different outcomes. In A. J. Stunkard & E. Stellar (Eds.), *Eating and its disorders.* New York: Raven Press.

Agras, W. S., Rossiter, E. M., Arnow, B., Schneider, J. A., Telch, C. F., Raeburn, S. D., Bruce, B., Perl, M., & Koran, L. M. (1992). Pharmacologic and cognitive-behavioral treatment for bulimia nervosa: A controlled comparison. *American Journal of Psychiatry, 149,* 82–87.

Agras, W. S., Rossiter, E. M., Arnow, B., Telch, C. F., Raeburn, S. D., Bruce, B., & Koran, L. (1994). One-year follow-up of psychosocial and pharmacologic treatments for bulimia nervosa. *Journal of Clinical Psychiatry, 55,* 179–183.

Agras, W. S., Schneider, J. A., Arnow, B., Raeburn, S. D., & Telch, C. F. (1989). Cognitive-behavioral and response-prevention treatments for bulimia nervosa. *Journal of Consulting and Clinical Psychology, 57,* 215–221.

Agras, W. S., Telch, C. F., Arnow, B., Eldredge, K., Wilfley, D. E., Raeburn, S. D., Henderson, J., & Marnell, M. (1994). Weight loss, cognitive-behavioral, and desipramine treatments in binge eating disorder: An additive design. *Behavior Therapy, 25,* 225–238.

Agras, W. S., Telch, C. F., Arnow, B., Eldredge, K., Henderson, J., & Marnell, M. (1995). Does interpersonal therapy help patients with binge eating disorder who fail to respond to cognitive-behavioral therapy? *Journal of Consulting and Clinical Psychology, 63,* 356–360.

Alger, S. A., Schwalberg, M. D., Bigaouette, J. M., Michalek, A. V., & Howard, L. J. (1991). Effect of tricyclic antidepressants and opiate agonist on binge-eating behavior in normoweight bulimic and obese, binge-eating subjects. *American Journal of Clinical Nutrition, 53,* 865–871.

American Psychiatric Association. (1994). *Diagnostic and statistical manual of mental disorders.* Washington. D.C.: Author.

Barlow, J., Blouin, J., Blouin, A., & Perez, E. (1988). Treatment of bulimia with desipramine: a double-blind crossover study. *Canadian Journal of Psychiatry, 33,* 129–133.

Beaumont, P. J. V., Russell, J. D., Touyz, S. W., Buckley, C., Lowinger, K., Talbot, P., & Johnson, G. F. S. (in press). Intensive nutritional counselling in bulimia nervosa: A role for supplementation with fluoxetine? *Australian and New Zealand Journal of Psychiatry*.

Blouin, A. G., Blouin, J. H., Iversen, H., Carter, J., Goldstein, C., Goldfried, G. & Perez, E. (1996). Light therapy in bulimia nervosa: A double-blind, placebo-controlled study. *Psychiatry Research, 60*, 1–9.

Blouin, A. G., Blouin, J. H., Perez, E. L., Bushnik, T., Zuro, C., & Mulder, E. (1988). Treatment of bulimia with fenfluramine and desipramine. *Journal of Clinical Psychopharmacology, 8*, 261–269.

Blouin, J. H., Carter, J., Blouin, A. G., Tener, L., Schnare-Hayes, K., Zuro, C., Barlow, J., & Perez, E. (1994). Prognostic indicators in bulimia nervosa treated with cognitive-behavioral group therapy. *International Journal of Eating Disorders, 15*, 113–124.

Carter, J. C., & Fairburn, C. G. (1996). Treating binge eating problems in primary care. *Addictive Behaviors, 20*, 765–772.

Carter, J. C., & Fairburn, C. G. (in press). Cognitive-behavioural self-help for binge eating disorder: A controlled effectiveness study. *Journal of Consulting and Clinical Psychology*.

Ceccherini-Nelli, A. & Guidi, L. (1993). Fluoxetine: The relationship between response, adverse events, and plasma concentrations in the treatment of bulimia nervosa. *International Clinical Psychopharmacology, 8*, 311–313.

Channon, S., De Silva, P., Helmsley, D., & Perkins, R. (1989). A controlled trial of cognitive behavioural and behavioural treatment of anorexia nervosa. *Behaviour Research and Therapy, 27*, 529–535.

Clark, D. M., Salkovskis, P. M., Hackmann, A., Middleton, H., Anastasiades, P., & Gelder, M. (1994). A comparison of cognitive therapy, applied relaxation and imipramine in the treatment of panic disorder. *British Journal of Psychiatry, 6*, 759–769.

Coker, S., Vize, C., Wade, T., & Cooper, P. J. (1993). Patients with bulimia nervosa who fail to engage in cognitive behavior therapy. *International Journal of Eating Disorders, 13*, 35–40.

Cooper, P. J. (1995). *Bulimia nervosa and binge-eating: A guide to recovery*. London: Robinson.

Cooper, P. J., Coker, S., & Fleming, C. (1995). An evaluation of the efficacy of cognitive behavioural self-help for bulimia nervosa. *Journal of Psychosomatic Research, 40*, 281–287.

Cooper, P. J., & Fairburn, C. G. (1993). Confusion over the core psychopathology of bulimia nervosa. *International Journal of Eating Disorders, 13*, 385–389.

Cooper, P. J., & Steere, J. (1995). A comparison of two psychological treatments for bulimia nervosa: Implications for models of maintenance. *Behaviour Research and Therapy, 33*, 875–886.

Cowen, P. J., Clifford, E. M., Williams, C., Walsh, A. E. S., & Fairburn, C. G. (1995). Why is dieting so difficult? *Nature, 376*, 557.

Craighead, L. W., & Agras, W. S. (1991). Mechanisms of action in cognitive-behavioral and pharmacological interventions for obesity and bulimia nervosa. *Journal of Consulting and Clinical Psychology, 59*, 115–125.

Crisp, A. H., Norton, K., Gowers, S., Halek, C., Bowyer, C., Yeldham, D., Levett, G., & Bhat, A. (1991). A controlled study of the effect of therapies aimed at adolescent and family psychopathology in anorexia nervosa. *British Journal of Psychiatry, 159*. 325–333.

Dare, C., & Eisler, I. (1995). Family therapy and eating disorders. In K. D. Brownell & C. G. Fairburn (Eds.), *Eating disorders and obesity* (pp. 318–323). New York: Guilford Press.

Davis, R., Olmsted, M. P., & Rockert, W. (1992). Brief group psychoeducation for bulimia nervosa. II: Prediction of clinical outcome. *International Journal of Eating Disorders, 11*, 205–211.

Derogatis, L. R., Rickels, K., & Rock, A. (1976). The SCL-90 and the MMPI: A step in the validation of a new self-report scale. *British Journal of Psychiatry, 128*, 280–289.

Devlin, M. J., & Walsh, B.T. (1995). Medication treatment for eating disorders. *Journal of Mental Health, 4*, 459–469.

de Zwaan, M., Nutzinger, D. O., & Schoenbeck G. (1992). Binge eating in overweight women. *Comprehensive Psychiatry, 33*, 256–261.

Fahy, T. A., Eisler, I., & Russell, G. F. M. (1993). A placebo-controlled trial of d-fenfluramine in bulimia nervosa. *British Journal of Psychiatry, 162*, 597–603.

Fahy, T. A., & Russell, G. F. M. (1993). Outcome and prognostic variables in bulimia nervosa. *International Journal of Eating Disorders, 14*, 135–146.

Fairburn, C. G. (1981). A cognitive behavioural approach to the management of bulimia. *Psychological Medicine, 11*, 707–711.

———. (1985). Cognitive-behavioral treatment for bulimia. In D. M. Garner & P. E. Garfinkel (Eds.), *Handbook of psychotherapy for anorexia nervosa and bulimia* (pp. 160–192). New York: Guilford Press.

———. (1995). *Overcoming binge eating*. New York: Guilford Press.

———. (1997a). Eating disorders. In D. M. Clark & C. G. Fairburn (Eds.), *The science and practice of cognitive behaviour therapy*. Oxford, U.K.: Oxford University Press.

———. (1997b). Interpersonal psychotherapy for bulimia nervosa. In D. M. Garner & P. E. Garfinkel (Eds.), *Handbook of treatment for eating disorders* (pp. 278–294). New York: Guilford Press.

Fairburn, C. G., Agras, W. S., & Wilson, G. T. (1992). The research on the treatment of bulimia nervosa: Practical and theoretical implications. In G. H. Anderson & S. H. Kennedy (Eds.), *The biology of feast and famine: Relevance to eating disorders* (pp. 317–340). New York: Academic Press.

Fairburn, C. G., & Carter, J. C. (1997). Self-help and guided self-help for binge eating problems. In D. M. Garner & P. E. Garfinkel (Eds.), *Handbook of treatment for eating disorders* (pp. 494–500). New York: Guilford Press.

Fairburn, C. G., & Cooper, P. J. (1993). The Eating Disorder Examination. In C. G. Fairburn & G. T. Wilson (Eds.), *Binge eating: Nature, assessment, and treatment* (pp. 317–360). New York: Guilford Press.

Fairburn, C. G., Hay, P. J., & Welch, S. L. (1993). Binge eating and bulimia nervosa: Distribution and determinants. In C. G. Fairburn & G. T. Wilson (Eds.), *Binge eating: Nature, assessment, and treatment* (pp. 123–143). New York: Guilford Press.

Fairburn, C. G., Kirk, J., O'Connor, M., & Cooper, P. J. (1986). A comparison of two psychological treatments for bulimia nervosa. *Behaviour Research and Therapy, 24,* 629–643.

Fairburn, C. G., Jones, R., Peveler, R. C., Carr, S. J., Solomon, R. A., O'Connor, M. E., Burton, J., & Hope, R. A. (1991). Three psychological treatments for bulimia nervosa. *Archives of General Psychiatry, 48,* 463–469.

Fairburn, C. G., Jones, R., Peveler, R. C., Hope, R. A., & O'Connor, M. (1993). Psychotherapy and bulimia nervosa: The longer-term effects of interpersonal psychotherapy, behaviour therapy and cognitive behaviour therapy. *Archives of General Psychiatry, 50,* 419–428.

Fairburn, C. G., Marcus, M. D., & Wilson, G. T. (1993). Cognitive behaviour therapy for binge eating and bulimia nervosa: A comprehensive treatment manual. In C. G. Fairburn & G. T. Wilson (Eds.), *Binge eating: Nature, assessment and treatment* (pp. 361–404). New York: Guilford Press.

Fairburn, C. G., Norman, P. A., Welch, S. L., O'Connor, M. E., Doll, H. A., & Peveler, R. C. (1995). A prospective study of outcome in bulimia nervosa and the long-term effects of three psychological treatments. *Archives of General Psychiatry, 52,* 304–312.

Fairburn, C. G., & Walsh, B. T. (1995). Atypical eating disorders. In K. D. Brownell & C. G. Fairburn (Eds.), *Eating disorders and obesity* (pp. 135–140). New York: Guilford Press.

Fichter, M. M. (1995). Inpatient treatment of anorexia nervosa. In K. D. Brownell & C. G. Fairburn (Eds.), *Eating disorders and obesity* (pp. 336–343). New York: Guilford Press.

Fichter, M. M., Kruger, R., Rief, W., Holland, R., & Dohne, J. (1996). Fluvoxamine in prevention of relapse in bulimia nervosa: Effects on eating-specific psychopathology. *Journal of Clinical Psychopharmacology, 16,* 9–18.

Fichter, M. M., Leibl, K., Rief, W., Brunner, E., Schmidt-

Auberger, S., & Engel, R. R. (1991). Fluoxetine versus placebo: A double-blind study with bulimic inpatients undergoing intensive psychotherapy. *Pharmacopsychiatry, 24,* 1–7.

Fluoxetine Bulimia Nervosa Collaborative Study Group. (1992). Fluoxetine in the treatment of bulimia nervosa: A multicenter, placebo-controlled, double-blind trial. *Archives of General Psychiatry, 49,* 139–147.

Freeman, C. P. L., Barry, F., Dunkeld-Turnbull, J., & Henderson, A. (1988).Controlled trial of psychotherapy for bulimia nervosa. *British Medical Journal, 296,* 521–525.

Garner, D. M. (1995). Measurement of eating disorder psychopathology. In K. D. Brownell & C. G. Fairburn (Eds.). *Eating disorders and obesity: A comprehensive handbook* (pp. 117–121). New York: Guilford Press.

Garner, D. M. & Bemis, K. M. (1985). A cognitive-behavioral approach to anorexia nervosa. In D. M. Garner & P. E. Garfinkel (Eds.), *Handbook of psychotherapy for anorexia nervosa and bulimia* (pp. 107–146). New York: Guilford Press.

Garner, D. M., Olmstead, M. P., Bohr, Y., & Garfinkel, P. E. (1982). The eating attitudes test: Psychometric features and clinical correlates. *Psychological Medicine, 12,* 871–878.

Garner, D. M., Rockert, W., Davis, R., Garner, M. V., Olmsted, M. P., & Eagle, M. (1993). Comparison of cognitive-behavioral and supportive-expressive therapy for bulimia nervosa. *American Journal of Psychiatry, 150,* 37–46.

Garner, D. M., & Wooley, S. C. (1991). Confronting the failure of behavioral and dietary treatments for obesity. *Clinical Psychology Review, 11,* 729–780.

Goldbloom, D. S., & Olmsted, M. P. (1993). Pharmacotherapy of bulimia nervosa with fluoxetine: Assessment of clinically significant attitudinal change. *American Journal of Psychiatry, 150,* 770–774.

Goldbloom, D. S., Olmsted, M., Davis, R., Clewes, J., Heinmaa, M., Rockert, W., & Shaw, B. (in press). A randomized controlled trial of fluoxetine and cognitive behavioral therapy for bulimia nervosa: Short-term outcome. *Behaviour Research and Therapy.*

Gormally, J., Black, S., Daston, S., & Rardin, E. (1982). The assessment of binge eating severity among obese persons. *Addictive Behaviors, 7,* 47–55.

Gowers, S., Norton, K., Halek, C., & Crisp, A. H. (1994). Outcome of outpatient psychotherapy in a random allocation treatment study of anorexia nervosa. *International Journal of Eating Disorders, 15,* 165–178.

Griffiths, R. A. (1996, April 27). *The short-term follow-up effects of hypnobehavioural and cognitive-behavioural treatment for bulimia nervosa.* Paper presented at the Seventh New York International Conference on Eating Disorders, New York.

Griffiths, R. A., Hadzi-Pavlovic, D., & Channon-Little, L. (1994). A controlled evaluation of hypnobehavioural treatment for bulimia nervosa: Immediate pre-post treatment effects. *European Eating Disorders Review*, 2, 202–220.

Hall, A., & Crisp, A. H. (1987). Brief psychotherapy in the treatment of anorexia nervosa. *British Journal of Psychiatry*, 151, 185–191.

Hamilton, M. (1967). Development of a rating scale for primary depressive illness. *British Journal of Clinical Psychology*, 6, 278–296.

Horne, R. L., Ferguson, J. M., Pope, H. G., Hudson, J. I., Lineberry, C. G., Ascher, J., & Cato, A. (1988). Treatment of bulimia with bupropion: A multicenter controlled trial. *Journal of Clinical Psychiatry*, 49, 262–266.

Hsu, L. K. G. (1990). *Eating disorders*. New York: Guilford Press.

Hughes, P. L., Wells, L. A., Cunningham, C. J., & Ilstrup, D. M. (1986). Treating bulimia with desipramine: a double-blind, placebo-controlled study. *Archives of General Psychiatry*, 43, 182–186.

Ilardi, S. S., & Craighead, W. E. (1994). The role of nonspecific factors in cognitive-behavior therapy for depression. *Clinical Psychology*, 1, 138–156.

Johnson, C., Tobin, D. L., & Dennis, A. (1990). Differences in treatment outcome between borderline and nonborderline bulimics at 1-year follow-up. *International Journal of Eating Disorders*, 9, 617–627.

Kaye, W. H., Weltzin, T. E., Hsu, L. K. G., Sokol, M. S., McConana, C., & Piotnicov, K. H. (1997). Relapse prevention with fluoxetine in anorexia nervosa: A double-blind placebo-controlled study. (Abstract) 150th Annual Meeting of the American Psychiatric Association, San Diego, CA, May 17–22.

Keller, M. B., Herzog, D. B., Lavori, P. W., Bradburn, I. S., & Mahoney, E. M. (1992). The naturalistic history of bulimia nervosa: Extraordinarily high rates of chronicity, relapse recurrence, and psychosocial morbidity. *International Journal of Eating Disorders*, 12, 1–10.

Kennedy, S. H., Goldbloom, D. S., Ralevski, E., Davis, C., D'Souza, J., & Lofchy, J. (1993). Is there a role for selective MAO-inhibitor therapy in bulimia nervosa? A placebo-controlled trial of brofaromine. *Journal of Clinical Psychopharmacology*, 13, 415–422.

Kennedy, S. H., Piran, N., Warsh, J. J., Prendergast, P., Mainprize, E., Whynot, C., & Garfinkel, P. E. (1988). A trial of isocarboxazid in the treatment of bulimia nervosa. *Journal of Clinical Psychopharmacology*, 8, 391–396.

Kirkley, B. G., Schneider, J. A., Agras, W. S., & Bachman, J. A. (1985). Comparison of two group treatments for bulimia. *Journal of Consulting and Clinical Psychology*, 53, 43–48.

Klerman, G. L., Weissman, M. M., Rounsaville, B. J., & Chevron, E. S. (1984). *Interpersonal psychotherapy of depression*. New York: Basic Books.

Laessle, R. G., Beumont, P. J. V., Butow, P., Lennerts, W., O'Connor, M., Pirke, K. M., Touyz, S. W., & Waadi, S. (1991). A comparison of nutritional management with stress management in the treatment of bulimia nervosa. *British Journal of Psychiatry*, 159, 250–261.

Lam, R. W., Goldner, E. M., Solyom, L., & Remick, R. A. (1994). A controlled study of light therapy for bulimia nervosa. *American Journal of Psychiatry*, 151, 744–750.

Lee, N. F., & Rush, A. J. (1986). Cognitive-behavioral group therapy for bulimia. *International Journal of Eating Disorders*, 5, 599–615.

le Grange, D., Eisler, I., Dare, C., & Russell, G. F. M. (1992). Evaluation of family treatments in adolescent anorexia nervosa: A pilot study. *International Journal of Eating Disorders*, 12, 347–358.

Leitenberg, H., & Rosen, J. C. (1985). Exposure plus response prevention treatment of bulimia. In D. M. Garner & P. E. Garfinkel (Eds.), *Handbook of psychotherapy for anorexia nervosa and bulimia* (pp. 193–209). New York: Guilford Press.

Leitenberg, H., Rosen, J. C., Gross, J., Nudelman, S., & Vara, L. S. (1988). Exposure plus response-prevention treatment of bulimia nervosa. *Journal of Consulting and Clinical Psychology*, 56, 535–541.

Leitenberg, H., Rosen, J. C., Wolf, J., Vara, L. S., Detzer, M. J., & Srebnik, D. (1994). Comparison of cognitive-behavior therapy and desipramine in the treatment of bulimia nervosa. *Behaviour Research and Therapy*, 32, 37–46.

Levy, A. B., Dixon, K. N., & Stern, S. I. (1989). How are depression and bulimia related? *American Journal of Psychiatry*, 146, 162.

Linehan, M., Armstrong, H. E., Suarez, A., Allmon, D., & Heard, H. L. (1991). Cognitive-behavioral treatment of chronically parasuicidal borderline patients. *Archives of General Psychiatry*, 48, 1060–1064.

Marcus, M. D., Wing, R. R., Ewing, L., Kern, E., Gooding, W., & McDermott, M. (1990). A double-blind, placebo-controlled trial of fluoxetine plus behavior modification in the treatment of obese binge eaters and non-binge eaters. *American Journal of Psychiatry*, 147, 876–881.

Marcus, M. D., Wing, R. R., & Fairburn, C. G. (1995). Cognitive treatment of binge eating versus behavioral weight control in the treatment of binge eating disorder. *Annals of Behavioral Medicine*, 17, S090.

McCann, U. D., & Agras, W. S. (1990). Successful treatment of nonpurging bulimia nervosa with desipramine: A double-blind, placebo-controlled study. *American Journal of Psychiatry*, 147, 1509–1513.

Mitchell, J. E., & de Zwaan, M. (1993). Pharmacological treatments of binge eating. In C. G. Fairburn & G. T. Wilson (Eds.), *Binge eating: Nature, assessment and treatment.* (pp. 250–269). New York: Guilford Press.

Mitchell, J. E., & Groat, R. (1984). A placebo-controlled, double-blind trial of amitriptyline in bulimia. *Journal of Clinical Psychopharmacology, 4,* 186–193.

Mitchell, J. E., Pyle, R. L., Eckert, E. D., Hatsukami, D., Pomeroy, C., & Zimmerman, R. (1989). Response to alternative antidepressants in imipramine nonresponders with bulimia nervosa. *Journal of Clinical Psychopharmacology, 9,* 291–293.

Mitchell, J. E., Pyle, R. L., Eckert, E. D., Hatsukami, D., Pomeroy, C., & Zimmerman, R. (1990). A comparison study of antidepressants and structured intensive group psychotherapy in the treatment of bulimia nervosa. *Archives of General Psychiatry, 47,* 149–157.

Mussell, M. P., Mitchell, J. E., Weller, C. L., Raymond, N. C., Crow, S. J., & Crosby, R. D. (1995). Onset of binge eating, dieting, obesity, and mood disorders among subjects seeking treatment for binge eating disorder. *International Journal of Eating Disorders, 17,* 395–402.

National Task Force on the Prevention and Treatment of Obesity. (1996). Long-term pharmacotherapy in the management of obesity. *Journal of the American Medical Association, 276,* 1907–1915.

Olmsted, M. P., Davis, R., Garner, D. M., Eagle, M., Rockert, W., & Irvine, M. J. (1991). Efficacy of a brief group psychoeducational intervention for bulimia nervosa. *Behaviour Research and Therapy, 29,* 71–84.

Peveler, R. C., & Fairburn, C. G. (1992). The treatment of bulimia nervosa in patients with diabetes mellitus. *International Journal of Eating Disorders, 11,* 45–53.

Pike, K. M., Loeb, K. & Vitousek, K. (1996). Cognitive-behavioral therapy for anorexia nervosa and bulimia nervosa. In J. K. Thompson (Ed.), *Eating disorders, obesity and body image: A practical guide to assessment and treatment.* Washington: American Psychological Association.

Polivy, J., & Herman, C. P. (1993). Etiology of binge eating: Psychological mechanisms. In C. G. Fairburn & G. T. Wilson (Eds.), *Binge eating: Nature, assessment and treatment.* New York: Guilford Press.

Pope, H. G., Hudson, J. I., Jonas, J. M., & Yurgelun-Todd, D. (1983). Bulimia treated with imipramine: A placebo-controlled, double-blind study. *American Journal of Psychiatry, 140,* 554–558.

Pope, H. G., Hudson, J. I., Jonas, J. M., & Yurgelun-Todd, D. (1985). Antidepressant treatment of bulimia: A two-year follow-up study. *Journal of Clinical Psychopharmacology, 5,* 320–327.

Pope, H. G., Keck, P. E., McElroy, S. L., & Hudson, J. I. (1989). A placebo-controlled study of trazodone in bulimia nervosa. *Journal of Clinical Psychopharmacology, 9,* 254–259.

Porzelius, L. K., Houston, C., Smith, M., Arfken, C., & Fisher, E., Jr. (1995). Comparison of a standard behavioral weight loss treatment and a binge eating weight loss treatment. *Behavior Therapy, 26,* 119–134.

Pyle, R. L., Mitchell, J. E., Eckert, E. D., Hatsukami, D. K., Pomeroy, C., & Zimmerman, R. (1990). Maintenance treatment and 6-month outcome for bulimic patients who respond to initial treatment. *American Journal of Psychiatry, 147,* 871–875.

Robin, A. L., Siegel, P. T., & Moye, A. (1995). Family versus individual therapy for anorexia: Impact on family conflict. *International Journal of Eating Disorders, 17,* 313–322.

Rosen, B. (1979). A method of structured brief psychotherapy. *British Journal of Medical Psychology, 52,* 157–162.

Rossiter, E. M., Agras, W. S., Losch, M., & Telch, C. F. (1988). Dietary restraint of bulimic subjects following cognitive-behavioral or pharmacological treatment. *Behaviour Research and Therapy, 26,* 495–498.

Rossiter, E. M., Agras, W. S., Telch, C. F., & Schneider, J. A. (1993). Cluster B personality disorder characteristics predict outcome in the treatment of bulimia nervosa. *International Journal of Eating Disorders, 13,* 349–358.

Russell, G. F. M., Checkley, S. A., Feldman, J., & Eisler, I. (1988). A controlled trial of d-fenfluramine in bulimia nervosa. *Clinical Neuropharmacology, 11,* S146–S159.

Russell, G. F. M., Szmukler, G. I., Dare, C., & Eisler, I. (1987). An evaluation of family therapy in anorexia nervosa and bulimia nervosa. *Archives of General Psychiatry, 44,* 1047–1056.

Sabine, E. J., Yonace, A., Farrington, A. J., Barratt, K. H., & Wakeling, A. (1983). Bulimia nervosa: A placebo controlled double-blind therapeutic trial of mianserin. *British Journal of Clinical Pharmacology, 15,* 195S–202S.

Smith, D. E., Marcus, M. D., & Kaye, W. (1992). Cognitive-behavioral treatment of obese binge eaters. *International Journal of Eating Disorders, 12,* 257–262.

Solanto, M. V., Jacobson, M. S., Heller, L., Golden, N. H., & Hertz, S. (1994). Rate of weight gain of inpatients with anorexia nervosa under two behavioral contracts. *Pediatrics, 93,* 989–991.

Spedding, M., Ouvry, C., Millan., Duhault, J., Dacquet, C., Wurtman, R. (1996). Neural control of dieting. *Nature, 380,* 488.

Steinhausen, H.-C. H., Rauss-Mason, C., & Seidel, R. (1991). Follow-up studies of anorexia nervosa: A review of four decades of outcome research. *Psychological Medicine, 21,* 447–454.

Stevens, J. (1990). *Intermediate statistics.* Hillsdale, N.J.: Erlbaum.

Strober, M., Freeman, R., DeAntonio, M., Lampert, C., & Diamond, J. (1997). Does adjunctive fluoxetine influence the post-hospital course of anorexia nervosa? Unpublished manuscript, UCLA Neuropsychiatric Institute.

Stunkard, A. J., Berkowitz, R., Tanrikut, C., Reiss, E., & Young, L. (1997). d-Fenfluramine treatment of binge eating disorder. *American Journal of Psychiatry, 153,* 1455–1459.

Stunkard, A. J. (1980). Psychoanalysis and psychotherapy. In A. J. Stunkard (Ed.), *Obesity* (pp. 355–368). Philadelphia: Saunders.

Stunkard, A. J., & Messick, S. (1985). The three-factor eating questionnaire to measure dietary restraint and hunger. *Journal of Psychosomatic Research, 29,* 71–83.

Szmukler, G. I., Young, G. P., Miller, G., Lichtenstein, M., & Binns, D. S. (1985). A controlled trial of cisapride in anorexia nervosa. *International Journal of Eating Disorders, 17,* 347–358.

Telch, C. F., & Agras, W. S. (1993). The effects of a very low calorie diet on binge eating. *Behavior Therapy, 24,* 177–194.

Telch, C. F., Agras, W. S., & Rossiter, E. M. (1988). Binge eating increases with increasing adiposity. *International Journal of Eating Disorders, 7,* 115–119.

Telch, C. F., Agras, W. S., Rossiter, E. M., Wilfley, D., & Kenardy, J. (1990). Group cognitive-behavioral treatment for the non-purging bulimic: An initial evaluation. *Journal of Consulting and Clinical Psychology, 58,* 629–635.

Thackwray, D. E., Smith, M. C., Bodfish, J. W., & Meyers, A. W. (1993). A comparison of behavioral and cognitive-behavioral interventions for bulimia nervosa. *Journal of Consulting and Clinical Psychology, 61,* 639–645.

Tobin, D. L. (1993). Psychodynamic psychotherapy and binge eating. In C. G. Fairburn & G. T. Wilson (Eds.), *Binge eating: Nature, assessment, and treatment* (pp. 297–313). New York: Guilford Press.

Touyz, S. W., Beumont, P. J. V., & Dunn, S. M. (1987). Behaviour therapy in the management of patients with anorexia nervosa: A lenient, flexible approach. *Psychotherapy and Psychosomatics, 48,* 151–156.

Touyz, S. W., Beumont, P. J. V., Glaun, D., Philips, T., & Cowie, I. (1984). A comparison of lenient and strict operant conditional conditioning programmes in refeeding patients with anorexia nervosa. *British Journal of Psychiatry, 144,* 517–520.

Touyz, S. W., Lennerts, W., Freeman, R. J., Beumont,

P. J. V. (1990). To weight or not to weight? Frequency of weighing and rate of weight gain in patients with anorexia nervosa. *British Journal of Psychiatry, 157,* 752–754.

Treasure, J., Schmidt, U., Troop, N., Tiller, J., Todd, G., Keilen, M., & Dodge, E. (1994). First step in managing bulimia nervosa: Controlled trial of therapeutic manual. *British Medical Journal, 308,* 686–689.

Treasure, J., Todd, G., Brolly, M., Tillo, J., Nehmed, A., & Denman, F. (1995). A pilot study of a randomized trial of cognitive analytical therapy vs. educational behavioral therapy for adult anorexia nervosa. *Behaviour Research and Therapy, 33,* 363–367.

Treasure, J., Schmidt, U., Troop, N., Tiller, J., Todd, G., & Turnbull S. (1996). Sequential treatment for bulimia nervosa incorporating a self-care manual. *British Journal of Psychiatry, 168,* 94–98.

Vandereycken, W., Kog, E., & Vanderlinden, J. (Eds.). (1989). *The family approach to eating disorders.* New York: PMA Publishing.

Vandereycken, W., & Meerman, R. (1984). *Anorexia nervosa: A clinician's guide to treatment.* Berlin: Walter de Gruyter & Co.

Waller, D., Fairburn, C. G., McPherson, A., Lee, A., & Nowell, T. (1996). Treating bulimia nervosa in primary care: A pilot study. *International Journal of Eating Disorders, 19,* 99–103.

Walsh, B. T. (1992). Pharmacological treatment of eating disorders. In K. Halmi (Ed.), *The psychobiology and treatment of anorexia nervosa and bulimia nervosa* (pp. 329–340). Washington, D.C.: American Psychiatric Press.

Walsh, B. T., Gladis, M., Roose, S. P., Stewart, J. W., Stetner, F., & Glassman, A. H. (1988). Phenelzine versus placebo in 50 patients with bulimia. *Archives of General Psychiatry, 45,* 471–475.

Walsh, B. T., Hadigan, C. M., Devlin, M. J., Gladis, M., & Roose, S. P. (1991). Long-term outcome of antidepressant treatment for bulimia nervosa. *American Journal of Psychiatry, 148,* 1206–1212.

Walsh, B. T., Wilson, G. T., Loeb, K. L., Devlin, M. J., Pike, K. M., Roose, S. P., Fleiss, J., & Waternaux, C. (1966). Medication and psychotherapy in the treatment of bulimia nervosa. *American Journal of Psychiatry, 154,* 523–531.

Wilfley, D. E., Agras, W. S., Telch, C. F., Rossiter, E. M., Schneider, J. A., Cole, A. G., Sifford, K., & Raeburn, S. D. (1993). Group cognitive-behavioral therapy and group interpersonal psychotherapy for the nonpurging bulimic individual: A controlled comparison. *Journal of Consulting and Clinical Psychology, 61,* 296–305.

Wilson, G. T. (1995). The controversy over dieting. In

K.D. Brownell & C. G. Fairburn (Eds.), *Comprehensive textbook of eating disorders and obesity* (pp. 87–92). New York: Guilford Press.

———. (1996). Treatment of bulimia nervosa: When CBT fails. *Behaviour Research and Therapy, 34,* 197–212.

Wilson, G. T., Fairburn, C. G., & Agras, W. S. (1997). Cognitive-behavioral therapy for bulimia nervosa. In D. M. Garner & P. Garfinkel (Eds.), *Handbook of treatment for eating disorders* (pp. 67–93). New York: Guilford Press.

Wilson, G. T., Nonas, C., & Rosenblum, G. D. (1993). Assessment of binge-eating in obese patients. *International Journal of Eating Disorders, 13,* 25–34.

Wilson, G. T., Rossiter, E., Kleifield, E. I., & Lindholm, L. (1986). Cognitive-behavioral treatment of bulimia nervosa: a controlled evaluation. *Behaviour Research and Therapy, 24,* 277–288.

Wilson, G. T., & Smith, D. (1989). Assessment of bulimia nervosa: An evaluation of the Eating Disorder Examination. *International Journal of Eating Disorders, 8,* 173–179.

Wolf, E. M., & Crowther, J. H. (1992). An evaluation of behavioral and cognitive-behavioral group interventions for the treatment of bulimia nervosa in women. *International Journal of Eating Disorders, 11,* 3–16.

Yanovski, S. Z., & Sebring, N. G. (1994). Recorded food intake of obese women with binge eating disorders before and after weight loss. *International Journal of Eating Disorders, 15,* 135–50.

26

Effective Treatments for Selected Sleep Disorders

Peter D. Nowell
Daniel J. Buysse
Charles M. Morin
Charles F. Reynolds III
David J. Kupfer

Nearly one third of adults reports at least occasional insomnia within a 1-year time period and up to 50% report insomnia during their lives. There is evidence that multiple psychological and medical consequences are associated with insomnia. In the *Diagnostic and Statistical Manual of Mental Disorders*, fourth edition (*DSM-IV*; American Psychiatric Association, 1994), insomnia is subcategorized: primary insomnia; insomnia related to another mental disorder; sleep disorder due to a general medical condition; and substance-induced sleep disorder, insomnia type. At least 14 medications have been studied in 117 separate reports of the treatment of insomnia. There are at least 33 studies of behavioral interventions for insomnia. Benzodiazepines and zolpidem are effective pharmacological agents, while melatonin and delta-sleep-inducing peptide (DSIP) are interesting experimental agents. Of the behavioral strategies, stimulus control, sleep restriction, relaxation, and cognitive-behavioral therapy are effective.

INSOMNIA

In this chapter, we review the treatment literature concerning the *Diagnostic and Statistical Manual of Mental Disorders*, fourth edition (*DSM-IV*; American Psychiatric Association [APA], 1994), insomnia disorders. We first present the prevalence of insomnia symptoms and the distress and impairments that are associated with them. We then discuss the *DSM-IV* diagnostic criteria that define specific insomnia disorders. We focus much of this chapter on the research methodology for insomnia and its relevance for interpreting the results of specific outcome studies. The clinical practice that emerges from these studies is best appreciated in relationship to the details of the research designs involved. This emphasis on how we identified and selected treatment studies and our discussion of clinical trial design will provide the reader with an appreciation of the complexity, as well as the limitations, behind summary findings such as: "Medication is effective for the treatment of insomnia." The chapter concludes with treatment recommendations supported by the reviewed literature and a discussion of the possible direction of future research of insomnia disorders and their management.

Scope of Insomnia

One in three adults reports at least occasional insomnia within a 1-year time period and up to 50% of adults report insomnia sometime in their lives (Balter & Uhlenhuth, 1992; Ford & Kamerow, 1989; Gallup

Organization, 1991; Partinen, Kaprio, Koskenvuo, Putkonen, & Langinvaino, 1983). Approximately 1 in 10 adults reports chronic insomnia, and 1 in 10 considers their insomnia to be a serious problem (Balter & Uhlenhuth, 1992; Mellinger, Balter, & Uhlenhuth, 1985). Despite this prevalence, only a minority of patients with insomnia presents to health care providers specifically for their sleep complaint (Gallup Organization, 1991; Welstein, Dement, Redington, Guilleminault, & Mitler, 1983). Instead, between 10% and 20% of patients with insomnia use nonprescription drugs, aspirin, or alcohol for their sleep difficulties (Mellinger et al., 1985; Welstein et al., 1983). Prescription sleeping pills have been reported to be used by about 5% of the population, with about 0.5% of the population using them for over 1 year (Mellinger et al., 1985). The annual cost for the management of insomnia in the United States is estimated at between $92.5 billion and $107.5 billion (Stoller, 1994).

Demographic and Natural History of Insomnia

Insomnia complaints increase with age (Gallup Organization, 1991; Mellinger et al., 1985; Morin & Gramling, 1989). Women report insomnia more than men (Karacan, Thornby, & Williams, 1983; Mellinger et al., 1985). Older men demonstrate more disrupted sleep on polysomnography (PSG) than do older women (Reynolds et al., 1986). Divorced, widowed, or separated individuals are more likely to report insomnia than are married individuals, and insomnia is reported more often in people of lower socioeconomic status than in those of upper socioeconomic status (Karacan et al., 1976; Karacan & Williams, 1983). In a prospective study of rural elderly subjects, approximately 1 in 3 reported either difficulty falling asleep, difficulty staying asleep, or early morning awakening (Ganguli, Reynolds, & Gilby, in press).

Transient symptoms of insomnia are reported more often than are persistent ones. However, prevalence estimates become complicated when insomnia syndromes are defined only by descriptions of duration such as acute insomnia or chronic insomnia. For example, a 7-year longitudinal study of young adults found that 15% reported occasional episodes of transient insomnia, 16% reported recurrent episodes of transient insomnia, and 9% reported chronic insomnia (Angst, Vollrath, Koch, & Dobler-Mikola, 1989;

Vollrath, Wicki, & Angst, 1989). It is unclear whether the recurrent forms of transient insomnia would be classified as acute or chronic in cross-sectional studies or surveys. Also, a boundary that defines acute insomnia from chronic insomnia has not been empirically demonstrated. Depending on the study or the classification scheme, this boundary may vary from 1 to several weeks. Much of the epidemiological and demographic data presented above most likely reflect the symptom of insomnia as it presents in various acute, recurrent, and chronic forms.

Longitudinal studies provide information on the evolution and stability of insomnia symptoms over time. Follow-up of young adult subjects over 2 to 7 years revealed that half of those with occasional episodes of transient insomnia had developed recurrent or persistent insomnia (Angst et al., 1989). In another study, most patients diagnosed with chronic insomnia continued to suffer from symptoms of insomnia 64 months later (Mendelson, 1995). In a third study, approximately 2 of 3 rural elderly subjects who reported insomnia symptoms at baseline continued to report them at 2-year follow-up (Ganguli et al., in press). Efforts to subtype insomnia by sleep onset insomnia difficulties or sleep maintenance difficulties demonstrated little stability over time (Hohagen et al., 1994).

Morbidity and Comorbidity

In addition to the high prevalence of insomnia symptoms, there is evidence suggesting multiple psychological and medical consequences associated with insomnia. In general, patients report elevated levels of distress, anxiety, depression, and medical illness compared with asymptomatic individuals (Healey et al., 1981; Kuppermann et al., 1995; National Institutes of Health, 1984). Patients with insomnia more often receive elevated scores on self-report psychological inventories (Hauri & Fisher, 1986; Kales, Caldwell, Soldatos, Bixler, & Kales, 1983), and they have been shown to demonstrate higher cognitive arousal that interferes with sleep in some, but not all, studies (Lichstein, 1980; Haynes et al., 1985). Patients with insomnia are at an increased risk for developing psychiatric disorders within a 1-year time period (Charon, Dramaix, & Mendlewicz, 1989; Ford & Kamerow, 1989), and a comorbid psychiatric diagnosis is seen in the majority of patients complaining of insomnia (Jacobs, Reynolds, Kupfer, Lovin, & Ehrenpreis, 1988;

Tan, Kales, Kales, Soldatos, & Bixler, 1984). In one study, poor sleepers in the Navy received fewer promotions, remained at lower pay grades, had higher rates of attrition, and had more frequent hospitalizations than good sleepers in the Navy (Johnson & Spinweber, 1983). Chronic insomnia has been reported to lead to deterioration of mood, motivation, attention, and concentration and level of energy. Interpersonal and occupational problems may develop as a result of concern with sleep, increased irritability, and poor concentration (Mendelson, Garnett, Gillin, & Weingartner, 1984a; Mendelson, Garnett, & Linnoila, 1984b; Seidel, Roth, Roehrs, Zorick, & Dement, 1984; Stepanski et al., 1989).

Patients with insomnia demonstrate physiological correlates of high arousal such as increased muscle tension and greater autonomic reactivity to stress (Mendelson et al., 1984a, 1984b; Haynes et al., 1985), and they have an increase in stress-related illnesses such as headaches and gastrointestinal upset (Moldofsky, 1989a, 1989b, 1989c; Gislason & Almqvist, 1987; Partinen, 1988; Vollrath et al., 1989; Whorwell, McCallum, & Creed, 1986). It has been suggested that such psychophysiological arousal comes to be associated with the patient's sleeping environment, and that this negative conditioning explains why patients with insomnia often sleep better in unexpected or unfamiliar sleep environments where these conditioned cues are absent. This is in contrast to subjects without insomnia, who tend to sleep more poorly in unfamiliar surroundings (Hauri & Fisher, 1986; Kales et al., 1983). Despite reports of poor or limited sleep and of daytime fatigue, most patients with insomnia have not been shown to have excessive daytime sleepiness (Mendelson et al., 1984a, 1984b; Seidel et al., 1984; Seidel & Dement, 1982; Sugarman, Stern, & Walsh, 1985).

DSM-IV INSOMNIA DIAGNOSES

The preceding discussion focused on the symptoms of insomnia. One of the goals of psychiatric classifications has been to improve the reliability of diagnoses. Insomnia symptoms have been classified in different ways by several systems, such as the Diagnostic Classification of Sleep and Arousal Disorders (DCSAD; Association of Sleep Disorders Centers, 1979), the International Classification of Sleep Disorders (ICSD; Diagnostic Classification Steering Committee & Thor-

py, 1990), and the International Classification of Diseases (ICD). In the *DSM-IV* (APA, 1994), the symptoms of insomnia have been combined with other symptoms to define syndromes grouped by presumed etiology. These diagnostic criteria have demonstrated moderate interrater reliability from unstructured diagnostic interviews (Buysse et al., 1994). The following overview describes these *DSM-IV* insomnia diagnoses.

The essential diagnostic feature of *primary insomnia* is a complaint of difficulty initiating or maintaining sleep or of nonrestorative sleep; the complaint lasts for at least 1 month and causes clinically significant distress or impairment in social, occupational, or other important areas of functioning. The disturbance in sleep does not occur exclusively during the course of another sleep disorder or mental disorder and is not due to the direct physiological effects of a substance or a general medical condition.

Insomnia related to another mental disorder describes insomnia that is judged to be related temporally and causally to another mental disorder. Because sleep disturbances are common features of other mental disorders, an additional diagnosis of insomnia related to another mental disorder is made only when the sleep disturbance is a predominant complaint and is sufficiently severe to warrant independent clinical attention. Most commonly, mood and anxiety disorders are considered when a chronic insomnia syndrome is being evaluated.

Sleep disorder due to a general medical condition, insomnia type, requires a prominent disturbance in sleep that is severe enough to warrant independent clinical attention and evidence from the history, physical examination, or laboratory findings that the sleep disturbance is the direct physiological consequence of a general medical condition. Most commonly, pain syndromes are considered when chronic insomnia is being evaluated.

Substance-induced sleep disorder, insomnia type, results from the direct physiological effects of a substance (e.g., a drug of abuse, a medication, or toxin exposure). This diagnosis should be made instead of a diagnosis of substance intoxication or substance withdrawal only when the symptoms are in excess of those usually associated with the intoxication or withdrawal syndrome and when the symptoms are sufficiently severe to warrant independent clinical attention. Most commonly, caffeine, nicotine, and alcohol use are considered when chronic insomnia is being evaluated. The list of medications reported to cause insomnia is lengthy, but among the more common agents to be considered are antidepressant medications and stimulant medications. *Dyssomnia not otherwise specified (NOS)* describes insomnias that do not meet criteria for other specific *DSM-IV* dyssomnia diagnoses. Restless legs syndrome that results in insomnia would be diagnosed as dyssomnia NOS.

REVIEW OF EFFECTIVE TREATMENTS

Source of Evidence

The most rigorous evidence for treatment efficacy in chronic insomnia derives from well-designed clinical trials. Such trials would ideally include a prospective design, adequate sample sizes, reliable diagnostic methods, well-defined inclusion and exclusion criteria, randomized treatment assignment, placebo-controlled groups, and blinded assessments.

Establishing a Diagnosis

Reliable diagnostic methods and well-defined inclusion and exclusion criteria improve the internal validity of the trial. However, operationalizing such standards for patients with insomnia has varied widely across studies. The use of a structured psychiatric sleep disorders interview to assign *DSM-III-R* (APA, 1987) sleep diagnoses (Schramm, Hohagen, Kappler, Grasshoff, & Berger, 1995) has been a step toward improving trial design, but no such instrument exists for *DSM-IV*.

Inclusion Criteria

Patients with clinically established insomnia diagnoses often, though not always, demonstrate disrupted continuity measures on PSG (Coates et al., 1981; Mendelson et al., 1984a, 1984b; Seidel et al., 1984; Sugarman et al., 1985). Patients with insomnia also demonstrate more variability in sleep measures than do patients without insomnia complaints (Frankel, Coursey, Buchbinder, & Snyder, 1976; Roehrs et al., 1985). Many treatment studies use the results of polysomnography as inclusion or exclusion criteria by "confirming" an insomnia diagnosis, by establishing a baseline "severity" for inclusion, or by documenting a different illness for the cause of the insomnia complaint (e.g., obstructive sleep apnea). However, none

of the classification systems currently requires the results of polysomnography as a minimal criterion in establishing an insomnia diagnosis. Furthermore, the American Sleep Disorders Association has published practice guidelines addressing the role of PSG in the evaluation of insomnia (Reite, Buysse, Reynolds, & Mendelson, 1995). Essentially, polysomnography is not recommended in the clinical assessment of insomnia unless certain conditions are met, such as suspicion of a different primary sleep disorder as the cause of the insomnia symptom, an insomnia that follows an unusual treatment course, or treatment nonresponse. Consequently, while PSG may provide information that is potentially useful when evaluating insomnia (Coleman, 1982), it is not considered essential to establish or confirm a diagnosis. Its ability to document the severity of an insomnia disorder or to measure outcomes in chronic insomnia remains to be established despite its widespread use for these purposes.

Outcome Measures

There is a poorly defined relationship between subjective complaints of insomnia and objective measures of good and bad sleep (Akerstedt, Hume, Minors, & Waterhouse, 1994; Barnes et al., 1983; Carskadon et al., 1976; Buysse, 1989). Some researchers have suggested that alterations in the perception of sleep might be one of the primary deficits resulting in insomnia (Mendelson et al., 1984a, 1984b). Accordingly, measures of subjective appraisals about sleep might be a more valid assessment of treatment effects than would polysomnographic changes in sleep. Moreover, studies with inclusion and exclusion criteria or outcome measures that rely solely on PSG variables may not generalize to studies with subjects that are defined by clinical measures alone. As a result, recent research has included both subjective and objective measures while emphasizing one or the other, depending on the study.

In addition to issues of subjective or objective outcome measures, little consensus exists as to which type of outcome measures will classify patients as "responders." Improved sleep efficiency, relief of subjective distress, reduced daytime impairment, or a combination of these (or other) measures may reflect treatment response. In general, studies have focused on sleep continuity measures and global subjective evaluations. Whether one obtains these outcome measures from the sleep laboratory or from actigraphy (ambulatory monitoring of sleep and wake states based on motion) adds additional complexities to the design of treatment studies.

Control Groups

There is a large night-to-night variability in sleep measures in patients with insomnia (Frankel et al., 1976). Patients selected for extremes of continuity disturbance demonstrate improvement over time that reflects regression toward the mean rather than the effects of treatment (Roehrs et al., 1985). Even after taking extremes of selection into account, patients with insomnia tend to demonstrate improvement over time that has been explained as resulting from the demand characteristics of the experiment (Carr-Kaffashan & Woolfolk, 1979; Lacks, Bertelson, Sugerman, & Kunkel, 1983; Steinmark & Borkovec, 1974). These effects can be seen in within-subject analysis of wait-list groups, sham treatment groups, and placebo groups. On one hand, these factors taken together suggest that a valid control group and between-group comparisons are needed to isolate the effects of treatment from other factors. On the other hand, the improvements that result from nonspecific effects of treatment protocols such as self-monitoring or support tend to be modest in magnitude and not sustained relative to the chronicity of the disorder overall.

Treatment and the Course of Insomnia

A final issue in evaluating outcomes in chronic insomnia concerns the benefits of treatment in relationship to the natural history of the illness. Most studies have addressed an acute intervention and its immediate response, that is, several nights of medication and the resulting changes in sleep continuity on those nights. There is little information about acute interventions and their ability to produce sustained effects over time. For instance, what benefits from 1 month of treatment are expected to be maintained over a 1-year follow-up period? Likewise, few studies have assessed the benefits of maintenance interventions such as low-dose medication on a nightly basis for 1 year and its cumulative effects on insomnia. Usually, behavioral treatments are compared to acute, short-term medication trials. In general, such behavioral interventions have a more durable impact on outcome when the

longitudinal course of the disorder is considered (Morin, Colecchi, Stone, Sood, & Brink, 1995); however, more studies are needed to resolve the issue in more detail.

PHARMACOLOGICAL AGENTS

A wide variety of agents have been used for the treatment of insomnia (see Table 26.2). This review focuses on agents that are commonly used in the United States and that have been established as efficacious based on randomized, controlled clinical trials. Agents related to gamma-aminobutyric acid, antidepressants, tryptophan, antihistamines, delta-sleep-inducing peptide (DSIP), and melatonin are discussed. Agents such as benzodiazepines (Greenblatt, 1992), imidazopyridines, or cyclopyrrolones are believed to work via GABA modulation. These agents can be classified by receptor pharmacology, that is, specificity for the benzodiazepine receptor or pharmacokinetics (e.g., absorption, distribution, or metabolism).

Antidepressant agents studied in the treatment of primary insomnia have included imipramine, trimipramine, and trazodone. Their mechanism of action may include serotonin regulation, histamine regulation, alpha-adrenergic receptor action, or anticholinergic changes. Tryptophan is a dietary amino acid and a precursor of serotonin.

Antihistamines are available in many over-the-counter preparations and antagonize receptors for histamine, a modulator for wakefulness. Delta-sleep-inducing peptide has been isolated and used experimentally in sleep research, but its clinical applications remain to be further clarified. Melatonin is a naturally occurring hormone produced by the pineal gland that has received considerable attention for its effects on circadian rhythms. Its effects on chronic insomnias unrelated to circadian disturbances have received less attention.

TABLE 26.1 Behavioral Treatments

Stimulus control therapy
Sleep restriction therapy
Relaxation therapies
Sleep hygiene education
Cognitive-behavioral therapy

BEHAVIORAL INTERVENTIONS

Both nonspecific and specific behavioral treatments have been studied in patients with insomnia (Guilleminault et al., 1995). *Stimulus control therapy* consists of a set of instructional procedures designed to curtail sleep-incompatible behaviors and to regulate sleep-wake schedules. This method targets both negative conditioning and circadian factors. These procedures are (Bootzin & Perlis, 1992)

1. Go to bed only when sleepy.
2. Use the bed and bedroom only for sleep and sex (i.e., no reading, television watching, eating, or working during the day or at night).
3. Get out of bed and go into another room whenever you are unable to sleep for 15–20 minutes and return only when sleepy again.
4. Arise in the morning at the same time regardless of the amount of sleep during the previous night.
5. Do not nap during the day.

Sleep restriction therapy consists of prescribing an initial restricted duration of time at night during which a patient has an opportunity to attempt sleep. The amount of the restriction is determined from two-week sleep diaries. Once a patient's sleep becomes more efficient, then the allowable time in bed is increased gradually to allow for the greatest total amount of sleep time while preserving the newly achieved capacity for more efficient sleep (Spielman, Saskin, & Thorpy, 1987). This method uses the homeostatic regulation of sleep to allow a sleep debt to facilitate sleep initiation and maintenance.

Relaxation therapies are designed to alleviate somatic or cognitive arousal; they consist of techniques such as progressive muscular relaxation, autogenic training, and biofeedback (Hauri, 1981; Freedman & Papsdorf, 1976).

Sleep hygiene education is concerned with health practices such as diet, exercise, and substance use and with environmental factors such as light, noise, and temperature that may be either detrimental or beneficial to sleep (Borkovec & Fowles, 1973; Hauri, 1981).

Cognitive-behavioral treatment for insomnia targets maladaptive cognitions that perpetuate insomnia (Morin, Colecchi, Stone, et al., 1995b). These behavioral interventions have been used as single interventions or, more typically, as combined or multimodal approaches.

GENERAL METHODS OF LITERATURE REVIEW

A review of the published literature was conducted by MEDLINE for the period 1966–1995. The medical subject heading (MeSH) "insomnia" restricted to "drug therapy" produced 1,291 citations. These 1,291 citations crossed with "double-blind" and with "placebos" produced a final 215 citations in the English language that were further reviewed. Likewise, the MeSH "insomnia" restricted to "behavioral therapy" resulted in a final 116 citations in the English language that were further reviewed. The *Journal of Sleep Research* (not indexed in MEDLINE) was reviewed manually from Volume 1 to Volume 4, June 1995. Abstracts were not reviewed.

The *DSM-IV* was published in 1994, and, as a result, insomnia studies prior to its release used diagnostic criteria available at the time. Efforts to classify earlier studies by *DSM-IV* diagnoses revealed several problems. Inclusion criteria that failed to address daytime impairment or fatigue were difficult to classify as primary insomnia. This is because the only remaining inclusion criterion for primary insomnia is "clinically significant distress." When subjects are drawn from university and community volunteers or from patients in institutionalized settings, the remaining criterion of "clinically significant" becomes more ambiguous. This ambiguity is compounded by differences that may exist between help-seeking patients with insomnia and non-help-seeking subjects with sleep difficulties (Stepanski et al., 1989). Another problem in classifying primary insomnia resulted from the lack of documentation in many studies regarding the method used to evaluate psychiatric disorders or substance use disorders. Likewise, there rarely was information to exclude circadian rhythm disorders in subjects with insomnia.

There were several difficulties in trying to classify insomnia related to another mental disorder. In studies of patients drawn from medically or psychiatrically ill populations, there was little documentation that clarified whether the insomnia syndrome was considered to be causally related to the primary illness and to what extent the insomnia complaint exceeded a threshold for sleep disturbance commonly associated with the primary illness. In many cases, insomnia appeared to be a symptom available for treatment that was part of the expected course of the illness. For example, studies of patients with depression and poor sleep seldom clarified what criteria were used to determine whether the insomnia difficulty was to be considered an independent sleep disorder.

Several problems emerged in trying to include or exclude studies based on research design. Randomized, double-blind, placebo-controlled trials were sought, but few studies clearly met all criteria. Double-blind conditions and placebo-controlled groups are difficult to provide, generally, in studies of behavioral interventions. The use of placebo controls may be easier to implement in pharmacological studies, but the actual degree of blinding achieved in studies of hypnotics may limit such design efforts (Morin, Colecchi, & Brink, 1995). Wait-list control groups or control groups giving "pseudo-" or "partial" behavioral interventions may represent analogies to placebo-controlled conditions of hypnotic trials. However, blinding of clinicians remained unresolved for these designs. To balance these design factors, we retained for review the medication studies that used a placebo-control group and double-blinded evaluation and behavioral studies that used a waiting list or pseudobehavioral intervention for a control group. All studies used prospective designs.

Another difficulty in selecting adequate studies was interpreting a report of a positive finding. In general, time to fall asleep, time awake in bed, number of awakenings, total sleep time, global subjective report, and daytime impairment were considered measures of treatment response. However, most studies reported on one or another measure, and, in many cases, one measure improved when another did not. Thus, studies with a positive result based on a reduced sleep latency may have had a negative result based on changes in total sleep time. Because there is no gold standard for determining treatment response, we considered the authors' report of positive treatment outcome as the conclusion of the study. It should be noted, however, that the overwhelming reporting of positive outcomes despite large variations in subject numbers, in inclusion and exclusion criteria, in outcome measures, and in definitions of response raises the possibility of publication bias and reporting that enhances the apparent effects of treatment.

CONCLUSIONS

Table 26.2 summarizes the clinical efficacy trials for chronic insomnia. Given the limitations, what conclu-sions can be drawn regarding the effective treatments for *DSM-IV* insomnia diagnoses as supported by the available clinical trials?

1. *The subjective symptoms and objective signs of chronic insomnia respond to acute behavioral and pharmacological interventions.* Typically, both behavioral and pharmacological interventions reduce sleep onset by 15–30 minutes from pretreatment levels or close to an absolute duration of 30 minutes. The number of awakenings typically decreases to an absolute level of 1–3 per night. On average, both behavioral and pharmacological interventions increase total sleep time about 15–45 minutes, with pharmacological agents acting more reliably in the short term and behavioral interventions producing more-sustained effects. The majority of patients report improved sleep quality after treatment. While there is little support for choosing one medication over another based solely on efficacy, tailoring an agent with rapid-acting properties for sleep-onset difficulties or a longer acting agent for sleep-maintenance difficulties does have empirical support. Subjective measures, taken as a whole, seem to correlate with the direction of objective measure, but the magnitude differs considerably and inconsistently.

2. *Effective pharmacological agents include benzodiazepines and zolpidem. Effective behavioral interventions include stimulus control, sleep restriction, relaxation strategies, and cognitive-behavioral therapy for acute management.* Of the medications, antihistamines and tryptophan have the least clear benefit, while melatonin and DSIP agents remain experimental agents. Of the behavioral strategies, sleep hygiene and paradoxical intention have the least clear benefit, while the remaining interventions provide acute beneficial effects, albeit less consistently than pharmacological agents.

Benzodiazepines, as a class, have been the most extensively studied hypnotic agents, both in terms of individual trials and in terms of patient numbers. In addition, benzodiazepines have been studied for more than 20 years with very different strategies. While the heterogeneity of trial design and outcome measures presents certain limits in combining findings to identify exactly what responds to treatment, this diversity can be useful in the sense that the vast majority of these studies (roughly more than 90%) report clinically significant results despite the heterogeneity of designs.

Zolpidem studies, while fewer in trial and patient

TABLE 26.2 Summary of Clinical Efficacy Trials in Chronic Insomnia

Intervention	No. of studies	Pooled N	Usual Dose (mg)	Dose Range (mg)	Duration Range (Days)
Chloral hydrate	2	131	500	250–500	1–2
Delta peptide	1	16	25 nmol/Kg iv	N/A	3
Deiphenhydramine	2	255	50	50	7–14
Estazolam	5	616	1 or 2	1–2	7–28
Flurazepam	22	1,372	15 or 30	15–30	2–28
Melatonin	2	23	Not established	1 mg–75 mg/os	1–14
Midazolam	9	373	15	5–30	1–84
Oxazepam	6	219	15	15–50	1–11
Quazepam	10	446	15 or 30	15–60	3–14
Temazepam	9	540	30	7.5–30	3–84
Triazolam	24	2,801	0.25	0.125–1.0	1–35
Tryptophan	3	155	Not established	1–3 grams	6–28
Zolpidem	4	497	5 or 10	1–20	14–28
Zopiclone	18	2,148	7.5	5–7.5	1–42
Behavioral[a]	33	1,324	5 hours	1–20 hours	1–16 weeks

[a]See text for specific interventions; time parameters based on Morin, Culbert, and Steven (1994).

numbers, have the advantage of being studied more recently with designs that have improved through development of strategies to evaluate benzodiazepines. As a result, zolpidem has been compared to both the gold standard of benzodiazepines and also to placebo conditions. Most of the studies have also included subjective measures like sleep quality, sleep quantity, and daytime functioning, as well as objective measures such as polysomnography. These studies, despite a diversity of assessment instruments and definitions of response, have also reported positive responses in almost all cases.

Diphenhydramine is a common agent in over-the-counter sleep preparations, yet our literature search identified only one placebo-controlled, double-blind clinical trial for patients with chronic insomnia (Rickels et al., 1983) and none for hydroxazine, another antihistamine available in hospital formularies. Other antihistamine studies identified failed to use a placebo control, and the characterization of the insomnia syndromes made generalizability difficult (Kudo & Kurihara, 1990). While the study by Rickels et. al. found support for the use of diphenhydramine at a 50 mg dose, additional well-designed trials would seem an important public health issue given the widespread availability of this agent.

Melatonin deserves mention because, unlike the other hypnotics reviewed, it is a naturally occurring hormone; because it affects circadian rhythms, which represent a potential mechanism of action distinct from the hypnotics; and because, like diphenhydramine, it is available in over-the-counter preparations. In evaluating the effects of melatonin, it is important to remember that the insomnia syndromes reviewed in this chapter are different from the sleep changes attributed to distinct disruptions of circadian systems such as shift work, jet lag, or delayed sleep phase syndrome. Our literature search identified two randomized, placebo-controlled clinical trials for patients with chronic insomnia (James, Sack, Rosenthal, & Mendelson, 1990; MacFarlane, Cleghorn, Brown, & Streiner, 1991). Both trials used supraphysiological doses of melatonin, and the results are difficult to interpret in that some subjective measures, like total sleep time, worsened, while others, like sleep quality, improved. There were no objective improvements on polysomnography. The role of melatonin in poor sleep continues to be evaluated, with more promising results in types of insomnia not specified by the DSM-IV (e.g., patients with "deficient" melatonin levels, which predicts a better response to melatonin replacement) (Garfinkel, Laudon, Nof, & Zisapel, 1995).

There has been no meta-analysis of pharmacological interventions for insomnia. However, Morin et al. (1994), using sleep onset, maintenance, or mixed insomnia, performed a meta-analysis of nonpharmacological interventions that included stimulus control, sleep restriction therapy, relaxation therapies, and sleep hygiene education. The 59 treatment studies involved 2,102 patients. Psychological interventions averaging 5 hours of therapy time produced reliable changes on sleep latency and time awake after sleep onset. Stimulus control and sleep restriction were the most effective single-therapy procedures. After stimulus control and sleep restriction, relaxation was most effective for sleep onset reductions, and biofeedback was most effective for wake-after-sleep onset reductions. While our literature review focused on insomnia syndromes defined in *DSM-IV* and included only studies with control groups, generally we obtained similar results. A qualitative literature review makes summary conclusions more difficult without the support of quantitative methods such as meta-analysis to help make finer distinctions among treatments, such as discriminating stimulus control, sleep restriction therapy, and relaxation therapies from the less-helpful sleep hygiene education and other behavioral approaches.

RECOMMENDATIONS

Identifying the disorder is the starting point in determining a treatment strategy for insomnia (Kupfer & Reynolds, 1997). Despite the prevalence of insomnia symptoms, it remains relatively underdiagnosed and undertreated. Clinicians need basic knowledge of sleep medicine and need to recognize the importance of sleep-related symptoms in the delivery of general medical treatment. Patients need to be educated about the relevance of sleep disorders to their general health. A clinical history is the cornerstone of establishing an insomnia diagnosis and planning treatment. In addition to an initial clinical evaluation, additional procedures such as patient self-monitoring with a sleep diary, consultation with a sleep specialist, psychological testing, psychiatric evaluation, or polysomnography may provide more diagnostic and treatment information. Polysomnography is often not indicated for routine evaluation of the young patient with chronic insomnia. It remains to be more clearly determined whether PSG is routinely indicated in the elderly

patient with insomnia. In summary, basic knowledge of sleep medicine and a clinical history are generally sufficient to establish an insomnia diagnosis and to develop an effective treatment strategy.

Sleep hygiene, health habits, substance and medication use, beliefs and expectations about sleep, psychiatric and medical status, and provider preference all play a role in treatment planning. A sleep diary has an educational and a potential therapeutic role. The role of bibliotherapy or patient-directed education and treatment remains to be researched.

Primary insomnia is best approached in a problem-solving format that unfolds over time as patients identify and modify various factors and track the effects on symptoms such as sleep quality and daytime impairment. Unfortunately, attempts to match patient variables to tailored treatments have not demonstrated robustly superior outcomes (Espie et al., 1989; Lilie & Lahmeyer, 1991; Sanavio, 1988). Nonetheless, it is still generally accepted that different patients with primary insomnia will require different treatment components. In general, a behavioral approach of stimulus control therapy, sleep restriction therapy, or cognitive-behavioral therapy for insomnia would serve as first-line interventions. A valuable component of cognitive-behavioral treatment is conceptualizing primary insomnia as a chronic illness and working with patients to develop skills to manage symptom recurrence. A benzodiazepine or an imidazopyridine (e.g., zolpidem) may be used as an adjuvant intervention, and by available evidence should be prescribed for no more than 4 weeks.

While dose effect studies are available for most of the medications discussed in this chapter, guidelines for each particular agent and particular patient demographics (e.g., the elderly, patients with liver dysfunction, etc.) should be directed toward standard pharmacology texts. As a rule, the lowest effective dose should be used. The efficacy of combined behavioral and pharmacological approaches as compared to single-intervention approaches has not been sufficiently addressed in the research literature. Moreover, the 4-week time frame for medication interventions requires empirical assessment because many patients will likely have persistent symptoms and require treatment for a longer term. While intermittent dosing strategies have been used to avoid chronic nightly exposure to benzodiazepines, our search identified only one randomized, placebo-controlled trial for patients with insomnia designed to evaluate an every-other-night regimen

(Scharf, 1994). This particular study used quazepam, which has a long half-life and makes generalizations to other agents difficult.

The chronic insomnias, other than primary insomnia, require treatment of the underlying illness (e.g., major depression).

DIRECTIONS FOR THE FUTURE

Research is required regarding preventive strategies, maintenance treatments, long-term management strategies, multimodal behavioral interventions, and combined pharmacological and behavioral approaches. While studies of behavioral interventions have been more sensitive to long-term gains and follow-up assessments, longitudinal studies are greatly needed, especially for pharmacological interventions, given that the vast majority of medication trials have lasted less than 1 month. Substantial research is needed to relate specific diagnoses to differential treatment strategies. There has been a trend toward improved clinical trial design, but researchers need to be particularly sensitive to reliable diagnostic inclusion criteria for future clarification of this issue. Consensus on which outcome variables constitute treatment response is needed, as is clarification of definitions such as partial response, relapse, and recurrence.

Efficacy is, of course, one of the most significant aspects in selecting a particular intervention and has been the organizing feature of this review. Side effects of treatment, however, present a major factor in addition to efficacy when choosing one intervention over another. The basic concerns with benzodiazepines and zolpidem are daytime sedation; psychomotor effects such as memory disturbances and incoordination; tolerance, abuse, and dependence; and discontinuation syndromes ranging from rebound insomnia to withdrawal delirium and seizures. In general, high-potency benzodiazepines such as triazolam are associated with a greater risk of amnesic effects, and agents with a rapid onset of action such as diazepam are associated with a greater abuse potential. Likewise, higher doses and longer exposure to these agents increase the likelihood of tolerance, dependence, and discontinuation syndromes. However, these generalities are not without controversy. A detailed account is beyond the scope of this chapter, and the interested reader is referred to excellent reviews by Woods and

Winger, 1995, and Linsen, Zitman, and Breteler, 1995.

Additional considerations include a multitude of other factors, including interaction with other illnesses and medications, ease of application, cost, and applicability to special populations such as the elderly or the institutionalized. Health services research and outcome studies are needed to determine how well the interventions established in clinical trials perform in various settings, such as primary care settings and sleep centers, or as implemented by various providers, such as family practitioners or sleep disorder specialists. This point is worth emphasizing because most patients with insomnia are seen in primary care settings in which providers may be less likely to implement behavioral treatments. Thus, interventions developed in tertiary settings need to be transferred adequately to community settings in order to deliver optimal treatment to the majority of patients with insomnia. With all these issues, however, the principles outlined above, such as reliable diagnoses and adequate trial design, continue to be essential factors from which treatment and assessment decisions can be appropriately evaluated.

References

Akerstedt, T., Hume, K., Minors, D., & Waterhouse, J. (1994). The subjective meaning of good sleep, an intraindividual approach using the Karolinska Sleep Diary. *Perceptual & Motor Skills, 79*(1, Pt. 1), 287–296.

American Psychiatric Association. (1987). *Diagnostic and statistical manual of mental disorders* (3rd ed., revised). Washington, D.C.: Author.

————. (1994). *Diagnostic and statistical manual of mental disorders* (4th ed.). Washington, D.C.: Author.

Angst, J., Vollrath, M., Koch, R., & Dobler-Mikola, A. (1989). The Zurich Study: VII. Insomnia: symptoms, classification and prevalence. *European Archives of Psychiatry and Clinical Neuroscience, 238*, 285–293.

Association of Sleep Disorders Centers, Sleep Disorders Classification Committee, & Roffwarg, H. P., Chairman. (1979). Diagnostic classification of sleep and arousal disorders. *Sleep, 2*, 1–137.

Balter, M. B., & Uhlenhuth, E. H. (1992). New epidemiologic findings about insomnia and its treatment. *Journal of Clinical Psychiatry, 53*(Suppl.), 34–39; discussion 40–42.

Barnes, R. F., Veith, R. C., Borson, S., Vershey, J., Raskind, M. A., & Halter, J. B. (1983). High levels of plasma catecholamines in dexamethasone-resistant depressed patients. *American Journal of Psychiatry, 140*, 1623–1625.

Bootzin, R. R., & Perlis, M. L. (1992). Nonpharmacologic treatments of insomnia [Review]. *Journal of Clinical Psychiatry, 53*(Suppl.), 37–41.

Borkovec, T. D., & Fowles, D. C. (1973). Controlled investigation of the effects of progressive and hypnotic relaxation on insomnia. *Journal of Abnormal Psychology, 82*(1), 153–158.

Buysse, D. J., Reynolds, C. F., Hauri, P. J., Roth, T., Stepanski, E. J., Thorpy, M. J., Bixler, E. O., Kales, A., Manfedi, R. L., Vgontzas, A. N., Messiano, D. A., Houck, P. R., & Kupfer, D. J. (1994). Diagnostic concordance for sleep disorders using proposed DSM-IV categories: A report from the APA/NIMH DSM-IV field trial. *American Journal of Psychiatry, 151*, 1351–1360.

Buysse, D. J., Reynolds, C. F., Monk, T. H., Berman, S. R., & Kupfer, D. J. (1989). The Pittsburgh Sleep Quality Index (PSQI): A new instrument for psychiatric research and practice. *Psychiatry Research, 28*, 193–213.

Carr-Kaffashan, L., & Woolfolk, R. L. (1979). Active and placebo effects in treatment of moderate and severe insomnia. *Journal of Consulting & Clinical Psychology, 47*(6), 1072–1080.

Carskadon, M. A., Dement, W. C., Mitler, M. M., Guilleminault, C., Zarcone, V. P., & Spiegel, R. (1976). Self-reports versus sleep laboratory findings in 122 drug-free subjects with complaints of chronic insomnia. *American Journal of Psychiatry, 133*(12), 1382–1388.

Charon, F., Dramaix, M., & Mendlewicz, J. (1989). Epidemiological survey of insomniac subjects in a sample of 1,761 outpatients. *Neuropsychobiology, 21*(3), 109–110.

Coates, T. J., George, J. M., Killen, J. D., Marchini, E., Hamilton, S., & Thorensen, C. E. (1981). First night effects in good sleepers and sleep-maintenance insomniacs when recorded at home. *Sleep, 4*(3), 293–298.

Coleman, R. M. (1982). Periodic movements in sleep (nocturnal myoclonus) and restless legs syndrome. In C. Guilleminault (Ed.), *Sleeping and waking disorders: Indications and techniques* (pp. 225–244). Boston: Butterworths.

Diagnostic Classification Steering Committee, & Thorpy, M. J. (1990). *International classification of sleep disorders: Diagnostic and coding manual.* Rochester, Minn.: American Sleep Disorders Association.

Espie, C. A., Brooks, D. N., & Lindsay, W. R. (1989). An evaluation of tailored psychological treatment of insomnia. *Journal of Behavior Therapy and Experimental Psychiatry, 20*(2), 143–153.

Ford, D. E., & Kamerow, D. B. (1989). Epidemiologic study of sleep disturbances and psychiatric disorders. *Journal of the American Medical Association, 262*, 1479–1484.

Frankel, B. L., Coursey, R. D., Buchbinder, R., & Snyder, F. (1976). Recorded and reported sleep in chronic primary insomnia. *Archives of General Psychiatry, 33*(5), 615–623.

Freedman, R., & Papsdorf, J. D. (1976). Biofeedback and progressive relaxation treatment of sleep-onset insomnia: A controlled, all-night investigation. *Biofeedback & Self Regulation, 1*(3), 253–271.

Gallup Organization. (1991). *Sleep in America.* Princeton, N.J.: Author.

Ganguli, M., Reynolds, C. F., & Gilby, J. E. (in press). Prevalence and persistence of sleep complaints in a rural elderly community sample: The MoVIES Project. *Journal of American Geriatrics Society.*

Garfinkel, D., Laudon, M., Nof, D., & Zisapel, N. (1995). Improvement of sleep quality in elderly people by controlled-release melatonin. *Lancet, 346*(8974), 541–544.

Gislason, T., & Almqvist, M. (1987). Somatic diseases and sleep complaints. An epidemiological study of 3,201 Swedish men. *Acta Medica Scandinavica, 221*(5), 475–481.

Greenblatt, D. J. (1992). Pharmacology of benzodiazepine hypnotics [Review]. *Journal of Clinical Psychiatry, 53*(Suppl.), 7–13.

Guilleminault, C., Clerk, A., Black, J., Labanowski, M., Pelayo, R., & Claman, D. (1995). Nondrug treatment trials in psychophysiologic insomnia. *Archives of Internal Medicine, 155*(8), 838–844.

Hauri, P. (1981). Treating psychophysiologic insomnia with biofeedback. *Archives of General Psychiatry, 38*(7), 752–758.

Hauri, P., & Fisher, J. (1986). Persistent psychophysiologic (learned) insomnia. *Sleep, 9*, 38–53.

Haynes, S. N., Fitzgerald, S. G., Shute, G., & O'Meary, M. (1985). Responses of psychophysiologic and subjective insomniacs to auditory stimuli during sleep: A replication and extension. *Journal of Abnormal Psychology, 94*(3), 338–345.

Healey, E. S., Kales, A., Monroe, L. J., Bixler, E. O., Chamberlin, K., & Soldatos, C. R. (1981). Onset of insomnia: Role of life-stress events. *Psychosomatic Medicine, 43*, 439–451.

Hohagen, F., Montero, R. F., Weiss, E., Lis, S., Schonbrunn, E., Dressing, H., Riemann, D., & Berger, M. (1994). Treatment of primary insomnia with trimipramine: An alternative to benzodiazepine hypnotics? *European Archives of Psychiatry & Clinical Neuroscience, 244*(2), 65–72.

Jacobs, E. A., Reynolds, C. F., Kupfer, D. J., Lovin, P. A., & Ehrenpreis, A. B. (1988). The role of polysomnography in the differential diagnosis of chronic insomnia. *American Journal of Psychiatry, 145*(3), 346–349.

James, S., Sack, D., Rosenthal, N., & Mendelson, W. (1990). Melatonin administration in insomnia. *Neuropsychopharmacology, 3*(1), 19–23.

Johnson, L. C., & Spinweber, C. L. (1983). Good and poor sleepers differ in navy performance. *Military Medicine, 148*(9), 727–731.

Kales, A., Caldwell, A., Soldatos, C., Bixler, E., & Kales, J. (1983). Biopsychobehavioral correlates of insomnia. II. Pattern specificity and consistency with the Minnesota Multiphasic Personality Inventory. *Psychosomatic Medicine, 45*(4), 341–356.

Karacan, I., Thornby, J. I., Anch, M., Holzer, C. E., Warheit, G. J., Schwab, J. J., & Williams, R. L. (1976). Prevalence of sleep disturbance in a primarily urban Florida county. *Social Science and Medicine, 10,* 239–244.

Karacan, I., Thornby, J. I., & Williams, R. L. (1983a). Sleep disturbance: A community survey. In C. Guilleminault & E. Lugaresi (Eds.), *Sleep/wake disorders: Natural history, epidemiology, and long-term evolution* (pp. 37–60). New York: Raven Press.

Karacan, I., & Williams, R. L. (1983). Sleep disorders in the elderly. *American Family Physician, 27*(3), 143–152.

Kudo, Y., & Kurihara, M. (1990). Clinical evaluation of diphenhydramine hydrochloride for the treatment of insomnia in psychiatric patients: A double-blind study. *Journal of Clinical Pharmacology, 30*(11), 1041–1048.

Kupfer, D. J., & Reynolds, C. F. (1997). Management of insomnia. *New England Journal of Medicine, 336*(5), 341–346.

Kuppermann, M., Lubeck, D. P., Mazonson, P. D., Patrick, D. L., Stewart, A. L., Buesching, D. P., & Fifer, S. K. (1995). Sleep problems and their correlates in a working population. *Journal of General Internal Medicine, 10*(1), 25–32.

Lacks, P., Bertelson, A. D., Sugerman, J., & Kunkel, J. (1983). The treatment of sleep-maintenance insomnia with stimulus-control techniques. *Behaviour Research & Therapy, 21*(3), 291–295.

Lichstein, K. L. (1980). Patients with insomnia perception of cognition versus somatic determinants of sleep disturbance. *Journal of Abnormal Psychology, 89*(1), 105–107.

Lilie, J. K., & Lahmeyer, H. (1991). Psychiatric management of sleep disorders. [Review]. *Psychiatric Medicine, 9*(2), 245–260.

Linsen, S. M., Zitman, F. G., & Breteler, M. H. (1995).

Defining benzodiazepine dependence: The confusion persists. *European Psychiatry, 10,* 306–311.

MacFarlane, J., Cleghorn, J., Brown, G., & Streiner, D. (1991). The effects of exogenous melatonin on the total sleep time and daytime alertness of chronic insomniacs: A preliminary study. *Biological Psychiatry, 30*(4), 371–376.

Mellinger, G. D., Balter, M. B., & Uhlenhuth, E. H. (1985). Insomnia and its treatment. *Archives of General Psychiatry, 42,* 225–232.

Mendelson, W. B. (1995). Long-term follow-up of chronic insomnia. *Sleep, 18*(8), 698–701.

Mendelson, W. B., Garnett, D., Gillin, J. C., & Weingartner, H. (1984a). The experience of insomnia and daytime and nighttime functioning. *Psychiatry Research, 12*(3), 235–250.

Mendelson, W. B., Garnett, D., & Linnoila, M. (1984b). Do patients with insomnia have impaired daytime functioning? *Biological Psychiatry, 19*(8), 1261–1264.

Moldofsky, H. (1989a). Sleep and fibrositis syndrome [Review]. *Rheumatic Diseases Clinics of North America, 15*(1), 91–103.

———. (1989b). Sleep influences on regional and diffuse pain syndromes associated with osteoarthritis [Review]. *Seminars in Arthritis & Rheumatism, 18*(4, Suppl. 2), 18–21.

———. (1989c). Sleep-wake mechanisms in fibrositis [Review]. *Journal of Rheumatology, 19*(Suppl.), 47–48.

Morin, C. M., Colecchi, C., Brink, D., Astruc, M., Mercer, J., & Remsberg, S. (1995). How "blind" are double-blind placebo-controlled trials of benzodiazepine hypnotics? *Sleep, 18*(4), 240–245.

Morin, C. M., Colecchi, C. A., Stone, J., Sood, R. K., & Brink, D. (1995b). Cognitive-behavior therapy and pharmacotherapy for insomnia: Update of a placebo-controlled clinical trial. *Sleep Research, 24,* 303.

Morin, C. M., Culbert, J. P., & Steven, S. J. (1994). Nonpharmacological interventions for insomnia: A meta-analysis of treatment efficacy. *American Journal of Psychiatry, 151,* 1172–1180.

Morin, C. M., & Gramling, S. E. (1989). Sleep patterns and aging: Comparison of older adults with and without insomnia complaints. *Psychology and Aging, 4,* 290–294.

National Institutes of Health. (1984). Drugs and insomnia. NIH Consensus Development Conference [Review]. *National Institutes of Health Consensus Development Conference Summary, 4*(10), 1–9.

Partinen, M. (1988). Stress and the heart: The sleep factor. *Stress Medicine, 4,* 253–363.

Partinen, M., Kaprio, J., Koskenvuo, M., Putkonen, P., & Langinvainio, H. (1983). Genetic and environmental determination of human sleep. *Sleep, 6*(3), 179–185.

Reite, M., Buysse, D., Reynolds, C., & Mendelson, W. (1995). The use of polysomnography in the evaluation of insomnia [Review]. *Sleep, 18*(1), 58–70.

Reynolds, C. F., Kupfer, D. J., Hoch, C. C., Stack, J. A., Houck, P. R., & Sewitch, D. E. (1986). Two-year follow up of elderly patients with mixed depression and dementia: Clinical and EEG sleep findings. *Journal of the American Geriatrics Society, 34*, 793–799.

Rickels, K., Morris, R. J., Newman, H., Rosenfeld, H., Schiller, H., & Weinstock, R. (1983). Diphenhydramine in insomniac family practice patients: A double-blind study. *Journal of Clinical Pharmacology, 23*(5–6), 234–242.

Roehrs, T., Vogel, G., Vogel, F., Wittig, R., Zorick, F., Paxton, C., Lamphere, J., & Roth, T. (1985). Eligibility requirements in hypnotic trials. *Sleep, 8*(1), 34–39.

Sanavio, E. (1988). Pre-sleep cognitive intrusions and treatment of onset-insomnia. *Behaviour Research and Therapy, 26*(6), 451–459.

Scharf, M. (1994). Feasibility of an every-other-night regimen in insomniac patients: Subjective hypnotic effectiveness of quazepam, triazolam, and placebo. *Journal of Clinical Psychiatry, 54*(1), 33–38.

Schramm, E., Hohagen, F., Kappler, C., Grasshoff, U., & Berger, M. (1995). Mental comorbidity of chronic insomnia in general practice attenders using *DSM-III-R. Acta Psychiatrica Scandinavica, 91*(1), 10–17.

Seidel, W. F., & Dement, W. C. (1982). Sleepiness in insomnia: Evaluation and treatment. *Sleep, 5*(Suppl. 2), S182–S190.

Seidel, W. F., Roth, T., Roehrs, T., Zorick, F., & Dement, W. C. (1984). Treatment of a 12-hour shift of sleep schedule with benzodiazepines. *Science, 224*, 1262–1264.

Spielman, A. J., Saskin, P., & Thorpy, M. J. (1987). Treatment of chronic insomnia by restriction of time in bed. *Sleep, 10*, 45–56.

Steinmark, S. W., & Borkovec, T. D. (1974). Active and placebo treatment effects on moderate insomnia under counterdemand and positive demand instructions. *Journal of Abnormal Psychology, 83*(2), 157–163.

Stepanski, E., Koshorek, G., Zorick, F., Glinn, M., Roehrs, T., & Roth, T. (1989). Characteristics of individuals who do or do not seek treatment for chronic insomnia. *Psychosomatics, 30*(4), 421–427.

Stoller, M. K. (1994). Economic effects of insomnia [Review]. *Clinical Therapeutics, 16*(5), 873–897; discussion, 854.

Sugarman, J. S., Stern, J. A., & Walsh, J. K. (1985). Daytime alertness in subjective and objective insomnia: Some preliminary findings. *Biological Psychiatry, 20*, 741–750.

Tan, T. L., Kales, J. D., Kales, A., Soldatos, C. R., & Bixler, E. O. (1984). Biopsychobehavioral correlates of insomnia, IV: Diagnosis based on *DSM-III. American Journal of Psychiatry, 141*, 357–362.

Vollrath, M., Wicki, W., & Angst, J. (1989). The Zurich Study: VIII. Insomnia: Association with depression, anxiety, somatic syndromes, and course of insomnia. *European Archives of Psychiatry and Clinical Neuroscience, 239*(2), 113–124.

Welstein, L., Dement, W. C., Redington, D., Guilleminault, C., & Mitler, M. M. (1983). Insomnia in the San Francisco Bay area: A telephone survey. In C. Guilleminault & E. Lugaresi (Eds.), *SleepWake disorders: Natural history, epidemiology, and long-term evolution* (pp. 73–85). New York: Raven Press.

Whorwell, P. J., McCallum, M., & Creed, F. H. (1986). Non-colonic features of irritable bowel syndrome. *Gut, 27*, 37–40.

Woods, J., & Winger, G. (1995). Current benzodiazepine issues. *Psychopharmacology, 118*, 107–115.

27

Psychosocial Treatments for Personality Disorders

Paul Crits-Christoph

A Type 2 random clinical trial (RCT) of psychological treatment for avoidant personality disorder (APD) compared three group-administered behavioral interventions (graded exposure, standard social skills training, intimacy-focused social skills training) with a wait-list control; while all three treatments were more efficacious than the control condition, no differences among the treatments were identified after either the 10-week treatment period or at follow-up. A single Type 2 RCT of psychological treatment for borderline personality disorder (BPD) randomly assigned 44 women demonstrating parasuicidal behavior to either dialectical behavioral therapy (DBT; consisted of weekly group and individual sessions for a year) or treatment as usual in the community; DBT resulted in lower attrition, fewer and less severe episodes of parasuicidal behavior, and fewer days of hospitalization as compared to the control condition, but no differences in depression, hopelessness, or suicidal ideation. No RCTs of psychological treatment for other personality disorders have been reported. A Type 2 RCT of psychological treatment for mixed PDs (excluding Cluster A disorders) randomly assigned 81 patients to two forms of brief dynamic therapy averaging 40 weeks and a wait-list control condition averaging 15 weeks; the two forms of brief dynamic therapy yielded substantial symptomatic improvements at both the end of treatment and a 1.5-year follow-up. Two less adequate case control studies also produced positive outcomes for dynamic treatment lasting from 9 sessions to 2 years for mixed PDs. Several substantial review articles have found a consistent adverse impact of PDs on outcomes of treatment for a wide range of Axis I disorders.

DEFINITION, EPIDEMIOLOGY, AND ETIOLOGY OF PERSONALITY DISORDERS

The American Psychiatric Association's (APA's) *Diagnostic and Statistical Manual,* fourth edition (*DSM-IV*) defines personality traits in terms of enduring patterns of thinking about, perceiving, and relating to the environment and oneself (APA, 1994). A personality disorder (PD) (Axis II diagnosis) is present when such personality traits result in impairment in social or occupational functioning or distress to the person. The *DSM-IV* describes 10 specific Axis II diagnoses. These are grouped into three clusters: (a) the "odd" cluster (paranoid, schizoid, and schizotypal), (b) the dramatic cluster (histrionic, narcissistic, antisocial, and borderline), and (c) the anxious cluster (avoidant, dependent, obsessive compulsive). The final personality disorder, personality disorder not otherwise specified (NOS), is not in a cluster. This disorder is defined by either (a) the pattern meets general criteria for a personality disorder and traits of several personality disorders are evident, but the criteria for any one specific disorder are not met, or (2) the pattern meets the general criteria for a personality disorder, but the type of personality disorder is not included in the classification. In terms of this last criterion, two personality disorders, passive-aggressive and depressive, are listed in *DSM-IV*'s appendix as potential diagnoses requiring further study but can be used to assign a personality disorder NOS diagnosis.

Although personality disorders are apparently relatively common compared to many other psychiatric disorders, precise estimates of the prevalence of different personality disorders are hard to obtain. The primary problem is one of assessment. Strides have been made in the development of structured clinical interviews for assessing Axis II disorders, but to date these instruments have displayed limited validity (Perry, 1992). With the measurement limitations in mind, Weissman (1993) reviewed studies of the epidemiology of personality disorders. Early studies (pre-*DSM-III*) (APA, 1980) yielded overall rates of 6% to 10% of the population manifesting some type of personality disorder. Studies using *DSM-III* or *DSM-III-R* (APA, 1987) diagnoses have yielded rates of 10% to 13.5%.

In terms of specific personality disorders, the *DSM-III* and *DSM-III-R* studies found the prevalence of paranoid personality disorder to range from 0.4% to 1.8%. The other personality disorder types ranged as follows: schizoid, 0.5% to 0.9%; schizotypal, 0.6% to 5.6%; histrionic, 1.3% to 3.0%; narcissistic, 0% to 0.4%; borderline, 1.1% to 4.6%; antisocial, 0.2% to 3.7% (although there may be cultural variability in such rates; see Hwu, Yeh, & Chang, 1989); avoidant, 0% to 1.3%; dependent, 1.6% to 6.7%; obsessive compulsive, 1.7% to 6.4%; and passive-aggressive, 0% to 3.0% (Weissman, 1993). There is also an extensive amount of comorbidity with personality disorders, that is, having one disorder tends to be associated with having one or more additional Axis II diagnoses. For example, half of people diagnosed with avoidant personality disorder (APD) also receive a diagnosis of schizotypal personality disorder (Zimmerman & Coryell, 1990).

A recent epidemiological study (Samuels, Nestadt, Romanoski, Folstein, & McHugh, 1994) of 810 adults in the community found an overall rate of 5.9% with *DSM-III* personality disorders, slightly lower than previous estimates. The subjects with Axis II diagnoses had higher rates of alcohol and drug use disorders, suicidal thoughts and attempts, and general life events in the past year. However, only one fifth of those

people with an Axis II diagnosis was receiving treatment.

Comorbidity of Axis II with Axis I disorders is especially important for treatment planning. but few adequate studies of the epidemiological rates of such comorbidity have been performed. Ruegg and Frances (1995) recently reviewed the literature on comorbidity of Axis I and II disorders and found that methodological problems, particularly the use of convenience samples from treatment centers rather than randomly selected community samples, limit the conclusions that can be drawn at this time.

However, the studies that have been done show high rates of comorbidity. Of patients with bulimia, in two studies, 39% (Fahy, Eisler, & Russell, 1993) and 38% (Ames-Frankel et al., 1992) had personality disorders. Ruegg and Frances (1995) reported large percentages of patients with anxiety disorders (36–76%; six studies) and mood disorders (36–65%; eight studies) also have a personality disorder. Patients with obsessive compulsive disorder (OCD) were found to have high rates of compulsive personality disorder and other personality disorders, particularly the avoidant type (Ruegg & Frances, 1995). Comorbidity of Axis II disorders with substance use disorders is particularly high. Weiss, Mirin, Griffin, Gunderson, and Hufford (1993) found that 74% of hospitalized cocaine-dependent patients had at least one Axis II diagnosis. Similarly, Haller, Knisely, Dawson, and Schnoll (1993) found that 75% of perinatal substance abusers also received an Axis II diagnosis. Dinwiddle, Reich, and Cloninger (1992) found that injecting drugs increased the odds of a diagnosis of comorbid antisocial personality disorder 21-fold and that the diagnosis of antisocial personality disorder increased the odds of injecting drugs by 27-fold. Swartz, Blazer, George, and Winfield (1990) describe data on comorbidity of borderline personality disorder (BPD) with Axis I disorders using a community-based sample, the Epidemiologic Catchment Area Program. Individuals with borderline personality disorder were frequently found to have generalized anxiety disorder (56%), major depression (41%), agoraphobia (37%), social phobia (35%), post-traumatic stress disorder (34%), and alcohol abuse/dependence (22%), among others.

Little is known about the etiology of personality disorders. A number of studies have documented high rates of physical and sexual abuse or other trauma during childhood in patients later diagnosed with borderline personality disorder (Herman, Perry, & van der Kolk, 1989; Ogata et al., 1990; Westen, Lundolph, Misle, Ruffins, & Block, 1990). Other studies have found evidence for familial transmission of borderline personality disorder (Baron, Gruen, Asnis, Asnis, & Lord, 1985; Loranger, Olkham, & Tullis, 1982) and schizotypal personality disorder (Baron et al., 1985). Twin studies have supported a genetic component for schizotypal personality disorder but not borderline personality disorder (Torgersen, 1984).

HISTORICAL PERSPECTIVE

Early psychoanalytic writings devoted a considerable amount of attention to the treatment of "characterological" problems (Alexander, 1930; Fenichel, 1945). Although some of this literature influenced modern psychodynamic approaches, it is difficult to know the relevance of these early writings to the current classification system for psychiatric disorders. For example, the distinction between obsessive compulsive disorder and obsessive compulsive personality disorder was not made in early writings on "obsessive compulsive" character, and this distinction is likely to be important for treatment selection.

Within the psychodynamic literature, there has been voluminous writing on the nature and treatment of narcissistic and borderline personality types in particular (Kernberg, 1984; Kohut, 1984; see review by Aronson, 1989). Even in these more recent writings, however, there has remained a lack of use of a consensual definition of the target patient population. As a consequence of the varying definitions of characterological conditions, the research literature on the treatment of personality disorders begins with the advent of the DSM-III and DSM-III-R classification system for Axis II disorders.

This is not to say that the DSM definition of personality pathology is not without problems. A number of authors have described various problems with the DSM classification, including lack of discrimination of many of the DSM criteria (Svrakic & Divac-Jovanovic, 1994), problems in distinguishing normal from deviant personality (Lively, Schroeder, Jackson, & Jang, 1994), and general lack of empirical support (Widiger, 1993). Alternatives to the DSM system have been recently reviewed by Dyce (1994). These alternatives include interpersonal circumplex models, neurobiological learning theory, biosocial learning theory, and the five-factor model of personal-ity. Although these alternatives appear promising, they have not yet been developed to the extent that they have guided treatment research. It seems likely that the DSM system will not be modified or replaced until adequate data justifying an alternative system exist.

REVIEW OF TREATMENT
OUTCOME LITERATURE

Despite the relatively high prevalence of Axis II disorders, there have been very few outcome studies using patients with these disorders. No meta-analytic reviews have been published on the treatment of personality disorders. Shea (1993) conducted a qualitative review of treatment studies involving personality disorder patients. This review updates the one by Shea. In addition, Shea included discussion of studies that did not involve DSM-III personality disorders per se (e.g., socially shy patients rather than avoidant personality disorder patients). Here, we restrict our attention to those studies involving personality disorder patients.

Below we summarize the existing literature on the treatment of personality disorders using the Type 1 to Type 6 classification of studies employed in this volume. Our emphasis is on Type 1 and Type 2 studies that involve patients meeting DSM-III or DSM-III-R criteria (no studies with DSM-IV criteria have yet been published). Type 3 through Type 6 studies, including any study using pre-DSM-III criteria, are mentioned only when no Type 1 or 2 studies are available.

Avoidant Personality Disorder

The only randomized controlled trial of DSM-III avoidant personality disorder compared graded exposure, standard social skills training, intimacy-focused social skills training, and a wait-list control (Alden, 1989). The behavioral treatments were all administered in group format. All of the active treatments were better than the wait list, but no differences among the behavioral treatments were found at the end of the 10-week treatment period or at follow-up. Examination of the clinical significance of the outcomes revealed that, although positive changes had occurred in the active treatment conditions, patients were not functioning at the level of normative comparison samples. This study, however, had minimal statistical power for detecting differences among the treatments (less than 20 patients per group).

One Type 3 study (not controlled) has been reported of *DSM-III-R* avoidant personality disorder (Renneberg, Goldstein, Phillips, & Chambless, 1990). This study evaluated an intensive (4 full days) group behavioral treatment program with 17 patients. The treatment included group systematic desensitization, behavioral rehearsal, and self-image work. Outcome was evaluated at posttreatment and 1-year follow-up. The results showed evidence of positive changes, especially in terms of fear of negative evaluation. Gains were maintained over the follow-up period.

In a comparative study without a control group, Stravynski, Lesage, Marcouiller, and Elie (1989) compared social skills training with group discussion plus homework in a crossover design for patients with *DSM-III* avoidant personality disorder. Although significant improvements on most measures were found in general, no differences between the treatment modalities were found, questioning the centrality of skills acquisition as the mechanism of action of social skills training. Treatment, however, may have been too brief (5 sessions of each modality) to detect an effect. More recently, Stravynski, Belisle, Marcouiller, and Lavallee (1994) examined whether a combination of office-based and in vivo (real-life interactions with people in shopping malls, a cafeteria, etc.) social skills training enhanced the outcome of office-based social skills training for 28 patients with *DSM-III* avoidant personality disorder. Outcomes were generally equal in the two conditions, although the in vivo condition had a greater attrition rate.

Because avoidant personality disorder appeared to be equally responsive to different kinds of behavioral treatments, Alden and Capreol (1993) examined the hypothesis that different kinds of interpersonal problems would moderate treatment response to various therapies. To test this hypothesis, data from the Alden (1989) project described above were used. Several findings emerged. Avoidant PD patients who had greater problems related to distrustful and angry behavior benefited more from structured exercises that required them to approach and talk to others (graded exposure). Patients with problems involving resisting others' demands benefited from both graded exposure and social skills training but were particularly responsive to intimacy-focused social skills training. The results suggest that a comprehensive assessment of interpersonal problems may be important in planning what

type of treatment intervention is most likely to be beneficial to patients with avoidant personality disorder.

In a quantitative case study, Coon (1994) reported on the successful treatment of avoidant personality disorder using schema-focused cognitive therapy. Positive outcomes were evidenced not only at termination but also at 1-year follow-up.

Borderline Personality Disorder

Linehan, Hubert, Suarez, Douglas, and Heard (1991) reported on probably the best study yet performed using patients with a diagnosis of borderline personality disorder. In this study, 44 women who showed evidence of parasuicidal behavior and were diagnosed with borderline personality disorder were randomly assigned to either dialectical behavior therapy (DBT) or treatment as usual in the community. The dialectical behavior therapy is actually a complex treatment modality that is more accurately described as an eclectic, rather than a traditional, behavior therapy per se. The treatment consists of weekly group and individual sessions for 1 year. The group component is psychoeducational, teaching interpersonal skills, distress tolerance/reality acceptance, and emotion regulation skills. The individual therapy sessions involve directive, problem-solving techniques, as well as supportive techniques such as empathy and acceptance. Behavioral goals serve as the focus of the individual sessions and are addressed in a sequential order, but previous goals are readdressed if the problem returns. These goals include decreasing suicidal behaviors, decreasing therapy-interfering behaviors, decreasing behaviors that interfere with quality of life, increasing behavioral skills, decreasing behaviors related to post-traumatic stress, increasing respect for self, and achieving individual goals. The basic treatment strategies of DBT are organized into four categories: (a) dialectical strategies, (b) core strategies, (c) stylistic strategies, and (d) case management strategies. Dialectical strategies include a range of techniques that allow the therapist to hold both sides of important polarities, with the hope that a new synthesis and flexibility will arise out of the opposing positions. The core strategies consist of acceptance (validation) strategies and problem-solving strategies. Stylistic strategies involve the form and style of therapeutic communications. Two styles are balanced: reciprocal communication strategies (responsiveness, self-disclosure, warm engagement, and genuineness) and irreverent communication strategies that are intended to keep the patient off balance. The case management strategies involve interactions between the therapist and the community (e.g., consultants, family members, significant others). More details about DBT can be found in the published treatment manual (Linehan, 1993).

The Linehan et al. (1991) study found that DBT resulted in relatively fewer and less severe episodes of parasuicidal behavior and fewer days of hospitalization compared to treatment as usual, but no differences in depression, hopelessness, or suicidal ideation were found. The attrition rate for DBT (16.7%) was much lower than the attrition rate for treatment as usual (58.3%). Although this important study has yielded very promising information on DBT as a treatment for parasuicidal patients with borderline personality disorder, several aspects of the study lead to a Type 2 classification. These limitations include the fact that the therapists in the treatment-as-usual condition were not equated with the DBT therapists in terms of their experience in treating patients with borderline personality disorder and the fact that 27% of the control patients never actually began therapy, although they were referred to a therapist.

Dialectical behavior therapy has also been extended to the treatment of inpatients with a diagnosis of borderline personality disorder (Barley et al., 1993). The implementation of DBT in an inpatient unit decreased the rates of incident reports of self-inflicted injuries and overdoses. No information on the assessment of patient diagnosis, however, was presented in that report.

Psychodynamic therapy was evaluated as a treatment for borderline personality disorder by Stevenson and Meares (1992). The treatment was, broadly speaking, based on self-psychology. Therapy had a maturational goal accomplished through helping the patients discover and elaborate their inner lives. Attention to empathy, particularly disruptions in empathy, was a central aspect of the process of therapy (Meares, 1987). For 1 year, 30 patients with *DSM-III* borderline personality disorder were treated with therapy twice per week. Outcome was assessed 1 year after termination of treatment. Substantial reductions in violent behavior, drug use, medical visits, episodes of self-harm, time away from work, and symptoms were evident. The criteria for borderline personality disorder were no longer met by 30% of the patients.

Munroe-Blum and Marziali (1995) compared open-ended individual psychodynamic therapy with a manualized interpersonal group therapy for 110 patients with borderline personality disorder. The group treatment lasted 30 sessions. No differences at 1 year (termination) or 2 years were found, although patients in general benefited from both treatments.

Other Personality Disorders

No controlled treatment outcome studies have yet been performed for histrionic, dependent, schizotypal, schizoid, narcissistic, passive-aggressive, antisocial, or paranoid personality disorder. A case study with quantitative outcome data has been published showing positive effects of cognitive therapy for a paranoid personality disorder patient (Williams, 1988).

Mixed Axis II Samples

There has been one controlled study using a sample of those with mixed personality disorders (Winston et al., 1991, 1994). This study randomly assigned 81 patients with personality disorders to a wait-list control condition and to two forms of brief dynamic therapy, one more cognitively oriented (brief adaptive therapy) and one oriented more toward confronting defenses and eliciting affect (modeled after Davanloo, 1980). The sample consisted mostly of Cluster B and Cluster C personality disorder types, as well as patients diagnosed as personality disorder not otherwise specified (mostly with Cluster C features). However, paranoid, schizoid, schizotypal, narcissistic, and borderline personality disorders were excluded.

Treatment lasted on average 40 weeks, although the wait list averaged only 15 weeks. Because of this confound of treatment condition with time, this study is classified as a Type 2 study. The results showed that both forms of brief dynamic therapy produced substantial improvements across multiple outcome measures, including general psychiatric symptoms, social adjustment, and target complaints. At follow-up assessments obtained 1.5 years on average after the end of therapy, the gains in improvement were maintained for target complaints (the only outcome measured).

Monsen, Odland, Faugli, Daae, and Eilertsen (1995) reported on the results of treating 25 patients (23 of whom had a diagnosis of a personality disorder) with psychodynamic therapy based on object relations theory and self-psychology. Treatment lasted on average a little bit more than 2 years. Patients were assessed at termination and again 5 years after termination. At the end of treatment, substantial change was found on measures of symptoms, affect consciousness, and defenses. In addition, 75% of the patients that had an Axis I disorder at intake no longer qualified for an Axis I disorder at termination. Of the patients with Axis II disorders, 72% no longer qualified for the disorder at termination. The gains were maintained at the 5-year follow-up.

Høglend (1993) studied 15 patients with personality disorders in comparison to 30 patients without Axis II disorders. The treatment was psychodynamic therapy of brief to moderate length (9–53 sessions) that was based on the approaches of Sifneos (1979) and Malan (1976). At termination, the Axis II patients showed evidence of less change than the patients without Axis II diagnoses, but at 4-year follow-up there was no difference. For the Axis II patients, the number of treatment sessions was significantly related to the acquisition of insight and dynamic change at follow-up. Thus, length of treatment appeared to be a crucial factor in producing positive outcomes for the Axis II patients (but not the patients without personality disorders).

Axis II Personality Disorders as Moderators of Treatment of Axis I Disorders

Reich and Vasile (1993) have reviewed studies of the relation of personality traits and Axis II personality disorders to the outcome of treatments (both psychosocial and psychopharmacological) designed to benefit Axis I conditions. This review of 17 studies builds on an earlier review of 21 studies (Reich & Green, 1991) and found a consistent adverse impact of personality pathology on the treatment outcome of a wide range of Axis I disorders. Examination of the studies in these two reviews, plus some more recent studies, that investigate specific personality disorders and specific psychosocial treatments reveals the following findings:

1. Antisocial personality disorder (ASP) (without a co-occurring diagnosis of depression) predicted poor outcome from cognitive therapy and psychodynamic therapy for opiate addiction (Woody, McLellan, Luborsky, & O'Brien, 1985).

2. Avoidant personality disorder was associated with relatively poorer outcome from exposure therapy for agoraphobia (Chambless, Renneberg, Goldstein, & Gracely, 1992).
3. Schizotypal personality disorder is associated with poor outcome of behavior therapy for obsessive compulsive disorder (Minichiello, Baer, & Jenike, 1987).
4. Presence of a personality disorder predicted poor outcome of cognitive-behavioral group therapy for social anxiety (Turner, 1987).
5. Patients with personality disorders show slower response to imipramine plus interpersonal psychotherapy for recurrent unipolar depression (Frank, Kupfer, Jacob, & Jarrett, 1987).
6. Patients with a diagnosis in the anxious cluster of personality disorders showed evidence of much poorer outcome with imipramine plus interpersonal therapy for recurrent unipolar depression (Pilkonis & Frank, 1988).

Presence of a personality disorder, however, does not always uniformly lead to poor outcome. For example, Longabaugh et al. (1994) recently investigated the extent to which ASP moderated the treatment of alcohol abuse. In the study, 31 patients with ASP were compared to 118 non-ASP alcohol abusers randomly assigned to either a group-extended cognitive-behavioral treatment (including stimulus control, rearranging consequences, restructuring cognitions, assertion training, problem solving for alternatives to drinking, and dealing with slips/relapses) or to relationship-enhanced cognitive-behavioral treatment (involving functional analysis, enhancing reinforcements in relationships with partners, using partners' relationship to reinforce abstinence, and educational/didactic sessions for partners). A significant interaction was found for ASP by treatment modality for the average number of drinks consumed on a drinking day, with patients with ASP in the extended cognitive-behavioral treatment having the fewest drinks (about 2 on a drinking day) and patients with ASP in the relationship enhancement condition having the most (about 8). Non-ASP patients had an intermediate level of drinking on a drinking day in both treatment conditions. This interaction, however, was not found for percentage of days abstinent. At 13–18-month follow-up, a main effect for ASP emerged, with ASP patients showing more days abstinent compared to non-ASP patients.

Barber and Muenz (1996) reported on how features of two personality disorders, avoidant and obsessive compulsive, interact with type of psychotherapy in the treatment of depression. Using data from the Treatment of Depression Collaborative Study (Elkin et al., 1989), Barber and Muenz found that interpersonal psychotherapy produced better outcomes for depressed patients with features of obsessive compulsive personality disorder, but cognitive therapy produced better outcomes with depressed patients who also had features of avoidant personality disorder.

In the treatment of public speaking anxiety among patients with social phobia, the presence of avoidant personality disorder did not predict outcome (i.e., treatment was equally successful for those with and without avoidant personality disorder) in one study (Hofmann, Newman, Becker, Taylor, & Roth, 1995).

There may be ways in which standard treatment can be enhanced or improved to treat more effectively Axis I patients that have a comorbid Axis II condition. For example, a quantitative case study by Walker, Freeman, and Christensen (1994) used restricted environmental stimulation to enhance successfully the exposure treatment of obsessive compulsive disorder in a patient with schizotypal personality disorder. Although this treatment focused on the OCD and not the schizotypal personality disorder per se, the restricted environmental stimulation therapy was incorporated because of the attentional problems found with patients with schizotypal personality. Thus, this treatment may have other applications as a means of increasing attentional focus for schizotypal personality disorder patients.

Summary of Recommendations Based on Treatment Outcome Literature

It is obvious that the systematic study of treatment efficacy for personality disorders is in its infancy. With no Type 1 studies published yet, it is difficult to make recommendations with a high degree of confidence. Linehan's dialectical behavior therapy appears to be a promising treatment for parasuicidal patients with borderline personality disorders. Behavior therapy is promising for the treatment of avoidant personality disorder, but the specific form of behavior therapy may need to be tailored to patients' types of interpersonal problems, with graded exposure better when distrust is an issue and intimacy-focused social skills training preferable when resisting others' demands is the major

interpersonal problem. A structured cognitive-behavioral treatment appears to be best for patients with antisocial personality disorder. Psychodynamic therapy, particularly more intensive and longer term, appears useful for the treatment of borderline personality disorder (based on an uncontrolled trial) and mixed personality disorders (based on a controlled trial and two uncontrolled trials).

One clear recommendation can be made based on a consistent finding across many studies: standard brief treatments for Axis I conditions often fail when Axis II pathology is also present. Therefore, the clinician should be alert to the presence of a comorbid Axis II disorder and reevaluate the selection of treatment modality if progress is not made within the period of brief therapy.

FUTURE DIRECTIONS IN THE TREATMENT OF PERSONALITY DISORDERS

The studies reviewed above begin to point to some promising likely developments for the treatment of personality disorders. First, we can predict that there will likely need to be modification of the existing Axis I treatments to take into account the Axis II pathology. These modifications will include the lengthening of brief treatments and greater attention to the long-standing rigid belief systems of Axis II patients, rather than a focus on symptoms or recent triggers only. A second major direction will be the matching of patients to treatment modalities. This matching may occur at the level of the personality disorder syndrome, such as Barber and Muenz's (in press) finding that depressed patients with features of avoidant personality disorder do better in cognitive therapy, but depressed patients with features of obsessive compulsive personality disorders fare better in interpersonal therapy. Alternatively, matching patients to treatment may occur in regard to other patient attributes that either underlie the distinctions between personality disorders or are other salient patient variables not captured in the current system. For example, Beutler, Mohr, Grawe, & Engle (1991) suggest that impulsivity/external coping style and resistance/reactance are two important dimensions for which there is preliminary evidence for the matching of patients to treatments. Thus, rather than use the diagnosis of antisocial personality disorder as a basis for recommending a more structured treatment modality, the underlying dimensions of impulsivity and low socialization that characterize, but do not uniquely define, antisocial personality disorder might be more salient for treatment selection. Whether these patient dimensions are examined in addition to the *DSM* categories or eventually replace them in some form remains to be seen.

Another direction for the future is the movement toward psychotherapy integration. In fact, Linehan's dialectical behavior therapy already integrates techniques from a wide variety of approaches. With personality disorders, such integration might be especially necessary because of the diverse set of problems that characterize these patients. Thus, a successful treatment might need elements of exposure therapy, understanding and modification of long-standing cognitive/interpersonal patterns, practice of new behaviors, and attention to disruptions in the therapeutic relationship (transference). Psychosocial and psychopharmacological interventions will also be examined in combination for personality disorders as a way of managing the symptoms while also treating the underlying psychological processes.

Significant advances in the treatment of personality disorders can be expected to have important public health impacts given the prevalence of these disorders and the impairment in social and occupational functioning associated with them.

ACKNOWLEDGMENTS The preparation of this manuscript was funded in part by National Institute of Mental Health grants P30-MH-45178, K02-MH00756, and RO1-MH40472. Address reprint requests to Paul Crits-Christoph, Ph.D., Room 700, 3600 Market Street, Philadelphia, Pennsylvania 19104.

References

Alden, L. E. (1989). Short-term structured treatment for avoidant personality disorder. *Journal of Consulting and Clinical Psychology, 57,* 756–764.

Alden, L. E., & Capreol, M. J. (1993). Avoidant personality disorder: Interpersonal problems as predictors of treatment response. *Behavior therapy, 24,* 357–376.

Alexander, F. (1930). The neurotic character. *International Journal of Psychoanalysis, 11,* 292–280.

American Psychiatric Association. (1980). *Diagnostic and statistical manual of mental disorder* (3rd ed.). Washington, D.C.: Author.

———. (1987). *Diagnostic and statistical manual of mental disorders* (3rd ed., revised). Washington, D.C.: Author.

———. (1994). *Diagnostic and statistical manual of mental disorders* (4th ed.). Washington, D.C.: Author.

Ames-Frankel, J., Devlin, M. J., Walsh, B. T., Strasser, T. J., Sadik, C., Oldham, J. M., & Roose, S. P. (1992). Personality disorder diagnoses in patients with bulimia nervosa: Clinical correlates and changes with treatment. *Journal of Clinical Psychiatry, 53,* 90–96.

Aronson, T. A. (1989). A critical review of psychotherapeutic treatments of the borderline personality: Historical trends and future directions. *Journal of Nervous and Mental Disease, 177,* 511–527.

Barber, J., & Muenz, L. (1996). The role of avoidance and obsessiveness in matching patients to cognitive and interpersonal psychotherapy: Empirical findings from the Treatment for Depression Collaborative Research Program. *Journal of Consulting and Clinical Psychology, 64,* 951–958.

Barley, W. D., Buie, S. E., Peterson, E. W., Hollingsworth, A. S., Griva, M., Hickerson, S. C., Lawson, J. E., & Bailey, B. J. (1993). *Journal of Personality Disorders, 7,* 232–240.

Baron, J., Gruen, R., Asnis, L., & Lord, S. (1985). Familial transmission of schizotypal and borderline personality disorders. *American Journal of Psychiatry, 142,* 927–934.

Beutler, L. E., Mohr, D. C., Grawe, K., & Engle, D. (1991). Looking for differential treatment effects: Cross-cultural predictors of differential psychotherapy efficacy. *Journal of Psychotherapy Integration, 1,* 121–141.

Chambless, D. L., Renneberg, B., Goldstein, A., & Gracely, E. J. (1992). MCMI-diagnosed personality disorders among agoraphobic outpatients: Prevalence and relationship to severity and treatment outcome. *Journal of Anxiety Disorders, 6,* 193–211.

Coon, D. W. (1994). Cognitive-behavioral interventions with avoidant personality: A single case study. *Journal of Cognitive Psychotherapy: An International Quarterly, 8,* 243–253.

Davanloo, H. (1980). *Short-term dynamic psychotherapy.* New York: Jason Aronson.

Dinwiddle, S. H., Reich, T., & Cloninger, C. R. (1992). Psychiatric comorbidity and suicidality among intravenous drug users. *Journal of Clinical Psychiatry, 53,* 364–369.

Dyce, J. A. (1994). Personality disorders: Alternatives to the official diagnostic system. *Journal of Personality Disorders, 8,* 77–88.

Elkin, I., Shea, T., Watkins, J. T., Imber, S. D., Sotsky, S. M., Collins, J. F., Glass, D. R., Pilkonis, P. A., Leber, W. R., Docherty, J. P., & Parloff, M. B. (1989). NIMH Treatment of Depression Collaborative Research Program: General effectiveness of treatments. *Archives of General Psychiatry, 46,* 971–982.

Fahy, T. A., Eisler, I., & Russell, G. F. (1993). Personality disorder and treatment response in bulimia nervosa. *British Journal of Psychiatry, 162,* 765–770.

Fenichel, O. (1945). *The psychoanalytic theory of neurosis.* New York: Norton.

Frank, E., Kupfer, D. J., Jacob, M., & Jarrett, D. (1987). Personality features and response to acute treatment in recurrent depression. *Journal of Personality Disorders, 1,* 14–26.

Haller, D. L., Knisely, J. S., Dawson, K. S., & Schnoll, S. H. (1993). Perinatal substance abusers. Psychological and social characteristics. *Journal of Nervous and Mental Disease, 181,* 509–513.

Herman, J. L., Perry, J. C., & van der Kolk, B. A. (1989). Childhood trauma in borderline personality disorder. *American Journal of Psychiatry, 146,* 490–495.

Hofmann, S. G., Newman, M. G., Becker, E., Taylor, C. B., & Roth, W. T. (1995). Social phobia with and without avoidant personality disorder: Preliminary behavior therapy outcome findings. *Journal of Anxiety Disorders, 9,* 427–438.

Høglend, P. (1993). Personality disorders and long-term outcome after brief dynamic psychotherapy. *Journal of Personality Disorders, 7,* 168–181.

Hwu, H. G., Yeh, E. K., & Chang, L. Y. (1989). Prevalence of psychiatric disorders in Taiwan defined by the Chinese Diagnostic Interview Schedule. *Acta Psychiatrica Scandinavica, 79,* 136–147.

Kernberg, O. (1984). *Severe personality disorders: Psychotherapeutic strategies.* New Haven, Conn.: Yale University Press.

Kohut, H. (1984). *How does analysis cure?* Chicago: University of Chicago Press.

Linehan, M. M. (1993). *Cognitive-behavioral treatment of borderline personality disorder.* New York: Guilford Press.

Linehan, M. M., Hubert, A. E., Suarez, A., Douglas, A., & Heard, H. L. (1991). Cognitive-behavioral treatment of chronically parasuicidal borderline patients. *Archives of General Psychiatry, 48,* 1060–1064.

Livesly, W. J., Schroeder, M. L., Jackson, D. N., & Jang, K. L. (1994). Categorical distinctions in the study of personality disorder: Implications for classification. *Journal of Abnormal Psychology, 103,* 6–17.

Longabaugh, R., Rubin, A., Malloy, P., Beattie, M., Clifford, P. R., & Noel, N. (1994). Drinking outcomes of alcohol abusers diagnosed as antisocial personality disorder. *Alcoholism: Clinical and Experimental Research, 18,* 778–785.

Loranger, A., Oldham, J., & Tullis, E. (1982). Familial transmission of *DSM-III* borderline personality disorder. *Archives of General Psychiatry, 39,* 795–799.

Malan, D. H. (1976). *The frontier of brief psychotherapy.* New York: Plenum Press.

Meares, R. (1987). The secret and the self: On a new direction in psychotherapy. *Australian and New Zealand Journal of Psychiatry, 21,* 545–559.

Minichiello, W. E., Baer, L., & Jenike, M. A. (1987). Schizotypal personality disorder: A poor prognostic indicator for behavior therapy in the treatment of obsessive-compulsive disorder. *Journal of Anxiety Disorders, 1,* 273–276.

Monsen, J., Odland, T., Faugli, A., Daae, E., & Eilertsen, D. E. (1995). Personality disorders: Changes and stability after intensive psychotherapy focusing on affect consciousness. *Psychotherapy Research, 5,* 33–48.

Munroe-Blum, H., & Marziali, E. (1995). A controlled trial of short-term group treatment for borderline personality disorder. *Journal of Personality Disorders, 9,* 190–198.

Ogata, S. N., Silk, K. R., Goodrich, S., Lohr, N., Westen, D., & Hill, E. M. (1990). Childhood sexual and physical abuse in adult patients with borderline personality disorder. *American Journal of Psychiatry, 147,* 1008–1013.

Perry, J. C. (1992). Problems and considerations in the valid assessment of personality disorders. *American Journal of Psychiatry, 149,* 1645–1653.

Pilkonis, P. A., Frank, E. L. (1988). Personality pathology in recurrent depression: Nature, prevalence, and relationship to treatment response. *American Journal of Psychiatry, 145,* 435–441.

Reich, J. H., & Green, A. I. (1991). Effect of personality disorders on outcome of treatment. *Journal of Nervous and Mental Disease, 179,* 74–82.

Reich, J. H., & Vasile, R. G. (1993). Effect of personality-disorders on the treatment outcome of Axis-I conditions—an update. *Journal of Nervous and Mental Disease, 181,* 475–484.

Renneberg, B., Goldstein, A. J., Phillips, D., & Chambless, D. L. (1990). Intensive behavioral group treatment of avoidant personality disorder. *Behavior Therapy, 21,* 363–377.

Ruegg, R., & Frances, A. (1995). New research on personality disorders. *Journal of Personality Disorders, 9,* 1–48.

Samuels, J. F., Nestadt, G., Romanoski, A. J., Folstein, M. F., & McHugh, P. R. (1994). *DSM-III* personality disorders in the community. *American Journal of Psychiatry, 151,* 1055–1062.

Shea, M. T. (1993). Psychosocial treatment of personality disorder. *Journal of Personality Disorders, 7,* 167–180.

Sifneos, P. E. (1979). *Short-term dynamic psychotherapy.* New York: Plenum Press.

Stevenson, J., & Meares, R. (1992). An outcome study of psychotherapy for patients with borderline personality disorder. *American Journal of Psychiatry, 149,* 358–362.

Stravynski, A., Belisle, M., Marcouiller, M., & Lavallee, Y. (1994). The treatment of avoidant personality disorder by social skills training in the clinic or in real-life settings. *Canadian Journal of Psychiatry, 39*, 377–383.

Stravynski, A., Lesage, A., Marcouiller, M., & Elie, R. (1989). A test of the therapeutic mechanism in social skills training with avoidant personality disorder. *Journal of Nervous and Mental Disease, 177*, 739–744.

Svrakic, D., & Divac-Jovanovic, M. (1994). Personality disorders: Model for conceptual approach and classification: II. Proposed classification. *American Journal of Psychotherapy, 48*, 562–580.

Swartz, M., Blazer, D., George, L., & Winfield, I. (1990). Estimating the prevalence of borderline personality disorder in the community. *Journal of Personality Disorders, 4*, 257–272.

Torgersen, S. (1984). Genetic and nosological aspects of schizotypal and borderline personality disorders. *Archives of General Psychiatry, 41*, 546–554.

Turner, R. M. (1987). The effects of personality disorder diagnosis on the outcome of social anxiety symptom reduction. *Journal of Personality Disorders, 1*, 136–144.

Walker, W. R., Freeman, R. F., & Christensen, D. K. (1994). Restricting environmental stimulation (REST) to enhance cognitive behavioral treatment for obsessive compulsive disorder with schizotypal personality disorder. *Behavior Therapy, 25*, 709–719.

Weiss, R. D., Mirin, S. M., Griffin, M. L., Gunderson, J. G., & Hufford, C. (1993). Personality disorders in cocaine dependence. *Comprehensive Psychiatry, 34*, 145–149.

Weissman, M. M. (1993). The epidemiology of personality disorders: A 1990 Update. *Journal of Personality Disorders, 7*, 44–62.

Westen, D., Lundolph, P., Misle, B., Ruffins, S., & Block, J. (1990). Physical and sexual abuse in adolescent girls with borderline personality disorder. *American Journal of Orthopsychiatry, 60*, 55–66.

Widiger, T. (1993). The *DSM-III-R* categorical personality disorder diagnoses: A critique and an alternative. *Psychological Inquiry, 4*, 75–90.

Williams, J. G. (1988). Cognitive intervention for a paranoid personality disorder. *Psychotherapy, 25*, 570–575.

Winston, A., Laikin, M., Pollack, J., Samstag, L. W., McCullough, L., & Muran, J. C. (1994). Short-term psychotherapy of personality disorders. *American Journal of Psychiatry, 151*, 190–194.

Winston, A., Pollack, J., McCullough, L., Flegenheimer, W., Kestenbaum, R., & Trujillo, M. (1991). Brief psychotherapy of personality disorders. *Journal of Nervous and Mental Disease, 179*, 188–193.

Woody, G. E., McLellan, A. T., Luborsky, L., & O'Brien, C. P. (1985). Sociopathy and psychotherapy outcome. *Archives of General Psychiatry, 42*, 1081–1086.

Zimmerman, M., & Coryell, W. H. (1990). Diagnosing personality disorders in the community: A comparison of self-report and interview measures. *Archives of General Psychiatry, 47*, 527–531.

28

Psychopharmacological Treatment of Personality Disorders

Ann Marie Woo-Ming

Larry J. Siever

The use of medication to treat personality (Axis II) disorders is a relatively new undertaking with many methodologic problems to be solved. Personality disorders are commonly divided into three clusters: Cluster A disorders (odd cluster), Cluster B disorders (dramatic cluster), and Cluster C disorders (anxious cluster). For Cluster A disorders, mainly involving schizotypal disorder, two Type 1, two Type 2, and one Type 3 studies are available. These suggest that dopamine antagonists may be useful for some aspects of these disorders. For borderline personality disorder (BPD) (a Cluster B disorder), noradrenergic agents tend to improve mood but not irritability or dyscontrol, whereas serotonergic agents may act to decrease impulsivity. There is inconsistent data for the utility of antipsychotic agents and anticonvulsants. There are very few pharmacological studies for the Cluster C disorders. Case reports suggest that antidepressants may be helpful for the avoidant personality disorder.

The pharmacotherapy of personality disorders represents a relatively new frontier of psychopharmacology. Traditionally, personality disordered patients have been treated with psychotherapy and have not been thought responsive to pharmacological intervention. However, advances in the field over the past 15 years have challenged that perspective. A biological approach to the personality disorders questions the traditional separation of Axis I and Axis II diagnoses. However, clinical research investigations seeking to clarify the biological substrates of those disorders also pose some logistic difficulties. What follows is a summary of some of these methodologic problems and a description of the more well-documented clinical strategies in current use.

Attempts to investigate biological etiologies and treatments systematically for these disorders have been in part limited by the overlap in symptomatology among the various personality disorder diagnoses. Other conceptual problems include (a) the existence of significant clinical heterogeneity even within one personality disorder diagnosis, (b) the relationship between Axis I and Axis II disorders, and (c) limited reliability assessment of the diagnoses of personality disorders.

CLINICAL HETEROGENEITY AND OVERLAP OF AXIS II DISORDERS

Within each Axis II category, many combinations of clinical presentations are possible, and it is possible to have a clinically heterogeneous group of patients in any one study even though the patients may technically meet criteria for the same personality disorder. For example, some schizotypal patients have marked borderline features, while others appear more emotionally restricted. Different Axis II diagnoses may share similar criteria under the current *Diagnostic and Sta-*

tistical Manual of Mental Disorders, fourth edition (*DSM-IV*; American Psychiatric Association [APA], 1994), categorization, and often patients meet criteria for more than one type of personality disorder (Hyler et al., 1990), adding to the potential for clinical heterogeneity within a given study sample.

RELATIONSHIP BETWEEN AXIS I AND II DISORDERS

Overlap in symptomatology also exists between the Axis I and II disorders. For example, in the Cluster B disorders in which depressive and labile mood are often found, distinction between these Axis II symptoms and the symptoms of bipolar spectrum disorders, dysthymia, or major depression is often unclear. In the Cluster C disorders, avoidant personality disorder shares many criteria of Axis I's social phobia disorder, and some authors feel that they are actually the same disorder.

Frequent comorbidity is seen between Axis I and II syndromes; for example, up to 50% of patients with borderline personality disorder (BPD) or schizotypal personality disorder (SPD) are found to have concurrent diagnoses of a depressive disorder. Thus, evaluating a personality disordered patient's response to drug treatment can be confounded by drug effects on a comorbid Axis I disorder.

RELIABILITY OF ASSESSMENT TOOLS

Methodologic problems in designing studies of personality disordered patients include limited reliability assessment of the diagnoses and limited longitudinal stability with this population. Questionable efficacy exists for our assessment instruments, as seen by mediocre retest and intratest reliability (Gitlin, 1993). Many of these difficulties are related to our limited understanding of how a personality disorder trait differs from adaptive personality traits. Measuring or standardizing change in a personality disorder symptom poses a challenge given the "persistently transient" nature of many of these symptoms (e.g., mood lability in the borderline patient). Because of the environmental responsiveness of the symptoms, a cardinal feature of most of these disorders, nonpharmacological variables such as milieu of the research setting and interactions with the research team should ideally be consistent.

Due to the episodic nature of some personality traits, such as mood lability, studies spanning a greater length of time would ideally allow investigation of these traits over their natural course. However, chaotic interpersonal relationships or suspiciousness of others may interfere with the sometimes lengthy treatment alliance required to complete a research study, leading to high dropout rates.

THE NEED FOR MULTIPLE APPROACHES TO DEFINING AND TREATING PERSONALITY DISORDERS

Attempts to avoid the overlap in diagnoses inherent in *DSM-IV* categorization have led to dimensional models of personality disorders in the context of which psychobiological findings can be understood. This model is based on studies of biological correlates of these dimensions, and family studies that point to heritability of these dimensions (Trestman, deVegvar, & Siever, 1995). The model presumes that the target dimensions of personality can be conceptualized in terms of cognitive/perceptual distortions, affective lability and impulsivity/aggression, and anxiety. These three categories correspond to the odd, dramatic, and anxious clusters, respectively, in *DSM-IV*. One challenge in studying a particular personality dimension is that abnormalities in more than one neurotransmitter system may converge to provide the substrate for a specific dimension. Also, targeting one core dimension still leaves unaddressed the complex clinical syndrome that encompasses a personality disorder. Finally, in defining a core dimension in the personality disordered patient, a distinction must be made between a trait and a state symptom. Despite these hurdles, the dimensional approach allows consideration of the fluidity that is clinically recognized between Axis I and II symptoms and provides a framework for inquiry into the interrelationships among types of behavior, their modulatory neurotransmitters, and pharmacological interventions.

In summary, descriptive (i.e., Axis II categories) and biological approaches can be used for investigating psychopharmacological treatments for personality disorders. A descriptive approach allows a more clinical conceptualization of the personality disorders but may not allow for meaningful measurements of change in response to medication given the broad overlap of symptoms within Axis II, comorbidity with Axis I disorders, and an incomplete distinction between state versus trait phenomena. A dimensional approach allows for more precise "targeting" of phenomena to be examined, yet may fail to wholly capture the complex entity of human personality. Although each approach has recognized limitations, each can also offer valuable frameworks within which these disorders can be further investigated.

We now turn to a review of the pharmacological treatments of personality disorders and the psychobiological findings that prompted the use of such treatments.

CLUSTER A DISORDERS
(ODD CLUSTER)

Schizotypal personality disorder (SPD) has been the most carefully studied of the odd cluster (Cluster A) disorders. Clinical, genetic, and psychophysiologic studies have established its place within the schizophrenia spectrum disorders. Phenomenologically, the SPD patient can be described as having both the deficitlike and psychoticlike symptoms seen in schizophrenia but in an attenuated form. Family studies have revealed significantly higher rates of SPD in the relatives of schizophrenic patients in comparison to control patients (Silverman et al., 1993), and siblings of probands with schizophrenia have been found to be at higher risk for both SPD and schizophrenia if either one or both parents had SPD (Baron, Gruen, & Asnis, 1985).

Psychophysiological testing reveals abnormal performance on smooth pursuit eye movements, backward masking tests, and continuous performance tasks associated with both schizophrenia and SPD (Siever, 1991). These findings have strengthened the concept of a spectrum of schizophrenialike disorders that span both Axis I and II categories. Psychobiological investigations into SPD, based on a dimensional model of symptoms, have also supported the relationship between SPD and schizophrenia and provide a logical starting point for psychopharmacological interventions for this personality disorder.

Schizotypal personality disorder can be characterized by disturbances in the cognitive/perceptual domain, manifested by impairment in attending to the environment, discriminating among stimuli, or processing information. Clinically, this may translate into psychoticlike symptoms (such as magical thinking, ideas of reference, or perceptual distortion), deficitlike symptoms (such as poor interpersonal relatedness or social detachment), and cognitive disorganization (such as deficient performance on cognitive, psychophysiological, and attentional testing).

Psychoticlike Symptoms in
Schizotypal Personality Disorder

The commonalities between SPD and schizophrenia and the role of dopamine in psychotic symptoms spurred interest into dopaminergic function in SPD. Cerebrospinal fluid homovanillic acid (HVA; the major dopamine metabolite) concentrations in SPD patients correlate significantly with psychoticlike symptoms and were significantly elevated compared to levels in other types of personality disordered patients in one study from our center (Siever, 1991). Similarly, plasma HVA concentrations also correlated significantly with psychoticlike symptoms in SPD and were elevated compared to normal subjects in an overlapping sample (Siever et al., 1991).

These findings suggest the possibility that dopamine antagonism might be beneficial in these disorders. Given the known efficacy of antipsychotic medications in the schizophrenia spectrum disorders, their effect on SPD psychoticlike symptoms has also been investigated (see Table 28.1). However, the majority of these studies primarily targeted subjects with borderline personality disorder (BPD) and described findings for patients who also met criteria for SPD. The single study involving only SPD patients (Hymowitz et al., 1986) did find an improvement in psychoticlike symptoms following treatment with haloperidol; however, a single-blind study was used. The three double-blind, placebo-controlled studies of mixed populations of SPD and BPD patients (Cowdry & Gardner, 1988; Goldberg et al., 1986; Soloff et al., 1989) show an association between low-dose antipsychotic use and broad improvements in symptomatology, including scales of psychoticism, anxiety, depression, hostility, and rejection sensitivity. However, one study (Cowdry & Gardner, 1988) involved patients characterized by severe affective instability so that the applicability of these findings to the more typically emotionally constricted SPD subjects is in question. Other non-placebo-controlled studies (Jensen & Andersen, 1989; Serban & Siegel, 1984) described moderate, global improvements in mixed BPD and SPD populations with the use of antipsychotic medication.

TABLE 28.1 Table of Antipsychotic Studies: Borderline Personality Disorder and Schizotypal Personality Disorder

Study	Diagnosis	Study Design	Comment
Goldberg et al. (1986)	$n = 50$ BPD and/or SPD outpatients (BPD with at least one prior psychotic episode)	Type 1 study: thiothixene (average 8.6 mg), 12 weeks, double blind, placebo controlled	Thiothixene led to improvement of psychoticlike/obsessive/phobic anxiety symptoms; no effect on depression
Cowdry & Gardner (1988)	$n = 16$, female BPD outpatients; all characterized as "seriously ill with severe dysphoria in setting of rejection, and dyscontrol behavior such as assaultiveness, cutting, overdose"; of these, 6 patients were also SPD	Type 1 study: tranylcypromine, trifluoperazine, carbamazepine, alprazolam; 6 weeks; double blind, placebo controlled	Tranylcypromine led to improved global and mood scores, improved impulsivity, but no effect on behavioral dyscontrol; trifluoperazine showed a trend toward broad symptomatic improvement; carbamezapine showed improvement of impulsivity and behavioral dyscontrol; alprazolam led to increases in suicidality and dyscontrol
Soloff et al. (1989)	$n = 90$ inpatients with BPD, mixed BPD/SPD symptoms, and a small number of SPD patients	Type 2 study: amitriptyline (100–175 mg) or haloperidol (4–16 mg); 5 weeks; placebo controlled	Haloperidol led to global improvements including hostile depression and impulsive ward behavior, especially if patient had severe schizotypal symptoms, hostility, or suspiciousness. AMI not as effective as haloperidol for anxiety and hostility; not effective on core depressive symptoms
Serban & Siegel (1984)	$n = 52$ outpatients with SPD (14), BPD with prior psychotic episode (16), mixed BPD/SPD (16)	Type 2 study: haloperidol or thiothixene (4–12 mg), 6 weeks to 3 months, double blind	Thiothixene > haloperidol led to moderate-to-marked improvements in all patients for general symptoms, paranoid ideation, anxiety, ideas of reference, and depression regardless of diagnosis
Hymowitz et al. (1986)	$n = 17$ SPD outpatients	Type 2 study: haloperidol (up to 12 mg, average 3.6 mg); 6 weeks; single blind, 2-week placebo washout	Drug led to mild-to-moderate improvement in ideas of reference, social isolation, odd communication, and thought disorder; also GAS scores increased
Jensen & Andersen (1989)	$n = 5$ SPD, 5 BPD inpatients	Type 3 study: amoxapine (up to 300 mg); 3 weeks minimum; open label, no placebo; oxazepam prn agitation (36–42 mg QD)	SPD subjects showed broad improvement in BPRS (schizophrenia subscale) and HDRS scores. BPD subjects showed no improvement

AMI = amitriptyline; BPD = borderline personality disorder; BPRS = Brief Psychiatric Rating Scale; HDRS = Hamilton Depression Rating Scale; SPD = schizotypal personality disorder.

Conversely, a state of dopamine agonism might be expected to exacerbate the psychoticlike symptoms of SPD. Indeed, a study of eight SPD/BPD and eight BPD patients selected by virtue of affective lability showed that, when administered amphetamine, SPD subjects had significantly increased Brief Psychiatric Rating Scale scores of thought disturbance and self-rated psychoticism compared to BPD subjects (Schulz, Cornelius, Schulz, & Soloff, 1988). The authors concluded that this finding supported the hypothesis that SPD is included in the psychotic spectrum disorders. In contrast, 20 patients selected solely on the basis of meeting SPD criteria demonstrated no increase in psychoticlike symptoms with amphetamine administration (Siever et al., unpublished, 1994). Thus, it may be that certain SPD subjects with hyperdopaminergic states may be more responsive to treatment with dopa-antagonist agents and respond negatively to dopamine agonism, while those with normal or reduced dopaminergic activities (see below) may respond beneficially to dopamine agonism.

Thus, it appears that schizotypal symptomatology in mixed BPD/SPD populations is responsive, in modest and generalized ways, to low-dose antipsychotic medication. Given the state of dopamine antagonism induced by these medications and correlations between increased plasma and cerebrospinal fluid (CSF) HVA and psychoticlike symptoms in SPD, it is tempting to hypothesize that psychoticlike symptoms in SPD would be particularly responsive to antipsychotic medications. Future trials with primarily SPD subjects in double-blind, placebo-controlled settings would help to refine further the role for these agents in SPD.

Deficitlike Symptoms and Cognitive Disorganization in Schizotypal Personality Disorder

Neurobiological studies of the deficitlike symptoms of SPD have investigated their relationship to psychophysiological testing, neuroanatomy, and monoaminergic indices. Abnormal performance on smooth pursuit eye movements, backward masking tests, and continuous performance tasks correlate with deficit symptoms of SPD (Siever, 1991). Cognitive disorganization, as measured by performance on psychological testing, has also been described among SPD patients. These subjects have been shown to make significantly increased numbers of errors on the Wisconsin Card Sort Test (WCST) and California Verbal Learning

Test compared to normal subjects and other non–Cluster A personality disordered patients (Bergman et al., unpublished, 1996). These indices suggest roles for the frontal and temporal cortices in the deficit symptoms of SPD.

Correlations between neurotransmitter levels and deficitlike symptoms in SPD have been investigated. Whereas increased plasma HVA levels have been shown to correlate with psychoticlike symptoms in personality disordered patients, decreased plasma HVA levels may be associated with deficitlike symptoms in relatives of schizophrenic patients and cognitive deficits in SPD patients (Siever, Kalus, & Keefe, 1993). Investigations of cholinergic indices in schizophrenic patients have yielded mixed results (Karson, Casanova, Kleinman, & Griffin, 1993; Tandon & Greden, 1989); however, preliminary data from our laboratory suggest that the cholinergic agent physostigmine may improve visuospatial delayed-response attentional performance in SPD patients.

Thus, an interrelationship may exist among deficitlike symptoms, cognitive deficits as measured by psychological and psychophysiological tests, and decreased plasma HVA concentrations.

The above findings raise the possibility that dopaminergic agents may lead to improvement of deficit symptoms and cognitive disorganization in SPD subjects. One double-blind, placebo-controlled study of amphetamine in SPD/BPD patients found that in addition to worsening of psychoticlike symptoms among the SPD group, all subjects had increased activation scores on the Brief Psychiatric Rating Scale (BPRS) in response to amphetamine (Schulz et al., 1988). This might suggest an improvement in such deficit symptoms as anergia and withdrawal. Further, a preliminary study of amphetamine use in SPD patients showed improved performance on the Wisconsin Card Sort Test (Siever et al., 1995).

The monoamine oxidase inhibitor (MAOI) tranylcypromine has been associated with broad-based behavioral effects in one mixed BPD/SPD group (see Table 28.1). Among the changes observed was an increased capacity for pleasure. While this may reflect an improvement of deficitlike symptoms, the effect of comorbidity of affective symptoms for both groups is unclear in the study. The continued investigation of catecholaminergic agents for SPD patients would be of value, with special focus on their effect on cognitive performance, as well as deficitlike symptoms.

Treatment of Comorbid Diagnoses in Schizotypal Personality Disorder

The use of antidepressant agents for SPD has a basis in the observation that high rates of comorbidity exist between SPD and the depressive disorders: 30% to 50% of SPD patients seen in clinical settings have been found to have a concurrent major depressive disorder, and 50% of patients have a history of major depressive disorder (Kaplan & Sadock, 1995). So far, however, trials with antidepressant agents have only been conducted in groups of mixed BPD/SPD patients (see Tables 28.1 and 28.2). The use of fluoxetine, up to 80 mg over a 12-week period, was investigated in a mixed group and was found to decrease obsessive symptoms, rejection sensitivity, depressive symptoms, anxiety, and psychoticism (Markovitz et al., 1991). These improvements occurred regardless of whether subjects had a concurrent diagnosis of major depressive disorder. Such findings are limited by the fact that the study was open label and again by the heterogeneity of the subjects.

There have been attempts to "pharmacologically distinguish" between affective and psychoticlike symptoms, primarily in BPD groups with some SPD patients included. In one large, mixed sample, amitriptyline led to a significant improvement in anxiety and hostility for the whole group, although less effectively than haloperidol (Soloff et al., 1989). Tranylcypromine was used in a primarily BPD group with a small subset of SPD patients and was found to decrease significantly a broad array of symptoms, including depressive scores, anxiety, rejection sensitivity, and impulsivity (Cowdry & Gardner, 1988). However, the generalized response of symptoms has failed to elucidate a differential response of affective symptoms or psychoticlike symptoms to antidepressants in these patient populations.

Thus, in order to determine the efficacy of antidepressants for SPD symptomatology, replication studies using double-blind, placebo-controlled methods in homogeneous groups of SPD patients are needed.

CLUSTER B (DRAMATIC CLUSTER)

The disorders seen in Cluster B (dramatic cluster) have been defined dimensionally as being composed of impulsivity/aggression and affective/lability. The prototype diagnoses involving these traits are borderline personality disorder and antisocial personality disorder. There are numerous investigations into the neurobiological substrates that may underlie each of these dimensions and corresponding implications for pharmacological management of the disorders that incorporate these dimensions.

Psychobiology of Impulsivity/Aggression

Impulsivity/aggression has been associated with a number of determinants, including familial inheritance, disturbances of the serotonergic and noradrenergic systems, and nonspecific cerebral dysfunction.

Family Studies for Impulsivity/Aggression

First-degree relatives of BPD patients have been shown to have significantly greater prevalences of both impulsive/aggressive behaviors and affective/lability than relatives of other personality disordered or schizophrenic patients (Silverman & Pinkham, 1991). Furthermore, relatives of borderline probands appear to be at greater risk for BPD than the relatives of normal control subjects (Baron et al., 1985). Although such findings do not distinguish the role of environmental versus genetic influences on familial inheritance, preliminary results from a twin study show that single BPD criterion may be genetically determined. These criteria include instability in relationships, impulsivity, anger, and affective instability (Torgersen, 1992).

Serotonergic and Noradrenergic Indices in Impulsivity/Aggression

Diminished serotonergic indices have been implicated in impulsive/aggressive behavior directed toward the self (i.e., suicide attempts) and others. This association exists across diagnostic categories, lending support to the conceptualization of impulsivity/aggression as a dimensional trait. For example, decreased CSF 5-hydroxyindoleacetic acid (5-HIAA) levels have been shown to correlate inversely with a history of aggressive behavior and with rating scales of aggressive behavior. Decreased CSF 5-HIAA levels are also associated with depressed patients who have made suicide attempts compared to depressed patients who had never attempted suicide or to healthy controls (Brown et al., 1982).

Central serotonergic function is also diminished in association with impulsivity/aggression in affective

TABLE 28.2 Pharmacology of Borderline Personality Disorder: Antidepressant and Antipsychotic Agents

Study	Diagnosis	Study Design	Comment
Sheard et al. (1976)	$n = 66$, inmates characterized by extreme impulsivity, aggression, and hostility	Type 2 study: lithium versus placebo	Decrease in number of major prison infractions
Links et al. (1990)	$n = 15$ BPD	Type 1 study: lithium versus desipramine; double blind, placebo controlled	Lithium led to decrease in therapist's perception of patient irritability, anger, and suicidal symptoms; trend for desipramine to have no effect or to worsen symptoms of anger/suicide and to be less effective than lithium in decreasing depression scores
Coccaro & Kavoussi (1995)	$n = 40$ PD patients with histories of impulsive aggression	Type 1 study: fluoxetine 20–60 mg; double blind, placebo controlled; 12 weeks	Overt aggression scores reduced at weeks 4, 10, 12, and end point; irritability scores reduced at weeks 6–12 and end point
Norden (1989)	$n = 12$ BPD patients, all except one with histories of suicidality	Type 3 study: fluoxetine; open label	Very much or much improved; irritability and suicidality among the most responsive symptoms
Coccaro et al. (1990)	$n = 2$, BPD; $n = 1$, antisocial PD	Type 3 study: fluoxetine; open label; 6 weeks	Initial decrease in impulsivity-aggression scores for all 3 patients
Cornelius, Soloff, Perel, & Ulrich (1991)	$n = 5$, BPD inpatients who had failed phenelzine and at least one neuroleptic	Type 3 study: fluoxetine; open label	Decreases in impulsivity and suicidality
Markovitz et al. (1991)	$n = 22$ outpatients: 8 BPD, 10 BPD/SPD with mixed symptoms, 4 SPD; 13 patients also with MDD	Type 3 study: fluoxetine; open label; 20–80 mg over 12 weeks	Decrease in 50% of patients' self-mutilatory behavior; significant decrease in depression, rejection sensitivity, psychoticism, anxiety, and obsessive compulsive symptoms regardless of comorbid diagnosis of MDD
Soloff et al. (1986)	$n = 52$, BPD inpatients	Type 2 study: amitriptyline; placebo controlled	AMI nonresponders showed significantly more impulsive/assaultive behavior than placebo nonresponders; AMI responders showed improvement in impulsive behavior and depression scores
Soloff et al. (1993)	$n = 92$, BPD and mixed BPD/SPD features	Type 1 study: comparison between haloperidol and phenelzine; double blind, placebo controlled	Phenelzine less effective than haloperidol in decreasing impulsivity/hostile-belligerence; phenelzine did not improve atypical depressive symptoms but did decrease scores on Buss-Durkee Hostility Inventory
Parsons et al. (1989)	All patients had symptoms of atypical depression Group 1: $n = 40$ patients with > 5 *DSM-III* BPD criteria, $n = 61$ patients with > 4 criteria Group 2: $n = 19$ patients, BPD to a considerable extent, $n = 29$, patients BPD to only some extent as measured by the Personality Assessment Form	Type 1 study: double blind, placebo controlled; random assignment to phenelzine 60 mg or imipramine 200 mg for 3–6 weeks each medication	BPD patients with symptoms of atypical depression had significant improvement in CGI scores due to phenelzine, as compared to imipramine and placebo; imipramine felt to be minimally effective

AMI = amitriptyline; BPD = borderline personality disorder; CGI = Clinical Global Impression; MDD = major depressive disorder; SPD = schizotypal personality disorder.

disorders, BPD, and other personality disorders. Decreased central 5-hydroxytryptophan (5-HT) function appears to be associated with self- and other-directed aggression in personality disordered patients and associated with a history of suicide attempts in patients with major depression. One study compared subjects with major affective disorder (acute or remitted depression or bipolar type), personality disorders, and normal controls on subscales of impulsivity, history of alcohol abuse, and history of suicide attempts (Coccaro et al., 1990). Central serotonergic function was assessed using fenfluramine; a blunted prolactin response to fenfluramine is thought to reflect decreased central serotonergic function. Results showed that among all the personality disordered patients, those with BPD had significantly blunted peak prolactin response compared to the others, and that this was due to the impulsive/aggressive features of this disorder. Similarly, among all PD patients, impulsive/aggressive scores were negatively correlated with peak prolactin values. For subjects with PD or major depression, a history of a suicide attempt was associated with a significant blunting of prolactin when compared to patients who had never attempted suicide.

Noradrenergic function, in contrast to serotonergic indices, may be elevated in association with impulsivity/aggression across such diagnostic categories as pathological gambling, major affective disorders, and personality disorders. The CSF and plasma levels of the norepinephrine metabolite 3-methoxy-4-hydroxy-phenylglycol were found to be increased and associated with extraversion scores in pathological gamblers. The scores also correlated positively with urine concentrations of vanillylmandelic acid, a noradepinephrine metabolite, and the sum of urinary output of norepinephrine and its major metabolites (Roy, De Jon, & Linnoila, 1989).

Cerebral Dysfunction in Impulsivity/Aggression

Electroencephalogram (EEG) measures have been the focus of several investigations, with equivocal results, into cerebral dysfunction as another possible biologic substrate of impulsivity and aggression. For example, episodic/dyscontrol patients (defined as having impulsive, aggressive, and violent behavior) were shown in one study to have a significant increase in nonspecific EEG changes when contrasted with subjects with depression or headaches (Drake, Hiet-

ter, & Pakalnis, 1992). However, a comparison of BPD and other personality disordered patients has shown no significant differences in the number of EEG abnormalities, and no associations between EEG abnormalities and impulsivity (Cornelius et al., 1986).

Further evidence for generalized cerebral dysfunction in impulsive/aggressive traits was found in a study of neurological soft signs in BPD and antisocial PD patients (Stein, Hollander, Cohen, & Frenkel, 1993). Compared to control subjects, the personality disordered patients displayed a significantly greater number of left-sided neurological soft signs. Among the patients, nine were identified as "aggressive" based on the Brown-Goodwin lifetime aggression scale. Compared to the nonaggressive PD patients, those with aggression showed significantly greater right-sided soft signs. Patients also underwent neuropsychological testing. Left-sided neurological soft signs were found to correlate with errors on Trails A and B tests, as well as on the Matching Familiar Faces Test, which may indicate an impairment of complex information processing. Right-sided soft signs correlated with errors on the Wisconsin Card Sort Test, a measure of frontal lobe functioning. Thus, in this study, lateralized neurological soft signs that correlated with specific neuropsychological deficits were found to be significantly associated with impulsive/aggressive traits in personality disordered patients.

Psychobiology of Affective/Lability

The cluster of traits thought to define affective instability in BPD subjects includes marked shifts between baseline and depressed moods, irritability, and anxiety that may persist from a few hours to a few days (Steinberg, Trestman, & Siever, 1994). Knowledge of the biological correlates of Axis I mood disorders provided a foundation for investigations into the psychobiology of affective-related traits in personality disordered patients. However, the state-dependent markers associated with major affective disorder, such as blunted thyroid stimulating hormone (TSH) response to thyrotropin releasing hormone (TRH) and lack of plasma cortisol suppression in response to dexamethasone, have not been found to correlate consistently with affective-related traits in personality disordered patients (Coccaro & Siever, 1995). Noradrenergic and cholinergic systems, which appear to play pivotal roles in Axis I mood disorders, have also been a logical area of study for the personality disorders.

Cholinergic agents are known to create a depressivelike picture in animal and human studies and can increase the rapid eye movement sleep latency associated with depression (Steinberg et al., 1994). Physostigmine, a centrally active cholinergic agent, has been shown to produce greater depressive responses in BPD subjects compared to normal controls (Steinberg et al., 1995). The depressive responses correlated with affective instability, and results were independent of past or present history of major depressive disorder. Thus, the dysphoric response seen with physostigmine infusion in BPD subjects appears to be specifically associated with affective lability and not due to comorbid major depression.

The role of noradrenergic and dopaminergic systems in affective/lability has been investigated using dextroamphetamine (d-Amp), which releases and prevents reuptake of norepinephrine and dopamine. Following administration of d-Amp, a significant correlation between dysphoric/irritable mood response to the drug and measures of lifetime history of mood instability was observed in healthy volunteers (Kavoussi & Coccaro, 1993). However, neither of these variables correlated with plasma levels of homovanillic acid or 3-methoxy-4-hydroxyphenylglycol, metabolites of dopamine and norepinephrine, respectively. Irritability, another symptom associated with affective lability, has been shown to correlate with increased growth hormone (GH) response to clonidine in personality disordered patients and normal controls (Coccaro et al., in press). The growth hormone response to clonidine is thought to reflect activity of postsynaptic alpha-two adrenergic receptors. Thus, increased responsiveness of the central adrenergic system may be involved in affective instability in BPD and other personality disordered subjects.

In summary, initial investigations have suggested that excessive cholinergic availability may play a role in the transient dysphoria seen in borderline patients, and that a hyperresponsive noradrenergic system may contribute to irritability/mood instability among healthy volunteers and personality disordered subjects.

Pharmacology of Borderline Personality Disorder: Antidepressant Agents

The investigation of antidepressant agents for the treatment of borderline symptomatology poses particular methodologic challenges. First, the rates of comorbidity between BPD and Axis I depressive disorders may

be as high as 50%. Although there is evidence to suggest that the affective picture in BPD can be conceptualized as a distinct entity from comorbid Axis I depressive disorders (Kavoussi & Coccaro, 1993; Silverman & Pinkham, 1991), the depressive symptomatology of BPD may be so heterogeneous as to defy further definition. In studies of antidepressant effects on symptoms or traits of BPD, it is important to acknowledge that we are limited in our knowledge of how dimensions or symptom clusters overlap and impinge on each other. For example, a drug's effect on depressive symptoms may in turn affect impulsive/aggressive traits.

With these caveats in mind, a summary of antidepressant trials for BPD patients can be found in Table 28.2.

The clinical effects of antidepressant agents on BPD symptomatology are consistent with biological findings that associate increased noradrenergic responsiveness with affective lability and decreased serotonergic indices with impulsivity.

There is a trend for noradrenergic agents to improve mood but to be inconsistent in treating irritability and dyscontrol in BPD. Amitriptyline, for example, while significantly decreasing depression scores and impulsive behaviors in a group of BPD patients, was found to paradoxically worsen impulsivity, assaultiveness, paranoid ideation, and global functioning in a subset of patients compared to normal controls (Soloff et al., 1986). The authors concluded that the paradoxical worsening of the amitriptyline nonresponders was due to its effect on impulsive behaviors rather than on depressive symptoms. Desipramine was also shown to have no effect or actually to worsen anger and suicidality in comparison to lithium among a cohort of borderline subjects (Links, Steiner, Boiago, & Irwin, 1990). Similarly, the noradrenergic agent maprotiline may be associated with an increase in suicide-provoking potential in patients with histories of repeated suicidal behavior (Montgomery et al., 1992). The monoamine oxidase inhibitor phenelzine has been shown to have a good effect on BPD patients with atypical depressive features such as leaden paralysis, rejection sensitivity, and mood reactivity (Parsons et al., 1989). Tranylcypromine was also found to improve physician-rated mood scores, impulsivity, and global functioning in a cohort of primarily BPD patients, yet no improvement of behavioral dyscontrol was noted (Cowdry & Gardner, 1988).

Thus, while these medications were found to improve depressive features and, in the case of amitriptyline responders, impulsive behavior, there may also be the risk of worsening anger and impulsivity in a subset of BPD patients (amitriptyline and desipramine), worsening suicidality in other patients (maprotiline), or having no effect on dyscontrol (tranylcypromine).

In contrast, serotonergic agents such as fluoxetine may act to decrease impulsivity among borderline patients. Other symptoms such as anger, suicidality, and irritability have also been improved with these agents. Fluoxetine was shown to be effective in decreasing impulsive aggression (Coccaro & Kavoussi, 1995) and depression scores and improving a broad array of symptoms such as rejection sensitivity, anxiety, psychoticism, and obsessive compulsive symptoms in BPD subjects. A trend toward decreased self-mutilatory behavior was also noted (Markovitz et al., 1991). It must be stressed that all except one of the fluoxetine studies have been open label; further controlled trials are needed to establish its efficacy for BPD subjects. Lithium, which may act as a serotonin agonist, has been shown to be effective in decreasing impulsivity and aggression in a sample of highly impulsive prison inmates (Sheard, Marini, Brideges, & Wagner, 1976).

Lithium has also been shown to decrease therapists' perceptions of irritability, suicidality, and angry behavior in a cohort of borderline subjects. Interestingly, there was a clear trend in this study for lithium to be more effective than desipramine (a noradrenergic agent) in decreasing anger and suicidality, as well as depression (Links et al., 1990). This observation supports the hypothesis that hyperresponsivity of noradrenergic systems may contribute to affective lability in borderline subjects.

Thus, it appears that for both features of impulsivity, aggression, and depressive spectrum symptomatology, serotonergic agents such as fluoxetine and lithium would be reasonable first-line agents. Noradrenergic agents such as the tricyclic antidepressants or MAOIs are less desirable; although they may have an effect on depressive or atypical depressive features, results have been inconsistent in the trials conducted so far. If they are used, patients should be carefully monitored for the appearance of increased impulsivity.

Pharmacology of Borderline Personality Disorder: Antipsychotic Agents

Studies of antipsychotic medication use for BPD (Tables 28.1 and 28.2) have shown global, but modest,

improvement in symptoms. Among the symptoms described, improvements have been shown in depression, suicidal ideation, rejection sensitivity, and psychoticlike symptoms including paranoid ideation, ideas of reference, and derealization. One study also noted an effect for haloperidol in reducing impulsive ward behavior (Soloff et al., 1989).

Thus, traditional antipsychotic agents may be a reasonable choice if patients are unable to tolerate or do not respond to lithium or fluoxetine. Although one study of BPD and SPD subjects found no difference in response to neuroleptics among diagnoses (Serban & Siegel, 1984), another study found that in their sample of BPD and/or SPD subjects, those who did respond to thiothixene were likely to be more severely ill at baseline, with psychoticism, illusions, ideas of reference, phobic anxiety, and obsessive compulsivity (Goldberg et al., 1986). Further, schizotypal symptoms, hostility, and suspiciousness seemed to predict a good response to haloperidol in another study (Soloff et al., 1989). Thus, it may be reasonable to choose an antipsychotic medication for a borderline patient who has a predominance of psychoticlike features, such as transient paranoid ideation. Consideration of extrapyramidal side effects, including tardive dyskinesia, must also be weighed before instituting a trial with these agents. Risperidone and clozapine have yet to be examined for this population.

Pharmacology of Borderline Personality Disorder: Mood-Stabilizing Agents

The use of carbamazepine (CBZ) for patients with behavioral dyscontrol/impulsivity or borderline patients has yielded mixed results in placebo-controlled trials. Carbamazepine has been found to decrease assaultiveness and depression significantly in patients with frontal lobe dysfunction (Foster, Hillbrand, & Chi, 1989) and was initially found to improve impulsivity and behavioral dyscontrol among borderline patients (Cowdry & Gardner, 1988). However, this finding was not replicated in a later study, which suggested that CBZ may have no effect on dyscontrol and may in fact be associated with an increase in impulsive, violent behavior in some borderline subjects (De la Fuente & Lotstra, 1994). In comparison to propranolol, use of CBZ may be associated with a decrease in aggression in patients with intermittent explosive disorder (Mattes, 1990), although both medications tend to lead to fewer aggressive outbursts. In this study, however, subjects also received antipsychotic agents, other anticonvulsants, and antidepressants, limiting the applicability of the findings.

Several case reports describe the efficacy of both CBZ and valproic acid (VPA) for episodic dyscontrol and violence and dyscontrol in organic mental syndromes or dementia (Glakas, Seibyl, & Mazure, 1990; Keck, McElroy, & Friedman, 1992). Overall, the case reports point to the usefulness of both mood stabilizers for a wide array of syndromes characterized by episodic, uncontrolled aggressive acts. The generalizability of these results to subjects with borderline personality disorder remains unclear.

In summary, the use of anticonvulsants for BPD is in the investigatory phase. Anecdotal reports suggest that CBZ and VPA may be useful for a wide array of syndromes involving episodic aggression; however, two double-blind, placebo-controlled studies disagree as to whether CBZ is effective for borderline personality patients. Further controlled trials are needed to define the role of these agents on impulsivity, aggression, and affective lability in BPD subjects.

CLUSTER C (ANXIOUS CLUSTER)

The psychobiology of anxiety (Cluster C) has been investigated in greater depth recently. The guiding principle for much of the research is the assumption that the biological factors regulating anxiety provide a common basis for the anxiety spectrum disorders, superseding Axis I and Axis II distinctions.

This assumption is supported by the comorbidity seen clinically between avoidant personality disorder (APD) and social phobia (SP). A number of authors have demonstrated that there are high rates of association between these two disorders (Schneier, Spitzer, & Gibbon, 1991; Stein & Hollander, 1993). Specifically, generalized social phobia, which involves pervasive fear in most social situations, is felt to be more closely linked to APD than discrete social phobia, which involves fear in one or two specific social situations. One recent study of 50 patients diagnosed with SP found rates of APD in 89% of patients diagnosed with generalized social phobia (Schneier et al., 1991). Some investigators feel that these findings suggest that APD and SP are variations of a similar underlying pathophysiology.

Thus, a review of the psychobiology of anxiety spectrum personality disorder may be best represented by studies of SP and APD. Early studies have established the role of the noradrenergic system in arousal and anxiety. Investigations of the growth hormone (GH) response to clonidine, a marker of postsynaptic alpha-2 adrenergic function, have consistently shown a blunted GH response in panic disorder patients (Uhde, 1994).

A logical outgrowth of these findings was to study the clonidine-GH response in patients with social phobia. Two studies, one using intravenous clonidine and one using oral clonidine, found contrasting results. The first study of GH response to intravenous clonidine in normal controls, SP, and panic disorder patients found significant blunting in SP patients compared to normal controls. There was no difference in the blunting between SP subjects and the panic disorder group (Uhde, 1994). The second study found no GH response difference for 21 subjects with SP when compared to 22 healthy controls in a double-blind, placebo-controlled study (Tancer, 1993). Thus, replication studies are needed to establish whether the clonidine-GH response is an index of abnormal noradrenergic activity in social phobia.

There have been few other positive findings with the use of chemical probes or challenge studies to define a biological basis for social phobia. Studies using lactic acid, norepinephrine, and caffeine (chosen because of their use as chemical probes in panic disorder) failed to induce symptoms of social phobia in patients with social phobia (Tancer, 1993). Investigations into the hypothalamic-pituitary-adrenal axis, via measures of urinary free cortisol and response to the dexamethasone suppression test, showed no abnormalities (Uhde, 1994). Challenge studies examining neurotransmitter systems revealed no abnormality in prolactic response to l-dopamine or fenfluramine; however, an increased cortisol response to fenfluramine differentiated social phobia patients from normal controls in one study (Uhde, 1994). Thus, the serotonergic system may play a role in the etiology of fear and avoidance responses of SP subjects. Interestingly, in contrast to impulsive borderline patients, avoidant personality disordered patients demonstrate some suggestions of increased serotonergic activity and reduced noradrenergic activity.

Pharmacotherapy Trials for Social Phobia and Avoidant Personality Disorder

There have been few pharmacotherapy trials involving the anxious cluster disorders. There are a limited number of controlled studies looking at avoidant personality traits in patients with SP, while the use of medications for APD alone has been documented only in case reports.

The MAOI phenelzine has been shown, in two controlled trials, to decrease avoidant personality features significantly for patients with SP (Davidson et al., 1993; Versiani et al., 1992). Among the changes seen with phenelzine treatment were decreases in anxiety and avoidance in work and social settings. The reversible MAOI moclobemide has also been shown to be effective in reducing avoidant traits and social phobia symptoms (Versiani et al., 1992). The benzodiazepines clonazepam and alprazolam have also been found to decrease measures of avoidance in SP patients (Davidson et al., 1993; Reich, Noyes, & Yates, 1989). These studies are reviewed in greater depth in the chapter on pharmacological treatments of anxiety disorders.

Case reports have described the usefulness of the MAOIs phenelzine and tranylcypromine for subjects with APD: after 4 to 6 weeks of treatment, patients experienced marked improvements in their abilities to socialize. These gains were maintained at a 1-year follow-up when the patients continued to take the medications (Deltito & Stam, 1989). Two case reports document the efficacy of fluoxetine for APD (Deltito & Stam, 1989; Goldman & Grinspoon, 1990). Within several weeks of initiating treatment, subjects reported decreases in social sensitivity and improvements in socialization, self-confidence, and assertiveness. Doses ranged from 1 mg po every other day to 40 mg of fluoxetine per day. Further controlled studies with well-defined groups of APD and other anxious cluster subjects are needed to establish the clinical indications for pharmacotherapy in this group of patients.

CONCLUSION

The search for pharmacological treatments for personality disordered patients has led to an exciting expansion of our views of the Axis II disorders. Attempts to find a biological dimension that could be targeted by such treatments have enhanced the notion of a fluid boundary between Axis I and II symptomatology. Future research should be aimed toward clearer descriptions, either categorically or psychobiologically, of personality disorders. Controlled clinical trials are needed

to create and test hypotheses concerning the efficacy of medications in these disorders.

References

American Psychiatric Association. (1994). *Diagnostic and statistical manual of mental disorders* (4th ed.). Washington, D.C.: Author.

Baron, M., Gruen, R., & Asnis, L. (1985). Familial transmission of schizotypal and borderline personality disorders. *American Journal of Pscyhiatry, 142*(8), 927–933.

Brown, G. L., Ebert, M. H., Goyer, P. F., et al. (1982). Aggression, suicide and serotonin: Relationships to CSF amine metabolites. *American Journal of Psychiatry, 139*, 741–746.

Coccaro, E. F., Astill, J. L., Herbert, J. A., et al. (1990). Fluoxetine treatment of impulsive aggression in DSM-III-R personality disorder patients. *Journal of Clinical Psychopharmacology, 10*, 373–375.

Coccaro, E. F., & Kavoussi, R. J. (1995, May 20–25). *Fluoxetine in aggression in personality disorders* [New Research Abstracts]. Presented at the American Psychiatric Association 148th annual meeting, Miami, Florida.

Coccaro, E. F., Lawrence, T., Trestman, R. L., et al. (in press). Growth hormone response to IV clonidine challenge correlates with behavioral irritability in psychiatric patients and healthy volunteers. *Psychiatric Research* (in press).

Coccaro, E. F., & Siever, L. J. (1995). The neuropsychopharmacology of personality disorders. In F. E. Bloom & D. J. Kupfer (Eds.), *Psychopharmocology: The fourth generation of progress*. New York: Raven Press.

Coccaro, E. F., Siever, L. J., Klar, H. M., et al. (1989). Serotonergic studies in patients with affective and personality disorders: correlates with suicidal and impulsive aggressive behavior. *Archives of General Psychiatry, 46*, 587–599; [Correction] *47*, 124 (1990).

Cornelius, J. R., Brenner, R. P., et al. (1986). EEG abnormalities in borderline personality disorder: Specific or nonspecific? *Biological Psychiatry, 21*, 977–980.

Cornelius, J. R., Soloff, P. H., Perel, J. M., & Ulrich, R. F. (1991). A preliminary trial of fluoxetine in refractory borderline patients. *Journal of Clinical Psychopharmacology, 11*, 116–120.

Cowdry, R. W., & Gardner, D. L. (1988). Pharmacotherapy of borderline personality disorder: alprazolam, carbamazepine, trifluoperazine, and tranylcypromine. *Archives of General Psychiatry, 45*, 111–119.

Davidson, J. T., Potts, N. S., Richichi, E. A., et al. (1993). Treatment of social phobia with clonazepam and placebo. *Journal of Clinical Psychopharmacology, 13*(6), 423–428.

De la Fuente, J. M., & Lotstra, F. (1994). A trial of carbamazepine in borderline personality disorder. *European Neuropsychopharmacology*, 4(4), 479–486.

Deltito, J. A., & Stam, M. (1989). Psychopharmacological treatment of avoidant personality disorder. *Comprehensive Psychiatry*, 30, 498–504.

Drake, M. E., Hietter, S. A., & Pakalnis, A. (1992). EEG and evoked potentials in episodic-dyscontrol syndrome. *Neuropsychobiology*, 26(3), 125–128.

Foster, H. G., Hillbrand, M., & Chi, C. C. (1989). Efficacy of carbamazepine in assaultive patients with frontal lobe dysfunction. *Progress in Neuropsychopharmacology and Biological Psychiatry*, 13, 865–874.

Giakas, W. J., Seibyl, J. P., & Mazure, C. M. (1990). Valproate in the treatment of temper outbursts. *Journal of Clinical Psychiatry*, 51(12), 525.

Gitlin, M. J. (1993). Pharmacotherapy of personality disorders: conceptual framework and clinical strategies. *Journal of Clinical Psychopharmacology*, 13(5), 343–353.

Goldberg, S., Schulz, S., et al. (1986). Borderline and schizotypal personality disorder treatment with low-dose thiothixene versus placebo. *Archives of General Psychiatry*, 43, 680–686.

Goldman, M. J., & Grinspoon, L. (1990). Ritualistic use of fluoxetine by a former substance abuser. *American Journal of Psychiatry*, 147(10), 1377.

Hyler, S. E., Skodol, A. E., Kellman, H. D., et al. (1990). Validity of Personality Diagnostic Questionnaire: Comparison between two structured interviews. *American Journal of Psychiatry*, 147, 1043–1048.

Hymowitz, P., Frances, A., Jacobsberg, L. B., et al. (1986). Neuroleptic treatment of schizotypal personality disorder. *Comprehensive Psychiatry*, 27, 267–271.

Jensen, H. V., & Andersen, J. (1989). An open, noncomparative study of amoxapine in borderline disorders. *Acta Psychiatrica Scandinavica*, 79, 89–93.

Kaplan, H. I., & Sadock, B. J. (Eds.). (1995). *Comprehensive textbook of psychiatry*, Vol 6. Williams and Wilkins, Baltimore.

Karson, C. N., Casanova, M. F., Kleinman, J. E., & Griffin, W. S. (1993). Choline acetyltransferase in schizophrenia. *American Journal of Psychiatry*, 150, 454–459.

Kavoussi, R. J., & Coccaro, E. R. (1993). The amphetamine challenge test correlates with affective lability in healthy volunteers. *Psychiatry Research*, 48, 219–228.

Keck, P. E., McElroy, S. L., & Friedman, L. M. (1992). Valproate and carbamazepine in the treatment of panic and posttraumatic stress disorders, withdrawal states, and behavioral dyscontrol syndromes. *Journal of Clinical Psychopharmacology*, 12(1, Suppl.), 36–41.

Links, P. S., Steiner, M., Boiago, I., & Irwin, D. (1990). Lithium therapy for borderline patients: preliminary findings. *Journal of Personality Disorders*, 4, 173–181.

Markovitz, P. J., Calabrese, J. U., Schulz, S. C., et al. (1991). Fluoxetine in the treatment of borderline and schizotypal personality disorders. *American Journal of Psychiatry*, 148, 1064–1067.

Mattes, J. A. (1990). Comparative effectiveness of carbamazepine and propranolol for rage outbursts. *Journal of Neuropsychiatry and Clinical Neuroscience*, 2, 159–164.

Montgomery, S. A., Montgomery, D. B., Green, M., et al. (1992). Pharmacotherapy in the prevention of suicidal behavior. *Journal of Clinical Psychopharmacology*, 12(2, Suppl.), 27S–31S.

Norden, M. J. (1989). Fluoxetine in borderline personality disorder. *Progress in Neuropsychopharmacology and Biological Psychiatry*, 13, 885–893.

Parsons, B., Quitkin, F. M., McGrath, P. J., et al. (1989). Phenelzine, imipramine, and placebo in borderline patients meeting criteria for atypical depression. *Psychopharmacology Bulletin*, 25, 524–534.

Reich, J., Noyes, R., & Yates, W. (1989). Alprazolam treatment of avoidant personality traits in social phobic patients. *Journal of Clinical Psychiatry*, 50(3), 91–95.

Roy, A., De Jon, J., & Linnoila, M. (1989). Extroversion in pathological gamblers correlates with indices of noradrenergic function. *Archives of General Psychiatry*, 46, 679–681.

Schneier, F. R., Spitzer, R. L., & Gibbon, M. (1991). The relationship of social phobia subtypes and avoidant personality disorder. *Comprehensive Psychiatry*, 32(6), 496–502.

Schulz, S. C., Cornelius, J., Schulz, P. M., & Soloff, P. H. (1988). The amphetamine challenge test in patients with borderline personality disorder. *American Journal of Psychiatry*, 145, 809–814.

Serban, G., & Siegel, S. (1984). Response of borderline and schizotypal patients to small doses of thiothixene and haloperidol. *American Journal of Psychiatry*, 141, 1455–1458.

Sheard, M. J., Marini, J. L., Brideges, C. I., & Wagner, E. (1976). The effect of lithium on impulsive aggressive behavior in man. *American Journal of Psychiatry*, 133, 1409–1413.

Siever, L. J. (1991). The biology of the boundaries of schizophrenia. In C. A. Tamminga & S. C. Schulz (Eds.), *Schizophrenia: Advances in neuropsychiatry and neuropsychopharmacology, Vol. 1: Schizophrenia research*. New York: Raven Press.

Siever, L. J., et al. (1995). Brain structure/function and the dopamine system in schizotypal personality disorder. *Schizotypal Personality*, 12, 272–286.

Siever, L. J., Amin, F., Coccaro, E. F., et al. (1991). Plasma HVA in schizotypal personality disorders. *American Journal of Psychiatry*, 148, 1246–1248.

Siever, L. J., Kalus, O. F., & Keefe, R. S. (1993). The boundaries of schizophrenia. *Psychiatric Clinics of North America, 16*, 217–244.

Silverman, J. M., & Pinkham, L. (1991). Affective and impulsive personality disorder traits in the relatives of patients with borderline personality disorder. *American Journal of Psychiatry, 148*, 1378–1385.

Silverman, J. M., Siever, L. J., Horvath, T. B., et al. (1993). Schizophrenia related and affective personality disorder traits in relatives of probands with schizophrenia and personality disorders. *American Journal of Psychiatry, 150*, 435–442.

Soloff, P. H., Corneluis, J. R., George, A., et al. (1993). Efficacy of phenelzine and haloperidol in borderline personality disorder. *Archives of General Psychiatry, 50*, 377–385.

Soloff, P. H., George, A., et al. (1986). Paradoxical effects of amitriptyline in borderline patients. *American Journal of Psychiatry, 143*, 1603–1605.

Soloff, P. H., George, A., Nathan, R. S., et al. (1989). Amitriptyline versus haloperidol in borderlines: Final outcomes and predictors of response. *Journal of Clinical Psychopharmacology, 9*, 238–246.

Stein, D. J., & Hollander, E. (1993). Anxiety disorders and personality disorders. *Journal of Personality Disorders, 7*(2), 87–104.

Stein, D. J., Hollander, E., Cohen, L., & Frenkel, M. (1993). Neuropsychiatric impairment in impulsive personality disorders. *Psychiatry Research, 48*(3), 257–266.

Steinberg, B. J., Trestman, R., Mitropolous, V., et al. (1995). Depressive response to physostigmine challenge in borderline personality disorder patients. Manuscript in review.

Steinberg, B. J., Trestman, R. L., & Siever, L. J. (1994). The cholinergic and noradrenergic neurotransmitter systems affective instability in borderline personality disorder. In K. R. Silk (Ed.), *Biological and neurobehavioral studies in borderline personality disorder* (pp. 41–62). Washington, D.C.: American Psychiatric Association.

Tancer, M. E. (1993). Neurobiology of social phobia. *Journal of Clinical Psychiatry, 54*(12, Suppl.), 26–30.

Tandon, R., & Greden, J. F. (1989). Cholinergic hyperactivity and negative schizophrenic symptoms: A model of cholinergic/dopaminergic interactions in schizophrenia. *Archives of General Psychiatry, 46*, 745–753.

Torgersen, S. (1992, December 14–18). *The genetic transmission of borderline personality features displays multidimensionality* [New Abstracts]. Presented at the American College of Neuropsychopharmacology annual meeting, San Juan, Puerto Rico.

Trestman, R. L., deVegvar, M., & Siever, L. J. Treatment of personality disorders. (1995). In C. B. Nemeroff & A. F. Schatzberg (Eds.), *The APA textbook of psychopharmacology*. Washington, D.C.: American Psychiatric Press.

Uhde, T. W. (1994). A review of biological studies in social phobia. *Journal of Clinical Psychiatry, 55*(6, Suppl.), 17–27.

Versiani, M., Nardi, A. E., Mundim, F. D., et al. (1992). Pharmacotherapy of social phobia: A controlled study with moclobemide and phenelzine. *British Journal of Psychiatry, 161*, 353–360.

Afterword—A Plea

Martin E. P. Seligman

If I were a typical practicing clinician, I would have mixed feelings about the volume I just read. On one hand, I would be better informed and even grateful. I would know what continuing education workshops to take to update my repertoire. On the other hand, I would feel threatened. Much of my work is not recognizable in this book, and many, perhaps even a majority of, psychotherapists in the United States today carry out forms of therapy not tested and not reflected in the pages of this book.

The typical clinician would think that my therapy is often long term, not short term like all of the efficacy studies described here. My therapy is eclectic. I borrow techniques as needed from several schools. If one of my techniques fails, I drop it and switch to another. Sometimes I switch modalities altogether. I do not use the rigid manuals described in this book. My treatment is often derived from psychodynamic thinking and from family systems, and few of these modalities have emerged as having proven value from controlled outcome trials. The patients I see have multiple problems, but those in controlled outcome studies usually have but a single disorder. I am concerned about improving my patients' productivity at work, their interpersonal relations, and their growth and their zest for life as well as alleviating their *DSM*-defined disorder, whereas the efficacy studies concentrate on merely alleviating the symptoms of the disorder.

My patients choose to work with me because they believe in me. And they choose the modality of therapy I do because they believe it will help them. They are not randomly assigned to me and my treatment modality as are the subjects in all the efficacy studies.

Does this mean that what I do is not empirically valid? Even worse, does this mean I can be sued for malpractice if I do not use the strategies described in this volume?

These are the questions that have nagged at me since the inception of this work, and they came to the forefront when I began to collaborate with *Consumer Reports* (CR).

THE *CONSUMER REPORTS* STUDY AND ITS IMPLICATIONS

In early 1993, *Consumer Reports* departed from its usual venue and reviewed medications and psychotherapy for panic disorder. As a textbook writer, I was surprised and heartened to see just how up-to-date, scholarly, and accurate this article was—and better, unlike the journals, it would be read by more than 5 million people. This was followed by another article in June 1993 on the diet industry, exposing the failure of the majority of people to keep the weight lost off in the long run. The gray eminence behind these articles was Joel Gurin, the science editor of *CR*. I phoned him to congratulate him and to ask if *CR* would be interested in publishing the other product of the Task Force—the volume for the general public.

He was interested and mentioned that both his parents were psychologists (his mother is chair of psychology at the University of Michigan). He told me that CR was planning to evaluate the services carried out by doctors, lawyers, psychotherapists, and other professionals. *Consumer Reports* eventually declined the general public volume, but Joel—now promoted to editor in chief—called me about a year later and asked me to collaborate on a new undertaking.

He said that CR wanted to study the outcome of the use of drugs and psychotherapy among its readership and to do this by their annual survey method. Three things were clear to both of us: First, this would be the largest study of treatment ever done. Second, it would also study the outcome of treatment as it is actually administered in the field, in contrast to the outcome of treatment as distilled into controlled "efficacy" studies. Third, and most relevant to me, the survey method has quite a number of methodological hazards that might compromise what was done. I agreed to help with the design of the questionnaire and the statistical analysis of the complex data set that would result. I could not help with the inherent limitations of the survey method: self-report, retrospection, cross-sectional focus, and lack of external control groups.

As is now well known, the study was carried out and its results published in the November 1995 issue of CR. I will not detail the methodological niceties and flaws here, and I refer the reader to Seligman (1995) and a special issue of the *American Psychologist* (October 1996) for lively discussion of these issues. But, there were three results of substantial relevance to this volume.

Treatment worked very well. Most respondents got a lot better. Averaged over all mental health professionals, of the 426 people who were feeling "very poor" when they began therapy, 87% were feeling very good, good, or at least so-so by the time of the survey. Of the 786 people who were feeling "fairly poor" at the outset, 92% were feeling very good, good, or at least so-so by the time of the survey. These findings converge with meta-analyses of efficacy (Lipsey & Wilson, 1993; Shapiro & Shapiro, 1982; Smith, Glass, & Miller, 1980).

Long-term therapy produced much more improvement than short-term therapy. Roughly double the number of people in treatment over 6 months reported major improvement in the presenting problem than people in treatment under 6 months. This result was very robust and held up over all statistical models.

There was no difference between psychotherapy alone and psychotherapy plus medication for any disorder. No specific modality of psychotherapy did any better than any other for any problem. These results confirm the "dodo bird" hypothesis—that all forms of psychotherapies do about equally well (Luborsky, Singer, & Luborsky, 1975).

I confess that each of these findings surprised me. Moreover, they should come as a surprise to any student whose knowledge of outcomes is limited to the present volume. First, I did not expect treatment—either psychotherapy or drugs—to work with 90% of patients. In the present volume, you encounter 60% to 70% of patients being helped as the modal "good" result. Second, I did not expect long-term therapy to work so well, and CR's analysts and I spent a good deal of energy analyzing the data for any artifact that might have produced such robust benefits of long-term treatment. Third, I expected specific drugs and specific kinds of psychotherapy to work on specific disorders. This, if anything, is the underlying theme of the present volume. So, with CR's analysts, we created the $n \times n$ tables looking at outcome as a function of specific treatment and specific disorder. We found no specificity at all, and, even more convincing to me, we could not even find a data "massage" that would produce a hint of specificity.

Why does the present volume show high specificity, more modest patient gains, and few effective long-term treatments? There are two possibilities. The first is that the CR study and the kindred "effectiveness" (looking at the outcome of treatment as it is actually carried out in the field) studies are methodologically flawed. The second is that the "efficacy" (looking at outcome of treatment when it is distilled into a highly controlled design) studies are methodologically flawed.

I think the answer is that both are flawed and that creating a new method that has the virtues of both without the flaws is, I believe, the urgent project to which we must now turn. The flaws of the effectiveness design generally, and the CR study in particular, involve insufficiently tight control: possible sampling bias, lack of external control groups, lack of rigorous diagnosis, self-report inaccuracy, retrospective distortions, and the need for a full battery of tests.

The flaws of the efficacy design are flaws of ecological validity, in which the therapy is carried out under conditions so different from those of actual therapy as to make the inferential distance to actual therapy very long. Or, to put it another way, the laboratory nature of the efficacy design omits so many crucial elements of real therapy, and introduces others so alien to real therapy, that it masks, minimizes, and distorts the beneficial results that actual therapy produces. In particular, the following five properties characterize psychotherapy as it is performed in the field. Each of these properties is absent from an efficacy study done under controlled conditions. If these properties are important to patients' getting better, efficacy studies will underestimate or even miss altogether the value of psychotherapy done in the field:

1. Psychotherapy in the field is not of fixed duration. It usually keeps going until the patient is markedly improved or quits. In contrast, the intervention in efficacy studies stops after a limited number of sessions—usually between 8 and 12—regardless of how well or poorly the patient is doing.

2. Psychotherapy in the field is self-correcting. If one technique is not working, another technique or even another modality is usually tried. In contrast, the intervention in efficacy studies is confined to a small number of techniques, all within one modality and manualized to be delivered in a fixed order.

3. Patients in psychotherapy in the field often get there by active shopping, entering a kind of treatment they actively sought with a therapist they screened and decided to work with. In contrast, patients enter efficacy studies by the passive process of random assignment to treatment and acquiescence to whoever and whatever happens to be offered in the study. Moreover, the sample of patients willing to be guinea pigs in an efficacy study may be quite demographically different from the sample who enter actual therapy.

4. Patients in psychotherapy in the field usually have multiple problems (and perhaps not even just the usual comorbidities), and psychotherapy is geared to relieve parallel and interacting difficulties. Patients in efficacy studies are selected to have but one diagnosis by a long set of exclusion and inclusion criteria.

5. Psychotherapy in the field is almost always concerned with improvement in the general functioning of patients, as well as amelioration of a disorder and relief of specific, presenting symptoms. Efficacy studies usually focus only on specific symptom reduction and whether the disorder ends.

Most generally, efficacy studies minimize the role of clinical judgment on outcome, while effectiveness studies maximize the role of clinical judgment. To illustrate: In the CR study, individual therapy did not differ from group therapy for any outcome variable. Does this mean that we should rush in and assign people to group therapy all the time? It is much cheaper. If the CR study had been an efficacy study and had assigned people at random to group versus individual therapy, this would have implied that, on average, individuals will benefit equally from either therapy. But people were not assigned randomly in the CR study. Therapists, in conjunction with their patients, presumably used a great deal of clinical judgment to decide if the patients would do better in individual or group therapy. (Does the patient respond well to authority? Or does the patient change markedly when criticized by others?) So, the result means that, once clinical judgment filters out who gets individual therapy and who gets group therapy, then the two modalities do equally well.

Consider another example: the CR finding that drugs plus psychotherapy did no better than psychotherapy alone for any disorder (schizophrenia and bipolar depression were too rare for analysis in this sample). The most obvious interpretation is that drugs are useless and do nothing over and above psychotherapy. But, the absence of random assignment and the overwhelming presence of clinical judgment should prevent us from leaping to that conclusion. Assume, for the moment, that therapists are canny about who needs drugs plus psychotherapy and who can do well with psychotherapy alone. The therapists assign those patients accordingly, and so appropriate patients get appropriate treatment. This is just the same logic as a self-correcting trajectory of treatment in which techniques and modalities are modified with the patient's progress. This means that drugs plus psychotherapy may actually have done pretty well after all—but only in a cannily selected subset of people.

So, I have come to believe that the efficacy method and the effectiveness method taken alone are each seriously incomplete. Each answers different questions. The efficacy method, I believe, answers two questions well: (a) Is a new treatment likely to work when exported to the field and added to the clinical repertoire already in existence? (b) What is the mechanism by which a given treatment works? (For such a question, random assignment and control groups are essential.)

The efficacy method cannot answer the question, Does treatment as it is actually done in the field work? since the inferential distance is so great. The efficacy method cannot answer questions in which variables omitted from its design—like clinical judgment—play a large role in outcome. Efficacy methodology cannot even test, to say nothing of empirically validate, long and complicated psychotherapy, in principle: Manuals cannot be written for long or complicated treatment, and patients cannot be randomly assigned, ethically, to a placebo condition for the many months or years that long-term treatment takes. A control group of patients who have equally severe symptoms, but are willing to eschew therapy in favor of talking to sympathetic friends, ministers, or doing nothing, cannot be found.

On the other hand, the effectiveness method can answer the panoply of questions about whether treatment as it is actually done in the field works. The effectiveness method can answer the question of how much added benefit is gained when a new treatment found efficacious is added to actual practice. The effectiveness method can answer questions of whether long-term therapy works. But, the effectiveness method cannot answer questions of active ingredients nearly as well as the efficacy method nor is it an efficient way of testing out new therapies.

Parts of the two methods can be combined, however, to do a scientifically compelling study of treatments that involves a good deal of clinical judgment, has variable duration, has self-correcting improvisations, is aimed at improved quality of life as well as symptom relief, and is carried out with patients who choose the treatment, who are not randomly assigned, and who have multiple problems. Such a study would draw on the virtues of both the efficacy method and the effectiveness method, correcting for the most salient flaws of each:

1. It would be a total sample study in which all the patients from a wide and representative range of modalities of treatment would be entered.
2. It would be longitudinal, with patients looked at before, during, and long after treatment.
3. It would have four perspectives on outcome— the patient's self-report, the therapist's view, blind diagnosis, and a full battery of tests.
4. It would be ecologically valid, with patients choosing the modality they wanted, with duration of treatment the joint decision of patient and therapist, without manuals and with self-

correction of techniques, without exclusion of any patients based on multiple diagnosis or insufficient number of symptoms.

There are several pressing questions that such a design could answer more authoritatively than either an efficacy or an effectiveness design alone:

- How well does long-term treatment work in actual practice?
- Is there a dose–response curve for psychotherapy for any given disorder?
- Is there specificity of modality of medication or psychotherapy for particular disorders?
- What is the actual economic benefit of treatment as opposed to cost since absenteeism, salary changes, physical health costs, divorce, arrests, and so forth, as well as mental suffering, would be measured?
- What is the effect of amount of training, degree, and experience of the therapist on outcome?
- What is the effect of case management versus clinical judgment alone on outcome?

I conclude that efficacy methods and effectiveness methods are complementary. Neither is prior and both warrant the honorific "empirical validation." Efficacy studies do not have to be done first, before a new method is tried in the field. This may be an efficient route, but human desperation and invention usually do it the other way around. Combining the strengths of the two methods, however, will, in my opinion, answer the most urgent questions before us now about which treatments work.

References

Lipsey, M., & Wilson, D. (1993). The efficacy of psychological, educational, and behavioral treatment: Confirmation from meta-analysis. *American Psychologist*, 48, 1181–1209.

Luborsky, L., Singer, B., & Luborsky, L. (1975). Comparative studies of psychotherapies. *Archives of General Psychiatry*, 32, 995–1008.

Seligman, M. E. P. (1995). The effectiveness of psychotherapy: The *Consumer Reports* study. *American Psychologist*, 50, 965–974.

Shapiro, D., & Shapiro, D. (1982). Meta-analysis of comparative therapy outcome studies: A replication and refinement. *Psychological Bulletin*, 92, 581–604.

Smith, M., Glass, G., & Miller, T. (1980). *The benefit of psychotherapy*. Baltimore, Md.: Johns Hopkins University Press.

AUTHOR INDEX

SUBJECT INDEX

Acamprosate, 134, 136
Acetyl-L-carnitine, 101, 110
Acute depression. *See* Depression
Addiction. *See* Alcohol use disorders; Cocaine Dependence; Opioid Dependence; Substance use disorders
ADHD. *See* Attention deficit hyperactivity disorder
Adrenocorticotropic hormone, 101
Aged. *See* Elderly
Agoraphobia, xxv–xxvi, 288–91, 291–94
Alcohol use disorders, xix, 127, 129, 132–36, 156–62
  community reinforcement treatment for, 156
  inpatient treatment duration for, 161
  patient-treatment matching, 156
  pharmacological treatments for: acamprosate, 136; antidipsotropic medication, 129, 132; opioid antagonists (naltrexone), 126, 135, 136; serotonergic agents, 129, 133–34
  psychosocial treatments for, 155–63: behavioral marital therapy, 156; brief treatment, 160; cognitive-behavioral treatment, xix, 156; interpersonal therapy, 156; social skills training, 156; twelve-step programs, 156; therapist characteristics in, 156, 160; treatment effectiveness of, 158–160; treatment setting for, 162–63
Alpha-2 agonists, 384, 388–89
Alprazolam, 321–22, 325, 330
Alzheimer's disease, 90–115
Amantadine, 140
Amnesia, dissociative, 423–25, 429–31
Amytal narcosynthesis, xxiii
Anorexia nervosa, 502–6
Anticonvulsants
  for dissociative identity disorder, 436–37
  for post-traumatic stress disorder, 386, 389–90
Antidepressants, 212–17, 221
  for acute depression, xxii, 257–58
  for binge eating disorder, 520–21
  for bipolar disorders, xx
  for borderline personality disorder, 560, 562–63
  for bulimia, xxi, 506–8, 511–13
  for cocaine dependence, 136–41
  for generalized anxiety disorder, xxiv, 327
  for schizophrenia, 176–77, 179
  for somatoform pain disorder, xxix
  for unipolar depression, 210–15, 219
  See also MAO inhibitors; Selective serotonin reuptake inhibitors; Tricyclic antidepressants
Antihypertensives, 384
Anti-inflammatory agents, 93, 106
Antipsychotics
  for bipolar disorders, 255–56, 261–62
  for borderline personality disorder, 557, 563
  for schizophrenia, xxvii, 169–75
Anxiety, in elderly. *See* Elderly
Anxiety disorders *See* Agoraphobia; Generalized anxiety disorder; Panic disorder; Phobias; Social Phobia

Anxiety management training, 402–3
Apomorphine, 458
Appetite suppressants, 506, 520
Assisted covert sensitization, 484–85
Atenolol, 329
Attention deficit hyperactivity disorder (ADHD), xix–xx, 29–32, 35, 37–38, 55, 58
  in adults, 46–47, 51–52
  pharmacological treatments for: side effects of, 51–52; long-term multimodal treatment, 36–37; nonstimulant drugs, 26, 54–55; psychostimulants, xx–xxii, 45–55, 58; treatment limitations of, 53–54; tricyclic antidepressants, 42
  psychosocial treatments for: behavior therapy, 29–30, 32–36; contingency management, xxi, 29–32, 35
Aversive behavior reversal, 485
Avoidant personality, xix–xx, 546–47, 564–65
Azapirones, 326–27

Behavioral weight control treatment, 522–23
Behavior marital therapy, 228
Behavior therapy, xxv–xxiv, 29–30, 32–36, 304–6, 401–5
  for avoidant personality disorder, xix
  for bulimia, 515–17
  for insomnia, xxviii
  for major depression, xxiv, 227–28, 234
  for obsessive compulsive disorder, 368–69
  for paraphilias, xxvi, 483–87
  for schizophrenia, xxvii, 197–98
  See also Cognitive-behavior therapy
Benzodiazepines
  for anxiety in elderly, 280
  for bipolar disorders, 256, 262
  for dissociative identity disorder, 436
  for generalized anxiety disorder, xxiii, 325–28
  for insomnia, xxviii, 537
  for panic disorder, xxvi, 321–22
  for post-traumatic stress disorder, 384, 388
  for schizophrenia, 175–77
  for social phobias, xxix, 330–31
Beta blockers, 329–30, 384, 390–91, 437
Binge eating disorder, 523–24
  pharmacological treatments for: antidepressants, 520–21; selective serotonin reuptake inhibitors, 521
  psychosocial treatments for: behavioral weight control, 522–23; cognitive-behavioral treatment, 521–22; interpersonal therapy, 522
Bipolar disorders, xx, 240, 246, 249, 262–63
  pharmacological treatments for: 249; for acute depression, 257–62; for acute mania, 250, 252–57; antipsychotic, 249, 255–56, 261–62; benzodiazepines, 249, 256, 262; carbamazepine, xx, 249, 254, 258–61; lithium, xx, 249–53, 257–60; maintenance of, 249, 259–62; valproate, xx, 249, 253–54, 258–59, 261
  psychoeducation and medication adherence, 240–46